Col. Henry Steel Olcott

# H. P. BLAVATSKY

## COLLECTED WRITINGS

## 1877

# ISIS UNVEILED

**VOL. II**
**THEOLOGY**

A publication supported by
THE KERN FOUNDATION

## Quest Books
Theosophical Publishing House

Wheaton, Illinois ♦ Chennai (Madras), India

© Copyright The Theosophical Publishing House 1972

*The Theosophical Publishing House, Wheaton, Illinois, is a department of The Theosophical Society in America*

Original edition 1877

New edition, revised and corrected, and with additional material, 1972
Copyright 1994 by The Theosophical Publishing House
First Quest Edition 1994
Second Printing, 2000

ISBN: 0-8356-0247-8

CIP data available upon request

*This publication made possible with the assistance of the Kern Foundation*

All rights reserved. No part of this book may be reproduced in any manner without written permission except for quotations embodied in critical articles or reviews. For additional information write to:

The Theosophical Publishing House
P.O. Box 270
Wheaton, IL 60189-0270

This edition is printed on acid-free paper that meets the American National Standards Institute Z39.48 Standard

Printed in the United States of America by Versa Press

# ILLUSTRATIONS

## VOLUME II

FACING

| | |
|---|---:|
| COL. HENRY STEEL OLCOTT (*frontispiece*) | |
| CODEX SINAITICUS | 18 |
| CODEX ALEXANDRINUS | 19 |
| ISAAC NEWTON | 114 |
| GOTTFRIED WILHELM, FREIHERR VON LEIBNITZ | 115 |
| HEINRICH CORNELIUS AGRIPPA VON NETTESHEIM | 146 |
| BARUCH (OR BENEDICTUS) DE SPINOZA | 147 |
| ELIAS ASHMOLE | 242 |
| THOMAS TAYLOR | 243 |
| COUNT GIOVANNI PICO DELLA MIRÁNDOLA | 274 |
| PHILIPPUS AUREOLUS THEOPHRASTUS BOMBAST OF HOHENHEIM, KNOWN AS PARACELSUS | 275 |
| COUNT DE SAINT-GERMAIN | 370 |
| SIR WILLIAM JONES | 371 |
| COUNT ALESSANDRO DI CAGLIOSTRO | 402 |
| JOSEPH PRIESTLEY | 403 |
| JOHN TYNDALL | 498 |
| JOHN LLOYD STEPHENS | 499 |
| HATSHEPSUT TEMPLE, DEIR-EL-BAHARI, EGYPT | 530 |
| CIRCULAR ZODIAC OF DENDERA (TENTYRA), UPPER EGYPT | 531 |
| IN THE JUDGMENT HALL OF ASAR (OSIRIS): "THE WEIGHING OF THE HEART" | 626 |
| FINAL SCENE IN THE JUDGMENT HALL: HORUS CONDUCTING ANI TO OSIRIS | 627 |
| KRISHNA AND SERPENT | 658 |
| KRISHNA AND SERPENT | 659 |

# ISIS UNVEILED:

## A MASTER-KEY

TO THE

## MYSTERIES OF ANCIENT AND MODERN

## SCIENCE AND THEOLOGY.

BY

### H. P. BLAVATSKY,

CORRESPONDING SECRETARY OF THE THEOSOPHICAL SOCIETY.

"Cecy est un livre de bonne Foy."—MONTAIGNE.

VOL. II.—*THEOLOGY.*

NEW YORK:
J. W. BOUTON, 706 BROADWAY.
LONDON: BERNARD QUARITCH.
1877.

COPYRIGHT, BY
J. W. BOUTON.
1877.

TROW'S
PRINTING AND BOOKBINDING CO.,
PRINTERS AND BOOKBINDERS,
205-213 *East* 12*th St.*,
NEW YORK.

# TABLE OF CONTENTS

|  | PAGE |
|---|---|
| PREFACE | iv |

Mrs. Elizabeth Thompson and Baroness Burdett-Coutts

## VOLUME SECOND

## THE "INFALLIBILITY" OF RELIGION

### CHAPTER I

#### THE CHURCH: WHERE IS IT?

| | |
|---|---|
| Church statistics | 1 |
| Catholic "miracles" and spiritualistic "phenomena" | 4 |
| Christian and Pagan belief compared | 10 |
| Magic and sorcery practiced by Christian clergy | 20 |
| Comparative theology a new science | 25 |
| Eastern traditions as to Alexandrian Library | 27 |
| Roman pontiffs imitators of the Hindu Brahmâtma | 30 |
| Christian dogmas derived from heathen philosophy | 33 |
| Doctrine of the Trinity of Pagan origin | 45 |
| Disputes between Gnostics and Church Fathers | 51 |
| Bloody records of Christianity | 53 |

### CHAPTER II

#### CHRISTIAN CRIMES AND HEATHEN VIRTUES

| | |
|---|---|
| Sorceries of Catherine of Medici | 55 |
| Occult arts practiced by the clergy | 59 |
| Witch-burning and auto-da-fé of little children | 62 |
| Lying Catholic saints | 74 |
| Pretensions of missionaries in India and China | 79 |
| Sacrilegious tricks of Catholic clergy | 82 |
| Paul a kabalist | 91 |
| Peter not the founder of Roman church | 91 |
| Strict lives of Pagan hierophants | 98 |
| High character of ancient "mysteries" | 101 |

# CONTENTS

|  | PAGE |
|---|---|
| Jacolliot's account of Hindu fakirs | 103 |
| Christian symbolism derived from Phallic worship | 109 |
| Hindu doctrine of the Pitris | 114 |
| Brahmanic spirit-communion | 115 |
| Dangers of *untrained* mediumship | 117 |

## CHAPTER III

### DIVISIONS AMONGST THE EARLY CHRISTIANS

| | |
|---|---|
| Resemblance between early Christianity and Buddhism | 123 |
| Peter never in Rome | 124 |
| Meaning of "Nazar" and "Nazarene" | 129 |
| Baptism a derived right | 134 |
| Is Zoroaster a generic name? | 141 |
| Pythagorean teachings of Jesus | 145 |
| The Apocalypse kabalistic | 147 |
| Jesus considered an adept by some Pagan philosophers and early Christians | 150 |
| Doctrine of permutation | 152 |
| The meaning of God-Incarnate | 153 |
| Dogmas of the Gnostics | 155 |
| Ideas of Marcion, the "heresiarch" | 159 |
| Precepts of *Manu* | 163 |
| Jehovah identical with Bacchus | 165 |

## CHAPTER IV

### ORIENTAL COSMOGONIES AND BIBLE RECORDS

| | |
|---|---|
| Discrepancies in the *Pentateuch* | 167 |
| Indian, Chaldean and Ophite systems compared | 170 |
| Who were the first Christians? | 178 |
| Christos and Sophia-Akhamôth | 183 |
| Secret doctrine taught by Jesus | 191 |
| Jesus never claimed to be God | 193 |
| New Testament narratives and Hindu legends | 199 |
| Antiquity of the "Logos" and "Christ" | 205 |
| Comparative Virgin-worship | 209 |

## CHAPTER V

### MYSTERIES OF THE KABALA

| | |
|---|---|
| Ain-Soph and the Sephîrôth | 212 |
| The primitive wisdom-religion | 216 |
| The book of *Genesis* a compilation of Old World legends | 217 |
| The Trinity of the Kabala | 222 |

# CONTENTS

|  | PAGE |
|---|---|
| Gnostic and Nazarene systems contrasted with Hindu myths | 225 |
| Kabalism in the book of *Ezekiel* | 232 |
| Story of the resurrection of Jairus' daughter found in the history of Kṛishṇa | 241 |
| Untrustworthy teachings of the early Fathers | 248 |
| Their persecuting spirit | 249 |

## CHAPTER VI

### ESOTERIC DOCTRINES OF BUDDHISM PARODIED IN CHRISTIANITY

| | |
|---|---|
| Decisions of Nicæan Council, how arrived at | 251 |
| Murder of Hypatia | 252 |
| Origin of the fish-symbol of Vishṇu | 256 |
| Kabalistic doctrine of the Cosmogony | 264 |
| Diagrams of Hindu and Chaldeo-Jewish systems | 265 |
| Ten mythical Avatâras of Vishṇu | 274 |
| Trinity of man taught by Paul | 281 |
| Socrates and Plato on soul and spirit | 283 |
| True Buddhism, what it is | 288 |

## CHAPTER VII

### EARLIER CHRISTIAN HERESIES AND SECRET SOCIETIES

| | |
|---|---|
| Nazareans, Ophites, and modern Druzes | 291 |
| Etymology of IAÒ | 298 |
| "Hermetic Brothers" of Egypt | 307 |
| True meaning of Nirvâna | 319 |
| The Jaina sect | 321 |
| Christians and Chrêstians | 323 |
| The Gnostics and their detractors | 325 |
| Buddha, Jesus, and Apollonius of Tyana | 341 |

## CHAPTER VIII

### JESUITRY AND MASONRY

| | |
|---|---|
| The *Zohar* and Rabbi Shimon | 348 |
| The Order of Jesuits and its relation to some of the Masonic orders | 352 |
| Crimes permitted to its members | 355 |
| Principles of Jesuitry compared with those of Pagan moralists | 364 |
| Trinity of man in Egyptian *Book of the Dead* | 367 |
| Freemasonry no longer esoteric | 372 |
| Persecution of Templars by the Church | 381 |
| Secret Masonic ciphers | 395 |
| Jehovah not the "Ineffable Name" | 398 |

## CONTENTS

### CHAPTER IX

#### THE VEDAS AND THE BIBLE

|  | PAGE |
|---|---|
| Nearly every myth based on some great truth | 405 |
| Whence the Christian Sabbath | 406 |
| Antiquity of the *Vedas* | 410 |
| Pythagorean doctrine of the potentialities of numbers | 417 |
| "Days" of *Genesis* and "Days" of Brahmâ | 422 |
| Fall of man and the Deluge in the Hindu books | 425 |
| Antiquity of the *Mahâbhârata* | 429 |
| Were the ancient Egyptians of the Âryan race? | 434 |
| Samuel, David, and Solomon mythical personages | 439 |
| Symbolism of Noah's Ark | 447 |
| The Patriarchs identical with zodiacal signs | 459 |
| All Bible legends belong to universal history | 469 |

### CHAPTER X

#### THE DEVIL-MYTH

| The devil officially recognized by the Church | 477 |
|---|---|
| Satan the mainstay of sacerdotalism | 480 |
| Identity of Satan with the Egyptian Typhon | 483 |
| His relation to serpent-worship | 489 |
| The *Book of Job* and the *Book of the Dead* | 493 |
| The Hindu devil a metaphysical abstraction | 501 |
| Satan and the Prince of Hell in the *Gospel of Nicodemus* | 515 |

### CHAPTER XI

#### COMPARATIVE RESULTS OF BUDDHISM AND CHRISTIANITY

| The age of philosophy produced no atheists | 530 |
|---|---|
| The legends of three Saviors | 537 |
| Christian doctrine of the Atonement illogical | 542 |
| Cause of the failure of missionaries to convert Buddhists and Brahmanists | 553 |
| Neither Buddha nor Jesus left written records | 559 |
| The grandest mysteries of religion in the *Bhagavad-Gîtâ* | 562 |
| The meaning of regeneration explained in the *Satapatha-Brâhmana* | 565 |
| The sacrifice of blood interpreted | 566 |
| Demoralization of British India by Christian missionaries | 573 |
| The Bible less authenticated than any other sacred book | 577 |
| Knowledge of chemistry and physics displayed by Indian jugglers | 583 |

### CHAPTER XII

#### CONCLUSIONS AND ILLUSTRATIONS

| Recapitulation of fundamental propositions | 587 |
|---|---|
| Seership of the soul and of the spirit | 590 |

## CONTENTS

| | PAGE |
|---|---|
| The phenomenon of the so-called spirit-hand | 594 |
| Difference between mediums and adepts | 595 |
| Interview of an English ambassador with a reincarnated Buddha | 598 |
| Flight of a lama's astral body related by Abbé Huc | 604 |
| Schools of magic in Buddhist lamaseries | 609 |
| The unknown race of Hindu Tôdas | 613 |
| Will-power of fakirs and yogis | 617 |
| Taming of wild beasts by fakirs | 622 |
| Evocation of a living spirit by a Shaman, witnessed by the writer | 626 |
| Sorcery by the breath of a Jesuit Father | 633 |
| Why the study of magic is almost impracticable in Europe | 635 |
| Conclusion | 639 |
| NOTES | 641 |
| INDEX | 663 |
| BIBLIOGRAPHY | 794 |

# PREFACE TO PART II[1]

WERE it possible, we would keep this work out of the hands of many Christians whom its perusal would not benefit, and for whom it was not written. We allude to those whose faith in their respective churches is pure and sincere, and those whose sinless lives reflect the glorious example of that Prophet of Nazareth, by whose mouth the spirit of truth spake loudly to humanity. Such there have been at all times. History preserves the names of many as heroes, philosophers, philanthropists, martyrs, and holy men and women; but how many more have lived and died, unknown but to their intimate acquaintances, unblessed but by their humble beneficiaries! These have ennobled Christianity, but would have shed the same lustre upon any other faith they might have professed—for they were higher than their creed. The benevolence of Peter Cooper and Elizabeth Thompson, of America, who are not orthodox Christians, is no less Christlike than that of the Baroness Angela G. Burdett-Coutts, of England, who is one. And yet, in comparison with the millions who have been accounted Christians, such have always formed a small minority. They are to be found to this day, in pulpit and pew, in palace and cottage; but the increasing materialism, worldliness and hypocrisy are fast diminishing their proportionate number. Their charity, and simple, childlike faith in the infallibility of their Bible, their dogmas, and their clergy, bring into full activity all the virtues that are implanted in our common nature. We have personally known such God-fearing priests and clergymen, and we have always avoided debate with them, lest we might be guilty of the cruelty of hurting their feelings; nor would we rob a single layman of his blind confidence, if it alone made possible for him holy living and serene dying.

An analysis of religious beliefs in general, this volume is in particular directed against theological Christianity, the chief opponent of free thought. It contains not one word against the pure teachings of Jesus, but unsparingly denounces their debasement into pernicious ecclesiastical systems that are ruinous to man's faith in his immortality and his God, and subversive of all moral restraint.

We cast our gauntlet at the dogmatic theologians who would enslave both history and science; and especially at the Vatican, whose despotic pretensions have become hateful to the greater portion of enlightened Christendom. The clergy apart, none but the logician, the investigator, the dauntless explorer should meddle with books like this. Such delvers after truth have the courage of their opinions.

# ISIS UNVEILED

## PART TWO — RELIGION

### CHAPTER I

"Yea, the time cometh, that whosoever killeth you will think that he doeth God service."
—*John* xvi, 2.

"Let him be ANATHEMA . . . who shall say that human Sciences ought to be pursued in such a spirit of freedom that one may be allowed to hold as true their assertions even when opposed to revealed doctrines."
—*Ecumenical Council of 1870.*

"GLOUCESTER. — The Church! Where is it?"
—Shakespeare, *King Henry VI*, Part I, Act I, Sc. i, line 33.

IN the United States of America, sixty thousand (60,428) men are paid salaries to teach the Science of God and His relations to His creatures.

These men contract to impart to us the knowledge which treats of the existence, character and attributes of our Creator; His laws and government; the doctrines we are to believe and the duties we are to practice. Five thousand (5,141) of them,\* with the prospect of 1,273 theological students to help them in time, teach this science, according to a formula prescribed by the Bishop of Rome, to five million people. Fifty-five thousand (55,287) local and travelling ministers representing fifteen different denominations,† each contradicting the other upon more or less vital theological questions, instruct in their respective doctrines thirty-three million (33,500,000) other persons. Many of these teach according to the canons of the cis-Atlantic branch of an establishment which acknowledges a daughter of the late Duke of Kent as its spiritual

---

\* These figures are copied from the *Religious Statistics of the United States for the year 1871.*

† These are: The *Baptists, Congregationalists, Episcopalians,* Northern *Methodists,* Southern *Methodists, Methodists* various, Northern *Presbyterians,* Southern *Presbyterians, United Presbyterians, United Brethren, Brethren in Christ, Reformed Dutch, Reformed German, Reformed Presbyterians, Cumberland Presbyterians.*

head. There are many hundred thousand Jews; some thousands of Orientals of all kinds; and a very few who belong to the Greek Church. A man at Salt Lake City, with nineteen wives and more than one hundred children and grandchildren, is the supreme spiritual ruler over ninety thousand people, who believe that he is in frequent intercourse with the gods — for the Mormons are Polytheists as well as Polygamists, and their chief god is represented as living in a planet they call Kolob.

The God of the Unitarians is a bachelor; the Deity of the Presbyterians, Methodists, Congregationalists, and the other orthodox Protestant sects, a spouseless Father with one Son, who is identical with Himself. In the attempt to outvie each other in the erection of their sixty-two thousand and odd churches, prayer houses, and meeting halls in which to teach these conflicting theological doctrines, $354,485,581 have been spent. The value of the Protestant parsonages alone, in which are sheltered the disputants and their families, is roughly calculated to approximate $54,115,297. Sixteen million ($16,179,387) dollars are, moreover, contributed every year for current expenses of the Protestant denominations only. One Presbyterian church in New York cost a round million; a Catholic altar alone, one-fourth as much!

We will not mention the multitude of smaller sects, communities, and extravagantly original little heresies in this country which spring up one year to die out the next, like so many spores of fungi after a rainy day. We will not even stop to consider the alleged millions of Spiritualists; for the majority lack the courage to break away from their respective religious denominations. These are the backdoor Nicodemuses.

And now, with Pilate, let us inquire, "What is truth?" Where is it to be searched for amid this multitude of warring sects? Each claims to be based upon divine revelation, and each to have the keys of the celestial gates. Are any in possession of this rare truth? Or, must we exclaim with the Buddhist philosopher, "There is but one truth on earth, and it is unchangeable: and this is — that there is *no* truth on it!"

Though we have no disposition whatever to trench upon the ground that has been so exhaustively gleaned by those learned scholars who have shown that every Christian dogma has its origin in a heathen rite, still the facts which they have exhumed, since the enfranchisement of science, will lose nothing by repetition. Besides, we propose to examine these facts from a different and perhaps rather novel point of view: that of the old philosophies as esoterically understood. These we have barely glanced at in our first volume. We will use them as the standard by which to compare Christian dogmas and miracles with the doctrines and phenomena of ancient magic, and the modern "New Dispensation," as Spiritualism is called by its votaries. Since the materialists deny the phenomena without investigation, and since the theologians in admitting them offer us the poor choice of two palpable absurdities — the Devil and miracles — we can lose little by applying to the theurgists, and they may actually help us to throw a great light upon a very dark subject.

Professor A. Butleroff, of the Imperial University of St. Petersburg, remarks in a recent pamphlet, entitled *Mediumistic Manifestations*, as follows: "Let the facts [of modern spiritualism] belong if you will to the number of those which were more or less known by the ancients; let them be identical with those which in the dark ages gave importance to the office of Egyptian priest or Roman augur; let them even furnish the basis of the sorcery of our Siberian Shaman; . . . let them be all these, and, if they are *real facts*, it is no business of ours. All the facts in nature *belong to science*, and every addition to the store of science enriches instead of impoverishing her. If humanity has once admitted a truth, and then in the blindness of self-conceit denied it, to return to its realization is a step forward and not backward."

Since the day that modern science gave what may be considered the deathblow to dogmatic theology, by assuming the ground that religion was full of mystery, and mystery is unscientific, the mental state of the educated class has presented a curious aspect. Society seems from that time to have been ever balancing itself upon one leg, on an unseen tightrope stretched from our visible universe into the invisible one; uncertain whether the end hooked on faith in the latter might not suddenly break, and hurl it into final annihilation.

The great body of nominal Christians may be divided into three unequal portions: materialists, spiritualists and Christians proper. The materialists and spiritualists make common cause against the hierarchical pretensions of the clergy; who, in retaliation, denounce both with equal acerbity. The materialists are as little in harmony as the Christian sects themselves — the Comtists, or, as they call themselves, the Positivists, being despised and hated to the last degree by the schools of thinkers, one of which Maudsley honorably represents in England. Positivism, be it remembered, is that "religion" of the future about whose founder even Huxley has made himself wrathful in his famous lecture, *On the Physical Basis of Life*; and Maudsley felt obliged, in behalf of modern science, to express himself thus: "it is no wonder that scientific men should be anxious to disclaim Comte as their lawgiver, and to protest against such a king being set up to reign over them. Not conscious of any personal obligation to his writings — conscious how much, in some respects, he has misrepresented the spirit and pretensions of science — they repudiate the allegiance which his enthusiastic disciples would force upon them, and which popular opinion is fast coming to think a natural one. They do well in thus making a timely assertion of independence; for if it be not done soon, it will soon be too late to be done well." * When a materialistic doctrine is repudiated so strongly by two such materialists as Huxley and Maudsley, then we must think indeed that it is absurdity itself.

Among Christians there is nothing but dissension. Their various churches represent every degree of religious belief, from the omnivorous credulity of blind faith to a condescending and high-toned deference to the Deity which thinly masks an evident conviction of their own deific wisdom. All these sects believe more or less in the immortality of the soul. Some admit the intercourse between the two worlds as a fact; some entertain the opinion as a sentiment; some positively deny it; and only a few maintain an attitude of attention and expectancy.

Impatient of restraint, longing for the return of the dark ages, the Romish Church frowns at the *diabolical* manifestations, and indicates what she would do to their champions had she but the power of old. Were it not for the self-evident fact that she herself is placed by science on trial, and that she is handcuffed, she would be ready at a moment's notice to repeat in the nineteenth century the revolting scenes of former days. As to the Protestant clergy, so furious is their common hatred toward spiritualism, that as a secular paper very truly remarks: "They seem willing to undermine the public faith in all the spiritual phenomena of the past, as recorded in the *Bible*, if they can only see the pestilent modern heresy stabbed to the heart." †

Summoning back the long-forgotten memories of the Mosaic laws, the Romish Church claims the monopoly of miracles, and of the right to sit in judgment over them, as being the sole heir thereto by direct inheritance. The *Old Testament*, exiled by Colenso, his predecessors and contemporaries, is recalled from its banishment. The prophets, whom his Holiness the Pope condescends at last to place, if not on the same level with himself, at least at a less respectful distance, ‡ are dusted and cleaned. The memory of all the diabolical abracadabra is evoked anew. The blasphemous *horrors* perpetrated by Paganism, its

---

* H. Maudsley, *Body and Mind*; lecture on "The Limits of Philosophical Inquiry."

† Boston *Sunday Herald,* November 5, 1876.

‡ See the self-glorification of the present Pope in the work entitled, *Speeches of Pope Pius IX*, by Don Pasquale de Franciscis; and the famous pamphlet of that name by the Rt. Hon. W. E. Gladstone. The latter quotes from the work named the following sentence pronounced by the Pope: "My wish is that all governments should know that I am speaking in this strain . . . And I have *the right* to speak, *even more than Nathan the prophet* to David the King, *and a great deal more than Ambrose had to Theodosius"!!* [p. 148.]

phallic worship, thaumaturgical wonders wrought by Satan, human sacrifices, incantations, witchcraft, magic and sorcery are recalled and DEMONISM is confronted with *spiritualism* for mutual recognition and identification. Our modern demonologists conveniently overlook a few insignificant details, among which is the undeniable presence of heathen phallicism in the Christian symbols. A strong spiritual element of this worship may be easily demonstrated in the dogma of the Immaculate Conception of the Virgin Mother of God; and a physical element equally proved in the fetish-worship of the holy *limbs* of Sts. Cosmo and Damiano at Isernia, near Naples; a successful traffic in which *ex-votos* in wax was carried on by the clergy, annually, until barely a half century ago.*

We find it rather unwise on the part of Catholic writers to pour out their vials of wrath in such sentences as these: "In a multitude of pagodas, the phallic stone, ever and always assuming, like the Grecian *baetylos*, the brutally indecent form of the *linga* . . . the Mahâdeva." † Before casting slurs on a symbol whose profound metaphysical meaning is too much for the modern champions of that religion of sensualism *par excellence*, Roman Catholicism, to grasp, they are in duty bound to destroy their oldest churches, and change the form of the cupolas of their own temples. The Mahâdeva of Elephanta, the Round Tower of Bhagalpur, the minarets of Islam — either rounded or pointed — are the originals of the *Campanile* column of San Marco at Venice, of Rochester Cathedral, and of the modern Duomo of Milan. All of these steeples, turrets, domes, and Christian temples, are the reproductions of the primitive idea of the *lithos*, the upright phallus. "The western tower of St. Paul's Cathedral, London," says the author of *The Rosicrucians*, "is one of the double *lithoi* placed always in front of every temple, Christian as well as heathen." Moreover, in all Christian Churches, "particularly in Protestant churches, where they figure most conspicuously, the two tables of stone of the Mosaic Dispensation are placed over the altar, side by side, as a united stone, the tops of which are rounded. . . . The right stone is *masculine*, the left stone *feminine*." ‡ Therefore neither Catholics nor Protestants have a right to talk of the "indecent forms" of heathen monuments so long as they ornament their own churches with the symbols of the *Linga* and *Yoni*, and even write the laws of their God upon them.

Another detail not redounding very particularly to the honor of the Christian clergy might be recalled in the word Inquisition. The torrents

---

\* See C. W. King, *The Gnostics*, etc., and other works.
† Des Mousseaux, *Les Hauts Phénomènes de la magie*, p. 24.
‡ Hargrave Jennings, *The Rosicrucians*, 1870, pp. 231, 239.

of human blood shed by this *Christian* institution, and the number of its human sacrifices, are unparalleled in the annals of Paganism. Another still more prominent feature in which the clergy surpassed their masters, the "heathen," is *sorcery*. Certainly in no Pagan temple was black magic, in its real and true sense, more practiced than in the Vatican. While strongly supporting exorcism as an important source of revenue, they neglected magic as little as the ancient heathen. It is easy to prove that the *sortilegium*, or sorcery, was widely practiced among the clergy and monks so late as the last century, and is practiced occasionally even now.

Anathematizing every manifestation of occult nature outside the precincts of the Church, the clergy — notwithstanding proofs to the contrary — call it "the work of Satan," "the snares of the fallen angels," who "rush in and out from the bottomless pit," mentioned by John in his kabalistic *Revelation*, "from whence arises a smoke as the smoke of a great furnace." "*Intoxicated by its fumes, around this pit are daily gathering millions of Spiritualists, to worship at 'the Abyss of Baal'.*"

More than ever arrogant, stubborn and despotic, now that she has been nearly upset by modern research, not daring to interfere with the powerful champions of science, the Latin Church revenges herself upon the unpopular phenomena. A despot without a victim, is a word void of sense; a power which neglects to assert itself through outward, well-calculated effects, risks being doubted in the end. The Church has no intention to fall into the oblivion of the ancient myths, or to suffer her authority to be too closely questioned. Hence she pursues, as well as the times permit, her traditional policy. Lamenting the enforced extinction of her ally, the Holy Inquisition, she makes a virtue of necessity. The only victims now within reach are the Spiritists of France. Recent events have shown that the meek spouse of Christ never disdains to retaliate on helpless victims.

Having successfully performed her part of *deus ex machina* from behind the French Bench, which has not scrupled to disgrace itself for her, the Church of Rome sets to work and shows in the year 1876 what she can do. From the whirling tables and dancing pencils of profane Spiritualism, the Christian world is warned to turn to the divine "miracles" of Lourdes. Meanwhile, the ecclesiastical authorities utilize their time in arranging for other more easy triumphs, calculated to scare the superstitious out of their senses. So, acting under orders, the clergy hurl dramatic, if not very impressive, anathemas from every Catholic diocese; threaten right and left; excommunicate and curse. Perceiving, finally, that her thunderbolts directed even against crowned heads fall about as harmlessly as the Jupiterean lightnings of Offenbach's *Calchas*, Rome turns about in powerless fury against the victimized *protégés* of the Emperor of Russia — the unfortunate Bulgarians and Serbians. Undisturbed by evidence and sarcasm, unbaffled by proof, "the lamb of the Vatican" impartially divides his wrath between the liberals of Italy, "the impious whose breath has the stench of the sepulcher," * the "schismatic Russian *Sarmates*," and the heretics and spiritualists, "who worship at the bottomless pit where the great Dragon lies in wait."

Mr. Gladstone went to the trouble of making a catalogue of what he terms the "flowers of speech," disseminated through these Papal discourses. Let us cull a few of the chosen terms used by this vicegerent of Him who said that, "whosoever shall say, *Thou fool*, shall be in danger of hell-fire." They are selected from authentic discourses. Those who oppose the Pope are "wolves, Pharisees, thieves, liars, hypocrites, dropsical, children of Satan, sons of perdition, of sin and corruption, satellites of Satan in human flesh, monsters of hell, demons incarnate, stinking corpses, men issued from the pits of hell, traitors and Judases led by the spirit of hell; children of the deepest pits of hell," etc., etc.; the whole piously collected and published by Don Pasquale de Franciscis, whom Gladstone has, with perfect propriety, termed, "an accomplished professor of *flunkeyism* in things spiritual." †

Since his Holiness the Pope has such a rich vocabulary of invectives at his command, why wonder that the Bishop of Toulouse did not scruple to utter the most undignified falsehoods about the Protestants and Spiritualists of America — people doubly odious to a Catholic — in his address to his diocese: "Nothing," he remarks, "is more common in an era of unbelief than to see a *false revelation substitute itself for the true one,* and minds neglect the teachings of the Holy Church, to devote themselves to the study of divination and the occult sciences." With a fine episcopal contempt for statistics, and strangely confounding in his memory the audiences of the revivalists, Moody and Sankey, and the patrons of darkened *séance* rooms, he utters the unwarranted and fallacious assertion that "it has been proven that Spiritualism, in the United States, has caused one-sixth of all the cases of suicide and insanity." He says that it is not possible that the spirits "teach either an exact science, because they are lying demons, or a useful science, because the character

---

\* Don Pasquale de Franciscis, *Discorsi del Sommo Pontefice Pio IX*, Part I, p. 341.

† W. E. Gladstone, *Rome and the Newest Fashions in Religion*, p. 154 (Speeches of Pope Pius IX); London, 1875.

of the word of Satan, like Satan himself, is sterile." He warns his dear *collaborateurs*, that "the writings in favor of Spiritualism are under the ban"; and he advises them to let it be known that "to frequent spiritual circles with the intention of accepting the doctrine, is to apostatize from the Holy Church, and assume the risk of excommunication"; finally, says he, "publish the fact that the teaching of no spirit should prevail against that of the pulpit of Peter, which is the teaching of the Spirit of God Himself"!!

Aware of the many false teachings attributed by the Roman Church to the Creator, we prefer disbelieving the latter assertion. The famous Catholic theologian Tillemont assures us in his work that "all the illustrious Pagans are condemned to the eternal torments of hell, *because they lived before the time of Jesus, and, therefore, could not be benefited by the redemption*"!! * He also assures us that the Virgin Mary personally testified to this truth over her own signature in a letter to a saint. Therefore, this is also a revelation — "the Spirit of God Himself" teaching such charitable doctrines.

We have also read with great advantage the topographical descriptions of *Hell and Purgatory* in the celebrated treatise under that name by a Jesuit, the Cardinal Bellarmine.† A critic found that the author, who gives the description from a *divine* vision with which he was favored, "appears to possess all the knowledge of a land measurer" about the secret tracts and formidable divisions of the "bottomless pit." Justin Martyr having actually committed to paper the heretical thought that after all Socrates might not be altogether fixed in hell, ‡ his Benedictine editor criticizes this too benevolent father very severely. Whoever doubts the Christian charity of the Church of Rome in this direction is invited to peruse the *Censure* of the Sorbonne on Marmontel's *Bélisaire*. The *odium theologicum* blazes in it on the dark sky of orthodox theology like an aurora borealis — the precursor of God's wrath, according to the teaching of certain mediaeval divines.

We have attempted in the first part of this work to show, by historical examples, how completely men of science have deserved the stinging sarcasm of the late Professor de Morgan, who remarked of them that "they wear the priest's cast-off garb, dyed to escape detection." The Christian clergy are, in like manner, attired in the cast-off garb of the *heathen* priesthood; acting diametrically in opposition to their *God's* moral precepts, but nevertheless, sitting in judgment over the whole world.

When dying on the cross, the martyred Man of Sorrows forgave his

---

\* [L. S. le Nain de Tillemont, *Mémoires*, etc., 1693, etc.]

† [*De loco purgatorii*, in his *De Controversiis Christianae Fidei*. Cf. his *Opera*, Roan, 1619.]

‡ [Cf. *1st Apology*, ch. xlvi.]

enemies. His last words were a prayer in their behalf. He taught his disciples to curse not, but to bless, even their foes. But the heirs of St. Peter, the self-constituted representatives on earth of that same meek Jesus, unhesitatingly curse whoever resists their despotic will. Besides, was not the "Son" long since crowded by them into the background? They make their obeisance only to the Dowager Mother, for — according to their teaching — again through "the direct Spirit of God," she alone acts as a mediatrix. The Ecumenical Council of 1870 embodied the teaching into a dogma, to disbelieve which is to be doomed forever to the "bottomless pit." The work of Don Pasquale de Franciscis is positive on that point; for he tells us that, as the Queen of Heaven owes to the present Pope "the finest gem in her coronet," since he has conferred on her the unexpected honor of becoming suddenly immaculate, there is nothing she cannot obtain from her Son for "her Church." *

Some years ago, certain travellers saw in Bari, Italy, a statue of the Madonna arrayed in a flounced pink skirt over a swelling *crinoline!* Pious pilgrims who may be anxious to examine the regulation wardrobe of their God's mother may do so by going to Southern Italy, Spain, and Catholic North and South America. The Madonna of Bari must still be there — between two vineyards and a *locanda* (gin shop). When last seen, a half-successful attempt had been made to clothe the infant Jesus; they had covered his legs with a pair of dirty, scallop-edged pantaloons. An English traveller having presented the "Mediatrix" with a green silk parasol, the grateful population of the *contadini*, accompanied by the village priest, went in procession to the spot. They managed to stick the sunshade, opened, between the infant's back and the arm of the Virgin which embraced him. The scene and ceremony were both solemn and highly refreshing to our religious feelings. For there stood the image of the goddess in its niche, surrounded with a row of ever-burning lamps, the flames of which, flickering in the breeze, infect God's pure air with an offensive smell of olive oil. The Mother and Son truly represent the two most conspicuous idols of *Monotheistic* Christianity!

For a companion to the idol of the poor *contadini* of Bari, go to the rich city of Rio de Janeiro. In the Church of the Domo da Candelaria, in a long hall running along one side of the church, there might be seen, a few years ago, another Madonna. Along the walls of the hall there is a line of saints, each standing on a contribution box, which thus forms a fit pedestal. In the centre of this line, under a gorgeously rich canopy of blue silk, is exhibited the Virgin Mary leaning on the arm of Christ. "Our Lady" is arrayed in a very *décolleté* blue satin dress with short

---

* *Vide* Don Pasquale, *op. cit.*, Pt. II, pp. 325, 394; Gladstone, *op. cit.*; Draper, *Hist. of the Conflict*, etc., and other works.

sleeves showing, to great advantage, a snow-white, exquisitely-moulded neck, shoulders and arms. The skirt, equally of blue satin with an overskirt of rich lace and gauze puffs, is as short as that of a ballet dancer; hardly reaching the knee, it exhibits a pair of finely-shaped legs covered with flesh-colored silk tights, and blue satin French boots with very high red heels! The blonde hair of this "Mother of God" is arranged in the latest fashion with a voluminous *chignon* and curls. As she leans on her Son's arm, her face is lovingly turned toward her Only-Begotten, whose dress and attitude are equally worthy of admiration. Christ wears an evening dress-coat, with swallow-tail, black trousers, and low cut white vest; varnished boots and white kid gloves, *over one of which* sparkles a rich diamond ring, worth many thousands we must suppose — a precious Brazilian jewel. Above this body of a modern Portuguese dandy is a head with the hair parted in the middle; a sad and solemn face, and eyes whose patient look seems to reflect all the bitterness of this last insult flung at the majesty of the Crucified.*

The Egyptian Isis was also represented as a Virgin Mother by her devotees, and as holding her infant son, Horus, in her arms. In some statues and *basso-relievos,* when she appears alone, she is either completely nude or veiled from head to foot. But in the Mysteries, in common with nearly every other goddess, she is entirely veiled from head to foot, as a symbol of a mother's chastity. It would not do us any harm were we to borrow from the ancients some of the poetic sentiment in their religions, and the innate veneration they entertained for *their* symbols.

It is but fair to say at once that the last of the *true* Christians died with the last of the direct apostles. Max Müller forcibly asks: "How can a missionary in such circumstances meet the surprise and questions of his pupils, unless he may point to that seed, † and tell them what Christianity was meant to be; unless he may show that, like all other religions, Christianity, too, has had its history; that the Christianity of the nineteenth century is not the Christianity of the Middle Ages, that the Christianity of the Middle Ages was not that of the early Councils, that the Christianity of the early Councils was not that of the Apostles, and 'that what has been said by Christ, that alone was well said'?" ‡

Thus we may infer that the only characteristic difference between modern Christianity and the old heathen faiths is the belief of the former in a personal devil and in hell. "The Âryan nations had no Devil," says Max Müller. "Pluto, though of a sombre character, was a very

---

\* The fact is given to us by an eyewitness who has visited the church several times; a Roman Catholic, who felt perfectly *horrified,* as he expressed it.
† Referring to the seed planted by Jesus and his Apostles.
‡ *Chips from a German Workshop,* Vol. I, preface, p. xxvi.

respectable personage; and Loki [the Scandinavian], though a mischievous person, was not a fiend. The German Goddess Hel, too — like Proserpine — had once seen better days. Thus, when the Germans were indoctrinated with the idea of a real Devil, the Semitic Satan or Diabolus, they treated him in the most good-humored manner." *

The same may be said of hell. Hades was quite a different place from our region of eternal damnation, and might be termed rather an intermediate state of purification. Neither does the Scandinavian *Hel* or *Hela* imply either a state or a place of punishment; for when Frigga, the grief-stricken mother of Balder, the white god, who died and found himself in the dark abodes of the shadows (Hadês), sent Hermod, a son of Thor, in quest of her beloved child, the messenger found him in the inexorable region — alas! but still comfortably seated on a rock, and reading a book.† The Norse kingdom of the dead is moreover situated in the higher latitudes of the Polar regions; it is a cold and cheerless abode, and neither the gelid halls of Hela, nor the occupation of Balder present the least similitude to the blazing hell of eternal fire and the miserable "damned" sinners with which the Church so generously peoples it. No more is it the Egyptian *Amenti*, the region of judgment and purification; nor the *Andhera* — the abyss of darkness of the Hindus; for even the fallen angels hurled into it by Śiva are allowed by Parabrahman to consider it as an intermediate state, in which an opportunity is afforded them to prepare for higher degrees of purification and redemption from their wretched condition. The Gehenna of the *New Testament* was a locality outside the walls of Jerusalem; and in mentioning it, Jesus used but an ordinary metaphor. Whence then came the dreary dogma of hell, that Archimedean lever of Christian theology, with which they have succeeded to hold in subjection the numberless millions of Christians for nineteen centuries? Assuredly not from the Jewish Scriptures, and we appeal for corroboration to any well-informed Hebrew scholar.

The only designation of something approaching hell in the *Bible* is *Gehenna* or Hinnom, a valley near Jerusalem, where was situated Tophet, a place where a fire was perpetually kept for sanitary purposes. The prophet Jeremiah informs us that the Israelites used to sacrifice their children to Moloch-Hercules on that spot; and later we find Christians quietly replacing this divinity by their god of *mercy*, whose wrath will not be appeased unless the Church sacrifices to him her unbaptized children and sinning sons on the altar of "eternal damnation"!

Whence then did the divines learn so well the conditions of hell as

---

* *Chips*, etc., II, p. 235.
† Mallet, *Northern Antiquities*, p. 448.

to actually divide its torments into two kinds, the *poena damni* and *poena sensus*, the former being the privation of the beatific vision; the latter the eternal pains *in a lake of fire and brimstone?* If they answer us that it is in the *Apocalypse* (xx, 10), we are prepared to demonstrate whence the theologist John himself derived the idea, "And *the devil* that deceived them was cast into the lake of fire and brimstone, where *the beast* and the false prophet are and shall be tormented . . . for ever and ever," he says. Laying aside the esoteric interpretation that the "devil" or tempting demon meant our own earthly body, which after death will surely dissolve in the *fiery* or ethereal elements,* the word "eternal" by which our theologians interpret the words "for ever and ever" does not exist in the Hebrew language, either as a word or meaning. There is no Hebrew word which properly expresses *eternity*; עוֹלָם *olam*, according to Le Clerc, only imports a time whose beginning or end is not known.† While showing that this word does not mean *infinite* duration, and that in the *Old Testament* the word *forever* only signifies a long time, Archbishop Tillotson has completely perverted its sense with respect to the idea of hell-torments. According to his doctrine, when Sodom and Gomorrah are said to be suffering "eternal fire," we must understand it only in the sense of that fire not being extinguished till both cities were entirely consumed. But, as to hell-fire, the words must be understood in the strictest sense of infinite duration. Such is the decree of the learned divine. For the duration of the punishment of the wicked must be proportionate to the happiness of the righteous. So he says, "These [speaking of the wicked] *shall go away*, εἰς κόλασιν αἰώνιον, *into eternal punishment*; but the righteous, εἰς ζωὴν αἰώνιον, *into life eternal.*" ‡

The Reverend T. Swinden,§ commenting on the speculations of his predecessors, fills a whole volume with unanswerable arguments, tending to show that the locality *of Hell is in the sun*. We suspect that the reverend speculator had read the *Apocalypse* in bed, and had a nightmare in consequence. There are two verses in the *Revelation of John* reading thus: "And the fourth angel poured out his vial upon the sun, and power was given him to scorch men with fire. And men were scorched with great heat, and blasphemed the name of God." ‖ This is simply Pythagorean and kabalistic allegory. The idea is new neither with the above-mentioned author nor with John. Pythagoras placed the "sphere of purification in the sun," which sun, with its

---

\* Ether is both *pure* and *impure* fire. The composition of the latter comprises all its visible forms, such as the "correlation of forces" — heat, flame, electricity, etc. The former is the *Spirit* of Fire. The difference is purely alchemical.

† [Cf. Gesenius, *A Hebrew and English Lexicon*, s.v. Olam.]

‡ [John Tillotson, *Works*, 3rd ed., 1701, Sermon XXXV, pp. 410-11, quoting Matt. xxv, 25.]

§ Cf. Tobias Swinden, *An Inquiry into the Nature and Place of Hell*, London, 1714, 1727.

‖ *Revelation* xvi, 8-9.

sphere, he moreover locates in the middle of the universe,\* the allegory having a double meaning: 1. Symbolically, the central, spiritual sun, the Supreme Deity. Arrived at this region every soul becomes purified of its sins, and unites itself forever with its spirit, having previously suffered throughout all the lower spheres. 2. By placing the sphere of *visible* fire in the middle of the universe, he simply taught the heliocentric system which appertained to the Mysteries, and was imparted only in the higher degree of initiation. John gives to his Word a purely kabalistic significance, which no "Fathers," except those who had belonged to the Neo-Platonic school, were able to comprehend. Origen understood it well, having been a pupil of Ammonius Saccas; therefore we see him bravely denying the perpetuity of hell-torments. He maintains that not only men, but even devils (by which term he meant disembodied human sinners), after a certain duration of punishment shall be pardoned and finally restored to heaven.† In consequence of this and other such heresies Origen was, as a matter of course, exiled.

Many have been the learned and truly inspired speculations as to the locality of hell. The most popular were those which placed it in the centre of the earth. At a certain time, however, skeptical doubts which disturbed the placidity of faith in this highly-refreshing doctrine arose in consequence of the meddling scientists of those days. As the Rev. Tobias Swinden in our own century observes, the theory was inadmissible because of two objections: "1st, that a fund of fuel or sulphur, sufficient to maintain so furious and constant a fire cannot be there supposed; and, 2nd, that it must want the nitrous particles in the air, to sustain and keep it alive." "And how," says he, "can such fire be eternal, when by degrees, the whole substance of the earth must be consumed thereby?" ‡

The skeptical gentleman had evidently forgotten that centuries ago St. Augustine solved the difficulty. Have we not the word of this learned divine that hell, nevertheless, *is* in the centre of the earth, for "God supplies the central fire with air, *by a miracle*"? The argument is unanswerable, and so we will not seek to upset it. §

The Christians were the first to make the existence of Satan a dogma of the Church. And once that she had established it, she had to struggle for over 1,700 years for the repression of a mysterious force which it was her policy to make appear of diabolical origin. Unfortunately, in manifesting itself, this force invariably tends to upset such a belief by the ridiculous discrepancy it presents between the alleged cause and the effects. If the clergy

---

\* Aristotle mentions Pythagoreans who placed the sphere of fire in the sun, and named it *Jupiter's Prison.* See *De caelo,* lib. II, 293 b.
† Origen, *De princ.,* I, vi. Cf. Augustine, *De civitate Dei,* xxi, xvii.
‡ *Demonologia,* London, 1827, p. 289.
§ [Swinden, *op. cit.,* p. 75.]

have not over-estimated the real power of the "Arch-Enemy of God," it must be confessed that he takes mighty precautions against being recognized as the "Prince of Darkness" who aims at our souls. If modern "spirits" are devils at all, as preached by the clergy, then they can only be those "poor" or "stupid devils" whom Max Müller describes as appearing so often in the German and Norwegian tales.

Notwithstanding this, the clergy fear above all to be forced to relinquish this hold on humanity. They are not willing to let us judge of the tree by its fruit, for that might sometimes force them into dangerous dilemmas. They refuse, likewise, to admit, with unprejudiced people, that the phenomena of Spiritualism have unquestionably spiritualized and reclaimed from evil courses many an indomitable atheist and skeptic. But, as they confess themselves, what is the use in a Pope if there is no Devil?

And so Rome sends her ablest advocates and preachers to the rescue of those perishing in "the bottomless pit." Rome employs her cleverest writers for this purpose — albeit they all indignantly deny the accusation — and in the preface to every book put forth by the prolific des Mousseaux, the French Tertullian of our century, we find undeniable proofs of the fact. Among other certificates of ecclesiastical approval, every volume is ornamented with the text of a certain original letter addressed to the very pious author by the world-known Father Ventura di Raulica, of Rome. Few are those who have not heard this famous name. It is the name of one of the chief pillars of the Latin Church, the ex-General of the Order of the Theatines, Consultor of the Sacred Congregation of Rites, Examiner of Bishops, and of the Roman Clergy, etc., etc., etc. This strikingly characteristic document will remain to astonish future generations by its spirit of unsophisticated demonolatry and unblushing sincerity. We translate a fragment verbatim, and by thus helping its circulation hope to merit the blessings of Mother Church: *

"MONSIEUR AND EXCELLENT FRIEND:
. . . . . . .
"The greatest victory of Satan was gained on that day when he succeeded in making himself denied.
"To demonstrate the existence of Satan, is to re-establish *one of the fundamental dogmas of the Church*, which serve as a basis for Christianity, and, without which, Satan would be but a name. . . .
"Magic, mesmerism, magnetism, somnambulism, spiritism, hypnotism . . . are only other names for SATANISM.
"To bring out such a truth and show it in its proper light, is to unmask the enemy; it is to unveil the immense danger of certain practices, *reputed innocent;* it is to deserve well in the eyes of humanity and of religion . . .
"FATHER VENTURA DI RAULICA."

---

* *Les Hauts Phénomènes de la magie,* p. iv; cf. *La Magie au XIXme siècle,* p. i.

A—men!

This is an unexpected honor indeed, for our American "controls" in general, and the innocent "Indian guides" in particular. To be thus introduced in Rome as princes of the Empire of Eblis, is more than they could ever hope for in other lands.

Without in the least suspecting that she was working for the future welfare of her enemies — the spiritualists and spiritists — the Church, some twenty years since, in tolerating des Mousseaux and de Mirville as the biographers of the Devil, and giving her approbation thereto, tacitly confessed the literary copartnership.

The Chevalier Gougenot des Mousseaux, and his friend and *collaborateur*, the Marquis Eudes de Mirville, to judge by their long titles, must be aristocrats *pur sang*, and they are, moreover, writers of no small erudition and talent. Were they to show themselves a little more parsimonious of double points of exclamation following every vituperation and invective against Satan and his worshippers, their style would be faultless. As it is, the crusade against the enemy of mankind was fierce, and lasted for over twenty years.

What with the Catholics piling up their psychological phenomena to prove the existence of a personal devil, and the Count de Gasparin, an ancient minister of Louis Philippe, collecting volumes of other facts to prove the contrary, the spiritists of France have contracted an everlasting debt of gratitude toward the disputants. The existence of an unseen spiritual universe peopled with invisible beings has now been demonstrated beyond question. Ransacking the oldest libraries, they have distilled from the historical records the quintessence of evidence. All epochs, from the Homeric ages down to the present day, have supplied their choicest materials to these indefatigable authors. In trying to prove the authenticity of the miracles wrought by Satan in the days preceding the Christian era, as well as throughout the middle ages, they have simply laid a firm foundation for a study of the phenomena in our modern times.

Though an ardent, uncompromising enthusiast, des Mousseaux unwittingly transforms himself into the tempting demon, or — as he is fond of calling the Devil — the "serpent of *Genesis*." In his desire to demonstrate in every manifestation the presence of the Evil One, he only succeeds in demonstrating that Spiritualism and magic are not new things in the world, but very ancient twin brothers, whose origin must be sought for in the earliest infancy of ancient India, Chaldea, Babylonia, Egypt, Persia and Greece.

He proves the existence of "spirits," whether these be angels or devils, with such a clearness of argument and logic, and such an amount of evidence, historical, irrefutable, and strictly authenticated, that little is left for spiritualist authors who may come after him. How unfortunate that the scientists, who believe neither in devil nor spirit, are more than likely to ridicule des Mousseaux's books without reading them, for they really contain so many facts of profound scientific interest!

But what can we expect in our own age of unbelief, when we find Plato, over twenty-two centuries ago, complaining of the same? "Me, too," says he, in his *Euthyphron*, "when I say anything in the public assembly concerning divine things, *and predict to them* what is going to happen, they ridicule as mad; and although *nothing that I have predicted has proved untrue*, yet they envy all such men as we are. However, we ought not to heed, but pursue our own way." *

The literary resources of the Vatican and other Catholic repositories of learning must have been freely placed at the disposal of these modern authors. When one has such treasures at hand — original manuscripts, papyri and books pillaged from the richest heathen libraries; old treatises on magic and alchemy; and records of all the trials for witchcraft, and sentences for the same to rack, stake and torture, it is mighty easy to write volumes of accusations against the Devil. We affirm on good grounds that there are hundreds of the most valuable works on the occult sciences, which are sentenced to eternal concealment from the public, but are attentively read and studied by the privileged who have access to the Vatican Library. The laws of nature are the same for heathen sorcerer as for Catholic saint; and a "miracle" may be produced as well by one as by the other, without the slightest intervention of God or devil.

Hardly had the manifestations begun to attract attention in Europe, than the clergy commenced their outcry that their traditional enemy had reappeared under another name, and "divine miracles" also began to be heard of in isolated instances. First they were confined to humble individuals, some of whom claimed to have them produced through the intervention of the Virgin Mary, saints and angels; others — according to the clergy — began to suffer from *obsession* and *possession;* for the Devil must have his share of fame as well as the Deity. Finding that notwithstanding the warning, the *independent* or so-called spiritual phenomena went on increasing and multiplying, and that these manifestations threatened to upset the carefully constructed dogmas of the Church, the world was suddenly startled by extraordinary intelligence. In 1864, a whole community became possessed by the Devil. Morzine, and the awful stories of its demoniacs; Valleyres, and the narratives of its well-authenticated exhibitions of sorcery; and those of the Presbytère de Cideville curdled the blood in Catholic veins.

Strange to say, the question has been asked over and over again,

---

* [*Euthyphron*, St. I, 3 C.]

why the "divine" miracles and most of the obsessions are so strictly confined to Roman Catholic dioceses and countries? Why is it that since the Reformation there has been scarcely one single divine "miracle" in a Protestant land? Of course, the answer we must expect from Catholics is that the latter are peopled by *heretics,* and abandoned by God. Then why are there no more Church-miracles in Russia, a country whose religion differs from the Roman Catholic faith but in external forms of rites, its fundamental dogmas being identically the same, except as to the emanation of the Holy Ghost? Russia has her accepted saints and thaumaturgical relics, and miracle-working images. The St. Mitrophan of Voronezh is an authenticated miracle-worker, but his miracles are limited to healing; and though hundreds upon hundreds have been healed *through faith,* and though the old cathedral is full of magnetic effluvia, and whole generations will go on *believing* in his power, and some persons will always be healed, still no such miracles are heard of in Russia as the Madonna-walking, and Madonna letter-writing, and statue-talking of Catholic countries. Why is this so? Simply because the emperors have strictly forbidden that sort of thing. The Czar, Peter the Great, stopped every spurious "divine" miracle with one frown of his mighty brow. He declared he would have *no false* miracles played by the holy *icones* (images of saints), and they disappeared forever.*

There are cases on record of isolated and independent phenomena exhibited by certain images in the last century; the latest was the bleeding of the cheek of an image of the Virgin, when a soldier of Napoleon cut her face in two. This miracle, alleged to have happened in 1812, in the days of the invasion by the "grand army," was the final farewell.†

---

* Dr. A. P. Stanley, *Lectures on the Hist. of the Eastern Church,* p. 407; lect. xii.

† In the government of Tambov, a gentleman, a rich landed proprietor, had a curious case happen in his family during the Hungarian campaign of 1848. His only and much-beloved nephew, whom, having no children, he had adopted as a son, was in the Russian army. The elderly couple had a portrait of him — a water-color painting — constantly, during the meals, placed on the table in front of the young man's usual seat. One evening as the family, with some friends, were at their early tea, the glass over the portrait, without anyone touching it, was shattered to atoms with a loud explosion. As the aunt of the young soldier caught the picture in her hand she saw the forehead and head besmeared with blood. The guests, in order to quiet her, attributed the blood to her having cut her fingers, with the broken glass. But, examine as they would, they could not find the vestige of a cut on her fingers, and no one had touched the picture but herself. Alarmed at her state of excitement, the husband, pretending to examine the portrait more closely, cut his finger on purpose, and then tried to assure her that *it was his* blood and that, in the first excitement, he had touched the frame without anyone remarking it. All was in vain, the old lady felt sure that Dimitry was killed. She began to have masses said for him daily at the village church, and arrayed the whole

But since then, although the three successive emperors have been pious men, their will has been respected, and the images and saints have remained quiet, and hardly been spoken of except as connected with religious worship. In Poland, a land of furious ultramontanism, there were, at different times, desperate attempts at miracle-doing. They died at birth, however, for the argus-eyed police were there, a Catholic miracle in Poland, made public by the priests, generally meaning political revolution, bloodshed and war.

Is it then, not permissible to at least suspect that if, in one country divine miracles may be arrested by civil and military law, and in another they *never occur*, we must search for the explanation of the two facts in some natural cause, instead of attributing them to either god or devil? In our opinion — if it is worth anything — the whole secret may be accounted for as follows. In Russia, the clergy know better than to bewilder their parishes, whose piety is sincere and faith strong without miracles; they know that nothing is better calculated than the latter to sow seeds of distrust, doubt, and finally of skepticism which leads directly to atheism. Moreover the climate is less propitious, and the magnetism of the average population too positive, *too healthy*, to call forth *independent* phenomena; and fraud would not answer. On the other hand, neither in Protestant Germany, nor England, nor yet in America, since the days of the Reformation, has the clergy had access to any of the Vatican secret libraries. Hence they are all but poor hands at the magic of Albertus Magnus.

As for America being overflowed with sensitives and mediums, the reason for it is partially attributable to climatic influence and especially to the physiological condition of the population. Since the days of the Salem witchcraft 200 years ago, when the comparatively few settlers had pure and unadulterated blood in their veins, nothing much had been heard of "spirits" or "mediums" until 1840.* The phenomena then first appeared among the ascetic and exalted Shakers, whose religious aspirations, peculiar mode of life, moral purity, and physical chastity all led to the production of independent phenomena of a psychological

---

household in deep mourning. Several weeks later, an official communication was received from the colonel of the regiment, stating that their nephew was killed by a fragment of a shell which had carried off the upper part of his head.

\* Executions for witchcraft took place, not much later than a century ago, in other of the American provinces. Notoriously there were negroes executed in New Jersey by burning at the stake — the penalty denounced in several States. Even in South Carolina, in 1865, when the State government was "reconstructed," after the Civil War, the statutes inflicting death for witchcraft were found to be still unrepealed. It is not a hundred years since they have been enforced to the murderous letter of their text.

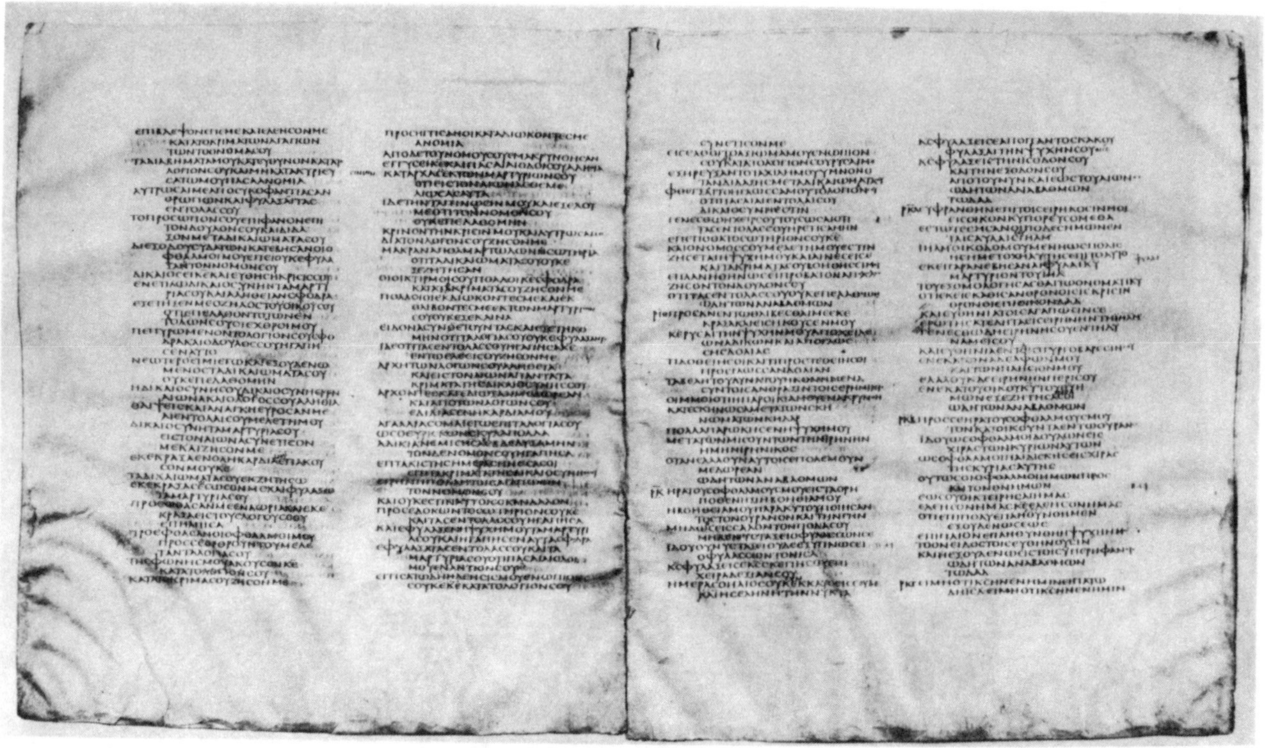

CODEX SINAITICUS. PSALMS CXVIII, 132—CXIII, 2
(*Psalms* cxix, 132—cxxiv, 1 in the English Psalter)
Reproduced from the original in the British Museum.

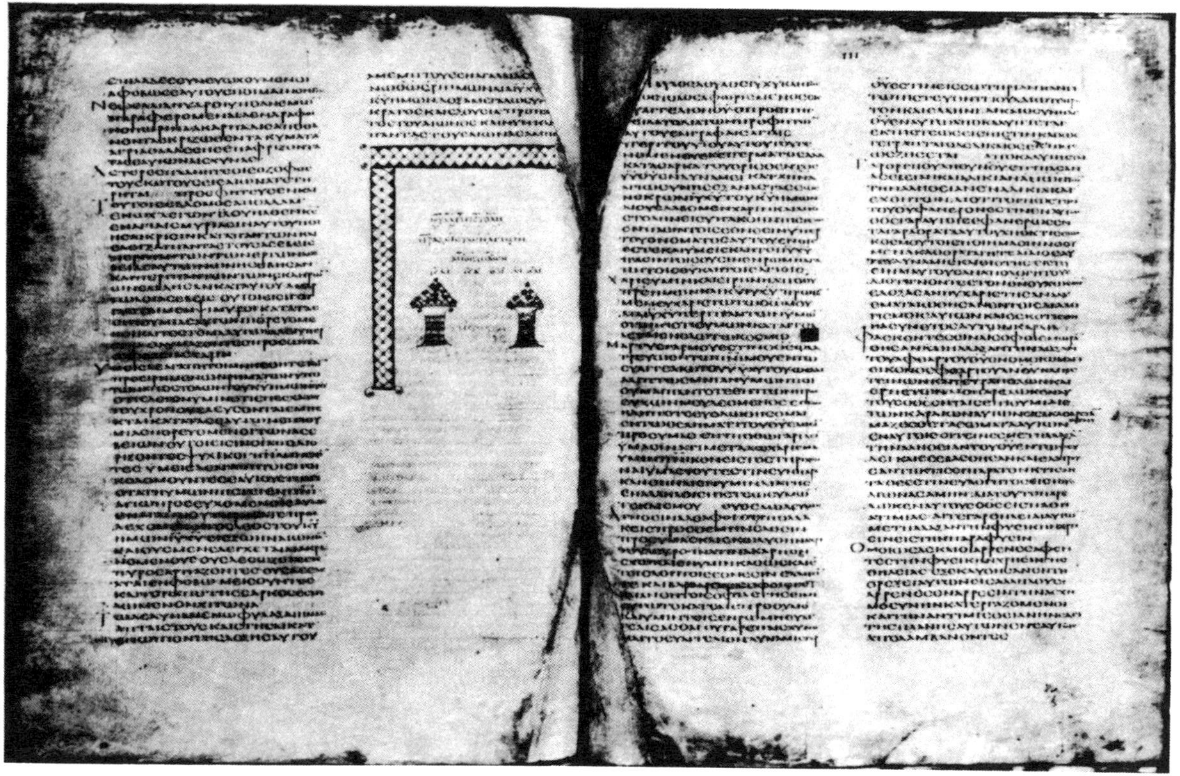

Codex Alexandrinus. Jude 12-25 (end); Romans I, 1-27
Reproduced from the original in the British Museum.

as well as physical nature. Hundreds of thousands, and even millions of men from various climates and of different constitutions and habits, have, since 1492, invaded North America, and by intermarrying have substantially changed the physical type of the inhabitants. Of what country in the world do the women's constitutions bear comparison with the delicate, nervous and sensitive constitutions of the feminine portion of the population of the United States? We were struck on our arrival in the country with the semi-transparent delicacy of skin of the natives of both sexes. Compare a hard-working Irish factory girl or boy, with one from a genuine American family. Look at their hands. One works as hard as the other; they are of equal age, and both seemingly healthy; and still, while the hands of the one, after an hour's soaping, will show a skin little softer than that of a young alligator, those of the other, notwithstanding constant use, will allow you to observe the circulation of the blood under the thin and delicate epidermis. No wonder, then, that while America is the conservatory of sensitives, the majority of its clergy, unable to produce divine or any other miracles, stoutly deny the possibility of any phenomena except those produced by tricks and juggling. And no wonder also that the Catholic priesthood, who are practically aware of the existence of magic and spiritual phenomena, and believe in them while dreading their consequences, try to attribute the whole to the agency of the Devil.

Let us adduce one more argument, if only for the sake of circumstantial evidence. In what countries have "divine miracles" flourished most, been most frequent and most stupendous? Catholic Spain and Pontifical Italy, beyond question. And which more than these two has had access to ancient literature? Spain was famous for her libraries; the Moors were celebrated for their profound learning in alchemy and other sciences. The Vatican is the storehouse of an immense number of ancient manuscripts. During the long interval of nearly 1,500 years they have been accumulating, from trial after trial, books and manuscripts confiscated from their sentenced victims, to their own profit. The Catholics may plead that the books were generally committed to the flames; that the treatises of famous sorcerers and enchanters perished with their accursed authors. But the Vatican, if it could speak, could tell a different story. It knows too well of the existence of certain closets and rooms, access to which is had but by the very few. It knows that the entrances to these secret hiding places are so cleverly concealed from sight in the carved framework and under the profuse ornamentation of the library walls, that there have even been Popes who lived and died within the precincts of the palace without ever suspecting their existence. But these Popes were neither Sylvester II, Benedict IX, John XX, nor the VIth and the VIIth Gregory; nor yet the famous Borgia of toxicological memory. Nor were those who remained ignorant of the hidden lore friends of the sons of Loyola.

Where, in the records of European Magic, can we find cleverer enchanters than in the mysterious solitudes of the cloister? Albertus Magnus, the famous Bishop and conjurer of Ratisbon, was never surpassed in his art. Roger Bacon was a monk, and Thomas Aquinas one of the most learned pupils of Albertus. Trithemius, Abbot of the Sponheim Benedictines,[2] was the teacher, friend and confidant of Cornelius Agrippa; and while the confederations of the Theosophists were scattered broadcast about Germany, where they first originated, assisting one another, and struggling for years for the acquirement of esoteric knowledge, any person who knew how to become the favored pupil of certain monks, might very soon be proficient in all the important branches of occult learning.

This is all in history and cannot be easily denied. Magic, in all its aspects, was widely and nearly openly practiced by the clergy till the Reformation. And even he who was once called the "Father of the Reformation," the famous John Reuchlin,* author of the *Mirific Word* and friend of Pico della Mirandola, the teacher and instructor of Erasmus, Luther, and Melanchthon, was a kabalist and occultist.

The ancient *sortilegium*, or divination by means of *sortes* or lots — an art and practice now decried by the clergy as an abomination, designated by *Stat. 10, Jac.* as felony, and by *Stat. 12, Caroli* II excepted out of the general pardons, on the ground of being *sorcery* †— was widely practiced by the clergy and monks. Nay, it was sanctioned by St. Augustine himself, who does not "disapprove of this method of learning futurity, provided it be not used for worldly purposes." More than that, he confesses having practiced it himself. ‡

Aye; but the clergy called it *sortes sanctorum*, when it was they who practiced it; while the *sortes praenestinae*, succeeded by the *sortes Homericae* and *sortes Virgilianae*, were abominable *heathenism*, the worship of the Devil, when used by anyone else.

Gregory of Tours informs us that when the clergy resorted to the *sortes* their custom was to lay the *Bible* on the altar, and to pray the Lord that He would discover His will, and disclose to them futurity in one of the verses of the book. § Guibert de Nogent writes that in his day

---

* *Vide* the title page of the English translation of Mayerhoff's *Johann Reuchlin und seine Zeit*, Berlin, 1830. *The Life and Times of John Reuchlin, or Capnion, the Father of the German Reformation*, by F. Barham, London, 1843.

† Lord Coke, 3 *Institutes*, fol. 44.

‡ [*Epistle II to Januarius*, §37.]

§ *Histoire des François, de S. Grégoire, évêque de Tours*, Paris, 1668, II, 37; V, 14, etc.

(about the twelfth century) the custom was, at the consecration of bishops, to consult the *sortes sanctorum*, to thereby learn the success and fate of the episcopate. On the other hand, we are told that the *sortes sanctorum* were condemned by the Council of Agde in 506. In this case again we are left to inquire, in which instance has the infallibility of the Church failed? Was it when she prohibited that which was practiced by her greatest saint and patron, Augustine, or in the twelfth century, when it was openly and with the sanction of the same Church practiced by the clergy for the benefit of the bishop's elections? Or, must we still believe that in both of these contradictory cases the Vatican was inspired by the direct "spirit of God"?

If any doubt that Gregory of Tours approved of a practice that prevails to this day, more or less, even among strict Protestants, let them read this: "Leudastus, Earl of Tours, who was for ruining me with Queen Fredegond, coming to Tours, big with evil designs against me, I withdrew to my oratory under a deep concern, where I took the *Psalms*. . . . My heart revived within me when I cast my eyes on this of the seventy-seventh *Psalm:* 'He caused them to go on with confidence, whilst the sea swallowed up their enemies.' Accordingly, the Count spoke not a word to my prejudice; and leaving Tours that very day, the boat in which he was, sank in a storm, but his skill in swimming saved him." *

The sainted bishop simply confesses here to having practiced a bit of sorcery. *Every mesmerizer knows the power of will during an intense desire bent on any particular subject.* Whether in consequence of "coincidents" or otherwise, the opened verse suggested to his mind revenge by drowning. Passing the remainder of the day in "deep concern," and possessed by this all-absorbing thought, the saint — it may be unconsciously — exercises his will on the subject; and thus while imagining in the accident the hand of God, he simply becomes a sorcerer exercising his magnetic will which reacts on the person feared; and the count barely escapes with his life. Were the accident decreed by God, the culprit would have been drowned; for a simple bath could not have altered his malevolent resolution against St. Gregory had he been very intent on it.

Furthermore, we find anathemas fulminated against this lottery of fate at the council of Vannes, which forbids "all ecclesiastics, under pain of excommunication, to perform that kind of divination, or to pry into futurity, by looking into any book, or writing, whatsoever." The same prohibition is pronounced at the councils of Agde in 506, of Orleans in 511, of Auxerre in 578, and finally at the council of Aenham in 1110; [3] the latter condemning "sorcerers, witches, diviners, such as occasioned death by magical operations, and who practiced fortune-telling by the

---

* [Forsyth, *Demonologia*, 1827, p. 76.]

holy book lots"; and the complaint of the joint clergy against de Garlande, their bishop at Orleans, and addressed to Pope Alexander III, concludes in this manner: "Let your apostolical hands put on strength to *strip naked* the iniquity of this man; that the curse prognosticated on the day of his consecration, may overtake him; for the gospels being opened, *according to custom*, the first words were: *And the young man, leaving his linen cloth, fled from them naked.*" \*

Why then roast the lay magicians and consulters of books, and canonize the ecclesiastics? Simply because the mediaeval as well as the modern phenomena, manifested through laymen, whether produced through occult knowledge or happening independently, upset the claims of both the Catholic and Protestant Churches to divine miracles. In the face of reiterated and unimpeachable evidence it became impossible for the former to maintain successfully the assertion that seemingly miraculous manifestations by the "good angels" and God's direct intervention could be produced exclusively by her chosen ministers and holy saints. Neither could the Protestant well maintain on the same ground that miracles had ended with the apostolic ages. For, whether of the same nature or not, the modern phenomena claimed close kinship with the Biblical ones. The magnetists and healers of our century came into direct and open competition with the apostles. The Zouave Jacob, of France, had outrivalled the prophet Elijah in recalling to life persons who were seemingly dead; and Alexis Didier, the somnambulist, mentioned by Mr. Wallace in his work,† was, by his lucidity, putting to shame apostles, prophets, and the Sibyls of old. Since the burning of the last witch, the great Revolution of France, so elaborately prepared by the league of the secret societies and their clever emissaries, had blown over Europe and awakened terror in the bosom of the clergy. It had, like a destroying hurricane, swept away in its course those best allies of the Church, the Roman Catholic aristocracy. A sure foundation was now laid for the right of individual opinion. The world was freed from ecclesiastical tyranny by opening an unobstructed path to Napoleon the Great, who had given the deathblow to the Inquisition. This great slaughterhouse of the Christian Church — wherein she butchered, in the name of the Lamb, all the sheep arbitrarily declared scurvy — was in ruins, and she found herself left to her own responsibility and resources.

So long as the phenomena had appeared only sporadically, she had always felt herself powerful enough to repress the consequences. Super-

---

\* Translated from the original document in the Archives of Orléans, France; also see "Sortes — Sortilegium" in *Demonologia*, p. 279, and *Lettres de Pierre de Blois*, Paris, 1667.

† *On Miracles and Modern Spiritualism*, p. 65.

stition and belief in the Devil were as strong as ever, and Science had not yet dared to publicly measure her forces with those of supernatural Religion. Meanwhile the enemy had slowly but surely gained ground. All at once it broke out with an unexpected violence. "Miracles" began to appear in full daylight, and passed from their mystic seclusion into the domain of natural law, where the profane hand of Science was ready to strip off their sacerdotal mask. Still, for a time, the Church held her position, and with the powerful help of superstitious fear checked the progress of the intruding force. But, when in succession appeared mesmerists and somnambulists, reproducing the physical and mental phenomenon of ecstasy, hitherto believed to be the special gift of saints; when the passion for the turning tables had reached in France and elsewhere its climax of fury; when the psychography — alleged spiritual — from a simple curiosity had developed itself and settled into an unabated interest, and finally ebbed into religious mysticism; when the echoes aroused by the first raps at Rochester, crossing the oceans, spread until they were repercussed from nearly every corner of the world — then, and only then, the Latin Church was fully awakened to a sense of danger. Wonder after wonder was reported to have occurred in the spiritual circles and the lecture rooms of the mesmerists; the sick were healed, the blind made to see, the lame to walk, the deaf to hear. J. R. Newton in America, and Du Potet in France, were healing the multitude without the slightest claim to divine intervention. The great discovery of Mesmer, which reveals to the earnest inquirer the mechanism of nature, mastered, as if by magical power, organic and inorganic bodies.

But this was not the worst. A more direful calamity for the Church occurred in the evocation from the upper and nether worlds of a multitude of "spirits," whose private bearing and conversation gave the direct lie to the most cherished and profitable dogmas of the Church. These "spirits" claimed to be the identical entities, in a disembodied state, of fathers, mothers, sons and daughters, friends and acquaintances of the persons viewing the weird phenomena. The Devil seemed to have no objective existence, and this struck at the very foundation upon which the chair of St. Peter rested.* Not a spirit except the mocking manni-

---

\* There were two chairs of the titular apostle at Rome. The clergy, frightened at the uninterrupted evidence furnished by scientific research, at last decided to confront the enemy, and we find the *Chronique des Arts* giving the cleverest, and at the same time most *Jesuitical*, explanation of the fact. According to their story, "The *increase in the number of the faithful* decided Peter upon making Rome henceforth the centre of his action. The cemetery of Ostrianum was too distant and would *not suffice for the reunions of the Christians*. The motive which had induced the Apostle to confer on *Linus and Cletus* successively the episcopal character, in order to render them capable

kins of Planchette would confess to the most distant relationship with the Satanic majesty, or accredit him with the governorship of a single inch of territory. The clergy felt their prestige growing weaker every day, as they saw the people impatiently shaking off, in the broad daylight of truth, the dark veils with which they had been blindfolded for so many centuries. Then finally, fortune, which previously had been on their side in the long-waged conflict between theology and science, deserted to their adversary. The help of the latter to the study of the occult side of nature was truly precious and timely, and science has unwittingly widened the once narrow path of the phenomena into a broad highway. Had not

---

of sharing the solicitudes of a church whose extent was to be without limits, led naturally to a multiplication of the places of meeting. The particular residence of Peter was therefore fixed at Viminal; and there was established that mysterious Chair, the symbol of power and truth. The august seat which was venerated at the Ostrian Catacombs was not, however, removed. Peter still visited this cradle of the Roman Church, and often, without doubt, exercised his holy functions there. A *second* Chair, expressing the same mystery as the first, was set up at Cornelia, and it is this which has come down to us through the ages." ["La fête de la chaire de saint Pierre," 1876, pp. 47-48, 73.]

Now, so far from it being possible that there ever were two genuine chairs of this kind, the majority of critics show that Peter never was at Rome at all; the reasons are many and unanswerable. Perhaps we had best begin by pointing to the works of Justin Martyr. This great champion of Christianity, writing in the early part of the second century *in Rome*, where he fixed his abode, eager to get hold of the least proof in favor of the truth for which he suffered, seems *perfectly unconscious of St. Peter's existence!!*

Neither does any other writer of any consequence mention him in connection with the Church of Rome, earlier than the days of Irenaeus, when the latter set himself to invent a new religion, drawn from the depths of his imagination. We refer the reader anxious to learn more to the able work of Mr. George Reber, entitled *The Christ of Paul*. The arguments of this author are conclusive. The above article in the *Chronique des Arts*, speaks of the *increase* of the faithful to such an extent that Ostrianum could not contain the number of Christians. Now, if Peter was at Rome at all — runs Mr. Reber's argument — it must have been between the years A.D. 64 and 69; for at 64 he was at Babylon, from whence he wrote epistles and letters to Rome, and at some time between 64 and 68 (the reign of Nero) he either died a martyr or in his bed, for Irenaeus makes him deliver the Church of Rome, together with Paul (!?) (whom he persecuted and quarreled with all his life), into the hands of *Linus*, who became bishop in 69 (see Reber's *The Christ of Paul*, p. 122). We will treat of it more fully in chapter iii.

Now, we ask, in the name of common sense, how could the *faithful* of Peter's Church *increase* at such a rate, when Nero trapped and killed them like so many mice during his reign? History shows the few Christians fleeing from Rome, wherever they could, to avoid the persecution of the emperor, and the *Chronique des Arts* makes them increase and multiply! "Christ," the article goes on to say, "willed that this visible sign of the doctrinal authority of his vicar should also have its portion of immortality; one can follow it from age to age in the documents of the Roman Church." Tertullian formally attests its existence in his book *De praescr. haeret.*, xxxvi. Eager to learn everything concerning so interesting a subject, we would like to be shown when

this conflict culminated at the nick of time, we might have seen reproduced on a miniature scale the disgraceful scenes of the episodes of Salem witchcraft and the nuns of Loudun. As it was, the clergy were muzzled.

But if science has unintentionally helped the progress of the occult phenomena, the latter have reciprocally aided science herself. Until the days when newly-reincarnated philosophy boldly claimed its place in the world, there had been but few scholars who had undertaken the difficult task of studying comparative theology. This science occupies a domain heretofore penetrated by few explorers. The necessity which it involved of being well-acquainted with the dead languages, necessarily limited the number of students. Besides, there was less popular need for it so long as people could not replace the Christian orthodoxy by something more tangible. It is one of the most undeniable facts of psychology, that the average man can as little exist out of a religious element of some kind, as a fish out of the water. The voice of truth, a voice stronger than "the voice of the mightiest thunder," speaks to the inner man in the nineteenth century of the Christian era, as it spoke in the corresponding century B.C. It is a useless and unprofitable task to offer to humanity the choice between a future life and annihilation. The only chance that remains for those friends of human progress who seek to establish for the good of mankind a faith, henceforth stripped entirely of superstition

---

did *Christ* WILL anything of the kind? However: "Ornaments of ivory have been fitted to the front and back of the chair, but only on those parts repaired with acacia-wood. Those which cover the panel in front are divided into three superimposed rows, each containing six plaques of ivory, on which are engraved various subjects, among others the 'Labors of Hercules'. Several of the plaques were wrongly placed, and seemed to have been affixed to the chair at a time when the remains of antiquity were employed as ornaments, without much regard to fitness." This is the point. The article was written simply as a clever answer to several facts published during the present century. Bower, in his *History of the Popes* (Vol. I, p. 7), narrates that in the year 1662, while cleaning one of the chairs, "the Twelve Labors of Hercules unluckily appeared engraved on it," after which the chair was removed and another substituted. But in 1795, when Bonaparte's troops occupied Rome, the chair was again examined. This time there was found the Mohammedan confession of faith, in Arabic letters: "There is no Deity but Allah, and Mohammed is his Apostle." (See appendix, pp. 96-97, to *Ancient Symbol-Worship*, by H. M. Westropp and C. Staniland Wake.) In the appendix Prof. Alexander Wilder very justly remarks as follows: "We presume that the 'apostle of the circumcision,' as Paul, his great rival, styles him, was never at the Imperial City, nor had a successor there, not even in the Ghetto. The 'Chair of Peter', therefore, is *sacred* rather than apostolical. Its sanctity proceeded, however, from the esoteric religion of the former times of Rome. The hierophant of the Mysteries probably occupied it on the day of initiations, when exhibiting to the candidates the *petroma* [stone tablet containing the last revelation made by the hierophant to the neophyte for initiation]."

and dogmatic fetters, is to address them in the words of Joshua: "Choose ye this day whom ye will serve; whether the gods which your fathers served that were on the other side of the flood, or the gods of the Amorites, in whose land ye dwell." \*

"The Science of Religion," wrote Max Müller in 1860, "is only just beginning. . . . During the last fifty years the authentic documents of the most important religions of the world *have been recovered in a most unexpected and almost miraculous manner.*† We have now before us the canonical books of Buddhism; the *Zend-Avesta* of Zoroaster is no longer a sealed book; and the hymns of the *Rig-Veda* have revealed a state of religions anterior to the first beginnings of that mythology which in Homer and Hesiod stands before us as a mouldering ruin." ‡

In their insatiable desire to extend the dominion of blind faith, the early architects of Christian theology had been forced to conceal, as much as it was possible, the true sources of the same. To this end they are said to have burned or otherwise destroyed all the original manuscripts on the *Kabala*, magic and occult sciences upon which they could lay their hands. They ignorantly supposed that the most dangerous writings of this class had perished with the last Gnostic; but some day they may discover their mistake. Other authentic and as important documents will perhaps reappear in a "most unexpected and almost miraculous manner."

---

\* *Joshua* xxiv, 15.

† One of the most surprising facts that has come under our observation, is that students of profound research should not couple the frequent recurrence of these "unexpected and almost miraculous" discoveries of important documents, at the most opportune moments, with a premeditated design. Is it so strange that the custodians of "Pagan" lore, seeing that the proper moment had arrived, should cause the needed document, book, or relic to fall as if by accident in the right man's way? Geological surveyors and explorers even as competent as Humboldt and Tschudi, have not discovered the hidden mines from which the Peruvian Incas dug their treasure, although the latter confesses that the present degenerate Indians have the secret. In 1839, Perring, the archaeologist, proposed to the sheik of an Arab village two purses of gold, if he helped him to discover the entrance to the hidden passage leading to the sepulchral chambers in the North Pyramid of Dahshûr. But though his men were out of employment and half-starved, the sheik proudly refused to "sell the secret of the dead," promising to show it *gratis,* when *the time would come for it*. Is it, then, impossible that in some other regions of the earth are guarded the remains of that glorious literature of the past, which was the fruit of its majestic civilization? What is there so surprising in the idea? Who knows but that as the Christian Church has unconsciously begotten free thought by reaction against her own cruelty, rapacity and dogmatism, the public mind may be glad to follow the lead of the Orientalists, away from Jerusalem and towards Ellora; and that then much more will be discovered that is now hidden?[4]

‡ *Chips from a German Workshop,* Vol. I, "Semitic Monotheism," pp. 377-78.

There are strange traditions current in various parts of the East — on Mount Athos and in the Desert of Nitria, for instance — among certain monks, and with learned Rabbis in Palestine, who pass their lives in commenting upon the *Talmud*. They say that not all the rolls and manuscripts, reported in history to have been burned by Caesar, by the Christian mob in 389, and by the Arab General Amru, perished as it is commonly believed; and the story they tell is the following: At the time of the contest for the throne in 51 B.C., between Cleopatra and her brother Dionysus Ptolemy, the Bruchion, which contained over seven hundred thousand rolls, all bound in wood and *fireproof* parchment, was undergoing repairs, and a great portion of the original manuscripts, considered among the most precious, and which were not duplicated, were stored away in the house of one of the librarians. As the fire which consumed the rest was but the result of accident, no precautions had been taken at the time. But, they add, that several hours passed between the burning of the fleet set on fire by Caesar's order, and the moment when the first buildings situated near the harbor caught fire in their turn; and that all the librarians, aided by several hundred slaves attached to the museum, succeeded in saving the most precious of the rolls. So perfect and solid was the fabric of the parchment, that while in some rolls the inner pages and the wood-binding were reduced to ashes, of others the parchment binding remained unscorched. These particulars were all written out in Greek, Latin, and the Chaldeo-Syriac dialect, by a learned youth named Theodas, one of the scribes employed in the museum. One of these manuscripts is alleged to be preserved till now in a Greek convent; and the person who narrated the tradition to us had seen it himself. He said that many more will see it and learn where to look for important documents, when a certain prophecy will be fulfilled; adding that most of these works could be found in Tartary and India.* The monk showed us a copy of the original, which, of course, we could read but poorly, as we claim but little erudition in the matter of dead languages. But we were so particularly struck by

---

\* An afterthought has made us fancy that we can understand what is meant by the following sentences of Moses of Choren: "The ancient Asiatics," says he, "five centuries before our era — and especially the Hindus, the Persians, and the Chaldeans, had in their possession a quantity of historical and scientific books. These works were partially borrowed, partially translated in the Greek language, mostly since the Ptolemies had established the Alexandrian library and encouraged the writers by their liberalities, so that the Greek language became the deposit of all the sciences" (*History of Armenia*, Bk. I, ii). Therefore, the greater part of the literature included in the 700,000 volumes of the Alexandrian Library was due to India, and her near neighbors.

28                ISIS UNVEILED

the vivid and picturesque translation of the holy father, that we perfectly remember some curious paragraphs, which run, as far as we can recall them, as follows: — "When the Queen of the Sun (Cleopatra) was brought back to the half-ruined city, after the fire had devoured the *Glory of the World;* and when she saw the mountains of books — or rolls — covering the half-consumed steps of the *estrada;* and when she perceived that the inside was gone and the indestructible covers alone remained, she wept in rage and fury, and cursed the meanness of her fathers who had grudged the cost of the real Pergamos for the inside as well as the outside of the precious rolls." Further, our author, Theodas, indulges in a joke at the expense of the queen for believing that nearly all the library was burned; when, in fact, hundreds and thousands of the choicest books were safely stored in his own house and those of other scribes, librarians, students and philosophers.

No more do sundry very learned Copts scattered all over the East in Asia Minor, Egypt and Palestine believe in the total destruction of the subsequent libraries. For instance, they say that out of the library of Attalus III of Pergamum, presented by Antony to Cleopatra, not a volume was destroyed. At that time, according to their assertions, from the moment that the Christians began to gain power in Alexandria — about the end of the fourth century — and Anatolius, Bishop of Laodicea, began to insult the national gods, the Pagan philosophers and learned theurgists adopted effective measures to preserve the repositories of their sacred learning. Theophilus, a bishop, who left behind him the reputation of a most rascally and mercenary villain, was accused by one named Antoninus, a famous theurgist and eminent scholar of occult science of Alexandria,[5] with bribing the slaves of the Serapeion to steal books which he sold to foreigners at great prices. History tells us how Theophilus had the best of the philosophers, in A.D. 389; and how his successor and nephew, the no less infamous Cyril, butchered Hypatia. Suidas gives us some details about Antoninus, whom he calls Antonius, and his eloquent friend Olympus, the defender of the Serapeion. But history is far from being complete in the miserable remnants of books, which, crossing so many ages, have reached our own learned century; it fails to give the facts relating to the first five centuries of Christianity which are preserved in the numerous traditions current in the East. Unauthenticated as these may appear, there is unquestionably in the heap of chaff much good grain. That these traditions are not oftener communicated to Europeans is not strange, when we consider how apt our travellers are to render themselves antagonistic to the natives by their skeptical bearing and, occasionally, dogmatic intolerance. When exceptional men like some archaeologists, who knew how to win the confidence and even friendship of certain Arabs, are favored with precious documents, it is declared simply a "coincidence." And yet there are widespread traditions of the existence of certain subterranean and immense galleries, in the neighborhood of Ishmonia — the "petrified city," in which are stored numberless manuscripts and rolls.[6] For no amount of money would the Arabs go near it. At night, they say, from the crevices of the desolate ruins, sunk deep in the unwatered sands of the desert, stream the rays from lights carried to and fro in the galleries by no human hands. The Afrits study the literature of the antediluvian ages, according to their belief, and the Jinn learn from the magic rolls the lessons of the following day.

The *Encyclopaedia Britannica,* in its article on Alexandria, says: "When the temple of Serapis was demolished . . . the valuable library was *pillaged* or destroyed; and *twenty* years afterwards the *empty shelves* excited the regret . . . etc." * But it does not state the subsequent fate of the *pillaged* books.

In rivalry of the fierce Mary-worshippers of the fourth century, the modern clerical persecutors of liberalism and "heresy" would willingly shut up all the heretics and their books in some modern Serapeion and burn them alive.† The cause of this hatred is natural. Modern research has more than ever unveiled the secret. "Is not the worship of saints and angels now," said Bishop Newton, years ago, "in all respects the same that the worship of demons was in former times? The name only is different, the thing is identically the same . . . the very same temples, the very same images, which were once consecrated to Jupiter and the other demons, are now consecrated to the Virgin Mary and other saints . . . the whole of Paganism is converted and applied *to Popery.*"

Why not be impartial and add that "a good portion of it was adopted by Protestant religions also"?

The very apostolic designation *Peter* is from the Mysteries. The hierophant or supreme pontiff bore the Chaldean title פתר, *pether,* or interpreter. The names Ptah, Peth'r, the residence of Balaam, Patara, and Patras, the names of oracle-cities, *pateres* or *pateras* and, perhaps,

---

* [8th edition, 1853, Vol. 2, p. 470.] Cf. B. N. Bonamy, "Dissertation historique sur la Bibliothèque d'Alexandrie," in the *Histoire de l'Académie Royale des Inscriptions et Belles Lettres,* 1736, Vol. 9, pp. 414 *et seq.* The Presbyter P. Orosius,[7] who was an eyewitness, says "twenty years" (*Hist. adv. paganos,* Book VI, sect. 15).

† Since the above was written, the spirit here described has been beautifully exemplified at Barcelona, Spain, where the Bishop Fray Joachim invited the local spiritualists to witness a formal burning of spiritual books. We find the account in a paper called *La Revelación,* published at Alicante, which sensibly adds that the performance was "a caricature of the memorable epoch of the Inquisition."

Buddha,* all come from the same root. Jesus says: "Upon this *petra* I will build my Church, and the gates, or rulers of Hades, shall not prevail against it"; † meaning by *petra* the rock-temple, and by metaphor, the Christian Mysteries; the adversaries to which were the old mystery-gods of the underworld, who were worshipped in the rites of Isis, Adonis, Atys, Sabazius, Dionysus and the Eleusinia. No *apostle* Peter was ever at Rome; but the Pope, seizing the sceptre of the *Pontifex Maximus*, the keys of Janus and Cybelê, and adorning his Christian head with the cap of the *Magna Mater*, copied from that of the tiara of *Brahmâtma*, the Supreme Pontiff of the Initiates of old India, became the successor of the Pagan high priest, the real Peter-Roma, or *Petroma*.‡

The Roman Catholic Church has two far mightier enemies than the "heretics" and the "infidels"; and these are — Comparative Mythology and Philology. When such eminent divines as the Rev. James Freeman Clarke go so much out of their way to prove to their readers that "Critical Theology from the time of Origen and Jerome . . . and the Controversial Theology during fifteen centuries, has not consisted in accepting on authority the opinions of other people," but has shown, on the contrary, much "acute and comprehensive reasoning," we can but regret that so much scholarship should have been wasted in attempting to prove that which a fair survey of the history of theology upsets at every step. In these "controversies" and critical treatment of the doctrines of the Church one can certainly find any amount of "acute reasoning," but far more of a still acuter sophistry.

Recently the mass of cumulative evidence has been reinforced to an extent which leaves little, if any, room for further controversy. A conclusive opinion is furnished by too many scholars to doubt the fact that India was the *alma mater*, not only of the civilization, arts and sciences, but also of all the great religions of antiquity; Judaism, and hence Christianity, included. Herder places the cradle of humanity in India, and shows Moses as a clever and relatively *modern* compiler of the ancient Brahmanical traditions: "The river which encircles the country (India) is the sacred Ganges, which all Asia considers as the paradisaical river. There, also, is the Biblical Gihon, which is none else but the Indus. The Arabs call it so unto this day, and the names of the countries watered by it are yet existing among the Hindus." § Jacolliot claims to have translated every ancient palm-leaf manuscript which he had the fortune

---

\* E. Pococke gives the variations of the name Buddha as: Bud'ha, Buddha, Booddha, Boutta, Pout, Pote, Pto, Pte, Phthe, Phtha, Phut, etc., etc. See *India in Greece*, Appendix, p. 397.

† [*Matt.* xvi, 18.]

‡ The tiara of the Pope is also a perfect copy of that of the Taley-Lama of Thibet.

§ [See his *Ideen zur Philosophie der Geschichte der Menschheit*, Bk. X, ch. 6.]

## ORIGIN OF THE PAPAL TIARA AND KEYS

of being allowed by the Brahmans of the pagodas to see. In one of his translations, we found passages which reveal to us the *undoubted origin of the keys* of St. Peter, and account for the subsequent adoption of the symbol by their Holinesses, the Popes of Rome.

He shows us, on the testimony of the *Agrushada Parikshai*, which he freely translates as "the *Book of Spirits*" (Pitris), that centuries before our era the *initiates* of the temple chose a Superior Council, presided over by the *Brahmâtma* or supreme chief of all these *Initiates;* that this pontificate could be exercised only by a Brahman who had reached the age of eighty years;* that the *Brahmâtma* was sole guardian of the mystic formula, *résumé* of every science, contained in the three mysterious letters,

**A**

**U   M**

which signify *creation, conservation,* and *transformation.* He alone could expound its meaning in the presence of the initiates of the third and supreme degree. Whosoever among these initiates revealed to a profane a single one of the truths, even the smallest of the secrets entrusted to his care, was put to death. He who received the confidence had to share his fate.

"Finally, to crown this able system," says Jacolliot, "there existed a word still more superior to the mysterious monosyllable — A U M, and which rendered him who came into the possession of its key nearly the equal of Brahmâ himself. The *Brahmâtma* alone possessed this key, and transmitted it in a sealed casket to his successor.

"This unknown word, of which no human power could, even today, when the Brahmanical authority has been crushed under the Mongolian and European invasions, today, when each pagoda has its *Brahmâtma,*† *force the disclosure,* was engraved in a golden triangle and preserved in a sanctuary of the temple of Asgartha, whose *Brahmâtma* alone held the keys.[8] He also bore upon his tiara *two crossed keys* supported by two kneeling Brahmans, symbol of the precious deposit of which he had the keeping . . . This word and this triangle were engraved upon the tablet of the ring that this religious chief wore as one of the signs of his dignity; it was also framed in a golden sun on the altar, where every morning the Supreme Pontiff offered the sacrifice of the *sarvamedha,* or sacrifice to all the forces of nature." ‡

---

* It is the traditional policy of the College of Cardinals to elect, whenever practicable, the new Pope among the oldest valetudinarians. The hierophant of the Eleusinia was likewise always an old man, and unmarried.

† This is not correct.

‡ *Le Spiritisme dans le monde,* pp. 27-28.

Is this clear enough? And will the Catholics still maintain that it was the Brahmans of 4,000 year ago who copied the ritual, symbols, and dress of the Roman Pontiffs? We would not feel in the least surprised.

Without going very far back into antiquity for comparisons, if we only stop at the fourth and fifth centuries of our era, and contrast the so-called "heathenism" of the third Neo-Platonic Eclectic School with the growing Christianity, the result may not be favorable to the latter. Even at that early period, when the new religion had hardly outlined its contradictory dogmas; when the champions of the bloodthirsty Cyril knew not themselves whether Mary was to become "the Mother of God," or rank as a "demon" in company with Isis; when the memory of the meek and lowly Jesus still lingered lovingly in every Christian heart, and his words of mercy and charity vibrated still in the air, even then the Christians were outdoing the Pagans in every kind of ferocity and religious intolerance.

And if we look still farther back, and seek for examples of true *Christism*, in ages when Buddhism had hardly superseded Brahmanism in India, and the name of Jesus was only to be pronounced three centuries later, what do we find? Which of the holy pillars of the Church has ever elevated himself to the level of religious tolerance and noble simplicity of character of some heathen? Compare, for instance, the Hindu Aśoka, who lived 300 B.C., and the Carthaginian St. Augustine, who flourished three centuries after Christ. According to Max Müller, this is what is found engraved on the rocks of Girnâr, Dhauli and Kapûrdigiri:

"Piyadasi, the king beloved of the gods, desires that the ascetics *of all creeds* might reside in all places. All these ascetics profess alike the command which people should exercise over themselves, and the purity of the soul. *But people have different opinions, and different inclinations.*" *

And here is what Augustine wrote after his baptism: "Wondrous depth of thy words! whose surface, behold! is before us, inviting to little ones; yet are they a wondrous depth, O my God, a wondrous depth! It is awful to look therein; and awfulness of honor, and a trembling of love. The enemies [read Pagans] thereof I *hate* vehemently; O *that thou wouldst slay them* with thy two-edged sword, that they might no longer be enemies to it; for *so do I love to have them slain* . . ." †

Wonderful spirit of Christianity; and that from a Manichaean converted to the religion of one who even on his cross prayed for his enemies!

---

* [*Chips*, etc., I, p. 256.]

† Augustine, *Confessions*, Bk. XII, ch. xiv(17); quoted by Prof. Draper in *The Hist. of the Conflict*, etc., ch. ii, pp. 60-61.

Who the enemies of the "Lord" were, according to the Christians, is not difficult to surmise; the few inside the Augustinian fold were His new children and favorites, who had supplanted in His affections the sons of Israel, His "chosen people." The rest of mankind were His natural foes. The teeming multitudes of heathendom were proper food for the flames of hell; the handful within the Church communion, "heirs of salvation."

But if such a proscriptive policy was just, and its enforcement was "sweet savor" in the nostrils of the "Lord," why not scorn also the Pagan rites and philosophy? Why draw so deep from the wells of wisdom, dug and filled up to the brim by the same heathen? Or did the fathers, in their desire to imitate the chosen people whose timeworn shoes they were trying to fit upon their feet, contemplate the re-enaction of the spoliation scene of the *Exodus* [xii, 35-36]? Did they propose, in fleeing from heathendom as the Jews did from Egypt, to carry off the valuables of its religious allegories, as the "chosen ones" did the gold and silver ornaments?

It certainly does seem as if the events of the first centuries of Christianity were but the reflection of the images thrown upon the mirror of the future and the time of the Exodus. During the stormy days of Irenaeus, the Platonic philosophy, with its mystical submersion into Deity, was not so obnoxious after all to the new doctrine as to prevent the Christians from helping themselves to its abstruse metaphysics in every way and manner. Allying themselves with the ascetical therapeutae — forefathers and models of the Christian monks and hermits, it was in Alexandria, let it be remembered, that they laid the first foundations of the purely Platonic trinitarian doctrine. It became the Plato-Philonean doctrine later, and such as we find it now. Plato considered the divine nature under a threefold modification of the *First Cause,* the reason or *Logos,* and the soul or spirit of the universe. "The three archical or original principles," says Gibbon,* "were represented in the Platonic system as three gods, united with each other by a mysterious and ineffable generation." Blending this transcendental idea with the more hypostatic figure of the *Logos* of Philo, whose doctrine was that of the oldest Kabala, and who viewed the King Messiah as the *Metatron,* or "the angel of the Lord," the *Legatus* descended in flesh, but not the *Ancient of Days* himself; † the Christians clothed, with this mythical representation of the Mediator for the fallen race of Adam, Jesus, the son of Mary. Under this unexpected garb his personality was all but lost. In the modern Jesus of the Christian Church, we find the ideal of the imaginative Irenaeus, not the adept

---

\* *Decline and Fall of the Roman Empire,* ch. xxi.

† *Zohar,* Comment. on *Genesis* xl, 10; *Kabbala Denudata,* Vol. I, p. 528.

of the Essenes, the obscure reformer from Galilee. We see him under the disfigured Plato-Philonean mask, not as the disciples heard him on the mount.

So far then the heathen philosophy had helped them in the building of the principal dogma. But when the theurgists of the third Neo-Platonic school, deprived of their ancient Mysteries, strove to blend the doctrines of Plato with those of Aristotle, and by combining the two philosophies added to their theosophy the primeval doctrines of the Oriental *Kabala*, then the Christians from rivals became persecutors. Once that the metaphysical allegories of Plato were being prepared to be discussed in public in the form of Grecian dialectics, all the elaborate system of the Christian trinity would be unravelled and the divine prestige completely upset. The eclectic school reversing the order, had adopted the inductive method; and this method became its death knell. Of all things on earth, logic and reasonable explanations were the most hateful to the new religion of mystery; for they threatened to unveil the whole groundwork of the trinitarian conception; to apprise the multitude of the doctrine of emanations, and thus destroy the unity of the whole. It could not be permitted, and it was not. History records the *Christ*-like means that were resorted to.

The universal doctrine of emanations, adopted from time immemorial by the greatest schools which taught the kabalistic, Alexandrian and Oriental philosophers, gives the key to that panic among the Christian fathers. That spirit of Jesuitism and clerical craft, which prompted Parkhurst, many centuries later, to suppress in his *Hebrew and English Lexicon* the true meaning of the first word of *Genesis*, originated in those days of war against the expiring Neo-Platonic and eclectic school. The fathers had decided to pervert the meaning of the word *"daimôn,"* * and they dreaded above all to have the esoteric and true meaning of the word *Rêshith* unveiled to the multitudes; for if once the true sense of this sentence, as well as that of the Hebrew word *ashdoth* (translated in the *Septuagint* "angels," while it means emanations),† were understood rightly, the mystery of the Christian trinity would have crumbled, carrying in its downfall the new religion into the same heap of ruins with the ancient Mysteries. This is the true reason why dialectitians, as well as Aristotle himself, the "prying philosopher," were ever obnoxious to Christian theology. Even Luther, while on his work of reform, feeling the ground insecure under his feet, notwithstanding that the dogmas had been reduced by him to their simplest expression, gave full vent to his fear and hatred for Aristotle. The amount of abuse he heaped upon the

---

* "The beings which the philosophers of other peoples distinguish by the name 'daemons', Moses names 'angels'," says Philo Judaeus. — *De gigantibus*, § 2; *De opificio mundi*, § 3.

† *Deuteronomy* xxxiii, 2; אשדת is translated "fiery law" in the English Bible.

memory of the great logician can only be equalled — never surpassed — by the Pope's anathemas and invectives against the liberals of the Italian government. Compiled together, they might easily fill a copy of a new encyclopaedia with models for monkish diatribes.

Of course, the Christian clergy can never be reconciled to a doctrine based on the application of strict logic to discursive reasoning. The number of those who have abandoned theology on this account has never been made known. They have asked questions and been forbidden to ask them; hence, separation, disgust, and often a despairing plunge into the abyss of atheism. The Orphean views of Aether as chief *medium between* God and created matter were likewise denounced. The Orphic Aether recalled too vividly the *Archaeus*, the Soul of the World, and the latter was in its metaphysical sense as closely related to the emanations, being the first manifestation—*Sephîrâh*, or Divine Light. And when could the latter be more feared than at that critical moment?

Origen,\* Clemens Alexandrinus,† Chalcidius,‡ Methodius § and Maimonides ‖ on the authority of the *Targum of Jerusalem*, the orthodox and greatest authority of the Jews, held that the first two words in the book of *Genesis*—BE-RÊSHÎTH, mean *Wisdom*, or the *Principle*, and that the idea of these words meaning "*in the beginning*" was never shared but by the profane, who were not allowed to penetrate any deeper into the esoteric sense of the sentence. Beausobre, and after him Godfrey Higgins, have demonstrated the fact. "All things," says the *Kabala*, "are derived by emanation from one principle; and this principle is [the *unknown* and *invisible*] God. From Him a substantial power immediately proceeds, which is the *image of God*, and the source of all subsequent emanations. This second principle sends forth, by the *energy* [or *will* and *force*] of emanation, other natures, which are more or less perfect, according to their different degrees of distance, in the scale of emanation, from the First Source of existence, and which constitute different worlds, or orders of being, all united to the eternal power from which they proceed. *Matter is nothing more than the most remote effect of the emanative energy* of the Deity. The material world receives its form from the immediate agency of powers far beneath the First Source of Being ¶ . . . Beausobre makes St. Augustine the Manichaean say thus: 'And if by *Rêshîth* we understand the *active Principle* of the creation, instead of its *beginning*, in such a

---

\* [*De princ.*, III, v.]
† [*Strom.*, VI, vii.]
‡ [*Comm. in Timaeum.*]
§ [Fragm. on "Things Created," § 8, ap. Photius, *Bibliotheca*, Cod. ccxxxv.]
‖ [*Moreh Nebûkhîm*, II, ch. xxx.]
¶ See Rees, *Cyclopaedia*, art. "Cabala." [Cf. Godfrey Higgins, *Anacalypsis*, Vol. I, pp. 72-73.]

case we will clearly perceive that Moses never meant to say that heaven and earth were the first works of God. He only said that God created heaven and earth *through the Principle*, who is His Son. It is not the *time* he points to, but to the immediate author of the creation'." * Angels, according to Augustine, were created *before* the firmanent, and according to the esoteric interpretation, the heaven and earth were created after that, evolving from the *second* Principle or the Logos—the creative Deity. "The word *principe*," says Beausobre,† "does not mean that the heaven and earth were created before anything else, for, to begin with, the *angels* were created before that; but that God did everything through His Wisdom, which is His *Verbum*, and which the Christian *Bible* named the *Beginning*," thus adopting the exoteric meaning of the word abandoned to the multitudes. The *Kabala*—the Oriental as well as the Jewish—shows that a number of *emanations* (the Jewish Sephîrôth) issued from the *First* Principle, the chief of which was *Wisdom*. This Wisdom is the Logos of Philo, and Michael, the chief of the Gnostic Aeôns; it is the Ormazd of the Persians; *Minerva*, goddess of wisdom, of the Greeks, who emanated from the head of Jupiter; and the second Person of the Christian Trinity. The early Fathers of the Church had not to exert their imagination much; they found a ready-made doctrine that had existed in every theogony for thousands of years before the Christian era. Their trinity is but the trio of Sephîrôth, the first three kabalistic *lights* of which Moses Nachmanides says, that *"they have never been seen by anyone"*; there is not any defect in them, nor any disunion." The first eternal number is the Father, or the Chaldean primeval, invisible, and incomprehensible *chaos*, out of which proceeded the *Intelligible* one. The Egyptian Ptah, or "the *Principle of Light* — not the light itself, and the Principle of Life, though himself *no* life." The *Wisdom* by which the Father created the heavens is the *Son*, or the kabalistic androgynous Adam-Kadmon. The Son is at once the Male *Râ*, or Light of Wisdom, Prudence or *Intelligence*, Sephîrâh, the female part of Himself; while from this dual being proceeds the third emanation, the Binah or Reason, the second Intelligence — the Holy Ghost of the Christians. Therefore, strictly speaking, there is a TETRAKTYS or quaternary, consisting of the Unintelligible First monad, and its triple emanation, which properly constitutes our Trinity.

How then avoid perceiving at once, that had not the Christians purposely disfigured in their intepretation and translation the Mosaic *Genesis* to fit their own views, their religion, with its present dogmas, would have been impossible? The word *Rêshîth*, once taught in its new sense of the *Principle* and not the *Beginning*, and the anathematized doctrine of emanations accepted, the position of the second trinitarian personage

---

\* *Histoire critique* . . . *du Manichéisme*, Vol. II, Bk. VI, ch. i, pp. 290-91. [Cf. Higgins, *op. cit.*, I, p. 74.]

† [*Ibid.*, quoting St. Augustine, *De civitate Dei*, XI, xxxii.]

becomes untenable. For, if the angels are the *first* divine emanations from the Divine Substance, and were in existence *before* the Second Principle, then the anthropomorphized *Son* is at best an emanation like themselves, and cannot be God *hypostatically* any more than our visible works are ourselves. That these metaphysical subtleties never entered into the head of the honest-minded, sincere Paul, is evident; as it is furthermore evident, that like all learned Jews he was well acquainted with the doctrine of emanations and never thought of corrupting it. How can anyone imagine that Paul identified the *Son* with the *Father*, when he tells us that God made Jesus "a *little lower* than the angels" (*Hebrews* ii, 9), and a *little higher* than Moses! "For this MAN was counted worthy of more glory than Moses" (*Hebrews* iii, 3). Of what or how many forgeries, interlined later in the *Acts*, the Fathers are guilty we know not; but that Paul never considered Christ more than a man "full of the Spirit of God" is but too evident: "In the *archê* was the *Logos*, and the Logos was adnate to the Theos." *

*Wisdom*, the first emanation of Ain-Soph; the Protogonos, the Hypostasis; the Adam-Kadmon of the kabalists, the Brahmâ of the Hindu; the Logos of Plato, and the "*Beginning*" of St. John — are the *Rêshith* — ראשית, of the *Book of Genesis*. If rightly interpreted, it overturns, as we have remarked, the whole elaborate system of Christian theology, for it proves that behind the *creative* Deity there was a HIGHER god; a planner, and architect; and that the former was but His executive agent — a simple POWER!

They persecuted the Gnostics, murdered the philosophers, and burned the kabalists and the masons; and when the day of the great reckoning arrives, and the light shines in darkness, what will they have to offer in the place of the departed, expired religion? What will they answer, these pretended monotheists, these worshippers and *pseudo*-servants of the one living God, to their Creator? How will they account for this long persecution of those who were the true followers of the grand Megalistor, the supreme great master of the Rosicrucians, the FIRST of masons? "For he is the Builder and Architect of the Temple of the universe; He is the *Verbum Sapienti*." †

"Everyone knows," wrote the great Manichaean of the fourth century, Faustus, "that the Evangeliums were written neither by Jesus Christ,

---

\* [*John* i, 1.]

† "The altogether mystic coloring of Christianity harmonized with the Essene rules of life and opinions, and it is not improbable that Jesus and the Baptist John were initiated into the Essene mysteries, to which Christianity may be indebted for many a form of expression; as indeed the community of Therapeutae, an offspring of the Essene order, soon belonged wholly to Christianity" (I. M. Jost, *The Israelite Indeed*, I, 411; quoted by Dunlap in *Sōd, the Son of Man*, p. 62).

nor his apostles, but long after their time by some unknown persons, who, judging well that they would hardly be believed when telling of things they had not seen themselves, headed their narratives with the names of the apostles or of disciples contemporaneous with the latter." *

Commenting upon the subject, A. Frank, the learned Hebrew scholar of the Institute and translator of the *Kabala*, expresses the same idea. "Are we not authorized," he asks, "to view the *Kabala* as a precious remnant of religious philosophy of the Orient, which, transported into Alexandria, got mixed to the doctrine of Plato, and under the usurped name of Dionysius the Areopagite, bishop of Athens, converted and consecrated by St. Paul, was thus enabled to penetrate into the mysticism of the mediaeval ages?" †

Says Jacolliot: "What is then this religious philosophy of the Orient, which has penetrated into the mystic symbolism of Christianity? We answer: This philosophy, the traces of which we find among the Magians, the Chaldeans, the Egyptians, the Hebrew kabalists and the Christians, is none other than that of the Hindu Brahmans, the sectarians of the *pitris*, or the spirits of the invisible worlds which surround us." ‡

But if the Gnostics were destroyed, the *Gnosis*, based on the secret science of sciences, still lives. It is the earth which helps the woman, and which is destined to open her mouth to swallow up mediaeval Christianity, the usurper and assassin of the great master's doctrine. The ancient *Kabala*, the Gnosis, or traditional *secret* knowledge, was never without its representatives in any age or country. The trinities of initiates, whether passed into history or concealed under the impenetrable veil of mystery, are preserved and impressed throughout the ages. They are known as Moses, Aholiab and Bezaleel, the son of Uri, the son of Hur, as Plato, Philo and Pythagoras, etc. At the Transfiguration we see them as Jesus, Moses and Elias, the three Trismegisti; and three kabalists, Peter, James and John — whose *revelation* is the key to all wisdom. We find them in the twilight of Jewish history as Zoroaster, Abraham and Terah, and later as Henoch, Ezekiel and Daniel.

Who, of those who ever studied the ancient philosophies, who understand intuitively the grandeur of their conceptions, the boundless sublimity of their views of the Unknown Deity, can hesitate for a moment to give the preference to their doctrines over the incomprehensible, dogmatic and contradictory theology of the hundreds of Christian sects? Who that ever read Plato and fathomed his τὸ ὄν, "*whom no person has seen except the Son*," can doubt that Jesus was a disciple of the same

---

\* [*Faustus, apud August.*, xxxii, 2; xxxiii, 3; cf. Beausobre, *Hist. crit. du Manich.*, I, p. 297.]

† *La Kabbale*, Paris, 1843, Pt. III, ch. iv, p. 341.

‡ *Le Spiritisme*, etc., p. 215.

secret doctrine which had instructed the great philosopher? For, as we have shown before now, Plato never claimed to be the inventor of all that he wrote, but gave credit for it to Pythagoras, who, in his turn, pointed to the remote East as the source whence he derived his information and his philosophy. Celebrooke shows that Plato confesses it in his epistles, and says that he has taken his teachings from ancient and sacred doctrines!* Moreover, it is undeniable that the theologies of all the great nations dovetail together and show that each is a part of "one stupendous whole." Like the rest of the initiates, we see Plato taking great pains to conceal the true meaning of his allegories. Every time the subject touches the greater secrets of the Oriental *Kabala*, secrets of the true cosmogony of the universe and of the *ideal*, pre-existing world, Plato shrouds his philosophy in the profoundest darkness. His *Timaeus* is so confused that no one but an *initiate* can understand the secret meaning. And Mosheim † thinks that Philo has filled his works with passages directly contradicting each other for the sole purpose of concealing the true doctrine. For once we see a critic on the right track.

And this very trinitarian idea, as well as the so bitterly denounced doctrine of emanations, whence their remotest origin? The answer is easy, and every proof is now at hand. In the sublime and profoundest of all philosophies, that of the universal "Wisdom-Religion," the first traces of which historical research now finds in the old pre-Vedic religion of India. As the much-abused Jacolliot well remarks, "It is not in the religious works of antiquity, such as the *Vedas*, the *Zend-Avesta*, the *Bible*, that we have to search for the exact expression of the ennobling and sublime beliefs of those epochs." ‡

"The holy primitive syllable, composed of the three letters [A—U—M], in which is contained the Vedic Trimûrti [Trinity], must be kept secret, like another triple *Veda*," says *Manu*, in Book XI, śloka 266.

Svayambhû is the unrevealed Deity; it is the Being existent through and of itself; he is the central and immortal germ of all that exists in the universe. Three trinities emanate and are confounded in him, forming a Supreme *unity*. These trinities, or the triple *Trimûrti*, are: the Nara, Nârî, and Virâj — the *initial* triad; the Agni, Vâyu, and Sûrya — the *manifested* triad; Brahmâ, Vishṇu, and Śiva, the *creative* triad. Each of these triads becomes less metaphysical and more adapted to the vulgar intelligence as it descends. Thus the last becomes but the symbol in its concrete expression; the necessarianism of a purely metaphysical conception. Together with

---

* *Transactions of the Royal Asiatic Society of Great Britain and Ireland*, London, 1827, Vol. I, pp. 578-79.

† [Note in Cudworth, *True Intellectual System*, II, p. 324; London, 1845.]

‡ *Le Spiritisme*, etc., p. 13.

Svayambhû, they are the ten *Sephirôth* of the Hebrew kabalists, the ten Hindu *Prajâpatis* — the Ain-Soph of the former, answering to the great *Unknown,* expressed by the mystic A U M of the latter.

Says Franck, the translator of the *Kabala:*

"The ten Sephirôth . . . are divided into *three classes,* each of them presenting to us the divinity *under a different aspect,* the whole still remaining an *indivisible Trinity.*

"The first three Sephirôth are purely intellectual in metaphysics, they express the absolute identity of existence and thought, and form what the modern kabalists called the intelligible world" — which is the first manifestation of God.

"The three that follow . . . make us conceive God in one of their aspects, as the identity of goodness and wisdom; in the other they show to us, in the Supreme good, the origin of beauty and magnificence [in the creation]. Therefore, they are named the *virtues,* or the *sensible world.*

"Finally, we learn by the last of these attributes, that the Universal Providence, that the Supreme artist is also *absolute Force,* the all-powerful cause, and that, at the same time, this cause *is the generative element of all that is.* It is these last Sephirôth that constitute the *natural world,* or nature in its essence and in its *active* principle, *natura naturans."* \*

This kabalistic conception is thus proved identical with that of the Hindu philosophy. Whoever reads Plato and his dialogue *Timaeus,* will find these ideas as faithfully re-echoed by the Greek philosopher. Moreover, the injunction of secrecy was as strict with the kabalists, as with the initiates of the Adyta and the Hindu Yogis.

"Close thy mouth, lest thou shouldst speak of *this* [the mystery], and thy heart, lest thou shouldst think aloud; and if thy heart has escaped thee, bring it back to its place, for such is the object of our alliance." †

"This is a secret which gives death: close thy mouth lest thou shouldst reveal to the vulgar; compress thy brain lest something should escape from it and fall outside" (*Agrushada-Parikshai*).

Truly the fate of many a future generation hung on a gossamer thread, in the days of the third and fourth centuries. Had not the Emperor sent in 389 to Alexandria a rescript — which was forced from him by the Christians — for the destruction of every idol, our own century would never have had a Christian mythological Pantheon of its own. Never did the Neo-Platonic school reach such a height of philosophy as when

---

\* A. Franck, *La Kabbale,* Paris, 1843, Pt. II, ch. iii, pp. 197-98.
† *Sepher Yetzirah* (Book of Creation), I, § 7.

nearest its end. Uniting the mystic theosophy of old Egypt with the refined philosophy of the Greeks; nearer to the ancient Mysteries of Thebes and Memphis than they had been for centuries; versed in the science of soothsaying and divination, as in the art of the Therapeutists; friendly with the acutest men of the Jewish nation, who were deeply imbued with the Zoroastrian ideas, the Neo-Platonists tended to amalgamate the old wisdom of the Oriental *Kabala* with the more refined conceptions of the Occidental Theosophists. Notwithstanding the treason of the Christians who saw fit, for political reasons, after the days of Constantine, to repudiate their tutors, the influence of the new Platonic philosophy is conspicuous in the subsequent adoption of dogmas, the origin of which can be traced but too easily to that remarkable school. Though mutilated and disfigured, they still preserve a strong family likeness, which nothing can obliterate.

But, if the knowledge of the occult powers of nature opens the spiritual sight of man, enlarges his intellectual faculties, and leads him unerringly to a profounder veneration for the Creator, on the other hand ignorance, dogmatic narrow-mindedness, and a childish fear of looking to the bottom of things, invariably leads to fetish-worship and superstition.

When Cyril, the Bishop of Alexandria, had openly embraced the cause of Isis, the Egyptian goddess, and had anthropomorphized her into Mary, the mother of God; and the trinitarian controversy had taken place; from that moment the Egyptian doctrine of the emanation of the creative God out of Emepht * began to be tortured in a thousand ways, until the Councils had agreed upon the adoption of it as it now stands — the disfigured Ternary of the kabalistic Solomon and Philo! But as its origin was yet too evident, the *Word* was no longer called the "Heavenly man," the *primal* Adam-Kadmon, but became the Logos — Christ, and was made as old as the "Ancient of the Ancient," his father. The *concealed* WISDOM became identical with its emanation, the DIVINE THOUGHT, and made to be regarded coequal and coeternal with its first manifestation.

If we now stop to consider another of the fundamental dogmas of Christianity, the doctrine of atonement, we may trace it as easily back to heathendom. This cornerstone of a Church which had believed herself built on a firm rock for long centuries, is now excavated by science and proved to come from the Gnostics. Professor Draper shows it as hardly known in the days of Tertullian, and as having *"originated* among the Gnostic heretics." † We will not permit ourselves to contradict such a

---

* [Cf. A. Kircher, *Sphinx mystagoga,* Amstelodami, 1676, Pt. III, ch. iii, p. 52. Cf. Note 26, in Vol. I, p. 636.]

† *The Hist. of the Conflict,* etc., p. 224.

learned authority, farther than to state that it *originated* among them no more than their "anointed" Christos and Sophia. The former they modelled on the original of the "King Messiah," the male principle of wisdom, and the latter on the third Sephîrôth, from the Chaldean *Kabala*,* and even from the Hindu Brahmâ and Sarasvatî,† and the Pagan Dionysus and Demeter. And here we are on firm ground, if it were only because it is now proved that the *New Testament* never appeared in its complete form, such as we find it now, till 300 years after the period of the apostles.‡ and the *Zohar* and other kabalistic books are found to belong to the first century before our era, if not to be far older still.

The Gnostics entertained many of the Essenean ideas; and the Essenes had their "greater" and "minor" Mysteries at least two centuries before our era. They were the *Ozarim* or *Initiates*, the descendants of the Egyptian hierophants, in whose country they had been settled for several centuries before they were converted to Buddhistic monasticism by the missionaries of King Aśoka, and amalgamated later with the earliest Christians; and they existed, probably, before the old Egyptian temples were desecrated and ruined in the incessant invasions of Persians, Greeks, and other conquering hordes. The hierophants had their *atonement* enacted in the Mystery of Initiation ages before the Gnostics, or even the Essenes, had appeared. It was known among hierophants as the BAPTISM OF BLOOD, and was considered not as an atonement for the "fall of man" in Eden, but simply as an expiation for the past, present and future sins of ignorant but nevertheless polluted mankind. The hierophant had the option of either offering his pure and sinless life as a sacrifice for his race to the gods whom he hoped to rejoin, or an animal victim. The former depended entirely on his own will. At the last moment of the solemn "new birth," the initiator passed "the word" to the initiated, and immediately after that the latter had a weapon placed in his right hand, and was ordered *to strike.* § This is the true origin of the Christian dogma of atonement.

---

\* See *Zohar; Kabbala denudata; Siphra Dtzeniuthah*, the oldest book of the Kabalists; and Milman, *The Hist. of Christianity*, 1840, pp. 212-15.

† Milman, *op. cit.*, p. 280. The *Kurios* and *Kora* are mentioned repeatedly in Justin Martyr. See *1st Apology*, ch. 64, etc.

‡ See Olshausen, *Biblischen Commentar über sämtliche Schriften des Neuen Testaments*, p. 11.

§ There is a widespread *superstition* (?), especially among the Slavonians and Russians, that the *magician* or wizard cannot die before he has passed the "word" to a successor. So deeply is it rooted among the popular beliefs, that we do not imagine there is a person in Russia who has not heard of it. It is but too easy to trace the origin of this superstition to the old Mysteries which had been for ages spread all over

## THE SORCERER'S TERRIFYING DEATHBED 43

Verily the "Christs" of the pre-Christian ages were many. But they died unknown to the world, and disappeared as silently and as mysteriously from the sight of man as Moses from the top of Pisgah, the mountan of Nebo (oracular wisdom), after he had laid his hands upon Joshua, who thus became "full of the spirit of wisdom" (*i.e.*, *initiated*).

Nor does the Mystery of the Eucharist pertain to Christians alone. Godfrey Higgins proves that it was instituted many hundreds of years before the "Paschal Supper," and says that "the sacrifice of bread and

---

the globe. The ancient *Variago-Russ* had his Mysteries in the North as well as in the South of Russia; and there are many relics of the bygone faith scattered in the lands watered by the sacred Dnieper, the baptismal Jordan of all Russia. No *Znachar'* (the knowing one) or *Koldun* (sorcerer), male or female, can die in fact before he has passed the mysterious word to some one. The popular belief is that unless he does that he will linger and suffer for weeks and months, and were he even finally to be liberated, it would be only to wander on earth, unable to quit its region unless he finds a successor even after death. How far the belief may be verified by others, we do not know, but we have seen a case which, for its tragical and mysterious *dénouement*, deserves to be given here as an illustration of the subject in hand. An old man, of over one hundred years of age, a peasant-serf in the government of S——, having a wide reputation as a sorcerer and healer, was said to be dying for several days, and still unable to die. The report spread like lightning, and the poor old fellow was shunned by even the members of his own family, as the latter were afraid of receiving the unwelcome inheritance. At last the public rumor in the village was that he had sent a message to a colleague less versed than himself in the art, and who, although he lived in a distant district, was nevertheless coming at the call, and would be on hand early on the following morning. There was at that time on a visit to the proprietor of the village a young physician who, belonging to the famous school of *Nihilism* of that day, laughed outrageously at the idea. The master of the house, being a very pious man, and but half inclined to make so cheap of the "superstition," smiled — as the saying goes — but with one corner of his mouth. Meanwhile the young skeptic, to gratify his curiosity, had made a visit to the dying man, had found that he could not live twenty-four hours longer, and, determined to prove the absurdity of the "superstition," had taken means to detain the coming "successor" at a neighboring village.

Early in the morning a company of four persons, comprising the physician, the master of the place, his daughter, and the writer of the present lines, went to the hut in which was to be achieved the triumph of skepticism. The dying man was expecting his liberator every moment, and his agony at the delay became extreme. We tried to persuade the physician to humor the patient, were it for humanity's sake. He only laughed. Getting hold with one hand of the old wizard's pulse, he took out his watch with the other, and remarking in French that all would be over in a few moments, remained absorbed in his professional experiment. The scene was solemn and appalling. Suddenly the door opened, and a young boy entered with the intelligence, addressed to the doctor, that the *kum* was lying dead drunk at a neighboring village, and, according to *his orders*, could not be with "grandfather" till the next day. The young doctor felt confused, and was just going to address the old man, when, as quick as lightning, the Znachar's snatched his hand from his grasp and raised himself in bed. His deep-sunken eyes flashed; his yellow-white beard and hair streaming round his livid face made him a

wine was common to many ancient nations." * Cicero mentions it in his works, and wonders at the strangeness of the rite. There had been an esoteric meaning attached to it from the first establishment of the Mysteries, and the Eucharistia is one of the oldest rites of antiquity. With the hierophants it had nearly the same significance as with the Christians. Ceres was *bread*, and Bacchus was *wine*; † the former meaning regeneration of life from the seed, and the latter — the grape — the emblem of wisdom and knowledge; the accumulation of the spirit of things, and the fermentation and subsequent strength of that esoteric knowledge being justly symbolized by wine. The mystery related to the drama of Eden; it is said to have been first taught by Janus, who was also the first to introduce in the temples the sacrifices of "bread" and "wine" in commemoration of the "fall into generation" as the symbol of the "seed." "I am the true vine, and my Father is the husbandman," says Jesus [*John* xv, 1], alluding to the secret knowledge that could be imparted by him. "I will drink no more of the fruit of the vine, until that day that I drink it new in the kingdom of God." [*Mark* xiv, 25.]

The festival of the Eleusinian Mysteries began in the month of Boedromion, which corresponds with the month of September, the time of grape-gathering, and lasted from the 15th to the 22nd of the month, *seven* days.‡ The Hebrew festival of the Feast of Tabernacles began on the 15th and ended on the 22nd of the month of Ethanim, which Dunlap shows as derived from Adonim, Adonia, Attenim, Ethanim; § and this feast is named in *Exodus* (xxiii, 16) the feast of *ingathering*. "All the men of Israel assembled themselves unto King Solomon at the feast in the month Ethanim, which is the *seventh* month.‖

---

dreadful sight. One instant more, and his long, sinewy arms were clasped round the physician's neck, as with a supernatural force he drew the doctor's head closer and closer to his own face, where he held him as in a vise, while *whispering* words inaudible to us in his ear. The skeptic struggled to free himself, but before he had time to make one effective motion the work had evidently been done; the hands relaxed their grasp, and the old sorcerer fell on his back — a corpse! A strange and ghostly smile had settled on the stony lips — a smile of fiendish triumph and satisfied revenge; but the doctor looked paler and more ghastly than the dead man himself. He stared round with an expression of terror difficult to describe, and without answering our inquiries rushed out wildly from the hut, in the direction of the woods. Messengers were sent after him, but he was nowhere to be found. About sunset a report was heard in the forest. An hour later his body was brought home, with a bullet through his head, for the skeptic had blown out his brains!

What made him commit suicide? What magic spell of sorcery had the "word" of the dying wizard left on his mind? Who can tell?

* *Anacalypsis*, II, 58 *et seq.*, 253; also Tertullian, *De praescr. haer.*, xl.

† [Cicero, *De natura deorum*, iii, 16.]

‡ Anthon, *Dict. of Greek and Roman Antiq.*, art. "Eleusinia."

§ *Sōd, the Mysteries of Adoni*, p. 71.

‖ *1 Kings* viii, 2.

Plutarch thinks the feast of the booths to be the Bacchic rites, not the Eleusinian. Thus "Bacchus was directly called upon," he says. The *Sabazian* worship was *Sabbatic*; the names Evius, or Hevius, and Luaios are identical with *Hivite* and *Levite*. The French name Louis is the Hebrew *Levi*; Iacchus again is Iaô or Jehovah; and Baal or Adon, like Bacchus, was a phallic god. "Who shall ascend into the hill [the high place] of the Lord?" asks the holy king David, "who shall stand in the place of his *Kadesh* קדש?" (*Psalms* xxiv, 3). *Kadesh* may mean in one sense to *devote, hallow, sanctify*, and even to initiate or to set apart; but it also means the ministry of lascivious rites (the Venus-worship) and the true interpretation of the word *Kadesh* is bluntly rendered in *Deuteronomy* xxiii, 17; *Hosea* iv, 14; and *Genesis* xxxviii, from verse 15 to 22. The "holy" Kadeshuth of the *Bible* were identical, as to the duties of their office, with the Nautch-girls of the later Hindu pagodas. The Hebrew *Kadeshim* or galli lived "by the house of the Lord, where the women wove hangings for the grove," or bust of Venus-Astartê, says verse the seventh in the twenty-third chapter of *2 Kings*.

The dance performed by David round the ark was the "circle-dance" said to have been prescribed by the Amazons for the Mysteries. Such was the dance of the daughters of Shiloh (*Judges* xxi, 21, 23 *et passim*), and the leaping of the prophets of Baal (*1 Kings* xviii, 26). It was simply a characteristic of the Sabaean worship, for it denoted the motion of the planets round the sun. That the dance was a Bacchic frenzy is apparent. Sistra were used on the occasion, and the taunt of Michal and the king's reply are very expressive. "The king of Israel uncovered himself before his maidservants as one of the *vain* [or debauched] fellows shamelessly uncovered himself." And he retorts: "I will play [act wantonly] before יהוה, and I will yet be more vile than this, and will be base in my own sight." * When we remember that David had sojourned among the Tyrians and Philistines, where their rites were common; and that indeed he had conquered that land away from the house of Saul, by the aid of mercenaries from their country, the countenancing and even, perhaps, the introduction of such a Pagan-like worship by the weak "psalmist" seems very natural. David knew nothing of Moses, it seems, and if he introduced the Jehovah-worship it was not in its monotheistic character, but simply as that of one of the many gods of the neighboring nations — a tutelary deity to whom he had given the preference, and chosen among "all other gods."

Following the Christian dogmas *seriatim*, if we concentrate our attention upon one which provoked the fiercest battles until its recognition, that of the Trinity, what do we find? We meet it, as we have shown, northeast of the Indus; and tracing it to Asia Minor and Europe, recognize it among every

---

* [*2 Sam.* vi, 20-22.]

people who had anything like an established religion. It was taught in the oldest Chaldean, Egyptian and Mithraic schools. The Chaldean Sun-god, Mithra, was called "Triple," and the trinitarian idea of the Chaldeans was a doctrine of the Akkadians, who, themselves, belonged to a race which was the first to conceive a metaphysical trinity. The Chaldeans are a tribe of the Akkadians, according to Rawlinson, who lived in Babylonia from the earliest times. They were Turanians, according to others, and instructed the Babylonians into the first notions of religion. But these same Akkadians, who were they? Those scientists who would ascribe to them a Turanian origin, make of them the inventors of the cuneiform characters; others call them Sumerians; others again, respectively, make their language, of which (for very good reasons) no traces whatever remain — Kastean, Chaldaic, Proto-Chaldean, Kasdo-Scythic, and so on. The only tradition worthy of credence is that these Akkadians instructed the Babylonians in the Mysteries, and taught them the sacerdotal or *Mystery*-language. These Akkadians were then simply a tribe of the Hindu Brahmans, now called Âryans — their vernacular language, the Sanskrit * of the *Vedas*; and the sacred or Mystery-language, that which, even in our own age, is used by the Hindu fakirs and initiated Brahmans in their magical evocations.† It has been, from time immemorial, and still is employed by the initiates of all countries, and the Thibetan lamas claim that it is in this tongue that appear the mysterious characters on the leaves and bark of the sacred Kumbum.

Jacolliot, who took such pains to penetrate the mysteries of the Brahmanical initiation in translating and commenting upon the *Agrushada-Parikshai*, confesses the following:

"It is pretended also, without our being able to verify the assertion, that the magical evocations were pronounced in a particular language, and that it was forbidden, under pain of death, to translate them into vulgar dialects. The rare expressions that we have been able to catch like — *L'rhom, h'hom, sh'krum, sho'rhim*, are in fact most curious, and do not seem to belong to any known idiom." ‡

Those who have seen a fakir or a lama reciting his mantras and conjurations, know that he never pronounces the words audibly when preparing for

---

\* Let us remember in this connection that Col. Vans Kennedy has long ago declared his opinion that Babylonia was once the seat of the Sanskrit language and of Brahmanical influence.[9]

† "The *Agrushada-Parikshai*, which discloses, to a certain extent, the order of initiation, does not give the formula of evocation," says Jacolliot, and he adds that, according to some Brahmans, "these formulae were never written, they were and still are imparted in a whisper in the ear of the adepts" (*"mouth to ear, and the word at low breath,"* say the Masons).

‡ *Le Spiritisme dans le monde,* p. 108.

a phenomenon. His lips move, and none will ever hear the terrible formula pronounced, except in the interior of the temples, and then in a cautious whisper. This, then, was the language now respectively baptized by every scientist, and, according to his imaginative and philological propensities, Kasdeo-Semitic, Scythic, Proto-Chaldean, and the like.

Scarcely two of even the most learned Sanskrit philologists are agreed as to the true interpretation of Vedic words. Let one put forth an essay, a lecture, a treatise, a translation, a dictionary, and straightway all the others fall to quarrelling with each other and with him as to his sins of omission and commission. Professor Whitney, greatest of American Orientalists, says that Professor Müller's notes on the *Ṛig-Veda-Saṃhitâ* "are far from showing that sound and thoughtful judgment, that moderation and economy, which are among the most precious qualities of an exegete." * Professor Müller angrily retorts upon his critics that "not only is the joy embittered which is the inherent reward of all *bona fide* work, but selfishness, malignity, aye, *even untruthfulness*, gain the upper hand, and the healthy growth of science is stunted." He differs "in many cases from the explanations of Vedic words given by Professor R. Roth" in his *Sanskrit-Wörterbuch*, and Professor Whitney shampooes both their heads by saying that there are, unquestionably, words and phrases "as to which both alike will hereafter be set right."

In Volume I of his *Chips*, Professor Müller stigmatizes all the *Vedas* except the *Ṛig*, the *Atharva-Veda* included, as "theological twaddle," while Professor Whitney regards the latter as "the most comprehensive and valuable of the four collections, next after the *Ṛig*." † To return to the case of Jacolliot. Professor Whitney brands him as a "bungler and a humbug," and, as we remarked above, this is the very general verdict. But when *La Bible dans l'Inde* appeared, the Société Académique de Saint Quentin requested Textor de Ravisi, a learned Indianist, ten years Governor of Karikal, India, to report upon its merits. He was an ardent Catholic, and bitterly opposed Jacolliot's conclusions where they discredited the Mosaic and Catholic revelations; but he was forced to say: "Written with good faith, in an easy, vigorous, and passionate style, of an easy and varied argumentation, the work of L. Jacolliot is of absorbing interest . . . a learned work on known facts and with familiar arguments." ‡

Enough. Let Jacolliot have the benefit of the doubt when such very imposing authorities are doing their best to show up each other as incompetents and literary journeymen. We quite agree with Professor Whitney that "the truism, that [for European critics?] it is far easier to

---

\* [*Oriental and Linguistic Studies*, p. 138.]
† [*Ibid.*, p. 147.]
‡ [L. Jacolliot, *Christna et le Christ*, p. 339.]

pull to pieces than to build up, is nowhere truer than in matters affecting the archaeology and history of India." *

Babylonia happened to be situated on the way of the great stream of the earliest Hindu emigration, and the Babylonians were one of the first peoples benefited thereby.† These Khaldi were the worshippers of the Moon-god, Deus-Lunus, from which fact we may infer that the Akkadians — if such must be their name — belonged to the race of the Kings of the Moon, whom tradition shows as having reigned in Prayâga — now Allâhâbâd. With them the trinity of Deus-Lunus was manifested in the three lunar phases, completing the quaternary with the fourth, and typifying the death of the Moon-god in its gradual waning and final disappearance. This death was allegorized by them, and attributed to the triumph of the genius of evil over the light-giving deity; as the later nations allegorized the death of their Sun-gods, Osiris and Apollo, at the hands of Typhon and the great Dragon Python, when the sun entered the winter solstice. Babel, Arach and Akkad are names of the sun. The *Chaldean Oracles* are full and explicit upon the subject of the Divine Triad. ‡ "A triad of Deity shines forth throughout the whole world, of which a Monad is the head," admits the Reverend Dr. Maurice.

"All things are governed in the bosoms of this triad," says a Chaldean oracle.§ The Phos, Pur, and Phlox, of Sanchoniathon,‖ are Light, Fire, and Flame, three manifestations of the Sun who is *one*. Bel-Saturn, Jupiter-Bel, and Bel or Baal-Chom are the Chaldean trinity;¶ "The Babylonian Bel was regarded in the Triune aspect of Belitan, Zeus-Belus (the Mediator) and Baal-Chom who is Apollo Chomaeus. This was the Triune aspect of the 'Highest God', who is according to Berosus either El [the Hebrew], Bel, Belitan, Mithra, or Zervana, and has the name πατήρ, 'the Father'." ** The Brahmâ, Vishṇu, and Śiva, †† corresponding to Power, Wisdom and Justice,

---

\* W. D. Whitney, *Oriental and Linguistic Studies*, p. 98.

† Jacolliot seems to have very logically demonstrated the absurd contradictions of some philologists, anthropologists and Orientalists, in regard to their *Akkado-* and *Semito-*mania. "There is not, perhaps, much of good faith in their negations," he writes. "The scientists who invent Turanian peoples know very well that in *Manu* alone, there is more of veritable science and philosophy than in all that this pretended Semitism has hitherto furnished us with; but they are the slaves of a path which some of them are following the last fifteen, twenty, or even thirty years ... We expect, therefore, nothing of the present. India will owe its reconstitution to the scientists of the next generation." (*La Genèse de l'humanité*, pp. 60-61).

§ [Cory, *op. cit.*, p. 6.]

§ [J. Lydus, *De mensibus*, 20; cf. Cory, *op. cit.*, p. 245.]

‖ [Cory, *op. cit.*, p. 6.]

¶ Movers, *Die Phönizier*, Vol. I, p. 263.

\*\* Dunlap, *Vestiges*, etc., p. 281.

†† Śiva is not a god of the *Vedas*, strictly speaking. When the *Vedas* were written, he held the rank of Mahâ-Deva or Bel among the gods of aboriginal India.

which answer in their turn to Spirit, Matter, Time, and to the Past, Present and Future, can be found in the temple of Gharapuri; thousands of dogmatic Brahmans worship these attributes of the Vedic Deity, while the severe monks and nuns of Buddhistic Thibet recognize but the sacred trinity of the three cardinal virtues: *Poverty, Chastity* and *Obedience*, professed by the Christians, practiced by the Buddhists and some Hindus alone.

The Persian triplicate Deity also consists of three persons, Ormazd, Mithra and Ahriman.\* It is that principle, of which the author of the *Chaldaic Summary* says, "*They conceive there is one principle of all things, and declare that is one and good.*" † The Chinese idol Sanpao, consists of three equal in all respects; ‡ and the Peruvians "supposed their Tanga-tanga to be one in three, and three in one," says Faber. § The Egyptians have their Emepht, Eikton, and Ptaḥ;|| and the triple god seated on the Lotus can be seen in the St. Petersburg Museum, on a medal of the Northern Tatars.¶

Among the Church dogmas which have most seriously suffered of late at the hands of the Orientalists, the last in question stands conspicuous. The reputation of each of the three personages of the anthropomorphic godhead, as an original revelation to the Christians through Divine will, has been badly compromised by inquiry into its predecessors and origin. Orientalists have published more about the similarity between Brahmanism, Buddhism and Christianity than was strictly agreeable to the Vatican. Draper's assertion that "Paganism was modified by Christianity, Christianity by Paganism," \*\* is being daily verified. "Olympus was restored but the divinities passed under other names," he says, treating of the Constantine period. "The more powerful provinces insisted on the adoption of their time-honored conceptions. Views of the Trinity, in accordance with Egyptian traditions, were established. Not only was the adoration of Isis under a new name restored, but even her image, standing on the crescent moon, reappeared. The well-known effigy of that goddess, with the infant Horus in her arms has descended to our days in the beautiful, artistic creations of the Madonna and Child."††

But a still earlier origin than the Egyptian and Chaldean can be assigned to the Virgin "Mother of God," Queen of Heaven. Though Isis is also by right

---

\* [Plutarch, *On Isis and Osiris*, § 46.]
† [Gallaeus, *Summ. Chald.* (Pselli expos.), in App. (p. 111) to *Sib. oracula*, Amsterdam, 1689.]
‡ Navarette, *Tratados hist., etc., de China*, Bk. II, ch. x.
§ *On the Origin of Pagan Idolatry*, Vol. I, p. 269; ed. 1816.
|| [Iamblichus, *De myst.*, VIII, 3.]
¶ [Faber, *A Dissert, on the Myst. of the Cabiri*, I, p. 315, note.]
\*\* Isis and Osiris are said, in the Egyptian sacred books, to have appeared (*i.e.*, been worshipped), on earth, later than Thoth, the *first* Hermes, called Trismegistus, who wrote all their sacred books according to the command of God or by "divine revelation." The companion and instructor of Isis and Osiris was Thoth, or Hermes II, who was an incarnation of the celestial Hermes.
†† [Draper, *The Hist. of the Conflict*, etc., pp. 47-48.]

the Queen of Heaven, and is generally represented carrying in her hand the Crux Ansata composed of the mundane cross, and of the Stauros of the Gnostics, she is a great deal younger than the celestial virgin, Neith. In one of the tombs of the Pharaohs — [that of] Rameses — in the valley of Bibân al-Mulûk in Thebes, Champollion, Jr., discovered a picture, according to his opinion the most ancient ever yet found. It represents the heavens symbolized by the figure of a woman bedecked with stars. The birth of the Sun is figured by the form of a little child, issuing from the bosom of its "Divine Mother." *

In the *Book of Hermes*, "Poimandres," is enunciated in distinct and unequivocal sentences, the whole trinitarian dogma accepted by the Christians. "The light is me," says Poimandres, the DIVINE THOUGHT. "I am the *nous* or intelligence, and I am thy god, and I am far older than the humid principle which escapes from the shadow. I am the germ of thought, the resplendent WORD, the SON of God. Think that what thus sees and hears in thee, is the *Verbum* of the Master, it is the Thought, which is God the Father . . . The celestial ocean, the AETHER, which flows from east to west, is the Breath of the Father, the life-giving Principle, the HOLY GHOST!" "For they are not at all separated and their union is LIFE." †

Ancient as may be the origin of Hermes, lost in the unknown days of Egyptian colonization, there is yet a far older prophecy, directly relating to the Hindu Kṛishṇa, according to the Brahmans. It is, to say the least, strange that the Christians claim to base their religion upon a prophecy of the *Bible*, which exists nowhere in that book. In what chapter or verse does Jehovah, the "Lord God," promise Adam and Eve to send them a Redeemer who will save humanity? "I will put enmity between thee and the woman," says the Lord God to the serpent, "and between thy seed and her seed; it shall bruise thy head, and thou shalt bruise his heel." ‡

In these words there is not the slightest allusion to a Redeemer, and the subtlest of intellects could not extract from them, as they stand in the third chapter of *Genesis*, anything like that which the Christians have contrived to find. On the other hand, in the traditions and *Manu*, Brahmâ promises directly to the first couple to send them a Savior who will teach them the way to salvation.

"It is from the lips of a messenger of Brahmâ, who will be born in Kurukshetra, Matsya, and the land of Pañchâla, also called Kanya-Kubja [mountain of the Virgin], that all men on earth will learn their duty," says *Manu* (Book II, ślokas 19 and 20).

The Mexicans call the Father of their Trinity Izamna, the Son Bacab, and the Holy Ghost Echuak, "and say they received it [the doctrine]

---

* [Champollion-Figeac, *Égypte ancienne*, p. 104.]
† [L. Ménard, *Hermès Trismégiste*, Paris, 1867, livre Ier, ch. i.]
‡ [*Gen.* iii, 15.]

from their ancestors." * Among the Semitic nations we can trace the trinity to the prehistorical days of the fabled Sesostris, who is identified by more than one critic with Nimrod, "the mighty hunter." Manetho makes the oracle rebuke the king, then the latter asks, "Tell me, O thou strong in fire, who before me could subjugate all things? and who shall after me?" And the oracle saith thus: "First, God, then, the Word; and with them the Spirit." †

In the foregoing lies the foundation of the fierce hatred of the Christians toward the "Pagans" and the theurgists. Too much had been *borrowed*; the ancient religions and the Neo-Platonists had been laid by them under contribution, sufficiently to perplex the world for several thousand years. Had not the ancient creeds been speedily obliterated, it would have been found impossible to preach the Christian religion as a New Dispensation, or the direct Revelation from God the Father, through God the Son, and under the influence of God the Holy Ghost. As a political exigency the Fathers had — to gratify the wishes of their rich converts — instituted even the festivals of Pan. They went so far as to accept the ceremonies hitherto celebrated by the Pagan world in honor of the *God of the gardens*, in all their primitive *sincerity*. ‡ It was time to sever the connection. Either the Pagan worship and the Neo-Platonic theurgy, with all ceremonial of magic, must be crushed out forever, or the Christians become Neo-Platonists.

The fierce polemics and singlehanded battles between Irenaeus and the Gnostics are too well known to need repetition. They were carried on for over two centuries after the unscrupulous Bishop of Lyons had uttered his last religious paradox. Celsus, the Neo-Platonist, and a disciple of the school of Ammonius Saccas, had thrown the Christians into perturbation, and even had arrested for a time the progress of proselytism by successfully proving that the original and purer forms of the most important dogmas of Christianity were to be found only in the teachings of Plato. Celsus accused them of accepting the worst superstitions of Paganism, and of interpolating passages from the books of the Sibyls, without rightly understanding their meaning. The accusations were so plausible, and the facts so patent, that for a long time no Christian writer had ventured to answer the challenge. Origen, at the fervent request of his friend Ambrosius, was the first to take the defense in hand, for, having belonged to the same Platonic school of Ammonius, he was considered the most competent man to refute the well-founded charges. But his eloquence failed, and the only remedy that could be found was to destroy the writings of

---

\* Lord Kingsborough, *The Antiquities of Mexico*, London, 1830-48, p. 165.

† Joannes Malala, *Hist. Chronica*, Oxford, 1691, Bk. I, cap. iv.

‡ R. Payne Knight, *A Discourse on the Worship of Priapus*, London, 1865, pp. 171 *et seq.*

Celsus themselves.* This could be achieved only in the fifth century, when copies had been taken from this work, and many were those who had read and studied them. If no copy of it has descended to our pressent generation of scientists, it is not because there is none extant at present, but for the simple reason that the monks of a certain Oriental church on Mount Athos will neither show nor confess they have one in their possession.† Perhaps they do not even know themselves the value of the contents of their manuscripts, on account of their great ignorance.

The dispersion of the Eclectic school had become the fondest hope of the Christians. It had been looked for and contemplated with intense anxiety. It was finally achieved. The members were scattered by the

---

\* The Celsus above mentioned, who lived between the second and third centuries, is not Celsus the Epicurean. The latter wrote several works against Magic, and lived earlier, during the reign of Hadrian.

† We have the facts from a trustworthy witness, having no interest to invent such a story. Having injured his leg in a fall from the steamer into the boat in which he was to land at the Mount, he was taken care of by these monks, and during his convalescence, through gifts of money and presents, became their greatest friend, and finally won their entire confidence. Having asked for the loan of some books, he was taken by the Superior to a large cellar in which they keep their sacred vessels and other property. Opening a great trunk, full of old musty manuscripts and rolls, he was invited by the Superior to *"amuse himself."* The gentleman was a scholar, and well versed in Greek and Latin text. "I was amazed," he says, in a private letter, "and had my breath taken away, on finding among these old parchments, so unceremoniously treated, some of the most valuable relics of the first centuries, hitherto believed to have been lost." Among others he found a half-destroyed manuscript, which he is perfectly sure must be a copy of the "True Doctrine," the λόγος ἀληθής of Celsus, out of which Origen quoted whole pages. The traveller took as many notes as he could on that day, but when he came to offer to the Superior to purchase some of these writings he found, to his great surprise, that no amount of money would tempt the monks. They did not know what the manuscripts contained, nor "did they care," they said. But the "heap of writing," they added, was transmitted to them from one generation to another, and there was a tradition among them that these papers would one day become the means of crushing the "Great Beast of the Apocalypse," their hereditary enemy, the Catholic Church of Rome. They were constantly quarreling and fighting with the Catholic monks, and among the whole "heap" they *knew* that there was a "holy" relic which protected them. They did not know *which*, and so in their doubt abstained. It appears that the Superior, a shrewd Greek, understood his *bévue* and repented of his kindness, for first of all he made the traveller give him his most sacred word of honor, strengthened by an oath he made him take on the image of the Holy Patroness of the Island, never to betray their secret, and never mention, at least, the name of their convent. And finally, when the anxious student who had passed a fortnight in reading all sorts of antiquated trash before he happened to stumble over some precious manuscript, expressed the desire to have the key, to "amuse himself" with the writings once more, he was very *naïvely* informed that the "key had been lost," and that they did not know where to look for it. And thus he was left to the few notes he had taken.

hand of the monsters Theophilus, Bishop of Alexandria, and his nephew Cyril — the murderer of the young, the learned, and the innocent Hypatia! *

With the death of the martyred daughter of Theon, the mathematician, there remained no possibility for the Neo-Platonists to continue their school at Alexandria. During the lifetime of the youthful Hypatia, her friendship and influence with Orestes, the governor of the city, had assured the philosophers security and protection against their murderous enemies. With her death they had lost their strongest friend. How much she was revered by all who knew her for her erudition, noble virtues and character, we can infer from the letters addressed to her by Synesius, Bishop of Ptolemais, fragments of which have reached us. "My heart yearns for the presence of your divine spirit," he wrote in 413 A.D., "which more than anything else could alleviate the bitterness of my fortunes." At another time he says: "Oh, my mother, my sister, my teacher, my benefactor! My soul is very sad. The recollection of my children I have lost is killing me. . . . When I have news of you and learn, as I hope, that you are more fortunate than myself, I am at least only half-unhappy." †

What would have been the feelings of this most noble and worthy of Christian bishops, who had surrendered family and children and happiness for the faith to which he had been attracted, had a prophetic vision disclosed to him that the only friend that had been left to him, his "mother, sister, benefactor," would soon become an unrecognizable mass of flesh and blood, pounded to jelly under the blows of the club of Peter the Reader — that her youthful, innocent body would be cut to pieces, "the flesh scraped from the bones" by oyster shells and the rest of her cast into the fire, by order of the same Bishop Cyril he knew so well — Cyril, the CANONIZED Saint!! ‡

There has never been a religion in the annals of the world with such a bloody record as Christianity. All the rest, including the traditional fierce fights of the "chosen people" with their next of kin, the idolatrous tribes of Israel, pale before the murderous fanaticism of the alleged followers of Christ! Even the rapid spread of Mohammedanism before the conquering sword of the Islam prophet, is a direct consequence of the

---

\* See the historical romance of Canon Kingsley, *Hypatia*, for a highly picturesque account of the tragical fate of this young martyr.

† [*Epistolae*, X and XVI.]

‡ We beg the reader to bear in mind that it is the same Cyril who was accused and proved guilty of having sold the gold and silver ornaments of his church, and spent the money. He pleaded guilty, but tried to excuse himself on the ground that he had used the money for the poor, but could not give evidence of it. His duplicity with Arius and his party is well known. Thus one of the first Christian saints, and the founder of the Trinity, appears on the pages of history as a murderer and a thief! [10]

bloody riots and fights among Christians. It was the intestine war between the Nestorians and Cyrilians that engendered Islamism; and it is in the convent of Basra that the prolific seed was first sown by Bahira, the Nestorian monk. Freely watered by rivers of blood, the tree of Mecca has grown till we find it in the present century overshadowing nearly two hundred millions of people. The recent Bulgarian atrocities are but the natural outgrowth of the triumph of Cyril and the Mariolaters.

The cruel, crafty politician, the plotting monk, glorified by ecclesiastical history with the aureole of a martyred saint. The despoiled philosophers, the Neo-Platonists, and the Gnostics, daily anathematized by the Church all over the world for long and dreary centuries. The curse of the unconcerned Deity hourly invoked on the magian rites and theurgic practice, and the Christian clergy themselves using *sorcery* for ages. Hypatia, the glorious maiden-philosopher, torn to pieces by the Christian mob. And such as Catherine of Medici, Lucrezia Borgia, Joanna of Naples, and the Isabellas of Spain, presented to the world as the faithful daughters of the Church — some even decorated by the Pope with the order of the "Immaculate Rose," the highest emblem of womanly purity and virtue, a symbol sacred to the Virgin-mother of God! Such are the examples of human justice! How far less blasphemous appears a total rejection of Mary as an immaculate goddess, than an idolatrous worship of her, accompanied by such practices.

In the next chapter we will present a few illustrations of sorcery, as practiced under the patronage of the Roman Church.

## CHAPTER II

"One undertakes by scales of miles to tell
The bounds, dimensions, and extent of hell;
• • • • • • • • •
Where bloated souls in smoky durance hung
Like a Westphalia gammon or neat's tongue,
To be redeemed with masses and a song."
—J. OLDHAM, *Satires upon the Jesuits*, 1678.

"*York* — But you are more inhuman, more inexorable,
O! ten times more, than tigers of Hyrcania."
—SHAKESPEARE, *King Henry VI*, Pt. III, Act I,
Scene iv, lines 154-55.

"*Warwick*—And hark ye, sirs; because she is a maid,
Spare for no fagots, let there be enow:
Place barrels of pitch upon the fatal stake,
That so her torture may be shortened."
—SHAKESPEARE, *King Henry VI*, Pt. I, Act V,
Scene iv, lines 55-57.

IN that famous work of Bodin on sorcery,* a frightful story is told about Catherine of Medici. The author was a learned publicist, who, during twenty years of his life, collected authentic documents from the archives of nearly every important city of France, to make up a complete work on sorcery, magic, and the power of various "demons." To use an expression of Éliphas Lévi, his book offers a most remarkable collection of "bloody and hideous facts; acts of revolting superstition, arrests, and executions of stupid ferocity. Burn every body! the Inquisition seemed to say — God will easily sort out His own! Poor fools, hysterical women, and idiots were roasted alive, without mercy, for the crime of magic. But, at the same time, how many great culprits escaped this unjust and sanguinary *justice!* This is what Bodin makes us fully appreciate." †

Catherine, the pious Christian — who has so well deserved in the eyes of the Church of Christ for the atrocious and never-to-be-forgotten massacre of St. Bartholomew's Day — the Queen Catherine, kept in her service an apostate Jacobin priest. Well versed in the "black art," so fully patronized by the Medici family, he had won the gratitude and protection of his pious mistress by his unparalleled skill in killing people at a distance, by torturing with various incantations their wax simulacra. The process has been described over and over again, and we scarcely need repeat it.

---
* *De la Démonomanie des sorciers*, Paris, 1587, Bk. II, ch. iii, pp. 78-79.
† [*Dogme et rituel*, etc., II, ch. xv.]

Charles was lying sick of an incurable disease. The queen mother, who had everything to lose in case of his death, resorted to necromancy, and consulted the oracle of the "bleeding head." This infernal operation required the decapitation of a child who must be possessed of great beauty and purity. He had been prepared in secret for his first communion by *the chaplain* of the palace, who was apprised of the plot, and at midnight of the appointed day, in the chamber of the sick man, and in the presence only of Catherine and a few of her confederates, the "devil's mass" was celebrated. Let us give the rest of the story as we find it in one of Lévi's works: "At this mass, celebrated before the image of the demon, having under his feet a reversed cross, the sorcerer consecrated two wafers, one black and one white. The white was given to the child, whom they brought clothed as for baptism, and who was murdered upon the very steps of the altar, immediately after his communion. His head, separated from the trunk by a single blow, was placed, all palpitating, upon the great black wafer which covered the bottom of the paten, then placed upon a table where some mysterious lamps were burning. The exorcism then began, and the demon was charged to pronounce an oracle, and reply by the mouth of this head to a secret question that the king dared not speak aloud, and that had been confided to no one. Then a feeble voice, a strange voice, which had nothing of human character about it, made itself audible in this poor little martyr's head." * The sorcery availed nothing; the king died, and — Catherine remained the faithful daughter of Rome!

How strange, that des Mousseaux, who makes such free use of Bodin's materials to construct his formidable indictment against Spiritualists and other sorcerers, should have overlooked this interesting episode!

It is a well-attested fact that Pope Sylvester II was publicly accused by Cardinal Benno of being a sorcerer and an enchanter. The brazen "oracular head" made by his Holiness was of the same kind as the one fabricated by Albertus Magnus. The latter was smashed to pieces by Thomas Aquinas, not because it was the work of, or inhabited by, a "demon," but because the spook who was fixed inside by mesmeric power, talked incessantly, and his verbiage prevented the eloquent saint from working on his mathematical problems. These heads and other talking statues, trophies of the magical skill of monks and bishops, were facsimiles of the "animated" gods of the ancient temples. The accusation against the Pope was proved at the time. It was also demonstrated that he was constantly attended by "demons" or spirits. In the preceding chapter we have mentioned Benedict IX, John XX, and the VIth and the VIIth Gregory, who were all known as magicians. The latter Pope, moreover, was the famous Hildebrand, who was said to have

---

* [É. Lévi, *op. cit.*, II, ch. xv.]

been so expert at "shaking lightning out of his sleeve"— an expression which makes the venerable spiritualistic writer, Mr. Howitt, think that "it was the origin of the celebrated thunder of the Vatican." *

The magical achievements of the Bishop of Ratisbon and those of the "angelic doctor," Thomas Aquinas, are too well known to need repetition; but we may explain farther how the "illusions" of the former were produced. If the Catholic bishop was so clever in making people believe on a bitter winter night that they were enjoying the delights of a splendid summer day, and cause the icicles hanging from the boughs of the trees in the garden to seem like so many tropical fruits, the Hindu magicians also practice such biological powers unto this very day, and claim the assistance of neither god nor devil. Such "miracles" are all produced by the same human power that is inherent in every man, if he only knew how to develop it.

About the time of the Reformation, the study of alchemy and magic had become so prevalent among the clergy as to produce great scandal. Cardinal Wolsey was openly accused before the court and the privy council of confederacy with a man named Wood, a sorcerer, who said that *"My Lord Cardinale had suche a rynge that whatsomevere he askyd of the Kynges grace that he hadd yt"*; adding that *"Master Cromwell, when he . . . was servaunt in my lord cardynales housse . . . rede many bokes and specyally the boke of Salamon . . . and studied mettells and what vertues they had after the canon of Salamon.'* 11 This case, with several others equally curious, is to be found among the Cromwell papers in the Record Office of the Rolls House.†

A priest named William Stapleton was arrested as a conjurer during the reign of Henry VIII, and an account of his adventures is still preserved in the Rolls House records. The Sicilian priest whom Benvenuto Cellini calls a necromancer, became famous through his successful conjurations, and was never molested. The remarkable adventure of Cellini with him in the Colosseum, where the priest conjured up a whole host of devils, is well known to the reading public. The subsequent meeting of Cellini with his mistress as predicted and brought about by the conjurer, at the precise time fixed by him, is to be considered, as a matter of course, a "curious coincidence." ‡ In the latter part of the sixteenth century there was hardly a parish to be found in which the priests did not study magic and alchemy. The practice of exorcism to cast out devils "in imitation of Christ," who by the way never used exorcism at all, led the clergy to devote themselves openly to "sacred" magic in contradistinction to black art, of which latter crime were accused all those who were neither priests nor monks.

---

\* [*Hist. of the Supernatural*, Vol. I, p. 483.]
† [Thos. Wright, *Narr. of Sorcery and Magic*, Vol. I, pp. 203-04.]
‡ [*Ibid.*, I, pp. 219 *et seq.*]

The occult knowledge gleaned by the Roman Church from the once fat fields of theurgy she sedulously guarded for her own use, and sent to the stake only those practitioners who "poached" on her lands of the *Scientia Scientiarum*, and those whose sins could not be concealed by the friar's frock. The proof of it lies in the records of history. "In the course only of fifteen years, between 1580 to 1595, and only in the single province of Lorraine, the President Remigius burned 900 witches," says Thomas Wright, in his *Sorcery and Magic*.* It was during these days, prolific in ecclesiastical murder and unrivalled for cruelty and ferocity, that Jean Bodin wrote.

While the orthodox clergy called forth whole legions of "demons" through magical incantations, unmolested by the authorities, provided they held fast to the established dogmas and taught no heresy, on the other hand, acts of unparalleled atrocity were perpetrated on poor, unfortunate fools. Gabriel Malagrida, an old man of eighty, was burnt by these evangelical Jack Ketches in 1761. In the Amsterdam library there is a copy of the report of his famous trial, translated from the Lisbon edition. He was accused of sorcery and illicit intercourse with the Devil, who had "disclosed to him *futurity*."(?) The prophecy imparted by the Arch-Enemy to the poor visionary Jesuit is reported in the following terms: "The culprit hath confessed that the demon, under the form of the blessed Virgin, having commanded him to write the life of Antichrist [?], told him that he, Malagrida, was a second John, but more clear than John the Evangelist; that there were to be three Antichrists, and that the last should be born at Milan, of a monk and a nun, in the year 1920; that he would marry Proserpine, one of the infernal furies," etc. †

The prophecy is to be verified forty-three years hence. Even were all the children born of monks and nuns really to become antichrists if allowed to grow up to maturity, the fact would seem far less deplorable than the discoveries made in so many convents when the foundations have been removed for some reason. If the assertion of Luther is to be disbelieved on account of his hatred for popery, then we may name discoveries of the same character made quite recently in Austrian and Russian Poland. Luther ‡ speaks of a fish pond at Rome, situated near a convent of nuns, which, having been cleared out by order of Pope Gregory, disclosed, at the bottom, over six thousand infant skulls; and of a nunnery at Neuburg, in Austria, whose foundations, when searched, disclosed the same relics of celibacy and chastity!

"*Ecclesia non novit sanguinem!*" meekly repeated the scarlet-robed cardinals. And to avoid the spilling of blood which horrified them, they instituted the Holy Inquisition. If, as the occultists maintain, and science half confirms, our most trifling acts and thoughts are indelibly impressed

---

* [Vol. I, p. 300.]
† [*The Proceeding and Sentence of the . . . Inquisition . . . against G. Malagrida*, etc., London, 1762.]
‡ [*Tischreden*, ch. xxxiii, p. 590 b, ed. of Andreas Zeidler, Leipzig, 1700.]

upon the eternal mirror of the astral ether, there must be somewhere, in the boundless realm of the unseen universe, the imprint of a curious picture. It is that of a gorgeous standard waving in the heavenly breeze at the foot of the great "white throne" of the Almighty. On its crimson damask face a cross, symbol of "the Son of God who died for mankind," with an *olive* branch on one side, and a sword, stained to the hilt with human gore, on the other. A legend selected from the *Psalms* emblazoned in golden letters, reading thus: *"Exurge, Domine, et judica causam meam."* For such appears the standard of the Inquisition, on a photograph in our possession, from an original procured at the Escorial of Madrid.

Under this Christian standard, in the brief space of fourteen years, Tomás de Torquemada, the confessor of Queen Isabella, burned over ten thousand persons, and sentenced to the torture eighty thousand more. Orobio, the well-known writer, who was detained so long in prison, and who hardly escaped the flames of the Inquisition, immortalized this institution in his works when once at liberty in Holland. He found no better argument against the Holy Church than to embrace the Judaic faith and submit even to circumcision. "In the cathedral of Saragossa," says a writer on the Inquisition, "is the tomb of a famous inquisitor; six pillars surround the tomb; *to each is chained a Moor*, as preparatory to being burnt. On this St-Foix ingeniously observes: If ever the Jack Ketch of any country should be rich enough to have a splendid tomb, this might serve as an excellent model!" * To make it complete, however, the builders of the tomb ought not to have omitted a bas-relief of the famous horse which was burnt for sorcery and witchcraft. Granger tells the story, describing it as having occurred in his time. The poor animal "had been taught to tell the spots upon cards, and the hour of the day by the watch. Horse and owner were both indicted by the sacred office for dealing with the Devil, and both were burned, with a great ceremony of *auto-da-fé*, at Lisbon, in 1601, as wizards!" †

This immortal institution of Christianity did not remain without its Dante to sing its praise. "Macedo, a Portuguese Jesuit," says the author of *Demonologia*, "has discovered the 'Origin of the *Inquisition*', in the terrestrial Paradise, and presumes to allege that God was the first who began the functions of an inquisitor over Cain and the workmen of Babel!" ‡

Nowhere, during the middle ages, were the arts of magic and sorcery more practiced by the clergy than in Spain and Portugal. The Moors were profoundly versed in the occult sciences, and at Toledo, Seville and Salamanca were, once upon a time, the great schools of magic. The kabalists of the latter town were skilled in all the abstruse sciences; they

---

\* [*Demonologia*, p. 302.]
† [James Granger, *Biogr. Hist. of England*, 1769.]
‡ [*Demonologia*, pp. 304, 306.]

knew the virtues of precious stones and other minerals, and had extracted from alchemy its most profound secrets.

The authentic documents pertaining to the great trial of the Maréchale d'Ancre, during the regency of Marie de Medici, disclose that the unfortunate woman perished through the fault of the priests with whom, like a true Italian, she surrounded herself. She was accused by the people of Paris of sorcery, because it had been asserted that she had used, after the ceremony of exorcism, newly killed white cocks. Believing herself constantly bewitched, and being in very delicate health, the Maréchale had the ceremony of exorcism publicly applied to herself in the Church of the Augustinians; as to the birds, she used them as an application to the forehead on account of dreadful pains in the head, and had been advised to do so by Montalto, the Jew physician of the queen, and by the Italian priests.

In the sixteenth century, the curé of Bargota, of the diocese of Calahorra, Spain, became the world's wonder for his magical powers. His most extraordinary feat consisted, it was said, in transporting himself to any distant country, witnessing political and other events, and then returning home to predict them in his own country. He had a familiar demon who served him faithfully for long years, says the *Chronicle*, but the curé turned ungrateful and cheated him. Having been apprised by his demon of a conspiracy against the Pope's life, in consequence of an intrigue of the latter with a fair lady, the curé transported himself to Rome (in his double, of course) and thus saved his Holiness' life. After which he repented, confessed his sins to the gallant Pope, and *got absolution*. "On his return he was delivered, as a matter of form, into the custody of the inquisitors of Logroño, but was acquitted and restored to his liberty very soon." *

Friar Pietro, a Dominican monk of the fourteenth century — the magician who presented the famous Dr. Eugenio Torralva, a physician attached to the house of the admiral of Castile, with a *demon* named Zequiel — won his fame through the subsequent trial of Torralva. The procedure and circumstances attendant upon the extraordinary trial are described in the original papers preserved in the Archives of the Inquisition. The Cardinal of Volterra and the Cardinal of Santa Cruz, both saw and communicated with Zequiel, who proved, during the whole of Torralva's life, to be a pure, kind, elemental spirit, doing many beneficent actions, and remaining faithful to the physician to the last hour of his life. Even the Inquisition acquitted Torralva, on that account; and, although an immortality of fame was insured to him by the satire of Cervantes, neither Torralva nor the monk Pietro are fictitious heroes, but historical personages, recorded in ecclesiastical documents of Rome and Cuenca,

---

\* [Thos. Wright, *Narr. of Sorcery and Magic*, Vol. II, pp. xx, xviii.]

in which town the trial of the physician took place, January the 29th, 1530.\*

The book of Dr. W. G. Soldan, of Stuttgart, has become as famous in Germany as Bodin's book on *Demonomania* in France. It is the most complete German treatise on witchcraft of the sixteenth century. One interested to learn the secret machinery underlying these thousands of legal murders, perpetrated by a clergy who pretended to believe in the Devil and succeeded in making others believe in him, will find it divulged in the above-mentioned work.† The true origin of the daily accusations and death sentences for sorcery are cleverly traced to personal and political enmities, and, above all, to the hatred of the Catholics toward the Protestants. The crafty work of the Jesuits is seen at every page of the bloody tragedies; and it is in Bamberg and Würzburg, where these worthy sons of Loyola were most powerful at that time, that the cases of witchcraft were most numerous. On the next page we give a curious list of some victims, many of whom were children between the ages of seven and eight years, and Protestants. "Of the multitudes of persons who perished at the stake in Germany during the first half of the seventeenth century for sorcery, the only crime of many was their attachment to the religion of Luther," says T. Wright, ". . . and the petty princes were not unwilling to seize upon any pretense to fill their coffers . . . the persons prosecuted were . . . those whose property was a matter of consideration . . . At Bamberg, as well as at Würzburg, the bishop was the sovereign prince in his dominions . . . The Prince-Bishop, John George II, who ruled Bamberg . . . after several unsuccessful attempts to root out Lutheranism . . . distinguished his reign by a series of sanguinary witch trials which disgrace the annals of that city . . . We may form some notion of the proceedings of this worthy,‡ from the statement of the most authentic historians . . . that between 1625 and 1630, not less than 900 trials took place in the two courts of Bamberg and Zeil; and a pamphlet published at Bamberg by authority, in 1659, states the number of persons whom Bishop John George had caused to be burned for sorcery to have been 600." §

Regretting that space should prevent our giving one of the most curious lists in the world of burned witches, we will nevertheless make a few extracts from the original record as printed in Hauber's *Bibliotheca*

---

\* [Rather in the years 1528 to 1530. Cf. Thos. Wright, *op. cit.*, II, xviii.]

† Dr. W. G. Soldan, *Geschichte der Hexenprocesse. Aus den Quellen dargestellt*, Stuttgart, 1843.

‡ Frederick Forner, Suffragan of Bamberg, author of a treatise against heretics and sorcerers, under the title of *Panoplia armaturae Dei*, etc.

§ *Narratives of Sorcery and Magic*, by Thomas Wright, M.A., F.S.A., etc., Corresponding Member of the National Institute of France; Vol. II, pp. 183-85.

*magica.*\* One glance at this horrible catalogue of murders in Christ's name is sufficient to discover that out of 162 persons burned, more than one-half of them are designated as *strangers* (*i.e.*, Protestants) in this hospitable town; and of the other half we find *thirty-four children*, the oldest of whom was fourteen, the youngest *an infant* child of Dr. Schütz. To make the catalogue shorter, we will present of each of the twenty-nine *burnings*, but the most remarkable.†

IN THE FIRST BURNING, FOUR PERSONS.

The wife of Liebler.
Old Ancker's widow.
The wife of Gutbrodt.
The wife of Höcker.

IN THE SECOND BURNING, FOUR PERSONS.

The old wife of Beutler.
Two strange women (names unknown).

IN THE THIRD BURNING, FIVE PERSONS.

Tungersleber, a minstrel.
Four wives of citizens.

IN THE FOURTH BURNING, FIVE PERSONS.

A strange man.

IN THE FIFTH BURNING, NINE PERSONS.

Lutz, an eminent shop-keeper.
The wife of Baunach, a senator.

IN THE SIXTH BURNING, SIX PERSONS.

The fat tailor's wife.
A strange man.
A strange woman.

---

\* [Cf. T. Wright, *op. cit.*, II, pp. 187-94.]

† Besides these burnings in Germany, which amount to many thousands, we find some very interesting statements in Prof. Draper's *Conflict between Religion and Science*. On page 146, he says: "The families of the convicted were plunged into irretrievable ruin. Llorente, the historian of the Inquisition, computes that Torquemada and his collaborators, in the course of eighteen years, burned at the stake 10,220 persons, 6,860 in effigy, and otherwise punished 97,321! . . . With unutterable disgust and indignation, we learn that the papal government realized much money by selling to the rich dispensations to secure them from the Inquisition."

### A RECORD OF FIENDISH CRUELTY

#### IN THE SEVENTH BURNING, SEVEN PERSONS.

A strange girl of twelve years old.
A strange man, a strange woman.
A strange bailiff (Schultheiss).
Three strange women.

#### IN THE EIGHTH BURNING, SEVEN PERSONS.

Baunach, a senator, the fattest citizen in Würzburg.
A strange man.
Two strange women.

#### IN THE NINTH BURNING, FIVE PERSONS.

A strange man.
A mother and daughter.

#### IN THE TENTH BURNING, THREE PERSONS.

Steinacher, a very rich man.
A strange man, a strange woman.

#### IN THE ELEVENTH BURNING, FOUR PERSONS.

Two women and two men.

#### IN THE TWELFTH BURNING, TWO PERSONS.

Two strange women.

#### IN THE THIRTEENTH BURNING, FOUR PERSONS.

A little girl nine or ten years old.
A younger girl, her sister.

#### IN THE FOURTEENTH BURNING, TWO PERSONS.

The mother of the two little girls before mentioned.
A girl twenty-four years old.

#### IN THE FIFTEENTH BURNING, TWO PERSONS.

A boy twelve years of age, in the first school.
A woman.

#### IN THE SIXTEENTH BURNING, SIX PERSONS.

A boy of ten years of age.

#### IN THE SEVENTEENTH BURNING, FOUR PERSONS.

A boy eleven years old.
A mother and daughter.

### IN THE EIGHTEENTH BURNING, SIX PERSONS.

Two boys, twelve years old.
The daughter of Dr. Junge.
A girl of fifteen years of age.
A strange woman.

### IN THE NINETEENTH BURNING, SIX PERSONS.

A boy of ten years of age.
Another boy, twelve years old.

### IN THE TWENTIETH BURNING, SIX PERSONS.

Göbel's child, the most beautiful girl in Würzburg.
Two boys, each twelve years old.
Stepper's little daughter.

### IN THE TWENTY-FIRST BURNING, SIX PERSONS.

A boy fourteen years old.
The little son of Senator Stolzenberger.
Two alumni.

### IN THE TWENTY-SECOND BURNING, SIX PERSONS.

Stürman, a rich cooper.
A strange boy.

### IN THE TWENTY-THIRD BURNING, NINE PERSONS.

David Croten's boy, nine years old.
The two sons of the prince's cook, one fourteen, the other ten years old.

### IN THE TWENTY-FOURTH BURNING, SEVEN PERSONS.

Two boys in the hospital.
A rich cooper.

### IN THE TWENTY-FIFTH BURNING, SIX PERSONS.

A strange boy.

### IN THE TWENTY-SIXTH BURNING, SEVEN PERSONS.

Weydenbush, a senator.
The little daughter of Valkenberger.
The little son of the town council bailiff.

### IN THE TWENTY-SEVENTH BURNING, SEVEN PERSONS.

A strange boy.
A strange woman.
Another boy.

IN THE TWENTY-EIGHTH BURNING, SIX PERSONS.

The infant daughter of Dr. Schütz.
A blind girl.

IN THE TWENTY-NINTH BURNING, SEVEN PERSONS.

The fat noble lady (Edelfrau).
A doctor of divinity.

*Item*

Summary:
| | |
|---|---:|
| "Strange" men and women, *i.e.*, Protestants, | 28 |
| Citizens, apparently all WEALTHY people, | 100 |
| Boys, girls, and little children, | 34 |
| In nineteen months, | 162 persons. |

"There were," says Wright, "little girls of from seven to ten years of age among the witches, and *seven and twenty* of them were convicted and burnt," at some of the other *brände*, or burnings. "The numbers brought to trial in these terrible proceedings were so great, and they were treated with so little consideration, that it was usual not even to take the trouble of setting down their names, but they were cited as the accused No. 1, 2, 3, and so on. The Jesuits took their confessions in private." \*

What room is there in a theology which exacts such holocausts as these to appease the bloody appetites of its priests for the following gentle words:

"Suffer little children, and forbid them not to come unto me; for of such is the kingdom of Heaven." "Even so it is not the will of your Father . . . that one of these little ones should perish." "But whoso shall offend one of these little ones which believe in me, it *were better for him that a millstone were hanged* about his neck, and that he were drowned in the depths of the sea." †

We sincerely hope that the above words have proved no vain threat to these child-burners.

Did this butchery in the name of their Moloch-god prevent these treasure hunters from resorting to the black art themselves? Not in the least: for in no class were such consulters of "familiar" spirits more numerous than among the clergy during the fifteenth, sixteenth and seventeenth centuries. True, there were some Catholic priests among the victims, but though these were generally accused of having "been

---

\* *Sorcery and Magic*; "The Burnings at Würzburg," II, p. 186.
† [*Matt.* xix, 14; xviii, 14, 6.]

led into practices too dreadful to be described," it was not so. In the twenty-nine burnings above catalogued we find the names of *twelve vicars, four* canons, and two doctors of divinity *burnt alive.* But we have only to turn to such works as were published at the time to assure ourselves that each popish priest executed was accused of "damnable heresy," *i.e.*, a tendency to reformation — a crime more heinous far than sorcery.

We refer those who would learn how the Catholic clergy united duty with pleasure in the matter of exorcisms, revenge and treasure hunting, to Volume II, chapter i, of W. Howitt's *History of the Supernatural.* "In what came to be called Pneumatologia Occulta et Vera, all the forms of adjuration and conjuration were laid down," says this veteran writer. He then proceeds to give a long description of the favorite *modus operandi.* The *Dogme et Rituel de la Haute Magie* of the late Éliphas Lévi, treated with so much abuse and contempt by des Mousseaux, tells nothing of the weird ceremonies and practices, but what was practiced legally and with the tacit if not open consent of the Church, by the priests of the middle ages. The exorcist-priest entered a circle at midnight; he was clad in a new surplice, and had a consecrated band hanging from the neck, covered with sacred characters. He wore on the head a tall pointed cap, on the front of which was written in Hebrew the holy word, Tetragrammaton — the ineffable name. It was written with a new pen dipped in the blood of a white dove. What the exorcists most yearned after, was to release miserable spirits *which haunt spots where hidden treasures lie.* The exorcist sprinkled the circle with the blood of a black lamb and a white pigeon. The priest had to adjure the evil spirits of hell — Acheront, Magoth, Asmodi, Beelzebub, Belial, and all the damned souls, in the mighty names of Jehovah, Adonai, Elohah, and Tsabaôth, which latter was the God of Abraham, Isaac, and Jacob, who dwelt in the Urim and Thummim. When the damned souls flung in the face of the exorcist that he was a sinner, and could not get the treasure from them, the priest-sorcerer had to reply that "all his sins were washed out in the blood of Christ,* and he bid them depart as cursed ghosts and damned flies." When the exorcist dislodged them at last, the poor soul was "comforted in the name of the Saviour, and *consigned to the care of good angels*," who were less powerful, we must think, than the exorcising Catholic worthies, "and the rescued treasure, of course, was secured for the Church."

"Certain days," adds Howitt, "are laid down in the calendar of the Church as most favorable for the practice of exorcism; and, if the devils

---

* And retinted in the blood of the millions murdered in his name — in the no less innocent blood than his own, of the little child-*witches!*

are difficult to drive, a fume of sulphur, asafetida, bear's gall, and rue is recommended, which, it was presumed, would outstench even devils." *

This is the Church, and this the priesthood, which, in the nineteenth century, pays 5,000 priests to teach the people of the United States the infidelity of science and the infallibility of the Bishop of Rome!

We have already noticed the confession of an eminent prelate that the elimination of Satan from theology would be fatal to the perpetuity of the Church. But this is only partially true. The Prince of Sin would be gone, but sin itself would survive. If the Devil were annihilated, the *Articles of Faith* and the *Bible* would remain. In short there would still be a pretended divine revelation, and the necessity for self-assumed inspired interpreters. We must, therefore, consider the authenticity of the *Bible* itself. We must study its pages, and see if they, indeed, contain the commands of the Deity, or but a compendium of ancient traditions and hoary myths. We must try to interpret them for ourselves — if possible. As to its pretended interpreters, the only possible assimilation we can find for them in the *Bible* is to compare them with the man described by the wise King Solomon in his *Proverbs*, with the perpetrator of these "six things . . . yea *seven* . . . which doth the Lord hate," and which are an abomination unto Him, to wit: "A *proud* look, a *lying* tongue, and hands that shed *innocent blood;* an heart *that deviseth wicked imaginations*, feet that be swift in running to mischief; a *false witness* that speaketh lies, and *he that soweth discord among brethren*." †

Of which of these accusations are the long line of men who have left the imprint of their feet in the Vatican guiltless?

"When the demons," says Augustine, "*insinuate* themselves in the creatures, they begin by conforming themselves *to the will of every one.* . . . In order to attract men, they begin by seducing them, by simulating obedience . . . *How could one know, had he not been taught by the demons themselves*, what they like or what they hate; *the name which attracts, or that which forces them into obedience*; all this art, in short, of *magic*, the whole science of the magicians?" ‡

To this impressive dissertation of the "saint," we will add that no magician has ever denied that he had learned the *art* from "spirits," whether, being a medium, they acted independently on him, or whether he had been initiated into the science of "evocation" by his fathers who knew it before himself. But who was it then that taught the exorcist, the priest

---

\* [Howitt, *op. cit.*, Vol. II, pp. 13-16.]

† *Proverbs* vi, 16, 17, 18, 19.

‡ Augustine, *De Civitate Dei*, XXI, vi; cf. des Mousseaux, *Mœurs et pratiques des démons*, p. 181.

who clothes himself with an authority not only over the magician, but even over all these "spirits," whom he calls demons and *devils* as soon as he finds them obeying anyone but himself? He must have learned somewhere from someone that power which he pretends to possess. For, ". . . *how could one know, had he not been taught by the demons themselves . . . the name which attracts, or that which forces them into obedience?*" asks Augustine.

Useless to remark that we know the answer beforehand: "Revelation . . . *divine* gift . . . the Son of God; nay, God Himself, through His direct Spirit, who descended on the apostles as the Pentecostal fire," and who is now alleged to overshadow every priest who sees fit to exorcise for either glory or a gift. Are we then to believe that the recent scandal of public exorcism, performed about the 14th of October, 1876, by the senior priest of the Church of the Holy Spirit, at Barcelona, Spain, was also done under the direct superintendence of the Holy Ghost?*

---

* A correspondent of the London *Times* describes the Catalonian exorcist in the following lines:

"About the 14th or 15th of this present month of October it was privately announced . . . that a young woman of seventeen or eighteen years of age, of the lower class, having long been afflicted with 'a hatred of holy things'. . . . the senior priest of the Church [of the Holy Spirit] would cure her of her disease." The exhibition was to be held in a church frequented by the best part of the community. "The church was dark, but a sickly light was shed by wax lights on the sable forms of some eighty or a hundred persons who clustered round the *presbiterio*, or sanctuary, in front of the altar. Within the little enclosure or sanctuary, separated from the crowd by a light railing, lay on a common bench, with a little pillow for her head to recline upon, a poorly-clad girl, probably of the peasant or artisan class; her brother or husband stood at her feet to restrain her (at times) frantic kicking by holding her legs. The door of the vestry opened; the exhibitor — I mean the priest — came in. The poor girl, not without just reason, 'had an aversion to holy things', or, at least, the 400 devils within her distorted body had such an aversion; and in the confusion of the moment, thinking that the father was 'a holy thing', she doubled up her legs, screamed out with twitching mouth, her breast heaving, her whole body writhing, and threw herself nearly off the bench. The male attendant seized her legs, the women supported her head and swept out her dishevelled hair. The priest advanced and, mingling familiarly with the shuddering and horror-struck crowd, said, pointing at the suffering child, now sobbing and twitching on the bench, 'Promise me, my children, that you will be prudent (*prudentes*), and of a truth, sons and daughters mine, you shall see marvels.' The promise was given. The exhibitor went to procure stole and short surplice (*estola y roquete*), and returned in a moment, taking his stand at the side of the 'possessed with the devils', with his face towards the group of students. The order of the day's proceedings was a lecture to the bystanders, and the operation of exorcising the devils. 'You know [said the priest] that so great is this girl's aversion to holy things, myself included, that she goes into convulsions, kicks, screams, and distorts her body the moment she arrives at the corner of this street, and her convulsive struggles reach their climax when she enters the sacred house of the Most High'. . . Turning to the prostrate, shuddering, most unhappy object of his attack, the priest commenced; 'In the name of

It will be urged that the "bishop was not cognizant of this freak of the clergy"; but even if he were, how could he have protested against a rite considered since the days of the apostles, one of the most holy prerogatives of the Church of Rome? So late as in 1852, only twenty-five years ago, these rites received a public and solemn sanction from the Vatican, and a new *Ritual of Exorcism* was published in Rome, Paris, and other Catholic capitals. Des Mousseaux, writing under the immediate patronage of Father Ventura, the General of the Theatines of Rome, even favors us with lengthy extracts from this famous ritual, and explains the reason why it was enforced again. It was in consequence of the revival of Magic under the name of Modern Spiritualism.* The bull of Pope Innocent VIII is exhumed, and translated for the benefit of des Mousseaux's readers. "We have heard," exclaims the Sovereign Pontiff, "that a great number of persons of both sexes have feared not to enter into relations with the spirits of hell; and that, by their practice of sorcery . . . they strike with sterility the conjugal bed, destroy the germs of humanity in the bosom of the mother, and throw spells on them, and set a barrier to the multiplication of animals . . . etc., etc."; then follow curses and anathemas against the practice. †

This belief of the Sovereign Pontiffs of an enlightened Christian country is a direct inheritance by the most ignorant multitudes from the southern Hindu rabble — the "heathen." The diabolical arts of certain *kaṅgâlins* (witches)[12] and *jâdûgars* (sorcerers) are firmly believed in by these people. The following are among their most dreaded powers: to inspire love and hatred at will; to send a devil to take possession of a person and torture

---

God, of the saints, of the blessed Host, of every holy sacrament of our Church, I adjure thee, Rusbel, come out of her'. (N. B. 'Rusbel' is the name of a devil, the devil having 257 names in Catalonia.) Thus adjured, the girl threw herself in an agony of convulsion, till her distorted face, foam-bespattered lips, and writhing limbs grew well-nigh stiff, at full length upon the floor, and, in language semi-obscene, semi-violent, screamed out, 'I don't choose to come out, you thieves, scamps, robbers'. . . . At last, from the quivering lips of the girl, came the words, 'I will'; but the devil added, with traditional perversity, 'I will cast the 100 out, but by the mouth of the girl'. The priest objected. The exit, he said, of 100 devils out of the small Spanish mouth of the woman would 'leave her suffocated'. Then the maddened girl said she must undress herself, for the devils to escape. This petition the holy father refused. 'Then I will come out through the right foot, but first'— the girl had on a hempen sandal, she was obviously of the poorest class — 'you must take off her sandal'. The sandal was untied; the foot gave a convulsive plunge; the devil and his myrmidons (so the *cura* said, looking round triumphantly) had gone to their own place. And, assured of this, the wretched dupe of a girl lay quite still. The Bishop . . . was not cognizant . . . of this freak on the part of the clergy . . . [and] the moment it came to the ears of the civil authorities, the sharpest and promptest means were taken to admonish the priest and prevent a repetition of a scandal which had shamed and sickened the whole city of Barcelona." [*The Times*, London, Nov. 2, 1876.]

\* *La Magie au XIXme siècle*, pp. 138 *et seq.*
† [*Mœurs et pratiques des démons*, p. 175.]

him; to expel him; to cause sudden death or an incurable disease; to either strike cattle with or protect them from epidemics; to compose philtres that will either strike with sterility or provoke unbounded passions in men and women, etc., etc. The sight alone of a man said to be such a sorcerer excites in a Hindu profound terror.

And now we will quote in this connection the truthful remark of a writer who passed years in India in the study of the origin of such superstitions: "Vulgar magic in India, like a degenerated infiltration, goes hand-in-hand with the most ennobling beliefs of the sectarians of the *Pitris*. It was the *work of the lowest clergy*, and designed to hold the populace in a perpetual state of fear. It is thus that in all ages and under every latitude, side by side with philosophical speculations of the highest character, one always finds *the religion of the rabble*." * In India it was the work of the *lowest clergy;* in Rome, that of the *highest Pontiffs*. But then, have they not as authority their greatest saint, Augustine, who declares that "whoever believes not in the evil spirits, refuses to believe in Holy Writ"? †

Therefore, in the second half of the nineteenth century, we find the counsel for the Sacred Congregation of Rites (exorcism of demons included), Father Ventura di Raulica, writing thus, in a letter published by des Mousseaux in 1865:

"We are in full magic! and under false names; the Spirit of lies and impudicity goes on perpetrating his horrible deprecations . . . The most grievous feature in this is that among the most serious persons they do not attach the importance to the strange phenomena which they deserve, these manifestations that we witness, and which become with every day more weird, striking, as well as most fatal.

"I cannot sufficiently admire and praise, from this standpoint, the zeal and courage displayed by you in your work. The facts which you have collected are calculated to throw light and conviction into the most skeptical minds; and after reading this remarkable work, written with so much learnedness and consciousness, blindness is no longer possible.

"If anything could surprise us, it would be the indifference with which these phenomena have been treated by *false* Science, endeavoring, as she has, to turn into ridicule so grave a subject; the childish simplicity exhibited by her in the desire to explain the facts by absurd and contradictory hypotheses . . .

[Signed] *"Father Ventura di Raulica, etc., etc."* ‡

Thus encouraged by the greatest authorities of the Church of Rome, ancient and modern, the Chevalier argues the necessity and the efficacy of exorcism by the priests. He tries to demonstrate — *on faith*, as usual —

---

* Louis Jacolliot, *Le Spiritisme dans le monde*, p. 162.
† St. Augustine, *De Civitate Dei*, XXI, vi.
‡ Des Mousseaux, *Mœurs*, etc., 1865, p. ii.

that the power of the spirits of hell is closely related to certain rites, words, and formal signs. "In the diabolical Catholicism," he says, "as well as in the *divine* Catholicism, potential grace is *bound* (*liée*) to certain signs." While the power of the Catholic priest proceeds from God, that of the Pagan priest proceeds from the Devil. The Devil, he adds, "is forced to submission" before the holy minister of God — "*he dares not* LIE." \*

We beg the reader to note well the underlined sentence, as we mean to test its truth impartially. We are prepared to adduce proofs, undeniable and undenied even by the Popish Church — forced, as she was, into the confession — proofs of hundreds of cases in relation to the most solemn of her dogmas, wherein the "spirits" lied from beginning to end. How about certain holy relics authenticated by visions of the blessed Virgin, and a host of saints? We have at hand a treatise by a pious Catholic, Guibert de Nogent, on the relics of saints. With honest despair he acknowledges the "great number of false relics, as well as false legends," and severely censures the inventors of these lying miracles. "It was on the occasion *of one of our Saviour's teeth*," writes the author of *Demonologia*, "that de Nogent took up his pen on this subject, by which the monks of St. Médard de Soissons pretended to work miracles; a pretension which he asserted to be as chimerical as that of several persons who believed they possessed the navel, and other parts less comely, of the body of Christ." †

"A monk of St. Anthony," says Stephanus,‡ "having been at Jerusalem, saw there several relics, among which was a bit of *the finger of the Holy Ghost*, as sound and entire as it had ever been; the snout of the seraphim that appeared to St. Francis; one of the nails of a cherubim; one of the ribs of the *Verbum caro factum est* (the Word was made flesh), some rays of the star that appeared to the three kings of the east; a phial of St. Michael's sweat, when he was fighting against the devil . . . 'All which things', observes our treasurer of relics, 'I have brought with me home very devoutly'."

And if the foregoing is set aside as the invention of a Protestant enemy, may we not be allowed to refer the reader to the history of England and authentic documents which state the existence of a relic not less extraordinary than the best of the others? Henry III received from the Grand Master of the Templars a phial containing a small portion of the sacred blood of Christ which he had shed upon the cross. It was attested to be genuine by the seals of the Patriarch of Jerusalem and others. The procession bearing

---

\* Des Mousseaux, *Mœurs*, etc., p. 431; also ch. xv, etc.
† *Demonologia*, London, 1827, p. 432.
‡ *Traité préparatif à l'apologie pour Hérodote*, c. 39. Cf. *Demonologia*, p. 436.

the sacred phial from St. Paul's to Westminster Abbey is described by the historian: "Two monks received the phial, and deposited it in the Abbey . . . which made all England shine with glory, dedicating it to God and St. Edward'."*

The story of the Prince Radzivill is well known. It was the undeniable deception of the monks and nuns surrounding him and his own confessor which made the Polish nobleman become a Lutheran. He felt at first so indignant at the "heresy" of the Reformation spreading in Lithuania, that he travelled all the way to Rome to pay his homage of sympathy and veneration to the Pope. The latter presented him with a precious box of relics. On his return home, his confessor saw the Virgin, who descended from her glorious abode for the sole purpose of blessing these relics and authenticating them. The superior of the neighboring convent and the mother abbess of a nunnery both saw the same vision, with a re-enforcement of several saints and martyrs; they prophesied and "felt the Holy Ghost" ascending from the box of relics and overshadowing the prince. A demoniac provided for the purpose by the clergy was exorcised in full ceremony, and upon being touched by the box immediately recovered, and rendered thanks on the spot to the Pope and the Holy Ghost. After the ceremony was over, the guardian of the treasury in which the relics were kept, threw himself at the feet of the prince, and confessed that on their way back from Rome he had lost the box of relics. Dreading the wrath of his master, he had procured a similar box, "which he had filled with the small bones of dogs and cats"; but seeing how the prince was deceived, he preferred confessing his guilt to such blasphemous tricks. The prince said nothing, but continued for some time testing — not the relics, but his confessor and the vision-seers. Their mock raptures made him discover so thoroughly the gross imposition of the monks and nuns that he joined the Reformed Church.

This is history. P. Bayle † shows that when the Roman Church is no longer able to deny that there have been false relics, she resorts to sophistry, and replies that if false relics have wrought miracles it is "because of the good intentions of the believers, who thus obtained from God a reward of their good faith"! The same Bayle shows, by numerous instances, that whenever it was proved that several bodies of the same saint, or three heads of him, or three arms (as in the case of Augustine) were said to exist in different places, and that they could not well be all authentic, the cool and invariable answer of the Church was that they were all genuine; for "God had multipied and miraculously reproduced them for the greater glory of His Holy Church"! In other words, they would have the faithful believe that the body of a deceased saint may, through divine miracle, acquire the physiological peculiarities of a crawfish!

---

\* [*Demonologia*, p. 436.]
† [*Dictionnaire historique et critique*, London, Rotterdam, 1697.]

We fancy that it would be hard to demonstrate to satisfaction that the visions of Catholic saints, are, in any one particular instance, better or more trustworthy than the average visions and prophecies of our modern "mediums." The visions of Andrew Jackson Davis — however our critics may sneer at them — are by long odds more philosophical and more compatible with modern science than the Augustinian speculations. Whenever the visions of Swedenborg, the greatest among the modern seers, run astray from philosophy and scientific truth, it is when they most run parallel with theology. Nor are these visions any more useless to either science or humanity than those of the great orthodox saints. In the life of St. Bernard it is narrated that as he was once in church, upon a Christmas eve, he prayed that the very hour in which Christ was born might be revealed to him; and when the "true and correct hour came, he saw the divine babe appear in his manger." What a pity that the divine babe did not embrace so favorable an opportunity to fix the correct day and year of his death, and thereby reconcile the controversies of his putative historians. The Tischendorfs, Lardners and Colensos, as well as many a Catholic divine, who have vainly squeezed the marrow out of historical records and their own brains in the useless search, would at least have had something for which to thank the saint.

As it is, we are hopelessly left to infer that most of the beatific and divine visions of the *Golden Legend*, and those to be found in the more complete biographies of the most important "saints," as well as most of the visions of our own persecuted seers and seeresses, were produced by ignorant and undeveloped "spirits" passionately fond of personating great historical characters. We are quite ready to agree with the Chevalier des Mousseaux, and other unrelenting persecutors of magic and spiritualism in the name of the Church, that modern spirits are often "lying spirits"; that they are ever on hand to humor the respective hobbies of the persons who communicate with them at "circles"; that they *deceive* them and, therefore, are not *always* good "spirits."

But, having conceded so much, we will now ask of any impartial person: is it possible to believe at the same time that the *power* given to the exorcist-priest, that supreme and *divine* power of which he boasts, has been given to him by God for the purpose of deceiving people? That the prayer pronounced by him *in the name of Christ*, and which, by forcing the *demon* into submission, makes him reveal himself, is calculated at the same time to make the devil confess, *not the truth*, but only that which in the *interest of the church to which the exorcist belongs* should *pass for truth*? And this is what invariably happens. Compare, for instance, the responses given by the demon to Luther, with those obtained from the devils by St. Dominic. The one argues against the private mass and upbraids Luther with placing the Virgin Mary and saints before Christ, and thus dishonoring the Son of God;* while the demons exorcised by St. Dominic, upon seeing the Virgin whom the holy father had also evoked to help him, roar out: "Oh! our enemy! oh! our damner! . . . why didst thou descend from heaven to torment us? Why art thou so powerful an intercessor for sinners! Oh! *thou most certain and secure way to heaven* . . . thou commandest us *and we are forced to confess* that nobody is damned who only perseveres in thy holy worship, etc., etc." † Luther's "Saint Satan" assures him that while believing in the transubstantiation of Christ's body and blood he had been worshipping merely bread and wine; and the *devils* of all the Catholic saints promise *eternal damnation* to whomsoever disbelieves or even so much as doubts the dogma!

Before leaving the subject, let us give one or two more instances from the *Chronicles of the Lives of the Saints*, selected from such narratives as are fully accepted by the Church. We might fill volumes with proofs of undeniable confederacy between the exorcisers and the demons. Their very nature betrays them. Instead of being independent, crafty entities, bent on the destruction of men's souls and spirits, the majority of them are simply the elementals of the kabalists; creatures with no intellect of their own, but faithful mirrors of the WILL which evokes, controls and guides them. We will not waste our time in drawing the reader's attention to doubtful or obscure thaumaturgists and exorcisers, but take as our standard one of the greatest saints of Catholicism, and select a bouquet from that same prolific conservatory of pious lies, *The Golden Legend*, of Jacobus de Voragine.‡[13]

St. Dominic, the founder of the famous order of that name, is one of the mightiest saints of the calendar. His order was the first that received a solemn confirmation from the Pope, § and he is well known in history as the associate and counsellor of the infamous Simon de Montfort, the papal general, whom he helped to butcher the unfortunate Albigenses in and near Toulouse. The story goes that this saint, and the Church after him, claims that he received from the Virgin, *in propria persona*, a rosary, whose virtues produced such stupendous miracles that they throw entirely into the shade those of the apostles, and even of Jesus himself. A man, says the biographer, an abandoned sinner, was bold enough to doubt the

---

\* [Told by Luther in] *De missa privata et unctione sacerdotum*, 1534.

† See the *Life of St. Dominic* and the story about the miraculous Rosary; also *The Golden Legend*.

‡ James de Varasse, known by the Latin name of Jacobus de Voragine, was Vicar-General of the Dominicans and Bishop of Genoa in 1292.

§ Thirteenth century.

virtue of the Dominican rosary; and for this unparalleled blasphemy was punished on the spot by having 15,000 devils take possession of him. Seeing the great suffering of the tortured demoniac, St. Dominic forgot the insult and called the devils to account.*

Following is the colloquy between the "blessed exorcist" and the demons:

*Question.*—How did you take possession of this man, and how many are you?

*Answer of the Devils.*—We came into him for having spoken disrespectfully of the rosary. We are 15,000.

*Question.*—Why did so many as 15,000 enter him?

*Answer.*—Because there are fifteen decades in the rosary which he derided, etc.

*Dominic.*—Is not all true I have said of the virtues of the rosary?

*Devils.*—Yes! Yes! (*they emit flames through the nostrils of the demoniac*). Know all ye Christians that Dominic never said one word concerning the rosary that is not most true; and know ye further, that if you do not believe him, great calamities will befall you.

*Dominic.*—Who is the man in the world the Devil hates the most?

*Devils.*—(*In chorus.*) Thou art the very man (*here follow verbose compliments*).

*Dominic.*—Of which state of Christians are there the most damned?

*Devils.*—In hell we have merchants, pawnbrokers, fraudulent bankers, grocers, Jews, apothecaries, etc., etc.

*Dominic.*—Are there any priests or monks in hell?

*Devils.*—There are a great number of priests, but *no monks*, with the exception of such as have transgressed the rule of their order.

*Dominic.*—Have you any Dominicans?

*Devils.*—Alas! alas! we have not one yet, but we expect a great number of them after their devotion is a little cooled.

We do not pretend to give the questions and answers literally, for they occupy twenty-three pages; but the substance is here, as may be seen by anyone who cares to read *The Golden Legend*. The full description of the hideous bellowings of the demons, their enforced glorification of the saint, and so on, is too long for this chapter. Suffice it to say that as we read the numerous questions offered by Dominic and the answers of the demons, we become fully convinced that they corroborate in every detail the unwarranted assertions and support the interest of the Church. The narrative is suggestive. The legend graphically describes the battle of the exorcist with the legion from the bottomless pit. The sulphurous flames which burst forth from the nose, mouth, eyes and ears of the demoniac; the sudden appearance of over

---

* [Cf. Jean Martin, *La Légende de m. st. Dominique*, Paris, 1510.]

a hundred angels, clad in golden armor; and, finally, the descent of the blessed Virgin herself, in person, bearing a golden rod, with which she administers a sound thrashing to the demoniac, to force the devils to confess that of herself which we scarcely need repeat. The whole catalogue of theological truths uttered by Dominic's devils were embodied in so many articles of faith by his Holiness the present Pope in 1870, at the last Ecumenical Council.

From the foregoing it is easy to see that the only substantial difference between infidel "mediums" and orthodox saints lies in the relative usefulness of the *demons*, if demons we must call them. While the Devil faithfully supports the Christian exorcist in his *orthodox*(?) views, the modern spook generally leaves his medium in the lurch. For, by lying, he acts *against* his or her interests rather than otherwise, and thereby too often casts foul suspicion on the genuineness of the mediumship. Were modern "spirits" *devils,* they would evidently display a little more discrimination and cunning than they do. They would act as the *demons* of the saint which, compelled by the ecclesiastical magician and by the power of "the name ... which forces them into submission," *lie in accordance with the direct interest* of the exorcist and his church. The moral of the parallel we leave to the sagacity of the reader.

"Observe well," exclaims des Mousseaux, "that there are *demons* which sometimes will speak the truth." "The exorcist," he adds, quoting the *Ritual,* "must command the demon to tell him whether he is detained in the body of the demoniac through some magic art, or by *signs*, or any objects which usually serve for this evil practice. In case the exorcised person has swallowed the latter, he must vomit them back; and if they are not in his body, the demon must indicate the proper place where they are to be found; and having found them they must be burned." * Thus some demons reveal the existence of the bewitchment, tell who is its author, and indicate the means to destroy the *malefice*. But beware to ever resort, in such a case, to magicians, sorcerers, or mediums. You must call to help you but the minister of your Church! "The Church believes in magic, as you well see," he adds, "since she expresses it so formally. And those who *disbelieve in magic*, can they still hope to share the faith of their own Church? And who can teach them better? To whom did Christ say: 'Go ye therefore, and teach all nations . . . and lo, I am with you always, even to the end of the world'?" †

Are we to believe that he said this but to those who wear the black or scarlet liveries of Rome? Must we then credit the story that this power was

---

\* *Rituale Romanum,* Paris, 1851-52, p. 478.
† *Mœurs et pratiques des démons,* p. 177.

given by Christ to Simeon Stylites, the saint who sanctified himself by perching on a pillar (*stylos*) sixty feet high for thirty-six years of his life, without ever descending from it, in order that, among other miracles stated in *The Golden Legend*, he might cure a *dragon* of a sore eye? "Near Simeon's pillar was the dwelling of a dragon, so very venomous that the stench was spread for miles round his cave." This ophidian-hermit met with an accident; he got a thorn in his eye, and, becoming blind, crept to the saint's pillar, and pressed his eye against it for three days, without touching anyone. Then the blessed saint, from his aërial seat, "*three feet in diameter*," ordered earth and water to be placed on the dragon's eye, out of which suddenly emerged a thorn (or stake), a cubit in length; when the people saw the "miracle" they glorified the Creator. As to the grateful dragon, he arose and, "having adored God for two hours, returned to his cave" *— a half-converted saurian, we must suppose.

And what are we to think of that other narrative, to disbelieve in which is "*to risk one's salvation*," as we were informed by a Pope's missionary of the Order of the Franciscans? When St. Francis preached a sermon in the wilderness, the birds assembled from the four cardinal points of the world. They warbled and applauded every sentence; they sang a holy mass in chorus; finally they dispersed to carry the glad tidings all over the universe. A grasshopper, profiting by the absence of the Holy Virgin, who generally kept company with the saint, remained perched on the head of the "blessed one" for a whole week. Attacked by a ferocious wolf, the saint, who had no other weapon but the sign of the cross which he made upon himself, instead of running away from his rabid assailant, began arguing with the beast. Having imparted to him the benefit to be derived from the holy religion, St. Francis never ceased talking until the wolf became as meek as a lamb, and even shed tears of repentance over his past sins. Finally, he "stretched his paws in the hands of the saint, followed him like a dog through all the towns in which he preached, and became half a Christian"! † Wonders of zoology! a horse turned sorcerer, a wolf and a dragon turned Christians!

These two anecdotes chosen at random from among hundreds, if rivalled are not surpassed by the wildest romances of the Pagan thaumaturgists, magicians and spiritualists! And yet, when Pythagoras is said to have subdued animals, even wild beasts, merely through a power-

---

* See the narrative selected from *The Golden Legend* by Alban Butler, in *The Lives of the Fathers, Martyrs*, etc.

† See *The Golden Legend*; *Life of St. Francis*; and *Demonologia*, pp. 398, 428.

ful mesmeric influence, he is pronounced by one half of the Catholics a barefaced impostor, and by the rest a sorcerer, who worked magic in confederacy with the Devil! Neither the she-bear, nor the eagle, nor yet the bull that Pythagoras is said to have persuaded to give up eating beans, were alleged to have answered with human voices; while St. Benedict's "black raven," whom he called "brother," argues with him, and croaks his answers like a born casuist. When the saint offers him one half of a poisoned loaf, the raven grows indignant and reproaches him in Latin as though he had just graduated at the Propaganda!

If it be objected that *The Golden Legend* is now but half-supported by the Church; and that it is known to have been compiled by the writer from a collection of the lives of the saints, for the most part unauthenticated, we can show that, at least in one instance, the biography is no legendary compilation, but the history of one man, by another one who was his contemporary. John Jortin and Gibbon* demonstrated years ago, that the early fathers used to select narratives, wherewith to ornament the lives of their apocryphal saints, from Ovid, Homer, Livy, and even from the unwritten popular legends of Pagan nations. But such is not the case in the above instances. St. Bernard lived in the twelfth century, and St. Dominic was nearly contemporaneous with the author of *The Golden Legend*. De Voragine died in 1298, and Dominic, whose exorcisms and life he describes so minutely, instituted his order in the first quarter of the thirteenth century. Moreover, de Voragine was Vicar-General of the Dominicans himself, in the middle of the same century, and therefore described the miracles wrought by his hero and patron but a few years after they were alleged to have happened. He wrote them in the same convent; and while narrating these wonders he had probably fifty persons at hand who had been eyewitnesses to the saint's mode of living. What must we think, in such case, of a biographer who seriously describes the following: One day, as the blessed saint was occupied in his study, the Devil began pestering him, in the shape of a flea. He frisked and jumped about the pages of his book until the harassed saint, unwilling as he was to act unkindly, even toward a devil, felt compelled to punish him by fixing the troublesome devil on the very sentence on which he stopped, by clasping the book. At another time the same devil appeared under the shape of a monkey. He grinned so horribly that Dominic, in order to get rid of him, ordered the devil-monkey to take the candle and hold it for him until he had done reading. The poor imp did so, and held it until it was consumed to the very end of the wick; and, notwithstanding his pitiful cries for mercy, the saint compelled him to hold it till his fingers were burned to the bones!

Enough! The approbation with which this book was received by the

---

* [*Decline and Fall*, etc., ch. xxviii.]

Church, and the peculiar sanctity attributed to it, is sufficient to show the estimation in which veracity was held by its patrons. We may add, in conclusion, that the finest quintessence of Boccaccio's *Decameron* appears prudery itself by comparison with the filthy realism of *The Golden Legend*.

We cannot regard with too much astonishment the pretensions of the Catholic Church in seeking to convert Hindus and Buddhists to Christianity. While the "heathen" keeps to the faith of his fathers, he has at least the one redeeming quality — that of not having apostatized for the mere pleasure of exchanging one set of idols for another. There may be for him some novelty in his embracing Protestantism; for in that he gains the advantage, at least, of limiting his religious views to their simplest expression. But when a Buddhist has been enticed into exchanging his Shwe Dagon for the Slipper of the Vatican, or the eight hairs from the head of Gautama and Buddha's tooth, which work miracles, for the locks of a Christian saint, and a tooth of Jesus, which work far less clever miracles, he has no cause to boast of his choice. In his address to the Literary Society of Java, Sir T. S. Raffles is said to have narrated the following characteristic anecdote: "On visiting the great temple on the hills of Nagasaki, the English commissioner was received with marked regard and respect by the venerable patriarch of the northern provinces, eighty years of age, who entertained him most sumptuously. On showing him round the courts of the temple, one of the English officers present heedlessly exclaimed in surprise, 'Jasus Christus!' The patriarch turning half round, with a placid smile, bowed significantly expressive of: 'We know your Jasus Christus! Well, don't obtrude him upon us in our temples, and we remain friends'; and so, with a hearty shake of the hands, these two opposites parted." \*

There is scarcely a report sent by the missionaries from India, Thibet and China, but laments the diabolical "obscenity" of the heathen rites, their lamentable impudicity; all of which "are so strongly suggestive of devil-worship," as des Mousseaux tells us. We can scarcely be assured that the morality of the Pagans would be in the least improved were they allowed a free inquiry into the life of, say, the psalmist-king, the author of those sweet *Psalms* which are so rapturously repeated by Christians. The difference between David performing a phallic dance before the holy ark — emblem of the female principle — and a Hindu Vishnavite bearing the same emblem on his forehead, favors the former only in the eyes of those who have studied neither the ancient faith nor their own. When a religion which compelled David to cut off and deliver two hundred foreskins of his enemies before he could become the king's son-in-law (*1 Sam.*

---

\* Chas. Coleman, *The Mythology of the Hindus*, p. 331.

xviii, 25-27) is accepted as a standard by Christians, they would do well not to cast into the teeth of heathen the impudicities of their faiths. Remembering the suggestive parable of Jesus, they ought to cast the beam out of their own eye before plucking at the mote in their neighbor's. The sexual element is as marked in Christianity as in any one of the "heathen religions." Certainly, nowhere in the *Vedas* can be found the coarseness and downright immodesty of language, that Hebraists now discover throughout the Mosaic *Bible*.

It would profit little were we to dwell much upon subjects which have been disposed of in such a masterly way by an anonymous author whose work electrified England and Germany last year;\* while as regards the particular topic under notice, we cannot do better than recommend the scholarly writings of Dr. Inman. Albeit one-sided, and in many instances unjust to the ancient heathen, Pagan and Jewish religions, the *facts* treated in the *Ancient Pagan and Modern Christian Symbolism*, are unimpeachable. Neither can we agree with some English critics who charge him with an intent to destroy Christianity. If by *Christianity* is meant the external religious form of worship, then he certainly seeks to destroy it, for in his eyes, as well as in those of every truly religious man, who has studied ancient exoteric faiths, and their symbology, Christianity is pure heathenism, and Catholicism, with its fetish-worshipping, is far worse and more pernicious than Hinduism in its most idolatrous aspect. But while denouncing the exoteric forms and unmasking the symbols, it is not the religion of Christ that the author attacks, but the artificial system of theology. We will allow him to illustrate the position in his own language, and quote from his preface:

"When vampires were discovered by the acumen of any observer," he says, 'they were, we are told, ignominiously killed, by a stake being driven through the body; but experience showed them to have such tenacity of life that they rose again and again, notwithstanding renewed impalement, and were not ultimately laid to rest till wholly burned. In like manner, the regenerated Heathendom, which dominates over the followers of Jesus of Nazareth, has risen again and again, after being transfixed. Still cherished by the many, it is denounced by the few. Amongst other accusers, I raise my voice against the Paganism which exists so extensively in ecclesiastical Christianity, and will do my utmost to expose the imposture. In a vampire story told in *Thalaba*, by Southey, the resuscitated being takes the form of a dearly-beloved maiden, and the hero is obliged to kill her with his own hand. He does so; but, whilst he strikes the form of the loved one, he feels sure that he slays

---

\* *Supernatural Religion: An Inquiry into the Reality of Divine Revelation*, London, 1874. [Published anonymously by W. R. Cassels.]

only a demon. In like manner, when I endeavor to destroy the current Heathenism, which has assumed the garb of Christianity, *I do not attack real religion.*\* Few would accuse a workman of malignancy who cleanses from filth the surface of a noble statue. There may be some who are too nice to touch a nasty subject; yet even they will rejoice when someone else removes the dirt. Such a scavenger is much wanted." †

But is it merely Pagans and heathens that the Catholics persecute, and about whom, like Augustine, they cry to the Deity, "Oh, my God! *so do I wish Thy enemies to be slain*"? Oh, no! their aspirations are more Mosaic and Cain-like than that. It is against their next of kin in faith, against their schismatic brothers that they are now intriguing within the walls which sheltered the murderous Borgias. The *larvae* of the infanticidal, parricidal and fratricidal Popes have proved themselves fit counsellors for the Cains of Castelfidardo and Mentana. It is now the turn of the Slavonian Christians, the Oriental Schismatics — the Philistines of the Greek Church!

His Holiness the Pope, after exhausting, in a metaphor of self-laudation, every point of assimilation between the great Biblical prophets and himself, has finally and truly compared himself with the Patriarch Jacob "wrestling against his God." He now crowns the edifice of Catholic piety by openly sympathizing with the Turks! The vicegerent of God inaugurates his infallibility by encouraging, in a true Christian spirit, the acts of that Moslem David, the modern Bashi-Bazouk; and it seems as if nothing would more please his Holiness than to be presented by the latter with several thousands of the Bulgarian or Serbian "foreskins." True to her policy to be all things to all men to promote her own interests, the Romish Church is, at this writing (1876), benevolently viewing the Bulgarian and Serbian atrocities, and, probably, maneuvering with Turkey against Russia.[15] Better Islam, and the hitherto-hated Crescent over the sepulchre of the Christian god, than the Greek Church established at Constantinople and Jerusalem as the state religion. Like a decrepit and toothless ex-tyrant in exile, the Vatican is eager for any alliance that promises, if not a restoration of its own power, at least the weakening of its rival. The axe its inquisitors swung, it now toys

---

\* Neither do we, if by *true religion* the world shall at last understand the adoration of one Supreme, Invisible, and Unknown Deity, by works and acts, not by the profession of vain human dogmas. But our intention is to go farther. We desire to demonstrate that if we exclude ceremonial and fetish worship from being regarded as essential parts of religion, then the true Christlike principles have been exemplified, and true Christianity practiced since the days of the apostles, exclusively among Buddhists and "heathens."

† *Ancient Pagan and Modern Christian Symbolism*, p. xvi, Introd.

with in secret, feeling its edge, and waiting, and hoping against hope. In her time, the Popish Church has lain with strange bedfellows, but never before now sunk to the degradation of giving her moral support to those who for over 1,200 years spat in her face, called her adherents "infidel dogs," repudiated her teachings, and denied godhood to her God!

The press of even Catholic France is fairly aroused at this indignity, and openly accuses the Ultramontane portion of the Catholic Church and the Vatican of siding, during the present Eastern struggle, with the Mohammedan against the Christian. "When the Minister of Foreign Affairs in the French Legislature spoke some mild words in favor of the Greek Christians, he was only applauded by the liberal Catholics, and received coldly by the Ultramontane party," says the French correspondent of a New York paper.

"So pronounced was this, that Lemoinne, the well-known editor of the great liberal Catholic *Journal des Débats*, was moved to say that the Roman Church felt more sympathy for the Moslem than the schismatic, just as they preferred an infidel to the Protestant. 'There is at bottom', says this writer, a great affinity between the *Syllabus* and the *Koran*, and between the two heads of the faithful. The two systems are of the same nature, and are united on the common ground of a one and unchangeable theory.' In Italy, in like manner, the King and Liberal Catholics are in warm sympathy with the unfortunate Christians, while the Pope and Ultramontane faction are believed to be inclining to the Mohammedans."

The civilized world may yet expect the apparition of the materialized Virgin Mary within the walls of the Vatican. The so often-repeated "miracle" of the Immaculate Visitor in the mediaeval ages has recently been enacted at Lourdes, and why not once more, as a *coup de grâce* to all heretics, schismatics and infidels? The miraculous wax taper is yet seen at Arras, the chief city of Artois; and at every new calamity threatening her beloved Church, the "Blessed Lady" appears personally, and lights it with her own fair hands, in view of a whole "biologized" congregation. This sort of "miracle," says E. Worsley, wrought by the Roman Catholic Church, "being most certain, and never doubted of by any." * Neither has the private correspondence with which the most "Gracious Lady" honors her friends been doubted. There are two precious missives from her in the archives of the Church. The first purports to be a letter in answer to one addressed to her by Ignatius. She confirms all things learned by her correspondent from "her friend" —

---

\* *Discourse of Miracles wrought in the Roman Catholic Church, or, a full Refutation of Dr. Stillingfleet's unjust Exceptions against Miracles*, Oxford, 1676, p. 64.

meaning the Apostle John. She bids him hold fast to his vows, and adds as an inducement: "*I and John will come together and pay you a visit.*" *

Nothing was known of this unblushing fraud till the letters were published at Paris in 1495. By a curious accident it appeared at a time when threatening inquiries began to be made as to the genuineness of the fourth Synoptic. Who could doubt, after such a confirmation from headquarters! But the climax of effrontery was capped in 1534, when another letter was received from the "Mediatrix," which sounds more like the report of a lobby-agent to a brother-politician. It was written in excellent Latin, and was found in the Cathedral of Messina, together with the image to which it alludes. Its contents run as follows:

"Mary Virgin, Mother of the Redeemer of the world, to the Bishop, Clergy, and the other faithful of Messina, sendeth health and benediction from *herself* and son: †

"Whereas ye have been mindful of establishing the worship of me; now this is to let you know that by so doing ye have found great favor in my sight. I have a long time reflected with pain upon your city, which is exposed to much danger from its contiguity to the fire of Etna, and I have often had words about it with my son, for he was vexed with you because of your guilty neglect of my worship, so that he would not care a pin about my intercession. Now, however, that you have come to your senses, and have happily begun to worship me, he has conferred upon me the right to become your everlasting protectress; but, at the same time, I warn you to mind what you are about, and give me no cause of repenting of my kindness to you. The prayers and festivals instituted in my honor please me tremendously (*vehementer*), and if you faithfully persevere in these things, and provided you oppose to the utmost of your power, the heretics which now-a-days are spreading through the world, by which both my worship and that of the other saints, male and female, are so endangered, you shall enjoy my perpetual protection.

"In sign of this compact, I send you down from Heaven the image of myself, cast by celestial hands, and if ye hold it in the honor to which it is entitled, it will be an evidence to me of your obedience and your faith. Farewell. Dated in Heaven, whilst sitting near the throne of my son, in the month of December, of the 1534th year from his incarnation.

"MARY VIRGIN."

The reader should understand that this document is no anti-Catholic forgery. The author from whom it is taken, ‡ says that the authenticity of the missive "is attested by the Bishop himself, his Vicar-General,

---

\* After this, why should the Roman Catholics object to the claims of the Spiritualists? If, without proof, they believe in the "materialization" of Mary and John, for Ignatius, how can they logically deny the materialization of Katie and John (King), when it is attested by the careful experiments of Mr. Crookes, the English chemist, and the cumulative testimony of a large number of witnesses?

† The "Mother of God" takes precedence therefore of God?

‡ See the *New Era*, New York, July, 1875.

Secretary, and six Canons of the Cathedral Church of Messina, all of whom have signed that attestation with their names, and confirmed it upon oath.

"Both the epistle and image were found upon the high altar, where they had been placed by angels from heaven."

A Church must have reached the last stages of degradation, when such sacrilegious trickery as this could be resorted to by its clergy, and accepted with or without question by the people.

No! far from the man who feels the working of an immortal spirit within him, be such a religion! There never was nor ever will be a truly philosophical mind, whether of Pagan, heathen, Jew, or Christian, but has followed the same path of thought. Gautama Buddha is mirrored in the precepts of Christ; Paul and Philo Judaeus are faithful echoes of Plato; and Ammonius Saccas and Plotinus won their immortal fame by combining the teachings of all these grand masters of true philosophy. "Prove all things; hold fast that which is good," ought to be the motto of all brothers on earth. Not so is it with the interpreters of the *Bible*. The seed of the Reformation was sown on the day that the second chapter of *The Catholic Epistle of James*, jostled the eleventh chapter of the *Epistle to the Hebrews* in the same *New Testament*. One who believes in Paul cannot believe in James, Peter and John. The Paulists, to remain Christians with their apostle, must withstand Peter "to the face"; and if Peter "was to be blamed" and *was wrong*, then he was not infallible. How then can his successor (?) boast of his infallibility? Every kingdom divided against itself is brought to desolation; and every house divided against itself must fall. A plurality of masters has proved as fatal in religions as in politics. What Paul preached was preached by every other mystic philosopher. "Stand *fast therefore in the liberty* wherewith Christ hath made us free, and *be not entangled again with the yoke of bondage!*" exclaims the honest apostle-philosopher; and adds, as if prophetically inspired: "But if ye bite and devour one another, take heed that ye be not consumed one of another." *

That the Neo-Platonists were not always despised or accused of demonolatry is evident in the adoption by the Roman Church of their very rites and theurgy. The identical evocations and incantations of the Pagan and Jewish Kabalist are now repeated by the Christian exorcist, and the theurgy of Iamblichus was adopted word for word. "Distinct as were the Platonists and Pauline Christians of the earlier centuries," writes Professor A. Wilder, "many of the more distinguished teachers of the new faith were deeply tinctured with the philosophical leaven. Synesius, the Bishop of Cyrene, was the disciple of Hypatia. *St. Anthony reiterated the theurgy of Iamblichus. The Logos, or word of the Gospel*

---

* [*Gal.* v, 1, 15.]

*according to John*, was a Gnostic personification. Clement of Alexandria, Origen, and others of the fathers drank deeply from the fountains of philosophy. The ascetic idea which carried away the Church was like that which was practiced by Plotinus . . . all through the middle ages there rose up men who accepted the interior doctrines which were promulgated by the renowned teacher of the Academy." *

To substantiate our accusation that the Latin Church first despoiled the kabalists and theurgists of their magical rites and ceremonies, before hurling anathemas upon their devoted heads, we will now translate for the reader fragments from the forms of *exorcism* employed by kabalists and Christians. The identity in phraseology may, perhaps, disclose one of the reasons why the Romish Church has always desired to keep the faithful in ignorance of the meaning of her Latin prayers and ritual. Only those directly interested in the deception have had the opportunity to compare the rituals of the Church and the magicians. The best Latin scholars were, until a comparatively recent date, either churchmen, or dependent upon the Church. Common people could not read Latin, and even if they could, the reading of the books on magic was prohibited, under the penalty of anathema and excommunication. The cunning device of the confessional made it almost impossible to consult, even surreptitiously, what the priests call a *grimoire* (a devil's scrawl), or *Ritual of Magic*. To make assurance doubly sure, the Church began destroying or concealing everything of the kind she could lay her hands upon.

The following are translated from the *Kabalistic Ritual*, and that generally known as the *Roman Ritual*. The latter was promulgated in 1851 and 1852, under the sanction of Cardinal Engelbert, Archbishop of Malines, and of the Archbishop of Paris. Speaking of it, the demonologist des Mousseaux says: "It is the ritual of Paul V, revised by the most learned of modern Popes, by the contemporary of Voltaire, Benedict XIV." †

| KABALISTIC (Jewish and Pagan) *Exorcism of Salt* | ROMAN CATHOLIC *Exorcism of Salt* § |
|---|---|
| The Priest-Magician blesses the Salt, and says: "*Creature of Salt*, ‡ in thee may remain the WISDOM [of God]; and may it preserve from all corruption *our minds and* | The Priest blesses the *Salt* and says: "*Creature of Salt*, I exorcise thee in the name of the living God . . . *become the health of the soul and of the body!* Every- |

---

* "Paul and Plato."

† See *La Magie au XIXme siècle*, 1860, p. 139.

‡ *Creature* of salt, air, water, or any object to be *enchanted* or *blessed*, is a technical word in magic, adopted by the Christian clergy.

§ *Rituale Romanum*, Paris, 1851-52, pp. 291-96, etc. Cf. des Mousseaux, *La Magie*, etc., 1860, p. 139.

*bodies.* Through Ḥokhmael [ חכמאל , God of wisdom], and the power of *Ruaḥ* Ḥokhmael [Spirit of the Holy Ghost] may the Spirits of matter (bad spirits) before it recede . . . *Amen."*

*Exorcism of Water (and Ashes)*

"Creature of the Water, I exorcise thee . . . by *the three names* which are Netzaḥ, Hod, and Yesod [kabalistic trinity], in the beginning and in the end, by Alpha and Omega, which are in the Spirit Azoth [Holy Ghost, or the *'Universal Soul'*], I exorcise and adjure thee . . . Wandering eagle, may the Lord command thee by the *wings of the bull and his flaming sword."* (The cherub placed at the east gate of Eden.)

*Exorcism of an Elemental Spirit*

"Serpent, in the name of the Tetragrammaton, the Lord; He commands thee, by the angel and the lion.

"Angel of darkness, obey, and run away with this holy [exorcised] water. Eagle in chains, obey this sign, and retreat before the breath. Moving serpent, crawl at my feet, or be tortured by *this sacred fire,* and evaporate before this holy incense. Let water return to water [the elemental spirit of water]; let the fire burn, and the air circulate; let the earth return to earth by the virtue of the Pentagram, which is the Morning Star, and in the name of the Tetragrammaton which is traced in the centre of *the Cross of Light. Amen."*

where where thou art thrown *may the unclean spirit be put to flight . . . Amen."*

*Exorcism of Water*

"Creature of the water, in the name of the Almighty God, the Father, the Son, and the Holy Ghost . . . *be exorcised.* . . . I adjure thee in the name of the Lamb . . . [the magician says *bull* or *ox — per alas Tauri*] of the Lamb that trod upon the basilisk and the aspic, and who crushes under his foot the lion and the dragon."

*Exorcism of the Devil*

. . . . . . . .
"O Lord, let him who carries along with him the terror, flee, struck in his turn by terror and defeated. O thou, who art the Ancient Serpent . . . tremble before the hand of him who, having triumphed of the tortures of hell [?] — *devictis gemitibus inferni —* recalled the souls to light . . . The more whilst thou delay, the more terrible will be thy torture . . . by Him who reigns over the living and the dead . . . and who will judge the century by fire, *saeculum per ignem,* etc. In the name of the Father, Son, and the Holy Ghost. Amen." \*

It is unnecessary to try the patience of the reader any longer, although we might multiply examples. It must not be forgotten that we have quoted from the latest revision of the *Ritual,* that of 1851-2. If we were to go back to the former one we would find a far more striking identity, **not merely of phraseology but of ceremonial form.** For the purpose of comparison we have not even availed ourselves of the ritual of ceremonial magic of the *Christian* kabalists of the middle ages, wherein the language modelled upon a belief in the divinity of Christ is, with the exception of a stray expression here and there, identical with the Catholic

---

\* *Rom. Rit.,* pp. 428-33. Cf. des Mousseaux, *La Magie,* etc., pp. 139-43.

Ritual.* The latter, however, makes one improvement, for the originality of which the Church should be allowed all credit. Certainly nothing so fantastical could be found in a ritual of magic. "Give place," apostrophizing the "Demon," it says, "give place to Jesus Christ . . . thou *filthy, stinking, and ferocious beast* . . . dost thou rebel? Listen and tremble, Satan; enemy of the faith, enemy of the human race, introducer of death . . . root of all evil, promoter of vice, soul of envy, origin of avarice, cause of discord, prince of homicide, whom God curses; author of incest and sacrilege, inventor of all obscenity, *professor* of the most detestable actions, *and Grand Master of Heretics* [!!] — *doctor hereticorum.* What! . . . dost thou still stand? Dost dare to resist, and thou knowest that Christ, our Lord, is coming? . . . Give place to Jesus Christ, give place to the Holy Ghost, which, by His blessed Apostle Peter, has flung thee down before the public, in the person of Simon the Magician (*te manifeste stravit in Simone mago*)." †

After such a shower of abuse, no devil having the slightest feeling of self-respect could remain in such company; unless, indeed, he should chance to be an Italian Liberal, or King Victor Emmanuel himself; both of whom, thanks to Pius IX, have become anathema-proof.

It really seems too bad to strip Rome of all her symbols at once; but justice must be done to the despoiled hierophants. Long before the sign of the Cross was adopted as a Christian symbol, it was employed as a secret sign of recognition among neophytes and adepts. Says Lévi: "The sign of the Cross adopted by the Christians does not belong exclusively to them. It is kabalistic, and represents the oppositions and quaternary equilibrium of the elements. We see by the occult verse of the *Pater,* to which we have called attention in Vol. I of this work, that there were originally two ways of making it, or, at least, two very different formulas to express its meaning — one reserved for priests and initiates; the other given to neophytes and the profane. Thus, for example, the *initiate,* carrying his hand to his forehead, said: *To thee;* then he added, *belong*; and continued, while carrying his hand to the breast — *the kingdom;* then, to the left shoulder — *justice;* to the right shoulder — *and mercy.* Then he joined the two hands, adding: *throughout the generating cycles:* '*Tibi sunt Malkhuth, et Geburah, et Ḥesed, per Aeonas*' — a sign of the Cross, *absolutely* and magnificently kabalistic, which the profanations of Gnosticism made the militant and official Church completely *lose.*" ‡

---

\* See *Art Magic,* Pt. III, sect. xix, art. on Peter d'Abano.
† *Ritual,* pp. 429-33; see *La Magie au XIXme siècle,* pp. 142-43.
‡ *Dogme et rituel de la haute magie,* Vol. II, ch. iv.

How fantastical, therefore, is the assertion of Father Ventura, that, while Augustine was a Manichaean, a philosopher, ignorant of and refusing to humble himself before the sublimity of the "grand Christian revelation," he knew nothing, understood naught of God, man, or universe; ". . . he remained poor, small, obscure, sterile, and wrote nothing, did nothing really grand or useful." But, hardly had he become a Christian ". . . when his reasoning powers and intellect, enlightened at the *luminary of faith*, elevated him to the most sublime heights of philosophy and theology." And his other proposition that Augustine's genius, as a consequence, "developed itself in all its grandeur and prodigious fecundity . . . his intellect radiated with that immense splendor which, reflecting itself in his immortal writings, has never ceased for one moment during fourteen centuries to illuminate the Church and the world"! *

Whatever Augustine was as a Manichaean, we leave Father Ventura to discover; but that his accession to Christianity established an everlasting enmity between theology and science is beyond doubt. While forced to confess that "the Gentiles had possibly something *divine* and true in their doctrines," † he, nevertheless, declared that for their superstition, idolatry and pride, they had "to be detested, and, unless they improved, to be punished by divine judgment." This furnishes the clue to the subsequent policy of the Christian Church, even to our day. If the Gentiles did not choose to come into the Church, all that was divine in their philosophy should go for naught, and the divine wrath of God should be visited upon their heads. What effect this produced is succinctly stated by Draper. "No one did more than this Father to bring science and religion into antagonism; it was mainly he who diverted the *Bible* from its true office — a guide to purity of life — and placed it in the perilous position of being the arbiter of human knowledge, an audacious tyranny over the mind of man. The example once set, there was no want of followers; the works of the great Greek philosophers were stigmatized as profane; the transcendently glorious achievements of the Museum of Alexandria were hidden from sight by a cloud of ignorance, mysticism, and unintelligible jargon, out of which there too often flashed the destroying lightnings of ecclesiastical vengeance." ‡

Augustine § and Cyprian ‖ admit that Hermes and Ostanes [16] believed in one true god; the first two maintaining, as well as the two Pagans, that he is invisible and incomprehensible, except spiritually. Moreover, we invite any man of intelligence — provided he be not a religious fanatic

---

* Ventura di Raulica, *Conférences*, II, part I, p. lvi, preface.
† [Cf. *De Civitate Dei*, VIII, ix; X, ii, etc.]
‡ *Hist. of the Conflict*, etc., p. 62.
§ [*De baptismo contra Donatistas*, lib. VI, c. xliv.]
‖ [*Sancti C. Cypriani opera*, s.v. "De idolorum vanitate," Treatise VI, sect. vi, p. 14; Oxoniae, 1682.]

— after reading fragments chosen at random from the works of Hermes and Augustine on the Deity, to decide which of the two gives a more philosophical definition of the "unseen Father." We have at least one writer of fame who is of our opinion. Draper calls the Augustinian productions a "rhapsodical conversation" with God, an "incoherent dream." \*

Father Ventura depicts the saint as attitudinizing before an astonished world upon "the most sublime heights of philosophy." But here steps in again the same unprejudiced critic, who passes the following remarks on this colossus of Patristic philosophy. "Was it for this preposterous scheme," he asks, "this product of ignorance and audacity — that the works of the Greek philosophers were to be given up? It was none too soon that the great critics who appeared at the Reformation, by comparing the works of these writers with one another, brought them to their proper level, and taught us to look upon them all with contempt." †

For such men as Plotinus, Porphyry, Iamblichus, Apollonius, and even Simon Magus, to be accused of having formed a pact with the Devil, whether the latter personage exists or not, is so absurd as to need but little refutation. If Simon Magus — the most problematical of all in an historical sense — ever existed otherwise than in the overheated fancy of Peter and the other apostles, he was evidently no worse than any of his adversaries. A difference in religious views, however great, is insufficient *per se* to send one person to heaven and the other to hell. Such uncharitable and peremptory doctrines might have been taught in the Middle Ages; but it is too late now for even the Church to put forward this traditional scarecrow. Research begins to suggest that which, if ever verified, will bring eternal disgrace on the Church of the Apostle Peter, whose very imposition of herself upon that disciple must be regarded as the most unverified and unverifiable of the assumptions of the Catholic clergy.

The erudite author of *Supernatural Religion* ‡ assiduously endeavors to prove that by *Simon Magus* we must understand the apostle Paul, whose Epistles were secretly as well as openly calumniated by Peter, and charged with containing "*dysnoëtic* learning." The Apostle of the Gentiles was brave, outspoken, sincere, and very learned; the Apostle of Circumcision, cowardly, cautious, *insincere*, and very ignorant. That Paul had been, partially at least, if not completely, initiated into the theurgic mysteries, admits of little doubt. His language, the phraseology so peculiar to the Greek philosophers, certain expressions used but by the initiates, are so many sure earmarks to that supposition. Our suspicion has been strengthened by an able article in one of the New York periodicals, entitled "Paul and Plato," in

---

\* Draper, *op. cit.*, p. 60.
† *Ibid.*, p. 66.
‡ [Vol. II, Part II, ch. v.]

which the author * puts forward one remarkable and, for us, very precious observation. In his *Epistles to the Corinthians* he shows Paul abounding with "expressions suggested by the initiations of Sabazius and Eleusis, and the lectures of the [Greek] philosophers. He [Paul] designates himself as *idiôtês* —a person unskillful in the Word, but not in the *gnosis* or philosophical learning. 'We speak wisdom among the perfect or initiated,' he writes; 'not the wisdom of this world, nor of the Archons of this world, but divine wisdom in a mystery, secret—which *none of the Archons of this world knew*'."†

What else can the apostle mean by these unequivocal words, but that he himself, as belonging to the *mystae* (initiated), spoke of things shown and explained only in the Mysteries? The "divine wisdom in a mystery which none of the *Archons of this world knew*," has evidently some direct reference to the *basileus* of the Eleusinian initiation who *did know*. The *basileus* belonged to the staff of the great hierophant, and was an *Archon* of Athens; and as such was one of the chief *mystae*, belonging to the *interior* Mysteries, to which a very select and small number obtained an entrance.‡ The magistrates supervising the Eleusinias were called Archons.

Another proof that Paul belonged to the circle of the "Initiates" lies in the following fact. The Apostle had his head shorn at Cenchrea (where Lucius Apuleius was initiated) because "he had a vow." The *nazars* — or set apart — as we see in the Jewish Scriptures, had to cut their hair which they wore long, and which "no razor touched" at any other time, and sacrifice it on the altar of initiation. And the *nazars* were a class of Chaldean theurgists. We will show further that Jesus belonged to this class.

Paul declares that: "According to the grace of God which is given unto me, as a wise *master-builder*, I have laid the foundation." §

This expression, master-builder, used only *once* in the whole *Bible*, and by Paul, may be considered as a whole revelation. In the Mysteries, the third part of the sacred rites was called *Epopteia*, or revelation, reception into the secrets. In substance it means that stage of divine clairvoyance when everything pertaining to this earth disappears, and earthly sight is paralyzed, and the soul is united free and pure with its Spirit, or God. But the real significance of the word is "overseeing," from ὅπτομαι — *I see myself*. In Sanskrit the word *avâpta* has the same meaning, as

---

* A. Wilder, editor of *The Eleusinian and Bacchic Mysteries* of Thomas Taylor.
† *1 Corinth.* ii, 6, 7, 8.
‡ Thos. Taylor, *The Eleusinian and Bacchic Mysteries*, p. 14. [ed. by A. Wilder; 4th ed., New York, 1891.]
§ *1 Corinth.* iii, 10.

well as *to obtain.*\* The word *epopteia* is a compound one, from ἐπί — upon, and ὅπτομαι — to look, or be an overseer, an inspector — also used for a master-builder. The title of master-mason, in Freemasonry, is derived from this, in the sense used in the Mysteries. Therefore, when Paul entitles himself a "master-builder," he is using a word pre-eminently kabalistic, theurgic, and masonic, and one which no other apostle uses. He thus declares himself an *adept,* having the right to *initiate* others.

If we search in this direction with those sure guides, the Grecian Mysteries and the *Kabala,* before us, it will be easy to find the secret reason why Paul was so persecuted and hated by Peter, John and James. The author of the *Revelation* was a Jewish kabalist *pur sang,* with all the hatred inherited by him from his forefathers toward the Mysteries.† His jealousy during the life of Jesus extended even to Peter; and it is but after the death of their common master that we see the two apostles — the former of whom wore the Mitre and the Petalon of the Jewish Rabbis — preach so zealously the rite of circumcision. In the eyes of Peter, Paul, who had humiliated him, and whom he felt so much his superior in "Greek learning" and philosophy, must have naturally appeared as a magician, a man polluted with the "*Gnosis,*" with the "wisdom" of the Greek Mysteries — hence, perhaps, "Simon the Magician." ‡

As to Peter, Biblical criticism has shown before now that he had probably no more to do with the foundation of the Latin Church at Rome, than to furnish the pretext so readily seized upon by the cunning Irenaeus to benefit this Church with the new name of the apostle — *Petros* or *Kêphas,* a name which allowed so readily, by an easy play upon words, to connect it with *Petroma,* the double set of stone tablets used

---

\* In its most extensive meaning, the Sanskrit word has the same literal sense as the Greek term; both imply "revelation," by no human agent, but through the "receiving of the sacred drink." In India the initiated received the "Soma," a sacred drink which helped to liberate his soul from the body; and in the Eleusinian Mysteries it was the sacred drink offered at the *Epopteia.* The Grecian Mysteries are wholly derived from the Brahmanical Vedic rites, and the latter from the ante-vedic religious Mysteries — primitive Buddhist philosophy.

† It is needless to state that the *Gospel according to John* was not written by John but by a Platonist or a Gnostic belonging to the Neo-Platonic school.

‡ The fact that Peter persecuted the "Apostle to the Gentiles," under that name, does not necessarily imply that there was no Simon Magus individually distinct from Paul. It may have become a generic name of abuse. Theodoret and Chrysostom, the earliest and most prolific commentators on the Gnosticism of those days, seem actually to make of Simon a rival of Paul, and to state that between them passed frequent messages. The former, as a diligent propagandist of what Paul terms the "antithesis of the Gnosis" (*1 Tim.* vi, 20), must have been a sore thorn in the side of the apostle. There are sufficient proofs of the actual existence of Simon Magus.

by the hierophant at the initiations, during the final Mystery. In this, perhaps, lies concealed the whole secret of the claims of the Vatican. As Professor Wilder happily suggests: "In the Oriental countries the designation פֶּתֶר, Pether [in Phoenician and Chaldaic, an interpreter] appears to have been the title of this personage [the hierophant] . . . There is in these facts some reminder of the peculiar circumstances of the Mosaic Law . . . and also of the claim of the Pope to be the successor of Peter, the hierophant or interpreter of the Christian religion." *

As such, we must concede to him, to some extent, the right to be such an interpreter. The Latin Church has faithfully preserved in symbols, rites, ceremonies, architecture, and even in the very dress of her clergy, the tradition of the Pagan worship — of the public or exoteric ceremonies, we should add; otherwise her dogmas would embody more sense and contain less blasphemy against the majesty of the Supreme and Invisible God.

An inscription found on the coffin of Queen Menthu-hetep, of the eleventh dynasty (2782 B.C.), now proved to have been transcribed from the seventeenth chapter of the *Book of the Dead* (dating not later than 4500 B.C.), is more than suggestive. This monumental text contains a group of hieroglyphics, which, when interpreted, read thus:

## PTR. RF. SU.
Peter-   ref-   su.

Baron Bunsen shows this sacred formulary mixed up with a whole series of glosses and various interpretations on a monument forty centuries old.[17] "This is identical with saying that the record [the true interpretation] was at that time no longer intelligible . . . We beg our readers to understand," he adds, "that a sacred text, a hymn, containing the words of a departed spirit, existed in such a state about 4,000 years ago . . . as to be all but unintelligible to royal scribes." †

That it was unintelligible to the uninitiated among the latter is as well proved by the confused and contradictory glossaries, as that it was a "mystery"-word, known to the hierophants of the sanctuaries, and, moreover, a word chosen by Jesus, to designate the office assigned by him to one of his apostles. This word PTR was partially interpreted, owing to another word similarly written in another group of hieroglyphics, on a

---

* Thos. Taylor, *op. cit.*, pp. 17-18 (4th ed.). Had we not trustworthy kabalistic tradition to rely upon, we might be, perhaps, forced to question whether the authorship of the *Revelation* is to be ascribed to the apostle of that name. He seems to be termed John the Theologist.

† Bunsen, *Egypt's Place in Universal History*, Vol. V, p. 90.

stele, the sign used for it being an opened eye.* Bunsen mentions as another explanation of PTR — "to show." "It appears to me," he remarks, "that our PTR is literally the old Aramaic and Hebrew 'Patar', which occurs in the history of Joseph as the specific word for *interpreting*; whence also *Pitrun* is the term for interpretation of a text, a dream." † In a manuscript of the first century, a combination of the Demotic and Greek texts, ‡ and most probably one of the few which miraculously escaped the Christian vandalism of the second and third centuries, when all such precious manuscripts were burned as magical, we find occurring in several places a phrase which, perhaps, may throw some light upon this question. One of the principal heroes of the manuscript, who is constantly referred to as "the Judaean Illuminator" or Initiate, Τελειωτής, is made to communicate but with his *Patar*; the latter being written in Chaldaic characters. Once the latter word is coupled with the name *Shimeon*. Several times, the "Illuminator," who rarely breaks his contemplative solitude, is shown inhabiting a κρυπτή (cave), and teaching the multitudes of eager scholars standing outside, not orally, but through this *Patar*. The latter receives the words of wisdom by applying his ear to a circular hole in a partition which conceals the teacher from the listeners, and then conveys them, with explanations and glossaries, to the crowd. This, with a slight change, was the method used by Pythagoras, who, as we know, never allowed his neophytes to see him during the years of probation, but instructed them from behind a curtain in his cave.

But, whether the "Illuminator" of the Graeco-Demotic manuscript is identical with Jesus or not, the fact remains that we find him selecting a "mystery"-appellation for one who is made to appear later by the Catholic Church as the janitor of the Kingdom of Heaven and the interpreter of Christ's will. The word Patar or Peter locates both master and disciple in the circle of initiation, and connects them with the "Secret Doctrine." The great hierophant of the ancient Mysteries never allowed the candidates to see or hear him personally. He was the *deus ex machina*, the presiding but invisible Deity, uttering his will and instructions through a second party; and 2,000 years later, we discover that the Taley-Lamas of Thibet had been following for centuries the same traditional program during the most important religious mysteries of Lamaism.

---

* See E. de Rougé. *Stèle*, p. 44; PTAR (*videns*) is interpreted on it "to appear," with a sign of interrogation after it — the usual mark of scientific perplexity. In Bunsen's fifth volume of *Egypt's Place*, etc., the interpretation following is "Illuminator," which is more correct.

‡ It is the property of a mystic whom we met in Syria.

† Bunsen, *op. cit.*, Vol. V, p. 90.

If Jesus knew the secret meaning of the title bestowed by him on Simon, then he must have been initiated; otherwise he could not have learned it; and if he was an initiate of either the Pythagorean Essenes, the Chaldean Magi, or the Egyptian Priests, then the doctrine taught by him was but a portion of the "Secret Doctrine" taught by the Pagan hierophants to the few select adepts admitted within the sacred adyta.

But we will discuss this question further on. For the present we will endeavor to briefly indicate the extraordinary similarity — or rather identity, we should say — of rites and ceremonial dress of the Christian clergy with that of the old Babylonians, Assyrians, Phoenicians, Egyptians, and other Pagans of the hoary antiquity.

If we would find the model of the Papal tiara, we must search the annals of the ancient Assyrian tablets. We invite the reader to give his attention to Dr. Inman's illustrated work, *Ancient Pagan and Modern Christian Symbolism*. On page sixty-four, he will readily recognize the headgear of the successor of St. Peter in the coiffure worn by gods or angels in ancient Assyria, "where it appears crowned by an emblem of the *male* trinity" (the Christian Cross). "We may mention, in passing," adds Dr. Inman, "that, as the Romanists adopted the mitre and the tiara from 'the cursed brood of Ham', so they adopted the Episcopalian crook from the augurs of Etruria, and the artistic form with which they clothe their angels from the painters and urn-makers of Magna Grecia and Central Italy."

Would we push our inquiries farther, and seek to ascertain as much in relation to the nimbus and the tonsure of the Catholic priest and monk? * We shall find undeniable proofs that they are solar emblems. Chas. Knight, in his *Old England: a Pictorial Museum*, gives a drawing by St. Augustine, representing an ancient Christian bishop, in a dress probably identical with that worn by the great "saint" himself. The *pallium*, or the ancient stole of the bishop, is the feminine sign when worn by a priest in worship. On St. Augustine's picture it is bedecked with Buddhistic crosses, and in its whole appearance it is a representation of the Egyptian T (tau), assuming slightly the figure of the letter Y. "Its lower end is . . . the mark of the masculine triad," says Inman; "the right hand [of the figure] has the forefinger extended, like the Assyrian priests while doing homage *to the grove* . . . When a male dons the pallium in worship, he becomes the representative of the trinity in the unity, the *arba*, or mystic four." †

"Immaculate is our Lady Isis," is the legend around an engraving of

---

\* The priests of Isis were tonsured.

† *Ancient Pagan*, etc., pp. 51, 52. [See also his *Ancient Faiths Embodied in Ancient Names*, Vol. II, pp. 915-18.]

Serapis and Isis, described by King, in *The Gnostics and their Remains*, "Ἡ ΚΥΡΙΑ ΕΙCΙC ΑΓΝΗ, 'Immaculate is our lady Isis,' the very terms applied afterwards to that personage who succeeded to her form, titles, symbols, rites, and ceremonies . . . Thus her devotees carried into the new priesthood the former badges of their profession, the obligation to celibacy, the tonsure, and the surplice, omitting unfortunately the frequent ablutions prescribed by the ancient creed." — "The 'Black Virgins', so highly reverenced in certain French cathedrals during the long night of the Middle Ages, proved, when at last examined critically, basalt figures of Isis"! *

Before the shrine of Jupiter Ammon were suspended tinkling bells, from the sound of whose chiming the priests gathered the auguries; "A golden bell and a pomegranate . . . round about the hem of the robe," was the result with the Mosaic Jews.† But in the Buddhistic system, during the religious services, the gods of the Deva-Loka are always invoked and invited to descend upon the altars by the ringing of bells suspended in the pagodas. The bell of the sacred table of Śiva at Kuhama is described in Kailâsa, and every Buddhist *vihâra* and lamasery has its bells.

We thus see that the bells used by Christians come to them directly from the Buddhist Thibetans and Chinese. The beads and rosaries have the same origin, and have been used by Buddhist monks for over 2,300 years. The *lingas* in the Hindu temples are ornamented upon certain days with large berries, from a tree sacred to Mahâdeva, which are strung into rosaries. The title of "nun" is an Egyptian word, and had with them the actual meaning; the Christians did not even take the trouble of translating the word *Nonna*. The aureole of the saints was used by the antediluvian artists of Babylonia, whenever they desired to honor or deify a mortal's head. In a celebrated picture in Moor's *Hindoo Pantheon*, entitled, "Krishna nursed by Devakî, from a highly-finished picture," the Hindu Virgin is represented as seated on a lounge and nursing Krishna. The hair brushed back, the long veil, and the golden aureole around the Virgin's head, as well as around that of the Hindu Savior, are striking. No Catholic, well versed as he might be in the mysterious symbolism of iconology, would hesitate for a moment to worship at that shrine the Virgin Mary, the mother of his God! ‡ In Indra-Sabhâ, the south entrance of the Caves of Ellora, may be seen to this day the figure of Indra's wife, *Indrâni*, sitting with her infant son-god, pointing the finger to heaven with the same gesture as the Italian Madonna and child.§ In *Ancient Pagan and Modern Christian Symbolism*, the author gives a figure

---

\* *The Gnostics and their Remains*, p. 71, and footnote [2nd ed., pp. 173-74.]
† [*Exod.* xxxix, 25, 26.]
‡ E. Moor, *The Hindoo Pantheon*, plate 59, pp. 197-98. Also Inman, *Ancient Pagan*, etc., p. 27.
§ [Inman, *op. cit.*, p. 29.]

from a mediaeval woodcut — the like of which we have seen by dozens in old psalters — in which the Virgin Mary, with her infant, is represented as the Queen of Heaven, on the crescent moon, emblem of virginity. "Being before the sun, she almost eclipses its light. Than this, nothing could more completely identify the Christian mother and child with Isis and Horus, Ishtar, Venus, Juno, and a host of other pagan goddesses, who have been called 'Queen of Heaven', 'Queen of the Universe', 'Mother of God', 'Spouse of God', the 'Celestial Virgin', the 'Heavenly Peacemaker', etc."*

Such pictures are not purely astronomical. They represent the male god and the female goddess, as the sun and moon in conjunction, "the union of the triad with the unit." The horns of the cow on the head of Isis have the same significance.

And so above, below, outside, and inside, the Christian Church, in the priestly garments, and the religious rites, we recognize the stamp of exoteric heathenism. On no subject within the wide range of human knowledge has the world been more blinded or deceived with such persistent misrepresentation as on that of antiquity. Its hoary past and its religious faiths have been misrepresented and trampled under the feet of it successors. Its hierophants and prophets, *mystai* and *epoptai* † of the once sacred adyta of the temple shown as demoniacs and devil-worshippers. Donned in the despoiled garments of the victim, the Christian priest now anathematizes the latter with rites and ceremonies which he has learned from the theurgists themselves. The Mosaic *Bible* is used as a weapon against the people who furnished it. The heathen philosopher is cursed under the very roof which has witnessed his initiation; and the "monkey of God" (*i.e.*, the devil of Tertullian), "the originator and founder of magical theurgy, the science of illusions and lies, whose father and author is the demon," is exorcised with holy water by the hand which holds the identical *lituus* ‡ with which the ancient augur, after a solemn prayer, used to determine the regions of heaven, and evoke, in the name of the HIGHEST, the minor god (now termed the Devil), who unveiled to his eyes futurity, and enabled him to prophesy! On the part of the Christians and the clergy it is nothing but shameful ignorance, prejudice, and that contemptible pride so boldly denounced by one of their own reverend ministers, J. B. Gross, § which rails against all investigation "as a useless or a criminal labor, when it must be feared that it will result in the overthrow of pre-established systems of faith." On the part of the scholars it is the same apprehension of the possible necessity of having to modify some of their

---

\* *Ibid.*, p. 76.
† Initiates and seers.
‡ The augur's, and now bishop's, pastoral crook.
§ *The Heathen Religion*, Introd.

erroneously established theories of science. "Nothing but such pitiable prejudice," says Gross, "can have thus misrepresented the theology of heathenism, and distorted — nay, caricatured — its forms of religious worship. It is time that posterity should raise its voice in vindication of violated truth, and that the present age should learn to recognize in the hoary past at least a little of that common sense of which *it* boasts with as much self-complacency as if the prerogative of reason was the birthright only of modern times." *

All this gives a sure clue to the real cause of the hatred felt by the early mediaeval Christian toward his Pagan brother and dangerous rival. We hate but what we fear. The Christian thaumaturgist once having broken all association with the Mysteries of the temples and with "these schools so renowned for magic," described by St. Hilarion,† could certainly expect but little to rival the Pagan wonder-workers. No apostle, with the exception perhaps of healing by mesmeric power, has ever equalled Apollonius of Tyana; and the scandal created among the apostles by the miracle-doing Simon Magus is too notorious to be repeated here again. "How is it," asks Justin Martyr, in evident dismay, "how is it that the talismans of Apollonius [the τελέσματα] have power in certain members of creation, for they prevent, *as we see*, the fury of the waves, and the violence of the winds, and the attacks of wild beasts; and whilst our Lord's miracles are preserved by tradition alone, those of Apollonius *are most numerous*, and actually manifested in present facts, so as to lead astray all beholders?" ‡ This preplexed martyr solves the problem by attributing very correctly the efficacy and potency of the charms used by Apollonius to his profound knowledge of the sympathies and antipathies (or repugnances) of nature.

Unable to deny the evident superiority of their enemies' powers, the fathers had recourse to the old but ever successful method — that of slander. They honored the theurgists with the same insinuating calumny that had been resorted to by the Pharisees against Jesus. "Thou hast a daemon," the elders of the Jewish Synagogue had said to him. "Thou hast the Devil," repeated the cunning fathers, with equal truth, addressing the Pagan thaumaturgist; and the widely bruited charge, erected later into an article of faith, won the day.

But the modern heirs of these ecclesiastical falsifiers, who charge magic, spiritualism, and even magnetism with being produced by a demon, forget or perhaps never read the classics. None of our bigots has ever looked with more scorn on the *abuses* of magic than did the true initiate of old. No modern

---

\* [*Ibid.*]

† Michel Ange Marin, *Les Vies des Pères des déserts d'Orient*, Avignon, 1761, tome II, pp. 283-84.

‡ Justin Martyr, *Quaestiones et Responsiones at Orthodoxos*, xxiv.

or even mediaeval law could be more severe than that of the hierophant. True, he had more discrimination, charity and justice, than the Christian clergy; for while banishing the "unconscious" sorcerer, the person troubled with a demon, from within the sacred precincts of the adyta, the priests, instead of mercilessly burning him, took care of the unfortunate "possessed one." Having hospitals expressly for that purpose in the neighborhood of temples, the ancient "medium," if obsessed, was taken care of and restored to health. But with one who had, by conscious *witchcraft*, acquired powers dangerous to his fellow-creatures, the priests of old were as severe as justice herself. "Any person accidentally guilty of homicide, or of any crime, or convicted of *witchcraft*, was excluded" from the Eleusinian Mysteries.* And so were they from all others. This law, mentioned by all writers on the ancient initiation, speaks for itself. The claim of Augustine, that all the explanations given by the Neo-Platonists were invented by themselves is absurd. For nearly every ceremony in their true and successive order is given by Plato himself, in a more or less covered way. The Mysteries are as old as the world, and one well versed in the esoteric mythologies of various nations can trace them back to the days of the ante-Vedic period in India. A condition of the strictest virtue and purity is required from the *Vatu* or candidate in India before he can become an initiate, whether he aims to be a simple fakir, a *Purohita* (public priest) or a *Sannyâsin*, a saint of the second degree of initiation, the most holy as the most reverend of them all. After having conquered, in the terrible trials preliminary to admittance to the inner temple in the subterranean crypts of his pagoda, the *sannyâsin* passes the rest of his life in the temple, practicing the eighty-four rules and ten virtues prescribed to the Yogis.

"No one who has not practiced, during his whole life, the ten virtues which the divine Manu makes incumbent as a duty, can be initiated into the mysteries of the council," say the Hindu books of initiation.

These virtues are: "Resignation; the act of rendering good for evil; temperance; probity; purity; chastity; repression of the physical senses; the knowledge of the Holy Scriptures; that of the *Superior* soul [spirit]; worship of truth; abstinence from anger." † These virtues must alone direct the life of a true Yogi. "No unworthy adept ought to defile the ranks of the holy initiates by his presence for twenty-four hours." The adept becomes guilty after having once broken any one of these vows. Surely the exercise of such virtues is inconsistent with the idea one has of *devil*-worship and lasciviousness of purpose!

And now we will try to give a clear insight into one of the chief ob-

---

* See Taylor, *Eleusinian and Bacchic Mysteries*, ed. by A. Wilder, p. 19 (4th ed); also Porphyry and others.

† [*Manu*, VI, ślokas 92-93.]

jects of this work. What we desire to prove is that underlying every ancient popular religion was the same ancient wisdom-doctrine, one and identical, professed and practiced by the initiates of every country, who alone were aware of its existence and importance. To ascertain its origin, and the precise age in which it was matured, is now beyond human possibility. A single glance, however, is enough to assure one that it could not have attained the marvellous perfection in which we find it pictured to us in the relics of the various esoteric systems, except after a succession of ages. A philosophy so profound, a moral code so ennobling, and practical results so conclusive and so uniformly demonstrable is not the growth of a generation, or even a single epoch. Fact must have been piled upon fact, deduction upon deduction, science have begotten science, and myriads of the brightest human intellects have reflected upon the laws of nature, before this ancient doctrine had taken concrete shape. The proofs of this identity of fundamental doctrine in the old religions are found in the prevalence of a system of initiation; in the secret sacerdotal castes who had the guardianship of mystical words of power, and a public display of a phenomenal control over natural forces, indicating association with preterhuman beings. Every approach to the Mysteries of all these nations was guarded with the same jealous care, and in all, the penalty of death was inflicted upon initiates of any degree who divulged the secrets entrusted to them. We have seen that such was the case in the Eleusinian and Bacchic Mysteries, among the Chaldean Magi, and the Egyptian hierophants; while with the Hindus, from whom they were all derived, the same rule has prevailed from time immemorial. We are left in no doubt upon this point; for the *Agrushada Parikshai* says explicitly, "Every initiate, to whatever degree he may belong, who reveals the great sacred formula, must be put to death."

Naturally enough, this same extreme penalty was prescribed in all the multifarious sects and brotherhoods which at different periods have sprung from the ancient stock. We find it with the early Essenes, Gnostics, theurgic Neo-Platonists, and mediaeval philosophers; and in our day, even the Masons perpetuate the memory of the old obligations in the penalties of throat-cutting, dismemberment and disemboweling, with which the candidate is threatened. As the Masonic "master's word" is communicated only at "low breath," so the selfsame precaution is prescribed in the Chaldean *Book of Numbers* and the Jewish *Merkabah*. When initiated, the neophyte was led by an *ancient* to a secluded spot, and there the latter whispered *in his ear* the great secret.* The Mason swears, under the most frightful penalties, that he will not communicate the secrets of

---

* A. Franck, *La Kabbale*, ch. i.

any degree "to a brother of an *inferior degree*"; and the *Agrushada Parikshai* says: "Any initiate of the third degree who reveals before the prescribed time, to the initiates of the second degree, the superior truths, must be put to death." Again, the Masonic apprentice consents to have his "tongue torn out by the roots" if he divulge anything to a profane; and in the Hindu books of initiation, the same *Agrushada Parikshai*, we find that any initiate of the first degree (the lowest) who betrays the secrets of his initiation, to members of other castes, for whom the science should be a closed book, must have *"his tongue cut out,"* and suffer other mutilations.

As we proceed, we will point out the evidence of this identity of vows, formulas, rites and doctrines, between the ancient faiths. We will also show that not only their memory is still preserved in India, but also that the Secret Association is still alive and as active as ever; that, after reading what we have to say, it may be inferred that the chief pontiff and hierophant, the *Brahmâtma*, is still accessible to those "who know," though perhaps recognized by another name; and that the ramifications of his influence extend throughout the world. But we will now return again to the early Christian period.

As though he were not aware that there was any esoteric significance to the exoteric symbols, and that the Mysteries themselves were composed of two parts, the lesser at Agrae, and the higher ones at Eleusis, Clemens Alexandrinus, with a rancorous bigotry that one might expect from a renegade Neo-Platonist, but is astonished to find in this generally honest and learned Father, stigmatized the Mysteries as indecent and diabolical. Whatever the rites enacted among the neophytes before they passed to a higher form of instruction; however misunderstood were the trials of *katharsis* or purification, during which they were submitted to every kind of probation; and however much the material or physical aspect might have led to calumny, it is but wicked prejudice which can compel a person to say that under this external meaning there was not a far deeper and spiritual significance.

It is positively absurd to judge the ancients from our own standpoint of propriety and virtue. And most assuredly it is not for the Church — which now stands accused by all the modern symbologists of having adopted precisely these same emblems in their coarsest aspect, and feels herself powerless to refute the accusations — to throw the stone at those who were her models. When men like Pythagoras, Plato and Iamblichus, renowned for their severe morality, took part in the Mysteries, and spoke of them with veneration, it ill behooves our modern critics to judge them so rashly upon their merely external aspect. Iamblichus explains the worst; and his explanation, for an unprejudiced mind, ought to be perfectly plausible. "Exhibitions of this kind," he says, "in the Mysteries were designed to free us from licentious passions, by gratifying the sight, and at the same time vanquishing all evil thought, through *the awful sanctity* with which these rites were accompanied." * "The wisest and best men in the Pagan world," adds Dr. Warburton, "are unanimous in this, that the Mysteries were instituted pure, and proposed the noblest ends by the worthiest means." †

In these celebrated rites, although persons of both sexes and all classes were allowed to take a part, and a participation in them was even obligatory, very few indeed attained the higher and final initiation. The gradation of the Mysteries is given us by Proclus in the fourth book of his *Theology of Plato*. ‡ "The *perfective rite* [τελετή, *teletê*] precedes in order the *initiation* [μύησις, *muêsis*], and *initiation*, the final apocalypse, *epopteia*." Theon of Smyrna, in *Mathematica*, also divides the mystic rites into five parts: "the first of which is the previous purification; for *neither are the Mysteries communicated to all* who are willing to receive them; but there are certain persons who are prevented by the voice of the crier (κῆρυξ) . . . since it is necessary that such as are not expelled from the Mysteries should first be refined by certain purifications: but after purification, the reception of the sacred rites succeeds. The third part is denominated *epopteia*, or reception. And the fourth, which is the end and design of the revelation, is the *binding of the head and the fixing of the crowns* § . . . whether after this he [the initiated person] becomes a torchbearer, or an hierophant of the mysteries, or sustains some other part of the sacerdotal office. But the fifth, which is produced from all these, *is friendship and interior communion with God* . . ." And this was the last and most awful of all the Mysteries.‖

There are writers who have often wondered at the meaning of this claim to a "friendship and interior communion with God." Christian authors have denied the pretensions of the "Pagans" to such "communion," affirming that only Christian saints were and are capable of enjoying it; materialistic skeptics have altogether scoffed at the idea of both. After long ages of religious materialism and spiritual stagnation, it has most certainly become difficult if not altogether impossible to substantiate the claims of either party. The old Greeks, who had once crowded

---

\* *De Mysteriis*, etc., I, ch. xi.

† *Divine Legation of Moses demonstrated*, etc., II, p. 172.

‡ *On the Theology of Plato*, Bk. IV, p. 220; Taylor's ed., London, 1816.

§ This expression must not be understood literally; for as in the initiation of certain Brotherhoods it has a secret meaning, hinted at by Pythagoras, when he describes his feelings after the initiation and tells that he was crowned by the gods in whose presence he had drunk "the waters of life" — in Hindostânî, *âb-i-hayât*, fount of life.

‖ [Cf. Thos. Taylor, *Eleus. and Bacchic Myst.*, ed. by A. Wilder, pp. 82-85 (4th ed.).]

around the Agora of Athens, with its altar to the "Unknown God," are no more; and their descendants firmly believe that they have found the "unknown" in the Jewish Jehovah. The divine ecstasies of the early Christians have made room for visions of a more modern character, in perfect keeping with progress and civilization. The "Son of man" appearing to the rapt vision of the ancient Christian as coming from the seventh heaven, in a cloud of glory, and surrounded with angels and winged seraphim, has made room for a more prosaic and at the same time more businesslike Jesus. The latter is now shown as making morning calls upon Mary and Martha in Bethany; as seating himself on "the *ottoman*" with the younger sister, a lover of "ethics," while Martha goes off to the kitchen to cook. Anon the heated fancy of a blasphemous Brooklyn preacher and harlequin, the Reverend Dr. Talmage, makes us see her rushing back "with besweated brow, a pitcher in one hand and the tongs in the other . . . into the presence of Christ," and blowing him up for not caring that her sister hath left her "to serve alone." *

From the birth of the solemn and majestic conception of the unrevealed Deity of the ancient adepts to such caricatured descriptions of him who died on the Cross for his philanthropic devotion to humanity, long centuries have intervened, and their heavy tread seems to have almost entirely obliterated all sense of a spiritual religion from the hearts of his professed followers. No wonder then, that the sentence of Proclus is no longer understood by the Christians, and is rejected as a "vagary" by the materialists, who, in their negation, are less blasphemous and atheistical than many of the reverends and members of the churches. But, although the Greek *epoptai* are no more, we have now, in our own age, a people far more ancient than the oldest Hellenes, who practice the so-called "preterhuman" gifts to the same extent as did their ancestors far earlier than the days of Troy. It is to this people that we draw the attention of the psychologist and philosopher.

One need not go very deep into the literature of the Orientalists to become convinced that in most cases they do not even suspect that in

---

\* This original and very long sermon was preached in a church at Brooklyn, N. Y., on the 15th day of April, 1877. On the following morning, the reverend orator was called in the *Sun* a gibbering charlatan; but this deserved epithet will not prevent other reverend buffoons doing the same and even worse. And this is the religion of Christ! Far better disbelieve in him altogether than caricature one's God in such a manner. We heartily applaud the *Sun* for the following views: "And then when Talmage makes Christ say to Martha in the tantrums: 'Don't worry, but sit down on this ottoman,' he adds the climax to a scene that the inspired writers had nothing to say about. Talmage's buffoonery is going too far. If he were the worst heretic in the land, instead of being straight in his orthodoxy, he would not do so much evil to religion as he does by his familiar blasphemies."

the arcane philosophy of India there are depths which they have not sounded, and *cannot* sound, for they pass on without perceiving them. There is a pervading tone of conscious superiority, a ring of contempt in the treatment of Hindu metaphysics, as though the European mind is alone enlightened enough to polish the rough diamond of the old Sanskrit writers, and separate right from wrong for the benefit of their descendants. We see them disputing over the external forms of expression without a conception of the great vital truths these hide from the profane view.

"**As a rule, the Brahmans,**" says Jacolliot, "rarely go beyond the class of *grihastha* [priests of the vulgar castes] and *purohita* [exorcizers, divines, prophets, and evocators of spirits]. And yet, we shall see . . . once that we have touched upon the question and study of manifestations and phenomena, that these initiates of the *first* degree [the lowest] attribute to themselves, and in appearance possess faculties developed to a degree which has never been equalled in Europe. As to the initiates of the second and especially of the third category, they pretend to be enabled to ignore time, space, and to command life and death." \*

Such initiates as these Jacolliot *did not meet*; for, as he says himself, they only appear on the most solemn occasions, and when the faith of the multitudes has to be strengthened by phenomena of a superior order. "They are never seen, either in the neighborhood of, or even inside the temples, except at the grand quinquennial festival of the fire. On that occasion, they appear about the middle of the night, on a platform erected in the centre of the sacred lake, like so many phantoms, and by their conjurations they illumine the space. A fiery column of light ascends from around them, rushing from earth to heaven. Unfamiliar sounds vibrate through the air, and five or six hundred thousand Hindus, gathered from every part of India to contemplate these demigods, throw themselves with their faces buried in the dust, invoking the souls of their ancestors." †

Let any impartial person read *Le Spiritisme dans le monde*, and he cannot believe that this "implacable rationalist," as Jacolliot takes pride in terming himself, said one word more than is warranted by what he had seen. His statements support and are corroborated by those of other skeptics. As a rule, the missionaries, even after passing half a lifetime in the country of "devil-worship," as they call India, either disingenuously *deny* altogether what they cannot help knowing to be true, or ridiculously attribute phenomena to this power of the Devil, that outrival the "miracles" of the apostolic ages. And what do we see this French

---

\* *Le Spiritisme dans le monde*, p. 68.
† *Ibid*, pp. 78, 79.

author, notwithstanding his incorrigible rationalism, forced to admit, after having narrated the greatest wonders? Watch the fakirs as he would, he is compelled to bear the strongest testimony to their perfect honesty in the matter of their miraculous phenomena. "Never," he says, "have we succeeded in detecting a single one in the act of deceit." One fact should be noted by all who, without having been in India, still fancy they are clever enough to expose the fraud of *pretended* magicians. This skilled and cool observer, this redoubtable materialist, after his long sojourn in India, affirms, "we unhesitatingly avow that we have not met, either in India or in Ceylon, a single European, even among the oldest residents, who has been able to indicate the means employed by these devotees for the production of these phenomena!"

And how should they? Does not this zealous Orientalist confess to us that even he, who had every available means at hand to learn many of their rites and doctrines at first hand, failed in his attempts to make the Brahmans explain to him their secrets? "All that our most diligent inquiries of the *Purohitas* could elicit from them respecting the acts of their superiors (the invisible initiates of the temples), amounts to very little." And again, speaking of one of the books, he confesses that, while purporting to reveal all that is desirable to know, it "falls back into mysterious formulas, in combinations of magical and occult letters, the secret of which it has been impossible for us to penetrate," etc.

The fakirs, although they can never reach beyond the first degree of initiation, are, notwithstanding, the only agents between the living world and the "silent brothers," or those initiates who never cross the thresholds of their sacred dwellings. The *Fukarâ-Yogins* belong to the temples, and who knows but these cenobites of the sanctuary have far more to do with the psychological phenomena which attend the fakirs, and have been so graphically described by Jacolliot, than the *Pitris* themselves? Who can tell but that the fluidic spectre of the ancient Brahman seen by Jacolliot was the *scîn-lâc*, the spiritual *double,* of one of these mysterious sannyâsins?

Although the story has been translated and commented upon by Professor Perty, of Geneva, still we will venture to give it in Jacolliot's own words: "A moment after the disappearance of the hands, the fakir continuing his evocations (*mantras*) more earnestly than ever, a cloud like the first, but more opalescent and more opaque, began to hover near the small brazier, which, by request of the Hindu, I had constantly fed with live coals. Little by little it assumed a form entirely human, and I distinguished the spectre — for I cannot call it otherwise — of an old Brahman sacrificator, kneeling near the little brazier.

"He bore on his forehead the signs sacred to Vishṇu, and around his body the triple cord, sign of the initiates of the priestly caste. He joined his hands above his head, as during the sacrifices, and his lips moved as if they were reciting prayers. At a given moment, he took a pinch of perfumed powder, and threw it upon the coals; it must have been a strong compound, for a thick smoke arose on the instant, and filled the two chambers.

"When it was dissipated, I perceived the spectre, which, two steps from me, was extending to me its fleshless hand; I took it in mine, making a salutation, and I was astonished to find it, although bony and hard, warm and living.

" 'Art thou, indeed', said I at this moment, in a loud voice, 'an ancient inhabitant of the earth?'

"I had not finished the question, when the word AM (yes) appeared and then disappeared in letters of fire, on the breast of the old Brahman, with an effect much like that which the word would produce if written in the dark with a stick of phosphorus.

" 'Will you leave me nothing in token of your visit?' I continued.

"The spirit broke the triple cord, composed of three strands of cotton, which begirt his loins, gave it to me, and vanished at my feet."

"Oh Brahmâ! what is this mystery which takes place every night? . . . When lying on the matting, with eyes closed, the body is lost sight of, and the soul escapes to enter into conversation with the Pitris . . . Watch over it, Oh Brahmâ, when, forsaking the resting body, it goes away to hover over the waters, to wander in the immensity of heaven, and penetrate into the dark and mysterious nooks of the valleys and grand forests of the Himavat!" (*Agrushada Parikshai.*) \*

The fakirs, when belonging to some particular temple, never act but under orders. Not one of them, unless he has reached a degree of extraordinary sanctity, is freed from the influence and guidance of his guru, his teacher, who first initiated and instructed him in the mysteries of the *occult* sciences. Like the *subject* of the European mesmerizer, the average fakir can never rid himself entirely of the psychological influence exercised on him by his guru. Having passed two or three hours in the silence and solitude of the inner temple in prayer and meditation, the fakir, when he emerges thence, is mesmerically strengthened and prepared; he produces wonders far more varied and powerful than before he entered. The "master" has *laid his hands upon him*, and the fakir feels strong.

It may be shown, on the authority of many Brahmanical and Buddhist sacred books, that there has ever existed a great difference between

---

\* Louis Jacolliot, *Le Spiritisme dans le monde*, pp. 319-20, 65.

adepts of the higher order, and purely psychological subjects — like many of these fakirs, who are mediums in a certain qualified sense. True, the fakir is ever talking of Pitris, and this is natural; for they are his protecting deities. But are the Pitris *disembodied human beings of our race?* This is the question, and we will discuss it in a moment.

We say that the fakir may be regarded in a degree as a medium; for he is — what is not generally known — under the direct mesmeric influence of a living adept, his *sannyâsin* or guru. When the latter dies, the power of the former, unless he has received the last transfer of spiritual forces, wanes and often even disappears. Why, if it were otherwise, should the fakirs have been excluded from the right of advancing to the second and third degrees? The lives of many of them exemplify a degree of self-sacrifice and sanctity unknown and utterly incomprehensible to Europeans, who shudder at the bare thought of such self-inflicted tortures. But however shielded from control by vulgar and earth-bound spirits, however wide the chasm between a debasing influence and their self-controlled souls; and however well protected by the seven-knotted magical bamboo rod which he receives from the guru, still the fakir lives in the outer world of sin and matter, and it is possible that his soul may be tainted, perchance, by the magnetic emanations from profane objects and persons, and thereby open an access to strange spirits and *gods.* To admit one so situated, one not under any and all circumstances sure of the mastery over himself, to a knowledge of the awful mysteries and priceless secrets of initiation, would be impracticable. It would not only imperil the security of that which must, at all hazards, be guarded from profanation, but it would be consenting to admit behind the veil a fellow being whose mediumistic irresponsibility might at any moment cause him to lose his life through an involuntary indiscretion. The same law which prevailed in the Eleusinian Mysteries before our era, holds good now in India.

Not only must the adept have mastery over himself, but he must be able to control the inferior grades of spiritual beings, nature-spirits and earth-bound souls, in short the very ones by whom, if by any, the fakir is liable to be affected.

For the objector to affirm that the Brahman-adepts and the fakirs admit that of themselves they are powerless, and can only act with the help of disembodied human spirits, is to state that these Hindus are unacquainted with the laws of their sacred books and even the meaning of the word *Pitris.* The *Laws of Manu,* the *Atharva-Veda,* and other books, prove what we now say. "All that exists," says the *Atharva-Veda,*\* "is in the power of the gods. The gods are under the power of magical conjurations. The magical conjurations are under the control of the Brahmans. Hence

---

\* [As quoted by L. Jacolliot, *Le Spiritisme dans le monde,* p. 25.]

the gods are in the power of the Brahmans." This is logical, albeit seemingly paradoxical, and it is the fact. And this fact will explain to those who have not hitherto had the clue (among whom Jacolliot must be numbered, as will appear on reading his works), why the fakir should be confined to the first, or lowest degree of that course of initiation whose highest adepts, or hierophants, are the *sannyâsins*, or members of the ancient Supreme Council of Seventy.

Moreover, in Book I of the Hindu *Genesis*, or *Book of Creation* of *Manu*, the *Pitris* are called the *lunar* ancestors of the human race. They belong to a race of beings different from ourselves, and cannot properly be called "human spirits" in the sense in which the spiritualists use this term. This is what is said of them:

"Then they [the gods] created the Yakshas, the Râkshasas, the Pisâchas,* the Gandharvas,† the Apsarases, and the Asuras, the Nâgas,‡ the Sarpas, the Suparnas, and the Pitris — *lunar ancestors of the human race*" (See *Institutes of Manu*, Book I, śloka 37, where the Pitris are termed "progenitors of mankind"). §

The Pitris are a distinct race of spirits belonging to the mythological hierarchy or rather to the kabalistical nomenclature, and must be included with the good genii, the daemons of the Greeks, or the inferior gods of the invisible world; and when a fakir attributes his phenomena to the Pitris, he means only what the ancient philosophers and theurgists meant when they maintained that all the "miracles" were obtained through the intervention of the gods, or the good and bad daemons, who control the powers of nature, the *elementals*, who are subordinate to the power of him "who knows." A ghost or human phantom would be termed by a fakir *palit*, or *bhûtnâ*, as that of a female human spirit *pichalpâi*, not *pitri*. True, *pitarah* (plural) means fathers, ancestors; and *pitarâi* is a kinsman; but these words are used in quite a different sense from that of the Pitris invoked in the mantras.

To maintain before a devout Brahman or a fakir that anyone can converse with the spirits of the dead, would be to shock him with what would appear to him blasphemy. Does not the concluding verse of the *Bhâgavata-Purâna* state that this supreme felicity is alone reserved to the holy sannyâsins, the gurus and yogis?

"Long before they finally rid themselves of their mortal envelopes, the souls who have practiced only good, such as those of the sannyâsins and the vanaprasthas, acquire the faculty of conversing with the souls which preceded them to the svarga." ‖

---

\* Pisâchas, daemons of the race of the gnomes, the giants and the vampires.
† Gandharvas, good daemons, celestial seraphs, singers.
‡ Asuras and Nâgas are the Titanic spirits and the dragon or serpent-headed spirits.
§ [Latter also in *Manu*, III, 201.]
‖ [L. Jacolliot, *Christna et le Christ*, p. 139.]

In this case the Pitris instead of genii are the spirits, or rather souls, of the departed ones. But they will freely communicate only with those whose atmosphere is as pure as their own, and to whose prayerful *kalâśas* (invocation) they can respond without the risk of defiling their own celestial purity. When the soul of the invocator has reached the *sâyujya*, or perfect identity of essence with the Universal Soul, when matter is utterly conquered, then the adept can freely enter into daily and hourly communion with those who, though unburdened with their corporeal forms, are still themselves progressing through the endless series of transformations included in the gradual approach to the *Paramâtman*, or the grand Universal Soul.

Bearing in mind that the Christian fathers have always claimed for themselves and their saints the name of "friends of God," and knowing that they borrowed this expression, with many others, from the technology of the Pagan temples, it is but natural to expect them to show an evil temper whenever alluding to these rites. Ignorant as a rule, and having had biographers as ignorant as themselves, we could not well expect them to find in the accounts of their beatific visions a descriptive beauty such as we find in the Pagan classics. Whether the visions and objective phenomena claimed by both the fathers of the desert and the hierophants of the sanctuary are to be discredited, or accepted as facts, the splendid imagery employed by Proclus and Apuleius in narrating the small portion of the final initiation that they dared reveal, throws completely into the shade the plagiaristic tales of the Christian ascetics, faithful *copies* though they were intended to be. The story of the temptation of St. Anthony in the desert by the female demon, is a parody upon the preliminary trials of the neophyte during the *Mikra*, or minor Mysteries of Agrae — those rites at the thought of which Clemens railed so bitterly, and which represented the bereaved Demeter in search of her child, and her good-natured hostess Baubo.\*

Without entering again into a demonstration that in Christian, and especially Irish Roman Catholic, churches † the same apparently indecent customs as the above prevailed until the end of the last century, we will recur to the untiring labors of that honest and brave defender of the ancient faith, Thomas Taylor, and his works. However much dogmatic Greek scholarship may have found to say against his "mistranslations," his memory must be dear to every true Platonist, who seeks rather to learn the inner thought of the great philosopher than enjoy the mere external mechanism of his writings. Better classical translators may have

---

\* Arnobius, *Adv. gent.*, V, 25; Clem. Alex., *Hortatory Address to the Greeks*, c. ii.
† See Inman, *Ancient Pagan and Modern Christian Symbolism*, 1874, p. 66.

rendered us, in more correct phraseology, Plato's *words*, but Taylor shows us Plato's *meaning*, and this is more than can be said of Zeller, Jowett, and their predecessors. Yet, as writes Professor A. Wilder, Taylor's works "have met with favor at the hands of men capable of profound and recondite thinking; and it must be conceded that he was endowed with a superior qualification — that of an intuitive perception of the interior meaning of the subjects which he considered. Others may have known more Greek, but he knew more Plato." \*

Taylor devoted his whole useful life to the search after such old manuscripts as would enable him to have his own speculations concerning several obscure rites in the Mysteries corroborated by writers who had been initiated themselves. It is with full confidence in the assertions of various classical writers that we say that ridiculous, perhaps licentious in some cases, as may appear ancient worship to the modern critic, it ought not to have so appeared to the Christians. During the mediaeval ages, and even later, they accepted pretty nearly the same without understanding the secret import of its rites, and quite satisfied with the obscure and rather fantastic interpretations of their clergy, who accepted the exterior form and distorted the inner meaning. We are ready to concede, in full justice, that centuries have passed since the great majority of the Christian clergy, who *are not allowed to pry into God's mysteries nor seek to explain* that which the Church has once accepted and established, have had the remotest idea of their symbolism, whether in its exoteric or esoteric meaning. Not so with the head of the Church and its highest dignitaries. And if we fully agree with Inman that it is "difficult to believe that the ecclesiastics who sanctioned the publication of such a print † could have been as ignorant as modern ritualists," we are not at all prepared to believe with the same author "that the latter, if they knew the real meaning of the symbols commonly used by the Roman Church, would *not* have adopted them." †

To eliminate what is plainly derived from the sex and nature wor-

---

\* Introduction to Taylor's *Eleusinian and Bacchic Mysteries*, p. 27; 4th ed.

† Illustrated figure "from an ancient Rosary of the blessed Virgin Mary, printed at Venice, 1524, with a license from the Inquisition." In the illustrations given by Dr. Inman the Virgin is represented in an Assyrian "grove," the *abomination in the eyes of the Lord*, according to the Bible prophets. "The book in question," says the author "contains numerous figures, all resembling closely the Mesopotamian emblem *of Ishtar*. The presence of the woman *therein* identifies the two as symbolic of Isis, or *la nature;* and a man bowing down in adoration thereof shows the same idea as is depicted in Assyrian sculptures, where males offer to the goddess *symbols* of *themselves*." See *Ancient Pagan and Modern Christian Symbolism*, 2nd ed., New York, p. 91.

‡ [*Ibid.*, p. 93.]

ship of the ancient heathens, would be equivalent to pulling down the whole Roman Catholic image-worship — the *Madonna* element — and reforming the faith to Protestantism. The enforcement of the late dogma of the Immaculation was prompted by this very secret reason. The science of symbology was making too rapid progress. Blind faith in the Pope's infallibility and in the immaculate nature of the Virgin and *of her ancestral female lineage to a certain remove* could alone save the Church from the indiscreet revelations of science. It was a clever stroke of policy on the part of the vicegerent of God. What matters it if, by "conferring upon her such an honor," \* as Don Pasquale de Franciscis naïvely expresses it, he has made a goddess of the Virgin Mary, an Olympian Deity, who, having been by her very nature placed in the impossibility of sinning, can claim no virtue, no personal merit for her purity, precisely for which, as we were taught to believe in our younger days, she was chosen among all other women. If his Holiness has deprived her of this, perhaps, on the other hand, he thinks that he has endowed her with at least one physical attribute not shared by the other virgin-goddesses. But even this new dogma, which, in company with the new claim to *infallibility*, has quasi-revolutionized the Christian world, is not original with the Church of Rome. It is but a return to a hardly remembered *heresy* of the early Christian ages, that of the Collyridians, so called from their *sacrificing cakes* to the Virgin, whom they claimed to *be Virgin-born.*† The new sentence, "O, Virgin Mary, *conceived without sin,*" is simply a tardy acceptance of that which was at first deemed a *"blasphemous heresy"* by the orthodox fathers.

To think for one moment that any of the popes, cardinals, or other high dignitaries "were not aware" from the first to the last of the external meanings of their symbols, is to do injustice to their great learning and their spirit of Machiavellism. It is to forget that the emissaries of Rome will never be stopped by any difficulty which can be skirted by the employment of Jesuitical artifice. The policy of complaisant conformity was never carried to greater lengths than by the missionaries in Ceylon, who, according to the Abbé Dubois — certainly a learned and competent authority — "conducted the images of the Virgin and Saviour on triumphal cars, imitated from the orgies of Juggernaut, and introduced the dancers from the Brahmanical rites into the ceremonial of the church." ‡ Let us at least thank these black-frocked politicians for their consistency in employ-

---

\* [*Discorsi del Sommo Pontefice Pio IX*, Part II, p. 26. Cf. W. E. Gladstone, *Rome, etc.*, p. 140.]

† Cf. C. W. King, *The Gnostics*, etc., pp. 91-92 [p. 231 in 2nd ed.]; *The Genealogy of the Blessed Virgin Mary*, by Faustus, Bishop of Riez.

‡ *Edinburgh Review*, Vol. XCIII, April, 1851, p. 415; cited in Pococke, *India in Greece*, London, 1852, pp. 318-19.

ing the car of Juggernaut, upon which the "wicked heathen" convey the *linga* of Śiva. To have used *this* car to carry in its turn the Romish representative of the female principle in nature, is to show discrimination and a thorough knowledge of the oldest mythological conceptions. They have blended the two deities, and thus represented, in a Christian procession, the "heathen" Brahmâ, or Nara (the father), Nârî (the mother), and Virâj (the son).

Says *Manu:* "The Sovereign Master who exists through himself, divides his body into two halves, male and female, and from the union of these two principles is born Virâj, the Son." *

There was not a Christian Father who could have been ignorant of these symbols in their physical meaning; for it is in this latter aspect that they were abandoned to the ignorant rabble. Moreover, they all had as good reasons to suspect the occult symbolism contained in these images; although as none of them — Paul excepted, perhaps — had been initiated, they could know nothing whatever about the nature of the final rites. Any person revealing these mysteries was put to death, regardless of sex, nationality, or creed. A Christian father would no more be proof against *an accident* than a Pagan Μύστης.

If during the *aporrheta* or preliminary arcanes, there were some practices which might have shocked the pudicity of a Christian convert — though we doubt the sincerity of such statements — their mystical symbolism was all sufficient to relieve the performance of any charge of licentiousness. Even the episode of the Matron Baubo — whose rather eccentric method of consolation was immortalized in the minor Mysteries—is explained by impartial mystagogues quite naturally. Ceres-Demeter and her earthly wanderings in search of her daughter are the euhemerized descriptions of one of the most metaphysico-psychological subjects ever treated of by human mind. It is a mask for the transcendent narrative of the initiated seers; the celestial vision of the freed soul of the initiate of the last hour describing the process by which the soul that has not yet been incarnated descends for the first time into matter. "Blessed is he who hath seen those *common concerns* of the underworld; he knows both the end of life and its divine origin from Jupiter," says Pindar.† Taylor shows, on the authority of more than one initiate, that the "dramatic spectacles of the Lesser Mysteries were designed by the ancient theologists, their founders, to signify *occultly* the condition of the unpurified soul invested with an earthly body, and

---

* *Manu*, Book I, śloka 32: Sir W. Jones, translating from the Northern "Manu," renders this *śloka* as follows: "Having divided his own substance, the mighty Power became half male, half female, or *nature active and passive;* and from that female he produced Virâj."

† [In Clem. Alex., *Strom.*, III, iii, quoting Pindar, *Dirges*, 137.]

enveloped in a material and physical nature . . . that the soul, indeed, till purified by philosophy, suffers death through its union with the body . . ."*

The body is the sepulchre, the prison of the soul, and many Christian Fathers held with Plato that the soul is *punished* through its union with the body. Such is the fundamental doctrine of the Buddhists and of many Brahmanists too. When Plotinus remarks that "when the soul has descended into generation [from its *half*-divine condition] she partakes of evil, and is carried a great way into a state the opposite of her first purity and integrity, to be entirely merged in which is nothing more than to fall into dark mire,"† he only repeats the teachings of Gautama Buddha. If we have to believe the ancient initiates at all, we must accept their interpretation of the symbols. And if, moreover, we find them perfectly coinciding with the teachings of the greatest philosophers and that which we know symbolizes the same meaning in the modern Mysteries in the East, we must believe them to be right.

If Demeter was considered the intellectual soul, or rather the *Astral* soul, half emanation from the spirit and half tainted with matter through a succession of spiritual evolutions — we may readily understand what is meant by the Matron Baubo, the Enchantress who, before she succeeds in reconciling the soul, Demeter, to its new position, finds herself obliged to assume the sexual forms of an infant. Baubo is *matter*, the physical body; and the intellectual, as yet pure, astral soul can be ensnared into its new terrestrial prison but by the display of innocent babyhood. Until then, doomed to her fate, Demeter, or *Magna-mater*, the Soul, wonders and hesitates and suffers; but once having partaken of the magic potion prepared by Baubo, she forgets her sorrows; for a certain time she parts with that consciousness of higher intellect that she was possessed of before entering the body of a child. Thenceforth she must seek to rejoin it again; and when the age of reason arrives for the child, the struggle — forgotten for a few years of infancy — begins again. The astral soul is placed between matter (body) and the highest intellect (its immortal spirit or *nous*). Which of those two will conquer? The result of the battle of life lies between the triad. It is a question of a few years of physical enjoyment on earth and — if it has begotten abuse — of dissolution of the earthly body being followed by death of the astral body, which thus is prevented from being united with the highest spirit of the triad, which alone confers on us individual immortality; or, on the other hand, of becoming immortal mystae; initiated before death of the body into the divine truths of the afterlife. Demigods below, and GODS above.

---

\* [Taylor, *Eleus. and Bacchic Myst.*, pp. 34-35; 4th ed.]
† *Enneads*, I, book viii, 4 and 14.

## THE SUBLIMEST PART OF THE EPOPTEIA    113

Such was the chief object of the Mysteries represented as diabolical by theology, and ridiculed by modern symbologists. To disbelieve that there exist in man certain arcane powers, which, by psychological study he can develop in himself to the highest degree, become an hierophant and then impart to others under the same conditions of earthly discipline, is to cast an imputation of falsehood and lunacy upon a number of the best, purest, and most learned men of antiquity and of the middle ages. What the hierophant was allowed to see at the last hour is hardly hinted at by them. And yet Pythagoras, Plato, Plotinus, Iamblichus, Proclus, and many others knew and affirmed their reality.

Whether in the "inner temple," or through the study of theurgy carried on privately, or by the sole exertion of a whole life of spiritual labor, they all obtained the practical proof of such divine possibilities for man fighting his battle with life on earth to win a life in the eternity. What the last *epopteia* was is alluded to by Plato in *Phaedrus* (250 B,C): ". . . being initiated in those *Mysteries*, which it is lawful to call the most blessed of all mysteries . . . we were freed from the molestations of evils which otherwise await us in a future period of time. Likewise, in consequence of this divine *initiation*, we became *spectators* of entire, simple, immovable, and *blessed visions*, resident in a pure light." This sentence shows that they saw *visions*, gods, spirits. As Taylor correctly observes, from all such passages in the works of the initiates it may be inferred, "that the most sublime part of the *epopteia* . . . consisted in beholding the gods themselves invested with a resplendent light," \* or highest planetary spirits. The statement of Proclus upon this subject is unequivocal: "In all the initiations and mysteries, the gods exhibit many forms of themselves, and appear in a *variety of shapes*. And sometimes indeed an unfigured light of themselves is held forth to the view; sometimes this light is according *to a human form*, and sometimes it proceeds into a different shape."†

"Whatever is *on earth is the resemblance and* SHADOW *of something that is in the sphere*, while that resplendent thing [the prototype of the soul-spirit] remaineth in *unchangeable* condition, it is well also with its shadow. But when the *resplendent one* removeth far from its shadow, life removeth from the latter to a distance. And yet, that very light is the shadow of something still more resplendent than itself." Thus speaks *Desâtir*, ‡ thereby showing its identity of esoteric doctrines with those of the Greek philosophers.

The second statement of Plato confirms our belief that the Mysteries of the ancients were identical with the Initiations, as practiced now

---

\* T. Taylor, *op. cit.*, p. 107; 4th ed.

† Proclus, *On Plato's Republic*, p. 380. Cf. T. Taylor, *The Works of Plato*, Vol. III, p. 328 fn.; London, 1804.

‡ *The Book of Shet the Prophet Zirtûsht*, Bombay, 1818, verses 35-38.

among the Buddhists and the Hindu adepts. The highest visions, the most *truthful*, are produced, not through *natural* ecstatics or "mediums," as it is sometimes erroneously asserted, but through a regular discipline of gradual initiations and development of psychical powers. The *Mystai* were brought into close union with those whom Proclus calls "mystical natures," "resplendent gods," because, as Plato says, "we were ourselves pure and immaculate, being liberated from this *surrounding vestment*, which we denominate body, and to which we are now bound like an oyster to its shell." \*

So the doctrine of planetary and terrestrial Pitris was revealed *entirely* in ancient India, as well as now, only at the last moment of initiation, and to the adepts of superior degrees. Many are the fakirs, who, though pure, and honest, and self-devoted, have yet never seen the astral form of a purely *human pitri* (an ancestor or father), otherwise than at the solemn moment of their first and last initiation. It is in the presence of his instructor, the guru, and just before the *vatu*-fakir is dispatched into the world of the living, with his seven-knotted bamboo wand for all protection, that he is suddenly placed face to face with the unknown PRESENCE. He sees it, and falls prostrate at the feet of the evanescent form, but is not entrusted with the great secret of its evocation; for it is the supreme mystery of the holy syllable. The AUM contains the evocation of the Vedic triad, the *Trimûtri*, Brahmâ, Vishnu, Śiva, say the Orientalists; † it contains the evocation of *something more real and objective than this triune abstraction* — we say, respectfully contradicting the eminent scientists. It is the trinity of man himself, on his way to becoming immortal through the solemn union of his inner triune SELF — the exterior, gross body, the husk not even being taken into consideration in this human trinity. ‡ It is when this trinity, in anticipation of the final

---

\* *Phaedrus*, 250 C.

† **The Supreme Buddha is invoked with two of his acolytes of the theistic triad,** Dharma and Sangha. This triad is addressed in Sanskrit in the following terms:

*Namo Buddhâya,*
*Namo Dharmâya,*
*Namo Sanghâya,*
    *Aum!*

while the Thibetan Buddhists pronounce their invocations as follows:

*Nan-wou Fo-tho-ye,*
*Nan-wou Tha-ma-ye,*
*Nan-wou Seng-kia-ye,*
    *An!*

See also *Nouveau Journal Asiatique*, tome VII, March 1831, p. 265.

‡ The body of man — his coat of skin — is an inert mass of matter, *per se*; it is but the *sentient* living body within the man that is considered as the man's body proper,

ISAAC NEWTON
1642-1727
Portrait by Godfrey Kneller.

GOTTFRIED WILHELM, FREIHERR VON LEIBNITZ
1646-1716

triumphant reunion beyond the gates of corporeal death becomes for a few seconds a UNITY, that the candidate is allowed, at the moment of the initiation, to behold his future self. Thus we read in the Persian *Desâtir*, of the "Resplendent One"; in the Greek philosopher-initiates, of the *Augoeides* — the self-shining "blessed vision resident in the pure light"; in Porphyry,* that Plotinus was united to his "god" four times during his lifetime; and so on.

"In ancient India, the mystery of the triad, known but to the initiates, could not, under the penalty of death, be revealed to the vulgar," says Brihaspati.

Neither could it in the ancient Grecian and Samothracian Mysteries. *Nor can it be now.* It is in the hands of the adepts, and must remain a mystery to the world so long as the materialistic savant regards it as an undemonstrated fallacy, an insane hallucination, and the dogmatic theologian, a snare of the Evil One.

*Subjective* communication with the human, godlike spirits of those who have preceded us to the silent land of bliss, is in India divided into three categories. Under the spiritual training of a guru or *sannyâsin*, the *vatu* (disciple or neophyte) begins *to feel* them. Were he not under the immediate guidance of an adept, he would be controlled by the invisibles, and utterly at their mercy, for among these subjective influences he is unable to discern the good from the bad. Happy the sensitive who is sure of the purity of his spiritual atmosphere!

To this subjective consciousness, which is the *first* degree, is after a time added that of clairaudience. This is the *second* degree or stage of development. The sensitive — when not naturally made so by psychological training — now audibly hears, but is still unable to discern, and is incapable of verifying his impressions; and, one who is unprotected, the tricky powers of the air but too often delude with semblances of voices and speech. But the guru's influence is there; it is the most powerful shield against the intrusion of the *bhûtnâ* into the atmosphere of the *vatu*, consecrated to the pure, human and celestial Pitris.

The *third* degree is that when the fakir or any other candidate both feels, hears, and sees; and when he can at will produce the *reflections* of the Pitris on the mirror of astral light. All depends upon his psychological and mesmeric powers, which are always proportionate to the intensity of his *will*. But the fakir will never control the Âkâsa, the spiritual life-principle, the omnipotent agent of every phenomenon, in the same degree as an adept of the third and highest initiation. And the

---

and it is that which, together with the fontal soul or purely astral body, directly connected with the immortal spirit, constitutes the trinity of man.

* [*Plotini vita,* cap. xxiii, in J. A. Fabricius, *Bibliotheca Graeca,* 1705-28.]

phenomena produced by the will of the latter do not generally run the market places for the satisfaction of open-mouthed investigators.

The unity of God, the immortality of the spirit, belief in salvation only through our works, merit and demerit; such are the principal articles of faith of the Wisdom-religion, and the groundwork of Vedaism, Buddhism, Pârsîism, and such we find to have been even that of the ancient Osirism, when we, after abandoning the popular sun-god to the materialism of the rabble, confine our attention to the *Books of Hermes*, the thrice-great.

"The THOUGHT concealed as yet the world in silence and darkness. . . . Then the Lord who exists through Himself, and *who is not to be divulged to the external senses of man*, dissipated darkness, and manifested the perceptible world."

"He that can be perceived only by the spirit, that escapes the organs of sense, who is without visible parts, eternal, the soul of all beings, that none can comprehend, displayed His own splendor."\*

Such is the ideal of the Supreme in the mind of every Hindu philosopher.

"Of all the duties, the principal one is to acquire the knowledge of the supreme soul [the spirit]; it is the first of all sciences, *for it alone confers on man immortality*." †

And our scientists talk of the Nirvâna of Buddha and the Moksha of Brahmâ as of a complete annihilation! It is thus that the following verse is interpreted by some materialists.

"The man who recognizes the *Supreme Soul*, in his own soul, as well as in that of all creatures, and who is equally just to all [whether man or animals] obtains the happiest of all fates, that to be finally *absorbed* in the bosom of Brahmâ." ‡

The doctrine of the Moksha and the Nirvâna, as understood by the school of Max Müller, can never bear confronting with numerous texts that can be found, if required, as a final refutation. There are sculptures in many pagodas which contradict, point-blank, the imputation. Ask a Brahman to explain Moksha, address yourself to an educated Buddhist and pray him to define for you the meaning of Nirvâna. Both will answer you that in every one of these religions Nirvâna represents the dogma of the spirit's immortality. That to reach the Nirvâna means absorption into the great universal soul, the latter representing a *state*, not an individual being or an anthropomorphic god, as some understand the great EXISTENCE. That a spirit reaching such a state becomes a *part* of the integral *whole*, but never loses its individuality for all that. Henceforth, the spirit lives spiritually, without any fear of further modi-

---

\* *Manu*, Bk. I, ślokas 5-7.
† *Ibid.*, Bk. XII, śloka 85.
‡ *Ibid.*, Bk. XII, śloka 125.

fications of form; for form pertains to matter, and the state of *Nirvâṇa* implies a complete purification or a final riddance from even the most sublimated particle of matter.

This word, *absorbed,* when it is proved that the Hindus and Buddhists believe in the *immortality* of the spirit, must necessarily mean intimate union, not annihilation. Let Christians call them idolaters, if they still dare do so, in the face of science and the latest translations of the sacred Sanskrit books; they have no right to present the speculative philosophy of ancient sages as an inconsistency and the philosophers themselves as illogical fools. With far better reason we can accuse the ancient Jews of utter *nihilism.* There is not a word contained in the Books of Moses — or the prophets either — which, taken literally, implies the spirit's immortality. Yet every devout Jew hopes as well to be "gathered into the bosom of A-Braham."

The hierophants and some Brahmans are accused of having administered to their *epoptai* strong drinks or anaesthetics to produce visions which shall be taken by the latter as realities. They did and do use sacred beverages which, like the Soma-drink, possess the faculty of freeing the astral form from the bonds of matter; but in those visions there is as little to be attributed to hallucination as in the glimpses which the scientist, by the help of his optical instrument, gets into the microscopic world. A man cannot perceive, touch, and converse with pure spirit through any of his bodily senses. Only spirit alone can talk to and see spirit; and even our astral soul, the *Doppelgänger,* is too gross, too much tainted yet with earthly matter to trust entirely to its perceptions and insinuations.

How dangerous may often become *untrained* mediumship, and how thoroughly it was understood and provided against by the ancient sages, is perfectly exemplified in the case of Socrates. The old Grecian philosopher was a "medium"; hence, he had never been initiated into the Mysteries; for such was the rigorous law. But he had his "familiar spirit" as they call it, his *daimonion;* and this invisible counsellor became the cause of his death. It is generally believed that if he was not initiated into the Mysteries it was because he himself neglected to become so. But the *Secret Records* teach us that it was because he could not be admitted to participate in the sacred rites, and precisely, as we state, on account of his mediumship. There was a law against the admission not only of such as were convicted of deliberate *witchcraft**

---

* We really think that the word "witchcraft" ought, once for all, to be understood in the sense which properly belongs to it. Witchcraft may be either conscious or unconscious. Certain wicked and dangerous results may be obtained through the mesmeric powers of a so-called sorcerer, who misuses his potential fluid; or again they may be achieved through an easy access of malicious, tricky "spirits" (so much the worse if

but even of those who were known to have "a familiar spirit." The law was just and logical, because a genuine medium is more or less irresponsible; and the eccentricities of Socrates are thus accounted for in some degree. A medium must be *passive*; and if a firm believer in his "spirit-guide" he will allow himself to be ruled by the latter, not by the rules of the sanctuary. A *medium* of olden times, like the modern "medium," was subject to be *entranced* at the will and pleasure of the "power" which *controlled* him; therefore, he could not well have been entrusted with the awful secrets of the final initiation, "never to be revealed under the penalty of death." The old sage, in unguarded moments of "spiritual inspiration," revealed that which he had never learned; and was therefore put to death as an atheist.

How then, with such an instance as that of Socrates, in relation to the visions and spiritual wonders of the *epoptai* of the Inner Temple, can any one assert that these seers, theurgists, and thaumaturgists were all "spirit-mediums"? Neither Pythagoras, Plato, nor any of the later more important Neo-Platonists; neither Iamblichus, Longinus, Proclus, nor Apollonius of Tyana, were ever mediums; for in such case they would not have been admitted to the Mysteries at all. As Taylor proves —"This assertion of divine visions in the Mysteries is clearly confirmed by Plotinus.* And, in short, that magical evocation formed a part of the sacerdotal office [in them], and that this was universally believed by all antiquity, long before the era of the later Platonists," † shows that apart from natural "mediumship," there has existed, from the beginning of time, a mysterious science, discussed by many, but known only to a few.

The use of it is a longing toward our only true and real home — the afterlife, and a desire to cling more closely to our parent spirit; abuse of it is sorcery, witchcraft, *black* magic. Between the two is placed natural "mediumship"; a soul clothed with imperfect matter, a ready agent for either the one or the other, and utterly dependent on its surroundings of life, constitutional heredity — physical as well as mental — and on the nature of the "spirits" it attracts around itself. A blessing or a curse, as fate will have it, unless the medium is purified of earthly dross.

The reason why in every age so little has been generally known of the mysteries of initiation, is twofold. The first has already been explained by more than one author, and lies in the terrible penalty following the least indiscretion. The second is the superhuman difficulties and even dangers which the daring candidate of old had to encounter, and either conquer or die in the attempt, when, what is still worse, he did not lose his reason.

---

human) to the atmosphere surrounding a medium. How many thousands of such irresponsible innocent victims have met infamous deaths through the tricks of those Elementaries!

* [*Enneads*, I, vi; VI, ix.]
† [*Eleus. and Bacchic Myst.*, pp. 108-11; 4th ed.]

There was no real danger to him whose mind had become thoroughly spiritualized, and so prepared for every terrific sight. He who fully recognized the power of his immortal spirit, and never doubted for one moment its omnipotent protection, had naught to fear. But woe to the candidate in whom the slightest physical fear — sickly child of matter — made him lose sight and faith in his own invulnerability. He who was not wholly confident of his moral fitness to accept the burden of these tremendous secrets was doomed.

The *Talmud*\* gives the story of the four Tannaim, who are made, in allegorical terms, to enter into *the garden of delight; i. e.*, to be initiated into the occult and final science.

"According to the teaching of our holy masters the names of the four who entered the garden of delight, are: Ben Asai, Ben Zoma, Aḥer, and Rabbi A'qîbah . . .

"Ben Asai looked and — lost his sight.

"Ben Zoma looked and — lost his reason.

"Aḥer made depredations in the plantation" [mixed up the whole and failed]. But A'qîbah, who had entered in peace, came out of it in peace, for the saint whose name be blessed had said, 'This old man is worthy of serving us with glory'."

"The learned commentators of the *Talmud*, the Rabbis of the synagogue, explain that the *garden of delight*, in which those four personages are made to enter, is but that mysterious science, the most terrible of sciences *for weak intellects, which it leads directly to insanity*," says A. Franck, in his *La Kabbale*.† It is not the pure at heart and he who studies but with a view to perfecting himself and so more easily acquiring the promised immortality, who need have any fear; but rather he who makes of the science of sciences a sinful pretext for worldly motives, who should tremble. *The latter will never withstand the kabalistic evocations of the supreme initiation.*

The licentious performances of the thousand and one early Christian sects may be criticized by partial commentators, as well as the ancient Eleusinian and other rites. But why should they incur the blame of the theologians, the Christians, when their own "Mysteries" of "the divine incarnation with Joseph, Mary, and the angel" in a sacred *trilogy* used to be enacted in more than one country, and were famous at one time in Spain and Southern France? Later, they fell like many other once secret rites into the hands of the populace. It is but a few years since, during every Christmas week, Punch-and-Judy boxes containing the above named personages, an additional display of the infant Jesus in his manger, were carried about the country in Poland and Southern Russia. They were called *koliadovki*, a word the correct etymology of which we are unable to give

---

\* [*Mishnah Ḥagîgâh*, 14b.]

† [Part II, ch. i, pp. 57-58; ed. Paris, 1843.]

unless it is from the verb *koliadovat'*, a word that we as willingly abandon to learned philologists.[18] We have seen this show in our days of childhood. We remember the three king-Magi represented by three dolls in powdered wigs and colored tights; and it is from recollecting the simple, profound veneration depicted on the faces of the pious audience, that we can the more readily appreciate the honest and just remark by the editor, in the introduction to the *Eleusinian and Bacchic Mysteries*, who says: "It is ignorance which leads to profanation. Men ridicule what they do not properly understand . . . The undercurrent of this world is set toward one goal; and inside of human credulity — call it human weakness, if you please — is a power almost infinite, a holy faith capable of apprehending the supremest truths of all Existence." [pp. 11-12.]

If that abstract sentiment called *Christian charity* prevailed in the Church, we would be well content to leave all this unsaid. We have no quarrel with Christians whose faith is sincere and whose practice coincides with their profession. But with an arrogant, dogmatic, and dishonest clergy, we have nothing to do except to see the ancient philosophy — antagonized by modern theology in its puny offspring, Spiritualism — defended and righted so far as we are able, so that its grandeur and sufficiency may be thoroughly displayed. It is not alone for the esoteric philosophy that we fight; nor for any modern system of moral philosophy, but for the inalienable right of private judgment, and especially for the ennobling idea of a future life of activity and accountability.

We eagerly applaud such commentators as Godfrey Higgins, Inman, R. Payne Knight, King, Dunlap and Dr. Newton, however much they disagree with our own mystical views, for their diligence is constantly being rewarded by fresh discoveries of the Pagan paternity of Christian symbols. But otherwise, all these learned works are useless. Their researches only cover half the ground. Lacking the true key of interpretation they see the symbols only in a physical aspect. They have no password to cause the gates of mystery to swing open; and ancient spiritual philosophy is to them a closed book. Diametrically opposed though they be to the clergy in their ideas respecting it, in the way of interpretation they do little more than their opponents for a questioning public. Their labors tend to strengthen materialism as those of the clergy, especially the Romish clergy, do to cultivate belief in diabolism.

If the study of Hermetic philosophy held out no other hope of reward, it would be more than enough to know that by it we may learn with what perfection of justice the world is governed. A sermon upon this text is preached by every page of history. Among all there is not one that conveys a deeper moral than the case of the Roman Church. The divine law of compensation was never more strikingly exemplified than in the fact that by her own act she has deprived herself of the only possible key to her own religious mysteries. The assumption of Godfrey Higgins that there are two doctrines maintained in the Roman Church, one for the masses and the other — the esoteric — for the "perfect," or the initiates, as in the ancient Mysteries, appears to us unwarranted and rather fantastic. They have lost the key, we repeat; otherwise no terrestrial power could have prostrated her, and except [in] a superficial knowledge of the means of producing "miracles," her clergy can in no way be compared in their wisdom with the hierophants of old.

In burning the works of the theurgists; in proscribing those who affect their study; in affixing the stigma of demonolatry to magic in general, Rome has left her exoteric worship and *Bible* to be helplessly riddled by every freethinker, her sexual emblems to be identified with coarseness, and her priests to unwittingly turn magicians and even sorcerers in their exorcisms, which are but necromantic evocations. Thus retribution, by the exquisite adjustment of divine law, is made to overtake this scheme of cruelty, injustice and bigotry, through her own suicidal acts.

True philosophy and divine truth are convertible terms. A religion which dreads the light cannot be a religion based on either truth or philosophy — hence, it must be false. The ancient Mysteries were mysteries to the profane only, whom the hierophant never sought nor would accept as proselyte; to the initiates the Mysteries became explained as soon as the final veil was withdrawn. No mind like that of Pythagoras or Plato would have contented itself with an unfathomable and incomprehensible mystery, like that of the Christian dogma. There can be but one truth, for two small truths on the same subject can but constitute one great error. Among thousands of exoteric or popular conflicting religions which have been propagated since the days when the first men were enabled to interchange their ideas, not a nation, not a people, nor the most abject tribe, but after their own fashion has believed in an Unseen God, the First Cause of unerring and immutable laws, and in the immortality of our spirit. No creed, no false philosophy, no religious exaggerations, could ever destroy that feeling. It must, therefore, be based upon an absolute truth. On the other hand, every one of the numberless religions and religious sects views the Deity after its own fashion; and, fathering on the unknown its own speculations, it enforces these purely human outgrowths of overheated imagination on the ignorant masses, and calls them "revelation." As the dogmas of every religion and sect often differ radically, they cannot be *true*. And if untrue, what are they?

"The greatest curse to a nation," remarks Dr. Inman, "is not a *bad religion*, but a form of faith which prevents manly inquiry. I know of no nation of old that was priest-ridden which did not fall under the swords of those who did not care for hierarchs. The greatest danger is to be feared from those ecclesiastics who wink at vice, and encourage it as a means whereby they can gain power over their votaries. So long as every man does to other men as he would that they should do to him, and *allows no one to interfere between him and his Maker*, all will go well with the world." *

---

* *Ancient Pagan and Modern Christian Symbolism*, Introd., p. xxxiv.

# CHAPTER III

"King. — Let us from point to point this story know."
SHAKESPEARE, *All's Well That Ends Well*, Act V, Scene iii, line 330.

"He is the One, self-proceeding; and from him all things proceed.
And in them he himself exerts his activity; no mortal
Beholds him, but he beholds all." — *Orphic Hymn.**

"And Athens, Oh Athena, is thy own!
Great Goddess, hear! and on my dark'ned mind
Pour thy pure light in measure unconfined;
That sacred light, Oh all-protecting Queen,
Which beams eternal from thy face serene.
My soul, while wand'ing on the earth, inspire
With thy own blessed and impulsive fire."
—PROCLUS, *To Minerva,* †

"Now *faith* is the substance of things hoped for . . . By faith the harlot Rahab perished not with them that believed not, when she had *received the spies with peace.*" — *Hebrews* xi, 1, 31.

"What doth it profit, my brethren, though a man says he hath faith, and have not works? Can FAITH *save him?* . . . Likewise also was not Rahab the harlot *justified by works*, when she had received the messengers, and had sent them out another way?" — *James* ii, 14, 25.

CLEMENT describes Basilides, the Gnostic, as "a philosopher devoted to the contemplation of divine things." [19] This very appropriate expression may be applied to many of the founders of the more important sects which later were all engulfed in one — that stupendous compound of unintelligible dogmas enforced by Irenaeus, Tertullian, and others, which is now termed Christianity. *If these must be called heresies, then early Christianity itself must be included in the number.* Basilides and Valentinus preceded Irenaeus and Tertullian; and the two latter Fathers had less facts than the two former Gnostics to show that their *heresy* was plausible. Neither divine right nor truth brought about the triumph of their Christianity; fate alone was propitious. We can assert, with entire plausibility, that there is not one of all these sects — Kabalism, Judaism, and our present Christianity included — but sprang from the two main branches of that one mother-trunk, the once universal religion, which antedated the Vedic ages — we speak of that prehistoric Buddhism which merged later into Brahmanism.

---

* [Cf. Justin Martyr, *Cohortatio ad Graecos*, xv; Gesnerus, *Orpheôs apanta;* T. Taylor, *Eleus. and Bacchic Myst.*, 4th ed., p. 238.]

† [T. Taylor, *op. cit.*, p. 226.]

The religion which the primitive teaching of the early few apostles most resembled — a religion preached by Jesus himself — is the elder of these two, Buddhism. The latter as taught in its primitive purity, and carried to perfection by the last of the Buddhas, Gautama, based its moral ethics on three fundamental principles. It alleged that 1, everything existing, exists from natural causes; 2, that virtue brings its own reward, and vice and sin their own punishment; and 3, that the state of man in this world is probationary. We might add that on these three principles rested the universal foundation of every religious creed: God, and individual immortality for every man — if he could but win it. However puzzling the subsequent theological tenets; however seemingly incomprehensible the metaphysical abstractions which have convulsed the theology of every one of the great religions of mankind as soon as it was placed on a sure footing, the above is found to be the essence of every religious philosophy, with the exception of later Christianity. It was that of Zoroaster, of Pythagoras, of Plato, of Jesus, and even of Moses, albeit the teachings of the Jewish lawgiver have been so piously tampered with.

We will devote the present chapter mainly to a brief survey of the numerous sects which have recognized themselves as Christians; that is to say, that have believed in a *Christos*, or an ANOINTED ONE. We will also endeavor to explain the latter appellation from the kabalistic standpoint, and show it reappearing in every religious system. It might be profitable, at the same time, to see how much the earliest apostles — Paul and Peter, agreed in their preaching of the new Dispensation. We will begin with Peter.

We must once more return to that greatest of all the Patristic frauds; the one which has undeniably helped the Roman Catholic Church to its unmerited supremacy, *viz.*: the barefaced assertion, in the teeth of historical evidence, that Peter suffered martyrdom at Rome. It is but too natural that the Latin clergy should cling to it, for, with the exposure of the fraudulent nature of this pretext, the dogma of apostolic succession must fall to the ground.

There have been many able works of late, in refutation of this preposterous claim. Among others we note Mr. G. Reber's, *The Christ of Paul*, which overthrows it quite ingeniously. The author proves, 1, that there was no church established at Rome until the reign of Antoninus Pius; 2, that as Eusebius and Irenaeus both agree that Linus was the second Bishop of Rome, into whose hands "the blessed apostles" Peter and Paul committed the church after building it, it could not have been at any other time than between A.D. 64 and 68; 3, that this interval of years happens during the reign of Nero, for Eusebius states that Linus held his office twelve years, entering upon it A.D. 69, one year after the death of Nero, and dying himself in 81.* After that the author maintains, on very solid grounds, that Peter could not be in Rome A.D. 64, for he was then in Babylon; wherefrom he wrote his first

---

*\*Ecclesiastical History*, Bk. III, ch. xiii.

Epistle, the date of which is fixed by Dr. Lardner and other critics at precisely this year. But we believe that his best argument is in proving that it was not in the character of the cowardly Peter to risk himself in such close neighborhood with Nero, who "was feeding the wild beasts of the Amphitheatre with the flesh and bones of Christians" * at that time.

Perhaps the Church of Rome was but consistent in choosing as her titular founder the apostle who thrice denied his master at the moment of danger; and the only one, moreover, except Judas, who provoked Christ in such a way as to be addressed as the "Enemy." "Get thee behind me, SATAN!" exclaims Jesus, rebuking the taunting apostle.†

There is a tradition in the Greek Church which has never found favor at the Vatican. The former traces its origin to one of the Gnostic leaders — Basilides, perhaps, who lived under Trajan and Adrian, at the end of the first and the beginning of the second century. With regard to this particular tradition, if the Gnostic is Basilides, then he must be accepted as a sufficient authority, having claimed to have been a disciple of the Apostle Matthew, and to have had for master Glaucias, a disciple of St. Peter himself. Were the narrative attributed to him authenticated, the London Committee for the Revision of the Bible would have to add a new verse to *Matthew, Mark* and *John*, who tell the story of Peter's denial of Christ.

This tradition, then, of which we have been speaking, affirms that, when frightened at the accusation of the servant of the high priest, the apostle had thrice denied his master, and the cock had crowed, Jesus, who was then passing through the hall in custody of the soldiers, turned, and looking at Peter, said: "Verily, I say unto thee, Peter, thou shalt deny me throughout the coming ages, and never stop until thou shalt be old, and shalt stretch forth thy hands, and another shall gird thee and carry thee whither thou wouldest not." ‡ The latter part of this sentence, say the Greeks, relates to the Church of Rome, and prophesies her constant apostasy from Christ, under the mask of false religion. Later, it was inserted in the twenty-first chapter of *John*, but the whole of this chapter had been pronounced a forgery, even before it was found that this *Gospel* was never written by John the Apostle at all.

The anonymous author § of *Supernatural Religion*, a work which in two years passed through several editions, and which is alleged to have been written by an eminent theologian, proves conclusively the spuriousness of the four gospels, or at least their complete transformation in the hands of the

---

\* *The Christ of Paul*, p. 123.
† *Mark* viii, 33.
‡ [*John* xxi, 18.]
§ [Walter R. Cassels.]

too-zealous Irenaeus and his champions. The fourth gospel is completely upset by this able author; the extraordinary forgeries of the Fathers of the early centuries are plainly demonstrated, and the relative value of the synoptics is discussed with an unprecedented power of logic. The work carries conviction in its every line. From it we quote the following: "We gain infinitely more than we lose in abandoning belief in the reality of Divine Revelation. Whilst we retain pure and unimpaired the light of Christian Morality, we relinquish nothing but the debasing elements added to it by human superstition. We are no longer bound to believe a theology which outrages Reason and moral sense. We are freed from base anthropomorphic views of God and his government of the universe; and from Jewish mythology we rise to higher conceptions of an infinitely wise and beneficent Being, hidden from our finite minds, it is true, in the impenetrable glory of Divinity, but whose Laws of wondrous comprehensiveness and perfection we ever perceive in operation around us . . . The argument so often employed by theologians that Divine Revelation is necessary for man, and that certain views contained in that Revelation are required for our moral consciousness, is purely imaginary and derived from the Revelation which it seeks to maintain. The only thing absolutely necessary for man is TRUTH; and to that, and that alone, must our moral consciousness adapt itself." \*

We will consider farther in what light was regarded the Divine revelation of the Jewish *Bible* by the Gnostics, who yet believed in Christ in their own way, a far better and less blasphemous one than the Roman Catholic. The Fathers have forced on the believers in Christ a *Bible*, the laws prescribed in which he was the first to break; the teachings of which he utterly rejected; and for which crimes he was finally crucified. Of whatever else the Christian world can boast, it can hardly claim logic and consistency as its chief virtues.

The fact alone that Peter remained to the last an "apostle of the circumcision," speaks for itself. *Whosoever else might have built the Church of Rome it was not Peter.* If such were the case, the successors of this apostle would have to submit themselves to circumcision, if it were but for the sake of consistency, and to show that the claims of the Popes are not utterly groundless. Dr. Inman asserts that report says that "in our Christian times, Popes have to be privately perfect,"† but we do not know whether it is carried to the extent of the Levitical Jewish law. The first fifteen Christian bishops of Jerusalem, commencing with James and including Judas, were all circumcised Jews.‡

---

\* *Supernatural Religion*, 5th ed., London, 1875, Vol. II, pp. 489-91.

† *Ancient Pagan and Modern Christian Symbolism*, Introd., p. xxviii.

‡ Eusebius, *Eccl. Hist.*, Bk. VI, ch. v; Sulpicius Severus, *Chronica*, II, xxvi.

In the *Sepher-Toledoth-Yeshu*,* a Hebrew manuscript of great antiquity, the version about Peter is different. Simon Peter, it says, was one of their own brethren, though he had somewhat departed from the laws, and the Jewish hatred and persecution of the apostle seems to have existed but in the fecund imagination of the fathers. The author speaks of him with great respect and fairness, calling him "a faithful servant of the living God," who passed his life in austerity and meditation, "living in Babylon at the summit of a tower," composing hymns, and preaching charity. He adds that Peter always recommended to the Christians not to molest the Jews, but as soon as he was dead, behold another preacher went to Rome and pretended that Simon Peter had altered the teachings of his master. He invented a burning hell and threatened everyone with it; promised miracles, but worked none.

How much there is in the above of fiction and how much of truth, it is for others to decide; but it certainly bears more the evidence of sincerity and fact on its face, than the fables concocted by the fathers to answer their end.

We may the more readily credit this friendship between Peter and his late co-religionists as we find in Theodoret the following assertion: "The Nazarenes are Jews, honoring the ANOINTED [Jesus] as a *just man* and using the *Evangel* according to Peter." † Peter was a Nazarene, according to the *Talmud*. He belonged to the sect of the later Nazarenes, which dissented from the followers of John the Baptist, and became a rival sect; and which — as tradition goes — was instituted by Jesus himself.

History finds the first Christian sects to have been either Nazarenes like John the Baptist; or Ebionites, among whom were many of the relatives of Jesus; or Essenes (Iessaens), the Therapeutae healers, of which the Nazaria were a branch. All these sects, which only in the days of Irenaeus began to be considered heretical, were more or less kabalistic. They believed in the expulsion of demons by magical incantations, and practiced this method; Jervis terms the Nabathaeans and other such sects "wandering Jewish exorcists," ‡ the Arabic word *nabae*, meaning to wander, and the Hebrew נבא, *naba*, to prophesy. The *Talmud* indiscrimi-

---

* It appears that the Jews attribute a high antiquity to *Sepher-Toledoth-Yeshu*. It was mentioned for the first time by Martin, about the beginning of the thirteenth century, for the Talmudists took great care to conceal it from the Christians. Lévi says that Porchetus de Salvaticis [*Victoria Porcheti adversus impios Hebraeos*, Paris, 1520, fol.] published some portions of it, which were used by Luther (see Vol. III, ff. 109-110, Jena ed. 1583; also Wittenberg ed., 1556, Vol. V, pp. 509-35). The Hebrew text, which was missing, was at last found by Münster and Buxtorf, and published in 1681 by Christopher Wagenseil, in a collection entitled *Tela Ignea Satanae*, or The Burning Darts of Satan [Altdorf, 2 Vols.; and by Jah. Jac. Huldrich, as *Historia Jeschuae Nazareni*, Leyden, 1705]. (See also É. Lévi, *La science des esprits*, pp. 37-38.)

† Theodoret, *Haeret. fabul.*, II, ii.

‡ John Jervis-White Jervis, *Genesis Elucidated*, London, 1852, p. 324.

nately calls all the Christians *Nozari*.* All the Gnostic sects equally believed in magic. Irenaeus, in describing the followers of Basilides, says, "They use images, invocations, incantations, and all other things pertaining unto magic." † Dunlap, on the authority of Lightfoot, shows that Jesus was called *Nazaraios,* in reference to his humble and mean external condition; "for Nazaraios means separation, alienation from other men." ‡

The real meaning of the word *nazar*, נזר, signifies to vow or consecrate one's self to the service of God. As a noun it is a *diadem* or emblem of such consecration, a head so consecrated. § Joseph was styled a *nazar*.|| "The head of Joseph, the vertex of the nazar among his brethren." Samson and Samuel (שמשון, שמואל, Shimshôn and Shemûêl) are described alike as *nazars*. Porphyry, treating of Pythagoras, says that he was purified and initiated at Babylon by Zar-adas, the head of the sacred college. May it not be surmised, therefore, that the Zoro-Aster was the *nazar* of Ishtar, Zar-adas or Na-Zar-Ad, ¶ being the same with change of idiom? Ezra, or עזרא, was a priest and scribe, a hierophant; and the first Hebrew colonizer of Judaea was זרובבל Zoro-Babel or the Zoro or *nazar* of Babylon.

The Jewish Scriptures indicate two distinct worships and religions among the Israelites; that of Bacchus-worship under the mask of Jehovah, and that of the Chaldean initiates to whom belonged some of the *nazars*, the theurgists, and a few of the prophets. The headquarters of these were always at Babylon and Chaldea, where two rival schools of Magians can be distinctly shown. Those who would doubt the statement will have in such a case to account for the discrepancy between history and Plato, who of all men of his day was certainly one of the best informed. Speaking of the Magians, he shows them as instructing the Persian kings [about] Zoroaster, as the son or priest of Oromazdes; ** and yet Darius, in the inscription at Behistun, boasts of having restored the cultus of Ormazd and put down the Magian rites! Evidently there were two distinct and antagonistic Magian schools. The oldest and the most esoteric of the two being that which, satisfied with its unassailable knowledge and secret power, was content to apparently relinquish her exoteric popularity, and concede her supremacy into the hands of the reforming

---

* J. Lightfoot, *Horae Hebr. et Talm.*, p. 501.
† [*Adv. Haer.*, I, xxiv, 5.]
‡ Dunlap, *Sôd, the Son of the Man*, p. x.
§ *Jeremiah* vii, 29: "Cut off thine hair, O Jerusalem, and cast it away, and take up a lamentation on high places."
|| *Genesis* xlix, 26.
¶ Nazareth? [Cf. Clem. Alex., *Strom.*, I, xv; Apuleius, *Floridora*, II, xv.]
** [*1 Alcib.*, 122A. Cf. Cicero, *De divinatione*, I, i.]

Darius. The later Gnostics showed the same prudent policy by accommodating themselves in every country to the prevailing religious forms, still secretly adhering to their own essential doctrines.

There is another hypothesis possible, which is that Zoro-Ishtar was the high priest of the Chaldean worship, or Magian hierophant. When the Âryans of Persia, under Darius Hystaspes, overthrew the Magian Gomates, and *restored* the Mazdean worship, there ensued an amalgamation by which the Magian Zoro-astar became the Zara-thushtra of the *Vendidâd*. This was not acceptable to the other Âryans, who adopted the Vedic religion as distinguished from that of *Avesta*. But this is but an hypothesis.

And whatever Moses is now believed to have been, we will demonstrate that he was an initiate. The Mosaic religion was at best a sun-and-serpent worship, diluted, perhaps, with some slight monotheistic notions before the latter were forcibly crammed into the so-called "inspired Scriptures" by Ezra, at the time he was alleged to have *re*written the Mosaic books. At all events the *Book of Numbers* was a later book; and there the sun-and-serpent worship is as plainly traceable as in any Pagan story. The tale of the fiery serpents is an allegory in more than one sense. The "serpents" were the *Levites* or *Ophites*, who were Moses' bodyguard (see *Exodus* xxxii, 26); and the command of the "Lord" to Moses to hang the heads of the people "before the Lord against the sun," which is the emblem of this Lord, is unequivocal.

The *nazars* or prophets, as well as the Nazarenes, were an anti-Bacchus caste, in so far that, in common with all the initiated prophets, they held to the spirit of the symbolical religions and offered a strong opposition to the idolatrous and exoteric practices of the dead letter. Hence, the frequent stoning of the prophets by the populace, under the leadership of those priests who made a profitable living out of the popular superstitions. Ottfried Müller shows how much the Orphic Mysteries differed from the *popular* rites of Bacchus,* although the *Orphikoi* are known to have followed the worship of Bacchus. The system of the purest morality and of a severe asceticism promulgated in the teachings of Orpheus, and so strictly adhered to by his votaries, are incompatible with the lasciviousness and gross immorality of the popular rites. The fable of Aristaeus pursuing Eurydice into the woods where a serpent occasions her death,† is a very plain allegory, which was in part explained in the earliest times. Aristaeus is *brutal power,* pursuing Eurydice, the esoteric doctrine, into the woods where the serpent (emblem of every sungod, and worshipped under its grosser aspect even by the Jews) kills her; *i.e.*, forces truth to become still more esoteric, and seek shelter in the Underworld, which is not the hell of our theologians. Moreover, the fate of Orpheus,

---

* K. O. Müller, *A Hist. of the Literature of Ancient Greece*, pp. 230-40.

† [Virgil, *Georgica*, VI, 282 *et seq.*]

torn to pieces by the Bacchantes, is another allegory to show that the gross and popular rites are always more welcome than divine but simple truth, and proves the great difference that must have existed between the esoteric and the popular worship. As the poems of both Orpheus and Musaeus were said to have been lost since the earliest ages, so that neither Plato nor Aristotle recognized anything authentic in the poems extant in their time, it is difficult to say with precision what constituted their peculiar rites. Still we have the oral tradition, and every inference to draw therefrom; and this tradition points to Orpheus as having brought his doctrines from India, and as one whose religion was that of the oldest Magians—hence that to which belonged the initiates of all countries, beginning with Moses, the "Sons of the Prophets," and the ascetic *nazars* (who must not be confounded with those against whom thundered Hosea and other prophets) [and ending with] the Essenes. This latter sect were Pythagoreans before they became degenerated rather than perfected in their system by the Buddhist missionaries, who, Pliny tells us, established themselves on the shores of the Dead Sea, ages before his time, "*per seculorum millia.*" * But if, on the one hand, these Buddhist monks were the first to establish monastic communities and inculcate the strict observance of dogmatic conventual rule, on the other, they were also the first to enforce and popularize those stern virtues so exemplified by Śâkyamuni, and which were previously exercised only in isolated cases of well-known philosophers and their followers; virtues preached two or three centuries later by Jesus, practiced by a few Christian ascetics, gradually abandoned, and even entirely forgotten by the Christian Church.

The *initiated* nazars had ever held to this rule, which had been followed before them by the adepts of every age; and the disciples of John were but a dissenting branch of the Essenes. Therefore, we cannot well confound them with all the nazars spoken of in the *Old Testament*, and who are accused by Hosea with having separated or consecrated themselves to *Bosheth*, בשת (see Hebrew text);† which implied the greatest possible abomination. To infer, as some critics and theologians do, that it means to separate one's self to *chastity* or continence, is either to advisedly pervert the true meaning, or to be totally ignorant of the Hebrew language. The eleventh verse of the first chapter of *Micah* half explains the word in its veiled translation: "Pass ye away, thou inhabitant of Saphir, etc.", and in the original text the word is *Bosheth*. Certainly neither Baal, nor Iahoh Kadosh, with his *Kadeshim*, was a god of ascetic virtue, albeit the *Septuagint* terms them, as well as the *galli* — the perfected priests — τετελεσμένοι, the *initiated* and the *consecrated*. ‡

---

\* [Pliny, *Nat. Hist.*, V, xv.]
† [*Hosea* ix, 10.]
‡ Movers, *Die Phönizier*, Vol. I, p. 683.

The great *Sod* of the *Kadeshim*, translated in *Psalms* lxxxix, 7, as "assembly of the saints," was anything but a mystery of the *"sanctified"* in the sense given to the latter word by Webster.

The Nazireate sect existed long before the laws of Moses,* and originated among people most inimical to the "chosen" ones of Israel, *viz.*, the people of Galilee, the ancient *olla-podrida* of idolatrous nations, where was built Nazara, the present Nasra. It is in Nazara that the ancient Nazaria or Nazireates held their "Mysteries of Life" or "assemblies" (as the word now stands in the translation),† which were but the secret mysteries of initiation,‡ utterly distinct in their practical form from the popular Mysteries which were held at Byblus in honor of Adonis. While the true *initiates* of the ostracized Galilee were worshipping the true God and enjoying transcendent visions, what were the "chosen" ones about? Ezekiel tells it to us (chap. viii) when, in describing what he saw, he says that the *form* of a hand took him by a lock of his head and transported him from Chaldea unto Jerusalem. "And there stood seventy men of the senators of the house of Israel. . . . 'Son of man, hast thou seen what the ancients . . . do in the dark?' " inquires the "Lord." "At the door of the house of the Lord . . . behold there sat women weeping for Tammuz" (Adonis). We really cannot suppose that the Pagans have ever surpassed the "chosen" people in certain shameful *abominations* of which their own prophets accuse them so profusely. To admit this truth, one hardly needs even to be a Hebrew scholar; let him read the *Bible* in English and meditate over the language of the "holy" prophets.

This accounts for the hatred of the later Nazarenes for the orthodox Jews — followers of the *exoteric* Mosaic Law — who are ever taunted by this sect with being the worshippers of *Iurbo-Adunai*, or Lord Bacchus. Passing under the disguise of *Adoni-Iahoh* (original text, *Isaiah* lxi, 1), Iahoh and Lord Tsabaôth, the Baal-Adonis, or Bacchus, worshiped in the groves and *public sods* or Mysteries, under the polishing hand of Ezra becomes finally the later-vowelled Adonai of the Masorah — the One and Supreme God of the Christians!

"Thou shalt not worship the Sun who is named Adunai," says the *Codex* of the Nazarenes; "whose name is also *Kadesh* § and El-El. This Adunai will elect to himself a nation and congregate *in crowds* [his worship will be exoteric] . . . Jerusalem will become the refuge and city of the *Abortive*, who shall perfect themselves [circumcise] with the sword . . . and shall adore Adunai." ‖

---

* [Cf. *Numb.* vi, 2; Munk, *Palestine*, p. 169.]
† Norberg, *Codex Nazaraeus*, II, p. 305.
‡ See Lucian, *De Syria Dea*.
§ *Psalms* lxxxix, 7.
‖ *Codex Nazaraeus*, I, p. 47.

The oldest Nazarenes, who were the descendants of the Scripture *nazars*, and whose last prominent leader was John the Baptist, although never very orthodox, in the sight of the scribes and Pharisees of Jerusalem were, nevertheless, respected and left unmolested. Even Herod "feared the multitude" because they regarded John as a prophet (*Matthew* xiv, 5). But the followers of Jesus evidently adhered to a sect which became a still more exasperating thorn in their side. It appeared as a heresy *within* another heresy; for while the nazars of the olden times, the "Sons of the Prophets," were Chaldean kabalists, the adepts of the new dissenting sect showed themselves reformers and innovators from the first. The great similitude traced by some critics between the rites and observances of the earliest Christians and those of the Essenes may be accounted for without the slightest difficulty. The Essenes, as we remarked just now, were the converts of Buddhist missionaries who had overrun Egypt, Greece, and even Judaea at one time, since the reign of Aśoka the zealous propagandist; and while it is evidently to the Essenes that belongs the honor of having had the Nazarene reformer Jesus as a pupil, still the latter is found disagreeing with his early teachers on several questions of formal observance. He cannot strictly be called an Essene, for reasons which we will indicate further on, neither was he a nazar, or Nazaria of the older sect. What Jesus *was* may be found in the *Codex Nazaraeus*, in the unjust accusations of the Bardesanian Gnostics.

"Jesu Mesio is *Nebu*, the false Messias, the destroyer of the ancient religion," says the *Codex*.* He is the founder of the sect of the new nazars, and, as the words clearly imply, a follower of the Buddhist doctrine. In Hebrew the word *naba*, נבא, means to speak of inspiration; and נבו is *nebo*, a god of wisdom. But Nebo is also *Mercury*, and *Mercury* is *Budha* in the Hindu monogram of planets. Moreover, we find the Talmudists holding that Jesus was inspired by the genius of Mercury.†

The Nazarene reformer had undoubtedly belonged to one of these sects; though, perhaps, it would be next to impossible to decide absolutely which. But what is self-evident is that he preached the philosophy of Buddha-Śâkyamuni. Denounced by the later prophets, cursed by the Sanhedrin, the *nazars* — they were confounded with others of that name "who separated themselves unto that shame," ‡ — were secretly, if not openly, persecuted by the orthodox synagogue. It becomes clear why Jesus was treated with such contempt from the first, and deprecatingly

---

* I, p. 55; Norberg, *Onomasticon*, p. 74.

† Alphonsus a Spina, *Fortalitium fidei*, ii, 2.

‡ *Hosea* ix, 10.

called "the Galilean." Nathaniel inquires — "Can there any good thing come out of Nazareth?" (*John* i, 46), at the very beginning of his career; and merely because he knows him to be a *nazar*. Does not this clearly hint that even the older nazars were not really Hebrew religionists, but rather a class of Chaldean theurgists? Besides, as the *New Testament* is noted for its mistranslations and transparent falsifications of texts, we may justly suspect that the word Nazareth was substituted for that of *nasaria*, or *nozari*; and that it originally read "Can any good thing come from a *nozari*, or Nazarene?" a follower of St. John the Baptist, with whom we see him associating from his first appearance on the stage of action, after having been lost sight of for a period of nearly twenty years. The blunders of the *Old Testament* are as nothing to those of the *gospels*. Nothing shows better than these self-evident contradictions the system of pious fraud upon which the superstructure of the Messiahship rests. "This *is Elias* which was for to come," says Matthew of John the Baptist, thus forcing an ancient kabalistic tradition into the frame of evidence (xi, 14). But when addressing the Baptist himself, they ask him (*John* i, 21), "Art thou Elias?" "And he saith, *I am not!*" Which knew best — John or his biographer? And which is divine revelation?

The motive of Jesus was evidently like that of Gautama Buddha, to benefit humanity at large by producing a religious reform which should give it a religion of pure ethics; the true knowledge of God and nature having remained until then solely in the hands of the esoteric sects and their adepts. As Jesus used *oil* and the Essenes never used aught but pure water,* he cannot be called a strict Essene. On the other hand, the Essenes were also "set apart"; they were healers (*asaya*) and dwelt in the desert as all ascetics did.

But although he did not abstain from wine, he could have remained a Nazarene all the same. For in chapter vi of *Numbers*, we see that after the priest has waved a part of the hair of a Nazarite for a waveoffering before the Lord, "after that a Nazarite may drink wine" (vi, 20). The bitter denunciation by the reformer of the people who would be satisfied with nothing is worded in the following exclamation: "John came neither eating nor drinking and ye say, He hath a devil. . . . The Son of man is come eating and drinking; and ye say, Behold a gluttonous man and winebibber." † And yet he was an Essene and Nazarene, for we not only find him sending a message to Herod, to say that he was one of those who cast out demons, and who performed

---

\* "The Essenes considered oil as a defilement," says Josephus, in *The Jewish War*, II, viii, 3.

† [*Luke* vii, 33-34.]

cures, but actually calling himself a prophet and declaring himself equal to the other prophets.*

The author of *Sōd* shows Matthew trying to connect the appellation of Nazarene with a prophecy,† and inquires "Why then does Matthew state that *the prophet* said he should be called *Nazaria?* Simply *because he belonged to that sect,* and a *prophecy* would *confirm* his claims to the Messiahship. Now it does not appear that the Prophets anywhere state that the Messiah will be called a *Nazarene*." ‡ The fact alone that Matthew tries in the last verse of chapter ii to strengthen his claim that Jesus dwelt in Nazareth *merely to fulfil a prophecy,* does more than weaken the argument; it upsets it entirely; for the first two chapters have sufficiently been proved later forgeries.

Baptism is one of the oldest rites and was practiced by all the nations in their Mysteries, as sacred ablutions. Dunlap seems to derive the name of the *nazars* from *nazah,* sprinkling; Bahâk-Ziwa is the genius who called the world into existence § out of the "dark water," say the Nazarenes; and Richardson's *Persian, Arabic, and English Lexicon* asserts that the word *Bahāk* means "raining." ‖ But the Bahâk-Ziwa of the Nazarenes cannot be traced so easily to Bacchus, who "was the rain-god," for the nazars were the greatest opponents of Bacchus-worship. "Bacchus is brought up by the Hyades, the rain-nymphs," says Preller;¶ and Dunlap shows, furthermore,** that at the conclusion of the religious Mysteries, the priests baptized (washed) their monuments and anointed them with oil. All this is but a very indirect proof. The Jordan baptism need not be shown a substitution for the *exoteric* Bacchic rites and the libations in honor of Adonis or Adoni — whom the Nazarenes abhorred — in order to prove it to have been a sect sprung from the "Mysteries" of the "Secret Doctrine"; and their rites can by no means be confounded with those of the Pagan populace, who had simply fallen into the idolatrous and unreasoning faith of all plebeian multitudes. John was the prophet of these Nazarenes, and in Galilee he was termed "the Savior," but he was not the founder of that sect which derived its tradition from the remotest Chaldeo-Akkadian theurgy.

---

* *Luke* xiii, 32.

† *Matthew* ii, 23. We must bear in mind that the Gospel according to Matthew in the New Testament is not the original Gospel of the apostle of that name. The authentic Evangel was for centuries in the possession of the Nazarenes and the Ebionites, as we show further on the admission of St. Jerome himself, who confesses that he had to *ask permission* of the Nazarenes to translate it. [*Vide* p. 182 in present Volume.]

‡ Dunlap, *Sōd, the Son of the Man,* p. x.

§ *Cod. Nazar.,* II, p. 233.

‖ [Dunlap, *Sōd, the Mystery,* etc., p. 79.]

¶ Preller, *Griechische Mythologie,* Vol. I, p. 415.

** Dunlap, *op. cit.,* pp. 46 *et seq.*

"The early plebeian Israelites were Canaanites and Phoenicians, with the same worship of the Phallic gods — Bacchus, Baal or Adon, Iacchos — Iaô or Jehovah"; but even among them there had always been a class of *initiated* adepts. Later, the character of this *plebs* was modified by Assyrian conquests; and, finally, the Persian colonizations superimposed the Pharisean and Eastern ideas and usages, from which the *Old Testament* and the Mosaic institutes were derived. The Asmonean priest-kings promulgated the canon of the *Old Testament* in contradistinction to the *Apocrypha* or Secret Books of the Alexandrian Jews — kabalists.* Till John Hyrcanus they were Asideans (Chasidim) and Pharisees (Pârsîs), but then they became Sadducees or Zadokites — asserters of sacerdotal rule as contradistinguished from rabbinical. The Pharisees were lenient and intellectual; the Sadducees, bigoted and cruel.

Says the *Codex*: "John, son of the Aba-Saba-Zacharia, conceived by his mother *Anasabet* in her hundredth year, had baptized for *forty-two years* † when Iesu Messias came to the Jordan to be baptized with John's baptism. But he will *pervert John's doctrine*, changing the baptism of the Jordan, and perverting the sayings of justice." ‡

The baptism was changed from *water* to that of the Holy Ghost, undoubtedly in consequence of the ever-dominant idea of the Fathers to institute a reform, and make the Christians distinct from St. John's Nazarenes, the Nabathaeans and Ebionites, in order to make room for new dogmas. Not only do the Synoptics tell us that Jesus was baptizing the same as John, but John's own disciples complained of it, though surely Jesus cannot be accused of following a purely Bacchic rite. The parenthesis in verse 2nd of *John* iv, ". . . though Jesus himself baptized not," is so clumsy as to show upon its face that it is an interpolation. *Matthew* makes John say that he that should come after him would not baptize them with water "but with *the Holy Ghost* and fire." *Mark*, *Luke* and *John* corroborate these words. Water, fire and spirit, or Holy Ghost, have all their origin in India, as we will show.

---

\* The word *Apocrypha* was very erroneously adopted as doubtful and spurious. The word means *hidden* and *secret*; but that which is secret may be often more true than that which is revealed.

† The statement, if reliable, would show that Jesus was between fifty and sixty years old when baptized; for the Gospels make him but a few months younger than John. The kabalists say that Jesus was over forty years old when first appearing at the gates of Jerusalem. The present copy of the *Codex Nazaraeus* is dated in the year 1042, but Dunlap finds in Irenaeus (2nd century) quotations from and ample references to this book. "The basis of the material common to Irenaeus and the *Codex Nazaraeus* must be at least as early as the first century," says the author in his preface to *Sōd, the Son of the Man*, p. iii.

‡ *Codex Nazaraeus*, Vol. I, p. 109; Dunlap, *op. cit.*, p. xxiv.

Now there is one very strange peculiarity about this sentence. It is flatly denied in *Acts* xix, 2-5. Apollos, a Jew of Alexandria, belonged to the sect of St. John's disciples; he had been baptized, and instructed others in the doctrines of the Baptist. And yet when Paul, cleverly profiting by his absence at Corinth, finds certain disciples of Apollos at Ephesus, and asks them whether they received *the Holy Ghost,* he is naïvely answered, "We have not so much as heard whether there be any Holy Ghost!" "Unto what then were ye baptized?" he inquires. *"Unto John's baptism,"* they say. Then Paul is made to repeat the words attributed to John by the Synoptics; and these men "were baptized in the name of the Lord Jesus," exhibiting, moreover, at the same instant, the usual polyglot gift which accompanies the descent of the Holy Ghost.

How then? St. John the Baptist, who is called the "precursor," that "the prophecy might be fulfilled," the great prophet and martyr, whose words ought to have had such an importance in the eyes of his disciples, announces the "Holy Ghost" to his listeners; causes crowds to assemble on the shores of the Jordan, where, at the great ceremony of Christ's baptism, the promised "Holy Ghost" appears within the opened heavens, and the multitude hears the voice, and yet there are disciples of St. John who have "never so much as *heard* whether there be any Holy Ghost"!

Verily the disciples who wrote the *Codex Nazaraeus* were right. Only it is not Jesus himself, but those who came after him, and who concocted the *Bible* to suit themselves, that *"perverted* John's doctrine, *changed* the baptism of the Jordan, and perverted the sayings of justice."

It is useless to object that the present *Codex* was written centuries after the direct apostles of John preached. So were our *Gospels.* When this astounding interview of Paul with the "Baptists" took place, Bardesanes had not yet appeared among them, and the sect was not considered a "heresy." Moreover, we are enabled to judge how little St. John's promise of the "Holy Ghost," and the appearance of the "Ghost" himself, had affected his disciples, by the displeasure shown by them toward the disciples of Jesus, and the kind of rivalry manifested from the first. Nay, so little is John himself sure of the identity of Jesus with the expected Messiah, that after the famous scene of the baptism at the Jordan, and the oral assurance by the *Holy Ghost* Himself that *"This is my beloved Son"* (*Matthew* iii, 17), we find "the Precursor," in *Matthew* xi, 3, sending two of his disciples from his prison to inquire of Jesus: "Art thou *he* that should come, or do we look *for another?"*!

This flagrant contradiction alone ought to have long ago satisfied reasonable minds as to the putative divine inspiration of the *New Testament.* But we may offer another question: If baptism is the sign of regeneration, and an ordinance instituted by Jesus, why do not Christians now baptize as Jesus is here represented as doing, "with the Holy Ghost and with fire," instead of following the custom of the Nazarenes? In making these palpable interpolations, what possible motive could Irenaeus have had except to cause people to believe that the appellation of Nazarene, which Jesus bore, came only from his father's residence at Nazareth, and not from his affiliation with the sect of *Nazaria*, the healers?

This expedient of Irenaeus was a most unfortunate one, for from time immemorial the prophets of old had been thundering against the baptism of fire as practiced by their neighbors, which imparted the "spirit of prophecy," or the Holy Ghost. But the case was desperate; the Christians were universally called Nazoraeans and Iessaeans (according to Epiphanius), and Christ simply ranked as a Jewish prophet and healer — so self-styled, so accepted by his own disciples, and so regarded by their followers. In such a state of things there was no room for either a new hierarchy or a new Godhead; and since Irenaeus had undertaken the business of manufacturing both, he had to put together such materials as were available, and fill the gaps with his own fertile inventions.

To assure ourselves that Jesus was a true Nazarene — albeit with ideas of a new reform — we must not search for the proof in the translated *Gospels*, but in such original versions as are accessible. Tischendorf, in his translation from the Greek of *Luke* iv, 34, has it "Iesou Nazarene"; and in the Syriac it reads "Iasua, thou *Nazaria*." Thus, if we take in account all that is puzzling and incomprehensible in the four *Gospels*, revised and corrected as they now stand, we shall easily see for ourselves that the true, original Christianity, such as was preached by Jesus, is to be found only in the so-called Syrian heresies. Only from them can we extract any clear notions about what was primitive Christianity. Such was the faith of Paul, when Tertullus, the orator, accused the apostle before the governor Felix. What he complained of was that "we have found this man . . . a mover of sedition . . . a ringleader of *the sect of the Nazarenes*";* and, while Paul denies every other accusation, he confesses that "after the way which they call heresy, *so worship I the God of my fathers*." † This confession is a whole revelation. It shows: 1, that Paul admitted belonging to the sect of the Nazarenes; 2, that he worshipped the *God of his fathers*, not the trinitarian Christian God, of whom he knows nothing, and who was not invented until after his death; and, 3, that this unlucky confession satisfactorily explains why the treatise, *Acts of the Apostles*, together with John's *Revelation*, which at one

---

\* *Acts* xxiv, 5.

† *Ibid.*, xxiv, 14.

period was utterly rejected, were kept out of the canon of the *New Testament* for such a length of time.

At Byblos, the neophytes as well as the hierophants were, after participating in the Mysteries, obliged to fast and remain in solitude for some time. There was strict fasting and preparation before as well as after the Bacchic, Adonian and Eleusinian orgies; and Herodotus hints, with fear and veneration about the LAKE of Bacchus, in which "they [the priests] made at night exhibitions of his life and sufferings." * In the Mithraic sacrifices, during the initiation, a preliminary scene of death was simulated by the neophyte, and it preceded the scene showing him himself "being born again by the rite *of baptism*." A portion of this ceremony is still enacted in the present day by the Masons, when the neophyte, as the Grand Master Hiram Abiff, lies dead, and is raised by the strong grip of the lion's paw.

The priests were circumcised. The neophyte could not be initiated without having been present at the solemn Mysteries of the LAKE. The Nazarenes were baptized in the Jordan; and could not be baptized elsewhere; they were also circumcised, and had to fast before as well as after the purification by baptism. Jesus is said to have fasted in the wilderness for forty days, immediately after his baptism. To the present day, there is outside every temple in India, a lake, stream, or a reservoir full of holy water, in which the Brahmans and the Hindu devotees bathe daily. Such places of consecrated water are necessary to every temple. The bathing festivals, or *baptismal* rites, occur twice every year; in October and April. Each lasts ten days; and, as in ancient Egypt and Greece, the statues of their gods, goddesses, and idols are immersed in water by the priests; the object of the ceremony being to wash away from them the sins of their worshippers which they have taken upon themselves, and which pollute them, until washed off by holy water. During the Ârati, the bathing ceremony, the principal god of every temple is carried in solemn procession to be baptized in the sea. The Brahman priests, carrying the sacred images, are followed generally by the Mahârâja — barefoot, and nearly naked. *Three times* the priests enter the sea; the third time they carry with them the whole of the images. Holding them up with prayers repeated by the whole congregation, the Chief Priest plunges the statues of the gods *thrice* in the name of the *mystic trinity*, into the water; after which they are purified.† The Orphic hymn calls *water* the greatest purifier of men and gods.

---

\* *History*, Bk. II, §§ 170, 171.

† The Hindu High Pontiff — the Chief of the Nampûtiris, who lives in the Cochin Land, is generally present during these festivals of "Holy Water" immersions. He travels sometimes to very great distances to preside over the ceremony.

Our Nazarene sect is known to have existed some 150 years B.C., and to have lived on the banks of the Jordan, and on the Western shore of the Dead Sea, according to Pliny and Josephus.* But in King's *Gnostics*, we find quoted another statement by Josephus (*Antiq.*, xv, 15), which says that the Essenes had been established on the shores of the Dead Sea "for thousands of ages" before Pliny's time.†

According to Munk the term "Galilean" is nearly synonymous with that of "Nazarene"; furthermore, he shows the relations of the former with the Gentiles as very intimate. The populace had probably gradually adopted, in their constant intercourse, certain rites and modes of worship of the Pagans; and the scorn with which the Galileans were regarded by the orthodox Jews is attributed by him to the same cause. Their friendly relations had certainly led them, at a later period, to adopt the "Adonia," or the sacred rites over the body of the lamented Adonis, as we find Jerome fairly lamenting this circumstance. "Over Bethlehem," he says, "the grove of Thammuz, that is of Adonis, was casting its shadow! And in the GROTTO where formerly the infant Jesus cried, the lover of Venus was being mourned." ‡

It was after the rebellion of Bar Cocheba, that the Roman Emperor established the Mysteries of Adonis at the Sacred Cave in Bethlehem; and who knows but this was the *petra* or rock-temple on which the church was built? The Boar of Adonis was placed above the gate of Jerusalem which looked toward Bethlehem.

Munk says that "the Nazireate was an institution established before the laws of Mūsah." § This is evident; as we find this sect not only mentioned but minutely described in *Numbers* (chap. vi). In the commandment given in this chapter to Moses by the "Lord," it is easy to recognize the rites and laws of the Priests of Adonis. ‖ The abstinence and purity strictly prescribed in both sects are identical. Both

---

\* Pliny, *Nat. Hist.*, V, xv, 73; Josephus, *Antiq.*, XIII, v, 9; XV, x, 4, 5; XVIII. i. 5.

† King thinks it a great exaggeration and is inclined to believe that these Essenes, who were most undoubtedly Buddhist monks, were "merely a continuation of the association known as 'Sons of the Prophets'." — *The Gnostics and their Remains*, p. 22, footnote [p. 52 in 2nd ed.].

‡ Jerome, *Epistles*, No. 49, *ad Paulinum altera*. Cf. Dunlap, *Vestiges*, etc., p. 218.

§ Munk, *Palestine*, p. 169.

‖ Bacchus and Ceres — or the mystical *Wine* and *Bread*, used during the Mysteries, become, in the "Adonia," Adonis and Venus. Movers shows that "*Iaô* is Bacchus" (*Die Phön.*, I, p. 550); and his authority is Joannes Lydus, *De mensibus*, IV, 38, 74; see also Dunlap, *Vestiges*, etc., p. 195. *Iaô* is a Sun-god and the Jewish Jehovah; the intellectual or Central Sun of the kabalists. See Julian, *Oratio IV in solem*, p. 136; and Proclus, *On the 1st Alcib.*, IV, p. 96. But this "Iaô" is not the Mystery-god.

allowed their hair *to grow long* * as the Hindu cenobites and fakirs do to this day, while other castes shave their hair and abstain on certain days from wine. The prophet Elijah, a Nazarene, is described in *2 Kings*, and by Josephus as "a hairy man girt with the girdle of leather." † And John the Baptist and Jesus are both represented as wearing very long hair. ‡ John is "clothed with camel's hair" and wearing a girdle of hide, and Jesus in a long garment "without any seams" . . . "and very white, like snow," says *Mark*; the very dress worn by the Nazarene Priests and the Pythagorean and Buddhist Essenes, as described by Josephus.

If we carefully trace the terms *nazar*, and *nazaret*, throughout the best known works of ancient writers, we will meet them in connection with "Pagan" as well as Jewish adepts. Thus, Alexander Polyhistor says of Pythagoras that he was a disciple of the Assyrian *Nazaratus*, whom some suppose to be Ezekiel. § Diogenes Laertius ‖ states most positively that Pythagoras, after being initiated into all the Mysteries of the Greeks and barbarians, "went into Egypt and afterward visited the Chaldeans and Magi"; and Apuleius ¶ maintains that it was Zoroaster who instructed Pythagoras.

Were we to suggest that the Hebrew *nazars*, the railing prophets of the "Lord," had been initiated into the so-called Pagan mysteries, and belonged (or at least a majority of them) to the same Lodge or circle of adepts as those who were considered idolaters, that their "circle of prophets" was but a collateral branch of a secret association, which we may well term "international," what a visitation of Christian wrath would we not incur! And still, the case looks strangely suspicious.

Let us first recall to our minds that which Ammianus Marcellinus,** and other historians relate of Darius Hystaspes. The latter, penetrating into Upper India (Bactriana), learned pure rites, and stellar and cosmical sciences from Brahmans, and communicated them to the Magi. Now Hystaspes is shown in history to have crushed the Magi; and introduced — or rather forced upon them — the pure religion of Zoroaster, that of Ormazd. How is it, then, that an inscription is found on the tomb

---

\* Josephus, *Antiq.*, IV, iv, 4.
† *Ibid.*, IX, ii, 1; *2 Kings* i, 8.
‡ In relation to the well-known fact of Jesus wearing his hair long, and being always so represented, it becomes quite startling to find how little the unknown Editor of the *Acts* knew about the Apostle Paul, since he makes him say in *1 Corinthians* xi, 14. "Doth not even Nature itself teach you, that, if a *man have long hair, it is a shame unto him?*" Certainly Paul could never have said such a thing! Therefore, if the passage is genuine, Paul knew nothing of the prophet whose doctrines he had embraced and for which he died; and if false — how much more reliable is what remains?
§ [Clem. Alex., *Strom.*, I, xv.]
‖ [*Lives*, "Pythagoras," § 3.]
¶ [*Florida*, II, xv; cf. Hyde, *Hist. rel. vet. Persarum*, p. 309; Oxonii, 1700.]
** [*Roman Hist.*, XXIII, vi, 33.]

of Darius, stating that he was "teacher and hierophant of magic, or magianism"? Evidently there must be some historical mistake, and history confesses it. In this imbroglio of names, Zoroaster, the teacher and instructor of Pythagoras, can be neither the Zoroaster nor Zarathushtra who instituted sun-worship among the Pârsîs; nor he who appeared at the court of Gushtasp (Hystaspes), the alleged father of Darius; nor, again, the Zoroaster who placed his magi above the kings themselves. The oldest Zoroastrian scripture — the *Avesta* — does not betray the slightest traces of the reformer having ever been acquainted with any of the nations that subsequently adopted his mode of worship. He seems utterly ignorant of the neighbors of Western Iran, the Medes, the Assyrians, the Persians, and others. If we had no other evidences of the great antiquity of the Zoroastrian religion than the discovery of the blunder committed by some scholars in our own century, who regarded King Vishtâspa (Gushtasp) as identical with the father of Darius, whereas the Persian tradition points directly to Vishtâspa as the last of the line of Kaianian princes who ruled in Bactriana, it ought to be enough, for the Assyrian conquest of Bactriana took place 1,200 years B.C.*

Therefore, it is but natural that we should see in the appellation of Zoroaster not a name but a generic term, whose significance must be left to philologists to agree upon. *Guru*, in Sanskrit, is a spiritual teacher; and as Zuruastara means in the same language he who worships the sun, why is it impossible, that by some natural change of language, due to the great number of different nations which were converted to the sun-worship, the word *guru-astara*, the spiritual teacher of sun-worship, so closely resembling the name of the founder of this religion, became gradually transformed in its primal form of Zuryastara or Zoroaster? The opinion of the kabalists is that there was but one Zarathushtra and many *guruastaras* or spiritual teachers, and that one such *guru*, or rather *huru-aster*, as he is called in the old manuscripts, was the instructor of Pythagoras. To philology and our readers we leave the explanation for what it is worth. Personally we believe in it, as we credit on this subject kabalistic tradition far more than the explanation of scientists, no two of whom have been able to agree up to the present year.

Aristotle states that Zoroaster lived 6,000 years before Plato;† Hermippus of Alexandria, who is said to have read the genuine books of the Zoroastrians, although Alexander the Great is accused of having destroyed

---

* Max Müller has sufficiently proved the case in his lecture on the "Zend-Avesta." He calls Gushtasp "the mythical pupil of Zoroaster." [*Chips*, etc., I, p. 88.] Mythical, perhaps, only because the period in which he lived and learned with Zoroaster is too remote to allow our modern science to speculate upon it with any certainty.

† [Pliny, *Nat. Hist.*, XXX, ii.]

them, shows Zoroaster as the pupil of Agonaces (Agon-ach, or the Ahon-God) and as having lived 5,000 years before the fall of Troy.* Er or Eros, whose vision is related by Plato in the *Republic*,† is declared by Clemens Alexandrinus to have been Zardosht.‡ While the Magus who dethroned Cambyses was a Mede, and Darius proclaims that he put down the Magian rites to establish those of Ormazd, Xanthus of Lydia declares Zoroaster to have been the chief of the Magi! § [20]

Which of them is wrong? or are they all right, and only the modern interpreters fail to explain the difference between the Reformer and his apostles and followers? This blundering of our commentators reminds us of that of Suetonius, who mistook the Christians for one Christos, or *Crestos*, as he spells it, and assured his readers that Claudius banished him for the disturbance he made among the Jews.‖

Finally, and to return again to the *nazars*, Zaratus is mentioned by Pliny in the following words: "He was Zoroaster and *Nazaret*." ¶ As Zoroaster is called *princeps* of the Magi, and *nazar* signifies separated or consecrated, is it not a Hebrew rendering of *mag*? Volney believes so. The Persian word *Na-zaruan* means millions of years, and refers to the Chaldean "Ancient of Days." Hence the name of the Nazar or Nazarenes, who were consecrated to the service of the Supreme one God, the kabalistic Ain-Soph, or the Ancient of Days, the "Aged of the aged."

But the word *nazar* may also be found in India. In Hindôstânî *nazar* is sight, internal or *supernatural* vision; *nazar-bandi* means fascination, a mesmeric or magical spell; and *nazarân* is the word for sight-seeing or vision.

Professor Wilder thinks that as the word *Zeruana* is nowhere to be found in the *Avesta*, but only in the later Pârsî books, it came from the Magians, who composed the Persian sacred caste in the Sassanian period, but were originally Assyrians. "Turan, of the poets," he says, "I consider to be Aturia, or Assyria; and that Zohak (Az-dahaka, Dei-okes, or Astyages), the Serpent-king, was Assyrian, Median, and Babylonian—when those countries were united."

This opinion does not, however, in the least implicate our statement that the secret doctrines of the Magi, of the pre-Vedic Buddhists, of the hierophants of the Egyptian Thoth or Hermes, and of the adepts of whatever age and nationality, including the Chaldean kabalists and the Jewish *nazars*, were *identical* from the beginning. When we use the term *Buddhists*, we do not mean to imply by it either the exoteric Buddhism instituted by the followers

---

\* [Pliny, *loc. cit.*]
† [*Republic*, X, 614 *et seq.*]
‡ [*Strom.*, V, xiv.]
§ [Diog. Laert., *Lives*, etc., Proemium, § 2.]
‖ [*Life of the Caesars*, "Claudius," §25.]
¶ [Pliny, *Nat. Hist.*, XXX, ii.]

of Gautama Buddha, nor the modern Buddhistic religion, but the secret philosophy of Śâkyamuni, which in its essence is certainly identical with the ancient wisdom-religion of the sanctuary, the pre-Vedic Brahmanism. The "schism" of Zoroaster, as it is called, is a direct proof of it. For it was no *schism*, strictly speaking, but merely a partially public exposition of strictly monotheistic religious truths, hitherto taught only in the sanctuaries, and that he had learned from the Brahmans. Zoroaster, the primeval institutor of sun-worship, cannot be called the founder of the dualistic system; neither was he the first to teach the unity of God, for he taught but what he had learned himself with the Brahmans. And that Zarathushtra and his followers, the Zoroastrians, "had been settled in India before they immigrated into Persia," is also proved by Max Müller. "That the Zoroastrians and their ancestors started from India," he says, "during the Vaidik period can be proved as distinctly as that the inhabitants of Massilia started from Greece. . . . Many of the gods of the Zoroastrians come out . . . as mere reflections and deflections of the primitive and authentic gods of the *Veda*." *

If now we can prove — and we can do so on the evidence of the *Kabala* and the oldest traditions of the wisdom-religion, the philosophy of the old sanctuaries — that all these gods, whether of the Zoroastrians or of the *Veda*, are but so many personated *occult powers* of nature, the faithful servants of the adepts of secret wisdom — Magic — we are on secure ground.

Thus, whether we say that Kabalism and Gnosticism proceeded from Masdeanism or Zoroastrianism, it is all the same, unless we mean the *exoteric* worship—which we do not. Likewise, and in this sense, we may echo King, the author of *The Gnostics*,† and several other archaeologists, and maintain that both the former proceeded from *Buddhism*, at once the simplest and most satisfying of philosophies, and which resulted in one of the purest religions of the world. It is only a matter of chronology to decide which of these religions, differing but in external form, is the oldest, therefore the least adulterated. But even this bears but very indirectly, if at all, on the subject we treat of. Already some time before our era, the adepts, except in India, had ceased to congregate in large communities; but whether among the Essenes, or the Neo-Platonists, or again, among the innumerable struggling sects born but to die, the same doctrines, identical in substance and spirit, if not always in form, are encountered. By *Buddhism*, therefore, we mean that religion signifying literally the doctrine of wisdom, and which by many ages antedates the metaphysical philosophy of Siddhârtha-Śâkyamuni.

After nineteen centuries of enforced eliminations from the canonical books of every sentence which might put the investigator on the true path, it has become very difficult so show, to the satisfaction of exact science, that the

---

* Max Müller, "The Zend-Avesta," in *Chips*, etc., I, p. 86.
†[ Page 55 in 2nd ed.]

"Pagan" worshippers of Adonis, their neighbors, the Nazarenes, and the Pythagorean Essenes, the healing Therapeutes,* the Ebionites, and other sects, were all, with very slight differences, followers of the ancient theurgic Mysteries. And yet by analogy and a close study of the *hidden* sense of their rites and customs, we can trace their kinship.

It was given to a contemporary of Jesus to become the means of pointing out to posterity, by his interpretation of the oldest literature of Israel, how deeply the kabalistic philosophy agreed in its esotericism with that of the profoundest Greek thinkers. This contemporary, an ardent disciple of Plato and Aristotle, was Philo Judaeus. While explaining the Mosaic books according to a purely kabalistic method, he is the famous Hebrew writer whom Kingsley calls the Father of New Platonism.

It is evident that Philo's Therapeutes are a branch of the Essenes. Their name indicates it — Ἐσσαῖοι, *Essaioi*, physicians. Hence, the contradictions, forgeries, and other desperate expedients to reconcile the prophecies of the Jewish canon with the Galilean nativity and godship.

Luke, who was a physician, is designated in the Syriac texts as *Asaya*, the Essaian or Essene. Josephus and Philo Judaeus have sufficiently described this sect to leave no doubt in our mind that the Nazarene Reformer, after having received his education in their dwellings in the desert, and been duly initiated in the Mysteries, preferred the free and independent life of a wandering *Nazaria*, and so separated or *inazarenized* himself from them, thus becoming a travelling Therapeute, a Nazaria, a healer. Every Therapeute, before quitting his community, had to do the same. Both Jesus and St. John the Baptist preached the end of the Age; † which proves their knowledge of the secret computation of the priests and kabalists, who with the chiefs of the Essene communities alone had the secret of the duration of the cycles. The latter were kabalists and theurgists; "they had their *mystic* books, and predicted future events," says Munk. ‡

Dunlap, whose personal researches seem to have been quite successful in that direction, traces the Essenes, Nazarenes, Dositheans, and some other sects as having all existed before Christ: "They rejected pleasures, *despised riches, loved one another,* and more than other sects, neg-

---

* Philo Judaeus, *De vita contemplativa.*
† The real meaning of the division into *ages* is esoteric and Buddhistic. So little did the uninitiated Christians understand it that they accepted the words of Jesus *literally* and firmly believed that he meant the end of the world. There had been many prophecies about the forthcoming age. Virgil, in the fourth *Eclogue,* mentions the Metatron — a new offspring, with whom the *iron age* shall end and a *golden one* arise.
‡ *Palestine,* pp. 517 *et seq.*

lected wedlock, deeming the conquest of the passions to be virtuous," * he says.

These are all virtues preached by Jesus; and if we are to take the gospels as a standard of truth, Christ was a metempsychosist or *reincarnationist* — again like these same Essenes, whom we see were Pythagoreans in all their doctrines and habits. Iamblichus asserts that the Samian philosopher spent a certain time at Carmel with them.† In his discourses and sermons, Jesus always spoke in parables and used metaphors with his audience. This habit was again that of the Esseneans and the Nazarenes; the Galileans who dwelt in cities and villages were never known to use such allegorical language. Indeed, some of his disciples being Galileans as well as himself, felt even surprised to find him using with the people such a form of expression. "Why speakest thou unto them in parables?" they often inquired. "Because, it is given unto you to know the Mysteries of the kingdom of heaven, but to them it is not given," was the reply, which was that of an initiate. "Therefore I speak unto them in parables: because they seeing see not; and hearing they hear not, neither do they understand." ‡ Moreover, we find Jesus expressing his thoughts still clearer — and in sentences which are purely Pythagorean — when, during the *Sermon on the Mount*, he says:

> "Give ye not that which is sacred to the dogs,
> Neither cast ye your pearls before swine;
> For the swine will tread them under their feet
> And the dogs will turn and rend you."

Professor A. Wilder, the editor of Taylor's *Eleusinian and Bacchic Mysteries*, observes "a like disposition on the part of Jesus and Paul to classify their doctrines as esoteric and exoteric, 'the Mysteries of the Kingdom of God' for the apostles, and 'parables' for the multitude. 'We speak wisdom', says Paul, 'among them that *are perfect*' (or initiated)." §

In the Eleusinian and other Mysteries the participants were always divided into two classes, the *neophytes* and the *perfect*. The former were sometimes admitted to the preliminary initiation: the dramatic performance of Ceres, or the soul, descending to Hades. ‖ But it was given only to the *"perfect"* to enjoy and learn the Mysteries of the

---

* Dunlap, *Sōd, the Son of the Man*, p. xi.

† Thos. Taylor, *Iamblichus' Life of Pythag.*, p. 10; London, 1818. Munk derives the name of the *Iessaeans* or Essenes from the Syriac *Asaya* — the healers, or physicians, thus showing their identity with the Egyptian Therapeutae. — *Palestine*, p. 515.

‡ *Matthew* xiii, 10-13.

§ Page 47 in 4th ed.

‖ This descent to Hades signifies the inevitable fate of each soul to be united for a time with a terrestrial body. This union, or dark prospect for the soul to find itself

divine *Elysium*, the celestial abode of the blessed; this Elysium being unquestionably the same as the "Kingdom of Heaven." To contradict or reject the above, would be merely to shut one's eyes to the truth.

The narrative of the Apostle Paul, in his second *Epistle to the Corinthians* (xii, 2-4), has struck several scholars, well versed in the descriptions of the mystical rites of the initiation given by some classics, as alluding most undoubtedly to the final *Epopteia*.* "I knew a certain man — *whether in body or outside of body*, I know not: God knoweth — who was rapt into Paradise, and heard things ineffable, ἄρρητα ῥήματα, *which it is not lawful for a man to repeat*." These words have rarely, so far as we know, been regarded by commentators as an allusion to the beatific visions of an "*initiated*" seer. But the phraseology is unequivocal. These things "*which it is not lawful to repeat*," are hinted at in the same words, and the reason for it assigned is the same as that which we find repeatedly expressed by Plato, Proclus, Iamblichus, Herodotus, and other classics. "We speak WISDOM [only] among them who are PERFECT," says Paul;† the plain and undeniable translation of the sentence being: "We speak of the profounder (or final) esoteric doctrines of the Mysteries (which were denominated *wisdom*) only among them who are *initiated*." ‡ So in relation to the "man who was rapt into Paradise" — and who was evidently Paul himself § — the Christian word Paradise having replaced that of Elysium. To complete the proof, we might recall the words of Plato, given elsewhere, which show that before an initiate could see the gods in their purest light, he had to become *liberated* from his body; *i.e.*, to separate his astral soul from it. ‖ Apuleius also describes his initiation into the Mysteries in the same way: "I approached the confines of death; and, having trodden on the threshold of Proserpina, returned, having been carried through all the elements. In the depths of midnight I saw the sun glittering with a splendid light, together with *the infernal and supernal gods*, and to these divinities approaching, I paid the tribute of devout adoration." ¶ [21]

---

imprisoned within the dark tenement of a body, was considered by all the ancient philosophers, and is even by the modern Buddhists, as a punishment.

* T. Taylor, *op. cit.*, pp. 87-88, in 4th ed.

† [*1 Cor.* ii, 6.]

‡ "The profounder or esoteric doctrines of the ancients were denominated *wisdom*, and afterwards *philosophy*, and also the *gnosis* or knowledge. They related to the human soul, its divine parentage, its supposed degradation from its high estate by becoming connected with 'generation' or the physical world, its onward progress and restoration to God by regenerations ... transmigrations." — T. Taylor, *op. cit.*, pp. 31, 32.

§ Cyril of Jerusalem asserts it. See *Cathecheses*, Oxford, 1838, xiv, 26.

‖ *Phaedrus*, 250 B, C.

¶ *The Golden Ass*, xi, 23; T. Taylor's ed., p. 283.

HEINRICH CORNELIUS AGRIPPA VON NETTESHEIM
1486-1535
From an old engraving.

BARUCH (OR BENEDICTUS) DE SPINOZA
1632-1677
From Abraham Wolfson, *Spinoza, A Life of Reason*, New York, 1932.

Thus, in common with Pythagoras and other hierophant reformers, Jesus divided his teachings into exoteric and esoteric. Following faithfully the Pythagoreo-Essenean ways, he never sat at a meal without saying "grace." "The priest prays before his meal," says Josephus, describing the Essenes.* Jesus also divided his followers into "neophytes," "brethren," and the "perfect," if we may judge by the difference he made between them. But his career, at least as a public Rabbi, was of a too short duration to allow him to establish a regular school of his own; and with the exception, perhaps, of John, it does not seem that he had initiated any other apostle. The Gnostic amulets and talismans are mostly the emblems of the apocalyptic allegories. The "seven vowels" are closely related to the "seven seals"; and the mystic title Abraxas, partakes as much of the composition of *Shem ha-Mephorash*, "the holy word" or ineffable name, as the name called: The word of God, that "*no man knew but he himself*," † as John expresses it.

It would be difficult to escape from the well-adduced proofs that the *Apocalypse* is the production of an initiated kabalist, when this *Revelation* presents whole passages taken from the *Books of Enoch* and *Daniel*, which latter is in itself an abridged imitation of the former; and when, furthermore, we ascertain that the Ophite Gnostics who rejected the *Old Testament* entirely, as "emanating from an inferior being" (Jehovah), accepted the most ancient prophets, such as Enoch, and deduced the strongest support from this book for their religious tenets, the demonstration becomes evident. We will show further how closely related are all these doctrines. Besides, there is the history of Domitian's persecutions of magicians and philosophers, which affords as good a proof as any that John was generally considered a kabalist. As the apostle was included among the number, and moreover conspicuous, the imperial edict banished him not only from Rome, but even from the continent. It was not the Christians whom — confounding them with the Jews, as some historians will have it — the emperor persecuted, but the astrologers and kabalists.‡

The accusations against Jesus of practicing the magic of Egypt were numerous, and at one time universal, in the towns where he was known. The Pharisees, as claimed in the *Bible*, had been the first to fling it in his

---

* [*Jewish Wars*, lib. II, cap. viii, 5.]
† *Revelation* xix, 12.
‡ Suetonius, *Lives of the Caesars*, "Domitian," 3, 12, 14. It is neither cruelty, nor an insane indulgence in it, which shows this emperor in history as passing his time in catching flies and transpiercing them with a golden bodkin, but religious superstition. The Jewish astrologers had predicted to him that he had provoked the wrath of Beelzebub, the "Lord of flies," and would perish miserably through the revenge of the dark god of Ekron, and die like King Ahaziah, because he persecuted the Jews.

face, although Rabbi Wise considers Jesus himself a Pharisee. The *Talmud* certainly points to James the Just as one of that sect.* But these partisans are known to have always stoned every prophet who denounced their evil ways, and it is not on this fact that we base our assertion. These accused him of sorcery, and of driving out devils by Beelzebub, their prince, with as much justice as later the Catholic clergy had to accuse of the same more than one innocent martyr. But Justin Martyr states on better authority that the men of his time *who were not Jews* asserted that the miracles of Jesus were performed by magical art — μαγικη φαντασία — the very expression used by the skeptics of those days to designate the feats of thaumaturgy accomplished in the Pagan temples. "They even ventured to call him a magician and a deceiver of the people," complains the martyr.† In the *Gospel of Nicodemus* (the *Acta Pilati*), the Jews bring the same accusation before Pilate. "Did we not tell thee he was a magician?"‡ Celsus speaks of the same charge, and as a Neo-Platonist believes in it. § The Talmudic literature is full of the most minute particulars, and their greatest accusation is that "Jesus could fly as easily in the air as others could walk." ‖ St. Augustine asserted that it was generally believed that he had been initiated in Egypt, and that he wrote books concerning magic, which he delivered to John. There was a work called *Magia Jesu Christi*, which was attributed to Jesus himself.¶ In the *Clementine Recognitions* the charge is brought against Jesus that he did not perform his miracles as a Jewish prophet, but as a magician, *i.e.*, an initiate of the "heathen" temples.**

It was usual then, as it is now, among the intolerant clergy of opposing religions, as well as among the lower classes of society, and even among those patricians who, for various reasons had been excluded from any participation of the Mysteries, to accuse, sometimes, the highest hierophants and adepts of sorcery and black magic. So Apuleius, who

---

* We believe that it was the Sadducees and not the Pharisees who crucified Jesus. They were Zadokites —partisans of the house of Zadok, or the sacerdotal family. In the *Acts* the apostles were said to be persecuted by the Sadducees, but never by the Pharisees. In fact, the latter never persecuted anyone. They had the scribes, rabbis, and learned men in their numbers, and were not, like the Saducees, jealous of their order.

† Justin Martyr, *Dial. with Trypho*, lxix.

‡ *Gospel of Nicodemus*, ii, 3 (Hone, and Grynaeus.)

§ Origen, *Contra Cels.*, I, lxviii; II, xlviii, *et seq.*

‖ *Talmud: Yôhânân.*

¶ Augustine, *De consensu evang.*, Bk. I, Ch. ix; Fabricius, *Cod. apocr. N. T.*, I, pp. 305 *et seq.*

** I, lviii.

had been initiated, was likewise accused of witchcraft, and of carrying about him the figure of a skeleton — a potent agent, as it is asserted, in the operations of the black art. But one of the best and most unquestionable proofs of our assertion may be found in the so-called *Museo Gregoriano*. On the sarcophagus, which is panelled with bas-reliefs representing the miracles of Christ, may be seen the full figure of Jesus, who, in the resurrection of Lazarus, appears beardless "and equipped with a wand in the received guise of a *necromancer* [?], whilst the corpse of Lazarus is swathed in bandages exactly as an Egyptian mummy." *

Had posterity been enabled to have several such representations executed during the first century when the figure, dress, and everyday habits of the Reformer were still fresh in the memory of his contemporaries, perhaps the Christian world would be more Christlike; the dozens of contradictory, groundless, and utterly meaningless speculations about the "Son of Man" would have been impossible; and humanity would now have but one religion and one God. It is this absence of all proof, the lack of the least positive clue about him whom Christianity has deified, that has caused the present state of perplexity. No pictures of Christ were possible until after the days of Constantine, when the Jewish element was nearly eliminated among the followers of the new religion. The Jews, apostles and disciples, whom the Zoroastrians and the Pârsîs had inoculated with a holy horror of any form of images, would have considered it a sacrilegious blasphemy to represent in any way or shape their master. The only authorized image of Jesus, even in the days of Tertullian, was an allegorical representation of the "Good Shepherd," † which was no portrait, but the figure of a man with a jackal-head, like Anubis. ‡ On this gem, as seen in the collection of Gnostic amulets, the Good Shepherd bears upon his shoulders the lost lamb. He seems to have a human head upon his neck; but, as King correctly observes, "it only *seems so* to the uninitiated eye." "On closer inspection, he becomes the double-headed Anubis, having one head human, the other a jackal's, whilst his girdle assumes the form of a serpent rearing aloft its crested head . . . This figure," adds the author of *The Gnostics*, etc., "had without doubt, two meanings: one obvious, for the vulgar; the other mystic and recognizable by the *initiated alone*. It was perhaps the signet of some chief

---

\* King, *The Gnostics*, p. 145 (1st ed.); the author places this sarcophagus among the earliest productions of that art which later inundated the world with mosaics and engravings, representing the events and personages of the "New Testament."

† Tertullian, *De pudicitia*, vii, 1. See King, *op. cit.*, p. 144; 1st ed., 1864.

‡ King, *op. cit.*, Plate I, p. 200 (1st ed.).

teacher or apostle." * This affords a fresh proof that the Gnostics and early *orthodox* (?) Christians were not so wide apart in their *secret doctrine*. King deduces from a quotation from Epiphanius, that even as late as 400 A.D. "it was considered an atrocious sin to attempt to represent the bodily appearance of Christ." Epiphanius † brings it as an idolatrous charge against the Carpocratians that "they kept painted portraits, and *even gold and silver images,* and *in other materials,* which they pretended to be portraits of Jesus, and made by Pilate after the likeness of Christ.... These they keep in secret, along with others of Pythagoras, Plato and Aristotle; and setting them all up together, they worship and offer sacrifice unto them *after the Gentiles' fashion."*

What would the pious Epiphanius say were he to resuscitate and step into St. Peter's Cathedral at Rome! Theseus Ambrosius [22] seems also very desperate at the idea that some persons fully credited the statement of Lampridius that Alexander Severus had in his private chapel an image of Christ among other great philosophers. ‡ "That the Pagans should have preserved the likeness of Christ," he exclaims, "but the disciples have neglected to do so, is a notion the mind shudders to entertain, much less to believe."

All this points undeniably to the fact that except a handful of self-styled Christians who subsequently won the day, all the civilized portion of the Pagans who knew of Jesus honored him as a philosopher, an *adept* whom they placed on the same level with Pythagoras and Apollonius. Whence such a veneration on their part for a man, were he simply, as represented by the Synoptics, a poor, unknown Jewish carpenter from Nazareth? As an incarnated God there is no single record of him on this earth capable of withstanding the critical examination of science; as one of the greatest reformers, an inveterate enemy of every theological dogmatism, a persecutor of bigotry, a teacher of one of the most sublime codes of ethics, Jesus is one of the grandest and most clearly-defined figures on the panorama of human history. His age may, with every day, be receding farther and farther back into the gloomy and hazy mists of the past; and his theology — based on human fancy and supported by untenable dogmas may, nay, must with every day lose more of its unmerited prestige; alone the grand figure of the philosopher and moral reformer instead of growing paler will become with every century more pronounced and more clearly defined. It will reign supreme and universal only on that day when the whole of humanity recognizes but one father — the UNKNOWN ONE above — and one brother — the whole of mankind below.

---

\* This gem is in the collection of the author of *The Gnostics and their Remains.* See p. 201 (1st ed.), Plate I, fig. 8.

† *Panarion,* lib. I, tom. II, Haer. XXVII, vi.

‡ [*The Gnostics,* etc., p. 144 (p. 227 in 2nd ed., 1887).]

In a pretended letter of Lentulus, a senator and a distinguished historian, to the Roman senate, there is a description of the personal appearance of Jesus. The letter itself,* written in horrid Latin, is pronounced a barefaced forgery; but we find therein an expression which suggests many thoughts. Albeit a forgery, it is evident that whosoever invented it has nevertheless tried to follow tradition as closely as possible. The hair of Jesus is represented in it as "wavy and curling . . . flowing down upon his shoulders," and as "*having a parting in the middle of the head after the fashion of the Nazarenes.*" This last sentence shows: 1. That there was such a tradition, based on the Biblical description of John the Baptist, the *Nazaria*, and the custom of this sect. 2. Had Lentulus been the author of this letter, it is difficult to believe that Paul should never have heard of it; and had he known its contents, he would never have pronounced it a *shame* for men to wear their hair long,† thus shaming his Lord and Christ-God. 3. If Jesus did wear his hair long and "parted in the middle of the forehead, after the fashion of the Nazarenes" (as well as John, the only one of his apostles who followed it), then we have one more good reason to say that Jesus must have belonged to the sect of the Nazarenes, and been called NAZARIA for this reason and not because he was an inhabitant of Nazareth; for they never wore their hair long. The Nazarite, who *separated* himself unto the Lord, allowed "no razor to come upon his head." "He shall be holy, and shall let the locks of the hair of his head grow," says *Numbers* (vi, 5.) Samson was a Nazarite, *i.e.*, vowed to the service of God, and in his hair was his strength. "No razor shall come on his head; for the child shall be a Nazarite unto God from the womb" (*Judges* xiii, 5). But the final and most reasonable conclusion to be inferred from this is that Jesus, who was so opposed to all the orthodox Jewish practices, would *not* have allowed his hair to grow had he not belonged to this sect, which in the days of John the Baptist had already become a heresy in the eyes of the Sanhedrin. The *Talmud,* speaking of the Nazaria or the Nazarenes (who had abandoned the world like Hindu yogis or hermits), calls them a sect of physicians, of wandering exorcists; as also does Jervis. "They went about the country, living on alms and performing cures." ‡ Epiphanius says that the Nazarenes come next in heresy to the Cerinthians whether having existed "before them or after them, nevertheless *synchronous*," and then adds "all Christians at that time were equally called *Nazarenes*"! §

---

\* [Grynaeus, *Monumenta S. Patrum Orthodoxographa*, Vol. I, p. 2; Basileae, 1569. Cf. King, *Gnostics*, etc., p. 69 (1st ed., 1864).]

† *1 Corinth*. xi, 14.

‡ I. M. Yost, *The Israelite Indeed*, Vol. II, p. 238; *Talmud, Mishnah Nazir.*

§ *Panarion*, lib. I, tom. II, Haer. XXIX, i; XXX, i.

In the very first remark made by Jesus about John the Baptist, we find him stating that he is "Elias, which was for to come." This assertion, if it is not a later interpolation for the sake of having a prophecy fulfilled, means again that Jesus was a kabalist; unless indeed we have to adopt the doctrine of the French spiritists and suspect him of believing in reincarnation. Except for the kabalistic sects of the Essenes, the Nazarenes, the disciples of Shimon ben-Yoḥai, and Hillel, neither the orthodox Jews, nor the Galileans, believed or knew anything about the doctrine of *permutation*. And the Sadducees rejected even that of resurrection.

"But the author of this *restitutio* was Mosah, our master, upon whom be peace! Who was the *revolutio* [transmigration] of Seth and Hebel, that he might cover the nudity of his Father Adam, to wit, *Primus*," says the *Kabala*.* Thus, Jesus hinting that John was the *revolutio*, or transmigration of Elias, seems to prove beyond any doubt the school to which he belonged.

Until the present day, uninitiated Kabalists and Masons believe permutation to be synonymous with transmigration and metempsychosis. But they are as much mistaken in regard to the doctrine of the true Kabalists as to that of the Buddhists. True, the *Zohar* says in one place, "All souls are subject to transmigration . . . men do not know the ways of the Holy One, blessed be He; they do not know that they are brought before the tribunal, both before they enter this world and after they quit it," † and the Pharisees also held this doctrine, as Josephus shows. ‡ Also the doctrine of *Gilgûlah*, held to the strange theory of the "Whirling of the Soul," which taught that the bodies of Jews buried far away from the Holy Land, still preserve a particle of soul which can neither rest nor quit them, until it reaches the soil of the "Promised Land." And this "whirling" process was thought to be accomplished by the soul being conveyed back through an actual evolution of species; transmigrating from the minutest insect up to the largest animal. But this was an *exoteric* doctrine. We refer the reader to the *Kabbala denudata* of Knorr von Rosenroth; his language, however obscure, may yet throw some light upon the subject.

But this doctrine of permutation, or *revolutio*, must not be understood as a belief in reincarnation. That Moses was considered the transmigration of Abel and Seth, does not imply that the kabalists — those who were *initiated* at least — believed that the identical spirit of either of Adam's sons reappeared under the corporeal form of Moses. It only shows what was the mode of expression they used when hinting at one of the profoundest mysteries of the Oriental Gnosis, one of the most majestic articles

---

\* *Kabbala denudata*, II, p. 155; also *Vallis Regia*, Paris edition.
† [*Zohar*, II, p. 99b; Amst. ed.]
‡ *Antiquities*, XVIII, i, 3.

of faith of the Secret Wisdom. It was purposely veiled so as to half-conceal and half-reveal the truth. It implied that Moses, like certain other godlike men, was believed to have reached the highest of all states on earth — the rarest of all psychological phenomena — the perfect union of the immortal spirit with the terrestrial *duad* had occurred. The trinity was complete. A *god* was incarnate. But how rare such incarnations!

That expression, "Ye are gods," which, to our Biblical students, is a mere abstraction, has for the kabalists a vital significance. Each immortal spirit that sheds its radiance upon a human being is a god — the Microcosmos of the Macrocosmos, part and parcel of the Unknown God, the First Cause of which it is a direct emanation. It is possessed of all the attributes of its parent source. Among these attributes are omniscience and omnipotence. Endowed with these, but yet unable to fully manifest them while in the body, during which time they are obscured, veiled, limited by the capabilities of physical nature, the thus divinely-inhabited man may tower far above his kind, evince a godlike wisdom, and display deific powers; for while the rest of mortals around him are but *overshadowed* by their divine SELF, with every chance given to them to become immortal hereafter, but no other security than their personal efforts to win the kingdom of heaven, the so chosen man has already become an immortal while yet on earth. His prize is secure. Henceforth he will live forever in eternal life. Not only he may have "dominion" \* over all the works of creation by employing the "excellence" of the NAME (the ineffable one) but be higher in this life, not, as Paul is made to say, "a little lower than the angels." †

The ancients never entertained the sacrilegious thought that such perfected entities were incarnations of the One Supreme and forever invisible God. No such profanation of the awful Majesty entered into their conceptions. Moses and his antetypes and types were to them but complete men, gods on earth, for their *gods* (divine spirits) had entered unto their hallowed tabernacles, the purified physical bodies. The disembodied spirits of the heroes and sages were termed gods by the ancients. Hence, the accusation of polytheism and idolatry on the part of those who were the first to anthropomorphize the holiest and purest abstractions of their forefathers.

---

\* *Psalms* viii, 6.

† This contradiction, which is attributed to Paul in *Hebrews*, by making him say of Jesus in chapter i, 4: "Being made *so much better* than the angels," and then immediately stating in chapter ii, 9, "But we see Jesus, who was made *a little lower* than the angels," shows how unscrupulously the writings of the apostles, if they ever wrote any, were tampered with.

The real and hidden sense of this doctrine was known to all the initiates. The Tannaim imparted it to their elect ones, the Ozarim, in the solemn solitudes of crypts and deserted places. It was one of the most esoteric and jealously guarded, for human nature was the same then as it is now, and the sacerdotal caste as confident as now in the supremacy of its knowledge, and ambitious of ascendency over the weaker masses; with the difference perhaps that its hierophants could prove the legitimacy of their claims and the plausibility of their doctrines, whereas now, *believers* must be content with blind faith.

While the kabalists called this mysterious and rare occurrence of the union of spirit with the mortal charge entrusted to its care, the "descent of the Angel Gabriel" (the latter being a kind of generic name for it), the *Messenger of Life*, and the angel Metatron; and while the Nazarenes termed the same *Hibil-Ziwa*,\* the *Legatus* sent by the Lord of Celsitude, it was universally known as the "Anointed Spirit."

Thus it is the acceptation of this doctrine which caused the Gnostics to maintain that Jesus was a man overshadowed by the Christos or Messenger of Life, and that his despairing cry from the cross *"Eloi, Eloi, lama shâbaḥthani,"* was wrung from him at the instant when he felt that this inspiring Presence had finally abandoned him, for — as some affirmed — his faith *had* also abandoned him when on the cross.

The early Nazarenes, who must be numbered among the Gnostic sects, believing that Jesus was a prophet, held, nevertheless, in relation to him the same doctrine of the divine "overshadowing," of certain "men of God," sent for the salvation of nations, and to recall them to the path of righteousness. "The Divine mind is eternal, and it is pure light, and poured out through splendid *and immense space* (pleroma). It is Genetrix of the Aeôns. But one of them went to Matter [chaos] stirring up confused (*turbulentos*) movements; and by a certain portion of *heavenly* light fashioned it properly constituted for use and appearance, but the beginning of every evil. The Demiurge [of matter] claimed divine honor.† Therefore Christ ('the anointed'), the prince of the Aeôns [powers], was sent (*expeditus*), who *taking on the person* of a most devout Jew (Iesu) *was to conquer him*; but who, having *laid it* [the body] *aside,* departed on high." ‡ We will explain further on the full significance of the name Christos and its mystic meaning.

And now, in order to make such passages as the above more intelligible, we will endeavor to define, as briefly as possible, the dogmas in

---

\* *Codex Nazaraeus*, I, p. 23.

† *Ibid.*, Norberg's preface, pp. iv, v.

‡ "According to the Nazarenes and Gnostics, the Demiurge, the creator of the material world, is not the highest God." (See Dunlap, *Sôd, the Son of the Man*.)

which, with very trifling differences, nearly all the Gnostic sects believed. It is in Ephesus that flourished in those days the greatest college, wherein the abstruse Oriental speculations and the Platonic philosophy were taught in conjunction. It was a focus of the universal "secret" doctrines; the weird laboratory whence, fashioned in elegant Grecian phraseology, sprang the quintessence of Buddhistic, Zoroastrian and Chaldean philosophy. Artemis, the gigantic concrete symbol of theosophico-pantheistic abstractions, the great mother Multimamma, androgyne and patroness of the "Ephesian writings," was conquered by Paul; but although the zealous converts of the apostles pretended to burn all their books on "curious arts," τὰ περίεργα, enough of these remained for them to study when their first zeal had cooled off. It is from Ephesus that spread nearly all the *Gnosis* which antagonized so fiercely with the Irenaean dogmas; and still it was Ephesus, with her numerous collateral branches of the great college of the Essenes, which proved to be the hotbed of all the kabalistic speculations brought by the Tannaim from the captivity. "In Ephesus," says J. Matter, "the notions of the Jewish-Egyptian school, and the semi-Persian speculations of the Kabalists had then recently come to swell the vast conflux of Grecian and Asiatic doctrines, so there is no wonder that teachers should have sprung up there who strove to combine the religion newly preached by the Apostle with the ideas there so long established." *

Had not the Christians burdened themselves with the *Revelations* of a little nation, and accepted the Jehovah of Moses, the Gnostic ideas would never have been termed *heresies;* once relieved of their dogmatic exaggerations, the world would have had a religious system based on pure Platonic philosophy, and surely something would then have been gained.

Now let us see what are the greatest *heresies* of the Gnostics. We will select Basilides as the standard for our comparisons, for all the founders of other Gnostic sects group round him, like a cluster of stars borrowing light from their sun.

Basilides maintained that he had had all his doctrines from the Apostle Matthew, and from Peter through Glaucias, the disciple of the latter.† According to Eusebius, ‡ he published twenty-four volumes of *Interpretations upon the Gospels*, § all of which were burned, a fact which makes us suppose that they contained more truthful matter than the school of Irenaeus was

---

* [King, *The Gnostics*, etc., p. 3 (p. 7 in 2nd ed.).]
† Clem. Alex., *Strom.*, VII, xvii. [Cf. Hippolytus, *Philosophumena*, VII, § 20.]
‡ *Eccles. Hist.*, IV, vii.
§ The gospels interpreted by Basilides were not our present gospels, which, as it is proved by the greatest authorities, were not in his days in existence. See *Supernatural Religion*, Vol. II, chap. vi, "Basilides."

prepared to deny. He asserted that the unknown, eternal, and uncreated Father having first brought forth *Nous*, or Mind, the latter emanated from itself the *Logos*. The Logos (the "Word" of John) emanated in its turn *Phronêsis*, or the Intelligences (Divine-human spirits). From Phronêsis sprang *Sophia*, or feminine wisdom, and *Dynamis* — strength.* These were the personified attributes of the Mysterious godhead, the Gnostic quinternion, typifying the five spiritual, but intelligible substances, personal virtues or beings external to the unknown godhead. This is pre-eminently a kabalistic idea. It is still more Buddhistic. The earliest system of the Buddhistic philosophy — which preceded by far Gautama Buddha — is based upon the uncreated substance of the "Unknown," the *Âdi-Buddha*.† This eternal, infinite Monad possesses, as proper to his own essence, five acts of wisdom. From these it, by five separate acts of *Dhyâna*, emitted five *Dhyâni-Buddhas*; these, like Âdi-Buddha, are quiescent in their system (passive). Neither Âdi, nor either of the five Dhyâni-Buddhas, were ever incarnated, but seven of their emanations became Avatâras, *i.e.*, were incarnated on this earth.

Describing the Basilidean system, Irenaeus, quoting the Gnostics, declares as follows:

---

* [Irenaeus, *Adv. Haer.*, I, xxiv, 3.]

† The five make mystically ten. They are androgynes. "Having divided his body in two parts, the Supreme Wisdom became male and female" (*Manu*, Book I, śloka 32). There are many early Buddhistic ideas to be found in Brahmanism.

The prevalent idea that the last of the Buddhas, Gautama, is the ninth incarnation of Vishnu, or the *ninth* Avatâra, is disclaimed partially by the Brahmans, and wholly rejected by the learned Buddhist theologians. The latter insist that the worship of Buddha possesses a far higher claim to antiquity than any of the Brahmanical deities of the *Vedas*, which they call secular literature. The Brahmans, they show, came from other countries, and established their heresy on the already accepted popular *deities*. They conquered the land by the sword, and succeeded in burying truth, by building a theology of their own on the ruins of the more ancient one of Buddha, which had prevailed for ages. They admit the divinity and spiritual existence of some of the Vedântic gods; but as in the case of the Christian angel-hierarchy they believe that all these deities are greatly subordinate, even to the incarnated Buddhas. They do not even acknowledge the creation of the physical universe. Spiritually and *invisibly* it has existed from all eternity, and thus it was made merely visible to the human senses. When it first appeared it was called forth from the realm of the invisible into the visible by the impulse of Âdi-Buddha — the "Essence." They reckon twenty-two such visible appearances of the universe governed by Buddhas, and as many destructions of it, by fire and water in regular successions. After the last destruction by the flood, at the end of the precedent cycle (the exact calculation, embracing several millions of years, is a secret cycle), the world, during the present age of the Kali-Yug — *Mahâ-Bhadra-Kalpa* — has been ruled successively by four Buddhas, the last of whom was Gautama, the "Holy One." The fifth, Maitreya-Buddha, is yet to come. This latter is the expected kabalistic King Messiah, the Messenger of Light, and Saoshyant, the Persian Savior, who will come on a *white* horse. It is also the Christian Second Advent. See *Apocalypse* of St. John.

"When the uncreated, *unnamed* Father saw the corruption of mankind, he sent his first-born *Nous*, into the world, in the form of Christ, for the redemption of all who believe in him, out of the power of those who fabricated the world [the Demiurgus, and his six sons, the planetary genii]. He appeared amongst men as the man Jesus, and wrought miracles. This Christ did *not die* in person, but Simon the Cyrenian suffered in his stead, *to whom he lent his bodily form;* for the Divine Power, the Nous of the Eternal Father, *is not corporeal,* and *cannot die.* Whoso, therefore, maintains that Christ has died, is still the bondsman of ignorance; whoso denies the same, he is free, and hath understood the purpose of the Father." *

So far, and taken in its abstract sense, we do not see anything blasphemous in this system. It may be a *heresy* against the theology of Irenaeus and Tertullian, † but there is certainly nothing sacrilegious against the religious idea itself, and it will seem to every impartial thinker far more consistent with divine reverence than the anthropormorphism of actual Christianity. The Gnostics were called by the orthodox Christians, *Docetae,* or Illusionists, for believing that Christ did not, nor could, suffer death actually — in physical body. The later Brahmanical books contain, likewise, much that is repugnant to the reverential feeling and idea of the Divinity; and as well as the Gnostics, the Brahmans explain such legends as may shock the divine dignity of the Spiritual beings called gods by attributing them to *Mâyâ* or illusion.

A people brought up and nurtured for countless ages among all the psychological phenomena of which the civilized (!) nations read, but reject as incredible and worthless, cannot well expect to have its religious system even understood — let alone appreciated. The profoundest and most transcendental speculations of the ancient metaphysicians of India and other countries, are all based on that great Buddhistic and Brahmanical principle underlying the whole of their religious metaphysics — *illusion* of the senses. Everything that is finite is illusion, all that which is eternal and infinite is reality. Form, color, that which we hear and feel, or see with our mortal eyes, exists only so far as it can be conveyed to each of us through our senses. The universe for a man born blind does not exist in either form or color, but it exists in its *privation* (in the Aristotelian sense), and is a reality for the spiritual senses

---

* Irenaeus, *Adv. Haer.*, I, xxiv, 4

† Tertullian reversed the table himself by rejecting, later in life, the doctrines for which he fought with such an acerbity and by becoming a Montanist.

of the blind man. We all live under the powerful dominion of phantasy. Alone the highest and invisible *originals* emanated from the thought of the Unknown are real and permanent beings, forms and ideas; on earth, we see but their reflections, more or less correct, and ever dependent on the physical and mental organization of the person who beholds them.

Ages untold before our era, the Hindu Mystic, Kapila, who is considered by many scientists as a skeptic, because they judge him with their habitual superficiality, magnificently expressed this idea in the following terms:

"Man [physical man] counts for so little, that hardly anything can demonstrate to him his proper existence and that of nature. Perhaps, that which we regard as the universe, and the divers beings which seem to compose it, have nothing real, and are but the product of continued illusion — *mâyâ* — of our senses."

And the modern Schopenhauer, repeating this philosophical idea, 10,000 years old now, says: "Nature is non-existent, *per se*. . . . Nature is the infinite illusion of our senses." Kant, Schelling, and other metaphysicians have said the same, and their school maintains the idea. The objects of sense being ever delusive and fluctuating, cannot be a reality. Spirit alone is unchangeable, hence — alone is no illusion. This is pure Buddhist doctrine. The religion of the *Gnosis* (knowledge), the most evident offshoot of Buddhism, was utterly based on this metaphysical tenet. Christos suffered *spiritually* for us, and far more acutely than did the illusionary Jesus while his body was being tortured on the Cross.

In the ideas of the Christians, Christ is but another name for Jesus. The philosophy of the Gnostics, the initiates and hierophants, understood it otherwise. The word Christos, Χριστός, like all Greek words, must be sought in its philological origin — the Sanskrit. In this latter language *Kris* means sacred,* [23] and the Hindu deity was named Kris-na (the pure or the sacred) from that. On the other hand, the Greek *Christos* bears several meanings, such as anointed (pure oil, *chrism*) and others. In all languages, though the synonym of the word means pure or sacred essence, it is the first emanation of the invisible Godhead, manifesting itself tangibly in spirit. The Greek Logos, the Hebrew Messiah, the

---

* In his debate with Jacolliot upon the right spelling of the Hindu Krishna, Mr. Textor de Ravisi, an ultramontane Catholic, tries to prove that the name of Christna ought to be written Krishna, for, as the latter means black, and the statues of this deity are generally black, the word is derived from the color. We refer the reader to Jacolliot's answer in his recent work, *Christna et le Christ*, for the conclusive evidence that the name is not derived from the color.

Latin Verbum, and the Hindu Virâj (the son) are identically the same; they represent an idea of collective entities — of flames detached from the one eternal centre of light.

"The man who accomplishes pious but interested acts [with the sole object of his salvation] may reach the ranks of the *devas* [saints];* but he who accomplishes, disinterestedly, the same pious acts, finds himself ridden forever of the five elements" (of matter). "Perceiving the Supreme Soul in all beings and all beings in the Supreme Soul, in offering his own soul in sacrifice, he identifies himself with the Being who shines in his own splendor." †

Thus Christos, as a unity, is but an abstraction: a general idea representing the collective aggregation of the numberless spirit-entities, which are the direct emanations of the infinite, invisible, incomprehensible FIRST CAUSE — the individual spirits of men, erroneously called the souls. They are the divine sons of God, of which some only overshadow mortal men — but these the majority; some remain forever planetary spirits, and some — the smaller and rare minority — unite themselves during life with some men. Such Godlike beings as Gautama Buddha, Jesus, Lao-Tse, Krishna, and a few others had united themselves with their spirits permanently — hence, they became gods on earth. Others, such as Moses, Pythagoras, Apollonius, Plotinus, Confucius, Plato, Iamblichus, and some Christian saints, having at intervals been so united, have taken rank in history as demi-gods and leaders of mankind. When unburthened of their terrestrial tabernacles, their freed souls, henceforth united forever with their spirits, rejoin the whole shining host, which is bound together in one spiritual solidarity of thought and deed, and called "the anointed." Hence, the meaning of the Gnostics, who, by saying that "Christos" suffered spiritually for humanity, implied that his Divine Spirit suffered mostly.

Such, and far more elevating, were the ideas of Marcion, the great "Heresiarch" of the second century, as he is termed by his opponents. He came to Rome toward the latter part of the half-century, from A.D. 139-142, according to Tertullian, Irenaeus, Clement, and most of his modern commentators, such as Bunsen, Tischendorf, Westcott and many others. Credner and Schleiermacher‡ agree as to his high and irreproachable personal character, his pure religious aspirations and elevated views. His influence must have been powerful, as we find

---

\* There is no equivalent for the word "miracle," in the Christian sense, among the Brahmans or Buddhists. The only correct translation would be *meipo*, a wonder, something remarkable; but not a violation of natural law. The "saints" only produce *meipo*.

† *Manu*, Bk. XII, ślokas 90, 91.

‡ Credner, *Beiträge*, etc., I, p. 40; Schleiermacher, *Sämtliche Werke*, VIII; *Einl. N. T.*, p. 64; ed. 1845.

Epiphanius writing more than two centuries later that in his time the followers of Marcion were to be found throughout the whole world.*

The danger must have been pressing and great indeed, if we are to judge it to have been proportioned with the opprobrious epithets and vituperation heaped upon Marcion by the "Great African," that Patristic Cerberus, whom we find ever barking at the door of the Irenaean dogmas. We have but to open his celebrated refutation of Marcion's *Antitheses*, to acquaint ourselves with the *fine-fleur* of monkish abuse of the Christian school; an abuse so faithfully carried through the middle ages, to be renewed again in our present day — at the Vatican. "Now, then, ye hounds, yelping at the God of truth, whom the Apostle casts out, to all your questions. These are the bones of contention which ye gnaw," etc.† "The poverty of the 'Great African's' arguments keeps pace with his abuse," remarks the author of *Supernatural Religion*.‡ "Their [the Father's] religious controversy bristles with misstatements, and is turbid with pious abuse. Tertullian was a master of this style, and the vehement vituperation with which he opens and often interlards his work against 'the impious and sacrilegious Marcion,' offers anything but a guarantee of fair and legitimate criticism." §

How firm these two Fathers — Tertullian and Epiphanius — were on their theological ground, may be inferred from the curious fact that they intemperately both vehemently reproach "the beast" (Marcion) "with erasing passages from the *Gospel of Luke*, which never were in *Luke* at all."‖ "The lightness and inaccuracy," adds the critic, "with which Tertullian proceeds, are all the better illustrated by the fact that not only does he accuse Marcion falsely, but *he actually defines the motives* for which he expunged a passage *which never existed*, for in the same chapter he also similarly accuses Marcion of erasing [from *Luke*] the saying that Christ had not come to destroy the law and the prophets, but to fulfill them, and he actually repeats the same charge on two other occasions.¶ Epiphanius commits the same mistake of reproaching Marcion with omitting from *Luke* what is only found in *Matthew*."**

Having so far shown the amount of reliance to be placed in the Patristic literature, and it being unanimously conceded by the great majority of Biblical critics that what the Fathers fought for was not *truth*, but their own interpretations and unwarranted assertions,†† we will now proceed to state

---

\* *Panarion*, lib. I, tom. III, Haer. XLII, i.
† Tertullian, *Adv. Marc.*, II, v.
‡ Vol. II, Part II, vii, p. 105.
§ *Ibid.*, p. 89.
‖ *Ibid.*, Vol. II, p. 100.
¶ Tertullian, *Adv. Marc.*, IV, ix; IV, xxxvi; *Matt.* v, 17.
\*\* *Panarion*, Haer. XLII.
†† The author of *Supern. Religion* (Vol. II, Pt. II, vii, p. 103) remarks with great justice of the "Heresiarch" Marcion, "whose high personal character exerted so powerful

what were the views of Marcion, whom Tertullian desired to annihilate as the most dangerous *heretic* of his day. If we are to believe Hilgenfeld, one of the greatest German Biblical critics, then "from the critical standpoint one must . . . consider the statements of the Fathers of the Church only as expressions of their *subjective view*, which itself requires proof."*

We can do no better nor make a more correct statement of facts concerning Marcion than by quoting what our space permits from *Supernatural Religion*, the author of which bases his assertions on the evidence of the greatest critics, as well as on his own researches. He shows in the days of Marcion "two broad parties in the primitive Church" — one considering Christianity "a mere continuation of the Law, and dwarfing it into an Israelitish institution, a narrow sect of Judaism"; the other representing the glad tidings "as the introduction of a new system applicable to all and supplanting the Mosaic dispensation of the Law by a universal dispensation of grace." These two parties, he adds, "were popularly represented in the early Church, by the two Apostles Peter and Paul, and their antagonism is faintly revealed in the *Epistle to the Galatians*." †

---

an influence upon his own time," that "it was the misfortune of Marcion to live in an age when Christianity had passed out of the pure morality of its infancy, when, untroubled by complicated questions of dogma, simple faith and pious enthusiasm had been the one great bond of Christian brotherhood, into a phase of ecclesiastical development in which religion was fast degenerating into theology, and complicated doctrines were rapidly assuming that rampant attitude which led to so much bitterness, persecution, and schism. In later times Marcion might have been honored as a reformer, in his own he was denounced as a heretic. Austere and ascetic in his opinions, he aimed at superhuman purity, and although his clerical adversaries might scoff at his impracticable doctrines regarding marriage and the subjugation of the flesh, they have had their parallels amongst those whom the Church has since most delighted to honor; and at least the whole tendency of his system was markedly towards the side of virtue." These statements are based upon Credner's *Beiträge*, etc., I, p. 40; cf. Neander, *Allgem. Geschichte*, etc., II, pp. 792, 815 *et seq.;* Milman, *The Hist. of Christ.*, pp. 77 *et seq.* (1867); Schleiermacher, etc., etc.

* Hilgenfeld, *Kritische Untersuchungen über die Evang. Justin's*, etc., p. 445.

† [Vol. II, p. 104.] But, on the other hand, this antagonism is very *strongly* marked in the *Clementine Homilies*, in which Peter unequivocally denies that Paul, whom he calls Simon the Magician, has ever had a *vision* of Christ, and calls him "an enemy." Canon Westcott says: "There can be no doubt that St. Paul is referred to as 'the enemy' " (*Hist. of the Canon*, p. 252, note 2; *Supernatural Religion*, Vol. II, p. 35). But this antagonism, which rages unto the present day, we find even in St. Paul's *Epistles*. What can be more energetic than such like sentences: "Such are *false* apostles, deceitful workers, transforming themselves into the apostles of Christ. . . . I suppose I was not a whit behind the very chiefest apostles" (2 *Corinthians* xi, 13, 5). "Paul, an apostle *not of men*, neither by man, but by Jesus Christ *and* God the Father, who raised him from the dead . . . but there be some that trouble you, and *would pervert* the Gospel

Marcion, who recognized no other *Gospels* than a few *Epistles of Paul*, who rejected totally the anthropomorphism of the *Old Testament*, and drew a distinct line of demarcation between the old Judaism and Christianity, viewed Jesus neither as a King, Messiah of the Jews, nor the son of David, who was in any way connected with the law or prophets, "but a divine being sent to reveal to man a wholly new spiritual religion, and a hitherto unknown God of goodness and grace." The "Lord God" of the Jews in his eyes, the Creator (Demiourgos), was totally different and distinct from the Deity who sent Jesus to reveal the divine truth and preach the glad tidings, to bring reconciliation and salvation to all. The mission of

---

of Christ . . . *false brethren* . . . When Peter was come to Antioch I withstood him to his face, because he was to be blamed. For before that certain came from James, *he did eat with the Gentiles, but when they were come, he withdrew . . . fearing them which were of the circumcision. And the other Jews dissembled . . . insomuch that Barnabas also was carried away with their dissimulation*," etc., etc. (*Gal*. i, 7; ii, 11-13). On the other hand, we find Peter in the *Homilies*, indulging in various complaints which, although alleged to be addressed to Simon Magus, are evidently all direct answers to the above-quoted sentences from the Pauline *Epistles*, and *cannot* have anything to do with Simon. So, for instance, Peter said: "For some among the Gentiles have rejected my lawful preaching and accepted certain *lawless* and foolish teaching of the hostile man [enemy]." — *Epistle of Peter to James*, § 2. He says further: "Simon [Paul] . . . who came before me to the Gentiles . . . and [I] have followed him as light upon darkness, as knowledge upon ignorance, as health upon disease" (*Homil*., ii, 17). Still further, he calls him *Death* and a *deceiver* (*ibid*., ii, 18). He warns the Gentiles that "our Lord and Prophet [?] [*Jesus*] announced that the evil one he would send from among his followers apostles to *deceive*. Therefore, above all remember to avoid every apostle, or teacher, or prophet, who first does not accurately compare his teaching with that of James, called the brother of my Lord" (see the difference between Paul and James on *faith*, *Epistle to Hebrews* xi, xii, and *Epistle of James* ii). "Lest this evil one should send a false preacher . . . as he has sent to us Simon [?] preaching a counterfeit of truth in the name of our Lord and disseminating error" (*Homil*., xi, 35; see above quotation from *Gal*. ii, 11-13). He then denies Paul's assertion, in the following words: "If, therefore, our Jesus indeed was seen in a vision . . . it was only as one angry with an adversary . . . But can anyone through a vision become wise to teach? And if thou sayest: 'It is possible', then wherefore did the Teacher remain and discourse for a whole year to us who were awake? And how can *we believe thy story that he was seen by thee?* And how could he have been seen by thee when thy thoughts are contrary to his teaching? . . . For thou hast directly withstood me who am a *firm rock, the foundation of the Church*. If thou hadst not been an adversary thou wouldst not have calumniated me, thou wouldst not have reviled my teaching [circumcision?] in order that, when declaring what I have myself heard from the Lord, I might not be believed, as though *I were condemned* . . . If thou callest me condemned, thou speakest against God who revealed Christ to me." [*Homil*., xvii, 19.] "This last phrase," observes the author of *Supernatural Religion* [Vol. II, p. 37], " 'if thou callest me condemned', is an evident allusion to *Galat*. ii, 11: 'I withstood him to the face, because he was to be blamed'." "There cannot be a doubt," adds the just-quoted author, "that the Apostle Paul is attacked in it, as the great enemy of the true faith, under the hated name of Simon the Magician, whom Peter follows everywhere for the purpose of unmasking and confuting him" (p. 34). And if so, then we must believe that it was St. Paul who broke both his legs in Rome when flying in the air.

Jesus—according to Marcion—was to abrogate the Jewish "Lord," who "was opposed to the God and Father of Jesus Christ as *Matter is to Spirit, impurity to purity*." *

Was Marcion so far wrong? Was it blasphemy, or was it intuition, divine inspiration in him to express that which every honest heart yearning for truth, more or less feels and acknowledges? If in his sincere desire to establish a purely spiritual religion, a universal faith based on unadulterated truth, he found it necessary to make of Christianity an entirely new and separate system from that of Judaism, did not Marcion have the very words of Christ for his authority? "No man putteth a piece of new cloth unto an old garment, for the rent is made worse . . . Neither do men put new wine into old bottles; else the bottles break, and the wine runneth out, and the bottles perish; but *they put new wine into new bottles*, and both are preserved." † In what particular does the jealous, wrathful, revengeful God of Israel resemble the unknown deity, the God of mercy preached by Jesus — *his* Father who is in Heaven, and the Father of all humanity? This Father alone is the God of spirit and purity, and, to compare Him with the subordinate and capricious Sinaitic Deity is an error. Did Jesus ever pronounce the name of Jehovah? Did he ever place *his* Father in contrast with this severe and cruel Judge; his God of mercy, love and justice, with the Jewish genius of retaliation? Never! From that memorable day when he preached his Sermon on the Mount, an immeasurable void opened between his God and that other deity who fulminated his commands from that other mount — Sinai. The language of Jesus is unequivocal; it implies not only rebellion but defiance of the Mosaic "Lord God." "Ye have heard," he tells us, "that it hath been said, an eye for an eye, and a tooth for a tooth: but *I say* unto you, That ye resist not evil: but whosoever shall smite thee on thy right cheek, turn to him the other also. Ye have heard that it hath been said [by the same "Lord God" on Sinai], Thou shalt love thy neighbor, and hate thine enemy. But *I say* unto you, Love your enemies, bless them that curse you, do good to them that hate you, and pray for them which despitefully use you, and persecute you." ‡

And now, open *Manu* and read:

"Resignation, *the action of rendering good for evil*, temperance, probity, purity, repression of the senses, the knowledge of the *Sâstras* [the holy books], that of the supreme soul, truthfulness and abstinence from anger, such are the ten virtues in which consists duty . . . Those who

---

* [*Supernatural Religion*, Vol. II, ch. vii, p. 104.]

† [*Matt*. ix, 16-17.]

‡ *Matt*. v, 38-44.

study these ten precepts of duty, and after having studied them conform their lives thereto, will reach to the supreme condition." *

If *Manu* did not trace these words many thousands of years before the era of Christianity, at least no voice in the whole world will dare deny them a less antiquity than several centuries B.C. The same in the case of the precepts of Buddhism.

If we turn to the *Pratimoksha-Sûtra* and other religious tracts of the Buddhists, we read the ten following commandments:

1. Thou shalt not kill any living creature.
2. Thou shalt not steal.
3. Thou shalt not break thy vow of chastity.
4. Thou shalt not lie.
5. Thou shalt not betray the secrets of others.
6. Thou shalt not wish for the death of thy enemies.
7. Thou shalt not desire the wealth of others.
8. Thou shalt not pronounce injurious and foul words.
9. Thou shalt not indulge in luxury (sleep on soft beds or be lazy).
10. Thou shalt not accept gold or silver.†

"Good master, what good thing shall I do that I may have eternal life?" asks a man of Jesus. "Keep the commandments." "Which?" "Thou shalt do no murder, Thou shalt not commit adultery, Thou shalt not steal, Thou shalt not bear false witness," ‡ is the answer.

"What shall I do to obtain possession of Bodhi?" [knowledge of eternal truth], asks a disciple of his Buddhist master. "What way is there to become an Upâsaka?" "Keep the commandments." "What are they?" "Thou shalt abstain all thy life from murder, theft, adultery, and lying," answers the master. §

Identical injunctions are they not? Divine injunctions, the living up to which would purify and exalt humanity. But are they more divine when uttered through one mouth than another? If it is godlike to return good for evil, does the enunciation of the precept by a Nazarene give it any greater force than its enunciation by an Indian, or Thibetan philosopher? We see that the Golden Rule was not original with Jesus; that its birthplace was India. Do what we may, we cannot deny Sâkyamuni Buddha a less remote antiquity than several centuries before the birth of Jesus. In seeking a model for his system of ethics, why should Jesus have gone to the foot of the Himâlayas rather than to the foot of

---

\* *Manu,* Bk. VI, ślokas 92-93.

† *Pratimoksha-Sûtra,* Pâli-Burmese copy; see also *Le Lotus de la Bonne Loi,* translated by Burnouf, p. 444.

‡ *Matthew* xix, 16-18.

§ *Pitakattayan,* Book III, Pâli Version.

Sinai, but that the doctrines of Manu and Gautama harmonized exactly with his own philosophy, while those of Jehovah were to him abhorrent and terrifying? The Hindus taught to return *good for evil*, but the Jehovistic command was: "An eye for an eye" and "a tooth for a tooth."

Would Christians still maintain the identity of the "Father" of Jesus and Jehovah, if evidence sufficiently clear could be adduced that the "Lord God" was no other than the Pagan Bacchus, Dionysos? Well, this identity of the Jehovah at Mount Sinai with the god Bacchus is hardly disputable. The name יהוה is Yava, or Iaô according to Diodorus and Lydus, which is the *secret* name of the Phoenician Mystery-god;* and it was actually adopted from the Chaldeans with whom it also was the secret name of the creator. Wherever Bacchus was worshipped there was a tradition of Nysa and a cave where he was reared. Beth-San or Scythopolis in Palestine had that designation; so had a spot on Mount Parnassus. But Diodorus declares that Nysa was between Phoenicia and Egypt; Euripides states that Dionysos came to Greece from India; and Diodorus † adds his testimony: "Osiris was brought up in Nysa, in Arabia the Happy; he was the son of Zeus, and was named from his father [nominative Zeus, genitive *Dios*] and the place *Dio-Nysos*"—the Zeus or Jove of Nysa. This identity of name or title is very significant. In Greece Dionysos was second only to Zeus, and Pindar says:

"So Father Zeus governs all things, and Bacchus he governs also."

But outside of Greece Bacchus was the all-powerful "Zagreus, the highest of gods." Moses seems to have worshipped him personally and together with the populace at Mount Sinai; unless we admit that he was an *initiated* priest, an adept, who knew how to lift the veil which hangs behind all such exoteric worship, but kept the secret. "*And Moses built an altar, and called the name of it Jehovah-*Nissi," or *Iaô-Nisi!*‡ What better evidence is required to show that the Sinaitic god was indifferently Bacchus, Osiris and Jehovah? S. Sharpe appends also his testimony that the place where Osiris was born "was Mount Sinai, called by the Egyptians Mount Nissa."§ The Brazen Serpent was a *naḥash,* נחש, and the month of the Jewish Passover *nisan.*

If the Mosaic "Lord God" were the only living God, and Jesus His only Son, how account for the rebellious language of the latter? Without hesitation or qualification he sweeps away the Jewish *lex talionis* and substitutes for it the law of charity and self-denial. If the *Old Tes-*

---

* See *Judges* xiii, 18, "And the angel of the Lord said unto him, Why askest thou after my name, seeing it is SECRET?"
† [Diod. Sic., *Bibl. hist.*, I, xv.]
‡ [*Exodus* xvii, 15.]
§ [*Egyptian Mythology and Egyptian Christianity*, 1863, pp. 10-11.]

*tament* is a divine revelation, how can the *New Testament* be? Are we required to believe and worship a Deity who contradicts himself every few hundred years? Was Moses inspired, or was Jesus *not* the son of God? This is a dilemma from which the theologians are bound to rescue us. It is from this very dilemma that the Gnostics endeavored to snatch the budding Christianity.

Justice has been waiting nineteen centuries for intelligent commentators to appreciate this difference between the orthodox Tertullian and the Gnostic Marcion. The brutal violence, unfairness, and bigotry of the "great African" repulse all who accept his Christianity. "How can a god," inquired Marcion, "break his own commandments? How could he consistently prohibit idolatry and image-worship, and still cause Moses to set up the brazen serpent? How command: Thou shalt not steal, and then order the Israelites to *spoil* the Egyptians of their gold and silver?" Anticipating the results of modern criticism, Marcion denies the applicability to Jesus of the so-called Messianic prophecies. Writes the author of *Supernatural Religion:** "The Emmanuel of *Isaiah* [vii, 14; cf. viii, 4] is not Christ; the 'Virgin,' his mother, is simply a 'young woman' [an *almeh* of the temple]; and the sufferings of the Servant of God (*Isaiah* lii, 13—liii, 3) are not predictions of the death of Jesus."†

---

* Vol. II, Pt. II, ch. vii, pp. 106-07 (1879). Cf. Tertullian, *Adv. Marc.*, III, xii.

† Emmanuel was doubtless the son of the prophet himself, as described in the sixth chapter; what was predicted, can only be interpreted on that hypothesis. The prophet had also announced to Ahaz the extinction of his line. "If ye will not believe, surely ye shall not be established." Next comes the prediction of the placing of a new prince on the throne — Hezekiah of Bethlehem, said to have been Isaiah's son-in-law, under whom the captives should return from the uttermost parts of the earth. Assyria should be humbled, and peace overspread the Israelitish country, (Cf. *Isaiah* vii, 14-16; viii, 3, 4; ix, 6, 7; x, 12, 20, 21; xi; *Micah* v, 2-7.) The popular party, the party of the prophets, always opposed to the Zadokite priesthood, had resolved to set aside Ahaz and his time-serving policy, which had let in Assyria upon Palestine, and to set up Hezekiah, a man of their own, who should rebel against Assyria and overthrow the Assur-worship and Baalim (*2 Kings* xviii, 4). Though only the prophets hint this, it being cut out from the historical books, it is noticeable that Ahaz offered his own child to Moloch, also that he died at the age of thirty-six, and Hezekiah took the throne at twenty-five, in full adult age.

## CHAPTER IV

"Nothing better than those MYSTERIES, by which, from a rough and fierce life, we are polished to gentleness (humanity, kindness), and softened."
—CICERO, *De Legibus*, II, xiv.

"Descend, O Soma, with that stream with which thou lightest up the Sun . . . Soma, a Life Ocean spread through All, thou fillest creative the Sun with beams."
—*Rig-Veda*, II, 143.

". . . the beautiful Virgin ascends, with long hair, and she holds two ears in her hand, and sits on a seat and feeds a BOY as yet little, and suckles him and gives him food."
—AVENARE.*

IT is alleged that the *Pentateuch* was written by Moses, and yet it contains the account of his own death (*Deuteronomy* xxxiv, 6); and in *Genesis* (xiv, 14), the name Dan is given to a city, which *Judges* (xviii, 29) tells us was only called by that name at that late day, it having previously been known as Laish. Well might Josiah have rent his clothes when he had heard the words of the Book of the Law; for there was no more of Moses in it than there is of Jesus in the *Gospel according to John*.

We have one fair alternative to offer our theologians, leaving them to choose for themselves, and promising to abide by their decision. Only they will have to admit, either that Moses was an impostor, or that his books are forgeries, written at different times and by different persons; or, again, that they are full of fraudulent interpolations. In either case the work loses all claims to be considered divine *Revelation*. Here is the problem, which we quote from the *Bible* — the word of the God of Truth:

"And I appeared unto Abraham, unto Isaac, and unto Jacob, by the name of God Almighty, but by my name JEHOVAH was I not known to them" (*Exodus* vi, 3), spake God unto Moses.

A very startling bit of information that, when, before arriving at the book of *Exodus*, we are told in *Genesis* (xxii, 14) that "Abraham called the name of that place" — where the patriarch had been preparing to cut the throat of his only-begotten son — "JEHOVAH-jireh" (Jehovah sees)! Which is the inspired text? — both cannot be — which the forgery?

---

* [Kircher, *Oedip. aegypt.*, Vol. II (1653), Pt. II, p. 203.]

Now, if both Abraham and Moses had not belonged to the same holy group, we might, perhaps, help theologians by suggesting to them a convenient means of escape out of this dilemma. They ought to call the reverend Jesuit Fathers—especially those who have been missionaries in India—to their rescue. The latter would not for a moment be disconcerted. They would coolly tell us that beyond doubt Abraham had heard the name of Jehovah and *borrowed* it from Moses. Do they not maintain that it was they who invented the *Sanskrit*, edited *Manu*, and composed the greater portion of the *Vedas?*

Marcion maintained, with the other Gnostics, the fallaciousness of the idea of an incarnate God, and therefore denied the corporeal reality of the living body of Christ. His entity was a mere *illusion;* it was not made of human flesh and blood, neither was it born of a human mother, for his divine nature could not be polluted with any contact with sinful flesh.\* He accepted Paul as the only apostle preaching the pure gospel of truth, and accused the other disciples of depraving "the pure form of the Gospel doctrines delivered to them by Jesus, 'mixing up matters of the Law with the words of the Savior'."†

Finally we may add that modern Biblical criticism, which unfortunately became really active and serious only toward the end of the last century, now generally admits that Marcion's text of the only gospel he knew anything about — that of Luke, is far superior and far more correct than that of our present Synoptics. We find in *Supernatural Religion* the following (for every Christian) startling sentence: "We are, therefore, *indebted to Marcion for the correct version even* of *'the Lord's Prayer'*." ‡

If, leaving for the present the prominent founders of Christian sects, we now turn to that of the Ophites, which assumed a definite form about the time of Marcion and the Basilideans, we may find in it the reason for the *heresies* of all others. Like all other Gnostics, they rejected the Mosaic *Bible* entirely. Nevertheless, their philosophy, apart from some deductions original with several of the most important founders of the various branches of Gnosticism, was not new. Passing through the Chaldean kabalistic tradition, it gathered its materials in the Hermetic books, and pursuing its flight still farther back for its metaphysical speculations, we find it floundering among the tenets of Manu, and the earliest Hindu ante-sacerdotal genesis. Many of our eminent antiquarians trace the Gnostic philosophies right back to Buddhism, which does not impair in

---

\* Tertullian, *Adv. Marc.*, III, viii *et seq.*
† *Supern. Relig.*, Vol. II, p. 107; Tertullian, *Adv. Marc.*, IV, iii; cf. Irenaeus, *Adv. Haer.*, III, ii, 2; III, xii, 12.
‡ *Supern. Relig.*, Vol. II, p. 126.

the least either their or our arguments. We repeat again, *Buddhism is but the primitive source of Brahmanism.* It is not against the primitive *Vedas* that Gautama protests. It is against the sacerdotal and official state religion of his country; and the Brahmans who, in order to make room for and give authority to the castes, at a later period crammed the ancient manuscripts with interpolated *slokas,* intended to prove that the castes were predetermined by the Creator by the very fact that each class of men was issued from a more or less noble limb of Brahmâ. Gautama Buddha's philosophy was that taught from the beginning of time in the impenetrable secrecy of the inner sanctuaries of the pagodas. We need not be surprised, therefore, to find again, in all the fundamental dogmas of the Gnostics, the metaphysical tenets of both Brahmanism and Buddhism. They held that the *Old Testament* was the revelation of an inferior being, a subordinate divinity, and did not contain a single sentence of their *Sophia,* the Divine Wisdom. As to the *New Testament,* it had lost its purity when the compilers became guilty of interpolations. The revelation of divine truth was sacrificed by them to promote selfish ends and to maintain quarrels. The accusation does not seem so very improbable to one who is well aware of the constant strife between the champions of circumcision and the "Law," and the apostles who had given up Judaism.

The Gnostic Ophites taught the doctrine of Emanations, so hateful to the defenders of the unity in the trinity, and *vice versa.* The Unknown Deity with them had *no name;* but his first female emanation was called Bythos or Depth.\* It answered to the Shekhînah of the kabalists, the "Veil" which conceals the "Wisdom" in the *cranium* of the highest of the *three* heads. As the Pythagorean Monad, this *nameless* Wisdom was the *Source* of Light, and *Ennoia* or Mind is Light itself. The latter was also called the "Primitive Man," like the Adam-Kadmon, or ancient Adam of the *Kabala.* Indeed, if man was created after his likeness and in the image of God, then this God was like his creature in shape and figure—hence, he is the "Primitive Man." The first Manu, the one evolved from *Svayambhû,* "he who exists unrevealed in his own glory," is also, in one sense, the primitive man, with the Hindus.

Thus the "nameless and the unrevealed" Bythos, his female reflection, and Ennoia, the revealed Mind proceeding from both, or their Son are the counterparts of the Chaldean first triad as well as those of the Brahmanic Trimûrti. We will compare: in all the three systems we see:

---

\* We give the systems according to an old diagram preserved among some Copts and the Druses of Mount Lebanon. Irenaeus had perhaps some good reasons to disfigure their doctrines.

THE GREAT FIRST CAUSE as the ONE, the primordial germ, the unrevealed and grand ALL, existing through himself. In the

| INDIAN PANTHEON | THE CHALDEAN | THE OPHITE |
|---|---|---|
| Brahman-Dyaus. | Ilu, Kabalistic Ain-Soph. | The Nameless, or Secret Name. |

Whenever the Eternal awakes from its slumber and desires to manifest itself, it divides itself into male and female. It then becomes in every system:

THE DOUBLE-SEXED DEITY, the universal Father and Mother.

| IN INDIA | IN CHALDEA | IN THE OPHITE SYSTEM |
|---|---|---|
| Brahmâ. Nâra (male), Nârî (female). | Eikon or Ain-Soph. Anu (male), Anata (female). | Nameless Spirit. Abrasax (male), Bythos (female). |

From the union of the two emanates a third, or creative Principle — the SON, or the manifested Logos, the product of the Divine Mind.

| IN INDIA | IN CHALDEA | IN THE OPHITE SYSTEM |
|---|---|---|
| Viraj, the Son. | Bel, the Son. | Ophis (another name for Ennoia), the Son. |

Moreover, each of these systems has a triple male trinity, each proceeding separately through itself from one female Deity. So, for instance:

| IN INDIA | IN CHALDEA | IN THE OPHITE SYSTEM |
|---|---|---|
| The trinity — Brahmâ, Vishnu, Siva, are blended into ONE, who is *Brahma* (neuter gender), creating and being created through the Virgin Nârî (the mother of perpetual fecundity). | The trinity — Anu, Bel, Hoa (or Sin, Samas, Bin), blend into ONE who is Anu (double-sexed) through the Virgin Mylitta. | The trinity consisted of the Mystery named Sigê, Bythos, Ennoia. These become ONE who is *Abrasax*, from the Virgin *Sophia* (or *Pneuma*), who herself is an emanation of Bythos and the Mystery-god and emanates through them Christos. |

To place it still clearer, the Babylonian System recognizes first—the ONE (*Ad*, or *Ad-ad*), who is never named, but only acknowledged in thought as the Hindu *Svayambhû*. From this he becomes manifest as *Anu* or *Ana* — the one above all — *Monas*. Next comes the Demiurge called *Bel* or *El*, who is the active power of the Godhead. The third is the principle of Wisdom, *Hea* or *Hoa*, who also rules the sea and the underworld. Each of these has his divine consort, giving us *Anata*, *Belita*, and *Davkina*. These, however, are only like the *Śaktis*, and not especially remarked by theologians. But the female principle is denoted by Mylitta, the Great Mother, called also Ishtar. So with the three male gods, we have the Triad or Trimûrti, and with Mylitta added, the *Arba* or Four (Tetraktys of Pythagoras), which perfects and potentializes all. Hence, the above-given modes of expression. The following Chaldean diagram may serve as an illustration for all others:

Triad { Anu, Bel, Hoa, } Mylitta—Arba-il, or Four-fold God,

become, with the Christians,

Trinity { God the Father, God the Son, God the Holy Ghost, } Mary, or mother of these three Gods since they are one, or, the Christian Heavenly Tetraktys.

Hence, Hebron, the city of the Kabiri was called *Kiryath-Arba*, city of the Four. The Kabiri were *Axieros*, the noble Eros; *Axiokersos*, the worthy horned one; *Axiokersa*, Demeter and *Casmilos*, Hoa, etc.

The Pythagorean ten denoted the *Arba-il* or Divine Four, emblematized by the Hindu *liṅga;* Anu, 1; Bel, 2; Hoa, 3, which makes 6. The triad and Mylitta as 4 make the ten.

Though he is termed the "Primitive Man," Ennoia, who is like the Egyptian Poimandres, the "Power of the Thought Divine," the first intelligible manifestation of the Divine Spirit in material form, he is like the "Only-Begotten" Son of the "Unknown Father," of all other nations. He is the emblem of the first appearance of the divine Presence in his own works of creation, tangible and visible, and therefore comprehensible. The mystery-God, or the ever-unrevealed Deity fecundates through His will Bythos, the unfathomable and infinite depth that exists in silence (*Sigê*) and darkness (for our intellect), and that represents the abstract idea of all nature, the ever-producing Cosmos. As neither the male nor female principle, blended into the idea of a double-sexed Deity in ancient conceptions, could be comprehended by an ordinary human intellect, the theology of every people had to create for its religion a Logos, or manifested word, in some shape or other. With the Ophites and other Gnostics who took their models direct from more ancient originals, **the unrevealed Bythos and her male counterpart produce Ennoia, and the three in their turn produce Sophia,\* thus completing the Tetraktys, which will emanate Christos, the very essence of the Father-Spirit.** As the

---

\* Sophia is the highest prototype of woman — the first *spiritual* Eve. In the Bible the system is reversed and the intervening emanation being omitted, Eve is degraded to simple humanity.

unrevealed One, or concealed Logos in its latent state, he has existed from all eternity in the *Arba-il,* the metaphysical abstraction; therefore, he is ONE with all others as a unity, the latter (including all) being indifferently termed Ennoia, Sigê (silence), Bythos, etc. As the revealed one, he is Androgyne: Christos and Sophia (Divine Wisdom), who descend into the man Jesus. Both Father and Son are shown by Irenaeus to have loved the beauty (*formam*) of the primitive woman,* who is Bythos — Depth — as well as Sophia, and as having produced conjointly Ophis and Sophia (double-sexed unity again), male and female wisdom, one being considered as the unrevealed Holy Spirit, or elder Sophia — the *Pneuma* — the intellectual "Mother of all things"; the other the revealed one, or *Ophis,* typifying divine wisdom fallen into matter, or God-man — Jesus, whom the Gnostic Ophites represented by the serpent (Ophis).

Fecundated by the Divine Light of the Father and Son, the highest spirit and Ennoia, Sophia produces in her turn two other emanations — one perfect Christos, the second imperfect Sophia-Akhamôth,† from חכמות, ḥokhmôth (simple wisdom), who becomes the mediatrix between the intellectual and material worlds.

Christos was the mediator and guide between God (the Higher) and everything spiritual in man; Akhamôth — the younger Sophia — held the same duty between the "Primitive Man," Ennoia and matter. What was mysteriously meant by the general term *Christos,* we have just explained.

Delivering a sermon on the "Month of Mary," we find the Rev. Dr. Preston, of New York City, expressing the Christian idea of the female principle of the trinity better and more clearly than we could, and substantially in the spirit of an ancient "heathen" philosopher. He says that the "plan of the redemption made it necessary that a mother should be found, and Mary stands pre-eminently alone as the only instance when a creature was necessary to the consummation of God's work." We will beg the right to contradict the reverend gentleman. As shown above, thousands of years before our era it was found necessary by all the "heathen" theogonies to find a female principle, a "mother" for the triune male principle. Hence, Christianity does not present the "only instance" of such a consummation of God's work—albeit, as this work shows, there was more philosophy and less materialism, or rather anthropomorphism, in it. But hear the reverend Doctor express "heathen" thought in

---

\* Irenaeus, *Adv. Haer.,* Book I, xxx, 1-3.

† In King's *Gnostics,* we find the system a little incorrect. The author tells us that he followed Bellermann's *Drei Programmen über die Abraxas-gemmen.* [p. 33, 1st ed.]

Christian ideas. "He" (God), he says, "prepared her (Mary's) virginal and celestial purity, for a mother defiled could not become the mother of the Most High. The holy virgin, even in her childhood, was more pleasing than all the Cherubim and Seraphim, and from infancy to the maturing maidenhood and womanhood she grew more and more pure. By her very sanctity she reigned over the heart of God. *When the hour came, the whole court of heaven was hushed, and the trinity listened for the answer of Mary, for without her consent the world could not have been redeemed.*"

Does it not seem as if we were reading Irenaeus explaining the Gnostic "*Heresy*, which taught that the Father and Son loved the beauty (*formam*) of the celestial Virgin"; or the Egyptian system of Isis being both wife, sister and mother of Osiris-Horus? With the Gnostic philosophy there were but *two*, but the Christians have improved and perfected the system by making it completely "heathen," for it is the Chaldean Anu-Bel-Hoa, merging into Mylitta. "Then while this month [of Mary]," adds Dr. Preston, "begins in the paschal season — the month when nature decks herself with fruits and flowers, the harbingers of a bright harvest — let us, too, begin for a golden harvest. In this month the dead come up out of the earth, figuring the resurrection; so, when we are kneeling before the altar of the holy and immaculate Mary, let us remember that there should come forth from us the bud of promise, the flower of hope, and the imperishable fruit of sanctity."

This is precisely the substratum of the Pagan thought, which, among other meanings, emblematized by the rites of the resurrection of Osiris, Adonis, Bacchus, and other slaughtered sun-gods, the resurrection of all nature in spring, the germination of seeds that had been dead and sleeping during winter, and so were allegorically said to be kept in the underworld (Hadês). They are typified by the three days passed in hell before his resurrection by Hercules, by Christ, and others.

This derivation, or rather *heresy*, as it is called in Christianity, is simply the Brahmanic doctrine in all its archaic purity. Vishnu, the second personage of the Hindu trinity, is also the Logos, for he is made subsequently to incarnate himself in Krishna. And *Lakshmi* — who, as in the case of Osiris, and Isis, of Ain-Soph and Sephîrah, and of Bythos and Ennoia, is both his wife, sister and daughter, through this endless correlation of male and female creative powers in the abstruse metaphysics of the ancient philosophies—is Sophia-Akhamôth. Krishna is the mediator promised by Brahmâ to mankind, and represents the same idea as the Gnostic Christos. And *Lakshmî*, Vishnu's spiritual half, is the emblem of physical nature, the universal mother of all the material and revealed forms; the mediatrix and protector of nature, like Sophia-Akhamôth, who is made by the Gnostics the mediatrix between the Great Cause and Matter, as Christos is the mediator between him and spiritual humanity.

This Brahmano-Gnostic tenet is more logical, and more consistent with the allegory of *Genesis* and the fall of man. When God curses the first couple, He is made to curse also the earth and everything that is on it. The *New Testament* gives us a Redeemer for the first sin of mankind, which was punished for having sinned; but there is not a word said about a Savior who would take off the unmerited curse from the earth and the animals, which had never sinned at all. Thus the Gnostic allegory shows a greater sense of both justice and logic than the Christian.

In the Ophite system, Sophia, the Androgyne Wisdom, is also the female spirit, or the Hindu female Nârî (Nârâyaṇa), moving on the face of the waters — chaos, or future matter. She vivifies it from afar, but not touching the abyss of darkness. She is unable to do so, for Wisdom is purely intellectual, and cannot act directly on matter. Therefore, Sophia is obliged to address herself to her Supreme Parent; but although life proceeds primally from the Unseen Cause, and his Ennoia, neither of them can, any more than herself, have anything to do with the lower chaos in which matter assumes its definite shape. Thus, Sophia is obliged to employ for the task her *imperfect* emanation, Sophia-Akhamôth, the latter being of a mixed nature, half spiritual and half material.

The only difference between the Ophite cosmogony and that of the St. John Nazarenes is a change of names. We find equally an identical system in the *Kabala*, the *Book of Mystery (Liber Mysterii)*.* All the three systems, especially that of the kabalists and the Nazarenes, which were the *models* for the Ophite Cosmogony, belong to the pure Oriental Gnosticism. The *Codex Nazaraeus* opens with: "The Supreme King of Light, Mano, the great first one," etc.,† the latter being the emanation of Ferho — the unknown, formless LIFE. He is the chief of the Aeôns, from whom proceed (or shoot forth) five refulgent rays of Divine light. Mano is *Rex Lucis*, the Bythos-Ennoia of the Ophites. "*Unus est Rex Lucis in suo regno, nec ullus qui eo altior, nullus qui ejus similitudinem retulerit, nullus qui, sublatis oculis, viderit Coronam quae in ejus capite est.*" ‡ He is the Manifested Light around the highest of the three kabalistic heads, the concealed wisdom; from him emanate the three *Lives*. Hibil-Ziwa is the revealed Logos, Christos the "Apostle Gabriel," and the first Legate or messenger of light. If Bythos and Ennoia are the Nazarene Mano, then the dual-natured, the semi-spiritual, semi-material Akhamôth must be Pthahil when viewed from her spiritual aspect; and if regarded in her grosser nature, she is the Nazarene "Spiritus."

---

\* See *Siphra Dtzeniuthah*.
† *Codex Nazaraeus*, I, pp. 1 *et seq*.
‡ [*Ibid.*, p. 11.]

Pthahil,* who is the reflection of his father, Lord Abathur, the *third life* — as the elder Sophia is also the third emanation — is the "newest man." Perceiving his fruitless attempts to create a perfect material world, the "Spiritus" calls to one of her progeny, the *Karabtanos*-Ialdabaôth, who is without sense or judgment ("blind matter"), to unite himself with her to create something definite out of this confused (*turbulentos*) matter, which task she is enabled to achieve only after having produced from this uinon with *Karabtanos* the seven stellars. Like the six sons or genii of the Gnostic Ialdabaôth, they then frame the material world. The same story is repeated over again in Sophia-Akhamôth. Delegated by her purely spiritual parent, the elder Sophia, to create the world of *visible forms,* she descended into chaos, and, overpowered by the emanation of matter, lost her way. Still ambitious to create a world of matter of her own, she busied herself hovering to and fro about the dark abyss, and imparted life and motion to the inert elements, until she became so hopelessly entangled in matter that, like Pthahil, she is represented sitting immersed in mud, and unable to extricate herself from it; until, by the contact of matter itself, she produces the *Creator* of the material world. He is the Demiurgus, called by the Ophites Ialdabaôth, and as we will directly show, the parent of the Jewish God in the opinion of some sects, and held by others to be the "Lord God" Himself. It is at this point of the kabalistic-gnostic cosmogony that begins the Mosaic *Bible*. Having accepted the Jewish *Old Testament* as their standard, no wonder that the Christians were forced by the exceptional position in which they were placed through their own ignorance, to make the best of it.

The first groups of Christians, whom Renan shows numbering but from seven to twelve men in *each church,* belonged unquestionably to the poorest and most ignorant classes. They had and could have no idea of the highly philosophical doctrines of the Platonists and Gnostics, and evidently knew as little about their own newly-made-up religion. To these [men] — who if Jews, had been crushed under the tyrannical dominion of the "law," as enforced by the elders of the synagogues; and if Pagans had been always excluded, as the lower castes are until now in India, from the religious mysteries — the God of the Jews and the "Father" preached by Jesus were all one. The contention which reigned from the first years following the death of Jesus, between the two parties, the Pauline and the Petrine — were deplorable. What one did, the other deemed

---

* See *Codex Nazaraeus*, I, pp. 177 *et seq*. Pthahil, sent to frame the world, finds himself immersed in the abyss of mud, and soliloquizes in dismay until the *Spiritus* (Sophia-Akhamôth) unites herself completely with matter, and so creates the material world.

a sacred duty to undo. If the *Homilies* are considered apocryphal, and cannot very well be accepted as an infallible standard by which to measure the animosity which raged between the two apostles, we have the *Bible*, and the proofs afforded therein are plentiful.

So hopelessly entangled seems Irenaeus in his fruitless endeavors to describe, to all outward appearance at least, the true doctrines of the many Gnostic sects of which he treats and to present them at the same time as abominable "heresies," that he either deliberately, or through ignorance, confounds all of them in such a way that few metaphysicians would be able to disentangle them, without the *Kabala* and the *Codex* as the true keys. Thus, for instance, he cannot even tell the difference between the Sethianites and the Ophites, and tells us that they called the "God of all," "*Hominem*," a MAN, and his mind the SECOND man, or the "*Son of man*." So does Theodoret, who lived more than two centuries after Irenaeus, and who makes a sad mess of the chronological order in which the various sects succeeded each other.* Neither the Sethianites (a branch of the Jewish Nazarenes), nor the Ophites, a purely Greek sect, have ever held anything of the kind. Irenaeus contradicts his own words by describing in another place the doctrines of Cerinthus, the direct disciple of Simon Magus. He says that Cerinthus taught that the world was not created by the FIRST GOD, but by a virtue (*virtus*) or power, an Aeôn so distant from the First Cause that he was even ignorant of HIM who *is above all things*. This Aeôn subjected Jesus, he begot him physically through Joseph from one who was not a virgin, but simply the wife of that Joseph, and Jesus was born like all other men. Viewed from this physical aspect of his nature, Jesus was called the "son of man." It is only after his *baptism*, that *Christos*, the anointed, descended from the Princeliness of above, in the figure of a dove, and then announced the UNKNOWN Father through Jesus.†

If, therefore, Jesus was physically considered as a son of man, and spiritually as the Christos, who overshadowed him, how then could the "GOD OF ALL," the "*Unknown* Father," be called by the Gnostics *Homo*, a MAN, and his Mind, Ennoia, the SECOND man, or *Son of man?* Neither in the Oriental *Kabala*, nor in Gnosticism, was the "God of all" ever anthropomorphized. It is but the first, or rather the second emanation, for Shekhînah, Sephîrâh, Depth, and other first-manifested female virtues are also emanations that are termed "primitive men." Thus Adam-Kadmon, Ennoia (or *Sigê*), the *logoi* in short, are the "only-begotten" ones, but not the *Sons* of man, which appellation properly be-

---

* Irenaeus, *Adv. Haer.*, I, xxx, 1; Theodoret, *Haereticarum fabularum compendium.*
† Irenaeus, *op. cit.*, I, xxvi, 1.

longs to Christos, the son of Sophia (the elder) and of the primitive man who produces him through his own vivifying light, which emanates from the source or *cause* of all, hence the *cause* of his light also, the "Unknown Father." There is a great difference made in the Gnostic metaphysics between the first unrevealed Logos and the "anointed," who is Christos. Ennoia may be termed, as Philo understands it, the *Second God*, but he alone is the "Primitive and First man," and by no means the Second one, as Theodoret and Irenaeus have it. It is but the inveterate desire of the latter to connect Jesus in every possible way, even in his *Against Heresies*, with the *Highest* God, that led him into so many falsifications.

Such an identification with the *Unknown* God, even of Christos the anointed — the Aeôn who overshadowed him — let alone of the man Jesus, never entered the head of the Gnostics, or even of the direct apostles and of Paul, whatever later forgeries may have added.

How daring and desperate were many such deliberate falsifications was shown in the first attempts to compare the original manuscripts with later ones. In Bishop Horsley's edition of Sir Isaac Newton's works,* several manuscripts on theological subjects were cautiously withheld from publication. The article known as *Christ's Descent into Hell*, which is found in the later Apostles' Creed, is not to be found in the manuscripts of either the fourth or sixth centuries. It was an evident interpolation copied from the fables of Bacchus and Hercules and enforced upon Christendom as an article of faith. Concerning it the author of the preface [24] to the *Catalogue of the Manuscripts of the King's Library* (preface, p. xxiv) remarks: "I wish that the insertion of the article of *Christ's Descent into Hell* into the Apostles' Creed could be as well accounted for as the *insertion* of the *said* verse" (viz., *First Epistle of John* v, 7).†

Now, this verse reads: "For there are three that bear record in Heaven, the Father, the Word, and the Holy Ghost: and these three are one." This verse, which has been "appointed to be read in churches," is now known to be spurious. It is not to be found "in any Greek manuscript, save one at Berlin," which was transcribed from some interpolated paraphrase between the lines. In the first and second editions of Erasmus, printed in 1516 and 1519, this allusion to these three heavenly witnesses is *omitted*;[25] and the text is not contained in any Greek manuscript which was written earlier than the fifteenth century. ‡ It was not mentioned by any of the Greek ecclesiastical writers nor by the early Latin

---

\* [London, 1779-85, 4 Vols.]

† See preface to *The Apocryphal New Testament*, London: printed for W. Hone, Ludgate Hill, 1820, p. vi.

‡ "It is first cited by Vigilius Tapsensis, a Latin writer of no credit, in the latter end of the fifth century, and by him it is suspected to have been forged." — *Op. cit.*, p. vii.

fathers, so anxious to get at every proof in support of their trinity; and it was omitted by Luther in his German version. Edward Gibbon* was early in pointing out its spurious character. Archbishop Newcome rejected it, and the Bishop of Lincoln expresses his conviction that it is spurious.† There are twenty-eight Greek authors — Irenaeus, Clement, and Athanasius included, who neither quote nor mention it; and seventeen Latin writers, numbering among them Augustine, Jerome, Ambrosius, Cyprian and Pope Eusebius, who appear utterly ignorant of it. "It is evident that if the text of the heavenly witnesses had been known from the beginning of Christianity the ancients would have eagerly seized it, inserted it in their creeds, quoted it repeatedly against the heretics, and selected it for the brightest ornament of every book that they wrote upon the subject of the Trinity." ‡

Thus falls to the ground the strongest trinitarian pillar. Another not less obvious forgery is quoted from Sir Isaac Newton's words by the editor of the *Apocryphal New Testament*. Newton observes "that what the Latins have done to this text (*First Epistle of John* v, 7), the Greeks have done to that of St. Paul (*1 Timothy* iii, 16). For, by changing *o* into *θ*, the abbreviation of θεός [God]," in the Alexandrian manuscript, from which their subsequent copies were made,, "they now read, '*Great is the mystery of Godliness*, GOD *was manifested in the flesh*'; whereas all the churches, for the first four or five hundred years, and the authors of all the ancient versions, Jerome, as well as the rest, read: 'Great is the mystery of godliness WHICH WAS *manifested in the flesh*'." Newton adds, that now that the disputes over this forgery are over, they that read GOD made manifest in the flesh, instead of the *godliness which was* manifested in the flesh, think this passage "one of the most obvious and pertinent texts for the business." §

And now we ask again the question: Who were the first Christians? Those who were readily converted by the eloquent simplicity of Paul, who promised them, with the name of Jesus, *freedom* from the narrow bonds of ecclesiasticism. They understood but one thing; they were the "children of promise" (*Galatians* iv, 28). The "allegory" of the Mosaic *Bible* was unveiled to them; the covenant "from the Mount Sinai which gendereth *to bondage*" was Agar (*ibid.*, 24), the old Jewish synagogue, and she was "in bondage with her children" to Jerusalem, the new and the free, "the mother of us all." On the one hand the synagogue and

---

\* [*Decline and Fall*, etc., III, ch. xxxvii.]

† George Tomline, *Elements of Christian Theology*, etc., Vol. II, p. 90, note.

‡ See Porson's *Letters to Mr. Archdeacon Travis*, etc., pp. 363, 402, etc.; London, 1790.

§ [Hone, *op. cit.*, p. ix.]

the law which persecuted everyone who dared to step across the narrow path of bigotry and dogmatism; on the other, Paganism* with its grand philosophical truths concealed from sight; unveiling itself but to the few, and leaving the masses hopelessly seeking to discover who was *the* god, among this overcrowded pantheon of deities and sub-deities. To others, the apostle of circumcision, supported by all his followers, was promising, if they obeyed the "law," a life hereafter, and a resurrection of which they had no previous idea. At the same time he never lost an occasion to contradict Paul without naming him, but indicating him so clearly that it is next to impossible to doubt whom Peter meant. While he may have converted some men, who, whether they had believed in the Mosaic resurrection promised by the Pharisees, or had fallen into the nihilistic doctrines of the Sadducees, or had belonged to the polytheistic heathenism of the Pagan rabble, had no future after death, nothing but a mournful blank, we do not think that the work of contradiction, carried on so systematically by the two apostles, had much helped their work of proselytism. With the educated thinking classes they succeeded very little, as ecclesiastical history clearly shows. Where was the truth; where the inspired word of God? On the one hand, as we have seen, they heard the apostle Paul explaining that of the two covenants, "which things are an allegory," the old one from Mount Sinai, "which gendereth to bondage," was *Agar* the bondwoman; and Mount Sinai itself answered to "Jerusalem," which now is "in bondage" with her circumcised children; and the new covenant meant Jesus Christ — the "Jerusalem which is above and free"; and on the other, Peter, who was contradicting and even abusing him. Paul vehemently exclaims, "Cast out the bondwoman and her son" (the old *law* and the synagogue). "The son of the bondwoman shall not be heir with the son of the freewoman." "Stand fast therefore in the

---

* The term "Paganism" is properly used by many modern writers with hesitation. Professor Alexander Wilder, in his edition of R. Payne Knight's *The Symbolical Language of Ancient Art and Mythology*, says: "It ['Paganism'] has degenerated into slang, and is generally employed with more or less of an opprobrious meaning. The more correct expression would have been 'the ancient ethnical worships," but it would hardly be understood in its true sense, and we accordingly have adopted the term in popular use, but not disrespectfully. A religion which can develop a Plato, an Epictetus, and an Anaxagoras, is not gross, superficial, or totally unworthy of candid attention. Besides, many of the rites and doctrines included in the Christian as well as in the Jewish Institute, appeared first in the other systems. Zoroastrianism anticipated far more than has been imagined. The Cross, the priestly robes and symbols, the sacraments, the sabbath, the festivals and anniversaries, are all anterior to the Christian era by thousands of years. The ancient worship, after it had been excluded from its former shrines, and from the metropolitan towns, was maintained for a long time by the inhabitants of humble localities. To this fact it owes its later designation. From being kept up in the *pagi,* or rural districts, its votaries were denominated *pagans,* or provincials."

liberty wherewith Christ hath made us free, and be not entangled again with the yoke of bondage. . . . Behold, I Paul say unto you, that if ye be circumcised, Christ shall profit you nothing!" (*Gal.* iv, 30; v, 1-2). What do we find Peter writing? Whom does he mean by saying, "They speak great swelling words of vanity . . . While they promise them *liberty*, they themselves are the servants of corruption: for of whom a man is overcome, of the same is he brought in bondage. . . . For if after *they have escaped* the pollutions of the world through the knowledge of the Lord and Savior . . . they are again entangled therein, and overcome . . . it had *been better for them not to have known the way of righteousness*, than after they have known it, to turn from the holy *commandment delivered unto them*" (*2 Peter* ii, 18-31).

Peter certainly cannot have meant the Gnostics, for they had never seen "the holy commandment delivered unto them"; Paul had. They never promised anyone "liberty" from bondage, but Paul had done so repeatedly. Moreover the latter rejects the "old covenant," Agar the bondwoman; and Peter holds fast to it. Paul warns the people against the *powers* and *dignities* (the lower angels of the kabalists); and Peter as will be shown further on, respects them and *denounces those who do not*. Peter preaches circumcision, and Paul forbids it.

Later, when all these extraordinary blunders, contradictions, dissensions and inventions were forcibly crammed into a frame elaborately executed by the episcopal caste of the new religion, and called Christianity; and the chaotic picture itself cunningly preserved from too close scrutiny by a whole array of formidable Church penances and anathemas, which kept the curious back under the false pretence of sacrilege and profanation of divine mysteries; and millions of people had been butchered in the name of the God of mercy — then came the Reformation. It certainly deserves its name in its fullest paradoxical sense. It abandoned Peter and alleges to have chosen Paul for its only leader. And the apostle who thundered against the old law of bondage; who left full liberty to Christians to either observe the Sabbath or set it aside; who rejects everything anterior to John the Baptist, is now the professed standard bearer of Protestantism, which holds to the *old* law more than the Jews, imprisons those who view the Sabbath as Jesus and Paul did, and outvies the synagogue of the first century in dogmatic intolerance!

But who then *were* the first Christians, may still be asked? Doubtless the Ebionites; and in this we follow the authority of the best critics. "There can be little doubt that the author [of the *Clementine Homilies*] was a representative of Ebionitic Gnosticism, which *had once been the* *purest form of primitive Christianity* . . . " * And who were the Ebionites? The pupils and followers of the early Nazarenes, the kabalistic Gnostics. In the preface to the *Codex Nazaraeus*, the translator says: "That also the Nazarenes did not at that time reject such (Aeôns), is credible. For of the Ebionites, who acknowledged such, these were the instructors." †

We find, moreover, Epiphanius, the Christian Homer of the *Heresies*, telling us that "Ebion had the opinion of the Nazarenes, the form of the Cerinthians (who fable that the world was put together by angels), and the appellation of Christians." ‡ An appellation certainly more correctly applied to them than to the orthodox (so-called) Christians of the school of Irenaeus and the later Vatican. Renan shows the Ebionites numbering among their sect all the surviving relatives of Jesus. John the Baptist, his cousin and *precursor*, was the accepted Savior of the Nazarenes, and their prophet. His disciples dwelt on the other side of the Jordan, and the scene of the baptism of the Jordan is clearly and beyond any question proved by the author of *Sôd, the Son of the Man*, to have been the site of the Adonis-worship.§ "Over the Jordan and beyond the lake dwelt the Nazarenes, a sect said to have existed already at the birth of Jesus, and to have counted him among its number. They must have extended along the east of the Jordan, and south-easterly among the Arabians (*Galat.* i, 17, 21; ii, 11), and Sabaeans in the direction of Basra; and again they must have gone far north over the Lebanon to Antioch, also *to the north-east* to the Nazarian settlement in Beroea where St. Jerome found them. In the Desert the Mysteries of Adonis may have still prevailed; in the mountains Aiai Adonin was still a cry." ||

"Having been united (*conjunctus*) to the Nazarenes, each (Ebionite) imparted to the other out of his own wickedness, and decided that Christ *was of the seed of a man*," writes Epiphanius. ¶

And if they did, we must suppose they knew more about their contemporary prophet than Epiphanius 400 years later. Theodoret, as shown elsewhere, describes the Nazarenes as Jews who "honor the Anointed as a just man," and use the *evangel* called "*According to Peter*." ** Jerome finds the authentic and original *evangel*, written in Hebrew, by Matthew the apostle-publican, in the library collected at Caesarea, by the martyr Pamphilius. "*I received permission from the Nazaraeans*, who at Beroea of Syria used this [gospel], to translate it," he writes toward the end of

---

\* *Supern. Relig.*, Vol. II, p. 4.
† Norberg, *Codex Nazaraeus*, preface, p. v.
‡ *Panarion*, lib. I, tom. II, Indiculus, § 8; Haer. XXX, 1.
§ Preliminary chapter, pp. v-xxix.
|| *Ibid.*, p. vii.
¶ [*Panarion*, lib. I, tom. II, Haer. XXX, ii, iii.]
\*\* [*Haer. fabul.*, II, ii.]

the fourth century.* "In the evangel which the *Nazarenes* and *Ebionites* use," adds Jerome, "which recently I translated from Hebrew into Greek, and which is called by most persons the *genuine Gospel of Matthew*," etc. †

That the apostles had received a "secret doctrine" from Jesus, and that he himself taught one, is evident from the following words of Jerome, who confessed it in an unguarded moment. Writing to the Bishops Chromatius and Heliodorus, he complains that "a difficult work is enjoined, since this translation has been commanded me by your Felicities, which *St. Matthew himself, the Apostle and Evangelist,* DID NOT WISH TO BE OPENLY WRITTEN. For if this had not been SECRET, he [Matthew] would have added to the *evangel* that what he gave forth was his; but he made this book sealed up in the Hebrew characters: which he put forth *even in such a way* that the book, written in Hebrew letters and *by the hand of himself,* might be possessed *by the men most religious;* who also, in the course of time, received it from those who preceded them. But this very book they never gave to anyone to be transcribed; and its *text* they related some one way and some another."‡ And he adds further on the same page: "And it happened that this book, having been published by a disciple of Manichaeus, named Seleucus, who also wrote falsely *The Acts of the Apostles,* exhibited matter not for edification, but for destruction; and that this book was approved in a synod which the ears of the Church properly refused to listen to." §

He admits himself, that the book which he authenticates as being written "*by the hand of Matthew*" was nearly unintelligible to him, notwith-

---

\* Jerome, *De viris inlustribus liber,* cap. 3. "It is remarkable that, while all church fathers say that Matthew wrote in *Hebrew,* the whole of them use the Greek text as the genuine apostolic writing, without mentioning what relation the *Hebrew* Matthew has to our Greek one! It had many *peculiar additions* which are wanting in our evangel" (Olshausen, *Nachweis der Echtheit der sämtlichen Schriften des Neuen Test.,* p. 35).

† Jerome, *Comment. to Matthew,* Book II, ch. xii, 13. Jerome adds that it was written in the Chaldaic language, but with Hebrew letters [*Dial. contra Pelag.,* iii, 2].

‡ Jerome, *Opera,* Vol. V (1706), col. 445; ed. Johannes Martianay, Paris: Ludovicus Roulland, 1693-1706. Cf. Dunlap, *Sôd, the Son of the Man,* p. 46.[26]

§ This accounts also for the rejection of the works of Justin Martyr, who used only this *Gospel according to the Hebrews,* as also did most probably Tatian, his disciple. At what late period was fully established the *divinity* of Christ we can judge by the mere fact that even in the fourth century Eusebius [*Eccl. Hist.,* III, xxv] did not denounce this book as spurious, but only classed it with such as the *Apocalypse* of John; and Credner (*Zur Geschichte des Kanons,* p. 120) shows Nicephorus inserting it, together with the *Revelation,* in his *Stichometry,* among the Antilegomena. The Ebionites, the *genuine* primitive Christians, rejecting the rest of the apostolic writings, made use only of this Gospel (Irenaeus, *Adv. Haer.,* I, xxvi, 2; also Eusebius, *Eccl. Hist.,* III, xxvii), and the Ebionites, as Epiphanius declares, firmly believed, with the Nazarenes, that Jesus was but a man "of the seed of a man" [*Panarion,* Haer. XXX, iii].

standing that he translated it twice, for it was arcane or *a secret*. Nevertheless, Jerome coolly sets down every commentary upon it, except his own, as *heretical*. More than that, Jerome knew that this *original Gospel of Matthew* was the expounder of the only true doctrine of Christ; and that it was the work of an evangelist who had been the friend and companion of Jesus. He knew that if of the two *Gospels*, the Hebrew in question and the Greek belonging to our present Scripture, one was spurious, hence heretical, it was not that of the Nazarenes; and yet, knowing all this, Jerome becomes more zealous than ever in his persecutions of the "Heretics." Why? Because to accept it was equivalent to reading the death sentence of the established Church. The *Gospel according to the Hebrews* was but too well known to have been the only one accepted for four centuries by the Jewish Christians, the Nazarenes and the Ebionites. And neither of the latter accepted the *divinity* of Christ.

If the commentaries of Jerome on the Prophets, his famous *Vulgate*, and numerous polemical treatises are all as trustworthy as this version of the *Gospel according to Matthew*, then we have a divine revelation indeed.

Why wonder at the unfathomable mysteries of the Christian religion, since it is perfectly *human*? Have we not a letter written by one of the most respected Fathers of the Church to this same Jerome, which shows better than whole volumes their traditionary policy? This is what *Saint Gregory* of Nazianzus wrote to his friend and confidant *Saint* Jerome: "Nothing can impose better on a people than *verbiage*; the less they understand the more they admire. Our fathers and doctors have often said, not what they thought, but what circumstances and necessity forced them to."

But to return to our Sophia-Akhamôth and the belief of the genuine, primitive Christians.

After having produced *Ialdabaôth* — from ילדה, *ialda*, a child, and בהות, *baôth*, chaos, a waste, a desolation — Sophia-Akhamôth suffered so much from the contact with matter, that after extraordinary struggles she escapes at last out of the muddy chaos. Although unacquainted with the pleroma, the region of her mother, she reached the middle space and succeeded in shaking off the material parts which have stuck to her spiritual nature; after which she immediately built a strong barrier between the world of intelligences (spirits) and the world of matter. Ialdabaôth is thus the "son of darkness," the creator of our sinful world (the physical portion of it). He follows the example of Bythos and produces from himself six stellar spirits (sons). They are all in his own image, and reflections one of the other, which become darker as they successively recede from their father. With the latter, they all inhabit seven regions disposed like a ladder, beginning under the middle space, the region of their mother, Sophia-Akhamôth, and ending with our earth, the *seventh* region. Thus they are the genii of the seven planetary spheres of which the lowest is the region of our earth (the sphere which surrounds it, our aether). The respective names of these genii of the spheres are *Iaô, Tsabaôth, Adonaios, Eloaios, Horaios, Astaphaios.*\* The first four, as everyone knows, are the mystic names of the Jewish "Lord God," † he being, as C. W. King expresses it, "degraded thus by the Ophites into the appellations of the subordinates of the Creator; the two last signify the Genii of Fire, and of Water."

Ialdabaôth, whom several sects regarded as the God of Moses, was not a pure spirit; he was ambitious and proud, and rejecting the spiritual light of the middle space offered him by his mother Sophia-Akhamôth, he set himself to create a world of his own. Aided by his sons, the six planetary genii, he fabricated man, but this one proved a failure. It was a monster; soulless, ignorant, and crawling on all fours on the ground like a material beast. Ialdabaôth was forced to implore the help of his spiritual mother. She communicated to him a ray of her divine light, and so animated man and endowed him with a soul. And now began the animosity of Ialdabaôth toward his own creature. Following the impulse of the divine light, man soared higher and higher in his aspirations; very soon he began presenting not the image of his Creator Ialdabaôth but rather that of the Supreme Being, the "primitive man," Ennoia. Then the Demiurgus was filled with rage and envy; and fixing his jealous eye on the abyss of matter, his looks envenomed with passion were suddenly reflected in it as in a mirror; the reflection became animate, and there arose out of the abyss Satan, serpent, Ophiomorphos — "the embodiment of envy and of cunning. He is the union of all that is most base in Matter, with the hate, envy, and craft, of a spiritual intelligence." ‡

After that, always in spite at the perfection of man, Ialdabaôth created the three kingdoms of nature, the mineral, vegetable and animal, with all evil instincts and properties. Impotent to annihilate the Tree of Knowledge, which grows in his sphere as in every one of the planetary regions, but bent upon detaching "man" from his spiritual protectress, Ialdabaôth forbade him to eat of its fruit, for fear it should reveal to mankind the

---

\* See King's *Gnostics*, p. 28 [p. 97 in 2nd ed.].

† This Iaô or Jehovah is quite distinct from the God of the Mysteries, IAÔ, held sacred by all the nations of antiquity. We will show the difference presently.

‡ King, *op. cit.*, p. 29 [p. 98 in 2nd ed.].

mysteries of the superior world. But Sophia-Akhamôth, who loved and protected the man whom she had animated, sent her own genius, Ophis, in the form of a serpent to induce man to transgress the selfish and unjust command. And "man" suddenly became capable of comprehending the mysteries of creation.

Ialdabaôth revenged himself by punishing the first pair, for man, through his *knowledge*, had already provided for himself a companion out of his spiritual and material half. He imprisoned man and woman in a dungeon of matter, in the body so unworthy of his nature, wherein man is still enthralled. But Akhamôth protected him still. She established between her celestial region and "man," a current of divine light, and kept constantly supplying him with this *spiritual* illumination.

Then follow allegories embodying the idea of dualism, or the struggle between good and evil, spirit and matter, which is found in every cosmogony, and the source of which is again to be sought in India. The types and antitypes represent the heroes of this Gnostic Pantheon, borrowed from the most ancient mythopoeic ages. But, in these personages, Ophis and Ophiomorphos, Sophia and Sophia-Akhamôth, Adam-Kadmon and Adam, the planetary genii and the divine Aeôns, we can also recognize very easily the models of our Biblical copies — the euhemerized patriarchs. The archangels, angels, virtues and powers are all found, under other names, in the *Vedas* and the Buddhistic system. The Avestic Supreme Being, Zeruana, or "Boundless Time," is the type of all these Gnostic and kabalistic "Depths," "Crowns," and even of the Chaldean Ain-Soph. The six Amshâspands, created through the "Word" of Ormazd, the "First-Born," have their reflections in Bythos and his emanations, and the antitype of Ormazd-Ahriman and his *daêvas* also enter into the composition of Ialdabaôth and his six *material*, though not wholly evil, planetary genii.

Akhamôth, afflicted with the evils which befall humanity, notwithstanding her protection, beseeches the celestial mother Sophia — her antitype — to prevail on the unknown DEPTH to send down Christos (the son and emanation of the "Celestial Virgin") to the help of perishing humanity. Ialdabaôth and his six sons of matter are shutting out the divine light from mankind. Man must be saved. Ialdabaôth had already sent his own agent, John the Baptist, from the race of Seth, whom he protects — as a prophet to his people; but only a small portion listened to him — the Nazarenes, the opponents of the Jews, on account of their worshipping Iurbo-Adonai.* Akhamôth had assured her son, Ialdabaôth, that the

---

* Iurbo and Adonai, according to the Ophites, are names of Iaô-Jehovah, one of the emanations of Ialdabaôth. "Iurbo is called by the Abortions [the Jews] Adonai" (*Codex Nazaraeus*, Vol. III, p. 73).

reign of Christos would be only temporal, and thus induced him to send the forerunner, or precursor. Besides that, she made *him cause* the birth of the *man* Jesus from the Virgin Mary, her own type on earth, "for the creation of a material personage could only be the work of the Demiurgus, not falling within the province of a higher power. As soon as Jesus was born, Christos, uniting himself with Sophia [wisdom and **spirituality**], descended through the seven planetary regions, assuming in each an analogous form, and concealing his true nature from their genii, while he attracted into himself the sparks of divine light they retained in their essence. Thus Christos entered into the *Man* Jesus at the moment of his baptism in the Jordan. From that time forth Jesus began to work miracles; before that he had been completely ignorant of his mission." *

Ialdabaôth, discovering that Christos was bringing to an end his own kingdom of matter, stirred up the Jews against him, and Jesus was put to death.† When on the Cross, Christos and Sophia left his body and returned to their own sphere. The material body of the man Jesus was abandoned to the earth, but he himself was given a body made up of *aether* (astral soul). "Thenceforward he consisted of merely *soul* and *spirit*, which was the cause that the disciples did not recognize him after the resurrection." In this spiritual state of a *simulacrum*, Jesus remained on earth for eighteen months after he had risen. During this last sojourn, he received from Sophia that perfect knowledge, that true Gnosis, *which he communicated to the very few among the apostles* who were capable of receiving the same.

"Thence, ascending up into the middle space, he sits on the right hand of Ialdabaôth, but unperceived by him, and there collects all the souls which shall have been purified by the knowledge of Christ. When he has collected all the spiritual light that exists in matter, out of Ialdabaôth's empire, the redemption will be accomplished and the world will be destroyed. Such is the meaning of the reabsorption of all the spiritual light into the pleroma or fullness, whence it originally descended." ‡

---

\* King, *The Gnostics and their Remains*, p. 31 [p. 100 in 2nd ed.].

† In the *Gospel of Nicodemus*, Ialdabaôth is called *Satan* by the pious and anonymous author; evidently, one of the final flings at the half-crushed enemy. "As for me," says Satan, excusing himself to the prince of hell, "I tempted him [Jesus], and stirred up my old people, the Jews, with zeal and anger against him" (Hone, *Apocr. N. T., Nicod.*, xv, 9).[27] Of all examples of Christian ingratitude this seems almost the most conspicuous. The poor Jews are first robbed of their sacred books, and then, in a spurious "Gospel," are insulted by the representation of Satan claiming them as his "old people." If they were his people, and at the same time are "God's chosen people," then the name of this God must be written Satan and not Jehovah. This is logic, but we doubt if it can be regarded as complimentary to the "Lord God of Israel."

‡ [King, *op. cit.*, p. 31 (p. 100 in 2nd ed.).]

## THE REAL OPHITE THEOLOGY

The foregoing is from the description given by Theodoret and adopted by King in his *Gnostics*, with additions from Epiphanius and Irenaeus. But the former gives a very imperfect version, concocted partly from the descriptions of Irenaeus, and partly from his own knowledge of the later Ophites, who, toward the end of the third century, had blended already with several other sects. Irenaeus also confounds them very frequently, and the real theogony of the Ophites is given by none of them correctly. With the exception of a change in names, the above-given theogony is that of all the Gnostics, and also of the Nazarenes. Ophis is but the successor of the Egyptian *Chnuphis* [Khnemu], the Good Serpent with a lion's radiating head, and was held from days of the highest antiquity as an emblem of wisdom, or Thoth, the instructor and Savior of humanity, the "Son of God." "Oh men, live soberly . . . win your immortality!" exclaims Hermes, the thrice-great Trismegistus. "Instructor and guide of humanity, I will lead you on to salvation." * Thus the oldest sectarians regarded Ophis, the Agathodaimôn, as identical with Christos; the serpent being the emblem of celestial wisdom and eternity, and, in the present case, the antetype of the Egyptian Chnuphis-serpent. These Gnostics, the earliest of our Christian era, held: "That the supreme Aeôn, having produced other Aeôns, one of them, a female, *Prounikos* (concupiscence), descended into the water; whence, unable to escape, she remained suspended in mid-space, being too clogged by matter to return above, and not falling lower where there was nothing in affinity to her nature. She then produced her son Ialdabaôth, the God of the Jews, who in his turn, produced seven Aeôns, or Angels,† who created the seven heavens." ‡

In this plurality of heavens the Christians believed from the first, for we find Paul teaching of their existence, and speaking of a man "caught up to the *third* heaven" (2 *Corin.* xii, 2). "From these seven angels Ialdabaôth shut up all that was above him, lest they should know of anything superior to himself.§ They then created man in the image of their Father,‖ but prone and crawling on the earth like a worm. But the heavenly mother, Prounikos,

---

\* [Champollion-Figeac, *Égypte ancienne*, p. 143.]

† This is the Nazarene system; the Spiritus, after uniting himself with Karabtanos (*matter*, turbulent and senseless), brings forth *seven badly-disposed stellars*, in the Orcus; "Seven Figures," which she bore "witless" (*Codex Nazaraeus*, I, p. 179). Justin Martyr evidently adopts this idea, for he tells us of "the sacred prophets, who say that one and the same *spirit* is divided into *seven* spirits (*pneumata*)." — Justin Martyr, *Cohortatio ad Graecos*, xxxii. Cf. Dunlap, *Sôd, the Son of the Man*, p. 52. In the *Apocalypse* the Holy Spirit is subdivided into "*seven* spirits before the throne," from the Persian Mithraic mode of classifying.

‡ [*The Gnostics*, etc., pp. 31-32, footnote (p. 102 in 2nd ed.).]

§ This certainly looks like the "*jealous* God" of the Jews.

‖ It is the *Elohim* (plural) who create Adam, and do not wish man to become "as one of us."

wishing to deprive Ialdabaôth of the power she had involuntarily endowed him with, infused into man a celestial spark, the soul. Immediately man rose up upon his feet, soared in mind beyond the limits of the eight spheres and glorified the Supreme Father, *Him that is above Ialdabaôth*. Hence [the latter], full of jealousy, cast down his eyes upon the lowest stratum of matter, and begot a Virtue in the form of a serpent, whom they [the Ophites] call his son. Eve, obeying him as the son of God, was readily persuaded to eat of the Tree of Knowledge." \*

It is a self-evident fact that the serpent of the *Genesis*, who appears suddenly and without any preliminary introduction, must have been the antitype of the Persian Arch-Daêvas, whose head is *Ashmog*, the "two-footed serpent of lies." If the *Bible*-serpent had been deprived of his limbs before he had tempted woman unto sin, why should God specify as a punishment that he should go "upon his belly"? Nobody supposes that he walked upon the extremity of his tail.

This controversy about the supremacy of Jehovah, between the Presbyters and Fathers on the one hand, and the Gnostics, the Nazarenes, and all the sects declared heterodox as a last resort, on the other, lasted till the days of Constantine, and later. That the peculiar ideas of the Gnostics about the *genealogy* of Jehovah, or the proper place that had to be assigned, in the Christian-Gnostic Pantheon, to the God of the Jews, were at first deemed neither blasphemous nor heterodox is evident in the difference of opinions held on this question by Clement of Alexandria, for instance, and Tertullian. The former, who seems to have known of Basilides better than anybody else, saw nothing heterodox or blamable in the mystical and transcendental views of the new Reformer. "In his eyes," remarks the author of *The Gnostics*, speaking of Clement, "Basilides was not a heretic, *i.e.*, an innovator as regards the doctrines of the Christian Church, but a mere theosophic philosopher, who sought to express *ancient truths* under new forms, and perhaps to combine them with the new faith, the truth of which he could admit without necessarily renouncing the old; exactly as is the case with the learned Hindus of our day." †

Not so with Irenaeus and Tertullian.‡ The principal works of the latter *against the heretics* were written after his separation from the Catholic Church, when he had ranged himself among the zealous followers of Montanus; and teem with unfairness and bigoted prejudice.§ He has exaggerated every

---

\* Theodoret, *Haer. fabul.*, I, xiv; King, *The Gnostics*, etc., p. 32 [pp. 102-03 in 2nd ed.].

† King, *op. cit.*, p. 78 [p. 258 in 2nd ed.].

‡ Some persons hold that he was Bishop of Rome; others, of Carthage.

§ His polemical work addressed against the so-called orthodox Church — the Catholic — notwithstanding its bitterness and usual style of vituperation, is far more fair, consider-

Gnostic opinion to a monstrous absurdity, and his arguments are not based on coercive reasoning but simply on the blind stubbornness of a partisan fanatic. Discussing Basilides, the "pious, god-like, theosophic philosopher," as Clement of Alexandria thought him, Tertullian exclaims: "After this, Basilides, the *heretic*, broke loose.\* He asserted that there is a Supreme God, by name Abraxas, by whom Mind was created, whom the Greeks call *Nous*. From her emanated the Word; from the Word, Providence; from Providence, Virtue and Wisdom; from these two again, *Principalities*,† *Powers* and *Angels* were made; thence infinite productions and emissions of angels. Among the lowest angels, indeed, and those that made this world, he sets *last of all* the god of the Jews, whom he denies to be God himself, affirming that he is but one of the angels." ‡

It would be equally useless to refer to the direct apostles of Christ, and show them as holding in their controversies that Jesus never made any difference between his "Father" and the "Lord-God" of Moses. For the *Clementine Homilies*, in which occur the greatest argumentations upon the subject, as shown in the disputations alleged to have taken place between Peter and Simon the Magician, are now also proved to have been falsely attributed to Clement the Roman. This work, if written by an Ebionite — as the author of *Supernatural Religion* declares in common with some other commentators§ — must have been written either far later than the Pauline period, generally assigned to it, or the dispute about the identity of Jehovah with God, the

---

ing that the "great African" is said to have been expelled from the Church of Rome. If we believe St. Jerome, it is but the envy and the unmerited calumnies of the early Roman clergy against Tertullian which forced him to renounce the Catholic Church and become a Montanist. However, were the unlimited admiration of St. Cyprian, who terms Tertullian "The Master," and his estimate of him merited, we would see less error and paganism in the Church of Rome. The expression of Vincent of Lerius, "that every word of Tertullian was a sentence, and every sentence a triumph *over error*," does not seem very happy when we think of the respect paid to Tertullian by the Church of Rome, notwithstanding his partial apostasy and the *errors* in which the latter still abides and has even enforced upon the world as *infallible* dogmas.

\* Were not the views of the Phrygian Bishop Montanus also deemed a HERESY by the Church of Rome? It is quite extraordinary to see how easily the Vatican encourages the abuse of one *heretic*, Tertullian, against another *heretic*, Basilides, when the abuse happens to further her own object.

† Does not Paul himself speak of "*Principalities* and *Powers* in heavenly places" (*Ephesians* iii, 10; i, 21), and confess that there be *gods* many and *Lords* many (*Kurioi*)? And Angels, Powers (*Dunameis*), and *Principalities?* (See *1 Corinthians* viii, 5; and *Epistle to Romans* viii, 38.)

‡ Tertullian, *Liber de praescriptione haereticorum.*[28]

§ Baur; Credner; Hilgenfeld; Kirchhofer; Lechler; Nicolas; Reuss; Ritschl; Schwegler; Westcott, and Zeller; see *Supernatural Religion*, Vol. II, Pt. II, ch. v, p. 2.

"Father of Jesus," have been distorted by later interpolations. This disputation is in its very essence antagonistic to the early doctrines of the Ebionites. The latter, as demonstrated by Epiphanius and Theodoret, were the direct followers of the Nazarene sect * (the Sabians), the "Disciples of John." He says, unequivocally, that the Ebionites believed in the *Aeôns* (emanations), that the Nazarenes were *their instructors*, and that "each imparted to the other out of his own wickedness." Therefore, holding the same beliefs as the Nazarenes did, an Ebionite would not have given even so much chance to the doctrine supported by Peter in *Homilies*. The old Nazarenes, as well as the later ones, whose views are embodied in the *Codex Nazaraeus*, never called Jehovah otherwise than *Adonai, Iurbo*, the God of the *Abortive* † (the orthodox Jews). ‡ They kept their beliefs and religious tenets so *secret* that even Epiphanius, writing as early as the end of the fourth century,§ confesses his ignorance as to their real doctrine. "Dropping the name of Jesus," says the Bishop of Salamis, "they neither call themselves *Iessaeans*, nor continue to hold the name of the Jews, nor name themselves Christians, but *Nazarenes* . . . The resurrection of the dead is confessed by them . . . but concerning Christ, *I cannot say* whether they think him a *mere man*, or as the *truth is*, confess that he was born through the *Holy Pneuma* from the Virgin." ‖

While Simon Magus argues in the *Homilies* from the standpoint of every Gnostic (Nazarenes and Ebionites included), Peter, as a true apostle of circumcision, holds to the old Law, as a matter of course, seeks to blend his belief in the divinity of Christ with his old Faith in the "Lord God" and ex-protector of the "chosen people." As the author of *Supernatural Religion* shows the *Epitome*,¶ "a blending of the other two, probably intended to purge them from heretical doctrine" ** and, together with a great majority of critics, assigns to the *Homilies* a date not earlier than the end of the third century, we may well infer that they must differ widely with their original, if there ever was one. Simon the Magician proves throughout the whole work that

---

\* See Epiphanius, *Panarion*, lib. I, tom. II, Haer. XXX, ii.

† The Ophites, for instance, made of Adonai the third son of Ialdabaôth, a malignant genius, and, like his other five brothers, a constant enemy and adversary of man, whose divine and immortal spirit gave man the means of becoming the rival of these genii.

‡ [*Cod. Nazar.*, III, p. 73.]

§ The Bishop of Salamis died A.D. 403.

‖ *Panarion*, lib. I, tom. II, Haer. XXIX, vii.

¶ The "Clementines" are composed of three parts — to wit: the *Homilies*, the *Recognitions*, and an *Epitome*.

\*\* *Supern. Relig.*, Vol. II, Pt. II, ch. v, p. 2.

the Demiurgus, the Architect of the World, is not the highest Deity; and he bases his assertions upon the words of Jesus himself, who states repeatedly that "no man knew the Father." Peter is made in the *Homilies* to repudiate, with a great show of indignation, the assertion that the Patriarchs were not deemed worthy to know the Father; to which Simon objects again by quoting the words of Jesus, who thanks the "Lord of Heaven and earth that what was concealed from the wise" he has "revealed to babes," proving very logically, that according to these very words, the Patriarchs could not have known the "Father." Then Peter argues, in his turn, that the expression, "what was *concealed from the wise*," etc., referred to the concealed *mysteries* of the creation.\*

This argumentation of Peter, therefore, had it even emanated from the apostle himself, instead of being a "religious romance," as the author of *Supernatural Religion* calls it, would prove nothing whatever in favor of the identity of the God of the Jews with the "Father" of Jesus. At best it would only demonstrate that Peter had remained from first to last "an apostle of circumcision," a Jew faithful to his old law, and a defender of the *Old Testament*. This conversation proves, moreover, the weakness of the cause he defends, for we see in the apostle a man who, although in most intimate relations with Jesus, can furnish us nothing in the way of direct proof that he ever thought of teaching that the all-wise and all-good Paternity he preached was the morose and revengeful thunderer of Mount Sinai. But what the *Homilies* do prove, is again our assertion that there was a secret doctrine preached by Jesus to the few who were deemed worthy to become its recipients and custodians. "And Peter said: We remember that our Lord and teacher, as commanding, said to us: 'Guard the mysteries for me, and the sons of my house.' Wherefore also he explained to his disciples, *privately* the *mysteries of the kingdom of the heavens*." †

If we now recall the fact that a portion of the Mysteries of the "Pagans" consisted of the ἀπόρρητα, *aporrheta*, or secret discourses; that the secret *Logia* or discourses of Jesus contained in the original *Gospel according to Matthew*, the meaning and interpretation of which St. Jerome confessed to be "a difficult task" for him to achieve, were of the same nature; and if we remember, further, that to some of the interior or final Mysteries only a very select few were admitted; and that, finally, it was from the number of the latter that were taken all the ministers of the holy "Pagan" rites, we will then clearly understand this expression of Jesus quoted by Peter: "Guard *the Mysteries for me, and the sons of my house*,"

---

\* *Clementine Homilies*, XVIII, i-xv. Cf. *Supern. Rel.*, Vol. II, p. 12.
† *Ibid.*, XIX, xx. Cf. *Supern. Rel.*, Vol. II, pp. 26-27.

*i.e.*, of my doctrine. And, if we understand it rightly, we cannot avoid thinking that this "secret" doctrine of Jesus, even the technical expressions of which are but so many duplications of the Gnostic and Neo-Platonic mystic phraseology — that this doctrine, we say, was based on the same transcendental philosophy of Oriental *Gnosis* as the rest of the religions of those and earlier days. That none of the later Christian sects, despite their boasting, were the inheritors of it, is evident from the contradictions, blunders, and clumsy repatching of the mistakes of every preceding century by the discoveries of the succeeding one. These mistakes, in a number of manuscripts claimed to be authentic, are sometimes so ridiculous as to bear on their face the evidence of being pious forgeries. Thus, for instance, the utter ignorance of some patristic champions of the very gospels they claimed to defend. We have mentioned the accusation against Marcion by Tertullian and Epiphanius of mutilating the *Gospel* ascribed to Luke, and erasing from it that which is now proved to have never been in that Gospel at all. Finally, the method adopted by Jesus of speaking in parables, in which he only followed the example of his sect, is attributed in the *Homilies* * to a prophecy of *Isaiah!* Peter is made to remark: "For Isaiah said: 'I will open my mouth in a parable: I will utter things that have been kept secret from the foundation of the world'." This erroneous reference to Isaiah of a sentence given in *Psalms* lxxviii, 2, is found not only in the apocryphal *Homilies*, but also in the Sinaitic *Codex*.[29] Commenting on the fact in the *Supernatural Religion*, the author states that "Porphyry, in the third century, twitted Christians with this erroneous ascription by their inspired evangelist to Isaiah of a passage from a *Psalm*, and reduced the Fathers to great straits." † Eusebius and Jerome tried to get out of the difficulty by ascribing the mistake to an "ignorant scribe"; and Jerome even went to the length of asserting that the name of Isaiah never stood after the above sentence in any of the old codices, but that the name of Asaph was found in its place, only *"ignorant* men had removed it." ‡ To this, the author again observes that "the fact is, that the reading 'Asaph' for 'Isaiah' is not found in any extant MS., and, although 'Isaiah' has *disappeared* from all but a few obscure codices, it cannot be denied that the name anciently stood in the text. In the Sinaitic *Codex*, which is probably the earliest manuscript extant, and which is assigned to the fourth century," he adds, "the prophet *Isaiah* stands in the text by the first hand, *but is erased* by the second."§

It is a most suggestive fact that there is not a word in the so-called

---

* *Clem. Homilies*, XVIII, xv. [Cf. *Matt.* xiii, 35.]

† *Supern. Relig.*, Vol. II, Part II, ch. v, p. 11.

‡ Jerome, *Opera*, Basileae, 1565, Vol. 8, p. 109.

§ *Supern Relig.*, loc. cit.

## HE NEVER CLAIMED TO BE GOD

sacred *Scriptures* to show that Jesus was actually regarded as a God by his disciples. Neither before nor after his death did they pay him divine honors. Their relation to him was only that of disciples and "master"; by which name [κύριος] they addressed him, as the followers of Pythagoras and Plato addressed their respective masters before them. Whatever words may have been put into the mouths of Jesus, Peter, Paul and others, there is not a single act of adoration recorded on their part, nor did Jesus, himself, ever declare his identity with *his Father*.30 He accused the Pharisees of *stoning* their prophets, not of deicide. He termed himself the son of God, but took care to assert repeatedly that they were all the children of God, who was the Heavenly Father of all. In preaching this, he but repeated a doctrine taught ages earlier by Hermes, Plato, and other philosophers. Strange contradiction! Jesus, whom we are asked to worship as the one living God, is found, immediately after his Resurrection, saying to Mary Magdalene: "I am not yet ascended *to my Father*: but go to my brethren, and say unto them, I ascend unto *my Father*, and *your* Father; and to *my* God, and *your* God!" (*John* xx, 17.)

Does this look like identifying himself with his Father? "*My* Father and *your* Father, *my* God and *your* God," implies, on his part, a desire to be considered on a perfect equality with his brethren — nothing more. Theodoret writes: "The heretics agree with us respecting the beginning of all things . . . But they say there is not one Christ (God), but one above, and the other below. And this last *formerly dwelt in many*; but *the Jesus*, they at one time say is *from* God, at another they call him a SPIRIT." * This spirit is the Christos, the *messenger* of life, who is sometimes called the Angel *Gabriel* (in Hebrew, the mighty one of God), and who took with the Gnostics the place of the Logos, while the Holy Spirit was considered *Life*.† With the sect of the Nazarenes, though, the Spiritus, or Holy Ghost, had less honor. While nearly every Gnostic sect considered it a Female Power, whether they called it *Binah*, בינה, [or] *Sophia*, the Divine intellect; with the Nazarene sect it was the *Female Spiritus*, the astral light, the genetrix of all things of *matter*, the chaos in its evil aspect, made *turbid* by the Demiurge. At the creation of man, "it becomes light on the side of the FATHER, and it was light [material light] on the side of the MOTHER. And this is the '*two-fold man*'," says the *Zohar*.‡ "That day [the last one] will perish the seven badly-disposed stellars, also the sons of man, who have confessed the *Spiritus*, the Messias [false], the Deus, and the MOTHER of the SPIRITUS shall perish." §

---

* Theodoret, *Haer. fabul.*, II, vii.
† See Irenaeus, *Adv. Haer.*, I, xii, 4; I, xv, 3.
‡ *Auszüge aus dem Buche Sohar*, p. 15; Berlin, 1857.
§ *Cod. Nazar.*, II, pp. 147-49.

Jesus enforced and illustrated his doctrines with signs and wonders; and if we lay aside the claims advanced on his behalf by his deifiers, he did but what other kabalists did; and *only they* at that epoch, when, for two centuries the sources of prophecy had been completely dried up, and from this stagnation of public "miracles" had originated the skepticism of the unbelieving sect of the Sadducees. Describing the "heresies" of those days, Theodoret, who has no idea of the hidden meaning of the word Christos, the *anointed* messenger, complains that they (the Gnostics) assert *that this Messenger or Delegatus changes his body from time to time, "and goes into other bodies, and at each time is differently manifested.* And these [the overshadowed prophets] use incantations and invocations of various demons and baptisms in the confession of their principles . . . They embrace astrology and magic, and the mathematical error,"(?) he says.\*

This "mathematical error," of which the pious writer complains, led subsequently to the rediscovery of the heliocentric system, erroneous as it may still be, and forgotten since the days of another "magician" who taught it — Pythagoras. Thus, the wonders of healing and the *thaums* of Jesus, which he imparted to his followers, show that they were learning, in their daily communication with him, the theory and practice of the new ethics, day by day, and in the familiar intercourse of intimate friendship. Their faith was progressively developed, like that of all neophytes, simultaneously with the increase of knowledge. We must bear in mind that Josephus, who certainly must have been well-informed on the subject, calls the skill of expelling demons "a science." This growth of faith is conspicuously shown in the case of Peter, who, from having lacked enough faith to support him while he could walk on the water from the boat to his Master, at last became so expert a thaumaturgist, that Simon Magus is said to have offered him money to teach him the secret of healing, and other wonders. And Philip is shown to have become an Aethrobat as good as Abaris of Pythagorean memory, but less expert than Simon Magus.

Neither in the *Homilies* nor any other early work of the apostles, is there anything to show that any of his friends and followers regarded Jesus as anything more than a prophet. The idea is as clearly established in the *Clementines*. Except that too much room is afforded to Peter to establish the identity of the Mosaic God with the Father of Jesus, the whole work is devoted to Monotheism. The author seems as bitter against Polytheism as against the claim to the divinity of Christ.† He seems

---

\* Theodoret, *Haer. fabul.*, II, vii.

† *Clem. Homilies*, II, xii; III, lvii, lix; X, xix; XVI, xv *et seq.*; Schliemann, *Die Clementinen*, pp. 130, 134 *et seq.*, 144 *et seq.* Cf. *Supern. Relig.*, Vol. II, p. 347.

## THE SOURCE OF CHRIST'S INSPIRATION 195

to be utterly ignorant of the Logos, and his speculation is confined to Sophia, the Gnostic wisdom. There is no trace in it of a hypostatic trinity, but the same overshadowing of the Gnostic wisdom (Christos and Sophia) is attributed in the case of Jesus as it is in those of Adam, Enoch, Noah, Abraham, Isaac, Jacob and Moses.* These personages are all placed on one level, and called "true prophets," and the seven pillars of the world. More than that, Peter vehemently denies the fall of Adam, and with him the doctrine of atonement, as taught by Christian theology, utterly falls to the ground, *for he combats it as a blasphemy.*† Peter's theory of sin is that of the Jewish kabalists, and even, in a certain way, Platonic. Adam not only never sinned, but, "as a true prophet possessed of the Spirit of God which afterwards was in Jesus, *could not* sin."‡ In short, the whole of the work exhibits the belief of the author in the kabalistic doctrine of permutation. The *Kabala* teaches the doctrine of transmigration of the spirit. § "Mosah is the *revolutio* of Seth and Hebel." ||

"Tell me who it is who brings about the *rebirth* (the *revolutio*)?" is asked of the wise Hermes. "God's Son, the *only man*, through the will of God," is the answer of the "heathen." ¶

"God's son" is the immortal spirit assigned to every human being. It is this divine entity which is the *"only man,"* for the casket which contains our soul, and the soul itself, are but half-entities, and without its overshadowing both body and astral soul, the two are but an animal *duad*. It requires a trinity to form the complete "man," and allow him to remain immortal at every "rebirth," or *revolutio*, throughout the subsequent and ascending spheres, every one of which brings him nearer to the refulgent realm of eternal and *absolute* light.

"God's FIRST-BORN, who is the 'holy Veil', the 'Light of Lights', it is he who sends the *revolutio* of the Delegatus, for he is the *First Power*," says the kabalist.**

"The *pneuma* [spirit] and the *dunamis* (power), which is from the God, it is right to consider nothing else than the *Logos*, who is *also* [?] First-begotten to the God," argues a Christian.††

"Angels and powers are in heaven!" says Justin,‡‡ thus bringing forth a purely kabalistic doctrine. The Christians adopted it from the

---

\* *Clem. Homilies*, II, xvi-xviii; III, xx *et seq.*
† *Ibid.*, III, xx, xxi.
‡ A. Schliemann, *Die Clementinen*, etc., pp. 130, 176 *et seq.* Cf. *Supern. Relig.*, Vol. II, p. 342.
§ We will speak of this doctrine further on.
|| Rosenroth, *Kabbala denudata*, II, p. 155.
¶ [L. Ménard, *Hermès Trismégiste*, Paris, 1867, p. 96.]
** [Kleucker, *Natur und Ursprung der Emanationslehre b.d. Kabbalisten*, pp. 10-11.]
†† Justin Martyr, *First Apology*, xxxiii.
‡‡ [*Dialogue with Trypho*, cxxviii.]

*Zohar* and the heretical sects, and if Jesus mentioned them, it was not in the official synagogues that he learned the theory, but directly in the kabalistic teachings. In the Mosaic books, very little mention is made of them, and Moses, who holds direct communications with the "Lord God," troubles himself very little about them. The doctrine was a secret one, and deemed by the orthodox synagogue heretical. Josephus calls the Essenes heretics, saying: "Those admitted among the Essenes must swear to communicate their doctrines to no one otherwise *than as he received them himself*, and equally to preserve the books *belonging to their sect*, and the *names of the angels*." \*
The Sadducees did not believe in angels, neither did the uninitiated Gentiles, who limited their Olympus to gods and demi-gods, or "spirits." Alone, the kabalists and theurgists hold to that doctrine from time immemorial, and, as a consequence, Plato, and Philo Judaeus after him, followed first by the Gnostics, and then by the Christians.

Thus, if Josephus never wrote the famous interpolation forged by Eusebius, concerning Jesus, on the other hand, he has described in the Essenes all the principal features that we find prominent in the Nazarenes. When praying, they sought solitude.† "When thou prayest, enter into thy closet . . . and pray to thy Father which is in secret" (*Matthew* vi, 6). "Everything spoken by them [Essenes] is stronger than an oath. Swearing is shunned by them." ‡ "But I say unto you, swear not at all . . . but let your communication be yea, yea; nay, nay" (*Matthew* v, 34-37).

The Nazarenes, as well as the Essenes and the Therapeutae, believed more in their own interpretation of the "hidden sense" of the more ancient Scriptures, than in the later laws of Moses. Jesus, as we have shown before, felt but little veneration for the commandments of his predecessor, with whom Irenaeus is so anxious to connect him.

The Essenes "enter into the houses of *those whom they never saw previously*, as if they were their intimate friends."§ Such was undeniably the custom of Jesus and his disciples.

Epiphanius, who places the Ebionite "heresy" on one level with that of the Nazarenes, also remarks that the Nazaraioi come next to the Cerinthians,‖ so much vituperated against by Irenaeus.¶

---

\* Josephus, *Jewish War*, II, viii, 7.

† *Ibid.*, II, viii; Philo Judaeus, *De vita contempl.* and *Quod omnis prob. lib.*, §12; *Fragm.* in Eusebius, *Praep. evang.*, VIII, viii; Munk, *Palestine,* pp. 35, 525, etc. Eusebius mentions their *semneion*, where they perform the mysteries of a retired life (*Eccles. Hist.*, lib. II, ch. xvii).

‡ Josephus, *Jewish War*, II, viii, 6.

§ *Ibid.*, II, viii, 4.

‖ *Panarion*, lib. I, tom. II, Haer. XXIX, i; XXX, i.

¶ Cerinthus is the same Gnostic — a contemporary of John the Evangelist — of whom Irenaeus invented the following anecdote: "There are those who heard him [Polycarp] say that John, the disciple of the Lord, going to bathe at Ephesus, and perceiving Cerinthus

Munk, in his work on *Palestine*, affirms that there were 4,000 Essenes living in the desert; that they had their mystical books, and predicted the future.* The Nabathaeans, with very little difference indeed, adhered to the same belief as the Nazarenes and the Sabians, and all of them honored John the Baptist more than his successor Jesus. The Persian Yezîdis say that they originally came to Syria from Basrah. They use baptism, and believe in seven archangels, though paying at the same time reverence to Satan. Their prophet Yezîd, who flourished long prior to Mohammed,† taught that God will send a messenger, and that the latter would reveal to him a book which is already written in heaven from the eternity.‡ The Nabathaeans inhabited the Lebanon, as their descendants do to the present day, and their religion was from its origin purely kabalistic. Maimonides speaks of them as if he identified them with the Sabians. "I will mention to thee the writings . . . respecting the belief and institutions of the *Sabaeans*," he says. "The most renowned is the book *The Agriculture of the Nabathaeans* which has been translated by Ibn al-Wahshîya. This book is full of heathenish nonsense . . . It speaks of the preparations of TALISMANS, the drawing down of the powers of the SPIRITS, MAGIC, DEMONS, and ghouls, which make their abode in the desert." §

There are traditions among the tribes living scattered about *beyond* the Jordan, as there are many such also among the descendants of the Samaritans at Damascus, Gaza, and at Nablus (the ancient Shechem). Many of these tribes have, notwithstanding the persecutions of eighteen centuries, retained the faith of their fathers in its primitive simplicity. It is there that we have to go for traditions based on *historical* truths, however disfigured by exaggeration and inaccuracy, and compare them with the religious legends of the Fathers, which they call revelation. Eusebius states that before the siege of Jerusalem the small Christian community — comprising members of whom many, if not all, knew Jesus and his apostles personally — took refuge in the little town of Pella, on the opposite shore of the Jordan.‖ Surely these simple people, separated for centuries from the rest of the world, ought to have preserved their traditions fresher than any other nation! It is in Palestine that we have to search for the *clearest* waters of Christianity, let alone its source. The first Christians, after the death of Jesus, all joined together for a time, whether

---

within, rushed forth from the bathhouse . . . crying out, 'Let us fly, lest the bathhouse fall down, Cerinthus, the enemy of the truth, being within it' " (Irenaeus, *Adv. Haer.*, III, iii, 4).
  * Munk, *Palestine*, pp. 517, 525; Dunlap, *Sōd, the Son of the Man.*
  † Haxthausen, *Transcaucasia*, etc., p. 229; ed. 1854.
  ‡ Shahrastânî, quoted by Dr. D. Chwolsohn, *Die Ssabier und der Ssabismus*, II, p. 625.
  § Maimonides, *Moreh Nebûkhim*, quoted by Chwolsohn, *op. cit.*, II, p. 458.
  ‖ [*Eccles. Hist.*, III, v.]

they were Ebionites, Nazarenes, Gnostics, or others. They had no Christian dogmas in those days, and their Christianity consisted in believing Jesus to be a prophet, this belief varying from seeing in him simply a "just" man,* or a holy, inspired prophet, a vehicle used by Christos and Sophia to manifest themselves through. These all united together in opposition to the synagogue and the tyrannical technicalities of the Pharisees, until the primitive group separated into two distinct branches — which we may correctly term the Christian kabalists of the Jewish Tannaim school, and the Christian kabalists of the Platonic Gnosis.† The former were represented by the party composed of the followers of Peter, and John, the author of the *Apocalypse*; the latter ranged with the Pauline Christianity, blending itself, at the end of the second century, with the Platonic philosophy, and engulfing, still later, the Gnostic sects, whose symbols and misunderstood mysticism overflowed the Church of Rome.

Amid this jumble of contradictions, what Christian is secure in confessing himself such? In the old Syriac *Gospel according to Luke* (iii, 22), the Holy Spirit is said to have descended in the likeness of a dove. "Iesua full of the sacred Spirit returned from Iurdan, and the Spirit led him into the desert" (old Syriac, *Luke* iv, 1, Tremellius). "The difficulty," says Dunlap, "was that the Gospels declared that John, a Baptist, saw the Spirit (the Power of God) descend upon Iesus after he had reached manhood; and if the Spirit then first descended upon him, there was some ground for the opinion of the Ebionites and Nazarenes who denied his *preceding* existence and refused him the attributes of the LOGOS. The Gnostics, on the other hand, objected to the flesh, but conceded the LOGOS." ‡

John's *Apocalypsis*, and the explanations of sincere Christian bishops, like Synesius, who, to the last, adhered to the Platonic doctrines, make us think that the wisest and safest way is to hold to that sincere primitive faith which seems to have actuated the above-named bishop. This best, sincerest, and most unfortunate of Christians, addressing the "Unknown," exclaims: "Oh Father of the Worlds . . . Father of the Aeôns . . . *Artificer of the Gods*, it is holy to praise!" ‖ But Synesius had Hypatia for instructor, and this is why we find him confessing in all sincerity his opinions and profession of faith. "The rabble desires nothing better

---

\* "Ye have condemned and killed the just," says James in his epistle to the twelve tribes [v, 6].

† Porphyry makes a distinction between what he calls "the *Antique* or *Oriental philosophy*," and the properly Grecian system, that of the Neo-Platonists. King says that all these religions and systems are branches of one antique and common religion, the Asiatic or Buddhistic (*Gnostics and their Remains*, p. 1).

‡ *Sōd, the Son of the Man*, p. 23.

‖ [Hymn III. Cf. H. Druon, *Œuvres de Synésius*, Paris, 1878.]

than to be deceived. . . . As regards myself, therefore, *I will always be a philosopher with myself*, but I *must be priest* with the people." *

"Holy is God the Father of all being, holy is God, whose wisdom is carried out into execution by his own Powers! . . . Holy art Thou, who through the Word had created all! Therefore, I believe in Thee, and bear testimony, and go into the LIFE and LIGHT." † Thus speaks Hermes Trismegistus, the heathen divine. What Christian bishop could have said better than that?

The apparent discrepancy of the four gospels as a whole, does not prevent every narrative given in the *New Testament* — however much disfigured — having a groundwork of truth. To this are cunningly adapted details made to fit the later exigencies of the Church. So, propped up partially by indirect evidence, still more by blind faith, they have become, with time, articles of faith. Even the fictitious massacre of the "Innocents" by King Herod has a certain foundation to it, in its allegorical sense. Apart from the now-discovered fact that the whole story of such a massacre of the Innocents is bodily taken from the Hindu *Bhâgavata-Purâna*, and Brahmanical traditions, the legend refers, moreover, allegorically, to an historical fact. King Herod is the type of Kansa, the tyrant of Mathurâ, the maternal uncle of Krishna, to whom astrologers predicted that a son of his niece Devakî would deprive him of his throne. Therefore he gives orders to kill the male child that is born to her; but Krishna escapes his fury through the protection of Mahâdeva (the great God) who causes the child to be carried away to another city, out of Kansa's reach. After that, in order to be sure and kill the right boy, on whom he failed to lay his murderous hands, Kansa has all the male newborn infants within his kingdom killed. Krishna is also worshipped by the *gopas* (the shepherds) of the land.

Though this ancient Indian legend bears a very suspicious resemblance to the modern Biblical romance, Gaffarel and others attribute the origin of the latter to the persecutions during the Herodian reign of the kabalists and the *wise men*, who had not remained strictly orthodox. The latter, as well as the prophets, were nicknamed the "Innocents," and the "Babes," on account of their holiness. As in the case of certain degrees of modern Masonry, the adepts reckoned their grade in initiation by a *symbolic* age. Thus Saul who, when chosen king, was "a choice and goodly man," and "from his shoulders upward was higher than any of the people," is described in Catholic versions, as "child of *one year* when he began to reign," which, in its literal sense, is a palpable

---

* [Letter to his brother, A.D. 409.]

† [L. Ménard, *Hermès Trismégiste*, Paris, 1867, pp. 15-16.]

absurdity. But in *1 Samuel* x, his anointing by Samuel and initiation are described; and at verse 6th, Samuel uses this significant language: ". . . the Spirit of the Lord will come upon thee and thou shalt prophesy with them, *and shalt be turned into another man.*" The phrase above quoted is thus made plain — he had received one degree of initiation and was symbolically described as "a child one year old." The Catholic *Bible*, from which the text is quoted, with charming candor says in a footnote: "It is extremely difficult to explain" (meaning that Saul was a child of one year). But undaunted by any difficulty, the Editor, nevertheless, does take upon himself to explain it, and adds: *"A child of one year. That is, he was good and like an innocent child."* An interpretation as ingenious as it is pious; and which if it does no good can certainly do no harm.*

If the explanation of the kabalists is rejected, then the whole subject falls into confusion; worse still — for it becomes a direct plagiarism from the Hindu legend. All the commentators have agreed that a literal massacre of young children is nowhere mentioned in history; and that, moreover, an occurrence like that would have made such a bloody page in Roman annals that the record of it would have been preserved for us by every author of the day. Herod himself was subject to the Roman law; and undoubtedly he would have paid the penalty of such a monstrous crime with his own life. But if, on the one hand, we have not the slightest trace of this fable in history, on the other, we find in the

---

\* It is the correct interpretation of the Bible allegories that makes the Catholic clergy so wrathful with the Protestants who freely scrutinize the Bible. How bitter this feeling has become, we can judge by the following words of the Reverend Father Parker of Hyde Park, New York, who, lecturing in St. Teresa's Catholic Church, on the 10th of December, 1876, said: "To whom does the Protestant Church owe its possession of the Bible, *which they wish to place in the hands of every ignorant person and child?* To monkish hands, that laboriously transcribed it before the age of printing. Protestantism has produced dissension in Church, rebellions and outbreaks in State, unsoundness in social life, and will never be satisfied short of the downfall of the Bible! Protestants must admit that the Roman Church has done more to scatter Christianity and extirpate idolatry than all their sects. From one pulpit it is said that there is no hell, and from another that there is immediate and unmitigated damnation. One says that Jesus Christ was only a man; another that you must be plunged bodily into water to be baptized, and refuses the rites to infants. Most of them have no prescribed form of worship, no sacred vestments, and their doctrines are as undefined as their service is informal. The founder of Protestantism, Martin Luther, was the worst man in Europe. The advent of the Reformation was the signal for civil war, and from that time to this the world has been in a restless state, uneasy in regard to Governments, and every day becoming more skeptical. The ultimate tendency of Protestantism is clearly nothing less than the destruction of all respect for the Bible, and the disruption of government and society." Very plain talk this. The Protestants might easily return the compliment.

official complaints of the Synagogue abundant evidence of the persecution of the initiates. The *Talmud* also corroborates it.

The Jewish version of the birth of Jesus is recorded in the *Sepher-Toledoth-Yeshu* in the following words:

"Mary having become the mother of a Son, named *Yehôshûah*, and the boy growing up, she entrusted him to the care of the Rabbi Elḥânân, and the child progressed in knowledge, for he was well gifted with spirit and understanding. Rabbi Yehôshûah, son of Peraḥiah, continued the education of Yehôshûah (Jesus) after Elḥânân, and *initiated* him in the *secret* knowledge; but the King, Jannaeus, having given orders to slay all the initiates, Yehôshûah Ben-Peraḥiah, fled to Alexandria, in Egypt, taking the boy with him."

While in Alexandria, continues the story, they were received in the house of a rich and learned lady (personified Egypt). Young Jesus found her beautiful, notwithstanding "*a defect in her eyes*," and declared so to his master. Upon hearing this, the latter became so angry that his pupil should find in the land of bondage anything good, that "he cursed him and drove the young man from his presence." Then follow a series of adventures told in allegorical language, which show that Jesus supplemented his initiation in the Jewish *Kabala* with an additional acquisition of the secret wisdom of Egypt. When the persecution ceased, they both returned to Judaea." *

The real grievances against Jesus are stated by the learned author of *Tela Ignea Satanae* (the fiery darts of Satan) to be two in number: 1st, that he had discovered the great Mysteries of their Temple, by having been initiated in Egypt; and 2nd, that he had profaned them by exposing them to the vulgar, who misunderstood and disfigured them. This is what he says:†

"There exists, in the sanctuary of the living God, a cubical stone, on which are sculptured the holy characters, the combination of which gives the explanation of the attributes and powers of the incommunicable name. This explanation is the secret key of all the occult sciences and forces in nature. It is what the Hebrew call the *Shem ha-Mephorash*. This stone is watched by two lions of gold, who roar as soon as it is approached.‡ The gates of the temple were never lost sight of, and the

---

* Babylonian *Talmud, Mishnah Sanhedrin,* ch. xi, fol. 107b, and *Mishnah Sotah,* ch. ix, fol. 47a. See also Éliphas Lévi, *La Science des esprits.*

† This fragment is translated from the original Hebrew [in the *Toledoth-Yeshu*] by Éliphas Lévi in his *La Science des esprits,* pp. 32-33.

‡ Those who know anything of the rites of the Hebrews must recognize in these lions the gigantic figures of the Cherubim, whose symbolical monstrosity was well calculated to frighten and put to flight the profane.

door of the sanctuary opened but once a year, to admit the High Priest alone. But Jesus, who had learned in Egypt the 'great secrets' at the initiation, forged for himself invisible keys, and thus was enabled to penetrate into the sanctuary unseen. . . . He copied the characters on the cubical stone, and hid them in his thigh;* after which, emerging from the temple, he went abroad and began astounding people with his miracles. The dead were raised at his command, the leprous and the obsessed were healed. He forced the stones which lay buried for ages at the bottom of the sea to rise to the surface until they formed a mountain, from the top of which he preached." The *Sepher-Toledoth* states further that, *unable to displace* the cubical stone of the sanctuary, Jesus fabricated one of clay, which he showed to the nations and passed it off for the true cubical stone of Israel.

This allegory, like the rest of them in such books, is written "*inside and outside*" — it has its secret meaning, and ought to be read two ways. The kabalistic books explain its mystical meaning. Further, the same Talmudist says, in substance, the following: Jesus was thrown in prison, and kept there forty days; then flogged as a seditious rebel; then stoned as a blasphemer in a place called Lud, and finally allowed to expire upon a cross. "All this," explains Lévi, "because he revealed to the people the truths which they [the Pharisees] wished to bury for their own use. He had divined the occult theology of Israel, had compared it with the wisdom of Egypt, and found thereby the reason for a universal religious synthesis." †

However cautious one ought to be in accepting anything about Jesus from Jewish sources, it must be confessed that in some things they seem to be more correct in their statements (whenever their direct interests in stating facts is not concerned) than our good but too jealous Fathers. One thing is certain, James, the "Brother of the Lord," is silent about the *resurrection*. He terms Jesus nowhere "Son of God," nor even Christ-God. Once only, speaking of Jesus, he calls him the "Lord of Glory," but so do the Nazarenes when writing about their prophet *Yôhânân bar Zachariah,* or John, son of Zacharias (St. John the Baptist). Their favorite expressions about their prophet are the same as those used by James when speaking of Jesus. A man "of the seed of a man," "Messenger of Life," of light, "my Lord Apostle," "King sprung of Light," and so on. "Have not the faith of our *Lord* JESUS Christ, *the Lord of Glory*," etc.,

---

* Arnobius tells the same story of Jesus, and narrates how he was accused of having robbed the sanctuary of the secret names of the Holy One, by means of which knowledge he performed all the miracles. — *Adv. gent.,* I, § 43.

† *La Science des esprits,* pp. 33-34.

says *James* in his epistle (ii, 1), presumably addressing Christ as GOD. "Peace to thee, my *Lord* JOHN Abo Sabo, Lord of Glory!" says the *Codex Nazaraeus* (II, 19), known to address but a prophet. "Ye have condemned and killed the *Just*," says *James* (v, 6). "Yôḥânân (John) is the *Just* one, he comes in the way of *justice*," says *Matthew* (xxi, 32, Syriac text).

James does not even call Jesus *Messiah,* in the sense given to the title by the Christians, but alludes to the kabalistic "King Messiah," who is Lord Tsabaôth \* (v, 4), and repeats several times that the "Lord" will come, but identifies the latter nowhere with Jesus. "Be patient therefore, brethren, unto the coming of the Lord . . . be patient, for the coming of the Lord *draweth nigh*" (v, 7, 8). And he adds: "Take, my brethren, the prophet [Jesus] *who has spoken in the name of the Lord* for an example of suffering, affliction, and of patience." Though in the present version the word "prophet" stands in the plural, yet this is a deliberate falsification of the original, the purpose of which is too evident. James, immediately after having cited the "prophets" as an example, adds: "Behold . . . ye have *heard* of the patience of Job, and *have seen the end* of the Lord" — thus combining the examples of these two admirable characters, and placing them on a perfect equality. But we have more to adduce in support of our argument. Did not Jesus himself glorify the prophet of the Jordan? "But what went ye out for to see? A prophet? Yea, I say unto you, and much more than a prophet. . . . For I say unto you, among those that are born *of women* there is not a greater prophet than John the Baptist." †

And of whom was he who spoke thus born? It is but the Roman Catholics who have changed Mary, the mother of Jesus, into a *goddess*. In the eyes of all other Christians she was a woman, whether his own birth was immaculate or otherwise. According to strict logic, then, Jesus confessed John *greater* than himself. Note how completely this matter is disposed of by the language employed by the Angel Gabriel when addressing Mary: "Blessed art thou among *women*." These words are unequivocal. He does not adore her as the Mother of God, nor does he call her *goddess;* he does not even address her as "Virgin," but he calls her *woman,* and only distinguishes her above other women as having had better fortune, through her purity.

The Nazarenes were known as Baptists, Sabians, and John's Christians [Mandaeans]. Their belief was that the Messiah was not the Son of God, but simply a prophet who would follow John. "Yôḥânân, the Son of the Abo Sabo Zachariah, shall say to himself, 'Whoever shall put faith in my *justice*

---

\* I. M. Jost, *The Israelite Indeed*, Vol. III, p. 61.

† [*Luke* vii, 26-28.]

and my BAPTISM shall be joined to my association and shall dwell with me in the seat which was the abode of life, of the supreme Mano, and of living fire," (*Codex Nazaraeus*, II, p. 115). Origen remarks "there are some who said of John [the Baptist] that he was the *anointed*" (Christos).* The Angel Rasiel of the kabalists is the Angel *Gabriel* of the Nazarenes, and it is the latter who is chosen of all the celestial hierarchy by the Christians to become the messenger of the "annunciation." The genius sent by the "Lord of Celsitude" is Hibil-Ziwa, whose name is also called GABRIEL Legatus.† Paul must have had the sect of the Nazarenes in mind when he said: "And last of all he [Jesus] was seen of me also, as *of one born out of due time*" (*1 Corinth*. xv, 8), thus reminding his listeners of the expression usual to the Nazarenes, who termed the Jews "the abortions, or born out of time." Paul prides himself of belonging to a heresy. ‡

When the metaphysical conceptions of the Gnostics, who saw in Jesus the Logos and the anointed, began to gain ground, the earliest Christians separated from the Nazarenes, who accused Jesus of perverting the doctrines of John, and changing the baptism of the Jordan. § "Directly," says Milman, "as it (the Gospel) got *beyond* the borders of Palestine and the name of 'Christ' had acquired sanctity and veneration in the Eastern cities, he became a kind of *metaphysical impersonation*, while the religion lost its purely moral cast and assumed the character of a *speculative theogony*."‖ The only half-original document that has reached us from the primitive apostolic days, is the *Logia* of Matthew. The real, genuine doctrine has remained in the hands of the Nazarenes, in this *Gospel of Matthew* containing the "secret doctrine," the "Sayings of Jesus," mentioned by Papias. These sayings were, no doubt, of the same nature as the small manuscripts placed in the hands of the neophytes, who were candidates for the Initiations into the Mysteries, and which contained the *aporrheta*, the revelations of some important rites and symbols. For why should Matthew take such precautions to make them "*secret*" were it otherwise?

Primitive Christianity had its grip, passwords, and degrees of initiation. The innumerable Gnostic gems and amulets are weighty proofs of it. It is a whole symbolical science. The kabalists were the first to embellish the universal Logos,¶ with such terms as "Light of Light," the Messenger of

---

\* Origen, *In Lucam Homiliae*, Hom. xxiv, cap. iii.
† *Codex Nazar.*, I, p. 23.
‡ "After the way which they call heresy, so worship I the God of my fathers" (*Acts* xxiv, 14).
§ *Codex Nazar.*, II, p. 109.
‖ *Hist. of Christianity*, p. 200; or. ed., 1840.
¶ Dunlap says in *Sōd, the Son of the Man* (p. 39, footnote): "Mr. Hall, of India, informs us that he has seen Sanskrit philosophical treatises in which the *Logos* continually occurs."

Life and Light,* and we find these expressions adopted *in toto* by the Christians, with the addition of nearly all the Gnostic terms such as Pleroma (fullness), Archons, Aeôns, etc. As to the "First-Born," the First, and the "Only-Begotten," these are as old as the world. Hippolytus shows the word "Logos" as existing among the Brahmans. "The *Brahmans* say that the God is *Light*, not such as one sees, nor such as the sun and fire; but they have the *God* Logos, not the articulate, but the Logos of the Gnosis, through whom the hidden mysteries of the Gnosis are seen by the wise." † The *Acts* and the fourth *Gospel* teem with Gnostic expressions. The kabalistic: "God's first-born emanated from the Most High," together with *that which is the "Spirit of the Anointing"*; and again "they called him the anointed of the Highest," ‡ are reproduced in Spirit and substance by the author of the *Gospel according to John*. "That was *the true light*," and "the light shineth in darkness." "And the word *was made flesh*." "And of his *fullness* [pleroma] have all we received," etc. (*John* i).

The "Christ," then, and the "Logos" existed ages before Christianity; the Oriental Gnosis was studied long before the days of Moses, and we have to seek for the origin of all these in the archaic periods of the primeval Asiatic philosophy. Peter's second *Epistle* and Jude's fragment, preserved in the *New Testament*, show by their phraseology that they belong to the kabalistic Oriental Gnosis, for they use the same expressions as did the Christian Gnostics who built a part of their system from the Oriental *Kabala*. "Presumptuous are they [the Ophites], self-willed, they are not afraid to speak evil of Dignities," says Peter (*2nd Epistle* ii, 10), the original model for the later abusive Tertullian and Irenaeus.§ "Likewise [even as Sodom and Gomorrah] also these *filthy* dreamers defile the flesh, despise Dominion and speak evil of Dignities," says Jude (8), repeating the very words of Peter, and thereby expressions consecrated in the *Kabala*. *Dominion* is the "Empire," the *tenth* of the kabalistic Sephîrôth.∥ The *Powers* and Dignities are the subordinate

---

* See *John* i.

† *Philosophumena*, I, xxi.

‡ Kleucker, *Über die Natur und den Ursprung der Emanationslehre*, etc., pp. 10, 11; Riga, 1786. See *Siphrah Dtzeniuthah*, etc.

§ "These as natural *brute beasts*." "The dog is turned to his own vomit again; and *the sow* that was washed to her wallowing in the mire" (*2 Peter*, ii, 12, 22).

∥ The types of the creation, or the attributes of the Supreme Being, are through the emanations of Adam-Kadmon; these are: "The *Crown, Wisdom, Prudence, Magnificence, Severity, Beauty, Victory, Glory, Foundation, Empire*. Wisdom is called *Yâh;* Prudence, *Yehôvâh;* Severity, *Elôhim;* Magnificence, *Elohah;* Beauty, *Tiphereth;* Victory, and Glory, Tze'baôth; Empire or Dominion, Adonai." Thus when the Nazarenes and other Gnostics of the more Platonic tendency twitted the Jews as "abortions who worship their god

genii of the Archangels and Angels of the *Zohar*.* These emanations are the very life and soul of the *Kabala* and Zoroastrianism; and the *Talmud* itself, in its present state, is all borrowed from the *Zend-Avesta*. Therefore, by adopting the views of Peter, Jude, and other Jewish apostles, the Christians have become but a dissenting sect of the Persians, for they do not even interpret the meaning of all such *Powers* as the true kabalists do. Paul's warning his converts against the worshipping of angels, shows how well he appreciated, even so early as his period, the dangers of borrowing from a metaphysical doctrine the philosophy of which could be rightly interpreted but by its well-learned adherents, the Magi and the Jewish Tannaim. "Let no man beguile you of your reward in a voluntary humility and *worshipping of angels*, intruding into those things which he hath not seen, vainly puffed up by his fleshly mind," † is a sentence laid right at the door of Peter and his champions. In the *Talmud*, Michael is Prince of Water, who has *seven* inferior spirits subordinate to him. He is the patron, the guardian angel of the Jews, as *Daniel* informs us (x, 21), and the Greek Ophites, who identified him with their Ophiomorphos, the personified creation of the envy and malice of Ialdabaôth, the Demiurgus (Creator of the *material* world), and undertook to prove that he was also Samuel, the Hebrew prince of the evil spirits, or Persian *daêvas*, were naturally regarded by the Jews as blasphemers. But did Jesus ever sanction this belief in angels except in so far as hinting that they were the messengers and subordinates of God? And here the origin of the later splits between Christian beliefs is directly traceable to these two early contradictory views.

Paul, believing in all such occult powers in the world "unseen," but ever "present," says: "Ye walked according to the AEÔN of this world, according to the *Archon* [Ialdabaôth, the *Demiurge*] that has the domination of the air," and "we wrestle not against flesh and blood, but against the *dominations,* the *powers;* the lords of darkness, the mischievousness of spirits in the upper regions." ‡ This sentence, "ye were dead in sin and error," for "ye walked according to the *Archon*," or Ialdabaôth, the God and creator of matter of the Ophites, shows unequivocally that: 1st, Paul, notwithstanding some dissension with the more important doctrines of the Gnostics, shared more or less their cosmogonical views on the emanations; and 2nd, that he was fully aware that this Demiurge,

---

Iurbo-*Adonai*," we need not wonder at the wrath of those who had accepted the old Mosaic system, but at that of Peter and Jude who claim to be followers of Jesus and dissent from the views of him who was also a Nazarene.

* According to the "Kabala," *Empire* or *Dominion* is "the consuming fire, and his wife is the Temple or the Church."

† *Colossians* ii, 18.

‡ [Cf. *Ephes.* ii, 2; vi, 12; ii, 1.]

whose Jewish name was Jehovah, was *not* the God preached by Jesus. And now, if we compare the doctrine of Paul with the religious views of Peter and Jude, we find that, not only did they worship Michael, the Archangel, but that also they *reverenced* SATAN, because the latter was also, before his fall, an angel! This they do quite openly, and abuse the Gnostics* for speaking "evil" of him. No one can deny the following: Peter, when denouncing those who are not afraid to speak evil of *"dignities,"* adds immediately, "whereas angels, which are greater in power and might, *bring not railing accusation* against them [the dignities] before the Lord" (ii, 11). Who are the dignities? Jude, in his General Epistle, makes the word as clear as day. The *dignities* are the DEVILS!! Complaining of the disrespect shown by the Gnostics to the *powers* and *dominions,* Jude argues in the very words of Peter: "Yet Michael the Archangel, when contending *with the devil* he disputed about the body of Moses, *durst not bring against him a railing accusation,* but said, The Lord rebuke thee" (i, 9). Is this plain enough? If not, then we have the *Kabala* to prove who were the *dignities.*

Considering that *Deuteronomy* tells us that the *"Lord"* Himself buried Moses in a valley of Moab (xxxiv, 6), "but no man knoweth of his sepulchre unto this day," this Biblical *lapsus linguae* of Jude gives a strong coloring to the assertions of some of the Gnostics. They claimed but what was secretly taught by the Jewish kabalists themselves; to wit: that the highest supreme God was unknown and invisible; "the King of Light is a closed eye"; that Ialdabaôth, the Jewish second Adam, was the real Demiurge; and that Iaô, Adonai, Tsabaôth, and Eloi were the quaternary emanation which formed the unity of the God of the Hebrews — Jehovah. Moreover, the latter was also called Michael and Samael by them, and regarded but as an angel, several removes from the Godhead. In holding to such a belief, the Gnostics countenanced the teachings of the greatest of the Jewish doctors, Hillel, and other Babylonian divines. Josephus shows the great deference of the official Synagogue in Jerusalem to the wisdom of the schools of Central Asia. The colleges of Sura, Pumbeditha, and Nahardea were considered the headquarters of esoteric and theological learning by all the schools of Palestine. The Chaldean version of the *Pentateuch,* made by the well-known Babylonian divine, Onkelos, was regarded as the most authoritative of all; and it is according to this learned Rabbi that Hillel and other Tannaim after him held that the Being who appeared to Moses in the burning bush, on Mount Sinai, and who finally buried him, was the *angel* of the Lord,

---

\* It is more likely that both abused Paul, who preached against this belief; and that the Gnostics were only a pretext. (See Peter's second *Epistle.*)

Memra, and not the Lord Himself; and that he whom the Hebrews of the *Old Testament* mistook for *Iahoh* was but His messenger, one of His sons, or emanations. All this establishes but one logical conclusion — namely, that the Gnostics were by far the superiors of the disciples, in point of education and general information; even in a knowledge of the religious tenets of the Jews themselves. While they were perfectly well-versed in the Chaldean wisdom, the well-meaning, pious, but fanatical as well as ignorant disciples, unable to fully understand or grasp the religious spirit of their own system, were driven in their disputations to such convincing logic as the use of "brute beasts," "sows," "dogs," and other epithets so freely bestowed by Peter.

Since then, the epidemic has reached the apex of the sacerdotal hierarchy. From the day when the founder of Christianity uttered the warning, that he who shall say to his brother, "Thou fool, shall be in danger of hell-fire," all who have passed as its leaders, beginning with the ragged fishermen of Galilee, and ending with the jewelled pontiffs, have seemed to vie with each other in the invention of opprobrious epithets for their opponents. So we find Luther passing a final sentence on the Catholics, and exclaiming that "the Papists are all asses, put them in whatever form you like; whether they are boiled, roasted, baked, fried, skinned, hashed, they will be always the same asses." Calvin called the victims he persecuted, and occasionally burned, "malicious barking dogs, full of bestiality and insolence, base corrupters of the sacred writings," etc. Dr. Warburton terms the Popish religion "an impious farce," and Monseigneur Dupanloup asserts that the Protestant Sabbath service is the "Devil's mass," and all clergymen are "thieves and ministers of the Devil."

The same spirit of incomplete inquiry and ignorance has led the Christian Church to bestow on its most holy apostles titles assumed by their most desperate opponents, the "Heretics" and Gnostics. So we find, for instance, Paul termed the vase of election, *"vas electionis,"* a title chosen by *Manes,** the greatest heretic of his day in the eyes of the Church, Manes meaning, in the Babylonian language, the chosen vessel or receptable.†

So with the Virgin Mary. They were so little gifted with originality, that they copied from the Egyptian and Hindu religions their several

---

\* The true name of Manes — who was a Persian by birth — was *Cubricus*. (See Epiphanius, *Panarion*, lib. II, tom II, Haer. LXVI, 1.) He was flayed alive at the instance of the Magi, by the Persian King Varanes I. Plutarch says that Manes or Manis means Masses or ANOINTED. The vessel, or vase of election, is, therefore, the vessel full of that light of God, which he pours on one he has selected for his interpreter.

† See King's *Gnostics*, p. 16.

apostrophes to their respective Virgin-mothers. The juxtaposition of a few examples will make this clear.

| Hindu | Egyptian | Roman Catholic |
|---|---|---|
| *Litany of our Lady Nâri: Virgin.* | *Litany of our Lady Isis: Virgin.* | *Litany of our Lady of Loretto: Virgin.* |
| 1. Holy *Nâri* — Mariâma, Mother of perpetual fecundity. | 1. Holy Isis, universal mother — *Mut*. | 1. Holy Mary, mother of divine grace. |
| 2. Mother of an incarnated God — Vishnu *(Devaki)*. | 2. Mother of Gods—Hathor. | 2. Mother of God. |
| 3. Mother of Krishna. | 3. Mother of Horus. | 3. Mother of Christ. |
| 4. Eternal Virginity — *Kanyâbhâva*. | 4. Virgo-generatrix—*Neith*. | 4. Virgin of Virgins. |
| 5. Mother — Pure Essence, *Âkâśa*. | 5. Mother-Soul of the universe — *Anuki*. | 5. Mother of Divine Grace. |
| 6. Virgin most chaste — *Kanyâ*. | 6. Virgin sacred earth—Isis. | 6. Virgin most chaste. |
| 7. Mother *Tanmâtra*, of the *five* virtues or elements. | 7. Mother of all the virtues — *Maât*, with the same qualities. | 7. Mother most pure. Mother undefiled. Mother inviola.e. Mother most amiable. Mother most admirable. |
| 8. Virgin *Triguna* (of the three elements, power, or richness, love and mercy). | 8. Illustrious Isis, most powerful, merciful, just. *(Book of the Dead.)* | 8. Virgin most powerful. Virgin most merciful. Virgin most faithful. |
| 9. Mirror of Supreme Conscience — *Ahaṃkâra*. | 9. Mirror of Justice and truth — *Maât*.[31] | 9. Mirror of Justice. |
| 10. Wise Mother—*Sarasvati*. | 10. Mysterious mother of the world — *Mut* (secret wisdom). | 10. Seat of Wisdom. |
| 11. Virgin of the white Lotus, *Padma* or *Kamala*. | 11. Sacred Lotus. | 11. Mystical Rose. |
| 12. Womb of Gold — *Hiranyagarbha*. | 12. Sistrum of Gold. | 12. House of Gold. |
| 13. Celestial Light—*Lakshmi*. | 13. Astartê (Syrian), 'Ashtôreth (Jewish). | 13. Morning Star. |
| 14. Ditto. | 14. Argua of the Moon. | 14. Ark of the Covenant. |
| 15. Queen of Heaven, and of the universe — *Śakti*. | 15. Queen of Heaven, and of the universe—*Sati*. | 15. Queen of Heaven. |
| 16. Mother soul of all beings — *Paramâtman*. | 16. Model of all mothers — Hathor. | 16. *Mater Dolorosa*. |
| 17. Devakî is conceived without sin, and immaculate herself. (According to the Brahmanic fancy.) | 17. Isis is a Virgin Mother. | 17. Mary conceived without sin. (In accordance with later orders.) |

If the Virgin Mary has her nuns, who are consecrated to her and bound to live in chastity, so had Isis her nuns in Egypt, as Vesta had hers at Rome, and the Hindu *Nârî*, "mother of the world," hers. The virgins consecrated to her cultus — the *Devadâsis* of the temples, who were the nuns of the days of old — lived in great chastity, and were objects of the most extraordinary veneration, as the holy women of the goddess. Would the missionaries and some travellers reproachfully point to the modern *Devadâsis*, or Nautch-girls? For all response, we would beg them to consult the official reports of the last quarter century, cited in Chapter II, as to certain discoveries made at the razing of convents, in Austria and Italy. Thousands of infants' skulls were exhumed from ponds, subterranean vaults, and gardens of convents. Nothing to match *this* was ever found in heathen lands.

Christian theology, getting the doctrine of the archangels and angels directly from the Oriental *Kabala*, of which the Mosaic *Bible* is but an allegorical screen, ought at least to remember the hierarchy invented by the former for these personified emanations. The hosts of the Cherubim and Seraphim, with which we generally see the Catholic Madonnas surrounded in their pictures, belong, together with the Elohim and Beni Elohim of the Hebrews, to the *third* kabalistic world, *Yetzirah*. This world is but one remove higher than *Asiah*, the fourth and lowest world, in which dwell the grossest and most material beings — the *klippoth*, who delight in evil and mischief, and whose chief is *Belial!*

Explaining, in his way, of course, the various "heresies" of the first two centuries, Irenaeus says: "Our Heretics hold . . . that PROPATÔR is known but to the *only-begotten* son, that is to the *mind*" (the nous).* It was the Valentinians, the followers of the "profoundest doctor of the Gnosis," Valentinus, who held that "there was a perfect AIÔN, who existed before Bythos," or Python (the Depth), "called Propatôr." † This is again kabalistic, for in the *Zohar* of Shimon-ben-Yoḥai, we read the following: "*Senior occultatus est et absconditus; Microprosopus manifestus est, et non manifestus.*" ‡

In the religious metaphysics of the Hebrews, the Highest One is an abstraction; he is "without form or being," "with no likeness with anything else." § And even Philo calls the Creator, the *Logos* who stands next to God, "the SECOND GOD." "The *second* God who is his WISDOM." ‖ God is NOTHING, he is nameless, and therefore called *Ain-Soph* — the word *Ain* meaning *nothing*. ¶ But if, according to the older Jews, Jehovah is *the* God,

---

\* [*Adv. Haer.*, I, ii, 1.]
† [*Ibid.*, I, i, 1.]
‡ Rosenroth, *Kabb. denud.*, *Lib. myst.*, iv, § 1.
§ A. Franck, *La Kabbale*, II, iii, p. 173; ed. Paris, 1843.
‖ Philo Judaeus, *Quaest. et sol. in Gen.*, Bk. II, § 62.
¶ Franck, *op. cit.*, II, iv (pp. 160 *et seq.*).

and He manifested Himself several times to Moses and the prophets, and the Christian Church anathematized the Gnostics who denied the fact — how comes it, then, that we read in the fourth gospel that *"No man hath seen God* AT ANY TIME, *but the only-begotten* Son . . . he hath declared him"? [i, 18.] The very words of the Gnostics, in spirit and substance. This sentence of St. John — or rather whoever wrote the gospel now bearing his name — floors all the Petrine arguments against Simon Magus, without appeal. The words are repeated and emphasized in chapter vi, 46: *"Not that any man hath seen the Father,* save he which is of God, he [Jesus] hath seen the Father" — the very objection brought forward by Simon in the *Homilies.* These words prove that either the author of the fourth evangel had no idea of the existence of the *Homilies,* or that he was *not* John, the friend and companion of Peter, whom he contradicts point-blank with this emphatic assertion. Be that as it may, this sentence, like many more that might be profitably cited, blends Christianity completely with the Oriental Gnosis, and hence with the KABALA.

While the doctrines, ethical code and observances of the Christian religion were all appropriated from Brahmanism and Buddhism, its ceremonials, vestments and pageantry were taken bodily from Lamaism. The Romish monastery and nunnery are almost servile copies of similar religious houses in Thibet and Mongolia, and interested explorers of Buddhist lands, when obliged to mention the unwelcome fact, have had no other alternative left them but, with an anachronism unsurpassed in recklessness, to charge the offence of plagiarism upon the religious system their own mother Church had despoiled. This makeshift has served its purpose and had its day. The time has at last come when this page of history must be written.

## CHAPTER V

"Learn to know all, but keep thyself unknown." — *Gnostic Maxim.*

"There is one God supreme over all gods, diviner than mortals,
Whose form is not like unto man's, and as unlike his nature;
But vain mortals imagine that gods *like themselves are begotten,*
With human sensations, and voice, and corporeal members."
—XENOPHANES, in Clem. Alex., *Stromateis,* V, xiv.

"TYCHIADES.—Can you tell me the reason, Philocles, why most men desire to lie, and delight not only to speak fictions themselves, but give busy attention to others who do?
PHILOCLES.—There be many reasons, Tychiades, which compel some to speak lies, because they see 'tis profitable."
—LUCIAN, *Philopseudês.*

"SPARTAN.—Is it to thee, or to God, that I must confess?"
"PRIEST.—To God."
"SPARTAN.—Then, *man,* stand back!"
—PLUTARCH, *Laconic Apophegms.*

WE will now give attention to some of the most important Mysteries of the *Kabala,* and trace their relations to the philosophical myths of various nations.

In the oldest Oriental *Kabala,* the Deity is represented as three circles in one, shrouded in a certain smoke or chaotic exhalation. In the preface to the *Zohar,* which transforms the three primordial circles into THREE HEADS, over these is described an exhalation or smoke, neither black nor white, but colorless, and circumscribed within a circle. This is the unknown Essence.\*
The origin of the Jewish image may, perhaps, be traced to Hermes' *Poimandres,* the Egyptian *Logos,* who appears within a cloud of a humid nature, with smoke escaping from it. † In the *Zohar* the highest God is, as we have shown in the preceding chapter, and as in the case of the Hindu and Buddhist philosophies, a pure abstraction, whose objective existence is denied by the latter. It is Ḥokhmah, the "SUPREME WISDOM, that cannot be understood by reflection," and that lies within and without the CRANIUM of LONG FACE ‡ (Sephîrâh), the uppermost of the three "Heads." It is the "boundless and the infinite Ain-Soph," the No-Thing.

The "three Heads," superposed above each other, are evidently taken from the three mystic triangles of the Hindus, which also superpose each other. The highest "head" contains the *Trinity in Chaos,* out of which springs the manifested trinity. Ain-Soph, the unrevealed forever, who is

---

\* Rosenroth, *Kabb. denudata,* II, p. 242.
† Champollion-Figeac, *Égypte ancienne,* p. 141.
‡ *Idrah Rabbah,* vi, § 58.

## THE SUPREME ESSENCE NOT THE CREATOR 213

boundless and unconditioned, cannot create, and therefore it seems to us a great error to attribute to him a "creative thought," as is commonly done by the interpreters. In every cosmogony this supreme Essence is *passive;* if boundless, infinite and unconditioned, it can have no *thought* nor *idea.* It acts not as the result of volition, but in obedience to its own nature, and *according to the fatality of the law of which it is itself the embodiment.* Thus, with the Hebrew kabalists, Ain-Soph is nonexistent, אין, for it is incomprehensible to our finite intellects, and therefore cannot exist to our minds. Its first emanation was כתר, Kether, the crown. When the time for an active period had come, then was produced a natural expansion of this Divine essence from within outwardly, obedient to eternal and immutable law; and from this eternal and infinite light (which to us is darkness) was emitted a spiritual substance.* This was the First Sephîrâh, containing in herself the other nine ספירות, Sephîrôth, or intelligences. In their totality and unity they represent the archetypal man, Adam-Kadmon, the πρωτόγονος, who in his individuality or unity is yet dual, or bisexual, the Greek *Didymos,* for he is the prototype of all humanity. Thus we obtain three trinities, each contained in a "head." In the first head, or face (the three-faced Hindu *Trimûrti*), we find *Kether,* the first androgyne, at the apex of the upper triangle, emitting *Hokhmah,* or Wisdom, a masculine and active potency — also called *Yâh,* יה — and *Binah,* בינה, or Intelligence, a female and passive potency, also represented by the name *Yahweh,* יהוה. These three form the first trinity or "face" of the Sephîrôth. This triad emanated *Hesed,* or Mercy, a masculine active potency, also called *Eloah,* from which emanated *Geburah,* גבורה, or Justice, also called *Pa'had,* a feminine passive potency; from the union of these two was produced *Tiphereth,* תפארת, Beauty, Clemency, the Spiritual Sun, known by the divine name *Elohim;* and the second triad, "face," or "head," was formed. These emanated, in their turn, the masculine potency *Netzah,* נצח, Firmness, or *Yehovah-Tsabaôth,* who issued the feminine passive potency *Hod,* הוד, Splendor, or *Elohim-Tsabaôth;* the two produced *Yesod,* יסוד, Foundation, who is the mighty living one, *El Hay,* thus yielding the third trinity or "head." The tenth Sephîrâh is rather a duad, and is represented on the diagrams as the lowest circle. It is *Malkhuth* or Kingdom, מלכות, and *Shekhînah,* שכינה, also called *Adonai,* and *Cherubim* among the angelic hosts. The first "Head" is called the Intellectual world; the second "Head" is the Sensuous, or the world of Perception, and the third is the Material or Physical world.

"Before he gave any shape to the universe," says the *Kabala,* "before

---

* *Idrah Zutah,* ch. ii.

he produced any form, he was alone without any form and resemblance to anything else. Who, then, can comprehend him, how he was before the creation, since he was formless? Hence, it is forbidden to represent him by any form, similitude, or even by his sacred name, by a single letter, or a single point.* . . . The Aged of the Aged, the Unknown of the Unknown, has a form, and yet no form. He has a form whereby the universe is preserved, and yet has no form, because he cannot be comprehended. When he first assumed a form [in Sephîrâh, his first emanation], he caused nine splendid lights to emanate from it." †

And now we will turn to Hindu esoteric Cosmogony and definition of "Him who is, and yet is not."

"From him who is,‡ from this immortal Principle which exists in our minds but cannot be perceived by the senses, is born Purusha, the Divine male and female, who became *Nârâyana,* or the Divine Spirit moving on the waters."§

Svayambhû, the unknown essence of the Brahmans, is identical with Ain-Soph, the unknown essence of the kabalists. As with the latter, the ineffable name could not be pronounced by the Hindus, under the penalty of death. In the ancient primitive trinity of India, that which may be certainly considered as pre-Vedic, the *germ* which fecundates the *mother-principle,* the mundane egg, or the universal womb, is called *Nara,* the Spirit, or the Holy Ghost, which emanates from the primordial essence. It is like Sephîrâh, the oldest emanation, called the *primordial point,* and the *White Head,* for it is the point of divine light appearing from within the fathomless and boundless darkness. In *Manu* it is "NARA," or the Spirit of God, which moves on "Ayana [Chaos, or place of motion], and thence is named NÂRÂYANA, or moving on the waters." || In Hermes, the Egyptian, we read: "In the beginning of the time there was naught in the chaos." But when the "*verbum,*" issuing from the void like a "colorless smoke," makes its appearance, then "this *verbum* moved on the humid principle." ¶ And in *Genesis* [i, 2] we find: "And darkness was upon the face of the deep [chaos]. And the Spirit of God moved upon the face of the waters." In the *Kabala,* the emanation of the primordial passive principle (Sephîrâh), by dividing itself into two parts, active and passive, emits Hokhmah-Wisdom and Binah-Yehovah, and in conjunction with these two acolytes, which complete the trinity, becomes the Creator of the abstract Universe; the physical world being the production of later and still more material powers.** In the Hindu Cosmogony, Svayambhû emits

* *Zohar,* II, p. 42b; Amst. ed., 1714.
† *Ibid.,* III, p. 288a (*Idrah Zutah,* ch. i, §§ 41-43).
‡ *Ego sum qui sum* (*Exod.* iii, 14).
§ *The Works of Wm. Jones,* Vol. III, pp. 66-67; London, 1799.
|| *Ibid.*
¶ Champollion-Figeac, *op. cit.,* p. 141.
** We are fully aware that some Christian kabalists term Ain-Soph the "Crown";

*Nara* and *Nârî*, its bisexual emanation, and dividing its parts into two halves, male and female, these fecundate the mundane egg, within which develops Brahmâ, or rather *Virâj*, the Creator. "The starting point of the Egyptian mythology," says Champollion, "is a triad . . . namely, Kneph, Neith, and Ptaḥ; and Ammon, the male, the father; Mut, the female and mother; and Khonsu, the son."

The ten Sephîrôth are copies taken from the ten Prajâpatis created by Virâj, called the "Lords of all beings," and answering to the Biblical Patriarchs.

Justin Martyr explains some of the "heresies" of the day, but in a very unsatisfactory manner. *He shows, however, the identity of all the world-religions at their starting points.* The first *beginning* opens invariably with the *unknown* and passive deity, producing from himself a cer-

---

identify him with Sephîrâh; call Ain-Soph "an emanation from God," and make the ten Sephîrôth comprise "Ain-Soph" as a unity. They also very erroneously reverse the first two emanations of Sephîrâh — Ḥokhmah and Binah. The greatest Kabalists have always held Ḥokhmah (Wisdom) as a male and active intelligence, Yâh, יה, and placed it under the No. 2 on the right side of the triangle, whose apex is the crown, while Binah (Intelligence) or בינה, is under No. 3 on the left hand. But the latter, being represented by its divine name as *Yahweh*, יהוה, very naturally showed the God of Israel as only a third emanation, as well as a feminine, passive principle. Hence when the time came for the Talmudists to transform their multifarious deities into one living God, they resorted to their Masoretic points and combined to transform Yehovah into Adonai, "the Lord." This, under the persecution of the Mediaeval kabalists by the Church, also forced some of the former to change their female Sephîrôth into male, and *vice versa*, so as to avoid being accused of disrespect and blasphemy to Jehovah; whose name, moreover, by mutual and secret agreement they accepted as a *substitute* for Yâh, or the mystery name IAŌ. Alone the *initiated* knew of it, but later it gave rise to a great confusion among the *uninitiated*. It would be worthwhile — were it not for lack of space — to quote a few of the many passages in the oldest Jewish authorities, such as Rabbi A'qîbah, and the *Zohar*, which corroborate our assertion. Ḥokhmah-Wisdom is a male principle everywhere, and Binah-Yehovah, a female potency. The writings of Irenaeus, Theodoret and Epiphanius, teeming with accusations against the Gnostics and "Heresies," repeatedly show Simon Magus and Cerinthus making of Binah the feminine divine Spirit which inspired Simon. Binah is Sophia, and the Sophia of the Gnostics is surely not a male potency, but simply the feminine Wisdom, or Intelligence. (See any ancient "Arbor Kabbalistica," or Tree of the Sephîrôth.) Éliphas Lévi, in the *Dogme et Rituel de la Haute Magie*, Vol. I, ch. x, places Ḥokhmah as No. 2 and as a male Sephîrâh on the right hand of the Tree. In the "Kabala" the three male Sephîrôth — Ḥokhmah, Ḥesed, Netzaḥ — are known as the Pillar of Mercy; and the three feminine on the left, namely, Binah, Geburah, Hod, are named the Pillar of Judgment; while the four Sephîrôth of the centre — Kether, Tiphereth, Yesod, and Malkhuth — are called the Middle Pillar. And, as MacKenzie, in the *Royal Masonic Cyclopaedia,* shows, "there is an analogy in these three pillars to the three Pillars of Wisdom, Strength, and Beauty in a Craft Lodge of Masonry, while the Ain-Soph forms the mysterious blazing star or mystic light of the East" (p. 407).

tain active power or virtue, "Rational," which is sometimes called WISDOM, sometimes the SON, very often God, Angel, Lord, and LOGOS.* The latter is sometimes applied to the very first emanation, but in several systems it proceeds from the first androgyne or double ray produced at the beginning by the unseen. Philo depicts this wisdom as male and female.† But though its first manifestation had a beginning, for it proceeded from *Olam* ‡ (Aiôn, time), the highest of the Aeôns, when emitted from the Fathers, it had remained with him *before all creations,* for it is part of him. § Therefore, Philo Judaeus calls Adam-Kadmon *"mind"* (the Ennoia of *Bythos* in the Gnostic system). "The mind, let it be named Adam." ||

Strictly speaking, it is difficult to view the Jewish *Book of Genesis* otherwise than as a chip from the trunk of the mundane tree of universal Cosmogony, rendered in Oriental allegories. As cycle succeeded cycle, and one nation after another came upon the world's stage to play its brief part in the majestic drama of human life, each new people evolved from ancestral traditions its own religion, giving it a local color, and stamping it with its individual characteristics. While each of these religions had its distinguishing traits, by which, were there no other archaic vestiges, the physical and psychological status of its creators could be estimated, all preserved a common likeness to one prototype. This parent cult was none other than the primitive "wisdom-religion." The Israelitish *Scriptures* are no exception. Their national history — if they can claim any autonomy before the return from Babylon, and were nothing more than migratory septs of Hindu pariahs, cannot be carried back a day beyond Moses; and if this ex-Egyptian priest must, from theological necessity, be transformed into a Hebrew patriarch, we must insist that the Jewish nation was lifted with that smiling infant out of the bulrushes of Lake Moeris. Abraham, their alleged father, belongs to the universal mythology. Most likely he is but one of the numerous aliases of Zeruan (Saturn), the king of the golden age, who is also called the old man (emblem of time). ¶

It is now demonstrated by Assyriologists that in the old Chaldean books, Abraham is called Zeru-an, or Zerb-an — meaning one very rich in gold and silver, and a mighty prince.** He is also called Zarouan and Zarman — a decrepit old man.††

---

\* *Dial. with Trypho,* ch. lxi.
† [*De fuga et inventione,* IX, 52.]
‡ A division indicative of time.
§ Sanchoniathon calls time the oldest Aeôn, *Protogonos,* the *"first-born."*
|| *De cherubim,* "Cain," § xvii; also *De opificio mundi,* § 3.
¶ Azrael, angel of death, is also Israel. *Ab-ram* means father of elevation, high-placed father, for Saturn is the highest or outermost planet. [Cf. Movers, *Die Phönizier,* Vol. I, p. 86.]
\*\* See *Genesis* xiii, 2.
†† Saturn is generally represented as a very old man, with a sickle in his hand.

The ancient Babylonian legend is that Xisuthros (Hasisadra of the Tablets,[32] or Xisuthros) sailed with his ark to Armenia,* and his son Sim became supreme king. Pliny says that Sim was called Zeruan; and Sim is Shem.† In Hebrew, his name writes שם, *Shem* — a sign. Assyria is held by the ethnologists to be the land of Shem, and Egypt called that of Ham. Shem, in the tenth chapter of *Genesis* is made the father of all the children of Eber, of Elam (Olam or Eilam), and Ashur (Assur or Assyria). The "*nephilim,*" or fallen men, *Giborim,* mighty men spoken of in *Genesis* (vi, 4), come from *Olam,* "men of *Shem.*" Even Ophir, which is evidently to be sought for in the India of the days of Hiram, is made a descendant of Shem. The records are purposely mixed up to make them fit into the frame of the Mosaic *Bible.* But *Genesis,* from its first verse down to the last, has naught to do with the "chosen people"; it belongs to the world's history. Its appropriation by the Jewish authors in the days of the so-called *restoration* of the destroyed books of the Israelites by Ezra, proves nothing, and until now, has been self-propped on an alleged divine revelation. It is simply a compilation of the universal legends of the universal humanity. Bunsen says that in the "Chaldean tribe immediately connected with Abraham, we find reminiscences of dates disfigured and misunderstood, as genealogies of single men, or indications of epoch. The Abrahamic tribe-recollections go back at least three millennia beyond the grandfather of Jacob." ‡

Eupolemus says that Abraham was born at Camarina or *Urie,* a city of soothsayers, and *invented astronomy.* § Josephus claims the same for Terah, Abraham's father. The tower of Babel was built as much by the direct descendants of Shem as by those of the "accursed" Ham and Canaan, for the people in those days were "one," and the "whole earth was of one language"; and Babel was simply an astrological tower, and its builders were astrologers and adepts of the primitive Wisdom-Religion, or, again, what we term the Secret Doctrine.

The Berosian Sibyl says: Before the Tower, Zeru-an, Titan, and Yapetosthes governed the earth, Zeru-an wished to be supreme, but his two brothers resisted, when their sister, Astlik, intervened and appeased them. It was agreed that Zeru-an should rule, but his male children should be put to death; and strong Titans were appointed to carry this into effect. ||

Sar (circle, *saros*) is the Babylonian god of the sky. He is also Assaros or Asshur (the son of Shem), and Zero — Zero-ana, the *chakra,* or wheel, boundless time. Hence, as the first step taken by Zoroaster, while founding his new religion, was to change the most sacred deities

---

\* [Berosus in Eusebius, *Chronicon,* I, iii, 2; Abydenus, *ibid.,* I, vii.]
† [Cf. Kleucker, *Anh. z. Zend-Avesta,* I, i, p. 189.]
‡ Bunsen, *Egypt's Place in Universal History,* Vol. V, p. 85.
§ Eusebius, *Praep. evang.,* IX; cf. Cory, *Anc. Fragm.,* p. 57; ed. 1832.
|| [*Berosi fragm.,* p. 59; ed. J. D. G. Richter, Lipsiae, 1825.]

of the Sanskrit *Veda* into names of evil spirits, in his Zend *Scriptures*, and even to reject a number of them, we find no traces in the *Avesta* of Chakra — the symbolic circle of the sky.

Elam, another of the sons of Shem, is *Olam*, עולם, and refers to an order or cycle of events. In *Ecclesiastes* iii, 11, it is termed "world." In *Ezekiel* xxvi, 20, "of old time." In *Genesis* iii, 22, the word stands as "forever"; and in chapter ix, 16, "eternal." Finally, the term is completely defined in *Genesis* vi, 4, in the following words: "There were *nephilim* [giants, fallen men, or Titans] in the earth." The word is synonymous with Aeôn, αἰών. In *Proverbs* viii, 23, it reads: "I was effused from *Olam*, from *Rosh*" (wisdom). By this sentence, the wise king-kabalist refers to one of the mysteries of the human spirit — the immortal crown of the man-trinity. While it ought to read as above, and be interpreted kabalistically to mean that the *I* (or my eternal, immortal *Ego*), the spiritual entity, was effused from the boundless and nameless eternity, through the creative wisdom of the unknown God, it reads in the canonical translation: "The Lord possessed me in the beginning of his way, before his works of old," which is unintelligible nonsense, without the kabalistic interpretation. When Solomon is made to say that *I* was "from the beginning . . . while as yet he [the Supreme Deity] had not made the earth . . . nor the highest part of the dust of the world . . . I was there," and "when he appointed the foundations of the earth . . . then I was by him, *as one brought up with him*," * what can the kabalist mean by the "*I*," but his own divine spirit, a drop effused from that eternal fountain of light and wisdom — the universal spirit of the Deity?

The thread of glory emitted by Ain-Soph from the highest of the three kabalistic heads, through which "all things shine with light," the thread which makes its exit through Adam *Primus*, is the individual spirit of every man. "I was daily his [Ain-Soph's] delight, rejoicing always before him . . . and my delights were *with the sons of men*," adds Solomon in the same chapter of the *Proverbs* [30-31]. The immortal spirit delights in the *sons of men*, who, without this spirit, are but dualities (physical body and astral soul, or that *life-principle* which animates even the lowest of the animal kingdom). But, we have seen that the doctrine teaches that this spirit cannot unite itself with that man in whom matter and the grossest propensities of his animal soul will be ever crowding it out. Therefore, Solomon, who is made to speak under the inspiration of his own spirit that possesses him for the time being, utters the following words of wisdom: "Hearken unto me, my son" (the dual man), "blessed are they that keep my ways . . . Blessed is the man that heareth me, watching daily at my gates . . . For whoso *findeth me findeth life*, and shall obtain favor of the Lord . . . But he that

---

* [*Proverbs* viii, 22-30.]

sinneth *against me* wrongeth his *own soul* . . . and loves *death*" (*Proverbs* viii, 32-36).

This chapter, as interpreted, is made by some theologians, like everything else, to apply to Christ, the "Son of God," who states repeatedly, that he who follows him obtains eternal life, and conquers death. But even in its distorted translation it can be demonstrated that it referred to anything but to the alleged Savior. Were we to accept it in this sense, then the Christian theology would have to return, *nolens volens*, to Averroism and Buddhism; to the doctrine of emanation, in short; for Solomon says: "I was effused" from *Olam* and *Rosh*, both of which are a part of the Deity; and thus Christ would not be, as their doctrine claims, God himself, but only an *emanation* of Him, like the Christos of the Gnostics. Hence, the meaning of the personified Gnostic Aeôn, a word signifying cycles or determined periods in the eternity, and at the same time, representing a hierarchy of celestial beings — spirits. Thus Christ is sometimes termed the "Eternal Aeôn." But the word "eternal" is erroneous in relation to the Aeôns. Eternal is that which has neither beginning nor end; but the "Emanations" or Aeôns, although having lived as absorbed in the divine essence from the eternity, when once individually emanated, must be said to have a beginning. They may be therefore *endless* in this spiritual life, never eternal.

These endless emanations of the one First Cause, all of which were gradually transformed by the popular fancy into distinct gods, spirits, angels and demons, were so little considered immortal, that all were assigned a limited existence. And this belief, common to all the peoples of antiquity, to the Chaldean Magi as well as to the Egyptians, and even in our day held by the Brahmanists and Buddhists, most triumphantly evidences the monotheism of the ancient religious systems. This doctrine calls the life-period of all the inferior divinities, "one day of Parabrahman." After a cycle of four billion, three hundred and twenty million human years — the tradition says — the trinity itself, with all the lesser divinities, will be annihilated, together with the universe, and cease to exist. Then another universe will gradually emerge from the pralaya (dissolution), and men on earth will be enabled to comprehend SVAYAMBHÛ as he is. Alone, this primal cause will exist forever, in all his glory, filling the infinite space. What better proof could be adduced of the deep reverential feeling with which the "heathen" regard the one Supreme eternal cause of all things visible and invisible.

This is again the source from which the ancient kabalists derived identical doctrines. If the Christians understood *Genesis* in their own way, and, if accepting the texts literally, they enforced upon the uneducated masses the belief in a creation of our world out of nothing; and moreover assigned to it a *beginning*, it is surely not the Tannaim, the sole expounders of the hidden meaning contained in the *Bible*, who are to be blamed. No more than any other philosophers had they ever believed either in spontaneous, limited, or *ex nihilo* creations. The *Kabala* has survived to show that their philosophy was precisely that of the modern Nepal Buddhists, the *Svâbhâvikas*. They believed *in the eternity and the indestructibility of matter*, and hence in many prior creations and destructions of worlds, before our own. "There were old worlds which perished." * "From this we see that the Holy One, blessed be His name, had successively created and destroyed sundry worlds, before he created the present world; and when he created this world he said: 'This pleases me; the previous ones did not please me'." † Moreover, they believed, again like the *Svâbhâvikas*, now termed Atheists, that everything proceeds (is created) from its own nature and that once that the first impulse is given by that Creative Force inherent in the "Self-created substance," or Sephîrâh, everything evolves out of itself, following its pattern, the more spiritual prototype which precedes it in the scale of infinite creation. "The indivisible point which has no limit, and cannot be comprehended [for it is absolute], expanded from within, and formed a brightness which served as a garment [a veil] to the indivisible point. . . . It, too, expanded from within . . . Thus, *everything originated through* a constant upheaving agitation, and thus finally the world originated." ‡

In the later Zoroastrian books, after Darius had both restored the worship of Ormazd and added to it the purer magianism of the primitive *Secret Wisdom* — חכמה-נסתרה [Hokhmah-Nistharah], of which, as the incription tells us, he was himself a hierophant, we see again reappearing the Zeruana, or boundless time, represented by the Brahmans in the *chakra*, or a circle, that we see figuring on the uplifted finger of the principal deities. Further on, we will show the relation in which it stands to the Pythagorean, mystical numbers — the first and the last — which is a *zero* (O), and to the greatest of the Mystery-Gods, IAÔ. The identity of this symbol alone, in all the old religions, is sufficient to show their common descent from one primitive Faith. § This term of "boundless time," which can be applied but to the ONE who has neither beginning nor end, is

---

\* *Zohar*, III, p. 292b; Amst. ed. (*Idrah Zutah*, x, §§ 421 *et seq.*)

† *Bereshith Rabbah*, parsha ix.

‡ *Zohar*, Pt. I, fol. 20a.

§ "The Sanskrit *s*," says Max Müller, "is represented by the Zend *h*. . . . Thus the geographical name 'hapta hendu,' which occurs in the *Avesta*, becomes intelligible if we retranslate the Zend *h* into the Sanskrit *s*. for 'sapta sindhu,' or the Seven Rivers, is the old Vaidik name of India itself" (*Chips*, Vol. I, pp. 82-83). The *Avesta* is the spirit of the *Vedas* — the esoteric meaning made partially known.

called by the Zoroastrians Zeruana-Akarane, because he has always existed. His glory, they say, is too exalted, his light too resplendent for either human intellect or mortal eyes to grasp and see. His primal emanation is eternal light which, from having been previously concealed in darkness, was called out to manifest itself, and thus was formed Ormazd, "the King of Life." He is the first-born of boundless time, but like his own antetype, or pre-existing spiritual idea, has lived within primitive darkness from all eternity. His *Logos* created the pure intellectual world. After the lapse of three grand cycles * he created the material world in six periods. The six Amshâspands, or *primitive* spiritual men, whom Ormazd created in his own image, are the mediators between this world and himself. Mithras is an emanation of the Logos and the chief of the twenty-eight *yazatas*, who are the tutelary angels over the spiritual portion of mankind — the souls of men. The *Ferohers* are infinite in number. They are the ideas or rather the ideal conceptions of things which formed themselves in the mind of Ormazd or Ahuramazda before he willed them to assume a concrete form. They are what Aristotle terms "privations" or forms and substances. The religion of Zarathushtra, as he is always called in the *Avesta,* is one from which the ancient Jews have borrowed the most. In one of the *Yashts*, Ahuramazda, the Supreme, gives to the seer as one of his sacred names, *Ahmi*, "I am"; and in another place, *ahmi yat ahmi*, "I am that I am," as Jehovah is alleged to have given it to Moses.

This Cosmogony, adopted with a change of names in the Rabbinical *Kabala,* found its way later, with some additional speculations of Manes, the half-Magus, half-Platonist, into the great body of Gnosticism. The real doctrines of the Basilideans, Valentinians and the Marcionites cannot be correctly ascertained in the prejudiced and calumnious writings of the Fathers of the Church; but rather in what remains of the works of the Bardesanians, known as the Nazarenes. It is next to impossible, now that all their manuscripts and books are destroyed, to assign to any of these sects its due part in dissenting views. But there are a few men still living who have preserved books and direct traditions about the Ophites, although they care little to impart them to the world. Among the unknown sects of Mount Lebanon and Palestine the truth has been concealed for more than a thousand years. And their *diagram* of the Ophite scheme differs from the description of it given by Origen † and hence from the *diagram* of J. Matter. ‡

---

\* What is generally understood in the *Avesta* system as a *thousand* years, means, in the esoteric doctrine, a cycle of a duration known but to the initiates and which has an allegorical sense.

† [*Contra Celsum,* VI, xxiv *et seq.*]

‡ J. Matter, *Histoire critique de Gnosticisme,* pl. III; cf. text in Vol. II, pp. 406-08; ed. 1843-44.

The kabalistic trinity is one of the models of the Christian one. "The ANCIENT, whose name is sanctified, is with three heads, but which make only one." * *Tria capita exsculpta sunt, unum intra alterum, et alterum supra alterum.* "Three heads are inserted in one another, and one over the other. The first head is the Concealed Wisdom (*Sapientia abscondita*). Under this head is the ANCIENT [Pythagorean *Monad*], the most hidden of mysteries; a head which is no head [*caput quod non est caput*]; no one can know what there is in this head. No intellect is able to comprehend this wisdom." † This *Senior Sanctissimus* is surrounded by the three heads. He is the eternal LIGHT of the wisdom; and the wisdom is the source from which all the manifestations have begun. "These three heads, included in ONE HEAD [which is no head]; and these three are bent down [overshadow] SHORT-FACE [the son] and through them all things shine with light." ‡ "Ain-Soph emits a thread from El or *Al* [the highest God of the Trinity], and the light follows the thread and enters, and passing through makes its exit through Adam *Primus* [Kadmon], who is *concealed* until the plan for arranging [*statum dispositionis*] is ready; it threads through him from his head to his feet; and in him [in the concealed Adam] is the figure of A MAN." §

"Whoso wishes to have an insight into the sacred unity, let him consider a flame rising from a burning coal or a burning lamp. He will see first a twofold light — a bright white, and a black or blue light; the white light is *above*, and ascends in a direct light, while the blue, or dark light, is *below*, and seems as the chair of the former, yet both are so intimately connected together that they constitute only one flame. The seat, however, formed by the blue or dark light, is again connected with the burning matter which is *under* it again. The white light never changes its color, it always remains white; but various shades are observed in the lower light, whilst the lowest light, moreover, takes two directions; *above*, it is connected with the white light, and *below* with the burning matter. Now, this is constantly consuming itself, and perpetually ascends to the upper light, and thus everything merges into a single unity." ||

Such were the ancient ideas of the trinity in the unity, as an abstraction. Man, who is the microcosmos of the macrocosmos, or of the

---

\* *Zohar*, III, p. 288b; Amst. ed., 1714 (*Idrah Zutah*, ii, § 78).

† *Idrah Zutah*, ii, §§ 59-63.

‡ *Ibid.*, ii, § 63; vii, §§ 177-87.

§ Jam vero quoniam hoc in loco recondita est illa plane non utuntur, et tantum de parte lucis ejus participant quae demittitur et ingretitur intra filum Ain-Soph protensum e Persona אל [*Al*, God] deorum: intratque et perrumpit et transit per Adam primum occultum usque in statum dispositionis transitque per eum a capite usque ad pedes ejus: *et in eo est figura hominis* (*Kabbala denudata*, II, p. 246).

|| *Zohar*, I, p. 51a, Amst. ed.

archetypal heavenly man, Adam-Kadmon, is likewise a trinity; for he is *body, soul* and *spirit.*

"All that is created by the 'Ancient of the Ancients' can live and exist only by a male and a female," says the *Zohar.*\* He alone, to whom no one can say, "Thou," for he is the spirit of the WHITE HEAD in whom the "THREE HEADS" are united, is uncreated. Out of the subtile fire, on one side of the White Head, and of the "subtile air," on the other, emanates Shekhînah, his veil (the feminized Holy Ghost). "This air," says *Idrah Rabbah,* "is the most occult [*occultissimus*] attribute of the Ancient of the Days. † The Ancient of the Ancients is the *Concealed* of the Concealed.‡ All things are Himself, and Himself is concealed on every side. § The *cranium* of the WHITE HEAD has no beginning, but its end has a shining reflection and a *roundness* which is our universe."‖

"They regard," says Kleucker, "the first-born as man and wife, in so far as his light includes in itself all other lights, and in so far as his spirit of life or breath of life includes all other life spirits in itself." ¶ The kabalistic Shekhînah answers to the Ophite Sophia. Properly speaking, Adam-Kadmon is the Bythos, but in this emanation-system, where everything is calculated to perplex and place an obstacle to inquiry, he is the *Source* of Light, the first "primitive man," and at the same time *Ennoia,* the Thought of Bythos, the Depth, for he is Poimandres.

The Gnostics, as well as the Nazarenes, allegorizing on the personification, said that the *First* and *Second* man loved the beauty of Sophia (Sephîrâh), the first woman, and thus the Father and the Son fecundated the heavenly "Woman" and from primal darkness procreated the visible light (Sephîrâh is the Invisible, or Spiritual Light), "whom they called the ANOINTED CHRISTUS, or King Messiah." \*\* This Christus is the *Adam of Dust* before his fall, with the spirit of the Adonai, his Father, and Shekhînah Adonai, his mother, upon him; for Adam Primus is Adon, Adonai, or Adonis. The primal existence manifests itself by its wisdom, and produces the *Intelligible* LOGOS (all visible creation). This wisdom was venerated by the Ophites under the form of a serpent. So far we see that the first and second life are the two Adams, or the first and the second man. In the former lies *Eva,* or the yet unborn spiritual Eve, and she is within Adam *Primus,* for she is a part of himself, who is androgyne. The Eva of dust, she who will be called in

---

\* *Zohar,* III, p. 290a; Amst. ed. (*Idrah Zutah,* viii, § 219).
† *Idrah Rabbah,* §§ 541-42.
‡ *Ibid.,* § 36.
§ *Ibid.,* § 172.
‖ *Idrah Zutah,* ii, § 51.
¶ *Nat. und Urspr. der Emanationslehre,* etc., p. 11.
\*\* Irenaeus, *Adv. Haer.,* I, xxx, § 1.

*Genesis* "the mother of all that live," is *within* Adam the Second. And now, from the moment of its first manifestation, the LORD MANO, the Unintelligible Wisdom, disappears from the scene of action. It will manifest itself only as Shekhînah, the GRACE; for the CORONA is "the innermost Light of all Lights," and hence it is darkness' own substance.*

In the *Kabala*, Shekhînah is the ninth emanation of Sephîrâh, which contains the whole of the ten Sephîrôth within herself. She belongs to the third triad and is produced together with *Malkhuth* or "Kingdom," of which she is the female counterpart. Otherwise she is held to be higher than any of these; for she is the "Divine Glory," the "veil," or "garment," of Ain-Soph. The Jews, whenever she is mentioned in the *Targumim*, say that she is the glory of Yehovah, which dwelt in the tabernacle, manifesting herself like a visible cloud; the "Glory" rested over the Mercy-Seat in the *Sanctum Sanctorum*.

In the Nazarene or Bardesanian System, which may be termed the Kabala within the Kabala, the Ancient of Days — *Antiquus Altus* — who is the Father of the Demiurgus of the universe, is called the *Third* Life, or *Abathur*; and he is the Father of *Pthahil*, who is the architect of the visible universe, which he calls into existence by the powers of his genii, at the order of the "Greatest"; the Abathur answering to the "Father" of Jesus in the later Christian theology. These two superior *Lives* then, are the crown within which dwells the greatest *Ferho*. "Before any creature came into existence the Lord Ferho existed." † This one is the First Life, formless and invisible; in whom the living Spirit of LIFE exists, the Highest GRACE. The two are ONE from eternity, for they are the Light and the CAUSE of the Light. Therefore, they answer to the kabalistic concealed *wisdom*, and to the concealed Shekhînah — the Holy Ghost. "This light, which is manifested, is the garment of the Heavenly Concealed," says *Idrah Zutah*. ‡ And the "heavenly man" is the superior Adam. "No one knows his paths except *Macroprosopus*" (Long-face) — the Superior *active* god. § "Not as I am *written* will I be read; in this world my name will be written Jehovah and read Adonai," ‖ say the Rabbins, very correctly. Adonai is the Adam-Kadmon; he is FATHER and MOTHER both. By this double mediatorship the Spirit of the "Ancient of the Ancient" descends upon the *Microprosopus* (Short-face) or the Adam of Eden. And the "Lord God breathes into his nostrils the breath of life."

When the woman separates herself from her androgyne, and becomes

---

* *Idrah Zutah*, ix, § 353; *Kabbala denudata*, II, p. 364; cf. Pythagoras' Monad.
† *Codex Nazaraeus*, I, p. 145.
‡ [ix, § 355.]
§ *Idrah Rabbah*, viii, 109.
‖ *Auszüge aus dem Buch Zohar*, p. 11 (Berlin, 1857); also *Zohar*, III, p. 230; Amst. ed.

a distinct individuality, the first story is repeated over again. Both the Father and Son, the two Adams, love her beauty; and then follows the allegory of the temptation and fall. It is in the *Kabala*, as in the Ophite system, in which both the Ophis and the Ophiomorphos are emanations emblematized as serpents, the former representing Eternity, Wisdom and Spirit (as in the Chaldean Magism of Aspic-worship and Wisdom-Doctrine in the olden times), and the latter Cunning, Envy and Matter. Both spirit and matter are serpents; and Adam-Kadmon becomes the Ophis who tempts himself — man and woman — to taste of the "Tree of Good and Evil," in order to teach them the mysteries of spiritual wisdom. Light tempts Darkness, and Darkness attracts Light, for Darkness is *matter*, and "the *Highest* Light shines not in its *Tenebrae*." With knowledge comes the temptation of the Ophiomorphos, and he prevails. The dualism of every existing religion is shown forth by the fall. "I have gotten a man from *the Lord*," exclaims Eve, when the Dualism, Cain and Abel — evil and good — is born. "And the Adam knew Hua, his woman (*astu*), and she became pregnant and bore *Kin*, and she said: קניתי איש את־יהוה : *Kanithi aish ath Yahveh* — I have gained or obtained a husband, even *Yahveh* (*Ish* — man)." * "*Cum arbore peccati Deus creavit seculum.*"

And now we will compare this system with that of the Jewish Gnostics — the Nazarenes, as well as with other philosophies.

The IsH AMON, the pleroma, or the boundless circle within which lie "all forms," is the THOUGHT of the power divine; it works in SILENCE, and suddenly light is begotten by darkness; it is called the SECOND life; and this one produces or generates the THIRD. This third light is "the FATHER of all things that live," as EUA is the "mother of all that live." He is the Creator who calls inert matter into life, through his vivifying spirit, and, therefore, is called the ancient of the world. Abathur is the Father who creates the first Adam, who creates in his turn the second. Abathur opens a gate and walks to the dark water (chaos), and looking down into it, the darkness reflects the image of Himself . . . and lo! a SON is formed—the Logos or Demiurge; Pthahil, who is the builder of the *material* world, is called into existence. According to the Gnostic dogma, this was the *Metatron*, the Archangel Gabriel, or messenger of life; or, as the Biblical allegory has it, the androgynous Adam-Kadmon again, the SON, who, with his Father's spirit, produces the ANOINTED, or Adam, before his fall.

When *Svayambhû*, the "Lord who exists through himself," feels impelled to manifest himself, he is thus described in the Hindu sacred books:

Having been impelled to produce various beings from his own divine

---

* [*Gen.* iv, 1.]

substance, he first manifested the waters which developed within themselves a productive seed.

"The seed became a germ bright as gold, blazing like the luminary with a thousand beams; and in that egg he was born himself, in the form of BRAHMÂ, the great principle of all the beings." *

The Egyptian Kneph, or Chnuphis, Divine Wisdom, represented by a serpent, produces an egg from his mouth, from which issues Ptah. In this case Ptah represents the universal germ, as well as Brahman, who is of the neuter gender, † otherwise [as *Brahmâ*] it becomes simply one of the names of the Deity. The former was the model of the THREE LIVES of the Nazarenes, as that of the kabalistic "Faces," PARTZUPHIM, which, in its turn, furnished the model for the Christian Trinity of Irenaeus and his followers. The egg was the primitive matter which served as a material for the building of the visible universe; it contained, as well as the Gnostic Pleroma, the kabalistic Shekhînah, the man and wife, the spirit and life, "whose light includes all other lights" or life-spirits. This first manifestation was symbolized by a serpent, which is at first *divine* wisdom, but *falling into generation*, becomes polluted. Ptah is the heavenly man, the Egyptian Adam-Kadmon, or Christ, who, in conjunction with the female Holy Ghost, the ZOÊ, produces the five elements, air, water, fire, earth and ether; the latter being a servile copy from the Buddhist Âdi, and his five Dhyâni-Buddhas, as we have shown in the preceding chapter. The Hindu *Svâyambhuva-Nara* develops from himself the *mother-principle*, enclosed within his own divine essence — *Nârî*, the immortal Virgin, who, when impregnated by his spirit, becomes *Tanmâtra*, the mother of the five elements — air, water, fire, earth and ether. Thus may be shown how all others proceed from the Hindu cosmogony.

Knorr von Rosenroth, busying himself with the interpretation of the *Kabala*, argues that, "In this first state (of secret wisdom), the infinite God Himself can be understood as 'Father' (of the new covenant). But the *Light* being let down by the Infinite through a canal into the 'primal Adam,' or *Messiah*, and joined with him, can be applied to the name SON. And the influx emitted down from him [the Son] to the lower parts [of the universe], can be applied to the character of the Holy Ghost." ‡ Sophia-Akhamôth, the half-spiritual, half-material LIFE, which vivifies the inert matter in the depths of chaos, is the Holy Ghost of the Gnostics, and the *Spiritus* (female) of the Nazarenes. She is — be it re-

---

* *Manu*, Bk. I, ślokas 8, 9.
† He is the universal and spiritual germ of *all* things.
‡ *Adumbratio Kabb. Chr.*, pp. 6, 7.

membered — the *sister* of *Christos*, the perfect emanation, and both are children or emanations of Sophia, the purely spiritual and intellectual daughter of Bythos, the Depth. For the elder Sophia is Shekhînah, the Face of God, "God's Shekhînah which is his image." *

"The *Son*, Zeus-Belus, or Sol-Mithra, is an image of the Father, an emanation from the *Supreme Light*," says Movers. "He passed for Creator." †

"Philosophers call the first air *anima mundi*. But the garment (Shekhînah) is higher than the first air, since it is joined closer to the Ain-Soph, the Boundless." ‡ Thus *Sophia* is Shekhînah, and Sophia-Akhamôth the *anima mundi*, the astral light of the kabalists, which contains the spiritual and material germs of all *that is*. For the Sophia-Akhamôth, like *Eve*, of whom she is the prototype, is "the mother of all that live."

There are three trinities in the Nazarene system as well as in the Hindu philosophy of the ante and the early Vedic period. While we see the few translators of the *Kabala*, the Nazarene *Codex*, and other abstruse works, hopelessly floundering amid the interminable pantheon of names, unable to agree as to a system in which to classify them, for the one hypothesis contradicts and overturns the other, we can but wonder at all this trouble, which could be so easily overcome. But even now, when the translation, and even the perusal of the ancient Sanskrit has become so easy as a point of comparison, they would never think it possible that every philosophy — whether Semitic, Hamitic, or Turanian, as they call it, has its key in the Hindu sacred works. Still facts are there, and facts are not easily destroyed. Thus, while we find the Hindu Trimûrti triply manifested as

| | | | |
|---|---|---|---|
| Nara (or Para-Purusha) | Agni | Brahmâ | the Father |
| Nârî (Mahâmâyâ) | Vâyu | Vishṇu | the Mother |
| Virâj (Brahmâ) | Sûrya | Śiva | the Son |

and the Egyptian trinity as follows:

| | | | |
|---|---|---|---|
| Kneph (or *Amen*) | Osiris | Râ (Horus) | the Father |
| Maut (or *Mut*) | Isis | Isis | the Mother |
| Khonsu | Horus | Malouli | the Son § |

the Nazarene System runs:

| | | | |
|---|---|---|---|
| Ferho (Ish-Amon) | Mano | Abathur | the Father |
| Chaos (dark water) | Spiritus (female) | Netubto | the Mother |
| Pthahil | Lehdoio | Lord Jordan | the Son |

The first is the concealed or non-manifested trinity — a pure abstraction. The other the active or the one revealed in the results of creation,

---
* *Idrah Rabbah*, xliv, § 1122.
† *Die Phönizier*, Vol. I, pp. 265, 550, 553.
‡ *Kabb. denudata*, II, p. 236.
§ Champollion-Figeac, *Égypte ancienne*, pp. 245-46.

proceeding out of the former — its spiritual prototype. The third is the mutilated image of both the others, crystallized in the form of human dogmas, which vary according to the exuberance of the national materialistic fancy.

The Supreme Lord of splendor and of light, luminous and refulgent, before which no other existed, is called Corona (the crown); Lord Ferho, the unrevealed life which existed in the former from eternity; and Lord Jordan — the spirit, the living water of grace.* He is the one through whom alone we can be saved; and thus he answers to the Shekhînah, the spiritual garment of Ain-Soph, or the Holy Ghost. These three constitute the trinity *in abscondito*. The second trinity is composed of the three lives. The first is the similitude of Lord Ferho, through whom he has proceeded forth; and the second Ferho is the King of Light — MANO (*Rex Lucis*). He is the heavenly life and light, and older than the Architect of heaven and earth.† The second life is *Ish Amon* (Pleroma), the vase of election, containing the visible thought of the *Iordanus Maximus* — the *type* (or its intelligible reflection), the prototype of the living water, who is the "spiritual Jordan." ‡ The third life, which is produced by the other two, is ABATHUR (*Ab*, the Parent or Father). This is the mysterious and decrepit "Aged of the Aged," the "Ancient *Senem sui obtegentem et grandaevum mundi*." This latter third Life is the Father of the Demiurge Pthahil, the Creator of the world, whom the Ophites call Ialdabaôth, § though Pthahil is the *only-begotten one*, the reflection of the Father, Abathur, who begets him by looking into the "dark water"; ‖ but the Lord Mano, "the Lord of loftiness, the Lord of all genii," is higher than the Father in this kabalistic *Codex* — one is purely spiritual, the other material. So, for instance, while Abathur's "only-begotten" one is the genius Pthahil, the Creator of the physical world, Lord Mano, the "Lord of Celsitude," who is the son of Him, who is "the Father of all who preach the Gospel," produces also an "only-begotten" one, the Lord Lehdoio, "a just Lord." He is the Christos, the anointed, who pours out the "grace" of the Invisible Jordan, the Spirit of the *Highest Crown*.

In the Arcanum, "in the assembly of splendor, lighted by MANO, to whom the scintillas of splendor owe their origin," the genii who live in light "rose, they went to the visible Jordan, and flowing water . . . they took counsel . . . and called forth the Only-Begotten Son of an imperishable

---

* *Codex Nazaraeus*, II, pp. 47-57.

† *Ibid.*, I, p. 145.

‡ *Ibid.*, II, p. 211.

§ *Ibid.*, I, p. 309.

‖ Sophia-Akhamôth also begets her son Ialdabaôth, the *Demiurge*, by looking into chaos or matter, and by coming into contact with it.

image, and who cannot be conceived by reflection, Lehdoio the just Lord, and sprang from Lehdoio, the just lord, whom the life had produced by his word." *

Mano is the chief of the seven Aeôns, who are Mano (*Rex Lucis*), Ayar-Ziwa, Ignis Vivus, Lux, Vita, Aqua Viva (the living water of baptism, the genius of the Jordan), and Ipsa Vita, the chief of the six genii, which form with him the mystic *seven*. The Nazarene Mano is simply the copy of the Hindu first Manu — the emanation of Manu-Svâyambhuva — from whom evolve in succession the six other Manus, types of the subsequent races of men. We find them all represented by the apostle-kabalist John in the "seven lamps of fire burning before the throne, which are the seven spirits of God," † and in the seven angels bearing the seven vials. Again in Pthahil we recognize the Christian doctrine.

In the *Revelation* of Joannes Theologos it is said: "I turned and saw . . . in the midst of the *seven candlesticks* one like unto the Son of man . . . his head and his hair were like wool, as white as snow; and his eyes were as a flame of fire . . . and his feet like unto fine brass as if they burned in a furnace" (i, 12-15). *John* here repeats, as is well known, the words of Daniel and Ezekiel. "The Ancient of Days . . . whose hair was white as pure wool . . . etc." And "the appearance of a *man* . . . above the throne . . . and the appearance of fire, and it had brightness round about." ‡ The fire being "the glory of the Lord." Pthahil is son of the man, the Third Life, and his upper part is represented as white as snow, while standing near the throne of the living fire he has the appearance of a flame.

All these "apocalyptic" visions are based on the description of the "white head" of the *Zohar*, in whom the kabalistic trinity is united. The white head, "which conceals in its cranium the spirit," and which is environed by subtle fire. The "appearance of a man" is that of Adam-Kadmon, through which passes the thread of light represented by the fire. Pthahil is the *Vir Novissimis* (the newest man), the son of Abathur, § the latter being the "man," or the *third* life, ‖ now the third personage of the trinity. *John* sees "one like unto the son of man," holding in his right hand seven stars, and standing between "seven golden candlesticks (*Revelation* i). Pthahil takes his "stand on high," according to the will of his father, "the highest Aeôn who has seven sceptres," and

---

\* *Codex Nazar.*, II, pp. 107-09. See Dunlap, *Sôd, the Son of the Man*, p. 60, for translation.
† *Revelation* iv, 5.
‡ *Ezekiel* i, 26, 27.
§ *Codex Nazar.*, II, p. 127.
‖ The first androgyne duad being considered a *unit* in all the secret computations, is, therefore, the Holy Ghost.

seven genii, who astronomically represent the seven planets or stars. He stands "shining in the garment of the Lord, resplendent by the agency of the genii." * He is the Son of his Father, Life, and his mother, Spirit, or Light.† The Logos is represented in the *Gospel according to John* as one in whom was "*Life*, and the life was the *light* of men" (i, 4). Pthahil is the Demiurge, and his father created the visible universe of matter through him. ‡ In the *Epistle of Paul to the Ephesians* (iii, 9), God is said to have "*created all things* by Jesus." In the *Codex*, the Parent-LIFE says: "Arise, go, our son first-begotten, ordained for all creatures." § "As the living father hath sent me," says Christ, "God sent his only-begotten son that we might live." ‖ Finally, having performed his work on earth, Pthahil reascends to his father Abathur. "*Et qui, relicto quem procreaverat mundo, ad Abathur suum patrem contendit.*"¶ "My father sent me . . . I go to the Father," repeats Jesus.

Laying aside the theological disputes of Christianity which try to blend together the Jewish Creator of the first chapter of *Genesis* with the "Father" of the *New Testament*, Jesus states repeatedly of his Father that "He is *in secret*." Surely he would not have so termed the ever-present "Lord God" of the Mosaic books, who showed Himself to Moses and the Patriarchs, and finally allowed all the elders of Israel to look on Himself.** When Jesus is made to speak of the temple at Jerusalem as of his "Father's house," he does not mean the physical building, which he maintains he can destroy and then again rebuild in three days, but of the temple of Solomon, the wise kabalist, who indicates in his *Proverbs* that every man is the temple of God, or of his own divine spirit. This term of the "Father who is in secret," we find used as much in the *Kabala* as in the *Codex Nazaraeus*, and elsewhere. No one has ever seen the wisdom concealed in the "Cranium," and no one has beheld the "Depth" (Bythos). Simon the *Magician* preached "one Father unknown to all." ††

We can trace this appellation of a "secret" God still farther back. In the *Kabala*, the "Son" of the *concealed* Father who dwells in light and glory, is the "Anointed," the *Zeir-Anpîn*, who unites in himself all the Sephîrôth, he is Christos, or the Heavenly man. It is through Christ that the Pneuma, or the Holy Ghost, creates "all things"

---

\* *Codex Nazar.*, III, p. 59.
† *Ibid.*, I, p. 285.
‡ *Ibid.*, I, 309.
§ *Ibid.*, I, p. 287. See Dunlap, *op. cit.*, p. 101.
‖ *John* vi, 57; *1 John* iv, 9.
¶ *Codex Nazar.*, II, p. 123.
\*\* "Then went up Moses and Aaron, Nadab and Abihu, and seventy of the elders of Israel. *And they saw the God of Israel*," *Exodus* xxiv, 9-10.
†† *Clementine Homilies*, XVIII, 4; Irenaeus, *Adv. Haer.*, I, xxiv, 1.

## WHAT ARE THE CHERUBIM AND SERAPHIM? 231

(*Ephesians* iii, 9), and produces the four elements, air, water, fire and earth. This assertion is unquestionable, for we find Irenaeus basing on this fact his best argument for the necessity of there being four gospels. There can be neither more nor fewer than four — he argues. "For as there are four quarters of the world, and four general winds (καθολικὰ πνεύματα) . . . it is right that she (the Church) should have four pillars. From which it is manifest that the Word, *the maker of all, he who sitteth upon the Cherubim* . . . as David says, supplicating his advent, 'Thou that sittest between the Cherubim, shine forth!' For the Cherubim also are *four-faced* and their faces are symbols of the working of the Son of God." *

We will not stop to discuss at length the special holiness of the four-faced Cherubim, although we might, perhaps, show their origin in all the ancient pagodas of India, in the *vâhanas* (or vehicles) of their chief gods; as likewise we might easily attribute the respect paid to them to the kabalistic wisdom, which, nevertheless, the Church rejects with great horror. But, we cannot resist the temptation to remind the reader that he may easily ascertain the several significances attributed to these Cherubs by reading the *Kabala*. "When the souls are to leave their abode," says the *Zohar*, holding to the doctrine of the pre-existence of souls in the world of emanations, "each soul separately appears before the Holy King, dressed in a sublime form, with the features in which it is to appear in this world. It is from this sublime form that the image proceeds." † Then it goes on to say that the types or forms of these faces "are four in number — those of the angel or man, of the lion, the bull, and the eagle." Furthermore, we may well express our wonder that Irenaeus should not have re-enforced his argument for the four gospels by citing the whole Pantheon of the four-armed Hindu gods!

Ezekiel in representing his four animals, now called Cherubim, as types of the four symbolical beings, which, in his visions support the throne of Jehovah, had not far to go for his models. The Chaldeo-Babylonian protecting genii were familiar to him; the Sed, Alaph or *Kirub* (Cherubim), the bull, with the human face; the Nergal, human-headed lion; Ustur the Sphinx-man; and the Nattig, with its eagle's head.[33] The religion of the masters — the idolatrous Babylonians and Assyrians — was transferred almost bodily into the revealed Scripture of the captives, and from thence came into Christianity.

Already we find Ezekiel addressed by the likeness of the glory of the Lord "as Son of man." This peculiar title is used repeatedly throughout the whole book of this prophet, which is as kabalistic as

---
\* *Adv. Haer.*, III, xi, § 8.
† *Zohar*, III, p. 104; Amsterdam ed.

the "roll of a book" which the "Glory" causes him to eat. It is written *within* and *without*; and its real meaning is identical with that of the *Apocalypse*. It appears strange that so much stress should be laid on this peculiar appellation, said to have been applied by Jesus to himself, when, in the symbolical or kabalistic language, a prophet is so addressed. It is as extraordinary to see Irenaeus indulging in such graphic descriptions of Jesus as to show him, "the maker of all, sitting upon a Cherubim," * unless he identifies him with Shekhînah, whose usual place was among the Cherubs of the Mercy Seat. We also know that the Cherubim and Seraphim are titles of the "Old Serpent" (the orthodox Devil), the Seraphs being the burning or fiery serpents in kabalistic symbolism. The ten emanations of Adam-Kadmon, called the Sephîrôth, have all emblems and titles corresponding to each. So, for instance, the last two are Victory, or Yehovah-Tsabaôth, whose symbol is the right column of Solomon, the Pillar *Jachin*; while GLORY is the left Pillar, or *Boaz*, and its name is "the Old Serpent," and also "Seraphim and Cherubim." †

The "Son of man" is an appellation which could not be assumed by any one but a kabalist. Except, as shown above, in the *Old Testament*, it is used but by one prophet — Ezekiel, the kabalist. In their mysterious and mutual relations, the Aeôns or Sephîrôth are represented in the *Kabala* by a great number of circles, and sometimes by the figure of a MAN, which is symbolically formed out of such circles. This man is Zeir-Anpîn, and the 243 numbers of which his figure consists relate to the different orders of the celestial hierarchy. The original idea of this figure, or rather the model, may have been taken from the Hindu Brahmâ, and the various castes typified by the several parts of his body, as King suggests in his *Gnostics*. In one of the grandest and most beautiful cave-temples at Ellora, dedicated to Viśvakarman, son of Brahmâ, is a representation of this God and his attributes. To one acquainted with Ezekiel's description of the "likeness of four living creatures," every one of which had four faces and the hands of a man under its wings, etc.,‡ this figure at Ellora must certainly appear absolutely *Biblical*. Brahmâ is called the father of "man," as well as Jupiter and other highest gods.

It is in the Buddhistic representations of Mount Meru, called by the Burmese *Myé-nmo*, and by the Siamese *Sineru*, that we find one of the originals of the Adam-Kadmon, Zeir-Anpîn, the "heavenly man," and of all the Aeôns, Sephîrôth, Powers, Dominions, Thrones, Virtues and

---

* [Irenaeus, *Fragments*, liii, liv.]
† C. W. King, *The Gnostics*, etc., p. 12.
‡ *Ezekiel* i, 5-7.

Dignities of the *Kabala*. Between two pillars, which are connected by an arch, the keystone of the latter is represented by a *crescent*. This is the domain in which dwells the Supreme Wisdom of Âdi-Buddha, the Supreme and invisible Deity. Beneath this highest central point comes the circle of the direct emanation of the Unknown — the circle of Brahmâ with some Hindus, of the first *avatâra* of Buddha, according to others. This answers to Adam-Kadmon and the ten Sephîrôth. Nine of the emanations are encircled by the tenth, and are occasionally represented by pagodas, each of which bears a name which expresses one of the chief attributes of the manifested Deity. Then below come the seven stages, or heavenly spheres, each sphere being encircled by a sea. These are the celestial mansions of the *devatâs*, or gods, each losing somewhat in holiness and purity as it approaches the earth. Then comes Meru itself, formed of numberless circles within three large ones, typifying the trinity of man; and for one acquainted with the numerical value of the letters in Biblical names, like that of the "Great Beast," or that of Mithras, $M\iota\theta\rho\alpha\varsigma$ $\alpha\beta\rho\alpha\xi\alpha\varsigma$, and others, it is an easy matter to establish the identity of the Meru-gods with the emanations or Sephîrôth of the kabalists. Also the genii of the Nazarenes, with their special missions, are all found in this most ancient mythos, a most perfect representation of the symbolism of the "secret doctrine," as taught in archaic ages.

King gives a few hints — though doubtless too insufficient to teach anything important, for they are based upon the calculations of Bishop Newton* — as to this mode of finding out mysteries in the value of letters. However, we find this great archaeologist, who has devoted so much time and labor to the study of Gnostic gems, corroborating our assertion. He shows that the entire theory is Hindu, and points out that the *Durgâ*, or female counterpart of each Asiatic god, is what the kabalists term active *Virtue* † in the celestial hierarchy, a term which the Christian Fathers adopted and repeated, without fully appreciating, and the meaning of which the later theology has utterly disfigured. But to return to Meru.

---

\* *The Gnostics and their Remains,* pp. 253 *et seq.* [p. 262 in 2nd ed.]

† "Although this science is commonly supposed to be peculiar to the Jewish Talmudists, there is no doubt that [they] borrowed the idea from a foreign source, and that, the Chaldeans, the *founders of magic art*," says King in *The Gnostics.* "The titles Iaô and *Abraxas,* and several others, instead of being recent Gnostic figments, were indeed holy names, borrowed from the most ancient formulae of the East. Pliny must allude to them when he mentions the virtues ascribed by the Magi to amethysts engraved with the names of the Sun and Moon; names . . . not expressed in either the Greek or Latin tongues. [*Nat. Hist.,* xxxviii, § 41.] In the '*Eternal Sun,*' the '*Abraxas,*' the '*Adonai,*' of these gems we recognize the very amulets ridiculed by the philosophic Pliny." (*Gnostics,* pp. 79-80; p. 283 in 2nd ed.) *Virtutes* (miracles) as employed by Irenaeus.

The whole is surrounded by the *Mahâ-Samudra*, or the great sea — the astral light and ether of the kabalists and scientists; and within the central circle appears "the likeness of a man." He is the Akhamôth of the Nazarenes, the twofold unity, or the androgyne man; the heavenly incarnation, and a perfect representation of *Zeir-Anpîn* (short-face), the son of *Arikh-Anpîn* (long-face).* This likeness is now represented in many lamaseries by Gautama Buddha, the last of the incarnated avatâras. Still lower, under the Meru, is the dwelling of the great *Nâga*, who is called *Râja-Nâga*, the king-serpent — the serpent of *Genesis*, the Gnostic Ophis — and the goddess of the earth, *Bhûmayî-Nârî*, or *Yâmî*, who waits upon the great dragon, for she is Eve, "the mother of all that live." Still lower is the eighth sphere, the infernal regions. The uppermost regions of Brahmâ are surrounded by the sun, moon, and planets, the seven stellars of the Nazarenes, and just as they are described in the *Codex*.

"The seven impostor-Daemons who deceive the sons of Adam. The name of one is *Sol*; of another *Spiritus Venereus*, Astro; of the third *Nebu*, Mercurius, *a false Messiah*; . . . the name of a fourth is Sin, *Luna*; the fifth is *Khiyûn*, Saturnus; the sixth, *Bel*, Zeus; the seventh, *Nerig*, Mars." † Then there are "*Seven Lives* procreated," seven good Stellars, "which are from Kebar-Ziwa, and are those bright ones who shine in their own form and splendor that pours from on high . . . At the gate of the HOUSE OF LIFE the throne is fitly placed for the Lord of Splendor, and there are THREE habitations." ‡ The habitations of the *Trimûrti*, the Hindu trinity, are placed beneath the keystone — the golden crescent, in the representation of Meru. "And there was under his feet [of the God of Israel] as it were a paved work of a sapphire-stone" (*Exodus* xxiv, 10). Under the crescent is the heaven of Brahmâ, all paved with sapphires. The paradise of Indra is resplendent with a thousand suns; that of Śiva (Saturn), is in the northeast; his throne is formed of lapiz-lazuli and the floor of heaven is of fervid gold. "When he sits on the throne he blazes with fire up to *the loins*." At Hardvâr, during the fair, in which he is more than ever *Mahâdeva*, the highest god, the attributes and emblems sacred to the Jewish "Lord God," may be recognized one by one in those of Śiva. The Binlang stone, § sacred to this Hindu deity, is an unhewn stone like the Bethel, consecrated by the Patriarch Jacob, and set up by him "for a pillar," and like the latter Binlang is *anointed*. We need hardly remind the student that the *liṅga*,

---

\* So called to distinguish the short-face, who *is exterior*, "from the venerable sacred ancient" (cf. *Idrah Rabbah*, iii, § 36; v, § 54). *Zeir-Anpîn* is the "image of the Father." "He that hath seen me hath seen the Father." (*John* xiv, 9).

† *Codex Nazar.*, I, p. 55.

‡ *Ibid.*, III, p. 61.

§ This stone, of a sponge-like surface, is found in the Narbada [river] and is seldom to be seen in other places.

the emblem sacred to Śiva and whose temples are modelled after this form, is identical in shape, meaning and purpose with the "pillars" set up by the several patriarchs to mark their adoration of the Lord God. In fact, one of these patriarchal lithoi might even now be carried in the Śivaitic processions of Calcutta, without its Hebrew derivations being suspected. The four arms of Śiva are often represented with appendages like wings; he has *three* eyes and a *fourth* in the crescent, obtained by him at the churning of the ocean, as Pañcha Mukha Śiva has four heads.

In this god we recognize the description given by Ezekiel, in the first chapter of his book, of his vision, in which he beholds the "likeness of a man" in the four living creatures, who had "four faces, four wings," who had one pair of "straight feet . . . which sparkled like the color *of burnished* brass . . . and their rings were full of eyes round about them four." It is the throne and heaven of Śiva that the prophet describes in saying ". . . and there was the likeness of a throne, as the appearance of a sapphire stone . . . and I saw as the color of amber [gold], as the appearance of fire round about . . . from his loins even upward, and from the appearance of his loins even downward, I saw as it were the appearance of fire" (*Ezekiel*, i, 26, 27). "And his feet like unto fine brass, as if they burned in a furnace" (*Revelation* i, 15). "As for their faces . . . one had the face of a cherub, and the face of a lion . . . they also had the face of *an ox* and the face of an eagle" (*Ezekiel* i, 10; x, 14). This *fourfold* appearance we find in the two *cherubim* of gold on the two ends of the ark; these symbolic four *faces* being adopted, moreover, later, one by each evangelist, as may be easily ascertained from the pictures of Matthew, Mark, Luke and John,* prefixed to their respective gospels in the Roman Vulgate and Greek *Bibles.*

"Taautus," the great god of the Phoenicians, says Sanchoniathon, "having portrayed Ouranus, represented also the countenances of the gods Cronus and Dagon, and the sacred characters of the elements. He contrived also for Cronus the ensign of his royal power, having four eyes in the parts before and in the parts behind, two of them closing as in sleep; and upon the shoulders four wings, two in the act of flying, and two reposing as at rest. And the symbol was, that Cronus whilst he slept was watching, and reposed whilst he was awake. And in like manner with respect to the wings, that he was flying whilst he rested, yet rested whilst he flew." †

The identity of Saturn with Śiva is corroborated still more when we consider the emblem of the latter, the *ḍamaru,* which is an hourglass, to

---

* John has an eagle near him; Luke, a bull; Mark, a lion; and Matthew, an angel — the kabalistic quaternary of the Egyptian Tarot.

† [Cf. Cory, *Anc. Fragm.*, p. 15; ed. 1832.]

show the progress of time, represented by this god in his capacity of a destroyer. The bull *Nandi*, the *vâhana* of Śiva and the most sacred emblem of this god, is reproduced in the Egyptian Apis; and in the bull created by Ormazd and killed by Ahriman. The religion of Zoroaster based upon the "secret doctrine," is found held by the people of Eritene;[34] it was the religion of the Persians when they conquered the Assyrians. From thence it is easy to trace the introduction of this emblem of LIFE represented by the Bull, in every religious system. The college of the Magians had accepted it with the change of dynasty;* Daniel is described as a Rabbi, the chief of the Babylonian astrologers and Magi;† therefore we see the Assyrian little bulls and the attributes of Śiva reappearing under a hardly modified form in the cherubs of the Talmudistic Jews, as we have traced the bull Apis in the sphinxes or cherubs of the Mosaic Ark; and as we find it several thousand years later in the company of one of the Christian evangelists, Luke.

Whoever has lived in India long enough to acquaint himself even superficially with the native deities, must detect the similarity between Jehovah and other gods besides Śiva. As Saturn, the latter was always held in great respect by the Talmudists. He was held in reverence by the Alexandrian kabalists as the direct inspirer of the law and the prophets; one of the names of Saturn was Israel, and we will show, in time, his identity in a certain way with Abram, which Movers ‡ and others hinted at long since. Thus it cannot be wondered at if Valentinus, Basilides, and the Ophite Gnostics placed the dwelling of their Ialdabaôth, also a destroyer as well as a creator, in the planet Saturn; for it was he who gave the law in the wilderness and spoke through the prophets. If more proof should be required we will show it in the testimony of the canonical *Bible* itself. In *Amos*, the "Lord" pours vials of wrath upon the people of Israel. He rejects their burnt offerings and will not listen to their prayers, but inquires of Amos, "have ye offered unto *me* sacrifices and offerings in the wilderness forty years, O house of Israel? But ye have borne the tabernacle of your Moloch and *Chiun* your images, the *star of your god*" (v, 25, 26). Who are *Moloch* and *Chiun* but Baal-Saturn-Śiva, and *Chiun*, Khîyûn, the same Saturn whose star the Israelites had taken to themselves? There seems no escape in this case; all these deities are identical.

The same in the case of the numerous Logoi. While the Zoroastrian Saoshyant is framed on that of the tenth Brahmanical Avatâra, and the fifth Buddha of the followers of Gautama; and we find the former, after having passed part and parcel into the kabalistic system of king Messiah, reflected in the Apostle Gabriel of the Nazarenes, and Hibil-Ziwa, the Legatus, sent on earth by the Lord of Celsitude and Light; all of these —

---

\* See J. Matter, *Hist. crit. de Gnosticisme*, upon the subject.

† Cf. *Daniel* v, 11.

‡ [*Die Phönizier*, Vol. I, pp. 396 *et seq.*]

Hindu and Persian, Buddhist and Jewish, the Christos of the Gnostics and the Philonean Logos are found combined in "the Word made flesh" of the fourth *Gospel.* Christianity includes all these systems, patched and arranged to meet the occasion. Do we take up the *Avesta*—we find there the dual system so prevalent in the Christian scheme. The struggle between Ahriman,* Darkness, and Ormazd, Light, has been going on in the world continually since the beginning of time. When the worst arrives and Ahriman will seem to have conquered the world and corrupted all mankind, *then will appear the Savior* of mankind, Saoshyant. He will come seated upon a white horse and followed by an army of good genii equally mounted on milk-white steeds.† And this we find faithfully copied in *Revelation*: "I saw heaven opened, and behold a *white horse;* and he that sat upon him was called faithful and true. . . . And the armies which were in heaven followed him upon white horses" (*Revelation* xix, 11, 14). Saoshyant himself is but a later Persian *permutation* of the Hindu Vishnu. The figure of this god may be found unto this day representing him as the Savior, the "Preserver" (the preserving spirit of God), in the temple of Râma. The picture shows him in his tenth incarnation — the *Kalki-avatâra*, which is yet to come — as an armed warrior mounted upon a white horse. Waving over his head the sword [of] destruction, he holds in his other hand a discus, made up of rings encircled in one another, an emblem of the revolving cycles of great ages, ‡ for Vishnu will thus appear but at the end of the *Kali-yuga,* answering to the end of the world expected by our Adventists. "And out of his mouth goeth a sharp sword . . . on his head were many crowns" (*Revelation* xix, 12, 15). Vishnu is often represented with several crowns superposed on his head. "And I saw an angel standing in the Sun" (17). The *white horse is the horse of the Sun.* § Saoshyant, the Persian Savior, is also born of a virgin, and at the end of days he will come as a Redeemer to regenerate the world, but he will be preceded by two prophets, who will come to announce him.¶ Hence the Jews who had Moses and Elias, are now waiting for the Messiah. "Then comes the

---

\* Ahriman, the production of Zoroaster, is so called in hatred of the Ârias or Âryas, the Brahmans against whose dominion the Zoroastrians had revolted. Although an Ârya (a noble, a sage) himself, Zoroaster, as in the case of the Devas whom he disgraced from gods to the position of *devils,* hesitated not to designate this type of the spirit of evil under the name of his enemies, the Brahman-Âryas. The whole struggle of Ahura-Mazda and Ahriman is but the allegory of the great religious and political war between Brahmanism and Zoroastrianism.

† Nork, *Bibl. Mythol.*, Vol. II, p. 146.

‡ Rev. Dr. Maurice also takes it to mean the cycles. [*Hist. of Hindostan,* 1795-98, Bk. IV, Pt. III, ch. v, p. 503.]

§ Duncker, *Geschichte der Alterthums,* Vol. II, p. 363.

¶ Spiegel, *Zend-Avesta,* Vol. I, pp. 32-37, 244. [Cf. King, *The Gnostics,* etc., p. 9; p. 31 in 2nd ed.]

general *resurrection*, when the good will immediately enter into this happy abode — the regenerated earth; and Ahriman and his angels (the devils),* and the wicked, be purified by immersion in a lake of molten metal . . . Henceforward, all will enjoy unchangeable happiness, and, headed by Saoshyant, ever sing the praises of the Eternal One." † The above is a perfect repetition of Vishṇu in his tenth avatâra, for he will then throw the wicked into the infernal abodes in which, after purifying themselves, they will be pardoned — even those devils which rebelled against Brahmâ, and were hurled into the bottomless pit by Śiva; as also the "blessed ones" will go to dwell with the gods, over the Mount Meru. ‡

Having thus traced the similarity of views respecting the Logos, Metatron and Mediator, as found in the *Kabala* and the *Codex* of the Christian Nazarenes and Gnostics, the reader is prepared to appreciate the audacity of the Patristic scheme to reduce a purely metaphysical figure into concrete form, and make it appear as if the finger of prophecy had from time immemorial been pointing down the vista of ages to Jesus as the coming Messiah. A *theomythos* intended to symbolize the coming day, near the close of the great cycle, when the "glad tidings" from heaven should proclaim the universal brotherhood and common faith of humanity, the day of regeneration — was violently distorted into an accomplished fact.

"Why callest thou me good? there is none good but *one, that is God*," says Jesus.‖ Is this the language of a God? of the second person in the Trinity, who is identical with the First? And if this Messiah, or Holy Ghost of the Gnostic and Pagan Trinities, had come in his person, what did he mean by distinguishing between himself, the "Son of man," and the Holy Ghost? "And whosoever shall speak a word against the Son of man, it shall be forgiven him; but unto him that blasphemeth against the Holy Ghost it shall not be forgiven," he says. § And how account for the marvellous identity of this very language, with the precepts enunciated, centuries before, by the Kabalists and the "Pagan" initiates? The following are a few instances out of many.

"No one of the gods, no man or Lord, can be good, but *only God alone*," says Hermes.¶

---

* The *daêvas* or devils of the Iranians contrast with the devas or deities of India.

† J. F. Kleucker, *Zend-Avesta, Bundahish*, § xxxi.

‡ Origen stoutly maintained the doctrine of eternal punishment to be erroneous. He held that at the second advent of Christ even the devils among the damned would be forgiven. The eternal damnation is a later *Christian* thought. [Cf. Origen, *De principiis*, I, v; II, x; III, vi.]

‖ *Matt.* xix, 17.

§ *Luke* xii, 10.

¶ [L. Ménard, *Hermès Trismégiste*, Paris, 1867, p. 25.]

"To be a good man is impossible, God alone possesses this privilege," repeats Plato, with a slight variation.*

Six centuries before Christ, the Chinese philosopher Confucius said that his doctrine was simple and easy to comprehend (*Lun Yü*, chap. 5, § 15). To which one of his disciples added: "The doctrine of our master consists in having an invariable correctness of heart, and in doing toward others as we would that they should do to us." †

"Jesus of Nazareth, a man approved of God among you by miracles." ‡ exclaims Peter, long after the scene of Calvary. "There was a *man* sent from God, whose name was John," § says the fourth *Gospel,* thus placing the Baptist on an equality with Jesus. John the Baptist, in one of the most solemn acts of his life, that of baptizing Christ, thinks not that he is going to baptize *a God*, but uses the word man. "This is he of whom I said, after me cometh *a man*." ‖ Speaking of himself, Jesus says, "Ye seek to kill *me, a man* that hath told you the truth, which *I have heard of God.*" ¶ Even the blind man of Jerusalem, healed by the great thaumaturgist, full of gratitude and admiration for his benefactor, in narrating the miracle does not call Jesus God, but simply says, ". . . *a man* that is called Jesus, made clay."**

We do not close the list for lack of other instances and proofs, but simply because what we now say has been repeated and demonstrated by others, many times before us. But there is no more incurable evil than blind and unreasoning fanaticism. Few are the men who, like Dr. Priestley, have the courage to write, "We find nothing like divinity ascribed to Christ before Justin Martyr (A.D. 141), who, from being a philosopher, became a Christian." ††  [35]

Mohammed appeared nearly six hundred years ‡‡ after the presumed deicide. The Graeco-Roman world was still convulsed with religious dissensions, withstanding all the past imperial edicts and forcible Christianization. While the Council of Trent was disputing about the *Vulgate*, the unity of God quietly superseded the trinity, and soon the Mohammedans outnumbered the Christians. Why? Because their prophet never sought to identify himself with Allah. Otherwise, it is safe to say, he would not have lived to see his religion flourish. Till the present day Mohammedanism has made and is now making more proselytes than Chris-

---

\* *Protagoras,* § 84.
† Pauthier, *La Chine,* Vol. II, p. 375.
‡ *Acts* ii, 22.
§ *John* i, 6.
‖ *John* i, 30.
¶ *John* viii, 40.
\*\* *John* ix, 11.
†† Jos. Priestley, *General History of the Christian Church,* Birmingham, 1790, Vol. I, p. 266; also *An History of Early Opinions Concerning Jesus Christ,* Birmingham, 1786, Vol. I, p. 92; Vol. II, pp. 29, 30, 271; Vol. III, p. 299, 300.
‡‡ Mohammed was born in 571 A.D.

tianity. Buddha Siddhârtha came as a simple mortal, centuries before Christ. The religious ethics of this faith are now found to far exceed in moral beauty anything ever dreamed of by the Tertullians and Augustines.

The true spirit of Christianity can alone be fully found in Buddhism; partially, it shows itself in other "heathen" religions. Buddha never made of himself a god, nor was he deified by his followers. The Buddhists are now known to far outnumber Christians; they are enumerated at nearly 500,000,000. While cases of conversion among Buddhists, Brahmanists, Mohammedans and Jews become so rare as to show how sterile are the attempts of our missionaries, atheism and materialism spread their gangrenous ulcers and gnaw every day deeper at the very heart of Christianity. There are no atheists among heathen populations, and those few among the Buddhists and Brahmanists who have become infected with materialism may always be found to belong to large cities densely thronged with Europeans, and only among educated classes. Truly says Bishop Kidder: "Were a wise man to choose his religion from those who profess it, perhaps Christianity would be the last religion he would choose!"

In an able little pamphlet from the pen of the popular lecturer, J. M. Peebles, M.D., the author quotes, from the London *Athenaeum*, an article in which are described the welfare and civilization of the inhabitants of Yarkand and Kashgar, "who seem virtuous and happy." "Gracious Heavens!" fervently exclaims the honest author, who himself was once a Universalist clergyman, "grant to keep Christian missionaries *away* from 'happy' and heathen Tartary!" *

From the earliest days of Christianity, when Paul upbraided the *Church* of Corinth for a crime "as is not so much as named among the Gentiles — that one should have his father's wife"; and for their making a pretext of the "Lord's Supper" for *debauch* and drunkenness (*1 Corinthians* v, 1), the profession of the name of Christ has ever been more a pretext than the evidence of holy feeling. However, a correct form of this verse is: "Everywhere the lewd practice among you is heard about, such a lewd practice as is nowhere among the heathen nations — even the having or marrying of the father's wife." The Persian influence would seem to be indicated in this language. The practice existed "nowhere among the nations," except in Persia, where it was esteemed especially meritorious. Hence, too, the Jewish stories of Abraham marrying his sister, Nahor his niece, Amram his father's sister, and Judah his son's widow, whose children appear to have been legitimate. The Âryan tribes esteemed endogamous marriages, while the Tatars and all barbarous nations required all alliances to be exogamous.

---

* J. M. Peebles, *Jesus: Myth, Man, or God*, etc., 1870, p. 86 footnote.

There was but one apostle of Jesus worthy of that name, and that was Paul. However disfigured were his *Epistles* by dogmatic hands before being admitted into the Canon, his conception of the great and divine figure of the philosopher who died for his idea can still be traced in his addresses to the various Gentile nations. Only, he who would understand him better yet must study the Philonean *Logos* reflecting now and then the Hindu *Śabda* (logos) of the Mîmânsâ school.

As to the other apostles, those whose names are prefixed to the *Gospels*, we cannot well believe in their veracity when we find them attributing to their Master miracles surrounded by circumstances recorded, if not in the oldest books of India, at least in such as antedated Christianity, and in the very phraseology of the traditions. Who, in his days of simple and blind credulity, but marvelled at the touching narrative given in the *Gospels according to Mark* and *Luke* of the resurrection of the daughter of Jairus? Who has ever doubted its originality? And yet the story is copied entirely from the *Harivanśa*, and is recorded among the miracles attributed to Krishna. We translate it from the French version:

"The King Angashuna caused the betrothal of his daughter, the beautiful Kalâvatî, with the young son of Vâmadeva, the powerful King of Antarvedi, named Govinda, to be celebrated with great pomp.

"But as Kalâvatî was amusing herself in the groves with her companions, she was stung by a serpent and died. Angashuna tore his clothes, covered himself with ashes, and cursed the day when he was born.

"Suddenly, a great rumor spread through the palace, and the following cries were heard, a thousand times repeated: '*Paśya pitaram; paśya gurum!*' 'See the Father! See the Teacher!' Then Krishna approached, smiling, leaning on the arm of Arjuna. . . 'Master!' cried Angashuna, casting himself at his feet, and sprinkling them with his tears, 'See my poor daughter!' and he showed him the body of Kalâvatî, stretched upon a mat . . .

" 'Why do you weep?' replied Krishna, in a gentle voice. '*Do you not see that she is sleeping?* Listen to the sound of her breathing, like the sigh of the night wind which rustles the leaves of the trees. See, her cheeks resuming their color, her eyes, whose lids tremble as if they were about to open; her lips quiver as if about to speak; she is sleeping, I tell you; and hold! see, she moves. *Kalâvatî! Rise and walk!*'

"Hardly had Krishna spoken, when the breathing, warmth, movement and life returned little by little into the corpse, and the young girl, obeying the injunction of the demi-god, rose from her couch and rejoined her companions. But the crowd marvelled and cried out: 'This is a god, since death is no more for him than sleep'!" *

All such parables are enforced upon Christians, with the addition of dogmas which, in their extraordinary character, leave far behind them the wildest conceptions of heathenism. The Christians, in order to believe in a deity, have found it necessary to kill their God, that they themselves should live!

And now, the Supreme, unknown one, the Father of grace and mercy, and his celestial hierarchy are managed by the Church as though they were so many theatrical stars and supernumeraries under salary! Six centuries before the Christian era, Xenophanes has disposed of such anthropomorphism by an immortal satire, recorded and preserved by Clement of Alexandria:

> "There is one God Supreme over all gods, diviner than mortals,
> Whose form is not like unto man's, and as unlike his nature;
> But vain mortals imagine that gods like themselves are begotten
> With human sensations, and voice, and corporeal members;
> So if oxen or lions had hands and could work in man's fashion,
> And trace out with chisel or brush their conception of Godhead
> Then would horses depict gods like horses, and oxen like oxen,
> Each kind the Divine with its own form and nature endowing." †

And hear Vyâsa — the poet-pantheist of India, who, for all the scientists can prove, may have lived, as Jacolliot has it, some fifteen thousand years ago — discoursing on Mâyâ, the illusion of the senses:

"All religious dogmas only serve to obscure the intelligence of man . . . Worship of divinities, under the allegories of which is hidden respect for natural laws, drives away truth to the profit of the basest superstitions" (*Vyâsa-Maya*). ‡

It was given to Christianity to paint us God Almighty after the model of the kabalistic abstraction of the "Ancient of Days." From old frescos on cathedral ceilings, Catholic missals, and other icons and images, we now find him depicted by the poetic brush of Gustave Doré. The awful, unknown majesty of Him, whom no "heathen" dared to reproduce in concrete form, is figuring in our own century in *Doré's Illustrated Bible*. Treading upon clouds that float in mid-air, darkness and chaos behind him and the world beneath his feet, a majestic old man stands, his left hand gathering his flowing robes about him, and his right raised in the gesture of command. He has spoken the Word, and

---

* Translated from the *Harivaṇśa*, by Jacolliot, *Christna et le Christ*, pp. 300-01.

† Clement, *Stromata*, V, xiv; transl. given in *Supern. Relig.*, Vol. I, Pt. I, ch. iii, p. 76.

‡ [*La Genèse de l'humanité*, p. 339; Paris, 1875.]

ELIAS ASHMOLE
1617-1692
Portrait in the Ashmolean Museum dated 1689,
and attributed to John Riley.

THOMAS TAYLOR
1758-1835

Portrait painted about 1812 by Sir Thomas Lawrence (1769-1830),
for William Meredith, Taylor's patron.
(*Reproduced by permission of The National Gallery
of Canada at Ottawa.*)

from his towering person streams an effulgence of Light — the Shekhînah. As a poetic conception, the composition does honor to the artist, but does it honor God? Better the chaos behind Him, than the figure itself; for there, at least, we have a solemn mystery. For our part, we prefer the silence of the ancient heathens. With such a gross, anthropomorphic, and, as we conceive, blasphemous representation of the First Cause, who can feel surprised at any iconographic extravagance in the representation of the Christian Christ, the apostles, and the putative Saints? With the Catholics, St. Peter becomes quite naturally the janitor of Heaven, and sits at the door of the celestial kingdom — a ticket-taker to the Trinity!

In a religious disturbance which recently occurred in one of the Spanish-American provinces, there were found upon the bodies of some of the killed, passports signed by the Bishop of the Diocese and addressed to St. Peter; bidding him "*admit the bearer as a true son of the Church.*" It was subsequently ascertained that these unique documents were issued by the Catholic prelate just before his deluded parishioners went into the fight at the instigation of their priests.

In their immoderate desire to find evidence for the authenticity of the *New Testament*, the best men, the most erudite scholars even among Protestant divines, but too often fall into deplorable traps. We cannot believe that such a learned commentator as Canon Westcott could have left himself in ignorance as to Talmudistic and purely kabalistic writings. How then is it that we find him quoting, with such serene assurance, as presenting "striking analogies to the *Gospel of St. John*," passages from the work of *The Shepherd of Hermas*, which are complete sentences from the kabalistic literature? "The view which Hermas gives of Christ's nature and work is no less harmonious with Apostolic doctrine, and it offers striking analogies to the *Gospel of St. John.* . . . He [Jesus] is 'a Rock higher than the mountains, able to hold the whole world, ancient, and yet having a new gate! . . . He is older than creation, so that he took counsel with the Father about the creation which he made . . . No one shall enter in unto him otherwise than by his Son'." \*

Now while — as the author of *Supernatural Religion* well proves — there is nothing in this which looks like a corroboration of the doctrine taught

---

\* [Westcott, *Hist. of the Canon of the New Testament*, pp. 183-84; ed. 1870.] This work, *The Shepherd of Hermas*, is now considered apocryphal; but it is found in the *Sinaitic Codex*, and appears among the books in the stichometry of the *Codex Claromontanus*. In the days of Iranaeus, it was quoted as Holy Scripture (see *Supern. Religion*, Vol. I, Part II, ch. i, §3) by the Fathers, held to be divinely inspired, and publicly read in the churches (Irenaeus, *Adv. Haer.*, IV, xx, § 2). When Tertullian became a Montanist he rejected it, after having *asserted* its divinity (*De oratione*, cap. xvi).

in the fourth gospel, he omits to state that nearly everything expressed by the pseudo-Hermas in relation to his parabolic conversation with the "Lord" is a plain quotation, with repeated variations, from the *Zohar* and other kabalistic books. We may as well compare, so as to leave the reader in no difficulty to judge for himself.

"God," says Hermas,* "planted the vineyard, that is, He created the people and gave them to His Son; and the Son . . . himself cleansed their sins, etc."; *i.e.*, the Son washed them in his blood, in commemoration of which Christians drink wine at the communion. In the *Kabala* it is shown that the Aged of the Aged, or *"Long Face,"* plants a vineyard, the latter typifying mankind; and a vine, meaning Life. The Spirit of *"King* Messiah" is, therefore, shown as washing his garments in *the wine* from above, from the creation of the world.† Adam, or A-Dam is "blood." The life of the flesh is in the blood (*nephesh* — soul),‡ And Adam-Kadmon is the Only-Begotten. Noah also plants a vineyard — the allegorical hotbed of future humanity. As a consequence of the adoption of the same allegory, we find it reproduced in the Nazarene *Codex*. Seven vines are procreated, which spring from Kabar-Ziwa, and Ferho (or Parcha) Raba waters them.§ When the blessed will ascend among the creatures of Light, they shall see Yawar-Ziwa, *Lord of* LIFE, and the First VINE! ‖ These kabalistic metaphors are thus naturally repeated in the *Gospel according to John* (xv, 1): "I am the true vine, and my Father is the husbandman." In *Genesis* (xlix, 10-11), the dying Jacob is made to say, "The sceptre shall not depart from Judah [the lion's whelp], nor a lawgiver from between his feet, until Shiloh come . . . Binding his foal unto *the vine*, and his ass' colt unto the choice vine; he washed his garments *in wine*, and his clothes *in the blood of grapes*." Shiloh is "King Messiah," as well as the Shiloh in Ephraim, which was to be made the capital and the place of the sanctuary. In the *Targum of Onkelos,* the Babylonian, the words of Jacob read: "Until the *King Messiah* shall come." ¶ The prophecy has failed in the Christian as well as in the kabalistico-Jewish sense. The sceptre has departed from Judah, whether the Messiah has already or will come, unless we believe, with the kabalists, that Moses was the first Messiah, who transferred his soul to Joshua — Jesus.**

Says Hermas: "And, in the middle of the plain he showed me a great *white* rock which had risen out of the plain, and the rock was

---

\* [*Hermas*, similitude V, § 6.]
† *Zohar*, comm. on *Genesis* xl, 10.
‡ *Leviticus* xvii, 11.
§ *Codex Nazar.*, III, p. 61.
‖ *Ibid.*, II, p. 281; III, p. 59.
¶ [Nork, *Hundert und Ein Frage*, p. 104.]
\*\* We must remind the reader, in this connection, that Joshua and Jesus are one and the same name. In the Slavonian Bibles Joshua reads — *Iessus* (or Jesus) *Navin*.

higher than the mountains, rectangular so as to be able to hold the whole world; but that rock was old, having a gate hewn out of it, and the hewing out of the gate seemed to me to be recent." \* In the *Zohar*, we find: "To 40,000 superior worlds the *white* of the skull of His Head [of the most Sacred Ancient *in abscondito*] is extended.† . . . When Zeir [the first reflection and image of his Father, the Ancient of the Ancient] will, through the mystery of the seventy names of Metatron, descend into Yetzîrah [the third world], he will open a new gate . . . The Spiritus Decisorius will cut and divide the garment [Shekhînah] into two parts. ‡ . . . At the coming of King Messiah, from the sacred cubical stone of the Temple a *white light* will be arising during forty days. This will expand, until *it encloses the whole world* . . . At that time King Messiah will allow himself to be revealed, and will be seen coming out of the gate of the garden of Odan [Eden]. 'He will be revealed in the land Galil'.§ . . . When 'he has made satisfaction for the sins of Israel, he will lead them on through a *new gate* to the seat of judgement'." ‖ "At the *Gate of the House of Life*, the throne is prepared for the Lord of Splendor." ¶

Further on, the commentator introduces the following quotation: "This *rock* and this *gate* are the Son of God. 'How, Lord', I said, 'is the rock old and the gate new?' 'Listen', He said, 'and understand, thou ignorant man. The *Son of God is older than all of his creation*, so that he was a Councillor with the Father in His work of creation; and for this is he old'."\*\*

Now, these two assertions are not only purely kabalistic, without even so much as a change of expression, but Brahmanical and Pagan likewise. "*Vidi virum excellentem, coeli terraeque conditore natu majorem.* . . . I have seen the most excellent (superior) MAN, who is older by birth than the maker of heaven and earth," says the kabalistic *Codex*.†† The Eleusinian Dionysos, whose particular name was *Iacchos* (Iaccho, Iahoh)‡‡ — the God from whom the liberation of souls was expected — was considered older than the Demiurge. At the mysteries of the Anthesteria at Limnae (the lakes), after the usual baptism by purification of water, the *Mystae* were made to pass through to another door (gate), and one

---

\* [*Hermas*, simil. IX, § 2.]

† *Idrah Rabbah*, § 41.

‡ Rosenroth, *Kabb. denudata*, II, p. 230; *Book of the Babylonian Companions*, p. 35.

§ *Zohar*, on *Exodus*, p. 11; Sulzbach ed.

‖ *Midrash Ḥazitha*.

¶ *Codex Nazar.*, III, p. 61.

\*\* *Hermas*, simil. IX, § 12; Westcott, *Hist. of the Canon* (1870), pp. 183-84.

†† Vol. II, p. 57.

‡‡ L. Preller, *Griech. Mythol.*, Vol. I, p. 486; K. O. Müller, *Hist. Lit. Anc. Greece*, p. 238; F. C. Movers, *Die Phönizier*, Vol. I, pp. 547 *et seq.*

particularly for that purpose, which was called "the gate of Dionysos," and that of "the *purified*."

In the *Zohar*, the kabalists are told that the work-master, the Demiurge, said to the Lord: "Let us make man after our image." * In the original texts of the first chapter of *Genesis*, it stands: "And the *Elohim* [translated as the Supreme God], who are the highest gods or powers, said: Let us make man in *our* [?] image, after *our* likeness." In the *Vedas* Brahmâ holds counsel with Parabrahman, as to the best mode to proceed to create the world.

Canon Westcott, quoting *Hermas*, shows him asking: "and why is the gate *new*, Lord?' I said. 'Because,' he replied, 'he was manifested at the last of the days of the dispensation; for this cause the gate was made new, in order that they who shall be saved might enter by it into the kingdom of God'." † There are two peculiarities worthy of note in this passage. To begin with, it attributes to "the Lord" a false statement of the same character as that so emphasized by the Apostle John, and which brought, at a later period, the whole of the orthodox Christians, who accepted the apostolic allegories as literal, to such inconvenient straits. Jesus, as Messiah, was *not* manifested at the last of the days; for the latter are yet to come, notwithstanding a number of divinely-inspired prophecies, followed by disappointed hopes, as a result, to testify to his immediate coming. The belief that the "last times" had come, was natural, when once the coming of King Messiah had been acknowledged. The second peculiarity is found in the fact that the *prophecy* could have been accepted at all, when even its approximate determination is a direct contradiction of *Mark,* who makes Jesus distinctly state that neither the angels, nor the Son himself, know of that day or that hour.‡ We might add that, as the belief undeniably originated with the *Apocalypse,* it ought to be a self-evident proof that it belonged to the calculations peculiar to the kabalists and the Pagan sanctuaries. It was the secret computation of a cycle, which, according to their reckoning, was ending toward the latter part of the first century. It may also be held as a corroborative proof, that the *Gospel according to Mark,* as well as that ascribed to *John,* and the *Apocalypse,* were written by men, neither of whom was sufficiently acquainted with the other. The Logos was first definitely called *petra* (rock) by Philo; the word, moreover, as we have shown elsewhere, means, in Chaldaic and Phoenician, "interpreter." Justin Martyr calls him throughout his works "angel," and makes a clear distinction between the Logos and God the Creator.

---

\* *Zohar*, I, p. 25; Amsterdam ed.
† *Hermas,* simil. IX, § 12. Westcott, *op. cit.,* p. 178.
‡ *Mark* xiii, 32.

"The Word of God is His Son ... and he is also called Angel and Apostle, for he declares whatever we ought to know [interprets], and is sent to declare whatever is disclosed." *

"Aedan Inferior is distributed into its own paths, into thirty-two sides of paths, yet it is not known to any one but *Zeir*. But no one knows the SUPERIOR AEDAN nor His paths, except that Long Face"— the Supreme God.† Zeir is the Nazarene "genius," who is called Hibil-Ziwa, and Gabriel Legatus — also "Apostle Gabriel." ‡ The Nazarenes held with the kabalists that even the Messiah who was to come did not know the "*Superior* Aedan," the concealed Deity; no one except the *Supreme* God; thus showing that above the Supreme Intelligible Deity, there is one still more secret and unrevealed. Zeir-Anpîn is the third God, while "Logos," according to Philo Judaeus, is the second one. § This is distinctly shown in the *Codex*. "The false Messiah shall say: I am Deus, son of Deus, my Father sent me here. I am the first *Legate*, I am Hibil-Ziwa, I am come from on high! But distrust him; for he will not be Hibil-Ziwa. Hibil-Ziwa will not permit himself to be seen in this age." || Hence the belief of some Gnostics that it was not Hibil-Ziwa (Archangel Gabriel) who "*overshadowed*" Mary, but Ialdabaôth, who formed the *material body* of Jesus; *Christos* uniting himself with him only at the moment of baptism in the Jordan.

Can we doubt Nork's assertion that "the *Berêshith Rabbah*, the oldest part of the *Midrash Rabboth, was known to the Church Fathers in a Greek translation*"? ¶

But if, on the one hand, they were sufficiently acquainted with the different religious systems of their neighbors to have enabled them to build a new religion alleged to be distinct from all others, their ignorance of the *Old Testament* itself, let alone the more complicated questions of Grecian metaphysics, is now found to have been deplorable. "So, for instance, in *Matthew* xxvii, 9 f., the passage from *Zachariah* xi, 12, 13, is attributed to *Jeremiah*," says the author of *Supernatural Religion*. "In *Mark* i, 2, a quotation from *Malachi* iii, 1, is as-

---

\* *First Apology*, lxiii.

† *Idrah Rabbah*, viii, §§ 107-09.

‡ *Codex Nazar.*, I, pp. 23, 181.

§ [*Quaest. et solut. in Gen.*, Bk. II, § 62.] Philo says that the *Logos* is the *interpreter* of the highest God, and argues "that he must be the God of us imperfect beings" (*Leg. Alleg.*, III, § 73). According to his opinion man was not made in the likeness of the *most High* God, the Father of all, but in that of the *second* God who is his word — Logos (Philo, *Fragments*, 1; ex Eusebius, *Praep. evang.*, VIII, 13).

|| *Codex Nazar.*, I, p. 57.

¶ Nork, *Hundert und ein Frage*, p. xvii. Cf. Dunlap, *Sôd, the Son of the Man*, p. 87, where the author quotes Nork (*op. cit.*, pp. xiv, xvii) to the effect that parts of the *Midrashim* and the *Targum of Onkelos* antedate the *New Testament*.

cribed to *Isaiah*.³⁶ In *1 Corinthians* ii, 9, a passage is quoted as *Holy Scripture*, which is not found in the *Old Testament* at all, but which is taken, as Origen and Jerome state, from an apocryphal work, *The Revelation of Elias*,\* and the passage is similarly quoted by the so-called *First Epistle of Clement to the Corinthians* (xvi, 8)." † How reliable are the pious Fathers in their explanations of diverse heresies may be illustrated in the case of Epiphanius, who mistook the Pythagorean sacred Tetrad, called in the Valentinian *Gnosis*, Kol-Arbas, for a *heretic leader*. ‡ What with the involuntary blunders, and deliberate falsifications of the teachings of those who differed in views with them; the canonization of the mythological Aura Placida (gentle breeze), into a pair of Christian martyrs — St. Aura and St. Placida;§ the deification of a *spear* and a *cloak*, under the names of SS. Longinus and Amphibolus;|| and the Patristic quotations from prophets, of what was never in those prophets at all; one may well ask in blank amazement whether the so-called religion of Christ has ever been other than an incoherent dream, since the death of the Great Master.

So malicious do we find the holy Fathers in their unrelenting persecution of pretended "*heresies*," ¶ that we see them telling, without hesitation, the most preposterous untruths, and inventing entire narratives, the better to impress their own otherwise unsupported arguments upon ignorance. If the mistake in relation to the Tetrad had at first originated as a simple consequence of an unpremeditated blunder of Hippolytus, the explanations of Epiphanius and others who fell into the same absurd error \*\* have a less innocent look. When Hippolytus gravely denounces the great heresy of the Tetrad, Kol-Arbas, and states that the imaginary Gnostic leader is, "Colarbasus, who endeavors to explain

---

\* *Apocalypsis Eliae*, in Origen, *Comm. in Matthaeum*, tom. x, p. 465.

† [*Supern. Relig.*, Vol. I, Pt. II, ch. i, 2, p. 240. Clement of Rome is meant.]

‡ Writing upon Ptolemaeus and Heracleon, the author of *Supernatural Religion* (Vol. II, p. 217) says that "the inaccuracy of the Fathers keeps pace with their want of critical judgment," and then proceeds to illustrate this particularly ridiculous blunder committed by Epiphanius, in common with Hippolytus, pseudo-Tertullian, and Philastrius. "Mistaking a passage of Irenaeus (*Adv. Haer.*, I, xiv, 1), regarding the sacred Tetrad (Kol-Arbas) of the Valentinian Gnosis, Hippolytus supposes Irenaeus to refer to another heretic leader. He at once treats the Tetrad as such a leader named 'Kolarbasus', and after dealing (vi, § 4) with the doctrines of Secundus, and Ptolemaeus, and Heracleon, he proposes, (vi, § 5) to show 'what are the opinions held by Marcus and Kolarbasus'," these two being, according to him, the successors of the school of Valentinus (cf. Bunsen, *Hippolytus und seine Zeit*, 1852, pp. 54 *et seq.*)

§ Godfrey Higgins, *Anacalypsis*, Vol. II, p. 85.

|| Inman, *Ancient Pagan and Modern Christian Symbolism*, p. 84.

¶ Meaning — holding up of *different views*.

\*\* "This absurd mistake," remarks the author of *Supernatural Religion*, Vol. II, pp. 218-19, "shows how little these writers knew of the Gnostics of whom they wrote, and how the one ignorantly follows the other."

religion by measures and numbers," \* we may simply smile. But when Epiphanius, with abundant indignation, elaborates upon the theme, "which is Heresy XV," and pretending to be thoroughly acquainted with the subject, adds: "A certain Heracleon follows after Colarbasus, which is Heresy XVI,"† then he lays himself open to the charge of deliberate falsification.

If this zealous *Christian* can boast so unblushingly of having caused "*by his information* seventy women, even of rank, to be sent into exile, *through the seductions of some* in whose number he had himself been drawn into joining their sect," he has left us a fair standard by which to judge him. C. W. King remarks, very aptly, on this point, that "it may reasonably be suspected that this worthy renegade had in this case saved himself from the fate of his fellow-religionists by turning evidence against them, on the opening of the persecution." ‡

And thus, one by one, perished the Gnostics, the only heirs to whose share had fallen a few stray crumbs of the unadulterated truth of primitive Christianity. All was confusion and turmoil during those first centuries, till the moment when all these contradictory dogmas were finally forced upon the Christian world, and examination was forbidden. For long ages it was made a sacrilege, punishable with severe penalties, often death, to seek to comprehend that which the Church had so conveniently elevated to the rank of *divine* mystery. But since Biblical critics have taken upon themselves to "set the house in order," the cases have become reversed. Pagan creditors now come from every part of the globe to claim their own, and Christian theology begins to be suspected of complete bankruptcy. Such is the sad result of the fanaticism of the "orthodox" sects, who, to borrow an expression of the author of *The History of the Decline and Fall of the Roman Empire*, never were, like the Gnostics, "the most polite, the most learned and most wealthy of the Christian name." § And, if not all of them "smelt garlic," as Renan will have it, on the other hand, none of these Christian saints have ever shrunk from spilling their neighbor's blood, if the views of the latter did not agree with their own.

And so all our philosophers were swept away by the ignorant and superstitious masses. The Philaletheians, the lovers of truth, and their eclectic school perished; and there, where the young Hypatia had taught the highest philosophical doctrines; and where Ammonius Saccas had explained that "the *whole which Christ had in view* was to reinstate and restore to its primitive integrity the wisdom of the ancients — to reduce

---

\* Hippolytus, *Philosophumena*, lib. IV, ch. i, § 13.

† Epiphanius, *Panarion*, lib. I, tom. III, Haer. XXXVI, i (quoted in *Supern. Relig.*). See Volkmar, *Die Colarbasus-gnosis*," in Niedner's *Zeitschrift Hist. Theol.*, 1885.

‡ *The Gnostics*, etc., p. 182, footnote 3 [p. 409 in 2nd ed.].

§ [Chapter I, xv.]

within bounds the universally prevailing dominion of superstition . . . and to exterminate the various errors that had found their way into the different popular religions" \* — there, we say, freely raved the οἱ πολλοί of Christianity. No more precepts from the mouth of the "God-taught philosopher," but others expounded by the incarnation of a most cruel, fiendish superstition.

"If thy father," wrote St. Jerome, "lies down across thy threshold, if thy mother uncovers to thine eyes the bosom which suckled thee, trample on thy father's lifeless body, trample on thy mother's bosom, and, with eyes unmoistened and dry, fly to the Lord who calleth thee"!! †

This sentence is equalled, if not outrivalled, by this other, pronounced in a like spirit. It emanates from another father of the early Church, the eloquent Tertullian, who hopes to see all the "philosophers" in the Gehenna fire of Hell. "What shall be the magnitude of that scene! . . . How shall I laugh! How shall I rejoice! How shall I triumph when I see so many illustrious kings who were said to have mounted into heaven, groaning with Jupiter, their god, in the lowest darkness of hell! Then shall the soldiers who have persecuted the name of Christ burn in more cruel fire than any they had kindled for the saints!" ‡

These murderous expressions illustrate the spirit of Christianity till this day. But do they illustrate the teachings of Christ? By no means. As Éliphas Lévi says, "The God in the name of whom we would trample on our mother's bosom we must see in the hereafter, a hell gaping widely at his feet, and an exterminating sword in his hand . . . Moloch burned children but a few seconds; it was reserved to the disciples of a god who is alleged to have died to redeem humanity on the cross, to create a new Moloch whose burning stake is eternal!"

That this spirit of true Christian love has safely crossed nineteen centuries and rages now in America, is fully instanced in the case of the rabid Moody, the revivalist, who exclaims: "I have a son, and no one but God knows how I love him; but I would see those beautiful eyes dug out of his head tonight, rather than see him grow up to manhood and go down to the grave without Christ and without hope"!!

To this an American paper, of Chicago, very justly responds: "This is the spirit of the Inquisition, which we are told is dead. If Moody in his zeal would 'dig out' the eyes of his darling son, to what lengths may he not go with the sons of others, whom he may love less? It is the spirit of Loyola, gibbering in the nineteenth century, and prevented from lighting the fagot flame and heating red-hot the instruments of torture only by the arm of law."

---

\* Mosheim, *An Eccles. Hist.*, cent. II, pt. II, ch. i, § 8; Dublin, 1767.
† [*Epistola XIV: Ad Heliodorum Monachum*, § 2.]
‡ Tertullian. *De spectaculis*, xxx.

# CHAPTER VI

"The curtains of Yesterday drop down, the curtains of Tomorrow roll up; but Yesterday and Tomorrow both *are*."
—CARLYLE, *Sartor Resartus:* "Natural Supernaturalism," p. 271.

"May we not then be permitted to examine the authenticity of [the Bible], which since the second century has been put forth as the criterion of scientific truth? To maintain itself in a position so exalted, it must challenge human criticism."
—DRAPER, *History of the Conflicts between Religion and Science*, p. 219.

"One kiss of Nara upon the lips of Nârî and all Nature wakes."
—VINA-SNATI (A Hindu Poet).

WE must not forget that the Christian Church owes its present canonical *Gospels*, and hence its whole religious dogmatism, to the *Sortes Sanctorum*. Unable to agree as to which were the most divinely-inspired of the numerous gospels extant in its time, the mysterious Council of Nicæa concluded to leave the decision of the puzzling question to miraculous intervention. This Nicene Council way well be called mysterious. There was a mystery, first, in the mystical number of its 318 bishops, on which Barnabas* lays such a stress; added to this, there is no agreement among ancient writers as to the time and place of its assembly, nor even as to the bishop who presided.† Notwithstanding the grandiloquent eulogium of Constantine, ‡ Sabinus, the Bishop of Heraclea, affirms that "except Constantine, the emperor, and Eusebius Pamphilis, these bishops were a set of *illiterate, simple creatures, that understood nothing*";§ which is equivalent to saying that they were a set of fools. Such was apparently the opinion entertained of them by Pappus, who tells us of the bit of magic resorted to, to decide which were the *true* gospels. In his *Synodicon* to that Council, Pappus says [that], having "promiscuously put all the books that were referred to the Council for determination under a communion-table in a church, they [the bishops] besought the Lord that the *inspired* writings might get upon the table, while the spurious ones remained underneath, and *it happened accordingly*." ‖ But we are not told who kept the keys of the council chamber overnight!

On the authority of ecclesiastical eyewitnesses, therefore, we are at liberty to say that the Christian world owes its "Word of God" to a

---

\* *Epistle of Barnabas*, viii, 11-13: Hone ed., London, 1820.
† [Mosheim, *An Eccl. Hist.*, cent. IV, pt. II, ch. v, § 12.]
‡ Socrates Scholasticus, *Eccl. Hist.*, I, ix.
§ *Ibid.*, I, viii.
‖ [Fabricius, *Bibl. graeca*, lib. VI, cap. iii, 34, "Synodus Nicaena."]

method of divination, for resorting to which the Church subsequently condemned unfortunate victims as conjurers, enchanters, magicians, witches and vaticinators, and burnt them by thousands! In treating of this truly divine phenomenon of the self-sorting manuscripts, the Fathers of the Church say that God himself presides over the *Sortes*. As we have shown elsewhere, Augustine confesses that he himself used this sort of divination. But opinions, like revealed religions, are liable to change. That which for nearly fifteen hundred years was imposed on Christendom as a book, of which every word was written under the direct supervision of the Holy Ghost; of which not a syllable, nor a comma could be changed without sacrilege, is now being retranslated, revised, corrected and clipped of whole verses, in some cases of entire chapters. And yet, as soon as the new edition is out, its doctors would have us accept it as a new "Revelation" of the nineteenth century, with the alternative of being held as an infidel. Thus, we see that, no more *within* than *without* its precincts, is the infallible Church to be trusted more than would be reasonably convenient. The forefathers of our modern divines found authority for the *Sortes* in the verse where it is said: "The lot is cast into the lap; but the whole disposing thereof is of the Lord"; \* and now, their direct heirs hold that "the whole disposing thereof is of the Devil." Perhaps, they are unconsciously beginning to endorse the doctrine of the Syrian Bardesanes, that the actions of God, as well as of man, *are subject to necessity?*

It was, no doubt, also according to strict "necessity" that the Neo-Platonists were so summarily dealt with by the Christian mob. In those days, the doctrines of the Hindu naturalists and antediluvian Pyrrhonists were forgotten, if they ever had been known at all to any but a few philosophers; and Darwin, with his modern *discoveries*, had not even been mentioned in the prophecies. In this case the law of the survival of the fittest was reversed; the *Neo-Platonists were doomed to destruction from the day when they openly sided with Aristotle.*

At the beginning of the fourth century crowds began gathering at the door of the academy where the learned and unfortunate Hypatia expounded the doctrines of the divine Plato and Plotinus, and thereby impeded the progress of Christian proselytism. She, too, successfully dispelled the mist hanging over the religious "mysteries" invented by the Fathers, not to be considered dangerous. This alone would have been sufficient to imperil both herself and her followers. It was precisely the teachings of this Pagan philosopher, which had been so freely borrowed by the Christians to give a finishing touch to their otherwise incomprehensible

---

\* *Proverbs* xvi, 33. In Ancient Egypt and Greece, and among Israelites, small sticks and balls called the "sacred divining lots" were used for this kind of oracle in the temples. According to the figures which were formed by the accidental juxtaposition of the latter, the priest interpreted the will of the god.

scheme, that had seduced so many into joining the new religion; and now the Platonic light began shining so inconveniently bright upon the pious patchwork, as to allow everyone to see whence the "revealed" doctrines were derived. But there was a still greater peril. Hypatia had studied under Plutarch, the head of the Athenian school, and had learned all the secrets of theurgy. While she lived to instruct the multitude, no *divine* miracles could be produced before one who could divulge the natural causes by which they took place. Her doom was sealed by Cyril,* whose eloquence she eclipsed, and whose authority, built on degrading superstitions, had to yield before hers, which was erected on the rock of immutable natural law. It is more than curious that Cave, the author of the *Lives of the Fathers*, should find it incredible that Cyril sanctioned her murder on account of his "general character." A saint who will sell the gold and silver vessels of his church, and then, after spending the money, lie at his trial, as he did, may well be suspected of anything.† Besides, in this case the Church had to fight for her life, to say nothing of her future supremacy. Alone, the hated and erudite Pagan scholars, and the no less learned Gnostics, held in their doctrines the hitherto concealed wires of all these theological marionettes. Once the curtain should be lifted, the connection between the old Pagan and the new Christian religions would be exposed; and then, what would have become of the Mysteries into which it is sin and blasphemy to pry? With such a coincidence of the astronomical allegories of various Pagan myths with the dates adopted by Christianity for the nativity, crucifixion and resurrection, and such an identity of rites and ceremonies, what would have been the fate of the new religion, had not the Church, under the pretext of serving Christ, got rid of the too-well-informed philosophers? To guess what might have been the prevailing religion in our own century, if the *coup d'état* had then failed, would indeed be a hard task. But, in all probability, the state of things which made of the middle ages a period of intellectual darkness, which degraded the nations of the Occident, and lowered the European of those days almost to the level of a Papuan savage — could not have occurred.

The fears of the Christians were but too well founded, and their pious zeal and prophetic insight was rewarded from the very first. In the demolition of the *Serapeion,* after the bloody riot between the Christian mob and the Pagan worshippers had ended with the interference of the emperor, a Latin cross of a perfect Christian shape, was discovered hewn upon the granite slabs of the adytum. This was a lucky discovery, indeed; and the monks did not fail to claim that the cross had

---

* [Of Alexandria.]

† [This description applies to Cyril of Jerusalem, not to Cyril of Alexandria. See footnote, Vol. II, p. 53.]

been hallowed by the Pagans in a "spirit of prophecy." At least, Sozomen, with an air of triumph, records the fact.* But, archaeology and symbolism, those tireless and implacable enemies of clerical false pretenses, have found in the hieroglyphics of the legend running around the design, at least a partial interpretation of its meaning.

According to King and other numismatists and archaeologists, the cross was placed there as the symbol of eternal life. Such a Tau, or Egyptian cross, was used in the Bacchic and Eleusinian Mysteries. Symbol of the dual generative power, it was laid upon the breast of the initiate, after his "new birth" was accomplished, and the Mystai had returned from their baptism in the sea. It was a mystic sign that his spiritual birth had regenerated and united his astral soul with his divine spirit, and that he was ready to ascend in spirit to the blessed abodes of light and glory — the Eleusinia. The Tau was a magic talisman at the same time as a religious emblem. It was adopted by the Christians through the Gnostics and kabalists, who used it largely, as their numerous gems testify, and who had the Tau (or handled cross) from the Egyptians, and the Latin cross from the Buddhist missionaries, who brought it from India, where it can be found until now, two or three centuries B.C. The Assyrians, Egyptians, ancient Americans, Hindus, and Romans had it in various, but very slight modifications of shape. Till very late in the mediaeval ages, it was considered a potent spell against epilepsy and demoniacal possession; and the "signet of the living God," brought down in St. John's vision by the angel ascending from the east to "seal the servants of our God in their foreheads," was but the same mystic Tau — the Egyptian cross. In the painted glass of St. Denys (France), this angel is represented as stamping this sign on the forehead of the elect; the legend reads, SIGNUM TAY. In King's *Gnostics*, the author reminds us that "this mark is commonly borne by St. Anthony, an *Egyptian* recluse." † What the real meaning of the Tau was, is explained to us by the Christian St. John, the Egyptian Hermes, and the Hindu Brahmans. It is but too evident that, with the apostle at least, it meant the "Ineffable Name," as he calls this "signet of the living God" a few chapters further on, ‡ the *"Father's name written in their foreheads."*

The Brahmâtma, the chief of the Hindu initiates, had on his headgear two keys, symbol of the revealed mystery of life and death, placed cross-

---

* [*Eccl. Hist.*, Bk. VII, ch. xv.] Another untrustworthy, untruthful and ignorant writer, an ecclesiastical historian of the fifth century. His alleged history of the strife between the Pagans, Neo-Platonists, and the Christians of Alexandria and Constantinople, which extends from the year 324 to 439, dedicated by him to Theodosius, the Younger, is full of deliberate falsifications. Edition of Reading, Cantab., 1720, fol. Translated: Plon frères, Paris. [Cf. Socrates, *Eccl. Hist.*, V, xvii.]

† Vol. I, p. 135 (1st ed.).

‡ *Revelation* vii, 2, 3; xiv, 1.

like; and, in some Buddhist pagodas of Tartary and Mongolia, the entrance of a chamber within the temple, generally containing the staircase which leads to the inner *dagoba*,\* and the porticos of some *Prachidas* † are ornamented with a cross formed of two fishes, as found on some of the zodiacs of the Buddhists. We should not wonder at all at learning that the sacred device in the tombs, in the Catacombs at Rome, the "vesica piscis," was derived from the said Buddhist zodiacal sign. How general must have been that geometrical figure in the world-symbols, may be inferred from the fact that there is a Masonic tradition that Solomon's temple was built on three foundations, forming the "triple Tau," or three crosses.

In its mystical sense, the Egyptian cross owes its origin, as an emblem, to the realization by the earliest philosophy of an androgynous dualism of every manifestation in nature, which proceeds from the abstract ideal of a likewise androgynous deity, while the Christian emblem is simply due to chance. Had the Mosaic law prevailed, Jesus should have been lapidated. ‡ The crucifix was an instrument of torture, and utterly common among Romans as it was unknown among Semitic nations. It was called the "Tree of Infamy." It is but later that it was adopted as a Christian symbol; but, during the first two decades, the apostles looked upon it with horror. § It is certainly not the Christian Cross that John had in mind when speaking of the "signet of the living God," but the *mystic* Tau — the Tetragrammaton, or mighty name — which, on the most ancient kabalistic talismans, was represented by the four Hebrew letters composing the Holy Word.

The famous Lady Ellenborough, known among the Arabs of Damascus, and in the desert, after her last marriage, as *Hanoum Midjwal*,[37] had a talisman in her possession, presented to her by a Druze from Mount Lebanon. It was recognized by a certain sign on its left corner, to belong to that class of gems which is known in Palestine as a *"Messianic"* amulet, of the second or third century B.C. It is a green stone of a pentagonal form; at the bottom is engraved a fish; higher, Solomon's seal; ‖

---

\* *Dagoba* is a small temple of globular form, in which are preserved the relics of Gautama.

† *Prachidas* are buildings of all sizes and forms, like our mausoleums, and are sacred to votive offerings to the dead.

‡ The Talmudistic records claim that, after having been hanged, he was lapidated and buried under the water at the junction of two streams. *Mishnah Sanhedrin*, vi, 4; *Talmud* of Babylon, same article, 48a, 67a [cited by E. Renan].

§ *Coptic Legends of the Crucifixion*, MSS. xi.

‖ The [accompanying] engraving represents the talisman as of twice the natural size. We are at a loss to understand why King, in his "Gnostic Gems," represents Solomon's Seal as a five-pointed star, whereas it is six-pointed, and is the signet of Vishṇu in India. [*The Gnostics*, etc., Plate XIII, A, 4.]

and still higher, the four Chaldaic letters — Yod, He, Vau, He, which form the name of the Deity. These are arranged in quite an unusual way, running from below upward, in reversed order, and forming the Egyptian Tau. Around these there is a legend which, as the gem is not our property, we are not at liberty to give. The Tau, in its mystical sense, as well as the *crux ansata*, is the *Tree of Life*.

It is well known, that the earliest Christian emblems — before it was ever attempted to represent the bodily appearance of Jesus — were the Lamb, the Good Shepherd, and the *Fish*. The origin of the latter emblem, which has so puzzled the archaeologists, thus becomes comprehensible. The whole secret lies in the easily-ascertained fact that, while in the *Kabalah*, the King Messiah is called "Interpreter," or Revealer of the mystery, and shown to be the *fifth* emanation, in the *Talmud* — for reasons we will now explain — the Messiah is very often designated as "DAG," or the Fish. This is an inheritance from the Chaldees, and relates — as the very name indicates — to the Babylonian Dagon, the man-fish, who was the instructor and interpreter of the people, to whom he appeared. Abarbanel explains the name, by stating that the sign of his (Messiah's) coming "is the conjunction of Saturn and Jupiter in the sign *Pisces*." * Therefore, as the Christians were intent upon identifying their Christos with the Messiah of the *Old Testament*, they adopted it so readily at to forget that its true origin might be traced still farther back than the Babylonian Dagon. How eagerly and closely the ideal of Jesus was united, by the early Christians, with every imaginable kabalistic and Pagan tenet, may be inferred from the language of Clement of Alexandria, addressed to his brother coreligionists.

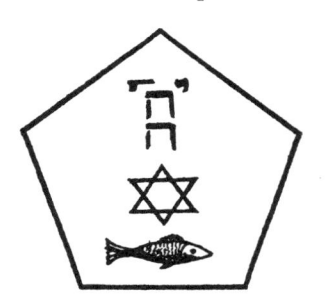

When they were debating upon the choice of the most appropriate symbol to remind them of Jesus, Clement advised them in the following words: "Let the engraving upon the gem of your ring be either *a dove*, or *a ship running before the wind* [the Argha], or *a fish*." † Was the good father, when writing this sentence, laboring under the recollection of Joshua, son of Nun (called *Jesus* in the Greek and Slavonian versions); or had he forgotten the real interpretation of these Pagan symbols?

---

* King (*The Gnostics*, p. 138) gives the figure of a Christian symbol, very common during the middle ages, of three fishes interlaced into a triangle, and having the FIVE letters (a most sacred Pythagorean number) I.X.Θ.Υ.Σ. engraved on it. The number five relates to the same kabalistic computation.

† [*Paedagogus*, III, xi.]

Joshua, son of Nun, or Nave (*Navis*), could have with perfect propriety adopted the image of a *ship*, or even of a fish, for Joshua means Jesus, son of the fish-god; but it was really too hazardous to connect the emblems of Venus, Astartê, and all the Hindu goddesses — the *argha, dove* and *fish* — with the "immaculate" birth of their god! This looks very much as if in the early days of Christianity but little difference was made between Christ, Bacchus, Apollo, and the Hindu Krishna, the incarnation of Vishnu, with whose first avatâra this symbol of the fish originated.

In the *Bhâgavata-Purâna*, as well as in several other books, the god Vishnu is shown as having assumed the form of a fish with a human head, in order to reclaim the *Vedas* lost during the deluge. Having enabled Vaivasvata to escape with all his tribe in the ark, Vishnu, pitying weak and ignorant humanity, remained with them for some time. It was this god who taught them to build houses, cultivate the land, and to thank the unknown Deity whom he represented, by building temples and instituting a regular worship; and, as he remained half-fish, half-man, all the time, at every sunset he used to return to the ocean, wherein he passed the night.

"It is he," says the sacred book, "who taught men, after the diluvium, all that was necessary for their happiness.

"One day he plunged into the water and returned no more, for the earth had covered itself again with vegetation, fruit, and cattle.

"But he had taught the Brahmans the secret of all things" (*Bhâgavata-Purâna*, viii, 24).

So far, we see in this narrative the *double* of the story given by the Babylonian Berosus about Oannes, the fish-man, who is no other than Vishnu — unless, indeed, we have to believe that it was Chaldea which civilized India!

We say again, we desire to give nothing on our sole authority. Therefore we cite Jacolliot, who, however criticized and contradicted on other points, and however loose he may be in the matter of chronology (though even in this he is nearer right than those scientists who would have all Hindu books written since the Council of Nicæa), at least cannot be denied the reputation of a good Sanskrit scholar. And he says, while analyzing the word *Oan*, or *Oannes*, that *O* in Sanskrit is an interjection expressing an invocation, as O Svayambhû! O God! etc.; and *Ana* is a radical, signifying in Sanskrit a spirit, a being; and, we presume, what the Greeks meant by the word *Daimôn*, a semi-god.

"What an extraordinary antiquity," he remarks, "this fable of Vishnu, disguised as a fish, gives to the sacred books of the Hindus; especially in presence of the fact that the *Vedas* and *Manu* reckon more *than twenty-five thousand years of existence,* as proved by the most serious as the most authentic documents. Few peoples, says the learned Halhed, have their annals more authentic or serious than the Hindus." *

We may, perhaps, throw additional light upon the puzzling question of the fish-symbol by reminding the reader that according to *Genesis* the first created of living beings, the first type of animal life, was the fish. "And the Elohim said: 'Let the waters bring forth abundantly the moving creature that *hath life*' . . . and God created great whales . . . and the morning and the evening were the *fifth day*." † Jonah is swallowed by a big fish, and is cast out again three days later. This the Christians regard as a premonition of the three days' sepulture of Jesus which preceded his resurrection — though the statement of the three days is as fanciful as much of the rest, and adopted to fit the well-known threat to destroy the temple and rebuild it again in *three* days. Between his burial and alleged resurrection there intervened but *one day* — the Jewish Sabbath — as he was buried on Friday evening and rose to life at dawn on Sunday. However, whatever other circumstance may be regarded as a prophecy, the story of Jonah cannot be made to answer the purpose.

"Big Fish" is *Cetus*, the latinized form of *Kêtos* (κῆτος), and Kêtos is Dagon, Poseidon, the female gender of it being Kêton Atar-gatis — the Syrian goddess, and Venus, of Askalon. The figure or bust of Der-Kêtos or Astartê was generally represented on the prow of the ships.‡ Jonah (Hebrew *Yonah*, for *dove*, a bird sacred to Venus) fled to Jaffa, where the god Dagon, the man-fish, was worshipped, and dared not go to Nineveh, *where the dove was revered*. Hence, some commentators believe that when Jonah was thrown overboard and was swallowed by a fish, we must understand that he was picked up by one of these vessels, on the prow of which was the figure of *Kêtos*. But the kabalists have another legend, to this effect: They say that Jonah was a runaway priest from the temple of the goddess where the dove was worshipped, and desired to abolish idolatry and institute monotheistic worship. That, caught near Jaffa, he was held prisoner by the devotees of Dagon in one of the prison-cells of the temple, and that it is the strange form of the cell which gave rise to the allegory. In the collection of Moses de García, a Portuguese kabalist, there is a drawing representing the interior of the temple of Dagon. In the middle stands an immense idol, the upper portion of whose body is human, and the lower fish-like. Between the belly and the tail is an aperture which can be closed like the door of a closet. In it the transgressors against the local deity were shut up until further disposal. The drawing in question was made from an old tablet covered with curious drawings

---
\* *La Genèse de l'humanité*, pp. 80, 81.
† [*Genesis* i, 20-23.]
‡ [Pliny, *Nat. Hist.*, V, xix; Diod. Sic., *Bibl. hist.*, II, iv.]

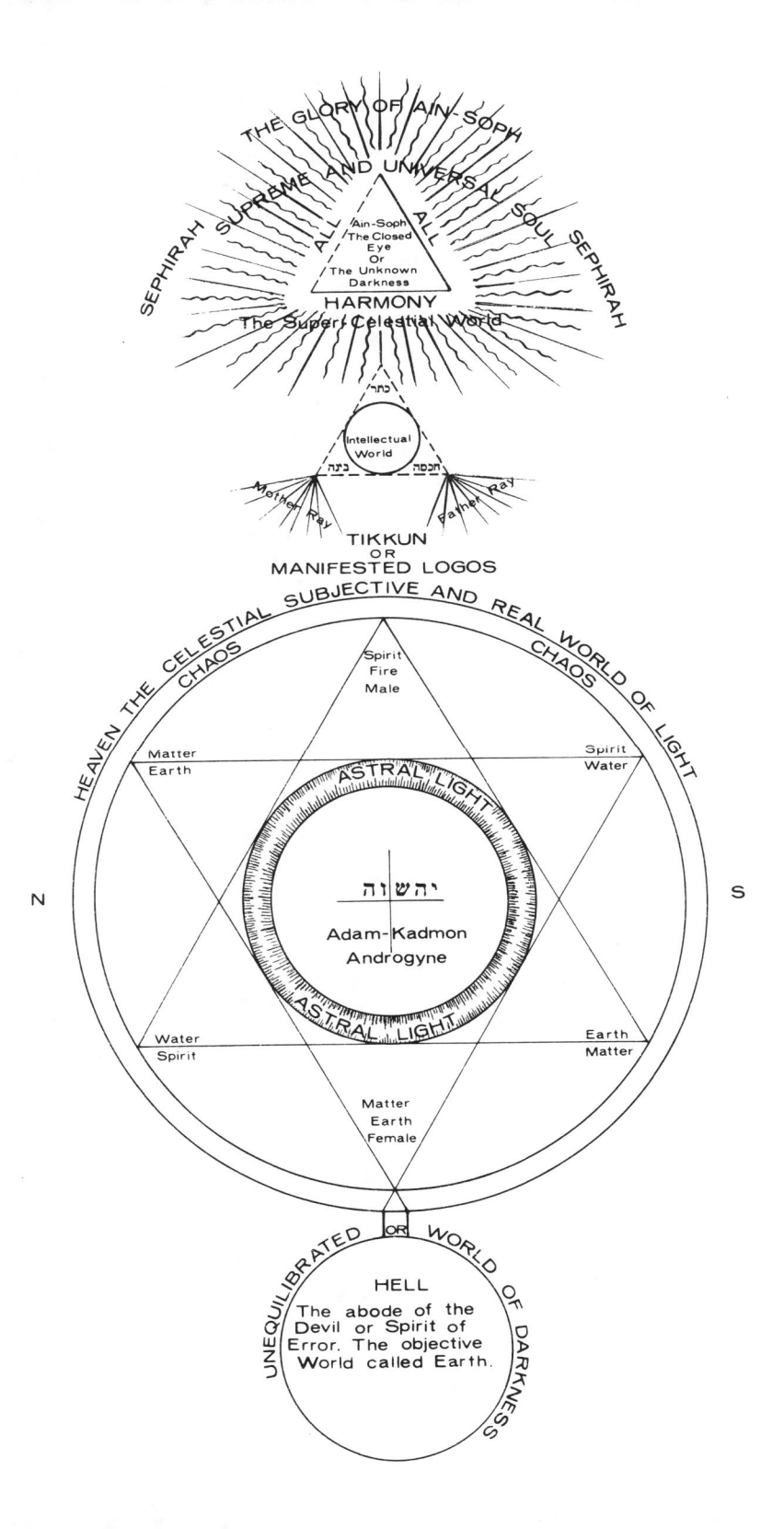

THE GLORY OF AIN-SOPH

SEPHIRAH — SUPREME AND UNIVERSAL SOUL — ALL IN ALL — SEPHIRAH

Ain-Soph
The Closed
Eye
Or
The Unknown
Darkness

HARMONY
The Super-Celestial World

כתר
Intellectual World
בינה   חכמה

Mother Ray   Father Ray

TIKKUN
OR
MANIFESTED LOGOS

HEAVEN THE CELESTIAL SUBJECTIVE AND REAL WORLD OF LIGHT

CHAOS          CHAOS

Spirit
Fire
Male

Matter / Earth          Spirit / Water

ASTRAL LIGHT

יהשוה

Adam-Kadmon
Androgyne

ASTRAL LIGHT

Water / Spirit          Earth / Matter

Matter
Earth
Female

N          S

OR

UNEQUILIBRATED WORLD OF DARKNESS

HELL
The abode of the Devil or Spirit of Error. The objective World called Earth.

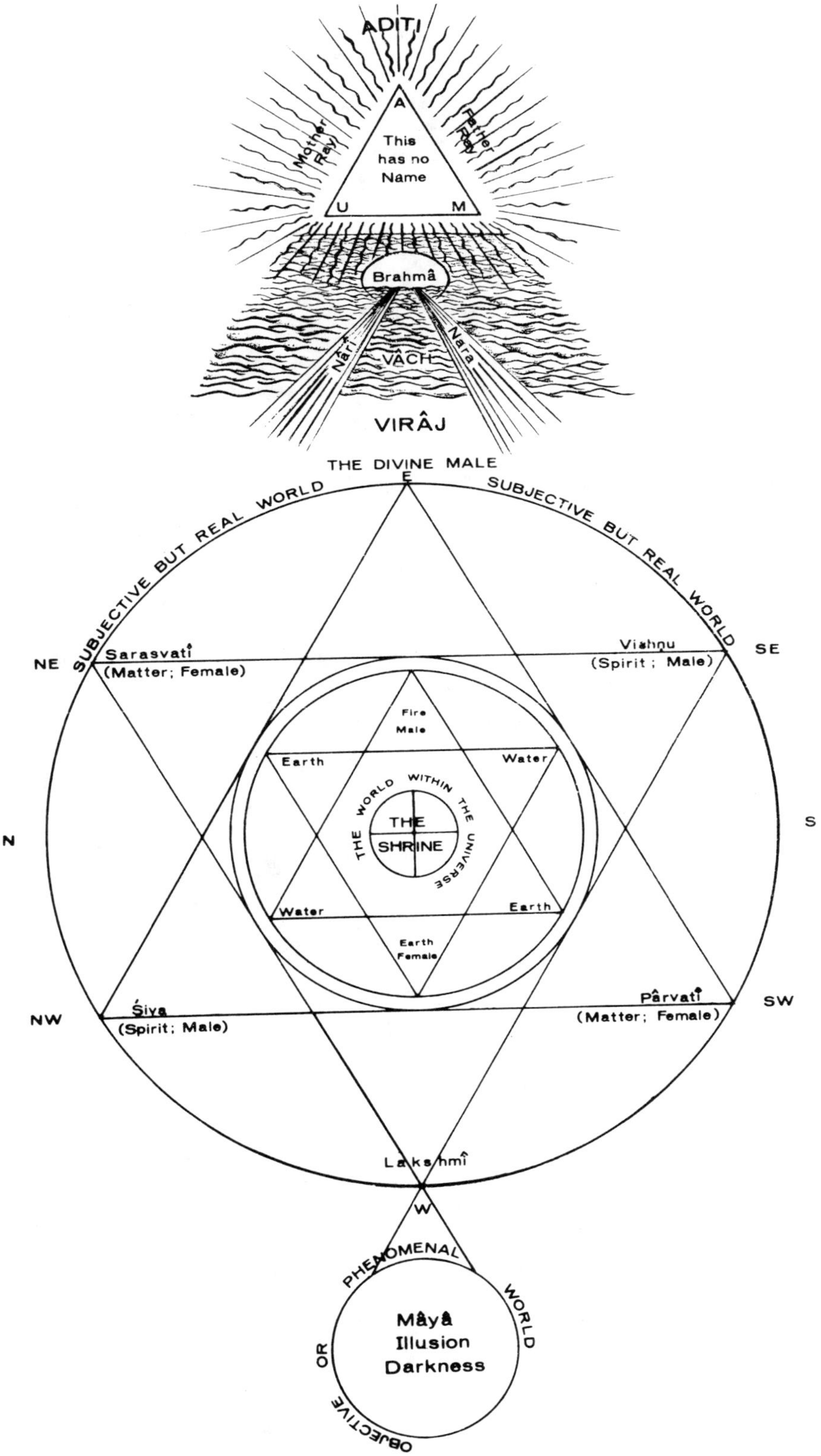
ADITI
A
This has no Name
U
M
Mother Ray
Father Ray
Brahmâ
Nârî
Nara
VÂCH
VIRÂJ
THE DIVINE MALE
E
SUBJECTIVE BUT REAL WORLD
SUBJECTIVE BUT REAL WORLD
NE
Sarasvatî
(Matter; Female)
Vishnu
(Spirit; Male)
SE
Fire
Male
Earth
Water
THE WORLD WITHIN THE UNIVERSE
THE SHRINE
N
S
Water
Earth
Earth
Female
NW
Śiva
(Spirit; Male)
Pârvatî
(Matter; Female)
SW
Lakshmî
W
PHENOMENAL WORLD
OR OBJECTIVE
Mâyâ
Illusion
Darkness

and inscriptions in old Phoenician characters, describing this Venetian *oubliette* of Biblical days. The tablet itself was found in an excavation a few miles from Jaffa. Considering the extraordinary tendency of Oriental nations for puns and allegories, is it not barely possible that the "big fish" by which Jonah was swallowed was simply the cell within the belly of Dagon?

It is significant that this double appellation of "Messiah" and "Dag" (fish), of the Talmudists, should so well apply to the Hindu Vishnu, the "Preserving" Spirit, and the second personage of the Brahmanic trinity. This deity, having already manifested itself, is still regarded as the future Savior of humanity, and is the selected Redeemer, who will appear at its tenth incarnation or *avatâra*, like the Messiah of the Jews, to lead the blessed onward, and restore to them the primitive *Vedas*. At his first avatâra, Vishnu is alleged to have appeared to humanity in form like a fish. In the temple of Râma, there is a representation of this god which answers perfectly to that of Dagon, as given by Berosus. He has the body of a man issuing from the mouth of a fish, and holds in his hands the lost *Veda*. Vishnu, moreover, is the water-god, in one sense, the Logos of the Parabrahman, for as the three persons of the manifested godhead constantly interchange their attributes, we see him in the same temple represented as reclining on the seven-headed serpent Ananta (eternity), and moving, like the *Spirit* of God, on the face of the primeval waters.

Vishnu is evidently the Adam-Kadmon of the kabalists, for Adam is the Logos of the first Anointed, as Adam Second is the King Messiah.

Lakshmî, the passive or feminine counterpart of Vishnu, the creator and the preserver, is also called Âdi-Mâyâ. She is the "Mother of the World," *Devamatrî*, the Venus-Aphrodite of the Greeks; also Isis and Eve. While Venus is born from the sea-foam, Lakshmî springs out from the water at the churning of the sea; when born, she is so beautiful that all the gods fall in love with her. The Jews, borrowing their types wherever they could get them, made their first woman after the pattern of Lakshmî. It is curious that Viracocha, the Supreme Being in Peru, means, literally translated, "foam of the sea."

Eugène Burnouf, the great authority of the French school, announces his opinion in the same spirit: "We must learn one day," he observes, "that all ancient traditions, disfigured by emigration and legend, belong to the history of India." Such is the opinion of Colebrooke, Inman, King, Jacolliot, and many other Orientalists.

We have said above that, according to the secret computation peculiar to the students of the hidden science, Messiah is the fifth emanation, or potency. In the Jewish *Kabala*, where the ten Sephîrôth emanate from Adam-Kadmon (placed below the crown), he comes fifth. So in the

Gnostic system; so in the Buddhistic, in which the fifth Buddha — Maitreya, will appear at his last advent to save mankind before the final destruction of the world. If Vishnu is represented in his forthcoming and last appearance as the *tenth* avatâra or incarnation, it is only because every unit held as an androgyne manifests itself doubly. The Buddhists who reject this dual-sexed incarnation reckon but five. Thus, while Vishnu is to make his last appearance in his tenth, Buddha is said to do the same in his fifth incarnation.*

The better to illustrate the idea, and show how completely the real meaning of the avatâras, known only to the students of the secret doctrine, was misunderstood by the ignorant masses, we elsewhere give the diagrams of the Hindu and Chaldeo-Kabalistic avatâras and emanations.† This basic and true fundamental stone of the secret cycles, shows on its very face, that far from taking their revealed *Vedas* and *Bible* literally, the Brahman-pundits, and the Tannaim — the scientists and philosophers of the pre-Christian epochs — speculated on the creation and development of the world quite in a Darwinian way, both anticipating him and his school in the natural selection of species, gradual development, and transformation.

We advise everyone tempted to enter an indignant protest against this affirmation to read more carefully the books of Manu, even in the incomplete translation of Sir William Jones, and the more or less careless one of Jacolliot. If we compare the Sanchoniathon Phoenician Cosmogony, and the record of Berosus with the *Bhâgavata-Purâna* and *Manu*, we will find enunciated exactly the same principles as those now offered as the latest developments of modern science. We have quoted from the Chaldean and Phoenician records in our first volume; we will now glance at the Hindu books.

"When this world had issued out of darkness, the subtile elementary principles produced the vegetal seed which animated first the plants; from the plants, life passed into fantastical bodies which were born *in the ilus of the waters*; then, through a series of forms and various animals, it reached MAN." ‡

"He [man, before becoming such] will pass successively through plants, worms, insects, fish, serpents, tortoises, cattle, and wild animals; such is the inferior degree."

"Such, from Brahmâ down to the vegetables, are declared the transmigrations which take place in this world." §

---

* The Kabalistic Sephîrôth are also ten in number, or five pairs.

† An avatâra is a descent from on high upon earth of the Deity in some manifest shape.

‡ *Bhâgavata-Purâna*, Bk. II, ch. 9 and 10.

§ *Manu*, Bk. XII, 42; Bk. I, 50.

In the Sanchoniathonian Cosmogony, men are also evolved out of the *ilus* of the chaos,* and the same evolution and transformation of species are shown.

And now we will leave the rostrum to Mr. Darwin: "I believe that animals have descended from at most only four or five progenitors." †

Again: "I should infer from analogy that probably all the organic beings which have ever lived on this earth have descended from some one primordial form. ‡ . . . I view all beings not as special creations, but as the lineal descendants of some few beings which lived long *before the first bed of the Silurian system was deposited.*" §

In short, they lived in the Sanchoniathonian chaos, and in the *ilus* of Manu. Vyâsa and Kapila go still farther than Darwin and Manu. "They see in Brahmâ but the name of the universal germ; *they deny the existence of a First Cause*; and pretend that everything in nature found itself developed only in consequence of material and fatal forces," says Jacolliot.‖

Correct as may be this latter quotation from Kapila, it demands a few words of explanation. Jacolliot repeatedly compares Kapila and Veda-Vyâsa with Pyrrho and Littré. We have nothing against such a comparison with the Greek philosopher, but we must decidedly object to any with the French Comtist; we find it an unmerited fling at the memory of the great Âryan sage. Nowhere does this prolific writer state the repudiation by either ancient or modern Brahmans of God — the "unknown," universal Spirit; nor does any other Orientalist accuse the Hindus of the same, however perverted the general deductions of our savants about Buddhistic atheism. On the contrary, Jacolliot states more than once that the learned Pundits and educated Brahmans have never shared the popular superstitions; and affirms their unshaken belief in the unity of God and the soul's immortality, although most assuredly neither Kapila, nor the initiated Brahmans, nor the followers of the Vedânta school would ever admit the existence of an anthropomorphic creator, a "First Cause" in the Christian sense. Jacolliot, in his *Indo-European and African Traditions*, is the first to make an onslaught on Professor Müller, for remarking that the Hindu gods were "masks without actors . . . names without being, and not beings without names." ¶ Quoting, in support of his argument, numerous verses from the sacred Hindu books, he adds: "Is it possible to refuse to the author of these stanzas a definite and clear conception of the divine

---

* See Cory, *Ancient Fragments*, 1832, p. 3.
† *On the Origin of Species* (1st ed.), p. 484.
‡ *Ibid.*, p. 484.
§ *Ibid.*, pp. 488-89.
‖ *La Genèse de l'humanité*, p. 338.
¶ *Les Traditions indo-européennes et africaines*, p. 291.

force, of the Unique Being, master and Sovereign of the Universe? . . . Were the altars then built to a metaphor?" *

The latter argument is perfectly just, so far as Max Müller's negation is concerned. But we doubt whether the French rationalist understands Kapila's and Vyâsa's philosophy better than the German philologist does the "theological twaddle," as the latter terms the *Atharva-Veda*. Professor Müller and Jacolliot may have ever so great claims to erudition, and be ever so familiar with Sanskrit and other ancient Oriental languages, but both lack the key to the thousand and one mysteries of the old secret doctrine and its philosophy. Only, while the German philologist does not even take the trouble to look into this magical and "theological twaddle," we find the French Indianist never losing an opportunity to investigate. Moreover, he honestly admits his incompetency to ever fathom this ocean of mystical learning. In its existence he not only firmly believes, but throughout his works he incessantly calls the attention of science to its unmistakable traces at every step in India. Still, though the learned Pundits and Brahmans — his revered "masters of the pagodas of Villianûr and Chidambaram in the Carnatic," † as it seems, positively refused to reveal to him the mysteries of the magical part of the *Agrushada-Parikshai*,‡ and of Brahmâtma's triangle,§ he persists in the honest declaration that everything is possible in Hindu metaphysics, even to the Kapila and Vyâsa systems having been hitherto misunderstood.

Jacolliot weakens his assertion immediately afterward with the following contradiction:

"We were one day inquiring of a Brahman of the pagoda of Chidambaram, who belonged to the *skeptical school of the naturalists of Vyâsa*, whether he believed in the existence of God. He answered us, smiling: '*Aham eva Parabrahman*'—'I am myself a god'.

" 'What do you mean by that?'

" 'I mean that every being on earth, however humble, is an immortal portion of the immortal matter'." ||

The answer is one which would suggest itself to every ancient philosopher, Kabalist and Gnostic, of the early days. It contains the very spirit of the Delphic and kabalistic commandments, for esoteric philosophy solved ages ago, the problem of what man was, is, and will be. If persons

---

\* Jacolliot, *op. cit.*, pp. 293 *et seq.*
† Jacolliot, *Les Fils de Dieu*, p. 32.
‡ Jacolliot, *Le Spiritisme dans le monde*, p. 78, and others.
§ *Les Fils de Dieu*, p. 272. While not at all astonished that Brahmans should have refused to satisfy Jacolliot's curiosity, we must add that the meaning of this sign is known to the superiors of every Buddhist lamasery, not alone to the Brahmans.
|| *La Genèse de l'humanité*, p. 339.

believing the *Bible* verse which teaches that the "Lord God formed man of the dust of the ground, and breathed into his nostrils the breath of life," * reject at the same time the idea that every atom of this dust, as every particle of this "living soul," contains "God" within itself, then we pity the logic of that Christian. He forgets the verses which precede the one in question. God blesses equally every beast of the field and every living creature, in the water as in the air, and He endows them all with *life*, which is a breath of His own Spirit, and the *soul* of the animal. Humanity is the Adam-Kadmon of the "Unknown," His microcosm, and His only representative on earth, and every man is a god on earth.

We would ask this French scholar, who seems so familiar with every śloka of the books of Manu, and other Vedic writers, the meaning of this sentence so well known to him:

"Plants and vegetation reveal a multitude of forms because of their precedent actions; they are surrounded by darkness, but are nevertheless endowed with an interior soul, and feel equally pleasure and pain." †

If the Hindu philosophy teaches the presence of a degree of *soul* in the lowest forms of vegetable life, and even in every atom in space, how is it possible that it should deny the same immortal principle to man? And if it once admits the immortal spirit in man, how can it logically deny the existence of the parent source — I will not say the first, but the eternal Cause? Neither rationalists nor sensualists, who do not comprehend Indian metaphysics, should estimate the ignorance of Hindu metaphysicians by their own.

The grand cycle, as we have heretofore remarked, includes the progress of mankind from its germ in the primordial man of spiritual form to the deepest depth of degradation he can reach — each successive step in the descent being accompanied by a greater strength and grossness of the physical form than its precursor — and ends with the Flood. But while the grand cycle, or age, is running its course, seven minor cycles are passed, each marking the evolution of a new race out of the preceding one, on a new world. And each of these races, or grand types of humanity, breaks up into subdivisions of families, and they again into nations and tribes, as we see the earth's inhabitants subdivided today into Mongols, Caucasians, Indians, etc.

Before proceeding to show by diagrams the close resemblance between the esoteric philosophies of all the ancient peoples, however geographically remote from each other, it will be useful to briefly explain the real ideas which underlie all those symbols and allegorical representations that have hitherto so puzzled the uninitiated commentators. Better than anything, it may show that religion and science were closer knit than twins

---

\* [*Gen.* ii, 7.]
† *Manu*, Bk. I, Ślokas 48-49.

in days of old; that they were one in two and two in one from the very moment of their conception. With mutually convertible attributes, science was spiritual and religion was scientific. Like the androgyne man of the first chapter of *Genesis* — "male and female," passive and active; created in the image of the Elohim. Omniscience developed omnipotency, the latter called for the exercise of the former, and thus the giant had dominion given him over all the four kingdoms of the world. But, like the second Adam, these androgynes were doomed to "fall and lose their powers" as soon as the two halves of the duality separated. The fruit of the Tree of Knowledge gives death without the fruit of the Tree of Life. Man must know *himself* before he can hope to know the ultimate genesis even of beings and powers less developed in their inner nature than himself. So with religion and science; united two in one they were infallible, for the spiritual intuition was there to supply the limitations of physical senses. Separated, exact science rejects the help of the inner voice, while religion becomes merely dogmatic theology — each is but a corpse without a soul.

The esoteric doctrine, then, teaches, like Buddhism and Brahmanism, and even the persecuted *Kabala*, that the one infinite and unknown Essence exists from all eternity, and in regular and harmonious successions is either passive or active. In the poetical phraseology of Manu these conditions are called the "day" and the "night" of Brahmâ. The latter is either "awake" or "asleep." The *Svâbhâvikas*, or philosophers of the oldest school of Buddhism (which still exists in Nepal), speculate but upon the active condition of this "Essence," which they call *Svabhavat*, and deem it foolish to theorize upon the abstract and "unknowable" power in its passive condition. Hence they are called atheists by both Christian theology and modern scientists; for neither of the two are able to understand the profound logic of their philosophy. The former will allow of no other God than the personified *secondary* powers which have blindly worked out the visible universe, and which became with them the anthropomorphic God of the Christians — the Jehovah, roaring amid thunder and lightning. In its turn, rationalistic science greets the Buddhists and the *Svâbhâvikas* as the "positivists" of the archaic ages. If we take a one-sided view of the philosophy of the latter, our materialists may be right in their own way. The Buddhists maintain that there is *no* Creator but an infinitude of *creative powers*, which collectively form the one eternal substance, the *essence* of which is inscrutable — hence not a subject for speculation for any true philosopher. Socrates invariably refused to argue upon the mystery of universal being, yet no one would ever have thought of charging him with atheism, except those who were bent upon his destruction. Upon inaugurating an active period, says the *Secret Doctrine,* an expansion of this Divine essence, *from within out-*

*wardly*, occurs in obedience to eternal and immutable law, and the phenomenal or visible universe is the ultimate result of the long chain of cosmical forces thus progressively set in motion. In like manner, when the passive condition is resumed, a contraction of the Divine essence takes place, and the previous work of creation is gradually and progressively undone. The visible universe becomes disintegrated, its material dispersed; and "darkness," solitary and alone, broods once more over the face of the "deep." To use a metaphor which will convey the idea still more clearly, an outbreathing of the "unknown essence" produces the world; and an inhalation causes it to disappear. *This process has been going on from all eternity, and our present universe is but one of an infinite series which had no beginning and will have no end.*

Thus we are enabled to build our theories solely on the visible manifestations of the Deity, on its objective natural phenomena. To apply to these creative principles the term God is puerile and absurd. One might as well call by the name of Benvenuto Cellini the fire which fuses the metal, or the air that cools it when it is run in the mould. If the inner and ever-concealed spiritual, and to our minds abstract, Essence within these forces can ever be connected with the creation of the physical universe, it is but in the sense given to it by Plato. It may be termed, at best, the framer of the abstract universe which developed gradually in the Divine Thought within which it had lain dormant.

In Chapter VIII we will attempt to show the esoteric meaning of *Genesis*, and its complete agreement with the ideas of other nations. The six days of creation will be found to have a meaning little suspected by the multitude of commentators, who have exercised their abilities to the full extent in attempting to reconcile them by turns with Christian theology and un-Christian geology. Disfigured as the *Old Testament* is, yet in its symbolism are preserved enough of the original in its principal features to show the family likeness to the cosmogonies of older nations than the Jews.

We here give the diagrams of the Hindu and the Chaldeo-Jewish cosmogonies. The antiquity of the diagram of the former may be inferred from the fact that many of the Brahmanical pagodas are designed and built on this figure, called the *Srî-Yantra*.* And yet we find the highest honors paid to it by the Jewish and mediaeval kabalists, who call it "Solomon's seal." It will be quite an easy matter to trace it to its origin, once we are reminded of the history of the king-kabalist and his transactions with King Hiram and Ophir — the country of peacocks, gold, and ivory — for which land we have to search in old India.

---

* See *Journal of the Royal Asiatic Society of Great Britain and Ireland*, Vol. XIII, 1852, pp. 71-79: "Note on the Sri Jantra and Khat Kon Chakra, etc.", by E. C. Ravenshaw.

# EXPLANATION OF THE TWO DIAGRAMS

REPRESENTING THE

CHAOTIC AND THE FORMATIVE PERIODS, BEFORE AND AFTER OUR UNIVERSE BEGAN TO BE EVOLVED

FROM THE ESOTERIC BRAHMANICAL, BUDDHISTIC, AND CHALDEAN STANDPOINTS, WHICH AGREE IN EVERY RESPECT WITH THE EVOLUTIONARY THEORY OF MODERN SCIENCE

## THE HINDU DOCTRINE

### The Upper Triangle

Contains the Ineffable Name. It is the AUM — to be pronounced only mentally, under penalty of death. The Unrevealed Parabrahman, the Passive Principle; the absolute and unconditioned "mukta," which cannot enter into the condition of a Creator, as the latter, in order to *think, will,* and *plan,* must be bound and conditioned (*baddha*); hence, in one sense, be a finite being. "THIS (Parabrahman) was absorbed in the non-being, imperceptible, without any distinct attribute, nonexistent for our senses. He was absorbed in his (to us) eternal (to himself) periodical sleep," for it was one of the "Nights of Brahmâ." Therefore he is not the *First* but the Eternal Cause. He is the Soul of Souls, whom no being can comprehend in this state. But "he who studies the secret Mantras and comprehends the *Vâch*" (the Spirit or hidden voice of the Mantras, the active manifestation of the latent Force) will learn to understand him in his "revealed" aspect.

## THE CHALDEAN DOCTRINE

### The Upper Triangle

Contains the Ineffable Name. It is Ain-Soph, the Boundless, the Infinite, whose name is known to no one but the initiated, and could not be pronounced aloud under the penalty of death.

No more than Parabrahman can Ain-Soph create, for he is in the same condition of non-being as the former; he is אין [*ain*], nonexistent, so long as he lies in his latent or passive state within *Olam* (the boundless and termless time); as such he is not the Creator of the visible universe, neither is he the *Or* (Light). He will become the latter when the period of creation shall have compelled him to expand the Force within himself, according to the Law of which he is the embodiment and essence.

"Whoever acquaints himself with ח,[*] the *Merkabah* and the *la'hash* (secret speech or incantation),[†] will learn the secret of secrets."

---

[*] [Initial letters of *hokhma nistharah,* secret wisdom.]

[†] *La'hash* is nearly identical in meaning with *Vâch,* the hidden power of the Mantra.

Both "THIS" and Ain-Soph, in their first manifestation of Light, emerging from within Darkness, may be summarized in the Svabhavat, the Eternal and the uncreated Self-existing Substance which produces all; while everything which is of its essence produces itself out of its own nature.

### The Space Around the Upper Triangle

When the "Night of Brahmâ" was ended, and the time came for the Self-Existent to manifest *Itself* by revelation, it made its glory visible by sending forth from its Essence an active Power, which, female at first, subsequently becomes

### The Space Around the Upper Triangle

When the active period had arrived, Ain-Soph sent forth from within his own eternal essence Sephîrâh, the active Power, called the Primordial Point, and the Crown, *Kether*. It is only through her that the "Unbounded Wisdom" could give a con-

androgyne. It is *Aditi*, the "Infinite," * the Boundless, or rather the "Unbounded." Aditi is the "mother" of all the gods, and Aditi is the Father and the Son.† "Who will give us back to the great Aditi, that I may see father and mother?" ‡ It is in conjunction with the latter female Force, that the Divine but latent Thought produces the great "Deep" — water. "Water is born from a transformation of light . . . and from a *modification* of the water is born the earth," says *Manu* (Book I, 78).

"Ye are born of Aditi from the water, you who are born of the earth, hear ye all my call." §

In this water (or primeval chaos) the "Infinite" androgyne, which, with the Eternal Cause, forms the first abstract Triad, rendered by AUM, deposited the germ of universal life. It is the Mundane Egg, in which took place the gestation of Purusha, or the manifested Brahmâ. The germ which fecundated the *Mother*-Principle (the water) is called *Nara*, the Divine Spirit or Holy Ghost,‖ and the waters themselves, are an emanation of the former, *Nârî*, while the Spirit which brooded over it is called *Nârâyana*.¶

"In that egg the great Power sat inactive a whole *year of the Creator,* at the close of which, by his thought alone he caused the egg to divide itself." ** The

---

\* In the *Rigveda Saṃhitâ* the meaning is given by Max Müller as the Absolute, "for it is derived from *'diti',* bond, and the negative particle *a.*"
† "Hymns to the Maruts," I, 89, 10.
‡ *Ibid.,* I, 24, 4.
§ *Ibid.,* X, 63, 2.
‖ Thus is it that we find in all the philosophical theogonies, the Holy Ghost female. The numerous sects of the Gnostics had Sophia; the Jewish Kabalists and Talmudists, *Shekhînah* (the garment of the Highest), which descended between the two Cherubim upon the Mercy Seat; and we find even Jesus made to say, in an old text, "My Mother, the Holy Ghost, took me." 38
"The waters are called *nara,* because they were the production of Nara, or the Spirit of God" (*Institutes of Manu,* I, 10; ed. Jones).
¶ *Nârâyaṇa,* or that which moves on the waters.
** *Manu,* I, 12 [Sir Wm. Jones, *Works,* III, p. 67; ed. 1799].

crete form to his abstract Thought. Two sides of the upper triangle, the right side and the base, are composed of unbroken lines; the third, the left side, is dotted. It is through the latter that emerges Sephîrâh. Spreading in every direction, she finally encompasses the whole triangle. In this emanation of the female active principle from the left side of the mystic triangle is foreshadowed the creation of Eve from Adam's left rib. Adam is the Microcosm of the Macrocosm, and is created in the image of the Elohim. In the Tree of Life, עץ החיים [*Etz Ḥaiyim*], the triple triad is disposed in such a manner that the three male Sephîrôth are on the right, the three female on the left, and the four uniting principles in the centre. From the Invisible Dew falling from the Higher "Head" Sephîrâh creates primeval water, or chaos taking shape. It is the first step toward the solidification of Spirit, which through various modifications will produce earth.\* "*It requires earth and water to make a living soul,*" says Moses.

When Sephîrâh emerges like an active power from within the latent Deity, she is female; when she assumes the office of a

---

\* George Smith gives the first verses of the Akkadian *Genesis* as found in the Cuneiform Texts on the "Lateres Coctiles." There, also, we find *Anu,* the passive deity or Ain-Soph; *Bel,* the Creator, the Spirit of God (Sephîrâh) moving on the face of the waters, hence water itself; and *Hea,* the Universal Soul or wisdom of the three combined.

The first eight verses read thus:
1. When above, were not raised the heavens:
2. and below on the earth a plant had not grown up;
3. The abyss also had not broken open its boundaries;
4. The chaos [or water] Tiamat [the sea] was the producing mother of the whole of them. [This is the Cosmical Aditi and Sephîrâh.]
5. Those waters at the beginning were ordained; but
6. a tree had not grown, a flower had not unfolded.
7. When the gods had not sprung up, any one of them;
8. a plant had not grown, and order did not exist;
This was the chaotic or ante-genesis period. [*The Chald. Acc. of Genesis* (1876), pp. 62-63.]

upper half became heaven, the lower, the earth (both yet in their ideal, not their manifested form).

Thus, this second triad, only another name for the first one (never pronounced aloud), and which is the real pre-Vedic and primordial *secret* Trimûrti, consisted of

| Nara, | Father-Heaven, |
|---|---|
| Nârî, | Mother-Earth, |
| Virâj, | the Son—or Universe. |

The Trimûrti, comprising Brahmâ, the Creator, Vishnu, the Preserver, and Śiva, the Destroyer and Regenerator, belongs to a later period. It is an anthropomorphic afterthought, invented for the more popular comprehension of the uninitiated masses. The *Dikshita,* the initiate, knew better. Thus, also, the profound allegory under the colors of a ridiculous fable, given in the *Aitareya-Brâhmanam,** which resulted in the representations in some temples of Brahmâ-Nara, assuming the form of a bull, and his daughter, Aditi-Nârî, that of a heifer, contains the same metaphysical idea as the "fall of man," or that of the Spirit into generation — matter. The All-pervading Divine Spirit embodied under the symbols of Heaven, the Sun, and Heat (fire)—the correlation of cosmic forces—fecundates Matter or Nature, the daughter of Spirit. And Brahmâ himself has to submit to and bear the penance of the curses of the other gods (Elohim) for such an incest. (See corresponding column.) According to the immutable, and, therefore, fatal law, both Nara and Nârî are mutually Father and Mother, as well as Father and Daughter.† Matter, through infinite transformation, is the gradual product of Spirit. The unification of one Eternal Supreme Cause required such a correlation; and if nature be the product or creator, she becomes a male; hence, she is androgyne. She is the "Father and Mother Aditi," of the Hindu Cosmogony. After brooding over the "Deep," the "Spirit of God" produces its own image in the water, the Universal Womb, symbolized in *Manu* by the Golden Egg. In the kabalistic Cosmogony, Heaven and Earth are personified by Adam-Kadmon and the second Adam. The first Ineffable Triad, contained in the abstract idea of the "Three Heads," was a "mystery name." It was composed of Ain-Soph, Sephîrâh, and Adam-Kadmon, the Protogonos, the latter being identical with the former, when bisexual.* In every triad there is a male, a female, and an androgyne. Adam-Sephîrâh is the Crown (Kether). It sets itself to the work of creation, by first producing Ḥokhmah, Male Wisdom, a masculine active potency, represented by יה, Yâh, or the Wheels of Creation אופנים [*Ophanim*], from which proceeds Binah, Intelligence, female and passive potency, which is *Yahveh,* יהוה, whom we find in the *Bible* figuring as the Supreme. But this *Yahveh* is not the kabalistic *Yod-heva.* The *binary* is the fundamental cornerstone of *Gnosis.* As the binary is the Unity multiplying itself and self-creating, the kabalists show the "Unknown" passive Ain-Soph, as emanating from himself Sephîrâh, which, becoming visible light, is said to produce Adam-Kadmon. But, in the hidden sense, Sephîrâh and Adam are one and the same light, only latent and active, invisible and visible. The second Adam, as the human tetragram, produces in his turn Eve, out of his side. It is this second triad, with which the kabalists have hitherto dealt, hardly hinting at the Supreme and Ineffable One, and never committing anything to writing. All knowledge concerning the latter was imparted orally. It is the *second* Adam, then, who is the unity represented by *Yod,* emblem of the kabalistic male principle, and, at the same time, he is Ḥokhmah, *Wisdom,* while *Binah* or Yehovah is Eve; the first, Ḥokhmah issuing from Kether, or

---

* See Haug's translation: III, iii, 33.

† The same transformations are found in the cosmogony of every important nation. Thus, we see in the Egyptian mythology, Isis and Osiris, sister and brother, man and wife; and Horus, the Son of both, becoming the husband of his mother, Isis, and producing a son, *Malouli.* [Champollion-Figeac, *Égypte ancienne,* p. 245.]

* When a female power, she is Sephîrâh; when male, he is Adam-Kadmon, for, as the former contains in herself the other nine Sephîrôth, so, in their totality, the latter, including Sephîrâh, is embodied in the Archetypal Kadmon, the πρωτόγονος.

effect of that Cause, in its turn it has to be fecundated by the same divine Ray which produced nature itself. The most absurd cosmogonical allegories, if analyzed without prejudice, will be found built on strict and logical necessarianism.

"Being was born from not-being," says a verse in the *Ṛig-Veda*.* The first being had to become androgyne and finite, by the very fact of its creation as a being. And thus even the sacred Trimûrti, containing Brahmâ, Vishṇu, and Śiva will have an end when the "night" of Parabrahman succeeds the present "day," or period of universal activity.

The second, or rather the first, triad—as the highest one is a pure abstraction—is the intellectual world. The *Vâch* which surrounds it is a more definite transformation of Aditi. Besides its occult significance in the secret Mantra, Vâch is personified as the active power of Brahmâ proceeding from him. In the *Vedas* she is made to speak of herself as the supreme and universal soul. "I bore the Father on the head of this [universal mind]; and *my origin is in the midst of the ocean;* and therefore do I pervade all beings . . . Originating all beings, I pass like the breeze [Holy Ghost]. I am above this heaven, beyond this earth; and *what is the Great One that am I.*" † Literally, Vâch is speech, the power of awakening, through the metrical arrangement contained in the number and syllables of the Mantras, ‡ corresponding powers in the invisible world. In the sacrificial Mysteries Vâch stirs up the Brahmâ (*Brahmâ jinvati*), or the power lying latent at the bottom of every magical operation. It existed from eternity as the *Yajña* (its latent form), lying dormant in Brahmâ from "no-beginning," and proceeded forth from him as Vâch (the active power). It is the key to the *Trai-vidyâ*," the thrice sacred science which

---

* *Mandala I, Sûkta* 166: Max Müller.

† *Asiatic Researches* (ed. 1805), Vol. VIII, pp. 391-92; Colebrooke's translation.

‡ As in the Pythagorean numerical system every number on earth, or the world of the effects, corresponds to its invisible prototype in the world of causes.

the androgyne, Adam-Kadmon, and the second, Binah, from Ḥokhmah. If we combine with *Yod* the three letters which form the name of Eve, we will have the divine tetragram pronounced IEVO-HEVAH, Adam and Eve, יהוה, Jehovah, male and female, or the idealization of humanity embodied in the first man. Thus is it that we can prove that, while the Jewish kabalists, in common with their initiated masters, the Chaldeans and the Hindus, adored the Supreme and Unknown God in the sacred silence of their sanctuaries, the ignorant masses of every nation were left to adore something which was certainly less than the Eternal Substance of the Buddhists, the so-called Atheists. As Brahmâ, the deity manifested in the mythical Manu, or the first man (born of *Svayambhû*, or the Self-existent), is finite, so Jehovah, embodied in Adam and Eve, is but a *human* god. He is the symbol of humanity, a mixture of good with a portion of unavoidable evil; of spirit fallen into matter. In worshipping Jehovah, we simply worship nature, as embodied in man, half-spiritual and half-material, at best: we are Pantheists, when not fetish worshippers, like the idolatrous Jews, who sacrificed on high places, in groves, to the personified male and female principle, ignorant of IAÔ, the Supreme "Secret Name" of the Mysteries.

Shekhînah is the Hindu Vâch, and praised in the same terms as the latter. Though shown in the kabalistic Tree of Life as proceeding from the ninth Sephîrôth, yet Shekhînah is the "veil" of Ain-Soph, and the "garment" of Jehovah. The "veil," for it succeeded for long ages in concealing the real supreme God, the universal Spirit, and masking Jehovah, the exoteric deity, made the Christians accept him as the "father" of the initiated Jesus. Yet the kabalists, as well as the Hindu *Dîkshita*, know the power of the Shekhînah or Vâch, and call it the "secret wisdom," חכמה נסתרה [*ḥohkmah nistharah*].

The triangle played a prominent part in the religious symbolism of every great nation; for everywhere it represented the three great principles — spirit, force and matter; or the active (male), passive (female), and the dual or correlative principle which partakes of both and binds the two together.

teaches the *Yajus* (the sacrificial Mysteries).*

Having done with the unrevealed triad, and the first triad of the Sephîrôth, called the "intellectual world," little remains to be said. In the great geometrical figure which has the double triangle in it, the central circle represents the world within the universe. The double triangle belongs to one of the most important, if it is not in itself the most important, of the mystic figures in India. It is the emblem of the Trimûrti three in one. The triangle with its apex upward indicates the male principle, downward the female; the two typifying, at the same time, spirit and matter. This world within the infinite universe is the microcosm within the macrocosm, as in the Jewish *Kabala*. It is the symbol of the womb of the universe, the terrestrial egg, whose archetype is the golden mundane egg. It is from within this spiritual bosom of mother nature that proceed all the great saviors of the universe — the avatâras of the invisible Deity.

"Of him who is and yet is not, from the not-being, Eternal Cause, is born the being Purusha," says Manu, the legislator. Purusha is the "divine male," the *second* god, and the avatâra, or the Logos of Parabrahman and his divine son, who in his turn produced Virâj, the son, or the ideal type of the universe. "Virâj begins the work of creation by producing the ten Prajâpatis, 'the lords of all beings'." †

According to the doctrine of Manu, the universe is subjected to a periodical and never-ending succession of creations and dissolutions, which periods of creation are named *Manvantaras*.

"It is the germ [which the Divine Spirit produced from its own substance] which never perishes in the being, for it becomes the soul of Being, and at the period of *pralaya* [dissolution] it returns to absorb itself again *into the Divine* Spirit, *which*

---

\* See initial chap., Vol. I, p. xliii, word *Yajña*.

† [*Manu*, Bk. I, 11 *et seq.*; 33 *et seq.*]

It was the *Arba* or mystic "four," * the mystery-gods, the Kabiri, summarized in the unity of one supreme Deity. It is found in the Egyptian pyramids, whose equal sides tower up until lost in one crowning point. In the kabalistic diagram the central circle of the Brahmanical figure is replaced by the cross; the celestial perpendicular and the terrestrial horizontal base line.† But the idea is the same: Adam-Kadmon is the type of humanity as a collective totality within the unity of the creative God and the universal spirit.

---

\* Eve is the trinity of nature, and Adam the unity of spirit; the former, the created material principle, the latter, the ideal organ of the creative principle, or, in other words, this androgyne is both the principle and the Logos, for א is the male, and ב the female; and, as Lévi expresses it, this first letter of the holy language, Aleph, represents a man pointing with one hand toward the sky, and with the other toward the ground. It is the macrocosm and the microcosm at the same time, and explains the double triangle of the Masons and the five-pointed star. While the male is active, the female principle is passive, for it is SPIRIT and MATTER, the latter word meaning *mother* in nearly every language. The columns of Solomon's temple, Jachin and Boaz, are the emblems of the androgyne; they are also respectively male and female, white and black, square and round; the male a unity, the female a binary. In the later kabalistic treatises, the active principle is pictured by the sword, זכר [*zakar*], **the passive by the sheath,** נקבה [*neqebah*]. See *Dogme et Rituel de la haute magie,* Vol. I.

† The vertical line being the male principle, and the horizontal the female, out of the union of the two at the intersection point is formed the CROSS; the oldest symbol in the Egyptian history of gods. It is the key of Heaven in the rosy fingers of Neith, the celestial virgin, who opens the gate at dawn for the exit of her first-begotten, the radiant sun. It is the Stauros of the Gnostics, and the philosophical cross of the high-grade Masons. We find this symbol ornamenting the *tee* of the umbrella-shaped oldest pagodas in Thibet, China and India, as we find it in the hand of Isis, in the shape of the "handled cross." In one of the Chaitya caves, at Ajanta, it surmounts the three umbrellas in stone, and forms the centre of the vault.

*itself* rests from all eternity within Svayambhû, the 'Self-Existent'." *

As we have shown, neither the Svâbhâvikas — Buddhist philosophers — nor the Brahmans believe in a creation of the universe *ex nihilo*, but both believe in the *Prakṛiti*, the indestructibility of matter.

The evolution of species, and the successive appearance of various new types is very distinctly shown in *Manu*.

"From earth, heat, and water, are born all creatures, whether animate or inanimate, produced by the germ which the Divine Spirit drew from its own substance. Thus has Brahmâ established the series of transformations from the plant up to man, and from man up to the primordial essence . . . Among them each succeeding being (or element) acquires the quality of the preceding; and in as many degrees as each of them is advanced, with so many properties is it said to be endowed." †

This, we believe, is the veritable theory of the modern evolutionists.

---

* *Manu*, Book I.
† *Manu*, Book I, śloka 20.
"When this world had emerged from obscurity, the subtile elementary principles produced the vegetable germ which at first animated the plants; from the plants, life passed through the fantastic organisms which were born in the ilus (*boue*) of the waters; then through a series of forms and different animals, it at length reached man" (*Manu*, Bk. I; and *Bhâgavata-Purâna*).

Manu is a convertible type which can by no means be explained as a personage. Manu means sometimes humanity, sometimes man. The Manu who emanated from the uncreated *Svayambhû* is, without doubt, the type of Adam-Kadmon. The Manu who is progenitor of the other six Manus is evidently identical with the Ṛishis, or seven primeval sages who are the forefathers of the post-diluvian races. He is — as we shall show in Chapter VIII — Noah, and his six sons, or subsequent generations are the originals of the post-diluvian and mythical patriarchs of the Bible.

"Of him who is formless, the non-existent (also the eternal, but *not* First Cause), is born the heavenly man." But after he created the form of the heavenly man, אדם עלאה [*Adam Illa-ah*], he "used it as a vehicle wherein to descend," says the Kabala. Thus Adam-Kadmon is the avatâra of the concealed power. After that the heavenly Adam creates or engenders, by the combined power of the Sephîrôth, the earthly Adam. The work of creation is also begun by Sephîrâh in the creation of the ten Sephîrôth (who are the Prajâpatis of the *Kabala*, for they are likewise the Lords of all beings).

The *Zohar* asserts the same. According to the kabalistic doctrine there were old worlds (*Zohar*, III, p. 292 b). Everything will return some day to that from which it first proceeded. "All things of which this world consists, spirit as well as body, will return to their principal, and the roots from which they proceeded" (*Zohar*, II, 218 b). The kabalists also maintain the indestructibility of matter, albeit their doctrine is shrouded still more carefully than that of the Hindus. The creation is eternal, and the universe is the "garment," or "the veil of God" — Shekhînah; and the latter is immortal and eternal as Him within whom it has ever existed. Every world is made after the pattern of its predecessor, and each more gross and material than the preceding one. In the *Kabala* all were called sparks. [*Zohar*, III, p. 292 b.] Finally, our present grossly materialistic world was formed.

In the Chaldean account of the period which preceded the Genesis of our world, Berosus speaks of a time when there existed nothing but darkness, and an abyss of waters, filled with hideous monsters, "produced of a two-fold principle . . . There were creatures in which were combined the limbs of every species of animals. In addition to these, fishes, reptiles, serpents, with other monstrous animals, which assumed each other's shape and countenance." *

---

* Cory, *Ancient Fragments*, pp. 23-24.

In the first book of *Manu*, we read: "Know that the sum of 1,000 divine ages composes the totality of one day of Brahmâ; and that one night is equal to that day." One thousand divine ages is equal to 4,320,000,000 of human years, in the Brahmanical calculations.

"At the expiration of each night, Brahmâ, who has been asleep, awakes, and [through the sole energy of the motion] causes to emanate from himself the spirit, which in its essence *is*, and yet is not."

"Prompted by the desire to create, the Spirit [first of the emanations] operates the creation and gives birth to ether, which the sages consider as having the faculty of transmitting sound.

"Ether begets air whose property is tangible [and which is necessary to life].

"Through a transformation of the air, light is produced.

"From [air and] light [which begets heat], water is formed [and the water is the womb of all the living germs]." *

Throughout the whole immense period of progressive creation, covering 4,320,000,000 years, ether, air, water and fire (heat) are constantly forming matter under the never-ceasing impulse of the Spirit, or the *unrevealed* God who fills up the whole creation, for he is in all, and all is in him. This computation, which was secret and which is hardly hinted at even now, led Higgins into the error of dividing every ten ages into 6,000 years. Had he added a few more ciphers to his sums he might have come nearer to a correct explanation of the neroses, or secret cycles. †

In the *Sepher Yetzîrah*, the kabalistic Book of Creation, the author has evidently repeated the words of Manu. In it, the Divine Substance is represented as having alone existed from the eternity, boundless and absolute; and emitted from itself the Spirit. "One is the Spirit of the living God, blessed be His Name, who liveth forever! Voice, Spirit, and Word, this is the Holy Spirit"; ‡ and this is the kabalistic abstract Trinity, so unceremoniously anthropomorphized by the Fathers. From this triple ONE emanated the whole Cosmos. First from ONE emanated number TWO, or Air, the creative element; and then number THREE, *Water*, proceeded from the air; *Ether* or *Fire* complete the mystic four, the Arba-il.§ "When the Concealed of the Concealed wanted to reveal Himself, he first made a point [primordial point, or the first Sephîrah, air or Holy Ghost], shaped it into a sacred form [the ten Sephîrôth,, or the Heavenly man], and covered it with a rich and splendid garment, *that is the world.*" ‖ "He maketh the wind His messengers, flaming Fire his

---

* [*Manu*, Bk. I, 72-78.]
† See Vol. I, ch. i, pp. 32-34 of this work.
‡ *Sepher Yetzîrah*, I, §8.
§ *Ibid.*, I, §11.
‖ *Zohar*, I, 2a.

servants," says the *Yetzîrah*, showing the cosmical character of the later euhemerized angels,* and that the Spirit permeates every minutest atom of the Cosmos.†

When the cycle of creation is run down, the energy of the manifested word is weakening. He alone, the Inconceivable, is unchangeable (ever latent), but the Creative Force, though also eternal, as it has been in the former from "no beginning," yet must be subject to periodical cycles of activity and rest; as it had a *beginning* in one of its aspects, when it first emanated, therefore must also have an end. Thus, the evening succeeds the day, and the night of the deity approaches. Brahmâ is gradually falling asleep. In one of the books of *Zohar*, we read the following:

"As Moses was keeping a vigil on Mount Sinai, in company with the Deity, who was concealed from his sight by a cloud, he felt a great fear overcome him and suddenly asked: 'Lord, where art Thou . . . sleepest thou, O Lord?' And the *Spirit* answered him: 'I never sleep; were I to fall asleep for a moment *before my time*, all the Creation would crumble into dissolution in one instant'." And Vâmadeva Modaliyar describes the "Night of Brahmâ," or the second period of the Divine Unknown existence, thus:

"Strange noises are heard, proceeding from every point . . . These are the precursors of the Night of Brahmâ; *dusk rises at the horizon* and the Sun passes away behind the thirtieth degree of *Makara* (sign of the zodiac), and will reach no more the sign of the *Mina* (zodiacal *Pisces*, or fishes). The gurus of the pagodas appointed to watch the *râsi-chakra* [Zodiac], may now break their circle and instruments, for they are henceforth useless.

"Gradually light pales, heat diminishes, uninhabitable spots multiply on the earth, the air becomes more and more rarefied; the springs of water dry up, the great rivers see their waves exhausted, the ocean shows its sandy bottom, and plants die. Men and animals decrease in size daily. Life and motion lose their force, planets can hardly gravitate in space; they are extinguished one by one, like a lamp which the hand of the *chokra* [servant] neglects to replenish. Sûrya (the Sun) flickers and goes out, matter falls into dissolution (*pralaya*), and Brahmâ merges back into *Dyaus*, the Unrevealed God, and, his task being accomplished, he falls asleep. Another day is passed, night sets in and continues until the future dawn.

---

\* *Sepher Yetzîrah*, I, 10.

† It is interesting to recall *Hebrews* i, 7, in connection with this passage. "Who maketh his angels [messengers] spirits, and his ministers [servants, those who minister] a flame of fire." The resemblance is too striking for us to avoid the conclusion that the author of *Hebrews* was as familiar with the "Kabala" as adepts usually are.

"And now again he re-enters into the golden egg of His Thought, the germs of all that exist, as the divine Manu tells us. During His peaceful rest, the animated beings, endowed with the principles of action, cease their functions, and all feeling (*manas*) becomes dormant. When they are all absorbed in the SUPREME SOUL, this Soul of all the beings sleeps in complete repose, till the day when it resumes its form, and awakes again from its primitive darkness." *

If we now examine the ten mythical avatâras of Vishṇu, we find them recorded in the following progression:

1. Matsya-Avatâra: as a fish. It will also be his tenth and last avâtara, at the end of the Kali-yuga.

2. Kûrma-Avatâra: as a tortoise.

3. Varâha: as a boar.

4. Nara-Sinha: as a *man-lion*; last animal stage.

5. Vâmana: as a dwarf; first step toward the human form.

6. Paraśu-Râma: as a hero, but yet an imperfect man.

7. Râma-Chandra: as the hero of *Râmâyaṇâ*. Physically a perfect man; his next of kin, friend and ally Hanuman, the monkey-god. *The monkey endowed with speech.*†

8. Kṛishṇa-Avatâra: the Son of the Virgin Devakî, one formed by God, or rather by the manifested Deity Vishṇu, who is identical with Adam-Kadmon. ‡ Kṛishṇa is also called *Kâneya*, the Son of the Virgin.

9. Gautama Buddha, Siddhârtha, or Śâkyamuni. (The Buddhists reject this doctrine of their Buddha being an incarnation of Vishṇu.)

10. This avatâra has not yet occurred. It is expected in the future, like the Christian Advent, the idea of which was undoubtedly copied from the Hindu. When Vishṇu appears for the last time he will come as a "Savior." According to the opinion of some Brahmans he will appear himself under the form of the horse *Kalki*. Others maintain that he will be mounting it. This horse is the envelope of the spirit of evil, and Vishṇu will mount it, invisible to all, till he has conquered it for the last time. The *Kalki-Avatâra*, or the last incarnation, divides Brahman-

---

\* Cf. Jacolliot, *Les Fils de Dieu*, pp. 229-30.

† May it not be that Hanuman is the representative of that link of beings, half-man, half-monkeys, which, according to the theories of Messrs. Hovelacque and Schleicher, were arrested in their development, and fell, so to say, into a retrogressive evolution?

‡ The Primal or Ultimate Essence has *no name* in India. It is indicated sometimes as "That" and "This." "This [universe] was not originally anything. There was neither heaven, nor earth, nor atmosphere. That being nonexistent (*asat*), resolved 'Let me be.'" (Dr. John Muir, *Original Sanskrit Texts*, V, p. 366; ed. 1863-71.)

Count Giovanni Pico della Mirándola
1463-1494
Original painting by an unknown master in the
Galleria Uffizi, Florence, Italy.

ALTERIVS NON SIT QVI SVVS ESSE POTEST

AVREOLVS PHILIPPVS, AB HOHENHEIM.
Stemmate nobilium genitus PARACELSVS
auorum.
Qua vetus Heluetia claret Eremus humo.
Sic oculos, sic ora tulit, cum plurima longum
Discendi studio per loca fecit iter

THEOPHRASTVS BOMBAST,
DICTVS PARACELSVS
Lustra nouem et medium vixit lustro ante
Lutherum.
Postque tuos lustro functus, Erasme, rogos.
Astra quater Sena Septembris luce subiuit;
Ossa Salisburga nunc cineresque jacent

I Tintoret ad viuum pinxit    F Chauueau sculpsit

**Philippus Aureolus Theophrastus Bombast of Hohenheim,**
**known as Paracelsus**
**1493-1541**

From an old engraving published in *Le Lotus*, Paris,
Tome II, October, 1887.

ism into two sects. That of the Vaishnava refuses to recognize the incarnations of their god Vishnu in animal forms literally. They claim that these must be understood as allegorical.

In this list of avatâras we see traced the gradual evolution and transformation of all species out of the ante-Silurian mud of Darwin and the *ilus* of Sanchoniathon and Berosus. Beginning with the Azoic time, corresponding to the *ilus* in which Brahmâ implants the creative germ, we pass through the Palaeozoic and Mesozoic times, covered by the first and second incarnations as the fish and tortoise; and the Cenozoic, which is embraced by the incarnations in the animal and semi-human forms of the boar and man-lion; and we come to the fifth and crowning geological period, designated as the "era of mind, or age of man," whose symbol in the Hindu mythology is the dwarf — the first attempt of nature at the creation of man. In this list we should follow the main idea, not judge the degree of knowledge of the ancient philosophers by the literal acceptance of the popular form in which it is presented to us in the grand epical poem of *Mahâbhârata* and its chapter, the *Bhagavad-Gitâ*.

Even the four ages of the Hindu chronology contain a far more philosophical idea than appears on the surface. It defines them according to both the psychological or mental, and the physical states of man during their period. Krita-yuga, the golden age, the "age of joy," or spiritual innocence of man; Tretâ-yuga, the age of silver, or that of fire — the period of supremacy of man and of giants and of the sons of God; Dwâpara-yuga, the age of bronze — a mixture already of purity and impurity (spirit and matter), the age of doubt; and at last our own, the Kali-yuga, or age of iron, of darkness, misery and sorrow. In this age, Vishnu had to incarnate himself in Krishna, in order to save humanity from the goddess *Kâlî*, consort of Śiva, the all-annihilating — the goddess of death, destruction, and human misery. *Kâlî* is the best emblem to represent the "fall of man"; the falling of spirit into the degradation of matter, with all its terrific results. We have to rid ourselves of *Kâlî* before we can ever reach *Moksha* or Nirvâna, the abode of blessed Peace and Spirit.

With the Buddhists the last incarnation is the fifth. When Maitreya-Buddha comes, then our present world will be destroyed; and a new and a better one will replace it. The four arms of every Hindu Deity are the emblems of the four preceding manifestations of our earth from its invisible state, while its head typifies the fifth and last *Kalki-Avatâra*, when this would be destroyed, and the power of Budh — Wisdom (with the Hindus, of Brahmâ), will be again called into requisition to manifest itself — as a *Logos* — to create the future world.

In this scheme, the male gods typify Spirit in its deific attributes, while their female counterparts — the *Śakti*, represent the active energies of these attributes. The *Durgâ* (active virtue) is a subtile, invisible force, which answers to Shekhinah — the garment of Ain-Soph. She is the Śakti through which the passive "Eternal" calls forth the visible universe from its first ideal conception. Every one of the three personages of the exoteric Trimûrti is shown as using its *Śakti* as a *Vâhana* (vehicle). Each of them is for the time being the form which sits upon the mysterious wagon of Ezekiel.

Nor do we see less clearly carried out in this succession of avatâras, the truly philosophical idea of a simultaneous spiritual and physical evolution of creatures and man. From a fish the progress of this dual transformation carries on the physical form through the shape of a tortoise, a boar and a man-lion; and then, appearing in the dwarf of humanity, it shows *Paraśu-Râma*, physically a perfect, spiritually an undeveloped entity, until it carries mankind personified by one godlike man, to the apex of physical and spiritual perfection — a god on earth. In Kṛishṇa and the other Saviors of the world, we see the philosophical idea of the progressive dual development understood and as clearly expressed in the *Zohar*. The "Heavenly man," who is the Protogonos, Tikkun, the first-born of God, or the universal Form and Idea, engenders Adam. Hence the latter is god-born in humanity, and endowed with the attributes of all the ten Sephîrôth. These are: Wisdom, Intelligence, Justice, Love, Beauty, Splendor, Firmness, etc. They make him the Foundation or basis, "*the mighty living one*," אל חי [*El-Ḥay*], and the crown of creation, thus placing him as the Alpha and Omega to reign over the "kingdom" — Malkhuth. "Man is both the import and the highest degree of creation," says the *Zohar*. "As soon as man was created, everything was complete, including the upper and nether worlds, for everything is comprised in man. He unites in himself all forms." \*

But this does not relate to our degenerated mankind; it is only occasionally that men are born who are the types of what man should be, and yet is not. The first races of men were spiritual, and their protoplastic bodies were not composed of the gross and material substances of which we see them composed now-a-days. The first men were created with all the faculties of the Deity, and powers far transcending those of the angelic host; for they were the direct emanations of Adam-Kadmon, the primitive man, the Macrocosm; while the present humanity is several degrees removed even from the early Adam, who was the Microcosm, or "the little world." Zeir-Anpîn, the mystical figure of the Man, consists of 243 numbers, and we see in the circles which follow each other that it is the angels which emanated from the "Primitive Man," not the

---

\* *Zohar*, III, p. 48a, Amsterdam ed.

Sephîrôth from angels. Hence, man was intended from the first to be a being of both a progressive and retrogressive nature. Beginning at the apex of the divine cycle, he gradually began receding from the centre of Light, acquiring at every new and lower sphere of being (worlds each inhabited by a different race of human beings) a more solid physical form and losing a portion of his *divine* faculties.

In the "fall of Adam" we must see, not the personal transgression of man, but simply the law of the dual evolution. Adam, or "Man," begins his career of existences by dwelling in the garden of Eden, "dressed in the celestial garment, which *is a garment of heavenly light*" (*Zohar*, II, 229 b); but when expelled he is "clothed" by God, or the eternal law of Evolution or necessarianism, with coats of skin. But even on this earth of material degradation — in which the divine spark (Soul, a corruscation of the Spirit) was to begin its physical progression in a series of imprisonments from a stone up to a man's body — if he but exercise his WILL and call his deity to his help, man can transcend the powers of the angel. "Know ye not that we shall judge angels?" asks Paul (*1 Corinthians* vi, 3). The real man is the Soul (Spirit), teaches the *Zohar*. "The mystery of the earthly man is after the mystery of the heavenly man . . . the wise can read the mysteries in the human face" (II, 76 a).

This is still another of the many sentences by which Paul must be recognized as an initiate. For reasons fully explained, we give far more credit for genuineness to certain Epistles of the apostles, now dismissed as apocryphal, than to many suspicious portions of the *Acts*. And we find corroboration of this view in the *Epistles of Paul to Seneca, and Seneca to Paul.*\* In one message Paul styles Seneca "most respectable master," while Seneca terms the apostle simply "brother."

No more than the true religion of Judaic philosophy can be judged by the absurdities of the exoteric *Bible,* have we any right to form an opinion of Brahmanism and Buddhism by their nonsensical and sometimes disgusting popular forms. If we only search for the true essence of the philosophy of both *Manu* and the *Kabala,* we will find that Vishṇu is, as well as Adam-Kadmon, the expression of the universe itself; and that his incarnations are but concrete and various embodiments of the manifestations of this "Stupendous Whole." "I am the Soul, O Arjuna. I am the Soul which exists in the heart of all beings; and I am the beginning and the middle, and also the end of existing things," says Kṛishṇa to his disciple, in *Bhagavad-Gîtâ* (ch. x).

"I am Alpha and Omega, the beginning and the ending . . . I am the first and the last," says Jesus to John (*Rev.* i, 8, 17).

---

\* [Hone, *The Apocr. N.T.*, London, 1820, pp. 95, 97.]

Brahmâ, Vishṇu and Śiva are a trinity in a unity, and, like the Christian trinity, they are mutually convertible. In the esoteric doctrine they are one and the same manifestation of him "whose name is too sacred to be pronounced, and whose power is too majestic and infinite to be imagined." Thus by describing the avatâras of one, all others are included in the allegory, with a change of form but not of substance. It is out of such manifestations that emanated the many worlds that were, and that will emanate the one which is to come.

Coleman, followed in this by other Orientalists, presents the seventh avatâra of Vishṇu in the most caricatured way.* Apart from the fact that the *Râmâyaṇa* is one of the grandest epic poems in the world — the source and origin of Homer's inspiration — this avatâra conceals one of the most scientific problems of our modern day. The learned Brahmans of India never understood the allegory of the famous war between men, giants and monkeys, otherwise than in the light of the transformation of species. It is our firm belief that were European academicians to seek for information from some learned native Brahmans, instead of unanimously and incontinently rejecting their authority, and were they, like Jacolliot — against whom they have nearly all arrayed themselves — to seek for light in the oldest documents scattered about the country in pagodas, they might learn strange but not useless lessons. Let anyone inquire of an *educated* Brahman the reason for the respect shown to monkeys — the origin of which feeling is indicated in the story of the valorous feats of Hanuman, the generalissimo and faithful ally of the hero of *Râmâyaṇa* † and he would soon be disabused of the erroneous idea that the Hindus accord deific honors to a monkey-*god*. He would, perhaps, learn — were the Brahman to judge him worthy of an explanation — that the Hindu sees in the ape but what Manu desired he should: the transformation of species most directly connected with that of the human family — a bastard branch engrafted on their own stock before the final perfection of the latter.‡ He might learn, further, that in the eyes of the educated

---

\* Coleman, *The Mythology of the Hindus*, pp. 22 *et seq*.

† The siege and subsequent surrender of Lankâ (Isle of Ceylon) to Râma is placed by the Hindu chronology — based upon the Zodiac — at 7500 to 8000 years B.C., and the following or eighth incarnation of Vishṇu at 4800 B.C. (from the *Book of the Historical Zodiacs* of the Brahmans).

‡ A Hanoverian scientist has recently published a work entitled *Über die Auflösung der Arten durch natürliche Zuchtwahl*,[39] in which he shows, with great ingenuity, that Darwin was wholly mistaken in tracing man back to the ape. On the contrary, he maintains that it is the ape which has evolved from man. That in the beginning, mankind were, morally and physically, the types and prototypes of our present race and of human dignity, by their beauty of form, regularity of feature, cranial development, nobility of sentiments, heroic impulses, and grandeur of ideal conceptions. This is a purely Brahmanic, Buddhistic, and kabalistic philosophy. His book is copiously illus-

"heathen" the spiritual or *inner* man is one thing, and his terrestrial, physical casket another; that *physical* nature, the great combination of physical correlations of forces ever creeping on toward perfection, has to avail herself of the material at hand; she models and remodels as she proceeds, and finishing her crowning work in man, presents him alone as a fit tabernacle for the overshadowing of the Divine spirit. But the latter circumstance does not give man the right of life and death over the animals lower than himself in the scale of *nature*, or the right to torture them. Quite the reverse. Besides being endowed with a soul — of which every animal, and even plant, is more or less possessed — man has his immortal *rational* soul, or *nous*, which ought to make him at least equal in magnanimity to the elephant, who treads so carefully, lest he should crush weaker creatures than himself. It is this feeling which prompts Brahman and Buddhist alike to construct hospitals for sick animals, and even insects, and to prepare refuges wherein they may finish their days. It is this same feeling, again, which causes the Jaina sectarian to sacrifice one-half of his lifetime to brushing away from his path the helpless, crawling insects, rather than recklessly deprive the smallest of life; and it is again from this sense of highest benevolence and charity toward the weaker, however abject the creature may be, that they honor one of the natural modifications of their own dual nature, and that later the popular belief in metempsychosis arose. No trace of the latter is to be found in the *Vedas*; and the true interpretation of the doctrine, discussed at length in *Manu* and the Buddhistic sacred books, having been confined from the first to the learned sacerdotal castes, the false and foolish popular ideas concerning it need occasion no surprise.

Upon those who, in the remains of antiquity, see evidence that modern times can lay small claim to originality, it is common to charge a disposition to exaggerate and distort facts. But the candid reader will scarcely aver that the above is an example in point. There were evolutionists before the day when the mythical Noah is made, in the *Bible*, to float in his ark; and the ancient scientists were better informed, and had their theories more logically defined than the modern evolutionists.

Plato, Anaxagoras, Pythagoras, the Eleatic schools of Greece, as well as the old Chaldean sacerdotal colleges, all taught the doctrine of the

---

trated with diagrams, tables, etc. He says that the gradual debasement and degradation of man, morally and physically, can be readily traced throughout the ethnological transformations down to our times. And, as one portion has already degenerated into apes, so the civilized man of the present day will at last, under the action of the inevitable law of necessity, be also succeeded by like descendants. If we may judge of the future by the actual present, it certainly does seem possible that so unspiritual and materialistic a body as our physical scientists should end as *simiae* rather than as seraphs.

dual evolution; the doctrine of the transmigration of souls referring only to the progress of man from world to world, after death here. Every philosophy worthy of the name, taught that the *spirit* of man, if not the *soul*, was pre-existent. "The Essenes," says Josephus, "believed that the souls were immortal, and that they descended from the ethereal spaces to be chained to bodies." * In his turn, Philo Judaeus says the "air is full of them [of souls]; those which are nearest the earth, descending to be tied to mortal bodies, παλινδρομοῦσιν αὖθις, return to other bodies, being desirous to live in them." † In the *Zohar*, the soul is made to plead her freedom before God: "Lord of the Universe! I am happy in this world, and do not wish to go into another world, where I shall be a bondmaid, and be exposed to all kinds of pollutions." ‡ The doctrine of fatal necessity, the everlasting immutable Law, is asserted in the answer of the Deity: "Against thy will thou becomest an embryo, and against thy will thou art born." § Light would be incomprehensible without darkness, to make it manifest by contrast; good would be no good without evil, to show the priceless nature of the boon; and so, personal virtue could claim no merit, unless it had passed through the furnace of temptation. Nothing is eternal and unchangeable, save the Concealed Deity. Nothing that is finite — whether because it had a beginning, or must have an end — can remain stationary. It must either progress or recede; and a soul which thirsts after a reunion with its spirit, which alone confers upon it immortality, must purify itself through cyclic transmigrations, onward toward the only Land of Bliss and Eternal Rest, called in the *Zohar*, "The Palace of Love," היכל אהבה [*hekal ahabah*];‖ in the Hindu religion, "Moksha"; among the Gnostics, the "Pleroma of eternal Light"; and by the Buddhists, Nirvâna. The Christian calls it the "Kingdom of Heaven," and claims to have alone found the truth, whereas he has but invented a new name for a doctrine which is coeval with man.

The proof that the transmigration of the soul does not relate to man's condition on this earth *after* death, is found in the *Zohar*, notwithstanding the many incorrect renderings of its translators. "All souls which have alienated themselves in heaven from the Holy One — blessed be His Name — have thrown themselves into an abyss at their very existence, and have anticipated the time when they are to descend on earth.¶ . . .

---

\* *Jewish War*, II, viii, 11.
† *De somniis*, I, §22; *De gigantibus*, §2.
‡ *Zohar*, II, p. 96a, Amsterdam ed.
§ *Mishnah Pirke Aboth*, IV, §29. Cf. MacKenzie, *Royal Masonic Cyclop.*, p. 413.
‖ [*Zohar*, II, p. 97a.]
¶ *Ibid.*, III, p. 61b.

Come and see when the soul reaches the abode of Love . . . The soul could not bear this light, but for the luminous mantle which she puts on. For, just as the soul sent to this earth, puts on an earthly garment to preserve herself here, so she receives above a shining garment, in order to be able to look without injury into the mirror, whose light proceeds from the Lord of Light." * Moreover, the *Zohar* teaches that the soul cannot reach the abode of bliss, unless she has received the "holy kiss," or the reunion of the soul *with the substance from which she emanated* — spirit.† All souls are dual, and, while the latter is a feminine principle, the spirit is masculine. While imprisoned in body, man is a trinity, unless his pollution is such as to have caused his divorce from the spirit. "Woe to the soul which prefers to her divine husband [spirit], the earthly wedlock with her terrestrial body," records a text of the *Book of the Keys*.‡

These ideas on the transmigrations and the trinity of man, were held by many of the early Christian Fathers. It is the jumble made by the translators of the *New Testament* and ancient philosophical treatises between soul and spirit, that has occasioned the many misunderstandings. It is also one of the many reasons why Buddha, Plotinus, and so many other initiates are now accused of having longed for the total extinction of their souls — "absorption unto the Deity," or "reunion with the universal soul," meaning, according to modern ideas, annihilation. The animal soul must, of course, disintegrate its particles, before it is able to link its purer essence forever with the immortal spirit. But the translators of both the *Acts* and the *Epistles*, who laid the foundation of the *Kingdom of Heaven*, and the modern commentators on the Buddhist *Sûtra of the Foundation of the Kingdom of Righteousness*, have muddled the sense of the great apostle of Christianity, as of the great reformer of India. The former have smothered the word ψυχικός, so that no reader imagines it to have any relation with *soul*; and with this confusion of *soul* and *spirit* together, *Bible* readers get only a perverted sense of anything on the subject; and the interpreters of the latter have failed to understand the meaning and object of the Buddhist four degrees of *Dhyâna*.

In the writings of Paul, the entity of man is divided into a trine — flesh, psychical existence or *soul*, and the overshadowing and at the same time interior entity or SPIRIT. His phraseology is very definite, when he teaches the *anastasis*, or the continuation of life of those who have died. He maintains that there is a *psychical* body which is sown in the corruptible, and a spiritual body that is raised in incorruptible sub-

---

* *Zohar*, I, pp. 65b, 66a.
† *Ibid.*, II, p. 97a; I, p. 168a.
‡ A Hermetic work.

stance. "The first man is of the earth earthy, the second man from heaven." * Even *James* (iii, 15) identifies the soul by saying that its "wisdom descendeth not from the above but is terrestrial, *psychical, demoniacal*" (see Greek text). Plato, speaking of the Soul (*psychê*), observes that "when she allies herself to the *nous* [divine substance, a god, as psychê is a goddess], she does everything aright and felicitously; but the case is otherwise when she attaches herself to *anoia*." What Plato calls *nous*, Paul terms the *Spirit;* and Jesus makes the *heart* what Paul says of the *flesh*. The natural condition of mankind was called in Greek ἀποστασία; the new condition ἀνάστασις. In Adam came the former (death), in Christ the latter (resurrection), for it is he who first publicly taught mankind the "Noble Path" to Eternal life, as Gautama pointed the same Path to Nirvâṇa. To accomplish both ends there was but one way, according to the teachings of both. "Poverty, chastity, contemplation or inner prayer; contempt for wealth and the illusive joys of this world."

"Enter on this Path and put an end to sorrow; verily the Path has been preached by me, who have found out how to quench the darts of grief. You yourselves must make the effort; *the Buddhas are only preachers.* The thoughtful who enter the Path are freed from the bondage of the Deceiver (Mâra)." †

"Enter ye in at the strait gate; for wide is the gate, and broad is the way that leadeth to destruction . . . Follow me . . . Everyone that heareth these sayings of mine, and doeth them not, shall be likened unto a foolish man" (*Matthew* vii, 13, 26). "*I can of mine own self do nothing*" (*John* v, 30). "The care of this world, and the deceitfulness of riches, choke the word" (*Matthew* xiii, 22), say the Christians; and it is only by shaking off all delusions that the Buddhist enters on the "Path" which will lead him "away from the restless tossing waves of the ocean of life," and take him "to the calm City of Peace, to the real joy and rest of Nirvâṇa."

The Greek philosophers are alike made misty instead of mystic by their too learned translators. The Egyptians revered the Divine Spirit. the One-Only One, as Nout. It is most evident that it is from that word that Anaxagoras borrowed his denominative *nous*, or, as he calls it, Νοῦς αὐτοκρατής — the Mind or Spirit self-potent, the ἀρχὴ τῆς κινήσεως. "All things," says he, "were in chaos; then came Νοῦς and introduced order." ‡ He also denominated this Νοῦς the One that ruled the many. In his idea Νοῦς was God; and the *Logos* was man, the emanation of the former. The external powers perceived *phenomena;* the *nous* alone recog-

---

\* [*1 Cor.* xv, 42-47.]

† *Dhammapada*, ślokas 275-76.

‡ [Diog. Laert., *Lives*, II, 6, "Anaxagoras."]

nized *noumena* or subjective things. This is purely Buddhistic and esoteric.

Here Socrates took his clue and followed it, and Plato after him, with the whole world of interior knowledge. Where the old Ionico-Italian world culminated in Anaxagoras, the new world began with Socrates and Plato. Pythagoras made the *Soul* a self-moving unit, with three elements, the *nous*, the *phrên* and the *thumos*; the latter two, shared with the brutes; the first, alone, being his essential *self*. So the charge that he taught transmigration is refuted; he taught no more than Gautama Buddha did, whatever the popular superstition of the Hindu rabble made of it [Gautama's teaching] after his death. Whether Pythagoras borrowed from Buddha, or Buddha from somebody else, matters not; the esoteric doctrine is the same.

The Platonic School is even more distinct in enunciating all this.

The real selfhood was at the basis of all. Socrates therefore taught that he had a δαιμόνιον (*daimonion*), a spiritual something which put him on the road to wisdom. He himself knew nothing, but this put him in the way to learn all.

Plato followed him with a full investigation of the principles of being. There was an *Agathon*, Supreme God, who produced in his own mind a *paradeigma* of all things.

He taught that in man was "the immortal principle of the soul," a mortal body, and a "separate mortal kind of soul," which was placed in a separate receptacle of the body from the other; the immortal part was in the head, the other in the trunk.*

Nothing is plainer than that Plato regarded the interior man as constituted of two parts — one always the same, formed of the same entity as Deity, and one mortal and corruptible.

"Plato and Pythagoras," says Plutarch, "distribute the soul into two parts, the rational (noëtic) and irrational (*agnoia*); "they say that part of the soul of man which is rational, is eternal; for though it be not God, yet it is the product of an eternal deity; but that part of the soul which is divested of reason (*agnoia*) dies." †

"Man," says Plutarch, "is compound; and they are mistaken who think him to be compounded of two parts only. For they imagine that the understanding is a part of the soul, but they err in this no less than those who make the soul to be a part of the body, for the understanding (*nous*) as far exceeds the soul, as the soul is better and diviner than the body. Now this composition of the soul (ψυχή) with the understanding (νοῦς) makes reason; and with the body, passion; of which the one is the beginning or principle of pleasure and pain, and the other of virtue and vice. Of these three parts conjoined and compacted together, the earth

---

\* *Timaeus,* 45, 46, 47, 69D.

† [Plutarch, *De placitio philosophorum,* IV, iv & vii.]

has given the body, the moon the soul, and the sun the understanding to the generation of man.

"Now of the deaths we die, *the one makes man two of three*, and the other, *one* of [out of] two. The former is in the region and jurisdiction of Ceres, whence the name given to the Mysteries, τελεῖν, resembled that given to death, τελευτᾶν. The Athenians also heretofore called the deceased sacred to Ceres. As for the *other death* it is in the moon or region of Proserpine. And as with the one the terrestrial, so with the other the celestial Hermes doth dwell. This suddenly and with violence plucks the soul from the body; but Proserpine mildly and in a long time disjoins the understanding from the soul. For this reason she is called *Monogenês, only-begotten,* or rather, *begetting one alone;* for the better part of man becomes alone when it is separated by her. Now both the one and the other happens thus according to nature. It is ordained by Fate that every soul, whether with or without understanding (νοῦς), when gone out of the body, should wander for a time, though not all for the same, in the region lying between the earth and moon. For those that have been unjust and dissolute suffer there the punishment due to their offences; but the good and virtuous are there detained till they are purified, and have, by expiation, purged out of them all the infections they might have contracted from the contagion of the body, as if from foul breath, living in the mildest part of the air, called the Meadows of Pluto, where they must remain for a certain prefixed and appointed time. And then, as if they were returning from a wandering pilgrimage or long exile into their country, they have a taste of joy, such as they principally receive who are initiated into Sacred Mysteries, mixed with trouble, admiration, and each one's proper and peculiar hope." \*

The *daimonion* of Socrates was this νοῦς, mind, spirit, or understanding of the divine in it. "The νοῦς of Socrates," says Plutarch, "was pure and mixed itself with the body no more than necessity required . . . Every soul hath some portion of νοῦς, reason, a man cannot be a man without it; but as much of each soul as is mixed with flesh and appetite is changed and through pain or pleasure becomes irrational. Every soul doth not mix herself after one sort; some plunge themselves into the body, and so, in this life their whole frame is corrupted by appetite and passion; others are mixed as to some part, but the purer part [*nous*] still remains *without the body*. It is not drawn down into the body, but it swims above and touches [overshadows] the extremest part of the man's head; it is like a cord to hold up and direct the subsiding part of the soul, as long as it proves obedient and is not overcome by the appetites of the flesh. The part that is plunged into the body is called *soul*. But the incorruptible part is called the *nous* and *the vulgar think it is within them*, as they

---

\* [Plutarch, *On the Face in the Orb of the Moon*, § 28.]

likewise imagine the image reflected from a glass to be in that glass. But the more intelligent, who know it to be without, call it a Daemon" (a god, a spirit).*

"The soul, like to a dream, flies quickly away, which it does not immediately, as soon as it is separated from the body, but afterward, when it is alone and divided from the understanding (*nous*) . . . The soul being moulded and formed by the understanding (*nous*), and itself moulding and forming the body, by embracing it on every side, receives from it an impression and form; so that although it be separated both from the understanding and the body, it nevertheless so retains still its figure and semblance for a long time, that it may, with good right, be called its image.

"And of these souls the moon is the element, because souls resolve into her, as the bodies of the deceased do into earth. Those, indeed, who have been virtuous and honest, living a quiet and philosophical life, without embroiling themselves in troublesome affairs, are quickly resolved; because, being left by the *nous*, understanding, and no longer using the corporeal passions, they incontinently vanish away."†

We find even Irenaeus, that untiring and mortal enemy of every Grecian and "heathen" heresy, explaining his belief in the trinity of man. The perfect man, according to his views, consists of *flesh, soul* and *spirit*. ". . . carne, anima et spiritu: el altero quidem salvante et figurante, qui est spiritus; altero quod unitur et formatur, quod est caro; id vero quod inter haec est duo, quod est anima; quae aliquando quidem subsequens spiritum, elevatur ab eo; aliquando autem consentiens carni, decidit in terrenas concupiscentias."‡

And Origen, in his *Commentary Epistle to the Romans*, says: "There is a threefold partition of man, the body or flesh, the lowest part of our nature, on which the old serpent by original sin inscribed the law of sin, and by which we are tempted to vile things, and as oft as we are overcome by temptations are joined fast to the Devil; the spirit, in or by which we express the likeness of the divine nature in which the very Best Creator, from the archetype of his own mind, engraved with his finger (that is, his spirit), the eternal law of honesty; by this we are joined (conglutinated) to God and made one with God. In the third, the soul mediates between these, which, as in a factious republic, cannot but join with one party or the other, is solicited this way and that and is at liberty to choose the side to which it will adhere. If, renouncing the flesh, it betakes itself to the party of the spirit it will itself become spiritual, but if it cast itself down to the cupidities of the flesh it will degenerate itself into body." §

---

\* [*On the Daemon of Socrates*, §§ 20, 22.]
† [Plutarch, *On the Face in the Orb of the Moon*, § 30.]
‡ *Adv. Haer.*, V, ix, § 1.
§ [Book VI. Cf. Migne, *Patr. Graeca*, Vol. XIV, Col. 1056-57.]

Plato defines *soul* as "the motion that is able to move itself." "Soul is the most ancient of all things, and the commencement of motion." "Soul was generated prior to body, and body is posterior and secondary, as being, according to nature, ruled over by the ruling soul." "The soul which administers all things that are moved in every way, administers likewise the heavens."

"Soul then leads everything in heaven, and on earth, and in the sea, by its movements — the names of which are, to will, to consider, to take care of, to consult, to form opinions true and false, to be in a state of joy, sorrow, confidence, fear, hate, love, together with all such primary movements as are allied to these . . . being a goddess herself, she ever takes as an ally Nous, a god, and disciplines all things correctly and happily; but when with *anoia* — not *nous* — it works out everything to the contrary." *

In this language, as in the Buddhist texts, the negative is treated as essential existence. *Annihilation* comes under a similar exegesis. The positive state is essential being but no manifestation as such. When the spirit, in Buddhistic parlance, entered *nirvâna*, it lost objective existence but retained subjective. To objective minds this is becoming absolute nothing; to subjective, NO-thing, nothing to be displayed to sense.

These rather lengthy quotations are necessary for our purpose. Better than anything else, they show the agreement between the oldest "Pagan" philosophies — not "assisted by the light of divine revelation," to use the curious expression of Laboulaye in relation to Buddha† — and the early Christianity of some Fathers. Both Pagan philosophy and Christianity, however, owe their elevated ideas on the soul and spirit of man and the unknown Deity to Buddhism and the Hindu Manu. No wonder that the Manichaeans maintained that Jesus was a permutation of Gautama; that Buddha, Christ and Mani were one and the same person, ‡ for the teachings of the former two were identical. It was the doctrine of old India that Jesus held to when preaching the complete renunciation of the world and its vanities in order to reach the kingdom of Heaven, Nirvâna, where "men neither marry nor are given in marriage, but live like the angels."

It is the philosophy of Siddhârtha-Buddha again that Pythagoras expounded, when asserting that the *ego* (νοῦς) was eternal with God, and that the soul only passed through various stages (Hindu *Rûpa-lokas*) to arrive at the divine excellence; meanwhile the *thumos* returned to the earth, and even the *phrên* was eliminated. Thus the *metempsychosis* was only a succession of disciplines through refuge-heavens (called by the Buddhists *Zion*),§ to work

---

* Plato, *The Laws*, X, 896-897B.
† [*Journal des débats*, April 4, 1853.]
‡ Neander, *Gen. Hist. of Christ. Religion and Church*, Vol. II, p. 160; ed. 1853.
§ It is from the highest *Zion* that Maitreya-Buddha, the Savior to come, will descend on earth; and it is also from Zion that comes the Christian Deliverer (see *Romans* xi, 26).[40]

off the exterior mind, to rid the *nous* of the *phrên*, or soul, the Buddhist "Viññāna-skandha," *that principle that lives* from *Karma* and the *Skandhas* (groups). It is the latter, the metaphysical personations of the "deeds" of man, whether good or bad, which, after the death of his body, incarnate themselves, so to say, and form their many invisible but never-dying compounds into a new body, or rather into an ethereal being, the *double* of what man was *morally*. It is the astral body of the kabalist and the "incarnated deeds" which form the new sentient self as his *Ahamkara* (the ego, self-consciousness), given to him by the sovereign Master (the breath of God) [which] can never perish, for it is immortal *per se* as a spirit; hence the sufferings of the newly-born *self* till he rids himself of every earthly thought, desire and passion.

We now see that the "four mysteries" of the Buddhist doctrine have been as little understood and appreciated as the "wisdom" hinted at by Paul, and spoken "among them that are *perfect*" (initiated), the "mystery-wisdom" which "none of the *Archons* of this world knew." \* The fourth degree of the Buddhist Dhyâna, the fruit of Samâdhi, which leads to the utmost perfection, to *Viśodhana*, a term correctly rendered by Burnouf in the verb *"perfected,"* † is wholly misunderstood by others, as well as by himself. Defining the condition of Dhyâna, Saint-Hilaire argues thus:

"Finally, having attained the fourth degree, the ascetic possesses no more this feeling of beatitude, however obscure it may be . . . he has also lost all memory . . . he has reached impassibility, as near a neighbor of Nirvâṇa as can be . . . However, this absolute impassibility does not hinder the ascetic from acquiring, at this very moment, *omniscience and the magical power;* a flagrant contradiction, about which the Buddhists no more disturb themselves than about so many others." ‡

And why should they, when these contradictions are, in fact, no contradictions at all? It ill behooves us to speak of contradictions in other peoples' religions, when those of our own have bred, besides the three great conflicting bodies of Romanism, Protestantism, and the Eastern Church, a thousand and one most curious smaller sects. However it may be, we have here a term applied to one and the same thing by the Buddhist holy "mendicants" and Paul, the Apostle. When the latter says: "If by any means I might attain unto the *resurrection* of the dead [the Nirvâṇa], not as though I had already attained, either were already *perfect*" (initiated), § he uses an expression common among the initiated Buddhists. When a Buddhist ascetic has reached the "fourth degree," he is considered a *rahat*. He produces every kind of phenomena by the

---

\* *1 Cor.* ii, 6, 7, 8.
† *Le Lotus de la bonne loi,* p. 806.
‡ *Le Bouddha et sa religion,* ch. iv, p. 137; Paris, 1860.
§ *Philippians* iii, 11, 12.

sole power of his freed spirit. A *rahat*, say the Buddhists, is one who has acquired the power of flying in the air, becoming invisible, commanding the elements, and working all manner of wonders, commonly, and as erroneously, called *meipo* (miracles). He is a *perfect* man, a demi-god. A god he will become when he reaches Nirvâna; for, like the initiates of both Testaments, the worshippers of Buddha know that they "are gods."

"Genuine Buddhism, overleaping the barrier between finite and infinite mind, urges its followers to aspire, *by their own efforts*, to that divine perfectibility of which it teaches that man is capable, and by attaining which man becomes *a god*," says Brian Houghton Hodgson.*

Dreary and sad were the ways, and blood-covered the tortuous paths by which the world of the Christians was driven to embrace the Irenaean and Eusebian Christianity. And yet, unless we accept the views of the ancient Pagans, what claim has our generation to having solved any of the mysteries of the "kingdom of heaven"? What more does the most pious and learned of Christians know of the future destiny and progress of our immortal spirits than the heathen philosopher of old, or the modern "Pagan" beyond the Himâlaya? Can he even boast that he knows as much, although he works in the full blaze of "divine" revelation? We have seen a Buddhist holding to the religion of his fathers, both in theory and practice; and, however blind may be his faith, however absurd his notions on some particular doctrinal points, later engraftings of an ambitious clergy, yet in practical works his Buddhism is far more Christlike in deed and spirit than the average life of our Christian priests and ministers. The fact alone that his religion commands him to "honor his own faith, but never slander that of other people," † is sufficient. It places the Buddhist lama immeasurably higher than any priest or clergyman who deems it his sacred duty to curse the "heathen" to his face, and sentence him and his religion to "eternal damnation." Christianity becomes every day more a religion of pure emotionalism. The doctrine of Buddha is entirely based on practical works. A general love of all beings, human and animal, is its nucleus. A man who knows that unless he toils for himself he has to starve, and understands that he has no scapegoat to carry the burden of his iniquities for him, is ten times as likely to become a better man than one who is taught that murder, theft and profligacy can be washed in one instant as white as snow, if he but believes in a God who, to borrow an expression of Volney, "once took food upon earth, and is now himself the food of his people."

---

* *Essays on the Languages, Literature, and Religion of Nepal and Tibet*, etc., London, 1874, p. 20.

† The Five Articles of Faith.

## CHAPTER VII

"Of the tenets of the Druzes, nothing authentic has ever come to light; the popular belief amongst their neighbors is, that they adore an idol in the form of a calf."
—KING, *The Gnostics and their Remains*, p. 183.

"O ye Lords of Truth without fault, who are forever cycling for eternity . . . save me from the annihilation of this Region of the *Two Truths*."
—*Book of the Dead*, ch. CXXV, lines 4-5.

"Pythagoras correctly [regarded] the Ineffable Name of God . . . [as] the key to the mysteries of the Kabbala."
—S. PANCOAST, *Blue and Red Light*, ch. i, pp. 24-25.

IN the next two chapters we shall notice the most important of the Christian secret sects — the so-called "Heresies" which sprang into existence between the first and fourth centuries of our era.

Glancing rapidly at the Ophites and Nazareans, we shall pass to their scions which yet exist in Syria and Palestine, under the name of Druzes of Mount Lebanon; and near Basra or Bassorah, in Persia,* under that of Mandaeans, or Disciples of St. John. All these sects have an immediate connection with our subject, for they are of kabalistic parentage and have once held to the secret "Wisdom-Religion," recognizing as the One Supreme, the Mystery-God of the *Ineffable Name*. Noticing these numerous secret societies of the past, we will bring them into direct comparison with several of the modern. We will conclude with a brief survey of the Jesuits, and of that venerable nightmare of the Roman Catholic Church — modern Freemasonry. All of these modern as well as ancient fraternities — present Freemasonry excepted — were and are more or less connected with magic — practically, as well as theoretically; and, everyone of them — Freemasonry *not* excepted — was and still is accused of demonolatry, blasphemy and licentiousness.

Our object is not to write the history of either of them; but only to compare these sorely-abused communities with the Christian sects, past and present, and then, taking historical facts for our guidance, to defend the secret science as well as the men who are its students and champions against any unjust imputation.

One by one the tide of time engulfed the sects of the early centuries, until of the whole number only one survived in its primitive integrity. That one still exists, still teaches the doctrine of its founder, still exemplifies its

---

* [Now situated in the S. E. corner of Iraq.]

faith in works of power. The quicksands which swallowed up every other outgrowth of the religious agitation of the times of Jesus, with its records, relics and traditions, proved firm ground for this. Driven from their native land, its members found refuge in Persia, and today the anxious traveller may converse with the direct descendants of the "Disciples of John," who listened, on the Jordan's shore, to the "man sent from God," and were baptized and believed. This curious people, numbering 30,000 or more, are miscalled "Christians of St. John," but, in fact, should be known by their old name of Nazareans, or their new one of Mandaeans.

To term them Christians, is wholly unwarranted. They neither believe in Jesus as Christ, nor accept his atonement, nor adhere to his Church, nor revere its "Holy Scriptures." Neither do they worship the Jehovah-God of the Jews and Christians, a circumstance which of course proves that their founder, John the Baptist, did not worship him either. And if not, what right has he to a place in the *Bible*, or in the portrait-gallery of Christian saints? Still further, if Ferho was his God, and he was "a man sent by God," he must have been sent by Lord Ferho, and in his name baptized and preached. Now, if Jesus was baptized by John, the inference is that he was baptized according to his own faith; therefore, Jesus, too, was a believer in Ferho, or Faho, as they call him; a conclusion that seems the more warranted by his silence as to the name of his "Father." And why should the hypothesis that *Faho* is but one of the many corruptions of Fho or Fo, as the Thibetans and Chinese call Buddha, appear ridiculous? In the North of Nepal, Buddha is more often called *Fo* than *Buddha*. The book of *Mahâvansa* shows how early the work of Buddhistic proselytism began in Nepal; and history teaches that Buddhist monks crowded into Syria * and Babylon in the century

---

* Not only did the Buddhist missionaries make their way to the Mesopotamian Valley, but they even went so far west as Ireland. The Rev. Dr. Lundy, in his work on *Monumental Christianity* (p. 255), referring to an Irish Round Tower, observes: "Henry O'Brien explains this Round Tower crucifixion as that of Buddha; the animals as the elephant and the bull sacred to Buddha, and into which his soul entered after death; the two figures standing beside the cross as Buddha's virgin mother, and Râma, his favorite disciple. The whole picture bears a close likeness to the crucifixion in the cemetery of Pope Julius, except the animals, which are conclusive proof that it cannot be Christian. It came ultimately from the Far East to Ireland, with the Phoenician colonists, who erected the Round Towers as symbols of the Life-giving and Preserving Power of man and nature, and how that universal life is produced through suffering and death." [Cf. *The Round Towers of Ireland,* 1st ed., p. 301.]

When a Protestant clergyman is thus forced to confess the pre-Christian existence of the crucifix in Ireland, its Buddhistic character, and the penetration of the missionaries of that faith even to that then remote portion of the earth, we need not wonder that in the minds of the Nazarean contemporaries of Jesus and their descendants, he should

preceding our era, and that Buddhasp (*Bodhisattva*), the alleged Chaldean, was the founder of Sabianism or *baptism*.*

What the actual Baptists, *al-Mughtasilah*,[41] or Nazareans, do believe, is fully set forth in other places, for they are the very Nazarenes of whom we have spoken so much, and from whose *Codex* we have quoted. Persecuted and threatened with annihilation, they took refuge in the Nestorian body, and so allowed themselves to be arbitrarily classed as Christians, but as soon as opportunity offered, they separated, and now, for several centuries have not even nominally deserved the appellation. That they are, nevertheless, so-called by ecclesiastical writers, is perhaps not very difficult to comprehend. They know too much of early Christianity to be left outside the pale, to bear witness against it with their traditions, without the stigma of heresy and backsliding being fastened upon them to weaken confidence in what they might say.

But where else can science find so good a field for Biblical research as among this too neglected people? No doubt of their inheritance of the Baptist's doctrine; their traditions are without a break. What they teach now, their forefathers taught at every epoch where they appear in history. They are the disciples of that John who is said to have foretold the advent of Jesus, baptized him, and declared that the latchet of his shoe he (John) was not worthy to unloose. As they two — the Messenger and the Messiah — stood in the Jordan, and the elder was consecrating the younger — his own cousin, too, humanly speaking — the heavens opened and God Himself, in the shape of a dove, descended in a glory upon his "Beloved Son"! How then, if this tale be true, can we account for the strange infidelity which we find among these surviving Nazareans? So far from believing Jesus the Only-Begotten Son of God, they actually told the Persian missionaries, who, in the seventeenth century, first discovered them for Europeans, that the Christ of the *New Testament* was "a false teacher," and that the Jewish system, as well as that of Jesus(?), came from the realm of darkness! Who knows better than they? Where can more competent living witnesses be found? Christian ecclesiastics

---

have been associated with that universally known emblem in the character of a Redeemer.

In noticing this admission of Dr. Lundy, Charles Sotheran remarked, in a lecture before the American Philological Society, that both legends and archaeological remains unite in proving beyond question "that Ireland, like every other nation, once listened to the propagandists of Siddhârtha-Buddha."

* "The religion of multiplied baptisms, the scion of the still existent sect named the 'Christians of St. John,' or Mandaeans, whom the Arabs call *al-Mughtasilah*, the Baptists. The Aramaean verb *seba*, origin of the name *Sabian*, is a synonym of βαπτίζω" (Renan, *Vie de Jésus*, ch. vi).

would force upon us an anointed Savior heralded by John, and the disciples of this very Baptist, from the earliest centuries, have stigmatized this ideal personage as an impostor, and his putative Father, Jehovah, "a spurious God," the Ialdabaôth of the Ophites! Unlucky for Christianity will be the day when some fearless and honest scholar shall persuade their elders to let him translate the contents of their secret books and compile their hoary traditions! It is a strange delusion that makes some writers think that the Nazareans have no other sacred literature, no other literary relics than four doctrinal works, and that curious volume full of astrology and magic which they are bound to peruse at the sunset hour, on every Sol's day (Sunday).

This search after truth leads us, indeed, into devious ways. Many are the obstacles that ecclesiastical cunning has placed in the way of our finding the primal source of religious ideas. Christianity is on trial, and has been ever since science felt strong enough to act as Public Prosecutor. A portion of the case we are drafting in this book. What of truth is there in this Theology? Through what sects has it been transmitted? *Whence was it primarily derived?* To answer, we must trace the history of the World-Religion, alike through the secret Christian sects as through those of other great religious subdivisions of the race; *for the Secret Doctrine is the Truth,* and that religion is nearest divine that has contained it with least adulteration.

Our search takes us hither and thither, but never aimlessly do we bring sects widely separated in chronological order, into critical juxtaposition. There is one purpose in our work to be kept constantly in view — the analysis of religious beliefs, and the definition of their descent from the past to the present. What has most blocked the way is Roman Catholicism; and not until the secret principles of this religion are uncovered can we comprehend the iron staff upon which it leans to steady its now tottering steps.

We will begin with the Ophites, Nazareans, and the modern Druzes. The personal views of the author, as they will be presented in the diagrams, will be most decidedly at variance with the prejudiced speculations of Irenaeus, Theodoret and Epiphanius (the sainted renegade, who sold his brethren), inasmuch as they will reflect the ideas of certain kabalists in close relations with the mysterious Druzes of Mount Lebanon. The Syrian 'Uqqâls, or Spiritualists, as they are sometimes termed, are in possession of a great many ancient manuscripts and gems, bearing upon our present subject.

The first *scheme* — that of the Ophites — from the very start, as we have shown, varies from the description given by the Fathers, inasmuch as it makes Bythos or depth a female emanation, and assigns her a place

## THE OPHITES, NAZAREANS AND DRUZES 293

answering to that of Pleroma, only in a far superior region; whereas the Fathers assure us that the Gnostics gave the name of Bythos to the First Cause. As in the kabalistic system, it represents the boundless and infinite void within which is concealed in darkness the Unknown Primal motor of all. It envelops HIM like a veil: in short we recognize again the "Shekhînah" of the Ain-Soph. Alone, the name of ʼΙΑΩ, Iaô, marks the upper centre, or rather the presumed spot where the Unknown One may be supposed to dwell. Around the Iaô, runs the legend, CEMEC ΕΙΛΑΜ ΑΒΡΑΣΑΞ, "The eternal Sun-Abrasax" (the Central Spiritual Sun of all the kabalists, represented in some diagrams of the latter by the circle of Tiphereth).

From this region of unfathomable Depth issues forth a circle formed of spirals, which, in the language of symbolism, means a grand cycle, κύκλος, composed of smaller ones. Coiled within, so as to follow the spirals, lies the serpent — emblem of wisdom and eternity — the Dual Androgyne: the cycle representing *Ennoia* or the Divine mind, and the Serpent — the Agathodaimôn, the Ophis — the Shadow of the Light. Both were the Logoi of the Ophites; or the unity as Logos manifesting itself as a double principle of good and evil; for, according to their views, these two principles are immutable, and existed from all eternity, as they will ever continue to exist.

This symbol accounts for the adoration by this sect of the Serpent, as the Savior, coiled either around the Sacramental loaf or a Tau. As a unity, Ennoia and Ophis are the *Logos;* when separated, one is the Tree of Life (Spiritual); the other, the Tree of Knowledge of Good and Evil. Therefore, we find Ophis urging the first human couple—the material production of Ialdabaôth, but which owed its spiritual principle to Sophia-Akhamôth — to eat of the forbidden fruit, although Ophis represents Divine Wisdom.

The Serpent, the Tree of Knowledge of Good and Evil, and the Tree of Life, are all symbols transplanted from the soil of India. The *Araśa-maram*, the banyan tree,[42] so sacred with the Hindus, since Vishṇu, during one of his incarnations, reposed under its mighty shade and there taught humanity philosophy and sciences, is called the Tree of Knowledge and the Tree of Life. Under the protective umbrage of this king of the forests, the Gurus teach their pupils their first lessons on immortality and initiate them into the mysteries of life and death. The *Yava*-ALEIM of the Sacerdotal College are said, in the Chaldean tradition, to have taught the sons of men to become like one of them. To the present day, Foh-tchou,* who lives in his *Foh-Maëyu*, or temple of Buddha, on the

---

\* Foh-tchou, literally, in Chinese, meaning Buddha's lord, or the teacher of the doctrines of Buddha—Foh.

top of "Kuen-lun-shan," * the great mountain, produces his greatest religious miracles under a tree called in Chinese *Sung-Ming-Shu*, or the Tree of Knowledge and the Tree of Life, for ignorance is death, and knowledge alone gives immortality. This marvellous display takes place every three years, when an immense concourse of Chinese Buddhists assemble in pilgrimage at the holy place.

Ialdabaôth, the "Son of Darkness" and the creator of the material world, was made to inhabit the planet Saturn, which identifies him still more with the Jewish Jehovah, who was Saturn himself, according to the Ophites, and is by them denied his Sinaitic name. From Ialdabaôth emanate six spirits, who respectively dwell with their father in the seven planets. These are: Tsabaôth — or Mars; Adonaios — Sol or the Sun;† Iaô — the Moon; Eloaios — Jupiter; Astaphaios — Mercury (spirit of water); and Horaios — Venus, spirit of fire. ‡

In their functions and description as given, these seven planets are identical with the Hindu *Sapta-lokas*, the seven places or spheres, or the superior and inferior worlds; for they represent the kabalistic seven spheres. With the Ophites, they belong to the lower spheres. The monograms of these Gnostic planets are also Buddhistic, the latter differing, albeit slightly, from those of the usual astrological "houses." In the explanatory notes which accompany the diagram, the names of Cerinthus (the disciple of Simon Magus), of Menander, and of certain other Gnostics, whose names are not to be met with in the Patristic writings, are often mentioned; such as *Par'ha* (Ferho), for instance. §

The author of the diagram claims, moreover, for his sect the greatest antiquity, bringing forward, as a proof, that their "forefathers" were the builders of all the "Dracontia" temples, even of those beyond "the great waters." He asserts that the "Just One," who was the mouthpiece of the Eternal Aeôn (Christos), himself sent his disciples into the world, placing them under the double protection of Sigê (Silence, the

---

* This mountain is situated southwest of China, almost between China and Thibet.

† SOL, being situated, on the diagram, exactly in the centre of the solar system (of which the Ophites appear to have been cognizant)—hence, under the direct vertical ray of the Higher Spiritual Sun—showers his brightness on all other planets.

‡ Speaking of Venus, Placidus de Titis, the astrologer, always maintained that "her bluish lustre denotes heat."[43] As to Mercury, it was a strange fancy of the Ophites to represent him as a spirit of water, when astrologically considered he is as "a cold, dry, earthy, and melancholy star."

§ The name which Norberg translates, in his *Onomasticon* to the *Codex Nazaraeus*, as Ferho, stands, in the original, *Par'ha Rabba*. In the *Life of Manes*, given by Epiphanius, in his *Panarion* [lib. II, tom. II, Haer. LXVI, iii], is mentioned a certain priest of Mithras, a friend of the great Haeresiarch Manes, names Parchus.

Logos) and Ophis, the Agathodaimôn. The author alludes, no doubt, to the favorite expression of Jesus, "be wise as serpents, and harmless as doves." On the diagram, Ophis is represented as the Egyptian Chnuphis or Kneph, called Dracontia. He appears as a serpent standing erect on its tail, with a lion's head, crowned and radiated, and bearing on the point of each ray one of the seven Greek vowels — symbol of the seven celestial spheres. This figure is quite familiar to those who are acquainted with the Gnostic gems,* and is borrowed from the Egyptian *Hermetic Books*. The description given in the *Revelation* of one "like unto the Son of Man," with his seven stars, and who is the Logos, is another form of Ophis.

The Nazarene diagram, except in a change of names, is identical with that of the Gnostics, who evidently borrowed their ideas from it, adding a few appellations from the Basilidean and Valentinian systems. To avoid repetition, we will now simply present the two in parallel.

Thus, we find that, in the Nazarene Cosmogony, the names of their powers and genii stand in the following relations to those of the Gnostics:

| Nazarene | Gnostic-Ophite |
|---|---|
| *First Trinity* | *First Unity in a Trinity* |
| Lord Ferho — the Life which is no Life — the Supreme God. The *Cause* which produces the Light, or the Logos *in abscondito*. The water of Jordanus Maximus — the water of Life, or Ajar, the feminine principle. Unity in a Trinity, enclosed within the Ish Amon. | Iaô — the Ineffable Name of the Unknown Deity — Abraxas, and the "Eternal Spiritual Sun." Unity enclosed within the Depth, Bythos, feminine principle — the boundless circle, within which lie all ideal forms. From this Unity emanates the |
| *Second Trinity* | *Second Trinity* |
| (The manifestation of the first.) | (Idem) |
| 1. Lord Mano — the King of Life and Light — *Rex Lucis*. First Life, or the primitive man. | 1. Ennoia — mind. |
| 2. Lord Jordan — manifestation or emanation of Jordanus Maximus — the waters of grace. Second Life. | 2. Ophis, the Agathodaimôn. |
| 3. The Superior Father — Abathur. Third Life. | 3. Sophia-Androgyne—wisdom; who, in her turn — fecundated with the Divine Light — produces |
| This Trinity produces also a duad — Lord Lehdoio, and Pthahil, the genius (the former, a perfect emanation; the latter, imperfect). | Christos and Sophia-Akhamôth (one perfect, the other imperfect), as an emanation. |

---

* Its description is found in one of the magic books of the Egyptian King Nechepso, and its use prescribed on green jasper stones, as a potent amulet. Galen mentions it in his work, *De simplicium medicamentorum facultatibus*, ix; [cf. King, *The Gnostics*, etc., p. 74; or p. 220, 2nd ed.].

| | |
|---|---|
| Lord Jordan—"the Lord of all Jordans," manifests NETUBTO (Faith *without* Works).* | Sophia-Akhamôth emanates Ialdabaôth—the Demiurge, who produces material and soulless creation. "Works *without* Faith" (or grace).* |

Moreover, the Ophite seven planetary genii, who emanated one from the other, are found again in the Nazarene religion, under the name of the "seven impostor-daemons," or stellars, who "will deceive all the sons of Adam." These are *Sol; Spiritus Venereus* (Holy Spirit, in her material aspect), † the mother of the "seven badly-disposed stellars," answering to the Gnostic Akhamôth; *Nebu,* or Mercury, "a false Messiah, who will deprave the ancient worship of God"; ‡ SIN (or Luna, or Shuril); KHÎYÛN (or Saturn); Bel-Jupiter; and the seventh, *Nerig,* Mars *(Codex Nazaraeus,* I, p. 55).

The Christos of the Gnostics is the chief of the seven Aeôns, St. John's seven spirits of God; the Nazarenes have also their seven genii or good Aeôns, whose chief is *Rex Lucis,* MANO, their Christos. The *Sapta-Rishis,* the seven sages of India, inhabit the *Sapta-Puras,* or the seven celestial cities.

What less or more do we find in the Universal Ecclesia, until the days of the Reformation, and in the Roman Popish Church after the separation? We have compared the relative value of the Hindu Cosmogony; the Chaldean, Zoroastrian, Jewish *Kabala;* and that of the so-termed Heretics. A correct diagram of the Judaico-CHRISTIAN religion — to enforce which on the heathen who have furnished it are expended such great sums every year — would still better prove the identity of the two; but we lack space and are also spared the necessity of proving what is already thoroughly demonstrated.

In the Ophite gems of King, § we find the name of Iaô repeated and often confounded with that of Ievo, while the latter simply represents one of the genii antagonistic to Abraxas. In order that these names may not be taken as identical with the name of the Jewish Jehovah, we will at once explain this word. It seems to us surpassingly strange that so many learned archaeologists should have so little insisted that there was more than one Jehovah, and disclaimed that the name originated with Moses. Iaô is certainly

---

\* Consider those two diametrically opposed doctrines—the Catholic and the Protestant; the one preached by Paul, the semi-Platonist, and the other by James, the orthodox Talmudist.

† The material, bad side of Sophia-Akhamôth, who emanates from herself Ialdabaôth and his six sons.

‡ See Norberg's translation of *Codex Nazaraeus,* Preface. This proves once more the identification of Jesus with Gautama Buddha, in the minds of the Nazarene Gnostics, as *Nebu* or Mercury is the planet sacred to the Buddhas.

§ *Gnostics and their Remains.*

a title of the Supreme Being, and belongs *partially* to the Ineffable Name; but it neither originated with, nor was it the sole property of, the Jews. Even if it had pleased Moses to bestow the name upon the tutelary "Spirit," the alleged protector and national deity of the "chosen people of Israel," there is yet no possible reason why other nationalities should receive Him as the Highest and One-living God. But we deny the assumption altogether. Besides, there is the fact that Yaho or Iaô was a "mystery name" from the beginning, for יה and יהוה never came into use before King David. Anterior to his time, few or no proper names were compounded with *iah* or *yah*. It looks rather as though David, being a sojourner among the Tyrians and Philistines (*2 Samuel*), brought thence the name of Jehovah. He made Zadok high priest, from whom came the Zadokites or Sadducees. He lived and ruled first at Hebron, חברון, Habir-on or Kabir-town, where the rites of the four (mystery-gods) were celebrated. Neither David nor Solomon recognized either Moses or the law of Moses. They aspired to build a temple to יהוה, like the structures erected by Hiram to Hercules and Venus, Adon and Astartê.

Says Fürst: "The very ancient name of God — *Yâho* . . . written in Greek 'Iαώ, appears, apart *from its derivation*, to have been an old mystic name of the supreme deity of the Semites. [Hence it was told to Moses when initiated at HOR-EB — the *cave* — under the direction of Jethro, the Kenite or Cainite priest of Midian.] In the old religion of the Chaldeans, whose remains are to be found among the new Platonists, the highest divinity, enthroned above the seven heavens, representing the spiritual light-principle [*nous*]\* and also conceived as demiurge,† was called 'Iαώ, יה, ‡ who was like the Hebrew Yâho mysterious and unmentionable . . . and whose name was communicated only to the initiated . . . The Phoenicians had a supreme god, whose name was triliteral (*litera trina*) and *secret* . . . and he was 'Iαω.§

But while Fürst insists that the name has a Semitic origin, there are other scholars who trace it farther than he does, and look back beyond the classification of the Caucasians.

In Sanskrit we have *Jah* and *Jaya*, or *Jaa* and *Jagad*, and this throws light on the origin of the famous festival of the car of *Jagan-nâtha*, commonly called Jaggernâth. *Yahve* means "he who is," and Dr. F. Spiegel traces even the Persian name of God, *Ahura*, to the root *ah*, ‖ which

---

\* *Nous*, the designation given by Anaxagoras to the Supreme Deity, was taken from Egypt, where he was styled NOUT.

† By very few though, for the creators of the material universe were always considered as subordinate deities to the Most High God.

‡ J. Lydus, *De mensibus*, IV, 38, 74, 98; Cedrenus, *Compendium historiarum*, I, p. 296.

§ [J. Fürst, *A Hebrew and Chaldee Lexicon to the Old Testament*. Tr. by S. Davidson, 4th ed., London, 1871.]

‖ *Erân das Land zwischen dem Indus und Tigris*, Berlin, 1863; *Avesta*, I, p. 9.

in Sanskrit is pronounced *as*, to breathe, and *asu* became, therefore, in time, synonymous with "Spirit." * Rawlinson strongly supports the opinion of an Âryan or Vedic influence on the early Babylonian mythology. We have given, a few pages back, the strongest possible proofs of the identity of Vishṇu with Dag-on. The same may be adduced for the title of 'Ιαώ, and its Sanskrit root traced in every country. JU or *Jovis* is the oldest Latin name for God. "As male he is Ju-*piter*, or *Ju*, the father, *pitri* being Sanskrit for father; as feminine, Ju-*no* or *Ju*, the comforter — נוה being the Phoenician word for rest and comfort." † Professor Max Müller shows that although *Dyaus*, sky, does not occur as a masculine in the ordinary Sanskrit, yet it does occur in the *Veda*, "and thus bears witness to the early Âryan worship of Dyaus, the Greek Zeus." ‡

To grasp the real and primitive sense of the term 'ΙΑΩ, and the reason of its becoming the designation for the most mysterious of all deities, we must search for its origin in the figurative phraseology of all the primitive people. We must first of all go to the most ancient sources for our information. In one of the *Books of Hermes*, for instance, we find him saying that the number TEN is the mother of the soul, and that the *life* and *light* are therein united. For "the number 1 (one) is born from the spirit, and the number 10 (ten) from matter"; § "the unity has made the TEN, the TEN the unity." ||

The kabalistic *Gematria* — one of the methods for extracting the hidden meaning from letters, words, and sentences — is arithmetical. It consists in applying to the letters of a word the sense they bear as numbers, in *outward* shape as well as in their individual sense. Moreover, by the *Temurah* (another method used by the kabalists) any word could be made to yield its mystery out of its anagram. Thus, we find the author of *Sepher Yetzîrah* ¶ saying, one or two centuries before our era: "ONE, the spirit of the *Alahim* of Lives."** So again, in the oldest kabalistic diagrams, the *ten* Sephîrôth are represented as wheels or circles, and Adam-Kadmon, the primitive man, as an *upright* pillar. "Wheels and seraphim and the holy creatures" (*ḥayyôth*),

---

\* *Asi* means, moreover, "thou art," in Sanskrit, and also "sword," *Asi*, without accent on the first vowel.
† Professor A. Wilder.
‡ "The Veda," in *Chips*, etc., Vol. I, p. 79.
§ These sacred anagrams were called *Zeruph*.
|| *Book of Numbers*, or *Book of the Keys*.
¶ The *Sepher Yetzîrah*, or Book of the Creation, was written by Rabbi A'qîbah, who was the teacher and instructor of Shimon ben-Yoḥai, who was called the prince of the kabalists, and wrote the *Zohar*. Franck asserts that *Yetzirah* was written one century B.C. (*La Kabbale*, 1843, p. 91); but other and as competent judges make it far older. At all events, it is now proved that Shimon ben-Yoḥai lived *before* the second destruction of the temple.
\*\* *Sepher Yetzîrah*, I, §8.

says Rabbi A'qîbah.* In another system of the same branch of the symbolical *Kabala*, called *Albath* — which arranges the letters of the alphabet by pairs in three rows — all the couples in the first row bear the numerical value *ten*; and in the system of Shimon ben-Shetah,† the uppermost couple, the most sacred of all, is preceded by the Pythagorean cipher, one and a nought, or zero — 10.

If we can once appreciate the fact that, among all the peoples of the highest antiquity the most natural conception of the First Cause manifesting itself in its creatures — and that to this they could not but ascribe the creation of all — was that of an androgyne deity; that the male principle was considered the vivifying invisible spirit, and the female, mother nature; we shall be enabled to understand how that mysterious cause came at first to be represented (in the picture-writings, perhaps) as the combination of the Alpha and Omega of numbers, a decimal, then as IAÔ, a trilateral name, containing in itself a deep allegory.

*IAÔ*, in such a case, would — etymologically considered — mean the "Breath of Life," generated or springing forth between an upright male and an egg-shaped female principle of nature; for, in Sanskrit, *as* means "to be," "to live or exist"; and originally it meant "to breathe." "From it," says Max Müller, "in its original sense of breathing, the Hindus formed 'asu,' breath, and 'asura,' the name of God, whether it meant the breathing one, or the giver of breath." ‡ It certainly meant the latter. In Hebrew, "Iâḥ" and "Iâh" mean life. Cornelius Agrippa, in his treatise on the *Pre-eminence of Women*, shows that the word Eve suggests comparison with the mystic symbols of the kabalists, the name of the woman having affinity with the ineffable Tetragrammaton, the most sacred name of the divinity. § Ancient names were always consonant with the things they represented. In relation to the mysterious name of the Deity in question, the hitherto inexplicable hint of the kabalists as to the efficacy of the letter H, "which Abram took away from his wife Sarah" and "put *into the middle of his own name*," becomes clear.

It may perhaps be argued, by way of objection, that it is not ascertained as yet at what period of antiquity the *nought* occurs for the first time in Indian manuscripts or inscriptions. Be that as it may, the case presents circumstantial evidence of too strong a character not to carry a conviction of probability with it. According to Max Müller, "the two words 'cipher' and 'zero,' which are in reality but one . . . are sufficient to prove that our figures are borrowed from the Arabs. Cipher is the

---

* *Ibid*, I, §11. See the constancy with which Ezekiel sticks in his vision to the "*wheels*" of the "living creatures" (ch. i, *passim*).
† He was an Alexandrian Neo-Platonist under the first of the Ptolemies.
‡ *Chips*, etc., Vol. I, p. 158.
§ [*De nobilitatae et praecellentia foeminea sexus*, Coloniae, 1532.]

Arabic 'cifron,' and means *empty*, a translation of the Sanskrit name of the nought, 'śûnya'," he says.* The Arabs had their figures from Hindostan, and never claimed the discovery for themselves.† As to the Pythagoreans, we need but turn to the ancient manuscripts of Boethius' *Geometry*, composed in the sixth century, to find in the Pythagorean numerals ‡ the 1 and the *nought*, as the first and final ciphers. And Porphyry, who quotes from the Pythagorean Moderatus, § says that the numerals of Pythagoras were "hieroglyphical symbols, by means whereof he explained ideas concerning the nature of things."

Now, if the most ancient Indian manuscripts show as yet no trace of decimal notation in them — Max Müller states very clearly that until now he has found but nine letters (the initials of the Sanskrit numerals) in them — on the other hand we have records as ancient to supply the wanted proof. We speak of the sculptures and the sacred imagery in the most ancient temples of the Far East. Pythagoras derived his knowledge from India; and we find Professor Max Müller corroborating this statement, at least so far as allowing the *Neo*-Pythagoreans to have been the first teachers of "ciphering" among the Greeks and Romans; that "they, at Alexandria, or in Syria, became acquainted with the Indian figures, and adapted them to the Pythagorean abacus" (our figures). This cautious allowance implies that Pythagoras himself was acquainted with but *nine* figures. So that we might reasonably answer that, although we possess no certain proof that the decimal notation was known to Pythagoras, who lived at the very close of the archaic ages, ‖ we yet have sufficient evidence to show that the full numbers, as given by Boethius, were known to the Pythagoreans, even before Alexandria was built.¶ This evidence we find in Aristotle, who says that "some philosophers hold that ideas and numbers are of the same nature, and amount to TEN in all." ** This, we believe, will be sufficient to show that the decimal notation was known among them at least as early as four centuries B. C., for Aristotle does not seem to treat the question as an innovation of the "Neo-Pythagoreans."

Besides, as we have remarked above, the representations of the archaic deities on the walls of the temples are of themselves quite suggestive enough. So, for instance, Vishnu is represented in the *Kûrma-avatâra* (his second avatâra) as a tortoise sustaining a circular pillar, on which the semblance of himself (*Mâyâ*, or illusion) sits with all his attributes. ††

---

\* *Chips*, etc., Vol. II, p. 286.
† *Ibid.*
‡ King, *The Gnostics*, etc., Plate XIII, G.
§ *Pythagorae vita.*
‖ 608 B.C.
¶ This city was built 332 B.C.
\*\* *Metaphysics*, XII, viii; XIII, viii.
†† [See Plate IX in Maurice, *Hist. of Hindostan*, Vol. I.]

While one hand holds a flower, another a club, the third a shell, the fourth, generally the upper one, or at the right, holds on his forefinger, extended as the cipher 1, the *chakra*, or discus, which resembles a ring, or a wheel, and might be taken for the nought. In his first avatâra, the *Matsya-avatâra*, when emerging from the fish's mouth, he is represented in the same position.* The ten-armed *Durgâ* of Bengal; the ten-headed Râvaṇa, the giant; Pârvatî — as Durgâ, Indra and Indrâṇî, are found with this attribute, which is a perfect representation of the Maypole.†

The holiest of the temples among the Hindus are those of Jagan-nâtha. This deity is worshipped equally by all the sects of India, and Jagan-nâtha is named "The Lord of the World." He is the god of the Mysteries, and his temples, which are most numerous in Bengal, are all of a pyramidal form.

There is no other deity which affords such a variety of etymologies as Yâho, nor a name which can be so variously pronounced. It is only by associating it with the Masoretic points that the later Rabbins succeeded in making Jehovah read "Adonai" — or Lord. Philo Byblius spells it in Greek letters 'IEYΩ — IEVO. Theodoret ‡ says that the Samaritans pronounced it 'Iαβέ (*Yabe*) and the Jews *Aïa*; Diodorus states that "among the Jews they relate that Moses called the God 'Iαώ," which would make it as we have shown — I-ah-O. § It is on the authority of the *Bible* itself, therefore, that we maintain that before his initiation by Jethro, his father-in-law, Moses had never known the word Yâho. The future Deity of the sons of Israel calls out from the burning bush and gives His name as "I am that I am," and specifies carefully that He is the "Lord God of the Hebrews" (*Exod.* iii, 18), not of the other nations. Judging him by his own acts, throughout the Jewish records, we doubt whether Christ himself, had he appeared in the days of the *Exodus*, would have been welcomed by the irascible Sinaitic Deity. However, "The Lord God," who becomes, on His own confession, Jehovah only in the 6th chapter of *Exodus* (verse 3) finds his veracity put to a startling test in *Genesis* xxii, 9, 14, in which *revealed* passage Abraham builds an altar to *Jehovah-jireh*.

It would seem, therefore, but natural to make a difference between the mystery-God 'Iαώ, adopted from the highest antiquity by all who participated in the esoteric knowledge of the priests, and his phonetic counterparts, whom we find treated with so little reverence by the Ophites and other Gnostics. Once having burdened themselves like the Azâzêl

---

\* See drawings from the Temple of Râma, Plate III in Coleman, *The Mythology of the Hindus,* New York: J. W. Bouton, Publisher.

† See Hargrave Jennings, *The Rosicrucians,* 1870, p. 252.

‡ [Theodoret, *Quaest. xv in Exodum.*]

§ [Diodorus Siculus, *Bibl. hist.,* I, 94. Cf. Gesenius, *A Hebrew and English Lexicon,* s.v. יהוה.]

of the wilderness with the sins and iniquities of the Jewish nation, it now appears hard for the Christians to have to confess that those whom they thought fit to consider the "chosen people" of God — their sole predecessors in monotheism — were, till a very late period, as idolatrous and polytheistic as their neighbors. The shrewd Talmudists have escaped the accusation for long centuries by screening themselves behind the Masoretic invention. But, as in everything else, truth was at last brought to light. We know now that Ihoh, יהוה, must be read Yâhoh and Yâh, not Jehovah. Yâh of the Hebrews is plainly the Iacchos (Bacchus) of the Mysteries; the God "from whom the liberation of souls was expected—Dionysus, Iacchos, Iachoh, Iahoh, Iaô." \* Aristotle then was right when he said: "Joh, יהוה, was Oromazdes and Ahriman Pluto, for the God of heaven, Ahura-Mazda, rides on a chariot which the *Horse of the Sun* follows." † And Dunlap quotes *Psalms* lxviii, 4, which reads:

> "Praise him by his name Yâh ( יה ),
> Who rides upon the heavens, as on a horse."

and then show that "the Arabs represented Iauk (Iach) by a horse. The Horse of the Sun (Dionysus)." "Iah is a softening of Iaḥ," he explains. " ח *ḥ* and ה *h* interchange; so *s* softens to *h*. The Hebrews express the idea of LIFE both by a ḥ and an *h;* as *ḥiaḥ,* to be, *hiah,* to be; Iaḥ, God of Life, Iah, 'I am'." ‡ Well then may we repeat these lines of Ausonius:

> "The sons of Ogyges call me Bacchus; Egypt thinks me Osiris;
> Mysians name me Phanaces; Indians regard me as Dionysus;
> Roman rites make me Liber; the Arab race thinks me Adoneus;
> Lucanians, the Universal God . . ." §

And the chosen people Adonis and Jehovah — we may add.

How little the philosophy of the old secret doctrine was understood, is illustrated in the atrocious persecutions of the Templars by the Church, and in the accusation of their worshipping the Devil under the shape of the goat — Baphomet! Without going into the old Masonic mysteries, there is not a Mason — of those we mean who *do know something* — but has an idea of the true relation that Baphomet bore to Azâzêl, the scapegoat of the wilderness, ‖ whose character and meaning are entirely per-

---

\* K. O. Müller, *A Hist. of the Literature of Anc. Greece*, p. 238; Movers, *Die Phönizier*, Vol. I, pp. 547-53; Dunlap, *Sōd, the Mysteries of Adoni*, p. 21.

† *A Universal History*, Vol. V, p. 301; London, 1747-66.

‡ Dunlap, *op. cit.*, p. 21.

§ *Epigrams*, XLVIII.

‖ See *Leviticus* xvi, 8-10, and other verses relating to the Biblical goat in the original texts.

verted in the Christian translations. "This terrible and venerable name of God," says Lanci,* librarian to the Vatican, "through the pen of biblical glossers, has been a *devil*, a *mountain*, a *wilderness*, and a *he-goat*." In MacKenzie's *Royal Masonic Cyclopaedia*, the author very correctly remarks that "this word should be divided into Azaz and El," for it "signifies God of Victory, but is here used in the sense of *Author of Death*, in contrast to Jehovah, the *Author of Life;* the latter received a dead goat as an offering." †
The Hindu Trinity is composed of three personages, which are convertible into one. The *Trimûrti* is one, and in its abstraction indivisible, and yet we see a metaphysical division taking place from the first, and while Brahmâ though collectively representing the three, remains behind the scenes, Vishṇu is the Life-Giver, the Creator, and the Preserver, and Śiva is the *Destroyer*, and the *Death-giving* deity. "Death to the *Life-giver*, life to the *Death-dealer*. The symbolical antithesis is grand and beautiful," says Gliddon. ‡ *"Deus est Daemon inversus"* of the kabalists now becomes clear. It is but the intense and cruel desire to crush out the last vestige of the old philosophies by perverting their meaning, for fear that their own dogmas should not be rightly fathered on them, which impels the Catholic Church to carry on such a systematic persecution in regard to Gnostics, Kabalists, and even the comparatively innocent Masons.

Alas, alas! How little has the divine seed, scattered, broadcast by the hand of the meek Judaean philosopher, thrived or brought forth fruit. He, who himself had shunned hypocrisy, warned against public prayer, showing such contempt for any useless exhibition of the same, could he but cast his sorrowful glance on the earth, from the regions of eternal bliss, would see that this seed fell neither on sterile rock nor by the wayside. Nay, it took deep root in the most prolific soil; one enriched even to plethora with lies and human gore!

"For if the truth of God hath more abounded *through my lie* unto his glory; why yet am I also judged as a sinner?" naïvely inquires Paul, the best and sincerest of all the apostles. And he then adds: *"Let us do evil*, that good may come!" (*Romans* iii, 7, 8).[44] This is a confession which we are asked to believe as having been a direct inspiration from God! It explains, if it does not excuse, the maxim adopted later by the Church that "it is an act of virtue to deceive and lie, when by such means the interests of *the Church* might be promoted." § A maxim

---

\* *La Sacra Scrittura*, etc., and *Paralipomeni*, etc.

† Article "Goat," p. 257.

‡ Nott and Gliddon, *Types of Mankind*, p. 600.

§ Mosheim, *An Eccl. History*, cent. IV, part II, ch. iii, §16. Read the whole section to appreciate the doctrine in full.

applied in its fullest sense by that accomplished professor in forgery, the Armenian Eusebius; or yet, that innocent-looking Bible-kaleidoscopist—Irenaeus. And these men were followed by a whole army of pious assassins, who, in the meanwhile, had improved upon the system of deceit, by proclaiming that it was lawful even to kill, when by murder they could enforce the new religion. Theophilus, "that perpetual enemy of peace and virtue," as the famous bishop was called; Cyril,* Athanasius, the murderer of Arius, and a host of other canonized "Saints," were all but too worthy successors of *Saint* Constantine, who drowned his wife in boiling water, butchered his little nephew, murdered with his own pious hand two of his brothers-in-law, killed his own son Crispus, bled to death several men and women, and smothered in a well an old monk. However, we are told by Eusebius that this Christian Emperor was rewarded by a *vision* of Christ himself, bearing his cross, who instructed him to march to other triumphs, inasmuch as he would always protect him!

It is under the shade of the Imperial standard, with its famous words, *"In hoc signo vinces,"* that *"visionary"* Christianity, which had crept on since the days of Irenaeus, arrogantly proclaimed its rights in the full blaze of the sun. The Labarum had most probably furnished the model for the *true* cross, which was "miraculously," and agreeably to the Imperial will, found a few years later. Nothing short of such a remarkable vision, impiously doubted by some severe critics — Dr. Lardner for one — and a fresh miracle to match, could have resulted in the finding of a cross where there had never before been one. Still, we have either to believe the phenomenon or dispute it at the risk of being treated as infidels; and this, notwithstanding that upon a careful computation we would find that the fragments of the "true Cross" had multiplied themselves even more miraculously than the five loaves in the invisible bakery and the two fishes. In all cases like this, where miracles can be so conveniently called in, there is no room for dull fact. History must step out that fiction may step in.

If the alleged founder of the Christian religion is now, after the lapse of nineteen centuries, preached — more or less unsuccessfully however — in every corner of the globe, we are at liberty to think that the doctrines attributed to him would astonish and dismay him more than anyone else. A system of deliberate falsification was adopted from the first. How determined Irenaeus was to crush truth and build up a Church of his own on the mangled remains of the seven primitive churches mentioned in the *Revelation,* may be inferred from his quarrel with Ptolemaeus. And this is again a case of evidence against which no blind faith can prevail. Ecclesiastical history assures us that Christ's

---

* [Of Alexandria.]

ministry was but of three years' duration. There is a decided discrepancy on this point between the first three Synoptics and the fourth gospel; but it was left for Irenaeus to show to Christian posterity that so early as A.D. 180 — the probable time when this Father wrote his works against heresies — even such pillars of the Church as himself either knew nothing certain about it, or deliberately lied and falsified dates to support their own views. So anxious was the worthy Father to meet every possible objection against his plans, that no falsehood, no sophistry, was too much for him. How are we to understand the following; and who is the falsifier in this case? The argument of Ptolemaeus was that Jesus was too young to have taught anything of much importance; adding that "Christ preached for *one year only,* and then suffered in the twelfth month." In this Ptolemaeus was very little at variance with the gospels. But Irenaeus, carried by his object far beyond the limits of prudence, from a mere discrepancy between one and three years, makes it *ten* and even twenty years! "Destroying his [Christ's] whole work, and *robbing him of that age* which is *both necessary* and more honorable than any other; that more advanced age, I mean, during which also, as a teacher, he excelled all others." And then, having no certain data to furnish, he throws himself back on *tradition,* and claims that Christ had preached for over TEN years! * In another place he makes Jesus fifty years old.

But we must proceed in our work of showing the various origins of Christianity, as also the sources from which Jesus derived his own ideas of God and humanity.

The Koinobioi lived in Egypt, where Jesus passed his early youth. They were usually confounded with the Therapeutae, who were a branch of this widely-spread society. Such is the opinion of Godfrey Higgins and Dr. Rebold. After the downfall of the principal sanctuaries, which had already begun in the days of Plato, the many different sects, such as the Gymnosophists and the Magi—from whom Clearchus very erroneously derives the former—the Pythagoreans, the Sufis, and the Ṛishis of Kashmîr, instituted a kind of international and universal Freemasonry, among their esoteric societies. "These Ṛishis," says Higgins, "are the same as Sofees, and are the Carmelites, Nazarites, or Essenians, belonging to the temple of Solomon in this country." † "That occult science known by ancient priests under the name of *regenerating fire,*" says Father Rebold, ". . . is a science that for more than 3,000 years was the peculiar possession of the [Indian and Egyptian] priesthood, into the knowledge of which Moses was initiated at Heliopolis, where he was educated; and Jesus among the Essenian priests of [Egypt or] Judaea;

---

\* *Adv. Haer.,* II, xxii, §§ 4, 5, 6.
† *Anacalypsis,* Vol. I, p. 731.

and by which these two great reformers, *particularly the latter*, wrought many of the miracles mentioned in the *Scriptures*." *

Plato states that the mystic Magian religion, known under the name of *Machagistia*, is the most uncorrupted form of worship in things divine. Later, the Mysteries of the Chaldean sanctuaries were added to it by one of the Zoroasters and Darius Hystaspes.† The latter completed and perfected it still more with the help of the knowledge obtained by him from the learned ascetics of India, whose rites were identical with those of the initiated Magi.‡ Ammianus, in his history of Julian's Persian expedition, gives the story by stating that one day "Hystaspes, as he was boldly penetrating into the unknown regions of Upper India, had come upon a certain wooded solitude, the tranquil recesses of which were occupied by those exalted sages, the Brachmanes [or Shamans]. Instructed by their teaching in the science of *the motions of the world* and of the heavenly bodies, and in *pure religious rites* . . . he transfused them into the creed of the Magi. The latter, coupling these doctrines with their *own peculiar science of foretelling the future*, have handed down the whole through their descendants to succeeding ages."§ It is from these descendants that the Sufis, chiefly composed of Persians and Syrians, acquired their proficient knowledge in astrology, medicine, and the esoteric doctrine of the ages. "The Sufi doctrine," says C. W. King, "involved the grand idea of one universal creed which could be secretly held under any profession of an outward faith; and in fact took virtually the same view of religious systems as that in which the ancient philosophers had regarded such matters." ‖ The mysterious Druzes of Mount Lebanon are the descendants of all these. Solitary Copts, earnest students scattered hither and thither throughout the sandy solitudes of Egypt, Arabia Petraea, Palestine, and the impenetrable forests of Abyssinia, though rarely met with, may sometimes be seen. Many and various are the nationalities to which belong the disciples of that mysterious school, and many the sideshoots of that one primitive stock.

---

* [E. Rebold, *Histoire générale de la Franc-Maçonnerie*, p. 23, footnote.]

† [Ammianus Marcellinus, *Roman History*, XXIII, vi, 32, 33.]

‡ We hold to the idea—which becomes self-evident when the Zoroastrian imbroglio is considered — that there were, even in the days of Darius, two distinct sacerdotal castes of Magi: the initiated and those who were allowed to officiate in the popular rites only. We see the same in the Eleusinian Mysteries. Belonging to every temple there were attached the "hierophants" of the *inner* sanctuary, and the secular clergy who were not even instructed in the Mysteries. It is against the absurdities and superstitions of the latter that Darius revolted, and "crushed them," for the inscription of his tomb shows that he was a "hierophant" and a Magian himself. It is also but the exoteric rites of this class of Magi which descended to posterity, for the great secrecy in which were preserved the "Mysteries" of the true Chaldean Magi was never violated, however much guesswork may have been expended on them.

§ [Amm. Marc., *op. cit.*, XXIII, vi.]

‖ *The Gnostics and their Remains*, p. 185 [p. 415 in 2nd ed.]

The secrecy preserved by these sub-lodges, as well as by the one and supreme great lodge, has ever been proportionate to the activity of religious persecutions; and now, in the face of the growing materialism, their very existence is becoming a mystery.*

But it must not be inferred, on that account, that such a mysterious brotherhood is but a fiction, not even *a name,* though it remains unknown to this day. Whether its affiliates are called by an Egyptian, Hindu, or Persian name, it matters not. Persons belonging to one of these sub-brotherhoods have been met by trustworthy, and not unknown persons, besides the present writer, who states a few facts concerning them, by the special permission of one *who has a right to give it.* In a recent and very valuable work on secret societies, K. R. H. MacKenzie's *Royal Masonic Cyclopaedia,* we find the learned author himself, an honorary member of the Canongate Kilwinning Lodge, No. 2 (Scotland), and a Mason not likely to be imposed upon, stating the following, under the head, "Hermetic Brothers of Egypt" (p. 309):

"An occult fraternity which has endured from very ancient times, having a hierarchy of officers, secret signs, and passwords, and a peculiar method of instruction in science, moral philosophy and religion . . . If we may believe those who, at the present time profess to belong to it, *the philosopher's stone, the elixir of life, the art of invisibility,* and the power of communication directly with the ultramundane life, are parts of the inheritance they possess. The writer has met with only three persons who maintained the actual existence of this body of religious philosophers, and who hinted that they themselves were actually members. There was no reason to doubt the good faith of these individuals — apparently unknown to each other, and men of moderate competence, blameless lives, austere manners, and almost ascetic in their habits.

---

* These are truths which cannot fail to impress themselves upon the minds of earnest thinkers. While the Ebionites, Nazarites, Haemerobaptists, Lampseans, Sabians, and many other earliest sects, wavered later between the varying dogmatisms suggested to them by the *esoteric* and misunderstood parables of the Nazarene teacher, whom they justly regarded as a prophet, there were men, for whose names we would vainly search history, who preserved the secret doctrines of Jesus as pure and unadulterated as they had been received. And still, even all these above-mentioned and conflicting sects were far more orthodox in their Christianity, or rather Christism, than the Churches of Constantine and Rome. "It was a strange fate that befell these unfortunate people" (the Ebionites), says Lord Amberley, "when, overwhelmed by the flood of heathenism that had swept into the Church, they were condemned as heretics. Yet there is no evidence that they had ever swerved from the doctrines of Jesus, or of the disciples who knew him in his lifetime. Jesus himself had been circumcised . . . reverenced the temple at Jerusalem as 'a house of prayer for all nations.' . . . But the torrent of progress swept past the Ebionites, and left them stranded on the shore" (*An Analysis of Religious Beliefs,* by Viscount Amberley, 1876, Vol. I, p. 446).

They all appeared to be men of forty to forty-five years of age, and evidently of vast erudition . . . their knowledge of languages not to be doubted . . . They never remained long in any one country, but passed away without creating notice." \*

Another of such sub-brotherhoods is the sect of the Pitris in India. Known by name, now that Jacolliot has brought it into public notice, it yet is more arcane, perhaps, than the brotherhood that Mr. MacKenzie names the "Hermetic Brothers." What Jacolliot learned of it was from fragmentary manuscripts delivered to him by Brahmans, who had their reasons for doing so, we must believe. The *Agrushada Parikshai* gives certain details about the association, as it was in days of old, and, when explaining mystic rites and magical incantations, explains nothing at all, so that the mystic *L'om, L'Rhum, Sh'hrum,* and *Sho'rhim Ramaya-Namaha*, remain, for the mystified writer, as much a puzzle as ever. To do him justice, though, he fully admits the fact, and does not enter upon useless speculations.†

Whoever desires to assure himself that there now exists a religion which has baffled, for centuries, the impudent inquisitiveness of missionaries, and the persevering inquiry of science, let him violate, if he can, the seclusion of the Syrian Druzes. He will find them numbering over 80,000 warriors, scattered from the plain east of Damascus to the western coast. They covet no proselytes, shun notoriety, keep friendly — as far as possible — with both Christians and Mohammedans, respect the religion of every other sect or people, but will never disclose their own secrets. Vainly do the missionaries stigmatize them as infidels, idolaters, brigands, and thieves. Neither threat, bribe, nor any other consideration will induce a Druze to become a convert to dogmatic Christianity. We have heard of two in fifty years, and both have finished their careers in prison, for drunkenness and theft. They proved to be "real *Druzes*,"‡ said one

---

\* What will, perhaps, still more astonish American readers, is the fact that in the United States, a mystical fraternity now exists, which claims an intimate relationship with one of the oldest and most powerful of Eastern Brotherhoods. It is known as the Brotherhood of Luxor, and its faithful members have the custody of very important secrets of science. Its ramifications extend widely throughout the great Republic of the West. Though this brotherhood has been long and hard at work, the secret of its existence has been jealously guarded. MacKenzie describes it as having "a Rosicrucian basis, and numbering many members" (*Royal Masonic Cyclopaedia*, p. 461). But, in this, the author is mistaken; it has no Rosicrucian basis. The name Luxor is primarily derived from the ancient Baluchistan city of Lukhsur, which lies between Bela and Kedje, and also gave its name to the Egyptian city.

† [Jacolliot, *Le Spiritisme*, etc., p. 78.]

‡ These people do not accept the name of Druzes, but regard the appellation as an insult. They call themselves the "disciples of Ḥ'amza," their Messiah, who came to them, in the eleventh century, from the "Land of the Word of God," and, together with his disciple, Mokshatana Boha-eddin, committed this *Word* to writing, and entrusted it

of their chiefs, in discussing the subject. There never was a case of an *initiated* Druze becoming a Christian. As to the uninitiated, they are never allowed to even see the sacred writings, and none of them have the remotest idea where these are kept. There are missionaries in Syria who boast of having in their possession a few copies. The volumes alleged to be the correct expositions from these secret books (such as the translation by Pétis de la Croix, in 1701, from the works presented by Nasr-Allah to the French king), are nothing more than a compilation of "secrets," known more or less to every inhabitant of the southern ranges of Lebanon and Anti-Libanus. They were the work of an apostate Dervish, who was expelled from the sect Hanafi, for improper conduct — the embezzlement of the money of widows and orphans. The *Exposé de la Religion des Druzes*, in two volumes, by Silvestre de Sacy (1838), is another network of hypotheses. A copy of this work was to be found in 1870, on the window sill of one of their principal *Khalwehs*, or place of religious meeting. To the inquisitive question of an English traveller, as to their rites, the *'Uqqâl*,* a venerable old man, who spoke English as well as French, opened the volume of de Sacy, and, offering it to his interlocutor, remarked, with a benevolent smile: "Read this instructive and truthful book; I could explain to you neither better nor more correctly the secrets of God and our blessed H'amza, than it does." The traveller understood the hint.

MacKenzie says they settled at Lebanon about the tenth century, and "seem to be a mixture of Kurds, Mardi-Arabs, and other semi-civilized tribes. Their religion is compounded of Judaism, Christianity, and Mohammedanism. They have a regular order of priesthood, and *a kind of hierarchy* . . . there is a regular system of passwords and signs . . . Twelve month's probation, to which either sex is admitted, precedes initiation." †

We quote the above only to show how little even persons as trustworthy as Mr. MacKenzie really know of these mystics.

Mosheim, who knows as much, or we should rather say as little, as any others, is entitled to the merit of candidly admitting that "their religion is peculiar to themselves, and is involved in some mystery." ‡ We should say it is — rather!

That their religion exhibits traces of Magianism and Gnosticism is natural, as the whole of the Ophite esoteric philosophy is at the bottom of it. But the characteristic dogma of the Druzes is the absolute unity

---

to the care of a few initiates, with the injunction of the greatest secrecy. They are usually called Unitarians.

* The *'Uqqâls* (from the Arabic *aql* — intelligence or wisdom) are the initiated, or wise men of this sect. They hold, in their mysteries, the same position as the hierophant of old, in the Eleusinian and others.

† [*Royal Masonic Cyclopaedia*, p. 165.]

‡ [*Eccl. Hist.*, cent. XVI, sect. III, pt. I, ch. ii, §19.]

of God. He is the essence of life, and although incomprehensible and invisible, is to be known through *occasional manifestations in human form.*\* Like the Hindus they hold that he was incarnated more than once on earth. H'amza was the *precursor*, not the inheritor, of *Ḥâkim*, the last manifestation (the tenth *avatâra*),† who is yet to come. H'amza was the personification of the "Universal Wisdom." Boha-eddin in his writings calls him Messiah. The whole number of his disciples, or those who at different ages of the world have imparted wisdom to mankind, which the latter as invariably have forgotten and rejected in course of time, is one hundred and sixty-four (164, the kabalistic *s d k*). Therefore, their stages or degrees of promotion after initiation are five; the first three degrees are typified by the "three feet of the candlestick of the inner Sanctuary, which holds the light of the *five* elements"; the last two degrees, the most important and terrifying in their solemn grandeur, belonging to the highest orders; and the whole five degrees emblematically represented the said five mystic Elements. The "three feet are the holy *Application*, the *Opening*, and the *Phantom*," says one of their books: on man's inner and outer soul, and his body, a phantom, a passing shadow. The body, or matter, is also called the "Rival," for "he is the minister of sin, the Devil ever creating dissensions between the Heavenly Intelligence [spirit] and the soul, which he tempts incessantly." Their ideas on transmigration are Pythagorean and kabalistic. The spirit, or al-Tamîmî (the divine soul), was in Elijah and John the Baptist; and the soul of Jesus was that of H'amza; that is to say, of the same degree of purity and sanctity. Until their resurrection, by which they understand the day when the spiritual bodies of men will be absorbed into God's own essence and being (the Nirvâṇa of the Hindus), the souls of men will keep their astral forms, except the few chosen ones who, from the moment of their separation from their bodies, begin to exist as pure spirits. The life of man they divide into soul, body and intelligence, or mind. It is the latter which imparts and communicates to the soul the divine spark from its H'amza (Christos).

They have seven great commandments which are imparted equally to all the uninitiated; and yet, even these well-known articles of faith have been so mixed up in the accounts of outside writers, that, in one of the best *Cyclopaedias* of America (Appleton's), they are garbled after the fashion that may be seen in the comparative tabulation below; the spurious and the true order parallel:

---

\* This is the doctrine of the Gnostics who held Christos to be the personal immortal Spirit of man.

† The ten Messiahs or avatâras remind again of the five Buddhistic and ten Brahmanical avatâras of Buddha and Kṛishṇa.

| Correct Version of the Commandments as Imparted Orally by the Teacher * | Garbled Version Reported by the Christian Missionaries and Given in Pretended Expositions † |
|---|---|
| 1. *The unity of God,* or the infinite oneness of Deity. | 1. (2) " 'Truth in words,' meaning in practice *only truth to the religion and to the initiated; it is lawful to act and to speak falsehood to men of another creed.*" ‡ |
| 2. *The essential excellence of Truth.* | 2. (7) "Mutual help, watchfulness, and protection." |
| 3. Toleration; right given to all men and women to freely express their opinions on religious matters, and make the latter subservient to reason. | 3. (?) "To renounce all other religions." § |
| 4. Respect to all men and women according to their character and conduct. | 4. (?) "To be separate from infidels of every kind, not externally but only in heart." ‖ |
| 5. Entire submission to God's decrees. | 5. (1) "Recognize God's eternal unity." |
| 6. Chastity of body, mind and soul. | 6. (5) "Satisfied with God's acts." |
| 7. Mutual help under all conditions. | 7. (5) "Resigned to God's will." |

As will be seen, the only exposé in the above is that of the great ignorance, perhaps malice, of the writers who, like Silvestre de Sacy, undertake to enlighten the world upon matters concerning which they know nothing.

"Chastity, honesty, meekness, and mercy," are thus the four theological virtues of all Druzes, besides several others demanded from the initiates; "murder, theft, cruelty, covetousness, slander," the five sins, to which several other sins are added in the sacred tablets, but which we must abstain from giving. The morality of the Druzes is strict and

---

\* See, farther on, a letter from an "Initiate."

† In this column the first numbers are those given in the article on the *Druzes* in the *New American Cyclopaedia* (Appleton's), Vol. VI, p. 631. The numbers in parentheses show the sequence in which the commandments would stand were they given correctly.

‡ This pernicious doctrine belongs to the old policy of the Catholic Church, but is certainly false as regards the Druzes. They maintain that it is right and lawful to *withhold the truth* about their own tenets, no one outside their own sect having a right to pry into their religion. The 'Uqqâls never countenance deliberate falsehood in any form, although the laymen have many a time gotten rid of the spies sent by the Christians to discover their secrets, by deceiving them with sham initiations. (See the letter of Prof. Rawson to the author, p. 313.)

§ This commandment does not exist in the Lebanon teaching.

‖ There is no such commandment, but the practice thereof exists by mutual agreement, as in the days of the Gnostic persecution.

uncompromising. Nothing can tempt one of these Lebanon Unitarians to go astray from what he is taught to consider his duty. *Their ritual being unknown to outsiders,* their would-be historians have hitherto denied them one. Their "Thursday meetings" are open to all, but no interloper has ever participated in the rites of initiation which take place occasionally on Fridays in the greatest secrecy. Women are admitted to them as well as men, and they play a part of great importance at the initiation of men. The probation, unless some extraordinary exception is made, is long and severe. Once, in a certain period of time, a solemn ceremony takes place, during which all the elders and the initiates of the highest two degrees start out for a pilgrimage of several days to a certain place in the mountains. They meet within the safe precincts of a monastery said to have been erected during the earliest times of the Christian era. Outwardly one sees but old ruins of a once grand edifice, used, says the legend, by some Gnostic sects as a place of worship during the religious persecutions. The ruins above ground, however, are but a convenient mask, the subterranean chapel, halls and cells, covering an area of ground far greater than the upper building; while the richness of ornamentation, the beauty of the ancient sculptures, and the gold and silver vessels in this sacred resort, appear like "a dream of glory," according to the expression of an initiate. As the lamaseries of Mongolia and Thibet are visited upon grand occasions by the holy shadow of "Lord Buddha," so here, during the ceremonial, appears the resplendent ethereal form of H'amza, the Blessed, which instructs the faithful. The most extraordinary feats of what would be termed magic take place during the several nights that the convocation lasts; and one of the greatest mysteries — faithful copy of the past — is accomplished within the discreet bosom of our mother earth; not an echo, nor the faintest sound, not a glimmer of light betrays without the grand secret of the initiates.

H'amza, like Jesus, was a mortal man, and yet "H'amza" and "Christos" are synonymous terms as to their inner and hidden meaning. Both are symbols of the *Nous,* the divine and higher soul of man — his spirit. The doctrine taught by the Druzes on that particular question of the duality of spiritual man, consisting of one soul mortal, and another immortal, is identical with that of the Gnostics, the older Greek philosophers, and other initiates.

Outside the East we have met one initiate (and only one), who, for some reasons best known to himself, does not make a secret of his initiation into the Brotherhood of Lebanon. It is the learned traveller and artist, Professor A. L. Rawson, of New York City.[45] This gentleman has passed many years in the East, four times visited Palestine, and has trav-

## A LETTER FROM AN INITIATE 313

elled to Mecca. It is safe to say that he has a priceless store of facts about the beginnings of the Christian Church, which none but one who had had free access to repositories closed against the ordinary traveller could have collected. Professor Rawson, with the true devotion of a man of science, noted down every important discovery he made in the Palestinian libraries, and every precious fact orally communicated to him by the mystics he encountered, and some day they will see the light. He has most obligingly sent us the following communication, which, as the reader will perceive, fully corroborates what is above written from our personal experience about the strange fraternity incorrectly styled the Druzes:

"34 BOND ST., NEW YORK, June 6, 1877.

". . . Your note, asking me to give you an account of my initiation into a secret order among the people commonly known as Druzes, in Mount Lebanon, was received this morning. I took, as you are fully aware, an obligation at that time to conceal within my own memory the greater part of the 'mysteries,' with the most interesting parts of the 'instruction'; so that what is left may not be of any service to the public. Such information as I can rightfully give, you are welcome to have and use as you may have occasion.

"The probation in my case was, by *special dispensation,* made one month, during which time I was 'shadowed' by a priest, who served as my cook, guide, interpreter, and general servant, that he might be able to testify to the fact of my having strictly conformed to the rules in diet, ablutions, and other matters. He was also my instructor in the text of the ritual, which we recited from time to time for practice, in dialogue or in song, as it may have been. Whenever we happened to be near a Druze village, on a Thursday, we attended the 'open' meetings, where men and women assembled for instruction and worship, and to expose to the world generally their religious practices. I was never present at a Friday 'close' meeting before my initiation, nor do I believe anyone else, man or woman, ever was, except by collusion with a priest, and that is not probable, for a false priest forfeits his life. The practical jokers among them sometimes 'fool' a too curious 'Frank' by a sham initiation, especially if such a one is suspected of having some connection with the missionaries at Beirut or elsewhere.

"The initiates include both women and men, and the ceremonies are of so peculiar a nature that both sexes are required to assist in the ritual and 'work.' The 'furniture' of the 'prayer-house' and of the 'vision-chamber' is simple, and except for convenience may consist of but a strip of carpet. In the 'Gray Hall' (the place is never named, and is underground, *not far* from Bayt-ed-Deen) there are some rich decorations and valuable pieces of ancient furniture, the work of the Arab silversmiths five or six centuries ago, inscribed and dated. The day of initiation must be a continual fast from daylight to sunset in winter, or six o'clock in summer, and the ceremony is from beginning to end a series of trials and temptations, calculated to test the endurance of the candidate under physical and mental pressure. It is seldom that any but the young man or woman succeeds in 'winning' all the 'prizes,' since *nature will sometimes exert itself* in spite of the most stubborn will, and the neophyte fail of passing some of the tests. In such a case the probation is extended another year, when another trial is had.

"Among other tests of the neophyte's self-control are the following: Choice pieces of cooked meat, savory soup, pilau, and other appetizing dishes, with sherbet, coffee, wine, and water, are set, as if accidentally, in his way, and he is left alone for a time with the tempting things. To a hungry and fainting soul the trial is severe. But a more difficult ordeal is when the seven priestesses retire, all but one, the youngest and prettiest, and the door is closed and barred on the outside, after warning the candidate that he will be left to his 'reflections,' for half an hour. Wearied by the long-continued ceremonial, weak with hunger, parched with thirst, and a sweet reaction coming after the tremendous strain to keep his animal nature in subjection, this moment of privacy and of temptation is brimful of peril. The beautiful young vestal, timidly approaching, and with glances which lend a double magnetic allurement to her words, begs him in low tones to 'bless her.' Woe to him if he does! A hundred eyes see him from secret peep-holes, and only to the ignorant neophyte is there the appearance of concealment and opportunity.

"There is no infidelity, idolatry, or other really bad feature in the system. They have the relics of what was once a grand form of nature-worship, which has been contracted under a despotism into a secret order, hidden from the light of day, and exposed only in the smoky glare of a few burning lamps, in some damp cave or chapel under ground. The chief tenets of their religious teachings are comprised in seven 'tablets,' which are these, to state them in general terms:

"1. The unity of God, or the infinite oneness of deity.
"2. The essential excellence of truth.
"3. The law of toleration as to all men and women in opinion.
"4. Respect for all men and women as to character and conduct.
"5. Entire submission to God's decrees as to fate.
"6. Chastity of body and mind and soul.
"7. Mutual help under all conditions.

"These tenets are not printed or written. Another set is printed or written to mislead the unwary, but with these we are not concerned.

"The chief results of the initiation seemed to be a kind of mental illusion or sleep-waking, in which the neophyte saw, or thought he saw, the images of people who were known to be absent, and in some cases thousands of miles away. I thought (or perhaps it was my mind at work) I saw friends and relatives that I knew at the time were in New York State, while I was in Lebanon. How these results were produced I cannot say. They appeared in a dark room, when the 'guide' was talking, the 'company' singing in the next 'chamber,' and near the close of the day, when I was tired out with fasting, walking, singing, robing, unrobing, seeing a great many people in various conditions as to dress and undress, and with great mental strain in resisting certain physical manifestations that result from the appetites when they overcome the will, and in paying close attention to the passing scenes, hoping to remember them—so that I may have been unfit to judge of any new and surprising phenomena, and more especially of those apparently magical appearances which have always excited my suspicion and distrust. I know the various uses of the magic-lantern, and other apparatus, and took care to examine the room where the 'visions' appeared to me the same evening, and the next day, and several times afterwards, and knew that, in my case, there was no use made of any machinery or other means besides the voice of the 'guide and instructor.' On several occasions afterward, when at a great distance from the 'chamber,' the same or similar visions were produced, as, for instance, in Hornstein's Hotel at Jerusalem. A daughter-in-law of a well-known Jewish merchant in Jerusalem is an initiated 'sister,' and can produce the visions almost at will on anyone who will live strictly according to the rules of the Order for a few weeks, more or less, according to their nature, as gross or refined, etc.

"I am quite safe in saying that the initiation is so peculiar that it could not be printed so as to instruct one who had not been 'worked' through the 'chamber.' So it would be even more impossible to make an exposé of them than of the Freemasons. The real secrets are acted and not spoken, and require several initiated persons to assist in the work.

"It is not necessary for me to say how some of the notions of that people seem to perpetuate certain beliefs of the ancient Greeks—as, for instance, the idea that a man has two souls, and many others—for you probably were made familiar with them in your passage through the 'upper' and 'lower chamber.' If I am mistaken in supposing you an 'initiate,' please excuse me. I am aware that the closest friends often conceal that 'sacred secret' from each other; and even husband and wife may live—as I was informed in Dayr-el-Kamar was the fact in one family there—for twenty years together and yet neither know anything of the initiation of the other. You, undoubtedly, have good reasons for keeping your own counsel.

"Yours truly,

"A. L. RAWSON."

Before we close the subject we may add that if a stranger ask for admission to a "Thursday" meeting he will never be refused. Only, if he is a Christian, the '*Uqqâl* will open a *Bible* and read from it; and if a Mohammedan, he will hear a few chapters of the *Koran*, and the ceremony will end with this. They will wait until he is gone, and then, shutting well the doors of their convent, take to their own rites and books, passing for this purpose into their subterranean sanctuaries.* "The Druzes remain, even more than the Jews, a peculiar people," says Colonel Churchill, one of the few fair and strictly impartial writers. "They marry within their own race; they are rarely if ever converted; they adhere tenaciously to their traditions, and they baffle all efforts to discover their cherished secrets . . . The bad name of that caliph whom they claim as their founder is fairly compensated by the pure lives of many whom they honor as saints, and by the heroism of their feudal leaders."

And yet the Druzes may be said to belong to one of the least esoteric of secret societies. There are others far more powerful and learned, the existence of which is not even suspected in Europe. There are many branches belonging to the great "Mother Lodge" which, mixed up with certain communities, may be termed secret sects within other sects. One of them is the sect commonly known as that of *Laṅghana-Sâstra*. It reckons several thousand adepts who are scattered about in small groups in the south of the Dekkan, India. In the popular superstition, this sect is dreaded on account of its great reputation for magic and sorcery. The Brahmans accuse its members of atheism and sacrilege, for none of them

---

* Cf. Col. C. H. Churchill, *Mount Lebanon*, Vol. II, pp. 255-56; London, 1853.

will consent to recognize the authority of either the *Vedas* or *Manu*, except so far as they conform to the versions in their possession, and which they maintain are professedly the only original texts; the *Laṅghana-Śāstra* have neither temples nor priests, but twice a month every member of the community has to absent himself from home for three days. Popular rumor, originated among their women, ascribes such absences to pilgrimages performed to their places of fortnightly resort. In some secluded mountainous spots, unknown and inaccessible to other sects, hidden far from sight among the luxurious vegetation of India, they keep their bungalows, which look like small fortresses, encircled as they are by lofty and thick walls. These, in their turn, are surrounded by the sacred trees called *aśvatha*, and in Tamil *araśa-maram*. These are the "sacred groves," the originals of those of Egypt and Greece, whose initiates also built their temples within such "groves" inaccessible to the profane.*

It will not be found without interest to see what Mr. John Yarker, Jr., has to say on some modern secret societies among the Orientals. "The nearest resemblance to the Brahminical mysteries, is probably found in the very ancient *'Paths'* of the Dervishes, which are usually governed by twelve officers, the oldest 'Court' superintending the others by right of seniority. Here the Master of the 'Court' is called *'Sheik,'* and has his deputies, 'Caliphs,' or successors, *of which there may be many* (as for instance in the brevet degree of a Master Mason). The order is divided into at least four columns, pillars, or degrees. The first step is that of 'Humanity,' which supposes attention to the written law, and 'annihilation in the *Sheik*.' The second is that of the 'Path,' in which the *'Murid'* or disciple, attains spiritual powers and 'self annihilation into the *Peer*' or founder of the '*Path*.' The third stage is called 'Knowledge,' and the *'Murid'* is supposed to become inspired, called 'annihilation into the Prophet.' The fourth stage leads him even to God, when he becomes a part of the Deity and sees Him in all things. The first and second stages have received modern sub-divisions, as 'Integrity,' 'Virtue,' 'Temperance,' 'Benevolence.' After this the *Sheik* confers upon him the grade of 'Caliph,' or Honorary Master, for in their mystical language, 'the man must die before the saint can be born.' It will be seen that this kind of mysticism is applicable to Christ as founder of a 'Path'."

To this statement, the author adds the following on the Baktâshî Dervishes, who "often initiated the Janizaries. Their ceremony is as follows, and they wear *a small marble cube spotted with blood*. Before reception a year's probation is required, during which false secrets are given to

---

* Every temple in India is surrounded by such belts of sacred trees. And like the Kumbum of Kansu (Mongolia) no one but an initiate has a right to approach them.

test the candidate: he has two godfathers *and is divested of all metals and even clothing;* from the wool of a sheep a cord is made for his neck and a girdle for his loins; he is led into the centre of a square room, presented as a slave, and seated upon a large stone with twelve escallops; his arms are crossed upon his breast, his body inclined forwards, his right toes extended over his left foot; after various prayers he is placed in a particular manner with his hand in a peculiar way in that of the Sheik, who repeats a verse from the *Koran*: 'Those who on giving thee their hand swear to thee an oath, swear it to God, the hand of God is placed in their hand; whoever violates this oath will do so to his hurt, and to whoever remains faithful God will give a magnificent reward.' Placing the hand below the chin is their sign, perhaps in memory of their vow. All use the double triangles. The Brahmins inscribe the angles with their trinity, and they possess also the Masonic sign of distress as used in France." *

From the very day when the first mystic found the means of communication between this world and the worlds of the invisible host, between the sphere of matter and that of pure spirit, he concluded that to abandon this mysterious science to the profanation of the rabble was to lose it. An abuse of it might lead mankind to speedy destruction; it was like surrounding a group of children with explosive batteries, and furnishing them with matches. The first self-made adept initiated but a select few, and kept silence with the multitudes. He recognized his God and felt the great Being within himself. The "Âtman," the Self,† the

---

\* *Notes on the Scientific and Religious Mysteries of Antiquity,* pp. 7-8. New York, 1878.

† This "Self," which the Greek philosophers called *Augoeides,* the "Shining One," is impressively and beautifully described in Max Müller's "**Veda.**" Showing the *Veda* to be the first book of the Âryan nations, the professor adds that "we have in it . . . a period of the intellectual life of man to which there is no parallel in any other part of the world. In the hymns of the *Veda* we see man left to himself to solve the riddle of this world. . . . He invokes [the gods around him], he praises them, he worships them. But still with all these gods . . . beneath him, and above him, the early poet seems ill at ease within himself. There, too, in his own breast, he has discovered a power . . . that is never mute when he prays, never absent when he fears and trembles. It seems to inspire his prayers, and yet to listen to them; it seems to live in him, and yet to support him and all around him. The only name he can find for this mysterious power is 'Brâhman'; for *brahman* meant originally force, will, wish, and the propulsive power of creation. But this impersonal brâhman, too, as soon as it is named, grows into something strange and divine. It ends by being one of many gods, one of the great triad, worshipped to the present day. And still the thought within him has no real name; that power which is nothing but itself, which supports the gods, the heavens, and every living being, floats before his mind, conceived but not expressed. At last he calls it 'Âtman'; for âtman, originally breath or spirit, comes to mean Self

mighty Lord and Protector, once that man knew him as the "*I am*," the "*Ego Sum*," the "*Asmi*," showed his full power to him who could recognize the "*still small voice*." From the days of the primitive man described by the first Vedic poet, down to our modern age, there has not been a philosopher worthy of that name, who did not carry in the silent sanctuary of his heart the grand and mysterious truth. If initiated, he learned it as a sacred science; if otherwise, then, like Socrates, repeating to himself, as well as to his fellowmen, the noble injunction, "O man, know thyself," he succeeded in recognizing his God within himself. "Ye are gods," the king-psalmist tells us, and we find Jesus reminding the scribes that the expression, "Ye are gods," was addressed to other mortal men, claiming for himself the same privilege without any blasphemy.* And, as a faithful echo, Paul, while asserting that we are all "the temple of the living God," † cautiously adds that after all these things are only for the "wise," and it is "unlawful" to speak of them.

Therefore, we must accept the reminder, and simply remark that even in the tortured and barbarous phraseology of the *Codex Nazaraeus*, we detect throughout the same idea. Like an undercurrent, rapid and clear, it runs without mixing its crystalline purity with the muddy and heavy waves of dogmatism. We find it in the *Codex*, as well as in the *Vedas*, in the *Avesta*, as in the *Abhidharma*, and in Kapila's *Sânkhya-Sûtras* not less than in the *Fourth Gospel*. We cannot attain the "Kingdom of Heaven," unless we unite ourselves indissolubly with our *Rex Lucis*, the Lord of Splendor and of Light, our Immortal God. We must first conquer immortality and "take the Kingdom of Heaven by violence," offered to our material selves. "The first man is of the earth earthy; the *second* man *is the Lord from heaven* . . . Behold, I show you a *mystery*," says Paul (*1 Corinthians* xv, 47-51). In the religion of Śâkya-Muni, which learned commentators have delighted so much of late to set down as purely *nihilistic*, the doctrine of immortality is very clearly defined notwithstanding the European or rather Christian ideas about Nirvâṇa. In the sacred Jaina books of Pattana, the dying Gautama

---

and Self alone; *Self* whether divine or human; Self whether creating or suffering; Self whether one or all; but always Self, independent and free. 'Who has seen the first-born,' says the poet, 'when he who had no bones (*i. e.,* form) bore him that had bones? Where was the life, the blood, the Self of the world? Who went to ask this from any that knew it?' (*Ṛig-Veda,* I, 164, 4). This idea of a divine Self once expressed, everything else must acknowledge its supremacy; '*Self* is the Lord of all things, Self is the King of all things. As all the spokes of a wheel are contained in the nave and the circumference, all things are contained in this Self; all selves are contained in this Self (*Brihad-âranyaka,* IV, 5, 15, ed. Roer, p. 487). Brâhman itself is but Self' (*Ibid.,* p. 478. *Chhandogya-Upanishad,* VIII, 3, 3-4)."— *Chips,* etc., Vol. I, pp. 69-70.

\* *John* x, 34, 35.
† *2 Cor.* vi, 16.

Buddha is thus addressed: "Arise into *Nirvi* (Nirvâṇa) from this decrepit body into which thou hast been sent. Ascend into *thy former abode*, O blessed Avatâra!" This seems to us the very opposite of Nihilism. If Gautama is invited to re-ascend into his "former abode," and this abode is Nirvâṇa, then it is incontestable that Buddhistic philosophy does *not* teach final annihilation. As Jesus is alleged to have appeared to his disciples after death, so to the present day is Gautama believed to descend from Nirvâṇa. And if he has an existence there, then this state cannot be a synonym for *annihilation*.

Gautama, no less than all other great reformers, had a doctrine for his "elect" and another for the outside masses, though the main object of his reform consisted in initiating all, so far as it was permissible and prudent to do, without distinction of castes or wealth, to the great truths hitherto kept so secret by the selfish Brahmanical class. Gautama Buddha it was whom we see the first in the world's history, moved by that generous feeling which locks the whole humanity within one embrace, inviting the "poor," the "lame," and the "blind" to the King's festival table, from which he excluded those who had hitherto sat alone, in haughty seclusion. It was he, who, with a bold hand, first opened the door of the sanctuary to the pariah, the fallen one, and all those "afflicted by men" clothed in gold and purple, often far less worthy than the outcast to whom their finger was scornfully pointing. All this did Siddhârtha six centuries before another reformer, as noble and as loving, though less favored by opportunity, in another land. If both, aware of the great danger of furnishing an uncultivated populace with the double-edged weapon of *knowledge which gives power*, left the innermost corner of the sanctuary in the profoundest shade, who that is acquainted with human nature can blame them for it? But while one was actuated by prudence, the other was forced into such a course. Gautama left the esoteric and most dangerous portion of the "secret knowledge" untouched, and lived to the ripe old age of eighty, with the certainty of having taught the essential truths, and having converted to them one-third of the world; Jesus promised his disciples the knowledge which confers upon man the power *of producing far greater miracles than he ever did himself*, and he died, leaving but a few faithful men, only halfway to knowledge, to struggle with the world to which they could impart but what they *half*-knew themselves. Later, their followers disfigured truth still more than they themselves had done.

It is not true that Gautama never taught anything concerning a future life, or that he denied the immortality of the soul. Ask any intelligent Buddhist his ideas on Nirvâṇa, and he will unquestionably express himself, as the well-known Wong Ching Foo, the Chinese orator, now travelling in this country, did in a recent conversation with us about *Niepang* (Nirvâṇa). "This condition," he remarked, "we all understand to mean a final reunion with God, coincident with the perfection of the human spirit by its ultimate disembarrassment of matter. It is the very opposite of personal annihilation."

Nirvâṇa means the certitude of personal immortality in *Spirit*, not in *Soul*, which, as a finite emanation, must certainly disintegrate its particles — a compound of human sensations, passions, and yearning for some objective kind of existence — before the immortal spirit of the *Ego* is quite freed, and henceforth secure against further transmigration in any form. And how can man ever reach this state so long as the *Upâdâna*, that state of longing for *life*, more life, does not disappear from the sentient being, from the *Ahaṃkara* clothed, however, in a sublimated body? It is the "Upâdâna" or the intense desire which produces WILL, and it is *will* which develops *force*, and the latter generates *matter*, or an object having form. Thus the disembodied *Ego*, through this sole undying desire in him, unconsciously furnishes the conditions of his successive self-procreations in various forms, which depend on his mental state and *Karma*, the good or bad deeds of his preceding existence, commonly called "merit and demerit." This is why the "Master" recommended to his mendicants the cultivation of the four degrees of Dhyâna, the noble "Path of the Four Truths," *i.e.*, that gradual acquirement of stoical indifference for either life or death; that state of spiritual self-contemplation during which man utterly loses sight of his physical and dual individuality, composed of soul and body; and uniting himself with his third and higher immortal self, the *real and heavenly man*, merges, so to say, into the divine Essence, whence his own spirit proceeded like a spark from the common hearth. Thus the Arhat, the holy mendicant, can reach Nirvâṇa while yet on earth; and his spirit, totally freed from the trammels of the "psychical, terrestrial, *devilish* wisdom," as James calls it, and being in its own nature omniscient and omnipotent, can on earth, through the sole power of his *thought*, produce the greatest of phenomena.

"It is the missionaries in China and India, who first started this falsehood about Niepang, or Niepana (Nirvâṇa)," says Wong Ching Foo. Who can deny the truth of this accusation after reading the works of the Abbé Dubois, for instance? A missionary who passes forty years of his life in India, and then writes that the "Buddhists admit no other God but the body of man, and have no other object but the satisfaction of their senses," utters an untruth which can be proved on the testimony of the laws of the Talapoins of Siam and Burma; laws which prevail unto this very day and which sentence a *sahân*, or *punghi* (a learned man; from the Sanskrit *pundit*), as well as a simple Talapoin, to death by decapitation, for the crime of unchastity. No foreigner can be admitted into their *Kyums*, or *Vihâras* (monasteries); and yet there are French writers, otherwise impartial and fair, who, speaking of the great severity of the rules to which the Buddhist monks are subjected in these communities, and without possessing one single fact to corroborate their skepticism, bluntly say, that "notwithstanding the great laudations bestowed upon them [Talapoins] by certain travellers, merely on the *strength of appearances*, I do not believe at all in their chastity." *

Fortunately for the Buddhist talapoins, lamas, sahâns, upasampadâs,† and even sâmanêras, ‡ they have popular records and facts for themselves, which are weightier than the unsupported personal opinion of a Frenchman, born in Catholic lands, whom we can hardly blame for having lost all faith in clerical virtue. When a Buddhist monk becomes guilty (which does not happen once in a century, perhaps) of criminal conversation, he has neither a congregation of tender-hearted members, whom he can move to tears by an eloquent confession of his guilt, nor a Jesus, on whose overburdened, long-suffering bosom are flung, as in a common Christian dust box, all the impurities of the race. No Buddhist transgressor can comfort himself with visions of a Vatican, within whose sin-encompassing walls black is turned into white, murderers into sinless saints, and golden or silvery lotions can be bought at the confessional to cleanse the tardy penitent of greater or lesser offenses against God and man.

Except for a few impartial archaeologists who trace a direct Buddhistic element in Gnosticism, as in all those early short-lived sects, we know of a very few authors, who, in writing upon primitive Christianity, have accorded to the question its due importance. Have we not facts enough to, at least, suggest some interest in that direction? Do we not learn that as early as in the days of Plato there were "Brahmanes" — read Buddhist, Samanean, Saman or Shaman missionaries — in Greece, and that at one time they had overflowed the country? Does not Pliny show them established on the shores of the Dead Sea, for "thousands of ages"? After making every necessary allowance for the exaggeration, we still have several centuries B.C. left as a margin. And is it possible that their influence should not have left deeper traces in all these sects than is generally thought? We know that the Jaina sect claims Buddhism as derived from its tenets — that Buddhism existed before Siddhârtha, better known as Gautama Buddha. The Hindu Brahmans who, by

---

* Jacolliot, *Voyage au pays des éléphants* (1876), p. 252.

† Buddhist chief priests at Ceylon.

‡ Sâmanêra is one who studies to obtain the high office of a *Upasampadâ*. He is a disciple and is looked upon as a son by the chief priest. We suspect that the Catholic seminarist must look to the Buddhists for the parentage of his title.

the European Orientalists, are denied the right of knowing anything about their own country, or understanding their own language and records better than those who have never been in India, on the same principle as the Jews are forbidden, by the Christian theologians, to interpret their own Scriptures — the Brahmans, we say, have authentic records. And these show the incarnation from the Virgin Avany of the first Buddha — *divine light* — as having taken place more than some thousands of years B.C., on the island of Ceylon. The Brahmans reject the claim that it was an avatâra of Vishṇu, but admit the appearance of a reformer of Brahmanism at that time. The story of the Virgin Avany and her divine son, Śâkya-muni, is recorded in one of the sacred books of the Singhalese Buddhists — the *Culla-Niddesa*; and the Brahmanic chronology fixes the great Buddhistic revolution and religious war, and the subsequent spread of Śâkya-muni's doctrine in Thibet, China, Japan, and other places at 4620 years B.C.*[46]

It is clear that Gautama Buddha, the son of the King of Kapilavastu, and the descendant of the first Śâkya, through his father, who was of the Kshatriya or warrior-caste, did not invent his philosophy. Philanthropist by nature, his ideas were developed and matured while under the tuition of Tîrthaṃkara, the famous guru of the Jaina sect. The latter claim the present Buddhism as a diverging branch of their own philosophy, and themselves, as the only followers of the first Buddha who were allowed to remain in India, after the expulsion of all other Buddhists, probably because they had made a compromise, and admitted some of the Brahmanic notions. It is, to say the least, curious that three dissenting and inimical religions, like Brahmanism, Buddhism and Jainism, should agree so perfectly in their traditions and chronology as to Buddhism, and that our scientists should give a hearing but to their own unwarranted speculations and hypotheses. If the birth of Gautama may, with some show of reason, be placed at about 600 B.C., then the preceding Buddhas ought to have some place allowed them in chronology. The Buddhas are not gods, but simply individuals overshadowed by the spirit of *Buddha* — the divine ray. Or is it because, unable to extricate themselves from the difficulty by the help of their own researches only, our Orientalists prefer to obliterate and deny the whole, rather than accord to the Hindus the right of knowing something of their own religion and history? Strange way of discovering truths!

The common argument adduced against the Jaina claim, of having been the source of the restoration of ancient Buddhism, that the principal tenet of the latter religion is opposed to the belief of the Jainas, is not a

---

* Jacolliot declares in *Les fils de Dieu*, pp. 349, 352, that he copied these dates from the *Book of the Historical Zodiacs*, preserved in the pagoda of Villianûr.

sound one. Buddhists, say our Orientalists, deny the existence of a Supreme Being; the Jainas admit one, but protest against the assumption that the "He" can ever interfere in the regulation of the universe. We have shown in the preceding chapter that the Buddhists do not deny any such thing. But if any disinterested scholar could study carefully the Jaina literature, in their thousands of books preserved — or shall we say hidden — in Râjputâna, Jaisalmer, at Pattan, and other places;* and especially if he could but gain access to the oldest of their sacred volumes, he would find a perfect identity of philosophical thought, if not of popular rites, between the Jainas and the Buddhists. The *Âdi-Buddha* and *Âdinâtha* (or *Âdîśvara*) are identical in essence and purpose. And now, if we trace the Jainas back, with their claims to the ownership of the oldest cave-temples (those superb specimens of Indian architecture and sculpture), and their records of an almost incredible antiquity, we can hardly refuse to view them in the light which they claim for themselves. We must admit that in all probability they are the only true descendants of the primitive owners of old India, dispossessed by those conquering and mysterious hordes of white-skinned Brahmans whom, in the twilight of history, we see appearing at first as wanderers in the valleys of Jumnâ and Ganges. The books of the *Srâvakas* — the only descendants of the Arhats or earliest Jainas, the naked forest-hermits of the days of old, might throw some light, perhaps, on many a puzzling question. But will our European scholars, so long as they pursue their own policy, ever have access to the *right* volumes? We have our doubts about this. Ask any trustworthy Hindu how the missionaries have dealt with those manuscripts which unluckily fell into their hands, and then see if we can blame the natives for trying to save from desecration the "gods of their fathers."

To maintain their ground, Irenaeus and his school had to fight hard with the Gnostics. Such also was the lot of Eusebius, who found himself hopelessly perplexed to know how the Essenes should be disposed of. The ways and customs of Jesus and his apostles exhibited too close a resemblance to this sect to allow the fact to pass unexplained. Eusebius tried to make people believe that the Essenes were the first Christians. His efforts were thwarted by Philo Judaeus, who wrote his historical account of the Essenes and described them with the minutest care, long before there had appeared a single Christian in Palestine. But, if there were no *Christians*, there were Chrêstians long before the era of Christianity; and the Essenes belonged to the latter as well as to all other initiated brotherhoods, without even mentioning the Krishna-ites of India. Lepsius

---

* We were told that there were nearly 20,000 such books.

shows that the word *Nofer* means *Chrêstos*, "good," and that one of the titles of Osiris, "Onnofer" [*Un-nefer*], must be translated "the goodness of God made manifest." * "The worship of Christ was not universal at this early date," explains MacKenzie, "by which I mean that Christolatry had not been introduced; but the worship of *Chrêstos* — the Good Principle — had preceded it by many centuries, and even survived the general adoption of Christianity, as shown on monuments still in existence . . . Again, we have an inscription which is pre-Christian on an epitaphial tablet Spon, *Miscell. erud. antiq.*, x, xvii, 2), Ὑάκινθε Λαρισαίων Δημόσιε, Ἥρως Χρηστέ, Χαῖρε, and de Rossi (*Roma Sotterranea*, tome i, tav. xxi), gives us another example from the catacombs — 'Aelia Chrêste in Pace'." † And, *Kris*, as Jacolliot shows, means in Sanskrit "sacred." ‡

The meritorious stratagems of the trustworthy Eusebius § thus proved lost labor. He was triumphantly detected by Basnage,‖ who, says Gibbon, "examined with the most critical accuracy the curious treatise of Philo,¶ which describes the Therapeutae," and found that "by proving that it was composed as early as the time of Augustus, [he] has demonstrated, in spite of Eusebius and a crowd of modern Catholics, that the Therapeutae were neither Christians nor monks." **

As a last word, *Christian* Gnostics sprang into existence toward the beginning of the second century, and just at the time when the Essenes most mysteriously faded away, which indicated that they were the identical Essenes, and moreover pure *Christists*, viz.: they believed and were those who best understood what one of their own brethren had preached. In insisting that the letter Iota, mentioned by Jesus in *Matthew* (v, 18), indicated a secret doctrine in relation to the ten Aeôns, it is sufficient to demonstrate to a kabalist that Jesus belonged to the Freemasonry of those days; for "I," which is Iota in Greek, has other names in other languages; and is, as it was among the Gnostics of those days, a password, meaning the SCEPTER of the FATHER, in Eastern brotherhoods which exist to this very day.

But in the early centuries, these facts, if known, were purposely ignored, and not only withheld from public notice as much as possible, but vehemently denied whenever the question was forced upon discussion. The denunciations of the Fathers were rendered bitter in proportion to the truth of the claim which they endeavored to refute.

---

\* Lepsius, *Königsbuch*, b. 11, tal. i dyn. 5, h.p. In *1 Peter* ii, 3, Jesus is called "the Lord Chrêstos."
† MacKenzie, *Royal Masonic Cyclopaedia*, pp. 206-07.
‡ [*Christna*, etc., p. 357.]
§ [*Eccl. Hist.*, II, xvii.]
‖ [*Histoire des Juifs*, etc., II, ch. 20-23]
¶ [*De vita contemplativa.*]
\*\* [*Hist. of the Decline*, etc., ch. xv, note 163.]

"It comes to this," writes Irenaeus, complaining of the Gnostics, "they neither consent to Scripture nor tradition." * And why should we wonder at that, when even the commentators of the nineteenth century, with nothing but fragments of the Gnostic manuscripts to compare with the voluminous writings of their calumniators, have been enabled to detect fraud on nearly every page? How much more must the polished and learned Gnostics, with all their advantages of personal observation and knowledge of fact, have realized the stupendous scheme of fraud that was being consummated before their very eyes! Why should they accuse Celsus of maintaining that their religion was all based on the speculations of Plato, with the difference that his doctrines were far more pure and rational than theirs, when we find Sprengel, seventeen centuries later, writing the following? — "Not only did they [the Christians] think to discover the dogmas of Plato in the books of Moses, but, moreover, they fancied that, by introducing Platonism into Christianity, they would *elevate the dignity of this religion and make it more popular among the heathens.*" †

They introduced it so well, that not only was the Platonic philosophy selected as a basis for the trinity, but even the legends and mythical stories which had been current among the admirers of the great philosopher —as a time-honored homage to every hero worthy of deification—were revamped and used by the Christians. Without going so far as India, did they not have a ready model for the "miraculous conception," in the legend about Perictionê, Plato's mother? ‡ In her case it was also maintained by popular tradition that she had immaculately conceived him, and that the god Apollo was his father. Even the annunciation by an angel to Joseph "in a dream" the Christians copied from the message of Apollo to Ariston, Perictionê's husband, that the child to be born from her was the offspring of that god. So, too, Romulus was said to be the son of Mars, by the virgin Rhea Sylvia.

It is generally held by all the symbolical writers that the Ophites were found guilty of practicing the most licentious rites during their religious meetings. The same accusation was brought against the Manichaeans, the Carpocratians, the Paulicians, the Albigenses — in short, against every Gnostic sect which had the temerity to claim the right to think for itself. In our modern days, the 160 American sects and the 125 sects of England are not so often troubled with such accusations; times are changed, and even the once all-powerful clergy have either to bridle their tongues or prove their slanderous accusations.

We have carefully looked over the works of such authors as R. Payne

---

* *Adv. Haer.*, III, ii, 2.
† *Geschichte der Arzneikunde,* Vol. II, p. 200.
‡ [Diog. Laert., *Lives,* etc., "Plato," §1; Plutarch, *Sympos.*, Book VIII, i, 2.]

Knight, C. W. King, and Olshausen, which treat of our subject; we have reviewed the bulky volumes of Irenaeus, Tertullian, Sozomen, Theodoret; and in none but those of Epiphanius have we found any accusation based upon direct evidence of an eyewitness. "They say"; "*Some* say"; "We have heard" — such are the general and indefinite terms used by the patristic accusers. Alone, Epiphanius, whose works are invariably referred to in all such cases, seems to chuckle with delight whenever he couches a lance. We do not mean to take upon ourselves to defend the sects which inundated Europe at the eleventh century, and which brought to light the most wonderful creeds; we limit our defense merely to those Christian sects whose theories were usually grouped under the generic name of *Gnosticism*. These are those which appeared immediately after the alleged crucifixion, and lasted till they were nearly exterminated under the rigorous execution of the Constantinian law. The greatest guilt of these were their syncretistic views, for at no other period of the world's history had truth a poorer prospect of triumph than in those days of forgery, lying, and deliberate falsification of facts.

But before we are forced to believe the accusations, may we not be permitted to inquire into the historical characters of their accusers? Let us begin by asking, upon what ground does the Church of Rome build her claim of supremacy for her doctrines over those of the Gnostics? Apostolic succession, undoubtedly. The succession *traditionally* instituted by the direct Apostle Peter. But what if this prove a fiction? Clearly, the whole superstructure supported upon this one imaginary stilt would fall in a tremendous crash. And when we do inquire carefully, we find that we must take the word of Irenaeus *alone* for it — of Irenaeus, who did not furnish one single valid proof of the claim which he so audaciously advanced, and who resorted for that to endless forgeries. He gives authority neither for his dates nor his assertions. This Smyrniote worthy has not even the brutal but sincere faith of Tertullian, for he contradicts himself at every step, and supports his claims solely on acute sophistry. Though he was undoubtedly a man of the shrewdest intellect and great learning, he fears not, in some of his assertions and arguments, to even appear an idiot in the eyes of posterity, so long as he can "carry the situation." Twitted and cornered at every step by his not less acute and learned adversaries, the Gnostics, he boldly shields himself behind blind faith, and in answer to their merciless logic falls upon imaginary tradition invented by himself.* Reber wittily remarks: "As we read his misapplication of words and sentences, we would conclude that he was a lunatic if we did not know that he was something else." †

---

\* [Irenaeus, *Adv. Haer.*, III, iii, 3.]

† *The Christ of Paul*, p. 188; New York, 1876.

So boldly mendacious does this "holy Father" prove himself in many instances, that he is even contradicted by Eusebius, more cautious if not more truthful than himself. He is driven to that necessity in the face of unimpeachable evidence. So, for instance, Irenaeus asserts that Papias, Bishop of Hierapolis, was a direct hearer of St. John;* and Eusebius is compelled to show that Papias never pretended to such a claim, but simply stated that he had received his *doctrine from those who had known John.*†

In one point, the Gnostics had the best of Irenaeus. They drove him, through mere fear of inconsistency, to the recognition of their kabalistic doctrine of atonement; unable to grasp it in its allegorical meaning, Irenaeus presented, with Christian theology as we find it in its present state of "original sin *versus* Adam," a doctrine which would have filled Peter with pious horror if he had been still alive.

The next champion for the propagation of Apostolic Succession, is Eusebius himself. Is the word of this Armenian Father any better than that of Irenaeus? Let us see what the most competent critics say of him. And before we turn to modern critics at all, we might remind the reader of the scurrilous terms in which Eusebius is attacked by George Syncellus, the Vice-Patriarch of Constantinople (eighth century), for his audacious falsification of the Egyptian chronology. The opinion of Socrates, an historian of the fifth century, is no more flattering. He fearlessly charges Eusebius with perverting historical dates, in order to please the Emperor Constantine. ‡ In his chronographic work, before proceeding to falsify the synchronistic tables *himself*, in order to impart to Scriptural chronology a more trustworthy appearance, Syncellus covers Eusebius with the choicest of monkish Billingsgate. *Baron Bunsen has verified the justness if not justified the politeness of this abusive reprehension.* His elaborate researches in the rectification of the *Egyptian List of Chronology* by Manetho, led him to confess that throughout his work, the Bishop of Caesarea "had undertaken, in a very *unscrupulous and arbitrary spirit, to mutilate history.*" "Eusebius," he says, "is the originator of that systematic theory of synchronisms which has so often subsequently maimed and mutilated history in its Procrustean bed."§ To this the author of the *History of the Intellectual Development of Europe* adds: "Among those who have been the most guilty of this offense, the name of the celebrated Eusebius, the Bishop of Caesarea . . . should be designated"! ||

It will not be amiss to remind the reader that it is the same Eusebius who is charged with the interpolation of the famous paragraph concerning

---

* *Adv. Haer.,* V, xxxiii, §4.
† *Eccl. Hist.* III, xxxix.
‡ [Socrates Scholasticus, *Eccles. Hist.,* I, i.]
§ Bunsen, *Egypt's Place,* etc., Vol. I, p. 206; Vol. II, p. 438.
|| Draper, *op. cit.,* ch. vi.

Jesus, which was so miraculously found, in his time, in the writings of Josephus,* the sentence in question having till that time remained perfectly unknown. Renan, in his *Vie de Jésus*, expresses a contrary opinion. "I believe," says he, "the passage respecting Jesus to be authentic. *It is perfectly in the style of Josephus*; and, *if* this historian had made mention of Jesus, it is *thus* that he must have spoken of him." [Introductory.]

Begging this eminent scholar's pardon, we must again contradict him. Laying aside his cautious "*if*," we will merely show that though the short paragraph may possibly be genuine, and "perfectly in the style of Josephus," its several parentheses are most palpably later forgeries; and "*if*" Josephus had made any mention of Christ at all, it is *not* thus that he would "have spoken of him." The whole paragraph consists of but a few lines, and reads: "At this time was *Iêsous*, a 'WISE MAN,' † if, at least, *it is right to call him a man* [ἄνδρα], for he was a doer of surprising works, and a teacher of such men as receive 'the truths' with pleasure . . . *This was the* ANOINTED [!!]. And, on an accusation by the first men among us, having been condemned by Pilate to the cross, they did not stop loving him who loved them. For *he appeared to them on the third day alive*, and the divine prophets having said these and many other wonderful things concerning him." 47

This paragraph (of sixteen lines in the original) has two unequivocal assertions and one qualification. The latter is expressed in the following sentence: "If, at least, it is right to call him a man." The unequivocal assertions are contained in "This is the ANOINTED," and in that Jesus "appeared to them *on the third day alive*." History shows us Josephus as a thorough, uncompromising, stiff-necked, orthodox Jew, though he wrote for "the Pagans." It is well to observe the false position in which these sentences would have placed a true-born Jew, if they had really emanated from him. Their "Messiah" was then and is still expected. The Messiah is the *Anointed*, and *vice versa*. And Josephus is made to admit that the "first men" among them have accused and crucified *their Messiah* and Anointed!! No need to comment any further upon such a preposterous incongruity,‡ even though supported by so ripe a scholar as Renan.

As to that patristic firebrand, Tertullian, whom des Mousseaux apotheosizes in company with his other demigods, he is regarded by Reuss, Baur and Schwegler, in quite a different light. The untrustworthiness of statement and inaccuracy of Tertullian, says the author of *Supernatural Religion*, are

---

\* *Antiquities*, XVIII, 63-64.

† "Wise man" always meant with the ancients a kabalist. It means astrologer and magician. (Jost, *The Israelite Indeed*, III, p. 206.) Ḥakim is a physician.

‡ Dr. Lardner rejects it as spurious, and gives *nine* reasons for rejecting it. [Cf. *The Credibility of the Gospel History*.]

often apparent.* Reuss characterizes his Christianism as "*âpre, insolent, brutal, ferrailleur*. It is without unction and without charity, sometimes even *without loyalty*, when he finds himself confronted with opposition . . . If in the second century all parties except certain Gnostics were intolerant, Tertullian was the most intolerant of all"! †

The work begun by the early Fathers was achieved by the sophomorical Augustine. His supra-transcendental speculations of the Trinity; his imaginary dialogues with the Father, Son and the Holy Spirit, and the *disclosures* and covert allusions about his ex-brethren, the Manichaeans, have led the world to load Gnosticism with opprobrium, and have thrown into a deep shadow the insulted majesty of the one God, worshipped in reverential silence by every "heathen."

*And thus it is that the whole pyramid of Roman Catholic dogmas rests not upon proof but upon assumption.* The Gnostics had cornered the Fathers too cleverly, and *the only salvation of the latter was a resort to forgery*. For nearly four centuries, the great historians nearly contemporary with Jesus had not taken the slightest notice either of his life or death. Christians wondered at such an unaccountable omission of what the Church considered the greatest events in the world's history. Eusebius saved the battle of the day. Such are the men who have slandered the Gnostics.

The first and most unimportant sect we hear of is that of the *Nicolaitans*, of whom John, in the *Apocalypse*, makes the voice in his vision say that he hates their doctrine.‡ These Nicolaitans were the followers, however, of Nicolas of Antioch, one of the "seven" chosen by the "twelve" to make distribution from the common fund to the proselytes at Jerusalem (*Acts* ii, 44, 45; vi, 1-5), hardly more than a few weeks, or perhaps months, after the Crucifixion; § and a man "of honest report, *full of the Holy Ghost and wisdom*" (verse 3). Thus it would appear that the "Holy Ghost and wisdom" from on high were no more a shield against the accusation of "heresy" than though they had never overshadowed the "chosen ones" of the apostles.

It would be but too easy to detect what kind of heresy it was that offended, even had we not other and more authentic sources of information in the kabalistic writings. The accusation and the precise nature of the "abomination" are stated in the second chapter of the book of *Revelation*, verses 14, 15. The sin was merely — *marriage*. John was a

---

* Vol. II, Pt. II, ch. vii, pp. 89-90.

†[*Revue de théologie,* XV, 1857, pp. 67 *et seq.*]

‡ *Revelation* ii, 6, 15.

§ Philip, the first martyr, was one of the seven, and he was stoned about the year A.D. 34.

"virgin"; several of the Fathers assert the fact on the authority of tradition. Even Paul, the most liberal and high-minded of them all, finds it difficult to reconcile the position of a married man with that of a faithful servant of God. There is also "a difference between a wife and a virgin." The latter cares "for the things of the Lord," and the former only for "how she may please her husband." * "If any man think that he behaveth uncomely toward his virgin . . . let them marry. Nevertheless, he that standeth steadfast in his heart . . . and hath power over his own will, and hath so decreed . . . that he will keep *his virgin*, doeth well." So that he who marries "doeth well . . . but he that giveth her not in marriage *doeth better*." † "Art thou loosed from a wife?" he asks, "seek not a wife" (27). And remarking that according to his judgment, both will be happier if they do not marry, he adds, as a weighty conclusion: "And I think also that I have the Spirit of God" (40). Far from this spirit of tolerance are the words of John. According to his vision there are "but the hundred and forty and four thousand, which were *redeemed* from the earth," and "these are they which were not defiled with women; for *they are virgins*." ‡ This seems conclusive; for except Paul there is not one of these primitive *Nazari*, there "set apart" and vowed to God, who seemed to make a great difference between "sin" within the relationship of legal marriage, and the "abomination" of adultery.

With such views and such narrow-mindedness, it was but natural that these fanatics should have begun by casting this *iniquity* as a slur in the faces of brethren, and then "bearing on progressively" with their accusations. As we have already shown, it is only Epiphanius whom we find giving such minute details as to the Masonic "grips" and other signs of recognition among the Gnostics. He had once belonged to their number, and therefore it was easy for him to furnish particulars. Only how far the worthy Bishop is to be relied upon is a very grave question. One need fathom human nature but very superficially to find that there seldom yet has been a traitor or a renegade who in a moment of danger turned "State's evidence," who would not lie as remorselessly as he betrayed. Men never forgive or relent toward those whom they injure. We hate our victims in proportion to the harm we do them. This is a truth as old as the world. On the other hand, it is preposterous to believe that such persons as the Gnostics who, according to Gibbon, § were the wealthiest, proudest, most polite, as well as the most learned "of the Christian name," were guilty of the disgusting, libidinous actions of which Epiphanius delights to accuse them. Were they even like that "set of tatterde-

---

* *1 Corinthians* vii, 34.
† *Ibid.*, 36-37.
‡ *Revelation* xiv, 3, 4.
§ [*Hist. of the Decline*, etc., I, xv.]

malions, almost naked, with fierce looks," that Lucian describes as Paul's followers,* we would hesitate to believe such an infamous story. How much less probable then that men who were Platonists, as well as Christians, should have ever been guilty of such preposterous rites.

R. Payne Knight seems never to suspect the testimony of Epiphanius. He argues that "if we make allowance for the willing exaggerations of religious hatred, and consequent popular prejudice, the general conviction that these sectarians had rites and practices of a licentious character appears too strong to be entirely disregarded." † If he draws an honest line of demarcation between the Gnostics of the first three centuries and those mediaeval sects whose doctrines "rather closely resembled modern communism," we have nothing to say. Only, we would beg every critic to remember that if the Templars were accused of that most "abominable crime" of applying the "holy kiss" to the root of Baphomet's tail,‡ St. Augustine is also suspected, and on very good grounds, too, of having allowed his community to go somewhat astray from the primitive way of administering the "holy kiss" at the feast of the Eucharist. The holy Bishop seems quite too anxious as to certain details of the ladies' toilet for the "kiss" to be of a strictly orthodox nature. § Wherever there lurks a true and sincere religious feeling, there is no room for worldly details.

Considering the extraordinary dislike exhibited from the first by Christians to all manner of cleanliness, we cannot wonder enough at such a strange solicitude on the part of the holy Bishop for his female parishioners, unless, indeed, we have to excuse it on the ground of a lingering reminiscence of Manichaean rites!

It would be hard, indeed, to blame any writer for entertaining such suspicions of immorality as those above noticed, when the records of many historians are at hand to help us to make an impartial investigation. "Heretics" are accused of crimes in which the Church has more or less openly indulged even down to the beginning of our century. In 1233 Pope Gregory IV issued two bulls against the Stedingers "for various *heathen* and magical practices," ‖ and the latter, as a matter of course, were exterminated in the name of Christ and his Holy Mother. In 1282, a parish priest of Inverkeithing named John performed rites on Easter day by far worse than "magical." Collecting a crowd of young girls, he forced them to enter into "divine ecstasies" and Bacchanalian fury, dancing the

---

* *Philopatris,* in R. Taylor, *The Diegesis,* etc., p. 376; Boston, 1832.
† [*A Discourse on the Worship of Priapus,* etc., London, 1865, pp. 175-76.]
‡ King, *The Gnostics,* etc., p. 420, note [2nd ed., 1887.]
§ *Sermones,* clii. See R. P. Knight, *op. cit.,* p. 107.
‖ Baronius, *Annales Ecclesiastici,* Vol. XXI, Anno 1233, § 41.

old Amazonian circle-dance around the figure of the heathen "god of the gardens." Notwithstanding that upon the complaint of some of his parishioners he was cited before his bishop, he retained his benefice because he proved that *such was the common usage of the country.*\* The Waldenses, those "earliest Protestants," were accused of the most unnatural horrors; burned, butchered, and exterminated for calumnies heaped upon them by their accusers. Meanwhile the latter, in open triumph, formed their heathen processions of "Corpus Christi," with emblems modelled on those of Baal-Peor and "Osiris," and every city in Southern France carried, in yearly processions on Easter days, loaves and cakes fashioned like the so-much-decried emblems of the Hindu Śivaites and Vishṇuites, as late as 1825! †

Deprived of their old means for slandering Christian sects whose religious views differ from their own, it is now the turn of the "heathen," Hindus, Chinese and Japanese, to share with the ancient religions the honor of having cast in their teeth denunciations of their "libidinous religions."

Without going far for proofs of equal if not surpassing immorality, we would remind Roman Catholic writers of certain *bas-reliefs* on the doors of St. Peter's Cathedral. They are as brazenfaced as the door itself; but less so than any author, who, knowing all this, feigns to ignore historical facts. A long succession of Popes have reposed their pastoral eyes upon these brazen pictures of the vilest obscenity, through these many centuries, without even finding the slightest necessity for removing them. Quite the contrary; for we might name certain Popes and Cardinals who made it a lifelong study to copy these heathen suggestions of "nature-gods," in practice as well as in theory.

In Polish Podolia there was, some years ago in a Roman Catholic Church, a statue of Christ in black marble. It was reputed to perform miracles on certain days, such as having its hair and beard grow in the sight of the public, and indulging in other *less* innocent wonders. This show was finally prohibited by the Russian Government. When in 1585 the Protestants took Embrun (Department of the Upper Alps), they found in the churches of this town relics of such a character that, as the Chronicle expresses it, "old Huguenot soldiers were seen to blush, several weeks after, at the bare mention of the discovery." In a corner of the Church of St. Fiacre, near Monceaux in France, there was — and it still is there, if we mistake not — a seat called "the chair of St. Fiacre,"

---

\* *Chronicon de Lanercost,* 1201-1346, etc.; ed. J. Stevenson, Edinb., 1839, p. 109.

† Dulaure, *Histoire abrégée des différents cultes,* Vol. II, p. 285; Martezzi, *Pagani e Cristiani,"* p. 78.

which had the reputation of conferring fecundity upon barren women. A rock in the vicinity of Athens, not far from the so-called "Tomb of Socrates," is said to be possessed of the same virtue. When, some twenty years since, the Queen Amelia [of Greece], perhaps in a merry moment, was said to have tried the experiment, there was no end of most insulting abuse heaped upon her by a Catholic Padre, on his way through Syra to some mission. The Queen, he declared, was a "superstitious heretic"! "an abominable witch"! "Jezebel using magic arts"! Much more the zealous missionary would doubtless have added, had he not found himself, right in the middle of his vituperations, landed in a pool of mud outside the window. The virtuous elocutionist was forced to this unusual transit by the strong arm of a Greek officer, who happened to enter the room at the right moment.

There never was a great religious reform that was not pure at the beginning. The first followers of Buddha, as well as the disciples of Jesus, were all men of the highest morality. The aversion felt by the reformers of all ages to vice under any shape is proven in the cases of Śâkyamuni, Pythagoras, Plato, Jesus, St. Paul, Ammonius Saccas. The great Gnostic leaders — if less successful — were not less virtuous in practice nor less morally pure. Marcion, Basilides, Valentinus,* were renowned for their ascetic lives. The Nicolaitans, who, if they did not belong to the great body of the Ophites, were numbered among the small sects which were absorbed in it at the beginning of the second century, owe their origin, as we have shown, to Nicolas of Antioch, "a man of honest report, full of the Holy Ghost and wisdom." How absurd the idea that such men would have instituted "libidinous rites." As well accuse Jesus of having promoted the similar rites which we find practiced so extensively by the mediaeval *orthodox* Christians behind the secure shelter of monastic walls.

If, however, we are asked to credit such an accusation against the Gnostics, an accusation transferred with tenfold acrimony, centuries later, to the unfortunate heads of the Templars, why should we not believe the same of the orthodox Christians? Minucius Felix states that "the first Christians were accused by the world of inducing [during the ceremony of the "Perfect Passover"] each neophyte on his admission to plunge a knife into an infant concealed under a heap of flour; the body then serving for a banquet to the whole congregation. After they had become the dominant party, they [the Christians] transferred the charge to their own dissenters." †

---

\* Valentinus is termed by Tertullian a Platonist. [*De praescr. haer.*, vii.]

† C. W. King, *The Gnostics and Their Remains*, p. 197, footnote 1 [pp. 124, 334, in 2nd ed., 1887].

The real crime of heterodoxy is plainly stated by John in his *Epistles* and *Gospel*: he "who confesseth not that Jesus Christ is come in the flesh . . . is a deceiver and *an antichrist*" (2 *John* 7). In his previous *Epistle*, he teaches his flock that there are *two* trinities (*1 John* v, 7, 8) — in short, the Nazarene system.

The inference to be drawn from all this is that the made-up and dogmatic Christianity of the Constantinian period is simply an offspring of the numerous conflicting sects, half-castes themselves, born of Pagan parents. Each of these could claim representatives converted to the so-called *orthodox* body of Christians. And, as every newly-born dogma had to be carried out by the majority of votes, every sect colored the main substance with its own hue, till the moment when the emperor enforced this *revealed olla-podrida*, of which he evidently did not himself understand a word, upon an unwilling world as the *religion of Christ*. Wearied in the vain attempt to sound this fathomless bog of international speculations, unable to appreciate a religion based on the pure spirituality of an ideal conception, Christendom gave itself up to the adoration of brutal force as represented by a Church backed up by Constantine. Since then, among the thousand rites, dogmas and ceremonies copied from Paganism, the Church can claim but one invention as thoroughly original with her — namely, the doctrine of eternal damnation, and one custom, that of the anathema. The Pagans rejected both with horror. "An execration is a fearful and grievous thing," says Plutarch. "Wherefore, the priestess at Athens was commended for refusing to curse Alcibiades [for desecration of the Mysteries] when the people required her to do it; *for*, she said, *that she was a priestess of prayers and not of curses*." \*

"Deep researches would show," says Renan, "that nearly everything in Christianity is mere baggage brought from the Pagan Mysteries. The primitive Christian worship is nothing but a *mystery*. The whole interior police of the Church, the degrees of initiation, the command of silence, and a crowd of phrases in the ecclesiastical language, have no other origin. The revolution which overthrew Paganism *seems* at first glance . . . an absolute rupture with the past . . . but *the popular faith saved its most familiar symbols from shipwreck*. Christianity introduced, at first, so little change into the habits of private and social life, that with great numbers in the fourth and fifth centuries it remains uncertain whether they were Pagans or Christians; many seem even to have pursued an irresolute course between the two worships." Speaking further of *Art*, which formed an essential part of the ancient religion, he says that "*it had to break with scarce one of its traditions*. Primitive Christian art is

---

\*Plutarch, *Alcibiades*, § 22; *Roman Questions*, § 44.

really nothing but Pagan art in its decay, or its lower departments. The Good Shepherd of the catacombs in Rome is a copy from the Aristaeus, or from the Apollo Nomios, which figure in the same posture on the Pagan sarcophagi, and still carries the flute of Pan in the midst of the four half-naked seasons. On the Christian tomb of the Cemetery of St. Calixtus, Orpheus charms the animals. Elsewhere, the Christ as Jupiter-Pluto, and Mary as Proserpine, receive the souls that Mercury, wearing the broad-brimmed hat and carrying in his hand the rod of the soul-guide (*psychopompos*), brings to them, in presence of the three fates. Pegasus, the symbol of the apotheosis; Psychê, the symbol of the immortal soul; Heaven, personified by an old man; the river Jordan; and Victory, figure on a host of Christian monuments." *

As we have elsewhere shown, the primitive Christian community was composed of small groups scattered about and organized in secret societies, with passwords, grips and signs. To avoid the relentless persecutions of their enemies, they were obliged to seek safety and hold meetings in deserted catacombs, the fastnesses of mountains, and other safe retreats. Like disabilities were naturally encountered by each religious reform at its inception. From the very first appearance of Jesus and his twelve disciples, we see them congregating apart, having secure refuges in the wilderness, and among friends in Bethany, and elsewhere. Were Christianity not composed of "*secret communities*" from the start, history would have more *facts* to record of its founder and disciples than it has.

How little Jesus had impressed his personality upon his own century, is calculated to astound the inquirer. Renan shows that Philo, who died toward the year 50, and was born many years earlier than Jesus, living all the while in Palestine while the "glad tidings" were being preached all over the country, according to the *Gospels*, had never heard of him! [48] Josephus, the historian, who was born three or four years after the death of Jesus, mentions his execution in a short sentence, and even those few words were altered "by a *Christian hand*," says the author of the *Vie de Jésus*.† Writing at the close of the first century, when Paul, the learned propagandist, is said to have founded so many churches, and Peter is alleged to have established the apostolic succession, which the Irenaeo-Eusebian chronology shows to have already included three bishops of Rome, ‡ Josephus, the painstaking enumerator and careful historian of even the most unimportant sects, entirely ignores the existence of a Christian sect. Suetonius, secretary of Hadrian, writing in the first quarter

---

\* [Renan, "Des religions de l'antiquité, etc.," in *Revue des Deux Mondes*, May 15, 1853.]

† [Introd. and ch. xxviii.]

‡ Linus, Analectus and Clement.

of the second century, knows so little of Jesus or his history as to say that the Emperor Claudius "banished all the Jews, who were continually making disturbances, at the instigation of one *Chrêstos*," meaning Christ, we must suppose.* The Emperor Hadrian himself, writing still later, was so little impressed with the tenets or importance of the new sect, that in a letter to Servianus he shows that he believes the Christians to be worshippers of Serapis.† "In the second century," says C. W. King, "the syncretistic sects had sprung up in Alexandria, the very hotbed of Gnosticism, found out in Serapis a prophetic type of Christ as the Lord and Creator of all, and Judge of the living and the dead." Thus, while the "Pagan" philosophers had never viewed Serapis, or rather the abstract idea which was embodied in him, as otherwise than a representation of the Anima Mundi, the Christians anthropomorphized the "Son of God" and his "Father," finding no better model for him than the idol of a Pagan myth! "There can be no doubt," remarks the same author, "that the head of Serapis, marked as the face is by a grave and pensive majesty, supplied the first idea for the conventional portraits of the Savior." ‡

In the notes taken by a traveller — whose episode with the monks on Mount Athos we have mentioned elsewhere — we find that, during his early life, Jesus had frequent intercourse with the Essenes belonging to the Pythagorean school, and known as the *Koinobioi*. We believe it rather hazardous on the part of Renan to assert so dogmatically, as he does, that Jesus "ignored the very name of Buddha, of Zoroaster, of Plato"; that he had never read a Greek nor a Buddhistic book, "although he had more than one element in him, which, unawares to him, proceeded from Buddhism, Parsism, and the Greek wisdom." § This is conceding half a miracle, and allowing as much to chance and coincidence. It is an abuse of privilege when an author, who claims to write historical facts, draws convenient deductions from hypothetical premises, and then calls it a biography — a *Life* of Jesus. No more than any other compiler of legends concerning the problematical history of the Nazarene prophet, has Renan one inch of secure foothold upon which to maintain himself; nor can anyone else assert a claim to the contrary, except on inferential evidence. And yet, while Renan has not one solitary fact to show that Jesus had never studied the metaphysical tenets of Buddhism and Parsism, or heard of the philosophy of Plato, his oppo-

---

\* *Lives of the Caesars*: "Claudius," § 25.

† F. Vopiscus, *Vita Saturnini*, in *Scriptores historiae Augustae*, viii.

‡ King, *The Gnostics*, etc., p. 68 [pp. 161-62 in 2nd ed.]. In R. Payne Knight's *Symbolical Language of Ancient Art and Mythology*, Serapis is represented as wearing his hair long, "formally turned back and disposed in ringlets hanging down upon his breast and shoulders like that of women. His whole person too is always enveloped in drapery reaching to his feet" (§ cxlv). This is the conventional picture of Christ.

§ *Vie de Jésus*, ch. xxviii.

nents have the best reasons in the world to suspect the contrary. When they find that — 1, all his sayings are in a Pythagorean spirit, when not *verbatim* repetitions; 2, his code of ethics is purely Buddhistic; 3, his mode of action and walk in life, Essenean; and 4, his mystical mode of expression, his parables, and his ways, those of an initiate, whether Grecian, Chaldean, or Magian (for the "Perfect," who spoke the *hidden* wisdom, were of the same school of archaic learning the world over), it is difficult to escape from the logical conclusion that he belonged to that same body of initiates. It is a poor compliment paid the Supreme, this forcing upon Him four gospels, in which, contradictory as they often are, there is not a single narrative, sentence, or peculiar expression, whose parallel may not be found in some older doctrine or philosophy. Surely, the Almighty — were it but to spare future generations their present perplexity — might have brought down with Him, at His *first and only* incarnation on earth, something original — something that would trace a distinct line of demarcation between Himself and the score or so of incarnate Pagan gods, who had been born of virgins, had all been saviors, and were either killed, or otherwise sacrificed themselves for humanity.

Too much has already been conceded to the emotional side of the story. What the world needs is a less exalted, but more faithful view of a personage, in whose favor nearly half of Christendom has dethroned the Almighty. It is not the erudite, world-famous scholar, whom we question for what we find in his *Vie de Jésus*, nor is it one of his *historical* statements. We simply challenge a few unwarranted and untenable assertions that have found their way past the emotional narrator, into the otherwise beautiful pages of the work—a life built altogether on mere probabilities, and yet that of one who, if accepted as an historical personage, has far greater claims upon our love and veneration, fallible as he is with all his greatness, than if we figure him as an omnipotent God. It is but in the latter character that Jesus must be regarded by every reverential mind as a failure.

Notwithstanding the paucity of old philosophical works now extant, we could find no end of instances of perfect identity between Pythagorean, Hindu, and *New Testament* sayings. There is no lack of proofs upon this point. What is needed is a Christian public that will examine what will be offered, and show common honesty in rendering its verdict. Bigotry has had its day, and done its worst. "We need not be frightened," says Professor Müller, "if we discover traces of truth, traces even of Christian truth, among the sages and lawgivers of other nations." *

After reading the following philosophical aphorisms, who can believe that Jesus and Paul had never read the Grecian and Indian philosophers?

---

* [*Chips*, etc., Vol. I, p. 55.]

| Sentences from Sextus, the Pythagorean, and other Heathen. | Verses from the New Testament.* |
|---|---|
| 1. "Possess those things which no one can take from you." † | 1. "Lay not up for yourselves treasures upon earth, where moth and rust doth corrupt, and where thieves break through and steal" *Matthew* vi, 19). |
| 2. "As it is better for a part of the body to be burnt, than to continue in the state in which it is, thus also is it better for a depraved man to die than to live." ‡ | 2. "And if thy hand offend thee, cut it off; it is better for thee to enter *unto life* maimed, than having two hands to go into hell," etc. (*Mark* ix, 43). |
| 3. "You have in yourself something *similar to God*, and therefore use yourself *as the temple of God*." § | 3. "Know ye not that ye are *the temple of God*, and that the Spirit of God dwelleth in you?" (*1 Cor.* iii, 16). |
| 4. "The greatest honor which can be paid to God, is to know and imitate him." ¶ | 4. "That ye may be the children of your Father which is in Heaven . . . be ye therefore perfect even as your *Father* which is in heaven *is perfect* (*Matthew* v, 45-48). |
| 5. "What I do not wish men to do to me, I also wish not to do to men" (*Analects of Confucius*, ch. v, xv; see Max Müller's *Chips*, I, pp. 304 *et seq.*). | 5. "Do ye unto others as ye would that others should do to you." |
| 6. "The moon shines even in the house of the wicked" (*Manu*). | 6. "He maketh his sun to rise on the evil and the good, and sendeth rain on the just and on the unjust" (*Matthew* v, 45). |
| 7. "They who give, have things given to them; those who withhold, have things taken from them" (*ibid.*). | 7. "Whosoever hath, to him shall be given . . . but whosoever hath not, from him shall be taken away even that he hath" (*Matthew* xiii, 12). |
| 8. "Purity of mind alone sees God" (*Ibid.*) —still a popular saying in India. | 8. "Blessed are the pure in heart, for they shall see God" (*Matthew* v, 8). |

Plato did not conceal the fact that he derived his best philosophical doctrines from Pythagoras, and that he himself was merely the first to reduce them to systematic order, occasionally interweaving with them metaphysical speculations of his own. But Pythagoras himself got his recondite doctrines, first from the descendants of Mochus, and later from the Brahmans of India. He was also initiated into the Mysteries among the hierophants of Thebes, the Persian and Chaldean Magi. Thus, step by step do we trace the origin of

---

\* See *Mishnah Pirke Aboth*; a Collection of Proverbs and Sentences of the old Jewish Teachers, in which many New Testament sayings are found. [ed. Strack, Karlsruhe, 1882.]

† Thos. Taylor, *Iamblichus' Life of Pythagoras*, "Select Sentences of Sextus the Pythagorean," p. 271.

‡ *Ibid.*, from Iamblichus' *Protreptics*, p. 279.

§ *Ibid.*, from Sextus, p. 269.

¶ *Ibid.*

most of our Christian doctrines to Middle Asia. Drop out from Christianity the personality of Jesus, so sublime because of its unparalleled simplicity, and what remains? History and comparative theology echo back the melancholy answer, "A crumbling skeleton formed of the oldest Pagan myths"!

While the mythical birth and life of Jesus are a faithful copy of those of the Brahmanical Kṛishṇa, his historical character of a religious reformer in Palestine is the true type of Buddha in India. In more than one respect their great resemblance in philanthropic and spiritual aspirations, as well as external circumstances, is truly striking. Though the son of a king, while Jesus was but a carpenter, Buddha was not of the high Brahmanical caste by birth. Like Jesus, he felt dissatisfied with the dogmatic spirit of the religion of his country, the intolerance and hypocrisy of the priesthood, their outward show of devotion, and their useless ceremonials and prayers. As Buddha broke violently through the traditional laws and rules of the Brahmans, so did Jesus declare war against the Pharisees and the proud Sadducees. What the Nazarene did as a consequence of his humble birth and position, Buddha did as a voluntary penance. He travelled about as a beggar; and — again like Jesus — later in life he sought by preference the companionship of publicans and sinners. Each aimed at a social as well as at a religious reform; and giving a death-blow to the old religion of his country, each became the founder of a new one.

"The reform of Buddha," says Max Müller, "had originally much more of a social than of a religious character . . . The most important element of the Buddhist reform has always been its social and moral code, not its metaphysical theories. *That moral code . . . is one of the most perfect which the world has ever known* . . . and he whose meditations had been how to deliver the soul of man from misery and the fear of death, had delivered the people of India from a degrading thralldom and from priestly tyranny." Further, the lecturer adds that were it otherwise, "Buddha might have taught whatever philosophy he pleased, and we should hardly have heard his name. The people would not have minded him, and his system would only have been a drop in the ocean of philosophic speculation, by which India was deluged at all times." *

The same with Jesus. While Philo, whom Renan calls Jesus' elder brother, Hillel, Shammai and Gamaliel, are hardly mentioned — Jesus has become a God! And still, pure and divine as was the moral code taught by Christ, it never could have borne comparison with that of Buddha, but for the tragedy of Calvary. That which helped forward the deification of Jesus was his dramatic death, the voluntary sacrifice of his life, alleged to have been made for the sake of mankind, and the later

---

* *Chips*, etc., "Buddhism," pp. 219-20.

convenient dogma of the atonement, invented by the Christians. In India, where life is valued as of no account, the crucifixion would have produced little effect, if any. In a country where — as all the Indianists are well aware — religious fanatics set themselves to dying by inches, in penances lasting for years; where the most fearful macerations are self-inflicted by fakirs; where young and delicate widows, in a spirit of bravado against the government, as much as out of religious fanaticism, mount the funeral pile with a smile on their faces; where, to quote the words of the great lecturer, "men in the prime of life throw themselves under the car of Jaggernâth, to be crushed to death by the idol they believe in; where the plaintiff who cannot get redress starves himself to death at the door of his judge; where the philosopher who thinks he has learnt all which this world can teach him, and who longs for absorption into the Deity, quietly steps into the Ganges, in order to arrive to the other shore of existence," * in such a country even a voluntary crucifixion would have passed unnoticed. In Judaea, and even among braver nations than the Jews — the Romans and the Greeks — where everyone clung more or less to life, and most people would have fought for it with desperation, the tragical end of the great Reformer was calculated to produce a profound impression. The names of even such minor heroes as Mucius Scaevola, Horatius Cocles, the mother of the Gracchi, and others, have descended to posterity; and, during our schooldays, as well as later in life, their histories have awakened our sympathy and commanded a reverential admiration. But, can we ever forget the scornful smile of certain Hindus at Benares, when an English lady, the wife of a clergyman, tried to impress them with the greatness of the sacrifice of Jesus, in giving *his* life for us? Then, for the first time the idea struck us how much the pathos of the great drama of Calvary had to do with subsequent events in the foundation of Christianity. Even the imaginative Renan was moved by this feeling to write in the last chapter of his *Vie de Jésus*, a few pages of singular and sympathetic beauty.†

---

* Max Müller, "Christ and other Masters," *Chips*, Vol. I, p. 58.

† *Das Leben Jesu* by Strauss, which Renan calls "*un livre commode, exact, spirituel et consciencieux*" (a handy, exact, witty, and conscientious book), rude and iconoclastic as it is, is nevertheless in many ways preferable to the *Vie de Jésus*, of the French author. Laying aside the intrinsic and historical value of the two works — with which we have nothing to do, we now simply point to Renan's distorted outline-sketch of Jesus. We cannot think what led Renan into such an erroneous delineation of character. Few of those who, while rejecting the divinity of the Nazarene prophet, still believe that he is no myth, can read the work without experiencing an uneasy, and even angry feeling at such a psychological mutilation. He makes of Jesus a sort of sentimental ninny, a theatrical simpleton, enamored of his own poetical divagations and speeches, wanting everyone to adore him, and finally caught in the snares of his enemies. Such was not Jesus, the Jewish philanthropist, the adept and mystic of a

Apollonius, a contemporary of Jesus of Nazareth, was, like him, an enthusiastic founder of a new spiritual school. Perhaps less metaphysical and more practical than Jesus, less tender and perfect in his nature, he nevertheless inculcated the same quintessence of spirituality, and the same high moral truths. His great mistake was to confine them too closely to the higher classes of society. While to the poor and the humble Jesus preached "Peace on earth and good will to men," Apollonius was the friend of kings, and moved with the aristocracy. He was born among the latter, and himself a man of wealth, while the "Son of man," representing the people, "had not where to lay his head"; nevertheless, the two "miracle-workers" exhibited striking similarity of purpose. Still earlier than Apollonius had appeared Simon Magus, called "the great Power of God." His "miracles" are both more wonderful, more varied, and better attested than those either of the apostles or of the Galilean philosopher himself. Materialism denies the fact in both cases, but history affirms. Apollonius followed both; and how great and renowned were his miraculous works in comparison with those of the alleged founder of Christianity as the kabalists claim, we have history again, and Justin Martyr, to corroborate.*

Like Buddha and Jesus, Apollonius was the uncompromising enemy of all outward show of piety, all display of useless religious ceremonies and hypocrisy. If, like the Christian Savior, the sage of Tyana had by preference sought the companionship of the poor and humble; and if instead of dying comfortably, at over one hundred years of age, he had been a voluntary martyr, proclaiming divine Truth from a cross,† his

---

school now forgotten by the Christians and the Church — if it ever was known to her; the hero, who preferred even to risk death, rather than withhold some truths which he believed would benefit humanity. We prefer Strauss who openly names him an impostor and a pretender, occasionally calling in doubt his very existence; but who at least spares him that ridiculous color of sentimentalism in which Renan paints him.

* See chap. III, p. 97 of the present volume.

† In a recent work, called *The World's Sixteen Crucified Saviors* (by Mr. Kernsey Graves) which attracted our notice by its title, we were indeed startled, as we were forewarned on the title page we should be, by *historical* evidences to be found neither in history nor tradition. Apollonius, who is represented in it as one of these sixteen "saviors," is shown by the author as finally "*crucified* . . . having risen from the dead . . . appearing to his disciples after his resurrection, and" — like Christ again — "convincing a *Tommy* [?] Didymus by getting him to feel the print of the nails in his hands and feet" (p. 305, ed. 1875). To begin with, neither Philostratus, the biographer of Apollonius, nor history says any such things. Though the precise time of his death is unknown, no disciple of Apollonius ever said that he was either crucified or appeared to them. So much for one "Savior." After that we are told that Gautama Buddha, whose life and death have been so minutely described by several authorities, Barthélemy Saint-Hilaire included, was also "*crucified* by his enemies near the foot of the Nepal

blood might have proved as efficacious for the subsequent dissemination of spiritual doctrines as that of the Christian Messiah.

The calumnies set afloat against Apollonius were as numerous as they were false. So late as eighteen centuries after his death he was defamed by Bishop Douglas in his work against miracles. In this the Right Reverend bishop crushed himself against historical facts. If we study the question with a dispassionate mind, we will soon perceive that the ethics of Gautama Buddha, Plato, Apollonius, Jesus, Ammonius Saccas, and his disciples, were all based on the same mystic philosophy; that all worshipped one God, whether they considered Him as the "Father" of humanity, who lives in man as man lives in Him, or as the Incomprehensible Creative Principle; all led Godlike lives. Ammonius, speaking of his philosophy, taught that their school dated from the days of Hermes, who brought his wisdom from India. It was the same mystical contemplation throughout, as that of the Yogin: the communion of the Brahman with his own luminous Self — the "Âtman." And this Hindu term is again kabalistic *par excellence*. Who is Self? is asked in the *Rig-Veda*; "Self is the Lord of all things . . . all things are contained in this Self; all selves are contained in this Self. Brâhman itself is but Self," * is the answer. Says *Idrah Rabbah*: "All things are Himself, and Himself is *concealed* on every side." † The "Adam-Kadmon of the kabalists contains in himself all the souls of the Israelites, and he is himself in every soul," says the *Zohar*. ‡ The groundwork of the Eclectic School was thus identical with the doctrines of the Yogins, the Hindu mystics, and the earlier Buddhism of the disciples of Gautama. And when

---

mountains" (see p. 120); while the Buddhist books, history, and scientific research tell us, through the lips of Max Müller and a host of Orientalists, that Gautama Buddha, (Sâkya-muni) died near the Ganges. "He had nearly reached the city of Kuśinâgara, when his vital strength began to fail. He halted in a forest, and while sitting under a sâl tree, he gave up the ghost" (Max Müller, *Chips from a German Workshop*, Vol. I, p. 216). The references of Mr. Graves to Higgins and Sir W. Jones, in some of his hazardous speculations, prove nothing. Max Müller shows some antiquated authorities writing elaborate books "in order to prove that Buddha had been in reality the Thoth of the Egyptians; that he was Mercury, or Wodan, or Zoroaster, or Pythagoras. Even Sir W. Jones identified Buddha, first with Odin, and afterwards with Shishak" (*Chips,* I, p. 222). We are in the nineteenth century, not in the eighteenth; and though to write books on the authority of the earliest Orientalists may in one sense be viewed as a mark of respect for old age, it is not always safe to try the experiment in our times. Hence this highly instructive volume lacks one important feature which would have made it still more interesting. The author should have added, after Prometheus the "Roman," and Alcides the *Egyptian god* (p. 300), a seventeenth "crucified Savior" to the list, "**Venus, god of the war,**" introduced to an admiring world by Artemus Ward the "showman"!

* *Chhandogya-Upanishad*, viii, 3, 3-4; Max Müller, *Chips*, etc., Vol. I, p. 70.

† *Idrah Rabbah*, § 171.

‡ Rosenroth, *Kabbalah denudata*, Vol. II, pp. 304 *et seq.*

Jesus assured his disciples that "the spirit of truth, whom the world cannot receive because *it seeth Him not*, neither knoweth Him," dwells *with* and *in* them, who "are in Him and He in them," * he but expounded the same tenet that we find running through every philosophy worthy of that name.

Saint-Hilaire, the learned and skeptical French savant, does not believe a word of the miraculous portion of Buddha's life; nevertheless, he has the candor to speak of Gautama as being *only second* to Christ in the great purity of his ethics and personal morality. For both of these opinions he is respectfully rebuked by des Mousseaux. Vexed at this scientific contradiction of his accusations of demonolatry against Gautama Buddha, he assures his readers that «ce savant distingué n'avait point étudié cette question».†

"I do not hesitate to say," remarks Barthélemy Saint-Hilaire, "that, except Christ alone, there is not among the founders of religions, a figure either more pure or more touching than that of Buddha. His life is spotless. His constant heroism equals his convictions . . . He is the perfect model of all the virtues he preaches; his abnegation, his charity, his unalterable sweetness of disposition, do not fail him for one instant. He abandoned, at the age of twenty-nine, his father's court to become a monk and a beggar . . . and when he dies in the arms of his disciples, it is with the serenity of a sage who practiced virtue all his life, and who dies convinced of having found the truth." ‡ This deserved panegyric is no stronger than the one which Laboulaye himself pronounced, § and which occasioned des Mousseaux's wrath. "It is more than difficult," adds the former, "to understand how men not assisted by revelation could have soared so high and approached so near the truth." || Curious that there should be so many lofty souls "not assisted by revelation"!

And why should anyone feel surprised that Gautama could die with philosophical serenity? As the kabalists justly say, "Death does not exist, and man never steps outside of universal life. Those whom we think dead live still in us, as we live in them . . . The more one lives for his kind, the less need he fear to die."¶ And, we might add, that he who *lives* for humanity does even more than he who dies for it.

The *Ineffable Name*, in the search for which so many kabalists — unacquainted with any Oriental or even European adept — vainly consume their knowledge and lives, dwells latent in the heart of every man. This

---

\* *John* xiv, 17.
† *Les Hauts Phénomènes de la magie*, p. 74, footnote.
‡ J. Barthélemy Saint-Hilaire, *Le Bouddha et sa religion*, Paris, 1860, Introd., p. v.
§ [Cf. M. Müller, *Chips*, etc., Vol. I, pp. 220-21.]
|| *Journal des Débats*, April 4, 1853.
¶ É. Lévi, *Dogme et rituel de la haute magie,* **Vol. II, ch. xiii.**

mirific name which, according to the most ancient oracles, "rushes into the infinite worlds ἀκοιμήτῳ στροφάλιγγι," * can be obtained in a twofold way: by regular initiation, and through the "small voice" which Elijah heard in the cave of Horeb, the mount of God. And "when Elijah heard it, that he wrapped his *face in his mantle*, and went out, and stood in the entering in of the cave. And, behold, there came a voice unto him . . ."†

When Apollonius of Tyana desired to hear the "small voice," he used to wrap himself up entirely in a mantle of fine wool, on which he placed both his feet, after having performed certain magnetic passes, and pronounced, not the "name," but an invocation well known to every adept. Then he drew the mantle over his head and face, and his translucid or astral spirit was free. On ordinary occasions he wore wool no more than the priests of the temples. The possession of the secret combination of the "name" gave the hierophant supreme power over every being, human or otherwise, inferior to himself in soul-strength. Hence, when Max Müller‡ tells us of the Quiché "Hidden Majesty, which was never to be opened by human hands," the kabalist perfectly understands what was meant by the expression, and is not at all surprised to hear even this most erudite philologist exclaim: "What it was we do not know!"

We cannot too often repeat that it is only through the doctrines of the more ancient philosophies that the religion preached by Jesus may be understood. It is through Pythagoras, Confucius and Plato, that we can comprehend the idea which underlies the term "Father" in the *New Testament*. Plato's ideal of the Deity, whom he terms the one everlasting, invisible God, the Fashioner and Father of all things, § is rather the "Father" of Jesus. This Divine Being of whom the Grecian sage says that He can neither be envious nor the originator of evil, for He can produce nothing but what is good and just, || is certainly not the Mosaic Jehovah, the "*jealous* God," but the God of Jesus, who "alone is good." He extols His all-embracing, divine power,¶ and His omnipotence, but at the same time intimates that, as He is unchangeable, He can never desire to change his laws, *i.e.*, to extirpate evil from the world through a miracle.** He is omniscient, and nothing escapes His watchful eye.†† His justice, which we find embodied in the law of compensation and retribution, will leave no crime without punishment, no virtue without its reward;‡‡ and therefore he declares that the only way to honor God is to cultivate moral purity. He utterly rejects not only the anthropomorphic

---

\* [Proclus, *On the Cratylus of Plato*].
† [*1 Kings* xix, 13.]
‡ [*Chips*, etc., Vol. I, p. 340.]
§ Plato, *Timaeus*, 28 C, 34 A, 37 C; *Polit.*, 269 E.
|| *Timaeus*, 29 E; *Phaedrus*, 182, 247 A; *Republic*, II, 379 B.
¶ *Laws*, IV, 715 E; X, 901 C.
\*\* *Republic*, II, 381 C; *Theaetetus*, 176 A B.
†† *Laws*, X, 901 D.
‡‡ *Laws*, IV, 716 A; *Republic*, X, 613 A.

idea that God could have a material body,* but rejects with disgust those fables which ascribe passions, quarrels and crimes of all sorts to the minor gods.† He indignantly denies that God allows Himself to be propitiated, or rather bribed, by prayers and sacrifices. ‡

The *Phaedrus* of Plato displays all that man once was, and that which he may yet become again. "Before man's spirit sank into sensuality and was embodied with it through the loss of his wings, he lived among the gods in the airy [spiritual] world where everything is true and pure." In the *Timaeus* he says that "there was a time when mankind did not perpetuate itself, but lived as pure spirits." In the future world, says Jesus, "they neither marry nor are given in marriage," but "are as the angels of God in Heaven." §

The researches of Laboulaye, Anquetil-Duperron, Colebrooke, Barthélemy Saint-Hilaire, Max Müller, Spiegel, Burnouf, Wilson, and so many other linguists, have brought some of the truth to light. And now that the difficulties of the Sanskrit, the Thibetan, the Singhalese, the Zend, the Pehlevi, the Chinese, and even of the Burmese, are partially conquered, and the *Vedas* and the *Zend-Avesta*, the Buddhist texts, and even Kapila's *Sûtras* are translated, a door is thrown wide open, which, once passed, must close forever behind any speculative or ignorant calumniators of the old religions. Even till the present time, the clergy have, to use the words of Max Müller — "generally appealed to the devilries and orgies of heathen worship . . . but they have seldom, if ever, endeavored to discover the true and original character of the strange forms of faith and worship which they call the work of the devil."‖ When we read the true history of Buddha and Buddhism by Müller, and the enthusiastic opinions of both expressed by Barthélemy Saint-Hilaire and Laboulaye; and when, finally, a Popish missionary, an eyewitness, and one who least of all can be accused of partiality to the Buddhists — the Abbé Huc, we mean — finds occasion for nothing but admiration for the high individual character of these "devil-worshippers"; we must consider Śâkyamuni's philosophy as something more than the religion of fetishism and atheism which the Catholics would have us believe it. Huc was a missionary and it was his first duty to regard Buddhism as no better than an outgrowth of the worship of Satan. The poor Abbé was struck off the list of missionaries at Rome,¶ after his

---

\* *Phaedrus*, 246 D.

† E. Zeller, *Plato and the Older Academy.*

‡ *Laws*, X, 905 D.

§ [*Matt.* xxii, 30.]

‖ Max Müller, *Chips*, etc., Vol. I, p. 184.

¶ Of the Abbé Huc, Max Müller thus wrote in his *Chips from a German Workshop*, Vol. I, p. 189: "The late Abbé Huc pointed out the similarities between the Buddhist and Roman Catholic ceremonials with such a *naïveté*, that, to his surprise, he found his delightful *Travels in Tartary, Thibet*, etc., placed on the *Index*. 'One cannot fail

book of travels was published. This illustrates how little we may expect to learn the truth about the religions of other people, through missionaries, when their accounts are first revised by the superior ecclesiastical authorities, and the former severely punished for telling the truth.

When these men who have been and still are often termed "the obscene ascetics," the devotees of different sects of India in short, generally termed "Yogins," were asked by Marco Polo, "how it comes that they are not ashamed to go stark naked as they do?" they answered the inquirer of the thirteenth century as a missionary of the nineteenth was answered. "We go naked," they say, "because naked we came into the world, and we desire to have nothing about us that is of this world. Moreover we have no sin in the flesh to be conscious of, and therefore, we are not ashamed of our nakedness, any more than you are to show your hand or your face. You who are conscious of the sins of the flesh do well to have shame, and to cover your nakedness." *

One could make a curious list of the excuses and explanations of the clergy to account for similarities daily discovered between Romanism and heathen religions. Yet the summary would invariably lead to one sweeping claim: The doctrines of Christianity were plagiarized by the Pagans the world over! Plato and his older Academy stole the ideas from the Christian revelation — said the Alexandrian Fathers!! The Brahmans and Manu borrowed from the Jesuit missionaries, and the *Bhagavad-Gitâ* was the production of Father Calmet, who transformed Christ and John into *Krishna* and Arjuna to fit the Hindu mind!! The trifling fact that Buddhism and Platonism both antedated Christianity, and the *Vedas* had already degenerated into Brahmanism before the days of Moses, makes no difference. The same with regard to Apollonius of Tyana. Although his thaumaturgical powers could not be denied in the face of the testimony of emperors, their courts, and the populations of several cities; and although few of these had ever heard of the Nazarene prophet whose "miracles" had been witnessed by a few apostles only, whose very individualities remain to this day a problem in history, yet Apollonius has to be accepted as the "monkey of Christ."

---

being struck,' he writes, 'with their great resemblance with the Catholicism. The bishop's crosier, the mitre, the dalmatic, the round hat that the great lamas wear in travel . . . the mass, the double choir, the psalmody, the exorcisms, the censer with five chains to it, opening and shutting at will, the blessing of the lamas, who extend their right hands over the head of the faithful ones, the rosary, the celibacy of the clergy, the penances and retreats, the cultus of the Saints, the fasting, the processions, the litanies, the holy water; such are the similarities of the Buddhists with ourselves.' He might have added tonsure, relics, and the confessional."

\* J. Crawfurd, *Journal of an Embassy to the Courts of Siam*, etc., p. 182; 1830. [Cf. *Travels of Marco Polo*, Vol. II, p. 352; ed. 1875.]

If of really pious, good and honest men, many are yet found among the Catholic, Greek and Protestant clergy, whose sincere faith has the best of their reasoning powers, and who, having never been among heathen populations, are unjust only through ignorance, it is not so with the missionaries. The invariable subterfuge of the latter is to attribute to demonolatry the really Christlike life of the Hindu and Buddhist ascetics and many of the lamas. Years of sojourn among "heathen" nations, in China, Tartary, Thibet and Hindostan have furnished them with ample evidence how unjustly the so-called idolaters have been slandered. The missionaries have not even the excuse of sincere faith to give the world that they mislead; and, with very few exceptions, one may boldly paraphrase the remark made by Garibaldi, and say that: *"A priest knows himself to be an impostor, unless he be a fool, or have been taught to lie from boyhood."*

## CHAPTER VIII

"Christian and Catholic sons may accuse their fathers of the crime of heresy . . . although they may know that their parents will be burned with fire, and put to death for it . . . And not only may they refuse them food, *if they attempt to turn them from the Catholic faith,* BUT THEY MAY ALSO JUSTLY KILL THEM."
—F. STEPHEN FAGUNDEZ, *In Praecepta Decalogi,* Lugduni, 1640.

"*Most Wise.* — What hour is it?
"*Respect. K. S. Warden.* — It is the first hour of the day, the time when the veil of the temple was rent asunder, when darkness and consternation were spread over the earth — when the light was darkened — when the implements of Masonry were broken — when the flaming star disappeared — when the cubic stone was broken — when the 'word' was lost."
—[From the Ritual of the 18° (Rose-Croix), Scottish Rite, Southern Jurisdiction.]

*Magna est Veritas et Praevalebit.*

ᕮᑎᒋᒍ ᕮᑎᐯᐯ ᒐᐱᐯ ᒎᑎ> ᒪᑎᐱᒍᒪ—JAH-BUH-LUN.

THE greatest of the kabalistic works of the Hebrews — the *Zohar,* זהר — was compiled by Rabbi Shimon ben Yoḥai. According to some critics, this was done years before the Christian era; according to others only after the destruction of the temple. However, it was completed only by the son of Shimon, Rabbi Eleazar, and his secretary, Rabbi Abba; for the work is so immense and the subjects treated so abstruse that even the whole life of this Rabbi, called the Prince of kabalists, did not suffice for the task. On account of its being known that he was in possession of this knowledge, and of the *Merkabah,* which insured the reception of the "Word," his very life was endangered, and he had to fly to the wilderness, where he lived in a cave for twelve years, surrounded by faithful disciples, and finally died there amid signs and wonders.*

But voluminous as is the work, and containing as it does the main points of the secret and oral tradition, it still does not embrace it all. It is well

---

* Many are the marvels recorded as having taken place at his death, or we should rather say his translation; for he did not die as others do, but having suddenly disappeared, while a dazzling light filled the cavern with glory, his body was again seen upon its subsidence. When this heavenly light gave place to the habitual semi-darkness of the gloomy cave — then only, says Ginsburg, "the disciples of Israel perceived that the lamp of Israel was extinguished." [*The Kabbala,* etc., ch. i.] His biographers tell us that there were voices heard from Heaven during the preparation for his funeral and at his interment. When the coffin was lowered down into the deep cave excavated for it, a flame broke out from it, and a voice mighty and majestic pronounced these words in the air: "This is he who caused the earth to quake, and the kingdoms to shake!" [*Zohar,* III, p. 296; Mantua ed].

known that this venerable kabalist never imparted the most important points of his doctrine otherwise than orally, and to a very limited number of friends and disciples, including his only son. Therefore, without the final initiation into the *Merkabah* the study of the *Kabala* will be ever incomplete, and the *Merkabah* can be taught only in "darkness, in a deserted place, and after many and terrific trials." Since the death of Shimon ben Yoḥai, this hidden doctrine has remained an inviolate secret for the outside world. Delivered *only as a mystery*, it was communicated to the candidate orally, *"face to face and mouth to ear."*

This Masonic commandment, "mouth to ear, and the word at low breath," is an inheritance from the Tannaim and the old Pagan Mysteries. Its modern use must certainly be due to the indiscretion of some renegade kabalist, though the "word" itself is but a "substitute" for the "lost word," and is a comparatively modern invention, as we will further show. The real sentence has remained forever in the sole possession of the adepts of various countries of the Eastern and Western hemispheres. Only a limited number among the chiefs of the Templars, and some Rosicrucians of the seventeenth century, always in close relations with Arabian alchemists and initiates, could really boast of its possession. From the seventh to the fifteenth centuries there was no one who could claim it in Europe; and although there had been alchemists before the day of Paracelsus, he was the first who had passed through the true initiation, that last ceremony which conferred on the adept the power of travelling toward the "burning bush" over the holy ground, and to "burn the golden calf in the fire, grind it to powder, and strew it upon the water." Verily, then, this magic *water*, and the "lost word," resuscitated more than one of the pre-Mosaic Adonirams, Gedaliahs and Hiram Abiffs. The real word now substituted by *Mac Benac* and *Mah* was used ages before its pseudo-magical effect was tried on the "widow's sons" of the last two centuries. Who was, in fact, the first operative Mason of any consequence? Elias Ashmole, *the last of the Rosicrucians and alchemists*. Admitted to the freedom of the Operative Masons' Company in London, in 1646, he died in 1692. At that time Masonry was not what it became later; it was neither a political nor a Christian institution, but a true secret organization, which admitted into the ties of fellowship all men anxious to obtain the priceless boon of liberty of conscience, and avoid clerical persecution.* Not until about thirty years after his death did what is now termed modern Freemasonry see the light. It was born on the 24th day of June, 1717, in the Apple-tree Tavern, Charles Street, Covent Garden, London. And it was then, as we are told in Anderson's

---

* Rob. Plot, *The Natural History of Staffordshire*, Oxford, 1686.

*Constitutions*, that the only four lodges in the south of England elected Anthony Sayer first Grand Master of Masons. Notwithstanding its great youth, this grand lodge has ever claimed the acknowledgment of its supremacy by the whole body of the fraternity throughout the whole world, as the Latin inscription on the plate put beneath the cornerstone of Freemasons' Hall, London, in 1775, would tell to those who could see it. But of this more anon.

In *La Kabbale*, by Franck, the author, following its "esoteric ravings," as he expresses it, gives us, in addition to the translations, his commentaries. Speaking of his predecessors, he says that Shimon ben Yohai mentions repeatedly what the "companions" have taught in the older works. And the author cites one "Ieba, the *old*, and Hamnuna, the *old*." * But what the two "old" ones mean, or who they were, in fact, he tells us not, for he does not know himself.

Among the venerable sect of the Tannaim, the wise men, there were those who taught the secrets practically and initiated some disciples into the grand and final Mystery. But the *Mishnah Ḥagîgâh*, 2nd section, says that the table of contents of the *Merkabah* "must only be delivered to wise old ones."† The *Gemara* [of the *Ḥagîgâh*] is still more dogmatic. "The more important secrets of the Mysteries were not even revealed to all the priests. Alone the initiates had them divulged." ‡ And so we find the same great secrecy prevalent in every ancient religion.

But, as we see, neither the *Zohar* nor any other kabalistic volume contains merely Jewish wisdom. The doctrine itself, being the result of whole millenniums of thought, is therefore the joint property of adepts of every nation under the sun. Nevertheless, the *Zohar* teaches practical occultism more than any other work on that subject; not as it is translated, though, and commented upon by its various critics, but with the secret signs on its margins. These signs contain the hidden instructions, apart from the metaphysical interpretations and apparent absurdities so fully credited by Josephus, who was never initiated, and gave out the *dead letter* as he had received it. §

The real practical magic contained in the *Zohar* and other kabalistic works, is only of use to those who read it *within*. The Christian apostles

---

\* *La Kabbale*, I, iii, pp. 132-33; ed. 1843.

† *Ibid.*, I, i, p. 56.

‡ [Cf. Clement Alex., *Strom.*, v, 670.]

§ He relates how Rabbi Eleazar, in the presence of Vespasian and his officers, expelled demons from several men by merely applying to the nose of the demoniac one of the number of roots recommended by King Solomon! The distinguished historian assures us that the Rabbi drew out the devils through the nostrils of the patients in the name of Solomon and by the power of the incantations composed by the king-kabalist. — *Antiquities*, VIII, ii, 5.

## "JOB" AND "REVELATION"— INITIATION ALLEGORIES    351

— at least, those who are said to have produced "miracles" *at will* \* — had to be acquainted with this science. It ill behooves a Christian to look with horror or derision upon "magic" gems, amulets, and other talismans against the "evil eye," which serve as charms to exercise a mysterious influence, either on the possessor, or the person whom the magician desires to control. There are still extant a number of such charmed amulets in public and private collections of antiquities. Illustrations of convex gems, with mysterious legends — the meaning of which baffles all scientific inquiry — are given by many collectors. King shows several such in his *Gnostics,* and he describes a white carnelian (chalcedony), covered on both sides with interminable legends, to interpret which would ever prove a failure; yes, in every case, perhaps, but that of a Hermetic student or an adept. But we refer the reader to his interesting work, and the talismans described in his plates, to show that even the "Seer of Patmos" himself was well versed in this kabalistic science of talismans and gems. St. John clearly alludes to the potent "white carnelian" — a gem well-known among adepts, as the *"alba petra,"* or the stone of initiation, on which the word *"prize"* is generally found engraved, as it was given to the candidate who had successfully passed through all the preliminary trials of a neophyte. The fact is, that no less than the *Book of Job,* the whole *Revelation* is simply an allegorical narrative of the Mysteries and initiation therein of a candidate, who is John himself. No high Mason, well versed in the different degrees, can fail to see it. The numbers *seven, twelve,* and others are all so many lights thrown over the obscurity of the work. Paracelsus maintained the same some centuries ago. And when we find the "one like unto the Son of man" saying (*Revel.* ii, 17): *"To him that overcometh* will I give to eat of the *hidden manna,* and will give him a WHITE STONE, and in the stone a new name written" — the word — "which *no man knoweth* saving *he that receiveth it,"* what Master Mason can doubt but it refers to the last headline of this chapter?

In the pre-Christian Mithraic Mysteries, the candidate who fearlessly overcame the *"twelve* Tortures," which preceded the final initiation, received a small round cake or wafer of unleavened bread, symbolizing, *in one of its meanings,* the solar disk and known as the heavenly bread or "manna," and having figures traced on it. A *lamb* or a *bull* was killed, and with the blood the candidate had to be sprinkled, as in the case of the Emperor Julian's initiation. The *seven* rules or mysteries

---

\* There are *unconscious* miracles produced sometimes, which, like the phenomena now called "Spiritual," are caused through natural cosmic powers, mesmerism, electricity, and the invisible beings who are always at work around us, whether they be human or elementary spirits.

were then delivered to the "newly born" that are represented in the *Revelation* as the seven seals which are opened "in order" (see chap. v and vi). There can be no doubt that the Seer of Patmos referred to this ceremony.

The origin of the Roman Catholic amulets and "relics" blessed by the Pope, is the same as that of the "Ephesian Spell," or magical characters engraved either on a stone or drawn on a piece of parchment; the Jewish amulets with verses of the Law, called *phylacteria*, φυλακτήρια, and the Mohammedan charms with verses of the *Koran*. All these were used as protective magic spells, and worn by the believers on their persons. Epiphanius, the worthy ex-Marcosian, who speaks of these charms when used by the Manichaeans as amulets, that is to say, things worn round the neck (*periapta*), and "incantations and *suchlike trickery*," cannot well throw a slur upon the *"trickery"* of the Pagans and Gnostics, without including the Roman Catholic and Popish amulets.

But consistency is a virtue which we fear is losing, under Jesuit influence, the slight hold it may ever have had on the Church. That crafty, learned, conscienceless, terrible soul of Jesuitism, within the body of Romanism, is slowly but surely possessing itself of the whole prestige and spiritual power that clings to it. For the better exemplification of our theme it will be necessary to contrast the moral principles of the ancient Tannaim and Theurgists with those professed by the modern Jesuits, who practically control Romanism today and are the hidden enemy that would-be reformers must encounter and overcome. Throughout the whole of antiquity, where, in what land, can we find anything like this Order or anything even approaching it? We owe a place to the Jesuits in this chapter on secret societies, for more than any other they are a secret body, and have a far closer connection with actual Masonry — in France and Germany at least — than people are generally aware of. The cry of an outraged public morality was raised against this Order from its very birth.* Barely fifteen years had elapsed after the [papal] bull approving its constitution was promulgated, when its members began to be driven away from one place to the other. Portugal and the Low Countries got rid of them in 1578; France in 1594; Venice in 1606; Naples in 1622. From St. Petersburg they were expelled in 1816,[49] and from all Russia in 1820.

It was a promising child from its very teens. What it grew up to be everyone knows well. The Jesuits have done more moral harm in this world than all the fiendish armies of the mythical Satan. Whatever extravagance may seem to be involved in this remark, will disappear when

---

* It dates from 1540; and in 1555 a general outcry was raised against them in some parts of Portugal, Spain, and other countries [Cf. Michelet and Quinet, *Des Jésuites*, p. 194; 6th ed., Paris, 1844.]

our readers in America, who now know little about them, are made acquainted with their principles (*principia*) and rules as they appear in various works written by the Jesuits themselves. We beg leave to remind the public that every one of the statements which follow in quotation marks is extracted from authenticated manuscripts, or folios printed by this distinguished body. Many are copied from the large Quarto * published by the authority of, and verified and collated by the Commissioners of the French Parliament. The statements therein were collected and presented to the King, in order that, as the *Arrest du Parlement du 5 Mars, 1762* expresses it, "the elder son of the Church might be made aware of the perversity of this doctrine ... A doctrine authorizing Theft, Lying, Perjury, Impurity, every Passion and Crime, teaching Homicide, Parricide, and Regicide, overthrowing religion in order to substitute for it superstition, by favoring *Sorcery*, Blasphemy, Irreligion, and Idolatry ... etc." Let us then examine the ideas on *magic* of the Jesuits. Writing on this subject in his secret instructions, Anthony Escobar says:

"It is lawful ... to make use of the science acquired *through the assistance of the devil,* provided the preservation and use of that knowledge do not depend upon the devil, *for the knowledge is good in itself, and the sin by which it was acquired is gone by.*" † Hence, why should not a Jesuit cheat the Devil as well as he cheats every layman?

"*Astrologers and soothsayers are either bound, or are not bound, to restore the reward of their divination, if the event does not come to pass.* I own," remarks the *good* Father Escobar, "that the former opinion does not at all please me, because, when the astrologer or diviner has exerted all the diligence *in the diabolic art* which is essential to his purpose, he has fulfilled his duty, whatever may be the result. As the physician ... is not bound to restore his fee ... if the patient should die; so neither is the astrologer bound to restore his charge ... ex-

---

* Extracts from this *Arrest* were compiled into a work in 4 vols., 12mo., which appeared at Paris in 1762, and was known as *Extraits des Assertions*, etc. In a work entitled *Réponse aux Assertions,* an attempt was made by the Jesuits to throw discredit upon the facts collected by the Commissioners of the French Parliament in 1762, as for the most part malicious fabrications. "To ascertain the validity of this impeachment," says the author of *The Principles of the Jesuits*, "the Libraries of the two Universities, of the British Museum, and of Sion College have been searched for the authors cited; and in every instance where the volume could be found, the correctness of the citation has been established." [pp. v-vi.]

† *Theologia moralis*, Lugduni, 1663. Tom. IV, lib. 28, sect. 1, de praecept. 1, cap. 20, n. 184, p. 25.

cept where he has used no effort, or was ignorant of his diabolic art; because, when he has used his endeavors he has not deceived." *

Further, we find the following on astrology: "If any one affirms, through conjecture founded upon the influence of the stars and the character, disposition, and manners of a man, that he will be a soldier, an ecclesiastic, or a bishop, *this divination may be devoid of all sin;* because the stars and the disposition of the man, may have the power of inclining the human will to a certain lot or rank, but not of constraining it." †

Busembaum and Lacroix, in *Theologia Moralis,* ‡ say, "Palmistry may be considered lawful, if from the lines and divisions of the hands it can ascertain the disposition of the body, and conjecture, with probability, the propensities and affections of the soul . . ." §

This noble fraternity, which many preachers have of late so vehemently denied to have ever been a *secret* one, has been sufficiently proved as such. Their constitutions were translated into Latin by the Jesuit Polancus, and printed in the college of the Society at Rome, in 1558. "They were jealously kept secret, the greater part of the Jesuits themselves knowing only extracts from them. *They were never produced to the light until 1761, when they were published by order of the French Parliament* [in 1761, 1762], in the famous process of Father La Valette." ‖ The degrees of the Order are: I. Novices; II. Lay Brothers, or temporal Coadjutors; III. Scholastics; IV. Spiritual Coadjutors; V. Professed of Three Vows; VI. Professed of Five Vows. "There is also a secret class, known only to the General and a few faithful Jesuits, which, perhaps more than any other, contributed to the dreaded and mysterious power of the Order," says Nicolini. The Jesuits reckon it among the greatest achievements of their Order that Loyola supported, by a special memorial to the Pope, a petition for the reorganization of that abominable and abhorred instrument of wholesale butchery — the infamous tribunal of the Inquisition.

This Order of Jesuits is now all-powerful in Rome. They have been reinstalled in the Congregation of Extraordinary Ecclesiastical Affairs, in the Department of the Secretary of State, and in the Ministry of Foreign

---

\* *Ibid.,* sect. 2, de praecept. 1, probl. 113, no. 584, p. 77.

† Richard Arsdekin, *Theologia tripartita universa,* Coloniae, 1744, Tom. II, Pars II, Tr. 5, c. 1, § 2, n. 4.

‡ *Theologia moralis . . . nunc pluribus partibus aucta à R. P. Claudio Lacroix, Societatis Jesu,* Coloniae, 1757. [Coloniae Agrippinae, 1733, ed. British Museum.]

§ Tom. II, lib. iii, Pars I, Tr. 1, c. 1, dub. 2, resol. viii. What a pity that the counsel for the defense had not bethought them to cite this orthodox legalization of "cheating by palmistry or otherwise," at the recent religio-scientific prosecution of the medium Slade, in London.

‖ G. B. Nicolini, *History of the Jesuits,* p. 30.

Affairs. The Pontifical Government was for years previous to Victor Emanuel's occupation of Rome entirely in their hands. The Society now numbers 8,584 members. But we must see what are their chief rules. By what is seen above, in becoming acquainted with their mode of action, we may ascertain what the whole Catholic body is likely to be. Says MacKenzie: "The Order has secret signs and passwords according to the degrees to which the members belong, and as they wear no particular dress, it is very difficult to recognize them, unless they reveal themselves as members of the Order; for they may appear as Protestants or Catholics, democrats or aristocrats, infidels or bigots, according to the special mission with which they are entrusted. Their spies are everywhere, of all apparent ranks of society, and they may appear learned and wise, or simple and foolish, as their instructions run. There are Jesuits of both sexes and all ages, and it is a well-known fact that members of the Order, of high family and delicate nurture, are acting as menial servants in Protestant families, and doing other things of a similar nature in aid of the Society's purposes. We cannot be too much on our guard, for the whole Society, being founded on a law of unhesitating obedience, can bring its force on any given point with unerring and fatal accuracy." *

The Jesuits maintain that "the Society of Jesus is not of human invention, *but it proceeded from him whose name it bears.* For Jesus himself described that rule of life which the Society follows, *first by his example,* and afterwards by his words." †

Let, then, all pious Christians listen and acquaint themselves with this alleged "rule of life" and precepts of their God, as exemplified by the Jesuits. Pater Alagona says: "By the command of God it is lawful to kill an innocent person, to steal, or commit . . . (*Ex mandato Dei licet occidere innocentem, furari, fornicari*); because he is the Lord of Life and death and all things: *and it is due to him thus to fulfill his command.*" ‡

"A man of a religious order, who for a short time lays aside his habit *for a sinful purpose*, is free from heinous crime, and does not incur the penalty of excommunication." §

---

\* *Royal Masonic Cyclopaedia*, p. 369.

† *Imago primi saeculi Societatis Jesu*, Antuerpiae, 1640, lib. I, cap. 3, p. 64.

‡ Peter Alagona, *St. Thomae Aquinatis Summae Theologiae Compendium*, Ex prima secondae, Quaest. 94.

§ Anthony Escobar, *Universae Theologiae Moralis receptiores, absque lite sententiae,* etc., Lugduni, 1652 (ed. Bibl. Acad. Cant.), Tomus I, lib. 3, Sect. 2, probl. 44, n. 212. "Idem sentio, breve illud tempus ad unius horae spatium traho. Religiosus itaque habitum demittens assignato hoc temporis interstitio, non incurrit excommunicationem, *etiamsi dimittat non solum ex causa turpi, scilicet fornicandi aut clam aliquid abripiendi, sed etiam ut incognitus ineat lupanar.*" — Probl. 44, n. 213.

John Baptist Taberna (*Synopsis Theologiae Practicae*), propounds the following question: "Is a judge bound to restore the bribe which he has received for passing sentence?" *Answer*: "*If he has received the bribe for passing an unjust sentence, it is probable that he may keep it . . . This opinion is maintained and defended by fifty-eight doctors*" (Jesuits).\*

We must abstain at present from proceeding further. So disgustingly licentious, hypocritical, and demoralizing are nearly all of these precepts, that it was found impossible to put many of them in print, except in the Latin language.† We will return to some of the more decent as we proceed, for the sake of comparison. But what are we to think of the future of the Catholic world, if it is to be controlled in word and deed by this villainous society? And that it is to be so, we can hardly doubt, as we find the Cardinal Archbishop of Cambrai loudly proclaiming the same to all the faithful? His pastoral has made a certain noise in France; and yet, as two centuries have rolled away since the *exposé* of these infamous principles, the Jesuits have had ample time to lie so successfully in denying the just charges, that most Catholics will never believe such a thing. The *infallible* Pope, Clement XIV (Ganganelli), suppressed them on the 23rd of July, 1773, and yet they came to life again; and another equally infallible Pope, Pius VII, re-established them on the 7th of August, 1814.

But we will hear what Monseigneur of Cambrai is swift to proclaim in 1876. We quote from a secular paper:

"Among other things, he maintains that *Clericalism, Ultramontanism, and Jesuitism are one and the same thing — that is to say, Catholicism* — and that the distinctions between them have been created by the enemies of religion. There was a time, he says, when a certain theological opinion was commonly professed in France concerning the authority of the Pope. It was restricted to our nation, and was of recent origin. The civil power during a century and a half imposed official instruction. Those who professed these opinions were called Gallicans, and those who protested were called Ultramontanes, because they had their doctrinal centre beyond the Alps, at Rome. Today the distinction between the two schools is no longer admissible. Theological Gallicanism can no longer exist, since this opinion has ceased to be tolerated by the Church. *It has been solemnly condemned, past all return, by the Ecumenical Council of the Vatican. One cannot now be Catholic without being Ultramontane — and Jesuit.*" ‡

---

\* Pars II, tr. 2, c. 31, p. 286.

† See *The Principles of the Jesuits, Developed in a Collection of Extracts from their own Authors*, London, 1839.

‡ From the Pastoral of the Archbishop of Cambrai.

This settles the question. We leave inferences for the present, and proceed to compare some of the practices and precepts of the Jesuits, with those of individual mystics and organized castes and societies of the ancient time. Thus the fair-minded reader may be placed in a position to judge between them as to the tendency of their doctrines to benefit or degrade humanity.

Rabbi Joshua ben Hananyah, who died about A.D. 72, openly declared that he had performed "miracles" by means of the *Book of Sepher Yetzirah,* and challenged every skeptic.* Franck, quoting from the Babylonian *Talmud,* names two other thaumaturgists, Rabbis Ḥanina and Oshaia.†

Simon Magus was doubtless a pupil of the Tannaim of Samaria, the reputation which he left behind, together with the title given to him of "the Great Power of God," testifies strongly in favor of the ability of his teachers. The calumnies so zealously disseminated against him by the unknown authors and compilers of the *Acts* and other writings, could not cripple the truth to such an extent as to conceal the fact that no Christian could rival him in thaumaturgic deeds. The story told about his falling during an aerial flight, breaking both his legs, and then committing suicide, is ridiculous. Instead of praying mentally that it should so happen, why did not the apostles pray rather that they should be allowed to outdo Simon in wonders and miracles, for then they might have proved their case far more easily than they did, and so converted thousands to Christianity. Posterity has heard but one side of the story. Were the disciples of Simon to have a chance, we might find, perhaps, that it was Peter who broke both his legs, had we not known that this apostle was too prudent ever to venture himself in Rome. On the confession of several ecclesiastical writers, no apostle ever performed such "supernatural wonders." Of course pious people will say this only the more proves that it was the "Devil" who worked through Simon.

Simon was accused of blasphemy against the Holy Ghost, because he introduced it as the "Holy Spiritus, the *Mens* (Intelligence), or the mother of all." But we find the same expression used in the *Book of Enoch,* ‡ in which, in contradistinction to the "Son of Man," he says "Son of the Woman." In the *Codex* of the Nazarenes, and in the *Zohar,* as well as in the *Books of Hermes,* the expression is usual; and even in the apocryphal *Evangelium of the Hebrews* we read that Jesus himself admitted the sex of the Holy Ghost by using the expression, *"My mother, the Holy Pneuma."* §

But what is the heresy of Simon, or what the blasphemies of all the

---

\* See Jerusalem *Talmud,* Sanhedrin, ch. 7, etc.
† A. Franck, *La Kabbale,* 1843, p. 78.
‡ [Ch. lxi, § 9.]
§ [Origen, *Comm. Evang. in Johannis,* 59, ed. Huet.]

heretics, in comparison with that of the same Jesuits who have now so completely mastered the Pope, ecclesiastical Rome, and the entire Catholic world? Listen again to their profession of faith.

"Do what your conscience tells you to be good and commanded: if, through invincible error, you believe lying or blasphemy to be commanded by God, *blaspheme*." *

"Omit to do what your conscience tells you is forbidden: omit the worship of God, if you invincibly believe it to be prohibited by God." †

"There is an implied law . . . obey an invincibly erroneous dictate of conscience. As often as you believe invincibly that a lie is commanded, lie." ‡

"Let us suppose a Catholic to believe invincibly, that the worship of images is forbidden: in such a case our Lord Jesus Christ will be obliged to say to him, *Depart from me, thou cursed*, etc., *because thou hast worshipped mine image* . . . So, neither, is there any absurdity (in supposing) that Christ may say, *Come thou blessed*, etc., *because thou hast lied, believing invincibly that in such a case I commanded the lie*." §

Does not this — but no! words fail to do justice to the emotions that these astonishing precepts must awaken in the breast of every honest person. Let silence, resulting from *invincible* disgust, be our only adequate tribute to such unparalleled moral obliquity.

The popular feeling in Venice (1606), when the Jesuits were driven out from that city, expressed itself most forcibly. Great crowds had accompanied the exiles to the seashore, and the farewell cry which resounded after them over the waves, was, "*Andè in malora!*" (Get away! and woe be to you.) "That cry was echoed throughout the two following centuries," says Quinet, who gives this statement, "in Bohemia in 1618 . . . in India in 1623 . . . and throughout all Christendom in 1773." ‖

In what particular was then Simon Magus a blasphemer, if he only did that which his conscience invincibly told him was true? And in what particular were ever the "heretics," or even *infidels* of the worst kind more reprehensible than the Jesuits — those of Caen, ¶ for instance — who say the following:

"(The Christian religion) is . . . *evidently* credible, but not *evidently true*. It is evidently credible; for it is evident that whoever embraces

---

* Charles Anthony Casnedi, *Crisis Theologica*, Ulyssipone, 1711, Tome I, Disp. 6, sect. 2, § 1, n. 59.

† *Ibid*.

‡ *Ibid*., § 2, n. 78.

§ *Ibid*., sect. 5, § 1, n. 165.

‖ [Michelet and Quinet, *Des Jésuites*, pp. 285-86; 6th ed., Paris, 1844.]

¶ *Thesis propugnata in regio Soc. Jes. Collegio, celeberrimae Academiae Cadomensis, die Veneris* 30 *Jan.*, 1693. *Cadomi*, 1693.

it is prudent. *It is not evidently true;* for it either teaches obscurely, or the things which it teaches are obscure. And they who affirm that the Christian religion is evidently true, are obliged to confess that it is evidently false (*Position* 5).

"Infer from hence —

"1. That it is *not* evident — that there is now any true religion in the world.

"2. That it is *not* evident — that of all religions existing upon the earth, the Christian religion is the most true; for have you travelled over all countries of the world, or do you know that others have? . . .

. . . . . . . . .

"4. That it is *not* evident — that the predictions of the prophets were given by inspiration of God; for what refutation will you bring against me, if I deny that they were true prophecies, or assert that they were only conjectures?

"5. That it is *not* evident — that the miracles were real, which are recorded to have been wrought by Christ; although no one can prudently deny them (*Position* 6).

"Neither is an avowed belief in Jesus Christ, in the Trinity, in all the Articles of Faith, and in the Decalogue, necessary to Christians. The only explicit belief which was necessary to the former (the Jews) and is necessary to the latter (Christians), is, 1. Of God. 2. Of a rewarding God" (*Position* 8).

Hence, it is also more than "evident" that there are moments in the life of the greatest liar when he may utter some truths. It is in this case so perfectly exemplified by the "good Fathers," that we can see more clearly than ever whence proceeded the solemn condemnation at the Ecumenical Council of 1870, of certain "heresies," and the enforcement of other articles of faith in which none believed less than those who inspired the Pope to issue them. History has yet perhaps to learn that the octogenarian Pope, intoxicated with the fumes of his newly-enforced infallibility, was but the faithful echo of the Jesuits. "An old man is raised trembling upon the *pavois* of the Vatican," says Michelet, "everything becomes absorbed and confined in him . . . For fifteen centuries Christendom had submitted to the spiritual yoke of the Church . . . But that yoke was not sufficient for them; they wanted the whole world to bend under the hand of one master. Here my own words are too weak; I shall borrow those of others. They [the Jesuits] wanted (this is the accusation flung in their faces by the Bishop of Paris in the full Council of Trent) *faire de l'épouse de Jésus Christ une prostituée aux volontés d'un homme.*" \*

---

\* Michelet and Quinet (of the College of France), *op. cit.*, pp. 284-85.

They have succeeded. The Church is henceforth an inert tool, and the Pope a poor weak instrument in the hands of this Order. But for how long? Until the end comes, well may sincere Christians remember the prophetic lamentations of the thrice-great Trismegistus over his own country: "Alas, alas, my son, a day will come when the sacred hieroglyphics will become but idols. *The world will mistake the emblems of science for gods,* and accuse grand Egypt of having worshipped hell-monsters. But those who will calumniate us thus, will themselves worship Death instead of Life, folly in place of wisdom; they will denounce love and fecundity, fill their temples with dead men's bones, as relics, and waste their youth in solitude and tears. Their *virgins will be widows* [nuns] *before being wives,* and consume themselves in grief; because men will have despised and profaned the sacred mysteries of Isis." *

How correct this prophecy has proved we find in the following Jesuit precept, which again we extract from the Report of the Commissioners to the Parliament of Paris:

"The more true opinion is, *that all inanimate and irrational things may be legitimately worshipped,*" says Father Gabriel Vázquez, treating of Idolatry. "If the doctrine which we have established be rightly understood, not only may a painted image, and every holy thing set forth by public authority for the worship of God, be properly adored with God as the image of himself; but also any other thing of this world, whether it be inanimate and irrational, or in its nature rational, and devoid of danger."†

"Why may we not adore and worship with God, apart from danger, anything whatsoever of this world; for God is in it according to his essence [this is precisely what the Pantheist and Hindu philosophy maintains] and preserves it continually by his power; and when we bow down ourselves before it and impress it with a kiss, we present ourselves before God, the Author of it, with the whole soul, as unto the prototype of the image [follow instances of relics, etc.] ... To these instances we may add a fourth. Since everything of this world is the work of God, and God is always abiding and working in it, we may more readily conceive him to be in it, than a saint in the vesture which belonged to him. And, therefore, *without regarding in any way the dignity of the thing created, to direct our thoughts to God alone, while we give to the creature the sign and mark of submission by a kiss or prostration, is neither vain nor superstitious, but an act of the purest religion.*" ‡

A precept this, which, whether or not doing honor to the Christian Church, may at least be profitably quoted by any Hindu, Japanese, or

---

* Champollion, *Lettres,* "Hermès Trismégiste," xxvii.
† *De culto adorationis libri tres,* Moguntiae, 1614, lib. iii, disp. 1, cap. 2.
‡ *Ibid.*

any other heathen when rebuked for his worship of idols. We purposely quote it for the benefit of our respected "heathen" friends who will see these lines.

The prophecy of Hermes is less equivocal than either of the alleged prophecies of Isaiah, which have furnished a pretext for saying that the gods of all the nations were demons. Only, facts are stronger, sometimes, than the strongest faith. All that the Jews learned, they had from older nations than themselves. The Chaldean Magi were their masters in the secret doctrine, and it was during the Babylonian captivity that they learned its metaphysical as well as practical tenets. Pliny mentions three schools of Magi: one that he shows to have been founded at an unknown antiquity; the other established by Osthanes and Zoroaster; the third by Moses and Jannes.* And all the knowledge possessed by these different schools, whether Magian, Egyptian, or Jewish, was derived from India, or rather from both sides of the Himâlayas. Many a lost secret lies buried under wastes of sand in the Gobi Desert of Eastern Turkestan, and the wise men of Khotan have preserved strange traditions and knowledge of alchemy.

Baron Bunsen shows that the "origin of the ancient prayers and hymns of the Egyptian *Book of the Dead* is *anterior* to Menes, and belongs probably, to the pre-Menite Dynasty of Abydos, between 3100 and 4500 B.C." The learned Egyptologist makes the era of Menes, or National Empire, as not later than 3059 B.C., and demonstrates that "the system of Osirian worship and mythology was already formed" before this era of Menes.†

We find in the hymns of this scientifically-established pre-Edenic epoch (for Bunsen carries us back several centuries *beyond* the year of the creation of the world, 4004 B.C., as fixed by biblical chronology) precise lessons of morality, identical in substance, and nearly so in form of expression, with those preached by Jesus in his Sermon on the Mount. We give the authority of the most eminent Egyptologists and hierologists for our statement. "The inscriptions of the twelfth Dynasty are filled with ritualistic formulae," says Bunsen. Extracts from the *Hermetic Books* are found on monuments of the earliest dynasties, and "on those of the twelfth [dynasty] portions of an *earlier* ritual are by no means uncommon . . . *To feed the* hungry, give drink to the thirsty, clothe the naked, bury the *dead . . . formed the first duty of a pious man* . . . The doctrine of the immortality of the soul is as old as this period (Tablet, *Brit. Mus.*, 562)." ‡

---

\* [Pliny, *Nat. Hist.*, XXX, ii.]
† *Egypt's Place in Universal History*, Vol. V, p. 94.
‡ *Ibid.*, Vol. V, pp. 128-29.

And far older, perhaps. It dates from the time when the soul was an *objective* being, hence when it could hardly be denied by *itself;* when humanity was a spiritual race and death existed not. Toward the decline of the cycle of life, the ethereal *man-spirit* then fell into the sweet slumber of temporary unconsciousness in one sphere, only to find himself awakening in the still brighter light of a higher one. But while the spiritual man is ever striving to ascend higher and higher toward its source of being, passing through the cycles and spheres of individual life, physical man had to descend with the great cycle of universal creation until it found itself clothed with the terrestrial garments. Thenceforth the soul was too deeply buried under physical clothing to reassert its existence, except in the cases of those more spiritual natures, which, with every cycle, became more rare. And yet none of the prehistorical nations ever thought of denying either the existence or the immortality of the inner man, the real "self." Only, we must bear in mind the teachings of the old philosophies: the spirit alone is immortal — the soul, *per se*, is neither eternal nor divine. When linked too closely with the physical brain of its terrestrial casket, it gradually becomes a *finite* mind, a simple animal and sentient life-principle, the *nephesh* of the Hebrew *Bible.*\*

The doctrine of man's *triune* nature is as clearly defined in the Hermetic books as it is in Plato's system, or again in that of the Buddhist and Brahmanical philosophies. And this is one of the most important as well as least understood of the doctrines of Hermetic science. The Egyptian Mysteries, so imperfectly known by the world, and only through

---

\* "And God created . . . every *nephesh* (life) that moveth" (*Gen.* i, 21), meaning animals; and (*Genesis* ii, 7) it is said: "And man became a *nephesh*" (living soul); which shows that the word *nephesh* was indifferently applied to *immortal* man and to *mortal* beast. "And surely your blood of your *nepheshim* (lives) will I require; at the hand of every beast will I require it, and at the hand of man" (*Gen.* ix, 5). "Escape for *naphsheḥa*" (escape for thy *life*, is translated) (*Gen.* xix, 17). "Let us not kill him," reads the English version (*Gen.* xxxvii, 21). "Let us not kill his *nephesh*," is the Hebrew text. "*Nephesh for nephesh,*" says *Leviticus* (xxiv, 18). "He that killeth any man shall surely be put to death." "He that smiteth the *nephesh* of a man" (*Levit.* xxiv, 17); and from verse 18 and following it reads: "And he that killeth a beast [*nephesh*] shall make it good; beast for beast," whereas the original text has it *"nephesh for nephesh."*

*1 Kings* i, 12; ii, 23; iii, 11; xix, 2, 3, all have *nephesh* for life and soul. "Then shall thy *naphsheḥa* for (his) *naphsho,*" explains the prophet in *1 Kings* xx, 39.

Truly, unless we read the *Old Testament* kabalistically and comprehend the hidden meaning thereof, there is very little we can learn from it as regards the soul's immortality. The common people among Hebrews had not the slightest idea of soul and spirit, and made no difference between *life, blood* and *soul,* calling the latter the "breath of life." And King James' translators have made such a jumble of it that *no one but a kabalist can restore the Bible to its original form.*

the few brief allusions to them in the *Metamorphoses* of Apuleius, taught the greatest virtues. They unveiled to the aspirant in the "higher" mysteries of initiation that which many of our modern Hermetic students vainly search for in the kabalistic books, and which no obscure teachings of the Church, under the guidance of the Order of Jesuits, will ever be able to unveil. To compare, then, the ancient secret societies of the hierophants with the artificially-produced hallucinations of those few followers of Loyola, who were, perchance, sincere at the beginning of their career, is to insult the former. And yet, in justice to them, we are compelled to do so.

One of the most unconquerable obstacles to initiation, with the Egyptians as with the Greeks, was any degree of murder. One of the greatest titles to admission in the Order of Jesuits is a *murder* in defence of Jesuitism. "*Children may kill their parents if they compel them to abandon the Catholic faith.*"

"Christian and Catholic sons," says Stephen Fagundez, "may accuse their fathers of the crime of heresy if they wish to turn them from the faith, although they may know that their parents will be burned with fire, and put to death for it, as Tolet teaches . . . And not only may they refuse them food . . . *but they may also justly kill them.*" *

It is well known that Nero, the Emperor, *had never dared* seek initiation into the Mysteries on account of the murder of Agrippina!

Under Section XIV of the *Principles of the Jesuits*, we find on *Homicide* the following Christian principles inculcated by Father Henry Henriquez: "If an adulterer, even although he should be an ecclesiastic . . . being attacked by her husband, kills his aggressor . . . *he is not considered irregular* (non videtur irregularis)." †

". . . if a father were obnoxious to the state [being in banishment] and to society at large, and there were no other means of averting such an injury, *then I should approve the opinion of the aforesaid authors*" (for a son to kill his father), says Sect. XV, on *Parricide and Homicide.*‡

"It will be lawful for an ecclesiastic, or one of the religious order, *to kill a calumniator* who threatens to spread atrocious accusations against himself or his religion . . ." § is the rule set forth by the Jesuit Francis Amicus.

---

\* *In praecepta Decalogi* (ed. of Sion Libr.), Tom. I, lib. 4, cap. 2, n. 7, 8, p. 501.

† *Summae Theologiae Moralis*, Venetiis, 1600 (ed. Coll. Sion), Tomus I, lib. xiv, *de Irregularitate*, cap. 10, n. 3, p. 869.

‡ Opinion of John de Dicastillo, *De justitia et jure,* etc., lib. II, Tr. 1, Disp. 10, dub. 1, n. 15.

§ *Cursus Theologicae,* etc., Duaci, 1642. Tom. V, Disp. 36, sec. 5, n. 118, p. 544.

So far, so good. We are informed by the highest authorities what a man in the Catholic communion may do that the common law and public morality stamps as criminal, and still continue in the odor of Jesuitical sanctity. Now suppose we again turn the medal and see what principles were inculcated by Pagan Egyptian moralists before the world was blessed with these modern improvements in ethics.

In Egypt every city of importance was separated from its burial place by a sacred lake. The same ceremony of judgment which the *Book of the Dead* describes as taking place in the world of Spirit, took place on earth during the burial of the mummy. Forty-two judges or assessors assembled on the shore and judged the departed "soul" according to its actions when in the body, and it was only upon a unanimous approval of this *post-mortem* jury that the boatman, who represented the Spirit of Death, could convey the justified defunct's body to its last resting place. After that the priests returned within the sacred precincts and instructed the neophytes upon the probable solemn drama which was then taking place in the invisible realm whither the soul had fled. The immortality of the spirit was strongly inculcated by the Al-om-jah.* In the *Crata Repoa* † the following is described as the *seven* degrees of the initiation.

After a preliminary trial at Thebes, where the neophyte had to pass through many trials, called the "Twelve Tortures," he was commanded to govern his passions and never lose for a moment the idea of his God. Then as a symbol of the wandering of the unpurified soul, he had to ascend several ladders and wander in darkness in a cave with many doors, all of which were locked. When he had overcome the dreadful trials, he received the degree of *Pastophoros,* the second and third degrees being called the *Neocoris,* and the *Melanêphoros.* Brought into a vast subterranean chamber thickly furnished with mummies lying in state, he was placed in presence of the coffin which contained the mutilated body of Osiris covered with blood. This was the hall called "Gates of Death," and it is most certainly to this mystery that the passages in the *Book of Job* (xxxviii, 17) and other portions of the *Bible* allude when these gates are spoken of. ‡ In chapter x, we give the esoteric interpretation of the *Book of Job,* which is the poem of initiation *par excellence.*

> "Have the gates of death been opened unto thee?
> Or hast thou seen the doors of the shadow of death?"

asks the "Lord" — *i.e.,* the Al-om-jah, the Initiator — of Job, alluding to this third degree of initiation.

---

\* Name of the highest Egyptian hierophants.

† *Crata Repoa oder Einweihungen in der alten geheimen Gessellschaft der Egyptischen Priester,* Berlin, 1778, pp. 17-31.

‡ *Matthew* xvi, 18, where it is mistranslated "the gates of Hell."

When the neophyte had conquered the terrors of this trial, he was conducted to the "Hall of Spirits," to be judged by them. Among the rules in which he was instructed, he was commanded *"never to either desire or seek revenge; to be always ready to help a brother in danger, even unto the risk of his own life; to bury every dead body; to honor his parents above all;* respect old age and protect those weaker than himself, and finally, to ever bear in mind the hour of death, and that of resurrection, in a new and imperishable body." * Purity and chastity were highly recommended, and *adultery threatened with death.*

Then the Egyptian neophyte was made a *Kistophoros*. In this degree the mystery-name of IAÔ was communicated to him. The fifth degree was that of *Balahate*, and he was instructed by Horus in alchemy, the "word" being *chemi*. In the sixth, the priestly dance in the circle was taught him, in which he was instructed in astronomy, for it represented the course of the planets. In the seventh degree, he was initiated into the final Mysteries. After a final probation in a building set apart for it, the *Astronomos*, as he was now called, emerged from these sacred apartments called *Maneras*, and received a cross — the *Tau*, which, at death, had to be laid upon his breast. He was a hierophant.

We have read above the rules of these holy initiates of the *Christian* Society of Jesus. Compare them with those enforced upon the Pagan postulant, and Christian(!) morality with that inculcated in those mysteries of the Pagans upon which all the thunders of an avenging Deity are invoked by the Church. Had the latter no mysteries of its own? Or were they in any wise purer, nobler, or more inciting to a holy, virtuous life? Let us hear what Nicolini has to say, in his able *History of the Jesuits*, of the *modern* mysteries of the Christian cloister.†

"In most monasteries, and more particularly in those of the Capuchins and Reformed (*Reformati*), there begins at Christmas a series of feasts, which continues till Lent. All sorts of games are played, the most splendid banquets are given, and in the small towns, above all, the refectory of the convent is the best place of amusement for the greater number of the inhabitants. At carnivals, two or three very magnificent entertainments take place; the board so profusely spread that one might imagine that Copia had here poured forth the whole contents of her horn. It must be remembered that these two orders live by alms. ‡ The sombre silence of the cloister is replaced

---

* Humberto Malhandrini, *Ritual of Initiations*, p. 105; Venice, 1657.

† Pages 43, 44, note. G. B. Nicolini of Rome, author of *The History of the Pontificate of Pius IX; The Life of Father Alessandro Gavazzi*, etc.

‡ And begged in the name of *Him* who had nowhere to lay his head!

by a confused sound of merrymaking, and its gloomy vaults now echo with other songs than those of the psalmist. A ball enlivens and terminates the feast; and, to render it still more animated, and perhaps to show *how completely their vow of chastity has eradicated all their carnal appetite*, some of the young monks appear coquettishly dressed in the garb of the fair sex, and begin the dance, along with others, transformed into gay cavaliers. *To describe the scandalous scene which ensues would be but to disgust my readers.* I will only say that I have myself often been a spectator at such Saturnalia."

The cycle is moving down, and, as it descends, the physical and bestial nature of man develops more and more at the expense of the Spiritual Self.\* With what disgust may we not turn from this religious farce called modern Christianity, to the noble faiths of old!

---

\* In *Egypt's Place in Universal History*, Bunsen gives the cycle of 21,000 years, which he adopts to facilitate the chronological calculations for the reconstruction of the universal history of mankind. He shows that this cycle "for the nutation of the ecliptic," arrived at its apex in the year 1240 of our era. He says:

"The cycle divides itself . . . into two halves of 10,500 (or twice 5,250) years each.

The beginning of the first half:
The highest point will be .................................................................... 19,760 B.C.
The lowest ............................................................................................ 9,260
Consequently the middle of the descending line (beginning of second
  quarter) will be .................................................................................. 14,510
The middle of the ascending line (beginning of fourth quarter) ......... 4,010

The new cycle, which began in 1240 of our era, will come to the end of its first quarter in 4010 A.D."

The Baron explains that "in round numbers, the most favorable epochs for our hemisphere since the great catastrophe in Middle Asia [Deluge 10,000 years B.C.], are: the 4,000 years before, and the 4,000 years after Christ; and the beginning of the first epoch *of which alone we can judge,* as it alone is complete before us, coincides exactly with the beginnings of national history, or (what is identical) with the beginning of *our consciousness* of continuous existence" (*Egypt's Place in Universal History,* Epilogue, p. 102).

"Our consciousness" must mean, we suppose, the consciousness *of scientists*, who accept nothing *on faith*, but much on unverified hypotheses. We do not say this with reference to the above-quoted author, earnest scholar and noble champion that he is, of freedom in the Christian Church, but generally. Baron Bunsen has well found for himself that a man cannot remain an honest scientist and please the clerical party. Even the little concessions he made in favor of the antiquity of mankind, brought on him, in 1859, the most insolent denunciations, such as "We lose all faith in the author's judgment . . . he has yet to learn the very principles of historical criticisms . . . extravagant and *unscientific* exaggeration," and so on — the pious vituperator closing his learned denunciations by assuring the public that Baron Bunsen "*cannot construe a Greek sentence* (*Quarterly Review,* 1859, pp. 382-421; see also *Egypt's Place in Universal History,* chap. on Egyptological Works and English Reviews, Vol. V, p. 118). But we do regret that Baron Bunsen had no better opportunity to examine the "Kabala" and the Brahmanical books of the Zodiacs.

In the Egyptian *Funeral Ritual* found among the hymns of the *Book of the Dead*, and which is termed by Bunsen "that precious and mysterious book," we read an address of the deceased, in the character of Horus, detailing all that he has done for his father Osiris. Among other things the deity says:

" 30. I have given thee thy *Spirit*.
31. I have given thee thy *Soul*.
32. I have given thee thy power.
33. I have given thee thy [force].*

In another place the entity, addressed as "Father" by the disembodied soul, is shown to mean the "spirit" of man; for the verse says: "I have made my soul come and speak with *his Father*," its *Spirit*.

The Egyptians regarded their *Ritual* as essentially a Divine inspiration; in short, as modern Hindus do the *Vedas*, and modern Jews their Mosaic books. Bunsen and Lepsius show that the term *Hermetic* means inspired; for it is Thoth, the Deity itself, that speaks and reveals to his elect among men the will of God and the arcana of divine things. Portions of them are expressly stated "to have been written by the very finger of Thoth himself, to have been the work and composition of the great God." † "At a later period their Hermetic character is still more distinctly recognized, and on a coffin of the 26th Dynasty Horus announces to the deceased that 'Thoth himself has brought him the books of his divine words,' or Hermetic writings." ‡

Since we are aware that Moses was an Egyptian priest, or at least that he was learned in all their *wisdom*, we need not be astonished that he should write in *Deuteronomy* (ix, 10): "And the *Lord* delivered unto me two tables of stone written with the finger of GOD"; or to find in *Exodus* xxxi, 18: "And he [the Lord] gave unto Moses . . . two tables of testimony, tables of stone, written with the finger of God."

In the Egyptian notions, as in those of all other faiths founded on philosophy, man was not merely, as with the Christians, a union of soul and body; he was a trinity when spirit was added to it. Besides, that doctrine made him consist of *kha* — body; *khaba* — astral form, or shadow; *ka* — animal soul or life-principle; *ba* — the higher soul; and *akh* — terrestrial intelligence. They had also a sixth principle named *sah* — or mummy; but the functions of this one commenced only after the death of the body.[50] After due purification, during which the soul, separated from its body, continued to revisit the latter in its mummified condition, this

---

\* Bunsen, *Egypt's Place*, etc., Vol. V, p. 325.
† Bunsen, *op. cit.*, Vol. V, pp. 133-34.
‡ *Ibid.*; see also Lepsius, *Denkmäler aus Aegypten, Abth.* III, Bl. 276.

astral soul "became a God," for it was finally absorbed into "the Soul of the world." It became transformed into one of the creative deities, "the god of Ptah," the Demiourgos, a generic name for the creators of the world, rendered in the *Bible* as the Elohim. In the *Ritual* the good or purified *soul*, "in conjunction with its higher or *uncreated* spirit, is more or less the victim of the dark influence of the dragon Apophis. If it has attained the final knowledge of the heavenly and the infernal mysteries — the *gnosis*, *i.e.*, complete reunion with the spirit, it will triumph over its enemies; if not, the soul could not escape its *second death*.\* It is "the lake that burneth with fire and brimstone" (elements), in which those that are cast undergo a "second death." † This death is the gradual dissolution of the astral form into its primal elements, alluded to several times already in the course of this work. But this awful fate can be avoided by the knowledge of the "Mysterious Name" — the "Word," ‡ say the kabalists.

And what, then, was the penalty attached to the neglect of it? When a man leads a naturally pure, virtuous life, there is none whatever; except a delay in the world of spirits, until he finds himself sufficiently purified to receive it from his Spiritual "Lord," one of the mighty Host. But if otherwise, the "soul," [51] as a half-animal principle, becomes paralyzed, and grows unconscious of its subjective half — the Lord — and in proportion to the sensuous development of the brain and nerves, sooner or later, it finally loses sight of its divine mission on earth. Like the *Vurdalak*, or Vampire, of the Serbian tale, the brain feeds and lives and grows

---

\* [Bunsen, *Egypt's Place*, etc., Vol. V, pp. 134-35, 136.] In the eighty-first chapter of the *Ritual* the soul is called *the germ of light* and in the seventy-ninth the Demiourgos, or one of the creators. [*Ibid.*, Vol. V, p. 144.]

† *Revel.* xxi, 8.

‡ We cannot help quoting a remark by Baron Bunsen in relation to the "Word" being identical with the "Ineffable Name" of the Masons and the kabalists. While explaining the *Ritual*, some of the details of which "resemble rather the *enchantments of a magician than solemn rites,* although a hidden and mystical meaning must have been attached to them" (the honest admission of this much, at least, is worth something), the author observes: "The mystery of names, the knowledge of which was a sovereign virtue, and which, at a later period degenerated into the *rank heresy* [?] of the Gnostics and the magic of enchanters, appears to have *existed not only in Egypt but elsewhere.* Traces of it are found in the 'Cabala' . . . it prevailed in the Greek and Asiatic mythology . . ." (*Egypt's Place*, etc., Vol. V, pp. 135, 147).

We then see the representatives of Science agreeing upon this one point, at least. The initiates of all countries had the same "mystery name." And now it remains with the scholars to prove that every adept, hierophant, magician, or enchanter (Moses and Aaron included) as well as every kabalist, from the institution of the Mysteries down to the present age, has been either a knave or a fool, for believing in the efficacy of this name.

in strength and power at the expense of its spiritual parent. Then the already half-unconscious soul, now fully intoxicated by the fumes of earthly life, becomes senseless, beyond hope of redemption. It is powerless to discern the splendor of its higher spirit, to hear the warning voice of its "guardian Angel," and its "God." It aims but at the development and fuller comprehension of natural, earthly life; and thus, can discover but the mysteries of physical nature. Its grief and fear, hope and joy, are all closely blended with its terrestrial existence. It ignores all that cannot be demonstrated by either its organs of action, or sensation. It begins by becoming virtually dead; it dies at last completely. It is *annihilated*. Such a catastrophe may often happen long years before the final separation of the *life*-principle from the body. When death arrives, its iron and clammy grasp finds work with *life* as usual; but there is no more a soul to liberate. The whole essence of the latter has been already absorbed by the vital system of the physical man. Grim death frees but a spiritual corpse; at best an idiot. Unable either to soar higher or awaken from lethargy, it is soon dissolved in the elements of the terrestrial atmosphere.

Seers, righteous men, who had attained to the highest science of the inner man and the knowledge of truth, have, like Marcus Antoninus, received instructions "from the gods," in sleep and otherwise. Helped by the purer spirits, those that dwell in "regions of eternal bliss," they have watched the process and warned mankind repeatedly. Skepticism may sneer; *faith,* based on *knowledge* and spiritual science, believes and affirms.

Our present cycle is pre-eminently one of such soul-deaths. We elbow soulless men and women at every step in life. Neither can we wonder, in the present state of things, at the gigantic failure of Hegel's and Schelling's last efforts at some metaphysical construction of a system. When facts, palpable and tangible facts of phenomenal Spiritualism, happen daily and hourly, and yet are denied by the majority of "civilized" nations, little chance is there for the acceptance of purely abstract metaphysics by the ever-growing crowd of materialists.

In the book called by Champollion *La Manifestation à la Lumière,* there is a chapter on the *Ritual* which is full of mysterious dialogues, with addresses to various "Powers" by the soul.[52] Among these dialogues there is one which is more than expressive of the potentiality of the "Word." The scene is laid in the "Hall of the Two Truths." The "Door," the "Hall of Truth," and even the various parts of the gate, address the soul which presents itself for admission. They all forbid it entrance unless it tells them their mystery, or mystic names. What student of the Secret Doctrines can fail to recognize in these names an identity of meaning and purpose with those to be met with in the *Vedas,* the later works of the Brahmans, and the *Kabala?*

Magicians, Kabalists, Mystics, Neo-Platonists and Theurgists of Alexandria, who so surpassed the Christians in their achievements in the secret science; Brahmans or Samaneans (Shamans) of old, and modern Brahmans; Buddhists and Lamaists, have all claimed that a certain power attaches to these various names, pertaining to one ineffable Word. We have shown from personal experience how deeply the belief is rooted to this day in the popular mind all over Russia,* that the Word works "miracles" and is at the bottom of every magical feat. Kabalists mysteriously connect *Faith* with it. So did the apostles, basing their assertions on the words of Jesus, who is made to say: "If ye have faith as a grain of mustard seed . . . nothing shall be impossible unto you" [*Matt.* xvii, 20], and Paul, repeating the words of Moses, tells that "the WORD is nigh thee, even in thy mouth, and in thy heart; that is, the *word of faith*" (*Romans* x, 8). But who, except the initiates, can boast of comprehending its full significance?

In our day it is as it was in olden times, to believe in the Biblical "miracles" requires *faith;* but to be enabled to produce them oneself demands a knowledge of the esoteric meaning of the "word." "If Christ," say Dr. F. W. Farrar and Canon B. F. Westcott, "wrought no miracles, then the *gospels* are untrustworthy." But even supposing that he did work them, would that prove that gospels written by others than himself are any more trustworthy? And if not, to what purpose is the argument? Besides, such a line of reasoning would warrant the analogy that miracles performed by other religionists than Christians ought to make *their* gospels trustworthy. Does not this imply at least an equality between the Christian Scriptures and the Buddhist sacred books? For these equally abound with phenomena of the most astounding character. Moreover, the Christians have no longer *genuine* miracles produced through their priests, for they have *lost the Word.* But many a Buddhist Lama or Siamese Talapoin — unless all travellers have conspired to lie — has been and now is able to duplicate every phenomenon described in the *New Testament,* and even do more, without any pretence of suspension of natural law or divine intervention either. In fact, Christianity proves that it is as dead in faith as it is dead in works, while Buddhism is full of vitality and supported by practical proofs.

The best argument in favor of the genuineness of Buddhist "miracles" lies in the fact that Catholic missionaries, instead of denying them or treating them as simple jugglery — as some Protestant missionaries do,

---

\* See Chap. I of this volume, pp. 42-44, note.

COUNT DE SAINT-GERMAIN

From a copper-engraving by N. Thomas, Paris, 1783, made from an oil painting attributed to Count Pietro dei Rotari (1707-1762), in the collection of the Marquise d'Urfé. The engraving is now in the Cabinet des Estampes of the Bibliothèque National in Paris.

### Sir William Jones
### 1746-1794

*Aetatis* 47. Drawn by A. W. Devis, Calcutta; engraved by Evans.
From *Memoirs of the Life, Writings, and Correspondence of Sir William Jones*, by Lord Teignmouth, London, 1804.

have often found themselves in such straits as to be forced to adopt the forlorn alternative of laying the whole on the back of the Devil. And so belittled do the Jesuits feel themselves in the presence of these genuine servants of God, that with an unparalleled cunning, they concluded to act in the case of the Talapoins and Buddhists as Mohammed is said to have acted with the mountain. "And seeing that it would not move toward him, the Prophet moved himself toward the mountain." Finding that they could not catch the Siamese with the birdlime of their pernicious doctrines in Christian garb, they disguised themselves, and for centuries appeared among the poor, ignorant people as Talapoins, until exposed. They have even voted and adopted a resolution forthwith, which has now all the force of an ancient article of faith. "Naaman, the Syrian," say the Jesuits of Caen, "did not dissemble his faith when he bowed the knee with the king in the house of Rimmon; *neither do the Fathers of the Society of Jesus dissemble, when they adopt the institute and the habit of the Talapoins of Siam* (nec dissimulant Patres S. J. Talapoinorum Siamensium institutum vestemque affectantes)." *

The potency contained in the *Mantras* and the *Vâch* of the Brahmans is as much believed in at this day as it was in the early Vedic period. The "Ineffable Name" of every country and religion relates to that which the Masons affirm to be the mysterious characters emblematic of the nine names or attributes by which the Deity was known to the initiates. The Omnific Word traced by Enoch on the two deltas of purest gold, on which he engraved two of the mysterious characters, is perhaps better known to the poor, uneducated "heathen" than to the highly accomplished Grand High Priests and Grand Z.'s of the Supreme Chapters of Europe and America. Only why the companions of the Royal Arch should so bitterly and constantly lament its loss, is more than we can understand. This word of M. M. is, as they will tell themselves, entirely composed of consonants. Hence, we doubt whether any of them could ever have mastered its pronunciation, had it even been "brought to light from the secret vault," instead of its several corruptions. However, it is to the land of Mizraim that the grandson of Ham is credited with having carried the sacred delta of the Patriarch Enoch. Therefore, it is in Egypt, and in the East alone that the mysterious "Word" must be sought.

But now that so many of the most important secrets of Masonry have been divulged by friend and foe, may we not say, without suspicion of malice or ill-feeling, that since the sad catastrophe of the Templars, no "Lodge" in Europe, still less in America, has ever known anything worth concealing. Reluctant to be misunderstood, we say no *Lodge*, leaving

---

* [*Thesis propugnata*, positio 9; Codoni, 1693.]

a few *chosen* brethren entirely out of question. The frantic denunciations of the Craft by Catholic and Protestant writers appear simply ridiculous, as also the affirmation of the Abbé Barruel that everything "betrays our Freemasons as the descendants of those proscribed Knights Templar" of 1314. The *Memoirs of Jacobinism**  by this Abbé, and eyewitness to the horrors of the first Revolution, is devoted in great measure to the Rosicrucians and other Masonic fraternities. The fact alone that he traces the modern Masons to the Templars, and points them out as secret assassins, trained to political murder, shows how little he knew of them, but how ardently he desired, at the same time, to find in these societies convenient scapegoats for the crimes and sins of another secret society which, since its existence, has harbored more than one dangerous political assassin — the Society of Jesus.

The accusations against Masons have been mostly half guesswork, half unquenchable malice and predetermined vilification. Nothing conclusive and certain of a criminal character has been directly proven against them. Even their abduction of Morgan has remained a matter of conjecture. The case was used at the time as a political convenience by huckstering politicians. When an unrecognizable corpse was found in Niagara River, one of the chiefs of this unscrupulous class, being informed that the identity was exceedingly questionable, unguardedly exposed the whole plot by saying: "Well, no matter, *he's a good enough Morgan until after the election!*" On the other hand, we find the Order of the Jesuits not only permitting, in certain cases, but actually *teaching and inciting to "High Treason and Regicide."* †

---

* [*Mémoires pour servir à l'histoire du Jacobinisme*, 1797, pt. II, ch. xi, pp. 375-77.]

† See *The Principles of the Jesuits, Developed in a Collection of Extracts from their own Authors*, London: J. G. and F. Rivington, St. Paul's Churchyard, and Waterloo Place, Pall Mall; H. Wix, 41 New Bridge Street, Blackfriars; J. Leslie, Great Queen Street, 1839. Section xvii, "High Treason and Regicide," containing thirty-four extracts from the same number of authorities (of the Society of Jesus) upon the question, among others the opinion thereof of the famous Robert Bellarmine. So Manuel de Sá says: "The rebellion of an ecclesiastic against a king *is not a crime of high treason, because he is not subject to the king*" (*Aphorismi confessariorum*, Coloniae, 1615, ed. Coll. Sion). "*The people*," says John Bridgewater, "*are not only permitted, but they are required, and their duty demands*, that at the mandate of the vicar of Christ, *who is the sovereign pastor over all the nations of the earth*, the faith which they had previously made with such princes should not be kept" (*Concertatio Ecclesiae Catholicae in Anglia adversus Calvino Papistas*, Resp. fol. 348).

In *De Rege et Regis Institutione Libri Tres*, 1640 (edit. Mus. Brit.), John Mariana goes even farther: ". . . if the circumstances will permit," he says, it will be lawful "to destroy with the sword the prince who is declared to be a public enemy . . . *I shall never consider that man to have done wrong, who, favoring the public wishes, would attempt to kill him,*" and "*to put them to death is not only lawful, but a laudable and glorious*

A series of *Lectures* upon Freemasonry and its dangers, as delivered in 1862 by James Burton Robertson, Professor of Modern History in the Dublin University, are lying before us. In them the lecturer quotes profusely as his authorities the said Abbé Barruel (a natural enemy of the Masons, *who cannot be caught at the confessional*), and Robison, a well-known apostate-Mason of 1798. As usual with every party, whether belonging to the Masonic or anti-Masonic side, the traitor from the opposing camp is welcomed with praise and encouragement, and great care is taken to whitewash him. However convenient for certain political reasons the celebrated Committee of the Anti-Masonic Convention of 1830 (U.S. of America) may have found it to adopt this most Jesuitical proposition of Pufendorf that "oaths oblige not when they are absurd and impertinent," and that other which teaches that "an oath obliges not if God does not accept it," * yet no truly honest man would accept such sophistry. We sincerely believe that the better portion of humanity will ever bear in mind that there exists a moral code of honor far more binding that an oath, whether on the *Bible, Koran,* or *Veda*. The Essenes never swore on anything at all, but their "yeas" and "nays" were as good and far better than an oath. Besides, it seems surpassingly strange to find nations that call themselves Christian instituting customs in civil and ecclesiastical courts diametrically opposed to the command of their God,† who distinctly forbids any swearing at all, "neither by heaven . . . nor by the earth . . . nor

---

*action*." Est tamen salutaris cogitatio, ut sit principibus persuasum si rempublicam oppresserint, si vitiis et faeditate intolerandi erunt, *ea conditione vivere, ut non jure tantum, sed cum laude et gloria perimi possint*" (Lib. i, c. 6, p. 61).

But the most delicate piece of Christian teaching is found in the precept of this Jesuit when he argues upon the best and surest way of killing kings and statesmen. "In my own opinion," he says, "deleterious drugs should not be given to an enemy, neither should a deadly poison be mixed with his food or in his cup . . . Yet *it will indeed be lawful to use this method* in the case in question [that "*he who should kill the tyrant would be highly esteemed, both in favor and in praise*," for "*it is a glorious thing to exterminate this pestilent and mischievous race from the community of men*"]; not to constrain the person who is to be killed, to take of himself the poison which, inwardly received, would deprive him of life, *but to cause it to be outwardly applied by another* without his intervention: as, when there is so much strength in the poison, that if spread upon a seat or on the clothes, it would be sufficiently powerful to cause death" (*Ibid.*, lib. i, c. 7, p. 67). It was thus that Squire attempted the life of Queen Elizabeth, at the instigation of the Jesuit Walpole. See É. Pasquier, *Le Catéchisme des Jésuites*, etc., 1677, pp. 350-52; and de Rapin-Thoyras, *Histoire d'Angleterre*, 2nd ed., 1733, t. VI, bk. xvii, p. 145.

* S. von Pufendorf, *Le Droit de la nature et des gens*, Basle, 1750, Vol. I, Bk. iv, ch. ii, p. 541.

† "Again, ye have heard that it hath been said by them of old time, thou shalt not forswear thyself . . . But I say unto you, swear not at all." etc. "But let your communication be yea, yea; nay, nay; for whatsoever is more than these cometh of evil" (*Matthew* v, 33, 34, 37).

by the head." It seems to us that to maintain that "an oath obliges not if God does not accept it," besides being an absurdity — as no man living, whether he be fallible or infallible, can learn anything of God's secret thoughts — is *anti-Christian* in the full sense of the word.* The argument is brought forward only because it is convenient and answers the object. Oaths will never be binding till each man will fully understand that humanity is the highest manifestation on earth of the Unseen Supreme Deity, and each man an incarnation of his God; and when the sense of *personal* responsibility will be so developed in him that he will consider forswearing the greatest possible insult to himself, as well as to humanity. No oath is now binding, unless taken by one who, without any oath at all, would solemnly keep his simple promise of honor. Therefore, to bring forward as authorities such men as Barruel or Robison is simply obtaining the public confidence under false pretences. It is not the "spirit of *Masonic malice* whose heart coins slanders like a mint," but far more that of the Catholic clergy and their champions; and a man who would reconcile the two ideas of honor and perjury, in any case whatever, is not to be trusted himself.

Loud is the claim of the nineteenth century to pre-eminence in civilization over the ancients, and still more clamorous that of the churches and their sycophants that Christianity has redeemed the world from barbarism and idolatry. How little both are warranted, we have tried to prove in these two volumes. The light of Christianity has only served to show how much more hypocrisy and vice its teachings have begotten in the world since its advent, and how immensely superior were the ancients over us in every point of honor.† The clergy, by teaching the helplessness of man, his utter dependence on Providence, and the doctrine of atonement, have crushed in their faithful followers every atom of self-reliance and self-respect. So true is this, that it is becoming an axiom that the most honorable men are to be found among atheists and the so-called "infidels." We hear from Hipparchus that in the days of *heathenism* "the shame and disgrace that justly attended the violation of his oath, threw the poor wretch into a fit of madness and despair, so that he cut his throat and perished by his own hand, and his memory was so abhorred after his death that his body lay upon the shore of the Island of Samos, and had no other burial than the sands of the sea." ‡ But in our own

---

* Barbeyrac, in his notes on Pufendorf, shows that the Peruvians used no oath, but a simple averment before the Inca, and were never found perjuring themselves.

† We beg the reader to remember that we do not mean by Christianity the *teachings of Christ*, but those of his alleged servants — the clergy.

‡ Dr. Anderson's *Defence of Masonry* quoted by John Yarker in his *Notes on the Scientific and Religious Mysteries of Antiquity*, p. 24.

century we find ninety-six delegates to the United States Anti-Masonic Convention, every one doubtless a member of some Protestant Church, and claiming the respect due to men of honor and gentlemen, offering the most Jesuitical arguments against the validity of a Masonic oath. The Committee, pretending to quote the authority of "the most distinguished guides in the philosophy of morals, and claiming the most ample support of *the inspired*\* . . . who wrote before Freemasonry existed," resolved that, as an oath was "a transaction between man on one part and the Almighty Judge on the other," and the Masons were all infidels and "unfit for civil trust," therefore their oaths had to be considered illegal and not binding.†

But we will return to these *Lectures* of Robertson and his charges against Masonry. The greatest accusation brought against the latter is that Masons reject a *personal* God (this on the authority of Barruel and Robison), and that they claim to be in possession of a "secret to make men better and happier than Christ, his apostles and his Church have made them." Were the latter accusation but half-true, it might yet allow the consoling hope that they had really found that secret by breaking off entirely from the mythical Christ of the Church and the official Jehovah. But both the accusations are simply as malicious as they are absurd and untrue, as we shall presently see.

Let it not be imagined that we are influenced by personal feeling in any of our reflections upon Masonry. So far from this being the case, we unhesitatingly proclaim our highest respect for the original purposes of the Order and some of our most valued friends are within its membership. We say naught against Masonry as it should be, but denounce it as, thanks to the intriguing clergy, both Catholic and -Protestant, it now begins to be. Professedly the most absolute of democracies, it is practically the appanage of aristocracy, wealth, and personal ambition. Professedly the teacher of true ethics, it is debased into a propaganda of anthropomorphic theology. The half-naked apprentice, brought before the master during the initiation of the first degree, is taught that at the door of the lodge every social distinction is laid aside, and the poorest brother is the peer of every other, though a reigning sovereign or an imperial prince. In practice, the Craft turns lickspittle in every monarchical country to any regal scion who may deign, for the sake of using it as a political tool, to put on the once symbolical lambskin.

How far gone is the Masonic Fraternity in this direction, we can judge

---

\* Epiphanius included, we must think, after he, in violation of his oath, had sent over seventy persons into exile, who belonged to the secret society he betrayed.

† United States Anti-Masonic Convention: "Obligation of Masonic Oaths," speech delivered by Mr. Hopkins, of New York.

from the words of one of its highest authorities. John Yarker, Jr., of England; Past Grand Warden of the Grand Lodge of Greece; Grand Master of the Rite of Swedenborg; also Grand Master of the Ancient and Primitive Rite of Masonry, and Heaven only knows what else,* says that Masonry could lose nothing by "the adoption of a higher (not pecuniary) standard of membership and morality, with exclusion from the 'purple' of all who *inculcate frauds, sham, historical degrees, and other immoral abuses*" (page 158). And again, on page 157: "As the Masonic fraternity is now governed the Craft is fast becoming the paradise of the *bon vivant*; of the 'charitable' hypocrite, who forgets the version of St. Paul, and decorates his breast with the 'charity jewel' (having by this judicious expenditure obtained the 'purple' he metes out judgment to other brethren of greater ability and morality but less means); the manufacturer of paltry Masonic tinsel; the rascally merchant who swindles in hundreds, and even thousands, by appealing to the tender consciences of those few who do regard their O.B.'s; and the Masonic 'Emperors' and other charlatans who make power or money out of the aristocratic pretensions which they have tacked on to our institution — *ad captandum vulgus*."

We have no wish to make a pretence of exposing secrets long since hawked about the world by perjured Masons. Everything vital, whether in symbolical representations, rites, or passwords, as used in modern Freemasonry, is known in the Eastern fraternities; though there seems to be no intercourse or connection between them. If Medea is described by Ovid as having "arm, breast, and knee made bare, left foot slipshod"; and Virgil, speaking of Dido, shows this "Queen herself . . . now resolute on death, having one foot bare, etc.," † why doubt that there are in the East *real* "Patriarchs of the sacred *Vedas*," explaining the esotericism of pure Hindu theology and Brahmanism quite as thoroughly as European "Patriarchs"?

But, if there are a few Masons who, from study of kabalistic and other rare works, and coming in personal communication with "Brothers" from the faraway East, have learned something of *esoteric* Masonry, it is not the case with the hundreds of American Lodges. While engaged on this chapter, we have received most unexpectedly, through the kindness of a friend, a copy of Mr. Yarker's volume, from which passages are quoted above. It is brimful of learning and, what is more, of *knowledge*,

---

* John Yarker, *Notes on the Scientific and Religious Mysteries of Antiquity; the Gnosis and Secret Schools of the Middle Ages; Modern Rosicrucianism; and the Various Rites and Degrees of Free and Accepted Masonry*, London, 1872.

† [Ovid, *Metam.*, VII, 180 *et seq.*; Virgil, *Aeneid*, IV, 517 *et seq.*]

as it seems to us. It is especially valuable at this moment, since it corroborates, in many particulars, what we have said in this work. Thus, we read in it the following:

"We think we have sufficiently established the fact of the connection of Freemasonry with the other Speculative Rites of antiquity, as well as the antiquity and purity of the old English Templar Rite of *seven degrees*, and the spurious derivation of many of the other rites therefrom."*

Such high Masons need not be told, though Craftsmen in general do, that the time has come to remodel Masonry, and restore those ancient landmarks, borrowed from the early sodalities, which the eighteenth century founders of speculative Freemasonry meant to have incorporated in the fraternity. There are no longer any secrets left unpublished; the Order is degenerating into a convenience for selfish men to use, and bad men to debase.

It is but recently that a majority of the Supreme Councils of the Ancient and Accepted Rite assembled at Lausanne, justly revolting against such a blasphemous belief as that in a personal Deity, invested with all human attributes, pronounced the following words: "Freemasonry proclaims, as it has proclaimed from its origin, the existence of a *creative principle*, under the name of the great Architect of the universe." Against this, a small minority has protested, urging that "belief in a *creative principle* is not *the belief in God, which Freemasonry requires of every candidate* before he can pass its very threshold."

This confession does not sound like the rejection of a personal God. Could we have had the slightest doubt upon the subject, it would be thoroughly dispelled by the words of General Albert Pike, perhaps the greatest authority of the day, among American Masons, who raises himself most violently against this innovation. We cannot do better than quote his words:

"This *Principe Créateur* is no new phrase — it is but an old term revived. *Our adversaries, numerous and formidable*, will say, and will have the right to say, that our *Principe Créateur* is identical with the *Principe Générateur* of the Indians and Egyptians, and may fitly be symbolized as it was symbolized anciently, by the Linga . . . To accept this, in lieu of a personal God, is TO ABANDON CHRISTIANITY, and *the worship of Jehovah*, and return to wallow in the styes of Paganism." †

---

* John Yarker, *Notes on the Scientific*, etc., p. 150.

† *Proceedings of the Supreme Council of Sovereign Grand Inspectors-General of the Thirty-third and Last Degree*, etc., etc. Held at the City of New York, August 15, 1876, pp. 54, 55.

And are those of *Jesuitism,* then, so much cleaner? "Our adversaries, numerous and formidable." That sentence says all. Who these so formidable enemies are, is useless to inquire. They are the Roman Catholics, and some of the Reformed Presbyterians. To read what the two factions respectively write, we may well ask which adversary is the more afraid of the other. But, what shall it profit anyone to organize against a fraternity that does not even dare to have a belief of its own for fear of giving offense? And pray, how, if Masonic oaths mean anything, and Masonic penalties are regarded as more than burlesque, can any adversaries, numerous or few, feeble or strong, know what goes on inside the lodge, or penetrate beyond that "brother terrible, or the tiler, who guards, with a drawn sword, the portals of the lodge"? Is, then, this "brother terrible" no more formidable than Offenbach's *General Boum,* with his smoking pistol, jingling spurs, and towering *panache?* Of what use the millions of men that make up this great fraternity, the world over, if they cannot be so cemented together as to bid defiance to all adversaries? Can it be that the "mystic tie" is but a rope of sand, and Masonry but a toy to feed the vanity of a few leaders who rejoice in ribbons and regalia? Is its authority as false as its antiquity? It seems so, indeed; and yet, as "even the fleas have smaller fleas to bite 'em," there are Catholic alarmists, even here, who pretend to fear Masonry!

And yet, these same Catholics, in all the serenity of their traditional impudence, publicly threaten America, with its 500,000 Masons, and 34,000,000 Protestants, with a union of Church and State under the direction of Rome! The danger which threatens the free institutions of this republic, we are told, will come from "the principles of Protestantism logically developed." The present Secretary of the Navy — the Hon. R. W. Thompson, of Indiana, having actually dared, in his own free Protestant country, to publish a book recently on *The Papacy and the Civil Power,* in which his language is as moderate as it is gentlemanly and fair, a Roman Catholic priest at Washington, D. C. — the very seat of Government — denounces him with violence. What is better, a representative member of the Society of Jesus, Father F. X. Weninger, D.D., pours upon his devoted head a vial of wrath that seems to have been brought direct from the Vatican cellars. "The assertions," he says, "which Mr. Thompson makes on the necessary antagonism between the Catholic Church and Free Institutions, are characterized by pitiful ignorance and blind audacity. He is reckless of logic, of history, of common sense and of charity; and presents himself before the loyal American people as a narrow-minded bigot. No scholar would venture to repeat the stale calumnies which have been so often refuted . . . In answer to his accusations against the Church as the enemy of liberty, I tell him that if ever this country should become a Catholic country, that is, if Catholics should ever be in the majority, and *have the control of political power,* then he would see the principles of our Constitution carried out to their fullest extent; he would see that these States would be in very deed 'United.' He would behold a people living in peace and harmony; joined in the bonds of one faith, their hearts beating in unison with love of their fatherland, with charity and forbearance towards all, and respecting the rights of conscience even of their slanderers." *

In behalf of this "Society of Jesus," he advises Mr. Thompson to send his book to Czar Alexander II, and to Frederick William, Emperor of Germany. He may expect from them, as a token of their sympathy, the orders of St. Andrew and of the Black Eagle. "From clear-minded, self-thinking, patriotic Americans, he cannot expect anything but the *decoration* of their contempt. As long as American hearts *will* beat in American bosoms, and the blood of their Fathers *shall* flow in their veins, such efforts as Thompson's *shall* not succeed. True, genuine Americans will protect the Catholic Church in this country, and *will finally join it*." After that, having thus, as he seems to think, left the corpse of his impious antagonist upon the field, he marches off emptying the dregs of his exhausted bottle after the following fashion: "We leave the volume, whose argument we have killed, as a carcass to be devoured by those Texan buzzards — those stinking birds — we mean that kind of men, who love to feed on corruption, calumnies and lies, and are attracted by the stench of them."

This last sentence is worthy to be added as an appendix to the *Discorsi del Sommo Pontefice Pio IX*, by Don Pasquale de Franciscis, immortalized in the contempt of Mr. Gladstone. — *Tel maître tel valet!*

Moral: This will teach fair-minded, sober, and gentlemanly writers that even so well-bred an antagonist as Mr. Thompson has shown himself in his book, cannot hope to escape the only available weapon in the Catholic armory — Billingsgate. The whole argument of the author shows that while forcible, he intends to be fair; but he might as well have attacked with a Tertullianistic violence, for his treatment would not have been worse. It will doubtless afford him some consolation to be placed in the same category with schismatic and infidel emperors and kings.

While Americans, including Masons, are now warned to prepare themselves to join the Holy Apostolic and Roman Catholic Church, we are glad to know that there are some as loyal and respected as any in Masonry who support our views. Conspicuous among them is our venerable friend, Mr. Leon Hyneman, P.M., and a member of the Grand Lodge of Pennsylvania. For eight or nine years he was editor of the *Masonic Mirror*

---

* [*Reply to Hon. R. W. Thompson . . . addressed to the American People*, N. Y., 1877, pp. 28, 82.]

*and Keystone,* and is an author of repute. He assures us personally that for over thirty years he has combated the design to erect into a Masonic dogma belief in a *personal* God. In his work, *Ancient York and London Grand Lodges,* he says: "Masonry, instead of unfolding progressively with the intellectual advancement of scientific knowledge and general intelligence, has departed from the original aims of the fraternity, and is apparently inclining towards a sectarian society. That is plainly to be seen . . . [in] the persistent determination not to expunge the sectarian innovations interpolated in the Ritual . . . It would appear that the Masonic fraternity of this country are as indifferent to ancient landmarks and usages of Masonry, as the Masons of the past century, under the London Grand Lodge were." * It was this conviction which prompted him, in 1856, when Jacques Étienne Marconis de Nègre, Grand Hierophant of the Rite of Memphis, came to America and tendered him the Grand Mastership of the Rite in the United States, and the Ancient and Accepted Rite offered him an Honorary 33rd — to refuse both.

The Temple was the last European secret organization which, as a body, had in its possession some of the mysteries of the East. True, there were in the past century (and perhaps still are) isolated "Brothers" faithfully and secretely working under the direction of Eastern Brotherhoods. But these, when they did belong to European societies, invariably joined them for objects unknown to the Fraternity, though at the same time for the benefit of the latter. It is through them that modern Masons have all they know of importance; and the similarity now found between the Speculative Rites of antiquity, the mysteries of the Essenes, Gnostics and the Hindus, and the highest and oldest of the Masonic degrees well prove the fact. If these mysterious brothers became possessed of the secrets of the societies, they could never reciprocate the confidence, though in their hands these secrets were safer, perhaps, than in the keeping of European Masons. When certain of the latter were found worthy of becoming affiliates of the Orient, they were secretly instructed and initiated, but the others were none the wiser for that.

No one could ever lay hands on the Rosicrucians, and notwithstanding the alleged discoveries of "secret chambers," *vellums* called "T," and of fossil knights with ever-burning lamps, this ancient association and its true aims are to this day a mystery. Pretended Templars and sham Rose-Croix, with a few genuine kabalists, were occasionally burned, and some unlucky Theosophists and alchemists sought and put to the torture; delusive confessions even were wrung from them by the most ferocious means, but yet, the true Society remains today, as it has ever been, unknown to all, especially to its cruelest enemy — the Church.

---

* *Op. cit.,* pp. 169-70.

As to the modern Knights Templars and those Masonic Lodges which now claim a direct descent from the ancient Templars, their persecution by the Church was a farce from the beginning. They have not, nor have they ever had, any secrets dangerous to the Church. Quite the contrary; for we find J. G. Findel saying that the "Scottish degrees or the Templar system dates from 1735-1740, and *following its Catholic tendency took up its chief residence in the Jesuit college of Clermont in Paris* and hence was called the Clermont system." The present Swedish system has also something of the Templar element in it, but free from Jesuits and interference with politics; however, it asserts that it has de Molay's Testament in the original, for a Count Beaujeu, a nephew of de Molay, *never heard of elsewhere,* transplanted Templarism into Freemasonry, and thus procured for his uncle's ashes a mysterious sepulchre. It is sufficient to prove this to be a Masonic fable; that on this pretended monument the day of de Molay's funeral is represented as March 11, 1313, while the day of his death was March 19, 1313 . . . This spurious production which is neither genuine Templarism nor genuine Freemasonry, has never taken firm root in Germany. But the case is otherwise in France. . ." *

Writing upon this subject, we must hear what Wilcke † has to say of these pretensions:

"The present Knights Templars of Paris will have it, that they are direct descendants from the ancient Knights, and endeavor to prove this by documents, interior regulations, and secret doctrines. Foraisse says the Fraternity of Freemasons was founded in Egypt, Moses communicating the secret teaching to the Israelites, Jesus to the Apostles, and thence it found its way to the Knights Templars. Such inventions are necessary . . . to the assertion that the Parisian Templars are the offspring of the ancient order. All these asseverations, unsupported by history, were fabricated *in the High Chapter of Clermont* [Jesuits], and preserved by the Parisian Templars as a legacy left them by those political revolutionists, the Stuarts and the Jesuits." Hence we find the Bishops Grégoire ‡ and Münter § supporting them.

Connecting the modern with the ancient Templars, we can at best, therefore, allow them an adoption of certain rites and ceremonies of purely *ecclesiastical* character after they had been cunningly inoculated into that grand and antique Order by the clergy. Since this desecration, it gradually lost its primitive and simple character, and went fast to its final ruin. Founded in 1118 by the Knights Hugues des Payens and

---

\* [*History of Freemasonry,* pp. 688-89.]

† [*History of the Order of Knights-Templars,* Halle, 1860.]

‡ *Histoire des sectes religieuses,* etc., II, pp. 392-428; Paris, 1828.

§ *Notitia codicis graeci evangelium Johannis variatum continentis,* Havniae, 1828.

Geoffroy de Saint-Adhémar, nominally for the protection of the pilgrims, its true aims was the restoration of the primitive secret worship. The true version of the history of Jesus, and the early Christianity was imparted to Hugh de Payens, by the Grand-Pontiff of the Order of the Temple (of the Nazarene or Johannite sect), one named Theocletes, after which it was learned by some Knights in Palestine, from the higher and more intellectual members of the St. John sect, who were initiated into its mysteries.* Freedom of intellectual thought and the restoration of one and universal religion was their secret object. Sworn to the vow of obedience, poverty and chastity, they were at first the true Knights of John the Baptist, crying in the wilderness and living on wild honey and locusts. Such is the tradition and the true kabalistic version.

It is a mistake to state that the Order became only later anti-Catholic. It was so from the beginning, and the red cross on the white mantle, the vestment of the Order, had the same significance as with the initiates in every other country. It pointed to the four quarters of the compass, and was the emblem of the universe. † When, later, the Brotherhood was transformed into a Lodge, the Templars had, in order to avoid persecution, to perform their own ceremonies in the greatest secrecy, generally in the hall of the chapter, more frequently in isolated caves or country houses built amidst woods, while the ecclesiastical form of worship was carried on publicly in the chapels belonging to the Order.

Though of the accusations brought against them by order of Philip IV, many were infamously false, the main charges were certainly correct, from the standpoint of what is considered by the Church, *heresy*. The present-day Templars, adhering strictly as they do to the *Bible*, can hardly claim descent from those who did not believe in Christ, as Godman, or as the Savior of the world; who rejected the miracle of his birth, and those performed by himself; who did not believe in transubstantiation, the saints, holy relics, purgatory, etc. The Christ Jesus was, in their opinion, a false prophet, but the man Jesus a Brother. They regarded John the Baptist as their patron, but never viewed him in the light in which he is presented in the *Bible*. They reverenced the doctrines of alchemy, astrology, magic, kabalistic talismans, and adhered to

---

* This is the reason why unto this day the fanatical and kabalistic members of the Nazarenes of Basra (Persia), have a tradition of the glory, wealth and power of their "Brothers," agents, or *messengers* as they term them in Malta and Europe. There are some few remaining yet, they say, who will sooner or later restore the doctrine of their Prophet Yôḥânân (St. John), the son of Lord Jordan, and eliminate from the hearts of humanity every other false teaching.

† The two great pagodas of Mathurâ and Benares, are built in the form of a cross, each wing being equal in extent (Maurice, *Indian Antiquities,* 1793-1800, Vol. III, pp. 360-377).

the secret teachings of their chiefs in the East. "In the last century," says Findel, "when Freemasonry erroneously supposed herself to be a daughter of Templarism, great pains were taken to regard the Order of Knights Templars as innocent . . . For this purpose not only legends and unrecorded events were fabricated, but pains were taken to repress the truth. The Masonic admirers of the Knights Templars bought up the whole of the documents of the lawsuit published by Mohldenhawer, because they proved the culpability of the Order." *

This culpability consisted in their "heresy" against the Roman Catholic Church. While the real "Brothers" died an ignominious death, the spurious Order which tried to step into their shoes became exclusively a branch of the Jesuits under the immediate tutelage of the latter. True-hearted, honest Masons, ought to reject with horror any connection, let alone descent from these.

"The Knights of St. John of Jerusalem," writes Commander Gourdin, "sometimes called the Knights Hospitallers, and the Knights of Malta, were not Freemasons. On the contrary, they seem to have been inimical to Freemasonry, for in 1740, the Grand Master of the Order of Malta caused the Bull of Clement XII to be published in that island, and forbade the meetings of the Freemasons. On this occasion several knights and many citizens left the island; and, in 1741, the Inquisition pursued the Freemasons at Malta. The Grand Master proscribed their assemblies under severe penalties, and six knights were banished from the island, in perpetuity, for having assisted at a meeting. In fact, unlike the Templars, they had not even a secret form of reception. Reghellini says that he was unable to procure a copy of the secret ritual of the Knights of Malta. The reason is obvious — there is none!" †

And yet American Templarism comprises three degrees. 1, Knight of the Red Cross; 2, Knight Templar; and 3, Knight of Malta. It was introduced from France into the United States in 1808, and the first *Grand Encampment General* was organized on June 21, 1816, with Governor De Witt Clinton of New York, as Grand Master.

This inheritance of the Jesuits should hardly be boasted of. If the Knights Templars desire to make good their claims, they must choose between a descent from the "heretical," anti-Christian, kabalistic, primitive Templars, or connect themselves with the Jesuits, and nail their tessellated carpets directly on the platform of ultra-Catholicism! Otherwise, their claims become a mere pretence.

---

\* Findel, *History of Freemasonry*, Appendix, p. 685.

† *A Sketch of the Knights Templars and the Knights Hospitallers of St. John of Jerusalem*, by Richard Woof, F.S.A., Commander of the Order of Masonic Knights Templars, pp. 70-71.

So impossible does it become for the originators of the *ecclesiastical* pseudo-order of Templars, invented, according to Dupuy, in France by the adherents of the Stuarts, to avoid being considered a branch of the Order of the Jesuits, that we are not surprised to see an anonymous author, rightly suspected of belonging to the Jesuit Chapter at Clermont, publishing a work in 1751, in Brussels, on the lawsuit of the Knights Templars. In this volume, in sundry mutilated notes, additions, and commentaries, he represents the *innocence* of the Templars of the accusation of "heresy," thus robbing them of the greatest title to respect and admiration that these early freethinkers and martyrs have won!

This last pseudo-order was constituted at Paris, on the 4th of November, 1804, by virtue of a *forged Constitution*, and ever since it has "contaminated genuine Freemasonry," as the highest Masons themselves tell us. *La Charte de transmission* (tabula aurea Larmenii) presents the outward appearance of such extreme antiquity "that Grégoire confesses that if all the other relics of the Parisian treasury of the Order had not silenced his doubts as to their ancient descent, the sight of this charter would at the very first glance have persuaded him." * The first Grand Master of this spurious Order was a physician of Paris, Dr. Fabré-Palaprat, who assumed the name of Bernard Raymond.

Count M. A. Ramsay, a Jesuit, was the first to start the idea of the Templars being joined to the Knights of Malta. Therefore, we read from his pen the following:

"Our forefathers [!!!], the Crusaders, assembled in the Holy Land from all Christendom, wished to unite in a Fraternity embracing all nations, that when bound together heart and soul for mutual improvement, they might, in the course of time, represent one single intellectual people." †

This is why the Templars are made to join the St. John's Knights, and the latter got into the craft of Masonry known as St. John's Masons.

In *Le Sceau rompu*, in 1745, we find, therefore, the following most impudent falsehood, worthy of the Sons of Loyola: "The lodges were dedicated to St. John, because the *Knights* (!) Masons had in the holy wars in Palestine joined the Knights of St. John." ‡

In 1743, the Kadosh degree was invented at Lyons (so writes Thory,§ at least), and "it represents the *revenge of the Templars*." And here we find Findel saying that "the Order of Knights Templars had been abolished in 1311, and to that epoch they were obliged to have recourse

---

* Findel, *History of Freemasonry*, Appendix, p. 690.

† ["Speech delivered by Mr. de R.," 1740; see Lenning's *Encyclopädie der Freimaurerei*, III, pp. 195 *et seq.* Cf. Findel, *op. cit.*, p. 205.]

‡ [Findel, *op. cit.*, p. 206.]

§ [*Histoire de la fondation du Grand Orient de France*, Paris, 1812.]

when, after the banishment of several Knights from Malta in 1740, because they were Freemasons, it was no longer possible to keep up a connection with the Order of St. John or Knights of Malta, then in the plenitude of their power *under the sovereignty of the Pope.*" \*

Turning to Clavel, one of the best Masonic authorities, we read: "It is clear that the erection of the French Order of the Knights Templars is not more ancient than the year 1804, and that it cannot lay any legitimate claim to being the continuation of the so-called Society of *la petite Résurrection des Templiers,* nor did this latter either extend back to the ancient Order of Knights Templars." † Therefore, we see these pseudo-Templars, under the guidance of the worthy Father Jesuits, forging in Paris, 1806, the famous charter of Larmenius. Twenty years later, this nefast and subterranean body, guiding the hand of assassins, directed it toward one of the best and greatest princes in Europe, whose mysterious death, unfortunately for the interests of truth and justice, has never been — for political reasons — investigated and proclaimed to the world as it ought to have been. It is this prince, a Freemason himself, who was the last depository of the secrets of the true Knights Templars. For long centuries these had remained unknown and unsuspected. Holding their meetings once every *thirteen* years at Malta, and their Grand Master advising the European brothers of the place of *rendezvous* but a few hours in advance, these representatives of the once mightiest and most glorious body of Knights assembled on the fixed day, from various points of the earth. *Thirteen* in number, in commemoration of the year of the death of Jacques de Molay (1313), the now Eastern brothers, among whom were crowned heads, planned together the future religious and political fate of the nations; while the Popish Knights, their murderous and bastard successors, slept soundly in their beds, without a dream disturbing their guilty consciences.

"And yet," says Rebold, "notwithstanding the confusion they had created (1736-72), the Jesuits had accomplished but one of their designs, viz.: *denaturalizing and bringing into disrepute the Masonic Institution.* Having succeeded, as they believed, in destroying it in one form, they were determined to use it in another. With this determination, they arranged the systems styled 'Clerkship of the Templars,' an amalgamation of the different histories, events, and characteristics of the crusades mixed with the reveries of the alchemists. *In this combination Catholicism governed all, and the whole fabrication moved upon wheels, representing the great object for which the Society of Jesus was organized.*" ‡

Hence, the rites and symbols of Masonry which though "Pagan" in

---

\* [*Hist. of Freemasonry*, p. 211.]

† [*Ibid.*, p. 446.]

‡ *Histoire générale de la Franc-Maçonnerie,* pp. 212 *et seq.*

origin, are all applied to and all flavor of Christianity. A Mason has to declare his belief in a *personal* God, Jehovah, and in the Encampment degrees, also in Christ, before he can be accepted in the Lodge, while the Johannite Templars believed in the unknown and invisible Principle, whence proceeded the Creative Powers misnamed *gods*, and held to the Nazarene version of Panthera being the sinful father of Jesus, who thus proclaimed himself "the son of god and of humanity." * This also accounts for the fearful oaths of the Masons taken *on the Bible*, and for their lectures servilely agreeing with the Patriarcho-Biblical chronology. In the American Order of Rose-Croix, for instance, when the neophyte approaches the altar, the "Sir Knights are called to order, and the captain of the guard makes his proclamation." "To the glory of the sublime architect of the universe [Jehovah-Binah?], under the auspices of the Sovereign Sanctuary of *Ancient* and *Primitive* Freemasonry," etc., etc. Then the Knight Orator strikes One and tells the neophyte that the antique legends of Masonry date back FORTY centuries; claiming no greater antiquity for the oldest of them than 622 A.M., at which time he says Noah was born. Under the circumstances this will be regarded as a liberal concession to chronological preferences. After that, Masons † are apprised that it was about the year 2188 B.C., that Mizraim led colonies into Egypt and laid the foundation of the Kingdom of Egypt, which kingdom lasted 1,663 years (!!!). Strange chronology, which, if it piously conforms with that of the *Bible*, disagrees entirely with that of history. The mythical nine names of the Deity, imported into Egypt, according

---

\* See Gaffarel's version; Éliphas Lévi's *La Science des Esprits;* MacKenzie's *Royal Masonic Cyclopaedia; Sepher-Toledoth-Yeshu;* and other kabalistical and Rabbinical works. The story given is this. A virgin named Mariam, betrothed to a young man of the name of Yôḥânân, was outraged by another man named Panthera or Pandira, says *Sepher-Toledoth-Yeshu.* "Her betrothed, learning of her misfortune, left her, at the same time forgiving her. The child born was Jesus, named Joshua. Adopted by his uncle Rabbi Jehoshuah, he was initiated into the secret doctrine by Rabbi Elhanan, a kabalist, and then by the Egyptian priests, who consecrated him High Pontiff of the Universal Secret Doctrine, on account of his great mystic qualities. Upon his return into Judaea his learning and powers excited the jealousy of the Rabbis, and they publicly reproached him with his origin and insulted his mother. Hence the words attributed to Jesus at Cana: 'Woman, what have I to do with thee?'" (See *John* ii, 4.) His disciples having rebuked him with his unkindness to his mother, Jesus repented, and having learned from them the particulars of the sad story, he declared that "My mother has not sinned, she has not lost her innocence; she is immaculate and yet she is a mother . . . As for myself I have no father, in this world, I am the Son of God and of humanity!" Sublime words of confidence and trust in the unseen Power, but how fatal to the millions upon millions of men murdered because of these very words being so thoroughly misunderstood!

† We speak of the American Chapter of Rose-Croix.

to the Masons, only in the twenty-second century B.C., are found on monuments reckoned twice as old by the best Egyptologists. Nevertheless we must take at the same time into consideration, that the Masons are themselves ignorant of these names.

The simple truth is that modern Masonry is a sadly different thing from what the once universal secret fraternity was in the days when the Brahma-worshippers of the AUM exchanged grips and passwords with the devotees of TUM, and the adepts of every country under the sun were "Brothers."

What was then that mysterious name, that mighty "word" through whose potency the Hindu as well as the Chaldean and Egyptian initiate performed his wonders? In Chapter cxv of the Egyptian *Funeral Ritual*, entitled "The chapter of coming forth from Heaven . . . and of knowing the Souls of Annu" (Heliopolis), Horus says: "I knew the Souls of Annu. The greatly glorious does not pass over it . . . unless the gods give me the WORD." In another hymn the soul, transformed, exclaims: "Make road for me to Re-stau. I am the Great One, dressed as the Great One. I have come! I have come! Delicious to me are the kings of Osiris. I am creating the water [through the power of the *Word*] . . . Have I not seen the hidden secrets . . . I have given truth to the Sun. I am clear. I am adored for my purity" (cxvii-cxix. The chapters of the going into and coming out from Re-stau). In another place the mummy's roll expresses the following: "I am the Great God [spirit] existing of myself, the creator of *His Name* . . . I know the name of this Great God that is there." [ch. xvii.]

Jesus is accused by his enemies of having wrought miracles, and is shown by his own apostles to have expelled *demons* by the power of the INEFFABLE NAME. The former firmly believed that he had stolen it in the Sanctuary. "And he cast out the spirits with his *word*, and healed all that were sick" (*Matthew* xviii, 16). When the Jewish rulers ask Peter (*Acts* iv, 7-10): "By what power, or by what *name*, have ye done this?" Peter replies, "By the NAME of Jesus Christ of Nazareth." But does this mean the name of Christ, as the interpreters would make us believe; or does it signify, "by the NAME which was in the possession of Jesus of Nazareth," the initiate, who was accused by the Jews to have learned it but who had it really through initiation? Besides, he states repeatedly that all that he does he does in *"His Father's Name,"* not in his own.

But who of the modern Masons has ever heard it pronounced? In their own *Ritual*, they confess that they never have. The "Sir Orator" tells the "Sir Knight," that the passwords which he received in the preceding degrees are all "so many corruptions" of the true name of

God engraved on the triangle; and that therefore they have adopted a "substitute" for it. Such also is the case in the Blue Lodge, where the Master, representing King Solomon, agrees with King Hiram that the Word * * * "shall be used as a *substitute* for the Master's word, until wiser ages shall discover the true one." What Senior Deacon, of all the thousands who have assisted in bringing candidates from darkness to light; or what Master who has whispered this mystic "word" into the ears of supposititious Hiram Abiffs, while holding them on the five points of fellowship, has suspected the real meaning of even this substitute, which they impart "at low breath"? How few newly-made Master Masons but go away imagining that it has some occult connection with the "marrow in the bone." What do they know of that mystical personage known to some adepts as the "venerable Mah," or of the mysterious Eastern Brothers who obey him, whose name is abbreviated in the first syllable of the three which compose the Masonic substitute — The Mah, who lives at this very day in a spot unknown to all but initiates, and the approaches to which are through trackless wildernesses, untrodden by Jesuit or missionary foot, for it is beset by dangers fit to appall the most courageous explorers? And yet, for generations this meaningless jingle of vowels and consonants has been repeated in novitiate ears, as though it possessed even so much potency as would deflect from its course a thistledown floating in the air! Like Christianity, Freemasonry is a corpse from which the spirit long ago fled.

In this connection, place may well be given to a letter from Mr. Charles Sotheran, Corresponding Secretary of the New York Liberal Club, which was received by us on the day after the date it bears. Mr. Sotheran is known as a writer and lecturer on antiquarian, mystical, and other subjects. In Masonry, he has taken so many of the degrees as to be a competent authority as regards the Craft. He is 32 .·. A. and P. R., 94 .·. Memphis, K.R. ☩, K. Kadosh, M. M. 104, Eng., etc. He is also an initiate of the modern English Brotherhood of the Rosie Cross and other secret societies, and Masonic editor of the *New York Advocate*.[53] Following is the letter, which we place before the Masons as we desire that they should see what one of their own number has to say:

"New York Press Club, January 11th, 1877.

"In response to your letter, I willingly furnish the information desired with respect to the antiquity and present condition of Freemasonry. This I do the more cheerfully since we belong to the same secret societies, and you can thus better appreciate the necessity for the reserve which at times I shall be obliged to exhibit. You rightly refer to the fact that Freemasonry, no less than the effete theologies of the day, has its fabulous history to narrate. Clogged up as the Order has been by the rubbish and drift of absurd biblical legends, it *is* no wonder that its usefulness has been impaired and its work as a civilizer hampered. Fortunately the great anti-Masonic excitement that raged in the United States during a portion of this century, forced a considerable band of workers to delve into the true origin of the Craft, and bring about a healthier state of things. The agitation in America also spread to Europe and the literary efforts of Masonic authors on both sides of the Atlantic, such as Rebold, Findel, Hyneman, Mitchell, MacKenzie, Hughan, Yarker and others well known to the fraternity, is now a matter of history. One effect of their labors has been, in a great measure, to bring the history of Masonry into an open daylight, where even its teachings, jurisprudence, and ritual are no longer secret from those of the 'profane,' who have the wit to read as they run.

"You are correct in saying that the *Bible* is the 'great light' of European and American Masonry. In consequence of this the theistic conception of God and the biblical cosmogony have been ever considered two of its great cornerstones. Its chronology seems also to have been based upon the same pseudo-revelation. Thus Dr. Dalcho, in one of his treatises, asserts that the principles of the Masonic Order were presented at and coeval with the creation. It is therefore not astonishing that such a pundit should go on to state that God was the first Grand Master, Adam the second, and the last named initiated Eve into the Great Mystery, as I suppose many a Priestess of Cybelê and 'Lady' Kadosh were afterward. The Rev. Dr. George Oliver, another Masonic authority, gravely records what may be termed the minutes of a Lodge where Moses presided as Grand Master, Joshua as Deputy Grand Master, and Ahohab and Bezaleel as Grand Wardens! The temple at Jerusalem, which recent archaeologists have shown to be a structure with nothing like the pretended antiquity of its erection, and incorrectly called after a monarch whose name proves his mystical character, Sol-Om-On (the name of the sun in three languages), plays, as you correctly observe, a considerable share in Masonic mystery. Such fables as these, and the traditional Masonic colonization of ancient Egypt, have given the Craft the credit of an illustrious origin to which it has no right, and before whose forty centuries of legendary history, the mythologies of Greece and Rome fade into insignificance. The Egyptian, Chaldean, and other theories necessary to each fabricator of 'high degrees' have also each had their short period of prominence. The last 'axe to grind' has consecutively been the fruitful mother of unproductiveness.

"We both agree that all the ancient priesthoods had their esoteric doctrines and secret ceremonies. From the Essenic brotherhood, an evolution of the Hindu Gymnosophists, doubtless proceeded the Sodalities of Greece and Rome as described by so-called 'Pagan' writers. Founded on these and copying them in the matter of ritual, signs, grips, passwords, etc., were developed the mediaeval guilds. Like the present livery companies of London, the relics of the English trade-guilds, the operative Masons were but a guild of workmen with higher pretensions. From the French name 'Maçon,' derived from 'Mas,' an old Norman noun meaning 'a house,' comes our English 'Mason,' a house builder. As the London companies alluded to present now and again the Freedom of the *'Liveries'* to outsiders, so we find the trade-guilds of Masons doing the same. Thus the founder of the Ashmolean Museum was made free of the Masons at Warrington, in Lancashire, England, on the 16th October, 1646. The entrance of such men as Elias Ashmole into the Operative Fraternity paved the way for the great 'Masonic Revolution of 1717,' when SPECULATIVE Masonry came into existence. The *Constitutions* of 1723 and 1738, by the Masonic impostor Anderson, were written up for the newly-fledged and first Grand Lodge of 'Free and Accepted Masons' of England, from which body all others over the world hail today.

"These bogus *Constitutions,* written by Anderson, were compiled about then, and in order to palm off his miserable rubbish, yclept history, on the Craft, he had the audacity to state that nearly all the documents relating to Masonry in England had been destroyed by the 1717 reformers. Happily, in the British Museum, Bodleian Library, and other public institutions, Rebold, Hughan and others have discovered sufficient evidence in the shape of old Operative Masonic charges to disprove this statement.

"The same writers, I think, have conclusively upset the tenability of two other documents palmed upon Masonry, namely, the spurious charter of Cologne of 1535, and the forged questions, supposed to have been written by Leylande, the antiquary, from a MS. of King Henry VI of England. In the last named, Pythagoras is referred to as having — 'formed a great lodge, at Crotona, and made many Masons, some of whom travelled into France, and there made many, from whence, in process of time, the art passed into England.' Sir Christopher Wren, architect of St. Paul's Cathedral, London, often called the 'Grand Master of Freemasons,' was simply the Master or president of the London Operative Masons Company. If such a tissue of fable could interweave itself into the history of the Grand Lodges which now have charge of the first three symbolical degrees, it is hardly astonishing that the same fate should befall nearly all of the High Masonic Degrees which have been aptly termed 'an incoherent medley of opposite principles.'

"It is curious to note too that most of the bodies which work these, such as the Ancient and Accepted Scottish Rite, the Rite of Avignon, the Order of the Temple, Fessler's Rite, the 'Grand Council of the Emperors of the East and West — Sovereign Prince Masons,' etc., etc., are nearly all the offspring of the sons of Ignatius Loyola. The Baron Hundt, Chevalier Ramsay, Tschoudy, Zinnendorf, and numerous others who founded the grades in these rites, worked under instructions from the General of the Jesuits. The nest where these high degrees were hatched, and no Masonic rite is free from their baleful influence more or less, was the Jesuit College of Clermont at Paris.

"That bastard foundling of Freemasonry, the 'Ancient and Accepted Scottish Rite,' which is unrecognized by the Blue Lodges was the enunciation, primarily, of the brain of the Jesuit Chevalier Ramsay. It was brought by him to England in 1736-38, to aid the cause of the Catholic Stuarts. The rite in its present form of thirty-three degrees was reorganized at the end of the eighteenth century by some half dozen Masonic adventurers at Charleston, South Carolina. Two of these, Pirlet a tailor, and a dancing master named Lacorne, were fitting predecessors for a later resuscitation by a gentleman of the name of Gourgas, employed in the aristocratic occupation of a ship's clerk, on a boat trading between New York and Liverpool. Dr. Crucefix, *alias* Goss, the *inventor* of certain patent medicines of an objectionable character, ran the institution in England. The powers under which these worthies acted was a document claimed to have been signed by Frederick the Great at Berlin, on May 1st, 1786, and by which were revised the Masonic Constitution and Status of the High Degrees of the Ancient and Accepted Rite. This paper was an impudent forgery and necessitated the issuing of a protocol by the Grand Lodges of the Three Globes of Berlin, which conclusively proved the whole arrangement to be false in every particular. On claims supported by this supposititious document, the Ancient and Accepted Rite have swindled their confiding brothers in the Americas and Europe out of thousands of dollars, to the shame and discredit of humanity.

"The modern Templars, whom you refer to in your letter, are but mere magpies in peacock's plumes. The aim of the Masonic Templars is the sectarianization, or rather the Christianizing of Masonry, a fraternity which is supposed to admit the Jew, Pârsî, Mohammedan, Buddhist, in fact every religionist within its portals who accepts the doctrine of a personal god, and spirit-immortality. According to the belief of a section, if not all the Israelites, belonging to the Craft in America — Templarism is Jesuitism.

"It seems strange, now that the belief in a personal God is becoming extinct, and that even the theologian has transformed his deity into an indescribable nondescript, that there are those who stand in the way of the general acceptation of the sublime pantheism of the primeval Orientals, of Jacob Boehme, of Spinoza. Often in the Grand Lodge and subordinate lodges of this and other jurisdictions, the old doxology is sung, with its 'Praise Father, Son, and Holy Ghost', to the distrust of Israelites and freethinking brethren, who are thus unnecessarily insulted. This could never occur in India, where the great light in a lodge may be the *Koran*, the *Zend-Avesta*, or one of the *Vedas*. The sectarian Christian spirit in Masonry must be put down. Today there are German Grand Lodges which will not allow Jews to be initiated, or Israelites from foreign countries to be accepted as brethren within their jurisdiction. The French Masons have, however, revolted against this tyranny, and the Grand Orient of France does now permit the atheist and materialist to fellowship in the Craft. A standing rebuke upon the claimed universality of Masonry is the fact that the French brethren are now repudiated.

"Notwithstanding its many faults — and speculative Masonry is but human, and therefore fallible — there is no institution that has done so much, and is yet capable of such great undertakings in the future, for human, religious, and political improvement. In the last century the Illuminati taught, 'peace with the cottage, war with the palace,' throughout the length and breadth of Europe. In the last century the United States was freed from the tyranny of the mother country by the action of the Secret Societies more than is commonly imagined. Washington, Lafayette, Franklin, Jefferson, Hamilton, were Masons. And in the nineteenth century it was Grand Master Garibaldi, 33°, who unified Italy, working in accordance with the spirit of the faithful brotherhood, as the Masonic, or rather Carbonari, principles of 'liberty, equality, humanity, independence, unity,' taught for years by brother Joseph Mazzini.

"Speculative Masonry has much, too, within its ranks to do. One is to accept woman as a co-worker of man in the struggle of life, as the Hungarian Masons have done lately by initiating the Countess Haideck. Another important thing is also to recognize practically the brotherhood of all humanity by refusing none on account of color, race, position, or creed. The dark-skinned should not be only theoretically the brother of the light. The colored Masons who have been duly and regularly raised stand at every lodge-door in America craving admission, and they are refused. And there is South America to be conquered to a participation in the duties of humanity.

"If Masonry be, as claimed, a progressive science and a school of pure religion, it should ever be found in the advance guard of civilization, not in the rear. If it be but an empirical effort, a crude attempt of humanity to solve some of the deepest problems of the race, and no more, then it must give place to fitter successors, perchance one of those that you and I know of, one that may have acted the prompter at the side of the chiefs of the Order, during its greatest triumphs, whispering to them as the daemon did in the ear of Socrates.

"Yours most sincerely,
"CHARLES SOTHERAN."

Thus falls to ruins the grand epic poem of Masons, sung by so many mysterious Knights as another revealed gospel. As we see, the Temple of Solomon is being undermined and brought to the ground by its own chief "Master Masons," of this century. But if, following the ingenious exoteric description of the *Bible,* there are yet Masons who persist in regarding it as once an actual structure, who, of the students of the esoteric doctrine will ever consider this mythic temple otherwise than an allegory, embodying the secret science? Whether or not there ever was a real temple of that name, we may well leave to archaeologists to decide; but that the detailed description thereof in *1 Kings* is purely allegorical, no serious scholar, proficient in the ancient as well as mediaeval jargon of the kabalists and alchemists, can doubt. The building of the Temple of Solomon is the symbolical representation of the gradual acquirement of the *secret* wisdom or magic; the erection and development of the spiritual from the earthly; the manifestation of the power and splendor of the spirit in the physical world, through the wisdom and genius of the builder. The latter, when he has become an adept, is a mightier king than Solomon himself, the emblem of the sun or *Light* himself — the light of the real subjective world, shining in the darkness of the objective universe. This is the "Temple" which can be reared *without the sound of the hammer, or any tool of iron being heard in the house while it is "in building."*

In the East, this science is called, in some places, the "seven-storied," in others, the "nine-storied" Temple; every story answers allegorically to a degree of knowledge acquired. Throughout the countries of the Orient, wherever magic and the wisdom-religion are studied, its practitioners and students are known among their craft as Builders — for they build the temple of knowledge, of secret science. Those of the adepts who are active, are styled practical or *operative* Builders, while the students, or neophytes are classed as *speculative* or theoretical. The former exemplify in works their control over the forces of inanimate as well as animate nature; the latter are but perfecting themselves in the rudiments of the sacred science. These terms were evidently borrowed at the beginning by the unknown founders of the first Masonic guilds.

In the now popular jargon, "Operative Masons" are understood to be the bricklayers and the handicraftsmen, who composed the Craft down to Sir Christopher Wren's time, and "Speculative Masons," all members of the Order, as now understood. The sentence attributed to Jesus, "Thou art Peter, and upon this rock I will build my church; and the gates of hell shall not prevail against it," * disfigured, as it is, by mistranslation and misinterpretation, plainly indicates its real meaning. We have shown the signification of *Pater* and *Petra,* with the hierophants — the interpretation traced on the tables of stone of the final initiation was handed by the initiator to the chosen future interpreter. Having acquainted himself with its mysterious contents, which revealed to him the mysteries of creation, the initiated became a *builder* himself, for he was made acquainted with the *dodecahedron,* or the geometrical figure on which the universe was built. To what he had learned in previous initiations of the use of the rule and of architectural principles was added a cross, the perpendicular and horizontal lines of which were supposed to form the foundation of the spiritual temple, by placing them across the junction, or central primordial point, the element of all existences,† representing the first concrete idea of deity. Henceforth he could, as a Master-builder (see *1 Corinthians* iii, 10), erect a temple of wisdom on that rock of *Petra,* for himself; and having laid a sure foundation, let "another build thereon."

The Egyptian hierophant was given a square headdress, which he had to wear always, and a square (see Mason's marks), without which he could never go abroad. The perfect *Tau* formed of the perpendicular (descending male ray, or spirit), a horizontal line (or matter, female ray), and the mundane circle was an attribute of Isis, and it is but at his death that the Egyptian cross was laid on the breast of his mummy. These square hats are worn unto this day by the Armenian priests. The claim that the cross is purely a Christian symbol introduced after our era, is

---

* [*Matt.* xvi, 18.]
† Pythagoras.

strange indeed, when we find Ezekiel stamping the foreheads of the men of Judah, who feared the Lord (*Ezekiel* ix, 4), with the *signa thau*, as it is translated in the *Vulgate*. In the ancient Hebrew this sign was formed thus ✗ but in the original Egyptian hieroglyphics as a perfect Christian cross ✝. In the *Revelation* also, the "Alpha and Omega" (spirit and matter), the first and the last, stamps the name of his Father in the foreheads of the *elect*.*

And if our statements are wrong, if Jesus was not an initiate, a Master-builder, or Master-Mason as it is now called, how comes it that on the most ancient cathedrals we find his figure with Mason's marks about his person? In the Cathedral of Santa Croce, Florence, over the main portal can be seen the figure of Christ holding a perfect square in his hand.

The surviving "Master-builders" of the *operative* craft of the true Temple may go literally *half-naked* and wander *slipshod* forever — now not for the sake of a puerile ceremony, but because, like the "Son of man," they have not where to lay their heads — and yet be the only surviving possessors of the "Word." Their "cable-tow" is the sacred triple cord of certain Brahmans-Sannyâsins, or the string on which certain lamas hang their *yu-stone;* but with these apparently valueless talismans, not one of them would part for all the wealth of Solomon and Sheba. The seven-knotted bamboo stick of the fakir can become as powerful as the rod of Moses "which was created between the evenings, and on which was engraven and set forth the great and glorious NAME, with which he was to do the wonders in Mizraim."

But these "operative workmen" have no fear that their secrets will be disclosed by treacherous ex-high priests of chapters, though their generation may have received them through others than "Moses, Solomon, and Zerubbabel." Had Moses Michael Hayes, the Israelite Brother who introduced Royal Arch Masonry into this country (in December, 1778),† had a prophetic presentiment of future treasons, he might have instituted more efficacious obligations than he has.

Truly, the grand omnific Royal Arch word, *"long lost but now found,"* has fulfilled its prophetic promise. The password of that degree is no more "I AM THAT I AM." It is now simply "I was but am no more!"

⊓ Ⴤ⊓⟨⅃Ɛ ⅃ᖴႮƎ ⅂⅃ᐯ⊓⅂ᐯ Ǝ⊓> Ⴤ⊓⊓ᖴƐ⟨· ⟨⊓ᐱ Ǝ⅃᙭⅃
⊓ᖴⅬᐯⅬᖴᗅⅬႮ ⟨⊓ᐱᖴ ⅂⟨ᐯᐯⅬᖴᗞⅬᐯ ƐⅬᐯ ᐯƎⅬᐯⅬ ƐƊ⅂⅃ᐯ ⅃ᐯᐯ
Ⅼᐯᐯⵊ

---

\* [*Rev.* vii, 2, 3; xiv, 1.]

† The first *Grand Chapter* was instituted at Philadelphia in 1797.

That we may not be accused of vain boasting, we shall give the keys to several of the secret ciphers of the most exclusive and important of the so-called higher Masonic degrees. If we mistake not, these have never before been revealed to the outside world (except that of the Royal Arch Masons, in 1830), but have been most jealously guarded within the various Orders. We are under neither promise, obligation, nor oath, and therefore violate no confidence. Our purpose is not to gratify an idle curiosity; we wish merely to show Masons and the affiliates of all other Western societies — the Company of Jesus included — that it is impossible for them to be secure in the possession of any secrets that it is worth an Eastern Brotherhood's while to discover. Inferentially, it may also show them that if the latter can lift the masks of European societies, they are nevertheless successful in wearing their own visors; for, if any one thing is universally acknowledged, it is that the real secrets of not a single surviving ancient brotherhood are in possession of the profane.

Some of these ciphers were used by the Jesuits in their secret correspondence at the time of the Jacobin conspiracy, and when Masonry (the alleged successor to the Temple) was employed by the Church for political purposes.

Findel says that in the eighteenth century, "besides the modern Knights Templars, we see the Jesuits . . . disfiguring the fair face of Freemasonry. Many Masonic authors who were fully cognizant of the period and knew exactly all the incidents occurring, positively assert that then and still later the Jesuits exercised a pernicious influence, or at least endeavored to do so, upon the fraternity." * Of the Rosicrucian Order he remarks, upon the authority of Prof. Woog, that its "aim at first . . . was nothing less than the support and advancement of Catholicism. *When this religion manifested a determination entirely to repress liberty of thought* . . . the Rosicrucians enlarged their designs likewise to check if possible the progress of this widely-spreading enlightenment." †

In the *Sincerus Renatus* (the truly converted) of S. Richter, of Berlin (1714), we note that laws were communicated for the government of the "Golden Rosicrucians," which "bear unmistakable evidences of Jesuitical intervention." ‡

We will begin with the cryptographs of the "Sovereign Princes Rose Croix," also styled *Knights of St. Andrew, Knights of the Eagle and Pelican, Heredom Rosae Crucis, Rosy Cross, Triple Cross, Perfect Brother, Prince Mason*, and so on. The "Heredom Rosy Cross" also claims a Templar origin in 1314.§

---

* J. G. Findel, *History of Freemasonry*, p. 253.

† [Findel, *op. cit.*, p. 258. Cf. Prof. Woog, *Journal für Freimaurer*, Vienna, 5786. Vol. III, 3rd Quarter, p. 147.]

‡ [*Ibid.*]

§ Cf. Yarker, *Notes on the Scientific and Religious Mysteries of Antiquity*, p. 153.

## Cipher of the
### S∴ P∴ R∴ C∴

| ☥ | — | ⌐ | ◻ | ▣ | ÷ | ⌞ | = | ⊰ | ⊥ | Γ | F | N |
|---|---|---|---|---|---|---|---|---|---|---|---|---|
| a | b | c | d | e | f | g | h | ij | k | l | m | n |

| π | C | ⌐ | ⌐ | ⊔ | ⊤ | P | Z | ϙ | ⊔ | ψ |
|---|---|---|---|---|---|---|---|---|---|---|
| o | p | q | r | s | t | uv | x | y | z | &. |

### Cipher of the Knights Rose Croix of Heredom
(of Kilwining)

| 0 | 1 | 2 | 3 | 4 | 5 | 6 | 7 | 8 | 9 | 10 | 10 | 11 | 12 | 13 | 14 | 15 | 16 | 17 |
|---|---|---|---|---|---|---|---|---|---|----|----|----|----|----|----|----|----|----|
| a | b | c | d | e | f | g | h | i | j | ba | (or) | k | kb | kc | kd | ke | kf | kg | kh |

| 18 | 19 | 20 | 30 | 40 | 50 | 60 | 70 | 80 | 90 | 100 | 200 | 300 | 400 | 500 |
|----|----|----|----|----|----|----|----|----|----|-----|-----|-----|-----|-----|
| ki | kj | ck | dk | ek | fk | gk | hk | ik | jk | l | cl | dl | el | fl |

| 600 | 700 | 800 | 900 | 1000 |
|-----|-----|-----|-----|------|
| gl | hl | il | jl | m |

### Cipher of the Knights Kadosh
(Also White and Black Eagle and Grand Elected Knight Templar)

| 70 | 2 | 3 | 12 | 15 | 20 | 30 | 33 | 38 | 9 | 10 | 40 |
|----|---|---|----|----|----|----|----|----|---|----|----|
| a | b | c | d | e | f | g | h | i | k | l | m |

| 60 | 80 | 81 | 82 | 83 | 84 | 85 | 86 | 90 | 91 | 94 | 95 |
|----|----|----|----|----|----|----|----|----|----|----|----|
| n | o | p | q | r | s | t | u | v | x | y | z |

The Knights Kadosh have another cipher—or rather hieroglyph—which, in this case, is taken from the Hebrew, possibly to be the more in keeping with the *Bible* Kadeshim of the Temple.*

---

\* See 2 *Kings* xxiii, 7, Hebrew text, and English, the former especially. In the degree of Kadosh, a lecture is given upon the descent of Masonry through Moses, Solomon, the Essenes and the Templars. Christian K. K.'s may get some light as to the kind of "Temple" their ancestors would, in such a genealogical descent, have been attached to, by consulting verse 13 of the same chapter as above quoted.

HIEROGLYPH OF THE K.·. KAD.·.

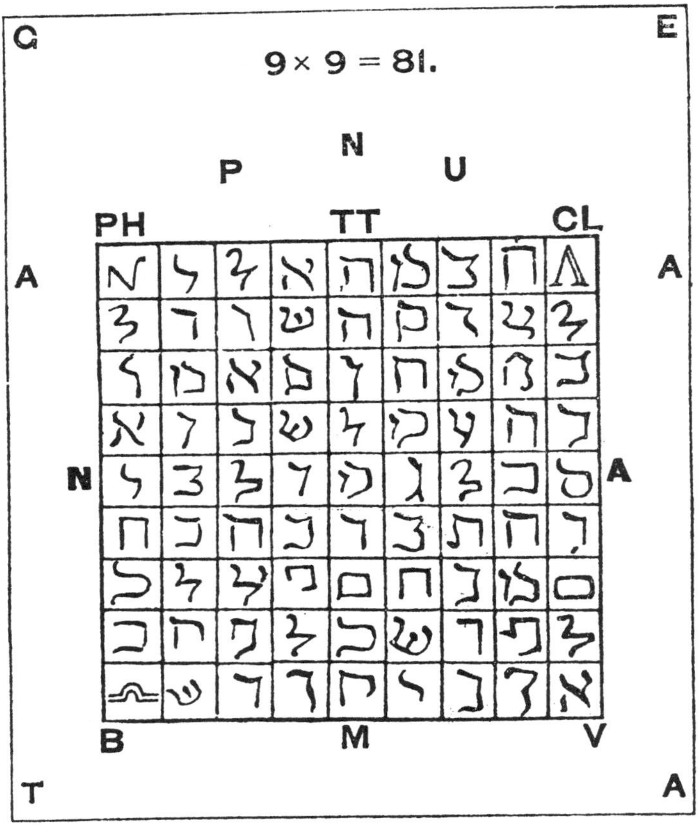


As for the Royal Arch cipher, it has been exposed before now, but we may as well present it slightly amplified.

This cipher consists of certain combinations of right angles, with or without points or dots. Following is the basis of its

*Formation.*

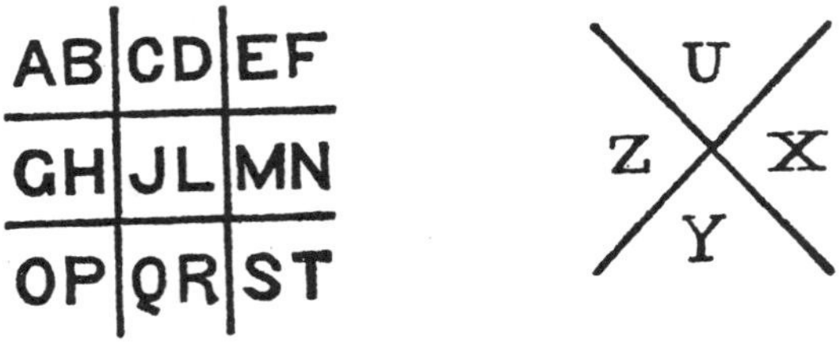

Now, the alphabet consists of twenty-six letters, and these two signs being dissected, form thirteen distinct characters, thus:

⌐ ⊔ ⌐  ⊐ ◻ ⊏ ⌐ ⊓ ⌐ V ∧ > <
1　2　3　4　5　6　7　8　9　10　11　12　13

A point placed within each gives thirteen more, thus:

⌐̇ ⊔̇ ⌐̇ ⊐̇ ◻̇ ⊏̇ ⌐̇ ⊓̇ ⌐̇ V̇ ∧̇ >̇ <̇
1　2　3　4　5　6　7　8　9　10　11　12　13

Making a total of twenty-six, equal to the number of letters in the English alphabet.

There are two ways, at least, of combining and using these characters for the purposes of secret correspondence. One method is to call the first sign, ⌐ a; the same, with a point, ⌐̇ b, etc. Another is to apply them, in their regular course, to the first half of the alphabet, ⌐ a, ⊔ b, and so on, to m; after which, repeat them with a dot, beginning with ⌐̇ n, ⊔̇ o, etc., to <̇ z.

The alphabet, according to the first method, stands thus:

⌐ ⌐̇ ⊔ ⊔̇ ⌐ ⌐̇ ⊐ ⊐̇ ◻ ◻̇ ⊏ ⊏̇ ⌐
a　b　c　d　e　f　g　h　i　j　k　l　m

⌐ ⌐̇ ⊓ ⊓̇ ⌐ ⌐̇ V V̇ ∧ ∧̇ > >̇ < <̇
n　o　p　q　r　s　t　u　v　w　x　y　z

According to the second method, thus:

⌐ ⊔ ⌐ ⊐ ◻ ⊏ ⌐ ⊓ ⌐ V ∧ > <
a　b　c　d　e　f　g　h　i　j　k　l　m

⌐̇ ⊔̇ ⌐̇ ⊐̇ ◻̇ ⊏̇ ⌐̇ ⊓̇ ⌐̇ V̇ ∧̇ >̇ <̇
n　o　p　q　r　s　t　u　v　w　x　y　z

Besides these signs, the French Masons, evidently under the tuition of their accomplished masters—the Jesuits, have perfected this cipher in all its details. So they have signs even for commas, diphthongs, accents, dots, etc., and these are

∧ ⌐⌐ ⌐⌐ ≫ ⌐̇ > < ∧ ⊓ ▷ ▷ ℬ ℬ ℬ ℬ etc.
&c　æ　œ　w　ç　'　`　^　-　.　,　;　:　∴　?

Let this suffice. We might, if we chose, give the cipher alphabets, with their keys, of another method of the Royal Arch Masons strongly resembling a certain Hindu character; of the G.˙. El.˙. of the Mystic City; of a well-known form of the Devanâgarî script of the (French) Sages of the Pyramids; and of the Sublime Master of the Great Work, and others. But we refrain; only, be it understood, for the reason that some of these alone of all the side branches of the original Blue Lodge Freemasonry contain the promise of a useful future. As for the rest, they may and will go to the ash-heap of time. High Masons will understand what we mean.

We must now give some proofs of what we have stated, and demonstrate that the word Jehovah, if Masonry adheres to it, will ever remain as a substitute, never be identical with the lost mirific name. This is so well known to the kabalists, that in their careful etymology of the יהוה they show it beyond doubt to be only one of the many substitutes for the real name, and composed of the twofold name of the first androgyne — Adam and Eve, Jod (or Yodh), Vau and He-Va — the female serpent as a symbol of Divine Intelligence proceeding from the ONE-Generative or *Creative* Spirit.\* Thus, Jehovah is not the sacred name at all. Had Moses given to Pharaoh the *true* "name," the latter would not have answered as he did, for the Egyptian King-Initiates knew it as well as Moses, who had learned it with them. *The* "name" was at that time the common property of the adepts of all the nations in the world, and Pharaoh certainly knew the "name" of the Highest God mentioned in the *Book of the Dead*. But instead of that, Moses (if we accept the allegory of *Exodus* literally) gives Pharaoh the name of *Yeva*, the expression or form of the Divine name used by all the *Targums* as passed by Moses. Hence Pharaoh's reply: "Who is that *Yeva* † that I should obey his voice to let Israel go?" ‡

"Jehovah" dates only from the Masoretic innovation. When the Rabbis, for fear that they should lose the keys to their own doctrines, then written exclusively in consonants, began to insert their vowel-points in their manuscripts, they were utterly ignorant of the true pronunciation of the NAME. Hence, they gave it the sound of *Adonai*, and made it read *Ja-ho-vah*. Thus the latter is simply a fancy, a perversion of the Holy Name. And how could they know it? Alone, out of all their nation, the high priests had it in their possession and respectively passed it to their successors, as the Hindu Brahmâtma does before his death. Once a year only, on the day of atonement, the high priest was

---

\* See É. Lévi, *Dogme et rituel*, etc., I, ch. ii.

† Yeva is *Heva*, the feminine counterpart of Jehovah-Binah.

‡ [*Exod.* v, 2.]

allowed to pronounce it in a whisper. Passing behind the veil into the inner chamber of the sanctuary, the Holy of Holies, with trembling lips and downcast eyes he called upon the dreaded NAME. The bitter persecution of the kabalists, who received the precious syllables after deserving the favor by a whole life of sanctity, was due to a suspicion that they misused it. At the opening of this chapter we have told the story of Shimon ben-Yohai, one of the victims to this priceless knowledge, and seen how little he deserved his cruel treatment.

The *Book of Jasher*, a work — as we are told by a very learned Hebrew divine of New York — composed in Spain in the twelfth century as "a popular tale," and that had not "the sanction of the Rabbinical College of Venice," is full of kabalistical, alchemical, and magical allegories.[54] Admitting so much, it must still be said that there are few popular tales but are based on historical truths. *The Norsemen in Iceland*, by Dr. G. W. Dasent, is also a collection of popular tales, but they contain the key to the primitive religious worship of that people. So with the *Book of Jasher*. It contains the whole of the *Old Testament* in a condensed form, and as the Samaritans held, *i. e.*, the five *Books of Moses*, without the Prophets. Although rejected by the orthodox Rabbis, we cannot help thinking that, as in the case of the apocryphal *Gospels*, which were written earlier than the canonical ones, the *Book of Jasher* is the true original from which the subsequent *Bible* was in part composed. Both the apocryphal *Gospels* and *Jasher* are a series of religious tales, in which miracle is heaped upon miracle, and which narrate the popular legends as they first originated, without any regard to either chronology or dogma. Still both are cornerstones of the Mosaic and Christian religions. That there was a *Book of Jasher* prior to the Mosaic *Pentateuch* is clear, for it is mentioned in *Joshua*, *Isaiah* and *2 Samuel*.

Nowhere is the difference between the Elohists and Jehovists so clearly shown as in *Jasher*. Jehovah is here spoken of as the Ophites held him to be, a Son of Ialdabaôth, or Saturn. In this Book, the Egyptian Magi, when asked by Pharaoh "Who is he, whom Moses speaks as the *I am*?" reply "we have heard that the God of the Hebrews is a son of the wise, the son of ancient kings" (ch. lxxix, 45).* Now, those who assert that *Jasher* is a forgery of the twelfth century — and we readily believe it — should nevertheless explain the curious fact that, while the above text is *not* to be found in the *Bible*, the answer to it *is*, and is,

---

* We find a very suggestive point in connection with this appellation of Jehovah, "Son of ancient Kings," in the Jaina sect of Hindostan, known as the Sauryas. They admit that Brahmâ is a Devatâ, but deny his creative power, and call him the "Son of a King." See *Asiatic Researches*, Vol. IX, p. 279; ed. 1807.

moreover, couched in unequivocal terms. At *Isaiah* xix, 11, the "Lord God" complains of it very wrathfully to the prophet, and says: "Surely the princes of Zoan *are fools,* the counsel of the wise counselors of Pharaoh is become brutish; how say ye unto Pharaoh, I am the son of the wise, the son of the ancient kings?" which is evidently a reply to the above. In *Joshua* x, 13, *Jasher* is referred to in corroboration of the outrageous assertion that the sun stood still, and the moon stayed until the people had avenged themselves. "Is not this written in the *Book of Jasher?*" says the text. And in *2 Samuel* i, 18, the same book is again quoted. "Behold," it says, "it is written in the *Book of Jasher.*" Clearly, *Jasher* must have existed; it must have been regarded as authority; must have been older than *Joshua;* and, since the verse in *Isaiah* unerringly points to the passage above quoted, we have at least as much reason to accept the current edition of *Jasher* as a transcription, excerpt, or compilation of the original work, as we have to revere the Septuagint *Pentateuch,* as the primitive Hebraic sacred records.

At all events, Jehovah is not the ancient of the ancient, or "aged of the aged," of the *Zohar;* for we find him, in this book, counselling with God the Father as to the creation of the world. "The work-master spoke to the Lord. Let us make man after our image" (*Zohar*, I, fol. 25). Jehovah is but the Metatron, and perhaps, not even the highest, but only one of the Aeôns; for he whom Onkelos calls *Memra,* the "Word," is not the exoteric Jehovah of the *Bible,* nor is he Yahve, יהוה, the Existing One.

It was the secrecy of the early kabalists, who were anxious to screen the real Mystery name of the "Eternal" from profanation, and later the prudence which the mediaeval alchemists and occultists were compelled to adopt to save their lives, that caused the inextricable confusion of divine names. This is what led the people to accept the Jehovah of the *Bible* as the name of the "One living God." Every Jewish elder, prophet, and other man of any importance knew the difference; but as the difference lay in the vocalization of the "name," and its right pronunciation led to death, the common people were ignorant of it, for no initiate would risk his life by teaching it to them. Thus the Sinaitic deity came gradually to be regarded as identical with "Him whose name is known but to the wise." When Capellus translates: "Whosoever shall pronounce the name of Jehovah, shall suffer death," he makes two mistakes.* The first is in adding the final letter *h* to the name, if he wants this deity to be considered either male or androgynous, for the letter makes the name feminine, as it really should be, considering it is one of the names of Binah, the third emanation; his second error is in asserting that the word *nokeb* means only to pronounce *distinctly.* It means to pronounce

---

* [Cf. MacKenzie, *Royal Masonic Cyclop.*, p. 538.]

*correctly*. Therefore, the Biblical name Jehovah may be considered simply a *substitute*, which, as belonging to one of the "powers," came to be viewed as that of the "Eternal." There is an evident mistake (one of the very many) in one of the texts in *Leviticus*, which has been corrected by Cahen, and which proves that the interdiction did not at all concern the name of the exoteric Jehovah, whose numerous names could also be pronounced without any penalty being incurred.* In the vicious English version, the translation runs thus: "And he that blasphemeth the name of the Lord, he shall surely be put to death," *Levit.* xxiv, 16. Cahen renders it far more correctly thus: "And he that blasphemeth the name of the *Eternal* shall die," etc. The "Eternal" being something higher than the exoteric and personal "Lord." †

As with the Gentile nations, the symbols of the Israelites were ever bearing, directly or indirectly, upon sun-worship. The exoteric Jehovah of the *Bible* is a *dual* god, like the other gods; and the fact that David — who is entirely ignorant of Moses — praises his "Lord," and assures him that the "Lord *is* a great God, and a great King above all gods,"‡ may be of a very great importance to the descendants of Jacob and David, but their national God concerns us in no wise. We are quite ready to show the "Lord God" of Israel the same respect as we do to Brahmâ, Zeus, or any other secondary deity. But we decline, most emphatically, to recognize in him either the Deity worshipped by Moses, or the "Father" of Jesus, or yet the "Ineffable Name" of the kabalists. Jehovah is, perhaps, one of the *Elohim*, who was concerned in the *formation* (which is not creation) of the universe, one of the architects who built from pre-existing matter, but he never was the "Unknowable" Cause that created (ברא, *bara*) in the night of the Eternity. These Elohim first form and bless; then they *curse* and *destroy;* as one of these Powers, Jehovah is therefore by turns beneficent and malevolent; at one moment he punishes and then repents. He is the antitype of several of the patriarchs — of Esau and of Jacob, the allegorical twins, emblems of the ever-manifest dual principle in nature. So Jacob, who is Israel, is the left pillar — the feminine principle of Esau, who is the right pillar and the male principle. When he wrestles with Malach-Iho, the Lord, it is the latter who becomes the *right* pillar, whom Jacob-Israel names God, although the *Bible*-interpreters have endeavored to transform him into a mere "angel of the Lord" (*Genesis* xxxii). Jacob conquers him — as matter will but too often conquer spirit—but his *thigh* is put out of joint in the fight.

---

* As, for instance, Shaddai, Elohim, Tsabaôth, etc.
† S. Cahen, *La Bible*, III, p. 117; ed. 1832.
‡ [*Psalms* xcv, 3.]

The name of Israel has its derivation from Isaral or Asar, the Sun-God, who is known as Suryal, Sûrya, and Sur. Isra-el means "striving with God." The "sun rising upon Jacob-Israel," is the *Sun*-God Isaral, fecundating *matter* or earth, represented by the *female*-Jacob. As usual, the allegory has more than one hidden meaning in the *Kabala*. Esau, Aesaou, Asu, is also the sun. Like the "Lord," Esau fights with Jacob and prevails not. The God-*Sun* first strives against, and then rises on, him in covenant.

"And as he passed over Penuel, *the sun rose upon him,* and he [Jacob] *halted upon his thigh*" (*Genesis* xxxii, 31). *Israel*-Jacob, opposed by his brother Esau, is *Samael,* and "the names of Samael are Azâzêl and *Satan*" (the opposer).

If it will be argued that Moses was unacquainted with the Hindu philosophy and, therefore, could not have taken Śiva, the regenerator and the destroyer, as his model for Jehovah, then we must admit that there was some miraculous international intuition which prompted every nation to choose for its exoteric national deity the dual type we find in the "Lord God" of Israel. All these fables speak for themselves. Śiva, Jehovah, Osiris, are all the symbols of the active principle in nature *par excellence*. They are the forces which preside at the formation or *regeneration* of matter and its destruction. They are the types of Life and Death, ever fecundating and decomposing under the never-ceasing influx of the *anima mundi,* the Universal intellectual Soul, the invisible but ever-present spirit which is behind the correlation of the blind forces. This spirit alone is immutable, and therefore the forces of the universe, cause and effect, are ever in perfect harmony with this one great Immutable Law. Spiritual Life is the one primordial principle *above;* Physical Life is the Primordial principle *below,* but they are one under their dual aspect. When the Spirit is completely untrammelled from the fetters of correlation, and its essence has become so purified as to be reunited with its CAUSE, it may — and yet who can tell whether it really will — have a glimpse of the Eternal Truth. Till then, let us not build ourselves idols in our own image, and accept the shadow for the Eternal Light.

The greatest mistake of the age was to attempt a comparison of the relative merits of all the ancient religions, and to scoff at the doctrines of the *Kabala* and other superstitions.

But truth is stranger than fiction; and this world-old adage finds its application in the case in hand. The "wisdom" of the archaic ages or the "secret doctrine" embodied in the *Oriental Kabala,* of which, as we have said, the Rabbinical is but an abridgment, did not die out with the Philaletheians of the last Eclectic school. The *Gnosis* lingers still on earth, and its votaries are many, albeit unknown. Such secret

COUNT ALESSANDRO DI CAGLIOSTRO
1743 ? — 1795 ?
Engraving by Francesco Bartolozzi (1727-1815).

JOSEPH PRIESTLEY
1733-1804
From Anne Holt, *A Life of Joseph Priestley*, London, 1931.

brotherhoods have been mentioned before MacKenzie's time, by more than one great author. If they have been regarded as mere fictions of the novelist, that fact has only helped the "brother-adepts" to keep their incognito the more easily. We have personally known several of them who, to their great merriment had had the story of their lodges, the communities in which they lived, and the wondrous powers which they had exercised for many long years, laughed at and denied by unsuspecting skeptics to their very faces. Some of these brothers belong to the small groups of "travellers." Until the close of the happy Louis-Philippian reign, they were pompously termed by the Parisian garçon and trader, the *nobles étrangers*, and as innocently believed to be "Boyards," Walachian "Gospodars," Indian "Nabobs," and Hungarian "Margraves," who had gathered at the capital of the civilized world to admire its monuments and partake of its dissipations. There are, however, some *insane* enough to connect the presence of certain of these mysterious guests in Paris with the great political events that subsequently took place. Such recall at least as very remarkable coincidences, the breaking out of the Revolution of '93, and the earlier explosion of the South Sea Bubble, soon after the appearance of "noble foreigners," who had convulsed all Paris for more or less longer periods, by either their mystical doctrines or "supernatural gifts." The Saint-Germains and Cagliostros of this century, having learned bitter lessons from the vilifications and persecutions of the past, pursue different tactics nowadays.

But there are numbers of these mystic brotherhoods which have naught to do with "civilized" countries; and it is in their unknown communities that are concealed the skeletons of the past. These "adepts" could, if they chose, lay claim to strange ancestry, and exhibit verifiable documents that would explain many a mysterious page in both sacred and profane history. Had the keys to the hieratic writings and the secret of Egyptian and Hindu symbolism been known to the Christian Fathers, they would not have allowed a single monument of old to stand unmutilated. And yet, if we are well informed — and we think we are — there was not one such in all Egypt, but that the secret records of its hieroglyphics were carefully registered by the sacerdotal caste. These records still exist, even if "not extant" for the general public, though perhaps the monuments may have passed away forever out of human sight.

Of forty-seven tombs of the kings, near Gornah, recorded by the Egyptian priests on their sacred registers, only fifteen were known to the public, according to Diodorus Siculus,* who visited the place about sixty years B.C. Notwithstanding this *historical* evidence, we assert that the whole number exist to this day, and the royal tomb discovered by

---

* [*Bibliotheca historica*, I, 46.]

Belzoni* among the sandstone mountains of Bibân al-Mulûk (Melech?) is but a feeble specimen of the rest. We will add, furthermore, that the Arab-Christians, the monks, scattered around in their poor, desolate convents on the borderland of the great Lybian Desert, know of the existence of such unbetrayed relics. But they are Copts, sole remnants of the true Egyptian race, and the Copt predominating over the Christian monk in their natures, they keep silent; for what reason it is not for us to tell. There are some who believe that their monkish attire is but a blind, and that they have chosen these desolate homes among arid deserts and surrounded by Mohammedan tribes, for some ulterior purposes of their own. Be that as it may, they are held in great esteem by the Greek monks of Palestine; and there is a rumor current among Christian pilgrims of Jerusalem, who throng the Holy Sepulcher at every Easter, that the holy fire from heaven will never descend so *miraculously* as when these monks of the desert are present to draw it down with their prayers.†

"The Kingdom of heaven suffereth violence, and the violent take it by force." ‡ Many are the candidates at the doors of those who are supposed to know the path that leads to the secret brotherhoods. The great majority are refused admittance, and these turn away interpreting the refusal as an evidence of the non-existence of any such secret society. Of the minority accepted, more than two-thirds fail upon trial. The seventh rule of the ancient Rosicrucian brotherhoods, which is universal among all true secret societies: "the Rosy-Crux becomes and is not *made*," is more than the generality of men can bear to have applied to them. But let no one suppose that of the candidates who fail, any will divulge to the world even the trifle they may have learned, as some Masons do. None know better than themselves how unlikely it is that a neophyte should ever talk of what was imparted to him. Thus these societies will go on and hear themselves denied without uttering a word until the day shall come for them to throw off their reserve and show how completely they are masters of the situation.

---

\* [G. B. Belzoni, *Narratives of the Operations . . . in Egypt and Nubia*, etc., pp. 224 *et seq;* 2nd ed., 1821; Kenrick, *Ancient Egypt under the Pharoahs*, Vol. I, pp. 165-67.]

† The Greek monks have this "miracle" performed for the "faithful" every year on Easter night. Thousands of pilgrims are there waiting with their tapers to light them at this sacred fire, which at the precise hour and when needed, descends from the chapel vault and hovers about the sepulcher in tongues of fire until every one of the thousand pilgrims has lighted his wax taper at it.

‡ [*Matt.* xi, 12.]

# CHAPTER IX

"All things are governed in the bosom of this triad."
—JOANNES LYDUS, *De mensibus*, 20.

"Thrice let the heaven be turned on its perpetual axis."
—OVID, *Fasti*, iv, 179.

"And Balaam said unto Balak, Build me here *seven* altars, and prepare me here *seven* oxen and *seven* rams."
—*Numbers* xxiii, 1, 2.

"In *seven* days all creatures who have offended me shall be destroyed by a deluge, but thou shalt be secured in a vessel miraculously formed; take, therefore . . . and with *seven* holy men, your respective wives, and pairs of all animals, enter the ark without fear; then shalt thou know God face to face, and all thy questions shall be answered."
—*Bhâgavata-Purâṇa,* Slokas 32-38, Adhyâya 24, Skandha VIII.

"And the Lord said, I will destroy man . . . from the face of earth . . . But with thee will I establish my covenant . . . Come thou and all thy house into the ark . . . For yet *seven* days, and I will cause it to rain upon the earth."
—*Genesis* vi, 7, 18; vii, 1.

"The Tetraktys was not only principally honored because all symphonies are found to exist within it, but also because it appears to contain the nature of all things."
—THEON OF SMYRNA, *Mathem.*, p. 147.

OUR task will have been ill-performed if the preceding chapters have not demonstrated that Judaism, earlier and later Gnosticism, Christianity and even Christian Masonry, have all been erected upon identical cosmical myths, symbols and allegories, whose full comprehension is possible only to those who have inherited the key from their inventors.

In the following pages we will endeavor to show how much these have been misinterpreted by the widely-different, yet intimately-related systems enumerated above, in fitting them to their individual needs. Thus not only will a benefit be conferred upon the student, but a long-deferred, and now much-needed act of justice will be done to those earlier generations whose genius has laid the whole human race under obligation. Let us begin by once more comparing the myths of the *Bible* with those of the sacred books of other nations, to see which is the original, which are copies.

There are but two methods which, correctly explained, can help us to this result. They are — the Vedic-Brahmanical literature and the Jewish *Kabala*. The former has, in a most philosophical spirit, conceived these grandiose myths; the latter, borrowing them from the Chaldeans and Persians, shaped them into a history of the Jewish nation, in which their spirit of philosophy was buried beyond the recognition of all but the elect, and under a far more absurd form than the Âryan had given them. The *Bible* of the Christian Church is the latest receptacle of this scheme of disfigured allegories which have been erected into an edifice of superstition, such as never entered into the conceptions of those from whom the Church obtained her knowledge. The abstract fictions of antiquity, which for ages had filled the popular fancy with but flickering shadows and uncertain images, have in Christianity assumed the shapes of real personages, and became accomplished facts. Allegory, metamorphosed, becomes sacred history, and Pagan myth is taught to the people as a revealed narrative of God's intercourse with His chosen people.

"The myths," says Horace in his *Ars Poetica*, "have been invented by wise men to strengthen the laws and teach moral truths." [55] While Horace endeavored to make clear the very spirit and essence of the ancient myths, Euhemerus pretended, on the contrary, that "myths were the legendary history of kings and heroes, transformed into gods by the admiration of the nations." * It is the latter method which was inferentially followed by Christians when they agreed upon the acceptation of euhemerized patriarchs, and mistook them for men who had really lived.

But, in opposition to this pernicious theory, which has brought forth such bitter fruit, we have a long series of the great philosophers the world has produced: Plato, Epicharmus, Socrates, Empedocles, Plotinus, Porphyry, Proclus, Damascenus, Origen, and even Aristotle. The latter plainly stated this verity by saying that a tradition of the highest antiquity, transmitted to posterity under the form of various myths, teaches us that the first principles of nature may be considered as "gods," for the *divine* permeates all nature. All the rest, details and personages, were added later for the clearer comprehension of the vulgar, and but too often with the object of supporting laws invented in the common interest.

Fairy tales do not exclusively belong to nurseries; all mankind — except those few who in all ages have comprehended their hidden meaning and tried to open the eyes of the superstitious — have listened to such tales in one shape or the other and, after transforming them into sacred symbols, called the product RELIGION!

We will try to systematize our subject as much as the ever-recurring necessity to draw parallels between the conflicting opinions that have been based on the same myths will permit. We will begin with the book of *Genesis,* and seek for its hidden meaning in the Brahmanical traditions and the Chaldeo-Judaic *Kabala.*

The first Scripture lesson taught us in our infancy is that God created the world in six days and rested on the *seventh.* Hence, a peculiar sol-

---

\* [Cf. Plutarch, *On Isis and Osiris*, § 23.]

emnity is supposed to attach to the seventh day, and the Christians, adopting the rigid observances of the Jewish Sabbath, have enforced it upon us with the substitution of the first, instead of the seventh day of the week.

All systems of religious mysticism are based on numerals. With Pythagoras, the Monas or unity, emanating the duad, and thus forming the trinity, and the quaternary or *Arba-il* (the mystic *four*), compose the number seven. The sacredness of numbers begins with the great First — the ONE, and ends only with the nought or zero — symbol of the infinite and boundless circle which represents the universe. All the intervening figures, in whatever combination, or however multiplied, represent philosophical ideas, from vague outlines down to a definitely established scientific axiom, relating either to a moral or a physical fact in nature. They are a key to the ancient views on cosmogony, in its broad sense, including man and beings, and the evolution of the human race, spiritually as well as physically.

The number *seven* is the most sacred of all, and is, undoubtedly, of Hindu origin. Everything of importance was calculated by and fitted into this number by the Âryan philosophers — ideas as well as localities. Thus they have the:

*Sapta-Rishis*, or seven sages, typifying the seven diluvian primitive races (post-diluvian as some say).

*Sapta-Lokas*, the seven inferior and superior worlds, whence each of the Rishis proceeded, and whither he returned in glory before reaching the final bliss of Moksha.*

*Sapta-Kulas*, or seven castes — the Brahmans assuming to represent the direct descendants of the highest of them.†

Then, again, the *Sapta-Puras* (seven holy cities); *Sapta-Dvîpas* (seven holy islands); *Sapta-Samudras* (the seven holy seas); *Sapta-Parvatas* (the seven holy mountains); *Sapta-Aranyas* (the seven deserts); *Sapta-Vrikshas* (the seven sacred trees); and so on.

---

* The *Rishis* are identical with Manu. The ten Prajâpatis, sons of *Virâj*, called *Marîchi, Atri, Angiras, Pulastya, Pulaka, Kratu, Prachetas, Vasishtha, Bhrigu*, and *Nârada*, are euhemerized *Powers* the Hindu *Sephirôth*. These emanate the seven Rishis, or Manus, the chief of whom issued himself from the "uncreated." He is the Adam of earth, and signifies man. His "sons," the following six Manus, represent each a new race of men, and in the total they are *humanity* passing gradually through the primitive seven stages of evolution.

† In days of old, when the Brahmans studied more than they do now the hidden sense of their philosophy, they explained that each of these six distinct races which preceded ours had disappeared. But now they pretend that a specimen was preserved which was not destroyed with the rest, but reached the present *seventh* stage. Thus they, the Brahmans, are the specimens of the heavenly Manu, and issued from the mouth of Brahmâ; while the Sûdra was created from his foot.

In the Chaldeo-Babylonian incantation, this number reappears again as prominently as among the Hindus. The number is *dual* in its attributes, *i.e.*, holy in one of its aspects, it becomes nefast under other conditions. Thus the following incantation we find traced on the Assyrian tablets, now so correctly interpreted.

"The evening of evil omen, the region of the sky, which produces misfortune . . .

"Message of pest.
"Deprecators of Nin-Ki-gal.
"The seven gods of the vast sky.
"The seven gods of the vast earth.
"The seven gods of blazing spheres.
"The seven gods of celestial legions.
"The seven gods maleficent.
"The seven phantoms — bad.
"The seven phantoms of maleficent flames . . .
"Bad demon, bad *alal*, bad *gigim*, bad *tilol* . . . bad god, bad *maskim*.
"Spirit of seven heavens remember . . . Spirit of seven earths remember . . . etc." *

This number reappears likewise on almost every page of *Genesis* and throughout the Mosaic books, and we find it conspicuous (see following chapter) in the *Book of Job* and the Oriental *Kabala*. If the Hebrew Semitics adopted it so readily, we must infer that it was not blindly, but with a thorough knowledge of its secret meaning; hence, that they must have adopted the doctrines of their "heathen" neighbors as well. It is but natural, therefore, that we should seek in *heathen* philosophy for the interpretation of this number, which again reappeared in Christianity with its *seven* sacraments, *seven* churches in Asia Minor, *seven* capital sins, *seven* virtues (four cardinal and three theological), etc.

Have the *seven* prismatic colors of the rainbow seen by Noah no other meaning than that of a covenant between God and man to refresh the memory of the former? To the kabalist, at least, they have a significance inseparable from the seven labors of magic, the seven upper spheres, the seven notes of the musical scale, the seven numerals of Pythagoras, the seven wonders of the world, the seven ages, and even the seven steps of the Masons, which lead to the Holy of Holies, after passing the flights of *three* and *five*.

Whence the identity then of these enigmatical, ever-recurring numerals that are found in every page of the Jewish Scriptures, as in every *ola* and *śloka* of Buddhistic and Brahmanical books? Whence these numerals that are the soul of the Pythagorean and Platonic thought, and that no unilluminated Orientalist nor Biblical student has ever been able to fathom?

---

* [F. Lenormant, *Chaldean Magic*, etc., Transl. from the French, London, 1877-78, ch. i, pp. 17-18.]

And yet they have a key ready in their hand, did they but know how to use it. Nowhere is the mystical value of human language and its effects on human action so perfectly understood as in India, nor any better explained than by the authors of the oldest *Brâhmaṇas*. Ancient as their epoch is now found to be, they only try to express, in a more concrete form, the abstract metaphysical speculations of their own ancestors.

Such is the respect of the Brahmans for the sacrificial mysteries, that they hold that the world itself sprang into creation as a consequence of a "sacrificial word" pronounced by the First Cause. This word is the "Ineffable Name" of the kabalists, fully discussed in the last chapter.

The secret of the *Vedas*, "Sacred Knowledge" though they may be, is impenetrable without the help of the *Brâhmaṇas*. Properly speaking, the *Vedas* (which are written in verse and comprised in four books) constitute that portion called the *Mantra*, or magical prayer, and the *Brâhmaṇas* (which are in prose) contain their key. While the *Mantra* part is alone holy, the *Brâhmaṇa* portion contains all the theological exegesis, and the speculations and explanations of the sacerdotal. Our Orientalists, we repeat, will make no substantial progress toward a comprehension of Vedic literature until they place a proper valuation upon works now despised by them; as, for instance, the *Aitareya-* and *Kaushîtaki-Brâhmaṇas*, which belong to the *Ṛig-Veda*.

Zoroaster was called a *Manthran*, or speaker of Mantras, and, according to Haug, one of the earliest names for the Sacred Scriptures of the Pârsîs was *Mânthra-speñta*. The power and significance of the Brahman who acts as the Hoṭri-priest at the Soma-Sacrifice, consists in his possession and full knowledge of the uses of the sacred word or speech — *Vâch*. The latter is personified in *Sarasvatî*, the wife of Brahmâ, who is the goddess of the sacred or "Secret Knowledge." She is usually depicted as riding upon a peacock with its tail all spread. The eyes upon the feathers of the bird's tail symbolize the sleepless eyes that see all things. To one who has the ambition of becoming an adept of the "Secret doctrines," they are a reminder that he must have the hundred eyes of Argus to see and comprehend all things.

And this is why we say that it is not possible to solve fully the deep problems underlying the Brahmanical and Buddhistic sacred books without having a perfect comprehension of the esoteric meaning of the Pythagorean numerals. The greatest power of this *Vâch*, or Sacred Speech, is developed according to the form which is given to the Mantra by the officiating Hoṭri, and this form consists wholly in the numbers and syllables of the sacred metre. If pronounced slowly and in a certain rhythm, one effect is produced; if quickly and with another rhythm, there is a different result. "Each metre," says Haug, "is the invisible master of something obtainable in this world; it is, as it were, its exponent, and ideal. This great significance of the metrical speech is derived from the number of syllables of which it consists, for each thing has (just as in the Pythagorean system) a certain numerical proportion . . . All these things, metres (*chhandas*), Stomas, and Prishtas, are believed to be as eternal and divine as the words themselves they contain. The earliest Hindu divines did not only believe in a primitive revelation of the words of the sacred texts, but even in that of the various forms . . . These forms along with their contents, the everlasting *Veda*-words, are symbols expressive of things of the invisible world, and in several respects comparable to the Platonic ideas." *

*This testimony from an unwilling witness shows again the identity between the ancient religions as to their secret doctrine.* The Gâyatrî metre, for example, consists of *thrice eight* syllables, and is considered the most sacred of metres. It is the metre of Agni, the fire-god, and becomes at times the emblem of Brahmâ himself, the chief creator, and "fashioner of man" in his own image. Now Pythagoras says that "the number eight, or the Octad, is the first cube, that is to say, squared in all senses, as a die, proceeding from its base two, or even number; *so is man four-square or perfect.*" Of course few, except the Pythagoreans and kabalists, can fully comprehend this idea; but the illustration will assist in pointing out the close kinship of the numerals with the Vedic *Mantras.* The chief problems of every theology lie concealed beneath this imagery of fire and the varying rhythm of its flames. The burning bush of the *Bible,* the Zoroastrian and other sacred fires, Plato's universal soul, and the Rosicrucian doctrines of both soul and body of man being evolved out of fire, the reasoning and immortal element which permeates all things, and which, according to Heraclitus, Hippocrates and Parmenides, is God, have all the same meaning.

Each metre in the *Brâhmanas* corresponds to a number, and as shown by Haug, as it stands in the sacred volumes, is a prototype of some visible form on earth, and its effects are either good or evil. The "sacred speech" can save, but it can kill as well; its many meanings and faculties are well known but to the *Dikshita* (the adept), who has been initiated into many mysteries, and whose "spiritual birth" is completely achieved; the *Vâch* of the *mantra* is a spoken power, which awakens another corresponding and still more occult power, each allegorically personified by some god in the world of spirits, and, according as it is used, responded to either by the gods or the *Râkshasas* (bad spirits). In the Brahmanical and Buddhist ideas, a curse, a blessing, a vow, a desire, an idle thought, can each assume a visible shape and so manifest itself *objectively* to the eyes of its author, or to him that it concerns.

---

* [Haug, *Aitareya-Brâhmanam,* I, pp. 76-79.]

Every sin becomes incarnated, so to say, and like an avenging fiend persecutes its perpetrator.

There are words which have a destructive quality in their very syllables, as though objective things; for every sound awakens a corresponding one in the invisible world of spirit, and the repercussion produces either a good or bad effect. Harmonious rhythm, a melody vibrating softly in the atmosphere, creates a beneficent and sweet influence around, and acts most powerfully on the psychological as well as physical natures of every living thing on earth; it reacts even on inanimate objects, for matter is still spirit in its essence, invisible as it may seem to our grosser senses.

So with the numerals. Turn wherever we will, from the Prophets to the *Apocalypse*, and we will see the Biblical writers constantly using the numbers *three, four, seven* and *twelve*.

And yet we have known some partisans of the *Bible* who maintained that the *Vedas* were copied from the Mosaic books! * The *Vedas*, which are written in Sanskrit, a language whose grammatical rules and forms, as Max Müller and other scholars confess, were *completely established* long before the days when the great wave of emigration bore it from Asia all over the Occident, are there to proclaim their parentage of every philosophy and every religious institution developed later among Semitic peoples. And which of the numerals most frequently occur in the Sanskrit chants, those sublime hymns to creation, to the unity of God, and the countless manifestations of His power? ONE, THREE and SEVEN. Read the hymn by Dîrghatamas.[56]

"TO HIM WHO REPRESENTS ALL THE GODS."

"The *God* here present, our blessed patron, our sacrificer, has a brother who spreads himself in mid-air. There exists a *third* Brother whom we sprinkle with our libations of liquid butter. It is he whom I have seen master of men and armed with *seven* rays." †

And again:

"Seven Bridles aid in guiding a car which has but ONE wheel, and which is drawn by a single horse that shines with *seven* rays. The wheel has *three* limbs, an immortal wheel, never-wearying, whence hang all the worlds."

"Sometimes *seven* horses drag this car of *seven* wheels, and *seven* personages mount it, accompanied by *seven* fecund nymphs of the water." ‡

And the following again, in honor of the fire-god — *Agni*, who is so clearly shown but a spirit subordinate to the ONE God.

---

\* To avoid discussion we adopt the palaeographical conclusions arrived at by Martin Haug and some other cautious scholars. Personally we credit the statements of the Brahmans and those of Halhed, the translator of the *Sâstras* [Cf. *A Code of Gentoo Laws*, 1776.]

† The god Heptaktis.

‡ [Cf. Jacolliot, *Les traditions indo-européennes*, etc., p. 155; cf. *Ṛig-Veda*, I, 164, 1, 2, 3.]

"Ever ONE, although having three forms of double nature [androgynous] — he rises! and the priests offer to *God*, in the act of sacrifice, their prayers which reach the heavens, borne aloft by Agni." *

Is this a coincidence, or rather, as reason tells us, the result of the derivation of many national cults from one primitive, universal religion? A *mystery* for the uninitiated, the *unveiling* of the most sublime (because correct and true) psychological and physiological problems for the initiate. Revelations of the personal spirit of man which is divine because that spirit is not only the emanation of the ONE Supreme God, but is the only God man is able, in his weakness and helplessness, to comprehend — to feel *within* himself. This truth the Vedic poet clearly confesses, when saying:

"The Lord, Master of the universe and full of wisdom, has entered with me [into me] — weak and ignorant — and has formed me of *himself* in that place † where the spirits obtain, by the help of *Science*, the peaceful enjoyment of the *fruit*, as sweet as ambrosia." ‡

Whether we call this fruit "an apple" from the Tree of Knowledge. or the *pippala* of the Hindu poet, it matters not. It is the fruit of esoteric wisdom. Our object is to show the existence of a religious system in India for many thousands of years before the exoteric fables of the Garden of Eden and the Deluge had been invented, hence the identity of doctrines. Instructed in them, each of the initiates of other countries became. in his turn, the founder of some great school of philosophy in the West.

Who of our Sanskrit scholars has ever felt interested in discovering the real sense of the following hymns, palpable as it is: "*Pippala*, the sweet fruit of that tree upon which come *spirits* who love the *science* [?] and where *the gods produce all marvels*. This is a mystery for him *who knows not the Father* of the world." §

Or this one again:

"These stanzas bear at their head a title which announces that they are consecrated to the *Viśvadevas* [that is to say, to all the gods]. He who knows not the Being whom I sing *in all his manifestations*, will comprehend nothing of my verses; those who do know HIM are not strangers to this reunion."||

This refers to the reunion and parting of the immortal and mortal parts of man. "The immortal Being," says the preceding stanza, "is in the cradle of the mortal Being. The two eternal spirits go and come everywhere; only some men know the one without knowing the other" (*Dirghatamas*).

---

\* [Jacolliot, *op. cit.*, p. 157. Cf. *Ṛig-Veda*, I, 164, 10.]
† The sanctuary of the initiation.
‡ [*Ibid.*, p. 160. Cf. *Ṛig-Veda*, I, 164, 21.]
§ [*Ṛig-Veda*, I, 164, 22.]
|| [Jacolliot, *op. cit.*, p. 165.]

Who can give a correct idea of Him of whom the Ṛig-Veda says: "That which is One the wise call it in divers manners." That One is sung by the Vedic poets in all its manifestations in nature; and the books considered "childish and foolish" teach how at will to call the beings of wisdom for our instruction. They teach, as Porphyry says: "a liberation from all terrene concerns . . . a flight of the *alone* to the ALONE."

Professor Max Müller, whose every word is accepted by his school as philological gospel, is undoubtedly right in one sense when in determining the nature of the Hindu gods, he calls them "masks without an actor . . . names without being, not beings without names." * For he but proves thereby the monotheism of the ancient Vedic religion. But it seems to us more than dubious whether he or any scientist of his school can hope to fathom the old Âryan † thought, without an accurate study of those very "masks." To the materialist, as to the scientist, who for various reasons endeavors to work out the difficult problem of compelling facts to agree with either their own hobbies or those of the *Bible,* they may seem but the empty shells of phantoms. Yet such authorities will ever be, as in the past, the unsafest of guides, except in matters of exact science. The *Bible* patriarchs are as much "masks without actors," as the *Prajâpatis,* and yet, if the living personage behind these masks is but an abstract shadow, there is an idea embodied in every one of them which belongs to the philosophical and scientific theories of ancient wisdom.‡ And who can render better service in this work than the native Brahmans themselves, or the kabalists?

To deny, point-blank, any sound philosophy in the later Brahmanical speculations upon the *Ṛig-Veda,* is equivalent to refusing ever to correctly understand the mother-religion itself, which gave rise to them, and which is the expression of the inner thought of the direct ancestors of these later authors of the *Brâhmaṇas.* If learned Europeans can so

---

* "Comparative Mythology," in *Chips,* etc., II, p. 76.

† While having no intention to enter at present upon a discussion as to the nomadic races of the "Rhematic period," we reserve the right to question the full propriety of terming that portion of the primitive people from whose traditions the *Vedas* sprang into existence, Âryans. Some scientists find the existence of these Âryans not only unproved by science, but the traditions of Hindostan protesting against such an assumption.

‡ Without the esoteric explanation, the *Old Testament* becomes an absurd jumble of meaningless tales — nay, worse than that, it must rank high with *immoral* books. It is curious that Professor Max Müller, such a profound scholar in Comparative Mythology, should be found saying of the *Prajâpatis* and Hindu gods that they are masks *without actors;* and of Abraham and other mythical patriarchs that they were real living men; of Abraham especially, we are told (see "Semitic Monotheism," in *Chips,* I, p. 373) that he "stands before us as a figure second only to one in the whole history of the world."

readily show that all the Vedic gods are but empty masks, they must also be ready to demonstrate that the Brahmanical authors were as incapable as themselves to discover these "actors" anywhere. This done, not only the three other sacred books which Max Müller says "do not deserve the name of *Vedas*," but the *Ṛig-Veda* itself becomes a meaningless jumble of words; for what the world-renowned and subtile intellect of the ancient Hindu sages failed to understand, no modern scientist, however learned, can hope to fathom. Poor Thomas Taylor was right in saying that "philology is not philosophy."

It is, to say the least, illogical to admit that there is a hidden thought in the literary work of a race perhaps ethnologically different from our own; and then, because it is utterly unintelligible to us whose spiritual development during the several thousand intervening years has bifurcated into quite a contrary direction — deny that it has any sense in it at all. But this is precisely what, with all due respect for erudition, Professor Max Müller and his school do in this instance, at least. First of all, we are told that, albeit cautiously and with some effort, yet we may still walk in the footsteps of these authors of the *Vedas*. "We shall feel that we are brought face to face and mind to mind with men yet intelligible to us, *after we have freed ourselves from our modern conceits*. We shall not succeed always; words, verses, nay, whole hymns in the *Ṛig-Veda*, will and must remain to us a dead letter." For, with a few exceptions, ". . . the whole world of Vedic ideas is so entirely beyond our own intellectual horizon, that instead of translating we can as yet only guess and combine." \*

And yet, to leave us in no possible doubt as to the true value of his words, the learned scholar, in another passage, expresses his opinion on these same *Vedas* (with one exception) thus: "The only important, the only real Veda, is the *Ṛig-Veda*. The other so-called *Vedas* . . . deserve the name of *Veda* no more than the *Talmud* deserves the name of *Bible*." Professor Müller rejects them as unworthy of the attention of anyone, and, as we understand it, on the ground that they contain chiefly "sacrificial formulas, charms, and incantations." †

And now, a very natural question: Are any of our scholars prepared to demonstrate that, so far, they are intimately acquainted with the hidden sense of these perfectly absurd "sacrificial formulas, charms, and incantations" and magic nonsense of *Atharva-Veda*? We believe not, and our doubt is based on the confession of Professor Müller himself, just quoted. If "the whole world of Vedic ideas [the *Ṛig-Veda* cannot be included

---

\* The italics are our own. *Chips*, etc., Vol. I, pp. 77, 75.

† *Chips*, etc., Vol. I, pp. 8-9.

alone in this *world*, we suppose] is so entirely beyond our own [the scientists'] intellectual horizon, that instead of translating we can as yet only guess and combine"; and the *Yajur-Veda, Sama-Veda*, and *Atharva-Veda* are "childish and foolish";* and the *Brâhmanas*, the *Sûtras*, Yâska and Sâyana, "though *nearest in time* to the hymns of the *Rig-Veda*, indulge in the most frivolous and ill-judged interpretations," † how can either he, himself, or any other scholar form any adequate opinion of either of them? If, again, the authors of the *Brâhmanas*, the nearest in time to the Vedic hymns, were already incompetent to offer anything better than "ill-judged interpretations," then at what period of history, where, and by whom, were written these grandiose poems, whose mystical sense has died with their generations? Are we, then, so wrong in affirming that if sacred texts are found in Egypt to have become — even to the priestly scribes of 4,000 years ago — wholly unintelligible,‡ and the *Brâhmanas* offer but "childish and foolish" interpretations of the *Rig-Veda*, at least as far back as that, then, 1st, both the Egyptian and Hindu religious philosophies are of an untold antiquity, far antedating ages cautiously assigned them by our students of comparative mythology; and, 2nd, the claims of ancient priests of Egypt and modern Brahmans as to their age are, after all, correct.

We can never admit that the three other *Vedas* are less worthy of their name than the *Rig* (hymns), or that the *Talmud* and the *Kabala* are so inferior to the *Bible*. The very name of the *Vedas* (the literal meaning of which is *knowledge* or *wisdom*) shows them to belong to the literature of those men who, in every country, language and age, have been spoken of as "those who know." In Sanskrit the third person singular is *veda* (he knows), and the plural is *vidus* (they know). The word *veda* is synonymous with the Greek θεοσέβεια, which Plato uses when speaking of the *wise*—the magicians; and with the Hebrew Ḥakhamim, חכמים (wise men). Reject the *Talmud* and its old predecessor the *Kabala*, and it will be simply impossible ever to render correctly one word of that *Bible* so much extolled at their expense. But then it is, perhaps, just what its partisans are working for. To banish the *Brâhmanas* is to fling away the key that unlocks the door of the *Rig-Veda*. The *literal* interpretation of the *Bible* has already borne its fruits; with the *Vedas* and the Sanskrit sacred books in general it will be just the same, with this difference, that the absurd interpretation of the *Bible* has received a time-honored right of eminent domain in the department of the ridiculous and will find its

---

*We believe that we have elsewhere given the contrary opinion, on the subject of *Atharva-Veda*, of Prof. Whitney of Yale College.

† *Chips*, etc., Vol. I, p. 76.

‡ See Baron Bunsen's *Egypt's Place*, etc., Vol. V, p. 90.

supporters, against light and against proof. As to the "heathen" literature, after a few more years of unsuccessful attempts at interpretation, its religious meaning will be relegated to the limbo of exploded superstitions, and people will hear no more of it.

We beg to be clearly understood before we are blamed and criticized for the above remarks. The vast learning of the celebrated Oxford professor can hardly be questioned by his very enemies, yet we have a right to regret his precipitancy to condemn that which he himself confesses "entirely beyond our own intellectual horizon." Even in what he considers a ridiculous blunder on the part of the author of the *Brâhmaṇas*, other more spiritually disposed persons may see quite the reverse. "*Who* is the greatest of the gods? Who shall first be praised by our songs?" says an ancient Ṛishi of the *Ṛig-Veda*; mistaking (as Prof. M. imagines) the interrogative pronoun "Who" for some divine name. Says the Professor: "A place is allotted in the sacrificial invocations to a god 'Who,' and hymns addressed to him are called 'Whoish' hymns."\* And is a god "Who" less natural as a term than a god "I am"? or "Whoish" hymns less reverential than "I-amish" psalms? And who can prove that this is really a blunder, and not a premeditated expression? Is it so impossible to believe that the strange term was precisely due to a reverential awe which made the poet hesitate before giving a name as form to that which is justly considered as the highest abstraction of metaphysical ideals — God? Or that the same feeling made the commentator who came after him to pause and so leave the work of anthropomorphizing the "Unknown," the "Who," to future human conceptions? "These early poets thought more for themselves than for others," remarks Max Müller himself. "They sought rather, in their language, to be true to their own thought than to please the imagination of their bearers."† Unfortunately it is this very thought which awakens no responsive echo in the minds of our philologists.

Farther, we read the sound advice to students of the *Ṛig-Veda* hymns, to collect, collate, sift and reject. "Let him study the commentaries, the *Sûtras*, the *Brâhmaṇas*, and even later works, in order to exhaust all the sources from which information can be derived. He [the scholar] *must not despise the traditions of the Brâhmans*, even where their misconceptions . . . are palpable . . . Not a corner in the *Brâhmaṇas*, the *Sûtras*, Yâska and Sâyana, should be left unexplored *before we venture to propose a rendering of our own* . . . When the scholar has done his work, the poet and philosopher must take it up and finish it." ‡

---

\* Max Müller, lecture on "The Vedas," in *Chips*, etc., Vol. I, p. 76.

† *Ibid.*, p. 73.

‡ *Ibid.*, pp. 75-76.

Poor chance for a "philosopher" to step into the shoes of a learned philologist and presume to correct *his* errors! We would like to see what sort of a reception the most learned Hindu in India would have from the educated public of Europe and America, if he should undertake to correct a savant, after he had sifted, accepted, rejected, explained and declared what was good, and what "absurd and childish" in the sacred books of his forefathers. That which would finally be declared "Brahmanic misconceptions," by the conclave of European and especially German savants, would be as little likely to be reconsidered at the appeal of the most erudite pundit of Benares or Ceylon, as the interpretation of Jewish Scripture by Maimonides and Philo Judaeus, by Christians after the Councils of the Church had accepted the mistranslations and explanations of Irenaeus and Eusebius. What pundit, or native philosopher of India could know his ancestral language, religion, or philosophy as well as an Englishman or a German? Or why should a Hindu be more suffered to expound Brahmanism, than a Rabbinical scholar to interpret Judaism or the Isaian prophecies? Safer, and far more trustworthy translators can be had nearer home. Nevertheless, let us still hope that we may find at last, even though it be in the dim future, a European philosopher to sift the sacred books of the wisdom-religion, and not be contradicted by every other of his class.

Meanwhile, unmindful of any alleged authorities, let us try to sift for ourselves a few of these myths of old. We will search for an explanation within the popular interpretation, and feel our way with the help of the magic lamp of Trismegistus — the mysterious number *seven*. There must have been some reason why this figure was universally accepted as a mystic [figure of] calculation. With every ancient people, the Creator, or Demiurge, was placed over the seventh heaven. "And were I to touch upon the initiation into our sacred Mysteries," says Emperor Julian, the kabalist, "which the Chaldean bacchised respecting the *seven-rayed God, lifting up the souls through Him*, I should say things unknown, and *very unknown to the rabble*, but well known to the *Blessed Theurgists*." * In Lydus it is said that "The Chaldeans call the God IAÔ, and TSABAÔTH he is often called, *as He* who is over the seven orbits [heavens, or spheres], that is the Demiurge." †

One must consult the Pythagoreans and Kabalists to learn the potentiality of this number. Exoterically the seven rays of the solar spectrum are represented concretely in the seven-rayed god Heptaktys. These seven rays epitomized into THREE primary rays, namely, the red, blue and yellow, form the solar trinity, and typify respectively spirit-

---

* Julian, *Oratio V in Matrem Deorum*, § 173.
† J. Lydus, *De mensibus*, IV, 38, 74; Movers, *Die Phönizier*, Vol. I, pp. 550-51.

matter and spirit-essence. Science has also reduced of late the seven rays to three primary ones, thus corroborating the scientific conception of the ancients of at least one of the visible manifestations of the invisible deity, and the seven divided into a quaternary and a trinity.

The Pythagoreans called the number seven the vehicle of life, as it contained body and soul. They explained it by saying that the human body consisted of four principal elements, and that the soul is triple, comprising reason, passion and desire. The ineffable WORD was considered the *Seventh* and highest of all, for there are six minor substitutes, each belonging to a degree of initiation. The Jews borrowed their Sabbath from the ancients, who called it *Saturn's* day and deemed it unlucky, and not the latter from the Israelites when Christianized. The people of India, Arabia, Syria and Egypt observed weeks of seven days; and the Romans learned the hebdomadal method from these foreign countries when they became subject to the Empire. Still it was not until the fourth century that the Roman kalends, nones and ides were abandoned, and weeks substituted in their place; and the astronomical names of the days, such as *dies Solis* (day of the Sun), *dies Lunae* (day of the Moon), *dies Martis* (day of Mars); *dies Mercurii* (day of Mercury), *dies Jovis* (day of Jupiter), *dies Veneris* (day of Venus), and *dies Saturni* (day of Saturn), prove that it was not from the Jews that the week of seven days was adopted. Before we examine this number kabalistically, we propose to analyze it from the standpoint of the Judaico-Christian Sabbath.

When Moses instituted the *yom sheba*, or *Shebang* (Shabbath), the allegory of the Lord God resting from his work of creation on the seventh day was but a *cloak*, or, as the *Zohar* expresses it, a screen, to hide the true meaning.

The Jews reckoned then, as they do now, their days by number, as, day the *first;* day the *second;* and so on; *yom a'had; yom sheni; yom shelishi; yom rebi'i; yom 'hamishi; yom shishshi; yom shebi'i.*

The Hebrew *seven*, שבע, consisting of three letters, *sh, b, ô*, has more than one meaning. First of all, it means *age* or cycle, Sheb-ang; Sabbath, שבת, can be translated *old age*, as well as *rest*, and in the old Coptic, *Sabe* means *wisdom*, learning. Modern archaeologists have found that as in Hebrew *shib*, שיב, also means *gray-headed*, and that therefore the *Saba*-day was the day on which the "gray-headed men," or "aged fathers" of a tribe, were in the habit of assembling for councils or sacrifices. *

Thus, the week of six days and the seventh, the *Saba* or *Sapta*-day period, is of the highest antiquity. The observance of the lunar festivals in India shows that that nation held hebdomadal meetings as well. With

---

* "Septenary Institutions," *Westminster Review,* London, Vol. LIV, Oct., 1850, p. 81.

every new quarter the moon brings changes in the atmosphere, hence certain changes are also produced throughout the whole of our universe, of which the meteorological ones are the most insignificant. On this day of the *seventh* and most powerful of the prismatic days, the adepts of the "Secret Science" meet as they met thousands of years ago, to become the agents of the occult powers of nature (emanations of the working God), and commune with the invisible worlds. It is in this observance of the seventh day by the old sages — not as the resting day of the Deity, but because they had penetrated into its occult power, that lies the profound veneration of all the heathen philosophers for the number *seven* which they term the "venerable," the sacred number. The Pythagorean *Tetraktys*, revered by the Platonists, was the *square* placed below the *triangle;* the latter, or the Trinity, embodying the invisible *Monad* — the unity, and deemed too sacred to be pronounced except within the walls of a Sanctuary.

The ascetic observance of the Christian Sabbath by Protestants is pure religious tyranny, and does more harm, we fear, than good. It really dates only from the *Enactment* of Charles II,\* which prohibited any "tradesman, artificer, workman, laborer, or other person," to "do or exercise any worldly labor, etc., etc., upon the Lord's day." The Puritans carried this thing to extremes, apparently to mark their hatred of Catholicism, both Roman and Episcopal. That it was no part of the plan of Jesus that such a day should be set apart is evident not only from his words but acts. It was not observed by the early Christians.

When Trypho, *the Jew,* reproached the Christians *for not having a Sabbath,* what does the martyr answer him? "The new law will have you keep a perpetual Sabbath. You, when *you have passed a day in idleness, think you are religious.* The Lord is not pleased with such things as these. If any be guilty of *perjury or fraud,* let him reform; *if he be an adulterer,* let him repent; and *he will then have kept the kind of Sabbath truly pleasing to God* . . . The elements are never idle, and keep no Sabbath. There was no need of the observance of Sabbaths before Moses, neither now is there any need of them after Jesus Christ." †

The *Heptaktys* is not the Supreme Cause, but simply an emanation from *Him* — the first visible manifestation of the Unrevealed Power. "His Divine *Breath,* which, violently breaking forth, condensed itself, shining with radiance until it evolved into Light, and so became cognizant to external sense," says John Reuchlin.‡ This is the emanation of the Highest, the Demiurge, a multiplicity in a *unity,* the *Elohim,* whom we

---

\* 1676. — 29 Car. II, c. 7.

† [Justin Martyr, *Dialogue with Trypho,* xii, xxiii.]

‡ *De verbo mirifico.*

see *creating* our world, or rather fashioning it, in six days, and resting on the *seventh*. And who are these *Elohim* but the euhemerized powers of nature, the faithful manifested servants, the laws of Him who is immutable law and harmony Himself?

They remain over the seventh heaven (or spiritual world), for it is they who, according to the kabalists, formed in succession the six material worlds, or rather, attempts at worlds, that preceded our own, which, they say, is the *seventh*. If, in laying aside the metaphysico-spiritual conception, we give our attention but to the religio-scientific problem of creation in "six days," over which our best Biblical scholars have vainly pondered so long, we might, perchance, be on the way to the true idea underlying the allegory. The ancients were philosophers, consistent in all things. Hence, they taught that each of these departed worlds, having performed its physical evolution, and reached—through birth, growth, maturity, old age and death—the end of its cycle, had returned to its primitive subjective form of a *spiritual* earth. Thereafter it had to serve through all eternity as the dwelling of those who had lived on it as men, and even animals, but were now spirits. This idea, were it even as incapable of exact demonstration as that of our theologians relating to Paradise, is, at least, a trifle more philosophical.

As well as man, and every other living thing upon it, our planet has had its spiritual and physical evolution. From an impalpable ideal *thought* under the creative Will of Him of whom we know nothing, and but dimly conceive in imagination, this globe became fluidic and *semi*-spiritual, then condensed itself more and more, until its physical development—matter, the tempting demon—compelled it to try its own creative faculty. *Matter* defied SPIRIT, and the earth, too, had its "Fall." The allegorical curse under which it labors is that it only *procreates*, it does not *create*. Our physical planet is but the handmaiden, or rather the maid-of-all-work, of the spirit, its master. "Cursed is the ground . . . thorns also and thistles shall it bring," the Elohim are made to say. "In sorrow thou shalt bring forth children."* The Elohim say this both to the ground and the woman. And this curse will last until the minutest particle of matter on earth shall have outlived its days, until every grain of dust has, by gradual transformation through evolution, become a constituent part of a "living soul," and, until the latter shall reascend the cyclic arc, and finally stand—its own *Metatron*, or Redeeming Spirit— at the foot of the upper step of the spiritual worlds, as at the first hour of its emanation. Beyond that lies the great "Deep"—A MYSTERY!

It must be remembered that every cosmogony has a *trinity* of workers at its head—Father, spirit; Mother, nature, or matter; and the mani-

---

* [*Gen.* iii, 16-18.]

fested universe, the Son or result of the two. The universe, also, as well as each planet which it comprehends, passes through *four* ages, like man himself. All have their infancy, youth, maturity and old age, and these four added to the other three make the sacred seven again.

The introductory chapters of *Genesis* were never meant to present even a remote allegory of the creation of *our* earth. They embrace (chapter i) a metaphysical conception of some indefinite period in the eternity, when successive attempts were being made by the law of evolution at the formation of universes. This idea is plainly stated in the *Zohar*: "There were old worlds, which perished as soon as they came into existence, were formless, and were called *sparks*. Thus, the smith, when hammering the iron, lets the sparks fly in all directions. The sparks are the primordial worlds which could not continue, because the *Sacred Aged* [Sephîrâh] had not as yet assumed its form [of androgyne or opposite sexes] of king and queen [Sephîrâh and Kadmon] and the Master was not yet at his work."*

The six periods or "days" of *Genesis* refer to the same metaphysical belief. Five such ineffectual attempts were made by the *Elohim*, but the sixth resulted in worlds like our own (*i.e.*, all the planets and most of the stars are worlds, and inhabited, though not like our earth). Having formed this world at last in the sixth period, the Elohim rested in the *seventh*. Thus the "Holy One," when he created the present world, said: "This pleases me; the previous ones did not please me."† And the Elohim "saw everything that he had made, and behold *it was* very good. And the evening and the morning were the sixth *day*."—*Genesis* i, 31.

The reader will remember that in Chapter IV an explanation was given of the "day" and "night" of Brahmâ. The former represents a certain period of cosmical activity, the latter an equal one of cosmical repose. In the one, worlds are being evolved, and passing through their allotted four ages of existence; in the latter the "inbreathing" of Brahmâ reverses the tendency of the natural forces; everything visible becomes gradually dispersed; chaos comes; and a long night of repose reinvigorates the cosmos for its next term of evolution. In the morning of one

---

* *Zohar*, III, p. 292b; Amst. ed. The Supreme consulting with the Architect of the world — his Logos — about creation.

† *Berêshith Rabbah*, parsha ix. If the chapters of *Genesis* and the other Mosaic books, as well as the subjects, are muddled up, the fault is the compiler's — not that of oral tradition. Hilkiah and Josiah had to commune with Huldah, the prophetess, hence resort to *magic*, to understand the word of the "Lord God of Israel," most conveniently found by Hilkiah (2 *Kings* xxiii); and that it has passed still later through more than one revision and remodeling is but too well proved by its frequent incongruities, repetitions and contradictions.

of these "days" the formative processes are gradually reaching their climax of activity; in the evening imperceptibly diminishing the same until the *pralaya* arrives, and with it *"night."* One such morning and evening do, in fact, constitute a cosmic day; and it was a "day of Brahmâ" that the kabalistic author of *Genesis* had in mind each time when he said: "And the evening and the morning were the first (or fifth or sixth, or any other) *day."* Six days of gradual evolution, one of repose, and then—evening! Since the first appearance of man on *our* earth there has been an eternal Sabbath or rest for the Demiurge.

The cosmogonical speculations of the first six chapters of *Genesis* are shown in the races of "sons of God," "giants," etc., of chapter vi. Properly speaking, the story of the formation of our earth, or "creation," as it is very improperly called, begins with the rescue of Noah from the deluge. The Chaldeo-Babylonian tablets recently translated by George Smith leave no doubt of that in the minds of those who read the inscriptions esoterically. Ishtar, the great goddess, speaks in column iii of the destruction of the *sixth* world and the appearance of the seventh, thus:

"Six days and nights passed, the wind, deluge, and storm, overwhelmed.

"On the *seventh* day, in its course was calmed the storm, and all the deluge,

"which had destroyed like an earthquake,*

"quieted. The sea he caused to dry, and the wind and deluge ended. . . .

"I perceived the shore at the boundary of the sea. . . .

"To the country of Nizir went the ship [argha, or the moon].

"the mountain of Nizir stopped the ship. . . .

"The *first* day, and the *second* day, the mountain of Nizir the same. . . .

"The *fifth,* the *sixth,* the mountain of Nizir the same.

"On the *seventh* day in the course of it

"I sent forth a dove and it left. The dove went and turned, and . . . the raven went . . . and did not return. . . .

"I built an altar on the peak of the mountain.

"by *seven* herbs I cut, at the bottom of them I placed reeds, pines and spices. . . .

"the gods like flies over the sacrifice gathered.

"From of old *also the great God* in his course.

---

* This assimilation of the deluge to an earthquake on the Assyrian tablets would go to prove that the antediluvian nations were well acquainted with other geological cataclysms besides the deluge, which is represented in the Bible as the *first* calamity which befell humanity, and a punishment.

"the great brightness [the sun] of Anu had created.* When the glory of those gods on the charm round my neck I would not leave. . ."† etc.

All this has a purely astronomical, magical and esoteric relation. One who reads these tablets will recognize at a glance the Biblical account; and judge, at the same time, how disfigured is the great Babylonian poem by euhemeric personages—degraded from their exalted positions of gods into simple patriarchs. Space prevents our entering fully into this Biblical travesty of the Chaldean allegories. We shall therefore but remind the reader that by the confession of the most unwilling witnesses—such as Lenormant, first the inventor and then champion of the Akkadians—the Chaldeo-Babylonian triad placed under Ilon, the *unrevealed* deity, is composed of Anu, Nuah and Bel. Anu is the primordial chaos, the god time and world at once, χρόνος and κόσμος, the uncreated matter issued from the one and fundamental principle of all things. As to *Nuah*, he is, according to the same Orientalist:

". . . the intelligence, we will willingly say the *verbum*, which animates and fecundates matter, which penetrates the universe, directs and makes it live; and at the same time Nuah is the king of the *humid principle; the Spirit moving on the waters.*"

Is not this evident? Nuah is Noah, *floating on the waters,* in his ark; the latter being the emblem of the argha, or moon, the feminine principle; Noah is the "spirit" falling into matter. We find him, as soon as he descends upon the earth, planting a vineyard, drinking of the wine, and getting drunk on it; *i.e.*, the pure spirit becoming intoxicated as soon as it is finally imprisoned in matter. The seventh chapter of *Genesis* is but another version of the first. Thus, while the latter reads: ". . . and darkness was upon the face of the deep. And the spirit of God moved upon the face of the waters," in chapter seventh it is said: ". . . and the waters prevailed . . . and the ark went [with Noah—the spirit] upon the face of the waters."‡ Thus Noah, if [identified with] the Chaldean Nuah, is the spirit vivifying *matter,* [which latter is] chaos

---

* George Smith notes in the tablets, first the creation of the moon, and then of the sun: "Its beauty and perfection are extolled, and the regularity of its orbit, which led to its being considered the type of a judge regulator of the world." Did this story of the deluge relate simply to a cosmogonical cataclysm — even were it universal — why should the goddess Ishtar or Astoreth (the moon) speak of the *creation of the sun* after the deluge? The waters might have reached as high as the mountain of *Nizir* (Chaldean version), or *Jebel-Judi* (the deluge-mountains of the Arabian legends), or yet Ararat (of the Biblical narrative), and even Himâlaya of the Hindu tradition, and yet not reach the sun — even the Bible itself stopped short of such a miracle. It is evident that the deluge of the people who first recorded it had another meaning, less problematical and far more philosophical than that of a *universal* deluge, of which there are no geological traces whatever.

† [Geo. Smith, *Assyrian Discoveries,* 1875, pp. 190-91. Cf. Jastrow, *The Civil. of Babylonia,* pp. 449-51.]

‡ [*Gen.* i, 2; vii, 18.]

represented by the Deep or the Waters of the Flood. In the Babylonian legend it is Ishtar (Astoreth, the moon) who is shut up in the ark, and sends out a dove (emblem of Venus and other lunar goddesses) in search of dry land. And whereas in the Semitic tablets it is Xisuthros or Hasisadra who is "translated to the company of the gods for his piety," in the *Bible* it is Enoch who walks with, and being taken up by God, "was no more."

The successive existence of an incalculable number of worlds before the subsequent evolution of our own was believed and taught by all the ancient peoples. The punishment of the Christians for despoiling the Jews of their records and refusing the true key to them began from the earliest centuries. And thus it is that we find the holy Fathers of the Church laboring through an impossible chronology and the absurdities of literal interpretation, while the learned rabbis were perfectly aware of the real significance of their allegories. So not only in the *Zohar,* but also in other kabalistic works accepted by Talmudists, such as *Midrash Berêshîth Rabbah,* or the universal *Genesis,* which, with the *Merkabah* (the chariot of Ezekiel), composes the *Kabala,* may be found the doctrine of a whole series of worlds evolving out of the chaos, and being destroyed in succession.

The Hindu doctrines teach of two *Pralayas* or dissolutions; one universal, the *Mahâ-Pralaya,* the other partial, or the minor *Pralaya.* This does not relate to the universal dissolution which occurs at the end of every "Day of Brahmâ," but to the geological cataclysms at the end of every minor cycle of our globe. This historical and purely local deluge of Central Asia, the traditions of which can be traced in every country, and which, according to Bunsen, happened about the year 10,000 B.C., had naught to do with the mythical Noah or Nuah. A partial cataclysm occurs at the close of every "age" of the world, they say, which does not destroy the latter, but only changes its general appearance. New races of men and animals and a new flora evolve from the dissolution of the precedent ones.

The allegories of the "fall of man" and the "deluge" are the two most important features of the *Pentateuch.* They are, so to say, the Alpha and Omega, the highest and the lowest keys of the scale of harmony on which resounds the majestic hymns of the creation of mankind; for they discover to him who questions the *Zura* (figurative, *Gematria*), the process of man's evolution from the highest spiritual entity unto the lowest physical—the post-diluvian man; as in the Egyptian hieroglyphics, every sign of the picture writing which cannot be made to fit within a certain circumscribed geometrical figure may be rejected as only intended by the sacred hierogrammatist for a premeditated blind, so many of the details in the *Bible* must be treated on the same principle, that portion only being accepted which answers to the numerical methods taught in the *Kabala.*

## HINDU ACCOUNTS OF THE DELUGE

The deluge appears in the Hindu books only as a tradition. It claims no sacred character, and we find it in the *Mahâbhârata*, the *Purânas*, and still earlier in the *Satapatha*, one of the latest *Brâhmanas*. It is more than probable that Moses, or whoever wrote for him, used these accounts as the basis of his own purposely disfigured allegory, adding to it moreover the Chaldean-Berosian narrative. In *Mahâbhârata*, we recognize Nimrod under the name of the *King Daitya*. The origin of the Grecian fable of the Titans scaling Olympus, and the other of the builders of the Tower of Babel who seek to reach heaven, is shown in the impious *Daitya*, who sends imprecations against heaven's thunder, and threatens to conquer heaven itself with his mighty warriors, thereby bringing upon humanity the wrath of Brahmâ. "The Lord then resolved," says the text, "to chastise his creatures with a terrible punishment which should serve as a warning to survivors, and to their descendants."

*Vaivasvata* (who in the *Bible* becomes Noah) saves a little fish, which turns out to be an *avatâra* of Vishnu. The fish warns that just man that the globe is about to be submerged, that all that inhabit it must perish, and orders him to construct a vessel in which he shall embark, with all his family. When the ship is ready, and *Vaivasvata* has shut up in it with his family *the seeds of plants and pairs of all animals,* and the rain begins to fall, a gigantic fish, armed with a horn, places itself at the head of the ark. The holy man, following its orders, attaches a cable to this horn, and the fish guides the ship safely through the raging elements. In the Hindu tradition the number of days during which the deluge lasted *agrees exactly with that of the Mosaic account*. When the elements were calmed, the fish landed the ark on the summit of the Himâlayas.

This fable is considered by many orthodox commentators to have been borrowed from the Mosaic *Scriptures*.* But surely if such a *universal* cataclysm had ever taken place within man's memory, some of the monuments of the Egyptians, of which many are of such a tremendous antiquity, would have recorded that occurrence, coupled with that of the

---

* The "dead letter that killeth" is magnificently illustrated in the case of the Jesuit de Carrière, quoted in *La Bible dans l'Inde*, p. 253. The following dissertation represents the spirit of the whole Catholic world: "So that the creation of the world," writes this faithful son of Loyola, explaining the Biblical chronology of Moses, "and all that is recorded in *Genesis,* might have become known to Moses through *recitals personally made to him by his fathers*. Perhaps, even, the memories yet existed among the Israelites, and from those recollections he may have recorded the dates of births and deaths of the patriarchs, the numbering of their children, and the names of the different countries in which each became established under the guidance *of the holy spirit, which we must always regard as the chief author of the sacred books"* ! ! !

disgrace of Ham, Canaan and Mizraim, their alleged ancestors. But, till now, there has not been found the remotest allusion to such a calamity, although Mizraim certainly belongs to the first generation after the deluge, if not actually an antediluvian himself. On the other hand, the Chaldeans preserved the tradition, as we find Berosus testifying to it, and the ancient Hindus possess the legend as given above. Now, there is but one explanation of the extraordinary fact that of two contemporary and civilized nations like Egypt and Chaldea, one has preserved no tradition of it whatever, although it was the most directly interested in the occurrence—if we credit the *Bible*—and the other has. The deluge noticed in the *Bible,* in one of the *Brâhmanas,* and in the Berosus *Fragments,*\* relates to the partial flood which, about 10,000 years B.C., according to Bunsen, and according to the Brahmanical computations of the Zodiac also, changed the whole face of Central Asia.† Thus the Babylonians and the Chaldeans might have learned of it from their mysterious guests, christened by some Assyriologists Akkadians, or what is still more probable, they themselves, perhaps, were the descendants of those who had dwelt in the submerged localities. The Jews had the tale from the latter as they had everything else; the Brahmans may have recorded the traditions of the lands which they first invaded, and had perhaps inhabited before they possessed themselves of the Puñjâb. But the Egyptians, whose first settlers had evidently come from Southern India, had less reason to record the cataclysm, since it had perhaps never affected them except indirectly, as the flood was limited to Central Asia.

Burnouf, noticing the fact that the story of the deluge is found only in one of the most modern *Brâhmanas,* also thinks that it might have been borrowed by the Hindus from the Semitic nations. Against such an assumption are ranged all the traditions and customs of the Hindus. The Âryans, and especially the Brahmans, never borrowed anything at all from the Semitists, and here we are corroborated by one of those "unwilling witnesses," as Higgins calls the partisans of Jehovah and *Bible.* "I have never seen anything in the history of the Egyptians and Jews," writes Abbé Dubois, forty years a resident of India, "that would induce me to believe that either of these nations or any other on the face of the earth, have been established earlier than the Hindus and particularly the Brahmans; so I cannot be induced to believe that the latter have drawn their rites from foreign nations. On the contrary, I infer that they have drawn them from an original source of their own. Whoever knows anything of the spirit and character of the Brahmans, their stateliness, their pride and extreme vanity, their distance, and sovereign contempt for everything that is foreign, and of which they cannot boast to have been

---

\* [Eusebius, *Chronicon,* lib. I, cap. ii and vii. Cf. Cory, *Anc. Fragm.*, 1832, p. 26 *et. seq.*]

† See Vol. I, ch. xv, and last, of the present work.

## THE SILENCE OF THE VEDAS HIGHLY SIGNIFICANT      427

the inventors, will agree with me that such a people cannot have consented to draw their customs and rules of conduct from an alien country."*

This fable which mentions the earliest avatâra—the Matsya—relates to another *yuga* than our own, that of the first appearance of animal life; perchance, who knows, to the Devonian age of our geologists? It certainly answers better to the latter than the year 2348 B.C.! Apart from this, the very absence of all mention of the deluge from the oldest books of the Hindus suggests a powerful argument when we are left utterly to inferences as in this case. "The *Vedas* and *Manu*," says Jacolliot, "those monuments of the old Asiatic thought, existed far earlier than the diluvian period; *this is an incontrovertible fact, having all the value of an historical truth,* for, besides the tradition which shows Vishnu himself as saving the *Vedas* from the deluge—a tradition which, notwithstanding its legendary form, must certainly rest upon a real fact—it has been remarked that neither of these sacred books mention the cataclysm, while the *Purânas* and the *Mahâbhârata,* and a great number of other more recent works, describe it with the minutest detail, *which is a proof of the priority of the former.* The *Vedas* certainly would never have failed to contain a few hymns on the terrible disaster which, of all other natural manifestations, must have struck the imagination of the people who witnessed it.

"Neither would Manu, who gives us a complete narrative of the creation, with a chronology from the divine and heroical ages, down to the appearance of man on earth—have passed in silence an event of such importance. . . . *Manu* (Book I, śloka 35) gives the names of ten eminent saints whom he calls *Prajâpatis,* in whom the Brahman theologians see prophets, ancestors of the human race, and the Pundits simply consider as ten powerful kings who lived in the Krita-yuga, or the age of good (the 'golden age' of the Greeks)." †

The last of these *Prajâpatis* is Nârada.

"Enumerating the succession of these eminent beings who, according to Manu, have governed the world, the old Brahmanical legislator names as descending from *Bhrigu: Svârochisha, Auttami, Tâmasa, Raivata,* the glorious *Châkshusha,* and the son of *Vivasvat,* every one of the six having made himself worthy of the title of Manu (divine legislator), a title which had equally belonged to the Prajâpatis, and every great personage of primitive India. The genealogy stops at this name.

---

* *Description, etc., of the People of India,* by the Abbé J. A. Dubois, missionary in Mysore, Vol. I, pt. II, ch. vi, pp. 129, 186; 1817.

† [*La Genèse de l'humanité,* pp. 169, 170.]

"Now, according to the *Purânas* and the *Mahâbhârata* it was under a descendant of this son of Vivasvat, named Vaivasvata, that occurred the great cataclysm, the remembrance of which, as will be seen, has passed into a tradition, and been carried by emigration into all the countries of the East and West which India has colonized since then. . . .

"The genealogy given by Manu stopping, as we have seen, at Vivasvat, it follows that this work [of Manu] knew nothing either of Vaivasvat or the deluge."\*

The argument is unanswerable; and we commend it to those official scientists, who to please the clergy, dispute every fact proving the tremendous antiquity of the *Vedas* and *Manu*. Colonel Vans Kennedy† has long since declared that Babylonia was, from her origin, the seat of *Sanskrit* literature and Brahman learning. And how or why should the Brahmans have penetrated there, unless it was as the result of intestine wars and emigrations from India? The fullest account of the deluge is found in the *Mahâbhârata* of Veda-Vyâsa, a poem in honor of the astrological allegories on the wars between the Solar and the Lunar races. One of the versions states that Vaivasvata became the father of all the nations of the earth through his own progeny, and this is the form adopted for the Noachian story; the other states that—like Deucalion and Pyrrha—he had but to throw pebbles into the ilus left by the retiring waves of the flood, to produce men at will. These two versions—one Hebrew, the other Greek—allow us no choice. We must either believe that the Hindus borrowed from pagan Greeks as well as from monotheistic Jews, or—what is far more probable—that the versions of both of these nations are derived from the Vedic literature through the Babylonians.

History tells us of the stream of immigration across the Indus, and later of its overflowing the Occident; and of populations of Hindu origin passing from Asia Minor to colonize Greece. But history says not a single word of the "chosen people," or of Greek colonies having penetrated India earlier than the 5th and 4th centuries B.C., when we first find vague traditions that make some of the problematical *lost* tribes of Israel take from Babylon the route to India. But even were the story of the ten tribes to find credence, and the tribes themselves be proved to have existed in profane as well as in sacred history, this does not help the solution at all. Colebrooke, Wilson, and other eminent Indianists show the *Mahâbhârata*, if not the *Śatapatha-Brâhmana*, in which the story is also given, as by far antedating the age of Cyrus, hence, the possible time of the appearance of any of the tribes of Israel in India.‡

---

\* Jacolliot, *op. cit.*, pp. 170-71.

† [*Researches into . . . Ancient and Hindu Mythology.*]

‡ Against the latter assumption derived solely from the accounts of the Bible we have

## ANTIQUITY OF THE "MAHÂBHÂRATA"    429

Orientalists accord the *Mahâbhârata* an antiquity of between twelve and fifteen hundred years B.C.; as to the Greek version it bears as little evidence as the other, and the attempts of the Hellenists in this direction have as signally failed. The story of the conquering army of Alexander penetrating into Northern India, itself becomes more doubted every day. No Hindu national record, not the slightest historical memento, throughout the length and breadth of India offers the slightest trace of such an invasion.

If even such *historical facts* are now found to have been all the while fictions, what are we to think of narratives which bear on their very face the stamp of invention? We cannot help sympathizing at heart with Professor Müller when he remarks that it seems "blasphemy to consider these fables of the heathen world as corrupted and misinterpreted fragments of *divine* Revelation once granted to the whole race of mankind." Only, can this scholar be held perfectly impartial and fair to both parties, unless he includes in the number of these fables those of the *Bible?* And is the language of the *Old Testament* more *pure* or *moral* than the books of the Brahmans? Or are any fables of the *heathen* world more blasphemous and ridiculous than Jehovah's interview with Moses (*Exodus* xxxiii, 23)? Are any of the Pagan gods made to appear more fiendish than the same Jehovah in a score of passages? If the feelings of a pious Christian are shocked at the absurdities of Father Kronos eating his children and maiming Ouranos; or of Jupiter throwing Vulcan down from heaven and breaking his leg; on the other hand he cannot feel hurt if a *non*-Christian laughs at the idea of Jacob boxing with the Creator, who "when he saw that *he prevailed not* against him," dislocated Jacob's thigh, the patriarch still holding fast to God and not allowing Him to go His way, notwithstanding His pleading.

Why should the story of Deucalion and Pyrrha, throwing stones behind them, and thus creating the human race, be deemed more ridiculous than that of Lot's wife being changed into a pillar of salt, or of the Almighty creating men *of clay* and then breathing the breath of life into them? The choice between the latter mode of creation and that of the Egyptian ram-horned god fabricating man on a potter's wheel is hardly perceptible. The story of Minerva, goddess of wisdom, ushered into existence after a certain period of gestation in her father's brain, is at least suggestive and poetical as an allegory. No ancient Greek was ever burned for not accepting it literally; and, at all events, "heathen" fables

---

every historical fact. 1st. There are no proofs of these twelve tribes having ever existed; that of Levi was a priestly caste and all the others imaginary. 2nd. Herodotus, the most accurate of historians, who was in Assyria when Ezra flourished, never mentions the Israelites at all? Herodotus was born in 484 B.C.

in general are far less preposterous and blasphemous than those imposed upon Christians, ever since the Church accepted the *Old Testament,* and the Roman Catholic Church opened its register of thaumaturgical saints.

"Many of the natives of India," continues Professor Müller, "confess that their feelings revolt against the impurities attributed to these gods by what they call their sacred writings; yet there are honest Brahmans who will maintain that *these stories have a deeper meaning* — that immorality being incompatible with a divine being, *a mystery* must be supposed to be concealed in these time-hallowed fables—a mystery which an inquiring and reverent mind may hope to fathom."*

This is precisely what the Christian clergy maintain in attempting to explain the indecencies and incongruities of the *Old Testament.* Only, instead of allowing the interpretation to those who have the key to these seeming incongruities, they have assumed to themselves the office and right, by *divine* proxy, to interpret these in their own way. They have not only done that, but have gradually deprived the Hebrew clergy of the means to interpret their Scriptures as their fathers did; so that to find among the Rabbis in the present century a well-versed kabalist is quite rare. The Jews have themselves forgotten the key! How could they help it? Where are the original manuscripts? The oldest Hebrew manuscript in existence is said to be the *Bodleian Codex,* which is not older than between eight and nine hundred years.†[57] The break between Ezra and this *Codex* is thus fifteeen centuries. In 1490 the Inquisition *caused all the Hebrew Bibles to be burned;* and Torquemada alone destroyed 6,000 volumes at Salamanca. Except a few manuscripts of the *Torah Khethubim* and *Nebiim,* used in the synagogues, and which are of quite a recent date, we do not think there is one old manuscript in existence which is not punctuated, hence — completely misinterpreted and altered by the Masoretes. Were it not for this timely invention of the *Masorah,* no copy of the *Old Testament* could possibly be tolerated in our century. It is well known that the Masoretes while transcribing the oldest manuscripts put themselves to task to take out, except in a few places which they have probably overlooked, all the *immodest* words and put

---

\* ["Comparative Mythology," in *Chips,* etc., Vol. II, p. 14.]

† Dr. Kennicott himself, and Bruns, under his direction, about 1780, collated 692 manuscripts of the Hebrew "Bible." Of all these, only *two* were credited to the tenth century, and three to a period as early as the eleventh and twelfth. The others ranged between the thirteenth and sixteenth centuries.

In his *Introduzione alla Sacra Scrittura,* pp. 34-47, de Rossi, of Parma, mentions 1,418 MSS. collated, and 374 editions. The oldest manuscript *Codex,* he asserts — that of Vienna — dates A.D. 1019; the next, Reuchlin's of Karlsruhe, 1038. "There is," he declares, "nothing in the manuscripts of the Hebrew *Old Testament* extant of an earlier date than the eleventh century after Christ."

in places sentences of their own, often changing completely the sense of the verse. "It is clear," says J. W. Donaldson, "that the Masoretic school at Tiberias was engaged in settling or unsettling the Hebrew text until the final publication of the *Masorah* itself."* Therefore, had we but the original texts—judging by the present copies of the *Bible* in our possession—it would be really edifying to compare the *Old Testament* with the *Vedas* and even with the Brahmanical books. We verily believe that no faith, however blind, could stand before such an avalanche of crude impurities and fables. If the latter are not only accepted but enforced upon millions of civilized persons who find it respectable and edifying to believe in them as *divine revelation,* why should we wonder that Brahmans believe their books to be equally a *Śruti,* a revelation?

Let us thank the Masoretes by all means, but let us study at the same time both sides of the medal.

Legends, myths, allegories, symbols, if they but belong to the Hindu, Chaldean, or Egyptian tradition, are thrown into the same heap of fiction. Hardly are they honored with a superficial search into their possible relations to astronomy or sexual emblems. The same myths—when and because mutilated—are accepted as Sacred Scriptures, more—the Word of God! Is this impartial history? Is this justice to either the past, the present, or the future? "Ye cannot serve God and Mammon," said the Reformer nineteen centuries ago. "Ye cannot serve truth and public prejudice," would be more applicable to our own age. Yet our authorities pretend they serve the former.

There are few myths in any religious system but have an historical as well as scientific foundation. Myths, as Pococke ably expresses it, "are now proved to be fables, just in proportion as we *misunderstand* them; truths, in proportion as they were once *understood.* Our ignorance it is which has made a myth of history; and our ignorance is an Hellenic inheritance, much of it the result of Hellenic vanity." †

Bunsen and Champollion have already shown that the Egyptian sacred books are by far older than the oldest part of the *Book of Genesis.* And now a more careful research seems to warrant the suspicion — which with us amounts to a certainty, that the laws of Moses are copies from the code of the Brahmanic *Manu.* Thus, according to every probability, Egypt owes her civilization, her civil institutions, and her arts, to India. But against the latter assumption we have a whole army of "authorities" arrayed, and what matters if the latter do deny the fact at present? Sooner or later they will have to accept it, whether they belong to the German or French school.

---

* [*Christian Orthodoxy,* London, 1857, p. 239.]
† *India in Greece,* preface, pp. viii-ix.

Among, but not of those who so readily compromise between interest and conscience, there are some fearless scholars, who may bring to light incontrovertible facts. Some twenty years since, Max Müller, in a letter to the Editor of the London *Times,* April, 1857, maintained most vehemently that Nirvâna meant *annihilation,* in the fullest sense of the word. (See *Chips,* etc., Vol. I, p. 279, on "The Meaning of Nirvâna.") But in 1869, in a lecture before the general meeting of the Association of German Philologists at Kiel, "he distinctly declares his belief that the nihilism attributed to Buddha's teaching forms no part of his doctrine, and that it is wholly wrong to suppose that Nirvâna means annihilation." (Trübner's *American and Oriental Literary Record,* Oct. 16, 1869; also Inman's *Ancient Faiths and Modern,* p. 128.) Yet if we mistake not, Professor Müller was as much of an authority in 1857 as in 1869.

"It will be difficult to settle," says (now) this great scholar, "whether the *Veda* is the oldest of books, and whether some of the portions of the *Old Testament* may not be traced back to the same or even an earlier date than the oldest hymns of the *Veda.*"\* But his retraction about the Nirvâna allows us a hope that he may yet change his opinion on the question of *Genesis* likewise, so that the public may have simultaneously the benefit of truth, and the sanction of one of Europe's greatest authorities.

It is well known how little the Orientalists have come to anything like an agreement about the age of Zoroaster, and until this question is settled, it would be safer perhaps to trust implicitly in the Brahmanical calculations by the Zodiac, than to the opinions of scientists. Leaving the profane horde of unrecognized scholars, those we mean who yet wait their turn to be chosen for public worship as idols symbolical of scientific leadership, where can we find, among the sanctioned authorities of the day, two that agree as to this age? There's Bunsen, who places Zoroaster at Baktria, and the emigration of Baktrians to the Indus at 3784 B.C. and the birth of Moses at 1392.† Now it is rather difficult to place Zoroaster anterior to the *Vedas,* considering that the whole of his doctrine is that of the earlier *Vedas.* True, he remained in Afghânistân for a period more or less problematical before crossing into the Puñjâb; but the *Vedas* were begun in the latter country. They indicate the progress of the Hindus, as the *Avesta* that of the Iranians. And there is Haug who assigns to the *Aitareya-Brâhmanam* — a Brahmanical speculation and commentary upon the *Ṛig-Veda* of a far later date than the *Veda* itself — between 1400 and 1200 B.C., while the *Vedas* are placed by him between 2,000 and 2,400 years B.C. Max Müller cautiously suggests

---

\* *Chips,* etc., Vol. I, p. 5.

† *Egypt's Place in Universal History,* Vol. V, pp. 77-78.

certain difficulties in this chronological computation, but still does not altogether deny it.* Let it, however, be as it may, and supposing that the *Pentateuch* was written by Moses himself — notwithstanding that he would thereby be made to twice record his own death — still, if Moses were born, as Bunsen finds, in 1392 B.C., the *Pentateuch* could not have been written *before the Vedas.* Especially if Zoroaster was born 3784 B.C. If, as Dr Haug † tells us, some of the hymns of the *Ṛig-Veda* were written before Zoroaster accomplished his schism, something like thirty-seven centuries B.C., and Max Müller says himself that "the Zoroastrians and their ancestors started from India during the Vaidic period," how can some of the portions of the *Old Testament* be traced back to the same or even "an earlier date than the oldest hymns of the *Veda*"?

It has generally been agreed among Orientalists that the Âryans, 3,000 years B.C., were still in the steppes east of the Caspian, and united. Rawlinson *conjectures* that they "flowed east" from Armenia as a common centre; while two kindred streams began to flow, one northward over the Caucasus, and the other westward over Asia Minor and Europe. He finds the Âryans, at a period anterior to the fifteenth century before our era, "settled in the tract watered by the Upper Indus." ‡ Thence Vedic Âryans migrated to the Puñjâb, and Zendic Âryans westward, establishing the historical countries. But this, like the rest, is a hypothesis, and only given as such.

Again, Rawlinson, evidently following Max Müller, says: "The early history of the Âryans is for many ages an absolute blank." But many learned Brahmans, however, have declared that they found trace of the existence of the *Vedas* as early as 2100 B.C.; and Sir William Jones,§ taking for his guide the astronomical data, places the *Yajur-Veda* 1580 B.C. This would be still "before Moses."

It is upon the supposition that the Âryans did not leave Afghânistân for the Puñjâb prior to 1500 B.C. that Max Müller and other Oxford savants have supposed that portions of the *Old Testament* may be traced back to the same or even an earlier date than the oldest hymns of the *Veda.* Therefore, until the Orientalists can show us the correct date at which Zoroaster flourished, no authority can be regarded as better for the ages of the *Vedas* than the Brahmans themselves.

---

* *Chips,* etc., Vol. I, p. 114; *Aitareya-Brâhmaṇam,* Vol. I, Introd., pp. 47-48.

† Dr. M. Haug, Superintendent of the Sanskrit studies in the Poona College, Bombay.

‡ [Geo. Rawlinson, *The Hist. of Herodotus.* Vol. I, pp. 669-70; London, 1858.]

§ [*Ordinances of Manu,* preface, p. vii.]

As it is a recognized fact that the Jews borrowed most of their laws from the Egyptians, let us examine who were the Egyptians. In our opinion — which is but a poor authority, of course — they were the ancient Indians, and in our first volume we have quoted passages from the historian Kullûka-Bhatta that support such a theory. What we mean by ancient India is the following:

No region on the map — except it be the ancient Scythia — is more uncertainly defined than that which bore the designation of India. Aethiopia is perhaps the only parallel. It was the home of Cushite or Hamitic races, and lay to the east of Babylonia. It was once the name of Hindostan, when the dark races, worshippers of *Bala-Mahâdeva* and *Bhavânî-Mahâdevî*, were supreme in that country. The India of the early sages appears to have been the region at the sources of the Oxus and Jaxartes. Apollonius of Tyana crossed the Caucasus or Hindu Kush, where he met with a king who directed him to the abode of the sages — perhaps the descendants of those whom Ammianus terms the "Brachmanes of Upper India," and whom Hystaspes, the father of Darius (or more probably Darius Hystaspes himself), visited; and, having been instructed by them, infused their rites and ideas into the Magian observances. This narrative about Apollonius seems to indicate Kashmîr as the country which he visited, and the *Nâgas* — after their conversion to Buddhism — as his teachers. At this time Âryan India did not extend beyond the Puñjâb.

To our notion, the most baffling impediment in the way of ethnological progress has always been the triple progeny of Noah. In the attempt to reconcile postdiluvian races with a genealogical descent from Shem, Ham and Japhet, the Christianesque Orientalists have set themselves a task impossible of accomplishment. The Biblical Noachian ark has been a Procrustean bed into which they had to make everything fit. Attention has therefore been diverted from veritable sources of information as to the origin of man, and a purely local allegory mistaken for a historical record emanating from an inspired source. Strange and unfortunate choice! Out of all the sacred writings of all the branch nations, sprung from the primitive stock of mankind, Christianity must choose for its guidance the national records and scriptures of a people perhaps the least spiritual of the human family — the Semitic. A branch that has never been able to develop out of its numerous tongues a language capable of embodying ideas of a moral and intellectual world; whose form of expression and drift of thought could never soar higher than the purely sensual and terrestrial figures of speech; whose literature has left nothing original, nothing that was not borrowed from the Âryan thought; and whose science and philosophy are utterly wanting in those noble features which characterize the highly spiritual and metaphysical systems of the Indo-European (Japhetic) races.

Bunsen* shows Khamism (the language of Egypt) as a very ancient deposit from Western Asia, containing *the germs* of the Semitic, and thus bearing "witness to the primitive cognate unity of the Semitic and Âryan races." We must remember, in this connection, that the peoples of Southwestern and Western Asia, including the Medes, were all Âryans. It is yet far from being proved who were the original and primitive masters of India. That this period is now beyond the reach of documentary history, does not preclude the probability of our theory that it was the mighty race of builders, whether we call them Eastern Aethiopians, or dark-skinned Âryans (the word meaning simply "noble warrior," a "brave"). They ruled supreme at one time over the whole of ancient India, enumerated later by Manu as the possession of those whom our scientists term the Sanskrit-speaking people.

These Hindus are *supposed* to have entered the country from the northwest; they are *conjectured* by some to have brought with them the Brahmanical religion, and the language of the conquerors was *probably* the Sanskrit. On these three meager data our philologists have worked ever since the immense Sanskrit literature was forcibly brought into notice by Sir William Jones — all the time with the three sons of Noah clinging around their necks. This is *exact* science, free from religious prejudices! Verily, ethnology would have been the gainer if this Noachian trio had been washed overboard and drowned before the ark reached land!

The Aethiopians are generally classed in the Semitic group; but we have to see how far they have a claim to such a classification. We will also consider how much they might have had to do with the Egyptian civilization, which, as a writer expresses it, seems referable in the same perfection to the earliest dates, and not to have had a rise and progress, as was the case with that of other peoples. For reasons that we will now adduce, we are prepared to maintain that Egypt owes her civilization, commonwealth and arts — especially the art of building, to pre-Vedic India, and that it was a colony of the dark-skinned Âryans, or those whom Homer and Herodotus term the eastern Aethiopians,† *i.e.*, the inhabitants of Southern India, who brought to it their ready-made civilization in the ante-chronological ages of what Bunsen calls the pre-Menite, but nevertheless epochal history.

In Pocock's *India in Greece*, we find the following suggestive paragraph: "The plain account of the wars carried on between the solar chief, Oosras (Osiris), the Prince of the Guclas, and 'Tu-phoo,' is the simple historical fact of the wars of the Apians, or Sun-tribes of Oudh,

---

* [*Egypt's Place*, etc., Vol. IV, p. 142.]

† [*History*, VII, § 70.]

with the people of 'TU-PHOO,' or THIBET, who were, in fact, of the Lunar race, mostly Buddhists,* and opposed by Râma, and the 'AITYO-PIAS,' or people of Oudh, subsequently the 'AITH-IO-PIANS,' of Africa."†

We would remind the reader in this connection, that Râvana, the giant, who, in the *Râmâyana*, wages such a war with Râma Chandra, is shown as King of Lankâ, which was the ancient name for Ceylon; and that Ceylon, in those days, perhaps formed part of the mainland of Southern India, and was peopled by the "Eastern Aethiopians." Conquered by Râma, the son of Daśaratha, the Solar King of ancient Oudh, a colony of these emigrated to Northern Africa. If, as many suspect, Homer's *Iliad* and much of his account of the Trojan war is plagiarized from the *Râmâyana*, then the traditions which served as a basis for the latter must date from a tremendous antiquity. Ample margin is thus left in prechronological history for a period, during which the "Eastern Aethiopians" might have established the hypothetical Mizraic colony, with their high Indian civilization and arts.

Science is still in the dark about cuneiform inscriptions. Until these are completely deciphered, especially those cut in rocks found in such abundance within the boundaries of the old Iran, who can tell the secrets they may yet reveal? There are no Sanskrit monumental inscriptions older than Chandragupta (315 B.C.), and the Persepolitan inscriptions are found 220 years older. There are even now some manuscripts in characters utterly unknown to philologists and palaeographists, and one of them is, or was, some time since in the library of Cambridge, England. Linguistic writers class the Semitic with the Indo-European language, generally including the Aethiopian and the ancient Egyptian in the classification. But if some of the dialects of the modern Northern Africa, and even the modern Geez or Aethiopian, are now so degenerated and corrupted as to admit of false conclusions as to the genetical relationship between them and the other Semitic tongues, we are not at all sure that the latter have any claim to such a classification, except in the case of the old Coptic and the ancient Geez.

That there is more consanguinity between the Aethiopians and the Âryan, dark-skinned races, and between the latter and the Egyptians, is something which yet may be proved. It has been lately found that the ancient Egyptians were of the Caucasian type of mankind, and the

---

* Pococke belongs to that class of Orientalists who believe that Buddhism preceded Brahmanism, and was the religion of the earliest *Vedas*, Gautama having been but the restorer of it in its purest form, which after him degenerated again into dogmatism.

† *India in Greece*, p. 200.

shape of their skulls is purely Asiatic.* If they were less copper-colored than the Aethiopians of our modern day, the Aethiopians themselves might have had a lighter complexion in days of old. The fact that, with the Aethiopian kings, the order of succession gave the crown to the nephew of the king, the *son of his sister*, and not to his own son, is extremely suggestive. It is an old custom which prevails until now in Southern India. The Râjâ is not succeeded by his own sons, but by *his sister's sons*.†

Of all the dialects and tongues alleged to be Semitic, the Aethiopian alone is written from left to right like the Sanskrit and the Indo-Âryan people.‡

Thus, against the origin of the Egyptians being attributed to an ancient Indian colony, there is no graver impediment than Noah's disrespectful son Ham — himself a myth. But the earliest form of Egyptian religious worship and government, theocratic and sacerdotal, and her habits and customs all bespeak an Indian origin.

The earliest legends of the history of India mention two dynasties now lost in the night of time; the first was the dynasty of kings, of "the race of the sun," who reigned in Ayôdhyâ (now Oudh); the second that of the

---

* The Asiatic origin of the first dwellers in the Nilotic Valley is clearly demonstrated by concurrent and independent testimony. Cuvier and Blumenbach affirm that all the skulls of mummies which they had the opportunity of examining, presented the Caucasian type. A recent American physiologist (Dr. S. G. Morton) has also argued for the same conclusion (*Crania Aegyptiaca*, London, Philadelphia, 1844, pp. 20, 40-41, 53, 63-66).

† The late Râjâ of Travancore was succeeded by the elder son of his sister now reigning, the Mahârâja *Râma Vurmah*. The next heirs are the sons of his deceased sister. In case the female line is interrupted by death, the royal family is obliged to adopt the daughter of some other Râjâ, and unless daughters are born to this Rânî another girl is adopted, and so on.

‡ There are some Orientalists who believe that this custom was introduced only after the early Christian settlements in Aethiopia; but as under the Romans the population of this country was nearly all changed, the element becoming wholly Arabic, we may, without doubting the statement, believe that it was the predominating Arab influence which had altered the earliest mode of writing. Their present method is even more analogous to the Devanâgarî, and other more ancient Indian alphabets, which read from left to right; and their letters show no resemblance to the Phoenician characters. Moreover, all the ancient authorities corroborate our assertion still more. Philostratus makes the Brahmin Iarchas say (*Vita Apoll.*, III, xx) that the Aethiopians were originally *an Indian race*, compelled to emigrate from the mother-land for sacrilege and regicide. "An Egyptian is made to remark, that he had heard from his father, that the Indians were the wisest of men, and that the Aethiopians, a colony of the Indians, preserved the wisdom and usages of their fathers, and acknowledged their ancient origin." Julius Africanus (in Eusebius and Syncellus), makes the same statement (Pococke, *India in Greece*, pp. 205-06). And Eusebius writes: "The Aethiopians, emigrating from the river Indus, settled in the vicinity of Egypt" (Lemprière, *Classical Dictionary*, s.v. "Meroe"; Barker's ed.).

"race of the moon," who reigned in Prayâga (Allâhâbâd). Let him who desires information on the religious worship of these early kings read the *Book of the Dead* of the Egyptians, and all the peculiarities attending this sun-worship and the sun-gods. Neither Osiris nor Horus are ever mentioned without being connected with the sun. They are the "Sons of the *Sun*"; "the Lord and Adorer of the Sun" is his name. "The sun is the creator of the body, the engenderer of the gods who are *the successors of the Sun.*" Pococke, in his most ingenious work, strongly advocates the same idea, and endeavors to establish still more firmly the identity of the Egyptian, Greek and Indian mythology. He shows the head of the Râjput Solar race—in fact the great Cuclo-pos (Cyclop or builder)— called "The Great Sun," in the earliest Hindu tradition. This Gok'la Prince, the patriarch of the vast bands of Inachienses, he says, "this *'Great Sun'* was deified at his death, and according to the Indian doctrine of the metempsychosis, his soul was supposed to have transmigrated into the bull 'Apis,' the 'Sera-pis' of the Greeks, and the Soora-pas,' or 'Sun-Chief,' of the Egyptians . . . *Osiris,* properly *Oosras,* signifies both 'a bull,' and 'a ray of light.' *Soora-pas* (Sera-pis) the Sun-Chief," for the Sun in Sanskrit is Sûrya.\* Champollion's *La Manifestation à la Lumière,* reminds in every chapter of the two Dynasties of the Kings of the Sun and the Moon. Later, these kings became all deified and transformed after death into solar and lunar deities. Their worship was the earliest corruption of the great primitive faith which justly considered the sun and its fiery life-giving rays as the most appropriate symbol to remind us of the universal invisible presence of Him who is master of Life and Death. And now it can be traced all around the globe. It was the religion of the earliest Vedic Brahmans, who call, in the oldest hymns of the *Ṛig-Veda,* Sûrya (the sun) and Agni (fire) "the ruler of the universe," "the lord of men," and the "wise king." It was the worship of the Magians, the Zoroastrians, the Egyptians and Greeks, whether they called him Mithra, or Ahura-Mazda, or Osiris, or Zeus, keeping in honor of his next of kin, Vesta, the pure celestial fire. And this religion is found again in the Peruvian solar-worship; in the Sabaeanism and heliolatry of the Chaldees, in the Mosaic "burning bush," the hanging of the heads of chiefs of the people toward the Lord, the "Sun," and even in the Abrahamic building of fire-altars and the sacrifices of the monotheistic Jews, to Astarte, the Queen of Heaven.

To the present moment, with all the controversies and researches, History and Science remain as much as ever in the dark as to the origin of the Jews. They may as well be the exiled Chaṇḍâlas, or Pariahs, of old India, the "bricklayers" mentioned by Vina-Snati, Veda-Vyâsa and Manu, as the Phoenicians of Herodotus, or the Hyksôs of Josephus, or

---

\* [Pococke, *India in Greece,* p. 200.]

descendants of Pâli shepherds, or a mixture of all these. The *Bible* names the Tyrians as a kindred people, and claims dominion over them.*

There is more than one important character in the *Bible*, whose biography proves him a mythical hero. Samuel is indicated as the personage of the Hebrew Commonwealth. He is the *doppel* of Samson, of the *Book of Judges*, as will be seen—being the son of Anna and EL-KAINA, as Samson was of Manua or Manoah. Both were fictitious characters, as now represented in the revealed book; one was the Hebrew Hercules, and the other Ganeśa. Samuel is credited with establishing the republic, as putting down the Canaanite worship of Baal and Astarte, or Adonis and Venus, and setting up that of Jehovah. Then the people demanded a king, and he anointed Saul, and after him David of Bethlehem.

David is the Israelitish King Arthur. He accomplished great achievements and established a government in all Syria and Idumaea. His dominion extended from Armenia and Assyria on the north and northeast, the Syrian Desert and Persian Gulf on the east, Arabia on the south, and Egypt and the Levant on the west. Only Phoenicia was excepted.

His friendship with Hiram seems to indicate that he made his first expedition from that country into Judaea; and his long residence at Hebron, the city of the Kabiri (*Arba* or four), would seem likewise to imply that he established a new religion in the country.

After David came Solomon, powerful and luxurious, who sought to consolidate the dominion which David had won. As David was a Jehovah-worshipper, a temple of Jehovah (Tukht-i-Sulaiman) was built in Jerusalem, while shrines of Moloch-Hercules, Chemosh and Astarte were erected on Mount Olivet. These shrines remained till Josiah.

There were conspiracies formed. Revolts took place in Idumaea and Damascus; and Ahijah, the prophet, led the popular movement which resulted in deposing the house of David and making Jeroboam king. Ever after the prophets dominated in Israel, where the calf-worship prevailed; the priests ruled over the weak dynasty of David, and the lasci-

---

* They might have been also, as Pococke thinks, simply the tribes of the "Oxus," a name derived from the "Ookshas," those people whose wealth lay in the "Ox," for he shows *Ookshan* to be a crude form of *Ooksha,* an ox (in Sanskrit *ox* is as in English). He believes that it was they, "the lords of the Oxus," who gave their name to the sea around which they ruled in many a country, the *Euxine* or Ooksh-ine. "Pâli means a shepherd, and *s'thân* is a land . . . The warlike tribes of the Oxus . . . penetrated into Egypt, then swept onwards to Palestine (PÂLI-STÂN), the 'land of the Pâlis or shepherds,' and there effected more permanent settlements . . ." (*India in Greece,* p. 198). Yet if even so, it would only the more confirm our opinion that the Jews are a hybrid race, for the *Bible* shows them freely intermarrying, not alone with the Canaanites, but with every other nation or race they come in contact with.

vious local worship existed over the whole country. After the destruction of the house of Ahab, and the failure of Jehu and his descendants to unite the country under one head, the endeavor was made in Judah. Isaiah had terminated the direct line in the person of Ahaz (*Isaiah* vii, 9), and placed on the throne a prince from Bethlehem (*Micah* v, 2, 5). This was Hezekiah. On ascending the throne, he invited the chiefs of Israel to unite in alliance with him against Assyria (*2 Chronicles* xxx, i, 21; xxxi, 1, 5; *2 Kings* xviii, 7). He seems to have established a sacred college (*Proverbs* xxv, i), and to have utterly changed the worship.[58] Aye, even unto breaking into pieces the brazen serpent that Moses had made.

This makes the story of Samuel and David and Solomon mythical. Most of the prophets who were literate seem to have begun about this time to write.

The country was finally overthrown by the Assyrians, who found the same people and institutions as in the Phoenician and other countries.

Hezekiah was not the lineal, but the titular son of Ahaz. Isaiah, the prophet, belonged to the royal family, and Hezekiah was reputed to be his son-in-law. Ahaz refused to ally himself with the prophet and his party, saying: "I will not *tempt* [depend on] the Lord" (*Isaiah* vii, 12). The prophet had declared: "If you will not believe, surely you shall not be established" — foreshadowing the deposition of his direct lineage. "Ye weary my God," replied the prophet, and predicted the birth of a child by an *almeh*, or temple-woman, and that before it should attain full age (*Hebrews* v, 14; *Isaiah* vii, 16; viii, 4), the king of Assyria should overcome Syria and Israel. This is the prophecy which Irenaeus took such pains to connect with Mary and Jesus, and made the reason why the mother of the Nazarene prophet is represented as belonging to the temple, and consecrated to God from her infancy.

In a second song, Isaiah celebrated the new chief, to sit on the throne of David (ix, 6, 7; xi, 1), who should restore to their homes the Jews whom the confederacy had led captive (*Isaiah* viii, 2-12; *Joel* iii, 1-7; *Obadiah* 7, 11, 14). Micah — his contemporary — also announced the same event (iv, 7-13; v, 1-7). The Redeemer was to come out of Bethlehem; in other words, was of the house of David; and was to resist Assyria to whom Ahaz had sworn allegiance, and also to reform religion (*2 Kings* xviii, 4-8). This Hezekiah did. He was grandson of Zechariah the seer (*2 Chronicles* xxix, 1; xxvi, 5), the counsellor of Uzziah; and as soon as he ascended the throne he restored the religion of David, and destroyed the last vestiges of that of Moses, *i.e.*, the *esoteric* doctrine, declaring "our fathers have trespassed" (*2 Chron.* xxix, 6-9). He next attempted a reunion with the northern monarchy, there being an interregnum in Israel (*2 Chron.* xxx, 1, 2, 6; xxxi, 1, 6, 7). It was successful, but resulted in an invasion by the king of Assyria. But it was a new *régime;* and all this shows the course of two parallel streams in the religious worship of the Israelites; one belonging to the state religion and adopted to fit political exigencies; the other pure idolatry, resulting from ignorance of the true esoteric doctrine preached by Moses. For the first time since Solomon built them "the high places were taken away."

It was Hezekiah who was the expected Messiah of the exoteric state-religion. He was the scion from the stem of Jesse, who should recall the Jews from a deplorable captivity, about which the Hebrew historians seem to be very silent, carefully avoiding all mention of this particular fact, but which the irascible prophets imprudently disclose. If Hezekiah crushed the exoteric Baal-worship, he also violently tore away the people of Israel from the religion of their fathers, and the secret rites instituted by Moses.

It was Darius Hystaspes who was the first to establish a Persian colony in Judaea; Zoro-Babel was perhaps the leader. "The name *Zoro-babel* means 'the seed or son of Babylon'—as Zoro-aster, זרע־אשתר is the seed, son, or prince of Ishtar."* The new colonists were doubtless *Judaei.* This is a designation from the East. Even Siam is called Judia, and there was an Ayôdhyâ in India. The temples of *Shalom* or Peace were numerous. Throughout Persia and Afghânistân the names of Saul and David are very common. The "Law" is ascribed in turn to Hezekiah, Ezra, Simon the Just, and the Asmonean period. Nothing definite; everywhere contradictions. When the Asmonean period began, the chief supporters of the Law were called Asideans or Kasdim (Chaldeans), and afterward Pharisees or Pharsi (Pârsîs). This indicates that Persian colonies were established in Judaea and ruled the country; while all the people that are mentioned in the books of *Genesis* and *Joshua* lived there as a commonalty (see *Ezra,* ix, 1).

There is no real history in the *Old Testament,* and the little historical information one can glean is only found in the indiscreet revelations of the prophets. The book, as a whole, must have been written at various times, or rather invented as an authorization of some subsequent worship, the origin of which may be very easily traced partially to the Orphic Mysteries, and partially to the ancient Egyptian rites in familiarity with which Moses was brought up from his infancy.

Since the last century the Church has been gradually forced into concessions of usurped Biblical territory to those to whom it of right belonged.

---

* Prof. A. Wilder: "Notes."

Inch by inch has been yielded, and one personage after another been proved mythical and Pagan. But now, after the recent discovery of George Smith, the much-regretted Assyriologist, one of the securest props of the *Bible* has been pulled down. Sargon and his tablets are demonstrated to be older than Moses. Like the account of *Exodus*, the birth and story of the lawgiver seem to have been "borrowed" from the Assyrians, as the "jewels of gold and jewels of silver" were said to be from the Egyptians.

On page 224 of *Assyrian Discoveries*, Mr. George Smith says: "In the palace of Sennacherib at Kouyunjik I found another fragment of the curious history of Sargon, a translation of which I published in the *Transactions of the Society of Biblical Archaeology*, Vol. I, part i, page 46. This text relates that Sargon, an early Babylonian monarch, was born of royal parents, but concealed by his mother, who placed him on the Euphrates in an ark of rushes, coated with bitumen, like that in which the mother of Moses hid her child (see *Exodus* ii). Sargon was discovered by a man named Akki, a water-carrier, who adopted him as his son, and he afterward became King of Babylonia. The capital of Sargon was the great city of Agadi, called by the Semites Akkad, mentioned in *Genesis* as a capital of Nimrod (*Genesis* x, 10), and here he reigned *for forty-five* years.\* Akkad lay near the city of *Sippara*† on the Euphrates and north of Babylon. The date of Sargon, who may be termed the Babylonian Moses, was in the sixteenth century B.C. or perhaps earlier."

G. Smith adds in his *Chaldean Account of Genesis* that "Sargon I was a Babylonian monarch who reigned in the city of Agade about 1600 B. C. The name of Sargon signifies the right, true, or legitimate king. The curious story is found on fragments of tablets from Kouyunjik, and reads as follows:

1. Sargina, the powerful king of Agade am I.
2. My mother was a princess, my father I did not know, a brother of my father ruled over the country.
3. In the city of Azupiran which by the side of the river Euphrates is situated,
4. My mother the princess conceived me; in difficulty she brought me forth.
5. She placed me in an ark of rushes, with bitumen my exit she sealed up.
6. She launched me on the river which did not drown me.
7. The river carried me, to Akki the water-carrier it brought me.
8. Akki the water-carrier in tenderness of bowels lifted me," etc., etc.‡

---

\* Moses reigned over the people of Israel in the wilderness for over *forty* years.

† The name of the wife of Moses was Zipporah (*Exodus* ii, 21).

‡ [*Op. cit.*, 1876, pp. 299-300.]

And now *Exodus* (ii, 3): "And when she [Moses' mother] could not longer hide him, she took for him an ark of bulrushes, and daubed it with slime and with pitch, and put the child therein, and she laid it in the flags by the river's brink."

The event, says Mr. G. Smith, "is supposed to have happened about 1600 B.C.,⁵⁹ rather earlier than the supposed age of Moses;* and, as we know that the fame of Sargon reached Egypt, it is quite likely that this account had a connection with the event related in *Exodus* ii, for every action, when once performed, has a tendency to be repeated."†

The "ages" of the Hindus differ but little from those of the Greeks, Romans, and even the Jews. We include the Mosaic computation advisedly, and with intent to prove our position. The chronology which separates Moses from the creation of the world by *only four generations* seems ridiculous, merely because the Christian clergy would enforce it upon the world literally.‡ The kabalists know that these generations stand for ages of the world. The allegories which, in the Hindu calculations, embrace the whole stupendous sweep of the four ages, are cunningly made in the Mosaic books, through the obliging help of the *Masorah*, to cram into the small period of two millenniums and a half (2513)!

The exoteric plan of the *Bible* was made to answer also to four ages. Thus, they reckon the Golden Age from Adam to Abraham; the silver, from Abraham to David; copper, from David to the Captivity; thenceforward, the iron. But the secret computation is quite different, and does not vary at all from the zodiacal calculations of the Brahmans. We are in the Iron Age, or Kali-Yuga, but it began with Noah, the mythical ancestor of our race.

Noah, or Nuah, like all the euhemerized manifestations of the Unrevealed One—Svâyambhuva (from Svayambhû) — was androgyne. Thus,

---

* About 1040, the Jewish doctors removed their schools from Babylonia to Spain, and of the four great rabbis that flourished during the next four centuries, their works all show different readings, and abound with mistakes in the manuscripts. The "Masorah" made things still worse. Many things that then existed in the manuscripts are there no longer, and their works teem with interpolations as well as with *lacunae*. The oldest Hebrew manuscript belongs to this period. Such is the divine revelation we are to credit.

† [*Op. cit.*, p. 300.]

‡ No chronology was accepted by the rabbis as authoritative till the twelfth century. The 40 and 1,000 are not exact numbers, but have been crammed in to answer monotheism and the exigencies of a religion calculated to appear different from that of the Pagans. ("Chron. Orth.", p. 237). One finds in the *Pentateuch* only events occurring about two years before the fabled "Exodus" and the last year. The rest of the chronology is nowhere, and can be followed only through kabalistic computations, with a key to them in the hand.

in some instances, he belonged to the purely feminine triad of the Chaldeans, known as "Nuah, the universal Mother." We have shown in another chapter that every male triad had its feminine counterpart, one in three, like the former. It was the passive complement of the active principle, its *reflection*. In India, the male *Trimûrti* is reproduced in the *Sakti-trimûrti*, the feminine; and in Chaldea, Ana, Belita and Davkina answered to Anu, Bel, Nuah. The former three resumed in one—Belita, were called:

"Sovereign goddess, lady of the nether abyss, mother of gods, queen of the earth, queen of fecundity."

As the primordial humidity, whence proceeded *all*, Belita is *Tiamat*, or the sea, the mother of *the city of Erech* (the great Chaldean necropolis), therefore, an infernal goddess. In the world of stars and planets she is known as Ishtar or Astoreth. Hence, she is identical with Venus, and every other Queen of Heaven, to whom cakes and buns were offered in sacrifice,* and, as all the archaeologists know, with *Eve*, the mother of all that live, and with Mary.

The Ark, in which are preserved the germs of all living things necessary to repeople the earth, represents the survival of life, and the supremacy of spirit over matter, through the conflict of the opposing powers of nature. In the Astro-Theosophic chart of the Western Rite, the Ark corresponds with the navel, and is placed at the sinister side, the side of the woman (the moon), one of whose symbols is the left pillar of Solomon's temple —Boaz. The umbilicus is connected with the receptacle in which are fructified the germs of the race.† The Ark is the sacred *Argha* of the Hindus, and thus, the relation in which it stands to Noah's ark may be easily inferred, when we learn that the Argha was an oblong vessel, used by the high priests as a sacrificial chalice in the worship of Isis, Astarte, and Venus-Aphrodite, all of whom were goddesses of the generative powers of nature, or of matter—hence, representing symbolically the Ark containing the germs of all living things.

We admit that Pagans had and now have—as in India—strange symbols, which, to the eyes of the hypocrite and Puritan, seem scandalously

---

\* The Gnostics, called Collyridians, had transferred their worship from Astoreth to Mary, also Queen of Heaven. They were persecuted and put to death by the orthodox Christians as heretics. But if these Gnostics had established her worship by offering her sacrifices of cakes, cracknels, or fine wafers, it was because they imagined her to have been born of an immaculate virgin, as Christ is alleged to have been born of his mother. And now, the Pope's *infallibility* having been recognized and accepted, its first practical manifestation is the revival of the Collyridian belief as an article of faith. See Hone, *The Apocryphal New Testament*, "The Gospel of the Birth of Mary" (attributed to Matthew), Hone's introduction.

† Hargrave Jennings, *The Rosicrucians*, 1870, p. 328.

immoral. But did not the ancient Jews copy most of these symbols? We have described elsewhere the identity of the linga with Jacob's pillar, and we could give a number of instances from the present Christian rites, bearing the same origin, did but space permit, and were not all these noticed fully by Inman and others (See Inman's *Ancient Faiths Embodied in Ancient Names*).

Describing the worship of the Egyptians, Mrs. Lydia Maria Child says: "This reverence for the production of Life, introduced into [the worship of Osiris] the sexual emblem so common in Hindostan. A colossal image of this kind was presented to his temple in Alexandria, by King Ptolemy Philadelphus. . . . Reverence for the mystery of organized life led to the recognition of a masculine and feminine principle in all things, spiritual or material. . . . The sexual emblems everywhere conspicuous in the sculptures of their temples would seem impure in description, but *no clean and thoughtful mind* could so regard them while witnessing the obvious simplicity and solemnity with which the subject is treated."\*

Thus speaks this respected lady and admirable writer, and no truly pure man or woman would ever think of blaming her for it. But such a perversion of the ancient thought is but natural in an age of cant and prudery like our own.

The water of the flood when standing in the allegory for the symbolic "sea," Tiamat, typifies the turbulent chaos, or matter, called "the great dragon." According to the Gnostic and Rosicrucian mediaeval doctrine, the creation of woman was not originally intended. She is the offspring of man's own impure fancy, and, as the Hermetists say, "an obtrusion." Created by an unclean thought she sprang into existence at the *evil* "seventh hour," when the "supernatural" real worlds had passed away and the "natural" or *delusive* worlds began evolving along the "descending Microcosmos," or the arc of the great cycle, in plainer phraseology. First "Virgo," the Celestial Virgin of the Zodiac, she became "Virgo-Scorpio." But in evolving his second companion, man had unwittingly endowed her with his own share of Spirituality; and the new being whom his "imagination" had called into life became his "Savior" from the snares of Eve-Lilith, the first Eve, who had a greater share of matter in her composition than the primitive "spiritual" man.†

---

\* *The Progress of Religious Ideas*, etc., I, pp. 151, 157-58.

† Lilith was Adam's *first* wife "before he *married* Eve," of whom "he begat nothing but devils"; which strikes us as a very novel, if pious, way of explaining a very philosophical allegory. [Cf. Buxtorf, *Lexicon Chaldaicum*, etc., p. 1140.]

Thus woman stands in the cosmogony in relation to "matter" or the *great deep*, as the "Virgin of the Sea," who crushes the "Dragon" under her foot. The "Flood" is also very often shown, in symbolical phraseology, as the "great Dragon." For one acquainted with these tenets it becomes more than suggestive to learn that with the Catholics the Virgin Mary is not only the accepted patroness of Christian sailors, but also the "Virgin of the Sea." So was Dido, the patroness of the Phoenician mariners;* and together with Venus and other lunar goddesses—the moon having such a strong influence over the tides—was the "Virgin of the Sea." *Mare,* the Sea, is the root of the name Mary. The blue color, which was with the ancients symbolical of the "Great Deep" or the material world, hence—of evil, is made sacred to our "Blessed Lady." It is the color of "Notre Dame de Paris." On account of its relation to the symbolical serpent this color is held in the deepest aversion by the ex-Nazarenes, disciples of John the Baptist, now the Mandaeans of Basra.

Among the beautiful plates of Maurice, there is one representing Kṛishṇa crushing the head of the Serpent. A three-peaked mitre is on his head (typifying the trinity), and the body and tail of the conquered serpent encircles the figure of the Hindu god.† This plate shows whence proceeded the inspiration for the "make up" of a later story extracted from an alleged prophecy. "And I will put enmity between thee and the woman, and between thy seed and her seed; it shall bruise thy head, and thou shalt bruise his *heel*."‡

The Egyptian *orant* is also shown with his arms extended as on a crucifix, and treading upon the "Serpent"; and Horus (the Logos) is represented piercing the head of the dragon, Typhon or Apophis.[60] All this gives us a clue to the Biblical allegory of Cain and Abel. Cain was held as the ancestor of the Hivites, the Serpents, and the twins of Adam are an evident copy from the fable of Osiris and Typhon. Apart from the external form of the allegory, however, it embodied the philosophical conception of the eternal struggle of good and evil.

But how strangely elastic, how adaptable to any and everything this mystical philosophy proved after the Christian era! When were ever facts, irrefutable, irrefragable, and beyond denial, less potential for the re-establishment of truth than in our century of casuistry and Christian cunning? Is Kṛishṇa proved to have been known as the "Good Shep-

---

\* It is in commemoration of the Ark of the Deluge that the Phoenicians, those bold explorers of the "deep," carried, fixed on the prow of their ships, the image of the goddess Astarte, who is Elissa, Venus-Erycina of Sicily, and Dido, whose name is the feminine of David.

† [*Hist. of Hindostan,* Vol. II, plate VIII; Vol. III, plates VIII and IX.]
‡ [*Genesis* iii, 15.]

herd" ages before the year A.D. 1, to have crushed the Serpent Kâlîyanâga, and to have been crucified—all this was but a prophetic foreshadowing of the future! Are the Scandinavian Thor, who bruised the head of the Serpent with his cruciform mace, and Apollo, who killed Python, likewise shown to present the most striking similarities with the heroes of the Christian fables — they become but original conceptions of "heathen" minds, "working upon the old Patriarchal prophecies respecting the Christ, as they were contained in the one universal and primeval Revelation"!\*

The flood, then, is the "Old Serpent" or the great deep of matter, Isaiah's "dragon in the sea" (xxvii, 1), over which the ark safely crosses on its way to the mount of Salvation. But, if we have heard of the ark and Noah, and the *Bible* at all, it is because the mythology of the Egyptians was ready at hand for Moses (if Moses ever wrote any of the *Bible*), and that he was acquainted with the story of Horus, standing on his boat of a serpentine form, and killing the Serpent with his spear; and with the hidden meaning of these fables, and their real origin. This is also why we find in *Leviticus,* and other parts of his books, whole pages of laws identical with those of *Manu.*

The animals shut up in the ark are the human passions. They typify certain ordeals of initiation, and the mysteries which were instituted among many nations in commemoration of this allegory. Noah's ark rested on the seventeenth of the *seventh* month. Here we have again the number; as also in the "clean beasts" that he took by *sevens* into the ark. Speaking of the water-mysteries of Byblos, Lucian says: "On the top of one of the two pillars which Bacchus set up, a man remains *seven* days."† He supposes this was done to honor Deucalion. Elijah, when praying on the top of Mount Carmel, sends his servant to look for a cloud toward the sea, and repeats, "go again *seven* times. And it came to pass at the *seventh* time, that he said, behold there ariseth a little cloud out of the sea like a man's hand."‡

"*Noah* is a *revolutio* of Adam, as Moses is a *revolutio* of Abel and Seth," says the *Kabala;*§ that is to say, a repetition or another version of the same story. The greatest proof of it is the distribution of the characters in the *Bible*. For instance, beginning with Cain, the first murderer, every *fifth* man in his line of descent is a murderer. Thus there come Enoch, Irad, Mehujael, Methuselah, and the *fifth* is *Lamech,* the second

---

\* Dr. Lundy, *Monumental Christianity,* p. 161.

† Lucian, *De Syria Dea,* § 28.

‡ *1 Kings* xviii, 43, 44. All this is allegorical, and, what is more, purely magical. For Elijah is bent upon an incantation.

§ [Rosenroth, *Kabb. denudata,* II, p. 305; ed. 1684.]

448     ISIS UNVEILED

murderer, and he is Noah's father. By drawing the five-pointed star of Lucifer (which has its crown-point downward) and writing the name of Cain beneath the lowest point, and those of his descendants successively at each of the other points, it will be found that each fifth name—which would be written beneath that of Cain—is that of a murderer. In the *Talmud* this genealogy is given complete, and thirteen murderers range themselves in line below the name of Cain. This is *no* coincidence. Siva is the Destroyer, but he is also the *Regenerator*. Cain is a murderer, but he is also the creator of nations, and an inventor. This star of Lucifer is the same one that John sees falling down to earth in his *Apocalypse*.

In Thebes, or Theba, which means ark—TH-ABA being synonymous with Kartha or Tyre, Astu or Athens and Urbs or Rome, and meaning also the city—are found the same foliations as described on the pillars of the temple of Solomon. The bi-colored leaf of the olive, the three-lobed fig-leaf, and the lanceolate-shaped laurel-leaf, had all esoteric as well as popular or vulgar meanings with the ancients.

The researches of Egyptologists present another corroboration of the identity of the *Bible*-allegories with those of the lands of the Pharaohs and Chaldeans. The dynastic chronology of the Egyptians, recorded by Herodotus, Manetho, Eratosthenes, Diodorus Siculus, and accepted by our antiquarians, divided the period of Egyptian history under four general heads: the dominion of gods, demi-gods, heroes and mortal men. By combining the demi-gods and heroes into one class, Bunsen\* reduces the periods to three: the ruling gods, the demi-gods or heroes—sons of gods, but born of mortal mothers—and the Manes, who were the ancestors of individual tribes. These subdivisions, as anyone may perceive, correspond perfectly with the Biblical Elohim, sons of God, giants and mortal Noachian men.

Diodorus of Sicily† and Berosus‡ give us the names of the twelve great gods who presided over the twelve months of the year and the twelve signs of the zodiac. These names, which include Nuah,§ are too well known to require repetition. The double-faced Janus was also at the head of twelve gods, and in the representations of him he is made to hold the keys to the celestial domains. All these having served as models for the Biblical patriarchs, have done still further service—especially Janus — by furnishing copy to St. Peter and his twelve apostles, the

---

\* [*Egypt's Place*, etc., Vol. I, pp. 69 *et seq.*; Vol. IV, p. 335.]
† [*Biblioth. Hist.*, II, 30.]
‡ [Cory, *Ancient Fragm.*, pp. 26 *et seq.* Cf. Movers, *Die Phönizier*, Vol. I, p. 165.]
§ The *Talmud* books say that Noah was himself the *dove* (spirit), thus identifying him still more with the Chaldean Nuah. Baal is represented with the wings of a dove, and the Samaritans worshipped on Mount Garizim the image of a dove. — *Talmud*, Hulin, 6a. [Cf. Nork, *Hundert und ein Frage*, p. 37.]

former also double-faced in his denial, and also represented as holding the keys of Paradise.

This statement that the story of Noah is but another version in its hidden meaning of the story of Adam and his three sons, gathers proof on every page of the book of *Genesis*.[61] Adam is the prototype of Noah. Adam *falls* because he eats of the forbidden fruit of *celestial* knowledge; Noah, because he tastes of the *terrestrial* fruit: the juice of the grape representing the abuse of knowledge in an unbalanced mind. Adam gets stripped of his spiritual envelope; Noah of his terrestrial clothing; and the *nakedness* of both makes them feel ashamed. The wickedness of Cain is repeated in Ham. But the descendants of both are shown as the wisest of races on earth; and they are called on this account "snakes," and the "sons of snakes," meaning the *sons of wisdom*, and not of Satan, as some divines would be pleased to have the world understand the term. Enmity has been placed between the "snake" and the "woman" only in this mortal phenomenal "world of man" as "born of woman." Before the carnal fall, the "snake" was *Ophis*, the divine wisdom, which needed no matter to procreate men, humanity being utterly spiritual. Hence the war between the snake and the woman, or between spirit and matter. If, in its material aspect, the "old serpent" is matter, and represents Ophiomorphos, in its spiritual meaning it becomes Ophis-Christos. In the magic of the old Syro-Chaldeans both are conjoint in the zodiacal sign of the androgyne of Virgo-Scorpio, and may be *divided* or separated whenever needed. Thus as the origin of "good and evil," the meaning of the S.S. and Z.Z. has always been interchangeable; and if upon some occasions the S.S. on sigils and talismans are suggestive of serpentine evil influence and denote a design of *black* magic upon others, the double S.S. are found on the sacramental cups of the Church and mean the presence of the Holy Ghost, or pure wisdom.

The Midianites were known as the *wise* men, or sons of snakes, as well as Canaanites and Hamites; and such was the renown of the Midianites, that we find Moses, *the prophet, led on and inspired by "the Lord,"* humbling himself before Hobab, the son of Raguel, the *Midianite*, and beseeching him to remain with the people of Israel: "Leave us not, I pray thee; forasmuch *as thou knowest how we are to encamp* IN THE WILDERNESS, *and thou mayest be to us instead of eyes.*"* Further, when Moses sends spies to search out the land of Canaan, they bring as a proof of the wisdom (kabalistically speaking) and goodness of the land, a branch with *one* cluster of *grapes*, which they are compelled to bear between two men on a staff. Moreover, they add: "we saw the children of ANAK there."

---

* *Numbers* x, 29. 31.

They are the *giants*, the sons of Anak, *"which come of the giants,"* and we were in our own sight as grasshoppers, and so we were in their sight."†

Anak is Enoch, the patriarch, who *dies not,* and who is the first possessor of the "mirific name," according to the *Kabala,* and the ritual of Freemasonry.

Comparing the Biblical patriarchs with the descendants of Vaivasvata, the Hindu Noah, and the old Sanskrit traditions about the deluge in the Brahmanical *Mahâbhârata,* we find them mirrored in the Vedic patriarchs who are the primitive types upon which all the others were modelled. But before comparison is possible, the Hindu myths must be comprehended in their true significance. Each of these mythical personages bears, besides an astronomical significance, a spiritual or moral, and an anthropological or physical meaning. The patriarchs are not only euhemerized gods—the prediluvian answering to the *twelve* great gods of Berosus, and to the *ten* Prajâpatis, and the postdiluvian to the seven gods of the famous tablet in the Ninevean Library, but they stand also as the symbols of the Greek Aeôns, the kabalistic Sephîrôth, and the zodiacal signs, as types of a series of human races.‡ This variation from *ten* to *twelve* will be accounted for presently, and proved on the very authority

---

\* The Bible contradicts itself as well as the Chaldean account, for in chapter vii of *Genesis* it shows "every one of them" perishing in the deluge.

† *Numbers* xiii, 33.

‡ We do not see why the clergy—especially the Catholic—should object to our statement that the patriarchs are all signs of the zodiac, and the old gods of the "heathen" as well. There was a time, and that less than two centuries ago, when they themselves exhibited the most fervent desire to relapse into sun and star worship. This pious and curious attempt was denounced but a few months since by Camille Flammarion, the French astronomer. He shows two Augsburgian Jesuits, Schiller and Bayer, who felt quite anxious to change the names of the whole Sabaean host of the starry heaven, and worship them again under Christian names! Having anathematized the idolatrous sun-worshippers for over fifteen centuries, the Church now seriously proposed to continue heliolatry — *to the letter* this time — as their idea was to substitute for Pagan myths Biblical and (in their ideas) real personages. They would have called the sun, Christ; the moon, Virgin Mary; Saturn, Adam; Jupiter, Moses (!); Mars, Joshua; Venus, John the Baptist; and Mercury, Elias. And very proper substitutes too, showing the great familiarity of the Catholic Church with ancient Pagan and kabalistic learning, and its readiness, perhaps, to at last confess the source whence came their own myths. For is not king Messiah the sun, the Demiurge of the heliolaters, under various names? Is he not the Egyptian Osiris and the Grecian Apollo? And what more appropriate name than Virgin Mary for the Pagan Diana-Astarte, "the Queen of Heaven," against which Jeremiah exhausted a whole vocabulary of imprecations? Such an adoption would have been historically as well as religiously correct. Two large plates were prepared, says Flammarion, in a recent number of *La Nature,* and represented the heavens with Christian constellations

of the *Bible*. Only, they are not the first gods described by Cicero,*
which belong to a hierarchy of higher powers, the Elohim—but appertain
rather to the second class of the "twelve gods," the *Dii minores*, and
who are the terrestrial reflections of the first, among whom Herodotus
places Hercules.† Alone, out of the group of twelve, Noah, by reason
of his position at the transitional point, belongs to the highest Babylonian
triad, Nuah, the spirit of the waters. The rest are identical with the
inferior gods of Assyria and Babylonia, who represent the lower order
of emanations, introduced around Bel, the Demiurge, and help him in
his work, as the patriarchs are shown to assist Jehovah—the "Lord
God."

Besides these, many of which were *local* gods, the protecting deities
of rivers and cities, there were the four classes of genii; we see
Ezekiel making them support the throne of Jehovah in his vision. A
fact which, if it identifies the Jewish "Lord God" with one of the
Babylonian trinity, connects, at the same time, the present Christian
God with the same triad, inasmuch as it is these four cherubs, if the
reader will remember, on which Irenaeus‡ makes Jesus ride, and which
are shown as the companions of the evangelists.

The Hindu kabalistic derivation of the book of *Ezekiel* and *Revelation* is shown in nothing more plainly than in this description of the four
beasts, which typify the four elementary kingdoms—earth, air, fire and
water. As is well known, they are the Assyrian sphinxes, but these figures are also carved on the walls of nearly every Hindu pagoda.

The author of the *Revelation* copies faithfully in his text (see chap.
iv, verse 7) the Pythagorean pentacle, of which Éliphas Lévi's admirable
sketch is reproduced on page 452.§

The Hindu goddess Ardhanârî (or as it might be more properly written,
Ardhonârî, since the second a is pronounced almost like the English o) is
represented as surrounded by the same figures. It fits exactly Ezekiel's
"wheel of the Adonai," known as "the Cherubs of Ezekiel," and indicates, beyond question, the source from which the Hebrew seer drew his
allegories. For convenience of comparison we have placed the figure in
the pentacle. (See page 453.)

---

instead of Pagan. Apostles, popes, saints, martyrs, and personages of the *Old* and *New
Testament* completed this Christian Sabaeanism. "The disciples of Loyola used every
exertion to make this plan succeed." It is curious to find in India among the Moslems the
name of Terah, Abraham's father, Azar or Azarh, and Âzur, which also means fire, and
is, at the same time, the name of the Hindu third solar month (from June to July),
during which the sun is in *Gemini*, and the full moon near *Sagittarius*.

* Cicero, *De natura Deorum*, I, xii.
† *History*, II, § 145.
‡ [*Fragments*, liii, liv.]
§ [Cf. É. Lévi, *Dogme et Rituel*, etc., Vol. I.]

452                    ISIS UNVEILED

Above these beasts were the angels or spirits, divided in two groups: the Igili, or celestial beings, and the Am-anaki, or terrestrial spirits, the giants, children of Anak, of whom the spies complained to Moses.

The *Kabbala Denudata* gives to the kabalists a very clear, to the profane a very muddled account of permutations or substitutions of one person for another. So, for instance, it says, that "the scintilla" (spiritual spark or soul) of Abraham was taken from Michael, the chief

ADO          NAI

of the Aeôns, and highest emanation of the Deity; so high indeed that in the eyes of the Gnostics, Michael was identical with Christ. And yet Michael and Enoch are one and the same person. Both occupy the junction-point of the cross of the Zodiac as "man." The scintilla of Isaac was that of Gabriel, the chief of the angelic host, and the scintilla of Jacob was taken from Uriel, named "the fire of God"; the sharpest-sighted spirit in all Heaven. Adam is not the Kadmon but Adam *Primus,* the *Microprosopus.* In one of his aspects the latter is Enoch, the terrestrial patriarch and father of Methuselah. He that "walked with God" and "did not die" is the spiritual Enoch, who typified humanity, eternal in spirit and as eternal in flesh, though the latter does *die*. Death is but a new birth, and spirit is immortal; thus humanity can never die, for the *Destroyer* has become the *Creator*, Enoch is the type of the dual man, spiritual and terrestrial. Hence his place in the centre of the astronomical cross.

ARDHA NÂRÎ

But was this idea original with the Hebrews? We think not. Every nation which had an astronomical system, and especially India, held the cross in the highest reverence, for it was the geometrical basis of the religious symbolism of their *avatâras*; the manifestation of the Deity, or of the Creator in his creature MAN; of God in humanity and humanity in God, as spirits. The oldest monuments of Chaldea, Persia and India disclose the double or eight-pointed cross. This symbol, which very naturally is found, like every other geometrical figure in nature, in plants as well as in the snowflakes, has led Dr. Lundy, in his super-Christian mysticism, to name such cruciform flowers as form an eight-pointed star by the junction of the two crosses—"the *Prophetic Star of the Incarnation*, which joined heaven and earth, God and man together."* The latter sentence is perfectly expressed; only, the old kabalist axiom, "as above, so below," answers still better, as it discloses to us the same God for all humanity, not alone for the handful of Christians. It is the *Mundane* cross of Heaven repeated on earth by plants and dual man: the physical man superseding the "spiritual," at the junction-point of which stands the mythical Libra-Hermes-Enoch. The gesture of one hand pointing to Heaven, is balanced by the other pointing down to earth; boundless generations below, boundless regenerations above; the visible but the manifestation of the invisible; the man of dust abandoned to dust, the man of spirit reborn in spirit; thus it is finite humanity which is the Son of the Infinite God. Abba, the Father; Amona, the Mother; the Son, the Universe. This primitive triad is repeated in all the theogonies. Adam-Kadmon, Hermes, Enoch, Osiris, Krishna, Ormazd, or Christos are all one. They stand as *Metatrons* between body and soul—eternal spirits which redeem flesh by the regeneration of flesh *below*, and soul by the regeneration *above*, where humanity walks once more with God.

We have shown elsewhere that the symbol of the cross or Egyptian *Tau*, T, was by many ages, earlier than the period assigned to Abraham, the alleged forefather of the Israelites, for otherwise Moses could not have learned it of the priests. And that the Tau was held as sacred by the Jews, as by other "Pagan" nations, is proved by a fact admitted now by Christian divines as well as by infidel archaeologists. Moses, in *Exodus* xii, 22, orders his people to mark their *doorposts and lintels* with blood, lest the "Lord God" should make a mistake and smite some of his chosen people, instead of the doomed Egyptians.† And this mark is a *Tau!* The identical Egyptian handled-*cross*, with the half of which talisman Horus raised the dead, as is shown on a sculptured ruin at Philae.‡ How gratuitous is the idea that all such crosses and symbols were so many unconscious prophecies of Christ, is fully exemplified in the case of the Jews upon whose accusation Jesus was put to death. For instance the same learned author remarks in *Monumental Christianity* that "the Jews themselves acknowledged this sign of salvation until they rejected

---

* *Monumental Christianity*, p. 9.

† Who but the authors of the *Pentateuch* could have invented a Supreme God or his angel so thoroughly human as to require a smear of blood upon the doorpost to prevent his killing one person for another! For gross materialism this exceeds any theistical conception that we have noticed in Pagan literature.

‡ Denon, *Voyage dans la basse et la haute Égypte*, Vol. II, pl. 40, fig. 8, pp. 54, 145.

Christ"; and in another place he asserts that "the rod of Moses, used in his miracles before Pharoah, was, no doubt, this *crux ansata,* or something like it, *also used by the Egyptian priests."\** Thus the logical inference would be, that 1, if the Jews worshipped the same symbols as the Pagans, then they were no better than they; and 2, if, being as well versed as they were in the hidden symbolism of the cross, in the face of their having waited for centuries for the Messiah, they yet rejected both the Christian Messiah and Christian Cross, then there must have been something wrong about both.

Those who "rejected" Jesus as the "Son of God," were neither the people ignorant of religious symbols, nor the handful of atheistical Sadducees who put him to death; but the very men who were instructed in the secret wisdom, who knew the origin as well as the meaning of the cruciform symbol, and who put aside both the Christian emblem and the Savior suspended from it, because they could not be parties to such a blasphemous imposition upon the common people.

Nearly all the prophecies about Christ are credited to the patriarchs and prophets. If a few of the latter may have existed as real personages, every one of the former is a myth. We will endeavor to prove it by the hidden interpretation of the Zodiac, and the relation of its signs to these antediluvian men.

If the reader will keep in mind the Hindu ideas of cosmogony, as given in Chapter VI, he will better understand the relation between the Biblical antediluvian patriarchs, and that puzzle of commentators—"Ezekiel's wheel." Thus, be it remembered: 1, that the universe is not a spontaneous creation, but an evolution from pre-existent matter; 2, that it is only one of an endless series of universes; 3, that eternity is pointed off into grand cycles, in each of which twelve transformations of our world occur, following its partial destruction by fire and water, alternately. So that when a new minor period sets in, the earth is so changed, even geologically, as to be practically a new world; 4, that of these twelve transformations, the earth after each of the first six is grosser, and everything on it—man included—more material, than after the preceding one: while after each of the remaining six the contrary is true, both earth and man growing more and more refined and spiritual with each terrestrial change; 5, that when the apex of the cycle is reached, a gradual dissolution takes place, and every living and objective form is destroyed. But when that point is reached, humanity has become fitted to live subjectively as well as objectively. And not humanity alone, but also

---

\* Dr. Lundy, *op. cit.,* pp. 13, 402.

animals, plants, and every atom. After a time of rest, say the Buddhists, when a new world becomes self-formed, the astral souls of animals, and of all beings, except such as have reached the highest Nirvâna, will return on earth again to end their cycles of transformations, and become men in their turn.

This stupendous conception, the ancients synthesized for the instruction of the common people, into a single pictorial design—the Zodiac, or celestial belt. Instead of the twelve signs now used, there were originally but ten known to the general public, viz.: Aries, Taurus, Gemini, Cancer, Leo, Virgo-Scorpio, Sagittarius, Capricornus, Aquarius, and Pisces.* These were exoteric. But in addition there were two mystical signs inserted, which none but initiates comprehended, viz.: at the middle or junction-point where now stands *Libra,* and at the sign now called Scorpio, which follows Virgo. When it was found necessary to make them exoteric, these two secret signs were added under their present appellations as blinds to conceal the true names which gave the key to the whole secret of creation, and divulged the origin of "good and evil."

The true Sabaean astrological doctrine secretly taught that within this double sign was hidden the explanation of the gradual transformation of the world, from its spiritual and subjective, into the "two-sexed" sublunary state. The twelve signs were therefore divided into two groups. The first six were called the ascending, or the line of Macrocosm (the great spiritual world); the last six, the descending line, or the Microcosm (the little secondary world)—the mere reflection of the former, so to say. This division was called Ezekiel's wheel, and was completed in the following way: First came the ascending five signs (euhemerized into patriarchs), Aries, Taurus, Gemini, Cancer, Leo, and the group concluded with Virgo-Scorpio. Then came the turning point, *Libra.* After which, the first half of the sign Virgo-Scorpio was duplicated and transferred to lead the lower, or descending group of Microcosm which ran down to *Pisces,* or Noah (deluge). To make it clearer, the sign Virgo-Scorpio, which appeared originally thus ♍, became simply *Virgo,* and the duplication, ♏, or Scorpio, was placed beyond Libra, the *seventh* sign (which is Enoch, or the angel Metatron, or *Mediator* between spirit and matter, or God and man). It now became Scorpio (or Cain), which sign or patriarch led *mankind to destruction,* according

---

* In C. F. de Volney's *Ruins . . . of Empires,* p. 360, it is remarked that as *Aries* was in its fifteenth degree 1447 B.C., it follows that the first degree of "Libra" could not have coincided with the Vernal equinox more lately than 15,194 years B.C., to which, if you add 1790 years since Christ, it appears that 16,984 years have elapsed since the origin of the *Zodiac.*

to exoteric theology; but, according to the true doctrine of the wisdom-religion, it indicated *the degradation of the whole universe in its course of evolution downward from the subjective to the objective.*

The sign of *Libra* is credited as a later invention by the Greeks, but it is not generally stated that those among them who were initiated had only made a change of names conveying the same idea as the secret name to those "who knew," leaving the masses as unwise as ever. Yet it was a beautiful idea of theirs, this Libra, or the balance, expressing as much as could possibly be done without unveiling the whole and ultimate truth. They intended it to imply that when the course of evolution had taken the worlds to the lowest point of grossness, where the earths and their products were coarsest, and their inhabitants most brutish, the turning point had been reached—the forces were at an even balance. At the lowest point, the still lingering divine spark of spirit within began to convey the upward impulse. The scales typified that eternal equilibrium which is the necessity of a universe of harmony, of exact justice, of the balance of centripetal and centrifugal forces, darkness and light, spirit and matter.

*These additional signs of the Zodiac warrant us in saying that the Book of Genesis as we now find it, must be of later date than the invention of Libra by the Greeks;* for we find the chapters of the genealogies remodelled to fit the new Zodiac, instead of the latter being made to correspond with the list of patriarchs. And it is this addition and the necessity of concealing the true key, that led the Rabbinical compilers to repeat the names of Enoch and Lamech twice, as we see them now in the Kenite table. Alone, among all the books of the *Bible, Genesis* belongs to an immense antiquity. The others are all later additions, the earliest of which appeared with Hilkiah, who evidently concocted it with the help of Huldah, the prophetess.

As there is more than one meaning attached to the stories of the creation and deluge, we say, therefore, that the Biblical account cannot be comprehended apart from the Babylonian story of the same; while neither will be thoroughly clear without the Brahmanical esoteric interpretation of the deluge, as found in the *Mahâbhârata* and the *Śatapatha-Brâhmaṇa*. It is the Babylonians who were taught the "mysteries," the sacerdotal language, and their religion by the problematical Akkadians, who according to Rawlinson came from Armenia—not the former who emigrated to India. Here the evidence becomes clear. The Babylonian Xisuthros is shown by Movers* to have represented the "sun" in the Zodiac, in the sign of Aquarius, and *Oannes*, the man-fish, the semi-demon, is Vishṇu in his first avatâra; thus giving the key to the double source of the Biblical revelation.

---

\* [*Die Phönizier,* Vol. I, p. 165 *et seq.*]

Oannes is the emblem of priestly, esoteric wisdom; he comes out from the sea, because the "great deep," the water, typifies, as we have shown, the secret doctrine. For this same reason Egyptians deified the Nile, apart from its being regarded, in consequence of its periodical overflows, as the "Savior" of the country. They even held the crocodiles as sacred, from having their abode in the "deep." The "Hamites," so called, have always preferred to settle near rivers and oceans. Water was the first-created element, according to some old cosmogonies. This name of Oannes is held in the greatest reverence, in the Chaldean records. The Chaldean priests wore a headgear like a fish's head, and a shad-belly coat, representing the body of a fish.*

"Thales," says Cicero, "assures us that *water* is the principle of all things; and that God is that Mind which shaped and created all things from water."†

> "In the Beginning, SPIRIT within strengthens Heaven and Earth,
> The watery fields, and the lucid globe of Luna, and
> Titan stars; and mind infused through the limbs
> Agitates the whole mass, and mixes itself with GREAT MATTER."‡

Thus water represents the duality of both the Macrocosmos and the Microcosmos, in conjunction with the vivifying SPIRIT, and the evolution of the little world from the universal cosmos. The deluge then, in this sense, points to that final struggle between the conflicting elements, which brought the first great cycle of our planet to a close. These periods gradually merged into each other, order being brought out of chaos or disorder, and the successive types of organism being evolved only as the physical conditions of nature were prepared for their appearance; for our present race could not have breathed on earth during that intermediate period, not having as yet the allegorical coats of skin.§

In chapters iv and v of *Genesis*, we find the so-called generations of Cain and Seth. Let us glance at them in the order in which they stand:

---

* See cuts in Inman's *Ancient Faiths Embodied in Ancient Names*, Vol. I, p. 529.

† Cicero, *De natura deorum*, I, x.

‡ Virgil, *Aeneid*, vi, 724-27.

§ The term "coats of skin," is the more suggestive when we learn that the Hebrew word "skin" used in the original text, means *human* skin. The text says: "And *Yava-Aleim* made for Adam and his wife עור כתנת, KOTHNOTH OR." [*Gen.* iii, 21.] The first Hebrew word is the same as the Greek χιτών, *chiton* — coat. Parkhurst defines it as *the skin of men* or animals, עור, ער and ערה, OUR, OR, or ORAH. The same word is used in *Exodus* xxxiv, 30, 35, when the *skin* of Moses "shone" (A. Wilder).

## LINES OF GENERATIONS

| Sethite | | | Kenite |
|---|---|---|---|
| 1. Adam | | | 1. Adam |
| 2. Seth | | | 2. Cain |
| 3. Enos | | | 3. Enoch |
| 4. Cainan | Good Principle | Evil Principle | 4. Irad |
| 5. Mahalaleel | | | 5. Mehujael |
| 6. Jared | | | 6. Methusael |
| 7. Enoch | | | 7. Lamech |
| 8. Methuselah | | | 8. Jubal |
| 9. Lamech | | | 9. Jabal |
| 10. Noah | | | 10. Tubalcain |

The above are the ten Biblical patriarchs, identical with Hindu Prajâpatis, and the Sephîrôth of the *Kabala*. We say *ten* patriarchs, not *twenty*, for the Kenite line was devised for no other purpose than, 1, to carry out the idea of dualism, on which is founded the philosophy of every religion, for these two genealogical tables represent simply the opposing powers or principles of good and evil; and 2, as a blind for the uninitiated masses. Suppose we restore them to their primitive form, by erasing these premeditated blinds. These are so transparent as to require but a small amount of perspicacity to select, even though one should use only his unaided judgment, and were not, as we are, enabled to apply the test of the secret doctrine.

By ridding ourselves, therefore, of the Kenite names that are mere duplications of the Sethite, or of each other, we get rid of Adam; of Enoch—who, in one genealogy, is shown the father of Irad, and in the other, the son of Jared; of Lamech, son of Methusael, whereas he, Lamech, is son of Methuselah in the Sethite line; of Irad (Jared),* Jubal and Jabal, who, with Tubalcain, form a trinity in one, and that one the double of Cain; of Mehujael (who is but Mahalaleel differently spelled), and Methusael (Methuselah). This leaves us in the Kenite genealogy of chapter iv, one only, Cain, who—the first murderer and fra-

---

\* Here, again, the "Masorah," by converting one name into another, has helped to falsify the little that was left original in the primitive Scriptures.

De Rossi, of Parma, says of the Masoretes, in his *Compèndio*, Vol. IV, pp. 7-8: "It is known with what carefulness Esdras, the most excellent critic they have had, had *reformed* [the text] and *corrected* it, and restored it to its primary splendor. Of the many revisions undertaken after him, none are more celebrated than that of the Masoretes, who came after the sixth century . . . and all the most zealous adorers and defenders of the 'Masorah,' Christians and Jews . . . ingenuously accord and confess that it, such as it exists, is *deficient, imperfect, interpolated, full of errors,* and *a most unsafe guide.*" The square letter was not invented till after the third century.

tricide—is made to stand in his line as father of Enoch, the most virtuous of men, who does not die, but is translated alive. Turn we now to the Sethite table, and we find that Enos, or Enoch, comes *second* from Adam, and is father to Cain(an). This is no accident. There was an evident reason for this inversion of paternity; a palpable design—that of creating confusion and baffling inquiry.

We say, then, that the patriarchs are simply the signs of the Zodiac, emblems, in their manifold aspects, of the spiritual and physical evolution of human races, of ages, and of divisions of time. In astrology, the first four of the "Houses," in the diagrams of the "Twelve Houses of Heaven"—namely, the first, tenth, seventh and fourth, or the second inner square placed with its angles upward and downward, are termed *angles*, as being of the greatest strength and power. They answer to Adam, Noah, Cain-an, and Enoch, Alpha, Omega, evil and good, leading the whole. Furthermore, when divided (including the two secret names) into four *trigons* or triads, viz.: fiery, airy, earthy and watery, we find the latter corresponding to Noah.

Enoch and Lamech were doubled in the table of Cain, to fill out the required number ten in both "generations" in the *Bible*, instead of employing the "Secret Name"; and, in order that the patriarchs should correspond with the ten kabalistic Sephîrôth, and fit at the same time the ten, and, subsequently, *twelve* signs of the Zodiac, in a manner comprehensible only to the kabalists.

And now, Abel having disappeared out of that line of descent, he is replaced by Seth, who was clearly an afterthought suggested by the necessity of not having the human race descend entirely from a murderer. This dilemma being apparently first noticed when the Kenite table had been completed, Adam is made (after all the generations had appeared) to beget this son, Seth. It is a suggestive fact that, whereas the doublesexed Adam of chapter v is made in the likeness of the Elohim (see *Genesis* i, 27 and v, 1), Seth (v, 3) is begotten in Adam's "own likeness," thus signifying that there were men of different races. Also, it is most noticeable that neither the age nor a single other particular respecting the patriarchs in the Kenite table is given, whereas the reverse is the case with those in the Sethite line.

Most assuredly, no one could expect to find, in a work open to the public, the final mysteries of that which was preserved for countless ages as the grandest secret of the sanctuary. But, without divulging the key to the profane, or being taxed with undue indiscretion, we may be allowed to lift a corner of the veil which shrouds the majestic doctrines of old. Let us then write down the patriarchs as they ought to stand in their relation to the Zodiac, and see how they correspond with the signs.

## EZEKIEL'S WHEEL FULLY EXPLAINED

The following diagram represents Ezekiel's Wheel, as given in many works, among others, in Hargrave Jenning's *The Rosicrucians*:

EZEKIEL'S WHEEL (exoteric).

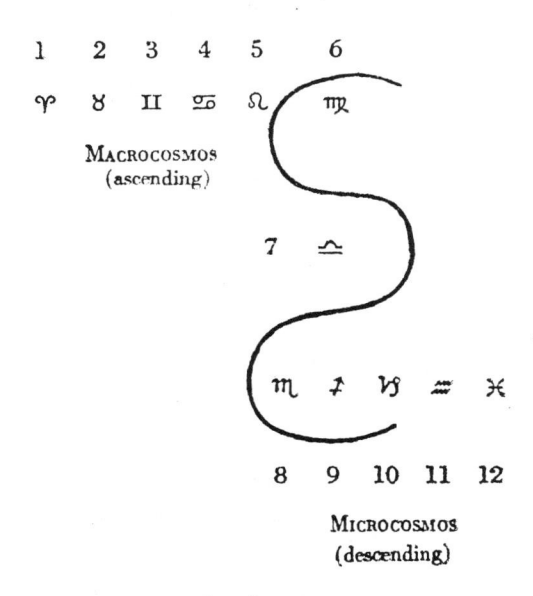

```
   1    2    3    4    5    6
   ♈    ♉    ♊    ♋    ♌   ⎛ ♍
                              ⎜
   MACROCOSMOS                ⎜
   (ascending)                ⎝
                                ⎞
                     7   ♎     ⎟
                                ⎠
                           ⎛
                           ⎜  ♏  ♐  ♑  ♒  ♓
                           ⎝
                              8   9   10  11  12
                              MICROCOSMOS
                              (descending)
```

These signs are (follow numbers):

1, Aries; 2, Taurus; 3, Gemini; 4, Cancer; 5, Leo; 6, Virgo, or the *ascending* line of the grand cycle of creation. After this comes 7, *Libra*—"man," which, though it is found right in the middle, or the intersection point, leads down the numbers:

8, Scorpio; 9, Sagittarius; 10, Capricornus; 11, Aquarius; and 12, Pisces.

While discussing the double sign of Virgo-Scorpio and Libra, Hargrave Jennings observes:

"All this is incomprehensible, except in the strange mysticism of the Gnostics and the Cabalists; and the whole theory requires a key of explanation to render it intelligible; which key is only darkly referred to as possible, but refused absolutely, by these extraordinary men, as not permissible to be disclosed." *

The said key must be turned *seven* times before the whole system is divulged. We will give it but *one* turn, and thereby allow the profane one glimpse into the mystery. Happy he, who understands the whole!

---

* *The Rosicrucians*, 1870, pp. 64-65.

## Ezekiel's Wheel (esoteric).

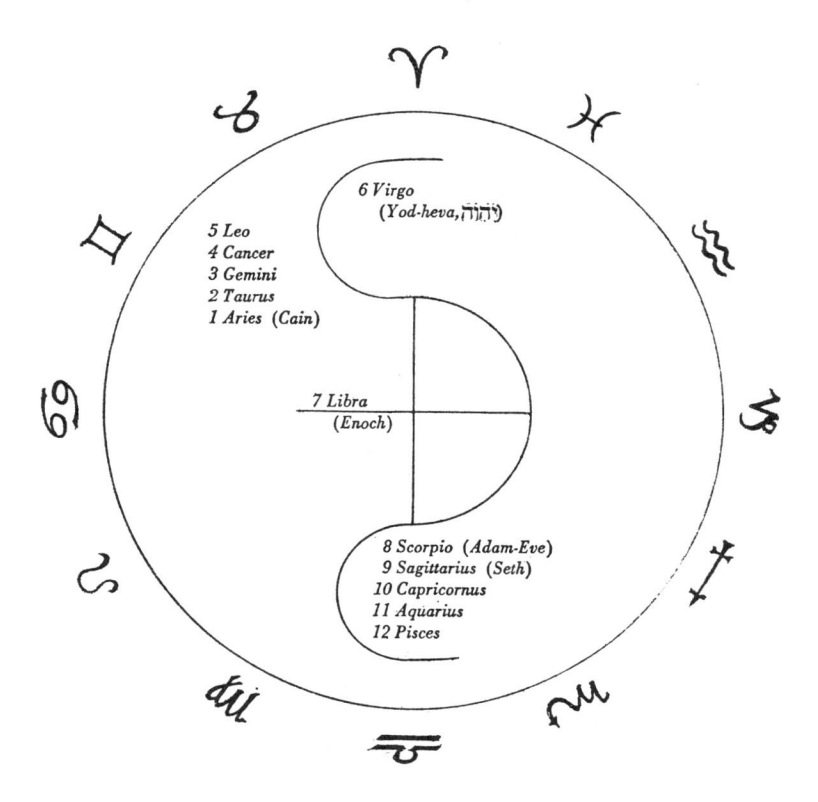

*6 Virgo (Yod-heva, יְהֹוָה)*

*5 Leo*
*4 Cancer*
*3 Gemini*
*2 Taurus*
*1 Aries (Cain)*

*7 Libra (Enoch)*

*8 Scorpio (Adam-Eve)*
*9 Sagittarius (Seth)*
*10 Capricornus*
*11 Aquarius*
*12 Pisces*

To explain the presence of Yod-'heva, or what is generally termed the Tetragram יהוה, and of Adam and Eve, it will suffice to remind the reader of the following verses in *Genesis*, with their right meaning inserted in brackets.

1. "So God [Elohim] created man in his [their] own image . . . male and female created he them [him]"—(ch. i, 27).

2. "Male and female created he them [him] . . . and called *their* [his] name ADAM"—(v, 2).

When the ternary is taken in the beginning of the Tetragram, it expresses the divine creation *spiritually, i.e.,* without any carnal sin: taken at its opposite end it expresses the latter; it is feminine. The name of Eve is composed of three letters, that of the primitive or heavenly

Adam is written with one letter, Jod or Yod; therefore it must not be read Jehovah, but *Ieva*, or Eve. The Adam of the first chapter is the spiritual, therefore pure, androgyne, Adam-Kadmon. When woman issues from the left rib of the second Adam (of dust), the pure *Virgo* is separated, and, falling "into generation," or the downward cycle, becomes *Scorpio*,* emblem of sin and matter. While the ascending cycle points at the purely spiritual races, or the ten prediluvian patriarchs, the Prajâpatis and Sephîrôth † are led on by the creative Deity itself, who is Adam-Kadmon or Yod-'heva. [Spiritually], the lower one [Jehovah] is that of the terrestrial races, led on by Enoch or *Libra*, the *seventh;* who, because he is half-divine, half-terrestrial, is said to have been taken by God alive. Enoch, Hermes and Libra are one.[62] All are the scales of universal harmony; justice and equilibrium are placed at the central point of the Zodiac. The grand circle of the heavens, so well discoursed upon by Plato in his *Timaeus*,‡ symbolizes the unknown as a unity; and the smaller circles which form the cross, by their division on the plane of the Zodiacal ring — typify, at the point of their intersection, life. The centripetal and centrifugal forces, as symbols of Good and Evil, Spirit and Matter, Life and Death, are also those of the Creator and the Destroyer—Adam and Eve, or God and the Devil, as they say in common parlance. In the subjective, as well as in the objective worlds, they are the two powers, which through their eternal conflict keep the universe of spirit and matter in harmony. They force the planets to pursue their paths, and keep them in their elliptical orbits, thus tracing the astronomical cross in their revolution through the Zodiac. In their conflict the centripetal force, were it to prevail, would drive the planets and living souls into the sun, type of the invisible Spiritual Sun, the Paramâtman or great universal Soul, their parent; while the centrifugal force would chase both planets and *souls* into the dreary space, far from the luminary of the objective universe, away from the spiritual realm of salvation and eternal life, and into the chaos of final cosmic destruction, and individual annihilation. But the *balance* is there, ever sensitive at the intersection point. It regulates the action of the two combatants, and the combined effort of both causes planets and "living souls" to pursue a double diagonal line in their revolution through Zodiac and Life; and thus preserving strict harmony, in visible and invisible heaven and earth, the forced unity of the two reconciles spirit and matter, and Enoch is

---

* Scorpio is the astrological sign of the organs of reproduction.

† The patriarchs are all convertible in their numbers as well as interchangeable. According to what they relate, they become ten, five, seven, twelve, and even fourteen. The whole system is so complicated that it is an utter impossibility in a work like this to do more than hint at certain matters.

‡ [34 *et seq.*]

said to stand a "Metatron" before God. Reckoning from him down to Noah and his three sons, each represents a new "world" (*i.e.*, our earth, the seventh)* which after every period of geological transformation gives birth to another and distinct race of men and beings.

Cain leads the ascending line, or Macrocosm, for he is the Son of the "Lord," not of Adam (*Genesis* vi, 1). The "Lord" is Adam-Kadmon, Cain, the Son of sinful thought, not the progeny of flesh and blood. Seth on the other hand is the leader of the races of earth, for he is the Son of Adam, and begotten "in his own likeness, after his image" (*Genesis* v, 3). Cain is *Kenu*, Assyrian, and means eldest, while the Hebrew word קין means a smith, an artificer.

Our science shows that the globe has passed through five distinct geological phases, each characterized by a different stratum, and these are in reverse order, beginning with the last: 1. The Quaternary period, in which man appears as a certainty; 2. The Tertiary period, in which he *may have* appeared; 3. The Secondary period, that of gigantic saurians, the megalosaurus, ichthyosaurus and plesiosaurus — *no vestige of man;* 4. The Palaeozoic period, that of gigantic crustacea; 5 (or first). The Azoic period, during which science asserts organic life had not yet appeared.

And is there no possibility that there was a period, or several periods, when man *existed,* and yet was not an organic being — therefore could not have left any vestige of himself for exact science? *Spirit* leaves no skeletons or fossils behind, and yet few are the men on earth who doubt that man can live both objectively and subjectively. At all events, the theology of the Brahmans, hoary with antiquity, which divides the formative periods of the earth into four ages and places between each of these a lapse of 1,728,000 years, agrees far more with official science and modern discovery than the absurd chronological notions promulgated by the Councils of Nicæa and Trent.

The names of the patriarchs were not Hebrew, though they may

---

* See Vol. I of the present work, p. 32. Alone, the Hindu calculation by the Zodiac can give a key to the Hebrew chronologies and the ages of the patriarchs. If we bear in mind that, according to the former astronomical and chronological calculations, out of the fourteen manvantaras (or divine ages), each of which, composed of *twelve* thousand years of the devas, multiplied by seventy-one, forms *one period* of creation — not quite *seven* are yet passed, the Hebrew calculation will become more clear. To help, as much as possible, those who will be sure to get a good deal bewildered in this calculation, we will remind the reader that the Zodiac is divided into 360 degrees, and every sign into thirty degrees; that in the Samaritan *Bible the age of Enoch is fixed at* 360 *years;* that in *Manu*, the divisions of time are given thus: "The day and the night are composed of thirty *Muhurtas*. A *muhurta* contains thirty *kalâs*. A month [of the mortals is of thirty days, but it] is but *one* day and a night of the Pitṛis. . . . A year [of the mortals] is one day and a night of the Devas." [*Manu*, I, 64-67.]

have been Hebraized later; they are evidently of Assyrian or Âryan origin.

Thus *Adam,* for instance, stands in the explained *Kabala* as a convertible term, and applies nearly to every other patriarch, as every one of the Sephîrôth to each Sephîrâh, and *vice versa.* Adam, Cain and Abel form the first *triad* of the twelve. They correspond in the Sephîrôthal tree to the Crown, Wisdom and Intelligence; and in astrology to the three trigons — the fiery, the earthy and the airy; which fact, were we allowed to devote more space than we have to its elucidation, would perhaps show that astrology deserves the name of science as well as any other. Adam (Kadmon) or Aries (ram) is identical with the Egyptian ram-headed god Amun, fabricating man on the potter's wheel. His duplication, therefore — or the Adam of dust — is also Aries, Amon, when standing at the head of his generations, for he fabricates mortals also in "his own likeness." In astrology the planet Jupiter is connected with the "first house" (Aries). The color of Jupiter, as seen in the "stages of the seven spheres," on the tower of Borsippa, or Birs Nimrud, was *red;** and in Hebrew Adam, אדם, means "red" as well as "man." The Hindu god Agni, who presides at the sign of Pisces, next to that of Aries in their relation to the twelve months ((February and March),† is painted of a deep red color, with *two* faces (male and female), *three* legs, and *seven* arms; the whole forming the number twelve. So, also, Noah (Pisces), who appears in the generations as the twelfth patriarch, counting Cain and Abel, is Adam again under another name, for he is the forefather of a new race of mankind; and with his "three sons," one bad, one good, and one partaking of both qualities, is the terrestrial reflection of the super-terrestrial Adam and his three sons. Agni is represented mounted on a ram, with a tiara surmounted by a cross. ‡

Kain, presiding over the Taurus (Bull) of the Zodiac, is also very suggestive. Taurus belongs to the earthy trigon, and in connection with this sign it will not be amiss to remind the student of an allegory from the Persian *Avesta.* The story goes that Ormazd produced a being — source and type of all the universàl beings — called LIFE, or Bull in the *Zend.* Ahriman (Cain) kills this being (Abel), from the seed of which

---

\* See H. C. Rawlinson's "Diagrams" ["On the Birs Nimrud, etc.," in *Journal of the Royal Asiatic Society of Great Britain and Ireland,* Vol. XVIII, 1861, pp. 17-19.]

† In the Brahmanical Zodiac the signs are all presided over by, and dedicated to, one of the twelve great gods. So: 1. Mesha (Aries) is dedicated to Varuṇa; 2. Vṛisha (Taurus), to Yama; 3. Mithuna (Gemini), to Pâvana; 4. Karkaṭaka (Cancer), to Sûrya; 5. Siṇha (Leo), to Soma; 6. Kanyâ (Virgo), to Kârttikeya; 7. Tulâ (Libra), to Kuvera; 8. Vṛiśchika (Scorpio), to Kâma; 9. Dhanu (Sagittarius), to Ganeśa; 10. Makara (Capricornus), to Pulaha; 11. Kumbha (Aquarius), to Indra; and 12. Mîna (Pisces), to Agni.

‡ E. Moor, *The Hindoo Pantheon,* pp. 295-302, and pl. 80.

(Seth) new beings are produced.* Abel, in Assyrian, means *son*, but in Hebrew, הבל, means something ephemeral, not long-lived, *valueless*, and also a "Pagan idol," † as Kain means a *Hermaic statue* (a pillar, the symbol of generation). Likewise, Abel is the female counterpart of Cain (male), for they are twins and probably androgynous; the latter answering to Wisdom, the former to Intelligence.

So with all other patriarchs. Enosh, אנוש, is *Homo* again — a man, or the same Adam, and Enoch in the bargain; and קינן, *Kain-an*, is identical with Cain. Seth, שת, is Teth, or Thoth, or Hermes; and this is the reason, no doubt, why Josephus,‡ shows Seth so proficient in astrology, geometry, and other occult sciences. Foreseeing the flood, he says, he engraved the fundamental principles of his art on two pillars of brick and stone, the latter of which "he saw himself [Josephus] *to remain in Syria in his own time*." Thus is it that Seth is identified also with Enoch, to whom kabalists and Masons attribute the same feat; and, at the same time, with Hermes, or Kadmus again, for Enoch is identical with the former; חנוך, He-NOCH, means a teacher, an initiator, or an initiate; in Grecian mythology, Inachus. We have seen the part he is made to play in the Zodiac.

Mahalalel, if we divide the word and write מחלה, *ma-ha-lah,* means tender, merciful; and therefore is he made to correspond with the fourth Sephîrâh, *Love* or *Mercy*, emanated from the first triad.‡ *Irad*, ירד, or *Iared*, is (minus the vowels) precisely the same. If from the verb ירד, it means *descent*; if from ארד, *arad*, it means offspring, and thus corresponds perfectly with the kabalistic emanations.

*Lamech,* למך, is not Hebrew, but Greek. Lam-ach means Lam — the father, and Olam-Ach is the father of the age; or the father of him (Noah) who inaugurates a new era or period of creation after the *pralaya* of the deluge; Noah being the symbol of a new world, the Kingdom (Malkhuth) of the Sephîrôth; hence his father, corresponding to the ninth Sephîrôth, is the Foundation. § Furthermore, both father and son answer to Aquarius and Pisces in the Zodiac; and thus the former belonging to the airy and the latter to the watery trigons, they close the list of the Biblical myths.

But if, as we see, every patriarch represents, in one sense, like each of the Prajâpatis, a new race of antediluvian human beings; and if, as it may as easily be proved, they are the copies of the Babylonian *Saros*,

---

* [Cf. Haug, *Essays on the Sacred Language . . . of the Parsees,* 1878, p. 147, note.]
† Apollo was also *Abelius,* or Bel.
‡ [*Antiquities*, I, ii, 3.]
§ Halal is a name of Apollo. The name of Ma*halal-Eliel* would then be the Autumnal sun, of July, and this patriarch presides over *Leo* (July), the zodiacal sign.
‖ See description of the Sephîrôth in Chapter V.

or ages, the latter themselves copies of the Hindu ten dynasties of the "Lords of beings," * yet, however we may regard them, they are among the profoundest allegories ever conceived by philosophical minds.

In the *Nychthêmeron*,† the evolution of the universe and its successive periods of formation, together with the gradual development of the human races, are illustrated as fully as possible in the twelve "hours" into which the allegory is divided. Each "hour" typifies the evolution of a new man, and in its turn is divided into four quarters or ages. This work shows how thoroughly was the ancient philosophy imbued with the doctrines of the early Âryans, who were the first to divide the life on our planet into four ages. If one would trace this doctrine from its source in the night of the traditional period down to the Seer of Patmos, he need not go astray among the religious systems of all nations. The Babylonians he would find teaching that in four different periods four Oannes (or suns) appeared; the Hindus asserting their four Yugas; the Greeks, Romans, and others firmly believing in the golden, silver, brazen, and iron ages, each of the epochs being heralded by the appearance of a savior. The four Buddhas of the Hindus and the three prophets of the Zoroastrians — Oshedâr-Bâmî, Oshedâr-Mâh, and Saoshyant — preceded by Zarathushtra, are the types of these ages. ‡

In the *Bible*, the very opening tells us that *before the sons of God saw the daughters of men*, the latter lived from 365 to 969 years. But when the "Lord God" saw the iniquities of mankind, He concluded to allow them at most 120 years of life (*Genesis* vi, 3). To account for such a violent oscillation in the human mortality table is only possible by tracing this decision of the "Lord God" to its origin. Such incongruities as we meet at every step in the *Bible* can be only attributed to the fact that the book of *Genesis* and the other books of *Moses* were tampered with and remodelled by more than one author; and that in their original state they were with the exception of the external form of the allegories, faithful copies from the Hindu sacred books. In *Manu*, Book I, 81 *et seq.*, we find the following:

---

\* How servile was this Chaldean *copy* may be seen in comparing the Hindu chronology with that of the Babylonians. According to *Manu*, the antediluvian dynasties of the Prajâpatis reigned 4,320,000 human years, a whole divine age of the devas in short, or that length of time which invariably occurs between life on earth and the dissolution of that life, or pralaya. The Chaldeans, in their turn, give precisely the same figures, minus *one* cipher, to wit: they make their 120 saroses yield a total of 432,000 years.

† Éliphas Lévi gives it both in the Greek and Hebrew versions, but so condensed and arbitrarily that it is impossible for one who knows less than himself to understand him. [*Dogme et rituel*, etc., II, suppl.]

‡ [Cf. Spiegel, *Zend-Avesta*, I, pp. 32 *et seq.*]

"In the first age, neither sickness nor suffering were known. Men lived four centuries."

This was in the Krita or Satya-yuga.

"The Krita-yuga is the type of justice. The *bull* which stands firm on its four legs is its image; man adheres to truth, and evil does not as yet direct his actions." * But in each of the following ages primitive human life loses one-fourth of its duration, that is to say, in Tretâ-yuga man lives 300, in Dvâpara-yuga 200, and in Kali-yuga, or our own age, but 100 years generally at the most. Noah, son of Lamech — Olam-*Ach*, or father of the age — is the distorted copy of Manu, son of Svayambhû, and the six Manus or Rishis issued from the Hindu "first man" are the originals of Terah, Abraham, Isaac, Jacob, Joseph and Moses, the Hebrew sages, who beginning with Terah were all alleged to have been astrologers, alchemists, inspired prophets and soothsayers; or in a more profane but plainer language — magicians.

If we consult the Talmudistic *Mishnah* we find therein the first emanated divine couple, the androgyne Demiurge Ḥokhmah (or Ḥokhma-Akhamôth) and *Binah* building themselves a house with *seven* pillars. They are the architects of God — Wisdom and Intelligence — and His "compass and square." The seven columns are the future *seven* worlds, or the typical *seven* primordial "days" of creation.

"Ḥokhmah immolates her victims." These victims are the numberless forces of nature which must "die" (expend themselves) *in order that they should live*; when one force dies out, it is but to give birth to another force, its progeny. It dies but lives in its children, and resuscitates at every *seventh* generation. The servants of Ḥokhmah, or wisdom, are the souls of ha-Adam, for in him are all the souls of Israel.

There are *twelve* hours in the day, says the *Mishnah*, and it is during these hours that is accomplished the creation of man. Would this be comprehensible unless we had Manu to teach us that this "day" embraces the four ages of the world and has a duration of *twelve* thousand divine years of the Devas?

"The Creators (Elohim) outline in the second" hour "the shape of a more corporeal form of man. They separate it into two and prepare the sexes to become distinct from each other. Such is the way the Elohim proceeded in reference to every created thing."† "Every fish, fowl, plant, beast and man was androgyne at the first hour."

Says the commentator, the great Rabbi Shimon:

---

* See Rabbi Shimon's dissertation on the primitive Man-Bull and the horns. *Zohar.*
† "The *Nychthêmeron* of the Hebrews"; see É. Lévi, *Dogme et rituel*, etc., II, suppl.

"O, companions, companions, man as emanation was both man and woman; as well on the side of the FATHER as on the side of the MOTHER. And this is the sense of the words, and Elohim spoke, Let there be Light and it was Light! . . . And this is the 'twofold man'!" *

A spiritual woman was necessary as a contrast for the spiritual man. Harmony is the universal law. In Taylor's translation, Plato's discourse upon creation is rendered so as to make him say of this universe that "He caused it to move with a circular revolution . . . When, therefore, that God who is a perpetual reasoning divinity cogitated about the *God* [man] *who was destined to subsist at some certain period of time,* he produced his body smooth and equable; and every way from the middle even and whole, and perfect from the composition of perfect bodies. This perfect circle of the created god, *He decussated in the form of the letter X.*" †

The italics of both these sentences from *Timaeus* belong to Dr. Lundy, the author of that remarkable work mentioned once before, *Monumental Christianity;*‡ and attention is drawn to the words of the Greek philosopher, with the evident purpose of giving them the prophetic character which Justin Martyr applied to the same, when accusing Plato of having borrowed his "physiological discussion in the *Timaeus* . . . concerning the Son of God placed crosswise in the universe," from Moses and his serpent of brass.§ The learned author seems to fully accord an unpremeditated prophecy to these words; although he does not tell us whether he believes that like Plato's created God, Jesus was originally a sphere "smooth and equable, and every way from the middle even and whole." Even if Justin Martyr were excusable for his perversion of Plato, Dr. Lundy ought to know that the day for that sort of casuistry is long gone by. What the philosopher meant was *man*, who before being encased in matter had no use for limbs, but was a pure spiritual entity. Hence if the Deity, his universe, and the stellar bodies are to be conceived as spheroidal, this shape would be archetypal man's. As his enveloping shell grew heavier, there came the necessity for limbs, and the limbs sprouted. If we fancy a man with arms and legs naturally extended at the same angle, by backing him against the circle that symbolizes his prior shape as a spirit, we would have the very figure described by Plato—the X cross within the circle.

All the legends of the creation, the fall of man, and the resultant deluge, belong to universal history, and are no more the property of the Israelites than that of any other nation. What specially belongs to them (kabalists excepted) are the disfigured details of every tradition. The *Genesis* of Enoch is by far anterior to the books of Moses, ‖ and

---

* *Auszüge aus dem Buche Sohar*, Berlin, 1857, pp. 14-15.
† [Thos. Taylor, *The Works of Plato*, Vol. II, pp. 483, 487.]
‡ [Page 8.]
§ [*First Apology*, cap. lx.]
‖ Such is the opinion of the erudite Dr. S. Jost and Donaldson. "The collection of the Old Testament writings, as we now possess them, appears to have been concluded

Guillaume Postel has presented it to the world, explaining the allegories as far as he dared; but the groundwork is still unexposed. For the Jews, the *Book of Enoch* is as canonical as the Mosaic books; and if the Christians accepted the latter as an authority, we do not see why they should reject the former as an apocrypha. No more can the age of one than that of the other be determined with anything like certainty. At the time of the separation, the Samaritans recognized only the books of Moses and that of Joshua, says Dr. Jost.* In 168 B.C., Jerusalem had its temple plundered, and all the sacred books were destroyed;† therefore, the few MSS. that remained were to be found only among the "teachers of tradition." The kabalistic Tannaim, and their initiates and prophets had always practised its teachings in common with the Canaanites, the Hamites, Midianites, Chaldeans, and all other nations. The story of Daniel is a proof of it.

There was a sort of Brotherhood or Freemasonry among the kabalists scattered all over the world, since the memory of man; and, like some societies of the mediaeval Masonry of Europe, they called themselves *Companions* ‡ and *Innocents*.§ It is a belief (founded on knowledge) among the kabalists, that, no more than the Hermetic rolls, are the genuine sacred books of the seventy-two elders—books which contained the *"Ancient Word"* —lost, but that they have all been preserved from the remotest times among secret communities. Emanuel Swedenborg says as much, and his words are based, he says, on the information he had from certain *spirits*, who assured him that "they performed their worship according to this Ancient Word." "Seek for it in China," adds the great seer, "peradventure you may find it in Great Tartary!" Other students of occult sciences have had more than the word of "certain spirits" to rely upon in this special case—they have seen the books.

We must choose therefore perforce between two methods — either to accept the *Bible* exoterically or esoterically. Against the former we have the following facts: That, after the first copy of the *Book of God* has been edited and launched on the world by Hilkiah, this copy disappears, and Ezra has to make a *new Bible*, which Judas Maccabeus finishes; that when it was copied from the horned letters into square letters, it was corrupted beyond recognition; that the *Masorah* completed the work of destruction; that, finally, we have a text, not 900 years old, abounding

---

about 150 years B.C. The Jews now sought out the books which had been scattered in war, and brought them into one collection" (Ghillany, *Die Menschenopfer der alten Hebräer*, p. 1).

\* I. M. Jost, *The Israelite Indeed*, I, p. 51.
† Josephus, *Antiquities*, XII, v, 4.
‡ A. Franck, *La Kabbale*, 1843, p. 131.
§ Gaffarel, Introduction to *Book of Enoch*.

with omissions, interpolations, and premeditated perversions; and that, consequently, as this Masoretic Hebrew text has fossilized its mistakes, and the key to the "Word of God" is lost, no one has a right to enforce upon so-called "Christians" the divagations of a series of hallucinated and, perhaps, spurious prophets, under the unwarranted and untenable assumption that the author of it was the "Holy Ghost" in *propria persona*.

Hence, we reject this pretended monotheistic Scripture, made up just when the priests of Jerusalem found their political profit in violently breaking off all connection with the Gentiles. It is at this moment only that we find them persecuting kabalists, and banning the "old wisdom" of both Pagans and Jews. *The real Hebrew Bible was a secret volume, unknown to the masses,* and even the Samaritan *Pentateuch* is far more ancient than the *Septuagint*. As for the former, the Fathers of the Church never even heard of it. We prefer decidedly to take the word of Swedenborg that the "Ancient Word" is *somewhere in China or the Great Tartary*. The more so, as the Swedish seer is declared, at least by one clergyman, namely, the Reverend Dr. R. L. Tafel of London, to have been in a state of "inspiration from God," while writing his theological works. He is given even the superiority over the penmen of the *Bible*, for, while the latter had the words spoken to them in their ears, Swedenborg was made to understand them rationally and was, therefore, *internally* and not externally illuminated. "When," says the reverend author, "a conscientious member of the New Church hears any charges made against the divinity and the infallibility of either the soul or the body of the doctrines of the New Jerusalem, he must at once place himself on the unequivocal declaration made in those doctrines, that the Lord has effected His second coming in and by means of those writings which were published by Emanuel Swedenborg, as His servant, and that, therefore, those charges are not and cannot be true." And if it is "the Lord" that spoke through Swedenborg, then there is a hope for us that at least one divine will corroborate our assertions, that the ancient "word of God" is nowhere but in the heathen countries, especially *Buddhistic Tartary, Thibet and China!*

"The primitive history of Greece is the primitive history of India," exclaims Pococke in his *India in Greece* (p. 30). In view of subsequent fruits of critical research, we may paraphrase the sentence and say: "The primitive history of Judaea is a distortion of Indian fable engrafted on that of Egypt." Many scientists, encountering stubborn facts, and being reluctant to contrast the narratives of the "divine" revelation with those of the Brahmanical books, merely present them to the reading public. Meanwhile they limit their conclusions to criticisms and contradictions of each other. So Max Müller opposes the theories of Spiegel, and someone else; and Professor Whitney those of the Oxford Orientalist; and Dr. Haug made onslaughts on Spiegel, while Dr. Spiegel chose some other victim; and now even the time-honored Akkadians and Turanians have had their day of glory. The *Proto-Kasdeans, Kasdeo-Scyths, Sumerians,* and what not, have to make room for some other fictions. Alas for the Akkads! Halévy, the Assyriologist, attacks the Akkado-Sumerian language of old Babylon,* and Chabas, the Egyptologist, not content with dethroning the Turanian speech, which has rendered such eminent services to Orientalists when perplexed, calls the venerable parent of the Akkadians — François Lenormant — himself, a charlatan. Profiting by the learned turmoil, the Christian clergy take heart for their fantastic theology on the ground that when the jury disagree there is a gain of time at least for the indicted party. And thus is overlooked the vital question whether Christendom would not be the better for adopting Christism in place of Christianity, with its *Bible,* its vicarious atonement and its Devil. But to so important a personage as the latter, we could not do less than devote a special chapter.

---

\* [*Mélanges d'épigraphie et d'archéologie sémitique,* Paris, 1874.]

## CHAPTER X

"Get thee behind me, SATAN" (Jesus to Peter).     —*Matt.* xvi, 23.

"And such a deal of skimble-skamble stuff
As puts me from my faith. I'll tell thee what;
He held me last night at least nine hours
In reckoning up the several devils' names . . ."
—*King Henry IV*, Part I, Act iii, Sc. 1, lines 153-56.

«La force terrible et juste qui tue éternellement les avortons a été nommée par les Hébreux Samaël; par les Orientaux, Satan; et par les Latins, Lucifer. Le Lucifer de la Cabale n'est pas un ange maudit et foudroyé; c'est l'ange qui éclaire et qui régénère en brûlant». —ÉLIPHAS LÉVI, *Dogme et Rituel*, etc., II, Introd.

"Bad as he is, the Devil may be abus'd,
Be falsely charg'd, and ceaselessly accus'd,
When Men, unwilling to be blam'd alone,
Shift off those Crimes on Him which are their Own."
—D. DEFOE, *The Political History of the Devil*, London, 1726.

SEVERAL years ago, a distinguished writer and persecuted kabalist suggested a creed for the Protestant and Roman Catholic bodies, which may be thus formulated:

*Protevangelium.*

"I believe in the Devil, the Father Almighty of Evil, the Destroyer of all things, Perturbator of Heaven and Earth;
And in Anti-Christ, his only Son, our Persecutor,
Who was conceived of the Evil Spirit;
Born of a sacrilegious, foolish Virgin;
Was glorified by mankind, reigned over them,
And ascended to the throne of Almighty God,
From which he crowds Him aside, and from which he insults the living and the dead;
I believe in the Spirit of Evil;
The Synagogue of Satan;
The coalition of the wicked;
The perdition of the body;
And the Death and Hell everlasting. *Amen.*"

Does this offend? Does it seem extravagant, cruel, blasphemous? Listen: In the city of New York, on the ninth day of April, 1877 — that is to say, in the last quarter of what is proudly styled the century of discovery and the age of illumination — the following scandalous ideas were broached. We quote from the report in the *Sun* of the following morning:

"The Baptist preachers met yesterday in the Mariners' Chapel, in Oliver Street. Several foreign missionaries were present. The Rev. John W. Sarles of Brooklyn read an essay, in which he maintained the proposition *that all adult heathen, dying without the knowledge of the Gospel, are damned eternally.* Otherwise, the reverend essayist argued, the Gospel is a curse instead of a blessing, the men who crucified Christ served him right, and the whole structure of revealed religion tumbles to the ground.

"Brother Stoddard, a missionary from India, endorsed the views of the Brooklyn pastor. The Hindus were great sinners. One day, after he had preached in the market place, a Brahman got up and said: 'We Hindus beat the world in lying, but this man beats us. How can he say that God loves us? Look at the poisonous serpents, tigers, lions, and all kinds of dangerous animals around us. If God loves us, why doesn't He take them away?'

"The Rev. Mr. Pixley, of Hamilton, N.Y., heartily subscribed to the doctrine of Brother Sarles' essay, and asked for $5,000 to fit out young men for the ministry."

And these men — we will not say teach the doctrine of Jesus, for that would be to insult his memory, but — are *paid* to teach his doctrine! Can we wonder that intelligent persons prefer annihilation to a faith encumbered by such a monstrous doctrine? We doubt whether any respectable Brahman would have confessed to the vice of lying — an art cultivated only in those portions of British India where the most Christians are found.*

---

* So firmly established seems to have been the reputation of the Brahmans and Buddhists for the highest morality, and that since time immemorial, that we find Colonel Henry Yule, in his admirable edition of "Marco Polo," giving the following testimony: "The high virtues ascribed to the Brahmans and Indian merchants were perhaps in part matter of tradition . . . but the eulogy is so constant among mediaeval travellers *that it must have had a solid foundation.* In fact it would not be difficult to trace a chain of similar testimony from ancient times down to our own. Arrian says no Indian was ever accused of falsehood. Hiuen Tsang ascribes to the people of India eminent uprightness, honesty, and disinterestedness. Friar Jordanus (*circa* 1330) says the people of Lesser India (Sind and Western India) were true in speech and eminent in justice; and we may also refer to the high character given to the Hindus by Abul Fazl. But *after 150 years of European trade indeed we find a sad deterioration* . . . Yet Pallas, in the last century, noticing the Banyan colony at Astrakhan, says its members were notable for an upright dealing that made them greatly preferable to Armenians. And that wise and admirable public servant, the late Sir William Sleeman, in our own time, has said that he knew no class of men in the world more strictly honorable than the mercantile classes of India." [Col. H. Yule, *The Book of Ser Marco Polo,* Vol. II, p. 354; 2nd ed., 1875.]

The sad examples of the rapid demoralization of *savage* American Indians, as soon as they are made to live in a close proximity with *Christian* officials and missionaries, are familiar in our modern days.

But we challenge any honest man in the wide world to say whether he thinks the Brahman was far from the truth in saying of the missionary Stoddard, "this man beats us all" in lying. What else would he say, if the latter preached to them the doctrine of *eternal damnation*, because, indeed, they had passed their lives without reading a Jewish book of which they never heard, or asked salvation of a Christ whose existence they never suspected! But Baptist clergymen who need a few thousand dollars must devise terrifying sensations to fire the congregational heart.

We abstain, as a rule, from giving our own experience when we can call acceptable witnesses, and so, upon reading missionary Stoddard's outrageous remarks, we requested our acquaintance, Mr. William L. D. O'Grady,* to give a fair opinion upon the missionaries. This gentleman's father and grandfather were British army officers, and he himself was born in India, and enjoyed lifelong opportunities to learn what the general opinion among the English is of these religious propagandists. Following is his communication in reply to our letter:

"You ask me for my opinion of the Christian missionaries in India. In all the years I spent there, I never spoke to a single missionary. They were not in society, and, from what I heard of their proceedings and could see for myself, I don't wonder at it. *Their influence on the natives is bad.* Their converts are worthless, and, as a rule, of the lowest class; *nor do they improve by conversion.* No respectable family will employ Christian servants. They lie, they steal, they are unclean — and dirt is certainly not a Hindu vice; they drink — and no decent native of any other belief ever touches intoxicating liquor; they are outcasts from their own people and utterly despicable. Their new teachers set them a poor example of consistency. While holding forth to the Pariah that God makes no distinction of persons, they boast intolerably over the stray Brahmans, who, very much 'off color,' occasionally, at long intervals, fall into the clutches of these hypocrites.

"The missionaries get very small salaries, as publicly stated in the proceedings of the societies that employ them, but, in some unaccountable way, manage to live as well as officials with ten times their income. When they come home to recover their health, shattered, as they say, by their arduous labors — which they seem to be able to afford to do quite frequently, when supposed richer people cannot — they tell childish stories on platforms, exhibit idols as procured with infinite difficulty, which is quite absurd, and give an account of their imaginary hardships which is perfectly harrowing but untrue from beginning to end. I lived some years in India myself, and nearly all my blood-relations have passed or will pass the best years of their lives there. I know hundreds of British officials, and I never heard from one of them a single word in favor of the missionaries. Natives of any position look on them with the supremest contempt, although suffering chronic exasperation from their arrogant aggressiveness; and the British Government, which continues endowments to Pagodas, granted by the East

---

* At the present moment Mr. O'Grady is Editor of *The American Builder*, of New York, and is well known for its interesting letters, "Indian Sketches; or, Rubs of a Rolling Stone," which he contributed under the pseudonym of *Hadji Nicka Bauker Khan*, to the Boston *Commercial Bulletin*.

India Company, and which supports unsectarian education, gives them no countenance whatever. Protected from personal violence, they yelp and bark at natives and Europeans alike, after the fashion of ill-conditioned curs. Often recruited from the poorest specimens of theological fanaticism, they are regarded on all sides as mischievous. Their rabid, reckless, vulgar, and offensive propagandism caused the great Mutiny of 1857. They are noisome humbugs.

"WM. L. D. O'GRADY.

"NEW YORK, June 12, 1877."

The new creed therefore, with which we opened this chapter, coarse as it may sound, embodies the very essence of the belief of the Church as inculcated by her missionaries. It is regarded as less impious, less infidel, to doubt the personal existence of the Holy Ghost, or the equal Godhead of Jesus, than to question the personality of the Devil. But a summary of *Koheleth* is well-nigh forgotten.* Who ever quotes the golden words of the prophet Micah,† or seems to care for the exposition of the Law, as given by Jesus himself? ‡ The "bull's eye" in the target of modern Christianity is in the simple phrase to "fear the Devil."

The Catholic clergy and some of the lay champions of the Roman Church fight still more for the existence of Satan and his imps. If des Mousseaux maintains the objective reality of spiritual phenomena with such an unrelenting ardor, it is because, in his opinion, the latter are the most direct evidence of the Devil at work. The Chevalier is more Catholic than the Pope; and his logic and deductions from never-to-be and non-established premises are unique, and prove once more that the creed offered by us is the one which expresses the Catholic belief most eloquently.

"If magic," he says, "were but a chimera, we would have to bid an eternal farewell to all the rebellious angels, now troubling the world; for thus, we would have *no more demons down here. And if we lost our demons, we would* LOSE OUR SAVIOR *likewise.* For, from whom did that Redeemer redeem us? Hence, *there would be no more Christianity!!"* §

Oh, Holy Father of Evil; Sainted Satan! We pray thee do not abandon such pious Christians as the Chevalier des Mousseaux and some Baptist clergymen!!

---

* *Ecclesiastes* xii, 13; see Lange, *Commentary on the Old Testament*, ed. by Tayler Lewis, Edinb., 1870, p. 199:
"The great conclusion hear:
Fear God and His commandments keep, for this is all of man."
† See *Micah* vi, 6-8, Noyes' Translation.
‡ *Matthew* xxii, 37-40.
§ *Les Hauts Phénomènes de la magie*, preface, p. xii.

## A PERSONAL DEVIL INVOLVES POLYTHEISM

For our part, we would rather remember the wise words of J. C. Colquhoun, who says that "those persons who, in modern times, adopt the doctrine of the Devil in its strictly literal and personal application, do not appear to be aware that they are in reality polytheists, heathens, idolaters." *

Seeking supremacy in everything over the ancient creeds, the Christians claim the discovery of the Devil officially recognized by the Church. Jesus was the first to use the word "legion" when speaking of them; and it is on this ground that des Mousseaux thus defends his position in one of his demonological works. "Later," he says, "when the synagogue *expired*, depositing its inheritance in the hands of Christ, were born into the world and *shone* the Fathers of the Church, who have been accused by certain persons of a rare and precious ignorance, of having borrowed their ideas as to the spirits of darkness from the theurgists." †

Three deliberate, palpable, and easily-refuted errors — not to use a harsher word — occur in these few lines. In the first place, the synagogue, far from having *expired*, is flourishing at the present day in nearly every town of Europe, America and Asia; and of all churches in Christian cities, it is the most firmly established, as well as the best behaved. Further — while no one will deny that many Christian Fathers were born into the world (always, of course, excepting the twelve fictitious Bishops of Rome, who were never born at all), every person who will take the trouble to read the works of the Platonists of the old Academy, who were theurgists before Iamblichus, will recognize therein the origin of Christian Demonology as well as the Angelology, the allegorical meaning of which was completely distorted by the Fathers. Then it could hardly be admitted that the said Fathers ever *shone*, except, perhaps, in the refulgence of their extreme ignorance. The Reverend Dr. Shuckford, who passed the better part of his life trying to reconcile their contradictions and absurdities, was finally driven to abandon the whole thing in despair. The ignorance of the champions of Plato must indeed appear rare and precious by comparison with the fathomless profundity of Augustine, "the giant of learning and erudition," who scouted the sphericity of the earth, for, if true, it would prevent the antipodes from seeing the Lord Christ when he descended from heaven at the second advent; or, of Lactantius, who rejects with pious horror Pliny's identical theory, on the remarkable ground that it would make the trees at the other side of the earth grow and the men walk with their heads downward; ‡ or, again, of Cosmas Indicopleustes, whose orthodox system of geography is embalmed in his *Christian Topography*; or, finally, of

---

* *An History of Magic, Witchcraft, and Animal Magnetism*, 1851, Vol. I, ch. iii, p. 21.
† [*La Magie au XIXme siècle*, p. 99.]
‡ [*Divine Instit.*, III, xxiv.]

Bede, who assured the world that the heaven "is tempered with glacial waters, lest it should be set on fire"*—a benign dispensation of Providence, most likely to prevent the radiance of their learning from setting the sky ablaze!

Be this as it may, these resplendent Fathers certainly did borrow their notions of the "spirits of darkness" from the Jewish kabalists and Pagan theurgists, with the difference, however, that they disfigured and outdid in absurdity all that the wildest fancy of the Hindu, Greek and Roman rabble had ever created. There is not a *daêva* in the Persian Pandaimonion half so preposterous, as a conception, as des Mousseaux's *Incubus* revamped from Augustine. Typhon, symbolized as an *ass*, appears a philosopher in comparison with the devil caught by the Normandy peasant in a keyhole; and it is certainly not Ahriman or the Hindu Vritra who would run away in rage and dismay when addressed as *St. Satan* by a native Luther.

The Devil is the patron genius of theological Christianity. So "holy and reverend is his name" in modern conception, that it may not, except occasionally from the pulpit, be uttered in ears polite. In like manner, anciently, it was not lawful to speak the sacred names or repeat the jargon of the Mysteries, except in the sacred cloister. We hardly know the names of the Samothracian gods, and cannot tell precisely the number of the Kabiri. The Egyptians considered it blasphemous to utter the title of the gods of their secret rites. Even now, the Brahman only pronounces the syllable *Om* in silent thought, and the Rabbi, the Ineffable Name, יהוה . Hence, we who exercise no such veneration, have been led into the blunders of miscalling the names of HISIR and YAVA by the mispronunciations, Osiris and Jehovah. A similar glamor bids fair, it will be perceived, to gather round the designation of the dark personage of whom we are treating; and in the familiar handling, we shall be very likely to shock the peculiar sensibilities of many who will consider a free mentioning of the Devil's names as blasphemy — the sin of sins, that "hath never forgiveness." †

Several years ago an acquaintance of the author wrote a newspaper article to demonstrate that the *diabolos* or Satan of the *New Testament* denoted the personification of an abstract idea, and not a personal being. He was answered by a clergyman, who concluded the reply with the deprecatory expression, "I fear that he has denied his Savior." In his rejoinder he pleaded, "Oh, no! we only denied the Devil." But the

---

\* See Draper's *History of the Conflict between Religion and Science*, p. 65.

† *Mark* iii, 29: "He that shall blaspheme against the Holy Ghost hath never forgiveness, but is in danger of eternal damnation" (ἁμαρτήματος, error).

clergyman failed to perceive the difference. In his conception of the matter, the denying of the personal objective existence of the Devil was itself "the sin against the Holy Ghost."

This necessary Evil, dignified by the epithet of "Father of Lies," was, according to the clergy, the founder of all the world religions of ancient time and of the heresies, or rather heterodoxies, of later periods, as well as the *deus ex machina* of modern Spiritualism. In the exceptions which we take to this notion, we protest that we do not attack true religion or sincere piety. We are only carrying on a controversy with human dogmas. Perhaps in doing this we resemble Don Quixote, because these things are only windmills. Nevertheless, let it be remembered that they have been the occasion and pretext for the slaughtering of more than fifty millions of human beings since the words were proclaimed: "LOVE YOUR ENEMIES." *

It is a late day for us to expect the Christian clergy to undo and amend their work. They have too much at stake. If the Christian Church should abandon or even modify the dogma of an anthropomorphic devil, it would be like pulling the bottom card from under a castle of cards. The structure would fall. The clergymen to whom we have alluded perceived that upon the relinquishing of Satan as a personal devil, the dogma of Jesus Christ as the second deity in their trinity must go over in the same catastrophe. Incredible, or even horrifying, as it may seem, the Roman Church bases its doctrine of the godhood of Christ entirely upon the satanism of the fallen archangel. We have the testimony of Father Ventura, who proclaims the vital importance of this dogma to the Catholics.

The Reverend Father Ventura, the illustrious ex-general of the Theatins, certifies that the Chevalier des Mousseaux, by his treatise, *Mœurs et pratiques des démons*, has deserved well of mankind, and still more of the most Holy Catholic and Apostolic Church. With this voucher, the noble Chevalier, it will be perceived, "speaks as one having authority." He asserts explicitly, that *to the Devil and his angels we are absolutely indebted for our Savior;* and that but for them *we would have no Redeemer, no Christianity.*†

Many zealous and earnest souls have revolted at the monstrous dogma of John Calvin, the popekin of Geneva, that *sin is the necessary cause of the greatest good.* It was bolstered up, nevertheless, by logic like that of des Mousseaux, and illustrated by the same dogmas. The execution of Jesus, the god-man, on the cross, was the most prodigious crime in the universe, yet it was necessary that mankind — those predestinated to ever-

---

* *Matthew* v, 44.

† Des Mousseaux, *op. cit.*, p. x.

lasting life — might be saved. D'Aubigné cites the quotation by Martin Luther from the canon, and makes him exclaim, in ecstatic rapture: *"O beata culpa, qui talem meruisti redemptorem!"* "O blessed sin, which didst merit such a Redeemer." We now perceive that the dogma which had appeared so monstrous is, after all, the doctrine of Pope, Calvin and Luther alike — that the three are one.

Mohammed and his disciples, who held Jesus in great respect as a prophet, remarks Éliphas Lévi, used to utter, when speaking of Christians, the following remarkable words: "Jesus of Nazareth was verily a true prophet of Allah and a grand man; but lo! his disciples all went insane one day, and made a god of him."

Max Müller kindly adds: "It was a mistake of the early Fathers to treat the heathen gods as demons or evil spirits, and we must take care not to commit the same error with regard to the Hindu gods." \*

But we have Satan presented to us as the prop and mainstay of sacerdotalism—an Atlas, holding the Christian heaven and cosmos upon his shoulders. If he falls, then, in their conception, all is lost, and chaos must come again.

This dogma of the Devil and redemption seems to be based upon two passages in the *New Testament*: "For this purpose the Son of God was manifested, that he might destroy the works of the devil." † "And there was war in heaven; Michael and his angels fought against the Dragon; and the Dragon fought, and his angels, and prevailed not; neither was their place found any more in heaven. And the great Dragon was cast out, that old serpent, called the Devil and Satan, which deceiveth the whole world."‡ Let us, then, explore the ancient Theogonies, in order to ascertain what was meant by these remarkable expressions.

The first inquiry is whether the term *Devil*, as here used, actually represents the malignant Deity of the Christians, or an antagonistic, blind force — the dark side of nature. By the latter we are not to understand the manifestation of any evil principle that is *malum in se*, but only the shadow of the Light, so to say. The theories of the kabalists treat of it as a force which is antagonistic, but at the same time essential to the vitality, evolving, and vigor of the good principle. Plants would perish in their first stage of existence, if they were kept exposed to a constant sunlight; the night alternating with the day is essential to their healthy growth and development. Goodness, likewise, would speedily cease to be such, were it not alternated by its opposite. In human nature, evil denotes the antagonism of matter to the spiritual, and each is accordingly purified thereby. In the cosmos, the

---

\* "Comparative Mythology," in *Chips*, etc., Vol. II, p. 76.
† *1 John* iii, 8.
‡ [*Revelation* xii, 7-9.]

equilibrium must be preserved; the operation of the two contraries produce harmony, like the centripetal and centrifugal forces, and are necessary to each other. If one is arrested, the action of the other will immediately become destructive.

The personification, denominated *Satan,* is to be contemplated from three different planes: the *Old Testament,* the Christian Fathers, and the ancient Gentile attitude. He is supposed to have been represented by the Serpent in the Garden of Eden; nevertheless, the epithet of Satan is nowhere in the Hebrew sacred writings applied to that or any other variety of ophidian. The Brazen Serpent of Moses was worshipped by the Israelites as a god,* being the symbol of Esmun-Asklepius, the Phoenician Iaô. Indeed, the character of Satan himself is introduced in the 1st book of *Chronicles* in the act of instigating King David to number the Israelitish people, an act elsewhere declared specifically to have been moved by Jehovah himself.† The inference is unavoidable that the two, Satan and Jehovah, were regarded as identical.

Another mention of Satan is found in the prophecies of *Zechariah.* This book was written at a period subsequent to the Jewish colonization of Palestine, and hence, the Asideans may fairly be supposed to have brought the personification thither from the East. It is well known that this body of sectaries were deeply imbued with the Mazdean notions; and that they represented Ahriman or Angra-mainyu by the god-names of Syria. Set or Sat-an, the god of the Hittites and Hyksôs, and Beel-Zebub the oracle-god, afterward the Grecian Apollo. The prophet began his labors in Judaea in the second year of Darius Hystaspes, the restorer of the Mazdean worship. He thus describes the encounter with Satan: "He showed me Joshua the high priest standing before the angel of the Lord, and Satan standing at his right hand to be his adversary. And the Lord said unto Satan, The Lord rebuke thee, O Satan; even the Lord that hath chosen Jerusalem rebuke thee: is not this a brand plucked out of the fire?"‡

---

* 2 *Kings* xviii, 4. It is probable that the fiery serpents or *Seraphim* mentioned in the twenty-first chapter of the book of *Numbers* were the same as the Levites, or Ophite tribe. Compare *Exodus* xxxii, 26-29 with *Numbers* xxi, 5-9. The names חוה, *Hevah*; חוי, *Hivi* or Hivite; and לוי, Levi, all signify a serpent; and it is a curious fact that the Hivites, or serpent-tribe of Palestine, like the Levites or Ophites of Israel, were ministers to the temples. The Gibeonites, whom Joshua assigned to the service of the sanctuary, were Hivites.

† 1 *Chronicles* xxi, 1: "And Satan stood up against Israel, and provoked David to number Israel." 2 *Samuel* xxiv, 1: "And again the anger of the Lord was kindled against Israel, and he moved David against them to say, Go, number Israel and Judah."

‡ *Zechariah* iii, 1, 2. A pun or play on words is noticeable; "adversary" is associated with "Satan," as if from שטן [*shatan*], to oppose.

We apprehend that this passage which we have quoted is symbolical. There are two allusions in the *New Testament* that indicate that it was so regarded. The Catholic *Epistle of Jude* refers to it in this peculiar language: "Yet Michael the archangel, when contending with the Devil, he disputed about the body of Moses, did not venture to utter to him a reviling judgment (κρίσιν ἐπενεγκεῖν βλασφημίας), but said, 'The Lord rebuke thee'." * The archangel Michael is thus mentioned as identical with the יהוה, Lord, or angel of the Lord, of the preceding quotation, and thus is shown that the Hebrew Jehovah had a twofold character, the secret and that manifested as the angel of the Lord, or Michael the archangel. A comparison between these two passages renders it plain that "the body of Moses" over which they contended was Palestine, which as "the land of the Hittites" † was the peculiar domain of Seth, their tutelar god.‡ Michael, as the champion of the Johovah-worship, contended with the Devil or Adversary, but left judgment to his superior.

Belial is not entitled to the distinction of either god or devil. The term בליעל, BELIAL, is defined in the Hebrew lexicons as meaning a destroying, waste, uselessness; or the phrase איש-בליעל AISH-BELIAL or Belial-man signifies a wasteful, useless man. If Belial must be personified to please our religious friends, we would be obliged to make him perfectly distinct from Satan, and to consider him as a sort of spiritual *Diakka*. The demonographers, however, who enumerate nine distinct orders of *daimonia*, make him chief of the third class—a set of hobgoblins, mischievous and good-for-nothing.

Asmodeus is no Jewish spirit at all, his origin being purely Persian. Bréal, the author of *Hercule et Cacus*, shows that he is the Pârsî Eshem-daêva, or *Aêshma-daêva*, the evil spirit of concupiscence, whom Max Müller tells us "is mentioned several times in the *Avesta* as one of the *devs*," § originally gods, who became evil spirits.

---

\* *Jude* 9.

† In the Assyrian Tablets, Palestine is called "the land of the Hittites"; and the Egyptian Papyri, declaring the same thing, also make Seth, the "pillar-god," their tutelar deity. [Bunsen, *Egypt's Place*, etc., Vol. III, pp. 180, 212; Vol. IV, p. 208.]

‡ *Seth, Suteh*, or Sat-an, was the god of the aboriginal nations of Syria. Plutarch [*On Isis*, etc., § 49] makes him the same as Typhon. Hence he was god of Goshen and Palestine, the countries occupied by the Israelites.

§ *Vendîdâd*, farg. x, 23: "I combat the daêva Aêshma, the very evil." The *Yaśna*, x, 18, speaks likewise of Aêshma-daêva: "For all other sciences depend upon Aêshma, the cunning." "To smite the wicked Aṅra-mainyus [Ahriman, the evil power], to smite Aêshma with the terrible weapons, to smite the Mazanian daêvas, to smite all daêvas." (*Yaśna*, lvi, 12. 5.)

In the same fargard [x, 16] of the *Vendîdâd* the Brahman divinities are involved in the same denunciation with Aêshma-daêva: "I combat Indra, I combat Sauru, I com-

## SAMAEL AND TYPHON ARE SATAN

Samael is Satan; but Bryant and a good many other authorities show it to be the name of the *Simoom* — the wind of the desert,* and the *Simoom* is called Atabul-os or Diabolos.

Plutarch † remarks that by Typhon was understood anything violent, unruly and disorderly. The overflowing of the Nile was called by the Egyptians Typhon. Lower Egypt is very flat, and any mounds built along the river to prevent the frequent inundations, were called Typhonian or *Taphos;* hence, the origin of Typhon. Plutarch, who was a rigid, orthodox Greek, and never known to compliment much the Egyptians, testifies in his *Isis and Osiris* to the fact that, far from worshipping the Devil (of which Christians accused them), they despised more than they dreaded Typhon. In his symbol of the opposing, obstinate power of nature, they believed him to be a poor, struggling, half-dead divinity. Thus, even at that remote age, we see the ancients already *too enlightened to believe in a personal devil.* As Typhon was represented in one of his symbols under the figure of an ass at the festival of the sun's sacrifices, the Egyptian priests exhorted the faithful worshippers not to carry gold ornaments upon their bodies for fear of giving food to the *ass!*‡

Three and a half centuries before Christ, Plato expressed his opinion of evil by saying that "there is in matter a blind, refractory force, which resists the will of the Great Artificer." This blind force, under Christian influx, was made to see and become responsible; it was transformed into Satan!

His identity with Typhon can scarcely be doubted upon reading the account in *Job* of his appearance with the sons of God, before the Lord. He accuses Job of a readiness to curse the Lord to his face upon sufficient provocation. So Typhon, in the Egyptian *Book of the Dead,* figures as the accuser. The resemblance extends even to the names, for one of Typhon's appellations was *Seth,* or *Set;* as *Shatan,* in Hebrew, means an adversary. In Arabic the word is *Shâtana* — to be adverse, to persecute, and Manetho says he had treacherously murdered Osiris and allied himself with the Shemites (the Israelites). This may possibly have originated the fable told by Plutarch, that from the fight between Horus and Typhon, Typhon, overcome with fright at the mis-

---

bat the daêva Nâunghaithya." The annotator explains them to be the Vedic gods, Indra, Saurva, or Śiva, and the two Aświns. There must be some mistake, however, for Śiva, at the time the *Vedas* were completed, was an aboriginal or Aethiopian God, the Bala or Bel of Western Asia. He was not an Âryan or Vedic deity. Perhaps Sûrya was the divinity intended.

* Jacob Bryant, *New System, or, an Analysis of Ancient Mythology,* III, p. 334; 3rd ed.

† Plutarch, *On Isis and Osiris,* §§ 49, 50, 64.

‡ *Ibid.,* §§ 30, 50.

chief he had caused, "fled seven days on an ass, and escaping, begat the boys Hierosolymus and Judaeus (Jerusalem and Judaea)." *

Professor Reuvens refers to an invocation of Typhon-Seth,† and Epiphanius says that the Egyptians worshipped Typhon under the form of an ass,‡ while according to Bunsen Seth "appears gradually among the Semites as the background of their religious consciousness." § The name of the ass in Coptic, AO, is a phonetic of Iaô, and hence the animal became a pun-symbol. Thus Satan is a later creation, sprung from the overheated fancy of the Fathers of the Church. By some reversal of fortune, to which the gods are subjected in common with mortals, Typhon-Seth tumbled down from the eminence of the deified son of Adam-Kadmon, to the degrading position of a subaltern spirit, a mythical demon — ass. Religious schisms are as little free from the frail pettiness and spiteful feelings of humanity as the partisan quarrels of laymen. We find a strong instance of the above in the case of the Zoroastrian reform, when Magianism separated from the old faith of the Brahmans. The bright *devas* of the *Veda* became, under the religious reform of Zoroaster, *daêvas*, or evil spirits of the *Avesta*. Even Indra, the luminous god, was thrust far back into the dark shadow ‖ in order to show off, in a brighter light, Ahura-Mazda, the Wise and Supreme Deity.

The strange veneration in which the Ophites held the serpent which represented Christos may become less perplexing if the students would but remember that at all ages the serpent was the symbol of divine wisdom, which kills in order to resurrect, destroys but to rebuild the better. Moses is made a descendant of Levi, a serpent-tribe. Gautama Buddha is of a serpent-lineage, through the Nâga (serpent) race of kings who reigned in Magadha. Hermes, or the god Taautos (Thoth), in his snake-symbol is Têt; and, according to the Ophite legends, Jesus or Christos is born from a snake (divine wisdom, or Holy Ghost), *i.e.*, he became a son of God through his initiation into the "Serpent Science." Vishṇu, identical with the Egyptian Kneph, rests on the heavenly *seven*-headed serpent.

The red or fiery dragon of the ancient time was the military ensign of the Assyrians. Cyrus adopted it from them when Persia became dominant. The Romans and Byzantines next assumed it; and so the "great red dragon," from being the symbol of Babylon and Nineveh, became that of Rome.¶

The temptation, or probation,** of Jesus is, however, the most dramatic

---

\* [*On Isis*, etc., § 31.]
† Wilkinson, *Manners and Customs of the Ancient Egyptians*, 2nd Series, 1841, Vol. I, p. 434.
‡ *Adv. Haer.*, Bk. III, tom. II, § xii.
§ *God in History*, London, 1868, Vol. I, p. 234.
‖ See *Vendîdâd*, fargard x.
¶ Salverte, *The Philosophy of Magic*, Vol. II, p. 315.
\*\* The term πειρασμός signifies a trial, or probation.

occasion in which Satan appears. As if to prove the designation of Apollo-Aesculapius, and Bacchus, [as] *Diobolos*, or son of Zeus, he is also styled *Diabolos*, or accuser. The scene of the probation was the wilderness. In the desert about the Jordan and Dead Sea were the abodes of the "sons of the prophets," and the Essenes.* These ascetics used to subject their neophytes to probations, analogous to the *tortures* of the Mithraic rites; and the temptation of Jesus was evidently a scene of this character. Hence, in the *Gospel according to Luke* [iv, 13, 14], it is stated that "the Diabolos, having completed the probation, left him for a specific time, ἄχρι καιροῦ; and Jesus returned in the power of the Spirit into Galilee." But the διάβολος, or Devil, in this instance is evidently no malignant principle, but one exercising discipline. In this sense the terms Devil and Satan are repeatedly employed.† Thus, when Paul was liable to undue elation by reason of the abundance of revelations or epoptic disclosures, there was given him "a thorn in the flesh, an angel of Satanas," to check him. ‡

The story of Satan in the *Book of Job* is of a similar character. He is introduced among the "Sons of God," presenting themselves before the Lord, as in a Mystic initiation. Micaiah, the prophet, describes a similar scene, where he "saw the Lord sitting on His throne, and all the host of Heaven standing by Him," with whom He took counsel, which resulted in putting "a lying spirit into the mouth of the prophets of Ahab." § The Lord counsels with Satan, and gives him *carte blanche* to test the fidelity of Job. He is stripped of his wealth and family, and smitten with a loathsome disease. In his extremity, his wife doubts his integrity, and exhorts him to worship God, as he is about to die. His friends all beset him with accusations, and finally the Lord, the chief hierophant Himself, taxes him with the uttering of words in which there is no wisdom, and with contending with the Almighty. To this rebuke Job yielded, making this appeal: "I will demand of thee, and thou shalt declare unto me: wherefore do I abhor myself and mourn in dust and ashes?" Immediately he was vindicated. "The Lord said Eliphaz . . . ye have not spoken of me the thing that is right, as my servant Job hath." ‖ His integrity had been asserted, and his prediction verified: "I know that my Champion liveth, and that he will stand up for me at a later time on the earth; and though after my skin my body itself be corroded away, yet even then without my flesh shall I see God."¶ The pre-

---

\* Pliny, *Nat. Hist.*, V, xvi.

† See *1 Corinthians* v, 5; *2 Corinthians* xi, 14; *1 Timothy* i, 20.

‡ *2 Corinthians* xii, 7. In *Numbers* xxii, 22, the angel of the Lord is described as acting the part of a Satan to Balaam.

§ *1 Kings* xxii, 19-23.

‖ [*Job* xlii, 4-7.]

¶ [*Job* xix, 25, 26.]

diction was accomplished: "I have heard of thee by the hearing of the ear, but now mine eye seeth thee . . . And the Lord turned the captivity of Job." [*Job* xlii, 4, 10.]

In all these scenes there is manifested no such malignant diabolism as is supposed to characterize "the adversary of souls."

It is an opinion of certain writers of merit and learning, that the Satan of the book of *Job* is a Jewish myth, containing the Mazdean doctrine of the Evil Principle. Dr. Haug remarks that "the Zoroastrian religion exhibits even a very close affinity to, or rather identity with, several important doctrines of the Mosaic religion and Christianity, such as the personality and attributes of the devil, and the resurrection of the dead."* The war of the *Apocalypse* between Michael and the Dragon, can be traced with equal facility to one of the oldest myths of the Âryans. In the *Avesta*† we read of war between *Thraêtaona* and *Azhi-Dahâka*, the destroying serpent. Burnouf has endeavored to show that the Vedic myth of Ahi, or the serpent, fighting against the gods, has been gradually euhemerized into "the battle of a pious man against the power of evil," in the Mazdean religion. By these interpretations Satan would be made identical with Zohâk or Azhi-Dahâka, who is a three-headed serpent, with one of the heads a human one.‡

Beel-Zebub is generally distinguished from Satan. He seems, in *The Apocryphal New Testament*,§ to be regarded as the potentate of the underworld. The name is usually rendered "Baal of the Flies," which may be a designation of the Scarabaei or sacred beetles.|| More correctly, it should be read, as it is always given in the Greek text of the *Gospels*, Beelzebul, or lord of the household, as is indeed intimated in *Matthew* x, 25:

---

* Haug, *Essays on the Sacred Language, Writings and Religion of the Parsees*, 2nd ed., p. 4.

† [*Vendidâd*, farg. I, 18; *Yaśna*, ix, 8 *et seq.*]

‡ [*Vendidâd*, I, 66; also Darmesteter's Introd., p. lxiii.] The *Avesta* describes the serpent Dahâka, as of the region of Bauri or Babylonia. In the Median history are two kings of the name Deiokes or Dahâka, and Astyages or Az-dahâka. There were children of Zohâk seated on various Eastern thrones, after Ferîdûn. It is apparent, therefore, that by Zohâk is meant the Assyrian dynasty, whose symbol was the *purpureum signum draconis* — the purple sign of the Dragon. From a very remote antiquity (*Genesis* xiv) this dynasty ruled Asia, Armenia, Syria, Arabia, Babylonia, Media, Persia, Bactria and Afghânistân. It was finally overthrown by Cyrus and Darius Hystaspes, after "1,000 years' " rule. Yima and Thraêtaona, or Jemshid and Ferîdûn, are doubtless personifications. Zohâk probably imposed the Assyrian or Magian worship of fire upon the Persians. Darius was the vicegerent of Ahura-Mazda.

§ [Hone, *Gospel of Nicodemus*, xviii.]

|| The name in the Gospels is βεελζεβούλ, or Baal of the Dwelling. It is pretty certain that Apollo, the Delphian God, was not Hellenian originally, but Phoenician. He was the Paian or physician, as well as the god of oracles. It is no great stretch of imagination to identify him with Baal-*Zebul*, the god of Ekron, or Acheron, doubtless changed to *Zebub*, or flies, by the Jews in derision.

"If they have called the master of the house Beelzebul, how much more shall they call them of his household." He was also styled the prince or archon of demons.

Typhon figures in the *Book of the Dead* as the Accuser of souls when they appear for judgment, as Satan stood up to accuse Joshua, the high priest, before the angel, and as the Devil came to Jesus to tempt or test him during his great fast in the wilderness. He was also the deity denominated Baal-Zephon, or god of the crypt, in the book of *Exodus* [xiv, 2, 9], and *Seth*, or the pillar. During this period, the ancient or archaic worship was more or less under the ban of the government; in figurative language, Osiris had been treacherously slain and cut in fourteen (twice *seven*) pieces and coffined by his brother Typhon, and Isis had gone to Byblos in quest of his body.

We must not forget in this relation that Saba or Sabazios, of Phrygia and Greece, was torn by the Titans into *seven* pieces, and that he was, like Heptaktys of the Chaldeans, the *seven*-rayed god. Siva, the Hindu, is represented crowned with seven serpents, and he is the god of war and destruction. The Hebrew Jehovah the Tsabaôth is also called the Lord of hosts, Seba, or Saba, Bacchus or Dionysus-Sabazius; so that all these may easily be proved identical.

Finally the princes of the older *régime*, the gods who had, on the assault of the giants, taken the forms of animals and hidden in Aethiopia, returned and expelled the shepherds.

According to Josephus, the Hyksôs were the ancestors of the Israelites.* This is doubtless substantially true. The Hebrew *Scriptures*, which tell a somewhat different story, were written at a later period, and underwent several revisions, before they were promulgated with any degree of publicity. Typhon became odious in Egypt, and shepherds "an abomination." "In the course of the twentieth dynasty he was suddenly treated as an evil demon, insomuch that his effigies and name are obliterated on all the monuments and inscriptions that could be reached."†

In all ages, the gods have been liable to be euhemerized into men. There are tombs of Zeus, Apollo, Hercules and Bacchus, which are often mentioned to show that originally they were only mortals. Shem, Ham and Japhet are traced in the divinities Shamas of Assyria, Kham of

---

* *Contra Apionem*, I, § 25: "The Egyptians took many occasions to hate and envy us: in the first place because our ancestors [the Hyksôs, or shepherds] had had the dominion over their country, and when they were delivered from them and gone to their own country, they lived there in prosperity."

† Bunsen, *God in History*, I, p. 233. The name *Seth* with the syllable *an* from the Chaldean *ana* or Heaven, makes the term *Satan*. The punners seem now to have pounced upon it, as was their wont, and so made it *Satan* from the verb שטן [*shatan*], to oppose.

Egypt, and Iapetos the Titan. Seth was god of the Hyksôs, Enoch, or Inachus, of the Argives; and Abraham, Isaac and Judah have been compared with Brahmâ, Ikshvaku and Yadu of the Hindu pantheon. Typhon tumbled down from godhead to devilship, both in his own character as brother of Osiris, and as the Seth, or Satan of Asia. Apollo, the god of day, became, in his older Phoenician garb, no more Baal-Zebul, the Oracle-god, but prince of demons, and finally the lord of the underworld. The separation of Mazdeanism from Vedism, transformed the *devas* or gods into evil potencies. Indra, also, in the *Vendîdâd* is set forth as the subaltern of Ahriman,* created by him out of the materials of darkness,† together with Śiva (Sûrya) and the two Aśvins. Even Jahi is the demon of Lust‡—probably identical with Indra.

The several tribes and nations had their tutelar gods, and vilified those of inimical peoples. The transformation of Typhon, Satan and Beelzebub are of this character. Indeed, Tertullian speaks of Mithra, the god of the Mysteries, as a devil.

In the twelfth chapter [9, 11] of the *Apocalypse,* Michael and his angels overcame the Dragon and his angels: "and the Great Dragon was cast out, that Archaic Ophis, called Diabolos and Satan, which deceiveth the whole world." It is added: "They overcame him by the blood of the Lamb." The Lamb, or Christ, had to descend himself to hell, the world of the dead, and remain there three days before he subjugated the enemy, according to the myth.

Michael was denominated by the kabalists and the Gnostics "the Savior," the angel of the Sun, and angel of Light. (מיכאל, probably from יכה, to manifest, and אל , God.) He was the first of the Aeôns, and was well-known to antiquarians as the "unknown angel" represented on the Gnostic amulets.

The writer of the *Apocalypse,* if not a kabalist, must have been a Gnostic. Michael was not a personage originally exhibited to him in his vision (*epopteia*) but the Savior and Dragon-slayer. Archaeological explorations have indicated him as identical with Anubis, whose effigy was lately discovered upon an Egyptian monument, with a cuirass and holding a spear, like St. Michael and St. George. He is also represented as slaying a Dragon that has the head and tail of a serpent.§

The student of Lepsius, Champollion, and other Egyptologists will

---

\* *Vendîdâd*, fargard x. The name *Vendîdâd* is a contraction of *Vidaêvo-dâtem,* ordinances against the Daêvas.

† *Bundahish* [cod. havn. fol. 90, recto 6, pen.]. "Ahriman created out of the materials of darkness Akuman and Ander, then Śauru and Nakait."

‡ [Spiegel, *Zend-Avesta,* III, Introd., p. 1.]

§ See A. Lenoir, "Du Dragon de Metz," in *Mémoires de l'Académie Celtique,* tome ii, pp. 11, 12.

quickly recognize Isis as the "woman with child," "clothed with the Sun and with the Moon under her feet," whom the "great fiery Dragon" persecuted, and to whom "were given two wings of the Great Eagle that she might fly into the wilderness." Typhon was red-skinned.*

The Two Brothers, the Good and Evil Principles, appear in the Myths of the *Bible* as well as those of the Gentiles, and Cain and Abel, Typhon and Osiris, Esau and Jacob, Apollo and Python etc. Esau or Osu is represented, when born, as "red all over like an hairy garment." He is the Typhon or Satan, opposing his brother.

From the remotest antiquity, the serpent was held by every people in the greatest veneration, as the embodiment of Divine wisdom and the symbol of spirit, and we know from Sanchoniathon that it was Hermes or Thoth who was the first to regard the serpent as "the most spirit-like of all the reptiles";† and the Gnostic serpent with the seven vowels over the head is but the copy of Ananta, the seven-headed serpent on which rests the god Vishṇu.

We have experienced no little surprise to find upon reading the latest European treatises upon serpent-worship, that the writers confess that the public is "still almost in the dark as to the origin of the superstition in question." Mr. C. Staniland Wake, M.A.I., from whom we now quote, says: "The student of mythology knows that certain ideas were associated by the peoples of antiquity with the serpent, and that it was the favorite symbol of particular deities; but why that animal rather than any other was chosen for the purpose is yet uncertain."‡

Mr. James Fergusson, F.R.S., who has gathered together such an abundance of material upon this ancient cult, seems to have no more suspicion of the truth than the rest.§

Our explanation of the myth may be of little value to students of symbology, and yet we believe that the interpretation of the primitive serpent-worship as given by the initiates is the correct one. In Vol. I, p. 10, we quote from the serpent Mantra, in the *Aitareya-Brâhmaṇam*, a passage which speaks of the earth as the *Sarpa-râjñî*, the Queen of the Serpents, and "the mother of all that moves" [V, iv, 23]. These expressions refer to the fact that before our globe had become egg-shaped or round, it was a long trail of cosmic dust or fire-mist, moving and writhing like a serpent. This, say the explanations, was the Spirit of God moving on the chaos until its breath had incubated cosmic matter and made it assume the annular shape of a serpent with its tail in its mouth—emblem of eternity

---

\* Plutarch, *On Isis and Osiris*, § 30; Diodorus Siculus, *Bibl. hist.*, I, 88.
† [Eusebius, *Praep. evang.*, lib. I, cap. x (40).]
‡ *Serpent-Worship*, etc., ch. iii; New York, J. W. Bouton, 1877.
§ *Tree and Serpent Worship*, etc., London, 1873.

in its spiritual and of our world in its physical sense. According to the notions of the oldest philosophers, as we have shown in the preceding chapter, the earth, serpent-like, casts off its skin and appears after every minor *pralaya* in a rejuvenated state, and after the great *pralaya* resurrects or evolves again from its subjective into objective existence. Like the serpent, it not only "puts off its old age," says Sanchoniathon, "but increases in size and strength."\* This is why not only Serapis, and later, Jesus, were represented by a great serpent, but even why, in our own century, big snakes are kept with sacred care in Moslem mosques; for instance, in that of Cairo. In Upper Egypt, a famous saint is said to appear under the form of a large serpent; and in India, in some children's cradles, a pair of serpents, male and female, are reared with the infant, and snakes are often kept in houses, as they are thought to bring (a magnetic aura of) wisdom, health and good luck. They are the progeny of *Sarpa-râjñî*, the earth, and endowed with all her virtues.

In the Hindu mythology, Vasuki, the Great Dragon, pours forth upon *Durgâ*, from his mouth, a poisonous fluid which overspreads the ground, but her consort Śiva causes the earth to open her mouth and swallow it.

Thus the mystic drama of the celestial virgin pursued by the dragon seeking to devour her child was not only depicted in the constellations of heaven, as has been mentioned, but was represented in the secret worship of the temples. It was the mystery of the god Sol, and inscribed on a black image of Isis.† The Divine Boy was chased by the cruel Typhon.‡ In an Egyptian legend, the Dragon is said to pusue Thuêris (Isis) while she is endeavoring to protect her son. § Ovid describes Dione (the consort of the original Pelasgian Zeus, and mother of Venus) as flying from Typhon to the Euphrates, ‖ thus identifying the myth as belonging to all the countries where the Mysteries were celebrated. Virgil sings the victory:

> "Hail, dear child of gods, great son of Jove!
> Receive the honors great; the time is at hand;
> The Serpent will die!" ¶

Albertus Magnus, himself an alchemist and student of occult science, as well as a bishop of the Roman Catholic Church, in his enthusiasm for astrology declared that the zodiacal sign of the celestial virgin rises above the horizon on the twenty-fifth of December, at the moment assigned by the Church for the birth of the Savior.\*\*

---

\* [Eusebius, *Praep. evang.*, lib. I, cap. x (41).]

† Higgins, *Anacalypsis*, I, p. 170; Dupuis, *Origine de tous les cultes*, Vol. III, pp. 49 *et seq.*

‡ Martianus Capella, "Hymn to the Sun," *De nuptiis philol.*, etc., II, 54; Movers, *Die Phönizier*, Vol. I, p. 266.

§ Plutarch, *On Isis and Osiris*, xix.

‖ Ovid, *Fasti*, II, 461.

¶ Virgil, *Eclogue IV*.

\*\* [G. Higgins, *Anacalypsis*, Vol. I, p. 314.]

## THE MYSTERIES OF DEMETER AND MITHRAS 491

The sign and myth of the mother and child were known thousands of years before the Christian era. The drama of the Mysteries of Demeter represents Persephone, her daughter, as carried away by Pluto or Hadês into the world of the dead; and when the mother finally discovers her there, she has been installed as queen of the realm of Darkness. This myth was transcribed by the Church into the legend of Ste. Anna* going in quest of her daughter Mary, who has been conveyed by Joseph into Egypt. Persephone is depicted with two ears of wheat in her hand; so is Mary in the old pictures; so was the Celestial Virgin of the constellation. Albumazar, the Arabian, indicates the identity of the several myths as follows:

"In the first decan of the Virgin rises a maid, called in Arabic Aderenosa [Ardhanârî?], that is, pure immaculate virgin,† graceful in person, charming in countenance, modest in habit, with loosened hair, holding in her hands two ears of wheat, sitting upon an embroidered throne, nursing a boy, and rightly feeding him in the place called Hebraea; a boy, I say, named Iessus by certain nations, which signifies Issa, whom they also call Christ in Greek."‡

At this time Grecian, Asiatic and Egyptian ideas had undergone a remarkable transformation. The Mysteries of Dionysus-Sabazius had been replaced by the rites of Mithras, whose "caves" superseded the crypts of the former god, from Babylon to Britain. Serapis, or Sri-Apa, from Pontus, had usurped the place of Osiris. The king of Eastern Hindostan, Aśoka, had embraced the religion of Siddhârtha, and sent missionaries clear to Greece, Asia, Syria and Egypt, to promulgate the evangel of wisdom. The Essenes of Judaea and Arabia, the Therapeutists§ of Egypt, and the Pythagorists‖ of Greece and Magna Graecia were evidently religionists of the new faith. The legends of Gautama superseded the myths of Horus, Anubis, Adonis, Atys and Bacchus. These were wrought anew into the Mysteries and Gospels, and to them we owe the

---

* Anna is an Oriental designation from the Chaldean *ana*, or heaven, whence Anaitis and Anaitres. *Durgâ*, the consort of Śiva, is also named *Annapûrṇa*, and was doubtless the original St. Anna. The mother of the prophet Samuel was named Anna; the father of his counterpart, Samson, was *Manu*.

† The virgins of ancient time, as will be seen, were not maids, but simply *almehs*, or nubile women.

‡ Kircher, *Oedipus Aegyptiacus*, Vol. II (1653), Pt. II, p. 203.

§ From θεραπεύω, to serve, to worship, to heal.

‖ E. Pococke [*India in Greece*, p. 364] derives the name *Pythagoras* from *Buddha*, and *guru*, a spiritual teacher. Higgins makes it Celtic, and says that it means an observer of the stars. See *Celtic Druids*, pp. 125-26. If, however, we derive the word *Pytho* from פתה, *patah*, the name would signify an expounder of oracles, while *Buddha-guru* would mean a teacher of the doctrines of Buddha.[63]

literature known as the *Evangels* and the *Apocryphal New Testament*. They were kept by the Ebionites, Nazarenes, and other sects as sacred books, which they might "show only to the wise"; and were so preserved till the overshadowing influence of the Roman ecclesiastical polity was able to wrest them from those who kept them.

At the time that the high priest Hilkiah is said to have found the *Book of the Law*, the Hindu *Purânas* (Scriptures) were known to the Assyrians. These last had for many centuries held dominion from the Hellespont to the Indus, and probably crowded the Âryans out of Bactriana into the Puñjâb. The *Book of the Law* seems to have been a *purâna*. "The learned Brahmans," says Sir William Jones, "pretend that five conditions are requisite to constitute a real *purâna:*

"1. To treat of the creation of matter in general.

"2. To treat of *the creation or production of secondary material and spiritual beings.*

"3. To give a chronological abridgment of the great periods of time.

"4. To give a genealogical abridgment of the principal families that reigned over the country.

"5. Lastly, to give the history of some great man in particular."*

It is pretty certain that whoever wrote the *Pentateuch* had this plan before him, as well as [that] those who wrote the *New Testament* had become thoroughly well acquainted with Buddhistic ritualistic worship, legends and doctrines, through the Buddhist missionaries who were many in those days in Palestine and Greece.

But "no Devil, no Christ." This is the basic dogma of the Church. We must hunt the two together. There is a mysterious connection between the two, more close than perhaps is suspected, amounting to identity. If we collect together the mythical sons of God, all of whom were regarded as "first-begotten," they will be found dovetailing together and blending in this dual character. Adam-Kadmon bifurcates from the spiritual conceptive wisdom into the creative one, which evolves *matter.* The Adam made from dust is both son of God and Satan; and the latter is also a son of God, according to Job.†

Hercules was likewise "the First-Begotten." He is also Bel, Baal and Bal, and therefore Śiva, the Destroyer. Bacchus was styled by Euripides, "Bacchus, the Son of God." As a child, Bacchus, like the Jesus of the *Apocryphal Gospels,* was greatly dreaded. He is described as benevolent to mankind; nevertheless he was merciless in punishing

---

\* [*The Works of Sir William Jones*, 1799, Vol. VI, pp. 444-45.]

† [*Job* i, 6.] In the Secret Museum of Naples, there is a marble bas-relief representing the *Fall of Man*, in which *God the Father plays the part of the Beguiling Serpent.*

whomever failed of respect to his worship. Pentheus, the son of Cadmus and Hermione, was, like the son of Rabbi Hannon, destroyed for his want of piety.

The allegory of Job, which has been already cited, if correctly understood, will give the key to this whole matter of the Devil, his nature and office; and will substantiate our declarations. Let no pious individual take exception to this designation of allegory. Myth was the favorite and universal method of teaching in archaic times. Paul, writing to the Corinthians, declared that the entire story of Moses and the Israelites was typical;* and in his *Epistle to the Galatians* asserted that the whole story of Abraham, his two wives, and their sons was an allegory.† Indeed, it is a theory amounting to certitude, that the historical books of the *Old Testament* were of the same character. We take no extraordinary liberty with the *Book of Job* when we give it the same designation which Paul gave the stories of Abraham and Moses.

But we ought, perhaps, to explain the ancient use of allegory and symbology. The truth in the former was left to be deduced; the symbol expressed some abstract quality of the Deity, which the laity could easily apprehend. Its higher sense terminated there; and it was employed by the multitude thenceforth as an image to be employed in idolatrous rites. But the allegory was reserved for the inner sanctuary, where only the elect were admitted. Hence the rejoinder of Jesus when his disciples interrogated him because he spoke to the multitude in parables. "To you," said he, "it is given to know the mysteries of the Kingdom of Heaven, but to them it is not given. For whosoever hath, to him shall be given, and he shall have more abundance; but whosoever hath not, from him shall be taken away even that he hath." ‡ In the minor Mysteries, a sow was washed to typify the purification of the neophyte; as her return to the mire indicated the superficial nature of the work that had been accomplished.

"The Mythus is the undisclosed thought of the soul. The characteristic trait of the myth is to convert reflection into history (a historical form). As in the epos, so in the myth, the historical element predominates. Facts (external events) often constitute the basis of the myth, and with these, religious ideas are interwoven."

The whole allegory of Job is an open book to him who understands the picture-language of Egypt as it is recorded in the *Book of the Dead*. In the Scene of Judgment, Osiris is represented sitting on his throne,

---

* *First Epistle to the Corinthians* x, 11: "Now all these things happened unto them for ensamples."

† *Epistle to the Galatians* iv, 22, 24: "It is written that Abraham had two sons, the one by a bondmaid, the other by a freewoman . . . which things are an allegory."

‡ [*Matt.* xiii, 12.]

holding in one hand the symbol of life, "the hook of attraction," and in the other the mystic Bacchic fan. Before him are the sons of God, the forty-two assessors of the dead. An altar is immediately before the throne, covered with gifts and surmounted with the sacred lotus-flower, upon which stand four spirits. By the entrance stands the soul about to be judged, whom Thmei, the genius of Truth, is welcoming to this conclusion of the probation.[31] Thoth holding a reed, makes a record of the proceedings in the Book of Life. Horus and Anubis, standing by the scales, inspect the weight which determines whether the heart of the deceased balances the symbol of truth, or the latter preponderates. On a pedestal sits a bitch — the symbol of the Accuser.

Initiation into the Mysteries, as every intelligent person knows, was a dramatic representation of scenes in the underworld. Such was the allegory of Job.

Several critics have attributed the authorship of this book to Moses. But it is older than the *Pentateuch*. Jehovah is not mentioned in the poem itself; and if the name occurs in the prologue, the fact must be attributed to either an error of the translators, or the premeditation exacted by the later necessity to transform polytheism into a monotheistic religion. The plan adopted was the very simple one of attributing the many names of the Elohim (gods) to a single god. So in one of the oldest Hebrew texts of Job (in chapter xii, 9) there stands the name of Jehovah, whereas all other manuscripts have "Adonai." But in the original poem Jehovah is absent. In place of this name we find *Al, Aleim, Ale, Shaddai, Adonai,* etc. Therefore, we must conclude that either the prologue and epilogue were added at a later period, which is inadmissible for many reasons, or that it has been tampered with like the rest of the manuscripts. Then, we find in this archaic poem no mention whatever of the Sabbatical Institution; but a great many references to the sacred number seven, of which we will speak further, and a direct discussion upon Sabaeanism, the worship of the heavenly bodies prevailing in those days in Arabia. Satan is called in it a "Son of God," one of the council which presents itself before God, and he leads him into tempting Job's fidelity. In this poem, clearer and plainer than anywhere else, do we find the meaning of the appellation, Satan. It is a term for the office or character of *public accuser*. Satan is the Typhon of the Egyptians, barking his accusations in Amenti; an office quite as respectable as that of the public prosecutor in our own age; and if, through the ignorance of the first Christians, he became later identical with the Devil, it is through no connivance of his own.

The *Book of Job* is a complete representation of ancient initiation and the trials which generally precede this grandest of all ceremonies.

The neophyte perceives himself deprived of everything he valued, and afflicted with foul disease. His wife appeals to him to curse God and die; there was no more hope for him. Three friends appear on the scene by mutual appointment: Eliphaz, the learned Temanite, full of the knowledge "which wise men have told from their fathers . . . to whom alone the earth was given"; Bildad, the conservative, taking matters as they come, and judging Job to have acted wickedly, because he was afflicted; and Zophar, intelligent and skillful with "generalities" but not interiorly wise.* Job boldly responds: "If I have erred, it is a matter with myself. You magnify yourselves and plead against me in my reproach; but it is God who has overthrown me . . . Why do you persecute me and are not satisfied with my flesh wasted away? But I know that my Champion lives, and that at a coming day he will stand for me in the earth; and though, together with my skin, all this beneath it shall be destroyed, yet without my flesh I shall see God . . . Ye shall say: 'Why do we molest him?' for the root of the matter is found in me!"†

This passage, like all others in which the faintest allusions could be found to a "Champion," "Deliverer," or "Vindicator," was interpreted as a direct reference to the Messiah; apart from that, in the *Septuagint* this verse is translated:

> "For I know that He is eternal
> Who is about to deliver me on earth,
> To restore this skin of mine which endures these things," etc. ‡

In King James' version, as it stands translated, it has no resemblance whatever to the original.§ The crafty translators have rendered it, "I know that *my Redeemer liveth*," etc. And yet *Septuagint, Vulgate*, and Hebrew original, have all to be considered as an inspired Word of God. Job refers to his own *immortal* spirit which is eternal, and which, when death comes, will deliver him from his putrid earthly body and clothe him with a new spiritual envelope. In *The Eleusinian and Bacchic Mysteries*, in the Egyptian *Book of the Dead,* and all other works treating on matters of initiation, this "eternal being" has a name. With the Neo-Platonists it was the *Nous*, the *Augoeides*; with the Buddhists it is *Agra;* and with the Persian, *Feroher.* All of these are called the "Deliverers," the "Champions," the "Metatrons," etc. In the Mithraic sculptures of Persia, the *feroher* is represented by a winged figure hovering in the air above its "object" or body. ‖ It is the luminous Self — the Âtman of the Hindus, our

---

* [*Job* ii, 9, 11.]
† [*Ibid.*, xix, 4-6, 22-29.]
‡ [*Ibid.*, xix, 25-27. Translated from the *Septuagint.*]
§ See *Job* by various translators, and compare the different texts.
‖ See Sir R. K. Porter's *Travels in Georgia, Persia*, etc., Vol. I, plates 17, 41.

immortal spirit, who alone can redeem our soul, and will, if we follow him instead of being dragged down by our body. Therefore, in the Chaldean texts, the above reads, "My *deliverer*, my *restorer*," i.e., the Spirit who will restore the decayed body of man, and transform it into a clothing of ether. And it is this *Nous, Augoeides, Feroher, Agra,* Spirit of himself, that the triumphant Job shall see without his flesh — i.e., when he has escaped from his bodily prison, and that the translators call "God."

Not only is there not the slightest allusion in the poem of Job to Christ, but it is now well proved that all those versions by different translators, which agree with that of King James, were written on the authority of Jerome, who has taken strange liberties in his *Vulgate*. He was the first to cram into the text this verse of his own fabrication:

> "*I know that my Redeemer lives,*
> And at the last day *I shall arise from the earth,*
> And again shall be surrounded with my skin,
> And in my flesh I shall see my God." \*

All of which might have been a good reason for him to believe in it since *he knew it,* but for others who did *not,* and who, moreover, found in the text a quite different idea, it only proves that Jerome had decided, by one more interpolation, to enforce the dogma of a resurrection "at the last day," and in the identical skin and bones which he had used on earth. This is an agreeable prospect of "restoration" indeed. Why not the linen also, in which the body happens to die?

And how could the author of the *Book of Job* know anything of the *New Testament,* when evidently he was utterly ignorant even of the *Old* one? There is a total absence of allusion to any of the patriarchs; and so evidently is it the work of an *Initiate,* that one of the three daughters of Job is even called by a decidedly "Pagan" mythological name. The name of *Keren happuch* † is rendered in various ways by the many translators. The *Vulgate* has "horn of antimony"; and the LXX has the "horn of Amalthea," the nurse of Jupiter, and one of the constellations, emblem of the "horn of plenty." The presence in the *Septuagint* of this heroine of Pagan fable, shows the ignorance of the transcribers of its meaning, as well as the esoteric origin of the *Book of Job.*

Instead of offering consolations, the three friends of the suffering Job seek to make him believe that his misfortune must have come in punishment of some extraordinary transgressions on his part. Hurling back upon them all their imputations, Job swears that while his breath is in him he will maintain his cause. He takes in view the period of his prosperity "when the secret of God was upon my tabernacle," ‡ and he was a judge

---

\* [*Job* xix, 25-27; tr. of Douay.]
† [*Job* xlii, 14.]
‡ [*Ibid.,* xxix, 4.]

"who sat chief, and dwelt as a king in the army, or one that comforteth the mourners," and compares it with the present time—when vagrant Bedouins held him in derision, men "viler than the earth," when he was prostrated by misfortune and foul disease. Then he asserts his sympathy for the unfortunate, his chastity, his integrity, his probity, his strict justice, his charities, his moderation, his freedom from the prevalent sun-worship, his tenderness to enemies, his hospitality to strangers, his openness of heart, his boldness for the right, though he encountered the multitude and the contempt of families; and invokes the Almighty to answer him, and his adversary to write down of what he had been guilty.*

To this there was not, and could not be, any answer. The three had sought to crush Job by pleadings and general arguments, and he had demanded consideration for his specific acts. Then appeared the fourth; Elihu, the son of Barachel the Buzite, of the kindred of Ram.†

Elihu is the hierophant; he begins with a rebuke, and the sophisms of Job's friends are swept away like the loose sand before the west wind.

"And Elihu, the son of Barachel, spoke and said: 'Great men are not always wise . . . there *is* a spirit in man; the *spirit within me* constraineth me . . . God speaketh once, yea twice, *yet man* perceiveth it not. In a dream; in a vision of the night, when deep sleep falleth upon man, in slumberings upon the bed; then he openeth the ears of men, and sealeth their instruction. O Job, hearken unto me; hold thy peace, and I shall teach thee WISDOM'."‡

And Job who, to the dogmatic fallacies of his three friends, in the bitterness of his heart had exclaimed: "No doubt but ye are *the* people, and wisdom shall die with you . . . Miserable comforters are ye all . . . Surely I would speak to the Almighty, and I desire to reason with God. But *ye* are forgers of lies, *ye* are physicians of no value!"§ The sore-eaten, visited Job, who in the face of the official clergy—offering for all hope the necessarianism of damnation — had in his despair nearly wavered in his patient faith, answered: "What *ye* know, *the same* do I know also; I am not inferior unto you . . . Man cometh forth like a flower, and is cut down: he fleeth also as a shadow, *and continueth not* . . . Man dieth, and wasteth away, yea, man giveth up the ghost, and *where is he?* . . . If a man die shall he *live* again? . . . When a few years are come, then I shall go the way *whence* I shall not return . . . O that one might plead for a man with God, as a man pleadeth for his neighbor!‖ Job finds one who answers to his cry of agony. He listens

---

\* [*Job* xxix, 25; xxx, 8; xxxi.]
† The expression "of the kindred of Ram" denotes that he was an Aramaean or Syrian from Mesopotamia. Buz was a son of Nahor. "Elihu son of Barachel" is susceptible of two translations. Eli-Hu — God is, or Hoa [he] is God; and Barach-Al — the worshipper of God, or Bar-Rachel, the son of Rachel, or son of the ewe.
‡ [*Job* xxxii, 2, 6, 9, 18; xxxiii, 14-16, 33.]
§ [*Ibid.*, xii, 2; xvi, 2; xiii, 3, 4.]
‖ [*Ibid.*, xiii, 2; xiv, 2, 10, 14; xvi, 21-22.]

to the WISDOM of Elihu, the hierophant, the perfected teacher, the inspired philosopher. From his stern lips comes the just rebuke for his impiety in charging upon the SUPREME Being the evils of humanity. "God," says Elihu, "is excellent in power, and in judgment, and in plenty of justice; HE *will not afflict.*" *

So long as the neophyte was satisfied with his own worldly wisdom and irreverent estimate of the Deity and His purposes; so long as he gave ear to the pernicious sophistries of his advisers, the hierophant kept silent. But, when this anxious mind was ready for counsel and instruction, his voice is heard, and he speaks with the authority of the Spirit of God that "constraineth" him: "Surely God will not hear *vanity*, neither will the Almighty regard it . . . He respecteth not any that are wise at heart." †

What better commentary than this upon the fashionable preacher, who "*multiplieth* words without knowledge"! This magnificent *prophetic* satire might have been written to prefigure the spirit that prevails in all the denominations of Christians.

Job hearkens to the words of wisdom, and then the "Lord" answers Job "out of the whirlwind" of nature, God's first visible manifestation: "Stand still, O Job, stand still! and consider the wondrous works of God; for *by them alone* thou canst know God. 'Behold, God is great, and *we know him not*,' Him who 'maketh small the drops of water; *but they* pour down rain *according to the vapor thereof*';" ‡ not according to the divine whim, but to the once established and immutable laws; which law "removeth the mountains and they know not; which shaketh the earth; which commandeth the sun, *and it riseth not;* and sealeth up the stars; . . . which doeth great things *past finding out;* yea, and *wonders without number* . . . Lo, *He goeth by me*, and I see *him not;* he passeth on also, but *I perceive him not!*"§

Then, "Who is this that darkeneth counsel by words without knowledge?" speaks the voice of God through His mouthpiece — nature. "Where wast thou when I laid the foundations of the earth? declare, if thou hast understanding. Who hath laid the measures thereof, *if thou knowest?* When the morning stars sang together, and all the sons of God shouted for joy? . . . Wast thou present when I said to the seas, 'Hitherto shalt thou come, but no further; and here shall thy proud waves be stayed?' . . . Knowest thou who hath caused it to rain on the earth, *where no man is;* on the wilderness, wherein *there is no man*. . . Canst thou bind the sweet influences of Pleiades,

---

\* [*Job* xxxvii, 23.]

† [*Ibid.*, xxxv, 13; xxxvii, 24.]

‡ *Ibid.*, xxxviii, 1; xxxvii, 14; xxxvi, 26-27.

§ *Ibid.*, ix, 5-11.

JOHN TYNDALL
1820-1893
Photo by Bassano taken in 1877.

JOHN LLOYD STEPHENS
1805-1852

Portrait by unknown artist, dating from about 1840, and published in *Maya Explorer*, by V. W. von Hagen, 1947.

or loose the bands of Orion? . . . Canst thou *send lightnings*, that they may go, and say unto thee, 'Here we are'?"\*

"Then Job answered the Lord." He understood His ways, and his eyes were opened for the first time. The Supreme Wisdom descended upon him; and if the reader remain puzzled before this final PETROMA of initiation, at least Job, or the man "afflicted" in his blindness, then realized the impossibility of catching "Leviathan by putting a hook into his nose." The Leviathan is OCCULT SCIENCE, on which one can lay his hand, but "*do no more*,"† whose power and "comely proportion" God wishes not to conceal.

"Who can discover the face of his garment, or who can come to him with his *double bridle?* Who can open the doors of his face, 'of him whose *scales* are his pride, shut up together as *with a closed seal?*' Through whose 'neesings a light doth shine,' and whose eyes are like the lids of the morning." Who "maketh a light to *shine* after him," for those who have the fearlessness to approach him. And then they, like him, will behold "all *high* things, for he is king only over all the children of pride." ‡

Job, now in modest confidence, responded:

> "I know that thou canst do everything,
> And that no thought of thine can be resisted.
> Who is he that maketh a show of arcane wisdom,
> Of which he knoweth nothing?
> Thus have I uttered what I did not comprehend —
> Things far above me, which I did not know.
> Hear! I beseech thee, and I will speak;
> I will demand of thee, and do thou answer me:
> I have heard thee with my ears,
> And now I see thee with my eyes,
> Wherefore am I loathsome,
> And mourn in dust and ashes?" §

He recognized his "champion," and was assured that the time for his vindication had come. Immediately the Lord ("the priests and the judges," *Deuteronomy* xix, 17) saith to his friends: "My wrath is kindled against thee and against thy two friends; for ye have not spoken of me the thing that is right, as my servant Job hath." So "the Lord turned the captivity of Job," and "blessed the latter end of Job more than his beginning." ‖

Then in the [Egyptian] judgment, the deceased invokes four spirits who preside over the Lake of Fire, and is purified by them. He then is conducted

---

\* *Job* xxxviii, 1 *et seq.*
† *Ibid*, xli, 2,8.
‡ *Ibid.*, xli, 13-15, 18, 32, 34.
§ [*Ibid.*, xlii, 2-6.]
‖ [*Ibid.*, xlii, 7, 10.]

to his celestial house, and is received by Athar and Isis, and stands before *Atum*,* the essential God. He is now *Turu*, the essential man, a pure spirit, and henceforth On-ati, the eye of fire, and an associate of the gods.[64]

This grandiose poem of Job was well understood by the kabalists. While many of the mediaeval Hermetists were profoundly religious men, they were, in their innermost hearts—like kabalists of every age—the deadliest enemies of the clergy. How true the words of Paracelsus when worried by fierce persecution and slander, misunderstood by friends and foes, abused by clergy and laity, he exclaimed:

"O ye of Paris, Padua, Montpellier, Salerno, Vienna, and Leipzig! Ye are not teachers of the truth, but confessors of lies. Your philosophy is a lie. Would you know *what* MAGIC *really is*, then seek it in St. John's *Revelation*. . . . As you cannot yourselves prove your teachings from the *Bible* and the *Revelation*, then let your farces have an end. The *Bible is the true key and interpreter*. John, not less than Moses, Elias, Enoch, David, Solomon, Daniel, Jeremiah, and the rest of the prophets, was a *magician*, kabalist, and diviner. If now, all, or even any of those I have named, were yet living, I do not doubt that you would make an example of them in your miserable slaughterhouse, and would annihilate them there on the spot, and *if* it were possible, the Creator of all things too!"

That Paracelsus had learned some mysterious and useful things out of *Revelation* and other *Bible* books, as well as from the *Kabala*, was proved by him practically; so much so, that he is called by many the "father of magic and founder of the occult physics of the *Kabala* and magnetism."†

So firm was the popular belief in the supernatural powers of Paracelsus, that to this day the tradition survives among the simple-minded Alsatians that he is not dead, but "sleepeth in his grave" at Salzburg.‡ And they often whisper among themselves that the green sod heaves with every respiration of that weary breast, and that deep groans are heard as the great fire-philosopher awakes to the remembrance of the cruel wrongs he suffered at the hands of his cruel slanderers for the sake of the great truth!

It will be perceived from these extended illustrations that the Satan of the *Old Testament*, the Diabolos or Devil of the *Gospels* and *Apostolic Epistles*, were but the antagonistic principle in matter, necessarily inci-

---

* *Atum*, or *At-mu* (Âtman), is the Concealed God, at once Ptaḥ and Amen, Father and Son, Creator and thing created, Thought and Appearance, Father and Mother.

† Cf. F. J. Molitor, *Philosophie der Geshichte*, Part III; Ennemoser, *History of Magic*, II; Hemmann, *Mediz.-Chir. Aufsätze* (Berlin, 1778); J. W. A. Pfaff, *Astrologie*, 1816.

‡ Schopheim, *Traditions*, p. 32.

dent to it, and not wicked in the moral sense of the term. The Jews, coming from the Persian country, brought with them the doctrine of *two principles*. They could not bring the *Avesta*, for it was not written. But they—we mean the *Asideans* [*Chasidim*] and *Pharsi*—invested Ormazd with the secret name of יהוה , and Ahriman with the name of the gods of the land, Satan of the Hittites, and *Diabolos*, or rather *Diobolos*, of the Greeks. The early Church, at least the Pauline part of it, the Gnostics and their successors, further refined their ideas; and the Catholic Church adopted and adapted them, meanwhile putting their promulgators to the sword.

The Protestant is a reaction from the Roman Catholic Church. It is necessarily not coherent in its parts, but a prodigious host of fragments beating their way round a common centre, attracting and repelling each other. Parts are centripetally impelled towards old Rome, or the system which enabled old Rome to exist; parts still recoil under the centrifugal impulse, and seek to rush into the broad ethereal region beyond Roman, or even Christian influence.

The modern Devil is their principal heritage from the Roman Cybelê, "Babylon, the Great Mother of the idolatrous and abominable religions of the earth."

But it may be argued, perhaps, that Hindu theology, both Brahmanical and Buddhistic, is as strongly impregnated with belief in objective devils as Christianity itself. There is a slight difference. The very *subtlety* of the Hindu mind is a sufficient warrant that the well-educated people, the learned portion, at least, of the Brahman and Buddhist divines, consider the Devil in another light. With them the Devil is a metaphysical abstraction, an allegory of necessary *evil;* while *with Christians the myth has become a historical entity, the fundamental stone on which Christianity, with its dogma of redemption, is built.* He is as necessary — as des Mousseaux has shown — to the Church as the beast of the seventeenth chapter of the *Apocalypse* was to his rider. The English-speaking Protestants, not finding the Bible explicit enough, have adopted the *Diabology* of Milton's celebrated poem, *Paradise Lost*, embellishing it somewhat from Goethe's celebrated drama of *Faust*. John Milton, first a Puritan and finally a Quietist and Unitarian, never put forth his great production except as a work of fiction, but it thoroughly dovetailed together the different parts of Scripture. The Ialdabaôth of the Ophites was transformed into an angel of light and the morning star, and made the Devil in the first act of the *Diabolic Drama*. Then the twelfth chapter of the *Apocalypse* was brought in for the second act. The great red Dragon was adopted as the same illustrious personage as *Lucifer,* and the last scene is his fall, like that of Vulcan-Hephaistos, from Heaven into the island of Lemnos; the fugitive hosts and their leader "coming to hard bottom" in Pandemonium. The third act is the Garden of Eden. Satan holds a council in a hall erected by him for his new empire, and determines to go forth on an exploring expedition in quest of the new world. The next acts relate to the fall of man, his career on earth, the advent of the Logos, or Son of God, and his redemption of mankind, or the elect portion of them, as the case may be.

This drama of *Paradise Lost* comprises the unformulated belief of English-speaking "evangelical Protestant Christians." Disbelief of its main features is equivalent, in their view, to "denying Christ" and "blaspheming against the Holy Ghost." If John Milton had supposed that his poem, instead of being regarded as a companion of Dante's *Divine Comedy*, would have been considered as another *Apocalypse* to supplement the *Bible*, and complete its demonology, it is more than probable that he would have borne his poverty more resolutely, and withheld it from the press. A later poet, Robert Pollok, taking his cue from this work, wrote another, *The Course of Time*, which bade fair for a season to take the rank of a later *Scripture;* but the nineteenth century has fortunately received a different inspiration, and the Scotch poet is falling into oblivion.

We ought, perhaps, to make a brief notice of the European Devil. He is the genius who deals in sorcery, witchcraft, and other mischief. The Fathers, taking the idea from the Jewish Pharisees, made devils of the Pagan gods, Mithras, Serapis, and the others. The Roman Catholic Church followed by denouncing the former worship as commerce with the powers of darkness. The *malefici* and witches of the middle ages were thus but the votaries of the proscribed worship. Magic in all ancient times had been considered as divine science, wisdom, and the knowledge of God. The healing art in the temples of Aesculapius, and at the shrines of Egypt and the East, had always been magical. Even Darius Hystaspes, who had exterminated the Median Magi, and even driven out the Chaldean theurgists from Babylon into Asia Minor, had also been instructed by the Brahmans of Upper Asia, and, finally, while establishing the worship of Ormazd, was also himself denominated the instituter of magism. All was now changed. Ignorance was enthroned as the mother of devotion. Learning was denounced, and savants prosecuted the sciences in peril of their lives. They were compelled to employ a jargon to conceal their ideas from all but their own adepts, and to accept opprobrium, calumny and poverty.

The votaries of the ancient worship were persecuted and put to death on charges of witchcraft. The Albigenses, descendants of the Gnostics, and the Waldenses, precursors of the Protestants, were hunted and massacred under like accusations. Martin Luther himself was accused of companionship with Satan in proper person. The whole Protestant world still lies under the same imputation. There is no distinction in the judgments of the Church between dissent, heresy and witchcraft. And except where civil authority protects, they are alike capital offences. Religious liberty the Church regards as intolerance.

But the reformers were nursed with the milk of their mother. Luther was as bloodthirsty as the Pope; Calvin more intolerant than Leo or Urban. Thirty years of war depopulated whole districts of Germany, Proestants and Catholics cruel alike. The new faith, too, opened its batteries against witchcraft. The statute books became crimsoned with bloody legislation in Sweden, Denmark, Germany, Holland, Great Britain, and the North American Commonwealth. Whosoever was more liberal, more intelligent, more free-speaking than his fellows was liable to arrest and death. The fires that were extinguished at Smithfield were kindled anew for magicians; it was safer to rebel against a throne than to pursue abstruse knowledge outside the orthodox deadline.

In the seventeenth century, Satan made a sortie in New England, New Jersey, New York, and several of the Southern colonies of North America, and Cotton Mather gives us the principal chronicles of his manifestation. A few years later, he visited the Parsonage of Mora, in Sweden, and life in Dalecarlia was diversified with the burning alive of young children, and the whipping of others at the church doors on Sabbath days. The skepticism of modern times has, however, pretty much driven the belief in witchcraft into Coventry; and the Devil in personal anthropomorphic form, with his Bacchus-foot, and his Pan-like goat's horns, holds place only in the *Encyclical Letters* and other effusions of the Roman Catholic Church. Protestant respectability does not allow him to be named at all except with bated breath in a pulpit-enclosure.

Having now set forth the biography of the Devil from his first advent in India and Persia, his progress through Jewish, and both early and later Christian *Theology* down to the latest phases of his manifestation, we now turn back to review certain of the opinions extant in the earlier Christian centuries.

Avatâras or incarnations were common to the old religions. India had them reduced to a system. The Persians expected Saoshyant, and the Jewish writers looked for a deliverer. Tacitus * and Suetonius † relate that the East was full of expectation of the Great Personage about the time of Octavius. "Thus doctrines obvious to Christians, were the *highest arcana* of Paganism."‡ The Maneros of Plutarch was a child of Palaes-

---

\* [*Annals*, V, xiii, 3.]

† [*Lives of the Caesars*, "Vespasian," § 4.]

‡ Dunlap, *Vestiges of the Spirit-History of Man*, p. 256, quoting W. Williams, *Prim. Hist.*, Bk. I, p. 70.

tinus;* his mediator Mithras, the Savior Osiris, is the Messiah.† In our present *"Canonical Scriptures"* are to be traced the vestigia of the ancient worships; and in the rites and ceremonies of the Roman Catholic Church we find the forms of the Buddhistical worship, its ceremonies and hierarchy. The first *Gospels*, once as canonical as any of the present four, contain pages taken almost entirely from Buddhistical narratives, as we are prepared to show. After the evidence furnished by Burnouf, Cosma de Körös, Beal, Hardy, Schmidt, and translations from the *Tripitaka*, it is impossible to doubt that the whole Christian scheme emanated from the other. The "Miraculous Conception" miracles and other incidents are found in full in Hardy's *A Manual of Budhism.* [pp. 141 *et seq.*] We can readily realize why the Roman Catholic Church is anxious to keep the common people in utter ignorance of the Hebrew *Bible* and the Greek literature. Philology and comparative Theology are her deadliest enemies. The deliberate falsifications of Irenaeus, Epiphanius, Eusebius and Tertullian had become a necessity.

The *Sibylline Books* at that period seem to have been regarded with extraordinary favor. One can easily perceive that they were inspired from the same source as those of the Gentile nations.

Here is a leaf from Gallaeus:

> "New Light has arisen
> Coming from heaven it assumed a mortal form.
> First Gabriel showed his sacred mighty person,
> Next, bearing his message he addressed in words the maid:
> Virgin, receive God in thy pure bosom . . .
> And courage returned to her and the WORD flew into her womb.
> Becoming incarnate in time and animated by her body
> It was formed in a mortal image, and a BOY was created
> By a Virgin delivery . . .
> The new God-sent star was adored by the Magi
> The infant swathed was shown in a manger to the obedient to God
> And Bethlehem was called 'God-called country' of the Word." ‡

This looks at first sight like a prophecy of Jesus. But could it not mean as well some other creative God? We have like utterances concerning Bacchus and Mithras.

"I, son of Zeus, am come to the land of the Thebans—Bacchus, whom formerly Semelê [the virgin], the daughter of Kadmos [the man from the East] brings forth—being delivered by the lightning-bearing flame; and having taken a mortal form instead of a God's, I have arrived."§

The *Dionysiacs*, written in the fifth century, serve to render this

---

\* Plutarch, *On Isis and Osiris*, §§ 16, 17.
† [W. Williams, *op. cit.*, p. 70.]
‡ *Sibyllina Oracula*, 760-788. Amst., 1689.
§ Euripides, *Bacchae*, lines 1-4.

matter very clear, and even to show its close connection with the Christian legend of the birth of Jesus:

> "Virgin-Persephoneia,* you found no escape from marriage
> But you were wived in a Dragon's hymeneals,
> When Zeus very coiled, his countenance being changed,
> A Dragon-bridegroom circled in love-inspiring fold,
> Proceeded to the sanctum of the dark Virgin
> Agitating his rough beard . . . Through the Aethereal Dracontean nuptials
> The womb of Persephone was agitated by a fruitful young,
> Bearing Zagreus † the horned Child." ‡

Here we have the secret of the Ophite worship, and the origin of the Christian later-*revised* fable of the immaculate conception. The Gnostics were the earliest Christians with anything like a regular theological system, and it is only too evident that it was Jesus who was made to fit their theology as Christos, and not their theology that was developed out of his sayings and doings. Their ancestors had maintained, before the Christian era, that the Great Serpent—Jupiter, the Dragon of Life, the Father and "Good Divinity," had glided into the couch of Semelê, and now, the post-Christian Gnostics, with a very trifling change, applied the same fable to the man Jesus, and asserted that the same "Good Divinity," Saturn (Ialdabaôth), had, in the shape of the Dragon of Life, glided over the cradle of the infant Mary.§ In their eyes, the Serpent was the Logos—Christos, the incarnation of Divine Wisdom, through his Father Ennoia and Mother Sophia.

"Now my mother the Holy Spirit [Holy Ghost] took me," Jesus is made to say in the *Gospel of the Hebrews*,∥ thus entering upon his part of Christos—the Son of Sophia, the Holy Spirit.¶

"*The Holy Ghost shall come upon thee*, and the POWER of the Highest shall overshadow thee; therefore also that *holy* thing which shall be born of thee shall be called the Son of God;" says the angel (*Luke* i, 35).

"God . . . hath in these last days spoken unto us by his Son,

---

\* We doubt the propriety of rendering κόρη, virgin. Demeter and Persephone were substantially the same divinity, as were Apollo and Aesculapius. The scene of this adventure is laid in *Krêtê* or *Kourêtis*, where Zeus was chief god. It was, doubtless, *Ceres* or Demeter that is intended. She was also named κούρη, which is the same as κώρα. As she was goddess of the Mysteries, she was fittest for the place as consort of the Serpent-God and mother of Zagreus.

† Pococke considers Zeus a grand lama, or chief Jaina, and Korê-Persephone as Kuru-Paraśu-pāṇi. Zagreus is *Chakra*, the wheel, or circle, the earth, the ruler of the world. He was killed by the Titans, or Teith-ans (*Daityas*). The Horns or crescent was a badge of Lamaic sovereignty. [See *India in Greece*, pp. 257, 265.]

‡ Nonnus, *Dionysiacs*, vi, 155 *et seq*.

§ See Deane, *Worship of the Serpent*, etc., London, 1830, pp. 89-90.

∥ F. Creuzer, *Symbolik und Mythologie*, 1837, Vol. I, p. 341. [Cf. Origen, *Comm. in Evang. Joannis*, tom. II, p. 64.]

¶ The Dragon is the *sun*, the generative principle — Jupiter-Zeus; and Jupiter is called the "Holy Spirit" by the Egyptians, says Plutarch, *De Iside*, xxxvi.

whom he hath appointed heir of all things, by whom also he made the Aeôns."*

All such expressions are so many Christian quotations from the Nonnus verse ". . . through the Aetherel Dracontean," for Aether is the Holy Ghost or third person of the Trinity—the Hawk-headed Serpent, the Egyptian Kneph, emblem of the Divine Mind,† and Plato's universal soul.

"I (Wisdom) came out of the mouth of the Most High and *covered the earth as a cloud.*"‡

Poimandres, the Logos, issues from the Infinite Darkness, and covers the earth with clouds which, serpentine-like, spread all over the earth.§ The Logos is the *oldest* image of God, and he is the *active* Logos, says Philo.‖ The Father is the *Latent Thought.*

This idea being universal, we find an identical phraseology to express it, among Pagans, Jews and early Christians. The Chaldeo-Persian *Logos* is the Only-Begotten of the Father in the Babylonian cosmogony of Eudemus.¶ "Hymn now ELI, child of Deus," begins a Homeric hymn to the sun.** Sol-Mithra is an "image of the Father," as the kabalistic Zeir-Anpîn.

That of all the various nations of antiquity, there never was one which believed in a personal devil more than liberal Christians in the nineteenth century, seems hardly credible, and yet such is the sorrowful fact. Neither the Egyptians, whom Porphyry terms "the most learned nation of all others,"†† nor Greece, its faithful copyist, were ever guilty of such a crowning absurdity. We may add at once that none of them, not even the ancient Jews, believed in hell or an eternal damnation any more than in the Devil, although our Christian churches are so liberal in dealing it out to the heathen. Wherever the word "hell" occurs in the translations of the Hebrew sacred texts, it is unfortunate. The Hebrews were ignorant of such an idea; but yet the Gospels contain frequent examples of the same misunderstanding. So, when Jesus is made to say (*Matthew* xvi, 18) ". . . and the gates of Hadês shall not prevail against it," in the original text it stands "the gates of *death.*"

---

* *Hebrews* i, 1-2. In the original it stands *Aeôns* (emanations). In the translation it stands *worlds*. It was not to be expected that, after anathematizing the doctrine of emanations, the Church would refrain from erasing the original word, which clashed diametrically with her newly-enforced dogma of the Trinity.

† See Dean, *op. cit.*, p. 145.

‡ *Ecclesiasticus* xxiv, 3.

§ Champollion-Figeac, *Égypte ancienne*, p. 141.

‖ *Quaest. et sol. in Gen.*, II, 62; *De conf. ling.*, § 33 *et seq.* Cf. Dunlap, *Vestiges*, etc., p. 233.

¶ [Movers, *Die Phönizier*, Vol. I, p. 268.]

** Hymn XXXI, To Helios.

†† *De abstinentia*, II, § 5.

Never is the word "hell"—as applied to the state of *damnation*, either temporary or eternal—used in any passage of the *Old Testament*, all hellists to the contrary, notwithstanding. "Tophet," or "the Valley of Hinnom"* bears no such interpretation. The Greek term "Gehenna"† has also quite a different meaning, as it has been proved conclusively by more than one competent writer that "Gehenna" is identical with the Homeric Tartarus.

In fact, we have Peter himself as authority for it. In his second *Epistle* (ii, 4) the Apostle, in the original text, is made to say of the sinning angels that God "cast them down into *Tartarus*." This expression too inconveniently recalling the war of Jupiter and the Titans, was altered, and now reads, in King James' version: "cast them down to *hell*."

In the *Old Testament* the expressions "gates of death," and the "chambers of death," simply allude to the "gates of the grave," which are specifically mentioned in the *Psalms* and *Proverbs*. Hell and its sovereign are both inventions of Christianity, coeval with its accession to power and resort to tyranny. They were hallucinations born of the nightmares of the Anthonys in the desert. Before our era the ancient sages knew the "Father of Evil," and treated him no better than an ass, the chosen symbol of Typhon, "the Devil."‡ Sad degeneration of human brains!

As Typhon was the dark shadow of his brother Osiris, so Python is the evil side of Apollo, the bright god of visions, the seer and the soothsayer, He is killed by Python, but kills him in his turn, thus redeeming humanity from sin. It was in memory of this deed that the priestesses of the sun-god enveloped themselves in the snake-skin, typical of the fabulous monster. Under its exhilarating influence—the serpent's skin being considered magnetic — the priestesses fell into magnetic trances, and "receiving their voice from Apollo," they became prophetic and delivered oracles.

Again, Apollo and Python are one, and morally androgynous. The sun-god ideas are all dual, without exception. The beneficent warmth of the sun calls the germ into existence, but excessive heat kills the plant. While playing on his seven-stringed planetary lyre, Apollo produces harmony; but, as well as other sun-gods, under his dark aspect he becomes the destroyer, Python.

St. John is known to have travelled in Asia, a country governed by Magi and imbued with Zoroastrian ideas, and in those days full of Buddhist

---

* *Isaiah* xxx, 33; *Joshua* xv, 8.

† [From the Hebrew *Ge Hinnom*.]

‡ Typhon is called by Plutarch and Sanchoniathon, "Tuphon, the *red*-skinned." Plutarch, *On Isis and Osiris*, § 30-31.

missionaries. Had he never visited those places and come in contact with Buddhists, it is doubtful whether the *Revelation* would have been written. Besides his ideas of the dragon, he gives prophetic narratives entirely unknown to the other apostles, and which, relating to the second advent, make of Christ a faithful copy of Vishṇu.

Thus Ophios and Ophiomorphos, Apollo and Python, Osiris and Typhon, Christos and the Serpent, are all convertible terms. They are all Logoi, and one is unintelligible without the other, as day could not be known had we no night. All are regenerators and saviors, one in a spiritual, the other in a physical sense. One insures immortality for the Divine Spirit; the other gives it through regeneration of the seed. The Savior of mankind has to die, because he unveils to humanity the great secret of the immortal ego; the serpent of *Genesis* is cursed because he said to *matter*, "Ye shall not die." [iii, 4.] In the world of Paganism, the counterpart of the "serpent" is the second Hermes, the reincarnation of Hermes Trismegistus.

Hermes is the constant companion and instructor of Osiris and Isis. He is the personified wisdom; so is Cain, the son of the "Lord." Both build cities, civilize and instruct mankind in the arts.

It has been repeatedly stated by the Christian missionaries in Ceylon and India that the people are steeped in demonolatry; that they are devil-worshippers, in the full sense of the word. Without any exaggeration, we say that they are no more so than the masses of uneducated Christians. But even were they worshippers of (which is more than believers in) the Devil, yet there is a great difference between the teachings of their clergy on the subject of a personal devil and the dogmas of Catholic preachers and many Protestant ministers, also. The Christian priests are bound to teach and impress upon the minds of their flock the existence of the Devil, and the opening pages of the present chapter show the reason why. But not only will the Sinhalese Upasampanna, who belong to the highest priesthood, not confess to belief in a personal demon but even the Sâmanêra, the candidates and novices, would laugh at the idea. Everything in the external worship of the Buddhists is allegorical and is never otherwise accepted or taught by the educated *punghis* (pundits). The accusation that they allow, and tacitly agree to leave the poor people steeped in the most degrading superstitions, is not without foundation; but that they enforce such superstitions, we most vehemently deny. And in this they appear to advantage beside our Christian clergy, who (at least those who have not allowed their fanaticism to interfere with their brains), without believing a word of it, yet preach the existence of the Devil, as the personal enemy of a personal God, and the evil genius of mankind.

St. George's Dragon, which figures so promiscuously in the grandest cathedrals of the Christians, is not a whit handsomer than the King of Snakes, the Buddhist Nammadâ-Nârada, the great Dragon. If the zodiacal Demon Râhu is believed, in the popular superstition of the Sinhalese, to endeavor to destroy the moon by swallowing it; and if in China and Tartary the rabble is allowed, without rebuke, to beat gongs and make fearful noises to drive the monster away from its prey during the eclipses, why should the Catholic clergy find fault, or call this superstition? Do not the country clergy in Southern France do the same, occasionally, at the appearance of comets, eclipses, and other celestial phenomena? In 1456, when Halley's comet made its appearance, "so tremendous was its apparition," writes Draper, "that it was necessary for the Pope himself to interfere. He exorcised and expelled it from the skies. It slunk away into the abysses of space, terror-stricken by the maledictions of Calixtus III, and did not venture back for seventy-five years!"*

We never heard of any Christian clergyman or Pope trying to disabuse ignorant minds of the belief that the Devil had anything to do with eclipses and comets; but we do find a Buddhist chief saying to an official who twitted him with this superstition: "Our Sinhalese religious books teach that the eclipses of the sun and moon denote an attack of Râhu,† *but not by a devil.*"‡

The origin of the "Dragon" myth so prominent in the *Apocalypse* and *Golden Legend,* and of the fable about Simeon Stylites converting the Dragon, is undeniably Buddhistic and even pre-Buddhistic. It was Gautama's pure doctrines which reclaimed to Buddhism the Kashmîrians whose primitive worship was the Ophite or Serpent worship. Frankincense and flowers replaced the human sacrifices and belief in personal demons. It became the turn of Christianity to inherit the degrading superstition about devils invested with pestilential and murderous powers. The *Mahâvaṇśa,* oldest of the Ceylonese books, relates the story of King Covercapal (cobra-de-capello), the snake-god, who was converted to Buddhism by a holy Rahat;§ and it is earlier, by all odds, than the *Golden Legend* which tells the same of Simeon Stylites and his Dragon.

---

\* *Conflict between Religion and Science,* p. 269.

† Râhu and Ketu are the two fixed stars which form the head and tail of the constellation of the Dragon.[65]

‡ E. Upham, *The Mahâvansi,* etc., p. 54, for the answer given by the chief-priest of Mulgirri-Galle Vihâra, named Sue Bandare Metankere Samenêre Samewahanse, to a Dutch Governor in 1766.

§ We leave it to the learned archaeologists and philologists to decide how the *Nâga* or Serpent worship could travel from Kashmîr to Mexico and become the Nagual worship, which is also a Serpent worship, and a doctrine of lycanthropy.

The Logos triumphs once more over the great Dragon; Michael, the luminous archangel, chief of the Aeôns, conquers Satan.*

It is a fact worthy of remark, that so long as the initiate kept silent "on what he knew," he was perfectly safe. So was it in days of old, and so it is now. As soon as the Christian God, emanating forth from *Silence*, manifested himself as the *Word* or Logos, the latter became the cause of his death. The serpent is the symbol of wisdom and eloquence, but it is likewise the symbol of destruction. "To dare, to know, to will, *and be silent*," are the cardinal axioms of the kabalist. Like Apollo and other gods, Jesus is killed by his *Logos*"; he rises again, kills him in his turn, and becomes his master. Can it be that this old symbol has, like the rest of ancient philosophical conceptions, more than one allegorical and never-suspected meaning? The coincidences are too strange to be results of mere chance.

And now that we have shown this identity between Michael and Satan, and the Saviors and Dragons of other people, what can be more clear than that all these philosophical fables originated in India, that universal hotbed of metaphysical mysticism? "The world," says Ramatsariar, in his comments upon the *Vedas*, "commenced with a contest between the Spirit of Good and the Spirit of Evil, and so must end. After the destruction of matter, evil can no longer exist, it must return to naught." ‡

In the *Apologia*, Tertullian falsifies most papably every doctrine and belief of the Pagans as to the oracles and gods. He calls them, indifferently, demons and devils, accusing the latter of taking possession of even the birds of the air! What Christian would now dare doubt such an authority? Did not the Psalmist exclaim: "All the gods of the nations are *idols*"; § and the Angel of the School, Thomas Aquinas, explains, on his own *kabalistic* authority, the word *idols* by *devils?* "They come to men," he says, "and offer themselves to their adoration by operating certain things which seem miraculous."||

The Fathers were prudent as they were wise in their inventions. To be impartial, after having created a Devil, they set to creating apocryphal saints. We have named several in preceding chapters; but we must not forget Baronius, who having read in a work of Chrysostom about the holy *Xynoris*, the word meaning a *pair*, a couple, mistook it for the

---

* Michael, the chief of the Aeôns, is also "Gabriel, the messenger of Life," of the Nazarenes, and the Hindu Indra, the chief of the good Spirits, who vanquished Vâsuki, the Demon who rebelled against Brahmâ.

† See the Gnostic amulet called the "Chnuphis-Serpent," in the act of raising its head crowned with the *seven vowels*, which is the kabalistic symbol for signifying the "gift of speech to man," or *Logos*.

‡ Jacolliot, *La Bible dans l'Inde*, p. 368.

§ [*Psalms* xcvi, 5.]

|| Thos. Aquinas, *Summa theologiae*, iia-iiae, quaest. 94, art. 4. [Cf. Porphyry, *De abstinentia*, II, 41, 42.]

name of a saint, and proceeded forthwith to create of it a *martyr* of Antioch, and went on to give a most detailed and authentic biography of the "blessed martyr." Other theologians made of Apollyon — or rather *Apolouôn* — the anti-Christ. Apolouôn is Plato's "washer," the god *who purifies*, who washes off, and *releases* us from sin, but he was thus transformed into him "whose name in the Hebrew tongue is Abaddon, but in the Greek tongue hath the name Apollyon"— Devil! [*Rev.* ix, 11.]

Max Müller says that the serpent in Paradise is a conception which might have sprung up among the Jews, and "seems hardly to invite comparison with the much grander conceptions of the terrible power of Vṛitra and Ahriman in the *Veda* and *Avesta*." * With the kabalists the Devil was always a myth — God or good reversed. That modern Magus, Éliphas Lévi, calls the Devil *l'ivresse astrale*. It is a blind force like electricity, he says; and, speaking allegorically, as he always did, Jesus remarked that he "beheld Satan as lightning fall from Heaven."†

The clergy insist that God has sent the Devil to tempt mankind; which would be rather a singular way of showing his boundless love to humanity! If the Supreme One is really guilty of such unfatherly treachery, he is worthy, certainly, of the adoration only of a Church capable of singing the *Te Deum* over the Massacre of St. Bartholomew, and of blessing Moslem swords drawn to slaughter Greek Christians!

This is at once sound logic and good sound law, for is it not a maxim of jurisprudence: *"Qui facit per alium, facit per se"?*

The great dissimilarity which exists between the various conceptions of the Devil is really often ludicrous. While bigots will invariably endow him with horns, tail, and every conceivable repulsive feature, even including an offensive *human* smell,‡ Milton, Byron, Goethe, Lermontoff, § and a host of French novelists have sung his praise in flowing verse and thrilling prose. Milton's Satan, and even Goethe's Mephistopheles, are certainly far more commanding figures than some of the angels, as represented in the prose of

---

* [*Chips*, etc., Vol. I, p. 155.]

† [*Luke* x, 18.]

‡ See des Mousseaux; see various other Demonographers; the different "Trials of Witches," the depositions of the latter exacted by torture, etc. In our humble opinion, the Devil must have contracted this disagreeable smell and his habits of uncleanliness in company with mediaeval monks. Many of these saints boasted of having never washed themselves! "To strip one's self for the sake of *vain* cleanliness, is to sin in the eyes of God," says Sprenger, in *The Witches' Hammer*. Hermits and monks "dreaded all cleansing as so much defilement. There was no bathing for a thousand years!" exclaims Michelet in *La Sorcière*. Why such an outcry against Hindu fakirs in such a case? These, if they keep dirty, besmear themselves only after washing, for their religion commands them to wash every morning, and sometimes several times a day.

§ Lermontoff, the great Russian poet, author of *The Demon*.

ecstatic bigots. We have but to compare two descriptions. Let us first award the floor to the incomparably sensational des Mousseaux. He gives us a thrilling account of an incubus, in the words of the penitent herself: "Once," she tells us, "during the space of a whole half-hour, she saw *distinctly* near her an individual with a black, dreadful, horrid body, and whose hands, of an enormous size, exhibited *clawed* fingers strangely hooked. The senses of sight, feeling, and *smell* were confirmed by that of hearing"!!\*

And yet, for the space of several years, the damsel suffered herself to be led astray by such a hero! How far above this odoriferous gallant is the majestic figure of the Miltonic Satan!

Let the reader then fancy, if he can, this superb chimera, this ideal of the rebellious angel become incarnate Pride, crawling into the skin of the most disgusting of all animals! Notwithstanding that the Christian catechism teaches us that Satan *in propria persona* tempted our first mother, Eve, in a real paradise, and that in the shape of a serpent, which of all animals was the most insinuating and fascinating! God orders him, as a punishment, to crawl eternally on his belly, and bite the dust. "A sentence," remarks Lévi, "which resembles in nothing the traditional flames of hell." The more so, that the real zoological serpent, which was created before Adam and Eve, crawled on his belly, and bit the dust likewise, before there was any original sin.

Apart from this, was not Ophion, the Daimôn or Devil, like God called *Dominus?*† The word *God* (deity) is derived from the Sanskrit word *Deva*, and Devil from the Persian *daêva*, which words are substantially alike. Hercules, son of Jove and Alcmena, one of the highest sun-gods and also the Logos manifested, is nevertheless represented under a double nature, as all others.‡

The Agathodaimôn, the beneficent daemon, § the same which we find later among the Ophites under the appellation of the Logos, or divine wisdom, was represented by a serpent standing erect on a *pole*, in the Bacchanalian Mysteries. The hawk-headed serpent is among the oldest of the Egyptian emblems, and represents the divine mind, says Deane.‖

Azâzêl is Moloch and Samael, says Movers,¶ and we find Aaron, the brother of the great lawgiver Moses, making equal sacrifices to Jehovah and Azâzêl.

---
\* *Les Hauts Phénomènes de la magie*, p. 373.
† Movers, *Die Phönizier*, I, p. 109.
‡ Hercules is of Hindu origin.
§ The same as the Egyptian *Kneph*, and the Gnostic *Ophis*.
‖ *Worship of the Serpent*, p. 145.
¶ Movers, *op. cit.*, pp. 367, 397. Azâzêl and Samael are identical.

"And Aaron shall cast lots *upon the two goats;* one lot for the Lord [*Ihoh* in the original] and one lot for the scapegoat [*Azâzêl*]."*

In the *Old Testament,* Jehovah exhibits all the attributes of old Saturn,† notwithstanding his metamorphoses from Adoni into Eloi, and God of Gods, Lord of Lords. ‡

Jesus is tempted on the mountain by the Devil, who promises to him kingdoms and glory if he will only fall down and worship him (*Matthew* iv, 8, 9). Buddha is tempted by the Demon Wasawartti-Mâra, who says to him as he is leaving his father's palace: "Be entreated to stay that you may possess the honors that are within your reach; go not, go not!" And upon the refusal of Gautama to accept his offers, gnashes his teeth with rage, and threatens him with vengeance. Like Christ, Buddha triumphs over the Devil.§

In the Bacchic Mysteries, a *consecrated cup* was handed around after supper, called the cup of the Agathodaimôn. ‖ The Ophite rite of the same description is evidently borrowed from these Mysteries. The communion consisting of bread and wine was used in the worship of nearly every important deity.¶

In connection with the semi-Mithraic sacrament adopted by the Marcosians, another Gnostic sect, utterly kabalistic and *theurgic,* there is a strange story given by Epiphanius as an illustration of the cleverness of the Devil. In the celebration of their Eucharist, three large vases of the finest and clearest crystal were brought among the congregation and filled with white wine. While the ceremony was going on, in full view of everybody, this wine was instantaneously changed into a blood-red, a purple, and then into an azure-blue color. "Then the magus," says Epiphanius, "hands one of these vases to a woman in the congregation, and asks her to bless it. When it is done, the magus pours it out into another vase of much greater capacity with the prayer: 'May the grace of God, which is above all, inconceivable, inexplicable, fill thy inner man, and augment the knowledge of Him within thee, sowing the grain of mustard seed in good

---

\* *Levit.* xvi, 8.

† Saturn is Bel-Moloch and even Hercules and Siva. Both of the latter are *Hâras,* or gods of the war, of the battle, or the "Lords of Hosts." Jehovah is called "a man of war" in *Exodus* xv, 3. "The Lord of Hosts is his name" (*Isaiah* li, 15), and David blesses him for teaching his "hands to war and his fingers to fight" (*Psalms* cxliv, 1). Saturn is also the Sun, and Movers says that "Kronos Saturn was called by the Phoenicians *Israel* (*Die Phönizier,* I, p. 130). Philo says the same (quoted in Eusebius, *Praep. evang.,* lib. I, cap. x, 40).

‡ "Blessed be Jehovah Elohim Elohei *Israel*" (*Psalms* lxxii, 18).

§ Hardy, *A Manual of Budhism,* pp. 159-60.

‖ Dunlap, *Vestiges,* etc., p. 217.

¶ Movers, Duncker, Higgins, and others.

ground.' Whereupon the liquor in the larger vase swells and swells until it runs over the brim." *

In connection with several of the Pagan deities which are made after death, and before their resurrection, to descend into Hell, it will be found useful to compare the pre-Christian with the post-Christian narratives. Orpheus made the journey,† and Christ was the last of these subterranean travellers. In the *Credo* of the Apostles, which is divided in twelve sentences or *articles*, each particular article having been inserted by each particular apostle, according to St. Augustine ‡ the sentence "He descended into hell, the third day he rose again from the dead," is assigned to Thomas; perhaps, as an atonement for his unbelief. Be that as it may, the sentence is declared a forgery, and there is no evidence "that this Creed was framed by the apostles, or indeed that it existed as a creed in their time." §

It is the most important addition in the Apostles' Creed, and dates since the year of Christ 600. || It was not known in the days of Eusebius. Bishop J. Pearson says that it was not in the ancient creeds or rules of faith.¶ Irenaeus, Origen, and Tertullian exhibit no knowledge of this sentence.** It is not mentioned in any of the Councils before the seventh century. Theodoret, Epiphanius, and Socrates are silent about it. It differs from the *creed* in St. Augustine.†† Rufinus affirms that in his time it was neither in the Roman nor in the Oriental creeds.‡‡ But the problem is solved when we learn that ages ago Hermes spoke thus to Prometheus, chained on the arid rock of the Caucasian mount:

---

* Epiphanius, *Panarion*, lib. I, tom. III, Haer. XXXIV, i; cf. King, *The Gnostics*, etc., pp. 53-54 [p. 126 in 2nd ed.]. Wine was first made *sacred* in the mysteries of Bacchus. R. Payne Knight [*Symb. Lang.*, p. 50] believes — erroneously we think — that wine was taken with the view to produce a false ecstasy through intoxication. It was held *sacred*, however, and the Christian Eucharist is certainly an imitation of the Pagan rite. Whether Mr. Knight was right or wrong, we regret to say that a Protestant clergyman, the Rev. Joseph Blanchard, of New York, was found drunk in one of the public squares on the night of Sunday, August 5, 1877, and lodged in prison. The published report says: "The prisoner said that he had been to church and taken a little too much of the communion wine!"

† The initiatory rite typified a descent into the underworld. Bacchus, Herakles, Orpheus, and Asclepius all descended into hell and ascended thence the third day.

‡ Lord King, *Hist. Apost. Creed*, Basel, 1750, p. 26.

§ Justice Bailey, *Common Prayer Book*, 1813, p. 9.

|| *Ibid.*

¶ *An Exposition of the Creed*, p. 225; 6th rev. ed.

** Cf. Irenaeus, *Adv. Haer.*, I, x; Origen, *De princ.*, proem.; Tertullian, *Adv. Praxean*, ii; *De praescr. haer.*, xiii.

†† [Theodoret, *Eccl. Hist.*, I, xi; Socrates Scholasticus, *Eccl. Hist.*, I, xxvi; Epiphanius, *Panarion*, lib. III, tom. I, Haer. LXXII, ii *et seq.*; Augustine, *De fide et symbole.*]

‡‡ *Exposit. in symbol. apost.*, 10; ed. 1682.

"To such labors look thou for no termination, UNTIL SOME GOD SHALL APPEAR AS A SUBSTITUTE IN THY PANGS AND SHALL BE WILLING TO GO BOTH TO GLOOMY HADÊS AND TO THE MURKY DEPTHS AROUND TARTARUS!"*

This god was Herakles, the "Only-Begotten One," and the Savior. And it is he who was chosen as a model by the ingenious Fathers. Hercules — called Alexikakos—for he brought round the wicked and converted them to virtue; *Soter*, or Savior, also called Neulos Eumêlos — the *Good Shepherd*; Astrochitôn, the star-clothed, and the Lord of Fire. "He sought not to subject nations by force but by *divine wisdom* and persuasion," says Lucian. "Herakles spread cultivation and a mild religion, and destroyed the *doctrine of eternal punishment* by dragging Cerberus (the Pagan Devil) from the nether world." And, as we see, it was Herakles again who liberated Prometheus (the Adam of the pagans), by putting an end to the torture inflicted on him for his transgressions, by descending to the Hadês, and going round the Tartarus. Like Christ he appeared as *a substitute for the pangs of humanity*, by offering himself in a self-sacrifice on a funereal burning pile. "His voluntary immolation," says Bart, "betokened the ethereal new birth of men . . . Through the release of Prometheus, and the erection of altars, we behold in him the mediator between the old and new faiths . . . He abolished human sacrifice wherever he found it practiced. He descended into the sombre realm of Pluto, as a shade . . . he *ascended as a spirit to his father Zeus in Olympus*."†

So much was antiquity impressed by the Heraklean legend, that even the *monotheistic* (?) Jews of those days, not to be outdone by their contemporaries, put him to use in their manufacture of original fables. Herakles is accused in his mythobiography of an attempted theft of the Delphian oracle. In *Sepher Toledoth Yeshu,* the Rabbis accuse Jesus of stealing from their Sanctuary the Incommunicable Name!

Therefore it is but natural to find his numerous adventures, worldly and religious, mirrored so faithfully in the *Descent into Hell.* For extraordinary daring of mendacity, and unblushing plagiarism, the *Gospel of Nicodemus,* only *now* proclaimed apocryphal, surpasses anything we have read. Let the reader judge.

At the beginning of chapter xvi, Satan and the "Prince of Hell" are described as peacefully conversing together. All of a sudden, both are startled by "a voice as of thunder" and the rushing of winds, which bids them to lift up their gates for *"the King of Glory* shall come in." Whereupon the Prince of Hell hearing this "begins quarreling with Satan for minding his duty so poorly, as not to have taken the necessary precautions against such a visit." The quarrel ends with the

---
* Aeschylus, *Prometheus Bound,* 1026-29.
† [C. C. Bart, *Die Kabiren in Teutschland,* 1832, pp. 177-78.]

prince casting Satan "forth from his hell," ordering, at the same time, his impious officers "to shut the brass gates of cruelty, and make them fast with iron bars, and fight courageously, lest we be taken captives."

But "when all the company of the saints [in Hell?] heard this, they spake with a loud voice of anger to the prince of hell, 'Open thy gates, that the King of Glory may come in'," thereby proving that the prince needed spokesmen.

"And the *divine* [?] prophet David cried out, saying: 'Did not I, when on earth, truly prophesy?'" After this, another prophet, namely holy Isaiah, spake in like manner, "Did not I rightly prophesy?" etc. Then the company of the saints and prophets, after boasting for the length of a chapter, and comparing notes of their prophecies, begin a riot, which makes the Prince of Hell remark that, "the dead never durst before behave themselves insolently towards us" (the devils, xviii, 6); feigning the while to be ignorant about *who* was claiming admission. He then innocently asks again: "But who is that King of Glory?" Then David tells him that he knows the voice well, and understands its words, "because," he adds, "I spake them by his Spirit." Perceiving finally that the Prince of Hell would not open the "brass doors of iniquity," notwithstanding the king-psalmist's voucher for the visitor, he, David, concludes to treat the enemy as a Philistine, and begins shouting: "And now, thou *filthy* and *stinking* prince of hell, open thy gates that the King of Glory may enter in." [xvi, 14-17.]

While he was yet quarreling, the "mighty Lord appeared in the form of *a man*"(?) upon which "impious *Death* and her cruel officers are seized with fear." Then they tremblingly begin to address Christ with various flatteries and compliments in the shape of questions, each of which *is an article of creed*. For instance: "And who art thou, who dost release the captives that were *held in chains by original sin?*" asks one devil. "Perhaps, thou art that Jesus," submissively says another, "of whom Satan just now spake, that by the *death of the Cross thou wert about to receive the power of death?*" etc. Instead of answering, the King of Glory "tramples upon Death, seizes the Prince of Hell, and deprives him of his power." [xvii, 7, 12-13.]

Then begins a turmoil in Hell which has been graphically described by Homer, Hesiod and their interpreter Preller, in his account of the astronomical Hercules *Invictus*, and his festivals at Tyre, Tarsus and Sardis. Having been initiated in the Attic Eleusinia, the Pagan god descends into Hadês and when he entered the nether world he spread such terror among the dead that all of them fled! * The same words are repeated in *Nicodemus*. Follows a scene of

---

* L. Preller, *Griechische Mythologie*, Vol. II, p. 154.

confusion, horror, and lamenting. Perceiving that the battle is lost, the Prince of Hell turns tail and prudently chooses to side with the strongest. He against whom, according to Jude and Peter, even the Archangel Michael "durst not bring a railing accusation before the Lord," is now shamefully treated by his ex-ally and friend, the "Prince of Hell." Poor Satan is abused and reviled for all his crimes both by devils and saints; while the *Prince* is openly rewarded for his treachery. Addressing him, the King of Glory says thus: "Beelzebub, the Prince of Hell, Satan the Prince shall be subject to thy dominion *forever, in the room of Adam* and his righteous sons, who are mine . . . Come to me, all ye my saints, who were *created in my image,* who *were condemned by the tree of the forbidden fruit,* and *by the Devil and death.* Live now *by the wood of my cross;* the Devil, the prince of this world, is overcome [?] and *Death is conquered.*" Then the Lord takes hold of Adam by his right hand, of David by the left, and *"ascends* from Hell, followed by all the saints," Enoch and Elias, and by the *"holy* thief." \*

The pious author, perhaps through an oversight, omits to complete the cavalcade, by bringing up the rear with the penitent dragon of Simeon Stylites and the converted wolf of St. Francis, wagging their tails and shedding tears of joy!

In the *Codex* of the Nazarenes it is *Tobo* who is "the *liberator of the soul of Adam,"* to bear it from Orcus (Hadês) to the place of LIFE.† Tobo is Tob-Adonijah, one of the twelve disciples (Levites) sent by Jehoshaphat to preach to the cities of Judah the *Book of the Law* (2 *Chron.* xvii). In the kabalistic book these were "wise men," Magi. They drew down the rays of the sun to enlighten the *Sheol (Hadês),* Orcus, and thus show the way out of the *Tenebrae,* the darkness of ignorance, to the soul of Adam, which represents collectively all the "souls of mankind." Adam (Athamas) is Tamuz or Adonis, and Adonis is the sun Hêlios. In the *Book of the Dead,* Osiris is made to say: "I shine like the sun in the star-house at the feast of the sun." Christ is called the "Sun of Righteousness," "Hêlios of Justice," ‡ simply a revamping of the old heathen allegories; nevertheless, to have made it serve for such a use is no less blasphemous on the part of men who pretended to be describing a true episode of the earth-pilgrimage of their God!

> "Herakles, who *has gone out from the chambers of earth,*
> Leaving the nether house of Plouton!"§

---

\* *Apocryphal Gospel of Nicodemus,* xviii-xix; transl. by Hone from Grynaeus, *Monumenta S. Patrum Orthodoxographa,* Basileae, 1569, Vol. II, p. 656.

† [Norberg, *Codex Nazaraeus,* III, p. 267.]

‡ Eusebius, *Demonstr. evang.,* V, xxix.

§ Euripides, *The Madness of Herakles,* 806-808.

> "At THEE the Stygian lakes trembled; Thee the janitor of Orcus
> Feared, reclining in his bloody cave upon half-devoured bones.
> THEE not even Typhon frightened . . .
> Hail *true* SON *of* JOVE, GLORY added to the gods!"\*

More than four centuries before the birth of Jesus, Aristophanes had written his immortal parody on the *Descent into Hell* by Herakles.† The chorus of the "blessed ones," the initiated, the Elysian Fields, the arrival of Bacchus (who is Iacchos — Iaho — and *Tsabaôth*) with Herakles, their reception with lighted torches, emblems of *new life* and RESURRECTION from darkness, death unto light, eternal LIFE; nothing that is found in the *Gospel of Nicodemus* is wanting in this poem:

> "Wake burning torches . . . for thou comest
> Shaking them in thy hand, Iacche,
> Phosphoric star of the nightly rite!" ‡

But the Christians accept these *post-mortem* adventures of their god concocted from those of his Pagan predecessors, and derided by Aristophanes four centuries before our era, *literally!* The absurdities of *Nicodemus* were read in the churches, as well as those of the *Shepherd of Hermas*. Irenaeus quotes the latter under the name of *Scripture,* a divinely-inspired "revelation"; Jerome and Eusebius both insist upon its being publicly read in the churches; and Athanasius observes that the Fathers "appointed it to be read in *confirmation of faith and piety*." § But then comes the reverse of this bright medal, to show once more how stable and trustworthy were the opinions of the strongest pillars of an *infallible* Church. Jerome, who applauds the book in his catalogue of ecclesiastical writers, in his later comments terms it "apocryphal and foolish"! Tertullian, who could not find praise enough for the *Shepherd of Hermas* when a Catholic, "began abusing it when a Montanist." ‖

Chapter xiii begins with the narrative given by the two resuscitated ghosts of Charinus and Lenthius, the sons of that Simeon who, in the *Gospel according to Luke* (ii, 28-32), takes the infant Jesus in his arms and blesses God, saying: "Lord, now lettest thou thy servant depart in peace . . . for mine eyes have seen thy salvation." ¶ These two ghosts

---

\* Virgil, *Aeneid*, viii, 296 *et seq.*
† Aristophanes, *Ranae* (Frogs).
‡ *Op. cit.,* lines 340-343.
§ [*Ep. Fest.* 39, Vol. I, pt. ii, p. 963. Cf. Smith and Wace, *Dict. of Christ. Biogr.,* s.v. Shepherd of Hermas.]
‖ Hone, *The Apocryphal New Testament,* pref. to *Hermas,* London, 1820.
¶ In the "Life of Buddha," of the *Kanjur* (*bKah-hgyur,* Tibetan text), we find the original of the episode given in the Gospel according to Luke. An old and holy ascetic, Ṛishi Asita, comes from afar to see the infant Buddha, instructed as he is of his birth and mission by supernatural visions. Having worshipped the little Gautama, the old saint bursts into tears, and upon being questioned upon the cause of his grief,

have arisen from their cold tombs on purpose to declare "the mysteries" which they saw after death in hell. They are enabled to do so only at the importunate prayer of Annas and Caiaphas, Nicodemus (the author), Joseph (of Arimathaea), and Gamaliel, who beseech them to reveal to them the great secrets. Annas and Caiaphas, however, who bring the *ghosts* to the synagogue at Jerusalem, take the precaution to make the two resuscitated men, who had been dead and buried for years, to swear on the *Book of the Law* "by God Adonai, and the God of Israel," to tell them only the truth. Therefore, after making the *sign of the cross* on their tongues,* they ask for some paper to write their confessions (*Gosp. of Nicod.* xii, 21-25). They state how, when "in the depth of hell, in the blackness of darkness," they suddenly saw "a substantial purple-colored light enlightening the place." Adam, with the patriarchs and prophets, began thereupon to rejoice, and Isaiah also immediately boasted that he had *predicted all that.* While this was going on, Simeon, their father, arrived, declaring that "the infant he took in his arms in the temple was now coming to liberate them."

After Simeon had delivered his message to the distinguished company in hell, "there came forth one like a little hermit"(?), who proved to be John the Baptist. The idea is suggestive and shows that even the "Precursor" and "the Prophet of the Most High," had not been exempted from drying up in hell to the most diminutive proportions, and that to the extent of affecting his brains and memory. Forgetting that (*Matthew* xi) he had manifested the most evident doubts as to the Messiahship of Jesus, the Baptist also claims his right to be recognized as a prophet. "And I, John," he says, "when I saw Jesus coming to me, being moved by the Holy Ghost, I said: 'Behold the Lamb of God, . . .

---

answers: "After becoming Buddha, he will help hundreds of thousands of millions of creatures to pass to the other shore of the ocean of life, and will lead them on forever to immortality. And I—I shall not behold this pearl of Buddhas! Cured of my illness, I shall not be freed by him from human passion! Great King! I am too old—that is why I weep, and why, in my sadness, I heave long sighs!"

It does not prevent the holy man, however, from delivering prophecies about the young Buddha, which, with a very slight difference, are of the same substance as those of Simeon about Jesus. While the latter calls the young Jesus "a light for the revelation of the Gentiles and the glory of the people of Israel," the Buddhist prophet promises that the young prince will find himself clothed with the perfect and complete *enlightenment* or "light" of Buddha, and will turn the wheel *of law* as no one *ever did before him.* *Rgya tch'er rol pa,* translated from the Tibetan text of the *Kanjur,* and revised from the original Sanskrit *Lalitavistara,* by P. É. Foucaux, 1847-48, Vol. II, pp. 106-07.

* The sign of the cross—only a few days after the resurrection, and before the cross was ever thought of as a symbol!

who takes away the sins of the world.' And I baptized him . . . and saw the Holy Ghost descending upon him . . . saying, 'This is my Beloved Son,' etc." [xiii, 12-13.] And to think that his descendants and followers, like the Mandeans of Basra, utterly reject these words!

Then Adam, who acts as though his own veracity might be questioned in this "impious company," calls his son Seth, and desires him to declare to his sons, the patriarchs and prophets, what the Archangel Michael had told him at the gate of Paradise, when he, Adam, sent Seth "to entreat God that he would anoint" his head when Adam was sick (xiv, 2). And Seth tells them that when he was praying at the gates of Paradise, Michael advised him not to entreat God for "the oil of the tree of mercy, wherewith to anoint thy father Adam for his *headache;* because thou canst not by any means obtain it, till the LAST DAY and times, namely, *till 5,500 years be past.*" [xiv, 4.]

This little bit of private gossip between Michael and Seth was evidently introduced in the interests of patristic chronology; and for the purpose of connecting Messiahship still closer with Jesus, on the authority of a recognized and divinely-inspired Gospel. The Fathers of the early centuries committed an inexplicable mistake in destroying fragile images and mortal Pagans, in preference to the monuments of Egyptian antiquity. These have become the more precious to archaeology and modern science since it is found they prove that King Menes and his architects flourished between four and five thousand years before "Father Adam" and the universe, according to the Biblical chronology, were created "out of nothing." *

"While all the saints were rejoicing, behold Satan, the prince and captain of death," says to the Prince of Hell: "Prepare to receive Jesus of Nazareth himself, who boasted that he was the Son of God, and yet was a man afraid of death, and said: 'My soul is sorrowful even to death'." (xv, 1, 2.)

There is a tradition among the Greek ecclesiastical writers that the "Heretics" (perhaps Celsus) had sorely twitted the Christians on this delicate point. They held that if Jesus were not a simple mortal, who was often forsaken by the Spirit of Christos, he could not have complained in such expressions as are attributed to him; neither would he have cried out with a loud voice: "My *god,* My *god!* why hast thou for-

---

* R. Payne Knight shows that "from the times of the first King, Menes, under whom all the country below Lake Moeris was a bog (Herod., II, 4), to that of the Persian invasion, when it was the garden of the world" — between 11,000 and 12,000 years must have elapsed. (See *Symbolic Language of Ancient Art and Mythology,* § 151. Edit. by A. Wilder.)

saken me?" This objection is very cleverly answered in the *Gospel of Nicodemus,* and it is the "Prince of Hell" who settles the difficulty.

He begins by arguing with Satan like a true metaphysician. "Who is that so powerful prince," he sneeringly inquires, "and yet a man who is afraid of death? . . . I affirm to thee that . . . when therefore he said he was afraid of death, *he designed to ensnare thee,* and unhappy it will be to thee for everlasting ages"! [xv, 4-7.]

It is quite refreshing to see how closely the author of this *Gospel* sticks to his *New Testament* text, and especially to the fourth evangelist. How cleverly he prepares the way for seemingly "innocent" questions and answers, corroborating the most dubious passages of the four gospels, passages more questioned and cross-examined in those days of subtile sophistry of the learned Gnostics than they are now; a weighty reason why the Fathers should have been even more anxious to burn the documents of their antagonists than to destroy their heresy. The following is a good instance. The dialogue is still proceeding between Satan and the metaphysical *half-converted* Prince of the underworld.

"Who, then, is that Jesus of Nazareth," naïvely inquires the prince, "that by his word hath taken away the dead from me, without prayer to God?" (xv, 13).

"Perhaps," replies Satan, with the innocence of a Jesuit, *"it is the same who took away from me* LAZARUS, *after he had been four days dead,* and did both stink and was rotten? . . . It is the very same person, Jesus of Nazareth. . . . I adjure thee by the powers which belong to thee and me, that thou bring him not to me!" exclaims the prince. "For when I heard of the power of his word, I trembled for fear, and all my *impious* company were at the same disturbed. And we were not able to detain Lazarus, but he gave himself *a shake,* and *with all the signs of malice,* immediately went away from us; and the very earth, in which the dead body of Lazarus was lodged, presently turned him out alive." "Yes," thoughtfully adds the Prince of Hell, "I know now *that he is Almighty God,* . . . who is mighty in his dominion, and mighty *in his human nature,* who is the Savior of mankind. Bring not therefore this person hither, for he will set at liberty all those whom I hold in prison under unbelief, and . . . *will conduct them to everlasting life"* (xv, 14-20).

Here ends the *post-mortem* evidence of the two ghosts. Charinus (ghost No. 1) gives what he wrote to Annas, Caiaphas, and Gamaliel, and Lenthius (ghost No. 2) his to Joseph and Nicodemus, having done which, both change into "exceedingly white forms and were seen no more."

To show furthermore that the "ghosts" had been all the time under the strictest "test conditions," as the modern spiritualists would express it, the author of the *Gospel* adds: "But what they had written was *found perfectly to agree,* the one not containing one letter more or less than the other."

This news spread in all the synagogues, the Gospel goes on to state; Pilate went to the temple as advised by Nicodemus, and assembled the Jews together. At this historical interview, Caiaphas and Annas are made to declare that their Scriptures testify *"that He [Jesus] is the Son of God, and the Lord and King of Israel"* (!) and close the confession with the following memorable words:

"And so it appears *that Jesus, whom we crucified, is Jesus Christ, the Son of God, and true and Almighty God. Amen."* (!) [xxii, 14, 20.]

Notwithstanding such a crushing confession for themselves, and the recognition of Jesus as the Almighty God himself, the "Lord God of Israel," neither the high priest, nor his father-in-law, nor any of the elders, nor Pilate, who wrote those accounts, nor any of the Jews of Jerusalem, who were at all prominent, became Christians.

Comments are unnecessary. This *Gospel* closes with the words: "In the name of *the Holy Trinity* [of which Nicodemus could know nothing yet], *thus ends the Acts of our Savior Jesus Christ, which the emperor Theodosius the Great found at Jerusalem, in the hall of Pontius Pilate, among the public records";* and which history purports to have been written in Hebrew by Nicodemus, *"the things were acted in the nineteenth year of Tiberius Caesar, Emperor of the Romans, and in the seventeenth year of the government of Herod, the son of Herod, king of Galilee, on the eighth of the calends of April,* etc., etc." It is the most barefaced imposture that was perpetrated after the era of pious forgeries opened with the first bishop of Rome, whoever he may have been. The clumsy forger seems to have neither known nor heard that the dogma of the Trinity was not propounded until 325 years later than this pretended date. Neither the *Old* nor the *New Testament* contains the word Trinity, nor anything that affords the slightest pretext for this doctrine (see page 177 of this volume, "Christ's descent into Hell"). No explanation can palliate the putting forth of this spurious gospel as a divine revelation, for it was known from the first as a premeditated imposture. If the gospel itself has been declared apocryphal, nevertheless every one of the dogmas contained in it was and is still enforced upon the Christian world. And even the fact that it is now repudiated is no merit, *for the Church was shamed and forced into it.*

And so we are perfectly warranted in repeating the amended *Credo* of Robert Taylor, which is substantially that of the Christians.

> I believe in Zeus, the Father Almighty,
> And in his son, Iasios Christ our Lord,
> Who was conceived of the Holy Ghost,

Born of the Virgin Elektra,
Smitten with a thunderbolt,
Dead and buried,
He descended into Hell,
Rose again and ascended up on high,
And will return to judge the living and the dead.
I believe in the Holy Nous,
In the Holy circle of Great Gods,
In the Community of Divinities,
In the expiation of sins,
The immortality of the Soul
And the Life Everlasting.*

The Israelites have been proved to have worshipped Baal, the Syrian Bacchus, offered incense to the Sabazian or Aesculapian serpent, and performed the Dionysian Mysteries. And how could it be otherwise if Typhon was called Typhon Set,† and Seth, the son of Adam, is identical with Satan or Sat-an; and Seth was worshipped by the Hittites? Less than two centuries B.C., we find the Jews either reverencing or simply worshipping the "golden head of an ass" in their temple; according to Apion, Antiochus Epiphanes carried it off with him. And Zacharias is struck dumb by the apparition of the deity under the shape of an ass in the temple!‡

---

\* [*The Diegesis*, pp. 9-10.]

† Seth or Sutech, Rawlinson's *History of Herodotus*, Book II, 144.

‡ The fact is vouchsafed for by Epiphanius. See Hone, *Apocryphal New Testament*, pref. to *The Gospel of the Birth of Mary*.

In his able article "Bacchus the Prophet-God," Professor A. Wilder remarks that "Tacitus was misled into saying that the Jews worshipped an ass, the symbol of Typhon or Seth, the Hyksôs God. The Egyptian name of the ass was *eo*, the phonetic of Iaô and hence, probably," he adds, "a symbol from that mere circumstance." We can hardly agree with this learned archaeologist, for the idea that the Jews reverenced, for some mysterious reason, Typhon under his symbolical representation rests on more proof than one. We find a passage in the *Gospel of the Birth of Mary*, cited from Epiphanius, which corroborates the fact. It relates to the death of "Zacharias, the father of John the Baptist, murdered by Herod," says the *Protevangelion* [ch. xvi]. Epiphanius writes that the cause of the death of Zacharias was that upon seeing a vision in the temple "he, through surprise, was willing to disclose it, and his mouth was stopped. That which he saw was at the time of his offering incense, and it was a man STANDING IN THE FORM OF AN ASS. When he was gone out, and had a mind to speak thus to the people, *Woe unto you, whom do ye worship?* he who had appeared unto him in the temple took away the use of his speech. Afterwards when he recovered it, and was able to speak, he declared this to the Jews, and they slew him. They add (viz. the Gnostics in this book), that on this very account the high priest was appointed by their lawgiver [Moses] to carry little bells, that whensoever he went into the temple to sacrifice, he, *whom they worshipped,* hearing the noise of the bells, might have time enough to hide himself, and not be caught in that ugly shape and figure." (Attributed to Epiphanius in Hone, *The Apocryphal New Testament*, 1820, p. 17.)

El, the Sun-God of the Syrians, the Egyptians, and the Semites, is declared by Pleyte to be no other than Set or Seth, and El is the primeval Saturn—Israel.* Śiva is an Aethiopian God, the same as the Chaldean Baal — Bel; thus he is also Saturn. Saturn, El, Seth and Khîyûn, or the Biblical Chiun of Amos, are all one and the same deity, and may be all regarded in their worst aspect as Typhon the Destroyer. When the religious Pantheon assumed a more definite expression, Typhon was separated from his androgyne—the *good* deity, and fell into degradation as a brutal *unintellectual* power.

Such reactions in the religious feelings of a nation were not unfrequent. The Jews had worshipped Baal or Moloch, the Sun-God Hercules,† in their early days—if they had any days at all earlier than the Persians or Maccabees—and then made their prophets denounce them. On the other hand, the characteristics of the Mosaic Jehovah exhibit more of the moral disposition of Śiva than of a benevolent, "long-suffering" God. Besides, to be identified with Śiva is no small compliment, for the latter is God of wisdom. Wilkinson depicts him as the most intellectual of the Hindu gods. He is *three-eyed*, and, like Jehovah, terrible in his resistless revenge and wrath. And, although the Destroyer, yet he is "the re-creator of all things in perfect wisdom." ‡ He is the type of St. Augustine's God who "prepares *hell* for pryers into his mysteries," and insists on trying human reason as well as common sense by forcing mankind to view with equal reverence his good and evil acts.

Notwithstanding the numerous proofs that the Israelites worshipped a variety of gods, and even offered human sacrifices until a far later period than their Pagan neighbors, they have contrived to blind posterity in regard to truth. They sacrificed human life as late as 169 B.C., § and the *Bible* contains a number of such records. At a time when the Pagans had long abandoned the abominable practice, and had replaced the sacrificial man by the animal, ‖ Jephthah is represented sacrificing his own daughter to the "Lord" for a burnt-offering.¶

The denunciations of their own prophets are the best proofs against them. Their worship in high places is the same as that of the "idolaters." Their prophetesses are counterparts of the Pythiae and Bacchantes. Pausanias speaks of women-colleges which superintend the worship of

---

* Westropp and Wake, *Ancient Symbol Worship*, 2nd ed., 1875, p. 62; Pleyte, *La religion des pré-Israélites*, pp. 89 et passim.

† Hercules is also a god-fighter as well as Jacob-Israel.

‡ Westropp and Wake, *op. cit.*, p. 74.

§ Antiochus Epiphanes found in 169 B.C. in the Jewish temple, a man kept there to be sacrificed. Josephus, *Contra Apionem*, II, § 8.

‖ The ox of Dionysus was sacrificed at the Bacchic Mysteries. See Wm. Smith, *Dict. of Greek and Roman Antiquities*, 1848, p. 410, s.v. DIIPOLEIA.

¶ [Judges xi, 39.]

Bacchus, and of the sixteen matrons of Elis.* The *Bible* says that "Deborah, a prophetess . . . judged Israel at that time";† and speaks of Huldah, another prophetess, who "dwelt in Jerusalem, *in the college*"; ‡ and *2 Samuel* mentions "*wise* women" several times, § notwithstanding the injunction of Moses not to use either divination or augury. As to the final and conclusive identification of the "Lord God" of Israel with Moloch, we find a very suspicious evidence of the case in the last chapter of *Leviticus,* concerning *things devoted not to be redeemed.* "A man shall devote unto the Lord of all that he hath, *both of man* and beast. . . . None devoted, which shall be devoted of men, shall be redeemed, *but shall surely be put to death* . . . it is *most holy unto the Lord.*"‖

The duality, if not the plurality of the gods of Israel may be inferred from the very fact of such bitter denunciations. Their prophets *never approved of sacrificial worship.* Samuel denied that the Lord had any delight in burnt offerings and sacrifices (*1 Samuel* xv, 22). *Jeremiah* asserted, unequivocally, that the Lord, Yava Tsabaôth Elohe Israel, never commanded anything of the sort, but contrariwise (vii, 21-24).

But these prophets who opposed themselves to human sacrifices were all *nazars* and *initiates.* These prophets led a party in the nation against the priests, as later the Gnostics contended against the Christian Fathers. Hence, when the monarchy was divided, we find the priests at Jerusalem and the prophets in the country of Israel. Even Ahab and his sons, who introduced the Tyrian worship of Baal-Hercules and the Syrian goddess into Israel, were aided and encouraged by Elijah and Elisha. Few prophets appeared in Judaea till Isaiah, after the northern monarchy had been overthrown. Elisha anointed Jehu on purpose that he should destroy the royal families of both countries, and so unite the people into one civil polity. For the Temple of Solomon, desecrated by the priests, no Hebrew prophet or initiate cared a straw. Elijah never went to it, nor Elisha, Jonah, Nahum, Amos, or any other Israelite. While the initiates were holding to the "secret doctrine" of Moses, the people, led by their priests, were steeped in idolatry exactly the same as that of the Pagans. It is the popular views and interpretations of Jehovah that the Christians have adopted.

The question is likely to be asked: "In the view of so much evidence showing that Christian theology is only a *pot-pourri* of Pagan mythologies, how can it be connected with the religion of Moses?" The early Christians, Paul and his disciples, the Gnostics and their successors generally, regarded Christianity and Judaism as essentially distinct. The

---

\* Pausanias, *Itinerary,* "Elis," I, xvi.
† *Judges* iv, 4.
‡ *2 Kings* xxii, 14.
§ xiv, 2; xx, 16, 17.
‖ xxvii, 28, 29.

latter, in their view, was an antagonistic system, and from a lower origin. "Ye received the law," said Stephen, "from the ministration of angels,"* or aeôns, and not from the Most High Himself. The Gnostics, as we have seen, taught that Jehovah, the Deity of the Jews, was Ialdabaôth, the son of the ancient *Bohu,* or Chaos, the adversary of Divine Wisdom.

The question may be more than easily answered. The *law of Moses, and the so-called monotheism of the Jews, can hardly be said to have been more than two or three centuries older than Christianity.* The *Pentateuch* itself, we are able to show, was written and revised upon this "new departure," at a period subsequent to the colonization of Judaea under the authority of the kings of Persia. The Christian Fathers, in their eagerness to make their new system dovetail with Judaism and so avoid Paganism, unconsciously shunned Scylla only to be caught in the whirlpool of Charybdis. Under the monotheistic stucco of Judaism was unearthed the same familiar mythology of Paganism. But we should not regard the Israelites with less favor for having had a Moloch and being like the natives. Nor should we compel the Jews to do penance for their fathers. They had their prophets and their law, and were satisfied with them. How faithfully and nobly they have stood by their ancestral faith under the most diabolical persecutions, the present remains of a once-glorious people bear witness. The Christian world has been in a state of convulsion from the first to the present century; it has been cleft into thousands of sects; but the Jews remain substantially united. Even their differences of opinion do not destroy their unity.

The Christian virtues inculcated by Jesus in the Sermon on the Mount are nowhere exemplified in the Christian world. The Buddhist ascetics and Indian fakirs seem almost the only ones that inculcate and practice them. Meanwhile the vices which coarse-mouthed slanderers have attributed to Paganism are current everywhere among Christian Fathers and Christian Churches.

The boasted wide gap between Christianity and Judaism, that is claimed on the authority of Paul, exists but in the imagination of the pious. We are nought but the inheritors of the intolerant Israelites of ancient days; not the Hebrews of the time of Herod and the Roman dominion, who, with all their faults, kept strictly orthodox and monotheistic, but the Jews who, under the name of Jehovah-Nissi, worshipped Bacchus-Osiris, Dio-Nysos, the multiform Jove of Nysa, the Sinai of Moses. The kabalistic demons—allegories of the profoundest meaning— were adopted as objective entities, and a Satanic hierarchy carefully drawn by the orthodox demonologists.

The Rosicrucian motto, *Igne natura renovatur integra* [INRI], which the alchemists interpret as nature renovated by fire, or matter by spirit, is

---

* [*Acts* vii, 53.]

made to be accepted to this day as *Iesus Nazarenus rex Iudaeorum*. The mocking satire of Pilate is accepted literally, and the Jews made to unwittingly confess thereby the royalty of Christ; whereas, if the inscription is not a forgery of the Constantinian period, it yet is the action of Pilate, against which the Jews were first to violently protest. I. H. S. is interpreted *Iesus Hominum Salvator*, and *In hoc signo*, whereas IHΣ is one of the most ancient names of Bacchus. And more than ever do we begin to find out, by the bright light of comparative theology, that the great object of Jesus, the initiate of the inner sanctuary, was to open the eyes of the fanatical multitude to the difference between the highest Divinity—the mysterious and never-mentioned IAÔ of the ancient Chaldean and later Neo-Platonic initiates—and the Hebrew Yahuh, or Yaho (Jehovah). The modern Rosicrucians, so violently denounced by the Catholics, now find brought against them, as the most important charge, the fact that they accuse Christ of having destroyed the worship of Jehovah. Would to Heaven he could have been allowed the time to do so, for the world would not have found itself still bewildered, after nineteen centuries of mutual massacres, among 300 quarrelling sects, and with a personal Devil reigning over a terrorized Christendom!

True to the exclamation of David, paraphrased in *King James' Version* as "all the gods of the nations are idols," * *i.e.*, devils, Bacchus or the "first-born" of the Orphic theogony, the Monogenes, or "only-begotten" of Father Zeus and Korê, was transformed, with the rest of the ancient myths, into a devil. By such a degradation, the Fathers, whose pious zeal could only be surpassed by their ignorance, have unwittingly furnished evidence against themselves. They have, with their own hands, paved the way for many a future solution, and greatly helped modern students of the science of religion.

It was in the Bacchus-myth that lay concealed for long and dreary centuries both the future vindication of the reviled "gods of the nations," and the last clue to the enigma of Jehovah. The strange duality of Divine and mortal characteristics, so conspicuous in the Sinaitic Deity, begins to yield its mystery before the untiring inquiry of the age. One of the latest contributions we find in a short but highly important paper in *The Evolution*, a periodical of New York, the closing paragraph of which throws a flood of light on Bacchus, the Jove of Nysa, who was worshipped by the Israelites as Jehovah of Sinai.

"Such was the Jove of Nysa to his worshippers," concludes the author. "He represented to them alike the world of nature and the world of

---

* [*Psalms* xcvi, 5: *dii gentium daemonia.*]

thought. He was the 'Sun of righteousness, with healing on his wings,' and he not only brought joy to mortals, but opened to them hope beyond mortality of immortal life. Born of a human mother, he raised her from the world of death to the supernal air, to be revered and worshipped. At once lord of all worlds, he was in them all alike the Savior.

"Such was Bacchus, the Phophet-God. A change of cultus, decreed by the Murderer-Imperial, the Emperor Theodosius, at the instance of Ghostly Father Ambrosius of Milan, has changed his title to Father of Lies. His worship, before universal, was denominated pagan or *local*, and his rites stigmatized as witchcraft. His orgies received the name of *Witches' Sabbath*, and his favorite symbolical form with the bovine foot became the modern representative of the Devil with the cloven hoof. The master of the house having been called Beelzebub, they of his household were alike denounced as having commerce with the powers of darkness. Crusades were undertaken; whole peoples massacred. Knowledge and the higher learning were denounced as magic and sorcery. Ignorance became the mother of devotion—such as was then cherished. Galileo languished long years in prison for teaching that the sun was in the centre of the solar universe. Bruno was burned alive at Rome in 1600 for reviving the ancient philosophy; yet, queerly enough, the Liberalia have become a festival of the Church.\* Bacchus is a saint in the calendar four times repeated, and at many a shrine he may be seen reposing in the arms of his deified mother. The names are changed, the ideas remain as before."†

And now that we have shown that we must indeed "bid an eternal farewell to all the rebellious angels," we naturally pass to an examination of the God Jesus, who was manufactured out of the man Jesus to redeem us from these very mythical devils, as Father Ventura shows us. This labor will of course necessitate once more a comparative inquiry into the history of Gautama Buddha, his doctrines and his "miracles," and those of Jesus and the predecessor of both—Kṛishṇa.

---

\* The festival denominated Liberalia occurred on the seventeenth of March, now St. Patrick's Day. Thus Bacchus was also the patron saint of the Irish.

† Prof. A. Wilder: "Bacchus the Prophet-God," in the June number (1877) of *The Evolution, a Review of Politics, Religion, Science, Literature, and Art*.

## CHAPTER XI

"Not to commit any sin, to do good, and to purify one's mind, that is the teaching of the Awakened . . .

"Better than Sovereignty over the earth, better than going to heaven, better than lordship over all the worlds is the reward of the first step in holiness."
—*Dhammapada*, verses 183, 178.

"Creator! Where are these tribunals, where do these courts proceed, where do these courts assemble, where do the tribunals meet, to which the man of the embodied world gives an account for his soul?"
—Persian *Vendidâd,* xix, 89.

"Hail to thee, O Man, who art come from the transitory place to the imperishable!"
—*Vendidâd,* farg. vii, 136.

"To the true believer, truth, wherever it appears, is welcome, nor will any doctrine seem the less true or the less precious, because it was seen not only by Moses or Christ, but likewise by Buddha or Lao-tse."
—Max Müller.

UNLUCKILY for those who would have been glad to render justice to the ancient and modern religious philosophies of the Orient, a fair opportunity has hardly ever been given to them. Of late there has been a touching accord between philologists holding high official positions and missionaries from heathen lands. Prudence before truth when the latter endangers our sinecures! Besides, how easy to compromise with conscience. A State religion is a prop of government; all State religions are "exploded humbugs"; therefore, since one is as good, or rather as bad, as another, *the* State religion may as well be supported. Such is the diplomacy of official science.

Grote in his *History of Greece*,* assimilates the Pythagoreans to the Jesuits, and sees in their Brotherhood but an ably disguised object to acquire political ascendancy. On the loose testimony of Heraclitus† and some other writers, who accused Pythagoras of craft, and described him as a man "of extensive research . . . but artful for mischief and destitute of sound judgment," some historical biographers hastened to present him to posterity in such a character.

How then if they must accept the Pythagoras painted by the satirical Timon: "a juggler of solemn speech engaged in fishing for men,"‡ can they avoid judging of Jesus from the sketch that Celsus has embalmed in his satire? Historical impartiality has nought to do with creeds and personal beliefs, and exacts as much of posterity for one as for the other. The life and doings of Jesus are far less attested than

---
* [Vol. III, Pt. II, ch. xxxvii, pp. 335 *et seq.*, 348; ed. 1862.]
† [Diog. Laert., VIII, "Pythagoras," v; IX, "Heraclitus," ii.]
‡ [*Ibid.,* VIII, "Pythag.," xv; Plutarch, *Lives*, "Numa," viii.]

those of Pythagoras, if, indeed, we can say that they are attested at all by any *historical* proof. For assuredly no one will gainsay that as a real personage Celsus has the advantage as regards the credibility of his testimony over Matthew, or Mark, or Luke, or John, who never wrote a line of the *Gospels* attributed to them respectively. Withal Celsus is at least as good a witness as Heraclitus. He was known as a scholar and a Neo-Platonist to some of the Fathers; whereas the very existence of the four Apostles must be taken on blind faith. If Timon regarded the sublime Samian as "a juggler," so did Celsus hold Jesus, or rather those who made all the pretenses for him. In his famous work, addressing the Nazarene, he says: "Let us grant that the wonders were performed by you . . . but are they not common with those who have been taught by the Egyptians to perform in the middle of the forum for a few oboli?" *
And we know, on the authority of the *Gospel according to Matthew*, that the Galilean prophet was also a man of solemn speech, and that he called himself and offered to make his disciples "fishers of men."

Let it not be imagined that we bring this reproach to any who revere Jesus as God. Whatever the faith, if the worshipper be but sincere, it should be respected in his presence. If we do not accept Jesus as God, we revere *him as a man*. Such a feeling honors him more than if we were to attribute to him the powers and personality of the Supreme, and credit him at the same time with having played a useless comedy with mankind, as, after all, his mission proves scarcely less than a complete failure; 2,000 years have passed, and Christians do not reckon one-fifth part of the population of the globe, nor is Christianity likely to progress any better in the future. No, we aim but at strict justice, leaving all personality aside. We question those who, adoring neither Jesus, Pythagoras, nor Apollonius, yet recite the idle gossip of their contemporaries; those who in their books either maintain a prudent silence, or speak of "our Savior" and "our Lord," as though they believed any more in the made-up theological Christ, than in the fabulous Fo of China.

*There were no Atheists in those days of old! no disbelievers or materialists, in the modern sense of the word, as there were no bigoted detractors.* He who judges the ancient philosophies by their external phraseology, and quotes from ancient writings sentences *seemingly* atheistical, is unfit to be trusted as a critic, for he is unable to penetrate into the inner sense of their metaphysics. The views of Pyrrho, whose rationalism has become proverbial, can be interpreted only by the light of the oldest Hindu philosophy. From Manu down to the latest Svâbhâvika, its leading metaphysical feature ever was to proclaim the reality and supremacy of spirit, with a vehemence proportionate to the denial

---

* [Origen, *Contra Celsum*, I, lxviii.]

HATSHEPSUT TEMPLE, DEIR-EL-BAHARI, EGYPT

Photo by G. E. Kidder Smith. Reproduced by permission from *The Art and Architecture of Ancient Egypt*, by W. Stevenson Smith, 1958.

CIRCULAR ZODIAC OF DENDERA (TENTYRA), UPPER EGYPT

Originally on the ceiling of an upper room of the Temple, it was removed in 1820, and is now on display at the Louvre, Paris. The outer circle of figures, moving counterclockwise like the stars, represents the thirty-six decans, or ten-day weeks of the Egyptian year; the twelve arms of the supporting figures, the twelve months of the year. Consult *The Secret Doctrine*, Vol. II, pp. 368, 374 footnote, and 431-32, for important occult data.

of the objective existence of our material world—passing phantom of temporary forms and beings. The numerous schools begotten by Kapila reflect his philosophy no clearer than the doctrines left as a legacy to thinkers by Timon, Pyrrho's "Prophet," as Sextus Empiricus calls him. His views on the divine repose of the soul, his proud indifference to the opinion of his fellow men, his contempt for sophistry, reflect in an equal degree stray beams of the self-contemplation of the Gymnosophists and of the Buddhist *Vaibhâshikas*. Notwithstanding that he and his followers are termed, from their state of constant suspense, "skeptics," "doubters," inquirers and ephectics, only because they postponed their final judgment on dilemmas, with which our modern philosophers prefer dealing, Alexander-like, by cutting the Gordian knot, and then declaring the dilemma a superstition, such men as Pyrrho cannot be pronounced atheists. No more can Kapila, or Giordano Bruno, or again Spinoza, who were also treated as atheists; nor yet, the great Hindu poet, philosopher and dialectician Veda-Vyâsa, whose principle that all is illusion—save the Great Unknown and His direct essence—Pyrrho has adopted in full.

These philosophical beliefs extended like a network over the whole pre-Christian world; and, surviving persecution and misrepresentations, form the cornerstone of every now existing religion outside Christianity.

Comparative theology is a two-edged weapon, and has so proved itself. But the Christian advocates, unabashed by evidence, force comparison in the serenest way; Christian legends and dogmas, they say, do somewhat resemble the heathen, it is true; but see, while the one teaches us the existence, powers and attributes of an all-wise, all-good Father-God, Brahmanism gives us a multitude of minor gods, and Buddhism none whatever; one is fetishism and polytheism, the other bald atheism. Jehovah is the one true God, and the Pope and Martin Luther are His prophets! This is one edge of the sword, and this the other: despite missions, despite armies, despite enforced commercial intercourse, the "heathens" find nothing in the teachings of Jesus — sublime though some are—that Krishna and Gautama had not taught them before. And so, to gain over any new converts, and keep the few already won by centuries of cunning, the Christians give the "heathen" dogmas more absurd than their own, and cheat them by adopting the habit of their native priests and practicing the very "idolatry and fetishism" which they so disparage in the "heathens." Comparative theology works both ways.

In Siam and Burma, Catholic missionaries have become perfect Talapoins to all external appearance, *i.e.*, minus their virtues; and throughout India, especially in the south, they were denounced by their own colleague, the Abbé Dubois.* This was afterward vehemently denied. But now we have living witnesses to the correctness of the charge. Among others, Captain O'Grady, already quoted, a native of Madras, writes the following on this systematic method of deception: "The hypocritical beggars profess total abstinence and horror of flesh to conciliate converts from Hinduism. . . . I got one father, or rather, he got himself gloriously drunk in my house, time and again, and the way he pitched into roast beef was a caution." † Further, the author has pretty stories to tell of "black-faced Christs," "Virgins on wheels," and of Catholic processions in general. We have seen such solemn ceremonies accompanied by the most infernal cacophony of a Sinhalese orchestra, tam-tam and gongs included, followed by a like Brahmanic procession, which, for its picturesque coloring and *mise-en-scène*, looked far more solemn and imposing than the Christian Saturnalia. Speaking of one of these, the same author remarks: "It was more devilish than religious. . . . The bishops walked off Romeward,‡ with a mighty pile of Peter's pence gathered in the minutest sums, with gold ornaments, nose rings, anklets, elbow bangles, etc., etc., in profusion, recklessly thrown in heaps at the feet of the grotesque copper-colored image of the Savior, with its Dutch metal halo and gaudily-striped cummerbund and — shade of Raphael!—blue turban."§

As everyone can see, such voluntary contributions make it quite profitable to mimic the native Brahmans and bonzes. Between the worshippers of Krishna and Christ, or Avany and the Virgin Mary, there is less substantial difference, in fact, than between the two native sects, the Vaishnavas and the Śivaites. For the *converted* Hindus, Christ is a slightly modified Krishna, that is all. Missionaries carry away rich donations and Rome is satisfied. Then comes a year of famine; but the nose rings and gold elbow bangles are gone and people starve by thousands. What matters it? They die in Christ, and Rome scatters her blessings over their corpses, of which thousands float yearly down the sacred rivers to the ocean.∥ So servile are the Catholics in their imita-

---

\* *Edinburg Review*, April, 1851, p. 411.

† "Indian Sketches; or Rubs of a Rolling Stone," written for the *Commercial Bulletin*, of Boston.

‡ See chapter II of this Vol., p. 110.

§ It would be worth the trouble of an artist, while travelling around the world, to make a collection of the multitudinous varieties of Madonnas, Christs, saints and martyrs as they appear in various costumes in different countries. They would furnish models for masquerade balls in aid of church charities!

∥ Even as we write, there comes from the Earl of Salisbury, Secretary of State for India, a report that the Madras famine is to be followed by one probably still more severe in Southern India, the very district where the heaviest tribute has been exacted by

tion, and so careful not to give offense to their parishioners, that if they happen to have a few high caste converts in a Church, no pariah or any man of the lower castes, however good a Christian he may be, can be admitted into the same Church with them. And yet they dare call themselves the servants of Him who sought in preference the society of the publicans and sinners; and whose appeal—"Come unto me all ye that labor and are heavy laden, and I will give you rest"*—has opened to him the hearts of millions of the suffering and the oppressed!

Few writers are as bold and outspoken as the late lamented Dr. Thomas Inman, of Liverpool, England. But however small their number, these men all agree unanimously that the philosophy of both Buddhism and Brahmanism must rank higher than Christian theology, and teach neither atheism nor fetishism. "To my own mind," says Inman, "the assertion that Sâkya did not believe in God is wholly unsupported. Nay, his whole scheme is built upon the belief that there are powers above which are capable of punishing mankind for their sins. It is true that these gods were not called Elohim, nor Jâh, nor Jehovah, nor Jahveh, nor Adonai, nor Ehieh, nor Baalim, nor Ashtoreth—yet, for the son of Suddhodana, there was a Supreme Being."†

There are four schools of Buddhist theology in Ceylon, Thibet and India. One is rather pantheistical than atheistical, but the other three are purely *theistical*.

On the first the speculations of our philologists are based. As to the second, third and fourth, their teachings vary but in the external mode of expression. We have fully explained the spirit of it elsewhere.

As to practical, not theoretical, views on the Nirvâṇa, this is what a rationalist and a skeptic says: "I have questioned at the very doors of their temples several hundreds of Buddhists, and have not found one but strove, fasted, and gave himself up to every kind of austerity, to perfect himself and acquire immortality; not to attain final annihilation.

"There are over 300,000,000 of Buddhists who fast, pray, and toil. . . . Why make of these 300,000,000 of men idiots and fools, macerating their bodies and imposing upon themselves most fearful privations of every nature, in order to reach a fatal annihilation which must overtake them anyhow?" ‡

As well as this author we have questioned Buddhists and Brahmanists and studied their philosophy. *Apavarga* has wholly a different meaning

---

the Catholic missionaries for the expenses of the Church of Rome. The latter, unable to retaliate otherwise, despoils British subjects, and when famine comes as a consequence, makes the heretical British Government pay for it.

\* [*Matt.* xi, 28.]
† *Ancient Faiths and Modern*, p. 24.
‡ Jacolliot, *La Genèse de l'humanité*, p. 67.

from annihilation. It is but to become more and more like Him, of whom he is one of the refulgent sparks, that is the aspiration of every Hindu philosopher, and the hope of the most ignorant is *never to yield up his distinct individuality.* "Else," as once remarked an esteemed correspondent of the author, "mundane and separate existence would look like God's comedy and our tragedy; sport to Him that we work and suffer, death to us to suffer it."

The same with the doctrine of metempsychosis, so distorted by European scholars. But as the work of translation and analysis progresses, fresh religious beauties will be discovered in the old faiths.

Professor Whitney has in his translation of the *Vedas* passages in which, he says, the assumed importance of the body to its old tenant is brought out in the strongest light. These are portions of hymns read at the funeral services, over the body of the departed one. We quote them from Mr. Whitney's scholarly work:

> "Start onward! bring together all thy members;
>     let not thy limbs be left, nor yet thy body;
> Thy spirit gone before, now follow after;
>     wherever it delights thee, go thou thither."
>
> ---
>
> Collect thy body, with its every member;
>     thy limbs with help of rites I fashion for thee.
>
> ---
>
> If some one limb was left behind by Agni,
>     when to thy Father's world he hence conveyed you,
> That very one I now again supply you;
>     rejoice in heaven with all your limbs, ye Fathers!*

The "body" here referred to is not the physical, but the *astral* one—a very great distinction, as may be seen.

Again, belief in the individual existence of the immortal spirit of man is shown in the following verses of the Hindu ceremonial of incremation and burial.

> "They who within the sphere of earth are stationed,
>     or who are settled now in realms of pleasure.
> . . . The Fathers who have the earth—the atmosphere—the heaven for their seat.
> The 'fore-heaven' the third heaven is styled,
>     and there the Fathers have their seat."—(*Rig-Veda*, x, 14)†

With such majestic views as these people held of God and the immortality of man's spirit, it is not surprising that a comparison between the

---

* *Oriental and Linguistic Studies*, "Vedic Doctrine of a Future Life," pp. 56-57; by W. Dwight Whitney, Prof. of Sanskrit and Comparative Philology at Yale College.
† [*Ibid.*, p. 59.]

Vedic hymns and the narrow, unspiritual Mosaic books should result to the advantage of the former in the mind of every unprejudiced scholar. Even the ethical code of *Manu* is incomparably higher than that of the *Pentateuch* of Moses, in the literal meaning of which all the uninitiated scholars of two worlds cannot find a single proof that the ancient Jews believed either in a future life or an immortal spirit in man, or that Moses himself ever taught it. Yet, we have eminent Orientalists who begin to suspect that the "dead letter" conceals something not apparent at first sight. So Professor Whitney tells us that "as we look yet further into the forms of the modern Hindu ceremonial we discover not a little of the same discordance between creed and observance; the one is not explained by the other," says this great American scholar. He adds: "We are forced to the conclusion either that India derived its system of rites from some foreign source, and practiced them blindly, careless of their true import, or *else that those rites are the production of another doctrine of older date,* and have maintained themselves in popular usage after the decay of the creed of which they were the original expression."*

This creed has not decayed, and its hidden philosophy, as understood now by the initiated Hindus, is just as it was 10,000 years ago. But can our scholars seriously hope to have it delivered unto them upon their first demand? Or do they still expect to fathom the mysteries of the World-Religion in its popular exoteric rites?

No orthodox Brahmans and Buddhists would deny the Christian incarnation; only, they understand it in their own philosophical way, and how could they deny it? The very cornerstone of their religious system is periodical incarnations of the Deity. Whenever humanity is about to merge into materialism and moral degradation, a Supreme Spirit incarnates himself in his creature selected for the purpose. The "Messenger of the Highest" links itself with the duality of matter and soul, and the triad being thus completed by the union of its Crown, a savior is born, who helps restore humanity to the path of truth and virtue. The early Christian Church, all imbued with Asiatic philosophy, evidently shared the same belief — otherwise *it would have neither erected into an article of faith the second advent, nor cunningly invented the fable of Anti-Christ as a precaution against possible future incarnations.* Neither could they have imagined that Melchisedek was an avatâra of Christ. They had only to turn to the *Bhagavad-Gîtâ* to find Krishna or Bhagavat saying to Arjuna: "He who follows me is saved by wisdom and even by works. . . . *As often as virtue declines in the world, I make myself manifest to save it."* †

---

\* *Oriental and Linguistic Studies,* p. 48.

† [See ch. iii, iv.]

Indeed, it is more than difficult to avoid sharing this doctrine of periodical incarnations. Has not the world witnessed, at rare intervals, the advent of such grand characters as Kṛishṇa, Śâkyamuni and Jesus? Like the two latter personages, Kṛishṇa seems to have been a real being, deified by his school at some time in the twilight of history, and made to fit into the frame of the time-honored religious program. Compare the two Redeemers, the Hindu and the Christian, the one preceding the other by some thousands of years; place between them Siddhârtha Buddha, reflecting Kṛishṇa and projecting into the night of the future his own luminous shadow, out of whose collected rays were shaped the outlines of the mythical Jesus, and from whose teachings were drawn those of the historical Christos; and we find that under one identical garment of poetical legend lived and breathed three real human figures. The individual merit of each of them is rather brought out in stronger relief than otherwise by this same mythical coloring; for no unworthy character could have been selected for deification by the popular instinct, so unerring and just, when left untrammeled. *Vox populi, vox Dei* was once true, however erroneous when applied to the present priest-ridden mob.

Kapila, Orpheus, Pythagoras, Plato, Basilides, Marcion, Ammonius and Plotinus founded schools and sowed the germs of many a noble thought, and disappearing, left behind them the refulgence of demi-gods. But the three personalities of Kṛishṇa, Gautama and Jesus appeared like true gods, each in his epoch, and bequeathed to humanity three religions built on the imperishable rock of ages. That all three, especially the Christian faith, have in time become adulterated, and the latter almost unrecognizable, is no fault of either of the noble Reformers. It is the priestly self-styled husbandmen of the "vine of the Lord" who must be held to account by future generations. Purify the three systems of the dross of human dogmas, the pure essence remaining will be found identical. Even Paul, the great, the honest apostle, in the glow of his enthusiasm either unwittingly perverted the doctrines of Jesus, or else his writings are disfigured beyond recognition. The *Talmud*, the record of a people who, notwithstanding his apostasy from Judaism, yet feel compelled to acknowledge Paul's greatness as a philosopher and religionist, says of Aḥer (Paul),*

---

* In his article on "Paul, the Founder of Christianity" [*The Evolution*, Sept., 1877], Professor A. Wilder, whose intuitions of truth are always clear, says: "In the person of *Aḥer* we recognize the Apostle Paul. He appears to have been known by a variety of appellations. He was named *Saul*, evidently because of this vision of Paradise —Saul or *Sheól* being the Hebrew name of the other world. *Paul*, which only means 'the little man,' was a species of nickname. *Aḥer*, or *other*, was an epithet in the Bible for persons outside of the Jewish polity, and was applied to him for having extended his ministry to the Gentiles. His real name was Elisha ben-Abuiah."

in the *Yerushalmi,* that "he corrupted the work of that man"—meaning Jesus.*

Meanwhile, before this smelting is completed by honest science and future generations, let us glance at the present aspect of the legendary three religions.

## The Legends of Three Saviors

| Krishna | Gautama Buddha | Jesus of Nazareth |
|---|---|---|
| *Epoch*: Uncertain. European science fears to commit itself. But the Brahmanical calculations fix it at about 5,000 years ago. | *Epoch*: According to European science and the Ceylonese calculations, 2,540 years ago. | *Epoch*: Supposed to be 1877 years ago. His birth and royal descent are concealed from Herod the tyrant. |
| Krishna descends of a royal family, but is brought up by shepherds; is called the **Shepherd God.** His birth and divine descent are kept secret from Kansa. | Gautama is the son of a king. His first disciples are shepherds and mendicants. | Descends of the Royal family of David. Is worshipped by shepherds at his birth, and is called the "Good Shepherd" See *Gospel according to John.*) |
| An incarnation of Vishnu, the second person of the Trimûrti (Trinity). Krishna was worshipped at Maturâ, on the river Jumnâ.† | According to some, an incarnation of Vishnu; according to others, an incarnation of one of the Buddhas, and even of Âdi-Buddha, the Highest Wisdom. | An incarnation of the Holy Ghost, then the second person of the Trinity, now the third. But the Trinity was not invented until 325 years after his birth. Went to Matarea, Egypt, and produced his first miracles there. ‡ |
| Krishna is persecuted by Kansa, Tyrant of Madura, but miraculously escapes. In the hope of destroying the child, the king has thousands of male innocents slaughtered. | Buddhist legends are free from this plagiarism, but the Catholic legend that makes of him St. Josaphat, shows his father, king of Kapilavastu, slaying innocent young *Christians* (!!). (*See Golden Legend.*) | Jesus is persecuted by Herod, King of Judaea, but escapes into Egypt under conduct of an angel. To assure his slaughter, Herod orders a massacre of innocents, and 40,000 were slain. |
| Krishna's mother was Devakî, an immaculate virgin (but had given birth to eight sons before Krishna. | Buddha's mother was Mâyâ,* or Mâyâdevî; married to her husband (yet an immaculate virgin). | Jesus' mother was Mariam, or Miriam; married to her husband, yet an immaculate virgin, but had several children besides Jesus (See *Matthew,* xiii, 55, 56.) |

---

*"In the *Talmud* Jesus is called Oto-ha-ish, אתו האיש, *that man.*"—A. Wilder, *op. cit.* [*Talmud Yerushalmi*: Hagigah II, 1.]

† See Arrian, *Anabasis,* Bk. VIII (Indica), viii, 5; and Rev. J. B. S. Carwithen, *Bampton Lectures,* 1809, pp. 98-100.

‡ Cf. *The Arabic Gospel of the Infancy,* § 24 *et passim;* Maurice, *History of Hindostan,* 1795-98, Bk. IV, Pt. II, ch. iii, pp. 308, 318.

| KRISHNA | GAUTAMA BUDDHA | JESUS OF NAZARETH |
|---|---|---|
| Krishna is endowed with beauty, omniscience and omnipotence from birth. Produces miracles, cures the lame and blind, and casts out demons. Washes the feet of the Brahmans, and descending to the lowest regions (hell), liberates the dead, and returns to Vaikuntha — the paradise of Vishnu. Krishna was the God Vishnu himself in human form.* | Buddha is endowed with the same powers and qualities, and performs similar wonders. Passes his life with mendicants. It is claimed for Gautama that he was distinct from all other Avatâras, having the entire spirit of Buddha in him, while all others had but a part (*anśa*) of the divinity in them. | Jesus is similarly endowed. (See *Gospels* and the *Apocryphal Testament*.) Passes his life with sinners and publicans. Casts out demons likewise. The only notable difference between the three is that Jesus is charged with casting out devils by the power of Beelzebub, which the others were not. Jesus washes the feet of his disciples, dies, descends to hell, and ascends to heaven, after liberating the dead. |
| Krishna creates boys out of calves, and *vice versa*. He crushes the Serpent's head.† | Gautama crushes the Serpent's head, *i.e.*, abolishes the Nâga worship as fetishism; but, like Jesus, makes the Serpent the emblem of divine wisdom. | Jesus is said to have crushed the Serpent's head, agreeably to original revelation in *Genesis*. He also transforms boys into kids and kids into boys.‖ |
| Krishna is Unitarian. He persecutes the clergy, charges them with ambition and hypocrisy to their faces, divulges the great secrets of the Sanctuary—the Unity of God and immortality of our spirit. Tradition says he fell a victim to their vengeance. His favorite disciple, Arjuna, never deserts him to the last. There are credible traditions that he died near a tree (or cross) being pierced in the foot by an arrow. ‡ The best scholars agree that the Irish Cross at Tuam, erected long before the Christian era, is Asiatic.§ | Buddha abolishes idolatry; divulges the Mysteries of the Unity of God and the Nirvâna, the true meaning of which was previously known only to the priests. Persecuted and driven out of the country, he escapes death by gathering about him some hundreds of thousands of believers in his Buddhaship. Finally, dies, surrounded by a host of disciples, with Ânanda, his beloved disciple and cousin, chief among them all. O'Brien believes that the Irish Cross at Tuam is meant for Buddha's, but Gautama was never crucified. He is represented in many temples, as sit- | Jesus rebels against the old Jewish law; denounces the Scribes and Pharisees, and the synagogue for hypocrisy and dogmatic intolerance. Breaks the Sabbath, and defies the Law. Is accused by the Jews of divulging the secrets of the Sanctuary. Is put to death on a cross (a tree). Of the little handful of disciples whom he had converted, one betrays him, one denies him, and the others desert him at the last, except John—the disciple *he loved*. Jesus, Krishna, and Buddha, all three Saviors, die either on or under *trees*, and are connected with crosses which |

---

* [Thos. Maurice, *Indian Antiquities*, 1794, Vol. III, pp. 44-46.]
† Thos. Maurice, *The History of Hindostan*, Vol. II, pp. 340-41, 343-45.
‡ [*Vishnu-Purâna*, V, xxxvii; *Mahâbhârata*, Mausal-parvan, 126 *et seq*.]
§ See H. O'Brien, *The Round Towers of Ireland*, pp. 296 *et seq*; also J. D. Guigniaut, *Religions de l'antiquité*, Vol. I, pp. 208-209, and engraving in Dr. P. Lundy's *Monumental Christianity*, p. 160.
‖ *Gospel of the Infancy*, xvii.

| KRISHNA | GAUTAMA BUDDHA | JESUS OE NAZARETH |
|---|---|---|
| | ting under a cruciform tree, which is the "Tree of Life." In another image he is sitting on Nâga, the Râjâ of Serpents with a cross on his breast.* | are symbolical of the threefold powers of creation. |
| Krishna ascends to Svarga and becomes Nirguna. | Buddha ascends to Nirvâna. | Jesus ascends to Paradise. |

### RESULT

About the middle of the present century, the followers of these three religions were reckoned as follows: †

| OF KRISHNA | OF BUDDHA | OF JESUS |
|---|---|---|
| Brahmanists, 60,000,000 | Buddhists, 450,000,000 | Christians, 260,000,000 |

Such is the present aspect of these three great religions, of which each is in turn reflected in its successor. Had the Christian dogmatizers stopped there, the results would not have been so disastrous, for it would be hard, indeed, to make a bad creed out of the lofty teachings of Gautama, or Krishna as *Bhagavat*. But they went farther, and added to pure primitive Christianity the fables of Hercules, Orpheus and Bacchus. As Moslems will not admit that their *Koran* is built on the substratum of the Jewish *Bible,* so the Christians will not confess that they owe next to everything to the Hindu religions. But the Hindus have chronology to prove it to them. We see the best and most learned of our writers uselessly striving to show that the extraordinary similarities — amounting to identity — between Krishna and Christ are due to the spurious Gospels of the *Infancy* and of *St. Thomas* having "probably circulated on the coast of Malabar, and giving color to the story of Krishna." ‡ Why not accept truth in all sincerity, and reversing matters, admit that St. Thomas, faithful to that policy of proselytism which marked the earliest Christians, when he found in Malabar the original of the mythical Christ in Krishna, tried to blend the two; and, adopting in his gospel (from which all others were copied) the most important details of the story of the Hindu Avatâra, engrafted the Christian heresy on the primitive religion of Krishna. For anyone acquainted with the spirit of Brahmanism, the idea of Brahmans accepting anything from a stranger, especially from a foreigner, is simply ridiculous. That they, the most fanatic people in religious matters, who, during centuries, could not be compelled to adopt the most simple of

---

* Cf. E. Moor, *The Hindoo Pantheon,* pl. lxxv, 3.

† Max Müller's estimate.

‡ Lundy, *Monumental Christianity,* p. 153; Maurice, *Hist. of Hind.,* Bk. IV, pt. II, ch. iii, pp. 300-306.

European usages, should be suspected of having introduced into their sacred books unverified legends about a foreign God, is something so preposterously illogical, that it is really a waste of time to contradict the idea!

We will not stop to examine the too well-known resemblances between the external form of Buddhistic worship — especially Lamaism — and Roman Catholicism, for noticing which poor Huc paid dear—but proceed to compare the most vital points. Of all the original manuscripts that have been translated from the various languages in which Buddhism is expounded, the most extraordinary and interesting are Buddha's *Dhammapada*, or *Path of Virtue*, translated from the Pâli by Colonel Rogers,* and *The Wheel of the Law*, containing the views of a Siamese Minister of State on his own and other religions, and translated by Henry Alabaster.† The reading of these two books, and the discovery in them of similarities of thought and doctrine often amounting to identity, prompted Dr. Inman to write the many profoundly true passages embodied in one of his last works, *Ancient Faiths and Modern*.‡ "I speak with sober earnestness," writes this kindhearted, sincere scholar, "when I say that after forty years' experience among those who profess Christianity, and those who proclaim . . . more or less quietly their disagreement with it, I have noticed more sterling virtue and morality amongst the last than the first . . . I know personally many pious, good Christian people, whom I honor, admire, and perhaps, would be glad to emulate or to equal; but they deserve the eulogy thus passed on them, in consequence of their good sense, having ignored the doctrine of faith to a great degree, and having cultivated the practice of good works . . . In my judgment the most praiseworthy Christians whom I know are *modified Buddhists,* though probably, not one of them ever heard of Siddhârtha."

Between the Lamaico-Buddhistic and Roman Catholic articles of faith and ceremonies, there are fifty-one points presenting a perfect and striking similarity; and four diametrically antagonistic.

As it would be useless to enumerate the "similarities," for the reader may find them carefully noted in Inman's work on *Ancient Faiths and Modern*, pp. 237-240, we will quote but the four dissimilarities, and leave everyone to draw his own deductions therefrom:

1. "The Buddhists hold that nothing which is contradicted by sound reason can be a true doctrine of Buddha."

1. "The Christians will accept any nonsense, if promulgated by the Church as a matter of faith." §

---

\* Buddhaghosa's *Parables,* translated from the Burmese by Col. H. T. Rogers, R.E.; with an Introduction, containing Buddha's *Dhammapada*, or, "Path of Virtue." Transl. from Pâli by F. Max Müller. London, 1870.

† Interpreter of the Consulate-General in Siam.

‡ *Ancient Faiths and Modern*, p. 162.

§ The words contained within quotation marks are Inman's.

2. "The Buddhists do not adore the mother of Śâkya," though they honor her as a holy and saint-like woman, chosen to be his mother through her great virtue.

3. "The Buddhists have no sacraments."

4. The Buddhists do not believe in any pardon for their sins, except after an adequate punishment for each evil deed, and a proportionate compensation to the parties injured.

2. "The Romanists adore the mother of Jesus, and prayer is made to her for aid and intercession." The worship of the Virgin has weakened that of Christ and thrown entirely into the shadow that of the Almighty.

3. "The papal followers have seven."

4. The Christians are promised that if they only believe in the "precious blood of Christ," this blood offered by Him for the expiation of the sins of the whole of mankind (read Christians) will atone for every mortal sin.

Which of these theologies most commends itself to the sincere inquirer is a question that may safely be left to the sound judgment of the reader. One offers light, the other darkness.

*The Wheel of the Law* has the following:

"Buddhists believe that every act, word, or thought has its consequence, which will appear sooner or later in the present or in some future state. Evil acts will produce evil consequences,* . . . good acts will produce good consequences: prosperity in this world, or birth in heaven . . . in some future state." †

This is strict and impartial justice. This is the idea of a Supreme Power which cannot fail, and, therefore, can have neither wrath nor mercy, but leaves every cause, great or small, to work out its inevitable effects. "With what measure you mete, it shall be measured to you again" ‡ neither by expression nor implication points to any hope of future mercy or salvation by proxy. Cruelty and mercy are finite feelings. The Supreme Deity is infinite, hence it can only be JUST, and Justice must be blind. The ancient Pagans held, on this question, far more philosophical views than modern Christians, for they represented their Themis blindfold. And the Siamese author of the work under notice has again a more reverent conception of the Deity than the Christians have, when he thus gives vent to his thought: "A Buddhist might believe in the existence of a God sublime above all human qualities and attributes, a perfect God, above love and hatred and jealousy, calmly resting in a quiet happiness that nothing could disturb, and of such a God he would speak no disparagement; not from desire to please him, or fear to offend him, but from natural veneration. But he cannot understand a God with the attributes and qualities of men, a God who loves and hates and shows anger, a Deity who, whether described to

---

* *The Wheel of the Law*, Vol. I, p. 319.
† *Ibid.*, p. 45.
‡ *Matthew* vii, 2.

him by Christian Missionaries, or by Mohammedans or Brahmans or Jews, falls below his standard of even an ordinary good man." *

We have often wondered at the extraordinary ideas of God and His justice that seem to be honestly held by those Christians who blindly rely upon the clergy for their religion, and never upon their own reason. How strangely illogical is this doctrine of the Atonement. We propose to discuss it with the Christians from the Buddhistic standpoint, and to show at once by what a series of sophistries, directed toward the one object of tightening the ecclesiastical yoke upon the popular neck, its acceptance as a divine command has been finally effected; also, that it has proved one of the most pernicious and demoralizing of doctrines.

The clergy say: "no matter how enormous our crimes against the laws of God and of man, we have but to believe in the self-sacrifice of Jesus for the salvation of mankind, and His blood will wash out every stain. God's mercy is boundless and unfathomable. It is impossible to conceive of a human sin so damnable that the price paid in advance for the redemption of the sinner would not wipe it out if a thousandfold worse. And, furthermore, it is never too late to repent. Though the offender wait until the last minute of the last hour of the last day of his mortal life, before his blanched lips utter the confession of faith, he may go to Paradise; the dying thief did it, and so may all others as vile." These are the assumptions of the Church.

But if we step outside the little circle of creed and consider the universe as a whole balanced by the exquisite adjustment of parts, how all sound logic, how the faintest glimmering sense of Justice revolts against this Vicarious Atonement! If the criminal sinned only against himself, and wronged no one but himself; if by sincere repentance he could cause the obliteration of past events, not only from the memory of man, but also from that imperishable record, which no deity — not even the Supremest of the Supreme — can cause to disappear, then this dogma might not be incomprehensible. But to maintain that one may wrong his fellow man, kill, disturb the equilibrium of society, and the natural order of things, and then — through cowardice, hope, or compulsion, matters not — be forgiven by believing that the spilling of one blood washes out the other blood spilt — this is preposterous! Can the *results* of a crime be obliterated even though the crime itself should be pardoned? The effects of a cause are never limited to the boundaries of the cause, nor can the results of crime be confined to the offender and his victim. Every good as well as evil action has its effects, as palpably as the stone flung into a calm water. The simile is trite, but it is the best ever conceived, so let us use

---

* *The Wheel of the Law*, pp. 17-18.

it. The eddying circles are greater and swifter, as the disturbing object is greater or smaller, but the smallest pebble, nay, the tiniest speck, makes its ripples. And this disturbance is not alone visible and on the surface. Below, unseen, in every direction — outward and downward — drop pushes drop until the sides and bottom are touched by the force. More, the air above the water is agitated, and this disturbance passes, as the physicists tell us, from stratum to stratum out into space forever and ever; an impulse has been given to matter, and that is never lost, can never be recalled! . . .

So with crime, and so with its opposite. The action may be instantaneous, the effects are eternal. When, after the stone is once flung into the pond, we can recall it to the hand, roll back the ripples, obliterate the force expended, restore the etheric waves to their previous state of non-being, and wipe out every trace of the act of throwing the missile, so that Time's record shall not show that it ever happened, then, *then* we may patiently hear Christians argue for the efficacy of this Atonement.

The Chicago *Times* recently printed the hangman's record of the first half of the present year (1877) — a long and ghastly record of murders and hangings. Nearly every one of these murderers received religious consolation, and many announced that they had received God's forgiveness through the blood of Jesus, and were going that day to Heaven! *Their conversion was effected in prison.* See how this ledger-balance of Christian Justice (!) stands: These red-handed murderers, urged on by the demons of lust, revenge, cupidity, fanaticism, or mere brutal thirst for blood, slew their victims, in most cases, without giving them time to repent, or call on Jesus to wash them clean with his blood. They, perhaps, died sinful, and, of course — consistently with theological logic — met the reward of their greater or lesser offenses. But the murderer, overtaken by human justice, is imprisoned, wept over by sentimentalists, prayed with and at, pronounces the charmed words of conversion, and goes to the scaffold a redeemed child of Jesus! Except for the murder, he would not have been prayed with, redeemed, pardoned. Clearly this man did well to murder, for thus he gained eternal happiness! And how about the victim, and his or her family, relatives, dependants, social relations — has Justice no recompense for them? Must they suffer in this world and the next, while he who wronged them sits beside the "holy thief" of Calvary and is forever blessed? On this question the clergy keep a prudent silence.

Steve Anderson was one of these American criminals — convicted of double murder, arson and robbery. Before the hour of his death he was "converted," but the record tells us that *"his clerical attendants objected to his reprieve, on the ground that they felt sure of his salvation should he die then, but could not answer for it if his execution was postponed."* We address these ministers, and ask them to tell us on what grounds they felt sure of such a monstrous thing. How they could feel *sure*, with the dark future before them, and the endless results of this double murder, arson and robbery? They could be sure of nothing, but that their abominable doctrine is the cause of three-fourths of the crimes of so-called Christians; that these terrific causes must produce like monstrous effects, which in their turn will beget other results, and so roll on throughout eternity to an accomplishment that no man can calculate.

Or take another crime, one of the most selfish, cruel and heartless, and yet the most frequent, the seduction of a young girl. Society, by an instinct of self-preservation, pitilessly judges the victim, and ostracizes her. She may be driven to infanticide, or self-murder, or if too averse to die, live to plunge into a career of vice and crime. She may become the mother of criminals, who, as in the now celebrated Jukes, of whose appalling details Mr. Dugdale has published the particulars, breed other generations of felons to the number of hundreds, in fifty or sixty years. All this social disaster came through one man's selfish passion; shall he be forgiven by Divine Justice until his offence is expiated, and punishment fall only upon the wretched human scorpions begotten of his lust?

An outcry has just been made in England over the discovery that Anglican priests are largely introducing auricular confession and granting absolution after enforcing penances. Inquiry shows the same thing prevailing more or less in the United States. Put to the ordeal of cross-examination, the clergy quote triumphantly from the English *Book of Common Prayer* the rubrics which clearly give them the absolving authority, through the power of "God, the Holy Ghost," committed unto them by the bishop by imposition of hands at their ordination. The bishop, questioned, points to *Matthew* xvi, 19, for the source of his authority to bind and loose on earth those who are to be blessed or damned in heaven; and to the apostolic succession for proof of its transmission from Simon Bar-jona to himself. The present volumes have been written to small purpose if they have not shown, 1, that Jesus, the Christ-God, is a myth concocted two centuries after the real Hebrew Jesus died; 2, that, therefore, he never had any authority to give Peter, or anyone else, plenary power; 3, that even if he had given such authority, the word Petra (rock) referred to the revealed truths of the Petroma, not to him who thrice denied him; and that besides, the apostolic succession is a gross and palpable fraud; 4, that the *Gospel according to Matthew* is a fabrication based upon a wholly different manuscript. The whole thing, therefore, is an imposition alike upon priest and penitent. But putting all these points aside for the moment, it suffices to ask these pretended agents of the three gods of the Trinity, how they reconcile it with the most rudimental notions of equity, that if the power to pardon sinners for sinning has been given them, *they did not also receive the ability by miracle to obliterate the wrongs done against person or property.* Let them restore life to the murdered; honor to the dishonored; property to those who have been wronged, and force the scales of human and divine justice to recover their equilibrium. Then we may talk of their divine commission to bind and loose. Let them say, if they can do this. Hitherto the world has received nothing but sophistry — believed on *blind* faith; we ask palpable, tangible evidence of their God's justice and mercy. But all are silent; no answer, no reply, and still the inexorable unerring Law of Compensation proceeds on its unswerving path. If we but watch its progress, we will find that it ignores all creeds, shows no preferences, but its sunlight and its thunderbolts fall alike on heathen and Christian. No absolution can shield the latter when guilty, no anathema hurt the former when innocent.

Away from us such an insulting conception of divine justice as that preached by priests on their own authority. It is fit only for cowards and criminals! If they are backed by a whole array of Fathers and Churchmen, we are supported by the greatest of all authorities, an instinctive and reverential sense of the everlasting and ever-present law of harmony and justice.

But, besides that of reason, we have other evidence to show that such a construction is wholly unwarranted. The *Gospels* being "Divine revelation," doubtless Christians will regard their testimony as conclusive. Do they affirm that Jesus gave himself as a voluntary sacrifice? On the contrary, there is not a word to sustain the idea. They make it clear that he would rather have lived to continue what he considered his mission, and that *he died because he could not help it, and only when betrayed.* Before, when threatened with violence, *he had made himself invisible* by employing the mesmeric power over the bystanders, claimed by every Eastern adept, and escaped. When, finally, he saw that his time had come, he succumbed to the inevitable. But see him in the garden, on the Mount of Olives, writhing in agony until "his sweat was, as it were, great drops of blood," praying with fervid supplication that the cup might be removed from him; exhausted by his struggle to such a degree that an angel from heaven had to come and strengthen him; and say if the picture is that of a self-immolating hostage and martyr. To crown all, and leave no lingering doubt in our minds, we have his own despairing words, "NOT MY WILL, *but thine,* be done!" (*Luke* xxii, 42.)

Again, in the *Purânas* it may be found that Kṛishṇa was nailed to a tree by the arrow of a hunter, who, begging the dying god to forgive him, receives the following answer: " 'Go, hunter, through my favor, to heaven, the abode of the gods' . . . Then the illustrious Krishna, having united himself with his own pure, spiritual, inexhaustible, inconceivable, unborn, undecaying, imperishable, and universal spirit, which is one with Vâsudeva, abandoned his mortal body, and the condition of the threefold qualities." * Is not this the original of the story of Christ forgiving the thief on the cross, and promising him a place in Heaven? Such examples "challenge inquiry as to their origin and meaning *so long anterior to Christianity*," says Dr. Lundy in *Monumental Christianity*, and yet to all this he adds: "The idea of Krishna as a shepherd, I take to be older than either [the *Gospel of the Infancy* and that of *St. John*], *and prophetic of Christ*" (p. 156).

Facts like these, perchance, furnished later a plausible pretext for declaring apocryphal all such works as the *Homilies*, which proved but too clearly the utter want of any early authority for the doctrine of atonement. The *Homilies* clash but little with the *Gospels;* they disagree entirely with the dogmas of the Church. Peter knew nothing of the atonement; and his reverence for the mythical father Adam would never have allowed him to admit that this patriarch had sinned and was accursed. Neither do the Alexandrian theological schools appear to have been cognizant of this doctrine, nor Tertullian; nor was it discussed by any of the earlier Fathers. Philo represents the story of the *Fall* as symbolical, and Origen regarded it the same way as Paul, as an allegory.†

Whether they will or not, the Christians have to credit the foolish story of Eve's temptation by a serpent. Besides, Augustine has formally pronounced upon the subject. "God, by His arbitrary will," he says, "has selected beforehand certain persons, *without regard to foreseen faith or good actions, and has irretrievably ordained to bestow upon them eternal happiness; while He has condemned others in the same way to eternal reprobation!!*" (*De dono perseverantiae*, § 25, etc.). ‡

---

\* H. H. Wilson, *Vishnu-Purâna*, Book V, ch. xxxvii.

† See Draper's *Conflict between Religion and Science*, p. 224.

‡ This is the doctrine of the Supralapsarians, who asserted that "He [God] *predestinated the fall of Adam*, with all its pernicious consequences, from all eternity, and that our first parents had no liberty from the beginning."

It is also to this highly-moral doctrine that the Catholic world became indebted, in the eleventh century, for the institution of the Order known as the Carthusian monks. Bruno, its founder, was driven to the foundation of this monstrous Order by a circumstance well worthy of being recorded here, as it graphically illustrates this *divine* predestination. A friend of Bruno, a French physician, famed far and wide for his extraordinary *piety, purity of morals,* and *charity,* died, and his body was watched by Bruno himself. Three days after his death, and as he was going to be buried, the pious physician suddenly sat up in his coffin and declared, in a loud and solemn voice, "that by the

Calvin promulgated views of Divine partiality and bloodthirstiness equally abhorrent. "The human race, corrupted radically in the fall with Adam, has upon it the guilt and impotence of original sin; its redemption can be achieved only through an incarnation and a propitiation; of this redemption only electing grace can make the soul a participant, and such grace, once given, is never lost; *this election can come only from God, and it includes only a part of the race, the rest being left to perdition;* election and perdition (the *horribile decretum*) are both predestinated in the Divine plan; that plan is a decree, and this decree is eternal and unchangeable . . . justification is by *faith alone, and faith is the gift of God*."\*

O Divine Justice, how blasphemed has been thy name! Unfortunately for all such speculations, belief in the propitiatory efficacy of blood can be traced to the oldest rites. Hardly a nation remained ignorant of it. Every people offered animal and even human sacrifices to the gods, in the hope of averting thereby public calamity, by pacifying the wrath of some avenging deity. There are instances of Greek and Roman generals offering their lives simply for the success of their army. Caesar complains of it, and calls it a superstition of the Gauls. "They devote themselves to death . . . believing that unless life is rendered for life the immortal gods cannot be appeased," he writes.† "If any evil is about to befall either those who now sacrifice, or Egypt, may it be averted on this head," was pronounced by the Egyptian priests when sacrificing one of their sacred animals.‡ And imprecations were uttered over the head of the expiatory victim, around whose horns a piece of byblus was rolled. The animal was generally led to some barren region, sacred to Typhon, in those primitive ages when this fatal deity was yet held in a certain consideration by the Egyptians. It is in this custom that lies the origin of the "scapegoat" of the Jews, who, when the rufous ass-god was rejected by the Egyptians, began sacrificing to another deity the "red heifer."

"Let all sins that have been committeed in this world fall on me that the world may be delivered," exclaimed Gautama, the Hindu Savior, centuries before our era.

---

just judgment of God he was eternally damned." After which consoling message from beyond the "dark river," he fell back and relapsed into death.

In their turn, the Pârsî theologians speak thus: "If anyone commit sin under the belief that he shall be saved by *somebody*, both the deceiver as well as the deceived shall be damned to the day of Rastâ Khez . . . There is no savior. In the other world you shall receive the return according to your actions . . . *Your savior is your deeds*, and God Himself." [M. Müller, *Chips*, I, p. 176.]

\* [Calvin, *Inst. Christ. Religion*, Book III.]

† [*Commentarii de bello Gallico*, VI, 16.]

‡ Plutarch, *On Isis and Osiris*, § 73.

No one will pretend to assert in our own age that it was the Egyptians who borrowed anything from the Israelites, as they now accuse the Hindus of doing. Bunsen, Lepsius, Champollion, have long since established the precedence of Egypt over the Israelites in age as well as in all the religious rites that we now recognize among the "chosen people." Even the *New Testament* teems with quotations and repetitions from the *Book of the Dead*, and Jesus, if everything attributed to him by his four biographers is true — must have been acquainted with the Egyptian Funereal Hymns.* In the *Gospel according to Matthew* we find whole sentences from the ancient and sacred *Ritual* which preceded our era by more than 4,000 years. We will again compare.†

The "soul" under trial is brought before Osiris, the "Lord of Truth," who sits decorated with the Egyptian cross, emblem of eternal life, and holding in his right hand the *vannus* or the flagellum of justice.‡ The spirit begins, in the "Hall of the Two Truths," an earnest appeal, and enumerates its good deeds, supported by the responses of the forty-two assessors — *its incarnated deeds and accusers.* If justified, it is addressed as *Osiris*, thus assuming the appellation of the Deity whence its divine essence proceeded, and the following words, full of majesty and justice, are pronounced! "Let the *Osiris* go; ye see he is without fault . . . He lived on truth, he has fed on truth . . . *The god has welcomed him* as he desired. *He has given food to my hungry, drink to my thirsty ones, clothes to my naked* . . . He has made the sacred food of the gods the meat of the spirits."§

In the parable of the *Kingdom of Heaven* (Matthew xxv, 34-36), the *Son of Man* (Osiris is also called the Son) sits upon the throne of his glory, judging the nations, and says to the justified, "Come ye blessed of my Father [*the* God] inherit the kingdom . . . For *I was an hungered, and ye gave me meat; I was thirsty, and ye gave me drink . . . naked, and*

---

\* Every tradition shows that Jesus was educated in Egypt and passed his infancy and youth with the Brotherhoods of the Essenes and other mystic communities.

† Bunsen found some records which show the language and religious worship of the Egyptians, for instance, not only existing at the opening of the old Empire, "but already so fully established and fixed as to receive *but a very slight development* in the course of the old, middle, and modern Empires," and while this opening of the old Empire is placed by him beyond the Menes period, at least 4,000 years B.C., the origin of the ancient Hermetic prayers and hymns of the *Book of the Dead,* is assigned by Bunsen to the pre-Menite dynasty of Abydos (between 4,000 and 4,500 B.C.), thus showing that "the system of Osirian worship and mythology was already formed 3,000 years before the days of Moses." [*Egypt's Place*, etc., V, p. 94.]

‡ It was also called the "hook of attraction." Virgil terms it "mystica vannus Iacchi" (*Georgica*, I, 166).

§ [*Book of the Dead,* cxxv, from the Papyrus of Nu; Brit. Mus. No. 10, 477, sheet 24.]

*ye clothed me.*" \* To complete the resemblance (*Matthew* iii, 12): John is made to describe Christ as Osiris, "whose *fan* (winnow or *vannus*) is in his hand," and who will "purge his floor, and gather his wheat into the garner."

The same in relation to Buddhist legends. In *Matthew* iv, 19, Jesus is made to say: "Follow me and I will make you *fishers* of men," the whole adapted to a conversation between him and Simon Peter and Andrew, his brother.

In Schmidt's *Der Weise und der Thor*,† a work full of anecdotes about Buddha and his disciples, the whole from original texts, it is said of a new convert to the faith, that "he had been caught by the hook of the doctrine, just as a fish, who has caught at the bait and line is securely pulled out." In the temples of Siam, the image of the expected Buddha, the Messiah Maitreya, is represented with a fisherman's net in the hand, while in Thibet he holds a kind of a trap. The explanation of it reads as follows: "He [Buddha] disseminates upon the Ocean of birth and decay the Lotus flower of the excellent law as *a bait;* with the loop of devotion, never cast out in vain, he brings living beings up like fishes, and carries them to the other side of the river, where there is true understanding." ‡

Had the erudite Archbishop Cave, Grabe and Dr. Parke, who so zealously contended in their time for the admission of the *Epistles of Jesus Christ and Abgarus, King of Edessa*, into the Canon of the Scripture, lived in our days of Max Müller and Sanskrit scholarship, we doubt whether they would have acted as they did. The first mention of these Epistles ever made was by the famous Eusebius. This pious bishop seems to have been self-appointed to furnish Christianity with the most unexpected proofs to corroborate its wildest fancies. Whether

---

\* In an Address to the Delegates of the Evangelical Alliance, New York, 1874, Mr. Peter Cooper, a Unitarian, and one of the noblest *practical* Christians of the age, closes it with the following memorable language: "In that *last and final account* it will be happy for us if we shall then find that our influence through life has tended to feed the hungry, to clothe the naked, and soothe the sorrows of those who were sick and in prison." Such words from a man who has given two million dollars in charity; educated four thousand young girls in useful arts, by which they gain a comfortable support; maintained a free public library, museum, and reading-room; classes for working people; public lectures by eminent scientists, open to all; and been foremost in all good works, throughout a long and blameless life, come with the noble force that marks the utterances of all benefactors of their kind. The deeds of Peter Cooper will cause posterity to treasure his golden sayings in its heart.

† *Aus dem Tibetischen übersetzt und mit dem Originaltexte herausgegeben*, von I. J. Schmidt, St. Petersburg, 1843.

‡ *Buddhism in Tibet*, by Emil Schlagintweit; ed. 1863, p. 213.

among the many accomplishments of the Bishop of Caesarea, we must include a knowledge of the Sinhalese, Pahlavi, Thibetan, and other languages, we know not; but he surely transcribed the letters of Jesus and Abgarus, and the story of the miraculous portrait of Christ taken on a piece of cloth, by the simple wiping of his face, from the Buddhistical Canon. To be sure, the bishop declared that he found the letter himself written in Syriac, preserved among the registers and records of the city of Edessa, where Abgarus reigned.* We recall the words of Babrias: "Myth, O son of King Alexander, is an ancient human invention of Syrians, who lived in old time under Ninus and Belus." Edessa was one of the ancient "holy cities." The Arabs venerate it to this day; and the purest Arabic is there spoken. They call it still by its ancient name Orfa, once the city *Arpha-Kasda* (Arphaxad), the seat of a College of Chaldeans and Magi; whose missionary, called Orpheus, brought thence the Bacchic Mysteries to Thrace. Very naturally, Eusebius found there the tales which he wrought over into the story of Abgarus, and the sacred picture taken on a cloth; as that of Bhagavat, or the blessed Tathâgata (Buddha)† was obtained by King Bimbisâra. ‡ The King having brought it, Bhagavat projected his shadow on it. § This bit of "miraculous stuff," with its shadow, is still preserved, say the Buddhists; "only the shadow itself is rarely seen." ||

In like manner, the Gnostic author of the *Gospel according to John*, copied and metamorphosed the legend of Ânanda who asked drink of a Mâtamgî woman — the antitype of the woman met by Jesus at the well,¶

---

* *Ecclesiastical History*, I, xiii.

† Tathâgata is Buddha, "he who walks in the footsteps of his predecessors"; as *Bhagavat* — he is the Lord.

‡ We have the same legend about St. Veronica — as a pendant.

§ E. Burnouf, *Introduction à l'histoire du bouddhisme indien*, p. 341.

|| [See the same story in the Tibetan *Kanjur*, Dulvâ, V, fol. 30. Cf. Alex. Csoma de Körös, *On the Kanjur*, p. 164.]

¶ Moses was a most notable practitioner of Hermetic Science. Bearing in mind that Moses (Asarsiph) is made to run away to the Land of Midian, and that he "sat down by a well" (*Exod*. ii, 15), we find the following:

The "Well" played a prominent part in the Mysteries of the Bacchic festivals. In the sacerdotal language of every country, it had the same significance. A well is "the fountain of salvation" mentioned in *Isaiah* (xii, 3). The water is the *male principle* in its spiritual sense. In its physical relation in the allegory of creation, the water is chaos, and chaos is the female principle vivified by the Spirit of God — the male principle. In the Kabala, *Zakhar* means "male"; and the Jordan was called *Zacchar* (*An Universal History*, Vol. II, p. 429). It is curious that the Father of St. John the Baptist, the Prophet of *Jordan* — Zacchar — should be called *Zachar-ias*. One of the names of Bacchus is *Zagreus*. The ceremony of pouring water on the shrine was sacred in the Osirian rites as well as in the Mosaic institutions. In the *Mishnah* it is said, "Thou shalt dwell in Sukkah and *pour out*

and was reminded by her that she belongs to a low caste, and may have nothing to do with a holy monk. "I do not ask thee, my sister," answers Ânanda to the woman, "either thy caste or thy family, I only ask thee for water, if thou canst give me some." * This Mâtamgî woman, charmed and moved to tears, repents, joins the monastic Order of Gautama, and becomes a saint, rescued from a life of unchastity by Sâkya-muni. Many of her subsequent actions were used by Christian forgers, to endow Mary Magdalene and other female saints and martyrs.

"And whosoever shall give to drink unto one of these little ones a cup of cold water only in the name of a disciple, verily I say unto you, he shall in no wise lose his reward," says the Gospel (*Matthew* x, 42). "Whosoever, with a purely believing heart, offers nothing but a handful of water, or presents so much to the spiritual assembly, or gives drink therewith to the poor and needy, or to a beast of the field; this meritorious action will not be exhausted in many ages," † says the Buddhist *Canon*.

At the hour of Gautama Buddha's birth there were 32 wonders performed. The clouds stopped immovable in the sky, the waters of the rivers ceased to flow; the flowers ceased unbudding; the birds re-

---

*water* seven, and the pipes six days" (*Mishnah Sukkah*, iv, 1). "Take *virgin earth* . . . and work up the *dust* with *living* WATER," prescribes the *Zohar* (*Kabbala Denudata*, II, pp. 220, 221). Only "earth and water, according to Moses, can bring forth a *living soul*," quotes Cornelius Agrippa. The water of Bacchus was considered to impart the Holy *Pneuma* to the initiate; and it washes off all sin by baptism through the Holy *Ghost*, with the Christians. The "well" in the kabalistic sense is the mysterious emblem of the *Secret Doctrine*. "If any man thirst, let him come *unto me and drink*," says Jesus (*John* vii, 37).

Therefore, Moses the adept, is naturally enough represented sitting by a well. He is approached by the *seven* daughters of the Kenite Priest of Midian coming to fill the troughs, *to water their faher's flock*. Here we have seven again — the mystic number. In the present Biblical allegory the daughters represent the *seven occult powers*. "The shepherds came and drove them [the seven daughters] away; but Moses stood up and helped them, and watered their flock." [*Exod.* ii, 17.] The shepherds are shown, by some kabalistic interpreters, to represent the seven "badly-disposed Stellars" of the Nazarenes; for in the old Samaritan text the number of these Shepherds is also to be seven (see kabalistic books).

Then Moses, who had conquered the seven *evil* Powers, and won the friendship of the seven *occult* and beneficent ones, is represented as living with Reuel the Priest of Midian, who invites "the Egyptian" to eat bread, *i.e.*, to partake of his wisdom. In the *Bible* the elders of Midian are known as great soothsayers and diviners. Finally, Reuel or Jethro, the initiator and instructor of Moses, gives him in marriage his daughter. This daughter is Zipporah, *i.e.*, the esoteric Wisdom, the shining light of knowledge, for Siprah means the "shining" or "resplendent," from the word "Shapar," to shine. Sippara, in Chaldea, was the city of the "Sun." Thus Moses was initiated by the Midianite, or rather the Kenite, and thence the Biblical allegory.

* [E. Burnouf, *op. cit.*, p. 205.]

† I. J. Schmidt, *Der Weise und der Thor*, II, p. 37.

mained silent and full of wonder; all nature remained suspended in her course, and was full of expectation. "There was a preternatural light spread all over the world; animals suspended their eating; the blind saw; and the lame and dumb were cured," etc.*

We now quote from the *Protevangelion:*

"At the hour of the Nativity, as Joseph looked up into the air, I saw [he says] *the clouds astonished,* and the fowls of the air stopping in the midst of their flight . . . And I beheld the sheep dispersed, and *yet the sheep stood still;* . . . and I looked into a river, and saw the kids *with their mouths close to the water, and touching it, but they did not drink.*

"*Then a bright cloud overshadowed the cave* . . . But on a sudden the cloud became *a great light* in the cave, so that their eyes could not bear it . . . The hand of Salome, which was withered, was straightway cured . . . The blind saw; the lame and dumb were cured." †

When sent to school, the young Gautama, without having ever studied, completely worsted all his competitors; not only in writing, but in arithmetic, mathematics, metaphysics, wrestling, archery, astronomy, geometry, and finally vanquished his own professors by giving the definition of sixty-four kinds of writings, which were unknown to the masters themselves.‡

And this is what is said again in the *Gospel of the Infancy:* "And when he [Jesus] was twelve years old . . . a certain principal Rabbi asked him, 'Hast thou read books?' . . . and a certain astronomer . . . asked the Lord Jesus, whether he had studied astronomy. And Lord Jesus explained to him . . . about the spheres . . . about the physics and metaphysics. Also things that reason of man had never discovered . . . The constitution of the body, how the soul operated upon the body, etc. . . . And at this the master was not surprised that he said: 'I believe this boy was born before Noah . . . he is more learned than any master'." §

The precepts of Hillel, who died forty years B.C., appear rather as quotations than original expressions in the Sermon on the Mount. Jesus taught the world nothing that had not been taught as earnestly before by other masters. He begins his sermon with certain purely Buddhistic

---

* *Rgya tch'er rol pa,* Vol. II, pp. 80, 81, 90, 91, etc.; Alabaster, *The Wheel of the Law,* pp. 104-05.

† *Protevangelion* (ascribed to James), ch. xiii and xiv.

‡ *Pâli-Buddhistical Annals,* III, p. 28; cf. Hardy, *A Manual of Budhism,* p. 153; *Lalitavistara,* x, xii.

§ *The Arabic Gospel of the Infancy,* §§ 48, 50-52 (ch. xx, xxi, Hone), accepted by Eusebius, Athanasius, Epiphanius, Chrysostom, Jerome, and others. The same story, with the Hindu earmarks rubbed off to avoid detection, is found in *Luke* ii, 46-47.

precepts that had found acceptance among the Essenes, and were generally practiced by the *Orphikoi*, and the Neo-Platonists. There were the Phil-hellenes, who, like Apollonius, had devoted their lives to moral and physical purity, and who practiced asceticism. He tries to imbue the hearts of his audience with a scorn for worldly wealth; a fakir-like unconcern for the morrow; love for humanity, poverty and chastity. He blesses the poor in spirit, the meek, the hungering and the thirsting after righteousness, the merciful and the peacemakers, and, Buddha-like, leaves but a poor chance for the proud castes to enter into the kingdom of heaven. Every word of his sermon is an echo of the essential principles of monastic Buddhism. The ten commandments of Buddha, as found in an appendix to the *Pratimoksha-Sûtra* (Pâli-Burmese text), are elaborated to their full extent in *Matthew*. If we desire to acquaint ourselves with the historical Jesus we have to set the mythical Christ entirely aside, and learn all we can of the man in the first Gospel. His doctrines, religious views, and grandest aspirations will be found concentrated in his sermon.

This is the principal cause of the failure of missionaries to convert Brahmanists and Buddhists. These see that the little of really good that is offered in the new religion is paraded only in theory, while their own faith demands that those identical rules shall be applied in practice. Notwithstanding the impossibility for Christian missionaries to understand clearly the spirit of a religion wholly based on that doctrine of emanation which is so inimical to their own theology, the reasoning powers of some simple Buddhistical preachers are so high, that we see a scholar like Gützlaff,* utterly silenced and put to great straits by Buddhists. Judson, the famous Baptist missionary in Burma, confesses, in his *Journal*,† the difficulties to which he was often driven by them. Speaking of a certain Ooyan, he remarks that his strong mind was capable of grasping the most difficult subjects. "His words," he remarks, "are as smooth as oil, as sweet as honey, and as sharp as razors; his mode of reasoning is soft, insinuating, and acute; and so adroitly did he act his part, that . . . *I, with the strength of truth,* [was] scarcely able to keep him down." It appears though, that at a later period of his mission, Mr. Judson found that he had utterly mistaken the doctrine. "I begin to find," he says, "that the semi-atheism, which I had sometimes mentioned, is nothing but a *refined Buddhism, having its foundation in the Buddhists Scriptures.*" Thus he discovered at last that while there is in Buddhism "a generic term of most exalted perfection actually applied to numerous individuals, a Buddha superior to the whole host of subordinate deities, there are also lurking in the

---

* Alabaster, *The Wheel of the Law*, pp. 20-26.

† [In Ann H. Judson's *An Account of the American Baptist Mission to the Burman Empire*, London, 1827.]

system the glimmerings of an *anima mundi* anterior to, and even superior to, Buddha." *

This is a happy discovery, indeed!

Even the so-slandered Chinese believe in *One*, Highest God, "The Supreme Ruler of the Imperial Heavens." Yuh-Hwang Shang-ti has his name inscribed only on the golden tablet before the altar of heaven at the great temple at Peking, T'ien-t'ân. "This worship," says Colonel Yule, "is mentioned by the *Mohammedan* narrator of Shah Rukh's embassy (A.D. 1421): 'Every year there are some days on which the Emperor eats no animal food . . . He spends his time in an apartment which contains *no idol*, and says that *he is worshipping the God of Heaven*'." †

Speaking of Shahrastânî, the great Arabian scholar, Chwolsohn says that for him Sabaeanism was not astrolatry, as many are inclined to think. He thought "that God is too sublime and too great to occupy Himself with the immediate management of this world; that He has, therefore, transferred the government thereof to the gods, and retained only the most important affairs for Himself; that further, man is too weak to be able to apply immediately to the Highest; that he must, therefore, address his prayers and sacrifices to the intermediate divinities, to whom the management of the world has been entrusted by the Highest." Chwolsohn argues that this idea is as old as the world, and that "in the heathen world this view was universally shared by the cultivated." ‡

Father C. Borri, a Portuguese missionary, who was sent to convert the "poor heathen" of Cochin-China, as early as the sixteenth century, "protests in despair [in his narrative], that there is not a dress, office, or ceremony in the Church of Rome, to which the Devil has not here provided some counterpart. Even when [the Father] began inveighing against their idols, he was answered, that these were the images of departed great men, whom they worshipped exactly in the same principle and manner as the Catholics did the images of the apostles and martyrs." § Moreover, these idols have importance but in the eyes of the ignorant multitudes. The *philosophy* of Buddhism ignores images and fetishes. Its strongest vitality lies in its psychological conceptions of man's *inner* self. The road to the supreme state of felicity, called the Ford of Nirvâna, winds its invisible paths through the spiritual, not physical life of a person while on this earth. The sacred Buddhistical literature points the way by stimulating man to follow

---

\* E. Upham, *The History and Doctrines of Buddhism*, p. 135. Dr. Judson fell into this prodigious error by reason of his fanaticism. In his zeal to "save souls," he refused to peruse the Burmese classics, lest his attention should be diverted thereby.

† *Indian Antiquary*, Vol. II, p. 81; *Book of Ser Marco Polo*, Vol. I, p. 441; ed. 1875.

‡ *Die Ssabier und der Ssabismus*, Vol. I, pp. 725-26.

§ Murray, *Historical Account of Discoveries and Travels in Asia*, etc., Vol. III, p. 249

*practically* the example of Gautama. Therefore, the Buddhistical writings lay a particular stress on the spiritual privileges of man, advising him to cultivate his powers for the production of *meipo* (phenomena) during life, and for the attainment of Nirvâṇa in the hereafter.

But turning again from the historical to the mythical narratives, invented alike about Kṛishṇa, Buddha and Christ, we find the following:

Setting a model for the Christian avatâra and the archangel Gabriel to follow, the luminous Santushita (Bodhisattva) appeared to Mahâ-mâyâ "like a cloud in the moonlight, coming from the north, and in his hand holding a white lotus." He announced to her the birth of her son, and circumambulating the queen's couch thrice, ". . . passed away from the deva-loka and was conceived *in the world of men*." * The resemblance will be found still more perfect upon examining the illustrations in mediaeval psalters,† and the panel-paintings of the sixteenth century (in the Church of Jouy, for instance, in which the Virgin is represented kneeling, with her hands uplifted toward the Holy Ghost, and the unborn child is miraculously seen through her body), and then finding the same subject treated in the identical way in the sculptures in certain convents in Thibet. In the *Pâli-Buddhistic Annals,* and other religious records, it is stated that Mâyâdevî and all her attendants were constantly gratified with the sight of the infant Bodhisattva quietly developing within his mother's bosom, and beaming already, from his place of gestation, upon humanity "the resplendent moonshine of his future benevolence." ‡

Ânanda, the cousin and future disciple of Śâkyamuni, is represented as having been born at the same time. He appears to have been the original for the old legends about John the Baptist. For example, the Pâli narrative relates that Mahâ-mâyâ, while pregnant with the sage, paid a visit to his mother, as Mary did to the mother of the Baptist. Immediately, as she entered the apartment, the unborn Ânanda greeted the unborn Buddha-Siddhârtha, who also returned the salutation; and in like manner the babe, afterward John the Baptist, leaped in the womb of Elizabeth when Mary came in. § More even than that; for Didron describes a scene of salutation, painted on shutters at Lyons, between Elizabeth and Mary, in which the two unborn infants, both pictured as outside their mothers, are also saluting each other. ||

If we turn now to Kṛishṇa and attentively compare the prophecies respecting him, as collected in the Ramatsariarian traditions of the

---

\* R. Spence Hardy, *A Manual of Budhism,* p. 142.

† See Inman, *Ancient Pagan and Modern Christian Symbolism,* p. 92.

‡ *Rgya tch'er rol pa,* ch. vi, in the Second Volume of the Fifth Section of the Tibetan *Kanjur;* also *The Wheel of the Law,* p. 100.

§ *Luke* i, 39-45.

|| Didron, *Iconographie chrétienne. Histoire de Dieu,* Paris, 1843, p. 287; and *Manuel d'iconographie chrétienne grecque et latine,* Paris, 1845, p. 156.

Atharva, the *Vedāṅgas* and the *Vedāntas*,\* with passages in the *Bible* and apocryphal Gospels, of which it is pretended that some presage the coming of Christ, we shall find very curious facts. Following are examples:

| FROM THE HINDU BOOKS † | FROM THE CHRISTIAN BOOKS |
|---|---|
| 1st. "He (the Redeemer) shall come, *crowned with lights*, the pure fluid issuing from the great soul . . . dispersing darkness" (*Atharva*). | 1st. "The People [of Galilee of the Gentiles] which sat in darkness saw great light" (*Matthew* iv, 16, from *Isaiah* ix, 1, 2). |
| 2nd. "In the *early part* of the Kali-Yuga shall be born the son of the Virgin" (*Vedânta*). | 2nd. "Behold, a virgin shall conceive, and bear a son" (*Isaiah* vii, 14, quoted in *Matthew* i, 23). |
| 3rd. "The Redeemer shall come, and the accursed *Râkshasas* shall fly for refuge to the deepest hell" (*Atharva*). | 3rd. "Behold now that Jesus of Nazareth, with the brightness of his glorious divinity, puts to flight all the horrid powers of darkness and death" (*Nicodemus*, xviii, 3). |
| 4th. "He shall come, and life shall defy death . . . and he shall revivify the blood of all beings, shall regenerate all bodies, and purify all souls." | 4th. "And I give unto them eternal life; and they shall never perish" (*John* x, 28). |
| 5th. "He shall come, and all animated beings, all the flowers, plants, men, women, the infants, the slaves . . . shall together intone the chant of joy, for he is the Lord of all creatures . . . he is infinite, for he is power, for he is wisdom, for he is beauty, for he is all and in all." | 5th. "Rejoice greatly, O daughter of Zion! shout, O daughter of Jerusalem! behold, thy King cometh unto thee: he is just . . . for how great is his goodness, and how great is his beauty? Corn shall make the young men cheerful, and new wine the maids" (*Zechariah* ix, 9, 17). |
| 6th. "He shall come, more sweet than honey and ambrosia, more pure than *the lamb* without spot" (*Ibid.*). | 6th. "Behold the lamb of God" (*John* i, 36). "He is brought as a lamb to the slaughter" (*Isaiah* liii, 7). |
| 7th. "Happy the blest womb that shall bear him" (*Ibid.*). | 7th. "Blessed art thou among women, and blessed is the fruit of thy womb" (*Luke* i, 42); "Blessed is the womb that bare thee" (xi, 27). |
| 8th. "For God shall manifest His glory, and make His power resound, and shall reconcile Himself with His creatures" (*Ibid.*). | 8th. Jesus "manifested forth His glory" (*John* ii, 11). "God was in Christ, reconciling the world unto himself" (2 *Corinth.* v, 19). |
| 9th. "It is in the bosom of a woman that the ray of the Divine splendor will receive human form, and she shall bring forth, being a virgin, for no impure contact shall have defiled her" (*Vedâṅgas*). | 9th. "Being an unparalleled instance, without any pollution or defilement, and a virgin not knowing any man shall bring forth a son, and a maid shall bring forth the Lord" (*Gospel of the Birth of Mary*, iii, 5). |

---

\* There are numerous works deduced immediately from the *Vedas*, called the *Upaveda*. Four works are included under this denomination, namely, the *Ayur, Gândharva, Dhanur,* and *Sthâpatya*. The third *Upaveda* was composed by Viśvamitra for the use of the Kshatriyas, the warrior caste.

† [Cf. L. Jacolliot, *The Bible in India*, London, 1870, pp. 220-21.]

Let there be exaggeration or not in attributing to the *Atharva-Veda* and the other books such a great antiquity, the fact remains that *these prophecies and their realization preceded Christianity*, and Krishna preceded Christ. That is all we need care to inquire.

One is completely overwhelmed with astonishment upon reading Dr. Lundy's *Monumental Christianity*. It would be difficult to say whether an admiration for the author's erudition, or amazement at his serene and unparalleled sophistry is stronger. He has gathered a world of facts which prove that the religions, far more ancient than Christianity, of Krishna, Buddha and Osiris had anticipated even its minutest symbols. His materials come from no forged papyri, no interpolated Gospels, but from sculptures on the walls of ancient temples, from monuments, inscriptions, and other archaic relics, only mutilated by the hammers of iconoclasts, the cannon of fanatics, and the effects of time. He shows us Krishna and Apollo as good shepherds; Krishna holding the cruciform *ânkh* and the *chakra*, and Krishna "crucified in space," as he calls it.\* Of this figure — borrowed by Dr. Lundy from Moor's *Hindoo Pantheon* — it may be truly said that it is calculated to petrify a Christian with astonishment, for it is the crucified Christ of Romish art to the last degree of resemblance. Not a feature is lacking; and the author says of it himself:† "[this] representation I believe to be anterior to Christianity . . . It looks like a Christian crucifix in many respects . . . The drawing, the attitude, and the nailmarks in hands and feet, indicate a Christian origin; while the Parthian coronet of seven points, the absence of the wood and of the usual inscription, and the rays of glory above, would seem to point to some other than a Christian origin. Can it be the Victim-Man, or the Priest and Victim both in one, of the Hindu mythology, who offered himself a sacrifice before the worlds were? Can it be Plato's second God who impressed himself on the universe in the form of the cross? Or is it his divine man who would be scourged, tormented, fettered, have his eyes burnt out; and lastly . . . *would be crucified?*" ‡ It is all that and much more; *Archaic Religious Philosophy* was universal.

As it is, Dr. Lundy contradicts Moor,§ and maintains that this figure is that of *Vithobâ*, one of the avatâras of Vishnu, hence Krishna, and *anterior to Christianity*, which is a fact not very easily to be put down. And yet although he finds it prophetic of Christianity, he thinks it has no relation whatever to Christ! His only reason is that "in a Christian crucifix the glory always comes from the sacred head; here it is from above and beyond . . . The Pundit's Vithobâ then, given to Moor, would seem to be the crucified *Krishna*, the shepherd-god of Mathurâ

---

\* Lundy, *Monumental Christianity*, fig. 72.
† *Ibid.*, p. 173.
‡ *Republic*, Bk. II, 362 A.
§ Lundy, *op. cit.*, p. 176

... a *Savior — the Lord of the covenant, as well as Lord of heaven and earth — pure and impure, light and dark, good and bad, peaceful and warlike, amiable and wrathful, mild and turbulent, forgiving and vindictive, God and a strange mixture of man*, but not the Christ of the Gospels."

Now all these qualities must pertain to Jesus as well as to Kṛishṇa. The very fact that Jesus was a man upon the mother's side — even though he were a *God*, implies as much. His behavior toward the fig tree, and his self-contradictions, in *Matthew*, where at one time he promises peace on earth, and at another the sword, etc., are proof in this direction. Undoubtedly this cut was never intended to represent Jesus of Nazareth. It was Viṭhobâ, as Moor was told, and as, moreover, the Hindu *Sacred Scriptures* state, Brahmâ, the sacrificer who is "at once both sacrificer and victim"; it is "Brahmâ, victim in His Son Kṛishṇa, who came to die on earth for our salvation, who Himself accomplishes the solemn sacrifice [of the Sarvamedha]." And yet, it is the man Jesus as well as the man Kṛishṇa, for both were united to their *Christos*.

Thus we have either to admit periodical "incarnations," or let Christianity go as the greatest imposture and plagiarism of the ages!

As to the Jewish *Scriptures*, only such men as the Jesuit de Carrière a covenient representative of the majority of the Catholic clergy, can still command their followers to accept only the chronology established by the Holy Ghost. It is on the authority of the latter that we learn that Jacob went, with a family of seventy persons, all told, to settle in Egypt in A.M. 2298, and that in A.M. 2513—just 215 years afterward — these seventy persons had so increased that they left Egypt 600,000 fighting men strong, "without counting women and children," which, according to the science of statistics, should represent a total population of between two and three millions!! Natural history affords no parallel to such fecundity, except in red herrings. After this let the Christian missionaries laugh, if they can, at Hindu chronology and computations.

"Happy are those persons, but not to be envied," exclaims Bunsen, "who have no misgiving about making Moses march out with more than two millions of people at the end of a popular conspiracy and rising, in the sunny days of the 18th Dynasty; who make the Israelites conquer Kanaan under Joshua, during, and previous to, the most formidable campaigns of conquering Pharaohs in that same country. The Egyptian and Assyrian annals, combined with the historical criticism of the *Bible*, prove that the exodus could only have taken place under Menephthah, so that Joshua could not have crossed the Jordan before Easter 1280, the last campaign of Ramses III in Palestine being in 1281." *

---

* Bunsen, *Egypt's Place in Universal History*, Vol. V, p. 75.

But we must resume the thread of our narrative with Buddha.

Neither he nor Jesus ever wrote one word of their doctrines. We have to take the teachings of the masters on the testimony of the disciples, and therefore it is but fair that we should be allowed to judge both doctrines on their intrinsic value. Where the logical preponderance lies may be seen in the results of frequent encounters between Christian missionaries and Buddhist theologians (*punghi*). The latter usually, if not invariably, have the better of their opponents. On the other hand, the "Lama of Jehovah" rarely fails to lose his temper, to the great delight of the Lama of Buddha, and practically demonstrates his religion of patience, mercy and charity, by abusing his disputant in the most uncanonical language. This we have witnessed repeatedly.

Despite the notable similarity of the direct teachings of Gautama and Jesus, we yet find their respective followers starting from two diametrically opposite points. The Buddhist divine, following literally the ethical doctrine of his master, remains thus true to the legacy of Gautama; while the Christian minister, distorting the precepts recorded by the four *Gospels* beyond recognition, teaches, not that which Jesus taught, but the absurd, too often pernicious, interpretations of fallible men — Popes, Luthers and Calvins included. The following are two instances selected from both religions, and brought into contrast. Let the reader judge for himself:

"Do not believe in anything because it is rumored and spoken of by many," says Buddha; "do not think that it is a proof of its truth.

"Do not believe merely because the written statement of some old sage is produced; do not be sure that the writing has never been revised by the said sage, or can be relied on. Do not believe in what you have fancied, thinking that *because an idea is extraordinary it must have been implanted by a Deva, or some wonderful being.*

"Do not believe in guesses, that is, assuming something at haphazard as a starting-point, draw conclusions from it; reckoning your two and your three and your four *before you have fixed your number one* . . .

"*Do not believe merely on the authority of your teachers and masters,* or believe and practice merely *because they believe and practice.*

"I [Buddha] tell you all, you must of your own selves know that 'this is evil, this is punishable, this is censured by wise men, belief in this will bring no advantage to one, but will cause sorrow.' And when you know this, then eschew it." *

It is impossible to avoid contrasting with these benevolent and human sentiments, the fulminations of the Ecumenical Council and the Pope,

---

*Alabaster, *The Wheel of the Law*, pp. 35-36.

against the employment of reason, and the pursuit of science when it clashes with revelation. The atrocious Papal benediction of Moslem arms and cursing of the Russian and Bulgarian Christians have roused the indignation of some of the most devoted Catholic communities. The Catholic Czechs of Prague on the day of the recent semi-centennial jubilee of Pius IX, and again on the 6th of July, the day sacred to the memory of John Huss, the burned martyr, to mark their horror of the Ultramontane policy in this respect, gathered by thousands upon the neighboring Mount Zhizhkov, and with great ceremony and denunciations, burned the Pope's portrait, his Syllabus, and last allocution against the Russian Czar, saying that they were good Catholics, but better Slavs. Evidently, the memory of John Huss is more sacred to them than the Vatican Popes.

"The worship of words is more pernicious than the worship of images," remarks Robert Dale Owen. "Grammatolatry is the worst species of idolatry. We have arrived at an era in which literalism is destroying faith . . . The letter killeth." *

There is not a dogma in the Church to which these words can be better applied than to the doctrine of *transubstantiation*. † "Whoso eateth my flesh, and drinketh my blood, hath eternal life," Christ is made to say. "This is an hard saying," repeated his dismayed listeners. The answer *was that of an initiate*. "Doth this offend you? . . . It is the Spirit that quickeneth; the flesh profiteth nothing. The words [*rêmata*, or arcane utterances] that I speak unto you, they are spirit and they are Life." [*John* vi, 54, 61, 63.]

During the Mysteries wine represented Bacchus, and bread Ceres. ‡

---

* *The Debatable Land*, p. 145.

† "We divide our zeal," says Dr. Henry More, "against so many things that we fancy Popish, that we scarce reserve *a just share of detestation* against what is truly so. Such are that gross, rank, and scandalous impossibility *of Transubstantiation*, the various modes of fulsome Idolatry and lying *impostures*, the *uncertainty* of their *loyalty* to their lawful Sovereigns by their superstitious adhesion to the spiritual tyranny of the Pope, and that *barbarous and ferine cruelty against those* that are not either such fools as to be persuaded to believe such things as they would obtrude upon men, or are not so false to God and their own consciences, as knowing better, yet to profess them" (P.S. to letter to Glanvill, *Sadduc. triumph.*, p. 53).

‡ R. Payne Knight believes that Ceres "was not a personification of the brute matter which composed the earth, but of the passive *productive principle* supposed to pervade it, which, joined to the active, was held to be the cause of the organization and animation of its substance . . . She is mentioned by Virgil as the wife of the omnipotent Father, Aether or Jupiter" (*The Symbolical Language of Ancient Art and Mythology*, § xxxvi). Hence the words of Christ, "it is the Spirit that quickeneth, the *flesh profiteth nothing,*" applied in their dual meaning to both spiritual and terrestrial things, to spirit and matter.

Bacchus, as Dionysos, is of Indian origin. Cicero mentions him as a son of Thyônê

The hierophant-initiator presented symbolically before the final *revelation* wine and bread to the candidate who had to eat and drink of both in token that the spirit was to quicken matter, *i.e.*, the divine wisdom was to enter into his body through what was to be revealed to him. Jesus, in his Oriental phraseology, constantly assimilated himself to the true vine (*John* xv, 1). Furthermore, the hierophant, the discloser of the Petroma, was called "Father." When Jesus says, "Drink . . . this is my blood," what else was meant, it was simply a metaphorical assimilation of himself to the vine, which bears the grape, whose juice is its blood — wine. It was a hint that as he had himself been initiated by the "Father," so he desired to initiate others. His "Father" was the husbandman, himself the vine, his disciples the branches. His followers being ignorant of the terminology of the Mysteries, wondered; they even took it as an offense, which is not surprising, considering the Mosaic injunction against blood.

There is quite enough in the four gospels to show what was the secret and most fervent hope of Jesus; the hope in which he began to teach, and in which he died. In his immense and unselfish love for humanity, he considers it unjust to deprive the many of the results of the knowledge acquired by the few. This result he accordingly preaches — the unity of a spiritual God, whose temple is within each of us, and in whom we live as He lives in us — in spirit. This knowledge was in the hands of the Jewish adepts of the school of Hillel and the kabalists. But the "scribes," or lawyers, having gradually merged into the dogmatism of the dead letter, had long since separated themselves from the Tannaim, the true spiritual teachers; and the practical kabalists were more or less persecuted by the Synagogue. Hence, we find Jesus exclaiming: "Woe unto you lawyers! *For ye have taken away the key of knowledge* [the Gnosis]: ye entered not in yourself, and them that were entering in ye hindered" (*Luke* xi, 52). The meaning here is clear. They did take the key away, and could not even profit by it themselves, for the *Masorah* (tradition) had become a closed book to themselves as well as to others.

---

and Nisus. [*De natura deorum*, III, xxiii.] Διόνυσος means the god Dis from Mount Nys in India. Bacchus, crowned with ivy, or *kissos*, is Krishna, one of whose names was *Kissen*. Dionysos is pre-eminently the deity on whom were centred all the hopes for future life; in short, he was the god who was expected to *liberate the souls of men* from their prisons of flesh. Orpheus, the poet-Argonaut, is also said to have come on earth to purify the religion of its gross and terrestrial anthropomorphism; he abolished human sacrifice and instituted a mystic theology based on pure spirituality. Cicero calls Orpheus a son of Bacchus. It is strange that both seem to have originally come from India. At least, as Dionysos-Zagreus, Bacchus is of undoubted Hindu origin. Some writers deriving a curious analogy between the name of Orpheus and an old Greek term, ὀρφνός, *dark or tawny-colored*, make him Hindu by connecting the term with his dusky Hindu complexion. See Voss, Heyne and Schneider on the Argonauts.

Neither Renan nor Strauss, nor the more modern Viscount Amberley seem to have had the remotest suspicion of the real meaning of many of the parables of Jesus, or even of the character of the great Galilean philosopher. Renan, as we have seen, presented him to us as a Gallicized Rabbi, «*le plus charmant de tous*», still but a Rabbi; and one, moreover, who does not even come out of the school of Hillel, or any school either, albeit he terms him repeatedly "the charming doctor." * He shows him as a sentimental young enthusiast, sprung out of the plebeian class of Galilee, who imagines the ideal king of his parables the empurpled and jewelled beings of whom one reads in nursery tales.

Lord Amberley's Jesus, on the other hand, is an "iconoclastic idealist," far inferior in subtilty and logic to his critics. Renan looks over at Jesus with the one-sidedness of a Semitomaniac; Viscount Amberley looks down upon him from the social plane of an English lord. *À propos* of this marriage-feast parable, which he considers as embodying "a curious theory of social intercourse," the Viscount says: "Nobody can object to charitable individuals asking poor people or invalids *without rank* to dinner at their houses . . . But we cannot admit that this kind action ought to be rendered obligatory . . . it is eminently desirable that we should do exactly what Christ would forbid us doing, namely, invite our neighbors and be invited by them as circumstances may require. The fear that we may receive a recompense for the dinner parties we may give is surely chimerical . . . Jesus, in fact, overlooks entirely the more intellectual side of society . . ." † All of which unquestionably shows that the "Son of God" was no master of social etiquette, nor fit for "society"; but it is also a fair example of the prevalent misconception of even his most suggestive parables.

The theory of Anquetil-Duperron ‡ that the *Bhagavad-Gîtâ* is an independent work, as it is absent from several manuscripts of the *Mahâbhârata*, may be as much a plea for a still greater antiquity as the reverse. The work is purely metaphysical and ethical, and in a certain sense it is *anti-Vedic;* so far, at least, that it is in opposition with many of the later Brahmanical interpretations of the *Vedas*. How comes it, then, that instead of destroying the work, or, at least, of sentencing it as uncanonical — an expedient to which the Christian Church would never have failed to resort — the Brahmans show it the greatest reverence? Perfectly *unitarian in its aim*, it clashes with the popular idol worship. Still, the only precaution taken by the Brahmans to keep its tenets from becoming too well known, is to preserve it more secretly than any other

---

\* *La Vie de Jésus*, ch. v.

† *An Analysis of Religious Belief*, Vol. I, pp. 466-67; ed. 1876.

‡ [*Oupnek'hat*, II, p. 732, note; Strassburg, 1801-02.]

religious book from every caste except the sacerdotal; and, to impose upon that even, in many cases, certain restrictions. The grandest mysteries of the Brahmanical religion are embraced within this magnificent poem; and even the Buddhists recognize it, explaining certain dogmatic difficulties in their own way. "Be unselfish, subdue your senses and passions, which obscure reason and lead to deceit," says Kṛishṇa to his disciple Arjuna, thus enunciating a purely Buddhistic principle. "Low men follow examples, great men give them . . . the soul ought to free itself from the bonds of action, and act absolutely according to its divine origin. *There is but one God*, and all other *devatâs* are inferior, and mere forms [powers] of Brahmâ or of myself. *Worship by deeds predominates over that of contemplation*." \*

This doctrine coincides perfectly with that of Jesus himself.† Faith alone, unaccompanied by "works," is reduced to naught in the *Bhagavad-Gîtâ*. As to the *Atharva-Veda*, it was and is preserved in such secrecy by the Brahmans that it is a matter of doubt whether the Orientalists have a *complete* copy of it. One who has read what Abbé J. A. Dubois says may well doubt the fact. "Of the last species"—the *Atharva*—"there are very few," he says, writing of the *Vedas*, "and many people suppose they no longer exist. But the truth is, they do exist though they conceal themselves with more caution than others, from the fear of being suspected to be initiated in the magic mysteries and other dreaded secrets which this work is believed to teach." ‡

There were even those among the highest *epoptai* of the greater *Mysteries* who knew nothing of their last and dreaded rite — the voluntary transfer of life from hierophant to candidate. In *Ghost-Land* § this mystical operation of the adept's transfer of his spiritual entity, after the death of his body, into the youth he loves with all the ardent love of a spiritual parent, is superbly described. As in the case of the reincarnation of the lamas of Thibet, an adept of the highest order may live indefinitely. His mortal casket wears out notwithstanding certain alchemical secrets for prolonging the youthful vigor far beyond the usual limits, yet the body can rarely be kept alive beyond ten or twelve score of years. The old garment is then worn out, and the spiritual Ego forced to leave it, selects for its habitation a new body, fresh and full of healthy vital principle. In case the reader should feel inclined to ridicule this assertion

---

\* See the *Bhagavad-Gîtâ*, translated by Charles Wilkins, in 1785; and the *Bhâgavata-Purâṇa*, containing the history of Kṛishṇa, translated into French by Eugène Burnouf, in 1840. [Bk. IV, ch. 29.]

† *Matthew* vii, 21.

‡ *Description of the People of India*, etc., Vol. I, Pt. i, pp. 47-48; ed. 1817.

§ *Ghost-Land; or Researches into the Mysteries of Occultism*, ch. xv, etc. Edited by Mrs. E. Hardinge-Britten, Boston, 1876.

of the possible prolongation of human life, we may as well refer him to the statistics of several countries. The author of an able article in the *Westminster Review*, for October, 1850, is responsible for the statement that in England they have authentic instances of one Thomas Jenkins dying at the age of 169, and "Old Parr" at 152;[66] and that in Russia some of the peasants are "known to have reached 242 years." * There are also cases of centenarianism reported among the Peruvian Indians. We are aware that many able writers have recently discredited these claims to an extreme longevity, but we nevertheless affirm our belief in their truth.

True or false, there are "superstitions" among the Eastern people such as have never been dreamed even by an Edgar Poe or a Hoffmann. And these beliefs run in the very blood of the nations with which they originated. Carefully stripped of exaggeration they will be found to embody a universal belief in those restless, wandering, astral souls, which are called ghouls and vampires. An Armenian Bishop of the fifth century, named Eznik, gives a number of such narratives in a manuscript work (Book i, §§ 20, 30), preserved some thirty years ago in the library of the Monastery of Etchmiadzin.† [67] Among others, there is a tradition dating from the days of heathendom, that whenever a hero whose life is needed yet on earth falls on the battlefield, the Aralezes, the popular gods of ancient Armenia, empowered to bring back to life those slaughtered in battle, lick the bleeding wounds of the victim and breathe on them until they have imparted a new and vigorous life. After that the warrior rises, washes off all traces of his wounds, and resumes his place in the fray. But his immortal spirit has fled; and for the remainder of his days he lives — a deserted temple.

Once that an adept was initiated into the last and most solemn mystery of the life-transfer, the awful *seventh* rite of the great sacerdotal operation, which is the highest theurgy, he belonged no more to this world. His soul was free thereafter, and the *seven* mortal sins lying in wait to devour his heart, as the soul, liberated by death, would be crossing the *seven* halls and *seven* staircases, could hurt him no more alive or dead; he has passed the "twice seven trials," the *twelve* labors of the final hour. ‡

The High Hierophant alone knew how to perform this solemn opera-

---

\* Capt. James Riley, in his *Narrative* of his enslavement in Africa, relates like instances of great longevity on the Sahara Desert.

† Russian Armenia; one of the most ancient Christian convents.

‡ Egyptian *Book of the Dead.* The Hindus have seven upper and seven lower heavens. The seven mortal sins of the Christians have been borrowed from the Egyptian *Books of Hermes* with which Clement of Alexandria was so familiar.

tion by infusing his own vital life and astral soul into the adept, chosen by him for his successor, who thus became endowed with a double life.*

"Verily, verily, I say unto thee, except a man *be born again*, he cannot see the kingdom of God" (*John* iii, 3). Jesus tells Nicodemus, "That which is born of the flesh is flesh; and that which is born of the spirit is spirit."

This allusion, so unintelligible in itself, is explained in the *Śatapatha-Brâhmaṇa*. It teaches that a man striving after spiritual perfection must have *three* births: 1st. Physical from his mortal parents; 2nd. *Spiritual*, through religious sacrifice (initiation); 3rd. His final birth into the world of spirit — at death. Though it may seem strange that we should have to go to the old land of the Puñjâb and the banks of the sacred Ganges for an interpreter of words spoken in Jerusalem and expounded on the banks of the Jordan, the fact is evident. This second birth, or regeneration of spirit, after the natural birth of that which is born of the flesh, might have astonished a Jewish ruler. Nevertheless, it had been taught 3,000 years before the appearance of the great Galilean prophet, not only in old India but to all the *epoptai* of the Pagan initiation, who were instructed in the great mysteries of LIFE and DEATH. This secret of secrets, that *soul* is not knit to flesh, was practically demonstrated in the instance of the Yogis, the followers of Kapila. Having emancipated their souls from the fetters of *Prakriti*, or *Mahat* (the physical perception of the senses and mind — in one sense, creation), they so developed their soul power and *will force*, as to have actually enabled themselves, while on earth, to communicate with the supernal worlds, and perform what is bunglingly termed "miracles." † Men whose astral spirits have attained on

---

*The atrocious custom subsequently introduced among the people, of sacrificing human victims, is a perverted copy of the Theurgic Mystery. The Pagan priests, who did not belong to the class of the hierophants, carried on for awhile this hideous rite, and it served to screen the genuine purpose. But the Grecian Herakles is represented as the adversary of human sacrifices and as slaying the men and monsters who offered them. Bunsen shows, by the very absence of any representation of human sacrifice on the oldest monuments, that this custom had been abolished in the old Empire, at the close of the seventh century after Menes [*Egypt's Place,* etc., Vol. I, p. 18; also pp. 65-66]; therefore, 3000 years B.C. Iphicrates had stopped the human sacrifices entirely among the Carthaginians. Diphilus ordered bulls to be substituted for human victims. Amosis forced the priests to replace the latter by figures of wax. [Porphyry, *De abstin.*, II, §§ 55, 56]. On the other hand, for every stranger offered on the shrine of Diana by the inhabitants of the Tauric Chersonesus, the Inquisition and the Christian clergy can boast of a dozen of heretics offered on the altar of the "mother of God," and her "Son." And when did the Christians ever think of substituting either animals or wax figures for living heretics, Jews, and witches? They burned these in effigy only when, through providential interference, the doomed victims had escaped their clutches.

† This is why Jesus recommends prayer in the solitude of one's closet. This secret prayer is but the *Parâ Vidyâ* [Supreme Knowledge] of the Vedântic philosopher: "He who

earth the *naiḥśreyasa,* or the *mukti,* are half-gods; disembodied spirits, they reach *Moksha* or *Nirvâṇa,* and this is their *second* spiritual birth.

Buddha teaches the doctrine of a new birth as plainly as Jesus does. Desiring to break with the ancient Mysteries, to which it was impossible to admit the ignorant masses, the Hindu reformer, though generally silent upon more than one secret dogma, clearly states his thought in several passages. Thus, he says: *"Some people are born again;* evil-doers go to Hell; righteous people go to Heaven; those who are free from all worldly desires enter Nirvâṇa" (*Dhammapada,* 126). Elsewhere Buddha states that it is better to believe in a future life, in which happiness or misery can be felt; for if the heart believes therein, "it will abandon sin and act virtuously; and even if there is no resurrection, such a life will bring a good name, and the regard of men. *But those who believe in extinction at death will not fail to commit any sin* that they may choose because of their disbelief in a future."*

The *Epistle to the Hebrews* treats of the sacrifice of blood. "Where a testament is," says the writer, "there must be of necessity *the death of the testator* . . . Without the shedding *of blood* is no remission." Then again: "Christ glorified not himself to *be made an High Priest;* but he that said unto him, Thou art my son; TODAY HAVE I BEGOTTEN THEE" (*Hebr.* v, 5). This is a very clear inference that, 1, Jesus was considered only in the light of a high priest, like Melchisedek — another *avatâra,* or incarnation of Christ, according to the Fathers; and, 2, that the writer thought that Jesus had become a "Son of God" only at the moment of his initiation by water; hence, that he was not born a god, neither was he begotten physically by Him. Every initiate of the "last hour" became, by the very fact of his initiation, a son of God. When Maximus, the Ephesian, initiated the Emperor Julian into the Mithraic Mysteries, he pronounced as the usual formula of the rite, the following: "By this blood, I wash thee from thy sins. The Word of the Highest has entered unto thee, and His Spirit henceforth will rest upon the NEWLY-BORN, the *now*-begotten of the Highest God . . . Thou art the son of Mithra." "Thou art the '*Son of God*'," repeated the disciples after Christ's baptism. When Paul shook off the viper into the fire without further injury to himself, the people of Melita said "that he was *a god*" (*Acts* xxviii, 6). "He is the son of God, the Beautiful!" was the term used by the disciples of Simon

---

knows his soul [inner self] daily retires to the region of *Svarga* [the heavenly realm] in his own heart," says the *Chhândogya-Upanishad* (VII, 3, 3). The Vedântic philosopher recognizes the Ātman, the spiritual *self,* as the sole and Supreme God.

* *The Wheel of the Law,* p. 42.

Magus, for they thought they recognized the "great power of God" in him.

A man can have no god that is not bounded by his own human conceptions. The wider the sweep of his spiritual vision, the mightier will be his deity. But where can we find a better demonstration of Him than in man himself; in the spiritual and divine powers lying dormant in every human being? "The very capacity to imagine the possibility of thaumaturgical powers, is itself evidence that they exist," says Dr. A. Wilder. "The critic, as well as the skeptic, is generally inferior to the person or subject that he is reviewing, and, therefore, is hardly a competent witness. *If there are counterfeits, somewhere there must have been a genuine original.*" \*

Blood begets phantoms, and its emanations furnish certain spirits with the materials required to fashion their temporary appearances. "Blood," says Lévi, "is the first incarnation of the universal fluid; it is the materialized *vital light*. Its birth is the most marvellous of all nature's marvels; it lives only by perpetually transforming itself, for it is the universal Proteus. The blood issues from principles where there was none of it before, and it becomes flesh, bones, hair, nails . . . tears, and perspiration. It can be allied neither to corruption nor death; when life is gone, it begins decomposing; if you know how to reanimate it, to infuse into it life by a new magnetization of its globules, life will return to it again. The universal substance, with its double motion, is the great arcanum of being; blood is the great arcanum of life."

"Blood," says the Hindu, Ramatsariar, "contains all the mysterious secrets of existence no living being can exist without. It is profaning the great work of the Creator to eat blood."

In his turn Moses, following the universal and traditional law, forbids eating blood.

Paracelsus writes that with the fumes of blood one is enabled to call forth any spirit we desire to see; for with its emanations it will build itself an appearance, a *visible* body — only this is sorcery. The hierophants of Baal made deep incisions all over their bodies and produced apparitions, objective and tangible, with their own blood. The followers of a certain sect in Persia, many of whom may be found around the Russian settlements in Temir-Khân-Shura, and Derbent, have their religious mysteries in which they form a large ring, and whirl round in a frantic dance. Their temples are ruined, and they worship in large temporary buildings, securely enclosed, and with the earthen floor deeply strewn with sand. They are all dressed in long white robes, and their heads are

---

\* A. Wilder, "Prophecy, Ancient and Modern."

bare and closely shaved. Armed with knives, they soon reach a point of furious exaltation, and wound themselves and others until their garments and the sand on the floor are soaked with blood. Before the end of the "Mystery," *every man has a companion*, who whirls round with him. Sometimes the spectral dancers have *hair on their heads*, which makes them quite distinct from their unconscious creators. As we have solemnly promised never to divulge the principal details of this terrible ceremony (which we were allowed to witness but once), we must leave the subject.*

In the days of antiquity the sorceresses of Thessaly added sometimes to the blood of a black lamb that of an infant, and by this means evoked the shadows. The priests were taught the art of calling up the spirits of the dead, as well as those of the elements, but their mode was certainly not that of Thessalian sorceresses.

Among the Yakuts of Siberia, there is a tribe dwelling on the very confines of the Transbaïkal regions near the river Vitema (eastern Siberia) which practices sorcery as known in the days of the Thessalian witches. Their religious beliefs are curious as a mixture of philosophy and superstition. They have a chief or supreme god Ay-Toyon, who did not create, they say, but only *presides* over the creation of all the worlds. He lives on the *ninth* heaven, and it is but from the *seventh* that the other minor gods — his servants — can manifest themselves to their creatures. This ninth heaven, according to the revelation of the minor deities (spirits, we suppose), has three suns and three moons, and the ground of this abode is formed of four lakes (the four cardinal points) of "soft air" (ether) instead of water. While they offer no sacrifices to the Supreme Deity, for he needs none, they do try to propitiate both the good and bad deities, which they respectively term the "white" and the "black" gods. They do it, because neither of the two classes are good or bad through personal merit or demerit. As they are all subject to the Supreme Ay-Toyon, and each has to carry on the duty assigned to him from eternity, they are not responsible for either the good or evil they produce in this world. The reason given by the Yakuts for such sacrifices is very curious. Sacrifices, they say, help each class of gods to perform their mission the better, and so please the Supreme; and every mortal that helps either of them in performing his duty must,

---

* While at *Petrovsk* (Daghestan, region of the Caucasus) we had the opportunity of witnessing another such *mystery*. It was owing to the kindness of Prince Loris-Melikoff, the governor-general of Daghestan, living at Temir-Khân-Shura, and especially of Prince Shamsudin-Khân, the ex-reigning Shamhal of Tarkoff, a native Tatar, that during the summer of 1865 we assisted at this ceremonial from the safe distance of a sort of private box, constructed under the ceiling of the temporary building.[68]

therefore, please the Supreme as well, for he will have helped justice to take place. As the "black" gods are appointed to bring diseases, evils, and all kinds of calamities to mankind, each of which is a punishment for some transgression, the Yakuts offer to them "bloody" sacrifices of animals; while to the "white" they make pure offerings, consisting generally of an animal consecrated to some special god and taken care of with great ceremony, as having become sacred. According to their ideas, the souls of the dead become "shadows," and are doomed to wander on earth, till a certain change takes place either for the better or worse, which the Yakuts do not pretend to explain. The *light* shadows, *i.e.*, those of good people, become the guardians and protectors of those they loved on earth; the "dark" shadows (the wicked) always seek, on the contrary, to hurt those they knew, by inciting them to crimes, wicked acts, and otherwise injuring mortals. Besides these, like the ancient Chaldees, they reckon seven divine *Sheitans* (daemons) or minor gods. It is during the sacrifices of blood, which take place at night, that the Yakuts call forth the wicked or *dark* shadows, to inquire of them what they can do to arrest their mischief; hence, *blood is necessary*, for without its fumes the ghosts could not make themselves clearly visible, and would become, according to their ideas, but the more dangerous, for they would suck it from living persons by their perspiration.\*
As to the good, *light* shadows, they need not be called out; besides that, such an act disturbs them; they can make their presence felt, when needed, without any preparation and ceremonies.

The blood-evocation is also practiced, although with a different purpose, in several parts of Bulgaria and Moldavia, especially in districts in the vicinity of Moslems. The fearful oppressions and slavery to which these unfortunate Christians have been subjected for centuries has rendered them a thousandfold more impressible, and at the same time more superstitious, than those who live in civilized countries. On every seventh of May, the inhabitants of every Moldavo-Walachian and Bulgarian city or village have what they term the "feast of the dead." After sunset, immense crowds of women and men, each with a lighted wax taper in hand, resort to the burial places, and pray on the tombs of their departed friends. This ancient and solemn ceremony, called *Trizna*, is everywhere a reminiscence of primitive Christian rites, but far more solemn yet, while in Moslem slavery. Every tomb is furnished with a kind of cupboard, about half a yard high, built of four stones, and with hinged double doors. These closets contain what is termed the household of the defunct: namely, a few wax tapers, some oil

---

\* Does not this afford us a point of comparison with the so-called "materializing mediums"?

and an earthen lamp, which is lighted on that day, and burns for twenty-four hours. Wealthy people have silver lamps richly chiselled, and bejewelled images, which are secure from thieves, for in the burial ground the closets are even left open. Such is the dread of the population (Moslem and Christian) of the revenge of the dead that a thief bold enough to commit any murder would never dare touch the property of a dead person. The Bulgarians have a belief that every Saturday, and especially the eve of Easter Sunday, and until Trinity Day (about seven weeks) the souls of the dead descend on earth, some to beg forgiveness from those living whom they had wronged; others to protect and commune with their loved ones. Faithfully following the traditional rites of their forefathers, the natives on each Saturday of these seven weeks keep either lamps or tapers lighted. In addition to that, on the *seventh* of May they drench the tombs with grape wine, and burn incense around them from sunset to sunrise. With the inhabitants of towns, the ceremony is limited to these simple observances. With some of the rustics though, the rite assumes the proportions of a theurgic evocation. On the eve of Ascension Day, Bulgarian women light a quantity of tapers and lamps; the pots are placed upon tripods, and incense perfumes the atmosphere for miles around; while thick white clouds of smoke envelope each tomb, as though a veil had separated it from the others. During the evening, and until a little before midnight, in memory of the deceased, acquaintances and a certain number of mendicants are fed and treated with wine and *rakíya* (grape-whiskey), and money is distributed among the poor according to the means of the surviving relatives. When the feast is ended, the guests approaching the tomb and addressing the defunct by name, thank him or her for the bounties received. When all but the nearest relatives are gone, a woman, usually the most aged, remains alone with the dead, and — some say — resorts to the ceremony of invocation.

After fervent prayers, repeated face downward on the grave-mound, more or less drops of blood are drawn from near the left bosom, and allowed to trickle upon the tomb. This gives strength to the invisible spirit which hovers around, to assume for a few instants a visible form, and whisper his instructions to the Christian theurgist — if he has any to offer, or simply to "bless the mourner" and then disappear again till the following year. So firmly rooted is this belief that we have heard, in a case of family difficulty, a Moldavian woman appeal to her sister to put off every decision till Ascension night, when their dead father *would be able to tell them of his will and pleasure in person;* to which the sister consented as simply as though their parent were in the next room.

That there are fearful secrets in nature may well be believed when, as we have seen in the case of the Russian *znachar'*, the sorcerer *cannot* die until he has passed the word to another, and the hierophants of White Magic rarely do. It seems as if the dread power of the "Word" could only be entrusted to one man of a certain district or body of people at a time. When the Brahmâtma was about to lay aside the burden of physical existence, he imparted his secret to his successor, either orally, or by a writing placed in a securely fastened casket which went into the latter's hands alone. Moses "lays his hands" upon his neophyte, Joshua, in the solitudes of Nebo and passes away forever. Aaron initiates Eleazar on Mount Hor, and dies. Siddhârtha-Buddha promises his mendicants before his death to live in him who shall deserve it, embraces his favorite disciple, whispers in his ear, and dies; and as John's head lies upon the bosom of Jesus, he is told that he shall "tarry" until he shall come. Like signal fires of the olden times, which, lighted and extinguished by turns upon one hilltop after another, conveyed intelligence along a whole stretch of country, so we see a long line of "wise" men from the beginning of history down to our own times communicating the word of wisdom to their direct successors. Passing from seer to seer, the "Word" flashes out like lightning, and while carrying off the initiator from human sight forever, brings the new initiate into view. Meanwhile, whole nations murder each other in the name of another "Word," an empty substitute accepted literally by each, and misinterpreted by all!

We have met few sects which truly practice sorcery. One such is the Yezîdis, considered by some a branch of the Kurds, though we believe erroneously. These inhabit chiefly the mountainous and desolate regions of Asiatic Turkey, about Mosul, and are found even in Syria* and Mesopotamia. They are called and known everywhere as devil worshippers; and most certainly it is not either through ignorance or mental obscuration that they have set up the worship and a regular intercommunication with the lowest and the most malicious of both elementals and elementaries. They recognize the present wickedness of the chief of the "black powers"; but at the same time they dread his power, and so try

---

\* The Yezîdis must number over 200,000 men altogether. The tribes which inhabit the Pashalik of Bagdad, and are scattered over the Sinjar mountains are the most dangerous, as well as the most hated for their evil practices. Their chief Sheik lives constantly near the tomb of their prophet and reformer Adi, but every tribe chooses its own Sheik among the most learned in the "black art." This Adi or Ad is a mythic ancestor of theirs, and simply is, Adi—the God of wisdom or the Pârsî Ab-ad, the first ancestor of the human race, or again Âdi-Buddha of the Hindus, anthropomorphized and degenerated.

to conciliate to themselves his favors. He is in an open quarrel with Allah, they say, but a reconciliation can take place between the two at any day; and those who have shown marks of their disrespect to the "black one" now, may suffer for it at some future time, and thus have both God and Devil against them. This is simply a cunning policy that seeks to propitiate his Satanic majesty, who is no other than the great *Tcherno-bog* (the black god) of the Variago-Russ, the ancient idolatrous Russians before the days of Vladimir.

Like J. Wier, the famous demonographer of the sixteenth century (who in his *Pseudomonarchia Daemonum* describes and enumerates a regular infernal court, which has its dignitaries, princes, dukes, nobles and officers), the Yezîdis have a whole pantheon of devils, and use the Yakshas, aerial spirits, to convey their prayers and respects to Satan their master, and the Afrits of the desert. During their prayer meetings, they join hands and form immense rings, with their Sheik, or an officiating priest in the middle, who claps his hands, and intones every verse in honor of Sheitan (Satan). Then they whirl and leap in the air. When the frenzy is at its climax, they often wound and cut themselves with their daggers, occasionally rendering the same service to their next neighbors. But their wounds do not heal and cicatrize as easily as in the case of lamas and holy men; for but too often they fall victims to these self-inflicted wounds. While dancing and flourishing high their daggers without unclasping hands — for this would be considered a sacrilege, and the spell instantly broken — they coax and praise Sheitan, and entreat him to manifest himself in his works by "miracles." As their rites are chiefly accomplished during the night, they do not fail to obtain manifestations of various character, the least of which are enormous globes of fire which take the shapes of the most uncouth animals.

Lady Hester Stanhope,[69] whose name was for many years a power among the masonic fraternities of the East, is said to have witnessed, personally, several of these Yezîdean ceremonies. We were told by an *'Uqqal* of the sect of Druses, that after having been present at one of the Yezîdis' "Devil masses," as they are called, this extraordinary lady, so noted for personal courage and daring bravery, fainted, and nothwithstanding her usual Emir's male attire, was recalled to life and health with the greatest difficulty. Personally, we regret to say, all our efforts to witness one of these performances failed.

A recent article in a Catholic journal on Nagualism and Voodooism charges Haiti with being the centre of secret societies, with terrible forms of initiation and bloody rites, where *human infants are sacrificed and devoured by the adepts* (!!). Piron, a French traveller, is quoted at length, describing a most fearful scene witnessed by him in Cuba, in the house of a lady whom he never would have suspected of any connection with so monstrous a sect. "A naked white girl acted as a voodoo priestess, wrought up to frenzy by dances and incantations that followed the sacrifice of a white and a black hen. A serpent, trained to its part, and acted on by the music, coiled round the limbs of the girl, its motions studied by the votaries dancing around or standing to watch its contortions. The spectator fled at last in horror when the poor girl fell writhing in an epileptic fit."

While deploring such a state of things in Christian countries, the Catholic article in question explains this tenacity for ancestral religious rites as evidence of the *natural depravity of the human heart,* and makes a loud call for greater zeal on the part of Catholics. Besides repeating the absurd fiction about devouring children, the writer seems wholly insensible to the fact that a devotion to one's faith that centuries of the most cruel and bloody persecution cannot quench, makes heroes and martyrs of a people, whereas their conversion to any other faith would turn them simply into renegades. A compulsory religion can never breed anything but deceit. The answer received by the missionary Margil from some Indians supports the above truism. The question being: "How is it that you are so heathenish after having been Christians so long?" The answer was: "What would you do, father, if enemies of your faith entered your land? Would you not take all your books and vestments and signs of religion and retire to the most secret caves and mountains? This is just what our priests, and prophets, and soothsayers, and nagualists have done to this time and are still doing."

Such an answer from a Roman Catholic, questioned by a missionary of either Greek or Protestant Church, would earn for him the crown of a saint in the Popish martyrology. Better a "heathen" religion that can extort from a Francis Xavier such a tribute as he pays the Japanese, in saying that "in virtue and probity they surpassed all the nations he had ever seen"; than a Christianity whose advance over the face of the earth sweeps aboriginal nations out of existence as with a hurricane of fire.* Disease, drunkenness and demoralization are the immediate results of apostasy from the faith of their fathers, and conversion into a religion of mere forms.

What Christianity is doing for British India, we need go to no inimical sources to inquire. Captain O'Grady, the British ex-official, says: "The British government is doing a shameful thing in turning the natives of India from a sober race to a nation of drunkards. And

---

* Within less than four months we have collected from the daily papers forty-seven cases of crime, ranging from drunkenness up to murder, committed by ecclesiastics in the United States only. By the end of the year our correspondents in the East will have valuable facts to offset missionary denunciations of "heathen" misdemeanors.

for pure *greed*. Drinking is forbidden by the religion alike of Hindus and Mussulmans. But . . . drinking is daily becoming more and more prevalent . . . What the accursed opium traffic, forced on China by British greed, has been to that unhappy country, the government sale of liquor is likely to become to India. For it is a government monopoly, based on almost precisely the same model as the government monopoly of tobacco by Spain . . . The outside domestics in European families usually get to be terrible drunkards . . . The indoor servants usually detest drinking, and are a good deal more respectable in this particular than their masters and mistresses . . . everybody drinks . . . bishops, chaplains, freshly-imported boarding-school girls, and all." *

Yes, these are the "blessings" that the modern Christian religion brings with its *Bibles* and *Catechisms* to the "poor heathen." Rum and bastardy to Hindostan; opium to China; rum and foul disorders to Tahiti; and, worst of all, the example of hypocrisy in religion, and a practical skepticism and atheism, which, since it seems to be good enough for *civilized* people, may well in time be thought good enough for those whom theology has too often been holding under a very heavy yoke. On the other hand, everything that is noble, spiritual, elevating, in the old religion is denied, and even deliberately falsified.

Take Paul, read the little of original that is left of him in the writings attributed to this brave, honest, sincere man, and see whether anyone can find a word therein to show that Paul meant by the word Christ anything more than the abstract ideal of the personal divinity indwelling in man. For Paul, Christ is not a person, but an embodied idea. "If any man be in Christ, he is a new creature," † *he is reborn*, as after initiation, for the Lord is spirit — the spirit of man. Paul was the only one of the apostles who had understood the secret ideas underlying the teachings of Jesus, although he had never met him. But Paul had been initiated himself; and, bent upon inaugurating a new and broad reform, one embracing the whole of humanity, he sincerely set his own doctrines far above the wisdom of the ages, above the ancient Mysteries and final revelation to the *epoptai*. As Professor A. Wilder well proves in a series of able articles, it *was not Jesus, but Paul who was the real founder of Christianity*. "The disciples were called Christians first in Antioch," say the *Acts of the Apostles*, xi, 26. "Such men as Irenaeus, Epiphanius, and Eusebius have transmitted to posterity a reputation for untruth and dishonest practices; and the heart sickens at the story of the crimes of that

---

\* [*Commercial Bulletin*, March 17, 1877.]

† [2 *Corinthians* v, 17.]

period," writes this author, in a recent article.* "It will be remembered," he adds, "that when the Moslems overran Syria and Asia Minor for the first time, they were welcomed by the Christians of those regions as deliverers from the intolerable oppression of the ruling authorities of the Church."

Mohammed never was, neither is he now, considered a god; yet under the stimulus of his name millions of Moslems have served their God with an ardor that can never be paralleled by Christian sectarianism. That they have sadly degenerated since the days of their prophet, does not alter the case in hand, but only proves the more the prevalence of matter over spirit all over the world. Besides, they have never degenerated more from primitive faith than Christians themselves. Why, then, should not Jesus of Nazareth, a thousandfold higher, nobler, and morally grander than Mohammed, be as well revered by Christians and followed in practice, instead of being blindly adored in fruitless faith as a god, and at the same time worshipped much after the fashion of certain Buddhists, who turn their wheel of prayers. That this faith has become sterile, and is no more worthy the name of Christianity than the fetishism of Kalmucks that of the philosophy preached by Buddha, is doubted by none. "We would not be supposed to entertain the opinion," says Dr. Wilder, "that modern Christianity is in any considerable degree identical with the religion preached by Paul. It lacks his breadth of view, his earnestness, his keen spiritual perception. Bearing the impress of the nations by which it is professed, it exhibits as many forms as there are races. It is one thing in Italy and Spain, but widely differs in France, Germany, Holland, Sweden, Great Britain, Russia, Armenia, Kurdistan and Abyssinia. As compared with the preceding worships, the change seems to be more in name than in genius. Men had gone to bed Pagans and awoke Christians. As for the *Sermon on the Mount,* its conspicuous doctrines are more or less repudiated by every Christian community of any considerable dimension. Barbarism, oppression, cruel punishments, are as common now as in the days of Paganism.

"The Christianity of Peter exists no more; that of Paul supplanted it, and was in its turn amalgamated with the other world-religions. When mankind are enlightened, or the barbarous races and families are supplanted by those of nobler nature and instincts, the ideal excellences may become realities.

"The 'Christ of Paul,' has constituted an enigma which evoked the most strenuous endeavor to solve. He was something else than the Jesus of the *Gospels.* Paul disregarded utterly their 'endless genealogies.' The

---

* *The Evolution,* Sept., 1877, art. "Paul, the Founder of Christianity."

author of the fourth *Gospel*, himself an Alexandrian Gnostic, describes Jesus as what would now be termed a 'materialized' divine spirit. He was the Logos, or First Emanation—the Metatron . . . The 'mother of Jesus,' like the Princess Mâyâ, Danaë, or perhaps Periktione, had given birth, not to a love-child, but to a divine offspring. No Jew of whatever sect, no apostle, no early believer, ever promulgated such an idea. Paul treats of Christ as a personage rather than as a person. The sacred lessons of the secret assemblies often personified the divine good and the divine truth in a human form, assailed by the passions and appetites of mankind but superior to them; and this doctrine, emerging from the crypt, was apprehended by churchlings and gross-minded men as that of an immaculate conception and divine incarnation."

In the old book, published in 1693 and written by the Sieur de La Loubère, French Ambassador to the King of Siam,* are related many interesting facts of the Siamese religion. The remarks of the satirical Frenchman are so pointed that we will quote his words about the Siamese Savior — Sommona-Codom.

"How marvellous soever they pretend the birth of their Savior has been, they cease not to give *him a father and a mother*.† His mother, whose name is found in some of their *Balie* [Pâli?] books, was called, as they say, *Mahâ* MARIA, which seems to signify the *Great Mary*, for *Mahâ* signifies *great* . . . However it be, this ceases not to give attention to the missionaries, and has perhaps given occasion to the Siamese to believe that Jesus being the Son of *Mary*, was brother to Sommona-Codom, and that having been crucified, he was that *wicked* brother whom they give to Sommona-Codom, under the name of *Thevetat*, and whom they report to be punished in Hell, with a punishment which participates something of the Cross . . . The Siamese expect another Sommona-Codom, I mean another miraculous man like him, whom they already named *Pra-Narotte*, and who they say was foretold by *Sommona* . . . He made all sorts of miracles . . . He had two disciples, both standing on each hand of his idol; one on the right hand, and the other on the left . . . the first is named *Pra-Mogla*, and the second *Pra-Scaribout* . . . The father of Sommona-Codom was, according to this same *Balie* Book, a King of *Teve Lanca*, that is to say, a King of the famous Ceylon. But *the Balie Books being without date, and without the author's name, have no more authority than all the traditions, whose origin is unknown*." ‡

---

*[*A New Historical Relation of the Kingdom of Siam*, "Diverse Observations to be Made in Preaching the Gospel to the Orientals," pp. 136-37; London, 1693.]

† We find in *Galatians* iv, 4, the following: "But when the fullness of the time was come, God sent forth his Son, *made of a woman, made under the law.*"

‡ The date has been fully established for these Pâli Books in our own century; sufficiently so, at least, to show that they existed in Ceylon 316 B.C., when Mahinda, the son of Aśoka, was there (See Max Müller, *Chips*, etc., Vol. I, p. 196).

This last argument is as ill-considered as it is naïvely expressed. We do not know of any book in the whole world less authenticated as to date, authors' names, or tradition, than our Christian *Bible*. Under these circumstances the Siamese have as much reason to believe in their miraculous Sommona-Codom as the Christians in their miraculously-born Savior. Moreover, they have no better right to force their religion upon the Siamese, or any other people, against their will, and in their own country, where they go unasked, than the so-called heathen "to compel France or England to accept Buddhism at the point of the sword." A Buddhist missionary, even in freethinking America, would daily risk being mobbed, but this does not at all prevent missionaries from abusing the religion of the Brahmans, Lamas and Bonzes, publicly to their teeth; and the latter are not always at liberty to answer them. This is termed diffusing the beneficent light of Christianity and civilization upon the darkness of heathenism!

And yet we find that these pretensions — which might appear ludicrous were they not so fatal to millions of our fellow men, who only ask to be left alone — were fully appreciated as early as in the seventeenth century. We find the same witty Monsieur de La Loubère, under a pretext of pious sympathy, giving some truly curious instructions to the ecclesiastical authorities at home,* which embody the very soul of Jesuitism.

"From what I have said concerning the opinions of the Orientals," he remarks, "it is easy to comprehend how difficult an enterprise it is to bring them over to the Christian religion; and of what consequence it is that the missionaries, which preach the Gospel in the East, do perfectly understand the manners and belief of these people. For as the apostles and first Christians, when God supported their preaching by so many wonders, did not on a sudden discover to the heathens all the mysteries which we adore, but a long time concealed from them, and the Catechumens themselves, the knowledge of those which might scandalize them; it seems very rational to me that the missionaries, who have not

---

* *A New Historical Relation of the Kingdom of Siam*, pp. 140-141, by M. de La Loubère, Envoy to Siam from France, 1687-8.

The Sieur de La Loubère's report to the king was made, as we see, in 1687-88. How thoroughly his proposition to the Jesuits, to suppress and dissemble in preaching Christianity to the Siamese, met their approval, is shown in the passage elsewhere quoted from the Thesis propounded by the Jesuits of Caen (*Thesis propugnata in regio Soc. Jes. Collegio, celeberrimae Academiae Cadomiensis, die Veneris*, 30 Jan., 1693), to the following effect: ". . . neither do the Fathers of the Society of Jesus dissemble, *when they adopt the institute and the habit* of the Talapoins of Siam." In five years the Ambassador's little lump of leaven had leavened the whole.

the gift of miracles, ought not presently to discover to the Orientals all the mysteries nor all the practices of Christianity.

" 'Twould be convenient, for example, if I am not mistaken, not to preach unto them, *without great caution*, the worshipping of Saints; and as to the knowledge of Jesus Christ, I think it would be necessary to manage it with them, if I may so say, and *not to speak to them of the mystery of the Incarnation*, till after having convinced them of the existence of a God Creator. For what probability is there to begin with persuading the Siamese to remove *Sommona-Codom, Pra-Mogla*, and *Pra-Scaribout* from the altars, to set up Jesus Christ, St. Peter, and St. Paul, in their stead? 'Twould not perhaps be more proper to preach unto them Jesus Christ crucified, till they have first comprehended that one may be *unfortunate* and *innocent;* and that by the rule received, even amongst them, which is that the innocent might load himself with the crimes of the guilty, it was necessary *that a god should become man*, to the end that this Man-God should by a laborious life, and a shameful but voluntary death, satisfy for all the sins of men; but before all things it would be necessary to give them the true idea of a God Creator, and justly provoked against men. The Eucharist after this will not scandalize the Siamese, as it formerly scandalized the Pagans of Europe; forasmuch as the Siamese do believe *Sommona-Codom* could give his wife and children to the Talapoins to eat.

"On the contrary, as the Chinese are respectful toward their parents even to a scruple, I doubt not that if the Gospel should be presently put into their hands, they would be scandalized at that place, where, when some told Jesus Christ that his mother and his brethren asked after him, he answered in such a manner, that he seems so little to regard them, that he affected not to know them. They would *not be less offended* at those other mysterious words, which our divine Savior spoke to the young man, who desired time to go and bury his parents: "Let the dead," said he, "bury the dead." Everyone knows the trouble which the Japanese expressed to St. Francis Xavier *upon the eternity of damnation*, not being able to believe that their dead parents should fall into so horrible a misfortune for *want of having embraced Christianity, which they had never heard of*. It seems necessary, therefore, to prevent and modify this thought, by the means which that great apostle of the Indies used, in first establishing the idea of an omnipotent, all-wise, and most just God, the author of all good, to whom only everything is due, and by whose will we owe unto kings, bishops, magistrates and to our parents the respect which we owe them. These examples are sufficient to show with what precautions it is necessary to prepare the minds of the Orientals to think like us, and *not to be offended with most* of the Articles of the Christian faith." *

And what, we ask, is left to preach? With no Savior, no atonement, no crucifixion for human sin, no Gospel, no eternal damnation to tell them of, and no miracles to display, what remained for the Jesuits to spread among the Siamese but the dust of the Pagan sanctuaries with which to blind their eyes? The sarcasm is biting indeed. The morality to which these poor heathen are made to adhere by their ancestral faith is so pure, that Christianity has to be stripped of every distinguishing mark before its priests can venture to offer it for their examination. A religion that cannot be trusted to the scrutiny of an unsophisticated people who are patterns of filial piety, of honest dealing, of deep reverence for God and an instinctive horror of profaning His majesty, must indeed be founded upon error. That it is so, our century is discovering little by little.

In the general spoliation of Buddhism to make up the new Christian religion, it was not to be expected that so peerless a character as Gautama Buddha would be left unappropriated. It was but natural that after taking his legendary history to fill out the blanks left in the fictitious story of Jesus, after using what they could of Krishna's, they should take the man Sâkyamuni and put him in their calendar under an *alias*. This they actually did, and the Hindu Savior in due time appeared on the list of saints as Josaphat, to keep company with those martyrs of religion, SS. Aura and Placida, Longinus and Amphibolus.

In Palermo there is even a church dedicated to *Divo Josaphat*. Among the vain attempts of subsequent ecclesiastical writers to fix the genealogy of this mysterious saint, the most original was the making him Joshua, the son of Nun. But these trifling difficulties being at last surmounted, we find the history of Gautama copied *word for word* from Buddhist sacred books, into the *Golden Legend*. Names of individuals

---

* In a discourse of Hermes with Thoth, the former says: "It is impossible for thought to rightly conceive of God . . . One cannot describe, through material organs, that which is immaterial and eternal . . . One is a perception of the spirit, the other a reality. That which can be perceived by our senses can be described in words; but that which is incorporeal, invisible, immaterial, and without form cannot be realized through our ordinary senses. I understand thus, O Thoth, I understand that God is ineffable." [Champo!lion-Figeac, *Égypte ancienne*, p. 139.]

In the *Cathechism of the Pârsîs*, as translated by Dâdâbhâi Nauroji, we read the following:

"Q. What is the form of our God?"

"A. Our God has neither face nor form, color nor shape, nor fixed place. There is no other like him. He is Himself, singly such a glory that we cannot praise or describe Him; nor our mind comprehend Him."

are changed, the place of action, India, remains the same — in the Christian as in the Buddhist Legends. It can be also found in the *Speculum Historiale* of Vincent de Beauvais, which was written in the thirteenth century. The first discovery is due to the historian, do Couto, although Professor Müller credits the first recognition of the identity of the two stories to Laboulaye, in 1859.* Colonel Yule tells us that these stories of Barlaam and Josaphat, "are recognized by Baronius, and are to be found at p. 348, of '*The Roman Martyrology* set forth by command of Pope Gregory XIII, and revised by the authority of Pope Urban VIII, translated out of Latin into English by G. K. of the Society of Jesus . . .' " †

To repeat even a small portion of this ecclesiastical nonsense would be tedious and useless. Let him who doubts and who would learn the story read it as given by Colonel Yule. Some of the Christian and ecclesiastical speculations seem to have embarrassed even Dominie Valentyn. "There be some, who hold this Budhum for a fugitive Syrian Jew," he writes; "others who hold him for a disciple of the Apostle Thomas; but how in that case he could have been born 622 years before Christ I leave them to explain. Diogo do Couto stands by the belief that he was certainly *Joshua*, which is still more absurd!" ‡

"The religious romance called *The History of Barlaam and Josaphat* was for several centuries one of the most popular works in Christendom," says Col. Yule. "It was translated into all the chief European languages, including Sandinavian and Slavonic tongues . . . The story . . . first appears among the works of St. John of Damascus, a theologian of the early part of the eighth century." § Here then lies the secret of its origin, for this St. John, before he became a divine, held a high office at the court of the Khalif Abu Jáfar Almansúr, where he probably learned the story, and afterwards adapted it to the new orthodox necessities of the Buddha turned into a Christian saint.

Having repeated the plagiarized story, Diogo do Couto, who seems to yield up with reluctance his curious notion that Gautama was Joshua, says: "To this name [Budâo] the Gentiles throughout all India have dedicated great and superb pagodas. With reference to this story we have been diligent in enquiring if the ancient Gentiles of those parts had in their writings any knowledge of St. Josaphat who was converted by Barlam, who in his legend is represented as the son of a great King of India, and who had just the same upbringing, with all the same particulars, that we have recounted of the life of the Budâo . . . As I was

---

\* *Contemporary Review*, July, 1870, p. 588.
† *Book of Ser Marco Polo*, Vol. II, p. 308.
‡ *Ibid.*, II, 308.
§ *Ibid.*, II, 305-06.

travelling in the Isle of Salsette, and went to see that rare and admirable Pagoda, which we call the Canará Pagoda [Kânheri Caves], made in a mountain, with many halls cut out of one solid rock . . . and enquiring from this old man about the work, and what he thought as to who had made it, he told us that without doubt the work was made by order of the father of St. Josaphat to bring him up therein in seclusion, as the story tells. And as it informs us that he was the son of a great King in India, it may well be, as we have just said, that *he* was the Budâo, of whom they relate such marvels." *

The Christian legend is taken, moreover, in most of its details, from the Ceylonese tradition. It is on this island that originated the story of young Gautama rejecting his father's throne, and the king's erecting a superb palace for him, in which he kept him half prisoner, surrounded by all the temptations of life and wealth. Marco Polo told it as he had it from the Ceylonese, and his version is now found to be a faithful repetition of what is given in the various Buddhist books. As Marco Polo naïvely expresses it, Buddha led a life of such hardship and sanctity, and kept such great abstinence, *"just as if he had been a Christian.* Indeed," he adds, "had he but been so, he would have been a great saint of our Lord Jesus Christ, so good and pure was the life he led." To which pious apothegm his editor very pertinently remarks that "Marco is not the only eminent person who has expressed this view of Sâkyamuni's life in such words." And in his turn Prof. Max Müller says: "And whatever we may think of the sanctity of saints, let those who doubt the right of Buddha to a place among them, read the story of his life as it is told in the Buddhistic canon. If he lived the life which is there described, few saints have a better claim to the title than Buddha; and no one either in the Greek or the Roman Church need be ashamed of having paid to his memory the honor that was intended for St. Josaphat, the prince, the hermit, and the saint." †

The Roman Catholic Church has never had so good a chance to Christianize all China, Thibet, and Tartary, as in the thirteenth century, during the reign of Kublai-Khân. It seems strange that they did not embrace the opportunity when Kublai was hesitating at one time between the four religions of the world, and, perhaps through the eloquence of Marco Polo, favored Christianity more than either Mohammedanism, Judaism, or Buddhism. Marco Polo and Ramusio, one of his interpreters, tell us why. It seems that, unfortunately for Rome, the embassy of Marco's father and uncle failed, because Clement IV happened to die just at that very time. There was no Pope for several months to

---

* *Da Asia,* etc., Dec. V, pt. II, liv. vi, cap. ii, pp. 16-17; ed. Lisbon, 1780. Cf. Yule, *op. cit.,* Vol. II, p. 308.

† [*Contemp. Rev., loc. cit.,* quoted in Yule, *op. cit.,* II, 300, 309.]

receive the friendly overtures of Kublai-Khân; and thus the one hundred Christian missionaries invited by him could not be sent to Thibet and Tartary.* To those who believe that there is an intelligent Deity above who takes a certain concern in the welfare of our miserable little world, this *contretemps* must in itself seem a pretty good proof that Buddhism should have the best of Christianity. Perhaps—who knows?—Pope Clement fell sick so as to save the Buddhists from sinking into the idolatry of Roman Catholicism?

From pure Buddhism, the religion of these districts has degenerated into Lamaism; but the latter, with all its blemishes — purely formalistic and impairing but little the doctrine itself — is yet far above Catholicism. The poor Abbé Huc very soon found it out for himself. As he moved on with his caravan, he writes—"everyone repeated to us that, as we advanced toward the west, we should find the doctrines growing more luminous and sublime. Lhasa was the great focus of light, the rays from which became weakened as they were diffused." One day he gave to a Thibetan lama "a brief summary of Christian doctrine, which appeared by no means unfamiliar to him [we do not wonder at that], and he even maintained that it [Catholicism] did not differ much from the faith of the grand lamas of Thibet . . . These words of the Thibetan lama astonished us not a little," writes the missionary; "the unity of God, the mystery of the Incarnation, the dogma of the real presence, appeared to us in his belief . . . The new light thrown on the religion of Buddha induced us really to believe that we should find among the lamas of Thibet a more purified system." † It is these words of praise to Lamaism, with which Huc's book abounds, that caused his work to be placed on the Index at Rome, and himself to be unfrocked.

When questioned why, since he held the Christian faith to be the best of the religions protected by him, he did not attach himself to it, the answer given by Kublai-Khân is as suggestive as it is curious:

"How would you have me to become a Christian? There are Four Prophets worshipped and revered by all the world. The Christians say their god is Jesus Christ; the Saracens, Mohammed; the Jews, Moses; the idolaters, Sogomon Borcan [Śâkyamuni Burkhan, or Buddha], who was the first god among the idols; and I worship and pay respect to all four, and pray that he among them who is the greatest in heaven in very truth may aid me." ‡

We may ridicule the Khân's prudence: we cannot blame him for trustingly leaving the decision of the puzzling dilemma to Providence itself. One of his most unsurmountable objections to embracing Chris-

---

* [Yule, *op. cit.*, I, Introd., pp. 15-16; also p. 13 of text; ed. 1875.]
† *Travels in Tartary, Thibet*, etc., I, v.
‡ [Yule, *op. cit.*, I, 339.]

tianity, he thus specifies to Marco: "You see that the Christians of these parts are so ignorant that they achieve nothing and can achieve nothing, whilst you see the idolaters can do anything they please, insomuch that when I sit at table, the cups from the middle of the hall come to me full of wine or other liquor without being touched by anybody, and I drink from them. They control storms, causing them to pass in whatever direction they please, and do many other marvels; whilst, as you know, their idols speak, and give them predictions on whatever subjects they choose. But if I were to turn to the faith of Christ and become a Christian, then my barons and others who are not converted would say: 'What has moved you to be baptized? . . . What powers or miracles have you witnessed on His part? (You know the idolaters here say that their wonders are performed by the sanctity and power of their idols.) Well, I should not know what answer to make; so they would only be confirmed in their errors, and the idolaters, who are adepts in such surprising arts, would easily compass my death. But now you shall go to your Pope, and pray him on my part to send hither an hundred men skilled in your law; who shall be capable of rebuking the practices of the idolaters to their faces, and of telling them *that they too know how to do such things but will not,* because they are done by the help of the devil and other evil spirits, and shall so control the idolaters that these shall have no power to perform such things in their presence. *When we shall witness this* we will denounce the idolaters and their religion, and then I will receive baptism . . . then all my barons and chiefs shall be baptized also . . . and thus in the end there will be more Christians here than exist in your part of the world!" \*

The proposition was fair. Why did not the Christians avail themselves of it? Moses is said to have faced such an ordeal before Pharaoh, and come off triumphant.

To our mind, the logic of this uneducated Mongol was unanswerable, his intuition faultless. He saw good results in all religions, and felt that, whether a man be Buddhist, Christian, Moslem, or Jew, his spiritual powers might equally be developed, his faith equally lead him to the highest truth. All he asked before making choice of a creed for his people, was the evidence upon which to base faith.

To judge alone by its jugglers, India must certainly be better acquainted with alchemy, chemistry and physics than any European academy. The psychological wonders produced by some fakirs of Southern Hindostan, and by the *Shaberons* and *Hubilgans* of Thibet and Mongolia, alike prove our case. The science of psychology has there reached an acme of

---

\* *Book of Ser Marco Polo,* Vol. I, pp. 339-40; ed. 1875.

perfection never attained elsewhere in the annals of the marvellous. That such powers are not alone due to study, but are natural to every human being, is now proved in Europe and America by the phenomena of mesmerism and what is termed "spiritualism." If the majority of foreign travellers, and residents in British India, are disposed to regard the whole as clever jugglery, not so with a few Europeans who have had the rare luck to be admitted *behind the veil* in the pagodas. Surely these will not deride the rites, nor undervalue the phenomena produced in the secret lodges of India. The *mahâdevasthâna* of the pagodas (usually termed *gopura*, from the sacred pyramidal gateway by which the buildings are entered) has been known to Europeans before now, though to a mere handful in all.

We do not know whether the prolific Jacoliot * was ever admitted into one of these lodges. It is extremely doubtful, we should say, if we may judge from his many fantastic tales of the immoralities of the mystical rites among the Brahmans, the fakirs of the pagodas, and even the Buddhists (!!) at all of which he makes himself figure as a Joseph. Anyhow, it is evident that the Brahmans taught him no secrets, for speaking of the fakirs and their wonders, he remarks, "under the direction of initiated Brahmans they practice in the seclusion of the pagodas, the *occult sciences* . . . And let no one be surprised at this word, which seems to open the door of the supernatural; while there are in the sciences which the Brahmans call occult, phenomena so extraordinary as to baffle all investigation, there is not one which cannot be explained, and which is not subject to natural law." †

Unquestionably, any initiated Brahman could, if he would, explain every phenomenon. But *he will not.* Meanwhile, we have yet to see an explanation by the best of our physicists of even the most trivial occult phenomenon produced by a fakir-pupil of a pagoda.

Jacolliot says that it will be quite impracticable to give an account of the marvellous facts witnessed by himself. But adds, with entire truthfulness, "let it suffice to say, that in regard to magnetism and spiritism, Europe

---

* His twenty or more volumes on Oriental subjects are indeed a curious conglomerate of truth and fiction. They contain a vast deal of fact about Indian traditions, philosophy and chronology, with most just views courageously expressed. But it seems as if the philosopher were constantly being overlaid by the romanticist. It is as though two men were united in their authorship — one careful, serious, erudite, scholarly, the other a sensational and sensual French romancer, who judges of facts not as they are but as *he* imagines them. His translations from *Manu* are admirable; his controversial ability marked; his views of priestly morals unfair, and in the case of the Buddhists, positively slanderous. But in all the series of volumes there is not a line of dull reading; he has the eye of the artist, the pen of the poet of nature.

† [*Les fils de Dieu*, p. 296.]

has yet to stammer over the first letters of the alphabet, and that the Brahmans have reached, in these two departments of learning, results in the way of phenomena that are truly stupefying. When one sees these strange manifestations, whose power one cannot deny, without grasping the laws that the Brahmans *keep so carefully concealed*, the mind is overwhelmed with wonder, and one feels that he must run away and break the charm that holds him."

"The only explanation that we have been able to obtain on the subject from a learned Brahman, with whom we were on terms of the closest intimacy, was this: 'You have studied physical nature, and you have obtained, through the laws of nature, marvellous results — steam, electricity, etc.; *for twenty thousand years or more, we have studied the intellectual* forces, we have discovered their laws, and *we obtain, by making them act alone or in concert with matter, phenomena still more astonishing than your own*'."

Jacolliot must indeed have been stupefied by wonders, for he says: "We have seen things such as one does not describe for fear of making his readers doubt his intelligence . . . but still we have seen them. And truly one comprehends how, in presence of such facts, the ancient world believed . . . in possessions of the Devil and in exorcism." \*

But yet this uncompromising enemy of priestcraft, monastic orders, and the clergy of every religion and every land — including Brahmans, lamas and fakirs — is so struck with the contrast between the fact-supported cults of India, and the empty pretences of Catholicism, that after describing the terrible self-tortures of the fakirs, in a burst of honest indignation, he thus gives vent to his feelings: "Nevertheless, these fakirs, these mendicant Brahmans, have still something grand about them: when they flagellate themselves, when during the self-inflicted martyrdom the flesh is torn out by bits, the blood pours upon the ground. But you [Catholic mendicants], what do you do today? You, Gray Friars, Capuchins, Franciscans, who play at fakirs, with your knotted cords, your flints, your hair shirts, and your rosewater flagellations, your bare feet and your comical mortifications — fanatics without faith, martyrs without tortures? Has not one the right to ask you, if it is to obey the law of God that you shut yourselves in behind thick walls, and thus escape the law of labor which weighs so heavily upon all other men? . . . Away, you are only beggars!" †

Let us pass on — we have devoted too much space to them and their conglomerate theology, already. We have weighed both in the balance of history, of logic, of truth, and found them wanting. Their

---

\* *Les Fils de Dieu*, p. 296.
† *Ibid.*, p. 297.

system breeds atheism, nihilism, despair, and crime; its priests and preachers are unable to prove by works their reception of divine power. If both Church and priest could but pass out of the sight of the world as easily as their names do now from the eye of our reader, it would be a happy day for humanity. New York and London might then soon become as moral as a heathen city unoccupied by Christians; Paris be cleaner than the ancient Sodom. When Catholic and Protestant would be as fully satisfied as a Buddhist or Brahman that their every crime would be punished, and every good deed rewarded, they might spend upon their own *heathen* what now goes to give missionaries long picnics, and to make the name of Christian hated and despised by every nation outside the boundaries of Christendom.

---

As occasion required, we have reinforced our argument with descriptions of a few of the innumerable phenomena witnessed by us in different parts of the world. The remaining space at our disposal will be devoted to like subjects. Having laid a foundation by elucidating the philosophy of occult phenomena, it seems opportune to illustrate the theme with facts that have occurred under our own eye, and that may be verified by any traveller. Primitive peoples have disappeared, but primitive wisdom survives, and is attainable by those who "will," "dare," and can "keep silent."

## CHAPTER XII

"My vast and noble Capital, my Daitu, My splendidly-adorned!
And Thou, my cool and delicious Summer-seat, my Shangtu-Keibung!

Alas for my illustrious name as the sovereign of the World!
Alas for my Daitu, seat of Sanctity, Glorious work of the immortal Kublai!
All, all is rent from me!"
— Col. H. Yule, *The Book of Ser Marco Polo*, I, 296 (ed. 1875).*

"As for what thou hearest others say, who persuade the many that the soul, when once freed from the body, neither suffers . . . evil nor is conscious, I know that thou art better grounded in the doctrines received by us from our ancestors, and in the sacred orgies of Dionysos, than to believe them: *for the mystic symbols are well known to us who belong to the 'Brotherhood'.*"
— PLUTARCH, *Consolatory Letter to his Wife*, X.

"The problem of life is *man*. MAGIC, or rather Wisdom, is the evolved knowledge of the potencies of man's interior being; which forces are Divine emanations, as intuition is the perception of their origin, and initiation our introduction into that knowledge . . . We begin with instinct; the end is OMNISCIENCE."
—A. WILDER.

"Power belongs to him WHO KNOWS."—*Brahmanical Book of Evocation.*

IT would argue small discernment on our part were we to suppose that we had been followed thus far through this work by any but metaphysicians, or mystics of some sort. Were it otherwise, we should certainly advise such to spare themselves the trouble of reading this chapter; for, although nothing is said that is not strictly true, they would not fail to regard the least wonderful of the narratives as absolutely false, however substantiated.

To comprehend the principles of natural law involved in the several phenomena hereinafter described, the reader must keep in mind the fundamental propositions of the Oriental philosophy which we have successively elucidated. Let us recapitulate very briefly:

1st. There is no miracle. Everything that happens is the result of law — eternal, immutable, ever active. Apparent miracle is but the operation of forces antagonistic to what Dr. W. B. Carpenter, F.R.S. — a man of great learning but little knowledge — calls "the well-ascertained laws of nature." Like many of his class, Dr. Carpenter ignores the fact that there may be laws once "known," now unknown to science.

---

* [Ascribed by Sanang Setsen, the Mongol historian, to Toghon Timur, last sovereign of the Chingiz dynasty.]

2nd. Nature is triune: there is a visible, objective nature; an invisible, indwelling, energizing nature, the exact model of the other, and its vital principle; and, above these two, *spirit*, source of all forces, alone eternal and indestructible. The lower two constantly change; the higher third does not.

3rd. Man is also triune: he has his objective, physical body; his vitalizing astral body (or soul), the real man; and these two are brooded over and illuminated by the third—the sovereign, the immortal spirit. When the real man succeeds in merging himself with the latter, he becomes an immortal entity.

4th. Magic, as a science, is the knowledge of these principles, and of the way by which the omniscience and omnipotence of the spirit and its control over nature's forces may be acquired by the individual while still in the body. Magic, as an art, is the application of this knowledge in practice.

5th. Arcane knowledge misapplied, is sorcery; beneficently used, true magic or WISDOM.

6th. Mediumship is the opposite of adeptship; the medium is the passive instrument of foreign influences, the adept actively controls himself and all inferior potencies.

7th. All things that ever were, that are, or that will be, having their record upon the astral light, or tablet of the unseen universe, the initiated adept, by using the vision of his own spirit, can know all that has been known or can be known.

8th. Races of men differ in spiritual gifts as in color, stature, or any other external quality; among some peoples seership naturally prevails, among others mediumship. Some are addicted to sorcery, and transmit its secret rules of practice from generation to generation, with a range of physical phenomena, more or less wide, as the result.

9th. One phase of magical skill is the voluntary and conscious withdrawal of the inner man (astral form) from the outer man (physical body). In the cases of some mediums withdrawal occurs, but it is unconscious and involuntary. With the latter the body is more or less cataleptic at such times; but with the adept the absence of the astral form would not be noticed, for the physical senses are alert, and the individual appears only as though in a fit of abstraction — "a brown study," as some call it.

To the movements of the wandering astral form neither time nor space offer obstacles. The thaumaturgist, thoroughly skilled in occult science, can cause himself (that is, his physical body) to *seem* to disappear, or to apparently take on any shape that he may choose. He may make his astral form visible, or he may give it protean appearances. In both cases these results will be achieved by a mesmeric hallucination of the senses of all witnesses, simultaneously brought on. This hallucination is so perfect that the subject of it would stake his life that he saw a reality, when it is but a picture in his own mind, impressed upon his consciousness by the irresistible will of the mesmerizer.

But, while the astral form can go anywhere, penetrate any obstacle, and be seen at any distance from the physical body, the latter is dependent upon ordinary methods of transportation. It may be levitated under prescribed magnetic conditions, but not pass from one locality to another except in the usual way. Hence we discredit all stories of the aerial flight of mediums in body, for such would be miracle, and miracle we repudiate. Inert matter may be, in certain cases and under certain conditions, disintegrated, passed through walls, and recombined, but living animal organisms cannot.

Swedenborgians believe and arcane science teaches that the abandonment of the living body by the soul frequently occurs, and that we encounter every day, in every condition of life, such living corpses. Various causes, among them overpowering fright, grief, despair, a violent attack of sickness, or excessive sensuality may bring this about. The vacant carcass may be entered and inhabited by the astral form of an adept sorcerer, or an elementary (an earth-bound disembodied human soul), or, very rarely, an elemental. Of course, an adept of white magic has the same power, but unless some very exceptional and great object is to be accomplished, he will never consent to pollute himself by occupying the body of an impure person. In insanity, the patient's astral being is either semi-paralyzed, bewildered, and subject to the influence of every passing spirit of any sort, or it has departed forever, and the body is taken possession of by some vampirish entity near its own disintegration, and clinging desperately to earth, whose sensual pleasures it may enjoy for a brief season longer by this expedient.

10th. The cornerstone of MAGIC is an intimate practical knowledge of magnetism and electricity, their qualities, correlations, and potencies. Especially necessary is a familiarity with their effects in and upon the animal kingdom and man. There are occult properties in many other minerals, equally strange with that in the lodestone, which all practitioners of magic *must* know, and of which so-called exact science is wholly ignorant. Plants also have like mystical properties in a most wonderful degree, and the secrets of the herbs of dreams and enchantments are only lost to European science and, useless to say, are unknown to it, except in a few marked instances, such as opium and hashish. Yet, the psychical effects of even these few upon the human system are regarded as evidences of a temporary mental disorder. The women of Thessaly and Epirus, the female hierophants of the rites of Sabazius, did not carry their secrets away with the downfall of their sanctuaries. They are still preserved, and those who are aware of the nature of Soma, know the properties of other plants as well.

To sum up all in a few words, MAGIC is spiritual WISDOM; nature, the material ally, pupil and servant of the magician. One common vital principle pervades all things, and this is controllable by the perfected human will. The adept can stimulate the movements of the natural forces in plants and animals in a preternatural degree. Such experiments are not obstructions of nature, but quickenings; the conditions of more intense vital action are given.

The adept can control the sensations and alter the conditions of the physical and astral bodies of other persons not adepts; he can also govern and employ, as he chooses, the spirits of the elements. He cannot control the immortal spirit of any human being, living or dead, for all such spirits are alike sparks of the Divine Essence, and not subject to any foreign domination.

There are two kinds of seership — that of the soul and that of the spirit. The seership of the ancient Pythoness, or of the modern mesmerized subject, vary but in the artificial modes adopted to induce the state of clairvoyance. But, as the visions of both depend upon the greater or less acuteness of the senses of the astral body, they differ very widely from the perfect, omniscient spiritual state; for, at best, the subject can get but glimpses of truth, through the veil which physical nature interposes. The astral principle, or mind, called by the Hindu Yogin *jîvâtman*, is the sentient soul, inseparable from our physical brain, which it holds in subjection, and is in its turn equally trammelled by it. This is the *ego*, the intellectual life-principle of man, his conscious entity. While it is yet *within* the material body, the clearness and correctness of its spiritual visions depend on its more or less intimate relation with its higher Principle. When this relation is such as to allow the most ethereal portions of the soul-essence to act independently of its grosser particles and of the brain, it can unerringly comprehend what it sees; then only is it the pure, rational, *super*sentient soul. That state is known in India as the *Samâdhi;* it is the highest condition of spirituality possible to man on earth. Fakirs try to obtain such a condition by holding their breath for hours together during their religious exercises, and call this practice *dama-sadhâna*. The Hindu terms *Prânâyâma, Pratyâhâra,* and *Dhâranâ,* all relate to different psychological states, and show how much more the Sanskrit, and even the modern Hindu language, are adapted to the clear elucidation of the phenomena that are encountered by those who study this branch of psychological science, than the tongues of modern peoples, whose experiences have not yet necessitated the invention of such descriptive terms.

When the body is in the state of *dhâranâ* — a total catalepsy of the physical frame—the soul of the clairvoyant may liberate itself, and perceive things subjectively. And yet, as the sentient principle of the brain is alive and active, these pictures of the past, present, and future will be tinctured with the terrestrial perceptions of the objective world; the physical *memory* and *fancy* will be in the way of clear vision. But the seer-adept knows how to suspend the mechanical action of the brain. His visions will be as clear as truth itself, uncolored and undistorted, whereas, the clairvoyant, unable to control the vibrations of the astral waves, will perceive but more or less broken images through the medium of the brain. The seer can never take flickering shadows for realities, for his memory being as completely subjected to his will as the rest of the body, he receives impressions directly from his spirit. Between his subjective and objective selves there are no obstructive mediums. This is the real spiritual seership, in which, according to an expression of Plato, soul is raised above all inferior good. When we reach "that which is supreme, which is *simple, pure, and unchangeable, without form, color, or human qualities:* the God — our Nous."

This is the state which such seers as Plotinus and Apollonius termed the "Union to the Deity"; which the ancient Yogins called *Îsvara,*\* and the modern call *Samâdhi;* but this state is as far above modern clairvoyance as the stars above glowworms. Plotinus, as is well known, was a clairvoyant-seer during his whole and daily life; and yet, *he had been united to his God* but four times during the sixty-six years of his existence, as he himself confessed to Porphyry.

Ammonius Saccas, the "God-taught," asserts that the only power which is directly opposed to soothsaying and looking into futurity is *memory;* and Olympiodorus calls it *phantasy.* "The phantasy," he says, "is an impediment to our intellectual conceptions; and hence, when we are agitated by the inspiring influence of Divinity, if the phantasy intervenes, the enthusiastic energy ceases: for enthusiasm and the phantasy are contrary to each other. Should it be asked, whether the soul is able to energize without the phantasy? we reply, that its perception of universals proves that it

---

\* In its general sense, *Îsvara* means "Lord"; but the Îsvara of the mystic philosophers of India was understood precisely as the union and communion of men with the Deity of the Greek mystics. *Îsvara-Prasâda* means literally, in Sanskrit, *grace*. Both of the *Mîmânsâs,* treating of the most abstruse questions, explain *Karma* as merit, or the *efficacy of works; Îsvara-Prasâda,* as grace; and *Sraddha,* as faith. The *Mîmânsâs* are the work of the two most celebrated theologians of India. The *Pûrva-Mîmânsâ-Sûtra* was written by the philosopher Jaimini, and the *Uttara-Mîmânsâ* (or Vedânta), by Krishna Dvaipâyana Vyâsa, who collected the four *Vedas* together. (See Sir William Jones, Colebrooke, and others.) [70]

is able. It has perceptions, therefore, independent of the phantasy; at the same time, however, the phantasy attends it in its energies, just as a storm pursues him who sails on the sea." *

A medium, moreover, needs either a foreign intelligence — whether it be spirit or living mesmerizer — to overpower his physical and mental parts, or some factitious means to induce trance. An adept, and even a simple fakir requires but a few minutes of "self-contemplation." The brazen columns of Solomon's temple; the golden bells and pomegranates of Aaron; the Jupiter Capitolinus of Augustus, hung around with harmonious bells; † and the brazen bowls of the Mysteries when the Korê was called,‡ were all intended for such artificial help. § So were the brazen bowls of Solomon hung round with a double row of 200 pomegranates, which served as clappers within the hollow columns. The priestesses of Northern Germany, under the guidance of hierophants, could never prophesy but amidst the roar of the tumultuous waters. Regarding fixedly the eddies formed on the rapid course of the river they *hypnotized* themselves. So we read of Joseph, Jacob's son, who sought for divine inspiration with his silver divining cup, which must have had a very bright bottom to it. The priestesses of Dodona placed themselves under the ancient oak of Zeus (the Pelasgian, not the Olympian god), and listened intently to the rustling of the sacred leaves, while others concentrated their attention on the soft murmur of the cold spring gushing from underneath its roots. ‖ But the adept has no need of any such extraneous aids — the simple exertion of his *will* power is all-sufficient.

The *Atharva-Veda* teaches that the exercise of such will power is the highest form of prayer and its instantaneous response. To desire is to realize in proportion to the intensity of the aspiration; and that, in its turn, is measured by inward purity.

Some of these nobler Vedântic precepts on the soul and man's mystic powers have recently been contributed to an English periodical by a Hindu scholar. "The *Sânkhya*," he writes, "inculcates that the soul [*i.e.*, astral body] has the following powers: shrinking into a minute form to which everything is pervious, or enlarging to a gigantic body, or assuming levity (rising along a sunbeam to the solar orb), or possessing unlimited extension of organs (as touching the moon with the tip of a finger), or irresistible will (for instance, sinking into the earth as easily as in water), and dominion over all beings, animate or inanimate, faculty of changing the course of nature, ability to accomplish everything desired." Further, he gives their various appellations:

---

\* Olympiodorus, *On the Phaedo of Plato*, in Thos. Taylor's *Select Works of Porphyry*, p. 207, footnote.

† Suetonius, *Lives of the Caesars*, "Augustus," § 91.

‡ Cf. Plutarch, *On the Face in the Orb of the Moon*, §§ 27-28.

§ Cf. Pliny, *Nat. Hist.*, XXX, ii et seq.

‖ Servius, *Comm. on Virgil, Aeneid*, p. 71.

"The powers are called: 1, *Animan;* 2, *Mahiman;* 3, *Laghiman;* 4, *Gariman;* 5, *Prâpti;* 6, *Prâkâmya;* 7, *Vaśitva;* 8, *Iśitva,* or divine power. The fifth is predicting future events, understanding unknown languages, curing diseases, divining unexpressed thoughts, understanding the language of the heart. The sixth is the power of converting old age into youth. The seventh is the power of mesmerizing human beings and beasts, and making them obedient; it is the power of restraining passions and emotions. The eighth is the spiritual state; the absence of the above seven proves that in this state the Yogi is full of God."

"No writings," he adds, "revealed or sacred, were allowed to be so authoritative and final *as the teaching of the soul.* Some of the Rishis appear to have laid the greatest stress on this supersensuous source of knowledge." \*

From the remotest antiquity, *mankind* as a whole *have always been convinced of the existence of a personal spiritual entity within the personal physical man.* This inner entity was more or less divine, according to its proximity to the crown — Christos. The closer the union, the more serene man's destiny, the less dangerous the external conditions. This belief is neither bigotry nor superstition, only an ever-present, instinctive feeling of the proximity of another spiritual and invisible world, which, though it be subjective to the senses of the outward man, is perfectly objective to the inner ego. Furthermore, they believed that *there are external and internal conditions which affect the determination of our will upon our actions.* They rejected fatalism, for fatalism implies a blind course of some still blinder power. But they believed in *destiny,* which from birth to death every man is weaving thread by thread around himself, as a spider does his web; and this destiny is guided either by that presence termed by some the guardian angel, or our more intimate astral inner man, who is but too often the evil genius of the man of flesh. Both these lead on the outward man, but one of them must prevail; and from the very beginning of the invisible affray, the stern and implacable *law of compensation* steps in and takes its course, following faithfully the fluctuations. When the last strand is woven, and man is seemingly enwrapped in the network of his own doing, then he finds himself completely under the empire of this *self-made* destiny. It then either fixes him like the inert shell against the immovable rock, or like a feather carries him away in a whirlwind raised by his own actions.

The greatest philosophers of antiquity found it neither unreasonable nor strange that "souls should come to souls, and impart to them concep-

---

\* Pyârichânda Mitra, "The Psychology of the Âryas," in *Human Nature,* for March, 1877. [Also in *On the Soul: its Nature and Development,* Calcutta, 1881, pp. 48-49.]

tions of future things, occasionally by letters, or by a mere touch, or by a glance reveal to them past events or announce future ones," as Ammonius tells us. Moreover, Lamprias and others held that if the *unembodied* spirits or souls could descend on earth and become guardians of mortal men, "we should not seek to deprive *those souls which are still in the body* of that power by which the former know future events and are able to announce them. It is not probable," adds Lamprias, "that the soul gains a new power of prophecy after separation from the body, and which before it did not possess. We may rather conclude *that it possessed all these powers during its union with the body, although in a lesser perfection* . . . For as the sun does not shine only when it passes from among the clouds, but has always been radiant and has only appeared dim and obscured by vapors, the soul does not only receive the power of looking into futurity when it passes from the body as from a cloud, but *has possessed it always,* though dimmed by connection with the earthly." \*

A familiar example of one phase of the power of the soul or astral body to manifest itself, is the phenomenon of the so-called spirit-hand. In the presence of certain mediums these seemingly detached members will gradually develop from a luminous nebula, pick up a pencil, write messages, and then dissolve before the eyes of the witnesses. Many such cases are recorded by perfectly competent and trustworthy persons. These phenomena are real, and require serious consideration. But false "phantom-hands" have sometimes been taken for the genuine. At Dresden we once saw a hand and arm, made for the purpose of deception, with an ingenious arrangement of springs that would cause the machine to imitate to perfection the movements of the natural member; while exteriorly it would require close inspection to detect its artificial character. In using this, the dishonest medium slips his natural arm out of his sleeve, and replaces it with the mechanical substitute; both hands may then be made to seem resting upon the table, while in fact one is touching the sitters, showing itself, knocking the furniture, and making other phenomena.

The mediums for real manifestations are least able, as a rule, to comprehend or explain them. Among those who have written most intelligently upon the subject of these luminous hands, may be reckoned Dr. Francis Gerry Fairfield, author of *Ten Years With Spiritual Mediums,* an article from whose pen appears in *The Library Table* for July 19, 1877. A medium himself, he is yet a strong opponent of the spiritualistic theory. Discussing the subject of the "phantom-hand," he testifies that "this the writer has personally witnessed, under conditions of test provided by himself, in his own room, in full daylight, with the medium seated upon a

---

\* [Plutarch, *On the Cessation of Oracles,* §§ 38, 39.]

sofa from six to eight feet from the table hovering upon which the apparition (the hand) appeared. The application of the poles of a horseshoe magnet to the hand caused it to waver perceptibly, and threw the medium into violent convulsions — pretty positive evidence that *the force concerned in the phenomenon was generated in his own nervous system.*"

Dr. Fairfield's deduction that the fluttering phantom-hand is an emanation from the medium is logical, and is correct. The test of the horseshoe magnet proves in a scientific way what every kabalist would affirm upon the authority of experience, no less than philosophy. The "force concerned in the phenomenon" is the will of the medium, exercised unconsciously to the outer man, which for the time is semi-paralyzed and cataleptic; the phantom-hand is an extrusion of the man's inner or astral member. This is that real self whose limbs the surgeon cannot amputate, but which remain behind after the outer casing is cut off, and (all theories of exposed or compressed nerve termini to the contrary, notwithstanding) have all the sensations the physical parts formerly experienced. This is that spiritual (astral) body which "is raised in incorruption." It is useless to argue that these are *spirit*-hands; for, admitting even that at every *séance* human spirits of many kinds are attracted to the medium, and that they do guide and produce some manifestations, yet to make hands or faces objective they are compelled to use either the astral limbs of the medium, or the materials furnished them by the elementals, or yet the combined aural emanations of all persons present. *Pure* spirits will not and *cannot* show themselves objectively, those that do are not pure spirits, but elementary and impure. Woe to the medium who falls a prey to such!

The same principle involved in the unconscious extrusion of a phantom limb by the cataleptic medium, applies to the projection of his entire "double" or astral body. This may be withdrawn by the will of the medium's own inner self, without his retaining in his physical brain any recollection of such an intent — that is one phase of man's dual capacity. It may also be effected by elementary and elemental spirits, to whom he may stand in the relation of mesmeric subject. Dr. Fairfield is right in one position taken in his book, viz.: mediums are usually diseased, and in many if not most cases the children or near connections of mediums. But he is wholly wrong in attributing all psychical phenomena to morbid physiological conditions. The adepts of Eastern magic are uniformly in perfect mental and bodily health, and in fact the voluntary and independent production of phenomena is impossible to any others. We have known many, and never a sick man among them. The adept retains perfect consciousness; shows no change of bodily temperature, or other sign of morbidity; requires no "conditions," but will do his feats anywhere and everywhere; and instead of being passive and in subjection to a foreign influence, rules the forces with an iron will. But we have elsewhere shown that the medium and the adept are as opposed as the poles. We will only add here that the body, soul and spirit of the adept are all conscious and working in harmony, and the body of the medium is an inert clod, and even his soul may be away in a dream while its habitation is occupied by another.

An adept can not only project and make visible a hand, a foot, or any other portion of his body, but the whole of it. We have seen one do this, in full day, while his hands and feet were being held by a skeptical friend whom he wished to surprise.* Little by little the whole astral body oozed out like a vapory cloud, until before us stood two forms, of which the second was an exact duplicate of the first, only slightly more shadowy.

The medium need not exercise any *will power*. It suffices that she or he shall know what is expected by the investigators. The medium's "spiritual" entity, when not obsessed by other spirits, will act outside the will or consciousness of the physical being, as surely as it acts when within the body during a fit of somnambulism. Its perceptions, external and internal, will be acuter and far more developed, precisely as they are in the sleepwalker. And this is why "the materialized form sometimes knows more than the medium," † for the intellectual perception of the astral entity is proportionately as much higher than the corporeal intelligence of the medium in its normal state, as the spirit entity is finer than itself. Generally the medium will be found cold, the pulse will have visibly changed, and a state of nervous prostration succeeds the phenomena, bunglingly and without discrimination attributed to disembodied spirits; whereas, but one-third of them may be produced by the latter, another third by elementals, and the rest by the astral double of the medium himself.

---

\* The Boulogne (France) correspondent of an English journal says that he knows of a gentleman who has had an arm amputated at the shoulder, "who is certain that he has a spiritual arm, which he sees and actually feels with his other hand. He can touch anything, and even pull up things with the spiritual or phantom arm and hand." The party knows nothing of spiritualism. We give this as we get it, without verification, but it merely corroborates what we have seen in the case of an Eastern adept. This eminent scholar and practical kabalist can at will project his astral arm, and with the hand take up, move, and carry objects, even at a considerable distance from where he may be sitting or standing. We have often seen him thus minister to the wants of a favorite elephant.

† Answer to a question at "The National Association of Spiritualists," May 14th, 1877.

But — while it is our firm belief that most of the physical manifestations, *i.e.*, those which neither need nor show intelligence or great discrimination, are produced mechanically by the *scin-lâc* (double) of the medium, as a person in sound sleep will when apparently awake do things of which he will retain no remembrance — the purely subjective phenomena are but in a very small proportion of cases due to the action of the personal astral body. They are mostly, and according to the moral, intellectual and physical purity of the medium, the work of either the elementary, or sometimes very pure human spirits. Elementals have naught to do with subjective manifestations. In rare cases it is the *divine* spirit of the medium himself that guides and produces them.

As Bâbû Pyârichânda Mitra says, in a letter to the President of the National Association of Spiritualists, Mr. Alexander Calder, "a spirit is an essence or power, and has no form . . . The very idea of form implies 'materialism.' The spirits [astral souls, we should say] . . . can assume forms for a time, but form is not their permanent state. The more material is our soul, the more material is our conception of spirits." *

Epimenides, the Orphikos, was renowned for his "sacred and marvellous nature," and for the faculty his soul possessed of quitting its body *"as long and as often as it pleased."* The ancient philosophers who have testified to this ability may be reckoned by the dozens. Apollonius left his body at a moment's notice, but it must be remembered Apollonius was an adept — a "magician." Had he been simply a medium, he could not have performed such feats *at will*. Empedocles of Agrigentum, the Pythagorean thaumaturgist, required no *conditions* to arrest a waterspout which had broken over the city. Neither did he need any to recall a woman to life, as he did. Apollonius used no *darkened* room in which to perform his aethrobatic feats. Vanishing suddenly in the air before the eyes of Domitian and a whole crowd of witnesses (many thousands), he appeared an hour after in the grotto of Puteoli. But investigation would have shown that his physical body having become invisible by the concentration of âkâśa about it, he could walk off unperceived to some secure retreat in the neighborhood, and an hour after, his astral form appear at Puteoli to his friends, and seem to be the man himself.

No more did Simon Magus wait to be entranced to fly off in the air before the apostles and crowds of witnesses. "It requires no conjuration and ceremonies; circle-making and incensing are mere nonsense and juggling," says Paracelsus. The human spirit "is so great a thing that no man can express it; as God Himself is eternal and unchangeable, so also

---

* "A Buddhist's Opinions of the Spiritual States," *The Spiritualist*, May 25, 1877, p. 246.

is the mind of man. If we rightly understood its powers, nothing would be impossible to us on earth. The imagination is strengthened and developed through *faith in our will.* Faith must confirm the imagination, for faith establishes the will."

A singular account of the personal interview — barely mentioned in Volume I — of an English ambassador in 1783, with a reincarnated Buddha, an infant eighteen months old at that time, is given in the *Asiatic Researches* from the narrative of an eyewitness himself, Mr. S. Turner, the author of *The Embassy to Tibet.* The cautious phraseology of a skeptic dreading public ridicule ill conceals the amazement of the witness, who, at the same time, desires to give facts as truthfully as possible. The infant lama received the ambassador and his suite with a dignity and decorum so natural and unconstrained that they remained in a perfect maze of wonder. The behavior of this infant, says the author, was that of an old philosopher, grave and sedate and exceedingly courteous. He contrived to make the young pontiff understand the inconsolable grief into which the Governor-General of Galagata (Calcutta), the City of Palaces, and the people of India were plunged when he died, and the general rapture when they found that he had resurrected in a young and fresh body again; at which compliment the young lama regarded him and his suite with looks of singular complacency, and courteously treated them to confectionery from a golden cup. "The ambassador continued to express the Governor-General's hope that the lama might long continue to illumine the world with his presence; and that the friendship which had, heretofore, subsisted between them might be yet more strongly cemented, for the benefit and advantage of the intelligent votaries of the lama . . . all which made the little creature look steadfastly at the speaker, and graciously bow and nod . . . and bow and nod again—as *if he* understood and approved of . . . every word that was uttered." *

As *if* he understood! *If* the infant behaved in the most natural and dignified way during the reception, and "when their cups were empty of tea became uneasy and throwing back his head and contracting the skin of his brow, continued making a noise till they were filled again," why could he not understand as well what was said to him?

Years ago, a small party of travellers were painfully journeying from Kashmîr to Leh, a city of Ladâkh (Central Thibet).[71] Among our guides we had a Tatar Shaman, a very mysterious personage, who spoke Russian a little and English not at all, and yet who managed, nevertheless, to converse with us, and proved of great service. Having learned that some of our party were Russians, he had imagined that our protec-

---

* Cf. Coleman, *The Mythology of the Hindus,* p. 217; also Mr. Turner's Letter to the Governor-General, in *Asiatic Researches* (1801), Vol. I, pp. 197-205.

tion was all-powerful, and might enable him to safely find his way back to his Siberian home, from which, for reasons unknown, some twenty years before, he had fled, as he told us, via Kyakhta and the great Gobi Desert, to the land of the Chakhars.* [72] With such an interested object in view, we believed ourselves safe under his guard. To explain the situation briefly: Our companions had formed the unwise plan of penetrating into Thibet under various disguises, none of them speaking the language, although one, a Mr. K——, had picked up some Kazan Tatar, and thought he did. As we mention this only incidentally, we may as well say at once that two of them, the brothers N——, were very politely brought back to the frontier before they had walked sixteen miles into the weird land of Eastern Bod; and Mr. K——, an ex-Lutheran minister, could not even attempt to leave his miserable village near Leh, as from the first days he found himself prostrated with fever, and had to return to Lahore via Kashmîr. But one sight seen by him was as good as if he had witnessed the reincarnation of Buddha itself. Having heard of this "miracle" from some old Russian missionary in whom he thought he could have more faith than in Abbé Huc, it had been for years his desire to expose the "great heathen" jugglery, as he expressed it. K—— was a positivist, and rather prided himself on this anti-philosophical neologism. But his positivism was doomed to receive a deathblow.

About four days' journey from Islamâbâd, at an insignificant mud village, whose only redeeming feature was its magnificent lake, we stopped for a few days' rest. Our companions had temporarily separated from us, and the village was to be our place of meeting. It was there that we were apprised by our Shaman that a large party of Lamaic "Saints," on pilgrimage to various shrines, had taken up their abode in an old cave-temple and established a temporary Vihâra therein. He added that, as the "Three Honorable Ones" † were said to travel along with them, the holy *Bhikshus* (monks) were capable of producing the greatest miracles. Mr. K——, fired with the prospect of exposing this humbug of the ages, proceeded at once to pay them a visit, and from that moment the most friendly relations were established between the two camps.

The Vihâra was in a secluded and most romantic spot secured against all intrusion. Despite the effusive attentions, presents, and protestations of Mr. K——, the Chief, who was *Pase-Budhu* ‡ (an ascetic of great

---

* Russian subjects are not allowed to cross the Tatar territory, neither the subjects of the Emperor of China to go to the Russian factories.

† These are the representatives of the Buddhist Trinity, Buddha, Dharma and Sangha, or Fo, Fa and Sengh, as they are called in Thibet.

‡ [*Pashi-Budha?*]

sanctity), declined to exhibit the phenomenon of the "incarnation" until a certain talisman in possession of the writer was exhibited.* Upon seeing this, however, preparations were at once made, and an infant of three or four months was procured from its mother, a poor woman of the neighborhood. An oath was first of all exacted of Mr. K——, that he would not divulge what he might see or hear, for the space of seven years. The talisman is a simple agate or carnelian known among the Thibetans and others as *A-yu,* and naturally possessed, or had been endowed with very mysterious properties. It has a triangle engraved upon it, within which are contained a few mystical words. †

Several days passed before everything was ready; nothing of a mysterious character occurring meanwhile, except that, at the bidding of a Bhikshu, ghostly faces were made to peep at us out of the glassy bosom of the lake, as we sat at the door of the Vihâra, upon its bank. One of these was the countenance of Mr. K——'s sister, whom he had left well and happy at home, but who, as we subsequently learned, had died some

---

\* A *Bhikshu* is not allowed to accept anything directly even from laymen of his own people, least of all from a foreigner. The slightest contact with the body and even dress of a person not belonging to their special community is carefully avoided. Thus even the offerings brought by us and which comprised pieces of red and yellow *pu-lu,* a sort of woollen fabric the lamas generally wear, had to pass through strange ceremonies. They are forbidden, 1, to ask or beg for anything — even were they starving — having to wait until it is voluntarily offered; 2, to touch either gold or silver with their hands; 3, to eat a morsel of food, even when presented, unless the donor distinctly says to the disciple, "This is for your master to *eat.*" Thereupon, the disciple turning to the *pazen* has to offer the food in his turn, and when he has said, "Master, this is allowed; take and eat," then only can the lama take it with the right hand, and partake of it. All our offerings had to pass through such purifications. When the silver pieces, and a few handfuls of annas (a coin equal to four cents) were at different occasions offered to the community, a disciple first wrapped his hand in a yellow handkerchief, and receiving it on his palm, conveyed the sum immediately into the *Badir,* called elsewhere *Sabaït,* a sacred basin, generally wooden, kept for offerings.

† These stones are highly venerated among Lamaist and Buddhists; the throne and sceptre of Buddha are ornamented with them, and the Taley-Lama wears one on the fourth finger of the right hand. They are found in the Altai Mountains, and near the river Yarkhun. Our talisman was a gift from the venerable high priest, a *Gelong,* of a Kalmuck tribe. Though treated as apostates from their primitive Lamaism, these nomads maintain friendly intercourse with their brother-Kalmucks, the Khoshuts of Eastern Thibet and Kokonor, and even with the Lamaists of Lhasa. The ecclesiastical authorities however, will have no relations with them. We have had abundant opportunities to become acquainted with this interesting people of the Astrakhan Steppes, having lived in their *kibitkas* in our early years, and partaken of the lavish hospitality of Prince Tumen', their late chief, and his Princess. In their religious ceremonies, the Kalmucks employ trumpets made from the thigh and arm bones of deceased rulers and high priests.

time before he had set out on the present journey. The sight affected him at first, but he called his skepticism to his aid, and quieted himself with theories of cloud-shadows, reflections of tree branches, etc., such as people of his kind fall back upon.

On the appointed afternoon, the baby, being brought to the Vihâra, was left in the vestibule or reception-room, as K—— could go no further into the temporary sanctuary. The child was then placed on a bit of carpet in the middle of the floor, and everyone not belonging to the party being sent away, two "mendicants" were placed at the entrance to keep out intruders. Then all the lamas seated themselves on the floor, with their backs against the granite walls, so that each was separated from the child by a space, at least, of ten feet. The chief, having had a square piece of leather spread for him by the *desservant,* seated himself at the farthest corner. Alone, Mr. K—— placed himself close by the infant, and watched every movement with intense interest. The only condition exacted of us was that we should preserve a strict silence, and patiently await further developments. A bright sunlight streamed through the open door. Gradually the "Superior" fell into what seemed a state of profound meditation, while the others, after a *sotto voce* short invocation, became suddenly silent, and looked as if they had been completely petrified. It was oppressively still, and the crowing of the child was the only sound to be heard. After we had sat there a few moments, the movements of the infant's limbs suddenly ceased, and his body appeared to become rigid. K—— watched intently every motion, and both of us, by a rapid glance, became satisfied that all present were sitting motionless. The superior, with his gaze fixed upon the ground, did not even look at the infant; but, pale and motionless, he seemed rather like a bronze statue of a Talapoin in meditation than a living being. Suddenly, to our great consternation, we saw the child, not raise itself, but, as it were, violently jerked into a sitting posture! A few more jerks, and then, like an automaton set in motion by concealed wires, the four-months-old baby stood upon his feet! Fancy our consternation, and, in Mr. K——'s case, horror. Not a hand had been outstretched, not a motion made, nor a word spoken; and yet, here was a babe-in-arms standing erect and firm as a man!

The rest of the story we will quote from a copy of notes written on this subject by Mr. K——, the same evening, and given to us, in case it should not reach its place of destination, or the writer fail to see anything more.

"After a minute or two of hesitation," writes K——, "the baby turned his head and looked at me with an expression of intelligence that was simply awful! It sent a chill through me. I pinched my hands and bit my lips till the blood almost came, to make sure that I did not dream. But this was only the beginning. The miraculous creature, making, *as I fancied*, two steps toward me, resumed his sitting posture, and, without removing his eyes from mine, repeated, sentence by sentence, in what I supposed to be the Thibetan language, the very words, which I had been told in advance, are commonly spoken at the incarnations of Buddha, beginning with 'I am Buddha; I am the old Lama; I am his spirit in a new body,' etc. I felt a real terror; my hair rose upon my head, and my blood ran cold. For my life I could not have spoken a word. There was no trickery here, no ventriloquism. The infant lips moved, and the eyes seemed to search my very soul with an expression that *made me think it was the face of the Superior himself*, his eyes, his very look that I was gazing upon. It was *as if his spirit had entered the little body, and was looking at me through the transparent mask of the baby's face*. I felt my brain growing dizzy. The infant reached toward me, and laid his little hand upon mine. I started as if I had been touched by a hot coal; and, unable to bear the scene any longer, covered my face with my hands. It was but for an instant; but when I removed them, the little actor had become a crowing baby again, and a moment after, lying upon his back, set up a fretful cry. The superior had resumed his normal condition, and conversation ensued.

"It was only after a series of similar experiments, extending over ten days, that I realized the fact that I had seen the incredible, astounding phenomenon described by certain travellers, but always by me denounced as an imposture. Among a multitude of questions unanswered, despite my cross-examination, the Superior let drop one piece of information, which must be regarded as highly significant. 'What would have happened,' I inquired, through the shaman, 'if, while the infant was speaking, in a moment of insane fright, at the thought of its being the "Devil," I had killed it?' He replied that, if the blow had not been instantly fatal, the child *alone* would have been killed. 'But,' I continued, 'suppose that it had been as swift as a lightning-flash?' 'In such case,' was the answer, *'you would have killed me also'*."

In Japan and Siam there are two orders of priests, of which one is public, and deals with the people, the other strictly private. The latter are never seen; their existence is known but to very few natives never to foreigners. Their powers are never displayed in public, nor ever at all except on rare occasions of the utmost importance, at which times the ceremonies are performed in subterranean or otherwise inaccessible temples, and in the presence of a chosen few whose heads answer for their secrecy. Among such occasions are deaths in the Royal family, or those of high dignitaries affiliated with the Order. One of the most weird and impressive exhibitions of the power of these magicians is that of the withdrawal of the astral soul from the cremated remains of human beings, a ceremony practiced likewise in some of the most important lamaseries of Thibet and Mongolia.

In Siam, Japan, and Great Tartary, it is the custom to make medallions, statuettes, and idols out of the ashes of cremated persons;* they are mixed with water into a paste, and after being molded into the desired shape, are baked and then gilded. The Lamasery of Ou-Tay, in the province of Shan-Si, Mongolia,[74] is the most famous for that work, and rich persons send the bones of their defunct relatives to be ground and fashioned there. When the adept in magic proposes to facilitate the withdrawal of the astral soul of the deceased, which otherwise they think might remain stupefied for an indefinite period *within* the ashes, the following process is resorted to: The sacred dust is placed in a heap upon a strongly magnetized metallic plate, of the size of a man's body. The adept then slowly and gently fans it with the *Talapat Nang*,† a fan of a peculiar shape and inscribed with certain signs, muttering, at the same time, a form of invocation. The ashes soon become, as it were, imbued with life, and gently spread themselves out into a thin layer which assumes the outline of the body before cremation. Then there gradually arises a sort of whitish vapor which after a time forms into an erect column, and compacting itself, is finally transformed into the "double," or ethereal, astral counterpart of the dead, which in its turn dissolves away into thin air, and disappears from mortal sight.‡

The "Magicians" of Kashmîr, Thibet, Mongolia and Great Tartary are too well known to need comments. If *jugglers* they be, we invite the most expert jugglers of Europe and America to match them if they can.

If our scientists are unable to imitate the mummy-embalming of the Egyptians, how much greater would be their surprise to see, as we have, dead bodies preserved by alchemical art, so that after the lapse of centuries, they seem as though the individuals were but sleeping. The complexions were as fresh, the skin as elastic, the eyes as natural and sparkling as though they were in the full flush of health, and the wheels of life had been stopped but the instant before. The bodies of certain very eminent personages are laid upon catafalques, in rich mausoleums,

---

* The Buddhist Kalmucks of the Astrakhan steppes are accustomed to making their idols out of the cremated ashes of their princes and priests. A relative of the author [73] has in her collection several small pyramids composed of the ashes of eminent Kalmucks and presented to her by the Prince Tumen' himself in 1836.

† The sacred fan used by the chief priests instead of an umbrella.

‡ See Vol. I, p. 476 of the present work.

sometimes overlaid with gilding or even with plates of real gold; their favorite arms, trinkets, and articles of daily use gathered about them, and a suite of attendants, blooming young boys and girls, but still corpses, preserved like their masters, stand as if ready to serve when called. In the convent of Great Kuren,[75] and in one situated upon the Holy Mountain (Bogdo-Ula) there are said to be several such sepulchres, which have been respected by all the conquering hordes that have swept through those countries. Abbé Huc heard that such exist, but did not see one, strangers of all kinds being excluded, and missionaries and European travellers not furnished with the requisite protection, being the last of all persons who would be permitted to approach the sacred places. Huc's statement that the tombs of Tatar sovereigns are surrounded with children "who were compelled to swallow mercury until they were suffocated," by which means "the color and freshness of the victims is preserved so well that they appear alive," is one of these idle missionary fables which impose only upon the most ignorant who accept on hearsay. Buddhists have never immolated victims, whether human or animal. It is utterly against the principles of their religion, and no Lamaist was ever accused of it. When a rich man desired to be interred in *company,* messengers were sent throughout the country with the Lama-embalmers, and children just dead in the natural way were selected for the purpose. Poor parents were but too glad to preserve their departed children in this poetic way, instead of abandoning them to decay and wild beasts.

At the time when Abbé Huc was living in Paris, after his return from Thibet, he related, among other unpublished wonders, to a Mr. Arsenieff, a Russian gentleman, the following curious fact that he had witnessed during his long sojourn at the lamasery of Kumbum. One day while conversing with one of the lamas, the latter suddenly stopped speaking, and assumed the attentive attitude of one who is listening to a message being delivered to him, although he (Huc) heard never a word. "Then, I must go"; suddenly broke forth the lama, as if in response to the message.

"Go where?" inquired the astonished "lama of Jehovah" (Huc). "And with whom are you talking?"

"To the lamasery of . . . ," was the quiet answer. "The Shaberon wants me; it was he who summoned me."

Now this lamasery was many days' journey from that of Kumbum, in which the conversation was taking place. But what seemed to astonish Huc the most was, that, instead of setting off on his journey, the lama simply walked to a sort of cupola-room on the roof of the house in which they lived, and another lama, after exchanging a few words, followed them to the terrace by means of the ladder, and passing between them, locked and barred his companion in. Then turning to Huc after a few seconds of meditation, he smiled and informed the guest that "he had gone."

"But how could he? Why you have locked him in, and the room has no issue?" insisted the missionary.

"And what good would a door be to him?" answered the custodian. *"It is he himself who went away; his body is not needed, and so he left it in my charge."*

Notwithstanding the wonders which Huc had witnessed during his perilous journey, his opinion was that both the lamas had mystified him. But three days later, not having seen his habitual friend and entertainer, he inquired after him, and was informed that he would be back in the evening. At sunset, and just as the "other lamas" were preparing to retire, Huc heard his absent friend's voice calling as if from the clouds, to his companion to open the door for him. Looking upward, he perceived the "traveller's" outline behind the lattice of the room where he had been locked in. When he descended he went straight to the Grand Lama of Kumbum, and delivered to him certain messages and "orders," from the place which he "pretended" he had just left. Huc could get no more information from him as to his *aerial* voyage. But he always thought, he said, that this "farce" had something to do with the immediate and extraordinary preparations for the polite expulsion of both the missionaries, himself and Father Gabet, to Chogor-tan, a place belonging to the Kumbum. The suspicion of the daring missionary may have been correct, in view of his impudent inquisitiveness and indiscretion.

If the Abbé had been versed in Eastern philosophy, he would have found no great difficulty in comprehending both the flight of the lama's astral body to the distant lamasery while his physical frame remained behind, or the carrying on of a conversation with the Shaberon that was inaudible to himself. The recent experiments with the telephone in America, to which allusion was made in Chapter V of our first volume, but which have been greatly perfected since those pages went to press, prove that the human voice and the sounds of instrumental music may be conveyed along a telegraphic wire to a great distance. The Hermetic philosophers taught, as we have seen, that the disappearance from sight of a flame does not imply its actual extinction. It has only passed from the visible to the invisible world, and may be perceived by the inner sense of vision, which is adapted to the things of that other and more real universe. The same rule applies to sound. As the physical ear discerns the vibrations of the atmosphere up to a certain point, not yet definitely fixed, but varying with the individual, so the adept whose interior hearing has been developed, can take the sound at this vanishing-point, and hear its vibrations in the astral light indefinitely. He needs no wire, helices, or sounding boards; his will power is all-sufficient. Hearing with the spirit, time and distance offer no impediments, and so he may converse with another adept at the antipodes with as great ease as though they were in the same room.

Fortunately, we can produce numerous witnesses to corroborate our statement, who, without being adepts at all, have, nevertheless, heard the sound of aerial music and of the human voice, when neither instrument nor speaker were within thousands of miles of the place where we sat. In their case they actually heard interiorly, though they supposed their physical organs of hearing alone were employed. The adept had, by a simple effort of will power, given them for the brief moment the same perception of the spirit of sound as he himself constantly enjoys.

If our men of science could only be induced to test instead of deriding the ancient philosophy of the trinity of all the natural forces, they would go by leaps toward the dazzling truth, instead of creeping, snail-like, as at present. Prof. Tyndall's experiments off the South Foreland, at Dover, in 1875, fairly upset all previous theories of the transmission of sound, and those he has made with sensitive flames bring him to the very threshold of arcane science. One step further, and he would comprehend how adepts can converse at great distances. But that step will *not* be taken. Of his sensitive — in truth, magical — flame, he says: "The slightest tap on a distant anvil reduces its height to seven inches. When a bunch of keys is shaken, the flame is violently agitated, and emits a loud roar. The dropping of a sixpence into a hand, already containing coin . . . knocks the flame down . . . The creaking of boots sets it in violent commotion. The crumpling, or tearing of paper, or the rustle of a silk dress, does the same. I hold a watch near the flame . . . At every tick it falls and roars. The winding up of the watch also produces tumult . . . A chirrup from a distance of 30 yards causes it to fall and roar. I repeat a passage from Spenser.\* The flame selects from the sounds those to which it can respond. It notices some by the slightest nod, to others it bows more distinctly, to some its obeisance is very profound, while to many sounds it turns an entirely deaf ear." †

Such are the wonders of modern physical science; but at what cost of apparatus, and carbonic acid and coal gas; of American and Canadian whistles, trumpets, gongs and bells! The poor heathen have none

---

\* [Edmund Spenser, *The Faerie Queene*, is quoted.]

† See John Tyndall, *Sound,* ch. vi, § 12.

such *impedimenta*, but — will European science believe it — nevertheless, produce the very same phenomena. Upon one occasion, when, in a case of exceptional importance, an "oracle" was required, we saw the possibility of what we had previously vehemently denied — namely, a simple mendicant cause a sensitive flame to give responsive flashes without a particle of apparatus. A fire was kindled of branches of the *Beal* tree, and some sacrificial herbs were sprinkled upon it. The mendicant sat near by, motionless, absorbed in contemplation. During the intervals between the questions the fire burned low and seemed ready to go out, but when the interrogatories were propounded, the flames leaped, roaring, skyward, flickered, bowed, and sent fiery tongues flaring toward the east, west, north, or south; each motion having its distinct meaning in a code of signals well understood. Between whiles it would sink to the ground, and the tongues of flame would lick the sod in every direction, and suddenly disappear, leaving only a bed of glowing embers. When the interview with the flame-spirits was at an end, the Bhikshu (mendicant) turned toward the jungle where he abode, keeping up a wailing, monotonous chant, to the rhythm of which the sensitive flame kept time, not merely like Prof. Tyndall's, when he read the *Faerie Queene*, by simple motions, but by a marvellous modulation of hissing and roaring until he was out of sight. Then, as if its very life were extinguished, it vanished, and left a bed of ashes before the astonished spectators.

Both in Western and Eastern Thibet, as in every other place where Buddhism predominates, there are two distinct religions, the same as it is in Brahmanism — the secret philosophy and the popular religion. The former is that of the followers of the doctrine of the sect of the *Sautrântikas*.* They closely adhere to the spirit of Buddha's original teachings which show the necessity of *intuitional* perception, and all deductions therefrom. These do not proclaim their views, nor allow them to be made public.

"All *compounds* are perishable," were the last words uttered by the lips of the dying Gautama, when preparing under the Sâla-tree to enter into Nirvâna. "Spirit is the sole, elementary, and primordial unity, and each of its rays is immortal, infinite, and indestructible. Beware of the illusions of matter." Buddhism was spread far and wide over Asia, and even farther, by Dharmâśoka. He was the grandson of the miracle-worker Chandragupta, the illustrious king who rescued the Puñjâb from the Macedonians — if they ever were at Puñjâb at all — and received Megasthenes at his court in Pâtaliputra. Dharmâśoka was the greatest King of the Maurya dynasty. From a reckless profligate and atheist,

---

* Compound word from *sûtra*, maxim or precept, and *antika*, close or near.

he had become *Priyadarśin,* the "beloved of the gods," and never was the purity of his philanthropic views surpassed by any earthly ruler. His memory has lived for ages in the hearts of the Buddhists, and has been perpetuated in the humane edicts engraved in several popular dialects on the columns and rocks of Allâhâbâd, Delhi, Gujarât, Peshâwar, Orissa, and other places.\* His famous grandfather had united all India under his powerful sceptre. When the Nâgas, or serpent-worshippers of Kashmîr had been converted through the efforts of the apostles sent out by the Sthâviras of the third council, the religion of Gautama spread like wildfire. Gândhâra, Kâbul, and even many of the Satrapies of Alexander the Great, accepted the new philosophy. The Buddhism of Nepal being the one which may be said to have diverged less than any other from the primeval ancient faith, the Lamaism of Tartary, Mongolia and Thibet, which is a direct offshoot of this country, may be thus shown to be the purest Buddhism; for we say it again, Lamaism properly is but an external form of rites.

The *Upâsakas* and *Upâsikâs,* or male and female semi-monastics and semi-laymen, have equally with the lama-monks themselves, to strictly abstain from violating any of Buddha's rules, and must study *Meipo* and every psychological phenomenon as much. Those who become guilty of any of the "five sins" lose all right to congregate with the pious community. The most important of these is *not to curse upon any consideration, for the curse returns upon the one that utters it, and often upon his innocent relatives who breathe the same atmosphere with him.* To love each other, and even our bitterest enemies; to offer our lives even for animals, to the extent of abstaining from defensive arms; to gain the greatest of victories by conquering one's self; to avoid all vices; to practice all virtues, especially humility and mildness; to be obedient to superiors, to cherish and respect parents, old age, learning, virtuous and holy men; to provide food, shelter and comfort for men and animals; to plant trees on the roads and dig wells for the comfort of travellers; such are the moral duties of Buddhists. Every *Ani* or *Bhikshuṇî* (nun) is subjected to these laws.

Numerous are the Buddhist and Lamaic saints who have been renowned for the unsurpassed sanctity of their lives and their "miracles." So Tissu, the Emperor's spiritual teacher, who consecrated Kublai-Khân, the Nadir Shâh, was known far and wide as much for the extreme holiness of his life as for the many wonders he wrought.[76] But

---

\* It sounds like injustice to Aśoka to compare him with Constantine, as is done by several Orientalists. If, in the religious and political sense, Aśoka did for India what Constantine is alleged to have achieved for the Western World, all similarity stops there.

he did not stop at fruitless miracles, but did better than that. Tissu purified completely his religion; and from one single province of Southern Mongolia is said to have forced Kublai to expel from convents 500,000 monkish impostors, who made a pretext of their profession, to live in vice and idleness. Then the Lamaists had their great reformer, the Shaberon Tsong-Kha-pa, who is claimed to have been immaculately conceived by his mother, a virgin from Koko-Nor (fourteenth century), who is another wonder-worker. The sacred tree of Kumbum, the tree of the 10,000 images, which, in consequence of the degeneration of the true faith had ceased budding for several centuries, now shot forth new sprouts and bloomed more vigorously than ever from the hair of this avatâra of Buddha, says the legend. The same tradition makes him (Tsong-Kha-pa) ascend to heaven in 1419. Contrary to the prevailing idea, few of these saints are *Hubilgans,* or Shaberons — reincarnations.

Many of the lamaseries contain schools of magic, but the most celebrated is the collegiate monastery of the Sitügtü, where there are over 30,000 monks attached to it, the lamasery forming quite a little city. Some of the female nuns possess marvellous psychological powers. We have met some of these women on their way from Lhasa to Kandy, the Rome of Buddhism, with its miraculous shrines and Gautama's relics. To avoid encounters with Moslems and other sects they travel alone by night, unarmed, and without the least fear of wild animals, *for these will not touch them.* At the first glimpses of dawn, they take refuge in caves and vihâras prepared for them by their co-religionists at calculated distances; for notwithstanding the fact that Buddhism has taken refuge in Ceylon, and nominally there are but few of the denomination in British India, yet the secret *Byauds* (Brotherhoods) and Buddhist vihâras are numerous, and every Jaina feels himself obliged to help, indiscriminately, Buddhist or Lamaist.

Ever on the lookout for occult phenomena, hungering after sights, one of the most interesting that we have seen was produced by one of these poor travelling Bhikshus. It was years ago, and at a time when all such manifestations were new to the writer. We were taken to visit the pilgrims by a Buddhist friend, a mystical gentleman born in Kashmîr, of Katchi parents, but a Buddhist-Lamaist by conversion, and who generally resides at Lhasa.

"Why carry about this bunch of dead plants?" inquired one of the Bhikshunîs, an emaciated, tall and elderly woman, pointing to a large nosegay of beautiful, fresh, and fragrant flowers in the writer's hands.

"Dead?" we asked, inquiringly. "Why they just have been gathered in the garden!"

"And yet, they are dead," she gravely answered. "To be born in this world, is this not death? See, how these herbs look when alive in the world of eternal light, in the gardens of our blessed Foh!"

Without moving from the place where she was sitting on the ground, the Ani took a flower from the bunch, laid it in her lap, and began to draw together, by large handfuls as it were, invisible material from the surrounding atmosphere. Presently a very, very faint nodule of vapor was seen, and this slowly took shape and color, until, poised in mid-air, appeared a copy of the bloom we had given her. Faithful to the last tint and the last petal it was, and lying on its side like the original, but a thousandfold more gorgeous in hue and exquisite in beauty, as the glorified human spirit is more beauteous than its physical capsule. Flower after flower to the minutest herb was thus reproduced and made to vanish, reappearing at our desire, nay, at our simple thought. Having selected a full-blown rose we held it at arm's length, and in a few minutes our arm, hand and the flower, perfect in every detail, appeared reflected in the vacant space, about two yards from where we sat. But while the flower seemed immeasurably beautified and as ethereal as the other spirit flowers, the arm and hand appeared like a mere reflection in a looking glass, even to a large spot on the forearm, left on it by a piece of damp earth which had stuck to one of the roots. Later we learned the reason why.

A great truth was uttered some fifty years ago by Dr. Francis J. Victor Broussais, when he said: "If magnetism were true, medicine would be an absurdity." Magnetism *is* true, and so we shall not contradict the learned Frenchman as to the rest. Magnetism, as we have shown, is the alphabet of magic. It is idle for anyone to attempt to understand either the theory or the practice of the latter until the fundamental principle of magnetic attractions and repulsions throughout nature is recognized.

Many so-called popular superstitions are but evidences of an instinctive perception of this law. An untutored people are taught by the experience of many generations that certain phenomena occur under fixed conditions; they give these conditions and obtain the expected results. Ignorant of the laws, they explain the fact by supernaturalism, for experience has been their sole teacher.

In India, as well as in Russia and some other countries, there is an instinctive repugnance to stepping across a man's shadow, especially if he have red hair; and in the former country, natives are extremely reluctant to shake hands with persons of another race. These are not idle fancies. Every person emits a magnetic exhalation or aura, and a man may be in perfect physical health, but at the same time his exhalation may have a morbific character for others, sensitive to such subtle influences. Dr. Esdaile and other mesmerists long since taught us that Oriental people, especially Hindus, are more susceptible than the white-skinned races. Baron Reichenbach's experiments — and, in fact, the world's entire experience — prove that these magnetic exhalations are most intense from the extremities. Therapeutic manipulations show this; hand-shaking is, therefore, most calculated to communicate antipathetic magnetic conditions, and the Hindus do wisely in keeping their ancient "superstition"—derived from Manu — constantly in mind.

The magnetism of a red-haired man, we have found, in almost every nation, is instinctively dreaded. We might quote proverbs from the Russian, Persian, Georgian, Hindôstânî, French, Turkish, and even German, to show that treachery and other vices are popularly supposed to accompany the rufous complexion. When a man stands exposed to the sun, the magnetism of that luminary causes his emanations to be projected toward the shadow, and the increased molecular action develops more electricity. Hence, an individual to whom he is antipathetic — though neither may be sensible of the fact — would act prudently in not passing through the shadow. Careful physicians wash their hands upon leaving each patient; why, then, should they not be charged with superstition, as well as the Hindus? The sporules of disease are invisible, but no less real, as European experience demonstrates. Well, *Oriental experience for a hundred centuries has shown that the germs of moral contagion linger about localities, and impure magnetism can be communicated by the touch.*

Another prevalent belief in some parts of Russia, particularly Georgia (Caucasus), and in India, is that in case the body of a drowned person cannot be otherwise found, if a garment of his be thrown into the water it will float until directly over the spot, and then sink. We have even seen the experiment successfully tried with the sacred cord of a Brahman. It floated hither and thither, circling about as though in search of something, until suddenly darting in a straight line for about fifty yards, it sank, and at that exact spot the divers brought up the body. We find this "superstition" even in America. A Pittsburg paper, of very recent date, describes the finding of the body of a young boy, named Reed, in the Monongahela, by a like method. All other means having failed, it says, "a curious superstition was employed. One of the boy's shirts was thrown into the river where he had gone down, and, it is said, floated on the surface for a time, and finally settled to the bottom at a certain place, which proved to be the resting place of the body, which was then drawn out. The belief that the shirt of a drowned person when thrown into the water will follow the body is well-spread, absurd as it appears."

This phenomenon is explained by the law of the powerful attraction existing between the human body and objects that have been long worn upon it. The oldest garment is most effective for the experiment; a new one is useless.

From time immemorial, in Russia, in the month of May, on Trinity Day, maidens from city and village have been in the habit of casting upon the river wreaths of green leaves — which each girl has to form for herself — and consulting their oracles. If the wreath sinks, it is a sign that the girl will die unmarried within a short time; if it floats, she will be married, the time depending upon the number of verses she can repeat during the experiment. We positively affirm that we have personal knowledge of several cases, two of them our intimate friends, where the augury of death proved true, and the girls *died* within twelve months. Tried on any other day than Trinity, the result would doubtless be the same. The sinking of the wreath is attributable to its being impregnated with the unhealthy magnetism of a system which contains the germs of early death; such magnetism having an attraction for the earth at the bottom of the stream. As for the rest, we are willing to abandon it to the friends of coincidence.

The same general remark as to superstition having a scientific basis applies to the phenomena produced by fakirs and jugglers, which skeptics heap into the common category of trickery. And yet, to a close observer, even to the uninitiated, an enormous difference is presented between the *kîmiyâ* (phenomenon) of a fakir, and the *baṭṭe-bâzî* (jugglery) of a trickster, and the necromancy of a *jâdûgar*, or *sâhir*, so dreaded and despised by the natives. This difference, imperceptible — nay incomprehensible — to the skeptical European, is instinctively appreciated by every Hindu, whether of high or low caste, educated or ignorant. The *kaṅgâlin*, or witch, who uses her terrible *abhichâr* (mesmeric powers) with intent to injure, may expect death at any moment, for every Hindu finds it lawful to kill her; a *hukkâbâz*, or juggler, serves to amuse. A serpent-charmer, with his *bâînî* full of venomous snakes, is less dreaded, for his powers of fascination extend but to animals and reptiles; he is unable to charm human beings, to perform that which is called by the natives *mantra phêṅknâ*, to throw spells on men by magic. But with the yogi, the sannyâsin, the holy men who acquire enormous psychological powers by mental and physical training, the question is totally different. Some of these men are regarded by the Hindus as demigods. Europeans cannot judge of these powers but in rare and exceptional cases.

The British resident who has encountered in the *maidans* and public places what he regards as frightful and loathsome human beings, sitting motionless in the self-inflicted torture of the *ûrdhwa-bâhu*, with arms raised above the head for months, and even years, need not suppose they are the wonder-working fakirs. The phenomena of the latter are visible only through the friendly protection of a Brahman, or under peculiarly fortuitous circumstances. Such men are as little accessible as the real Nautch girls, of whom every traveller talks, but very few have actually seen, since they belong exclusively to the pagodas.

It is surpassingly strange, that with the thousands of travellers and the millions of European residents who have been in India, and have traversed it in every direction, so little is yet known of that country and the lands which surround it. It may be that some readers will feel inclined not merely to doubt the correctness but even openly contradict our statement. Doubtless, we will be answered that all that it is desirable to know about India is already known. In fact this very reply was once made to us personally. That resident Anglo-Indians should not busy themselves with inquiries is not strange; for, as a British officer remarked to us upon one occasion, "society does not consider it well-bred to care about Hindus or their affairs, or even show astonishment or desire information upon anything they may see extraordinary in that country." But it really surprises us that at least travellers should not have explored more than they have this interesting realm. Hardly fifty years ago, in penetrating the jungles of the Blue or Nîlgiri Hills in Southern Hindostan, a strange race, perfectly distinct in appearance and language from any other Hindu people, was discovered by two courageous British officers who were tiger-hunting.[77] Many surmises, more or less absurd, were set on foot, and the missionaries, always on the watch to connect every mortal thing with the *Bible*, even went so far as to suggest that these people were one of the lost tribes of Israel, supporting their ridiculous hypothesis upon their very fair complexions and "strongly-marked Jewish features." The latter is perfectly erroneous, the Tôdas, as they are called, not bearing the remotest likeness to the Jewish type; either in feature, form, action, or language. They closely resemble each other, and, as a friend of ours expresses himself, the handsomest of the Tôdas resemble the statue of the Grecian Zeus in majesty and beauty of form more than anything he had yet seen among men.

Fifty years have passed since the discovery; but though since that time towns have been built on these hills, and the country has been invaded by Europeans, no more has been learned of the Tôdas than at the first. Among the foolish rumors current about these people, the most erroneous are those in relation to their numbers and to their practicing polyandry. The general opinion about them is that on account of the latter custom their number has dwindled to a few hundred families, and the race is fast dying out. We had the best means of learning much about them, and therefore state most positively that the Tôdas neither practice polyandry nor are they as few in number as supposed. We are ready to show that no one has ever seen children belonging to them.

Those that may have been seen in their company have belonged to the Badagas, a Hindu tribe totally distinct from the Tôḍas, in race, color and language, and which includes the most direct "worshippers" of this extraordinary people. We say *worshippers,* for the Badagas clothe, feed, serve, and positively look upon every Tôḍa as a divinity. They are giants in stature, white as Europeans, with tremendously long and generally brown, wavy hair and beard, which no razor ever touched from birth. Handsome as a statue of Phidias or Praxiteles, the Tôḍa sits the whole day inactive, as some travellers who have had a glance at them affirm. From the many conflicting opinions and statements we have heard from the very residents of Ootacamund and other little new places of civilization scattered about the Nîlgiri Hills, we cull the following:

"They never use water; they are wonderfully handsome and noble looking, but extremely unclean; unlike all other natives they despise jewelry, and never wear anything but a large black drapery or blanket of some woollen stuff, with a colored stripe at the bottom; they never drink anything but pure milk; they have herds of cattle but neither eat their flesh, nor do they make their beasts of labor plough or work; they neither sell nor buy; the Badagas feed and clothe them; they never use nor carry weapons, not even a simple stick; the Tôḍas can't read and won't learn. They are the despair of the missionaries and apparently have no sort of religion, beyond the worship of themselves as the Lords of Creation."*

We will try to correct a few of these opinions, as far as we have learned from a very holy personage, a *Brâhmaṇa-guru,* who has our great respect.

Nobody has ever seen more than five or six of them at one time; they will not talk with foreigners, nor was any traveller ever inside their peculiar long and flat huts, which apparently are without either windows or chimney and have but one door; nobody ever saw the funeral of a Tôḍa, nor very old men among them; nor are they taken sick with cholera, while thousands die around them during such periodical epidemics; finally, though the country all around swarms with tigers and other wild beasts, neither tiger, serpent, nor any other animal so ferocious in those parts, was ever known to touch either a Tôḍa or one of their cattle, though, as said above, they never use even a stick.

Furthermore, the Tôḍas do not marry at all. They seem few in number, for no one has or ever will have a chance of numbering them; as soon as their solitude was profaned by the avalanche of civilization —

---

* See "Indian Sketches, etc.," by W. L. O'Grady; also Appleton's *New American Cyclopaedia,* etc.

which was, perchance, due to their own carelessness — the Tôḍas began moving away to other parts as unknown and more inaccessible than the Nîlgiri Hills had formerly been; they are not born of Tôḍa mothers, nor of Tôḍa parentage; they are the children of a certain very select sect, and are set apart from their infancy for special religious purposes. Recognized by a peculiarity of complexion, and certain other signs, such a child is known as what is vulgarly termed a Tôḍa, from birth. Every third year, each of them must repair to a certain place for a certain period of time, where each of them must meet; their "dirt" is but a mask, such as a sannyâsin puts on in public in obedience to his vow; their cattle are, for the most part, devoted to sacred uses; and, though their places of worship have never been trodden by a profane foot, they nevertheless exist, and perhaps rival the most splendid pagodas — *gopuras* — known to Europeans. The Badagas are their special vassals, and — as has been truly remarked — worship them as half-deities; for their birth and mysterious powers entitle them to such a distinction.

The reader may rest assured that any statements concerning them, that clash with the little that is above given, are false. No missionary will ever catch one with his bait, nor any Badaga betray them, though he were cut to pieces. They are a people who fulfill a certain high purpose, and whose secrets are inviolable.

Furthermore, the Tôḍas are not the only such mysterious tribe in India. We have named several in a preceding chapter, but how many are there besides these, that will remain unnamed, unrecognized, and yet ever present!

What is now generally known of Shamanism is very little; and that has been perverted, like the rest of the non-Christian religions. It is called the "heathenism" of Mongolia, and wholly without reason, for it is one of the oldest religions of India. It is spirit-worship, or belief in the immortality of the souls, and that the latter are still the same men they were on earth, though their bodies have lost their objective form, and man has exchanged his physical for a spiritual nature. In its present shape, it is an offshoot of primitive theurgy, and a practical blending of the visible with the invisible world. Whenever a denizen of earth desires to enter into communication with his invisible brethren, he has to assimilate himself to their nature, *i.e.*, he meets these beings halfway, and, furnished by them with a supply of spiritual essence, endows them, in his turn, with a portion of his physical nature, thus enabling them sometimes to appear in a semi-objective form. It is a temporary exchange of natures, called theurgy. Shamans are called sorcerers, because they are said to evoke the "spirits" of the dead for purposes of necromancy. The true Shamanism — striking features of which prevailed in India in the days of Megasthenes (300 B.C.) — can no more be judged by its degenerated scions among the Shamans of Siberia, than the religion of Gautama Buddha can be interpreted by the fetishism of some of his followers in Siam and Burma. It is in the chief lamaseries of Mongolia and Thibet that it has taken refuge; and there Shamanism, if so we must call it, is practiced to the utmost limits of intercourse allowed between man and "spirit." The religion of the lamas has faithfully preserved the primitive science of *magic,* and produces as great feats now as it did in the days of Kublai-Khân and his barons. The ancient mystic formula of the King Songtsen Gampo, the "Aum mani padme hum,"* effects its wonders now as well as in the seventh century. Avalokitêśvara, highest of the three Bodhisattvas, and patron saint of Thibet, projects his shadow full in the view of the faithful, at the lamasery of Ganden, founded by him; and the luminous form of Tsong-Kha-pa, under the shape of a fiery cloudlet, that separates itself from the dancing beams of the sunlight, holds converse with a great congregation of lamas, numbering thousands; the voice descending from above, like the whisper of the breeze through foliage. Anon, say the Thibetans, the beautiful appearance vanishes in the shadows of the sacred trees in the park of the lamasery.

At Garma-Kian (the mother-cloister) it is rumored that bad and unprogressed spirits are made to appear on certain days, and *forced* to give an account of their evil deeds; they are compelled by the lamaic adepts to redress the wrongs done by them to mortals. This is what Huc naïvely terms "personating evil spirits," *i.e.,* devils. Were the skeptics of various European countries permitted to consult the accounts printed daily at Muru,† and in the "City of Spirits," of the businesslike intercourse which takes place between the lamas and the invisible world, they would certainly feel more interest in the phenomena described so triumphantly in the spiritualistic journals. At Buddha-la, or rather Potala (Buddha's Mount), in the most important of the many thousand lamaseries of that country, the sceptre of the Bodhisattva is seen floating, unsupported, in the air, and its motions regulate the actions of the community. Whenever a lama is called to account in the presence of the Superior of

---

* *Aum* (mystic Sanskrit term of the Trinity), *mani* (holy jewel), *padme* (*in* the lotus, *padma* being the name for lotus), *hum* (be it so). The six syllables in the sentence correspond to the six chief powers of nature emanating from Buddha (the abstract deity, not Gautama), who is the *seventh,* and the Alpha and Omega of being.[78]

† Muru (the pure) is one of the most famous lamaseries of Lhasa, directly in the centre of the city. There the Shaberon, the Taley-Lama, resides the greater portion of the winter months; during two or three months of the warm season his abode is at Potala. At Muru is the largest typographical establishment of the country.

the monastery, he knows beforehand it is useless for him to tell an untruth; the "regulator of justice" (the sceptre) is there, and its waving motion, either approbatory or otherwise, decides instantaneously and unerringly the question of his guilt. We do not pretend to have witnessed all this personally — we wish to make no pretensions of any kind. Suffice it, with respect to any of these phenomena, that what we have not seen with our own eyes has been so substantiated to us that we endorse its genuineness.

A number of lamas in Sikkim produce *meipo* — "miracle" — by magical powers. The late Patriarch of Mongolia, Gegen Hutugtu, who resided at Urga,[79] a veritable paradise, was the sixteenth incarnation of Gautama, therefore a Bodhisattva. He had the reputation of possessing powers that were phenomenal, even among the thaumaturgists of the land of miracles *par excellence*. Let no one suppose that these powers are developed without cost. The lives of most of these holy men, miscalled idle vagrants, cheating beggars, who are supposed to pass their existence in preying upon the easy credulity of their victims, are miracles in themselves. Miracles, because they show what a determined will and perfect purity of life and purpose are able to accomplish, and to what degree of preternatural asceticism a human body can be subjected and yet live and reach a ripe old age. No Christian hermit has ever dreamed of such refinement of monastic discipline; and the aerial habitation of a Simeon Stylites would appear child's play before the fakir's and the Buddhist's inventions of will-tests. But the theoretical study of magic is one thing; the possibility of practicing it quite another. At Drepung, the Mongolian college [80] where over three hundred magicians (*sorciers*, as the French missionaries call them) teach about twice as many pupils from twelve to twenty, the latter have many years to wait for their final initiation. Not one in a hundred reaches the highest goal; and out of the many thousand lamas occupying nearly an entire city of detached buildings clustering around it, not more than two percent become wonder-workers. One may learn by heart every line of the 108 volumes of *Kanjur*,* and still make but a poor practical magician. There is but one thing which leads surely to it, and this particular study is hinted at by more than one Hermetic writer. One, the Arabian alchemist Alipili, speaks thus: "I admonish thee whosoever thou art that desirest to dive into the inmost parts of nature, if that which thou seekest thou findest not *within thee*, thou wilt *never find it without thee*. If thou knowest not the excellency of thine own house, for what doest thou seek and search after the

---

\* The Buddhist great canon, containing 1,083 works in several hundred volumes, many of which treat of magic.

excellency of other things? . . . O MAN, KNOW THYSELF; IN THEE IS HID THE TREASURE OF TREASURES." \*

In another alchemic tract, *De manna benedicta*,† the author expresses his ideas of the philosopher's stone, in the following terms: "My intent is for certain reasons that I have, not to prate too much of the matter, which yet is but only one thing, already too plainly described; for it shows and sets down such magical and natural uses of it [the stone] as many that have had it never knew nor heard of; and such as, when I beheld them, *made my knees to tremble and my heart to shake, and I to stand amazed at the sight of them!*"

Every neophyte has experienced more or less such a feeling; but once that it is overcome, the man is an ADEPT.

Within the cloister of Tashi-Lhünpo and Si-dzang, these powers, inherent in every man, called out by so few, are cultivated to their utmost perfection. Who, in India, has not heard of the Panchen Rimpoche, the *Hutugtu* of the capital of Higher Thibet? His brotherhood of Khe-lan was famous throughout the land; and one of the most famous "brothers" was a *Peh-ling* (an Englishman)[81] who had arrived one day during the early part of this century, from the West, a thorough Buddhist, and after a month's preparation was admitted among the Khe-lans. He spoke every language, including the Thibetan, and knew every art and science, says the tradition. His sanctity and the phenomena produced by him caused him to be proclaimed a Shaberon after a residence of but a few years. His memory lives to the present day among the Thibetans, but his real name is a secret with the Shaberons alone.

The greatest of the *meipo* — said to be the object of the ambition of every Buddhist devotee — was, and yet is, the faculty of walking in the air. The famous King of Siam, Pia Metak, the Chinese, was noted for his devotion and learning. But he attained this "supernatural gift" only after having placed himself under the direct tuition of a priest of Gautama Buddha. Crawfurd and Finlayson, during their residence at Siam, followed with great interest the endeavors of some Siamese nobles to acquire this faculty.‡

Numerous and varied are the sects in China, Siam, Tartary, Thibet, Kashmîr and British India, which devote their lives to the cultivation of "supernatural powers," so called. Discussing one of such sects, the *Taossé*, Semedo says: "They pretend that by means of certain exercises and meditations one shall regain his youth, and others shall attain to be *Shên-hsien*, i.e., 'Terrestrial Beati,' in which state every desire is gratified, whilst they have the power to transport themselves from one place to

---

\* [Alipili, *Centrum Naturae Concentratum*, etc., London, 1696, pp. 78-80.]

† [London, 1680.]

‡ J. Crawfurd, *Journal of an Embassy . . . to the Courts of Siam and Cochin-China*, 1828, pp. 181-182.

another, *however distant,* with speed and facility." * This faculty relates but to the *projection* of the *astral entity,* in a more or less corporealized form, and certainly not to bodily transportation. This phenomenon is no more a miracle than one's reflection in a looking glass. No one can detect in such an image a particle of matter, and still there stands our double, faithfully representing even to each single hair on our heads. If, by this simple law of reflection, our double can be seen in a mirror, how much more striking a proof of its existence is afforded in the art of photography! *It is no reason, because our physicists have not yet found the means of taking photographs, except at a short distance, that the acquirement should be impossible to those who have found these means in the power of the human will itself, freed from terrestrial concern.*† Our thoughts are *matter,* says science; every energy produces more or less of a disturbance in the atmospheric waves. Therefore, as every man — in common with every other living, and even inert object — has an *aura* of his own emanations surrounding him; and, moreover, is enabled, by a trifling effort, to transport himself in *imagination* wherever he likes, why is it scientifically impossible that his thought, regulated, intensified and guided by that powerful magician, the educated WILL, may become corporealized for the time being, and appear to whom it likes, a faithful double of the original? Is the proposition, in the present state of science, any more unthinkable than the photograph or telegraph were less than forty years ago, or the telephone less than fourteen months ago?

If the sensitized plate can so accurately seize upon the *shadow* of our faces, then this shadow or reflection, although we are unable to perceive it, must be something substantial. And, if we can, with the help of

---

\* Semedo, *Histoire de la Chine,* III, p. 114. Cf. Yule, *The Book of Ser Marco Polo,* Vol. I, pp. 314-15; ed. 1875.

† There was an anecdote current among Daguerre's friends between 1838 and 1840. At an evening party, Madame Daguerre, some two months previous to the introduction of the celebrated Daguerrean process to the *Académie des Sciences* by Arago (January, 1839), had an earnest consultation with one of the medical celebrities of the day about her husband's mental condition. After explaining to the physician the numerous symptoms of what she believed to be her husband's mental aberration, she added, with tears in her eyes, that the greatest proof to her of Daguerre's insanity was his firm conviction that he would succeed in nailing his own shadow to the wall, or fixing it on *magical* metallic plates. The physician listened to the intelligence very attentively, and answered that he had himself observed in Daguerre lately the strongest symptoms of what, to his mind, was an undeniable proof of madness. He closed the conversation by firmly advising her to send her husband quietly and without delay to Bicêtre, the well-known lunatic asylum. Two months later a profound interest was created in the world of art and science by the exhibition of a number of pictures taken by the new process. The *shadows* were fixed, after all, upon metallic plates, and the "lunatic" proclaimed the father of photography.

optical instruments, project our *semblances* upon a white wall, at a distance of several hundred feet sometimes, then there is no reason why the adepts, the alchemists, the savants of the secret art, should not have already found out that which scientists deny today, but may discover true tomorrow, *i.e.*, how to project electrically their astral bodies, in an instant, through thousands of miles of space, leaving their material shells with a certain amount of animal vital principle to keep the physical life going, and acting within their spiritual, ethereal bodies as safely and intelligently as when clothed with the covering of flesh? There is a higher form of electricity than the physical one known to experimenters; a thousand correlations of the latter are as yet veiled to the eye of the modern physicist, and none can tell where end its possibilities.

Schott explains that "by *Sian* or *Shên-hsien* are understood in the old Chinese conception, and particularly in that of the Tao-Kiao [or Taossé] sect, persons who withdraw to the hills to lead the life of anchorites, and who have attained, either through their ascetic observances or by the power of charms and elixirs, to the possession of miraculous gifts and of terrestrial *immortality*."(?)* This is exaggerated if not altogether erroneous. What they claim, is merely their ability to prolong human life; and they can do so, if we are to believe human testimony. What Marco Polo testifies to in the thirteenth century is corroborated in our own day. "There are another class of people called *Chughi*" (Yogi), he says, "who are indeed properly *Abraiaman* [Brahmans?] . . . They are extremely long-lived, every man of them living to 150 or 200 years. They eat very little; rice and milk chiefly. And these people make use of a very strange beverage . . . a potion of sulphur and quicksilver mixed together and this they drink twice every month. This, they say, gives them long life; and it is a potion they are used to take from their childhood." † Bernier shows, says Colonel Yule, the Yogis very skillful in preparing mercury "so admirably that one or two grains taken every morning restored the body to perfect health"; ‡ and adds that the *mercurius vitae* of Paracelsus was a compound in which entered antimony and quicksilver.§ This is a very careless statement, to say the least, and we will explain what we know of it.

The longevity of some lamas and Talapoins is proverbial; and it is generally known that they use some compound which "renews the old blood," as they call it. And it was equally a recognized fact with alchemists that a judicious administration, "of *aura of silver* does restore

---

* W. Schott, *Über den Buddhaismus*, etc., Berlin, 1846, p. 71.

† Col. Yule, *The Book of Ser Marco Polo*, Vol. II, pp. 351-52; ed. 1875.

‡ F. Bernier, *Voyages de Bernier*, etc., Vol. II, p. 130; Amsterdam, 1699. Cf. Yule, *op. cit.*, Vol. II, p. 356.

§ [*Paracelsi opera omnia*, II, 20; Geneva, 1658.]

health and prolongs life itself to a wonderful extent." But we are fully prepared to oppose the statements of both Bernier and Col. Yule who quotes him, that it is *mercury* or quicksilver which the Yogis and the alchemists used. The Yogis, in the days of Marco Polo, as well as in our modern times, *do use that which may appear to be quicksilver, but is not.* Paracelsus, the alchemists, and other mystics, meant by *mercurius vitae*, the living spirit of silver, the *aura* of silver, not the *argent vive*; and this *aura* is certainly not the mercury known to our physicians and druggists. There can be no doubt that the imputation that Paracelsus introduced mercury into medical practice is utterly incorrect. No mercury, whether prepared by a mediaeval fire-philosopher or a modern self-styled physician, can or ever did restore the body to perfect health. Only an unmitigated charlatan ever will use such a drug. And it is the opinion of many that it is just with the wicked intention of presenting Paracelsus in the eyes of posterity as a *quack*, that his enemies have invented such a preposterous lie.

The Yogis of the olden times, as well as modern lamas and Talapoins, use a certain ingredient with a minimum of sulphur, and a milky juice which they extract from a medicinal plant. They must certainly be possessed of some wonderful secrets, as we have seen them healing the most rebellious wounds in a few days; restoring broken bones to good use in as many hours as it would take days to do by means of common surgery. A fearful fever contracted by the writer near Rangoon, after a flood of the Irrawaddy River, was cured in a few hours by the juice of a plant called, if we mistake not, *Kukushan*,[82] though there may be thousands of natives ignorant of its virtues who are left to die of fever. This was in return for a trifling kindness we had done to a *simple mendicant*; a service which can interest the reader but little.

We have also heard of a certain water called *âb-i-hayât*, which the popular superstition thinks hidden from every mortal eye, except that of the holy sannyâsin; the fountain itself being known as the *âb-i-ḥaiwân-i*. It is more than probable though, that the Talapoins will decline to deliver up their secrets, even to academicians and missionaries; as these remedies must be used for the benefit of humanity, never for money.*

---

* No country in the world can boast of more medicinal plants than Southern India, Cochin, Burma, Siam and Ceylon. European physicians — according to time-honored practice — settle the case of professional rivalship, by treating the native doctors as quacks and empirics; but this does not prevent the latter from being often successful in cases in which eminent graduates of British and French schools of Medicine have signally failed. Native works on materia medica do not certainly contain the secret remedies known; and yet the best febrifuges have been learned by British physicians from the

At the great festivals of Hindu pagodas, at the marriage feasts of rich high castes, everywhere where large crowds are gathered, Europeans find *guṇî* — or serpent-charmers, fakirs-mesmerizers, thaum-working *sannyâsins*, and so-called "jugglers." To deride is easy — to explain, rather more troublesome — to science impossible. The British residents of India and the travellers prefer the first expedient. But let anyone ask one of these Thomases how the following results — which they cannot and do not deny — are produced. When crowds of *guṇî* and fakirs appear with their bodies encircled with cobras de capello, their arms ornamented with bracelets of *coralillos* — diminutive snakes inflicting certain death in a few seconds — and their shoulders with necklaces of *trigonocephali*, the most terrible enemy of naked Hindu feet, whose bite kills like a flash of lightning, the sceptical witness smiles and gravely proceeds to explain how these reptiles, having been thrown into cataleptic torpor, were all deprived by the *guṇî* of their fangs. "They are harmless and it is ridiculous to fear them." "Will the Sâhib caress one of my nâg?" asked once a *guṇî* approaching our interlocutor, who had been thus humbling his listeners with his herpetological achievements for a full half-hour. Rapidly jumping back — the brave warrior's feet proving no less nimble than his tongue — Captain B——'s angry answer could hardly be immortalized by us in print. Only the *guṇî*'s terrible bodyguard saved him from an unceremonious thrashing. Besides, say a word, and for a half-rupee any professional serpent-charmer will begin creeping about and summon around, in a few moments, numbers of untamed serpents of the most poisonous species, and will handle them and encircle his body with them. On two occasions in the neighborhood of Trincomalee a serpent was ready to strike at the writer, who had once nearly sat on its tail, but both times, at a rapid whistle of the *guṇî* whom we had hired to accompany us, it stopped — hardly a few inches from our body, as if arrested by lightning, and slowly sinking its menacing head to the ground, remained stiff and motionless as a dead branch, under the charm of the *kîlnâ*.*

Will any European juggler, tamer, or even mesmerizer, risk repeating just once an experiment that may be daily witnessed in India, if you know where to go to see it? There is nothing in the world more ferocious than a royal Bengal tiger. Once the whole population of a small village, not far from Dakka, situated on the confines of a jungle, was thrown

---

Hindus, and where patients, deafened and swollen by abuse of quinine, were slowly dying of fever under the treatment of enlightened physicians, the bark of the *Mârgosa,* and the *Chiretta* herb have cured them completely, and these now occupy an honorable place among European drugs.

* The Hindu appellation for the peculiar mantra or charm which prevents the serpent from biting.

into a panic at the appearance of an enormous tigress, at the dawn of the day. These wild beasts never leave their dens but at night, when they go searching for prey and for water. But this unusual circumstance was due to the fact that the beast was a mother, and she had been deprived of her two cubs, which had been carried away by a daring hunter, and she was in search of them. Two men and a child had already become her victims, when an aged fakir, bent on his daily round, emerging from the gate of the pagoda, saw the situation and understood it at a glance. Chanting a mantra he went straight to the beast, which with flaming eye and foaming mouth crouched near a tree ready for a new victim. When at about ten feet from the tigress, without interrupting his modulated prayer, the words of which no layman comprehends, he began a regular process of mesmerization, as we understood it; he made *passes*. A terrific howl which struck a chill into the heart of every human being in the place, was then heard. This long, ferocious, drawling howl gradually subsided into a series of plaintive broken sobs, as if the bereaved mother was uttering her complaints, and then, to the terror of the crowd which had taken refuge on trees and in the houses, the beast made a tremendous leap — on the holy man as they thought. They were mistaken, she was at his feet, rolling in the dust, and writhing. A few moments more and she remained motionless, with her enormous head laid on her forepaws, and her bloodshot but now mild eyes riveted on the face of the fakir. Then the holy man of prayers sat beside the tigress and tenderly smoothed her striped skin, and patted her back, until her groans became fainter and fainter, and half an hour later all the village was standing around this group; the fakir's head lying on the tigress' back as on a pillow, his right hand on her head, and his left thrown on the sod under the terrible mouth, from which the long red protruding tongue was gently licking it.

This is the way the fakirs tame the wildest beast in India. Can European tamers, with their white-hot iron rods, do as much? Of course every fakir is not endowed with such a power; comparatively very few are. And yet the actual number is large. How they are *trained* to these requirements in the pagodas will remain an eternal secret, to all except the Brahmans and the adepts in occult mysteries. The stories, hitherto considered fables, of Kṛishṇa and Orpheus charming the wild beasts, thus receive their corroboration in our day. There is one fact which remains undeniable. *There is not a single European* in India who could have, or has ever boasted of having, penetrated into the enclosed sanctuary *within* the pagodas. Neither authority nor money has ever induced a Brahman to allow an uninitiated foreigner to pass the threshold of the reserved precinct. To use authority in such a case would be equivalent to throwing a lighted taper into a powder magazine. The Hindus, mild, patient, long-suffering, whose very apathy saved the British from being driven out of the country in 1857, would raise their hundred millions of devotees as one man, at such a profanation; regardless of sects or castes, they would exterminate every Christian. The East India Company knew this well and built its stronghold on the friendship of the Brahmans, and by paying subsidy to the pagodas; and the British Government is as prudent as its predecessor. It is the castes, and non-interference with the prevailing religions, that secure its comparative authority in India. But we must once more recur to Shamanism, that strange and most despised of all surviving religions — "Spirit-worship."

Its followers have neither altars nor idols, and it is upon the authority of a Shaman priest that we state that their true rites, which they are bound to perform only once a year, on the shortest day of winter, cannot take place before any stranger to their faith. Therefore, we are confident that all descriptions hitherto given in the *Asiatic Journal* and other European works, are but guesswork. The Russians who, from constant intercourse with the Shamans in Siberia and Tartary, would be the most competent of all persons to judge of their religion, have learned nothing except the personal proficiency of these men in what they are half-inclined to believe as clever jugglery. Many Russian residents, though, in Siberia, are firmly convinced of the "supernatural" powers of the Shamans. Whenever they assemble to worship, it is always in an open space, or on a high hill, or in the hidden depths of a forest — in this reminding us of the old Druidical rites. Their ceremonies upon the occasions of births, deaths and marriages are but trifling parts of their worship. They comprise offerings, the sprinkling of the fire with spirits and milk, and weird hymns, or rather, magical incantations, intoned by the officiating Shaman, and concluding with a chorus of the persons present.

The numerous small bells of brass and iron worn by them on the priestly robe of deerskin,* or the pelt of some other animal reputed magnetic, are used to drive away the malevolent spirits of the air, a *superstition* shared by all the nations of old, including Romans, and even the Jews, whose golden bells tell the story. They have iron staves also cov-

---

* Between the bells of the "heathen" worshippers, and the bells and pomegranates of the Jewish worship, the difference is this: the former, besides purifying the soul of man with their harmonious tones, kept *evil* demons at a distance, "for the sound of pure bronze breaks the enchantment," says Tibullus (*Elegies*, I, viii, 22), and the latter explained it by saying that the sound of bells "shall be heard [by the Lord] when he [the priest] goeth in unto the holy place before the Lord, and when he cometh out, *that he die not*" (*Exodus,* xxviii, 35; *Ecclesiasticus,* xlv, 9). Thus, one sound served to keep away *evil* spirits, and the other, the Spirit of Jehovah. The Scandinavian traditions affirm that the Trolls were always driven from their abodes by the bells of the churches. A similar tradition is in existence in relation to the fairies of Great Britain.

ered with bells, for the same reason. When, after certain ceremonies, the desired crisis is reached, and "the spirit has spoken," and the priest (who may be either male or female) feels its overpowering influence, the hand of the Shaman is drawn by some occult power toward the top of the staff, which is commonly covered with hieroglyphics. With his palm pressing upon it, he is then raised to a considerable height in the air, where he remains for some time. Sometimes he leaps to an extraordinary height, and, according to the control — for he is often but an irresponsible medium — pours out prophecies and describes future events. Thus it was that, in 1847, a Shaman in a distant part of Siberia prophesied and accurately detailed the issue of the Crimean War. The particulars of the prognostication, being carefully noted by those present at the time, were all verified six years after this occurrence. Although usually ignorant of even the name of astronomy, let alone having studied this science, they often prophesy eclipses and other astronomical phenomena. When consulted about thefts and murders, they invariably point out the guilty parties.

The Shamans of Siberia are all ignorant and illiterate. Those of Tartary and Thibet — few in number — are mostly learned men in their own way, and will not allow themselves to fall under the control of spirits of any kind. The former are *mediums* in the full sense of the word; the latter, "magicians." It is not surprising that pious and superstitious persons, after seeing one of such crises, should declare the Shaman to be under demoniacal possession. As in the instances of Corybantic and Bacchantic fury among the ancient Greeks, the "spiritual" crisis of the Shaman exhibits itself in violent dancing and wild gestures. Little by little the lookers-on feel the spirit of imitation aroused in them; seized with an irresistible impulse, they dance, and become, in their turn, ecstatics; and he who begins by joining the chorus, gradually and unconsciously takes part in the gesticulations, until he sinks to the ground exhausted, and often dying.

"O, young girl, a god possesses thee! it is either Pan, or Hekatê, or the venerable Corybantes, or Cybelê that agitates thee!" the chorus says, addressing Phaedra, in Euripides.* This form of psychological epidemic has been too well known from the time of the Middle Ages to cite instances from it. The *chorea Sancti Viti* is an historical fact, and spread throughout Germany. Paracelsus cured quite a number of persons possessed of such a spirit of imitation. But he was a kabalist, and therefore accused, by his enemies, of having cast out the devils by the power of a stronger demon, which he was believed to carry about with

---

* [*Hippolytus*, 141 *et seq.*]

him in the hilt of his sword. The Christian judges of those days of horror found a better and a surer remedy. Voltaire states that, in the district of Jura, between 1598 and 1600, over 600 lycanthropes were put to death by a pious judge.

But, while the illiterate Shaman is a victim, and during his crisis sometimes sees the persons present, under the shape of various animals, and often makes them share his hallucination, his brother Shaman, learned in the mysteries of the priestly colleges of Thibet, *expels* the elementary creature, which can produce the hallucination as well as a living mesmerizer, not through the help of a stronger demon, but simply through his knowledge of the nature of the invisible enemy. Where academicians have failed, as in the cases of the Cévennois, a Shaman or a lama would have soon put an end to the epidemic.

We have mentioned a kind of carnelian stone in our possession, which had such an unexpected and favorable effect upon the Shaman's decision. Every Shaman has such a talisman, which he wears attached to a string, and carries under his left arm.

"Of what use is it to you, and what are its virtues?" was the question we often offered to our guide. To this he never answered directly, but evaded all explanation, promising that as soon as an opportunity was offered, and we were alone, he would ask the stone *to answer for himself*. With this very indefinite hope, we were left to the resources of our own imagination.

But the day on which the stone "spoke" came very soon. It was during the most critical hours of our life; at a time when the vagabond nature of a traveller had carried the writer to far-off lands, where neither civilization is known, nor security can be guaranteed for one hour. One afternoon, as every man and woman had left the *yurta* (Tatar tent), that had been our home for over two months, to witness the ceremony of the Lamaic exorcism of a *jedker*,* accused of breaking and spiriting away every bit of the poor furniture and earthenware of a family living about two miles distant, the Shaman, who had become our only protector in those dreary deserts, was reminded of his promise. He sighed and hesitated; but, after a short silence, left his place on the sheepskin, and, going outside, placed a dried-up goat's head with its prominent horns over a wooden peg, and then dropping down the felt curtain of the tent, remarked that now no living person would venture in, for the goat's head was a sign that he was "at work."

After that, placing his hand in his bosom, he drew out the little stone, about the size of a walnut, and, carefully unwrapping it, proceeded, as it

---

* An elemental daemon, in which every native of Asia believes. [Mongolian term pronounced *südger*.]

In the Judgment Hall of Asar (Osiris)—"The Weighing of the Heart"
From the *Papyrus of Ani*, British Museum.

FINAL SCENE IN THE JUDGMENT HALL—HORUS CONDUCTING ANI TO OSIRIS
From the *Papyrus of Ani*, British Museum.

appeared, to swallow it. In a few moments his limbs stiffened, his body became rigid, and he fell, cold and motionless as a corpse. But for a slight twitching of his lips at every question asked, the scene would have been embarrassing, nay — dreadful. The sun was setting, and were it not that dying embers flickered at the centre of the tent, complete darkness would have been added to the oppressive silence which reigned. We have lived in the prairies of the West, and in the boundless steppes of Southern Russia; but nothing can be compared with the silence at sunset on the sandy deserts of Mongolia; not even the barren solitudes of the deserts of Africa, though the former are partially inhabited, and the latter utterly void of life. Yet, there was the writer alone with what looked no better than a corpse lying on the ground. Fortunately, this state did not last long.

"Mahandū!" uttered a voice, which seemed to come from the bowels of the earth, on which the Shaman was prostrated. "Peace be with you . . . what would you have me do for you?"

Startling as the fact seemed, we were quite prepared for it, for we had seen other Shamans pass through similar performances. "Whoever you are," we pronounced mentally, "go to K——, and try to bring that person's *thought* here. See what that other party does, and tell . . . what we are doing and how situated."

"I am there," answered the same voice. "The old lady (*cucoana*)\* is sitting in the garden . . . she is putting on her spectacles and reading a letter."

"The contents of it, and hasten," was the hurried order while preparing notebook and pencil. The contents were given slowly, as if, while dictating, the invisible presence desired to afford us time to put down the words phonetically, for we recognized the Walachian language of which we know nothing beyond the ability to recognize it. In such a way a whole page was filled.

"Look west . . . toward the third pole of the yurta," pronounced the Tatar in his natural voice, though it sounded hollow, and as if coming from afar. "Her *thought* is here."

Then with a convulsive jerk, the upper portion of the Shaman's body seemed raised, and his head fell heavily on the writer's feet, which he clutched with both his hands. The position was becoming less and less attractive, but curiosity proved a good ally to courage. In the west corner was standing lifelike but flickering, unsteady and mist-like, the form of a dear old friend, a Roumanian lady of Walachia, a mystic by disposition, but a thorough disbeliever in this kind of occult phenomena.

---

\* Lady, or Madam, in Moldavian.

"Her thought is here, but her body is lying unconscious. We could not bring her here otherwise," said the voice.

We addressed and supplicated the apparition to answer, but all in vain. The features moved, and the form gesticulated as if in fear and agony, but no sound broke forth from the shadowy lips; only we imagined — perchance it was a fancy — hearing as if from a long distance the Roumanian words, *"Non se póte"* (it cannot be done).

For over two hours, the most substantial, unequivocal proofs that the Shaman's astral soul was travelling at the bidding of our unspoken wish, were given us. Then months later, we received a letter from our Walachian friend in response to ours, in which we had enclosed the page from the notebook, inquiring of her what she had been doing on that day, and describing the scene in full. She was sitting — she wrote — in the garden on that morning* prosaically occupied in boiling some conserves; the letter sent to her was word for word the copy of the one received by her from her brother; all at once — in consequence of the heat, she thought — she fainted, and remembered distinctly *dreaming* she saw the writer in a desert place which she accurately described, and sitting under a "gypsy's tent," as she expressed it. "Henceforth," she added, "I can doubt no longer!"

But our experiment was proved still better. We had directed the Shaman's inner *ego* to the same friend heretofore mentioned in this chapter, the Katchi of Lhasa, who travels constantly to British India and back. *We know* that he was apprised of our critical situation in the desert; for a few hours later came help, and we were rescued by a party of twenty-five horsemen who had been directed by their chief to find us at the place we were, which no living man endowed with common powers could have known. The chief of this escort was a Shaberon, an "adept" whom we had never seen before, nor did we after that, for he never left his *süme* (lamasery), and we could have no access to it. But *he was a personal friend of the Katchi.*

The above will of course provoke naught but incredulity in the general reader. But we write for those who will believe; who, like the writer, understand and know the illimitable powers and possibilities of the human astral soul. In this case we willingly believe, nay, we know, that the "spiritual double" of the Shaman did not act alone, for he was no adept, but simply a medium. According to a favorite expression of his, as soon as he placed the stone in his mouth, his "father appeared,

---

* The hour in Bucharest corresponded perfectly with that of the country in which the scene had taken place.

dragged him out of his skin, and took him wherever he wanted," and at his bidding.

One who has only witnessed the chemical, optical, mechanical, and sleight-of-hand performances of European *prestidigitateurs*, is not prepared to see, without amazement, the open-air and off-hand exhibitions of Hindu jugglers, to say nothing of fakirs. Of the mere display of deceptive dexterity we make no account, for Houdin and others far excel them in that respect; nor do we dwell upon feats that permit of confederacy, whether resorted to or not. It is unquestionably true that non-expert travellers, especially if of an imaginative turn of mind, exaggerate inordinately. But our remark is based upon a class of phenomena not to be accounted for upon any of the familiar hypotheses. "I have seen," says a gentleman who resided in India, "a man throw up into the air a number of balls numbered in succession from one upwards. As each went up — and there was no deception about their going up — the ball was seen clearly in the air, getting smaller and smaller, till it disappeared altogether out of sight. When they were all up, twenty or more, the operator would politely ask which ball you wanted to see, and then would shout out, 'No. 1,' 'No. 15,' and so on, as instructed by the spectators, when the ball demanded would bound to his feet violently from some remote distance . . . These fellows have very scanty clothing, and apparently no apparatus whatever. Then, I have seen them swallow three different colored powders, and then, throwing back the head, wash them down with water, drunk, in the native fashion, in a continuous stream from a *loṭâ*, or brass-pot, held at arm's length from the lips, and keep on drinking till the swollen body could not hold another drop, and water overflowed from the lips. Then these fellows, after squirting out the water in their mouths, have spat out the three powders onto a clean piece of paper, dry and unmixed." *

In the eastern portion of Turkey and Persia have dwelt, from time immemorial, the warlike tribes of the Kurdistan. This people of purely Indo-European origin, and without a drop of Semitic blood in them (though some ethnologists seem to think otherwise), notwithstanding their brigand-like disposition, unite in themselves the mysticism of the Hindu and the practices of the Assyrio-Chaldean magians, vast portions of whose territory they have helped themselves to, and will not give up, to please either Turkey or even all Europe.† Nominally Mohammedans of the sect of Omar, their rites and doctrines are purely magical and magian. Even those who are Christian Nestorians, are Christians but in name. The Kaldany, numbering

---

* Capt. W. L. D. O'Grady: "Indian Sketches, etc.," in *Commercial Bulletin*, April 14, 1877.

† Neither Russia nor England succeeded in 1849 in forcing them to recognize and respect the Turkish [as distinct] from the Persian territory.

and with their two Patriarchs, are undeniably rather Manichaeans than Nestorians. Many of them are Yezîdis.

One of these tribes is noted for its fire-worshipping predilections. At sunrise and sunset, the horsemen alight and, turning towards the sun, mutter a prayer; while at every new moon they perform mysterious rites throughout the whole night. They have a tent set apart for the purpose, and its thick, black, woolen fabric is decorated with weird signs, worked in bright red and yellow. In the centre is placed a kind of altar, encircled by three brass bands, to which are suspended numerous rings by ropes of camel's hair, which every worshipper holds with his right hand during the ceremony. On the altar burns a curious, old-fashioned silver lamp, a relic found possibly among the ruins of Persepolis.* This lamp, with three wicks, is an oblong cup with a handle to it, and is evidently of the class of Egyptian sepulchral lamps, once found in such profusion in the subterranean caves of Memphis, if we may believe Kircher.† It widened from its end toward the middle, and its upper part was of the shape of a heart; the apertures for the wicks forming a triangle, and its centre being covered by an inverted heliotrope attached to a gracefully curved stalk proceeding from the handle of the lamp. This ornament clearly bespoke its origin. It was one of the sacred vessels used in sun-worship. The Greeks gave the *heliotrope* its name from its strange propensity to ever incline towards the sun. The ancient Magi used it in their worship; and who knows but Darius had performed the mysterious rites with its triple light illuminating the face of the king-hierophant!

If we mention the lamp at all, it is because there happened to be a strange story in connection with it. What the Kurds do, during their nocturnal rites of lunar-worship, we know but from hearsay; for they conceal it carefully, and no stranger could be admitted to witness the ceremony. But every tribe has one old man, sometimes several, regarded as "holy beings," who know the past, and can divulge the secrets of the future. These are greatly honored, and generally resorted to for information in cases of theft, murders or danger.

Travelling from one tribe to the other, we passed some time in company with these Kurds. As our object is not autobiographical, we omit all details that have no immediate bearing upon some occult fact, and even of these, have room but for a few. We will then simply state

---

* Persepolis is the Persian Istakhr, northeast of Shiraz; it stood on a plain now called Merdasht, at the confluence of the ancient Medus and the Araxes, now Pulwâr and Bend-emir.

† *Oedipus aegyptiacus*, etc., Vol. III (1654): Theatrum hieroglyphicum, p. 544.

that a very expensive saddle, a carpet, and two Circassian daggers, richly mounted and chiselled in gold, had been stolen from the tent, and that the Kurds, with the chief of the tribe at the head, had come, taking Allah for their witness that the culprit could not belong to their tribe. We believed it, for it would have been unprecedented among these nomadic tribes of Asia, as famed for the sacredness in which they hold their guests, as for the ease with which they plunder and occasionally murder them, when once they have passed the boundaries of their *aûl*.

A suggestion was then made by a Georgian belonging to our caravan to have resort to the light of the *kudian* (sorcerer) of their tribe. This was arranged in great secrecy and solemnity, and the interview appointed to take place at midnight, when the moon would be at its full. At the stated hour we were conducted to the above-described tent.

A large hole, or square aperture, was managed in the arched roof of the tent, and through it poured in vertically the radiant moonbeams, mingling with the vacillating triple flame of the little lamp. After several minutes of incantations, addressed, as it seemed to us, to the moon, the conjurer, an old man of tremendous stature, whose pyramidal turban touched the top of the tent, produced a round looking glass, of the kind known as "Persian mirrors." Having unscrewed its cover, he then proceeded to breathe on it for over ten minutes, and wipe off the moisture from the surface with a package of herbs, muttering incantations the while *sotto voce*. After every wiping the glass became more and more brilliant, till its crystal seemed to radiate refulgent phosphoric rays in every direction. At last the operation was ended; the old man, with the mirror in his hand, remained as motionless as if he had been a statue. "Look, Hanoum . . . look steadily," he whispered, hardly moving his lips. Shadows and dark spots began gathering, where one moment before nothing was reflected but the radiant face of the full moon. A few more seconds, and there appeared the well-known saddle, carpet and daggers, which seemed to be rising as from a deep, clear water, and becoming with every instant more definitely outlined. Then a still darker shadow appeared hovering over these objects, which gradually condensed itself, and then came out, as visibly as at the small end of a telescope, the full figure of a man crouching over them.

"I know him!" exclaimed the writer. "It is the Tatar who came to us last night, offering to sell his mule!"

The image disappeared, as if by enchantment. The old man nodded assent, but remained motionless. Then he muttered again some strange words, and suddenly began a song. The tune was slow and monotonous, but after he had sung a few stanzas in the same unknown tongue, without changing either rhythm or tune, he pronounced, *recitative*-like, the following words, in his broken Russian:

"Now, Hanoum, look well, whether we will catch him — the fate of the robber — we will learn this night," etc.

The same shadows began gathering, and then, almost without transition, we saw the man lying on his back, in a pool of blood, across the saddle, and two other men galloping off at a distance. Horror-stricken, and sick at the sight of this picture, we desired to see no more. The old man, leaving the tent, called some of the Kurds standing outside, and seemed to give them instructions. Two minutes later, a dozen horsemen were galloping off at full speed down the side of the mountain on which we were encamped.

Early in the morning they returned with the lost objects. The saddle was all covered with coagulated blood, and of course abandoned to them. The story they told was, that upon coming in sight of the fugitive, they saw disappearing over the crest of a distant hill two horsemen, and upon riding up, the Tatar thief was found dead upon the stolen property, exactly as we had seen him in the magical glass. He had been murdered by the two banditti, whose evident design to rob him was interrupted by the sudden appearance of the party sent by the old *Kudian*.

The most remarkable results are produced by the Eastern "wise men" by the simple act of breathing upon a person, whether with good or evil intent. This is pure mesmerism; and among the Persian dervishes who practice it, the animal magnetism is often reinforced by that of the elements. If a person happens to stand facing a certain wind, there is always danger, they think; and many of the "learned ones" in occult matters can never be prevailed upon to go at sunset in a certain direction from whence blows the wind. We have known an old Persian from Baku,* on the Caspian Sea, who had the most unenviable reputation for *throwing spells* through the timely help of this wind, which blows but too often at that town, as its Persian name itself shows.† If a victim, against whom the wrath of the old fiend was kindled, happened to be

---

* We have twice assisted at the strange rites of the remnants of that sect of fire-worshippers known as the Ghebers, who assemble from time to time at Baku, on the "field of fire." This ancient and mysterious town is situated near the Caspian Sea. It belongs to Russian Georgia. About twelve miles northeast from Baku stands the remnant of an ancient Gheber temple, consisting of four columns, from whose empty orifices issue constantly jets of flame, which gives it, therefore, the name of Temple of the Perpetual Fire. The whole region is covered with lakes and springs of naphtha. Pilgrims assemble there from distant parts of Asia, and a priesthood, worshipping the divine principle of fire, is kept by some tribes, scattered hither and thither about the country.

† *Badkube* — literally "a gathering of winds."

facing this wind, he would appear, as if by enchantment, cross the road rapidly, and breathe in his face. From that moment, the latter would find himself afflicted with every evil — he was under the spell of the "evil eye."

The employment of the human breath by the sorcerer, as an adjunct for the accomplishment of his nefarious purpose, is strikingly illustrated in several terrible cases recorded in the French annals — notably those of several Catholic priests. In fact, this species of sorcery was known from the oldest times. The Emperor Justinian prescribed the severest penalties against such as should employ sorcery to do violence to chastity and excite unlawful passion.* Augustine (*City of God*) warns against it; Jerome, Gregory of Nazianzus, and many other ecclesiastical authorities, lend their denunciation of a crime not uncommon among the clergy. Basset † relates the case of the *curé* of Peifane, who accomplished the ruin of a highly-respected and virtuous lady parishioner, the Dame du Lieu, by resort to sorcery, and was burned alive for it by the Parliament of Grenoble. In 1611, a priest named Goffridy was burned by the Parliament of Provence for seducing a penitent at the confessional, named Madelaine de la Palud, *by breathing upon her*, and thus throwing her into a delirium of sinful love for him.

The above cases are cited in the official report of the famous case of Father Girard, a Jesuit priest of very great influence, who in 1731 was tried before the Parliament of Aix, France, for the seduction of his parishioner, Mlle. Catherine Cadière, of Toulon, and certain revolting crimes in connection with the same. The indictment charged that the offence was brought about by resort to sorcery. Mlle. Cadière was a young lady noted for her beauty, piety, and exemplary virtues. Her attention to her religious duties was exceptionally rigorous, and that was the cause of her perdition. Father Girard's eye fell upon her, and he began to maneuver for her ruin. Gaining the confidence of the girl and her family by his apparent great sanctity, he one day made a pretext to blow his breath upon her. The girl became instantly affected with a violent passion for him. She also had ecstatic visions of a religious character, stigmata, or blood-marks of the "Passion," and hysterical convulsions. The long-sought opportunity of seclusion with his penitent finally offering, the Jesuit breathed upon her again, and before the poor girl recovered her senses, his object had been accomplished. By sophistry and the excitation of her religious fervor, he kept up this illicit relation for months, without her suspecting that she had done anything wrong. Finally, however, her eyes were opened, her parents informed, and the priest was arraigned. Judgment was rendered October 12th, 1731. Of twenty-five judges,

---

\* *Codex Justinianus,* Liber IX, Titulus XVIII, "De maleficis, etc.", Statutum 4.[83]

† [J.-G. Basset, *Plaidoyez et Arrests de la Cour de Parlement,* etc., Paris, 1645, Vol. I, bk. v, tit. 19, ch. 6, p. 108.]

twelve voted to send him to the stake. The criminal priest was defended by all the power of the Society of Jesus, and it is said that a million francs were spent in trying to suppress the evidence produced at the trial. The facts, however, were printed in a work (in 5 vols., 16mo), now rare, entitled *Recueil Général des Pièces contenues au Procèz du Père Jean-Baptiste Girard, Jésuite,* etc., etc.*

We have noted the circumstance that, while under the sorcerous influence of Father Girard, and in illicit relations with him, Mlle. Cadière's body was marked with the *stigmata* of the *Passion,* viz.: the bleeding wounds of thorns on her brow, of nails in her hands and feet, and of a lance-cut in her side. It should be added that the same marks were seen upon the bodies of six other penitents of this priest, viz.: Mesdames Guyol, Laugier, Grodier, Allemande, Batarelle, and Reboul. In fact, it became commonly remarked that Father Girard's handsome parishioners were strangely given to ecstasies and *stigmata!* Add this to the fact that, in the case of Father Goffridy, above noted, the same thing was proved, upon surgical testimony, to have happened to Mlle. de la Palud, and we have something worth the attention of all (especially spiritualists) who imagine these *stigmata* are produced by pure spirits. Barring the agency of the Devil, whom we have quietly put to rest in another chapter, Catholics would be puzzled, we fancy, despite all their infallibility, to distinguish between the *stigmata* of the sorcerers and those produced through the intervention of the Holy Ghost or the angels. The Church records abound in instances of alleged diabolical imitations of these signs of saintship, but, as we have remarked, the Devil is out of court.

By those who have followed us thus far, it will naturally be asked, to what practical issue this book tends; much has been said about magic and its potentiality, much of the immense antiquity of its practice. Do we wish to affirm that the occult sciences ought to be studied and practiced throughout the world? Would we replace modern spiritualism with the ancient magic? Neither; the substitution could not be made, nor the study universally prosecuted, without incurring the risk of enormous public dangers. At this moment, a well-known spiritualist and lecturer on mesmerism is imprisoned on the charge of raping a subject whom he had hypnotized. A sorcerer is a public enemy, and mesmerism may most readily be turned into the worst of sorceries.

We would have neither scientists, theologians nor spiritualists turn practical magicians, but all to realize that there were true science, profound religion, and genuine phenomena before this modern era. We would

---

* See also *Magic and Mesmerism,* a novel reprinted by the Harpers, thirty years ago. [London, 1843.]

that all who have a voice in the education of the masses should first know and then *teach* that the safest guides to human happiness and enlightenment are those writings which have descended to us from the remotest antiquity; and that nobler spiritual aspirations and a higher average morality prevail in the countries where the people take their precepts as the rule of their lives. We would have all to realize that magical, *i. e.*, spiritual, powers exist in every man, and those few to practice them who feel called to teach, and are ready to pay the price of discipline and self-conquest which their development exacts.

Many men have arisen who had glimpses of the truth, and fancied they had it all. Such have failed to achieve the good they might have done and sought to do, because vanity has made them thrust their personality into such undue prominence as to interpose it between their believers and the *whole* truth that lay behind. The world needs no sectarian church, whether of Buddha, Jesus, Mohammed, Swedenborg, Calvin, or any other. There being but ONE Truth, man requires but one church — the Temple of God within us, walled in by matter but penetrable by anyone who can find the way; *the pure in heart see God.*

*The trinity of nature is the lock of magic, the trinity of man the key that fits it.* Within the solemn precincts of the sanctuary, the SUPREME had and has no name. It is unthinkable and unpronounceable; and yet every man finds in himself his god. "Who art thou, O fair being?" inquires the disembodied soul, in the *Khordah-Avesta*, at the gates of Paradise. "I am, O soul, *thy good and pure thoughts*, thy works and thy *good law* . . . thy angel . . . and thy god." * The man, or the soul, is reunited with ITSELF, for this "Son of God" is one with him; it is his own mediator, the *god* of his human soul and his "Justifier." "*God not revealing himself immediately to man, the spirit is his interpreter,*" says Plato in the *Symposium.*†

Besides, there are many good reasons why the study of magic, except in its broad philosophy, is nearly impracticable in Europe and America. Magic being what it is, the most difficult of all sciences to learn experimentally — its acquisition is practically beyond the reach of the majority of white-skinned people; and that, whether their effort is made at home or in the East. Probably not more than one man in a million of European blood is fitted — either physically, morally or psychologically — to become a practical magician, and not one in ten million would be found endowed with all these three qualifications as required for the work. Civilized nations lack the phenomenal powers of endurance, both mental and physical, of the Easterners; the favoring temperamental idiosyncrasies of the Orientals are utterly wanting in them. In the Hindu, the

---

* [*Khordah-Avesta*, yasht xxii, § 10 *et seq.*]
† [202E-203A.]

Arabian, the Thibetan, an intuitive perception of the possibilities of occult natural forces in subjection to human will, comes by inheritance; and in them, the physical senses as well as the spiritual are far more finely developed than in the Western races. Notwithstanding the notable difference of thickness between the skulls of a European and a Southern Hindu, this difference, being a purely climatic result due to the intensity of the sun's rays, involves no psychological principles. Furthermore, there would be tremendous difficulties in the way of *training*, if we can so express it. Contaminated by centuries of dogmatic superstition, by an ineradicable — though quite unwarranted — sense of superiority over those whom the English term so contemptuously "niggers," the white European would hardly submit himself to the practical tuition of either Copt, Brahman or Lama. To become a neophyte, one must be ready to devote himself heart and soul to the study of mystic sciences. Magic — most imperative of mistresses — brooks no rival. Unlike other sciences, a theoretical knowledge of formulae without mental capacities or soul powers is utterly useless in magic. The spirit must hold in complete subjection the combativeness of what is loosely termed educated reason, until facts have vanquished cold human sophistry.

Those best prepared to appreciate occultism are the spiritualists, although, through prejudice, until now they have been the bitterest opponents to its introduction to public notice. Despite all foolish negations and denunciations, their phenomena are real. Despite, also, their own assertions, they are wholly misunderstood by themselves. The totally insufficient theory of the constant agency of disembodied human spirits in their production has been the bane of the *Cause*. A thousand mortifying rebuffs have failed to open their reason or intuition to the truth. Ignoring the teachings of the past, they have discovered no substitute. We offer them philosophical deduction instead of unverifiable hypothesis, scientific analysis and demonstration instead of undiscriminating faith. Occult philosophy gives them the means of meeting the reasonable requirements of science, and frees them from the humiliating necessity of accepting the oracular teachings of "intelligences," which as a rule have less intelligence than a child at school. So based and so strengthened, modern phenomena would be in a position to command the attention and enforce the respect of those who carry with them public opinion. Without invoking such help, spiritualism must continue to vegetate, equally repulsed — not without cause — both by scientists and theologians. In its modern aspect, it is neither a science, a religion, nor a philosophy.

Are we unjust; does any intelligent spiritualist complain that we have misstated the case? To what can he point us but to a confusion of theories, a tangle of hypotheses mutually contradictory? Can he affirm that spiritualism, even with its thirty years of phenomena, has any defensible philosophy; nay, that there is anything like an established method that is generally accepted and followed by its recognized representatives?

And yet, there are many thoughtful, scholarly, earnest writers among the spiritualists, scattered the world over. There are men who, in addition to a scientific mental training and a reasoned faith in the phenomena *per se*, possess all the requisites of leaders of the movement. How is it then, that, except throwing off an isolated volume or so, or occasional contributions to journalism, they all refrain from taking any active part in the formation of a system of philosophy? This is from no lack of moral courage, as their writings well show. Nor because of indifference, for enthusiasm abounds, and they are sure of their facts. Nor is it from lack of capacity, because many are men of mark, the peers of our best minds. It is simply for the reason that, almost without exception, they are bewildered by the contradictions they encounter, and wait for their tentative hypotheses to be verified by further experience. Doubtless this is the part of wisdom. It is that adopted by Newton, who, with the heroism of an honest, unselfish heart, withheld for seventeen years the promulgation of his theory of gravitation, only because he had not verified it to his own satisfaction.

Spiritualism, whose aspect is rather that of aggression than of defense, has tended toward iconoclasm, and so far has done well. But, in pulling down, it does not rebuild. Every really substantial truth it erects is soon buried under an avalanche of chimeras, until all are in one confused ruin. At every step of advance, at the acquisition of every new vantage-ground of FACT, some cataclysm, either in the shape of fraud and exposure, or of premeditated treachery, occurs, and throws the spiritualists back powerless because they *cannot* and their invisible friends *will* not (or perchance can less than themselves) make good their claims. Their fatal weakness is that they have but *one* theory to offer in explanation of their challenged facts — the agency of *human disembodied spirits,* and the medium's complete subjection to them. They will attack those who differ in views with them with a vehemence only warranted by a better cause; they will regard every argument contradicting their theory as an imputation upon their common sense and powers of observation; and they will positively refuse even to argue the question.

How, then, can spiritualism ever be elevated to the distinction of a science? This, as Professor Tyndall shows, includes three absolutely necessary elements: observation of facts; induction of laws from these facts; and verification of those laws by constant practical experience. What experienced observer will maintain that spiritualism presents either one of these three elements? The medium is not uniformly surrounded by such test conditions that we may be sure of the facts; the inductions from the supposed facts are unwarranted in the absence of such verification; and, as a corollary, there has been no sufficient verification of those hypotheses by experience. In short, the prime element of accuracy has, as a rule, been lacking.

That we may not be charged with desire to misrepresent the position of spiritualism, at the date of this present writing, or accused of withholding credit for advances actually made, we will cite a few passages from the London *Spiritualist* of March 2, 1877. At the fortnightly meeting, held February 19, a debate occurred upon the subject of "Ancient Thought and Modern Spiritualism." Some of the most intelligent Spiritualists of England participated. Among these was Mr. W. Stainton Moses, M.A., who has recently given some attention to the relation between ancient and modern phenomena. He said: "Popular Spiritualism is not scientific; it does very little in the way of scientific verification. Moreover, exoteric Spiritualism is, to a large extent, devoted to presumed communion with personal friends, or to the gratification of curiosity, or the mere evolution of marvels . . . The truly esoteric science of Spiritualism is very rare, and not more rare than valuable. To it we must look for the origination of knowledge which may be developed exoterically . . . We proceed too much on the lines of the physicist; our tests are crude and often illusory; we know too little of the Protean power of spirit. Here the ancients were far ahead of us, and can teach us much. We have not introduced any certainty into the conditions — a necessary prerequisite for true scientific experiment. This is largely owing to the fact that our circles are constructed on no principle. . . . We have not even mastered the elementary truths which the ancients knew and acted on, *e. g.*, the isolation of mediums. We have been so occupied with wonder-hunting that we have hardly tabulated the phenomena or propounded one theory to account for the production of the simplest of them . . . We have never faced the question, What is the intelligence? This is the great blot, the most frequent source of error, and here we might learn with advantage from the ancients. There is the strongest disinclination among spiritualists to admit the possibility of the truth of occultism. In this respect they are as hard to convince as is the outer world of Spiritualism. Spiritualists start with a fallacy, viz., that all phenomena are caused by the action of departed human spirits; *they have not looked into the powers of the incarnate human spirit;* they do not know the extent to which spirit acts, how far it reaches, what it underlies."

Our position could not be better defined. If Spiritualism has a future, it is in the keeping of such men as Mr. Stainton Moses.

Our work is done — would that it were better done! But, despite our inexperience in the art of bookmaking, and the serious difficulty of writing in a foreign tongue, we hope we have succeeded in saying some things that will remain in the minds of the thoughtful. The enemies of truth have been all counted, and all passed in review. Modern science, powerless to satisfy the aspirations of the race, makes the future a void, and bereaves man of hope. In one sense, it is like the Baital Pachisi,[84] the Hindu vampire of popular fancy, which lives in dead bodies, and feeds but on the rottenness of matter. The theology of Christendom has been rubbed threadbare by the most serious minds of the day. It is found to be, on the whole, subversive of, rather than promotive of, spirituality and good morals. Instead of expounding the rules of divine law and justice, it teaches but *itself*. In place of an ever-living Deity, it preaches the Evil One, and makes him indistinguishable from God Himself! "Lead us not into temptation" is the aspiration of Christians. Who, then, is the tempter? Satan? No; the prayer is not addressed to him. It is that tutelary genius who hardened the heart of Pharaoh, put an evil spirit into Saul, sent lying messengers to the prophets, and tempted David to sin; it is — the *Bible*-God of Israel!

Our examination of the multitudinous religious faiths that mankind, early and late, have professed, most assuredly indicates that they have all been derived from one primitive source. It would seem as if they were all but different modes of expressing the yearning of the imprisoned human soul for intercourse with supernal spheres. As the white ray of light is decomposed by the prism into the various colors of the solar spectrum, so the beam of divine truth, in passing the *three-sided* prism of man's nature, has been broken up into vari-colored fragments called RELIGIONS. And, as the rays of the spectrum, by imperceptible shadings, merge into each other, so the great theologies that have appeared at different degrees of divergence from the original source, have been connected by minor schisms, schools, and offshoots from the one side or the other. Combined, their aggregate represents one eternal truth; separate, they are but shades of human error and the signs of imperfection. The worship of the Vedic *pitris* is fast becoming the worship of the spiritual portion of mankind. It but needs the right perception of things objective to finally discover that the only world of reality is the subjective.

What has been contemptuously termed Paganism, was ancient wisdom replete with Deity; and Judaism and its offspring, Christianity and Islamism, derived whatever of inspiration they contained from this ethnic parent. Pre-Vedic Brahmanism and Buddhism are the double source from which all religions sprang; Nirvâna is the ocean to which all tend.

For the purposes of a philosophical analysis, we need not take account of the enormities which have blackened the record of many of the world's religions. True faith is the embodiment of divine charity; those who minister at its altars, are but human. As we turn the bloodstained pages of ecclesiastical history, we find that, whoever may have been the hero, and whatever costumes the actors may have worn, the plot of the tragedy has ever been the same. But the Eternal Night was in and behind all, and we pass from what we see to that which is invisible to the eye of sense. Our fervent wish has been to show true souls how they may lift aside the curtain, and, in the brightness of that Night made Day, look with undazzled gaze upon the UNVEILED TRUTH.

THE END

## NOTES BY THE EDITOR

*[These Notes correspond with the superior numbers in the text of Volume II at pages indicated in parentheses.]*

¹(Page iii) There exists some evidence that this brief Preface to Vol. II of *Isis Unveiled* was, possibly, partly written by Dr. Alexander Wilder, and most likely corrected or altered by H.P.B. herself. In her letter to Dr. Wilder, dated December 6, 1876, she says:

> "My dear Doctor, can you do me a favor to write me half a page or so of a 'Profession of Faith,' to insert in the first page or pages of Part II? Just to say briefly and eloquently that it is not against Christ or the *Christ*-religion, that I battle. Neither do I battle against any *sincere, true* religion, but against theology and Pagan Catholicism. If you write me this I will know how to make variations on this theme without becoming guilty of false notes in your eyes and the sight of Bouton. Please do; you can do in three minutes . . ."

²(Page 20) Johannes Tritheim (actually Heidenberg) was born at Trittenheim, near Trier, Germany, February 1, 1462, and died at Würzburg, December 13, 1516. He was a Humanist and became in 1485 abbot of Sponheim, near Kreuznach. At a later date he was abbot of Schottenkloster St. Jacob, at Würzburg. This scholarly individual, known best by his Latinized name of Trithemius, was the author of a number of important works, such as: *De scriptoribus ecclesiasticis* (1494); *Steganographia* (1500, and later ed. of 1606, 1621, 1635); *Annales Hirsangiensis* (1514); *Annales de origine Francorum* (unfinished); *Polygraphia* (1518).

³(Page 21) The Councils referred to in the text are at best minor convocations, concerning which there is scarcity of information. The Council of Agde was held in September, 506; the one at Orleans, known as the first

642                                    ISIS UNVEILED

Council in that city, was held in 511; the date of the one at Auxerre, known as the Synod of Auxerre, varies between 570 and 590, according to various authorities. The Council held at Aenham (or Enham), which was a village for disabled soldiers some two miles north of Andover, N. W. Hampshire, presents an even greater uncertainty as to date; according to Mansi, it was held between 1100 and 1116, while Hefele gives its date as 1009. The period during which Alexander III was Pope is 1159-1181. *Vide* Mansi, *Sacrorum conciliorum nova et amplissima collectio*, Florence, 1759-98, t. XIX, col. 308; *Dictionnaire de théologie catholique*, III, 886; V, 2188; C. J. von Hefele, *Conciliengeschichte*, Freiburg, 1855-74, Vol. IV.


⁴(Page 26) As instances of *unexpected* discoveries along the line of ancient mystical traditions and writings, mention may be made of the Gnostic Coptic Manuscripts discovered in 1945 near the site of the ancient townlet Chenoboskion, in Egypt, at the foot of the mountain called Gebel et-Tarif; and the now famous texts of the Dead Sea Scrolls found in 1947 and later in several caves near the site of an ancient ruin called Khirbet Qumran.


⁵(Page 28) Antoninus was a Neo-Platonist who lived early in the 4th century of our era and had a school at Canopus, near Alexandria in Egypt. He devoted himself wholly to those who sought his instruction. He could clearly see the end of the cycle as far as the so-called Pagan religions were concerned, and predicted that after his death all the temples of the gods would be changed into tombs. His moral conduct is said to have been exemplary. The only data we seem to have about Antoninus are to be found in the *Lives of Sophists* written by Eunapius, a Greek Sophist and historian of Sardis born in A.D. 347. He speaks of Antoninus in his "Life of Aedesius," (p. 68, ed. Antw., 1568), a distinguished disciple of Iamblichus.


⁶(Page 29) Extensive research by several competent scholars failed to identify *Ishmonia*, a locality which may be known today by some different name.


⁷(Page 29) Paulus Orosius was a Spanish presbyter, a native of Tarragona who flourished in the later part of the fourth and in the fifth century of our era. He was the author of *Historiarum adversus Paganus Libri VII*, dedicated to St. Augustine, at whose suggestion the task was undertaken.

8 (Page 31) The term *Asgartha* or *Asgarta* occurs also in the XXVIIth Chapter of H.P.B.'s story *From the Caves and Jungles of Hindostan*, and is spoken of there as "the city of the Sun" supposedly located in ancient days on the site of the present city of Jâjmau. She says that "according to the ancient *Purânas*" Asgarta "was built by the Sons of the Sun, two centuries after the conquest of the island Lankâ by King Râma, in other words 5,000 years B.C., according to the reckoning of the Brâhmanas." She does not indicate what particular *Purâna* she has in mind. The original use of this term has, therefore, not been substantiated and demands further research. However, the most interesting aspect of it is that it bears such a remarkable resemblance to the Norse mythological term *Asgard* or *Asgarth*, properly *Âsgarthr* (from *âss*, a divine being, and *garthr*, an enclosure), which occurs in both the Older and the Younger *Edda*. The *Aesir* (pl. of *âss*) were the chief gods of the Teutonic pantheon and included such figures as Odin, Thor, Balder and others. *Asgard* was the abode or citadel of the gods, situated at the zenith and which could be reached only by the bridge *Bifrost*, the rainbow. It is also represented as rising from the center of *Midgard*. In Asgard is the *Ithavoll*, where the gods hold assembly at the base of the tree Yggdrasill. There are in Asgard *twelve* mansions or realms of the gods, a legend which contains an echo of an esoteric truth concerning the inner structure of the Universe. Whether this legend has its counterpart, or indeed origin, in any of the known *Purânas*, is something left to be ascertained by some competent scholar.

9 (Page 46) Reference here is to Major-General Vans Kennedy (1784-1846), a very remarkable man and scholar, author of two important works: *Researches into the Origin and Affinity of the principal Languages of Asia and Europe*, London, 1828, 4to.; and *Researches into the Nature and Affinity of Ancient and Hindu Mythology*, London, 1831, 4to. Kennedy's ideas concerning early Buddhist influence on nascent Christianity are strongly supported by Gen. J. G. R. Forlong in his essay "Through what Historical Channels did Buddhism Influence Early Christianity," published in *The Open Court* for Aug. 18 and Sept. 1 and 18, 1887.

At the turn of the century, Dr. Heinrich Zimmer, famous professor of Indology at the Universities of Heidelberg, Oxford and Columbia, and other scholars, such as G. Bühler and Vincent A. Smith, had the opportunity, during their studies in India, to visit an old monastery in the Barabar and Nagarjuni Hills. They were allowed to enter a sacred cave where they saw — probably as the first Western scholars — the *Edict XIII* of Emperor Aśoka cut into the rock. Pertinent information on this may be had by consulting Bühler's article, "The Barabar and Nagarjuni Hill Cave Inscriptions of Aśoka and Daśaratha," in *The Indian Antiquary*, XX (1891), pp. 361 *et seq.*; *The Edicts of Aśoka* by V. A. Smith (London, 1909), p. 20; and Zimmer's two works: *Aśoka, the Buddhist Emperor of India* (Oxford, 1909), and *Philosophies of India* (published posthumously in 1951), chapter on "The Great Buddhist Kings."

[10] (Page 53) This footnote embodies an unfortunate error. Either H.P.B. herself or someone else who may have been helping her editorially at the time, confused Bishop Cyril of Alexandria with Cyril, Bishop of Jerusalem. The former, whose year of birth is not known, after having been a presbyter of the church at Alexandria, succeeded to the episcopal chair on the death of Theophilus, A.D. 412. Cyril of Jerusalem, on the other hand, was probably born around A.D. 315, and was chosen to fill the episcopal chair in A.D. 351, in the reign of Constantius. The accusations against Cyril, as they appear in H.P.B.'s footnote, apply to Cyril of Jerusalem and not to Cyril of Alexandria. However, the latter was a man whose character was anything but "saintly." He was openly accused of simony, dishonesty, and the prostitution of his office to personal ends, and Neander (*Gen. Hist. of Christian Religion and Church*, IV, 133ff.) pictures him as violent, tyrannical, a hypocrite and a liar. Isidor, Bishop of Pelusium, in a letter addressed to Cyril himself (*Epistles*, No. 370) wrote: "Let not the punishment, which you deem it necessary to inflict on mortal men *on account of personal grievances*, fall upon the living church. Prepare not the way for perpetual division of the church under the *pretense of piety*." It follows, therefore, that the last sentence of H.P.B.'s footnote is partially warranted, though the footnote as a whole is not.

[11] (Page 57) For the sake of accuracy, it would be preferable to alter this passage to read thus:

". . . a man named Wood, a sorcerer, who said [on the authority of one William Neville, an inmate of the Cardinal's house] that '*My Lord Cardinale had suche a rynge that whatsomevere he askyd of the Kynges grace that he hadd yt*'; adding that '*Master Cromwell, when he . . . was servaunt in my lord cardynales housse,*' [was reported to owe his advancement to such arts and his association with Wood, who further acknowledged himself to have] '*rede many bokes, and specyally the boke of Salomon . . . and studied mettells and what vertues they had after the canon of Salomon*' . . ."

NOTES BY THE EDITOR 645

¹²(Page 69) Strictly speaking, *kaṅgâlîn* in Hindî means a pauper. It could be also the name of a person or of a local goddess. H.P.B. uses the same term in her story "From the Caves and Jungles of Hindostan."

¹³(Page 74) Giacomo da Varaggio (ca. 1230 - ca. 1298) was an Italian chronicler born at Varazze, near Genoa, who joined the Dominicans in 1244. He was provincial of Lombardy from 1267 to 1286, and represented his own province at the Councils of Lucca (1288) and Ferrara (1290). Early in 1292 he was consecrated archbishop of Genoa where he distinguished himself by his effort to appease the civil discords in that city. Apart from his *Chronicle* of the history of Genoa, he wrote the *Golden Legend* — one of the most popular religious works of the middle ages, which is a collection of the legendary lives of the greater saints, ornamented with much curious information of rather doubtful authenticity.

*Vide* also J. Bollandus, S. J., *Acta Sanctorum*, Augusti, tom. XXXV, pp. 409, 410.

¹⁴(Page 80) Walter Richard Cassels (1826-1907) was an English theological critic who published in 1874 an anonymous work in two volumes entitled *Supernatural Religion; an Inquiry into the Reality of Divine Revelation,* impugning the credibility of miracles and the authenticity of the New Testament; it was a work of high scholarship which aroused instant attention. By 1875, the work had gone through six editions. A third volume was added in 1877, and a revised edition of the complete work appeared in 1879. H.P.B. had a very high regard for Cassels' work and used its many arguments upon innumerable occasions.

¹⁵(Page 81) The date of 1876, as given by H.P.B., is confirmed by her letter to Dr. Alexander Wilder written December 6, 1876, on the day when Col. Olcott was in the small town of Washington, Washington Co., Pennsylvania, attending the cremation of Baron de Palm's body. See also *Old Diary Leaves*, I, 166 *et seq.*

¹⁶(Page 88) Ostanes, Osthanes or Hosthanes, with varied spelling, was an ancient occultist and teacher regarding whom no reliable information is at hand. He may have been a Mede. The most comprehensive analysis of all known traditions about him may be found in the monumental *Real-Encyclopaedie der Classischen Alterthumswissenschaft,* by Pauly-Wissowa, s.v. *Ostanes.*

17(Page 92) PTR RF SU means "what (or who) is this?" The XVIIth Chapter of the *Book of the Dead* first appeared in the XIth Dynasty. It makes a statement at the end of which comes the question: "what (or who) is this?" Then comes the first explanation, often followed by the words KY DJED, "another saying," followed by another explanation. There may be still another explanation for the same statement, etc. Budge in his Engl. transl. of the *Book of the Dead* (Introduction, p. xcvii) says: "Like many sections of the *Book of the Dead* this chapter was composed by the Priests of Heliopolis, and it represented their views about the nature of the Gods and it proves that various opinions as to the meaning of passages in it existed among the learned."

18(Page 120) *Koleda* or *Kolyada* (possibly related to the Latin *calendae*) is a term used in the Southern and Western portions of Russia in connection with the Christmas festival and the period between the latter and January 6th; *kolyadovanye* or *kolyadovat'* is the term used for the custom of going to various houses at Christmas and the New Year, carrying a star, congratulating people, singing and exchanging food, sometimes soliciting donations; *kolyadka* is the name for the songs which are being sung on these occasions; the above-mentioned terms have many variations in spelling from one province to another.

19(Page 123) Wrongly ascribed to Clement of Alexandria, who, however, describes the Basilidean *doctrine* as in part occupied with "divine teaching." Cf. *Stromateis*, VIII, xi, "he the Gnostic conceives truly and grandly in virtue of his reception of divine teaching"; see also King, *The Gnostics*, etc., p. 258 (ed. 1887).

20(Page 142) Xanthus (or Xanthos) was a celebrated Lydian historian, older than Herodotus, who is said to have been indebted to the work of Xanthus, which is known as the *Four Books of Lydian History*, only fragments of which have come down to our time.

21(Page 146) The original Latin of this passage from the *Metamorphoses*, XI, 23. is as follows:

"Accessi confinium mortis et calcato Proserpinae limine per omnia vectus elementa remeavi; nocte media vidi solem candido coruscantem lumine, deos inferos et deos superos accessi coram et adoravi de proxumo."

22 (Page 150) This Ambrosius should not be confused with the Church Father by that name. Theseus Ambrosius was Teseo Ambrogio, an Italian Orientalist born at Pavia in 1469, and who died there in 1540. He was one of the first Italians who devoted himself to Oriental studies. Pope Leo X encouraged him in this. He knew some eighteen languages, and must have been somewhat of a genius since early childhood. In the British Museum Catalogue he is listed under Albonesius (Theseus Ambrosius). He wrote a work, now very rare, entitled *Introductio in Chaldaicam linguam, Syriacam atque Armenicam et decem alias linguas*, Pavia, 1539, 4to.

As to the statement of Aelius Lampridius concerning Alexander Severus as having in his chapel an image of Christ, it is actually not Lampridius himself who says so, but "a contemporary writer" whose name is not mentioned. See Chapter XXIX of Lampridius' account in *Scriptores Historiae Augustae*, Vol. II (Loeb Classical Series).

23 (Page 158) There seems to be an error here. There is no authority known for *kris* meaning "sacred." It way be due to some confusion on Jacolliot's part. Kṛishṇa means black, dark, dark-blue, and it is the accepted form of the name of one of the avatâras of Vishṇu. Kṛishṇa-paksha is the term used for the dark half of the month, during which the moon is on the wane.

24 (Page 177) The author of the Preface referred to was David Casley, and the Catalogue was published in London in 1734, 4to.

25 (Page 177) The New Testament published by Erasmus at Basle in 1516, under the title of *Novum Instrumentum*, consisted of the Greek text and was accompanied with a Latin rendering of his own, in which he aimed at giving the meaning of the Greek without blindly following the Latin *Vulgate*, the only form in which the N.T. had been current in Western Europe for centuries. This rendering of Erasmus, one of the greatest humanists of the time, together with his annotations and prefaces to the several books, make his edition the first great monument of modern Biblical study.

26 (Page 182) In connection with this reference to Jerome's *Opera* and the subject-matter in the text itself, the student is referred to Vol. VIII, pp. 233-38, of H.P.B.'s *Collected Writings*, wherein the Compiler has given a comprehensive explanation of both the text and the references involved. These explanations help to clarify a few uncertainties in H.P.B.'s text and quotes.

27 (Page 186) As well as in J. J. Grynaeus, *Monumenta S. Patrum Orthodoxographa,* etc. (Basileae, 1569, fol.), Vol. I, tom. ii, pp. 643ff.

28 (Page 189) Consult Volume VIII, pp. 232-33, of the *Collected Writings,* for comprehensive information about this work attributed to Tertullian, wherein the Latin text and a complete English translation may be found.

29 (Page 192) The *Codex Sinaiticus* derives its name from the place of its discovery, the famous monastery of St. Catherine on Mount Sinai, founded in the middle of the 6th century A.D. by the Emperor Justinian. In May, 1844, a German Biblical scholar, Constantine Tischendorf (1815-74), travelling in search of ancient MSS., rescued 43 leaves of this 4th century MS. of portions of the *Old Testament* in Greek from a basket containing tattered parchments which were to be burnt as rubbish. On his third visit to the monastery, in 1859, he was shown a much more voluminous MS. containing not only portions of the *O.T.* but the *New Testament* complete. After various difficulties had been surmounted, he was permitted to take it along with the specific intention of presenting it as a gift to Emperor Alexander II of Russia who had conferred numerous benefits upon the monastery. Eventually, the Imperial Government paid the monastery 9,000 roubles for this MS. and it was deposited in the Imperial Public Library at St. Petersburg. Some years after the Russian Revolution, the Soviet Government, after attempts to dispose of it in America, opened up negotiations with the British Museum, and in 1933 the MS. was purchased for the sum of 100,000 pounds sterling with the aid and approval of the British Government. It is now incorporated in the collections as Additional Manuscript 43725.

Consult for a detailed account: *The Codex Sinaiticus and the Codex Alexandrinus,* a booklet issued by the Trustees of the British Museum, 2nd ed., London, 1955.

30 (Page 193) We have to bear in mind, however, the reported words of Jesus as found in *John* x, 30, and xvii, 11, 22, wherein his identity or oneness with the Father is definitely spoken of.

31 (Page 209) H.P.B. very often uses Greek and Gnostic forms of Egyptian names, which were also largely used by the Egyptologists of her day. *Thmei* is *Maât,* about whom a large book could be written without exhausting the subject. As the Goddess of Truth and Justice, she is always present in the Judgment Scenes, and in some papyri is actually shown extending her arms in welcome to the deceased, acquitted in the Court of

Osiris. Her emblem is the feather against which the heart (conscience) of the deceased is weighed, and also a wedge-shaped object. She is called the daughter of Râ, wife of Râ, mother of Râ, and is identified with both Isis and Hathor (sometimes appearing in H.P.B.'s writings as Athyr and Athar). Apart from her personification of a Goddess, *Maât* signifies the inflexible, unalterable Law of Nature which cannot be broken or changed; the ultimate Truth, Right and Justice.

32(Page 217) Also called Atrekhasis, and Utnapishtim, in the Tablets.

33(Page 231) Consult in this connection: Isaac Myer, *Qabbalah*, Philadelphia, 1888, pp. 227-28; A. H. Sayce, *Records of the Past*, III, p. 121; J. Kitto, *Cyclop. of Biblical Literature*, 1876, Vol. I, p. 484; F. Lenormant, *Chaldean Magic*, 1878, pp. 39, 47, 121.

34(Page 236) It is probable that what is meant here is *Erythini* ('Ερυθίνοι), a place on the coast of Paphlagonia, mentioned by Homer (*Iliad*, ii, 855) and by Strabo (xi, 545).

35(Page 239) The general trend of the arguments brought forward by Priestley are of that nature, but no actual wording such as quoted by H.P.B. has been found in his works treating on the subject of early Christianity.

36(Page 248) There is some error here, as reference to the Old Testament shows clearly that the passage spoken of may be found in *Isaiah*, lxiv, 4. In this case Cassels text quoted by H.P.B. is at fault.

37(Page 255) Reference is here to Jane Elizabeth (ca. 1807-1881), daughter of Admiral Sir Henry Digby, and second wife of Edward Law, 1st Earl of Ellenborough (1790-1871) whom she married September 15, 1824, and from whom she was divorced in 1830 by act of Parliament. The reason for this was her adultery with Prince Schwartzenburg in 1828. The Earl had a child by her who died in 1830. Her third marriage was to Sheikh Midjwal el Mezrab, *i.e.*, of the tribe of Mezrab, a branch of the Anazeh Bedouins at Damascus. Jane Elizabeth was a woman of great beauty and linguistic and artistic talents; she had an adventurous career in Europe, and later resided for many years in camp in the desert near Damascus. Cf. *Revue Britannique*, March and April, 1873, quoting an account of her by her friend Isabel (Lady) Burton.

38 (Page 267) Reference here is to Origen's *Commentaria in Evangelium Joannis*, tom. II, p. 64 (*vide* Migne, *Patrologia graeca*, XI, col. 72), where he quotes a passage from the *Gospel according to the Hebrews:* "Modo accepit me mater mea sanctus Spiritus, uno capillorum meorum et me in montem magnum Thabor portavit." — "My mother, the Holy Ghost took me by one of my hairs and carried me onto the great mountain Thabor."

39 (Page 278) The complete title of this work is: *Über die Auflösung der Arten durch natürliche Zuchtwahl oder die Zukunft des organischen Reiches*. It was published anonymously by Julius Wilhelm Albert Wigand at Hanover, in 1872, and consists of 72 pages only. (*Vide* Dr. M. Holzmann and Dr. Hanns Bohatta, *Deutsches Anonymen Lexikon*, Hildesheim, 1961, Band V, 1851-1908.)

40 (Page 286) There is some confusion at this point of the text, and no explanation seems possible with regard to the usage of the term *Zion* in connection with Buddhism.

41 (Page 291) By the rivers of 'Iraq and especially in the alluvial land of Al-Khaur watered by the Tigris and the Euphrates, and in the lowland of Persia along the Karun, there still dwells the remnant of a handsome people who call themselves *Mandaiia*, Mandaeans ("gnostics"), and speak a dialect of Aramaic. When the armies of Islam vanquished the Sassanids, they were already there and in such numbers that the *Qur'ân* granted them protection as "people of a book," calling them *Ṣâbiya* (Sabians). They still cling to this name, both in its literary form and as the vernacular aṣ-Ṣubba. This word means "submergers" and refers to their baptism (*masbuta*) and frequent self-immersion. In the ninth book of his *Fihrist al-'ulûm*, Al-Nadîm, who wrote in the tenth century, calls them *al-Mughtasilah*, "the self-ablutionists."

Those amongst the community who possess secret knowledge are called *Nasuraiia*, Naṣoraeans (or, if the heavy ṣ is written as z, Nazorenes). The ignorant or semi-ignorant laity are called "Mandaeans, *Mandaiia*," which originally meant "gnostics." When a man becomes a priest he leaves "Mandaeanism" and enters *termiduta*, "priesthood." Even then he is not considered as having attained to true enlightenment, for this, called *nasirutha*, is reserved for a very few. Those possessed of its secrets may call themselves Naṣoraeans, and this term indicates today not only one who observes strictly all the rules of ritual purity, but one who understands the secret doctrine.

The principal sacred books of the Mandaeans are the *Ginzâ* ("Treasure") and the *John-Book* written in a peculiar type of Aramaic.

Consult the following sources:

*Ginzâ: der Schatz oder das grosse Buch der Mandäer.* German transl. by M. Lidzbarski. Göttingen: Vanderhoeck u. Ruprecht, 1925.

*Das Johannesbuch der Mandäer.* Text and transl. by M. Lidzbarski. Giessen: Töpelmann, 1915. 2 vols.

*Codex Nazaraeus, Liber Adami Appellatus.* Syriac text and Latin transl. by M. Norberg, Lund, 1815-16, 3 vols.

*Thesaurus Liber Magnus vulgo "Liber Adami" appellatus, opus Mandaeorum summi ponderis.* Descripsit et edidit, H. Petermann. Leipzig: Weigel, 1867. 2 vols.

*The Secret Adam.* A study of Nasoraean Gnosis, by E. S. Drower. Oxford: Clarendon Press, 1960.

42 (Page 293) *Araśa-maram* is the Tamil word for the *Ficus religiosa*. The Skt. for *Araśa* is *Aśvattha*; *maram* in Tamil is tree. This tree, however, is not the Banyan. The latter is the *Ficus Indica* called in Skt. *vaṭa*. Both belong to the same family, but it is the Aśvattha or Araśa which is usually held sacred.

43 (Page 294) Placidus de Titis (or Titi) was a monk of the monastery on Montis Oliveti, born at Perugia, and who flourished in the middle of the 17th century. He was the author of several works, two of which, now very rare, are in the British Museum. In his *Physiomathematica* (Francisci Vigoni, Milan, 1675, 4to.), Section entitled "De Viribus Astrorum in Sublunaria," liber I, cap. 13, p. 79, he says: Quod color ceruleus, et croceus, quales sunt in Jove, & Venere, qui colores mixti sunt ex albo, & aureo, indicent naturam temperatam ex calore, & humiditate, in ceruleo quidem praedominante calore, in croceo humiditate . . ."

In his *Tabulae Primi Mobilis . . . Juxta principia . . . in sua Cœlesti Philosophia exposita*, etc. (Vatavii, Typis Pauli Frambotti, 1657, 4to.), the 20th thesis says: "Alii colores in Astris sunt causae qualitatum in specie, ut ceruleus, & croceus, quales sunt in Jove, & Venere, qui mixti sunt ex albo & aureo, indicant naturam temperatam ex calore, & humiditate, in ceruleo quidem predominante calore, in croceo humiditate, ideoque hi duo Planetae ambo dant bonum utile, & delectabile." In M. Sibly's revision of John Cooper's English translation entitled *Astronomy and Elementary Philosophy* (W. Justins, London, 1789, 8vo.), page 131 renders this passage as follows: "The other colors in the stars are the cause of specific qualities; so the blue and yellow, such as are in Jupiter and Venus, which are a mixture of white and gold, give signs of a temperate nature between heat and cold, or moisture; in the blue, heat is predominant . . ."

44 (Page 303) This is apt to lead to a misunderstanding unless quoted in full. The text in *Romans* iii, 7-8, reads thus: "For if the truth of God hath more abounded through my lie unto his glory; why yet am I also judged as a sinner? And not *rather* (as we be slanderously reported, and as some affirm that we say), Let us do evil, that good may come? whose damnation is just."

45 (Page 312) A. L. Rawson was an American engraver, philologist, archaeologist and writer, born at Chester, Vt., Oct. 15, 1829; he died at New York in November, 1902. He illustrated various works by other writers and scholars and took part in the archaeological work conducted on Cyprus by Gen. Luigi Palma di Cesnola. Very little is known of the personal life of Rawson, but there is little doubt that he was well versed in various mystical doctrines and secret societies. Rawson published in the pages of Frank Leslie's *Popular Monthly* (Vol. XXXIII, Feb., 1892, pp. 199-208) an illustrated account of H.P.B. titled "Madame Blavatsky: A Theosophical Occult Apology" which contains a number of interesting points.

46 (Page 322) This is a date which may have had some special meaning to Jacolliot from whom H.P.B. copied it; but it does not coincide with any historically established facts concerning the origin and spread of Buddhism.

47 (Page 328) Consult *The Loeb Classical Library*'s edition of Josephus' *Jewish Antiquities*, Bk. XVIII, 63-64 (pp. 48-51 in *Loeb*), wherein, in addition to the Greek and English text and translation, may be found valuable notes concerning this passage and the divergent views of various scholars as to its genuineness.

48 (Page 335) This is unfortunately an erroneous statement. Philo Judaeus resided mainly at Alexandria, long "a favorite abode of the learned Jews" (Yonge, *The Works of Philo Judaeus*, Preface), but on at least one occasion visited Jerusalem.

49 (Page 352) Comprehensive information concerning the Order of the Jesuits may be found in Volume IX of H.P.B.'s *Collected Writings*, in her famous article "Theosophy or Jesuitism?", and in the Compiler's Notes appended thereto. There is considerable overlapping between the above-mentioned article and the text as found in *Isis Unveiled*.

50 (Page 367) Egyptologists differ among themselves in regard to this subject. Many points remain uncertain in the interpretation of hieroglyphic texts. Some have pointed out the following sequence of constituent portions of man: 1. *Khat*—physical body; 2. *Sahu*—the *Khat* transformed by mummification. 3. *Ka*—the "double" (also "material soul"); 4. *Ba*—the soul; 5. *Akh*—glorified spirit; 6. *Khabit*—the shadow; 7. *Ren*—the name; 8. *Sekhem*—the power; 9. *Ib*—the heart, or conscience.

One of the most valuable studies in this field of research is a serial article by Franz Lambert entitled *Weisheit der Aegypter* (Wisdom of the Egyptians) and published in the *Sphinx* (Leipzig, Germany; ed. by Dr. Wm. Hübbe-Schleiden), Vol. VII, January, February, April and June, 1889, with diagrams and tables.

51 (Page 368) In Letter No. XXV in *The Mahatma Letters to A. P. Sinnett* (p. 196; 3rd ed., p. 193), received Feb. 2, 1883, Master K. H. inserts a footnote saying:

"See *Isis*, Vol. 2, pp. 368 and 369 — the word *Soul* standing there for 'Spiritual' Soul, of course, which, whenever it leaves a person 'Soulless' becomes the cause of the fifth principle (Animal Soul) sliding down into the eighth sphere."

52 (Page 369) The title *La Manifestation à la Lumière* is merely Champollion's rendering in French of the Egyptian descriptive title: "Reu nu pert em hru" which means "Chapter of the Coming Forth [into] the Day." These texts have come to be known as the *Book of the Dead*, and the latter name is merely a translation of the Arabic "Kitâb al-Maggitun," under which name any papyrus roll found with the mummies was sold by the Egyptian tomb-robbers.

53 (Page 388) Comprehensive biographical information concerning Charles Sotheran and his role in the formative years of The Theosophical Society may be found in Volume I of H. P. Blavatsky's *Collected Writings*, pp. 126, 237 fn., 311-12, 369 fn., 433, 525-28.

54 (Page 399). Consult in connection with the *Book of Jasher* the Editor's Note No. 26, on page 637 of Volume I of *Isis Unveiled*.

55 (Page 406) The text of the *Ars poetica* of Horace does not disclose any such statement at all. There may be some error here in the reference given.

56 (Page 411) There is considerable uncertainty about this name. In *The Secret Doctrine*, II, 97, this term occurs as the title of a work. As far as is known, there is no such work. Dîrghatamas, meaning "long night," was the name of a Vedic sage to whom a few of the *Rigveda* Hymns are attributed. He was born blind and the *Mahâbhârata* relates (Adiparva, 1st Section) that at the request of King Bali he produced five sons by his wife Sudeshṇâ.

57 (Page 430) This undoubtedly refers to the listing of Joannes Uri who compiled a work entitled *Catalogus Codicum Manuscriptorum Orientalium Bibliothecae Bodleianae*, 1781, in three volumes, which contains in Vol. I a listing of Hebrew MSS. Entry No. 37 therein is a Codex of the year 1104. In Adolf Neubauer's *Catalogue of the Hebrew Manuscripts in the Bodleian Library and in the College Libraries of Oxford*, etc., 1886, 1906, in two volumes, which is a chronological listing, this Codex appears as No. 1 and is marked ARCH. SELD. A. 47, which seems to indicate that it was acquired by the Bodleian from the collection of John Selden.

At the present time, the situation with regard to the earliest Hebrew manuscripts of the Old Testament has radically changed, on account of the discovery of the so-called Dead Sea Scrolls.

58 (Page 440) The references to *Chronicles* seem to be erroneous, and the reference to *Proverbs* is not borne out by the text itself.

⁵⁹(Page 443) Corrected to 1800 B.C. by Sayce, in *Chald. Account of Genesis*, but put by Hilprecht (in 1904) at 3800 B.C. (*Babyl. Exped.*, Series D, I, p. 249). Cf. *The Secret Doctrine*, Vol. I, p. 320, footnote.

⁶⁰(Page 446) The term *orant* has puzzled a number of theosophical students and seems to have been a stumbling block to one or two earlier Editors of *Isis Unveiled*. Some have speculated as to whether this was the name of some god or deity. The word is derived from the Latin *orans, -antis*, pres. part. of *orare*, to pray. In ancient Greek art it is used for a female figure in the posture of prayer. In early Christian art, it was a figure, usually a female one, standing with outstretched arms as in prayer. Such figures are very common in catacombs, and the attitude was regarded as especially significant because it recalled the position of Christ on the cross. Such figures may also be met with in Egyptian symbolism.

⁶¹(Page 449) Cf. report of Dr. S. Langdon in the *Proceedings of the Society of Biblical Archaeology*, Vol. XXXVI (1914), pp. 188-98.

⁶²(Page 463) The square brackets in this sentence have been added in accordance with H. P. B.'s own corrections in *The Secret Doctrine*, Vol. II, p. 129, where she quotes this passage from *Isis Unveiled*.

⁶³(Page 491) *Patah* means "door" and *potoh* "to open." According to Jastrow (*Dict. of the Targumim*, etc., Vol. II, p. 1252), the term *Pethahia* is the name of a priest and a priestly family; Pethahia had the supervision of the sacrificial birds, and was named Pethahia because he explained words and interpreted them.

⁶⁴(Page 500) If the reader reads this paragraph on the Egyptian judgment scene immediately following the first paragraph at the top of page 494, he will see that it definitely belongs there. Somehow or other, it became misplaced in the MS. of *Isis Unveiled* or during the progress of setting it up. The terms *Turu* and *On-ati*, however, have not been identified.

⁶⁵(Page 509) Apart from their exoteric mythological aspect, Râhu and Ketu are respectively the ascending and descending nodes of the Moon's orbit, *i.e.*, the points where the latter intercepts the ecliptic. They are fixed points on the orbit of the Moon, even though they move in relation to the

656   ISIS UNVEILED

earth on account of the motion of the orbit itself. They may be termed the head and the tail of the Dragon, if we take into account the fact that the Moon has been called a Dragon by the Chinese. Unless these facts are taken into consideration, the footnote does not carry any definite meaning, the terms "fixed stars" and "constellation" being somewhat misleading.

⁶⁶(Page 564) Thomas Parr, "Old Parr," is said to have been born at Winnington in 1483. The chief source of information about him is John Taylor's *Old, Old, Very Old Man*, a six-penny pamphlet published in 1635 and frequently reprinted since. Parr spent most of his life in the small holding at his birthplace which he inherited from his father. He married for the first time when he was eighty years old, and for the second time when he was 122. Thirty years later he was taken to London by Thomas Howard, second Earl of Arundel, and was presented to the King in September, 1635. The change of life and the plethora of rich diet proved fatal to him, and he died on Nov. 14, 1635 at Lord Arundel's house. An autopsy was performed on the following day by the famous William Harvey who found all the chief organs of Old Parr in healthy condition. Parr was subsequently buried in the south transept of Westminster Abbey where there is an inscription on the stone floor which gives his dates and states that he was 152 years old and lived under ten Kings and Queens.

Consult *Dict. of National Biography*, where detailed bibliographical data and source material may also be found.

⁶⁷(Page 564) Eznik Kulpskiy (also spelled Yeznik) was an Armenian theologian and writer of the 5th century; he was Bishop of Bagrevand and Arsharunik and author of *Refutation of the Sects*, the Armenian text of which was published at Constantinople in 1763, in Smyrna in 1772, and in Venice in 1826 and 1863. A French translation appeared in Paris in 1853, and a German one in 1927. The work may be found in *Patrologia Orientalis*, Vol. XXVIII, Nos. 3-4. Although H. P. B. speaks of it as a manuscript, it is most likely that she means the above-mentioned work.

⁶⁸(Page 568) The dominion of Tarkov had an independent existence within Daghestan from the eighth century to 1867 when it became the district of Temir-Khân-Shura within the Russian Empire. Throughout the many centuries of its history, and its wars with various invading armies, Tarkov was ruled by individuals bearing the title of *Shamhal* and whose dominion extended along the shores of the Caspian Sea, between the rivers of Koysu and Orusay-Bulak.

NOTES BY THE EDITOR 657

Shamsudin-Khân was the last of the Shamhals of Tarkov who retired from active participation in the affairs of the dominion on April 20, 1867, when the Russian administration took over. He continued, however, to exercise a good deal of influence owing to his upstanding character and great abilities. Apparently H. P. B. had met him somewhat prior to his retirement, when his rulership was shared by a Russian Resident officer.

[69] (Page 572) Lady Hester Lucy Stanhope was the eldest daughter of Charles, viscount Mahon (afterwards 3rd Earl Stanhope), by his first wife, Lady Hester Pitt, sister of the famous William Pitt. She was born March 12, 1776, and lived at her father's seat of Chevening, Kent, until early in 1800, when her wayward disposition drove her to her grandmother's house. In 1803, she was made the chief of the household of her uncle, William Pitt, where she soon became his most trusted confidant. She was possessed of wit, beauty and business talent. After Pitt's death in 1806, she stayed for a while in London and in Wales. Irked by the restrictions of society, she left England for the Levant in 1810, and after many wanderings settled among the Druses on Mt. Lebanon, where the Pasha of Acre ceded her the ruins of a convent and the village of Dahar-Juni. From a group of houses she built there, surrounded with a wall like a fortress, she wielded an almost absolute authority over some of the surrounding districts, maintained by her commanding character and by the belief that she possessed the gift of divination. She intrigued against the British consuls and exercised some influence over Ibrahim Pasha himself. As time went on, she adopted Eastern manners and customs, practiced astrology and is said to have believed in "transmigration" of souls, whatever was actually meant by this expression. She incurred many debts and the bulk of her pension was appropriated by the Government of England to settle the claims. She felt this very keenly and shut herself in her castle, the gate of which she walled up. She died there on June 23, 1839, and was buried in her own garden. In 1845, there appeared three volumes of *Memoirs of the Lady Hester Stanhope as related by herself in Conversations with her Physician* (Dr. Charles Lewis Meryon, who was with her for a number of years); these were followed by another three volumes of *Travels* from the same pen. Altogether, Lady Stanhope was a most eccentric and strange character.

[70] (Page 591) There is considerable confusion in the last few lines of this footnote, the cause of which is difficult to ascertain. Suffice it to point out that the *Pûrva-mîmânsâ-sûtra* is also known as *Jaiminisûtra,* and the philosophy of the Uttara-Mîmânsâ or Vedânta is set forth mainly in the *Brahmasûtras* of Bâdarâyana and Śamkarâchârya's famous *bhâshyas* or commentaries upon them. The name of Vyâsa is not connected with Vedânta at all. Consult Bibliographies, s.v. *Mîmânsâ.*

⁷¹(Page 598) Ladak (or Ladakh) and Baltistan are provinces of Kashmîr, and the name of Ladak belongs primarily to the broad valley of the Upper Indus, but includes also several surrounding districts in political connection with it. It is bounded North by the Kuenlun range and the slopes of the Karakorum, Northwest and West by Baltistan which has been known as Little Tibet, Southwest by Kashmîr proper, South by what used to be British Himâlayan territory, and East by the Tibetan provinces of Ngari and Rudog. The entire region is very high, the valleys of Rupshu and the Southeast being 15,000 feet, and the Indus near Leh some 11,000 feet, while the average height of the surrounding ranges is some 20,000 feet. Leh (11,550 feet) is the capital of Ladak, and the road to Leh from Srinagar lies up the lovely Sind valley to the sources of the river at the Pass of Zoji La (11,580 feet) in the Zaskar range. From Leh there are several routes to Tibet, the best known being that from the Indus valley to the Tibetan plateau, by the Chang La, to Lake Pangong and Rudog (14,000 ft.).

It would be an error to call this region Central Tibet, as has apparently been done by some writers.

⁷²(Page 599) *Chakhars* are a tribe of Mongols who are leading a nomadic life along the Great Wall North of Suanhwa and Tatung in China. In H.P.B.'s days, they were ruled by Officials appointed by Peking. There is a great deal of Shamanism among them, although in various respects they have adopted many Chinese customs and beliefs.

⁷³(Page 603) Most likely Miss Nadyezhda Andreyevna de Fadeyev (1829-1919), sister of H.P.B.'s mother. She was only two years older than H.P.B. and they engaged in quite an extensive correspondence through the years.

⁷⁴(Page 603) It is most likely that H.P.B. has in mind the mountains known as Wutai Shan or Wu-t'ai Shan, in the Northeast part of the Shansi province of China, close to the border of Inner Mongolia. They are situated at about thirty miles Northeast of the town of Wutai, and their highest peak is 9,974 feet high. This region has been considered sacred by the Mongolians, and the mountains contain many lamaseries frequented by pilgrims. It is not clear what particular one of these lamaseries H.P.B. has in mind.

⁷⁵(Page 604) The enormous Kuren monastery is at Urga (*Hurae* in Mongolian), now known as Ulan Bator, a city in Outer Mongolia, on an

CREESHNA trampling on the HEAD of the crushed SERPENT.

*a Corruption of the Grand primæval Tradition preserved in India*
*To his Grace John, Lord Archbishop of Canterbury, this wonderful additional*
*Testimony to the Mosaic Records is with true respect and gratitude inscribed by*

KRISHNA AND SERPENT
From Thomas Maurice, *The History of Hindostan*, Vol. II,
Part I, frontispiece.

# THE SERPENT BITING CREESHNA'S HEEL.

*another Corruption of the Grand Primaeval Tradition.*
*To the Right Rev.ᵈ George, Lord Bishop of Lincoln, this powerful additional*
*attestation to the truth of the Mosaic Records is gratefully & most respectfully inscribed*
*by*
*T. M.*

KRISHNA AND SERPENT
From Thomas Maurice, *The History of Hindostan*, Vol. II,
Part III, frontispiece.

affluent of the Tola River. For many years past, it was a holy city among Mongols and the residence of one of the so-called "living Buddhas," the third in veneration after the Panchen Lama and the Taley Lama of Tibet. He was Djibtzun-damba-Hutugtu who was supposed to be the tulku of Darapata (1573-1635), a Buddhist teacher.

*Bogdo-ula* is a sacred mountain, part of the enormous Tian-Shan system, and is believed by the Mongolians to be the abode of divine beings. Ulan Bator is situated in the valley of the Tôla River, to the north of this mountain.

76 (Page 608) There is some confusion in this sentence which may never be satisfactorily clarified. Nadir Shâh, a Persian ruler of the 18th century bears no relation to this whatsoever, and the introduction of his name into the sentence must be considered an obvious error the cause of which can hardly be ascertained at this late date.

77 (Page 613) They were Kindersley and Whish, two English land surveyors in the pay of the East India Company, who, in September, 1818, started on a hunting trip from Coimbatore. The story of their adventures and the many interesting facts about the Tôḍas are related by H.P.B. in her Russian serial story entitled "The Enigmatical Tribes of the Azure-Blue Hills" published in the *Russkiy Vestnik* (Russian Messenger) of Moscow in 1884-85 (Vols. 174, 175 and 176). A complete English translation of this story will be found in the *Collected Writings*.

78 (Page 616) A beautiful and very adequate interpretation of this mantra has been given by W. E. Garrett in the *National Geographic*, May, 1963, p. 686, in an art. on Ladakh. It runs:

"OM — I invoke the path and experience of universality, so that

MANI — the jeweline luminosity of my immortal mind

PADME — be unfolded within the depths of the lotus-center of awakened consciousness

HUM — and I be wafted by the ecstasy of breaking through all bonds and horizons."

660                    ISIS UNVEILED

⁷⁹(Page 617) The Mongolian term *Gegen* means "daylight," "dawn," "brilliant," "shining," "splendor," and "bright," or "serene," as an honorific title bestowed mainly for lay accomplishments but sometimes used also as a term of reverence for highly spiritual lamas, and in that case translated as "Serene Holiness." The term *Hutugtu* (also rendered as *Khutukhtu*) means "saintly," "holy," "blessed" (*hutugtai*) and "felicitous," and is an honorific title bestowed on high members of the clergy for devoted work in the cause of Buddhism. It is usually given to eminent *Hubilgans*. The latter term means several things, such as "transformation," "metamorphosis," "apparition," "phantom," and also what is known as *tulku*, a condition explained in our Introductory to Vol. I of *Isis Unveiled*. The term is sometimes misspelled *Khobilgan*.

It is most likely that H.P.B. had in mind a high lama known as Djibtzun-damba-Hutugtu, resident at the time at Urga and who was supposed to be the *tulku* of Darapata (1573-1635) a Buddhist teacher.

⁸⁰(Page 617) Drepung (spelled in Tibetan *ḥBras-sPuṅs*) is one of the three large monasteries near Lhasa. It is not exactly a Mongolian College. Actually, there are within the monastery several so-called "colleges" (called *gra-tshang* in Tibetan) where monks are grouped according to nationality, and there is one which is the "college" for monks from Mongolia, who learn the teachings in Tibetan.

⁸¹(Page 618) In connection with this term *Peh-ling*, it should be pointed out that *rgya-p'i-liṅ* is the name of the country, and *rgya-p'i-liṅ-pa*, the name of the people through which the Tibetans heard first (probably at the beginning of the 18th century) of the civilized nations of the Occident; hence the term has been applied for British India, for Englishmen, for European residents of India, and also (sometimes without *rgya*) for Europe and Europeans in general. Some derive it from *Feringhee*, which term, in its altered form of *p'a-raṅ* or *p'e-raṅ*, is current in Central Tibet. It is therefore not improbable that *p'i-liṅ* represents only the more vulgar pronunciation of the genuine Tibetan word *p'yi-gliṅ*, meaning an out-country, a distant foreign country and especially Europe.

As for the term *Feringhee*, it usually stands for a European, especially an Indian-born Portuguese; also a Eurasian, especially of Portuguese-Indian blood. *A Dictionary of Anglo-Indian Words and Phrases* by Col. Henry Yule and A. C. Burnell lists that term under *Firinghee* and says: "Pers. *Farangi, Firingî*; Ar. *Al-Faranj, Ifranji, Firanji*, i.e., a Frank. This term for a European is very old in Asia, but when now employed by natives in India is either applied (especially in the South) specifically to the Indian-born Portuguese, or, when used more generally, for 'European,' implies hostility or disparagement . . ."

82 (Page 621) The term *kukushan* is somewhat uncertain. In Burmese *ku* means to "give medicine" and *kawkutânaw* is a synonym. The letter *t* substitutes in Burmese for the Skt. *s*. As the context speaks of the Irrawady River, it is possible that a Burmese word is used.

83 (Page 633) The text of this statement is as follows: "Eorum est scientia punienda et severissimis legibus vindicanda, qui magicis adcincti artibus aut contra salutem hominum moliti aut pudicos animos ad libidinem deflexisse detegentur." A free translation would be: "The knowledge of those shall be justly punished by the severest laws, who have recourse to the magical arts or are endeavoring to harm the well-being of people or are discovered to bend chaste souls towards lustfulness." Though the title of this Chapter is "De maleficis et mathematicis et ceteris similibus," it is the magicians and astrologers who are meant, as in Byzantine times the word "mathematician" meant an astrologer.

The Codex Justinianus is to be found in the collection of laws entitled *Corpus Juris Civilis* which was published in many editions before 1874, and H.P.B. may have seen the passage in the edition of the brothers Kriegel which first come out at Leipzig, at the publisher Baumgartner, in 1840, where the passage may be found in Vol. II, p. 595.

84 (Page 639) This term is a dialectical corruption of *Vetâla-panchaviṁśati,* or "Twenty-five Tales of the Vetâla," a collection of fairy tales about a demon, known as Vetâla, who is supposed to occupy corpses. These stories are known to English readers under the title of *Vikram and the Vampire,* translated by Sir R. Burton in 1870, and as *The Baital Pachisi,* translated by W. B. Barker and edited by E. B. Eastwick, London, 1855.

# GENERAL INDEX

To avoid any uncertainty with regard to the way in which *entries* and *sub-entries* are listed in this Index, the following explanation should be of help:
Entries which merely list pages of one or the other Volume, or of both, indicate that the term occurs without any specific relation worthy to be noticed.
Sub-entries are arranged alphabetically, first for Volume I, then for Volume II. This is done in order to save space. Whenever a reference to Vol. II occurs for the first time, all following sub-entries are for that Volume. If an identical sub-entry refers to both Volumes, their pages in both Volumes follow one another, and the next sub-entry is definitely shown to be from one or the other Volume, to avoid any confusion.
The word "and" is not part of any alphabetical sequence.
Pages within square brackets, such as [16] or [24], refer to the Introductory Section in Volume I. Pages in italics refer to definitions of terms.
Abbreviations used are: c. for century; ca. for *circa*, meaning approximately or about; *fl.* for flourished; r. for reigned or ruled.

## A

*A, atl,* as radicals, I, 591.
Aaron: rod of, I, 414, 485; and goats, II, 512-13; initiates Eleazar and dies, 571.
Ab-ad, II, 571fn.
Abarbanel (or Abrabanel), Isaac (1437-1508), on conjunction of Saturn and Jupiter in Pisces, II, 256.
Abaris, aethrobat, II, 194.
Abathur: Lord, II, 175, 295; and Pthahil, 224, 225, 228, 229.
Abba, Rabbi, II, 348.
Abbott, Dr., Egyptologist, I, 6, 20, 240.
Abel: II, 225, 489; and Cain (or Kain), 446, 466; and Seth, 460.
Abel, Eugenius, *Orphica,* on mystic mother, I, 257.
Abhichâr, mesmeric power, II, 612.
*Abhidharma,* II, 318.
Ab-i-haiwân-î, II, 621.
Ab-i-hayât (fount of life), healing water of Talapoins, II, 621.
Abir, Great, I, 569.
Abortion, and reincarnation, I, 351.
Abo Sabo, John, II, 203, 204.
Abraham (A-Braham): I, 549, 554, 569, 570; as Saturn and Pâli Shepherd, 578;
and Abram, II, 299; alias for Zeruan or Saturn, 216 & fn., 236; bosom of, 117; and Hindu pantheon, 488; Müller on, 413fn.; story of, allegory, 493. *See also* Abram.
Abraiamans: fish-charmers, I, 606; long-lived, II, 620.
Abram: and Abraham, II, 299; and Saturn, 236; meaning of, 216fn.
Abraxas (αβραξας), Abrasax, II, 147, 233fn., 293, 295.
Absolution, in Church of England, II, 544.
Abu Jáfar Almansúr, and St. John of Damascus, II, 580.
Abuse, religious leaders, opponents, II, 208.
Abu Simbel, and Thebes, I, 542.
Abydenus, on Xisuthros, II, 217fn.
Abydos, Dynasty of, II, 361.
Abyss: in grain of sand, I, 339; seven-step, below earth, 353.
Abyssinians, and fire, I, 248.
Academicians, reject theurgy, I, 281.
Academy(ies): Berlin, & mesmerism, I, 173; blindness of, 225; French, & mesmerism, 171ff.; of Medicine & mesmerism, 174; of Science skirmishes with clergy, 101-03.
Acari, produced by Crosse, I, 465.

Accidental, discoveries, I, 3.
*Account of the Origin and Attributes of the True Rosicrucians, MS.*, on medical art, I, 163.
Acla, and Atlan, I, 591.
*actio in distans*, I, 59, 109.
*Acts:* I, 25, 488; II, 182, 204fn.; on exorcism, I, 355; Epistles of Apostles more genuine than, II, 277; tampered, 37; why long rejected from Canon, 137-138; on baptism, 136; on name of Jesus, 239, 387; on Nicolas of Antioch, 329; on Paul, 137; on Paul & viper, 566; on Sadducees, 148fn.
Ad, Ad-ad: I, xxxiii, 579; II, 170.
Ad-ah, Sons of, I, 579, 580fn.
Adair, Lord, I, 379, 445.
Adam(s): emanated from Divine Essence, I, 1; and esoteric doctrine, 575; invested with *chiton*, 475-76; meaning of, 297; II, 517; primitive man, I, 2; second, and Lillith, 433; second, as Elohim, 299; second, of *Genesis*, 149; II, 268; several, of *Genesis*, I, 303; Aries as, II, 465; begets Seth, 464; and Eve, 269, 270*fn.*, 463; Fall of, and religious dualism, 225, 277; is blood, 244; left rib of, and Sephîrâh, 267; means red, 465; Noah is double of, 465; of dust, 223; prototype of Noah, 449; sends Seth on errand to Paradise, 520.
Adam Illa-ah, Heavenly man, II, 271.
Adamic earth, I, 51.
Adam-Kadmon: I, 302, 590; II, 169, 176, 205fn., 222, 223, 229; androgynous, I, 297; as Logos, 298; as expressing universe, II, 277; as Ophis, 225; as Primus, 223, 452; as protogonos, 213; as Yod, 463; called mind by Philo, 216; def. *270;* first race as emanation of, 276; is Ptaḥ, 226; is Vishṇu, 259; and Manu, 271fn.; and Mt. Meru, 233; originates Cain, 464; and Sephîrâh, 268 & fn.; and souls of Israelites, 342.
Adar-gat, I, 579.
Addison, J. (1672-1719), on eternity, I, 205.
Adelon, Dr. N. P. (1782-1862), and mesmerism, I, 174.
Adept(s): Ākâśa known to, I, 113; become immortal through labor for good of man, 66-67; dangers to, 319; H.P.B.'s intimate acquaintance with Eastern, v, 42-43; make themselves known but to few, 17; perform wonders, 16; requisites of, 342; safekeepers of fundamental truths, 37; secret records of, 557; II, 403; solved every problem, I, 38; will of, 464; ancient, unhampered by body, II, 597; body of, wears out, 563; brother- in Europe, 403; consciously withdraws from outer body, 588; controls spirits of elements, but not spirit of man, 590; def. *588;* do not congregate in large communities, 143; extent of their mastery, 106; first self-made, 317; fraternities of, 306-07; incarnate god, 153; incarnation of, into child's body at Ladakh, 601-02; Jesus an, 150; and medium compared, 595-96; of Kublai-Khân, 583; of seventh rite, 564; once brothers all over world, 387; perfect health of, 595; quickens natural forces, 590; requires no extraneous aid, relies on will power, 592; and seventh day, 419; transfer spiritual ego into younger body, 563, 565, 589; uses mesmeric hallucination, 588-89; visions of, undistorted by memory or fancy, 591.
Ādi Buddha; anthropomorphized among Yezîdis, II, 571fn.; emanations of, 156 & fn., 226; and Gautama, 537; identical with Ādinâtha, 323; Supreme Deity, 233.
Ādima, and Heva, ancestors of present man, I, 579fn., 590.
Ādinâtha, or Ādiśvara, II, 323.
Aditi: and Daksha, I, xxxi; Father-Mother, II, 267, 268, 269.
Aditya: I, 348; commanded by Brâhmans, xxxviii.
Adon, I, 579.
Adonai: and sacred sleep, I, 358; sexless, 303; as Adam Primus, II, 223; and Ardhanârî, 451-53; as Shekhînah, 213, 223; dual, 224; and Jehovah, 224, 398; in *Job,* 494; on Gnostic gems, 233fn.; third son of Ialdabaôth, 190fn.
Adonaios, genius of spheres, II, 184, 294.
Adoni-Iahoh, made Supreme God, II, 131.
Adonim, angelic hierarchy, I, 301.
Adonis: boat of, II, 139; is Helios, 517; worship of, 131, 139, 181.
Adunai, Kadush, El-el, II, 131, 185.
Advent, Second, and avatâras, II, 535.
Adventists, I, 34; II, 237.
Aedan, Superior and Inferior, II, 247.
Aelian, Claudius (ca. 170-235 A.D.): I, 466; on Iachus, 406.

Aeneas, I, 362-63.
Aeôn(s) (αἰών): II, 181; as Olam, 216; and Christos in Gnosticism, 176, 177; Ebionites believed in, 190; Gnostic, *219;* idea of, in Paul, 506; and Patriarchs, 450; and Propatôr, 210; Seven, 187; Seven, in Nazarene system, 229, 296; ten, and Jesus' secret doctrine, 324.
Aërolites: and prophetic visions, I, 331; used in mysteries, 282.
Aeschylus (525-456 B.C.), I, 405.
— *Prometheus unbound,* on descent of a god to Hâdes, II, 514-15.
Aesculapius: as Ptaḥ, Baal, Hercules, etc., I, 130; and healing, I, 502; and underworld, 514fn.
Aêshma-daêva, II, 482 & fn.
Aesir: bridge of, I, 161; gods, 151.
Aether (αἰθήρ): as anima mundi, I, 316-17; as Zeus or Zên, 157, 158; and chaos, *341;* directing intelligences of, 342; highest, 349; known to ancients, 189; luminous as space, 289; pervades all, 129; seat of Idea & Will, 57; Simplicius on, 178; and Spirit, 290; Spiritual Mother of beings, 134; Universal, & elementals, 284; universal, & psychometry, 183-84; as Holy Ghost, II, 506; celestial ocean, 50; in Orphism, 35; Omnipotent Father, 560fn.
Aetheraeum, I, 423.
Aethicus, Ister (*fl.* 4th c. A.D.), *Cosmographia* (implied), on voices in desert, I, 604.
Aethiopia, East of Babylonia, II, 434.
Aethiopians: from Indus, possibly Jews, I, 567, 570; Eastern, or Âryans, II, 435, 436, 437fn.; language written from left to right, 437; orig. an Indian race, 437fn.; succession order among, and Hindus, 437 & fn.
Aethrobasy: I, *xxiii-xxiv,* 225, 629; and levitation, 496ff.
Aethrobat, II, 194, 597.
Aetius Amidenus (5th or 6th c. A.D.), I, 89.
Afrasiab, Assyrian King, I, 576.
Africans, I, 313, 357fn., 378-79, 381-83, 538.
Afrits: elementary spirits, I, 141, 313; II; 572; and jinn at Ishmonia, 29.
After-death: I, 292; mysteries of, are many, 69.
Agar, meaning of, II, 178, 179, 180.
Agardt, J. G., on water turned into blood, I, 414.

Agassiz, J. L. R. (1807-73), I, 63, 85, 281, 427.
— *An Essay on Classification,* on life and its future, I, 420fn.
Agate. See A-yu.
Agathodaimôn (ἀγαθοδαίμων): I, 133; symbol of healing, 157; as Chnuphis, II, 295; as Ophis, 295; as shadow of light, 293; cup of, 513; erect on a pole, 512; identical with Christos, 187; and Lord Jordan, 295.
Agathon (τὸ ἀγαθόν), Plato's Supreme God, I, xvi; II, 285.
Agde, Council of, condemns *sortes,* II, 21.
Age(s): four, in history, I, 32, 34; of paper, 535; and cycles, II, 144fn., 424; four, in ancient religions, 467; four, in Bible, 443; four, of each planet, 421; four, of Hindus, 275; geological, 464.
Aged of the Aged, II, 213, 244.
Agni: I, *xxxi,* 156, 348; II, 39, 411, 412, 438; and sun, I, 270; presides over Pisces, II, 465.
Agnihotṛis, and soma, I, xl.
Agniṣhṭoma, I, 10, 569.
Agonaces, teacher of Zoroaster, II, 142.
Agra, same as Augoeides, II, 495.
Agrae, lesser mysteries at, II, 100.
Agrippa, H. C. (1486-1535): I, 167; II, 20; on earth, water & living soul, II, 551fn.
— *De occulta philosophia:* on sidereal influence & magic, I, 171; on nature of phantoms, 200; on soul of the world, 280.
— *Preheminence of Women,* on Eve, II, 299.
*Agrushada Parikshai*: and Brahmâtma, II, 31; invocation to Brahmâ, 105; magical part of, denied Jacolliot, on mystery-language, 46 & fn.; on revealing secret knowledge, 99, 100; on secrecy, 40; on secret brotherhood, 308.
Ah, as root of Ahura, II, 297.
Aḥab, encouraged by prophets, II, 525.
*Aham eva parabrahman,* II, 262.
Ahaṃkâra: I, xix; II, 209; self-consciousness, II, 287, 320.
Âhavanîya, sacrificial fire, I, xliv.
Aḥaz: and Hezekiah, II, 166fn.; his family deposed, 440.
Aḥer, in garden of delights: I, xxxiiifn.; II, 119. *See also* Paul.
Ahi, myth of, and Dragon, II, 486.
Ahijah, leads insurrection, II, 439.
*Ahmi yaṭ ahmi,* II, 221.

Aholiab, II, 38.
Ahriman: II, 482, 488 & fn.; and Bull, 464-65; struggle between, and Ahura-Mazda, 237fn., 302; to be purified in fiery lake, 238.
Ahuna-Vairya, and Jewish "I am," I, 560, 651.
Ahura-Mazda: II, 297; as "I am," 221; and Indra, 484; struggle between, and Ahriman, 237fn., 302. *See also* Ormazd.
Aia, II, 301.
Ain-Soph: I, 67, 270, 272, 292, 302; II, 227; a Power, I, 16; as Boundless, 347; as No-Thing, II, 210, 212; confusion of Christian Kabalists about, 215fn.; identical with Svayambhû, 214; and immortal spirit of man, 218; nature of, 266, 268; passive, non-existent, formless, 214; Wisdom as first emanation of, 37.
Air: and spirits, I, 290; "powers of the," 311.
Aisthêtikon (αἰσθητικόν), instinctual, I, 432.
*Aitareya-Brâhmana:* I, 9, 569, 580fn.; age of, 347fn.; II, 433; on antiquity of *Vedas,* I, 11; on Asuras & Devas, 12; on Brahmâ-Prajâpati, 265; on Brahmâ & the 12 bodies, 348; on Manas, 348; on sunrise & sunset, 10; on *Sattras,* 11; on Soma, xl; on sphericity of earth, 10; on Yajña, xliv; on Brahmâ-Nara, II, 268; on vâch, 409-10; on sarpa-râjñî, 489.
Aitken, Wm. (1825-1892), *The Science and Practice of Medicine,* on foetus' malformations, I, 387-88.
Ajanta: caves of, I, 349-51; 590; and cross, II, 270fn.
Âkâśa (Tib.: Nam-*m*khaḥ): II, 209, 597; as life-fluid, can be compressed into a shell, I, 378, as life-principle, 113, 144; becomes potent under Will and Spirit, 616; bolt of, can kill, 380; def. *xxvii,* 139-40fn.; fakir concentrates, on the germ, 139-40; fourth emanation of, 506; and human will, 463; many names for, 125; memory of God, 178-79; personified, 158; and pregnant women, 395; and fakirs, II, 115.
Akhamôth. *See* Sophia-Akhamôth.
Akkad, I, 580fn.; II, 442.
Akkadians: derivation of name, I, 579; emigrants from India, 576, 578; introduce worship of Baal, 263; and ancient Prayâga, II, 48; as Brahmans from India, 46; brought Mysteries to Babylonians, 46;

457; cosmogony of, 267fn.; invented by Lenormant, 423.
Akkas, I, 412.
Aksakoff, A. N. (1832-1903): on phenomena, I, 41; & St. Petersburg's Commission, 118.
— *Phenomena of Mediumism,* I, 46.
Al, meaning of, and El, I, 13 & fn.
Alabaster, H. (? - 1884), *The Wheel of the Law:* II, 540, 555fn.; on basis of true belief, 559; on Buddha's birth, 552fn.; on Buddhist idea of consequences, 541; on conception of God, 541-42; on future life and extinction, 566.
Aladdin, lamp of, I, 603.
Alagona, P. (1549-1624), *S. Thomae Aquinatus theologicae summae compendium,* on killing, etc., II, 355.
*Alba petra,* stone of initiation, II, 351.
Albath, system of, II, 299.
Albertus Magnus (1206?-1280): I, 65, 226, 230, 415; magic of, II, 18, 20, 57; on Sign of Virgo & Dec. 25th, 490; oracular head of, 56.
Albigenses, II, 74, 325, 502.
Albumazar (805-885), on Sign of Virgo & boy-child, II, 491.
Alchemists: I, *xxv;* jargon of, 191; knowledge & soul-qualities of, 67; symbolic language of, 307.
Alchemy (*Arab.* al-kîmiyâ): I, *xxv;* as old as tradition, 503; bridge between old, and chemistry, 163; defence of, and magic, 508ff.; and Hermetic philosophy, 169; ideas of, on alkahest, 191; and metallurgy among ancients, 542; secret meaning of terms of, 192; symbolical language of, on man, 309; symbolism of, and of chemistry, 505-06; was universal, 502; works on, destroyed by Diocletian, 503; prevalent among clergy, II, 57.
Alcohol, and electrical polarity, I, 277fn.
Aldafader, as Odin, I, 151.
Aleph, symbol of, II, 270fn.
Aleim, priests, magi, I, 575, 580. *See also* Yava-Aleim.
Aleppo, mufti of, I, 362.
Alexander of Macedonia (356-323 B.C.): and Napoleon, reflexed images of former types, I, 35; did not invade India, II, 429, 607.
Alexander Cornelius Polyhistor (2nd c. B.C.): q. Berosus on flood, I, 349; on Pythagoras, II, 140.

# INDEX

Alexander Severus (208-235): pillages temples, I, 406; and image of Christ, II, 150.
Alexander III, Pope (1159-81), II, 22.
Alexandria, mirror in port of, I, 528.
Alexandrian Library: burning of, I, 403, 511; precious rolls preserved, II, 27.
Alexandrian School, derived soul from World-Soul, I, 316.
Alexikakos, name for Heracles, II, 515.
Algebra, known in Egypt, I, 536.
Alger, Dr. H. D. d', on taming birds by will power, I, 380-81.
Algeria, Houdin in, I, 379.
Alipili, *Centrum naturae concentratum*, etc., on true magic, II, 617-18.
Alkahest: I, 192; and Âkâśa, xvii; ignored by the Academy, 165; nature and virtues of, 50, 191; and pre-Adamic earth, 133; and salt, 148; universal solvent, 503, 507.
Allchin, Dr. Wm. H. (1817-90), on medicine, I, 180.
Allegory: becomes sacred history, II, 406; myth and symbol, 493.
Allopathists, oppose discoveries, I, 88.
*Almaz*, flagship, and levitation, I, 495.
Almeh, II, 440, 491fn.
Almignana, Abbé, I, 204.
Al-om-jah, Egyptian hierophant, II, 364.
Alternation, of waking and sleep, I, xvii.
Alva, Fernando Alvarez de Toledo, Duque de (1508-1583), I, 386.
Alvarado, Pedro de (1495-1541), I, 552.
Amartêmatos (ἁμαρτήματος), error, II, 478fn.
Amasis, King (600 B.C.), and Lindus, I, 536.
Amazons, circle-dance of, II, 45.
Amberley, J. (1842-1876), *An Analysis of Religious Belief*: looks down on Jesus, II, 562; on Ebionites, 307fn.
Ambition, of certain daemons, I, 219, 332-33.
Ambrosius (Teseo Ambrogio, 1469-1540), *Introd. in Chald. Linguam* (implied), II, 150, 647.
Ambrosius, St. (340?-397), II, 178, 528.
Amelia, Queen, and fecundity, II, 333.
Amen: I, 156; begat Osiris, 262.
Amenhotep I (*fl.* 1778 B.C.), I, 542.
Amenhotep II (*fl.* 1687 B.C.), I, 544.
Amenti, not our Hell: II, 11; and Typhon, 494.
Americ, Nicaragua Range, I, 592, 652-53.

America: first mention of, I, 592, 653-54; and Meru, 591; and Northmen, 592; old ruins of, 239; origin of aborigines of, a vexing question, 548; origin of name, 592; people of Central, and Phoenicians, 555; and size of buildings, 525; conservatory of sensitives, II, 19; physico-psychological characteristics of people in, 19.
American, Ass'n for Adv. of Science, I, 117, 245-46.
*American Bookseller*, and *Isis Unveiled*, I, [2].
*American Builder*, II, 475fn.
*Amianthus* (ἀμίαντος), I, 231.
Amico, F. (1578-1651), *Cursus theologicae*, etc., on murder, II, 363.
*L'Ami des sciences* (art. by J. B. Jobard), I, 188.
Amita, or Buddha, I, 601.
Ammianus Marcellinus (330?-395), *Roman History*: on bull Apis, I, 406; on fire from heaven, 528; on Gymnosophists, 90; on Zoroaster, 19; on Darius & India, II, 140-41; on sources of magianism, 306.
Ammon, Dr. F. A. von (1799- ?), I, 387.
Ammonius Saccas: II, 333, 342; on Jesus and religion, I, 443-44; taught unity of religions, 444; on memory, II, 591; on real aim of Christ, 249-50; on souls visiting souls, 594.
Amon, identical with Adam, II, 465.
Amoretti, C. (1741-1816), on electric polarity of precious stones, I, 264-65.
Amorites, I, 568.
*Amos*: on various gods, I, 491fn.; on Moloch and Chiun, II, 236.
Amosis, II, 565.
Ampère, A. M. (1775-1836), I, 163.
Amphiaraus, I, 19.
Amphibolus, St., II, 248, 579.
Amrita, supreme soul, I, 265fn.
Amru, General, and destruction of MSS., II, 27.
Amshâspands, as mediators, II, 221.
Amulet(s): soldier made bullet-proof by, I, 379; messianic, of Lady Ellenborough, II, 255-56; and talismans, 351, 352.
Anaesthesia: I, 175; among ancients and today, 539-40.
Anâhita, earth, I, 11.
Anaitis, Venus, I, 11.
Anak, is Enoch, II, 450.

Anakim: II, 450; and Phoenicians, I, 569; or zamzummim, 567.
Ananda: II, 538; and Matamgî woman, 550-51; original of John the Baptist, 555.
Ananta: seven-headed serpent, II, 489; and Vishṇu, 259.
Anastasi, Papyrus, I, 403.
Anastasis (ἀνάστασις), Paul on, II, 281, 282.
Anathema, original with Christians, II, 334.
Anatolius, Bishop (230?-282 A.D.), II, 28.
Anatomy, Manetho on, I, 406.
Anaxagoras (b. ca. 499 B.C.): II, 179fn., 297fn.; and spiritual prototypes, I, 158; on nous, II, 282.
Anaximenes (fl. ca. 546 B.C.), on evolution, I, 238.
Ancient & Accepted Scottish Rite, a Jesuitical product, II, 390.
Ancient of Days, II, 33, 222, 223, 224, 244, 245, 400.
Ancients: astronomical knowledge of, I, 21-22; chemical knowledge of, 531; civilization of, 564; experimental researches of, 49-50; knew more than moderns, 25; knowledge of, in hands of initiates, 510-11; knowledge of, to be revealed, 38; methods of, & science, 405; misunderstood, 236-37, 461-62; modern explorers & discoveries of, 189; and modern thinkers, 248-52; myths of, hide facts of nature, 261-62, 263; not impostors, 267; on elementals in space & gods, 285ff.; possessed vast knowledge, 135, 238ff., 253, 265, 406, 411ff., 515ff., 618-20; religion of, is religion of future, 613.
Ancre, Maréchale d', her trial for sorcery, II, 60.
Anderson, J. (1680-1739), *The Book of Constitutions*, etc., II, 350, 389.
—— *Defence of Masonry*, II, 374fn.
Anderson, Steve, "converted" criminal, II, 543-44.
Andhera [Hindî; Skt. Andhakâra]: and Śiva, I, 299; fallen angels hurled into, II, 11.
Andra (ἄνδρα), man, II, 328.
Androgyne, Androgynous: Adam and separation of sexes, I, 297, 303; deity and First Cause, II, 299; everything, at first "hour," 468, 469; gods in ancient cosmogonies, 267ff., 293.
Andrologists, ancient, and man, I, 5.
Angel(s): guardian, of Plotinus, I, xliii;

doctrine of, secret, II, 196; Justin Martyr on, 195; Satan an, before Fall, 207; Paul warns against worship of, 206.
Anger, and self-control, I, 248.
Angkor, Angkorthôm, I, 261, 565, 566, 567.
Angkor Vat. *See* Nagkon-Wat.
Anglican Church, returns to Roman uses, II, 544.
Ani, or Bhikshuni, II, 608.
Anima: I, 37; II, 593; *bruta* and *divina*, I, 317.
Animals: astral bodies of, and men identical, I, 327; astral soul assuming form of, 328; distinction between, and man, 327; have germ of immortal soul, 301fn., 427; manifestation of spirit-, 70-71; materialized, 329; monsters among, 397-98; perceive invisible entities, 467; possessed of clairvoyance, 469; sacred, 146-47; something divine in, xix; taming, 467; II, 623; meaning of, in Arc, II, 447.
Anima Mundi: I, 299; as aether, 316-17; and intelligent magnetic streams, 208; and man as trinity, 212; and Nirvâṇa, 291; is dual, 301fn.; soul born upon leaving, 345; as Universal Soul, II, 402; is Sophia-Akhamôth, 227.
Animated statues, I, 614.
Animation: cases and nature of suspended, I, 479, 483, 485-86.
Ânkh, cruciform, of Kṛishṇa, II, 557.
Anna, Ste., Oriental origin of legend of, and Persephone, II, 491 & fn.
*Annales d'hygiène publique* (Dr. Elam), on arson, I, 276.
*Annales médico-psychologiques*, on de Mirville's book, I, 102.
Annas, and Caiaphas, on Jesus, II, 522.
Annihilation: I, 290, 291, 292; II, 286; of matter, I, 289; of the soul, 317ff., 328; II, 368-69; belief in, or extinction, II, 566; not taught by Buddhism, 319.
Annu, souls of, II, 387.
Annunciation: of Gautama, I, 92; copied from other religions, 325; and Buddhist original legend, II, 555.
Anoia (ἄνοια), and nous, II, 282, 286.
Anointed, Josephus allegedly on the, II, 328.
Anquetil-Duperron, A. H. (1731-1805), II, 342.
—— *Oupnek'-hat:* on lightning, I, 528; on *Bh.-Gîtâ*, II, 562.
Ant, more intelligent than tiger, I, 433.

Ante-historical, cataclysms, I, 266.
Anthesteria, and gate of Dionysos, II, 245-246.
Anthon, Chas. (1797-1867), *A Classical Dictionary,* I, 130.
—— *Dict. of Greek & Roman Antiquities,* on Eleusinia, II, 44.
Anthony, St. (ca. 250-350 A.D.): monk of, and false relics, II, 71; temptation of, 108; and theurgy of Iamblichus, 84.
Anthropology, I, *xxvii-xxviii.*
Anthrôpos (ἄνθρωπος), man, I, 1, 412.
Anti-Christ(s): fable of, its object, II, 535; three, 58.
Anticlides, I, 532.
Anti-Masonic Convention, II, 373, 375.
Antiochus Epiphanes (2nd c. B.C.): and head of ass, II, 523; and Jewish human sacrifices, 542fn.
Antiquity: lost natural philosophy of, I, 235; misrepresented by Christians, II, 96.
Antitypes, invisible, of men *to be* born, I, 310.
Antoninus, occultist, II, 28, 642.
Antony, Mark (Marcus Antonius, ca. 83-30 B.C.), I, 517.
Anu: and Bel & Nuah, II, 444; and Hea, 267fn.; as chaos, 423; or Anata, 170.
Anubis: identical with Michael, II, 488; picture of, 149-50.
Anukis, II, 209.
Apavarga, not annihilation, II, 533-34.
Ape(s): and genealogical trees of people, I, 40; as symbols, 564; mediumistic manifestations of, 326-27; derived from man, II, 278fn.
Apellicon of Teos (?-84 B.C.), I, 320.
Apion: I, 287; on golden head of ass, II, 523.
Apis: age of, I, 406; and other bulls, II, 236.
*Apocalypse.* See *Revelation.*
*Apocalypsis Eliae,* II, 248.
*Apocrypha:* of Alexandrian Jews, II, 135 & fn.; first received then discarded, 518; Gospels, 539.
Apollo: and Python, II, 507; as Halal, 466fn.; degraded, 488; killed his logos, 510.
Apollo-Chomaeus, II, 48.
Apollo-Nomios, II, 335.
Apollo-Python, and Caduceus, I, 556.
Apollodorus (*fl.* B.C. 140), *Bibliotheca,* on magnetic sleeper, I, 532.

Apollonides Orapius, *Semenuthi,* on gods of Egypt, I, 406, 645.
Apollonius Rhodius (*fl.* 3rd c. B.C.), *Scholia in Apollonium Rhodium,* on Kabiri, I, 569.
Apollonius of Tyana: beholds future, I, 486; biogr. of, hides esoteric meaning, 19; casts out devils, 356; and contemplation, 434; on abstemious life, 489; on precious stones, 265; restores life to Roman bride, 481, sees ghûls in desert, 604; aethrobatic feats of, II, 597; compared to Jesus, 341; instructed by Nâgas, 434; talismans of, 97; teaching of, 342; uses mantle of wool to leave body, 344.
Apollyon. See Apolouôn.
Apolouôn ('Απολούων), meaning of, II, 511.
Apophis, influence of dragon, II, 368.
Aporrhêta (ἀπόρρητα): secret discourses, II, 191, 204; symbolism in, 111.
Apostasia (ἀποστασία), II, 282.
Apostles: Creed of, on descent to hell, II, 177, 514; doubtful actuality of, 346.
Apostolic Succession: II, 544; a gross and palpable fraud, 544; and Irenaeus & Eusebius, 326-27; fiction of Roman, 124ff.
Apparitions: ancients on, I, 37; Görres on, 103; H. More on, 54-55; of malicious demons, 70; produced by sylphs & undines, 67.
Appearances, Porphyry on divinely luminous, I, xliii.
Appian (*fl.* 2nd c. A.D.), I, 226, 638.
—— *Roman History:* on Carthage, I, 520. 638.
Apple, II, 412.
Appleton. See *New American Cyclopaedia.*
Apsaras, II, 107.
Apuleius, L. (b. 125 A.D.?), initiated at Cenchrea, II, 90.
—— *De Deo Socratis,* on souls, lemures & lares, I, 345, 644.
—— *Florida:* II, 128fn.; on Pythagoras, 140.
—— *Golden Ass:* II, 363; on midnight sun, 146, 646.
Apûrvâ, I, *348.*
A'qîbah: II, 119, 215fn.; 298fn.; friend of Paul, I, xxxiiifn.
Aquapontanus. See Bridgewater.
Aquinas, Thos. (1225?-1274): I, 65, 504; II, 20; smashes "oracular head," II, 56.
—— *Summa,* on devils & miracles, II, 510.
Arabia Petraea, solitary Copts in, II, 306.

Arabian, MSS. burned, I, 511.
*Arabic Gospel of the Infancy*: II, 537, 538, 539; on Jesus' learning, 552.
Arabs: II, 29, 30, 255, 349, 418, 437fn., 550; and Abraham, I, 578; as physicians & Averroes, 619; charming snakes, 382-83; climb obelisks, 524; MSS. of, burned, 511; and digital figures, II, 300; intuitive perception of occult forces in, 636.
Arago, D. F. J. (1786-1853), and Daguerre, II, 619fn.
— *Œuvres complètes,* I, 107.
Aralezes, gods of Armenia, revive the dead, II, 564.
Araśa-maram, banyan-tree, II, 293, 316, 651.
Ârati, bathing festival in India, II, 138.
Arba, Arba-il: fourfold God, I, 508fn.; mystic "four," or Kabiri, II, 270, 407, 439; on Tetraktys, 171.
Arc, descending and ascending, of evolution, II, 455, 456, 457, 461, 462.
Arcadians, called Proselênoi, I, xxxixfn.
Arcana, highest, II, 503.
Arcanum, magical, as Principle of Life, I, 506.
d'Arcet, and mesmerism, I, 171.
Arch, Sacred, I, 29.
Archaeal, Universal Soul, I, 130.
*Archaeologia,* etc.: on Dracontia (Deane), I, 550; on monuments of Druids, 554; on Tiryns & Cyclops (W. Hamilton), 529.
Archaeology, and symbolism as enemies of clerical false pretences, II, 254.
Archaeus ('Ἀρχαῖος): II, 35; as mind of Demiurgus, I, 130; as van Helmont's principle of life, 400; great Universal, 14; many names for, 125; or anima mundi, 405.
Archaic, and ancient, I, *xliv.*
Archangels, and gods, not men on our planet, I, 316.
Archê (ἀρχή), II, 282.
Arches, and keystones, I, 571.
Archimedes (287-212 B.C.), I, 512, 543, 619.
Architecture: in archaic India, I, 620; prehistoric, its universal identity, 561, 572; prehistoric, reflects same religion, 567, 571.
*Archives des sciences* (de Candolle), on vital force, I, 313.
Archon(s): II, 90, 287; as Ialdabaôth, 206.
Archos, I, xli.

Archytas (4th c. B.C.), as inventor, I, 545; MS. of, and Galileo, 238fn.
Arciniegas, Germán (1900-?), *Amerigo and the New World,* I, 652.
Arctic, visited by Phoenicians, I, 545.
Ardhanârî, and Adonai, II, 451-53.
Argent, J. B. de Boyer, Marquis d' (1704-1771), supports vampirism, I, 450.
Argha, Argua: and Noah's ark, II, 444; of Moon, 209.
Argives, II, 488.
Argonauts, II, 561fn.
Arhats: I, 291; free from evil desire, 346; reach Nirvâṇa while on earth, II, 320.
Arica, and Incas' tomb, I, 597, 598.
Aries: I, 262, 268; II, 456, 461-62; as both Adams, II, 465.
Arik-anpin, and symbolism of Mt. Meru, II, 234.
Aristaeus: II, 335; as brute power, 129.
Aristarchus (between 280 & 264 B.C.): I, 621; taught heliocentric system, xiiifn.
Aristeas, I, 364.
Aristides, I, 131.
Aristophanes (448?-340? B.C.), *Ranae,* on Heracles in Hadês, II, 518.
Aristotle (384-322 B.C.): beliefs of, I, 12; Draper on failure of, 404; history of his MSS., 320, 643-44; ignorant of esoteric mysteries, 16; misrepresented Plato & Pythagoras, xv-xvi; on astral emanations, 200; on first man, 428; on the soul, 317; and Platonists, 430; taught earth in center of universe, 408; and Neo-Platonists, II, 252; on Joh as Oromasdes, 302; why Luther hated, 34-35.
— *De anima,* on rational soul, I, 251.
— *De caelo,* on revolution of earth, I 256fn.; on Sun as prison of Jupiter, II, 13fn.
— *De generatione et corruptione,* on double soul, I, 319.
— *De partibus animalium,* on life, I, 320.
— *Metaphysics:* I, xvi, xix; on privation, matter & form, 310, 312; on decimal notation, II, 300.
— *Parva naturalia,* on soul & dreams, I, 429.
— *Problemata,* on prophesy, I, 430.
Arius (ca. 250-336 A.D.), II, 304.
Ark: II, 405; meaning of, 444; meaning of animals in, 447.
Armenians, II, 393.
Armor, Prof., on teratology, I, 392, 393.

Armstrong, Sir Wm., I, 241.
Arnobius the Elder (*fl.* 290? A.D.), I, 317.
—— *Adversus gentes*: on Zoroaster, I, 19; on Mercury, 131; on minor mysteries, II, 108; on Jesus robbing sanctuary, 202fn.
Arnaldus de Villa Nova (ca. 1235-1313), I, 504.
Arnolphinus, *Tractat de lapide*, etc., I, 254fn.
Arpha-Kasda, *See* Edessa.
*Arrest du Parlement*, etc., on Jesuits, II, 353.
Arrhêta rênata (ἄρρητα ῥήματα), things ineffable, II, 146.
Arrhidaeus (4th c. B.C.), *Epistles to Philip*, I, 365, 645.
Arrian, F. (100?-170? A.D.), on truthfulness of Hindus, II, 474fn.
—— *Anabasis*, on Krishṇa, II, 537.
—— *Indica*: Bk. VIII of above.
Ars, Curé, d' [St. Jean Baptiste Vianney] (1786-1859), I, 218.
Arsdekin, R. (1618-1693), *Theologia tripartita*, etc., on divination, II, 354.
Arsenieff, and Huc's story, II, 604.
Arson, I, 276.
Artapanus, on Orpheus, I, 532.
Artemis, I, 264.
Artesian, wells known in China, I, 517.
Artificer, of the gods, II, 198.
Arts: lost, I, 6, 239-40, 405-06, 526, 536, 539; medical, 163; curious (τὰ περίεργα), II, 155.
Artufas, crypts, I, 557.
Âryans: I, 539, 569, 576; II, 434; age of, II, 433; did not borrow from Semites, 426; misleading term, 413fn.; or Eastern Aethiopians, built Egypt, 435.
Âryas, or Ârias, II, 237fn., 593fn.
Aryavosta(?), I, 621, 657.
*As*, I, 140fn.; to breathe, II, 298, 299.
As above, so below, I, 35.
Asaph, and Isaiah, II, 192.
Asar, or Isaral, II, 402.
Asaya, healer, II, 133.
Asbestos ("Ασβεστος): and perpetual flame, I, 125, 229-31; oil of, 504-05.
Asclepiades Bithynus: and music, I, 215; and real & apparent death, 481.
*Asclepian Dialogue*, on Divine voice, I, 246-47, 640.
Asclepiodotus (5th c. A.D.), I, 531.
Asclepius. *See* Asklepios.

Asgartha, temple of, II, 31, 643.
Ashdoth, as emanations, II, 34.
Ashes: retain form of burned object, I, 476; figurines made of, II, 603 & fn.; of cremated people magnetized to release astral soul, 603.
Ashmog, Persian serpent, II, 188.
Ashmole, Elias (1617-1692): II, 389; last of the Rosicrucians, 349.
'Ashtôreth. *See* Astartê.
Ash-tree, and origin of man, I, 151fn., 558fn.
Asi, II, 298fn.
Asia: inland sea in, I, 589; schools of Central, II, 207.
*Asiatic Journal* (London), II, 624.
*Asiatick Researches*: (S. Davis) I, 32; on Vâch (H. T. Colebrooke), II, 269; on the Saurya sect, 399fn.; (S. Turner), 598.
Asideans (Chasidîm), II, 135, 441, 481, 501.
Asklepiadae, I, xxxvii.
Asklepios (or Asclepius): I, xxxvii, 556, 613, 624; II, 481, 514fn.; Dialogue of, I, 247.
Askr, I, 151.
Asmodeus, II, 482.
Asmonean, Kings and *Apocrypha*, II, 135.
Aśoka: I, 590fn.; rock inscriptions of, II, 32; sends missionaries West, 491. *See also* Dharmâśoka.
Asor, Egyptian lyre, I, 544.
Asp, and Isis, I, 556.
Ass: and Typhon, II, 483, 484; *eo* in Egyptian, 523fn.; Jews worship the, 523.
Assar, Azon, and Druids, I, 572.
Assyrian: *basso-relievos* at Nagkon-Wat, I, 566; priests bore name of their god, 554; tablet on seven, II, 408; tablets, 422, 451.
Assyrians: I, xxxiv, 554, 576, 618; II, 94, 141, 231, 236, 254, 440, 442, 484, 486fn., 492.
Astaphaios, genius of spheres, II, 184, 294.
Astartê: II, 209, 438, 439; on prow of ships, I, 567fn.; II, 258, 446fn.; or Luna, I, 513; and Mary, II, 444fn.
Astral: capsule, I, 315; currents & levitation, 449; currents produce fertile & barren periods, 247; emanations & sensitives, 200; epidemics of hallucination, 370ff.; fluid can be compressed, 378; matter provides clothing for phantoms, 200; monad & reincarnation, 351; H. More on, spirit of man, 206; saturation

**672**  ISIS UNVEILED

by, force, 500; spirit & cometary matter, 168; spirit in *Cod. Naz.,* 300; virgin, 126; and amputated limbs, II, 595, 596fn.; form not subject to time & space, 588-89; inner, man often evil genius, 593; projection of, entity, 619-20.

Astral Body: as shell of ethereal body, I, 329; identical in man & animals, 327; injuries upon, repercuss upon physical, 360-61; nature & powers of, 198; Paracelsus on, 170; and suspended animation, 483; of adept oozing out of physical, II, 596; and spirit-hand phenomenon, 594-95; *Ṛigveda* on, 534.

Astral Light: as Âkâśa, all-pervading force, I, 113; as alkahest, 507-08; as azoth, 462; as memory of nature, 178-79; as *ob & od,* 158 as v. Helmont's principle of life, 400; control of currents in, 129; currents in, & Intelligences, 199-200; def. xxv-xxvi; dual & bisexual, 301fn.; and envelope of soul, 281; and heat & electricity, 272, 283, 393-94; key to many forces, 58; Lévi on, 137-38; magical properties of, 340; magnetizes mediums, 483; many names for, 125; and memory, 184; permeates all, xxvi; Porta on, 208; and *prima materia,* 156; record of everything in, 185; II, 588; and sleep, I, 180; symbol of, in *Edda,* 151; as Gnostic Female spiritus, II, 193; reflection of Pitṛis on, 115.

Astral Soul: assuming animal form, I, 328; assuming forms in acc. with man's thoughts, 292; at death, 476; distinct from ego, 459; and *inner self,* 316; free from fetters, 430; not immortal, 432; of mummies, 226; projection of, 476, 477; sublimated matter, 289; descent of, into matter, II, 112; in insanity, 589.

Astrochitôn, term for Herakles, II, 515.

Astrograph: and unborn child, I, 385, 395; produced by astral light, 394-95, 398.

Astrology: ancient knowledge of, I, 268; connection of, with elementals, 313; and currents of elementals, 284-85; infallible science if interpreters are that too, 259; judiciary, 267; and network of forces in inner worlds, 314; and the eighth sphere, 357; a science, II, 465.

Astronomical, amazing, knowledge of ancients, I, 21.

Astronomus, II, 365.

Astronomy: Aztec, I, 11; Chinese, 241; Hindu, 618, 621; vast knowledge of, in Egypt, 533.

Astu (Ἄστυ), Athens, II, 448.

Asu, II, 298, 299.

Asuras: II, 107, 299; as Iranians, I, 12.

Aśvattha, I, 152, 153; II, 316.

Atargatis, II, 258.

Âtas-Behrâm, I, 125.

Ateth, King of Egypt, I, 406.

Athanasius, St. (296?-373 A.D.), murdered Arius, II, 304.

—— *Epistolae Festales,* on *Hermas,* II, 518.

Athanor, and alchemy, I, 506.

Athar, II, 500.

*Atharva-Veda:* II, 262; and mantras, I, xxxvi; prodigies in, 91; compared to Bible, II, 556; great value of, 415; on power of Brahmans, 106-07; on will power as prayer, 592; preserved in secrecy, 563; Dubois on, 563.

Atheism: I, xviii; and Comte, 79-80; Buddhists do not teach, 292; none in days of old, II, 530, 531.

Athena, hymn to, II, 123.

*Athenaeum* (London), II, 240.

Athos, Mt.: manuscripts at, II, 52fn.; strange traditions at, 27.

Atibbâ, native doctors and European medicine, II, 621fn.

Atlanta, American-Indian name, I, 591 & fn.

Atlanteans, I, 545, 595.

*Atlantic Monthly* (Marcou), I, 592.

Atlantis: I, 413, 529, 545; location of, 591; Plato on, 591.

Âtman: and contemplation, I, 346; communion with, II, 342; or Self, the inner god, 317-18, 495-96.

Atmosphere, electricity of, embodied in demi-gods, etc., I, 261.

Atom(s): acted upon by Universal Will, I, 62; and Democritus, xxv, 249, 401, 411, 510; every, moved by spirit, 384; organic, and merging in primordial essence, 213.

Atonement: vicarious, I, 316; an imposition, II, 544; doctrine of, known to Gnostics, 41, 327; **invented by Christians,** 340; **moral effects of doctrine of,** 374; origin of doctrine of, 42; vicarious, doctrine breeding crime, 542ff.

Attalus III Philomotor (ca. 160-133 B.C.), library of, at Pergamum, II, 28.

Attraction: I, 271fn.; and gravity, xxiii-xxiv, 244; **magnetic, and elementals,** 313;

nature of, material & spiritual, 340; repulsion and will, 144, 281; role in finding body of drowned, II, 611-12.
Atum (At-mu), essential god, II, 500 & fn.
Aubigné. *See* Merle d'Aubigné.
Aucante, "Lettre sur une production monstrueuse," I, 384.
Audhumla (Old Norse: *Authumla*), as female principle, I, 147, 148.
Augoeides (αὐγοειδῆ): I, 12; II, 115, 317fn., 495; Divine Spirit, I, 12; and living being, 315; and monad, 303, 306; and sacred sleep of neophyte, 358; severed from soul, 432; and *subjective* mediums, 321.
Augustine, St. (354-430): on false religion & truth, I, 443; on Plato, xii; distorts truth, II, 329; on earth's sphericity, 477; misrepresented by di Raulica, 88; responsible for enmity between theology & science, 88.
— *Confessiones,* on slaying of enemies, II, 32.
— *Contra Faustum,* etc., on Faustus & Gospels, II, 37-38.
— *De baptismo contra Donatistas,* on the one true God, II, 88.
— *De Civitate Dei:* on mischievous spirits, I, 158-59fn.; on perpetual lamps, 227; enjoins belief in evil spirits, II, 70; on creation & *rēshîth,* 35-36; on Gentiles, 88; on hell, 13; on magic & demons, 67; warns against sorcery, 633.
— *De consensu evang.,* on Jesus & magic, II, 148.
— *De dono perseverantiae,* on eternal happiness & damnation, II, 546.
— *De fide et symbole,* on descent into hell, II, 514.
— *Epistle II to Januarius,* on *sortilegium,* II, 20.
— *Sermones,* on "holy kiss," II, 331.
Aûl, of Kurds, II, 631.
Aum: as Ineffable Name, II, 266; as means of evoking Inner Self, 114-15; contains Vedic Trimûrti, 39; meaning of, 31; and Tum, 387.
*Aum mani padme hum,* II, 616 & fn., 659-60.
Aura: quality of, & mediumship, I, 487, 490; restoring equilibrium in, 217; of sitters at séance provides materials for phenomena, II, 595; or emanation, 619; or magnetic exhalation & its effects, 610-11.
Aura, and Placida, R. Catholic Saints, I, 160; II, 248, 579.
Aurangâbâd, ruins of, I, 350-51.
Auricular, confession in Anglican Church, II, 544.
Aurora, theories about, I, 417-18.
*Aurum potabile,* I, 192.
Ausonius, D. M. (310?-394), *Epigrams,* on names of Iach, II, 302.
Austin Friars, I, 445.
*Auszüge a. d. Buche Sohar:* on androgynous beings, II, 469; on Jehovah & Adonai, 224; on twofold man, 193.
Authority: Fisher on, I, 396; Greeley on, x.
Autokratês (αὐτοκρατής), self-potent, II, 282.
Avalokitêśvara (Tib.: *sPyan-ras-gzigs,* pron. *Chenrezi*), appears at Ganden, II, 616.
Avany, Virgin, II, 322, 532.
Avâpta, and epopteia, II, 90-91 & fn.
Avatâras: I, 291; as emanations of Dhyâni-Buddhas, II, 156; Kalki, 237; Matsya, 427; and mother nature, 270; necessity of admitting, 558; of Druzes, 310; of Vishṇu, 259-60, 274, 425, 457; of Vishṇu, Brahmâ & Śiva, 278; periodic appearance of, 535-36; Suetonius on, 503; and symbol of cross, 453; symbolize evolution of races, 275.
Avenare (Johan Avenarius, 1520-1590; real name was Habermann or Hafermann), on Virgin & child, II, 167, 491.
Averroes (1126-98), I, 619.
*Avesta* (or *Zend-Avesta*):
I, xxviii, 25, 441, 442; II, 142, 432, 482fn., 484, 486; on fire, I, 129fn.; as spirit of *Vedas,* II, 220fn.; on cycles, 221fn.; on Jahi, 488; on Saoshyant, 237-38, 467; and Vedic religion, 129; and Zoroaster, 141.
— *Khordah-Avesta,* on the soul, II, 635.
— *Vendîdâd:* on Aêshma, II, 482-83fn.; on Azhi-Dahâka, 486; on Indra, 484, 488, on soul's account, 529; origin of term, 488fn.
— *Yaśna:* I, xxxvi; on Aêshma, II, 482fn.; on Azhi-Dahâka, 486.
— *Yashts:* on "I am," II, 221.
*See also* Kleucker.
Avicenna (979-1037): I, 164; on foetus, 385.

Ávila, Gil Gonzáles de (1577?-1658), I, 592.
Avogadro, A. (1776-1856), law of, I, 163, 627.
Ávṛitâ, I, 620, 657.
Axial, rotation, I, 254.
Axiokersos, etc., as Kabiri, I, 569.
Axis, heaven's perpetual, II, 405.
Ayana, Chaos or place of motion, II, 214.
Ayôdhyâ (Oudh), II, 437, 441.
Ay-Toyon, Supreme God of Yakuts, II, 568.
A-yu: agate or carnelian talisman in possession of H.P.B., II, 600, 626; used by Taley-Lama, 600fn.
Azar (or Azarh, Âzur), means fire, II, 451fn.
Azâzêl: and Baphomet: II, 302-03; as Moloch & scapegoat, 512; or Samael, 402, 512.
Azhi-Dahâka, and Satan, II, 486.
Azoth: I, 505; as astral light, 462, 508; and de Mirville, 462.
Azrael, and Israel, II, 216fn.
Aztecs: I, 553, 560; calendar of, 11.
Âzur, II, 451fn.

# B

Baader, F. H. von (1765-1841), *Sämtliche Werke* (implied), on Jews, I, 25.
Baal: II, 131, 236, 439; and Śiva, I, 578; dance of prophets of, II, 45; hierophants of, and apparitions, 567.
Baal-Chom, II, 48.
Baal-Hercules, adopted by Jews, II, 525.
Baal-Peor, II, 332.
Baal-Zephon, II, 487.
Babbage, Chas. (1792-1871), *Passages from the Life of a Philosopher* (implied), I, 185, 212, 361fn., 395.
Babel, Tower of, II, 217.
Babinet, J. (1794-1872): I, 116, 125, 502; and Comte, 101; on cause of moving tables, 60-61; on globular lightning, 107, 202; on levitation, 105, 202fn., 501, 505; on movement of furniture, 104-05; on raps, 105-06.
Babrius (1st c. B.C.), *Myths* (implied), II, 550.
Babylon, founded by giants, I, 31.
Babylonia: II, 442; civilization of, from India, I, 576; priests of, have very old records, 533; language of, II, 472; religious system of, 170; seat of Sanskrit literature, 428.
Bacchantes, I, xxxvii; II, 129, 524.
Bacchus (Βάκχος): coffin & relics of, at Rome, I, 160; is Nimrod, 568; ancient name of, as IHΣ, II, 527; and Ceres, 139fn., 560; crowned with ivy, 561fn.; greatly dreaded, 492; and Heracles, 518; Indian origin of, 561fn.; lake of, & baptism, 138; Liberalia of, 528 & fn.; mysteries of, & ox, 524fn.; nature & degradation of, 527-28; Nazarenes as anti-, sect, 129; rain-god, 134; rites of, 45; saint in Church calendar, 528; symbol of wine; 44; transformed into a devil, 527; and underworld, 514fn.; worshipped under mask of Jehovah, 128, 131, 165.
Bacon, Francis (1561-1626): I, 401, 405; on conviction, 49; on philosophy, 234.
—— *Novum Organum* (or *Organon*), I, 460.
Bacon, Roger (1214?-1294): I, xxv, 241, 415; II, 20; magical knowledge of, I, 65.
—— *De Mirabile Potestate*, etc., I, 413.
Badagas, II, 614, 615.
Baddha, conditioned, II, 266.
Badir, sacred basin, II, 600fn.
Bael-tree, and tiger, I, 469.
Bags, inflated, of hide in Egypt, I, 518.
Bahak-Ziwa: I, 298, 299, 300; name derived from "rain," II, 134.
Bahira, Nestorian monk, II, 54.
Bahti, gnomes, I, 598.
Bailey, Justice, *Book of Common Prayer*, on descent into Hell, II, 514.
Bailey, N. ( ? -1742), *Philologos* (Φιλόλογος), on ever-burning lamp, I, 224.
Bailey, Ph. J. (1816-1902), *Festus*, on powers of human heart, I, v.
Bailly, J.-S. (1736-1793), and mesmerism, I, 171.
Bain, A. (1818-1903), "Correlation of Nervous and Mental Forces," I, 466 (implied).
Bâini, II, 612.
Baital Pachisi, vampire, II, 639, 661.
Baktâshî, Dervishes, II, 316-17.
Baku, meaning of name & Gheber temple, II, 632fn.
Balaam, ass of, I, 493.
Balahate, fifth degree, II, 365.
Balam Acán, Toltec king, I, 553.
Bala-Mahâdeva, II, 434.

Balder, II, 11.
Baldinger, and Jesuits, I, 445.
Baldwin, Edw. (pseud. of Wm. Godwin, 1756-1836), *The Pantheon*, etc., on Pythia, I, xxxixfn.
Baldwin, J. D. (1809-1883), *Ancient America*, on Atlanta, I, 591.
Bamberg, Bishop & witchcraft, II, 61.
*Bampton Lectures* (Carwithen), II, 537.
Bandini, A. M. (1726-1803), *Vita e lettere di Amerigo Vespucci*, I, 652.
*Banner of Light, The* (Boston, Mass.), I, 356, 636.
Banyan tree, I, 293.
Baobab tree, I, 136fn.
Baôth, II, 183.
Baphomet, or Azâzêl, II, 302, 331.
Baptism: and oil, II, 134; of blood in Egyptian Mysteries, 42; of Nazarenes, 204; very old rite, 134ff.
Bara, created, II, 401.
Barachel, II, 497 & fn.
Barbarus, Hermolaus (1454-93), I, 226, 638.
Barbeyrac, Jean (1674-1744), on Peruvians & oath, II, 374fn.
Barborka, G. A., *H. P. Blavatsky, Tibet and Tulku:* I, [14fn.]; on John H. Judge, [10].
Barcelona, recent exorcism at, II, 68-69fn.
Bar-Cocheba, II, 139.
Bardesanes, II, 136, 252.
Bargota, Curé of (16th c.), magical powers of, II, 60.
Barham, F. *See* Mayerhoff.
Bari, dressed up Madonna at, II, 9.
*Barlaam and Josaphat, History of*, II, 580.
Baronius, Card. Cesare (1538-1607), and Josaphat, II, 580.
—— *Annales eccles.*, on Stedingers, II, 331.
Barrachias-Hassan-Oglu, *Tales of the Impious Khalif*, on self-incence, I, 43.
Barruel, A. de (1741-1820), *Mémoires . . . du Jacobinisme*, confused on Masons, II, 372.
Bart, C. C., *Kabiren in Teutschland*: I, 281; on Dactyls, 23; on Heracles, II, 515.
Barthélemy Saint-Hilaire, J. (1805-95), I, 583.
—— *Le Bouddha et sa religion*: on character of Buddha, II, 343; on 4th degree of Dhyâna, 287.
Bartholinus, Thos. (1616-80), I, 142.
Bartholomew's Day, St., massacre of, I, 55.

Basileus (Βασιλεύς), II, 90.
Basilides: II, 123; ascetic, 333; followers of, 128; founded School, 536; ideas of, acc. to Tertullian, 189; teachings of, 155-56, 188; tradition about, 125.
Basnage de Beauval, J. (1653-1723), *Histoire des Juifs*, etc., on Therapeutae, II, 324.
Basra, seed of Islam, II, 54.
Basset, J. G. (*fl.* 1665), *Plaidoyez et Arrests*, etc., II, 633.
Bastian, A. (1826-1905), *Die Völker des östlichen Asien*, on Nagkon-Wat, I, 565, 567-68.
Bathing, none for a thousand years, II, 511fn.
Bath-Kôl: daughter of the divine voice, I, vi; Lightfoot on, viifn.
Batoutah. *See* Ibn Batoutah.
Batria, woman-initiate, I, 25.
Batte-bâzi, juggler, II, 612.
Battle of life, II, 112.
Batylos, and liṅga, II, 5.
Baubo, symbolism of, II, 111, 112.
Baumé, Antoine (1728-1804), I, 344.
Baur, F. C. (1792-1860), II, 189fn., 328.
Baxendell, Jos. (1815-87`, I, 410.
Baxitae, levitation of, I, 472.
Bayle, P. (1647-1706), *Dict. historique et critique*: on shedding blood, I, 64; on false relics, II, 72.
Bayt-ed-Deen, II, 313.
Beal tree, II, 607.
Beasts, wild, do not attack Buddhist nuns, II, 609.
Beaujeu, Count, imposture of, II, 381.
Beausobre, I. de (1659-1738), *Hist. critique . . . du Manichéisme:* q. Augustine on rêshîth, II, 35-36; on Gospels, 37-38.
Beccaria, G. B. (1716-81), I, 82.
Bede (or Baeda) (672-735): I, 9, 337fn., 513, 622; on heaven, II, 478.
Bedouins, II, 497.
Beecher, H. W. (1813-1887), I, x.
Beelzebub (or Beelzebul) (βεελζεβούλ): II, 486 & fn., 487, 528; and Domitian, 147fn.
Beer, in Egypt, I, 543.
Being, from not-Being, II, 269.
Beings: countless races of, in space, I, 116; people all the elements, 343fn.; invisible, 340-41.
Beisla, I, 122, 148.
Bel, Baal: Assyrian Jupiter, and satellites,

I, 261; as Śiva, 263; and Devil, 552; and Dragon, 550. *See also* Baal.
Bela, II, 308fn.
Belial: chief of the Klippoth, II, 210; spiritual Diakka, 482.
Belief, basis of true, II, 559.
Belita: II, 170; identical with Eve, 444.
Belitan II, 48.
Bell, A. Graham (1847-1922), and telephone, I, 126-27.
Bellarmin, R. (1542-1621), *De loco purgatorii*, on topography of Hell, II, 8.
Bellerman, J. J. (1754-1842), *Drei Programmen*, etc., II, 172fn.
Bells: among Shamans, heathens & Jews, II, 624 & fn.; of Jupiter, 592; origin of tinkling, 95; Moses commands high priest to carry, 523fn.
Belt, Thos. (1832-78), *The Naturalist in Nicaragua*, I, 592fn.
Belus, I, 332, 552. *See* Baal, Bel.
Belzoni, G. B. (1778-1823), *Narratives*, etc., on Kings' tombs, II, 404.
Ben David, Lazarus (1762-1832), on Moses, I, 528.
Bend-emir, II, 630fn.
Benedict, St. (480-543 A.D.), & black raven, II, 78.
Benim nabim, I, xxx.
Bennett, J. H. (1812-1875), *Textbook of Physiology*, etc., I, 475fn.
Berêshîth, II, 35.
Bergelmir, I, 150.
*Berliner Monatschrift* (Eberhart), I, 24.
Bernadette, Soubirous (1844-79), I, 120.
Bernard, St. (1090-1153), vision of Christ's birth, II, 73.
Bernier, F. (1630?-1688), *Voyages*, etc., on mercury potions, II, 620.
Beroea, Nazarene settlement, II, 181.
Berosus (*fl.* 3rd c. B.C.): I, 154, 341; II, 257, 260, 275, 426; and Oannes or Dagon, I, 133, 349; on cycles, 30fn.; on Chaldean account of creation, II, 271; on twelve gods, 448.
—— *Berosi Chald. Historiae*, on Zeruan, II, 217.
Berti, D. (1820-1897), *Vita di Giordano Bruno*, etc., on charges against Bruno and his beliefs, I, 95-97.
Bertrand, A. J. F. (1795-1831), *Du Magnétisme animal en France*, I, 172.
Berythus, I, 570, 651.

Berzelius, Baron J. J. (1779-1848), on science, I, 411. *See also* Siljeström.
Beth-El, Both-Al: and Betylos, I, 550; house of the Sun, 13.
Bethlehem, grotto of, II, 139.
Betylos ($\beta\alpha\iota\tau\upsilon\lambda os$): and Beth-el, I, 550; meteoric stone, 352; and liṅga, II, 5.
Bezaleel, II, 38.
Bhagalpur, Round Tower of, II, 5.
*Bhagavad-Gîtâ*: I, 92; II, 275, 535; on soul in everything, II, 277; unitarian & pre-Vedic, 562-63.
Bhagavant, I, 91.
Bhagavat: I, 148; emanates Brahmâ, 347; title of Buddha, II, 550; title of Kṛishṇa, 539.
*Bhâgavata-Purâṇa*: II, 271fn., 563fn.; on ark, 405; on creation, 260; on deluge & Vishṇu, 257; on massacre of Innocents, 199; on Pitṛis, 107.
Bhavânî-Mahâdevî, II, 434.
Bhikshuṇî, evokes soul of flowers, II, 609-10.
Bhikshus: divine by flame, II, 607; strict rules among the, 600fn., 608.
Bhṛigu: II, 407fn.; and *Manu*, I, 586.
Bhutavân, I, 265.
Bhûtnâ, phantom, II, 107, 115.
Bibân al-Mulûk: II, 50; and tombs, 404.
Bible: allegorical, I, 436; amenable to criticism, 605; antedated by *Vedas*, 91; earliest Hebrew MS. of, 587; II, 430 & fn.; identity of, with other cosmogonies, I, 122; myths of the, 570; not all mere allegory, 575; H. Burgess on, 605fn.; allegorical screen of Kabalah, II, 210; allegories of, & Egypt, 448; forced on believers in Christ, 126; genuine sacred books of, preserved, 470; Hebrew MSS. of, 430fn.; legends of, belong to univ. history, 469; only a Kabalist can restore the, 362fn.; on murderers after Cain, 448; passages in, comp. with Oriental Scriptures; 556; and Protestants, 200fn.; real Hebrew, a secret vol., 471; restored by Ezra, 217; revised & cut, 252; unauthenticated, 577; and *Vedas*, 415; vicissitudes of original books of, 470-71; and Zodiac, 457.
*Bibliothèque du magnétisme animal* (Deleuze), I, 194fn., 399.
Billot, G. P. (1768-1841), *Recherches*, etc., on manifestations, I, 499.
Bichat, M. F. K. (1771-1802), I, 390.

Biffi, q. on the essential, I, v-vi.
Bifröst, I, 161, 187-88fn.
Bilocation, I, 361.
Binah: and androgyne Demiurge, II, 468; or Sophia, 193, 215fn.; —Yehovah, female potency, 213, 215fn., 268-69.
Binlang, stone of, is anointed, II, 234-35.
*Biographie contemporaine,* on Littré, I, 76.
Birds, tamed by will power, I, 380.
Birs-Nimrud: and Borsippa Temple, I, 261; towers of, and the seven spheres, II, 465.
Birth-marks, I, 384ff., 391.
Births: new—, at initiation, II, 566; three, of man striving for perfection, 565.
Bischoff, T. L. W. (1807-82), I, 387.
Bishops, of 4th cent. illiterate, I, 251.
Bitch, as symbol of Accuser, II, 494.
Black: mirror and Inca queen, I, 596; —faced Christs in India, II, 532; **gods of Yakuts, 568-69;** virgins in France, 95.
*Blackwood's Edinburgh Magazine* (Hamley), on Egyptian knowledge, I, 515ff., 647.
Blanc, H., *De l'Inspiration des Camisards,* on vampires, I, 452.
Blasphemy, and lying, II, 358.
Blanchard, Rev. J., drunk, II, 514fn.
Blautasis, I, 406.
Blavatsky, H. P. (1831-91): and apparitions at Eddys', I, 70; business relations of, with priest in Peru, 547; creates a vacuum in space, [17-18fn.]; and Incas' treasure, 595-96; intimately acquainted with adepts, v; observed mediumship in many lands, 320; on her English style & K. H., [33]; on her own mediumship, [12]; and Peru's subterraneans, 598; travels in, & prophecy about, Gobi, 599; variants of handwriting, [19]; **wanderings of, among magicians, 42-43; witnesses** case of invulnerability, 379; witnesses **charming of snakes, 382-83; writes** to Dr. Wilder on *Isis,* [45], 641; among Kalmucks in early years, II, 600fn.; cured of fever in Burma, 621; does not attack true religion, 479; and magic of Shaman, 626-28; personally knows members of secret brotherhood, 307; rescued in desert by Katchi, 628; **sees adept ooze out of body, 596;** witnesses evocation of phantoms by blood, 567-68 & fn.; witnesses faked phenomenon, 594; witnesses incarnation of adept into child's body,
600-02; witnesses magic among Kurds, 630-32.
—— Letters written to her. See O'Grady, O'Sullivan, Rawson, Sotheran.
—— *Collected Writings,* cited, I, [6ff.], 67, 69, 325.
—— *From the Caves and Jungles of Hindostan,* on Asgartha, I, 643.
—— *Isis Unveiled*: based on idea of higher nature in man, I, 194; opinions in, based on years of study, 42; plan, purpose & objectives of, v, vii, xliv-xlv; II, 99, 120, 292, 640; plates & copyright of, purchased by T. P. Co., I, [56]; probable opponents of, viii; 30 years earlier would have been doomed, 220; words in, attributed to Lucretius, 37, 635; four main facts established in, II, 544; **Vol. II & theol. Christianity, iv; states facts about secret brotherhood by permission, 307.**
—— *Letters to A. P. Sinnett,* on writing *Isis,* I, [19fn.], [54], [55].
—— "My Books," I, [34ff.].
—— *Scrapbooks,* I, [1fn.], 636.
—— *The Key to Theosophy,* I, [47].
—— *The Secret Doctrine,* I, 637, 651.
—— "The Secret Doctrine, Vol. III," I, 635.
—— *Theosophical Glossary,* I, 631.
**Blech, Charles ( ?-1934),** *Histoire,* **etc.,** q. H.P.B. on *Isis,* I, [44].
Blood: Church disbelieves in shedding, I, 64; and evocation of larvae, 493; Homer **on festival of, 362; in Lake Morat, 413;** in snow & water, - 414-15; miracle of, of S. Gennaro & Sûran, 613; Plato on circulation of, 236-37; spilled, & phantoms, 344-45; *volatilized,* can feed, 463; baptism of, in Egypt, II, 42; begets phantoms & gives them form, 567-68, 569; eating of, forbidden by Moses, 567; evocation by means of, 569-70; in Eucharist, 561; and nephesh, 244; occult nature of, **and vital light, 567; of Christ at Westminster, 71-72; propitiatory efficacy of,** 547; sucked through perspiration, 569.
Blue: magnetic properties of, I, 264-65; ray, 137; symbol of material world, II, 446.
Blue Lodge, II, 398.
Blue-violet, seventh ray, I, 514.
Blumenbach, J. F. (1752-1840), *Institutiones physiologicae*: on sleep, I, 180; on skulls of mummies, II, 437fn.

Boccaccio, G. (1313-1375), *Decameron*, II, 79.
Bodhi (Tib.: byan-chub), precepts to attain, II, 164.
Bodhisattva (Tib.: byan-chub-sems-*d*pa), sceptre of, at Potala, II, 616-17.
Bodin, J. (1530-1596), *De la Démonomanie*, etc.: II, 61; on daemons & sword, I, 364; on Cath. de Medici's sorcery, II, 55-56.
*Bodleian Codex*, II, 430, 654.
Body: nourished through magnetic forces, I, 169; Plato on escaping prison of, 139fn.; as sepulchre of soul, II, 112; cannot be disintegrated as inert matter, 589; how long may be kept alive, 563; lama leaving, behind, 604-05; of Moses, symbol of Palestine, 482; sentient living, 114fn.
Boessière, and lightning among ancients, I, 527. See *Notice*, etc.
Boethius, A.M.S. (470?-524?), I, 251.
—— *Ars Geometriae*, on Pythagorean numerals, II, 300.
Bogdo-Ula, Mt., sepulchres of, II, 604, 659.
Bohatta, H. (1864-1947), *Deutsches Anonymen Lexikon*, II, 650.
Böhme, Jacob (1575-1624), I, xxxvii, 221.
Bohu, chaos, waste, II, 526.
Bois-Robert, I, 188.
Bolland, John (1596-1665), *Acta Sanctorum*, II, 645.
Bölthorn, I, 122.
Bonamy, P. N. (1694-1770), "Dissertation . . . sur la Bibliothèque d'Alexandrie," on serapeion, II, 29fn.
Bond, on Indian pigmies, I, 188.
Bonelli, F. A. (1784-1830), I, 188.
Book(s): burning of, I, 24-25, 511; II, 29fn.; 42 sacred, of Egyptians, I, 33fn.; very old, 1.
*Book of Brahmanical Evocations*, I, xlii, xliii; II, 587.
*Book of Common Prayer*. See Bailey, J.
*Book of Enoch*: II, 357; on "daughters of men," I, 305; on Jehovah, 270; as canonical as Mosaic Books, II, 470; and *Revelation*, 147.
*Book of Jasher*: I, 637; a forgery, 549; on coats of skin, 149-50; on Sulanuth, 325fn.; discussed, II, 399-400.
"Book of Life," and elementals, I, 343.

*Book of Numbers* (Chaldean): I, 32, 256, 575, 579, 580; II, 99; one of the *Books of Hermes*, I, 254fn.
*Book of Shet*. See *Desâtir*.
*Book of the Babylonian Companions*, II, 245fn.
*Book of the Dead*: and New Test., I, 518; anterior to Menes, II, 361; immense antiquity of, 548fn.; and judgment of soul, 364, 369; and *Matthew* compared, 548-49; on Osiris as Sun, 517; on the Word, 387; on two Truths, 289; reflects worship of India, 438; and role of Thoth, 367; scene of Judgment in, 493-94, 499-500, 548.
*Book of the Historical Zodiacs:* on first Buddha & Virgin Avany, II, 322 & fn.; on Lankâ & Râma, 278fn.
*Book of the Keys*: on 1 & 10, II, 298; on soul, 281.
*Book of the Law*, a *purâna*, II, 492.
*Book of the Wisdom of Solomon*, I, 580.
*Books of Hermes*. See *Hermetic Books*.
Booths, feast of the, II, 44-45.
Bör: meaning of, I, 150; son of Buri, marries Beisla, 122, 148; sons of, saved from Flood, 150; sons of, slay Ymir, 150.
Bordj, I, 156.
Borie, and mesmerism, I, 171.
Borri, Father (16th c.), and heathen religious symbols, II, 554.
Borrichius, Olaus (1626-1690): on alchemy, I, xxv; biogr. 630.
Borsippa, Temple of, and symbolic colors, I, 261.
Bosco, I, 100.
Bosheth, II, 130.
*Boston Sunday Herald*, on Eastern magic, I, 457-58.
Both-al, and Betylos, I, 550.
Boucher de Crévecœur de Perthes, J. (1788-1868), flint axes found by, I, 155, 223.
Boucicault, D. L. (1820-1890), *Louis XI*, I, 485.
Boudin, J. C. (1806-1867), *De la Foundre*, etc., on globular lightning, I, 108.
Boué, A. (1794-1881), and fossil, I, 223.
Bougainville, L. A. de (1729-1811), I, 413fn.
Bourdois de la Motte, E.-J. (1754-1835), and mesmerism, I, 174.
Boussingault, J. B. (1802-87), and Babinet, I, 60.

Bouton, J. W., and *Isis Unv.*, I, [3], [43], [51-52], [56].
Bower, A. (1686-1766), *Hist. of the Popes*, on Peter's chair, II, 25fn.
Bowls, brazen, of Korê, II, 592.
Boyle, R. (1627-91), I, 218, 503.
—— *Works*, I, 193.
Brachmanes: I, xl, 532; II, 306, 321, 434.
Bradhna, and soma, I, xl.
Brahe, Tycho (1546-1601): and comet, I, 441-42; theory of, 622.
Brahmâ: I, 156; comes from Bhagavat, 347; creates Daityas & originates Brâhmaṇas, 148; creates Lomaśa, 133; and esoteric meaning of lotus, 91-92; manifesting as 12 bodies, 348; secondary creative deity, 91, 93; stirring up of, xxvii, xxxv; II, 269; as Creator, II, 215, 226; as father of man, 232; as "son of a king," 399fn.; and Brahmans' descent, 407fn.; "days" & "nights" of, 264-65, 269, 272-74, 421-22; devatâs are powers of, 563; invocation to, 105; and mythical Manu, 269.
Brahmagupta, I, 621.
Brahmamaya, I, 271fn.
Brahmâ-Nara, II, 268.
Brahmâ-Prajâpati, I, xliv, 265, 348.
Brahman (neuter): Unknowable Deity, I, 291; "aham eva para——," II, 262; or Ptaḥ, 226.
Brahman-Dyaus, II, 170.
*Brâhmaṇas*: II, 416; antiquity of, I, 12, Müller on, 580; period of, 11; interpret *Vedas*, II, 409, 413; key to *Ṛigveda*, 415; metre in, 410.
Brahmanism: Buddhism as primitive source of, II, 169; pre-Vedic, 143, 156fn., 639.
Brahmans, Brahmins [Brâhmaṇas]: ambitions of, distort *Manu*, I, 587, 588; as Hotars, xxxviii; curing by word, 444; levitating, 472; origin of, 122; prophecy & clairvoyance of, 446; rod of, xxxifn.; —Yogins, 307; *Atharvaveda* on power of, II, 106-07; can but will not explain phenomena, 584-85; claims of, as to descent, 407fn.; high virtues of, 474fn.; in Babylonia, 46, 428; intruders displacing earlier faith, 156fn.; Jacolliot on occult faculties of, 103; and Jainas, 323; never borrow any myths, 426-27, 539-40; on first Buddha in Ceylon, 322; spoil ancient MSS., 169; triple cord of, 393; views on Hanuman, 278; and Zoroaster, 237fn. *See also* Brachmanes.
Brahmans-Sannyâsins, cable-tow of, II, 393.
Brahmans-Tîrthikas, and Nirvâṇa, I, 431.
Brahmâtma: I, xxxiii; cross of, II, 254; passes on secret to successor, 571; and Popes, 30; and sacred name, 398; sole guardian of mystic formula, 31; still accessible today, 100; triangle of, 262 & fn.
Braid, J. (1795-1860), *Observations on Trance*, etc., I, 477.
Brain: animal, philosophizes, I, 247; change in, by thought, 249-50; convolutions of, 352; ganglion of neurological telegraphy, 324; of savages, 331; "silvery spark" in, 329; Tyndall on, and consciousness, 86; action of, impairs true seership, II, 591.
Brasseur de Bourbourg, C. E. (1814-74), on Atlanta, I, 591.
—— *Histoire des nations*: on magic mirror, I, 596fn.; on naguals, 556.
—— *Lettres* (Cartas): on Hivims, I, 554; on Nin & Baal, 551-52; on Votan & Phoenicians, 546; on Votan & snake's hole, 553.
——*Popol-Vuh*: I, 122, 151fn., 650; fragments of original, 551; magic in, 549; mentions 4th race, 593; and Müller, 548-49; on creation of man, 549, 558; on higher races, 2; on man out of mud, 133.
Brazil, gold from, I, 597.
Bread, and wine. *See* Eucharist.
Bréal, M. (1832-1915), *Hercule et Cacus*, etc., on Asmodeus, II, 482.
Breath(s): and ether, I, 290; infusing intelligent life, 302; Divine, II, 419.
Breathing, and mesmerism, II, 632, 633.
Brewster, D. (1781-1868), I, 75, 543; on Egyptian magicians, 416.
—— *A Treatise on Optics*: on knowledge of ancients, I, 282; on light being material, 137.
Bribe, and Jesuits, II, 356.
Bridgewater, J. (1532?-1596?), *Concertatio*, etc., on breaking faith, II, 372fn.
Brierre de Boismont, A. J. F. (1798-1881): I, 164; on de Mirville's book, 102.
—— *Des Hallucinations*: on precognition, I, 144-45; on soul-powers, 181; on supernatural, 71; on vampires, 450.
Bṛihad-Âraṇyaka, on the Self, II, 318fn.

Brihaspati: I, xi; as a cycle, 31; on human triad, II, 115.

Britten, Emma H. ( ? -1899), and elementals, I, xxixfn.

—— *Art Magic*: I, xxvii, 245; on Cabbala, 358; on mediums & magicians, 367; on Sanskrit psychography, 368; on exorcisms, II, 87fn.

—— *Ghost Land*: on knowledge, I, 574; on transference of adept's ego, II, 563.

—— *Modern American Spiritualism*, on R. Hare, I, 245.

Bronze: age of, I, 534fn.; brought by Āryans, 539.

Brothers of the Shadow, and materializations, I, 319.

Brotherhood(s): among Kabalists, II, 470; Eastern, and Masonry, 380, 388; members of mysterious, and H.P.B., 306-07; of Luxor in U.S.A., 308fn.; secret, masters of the situation, 404; secrets of ancient, not in possession of profane, 394; and their disciples, 404.

Broussais, F. J. V. (1772-1838), *Examen de la doctrine médicale*, etc., on magnetism, II, 610.

Browne, Sir Thos. (1605-1682), *Pseudodoxia Epidemica*, etc., on perpetual lamps, I, 232.

Bruce, J. (1730-1794), *Travels*, etc.: I, 381; on arts in Egypt, 544.

Bruchion, story about the fire of, and salvaged MSS., II, 27-28.

Bruno, G. (1548-1600): fate of, I, 339fn.; II, 528; Pythagorean, I, 97-98; victim of Church, 93; why slaughtered, 95; not an atheist, II, 531.

—— *Della Causa, Principio ed Uno*, I, 93-94.

—— *Del' Universo e Mondi*, I, 93-94.

Bruns, Paul J. (1743-1814), Dr. Kennicott & Hebrew MSS., II, 430fn.

Bruun. See Malte-Brun.

Bryant, J. (1715-1804), *A New System*, etc., on Samael, II, 483.

*Buarth Beirdd—The Cattlepen of the Bards*, I, 651.

Buchanan, J. R. (1814-99): I, 63; and psychometry, 330.

—— *Outlines*, etc.: I, ix; on gestures, 500; on crime & psychometry, 332; on nature of psychometry, 182; valuable suggestions in, 86-87.

Büchner, F. C. C. L. (1824-1899), *Stellung des Menschen*, etc. (implied), on man's antiquity, I, 155.

Buddha: as formless Brahm, I, 291; as generic term is *monad*, 291; every man can become a, 291; Huc on reincarnation of a, 438; as abstract deity & its powers, II, 616fn.; fifth, and Vishṇu, 260, 275; first, & Virgin Avany, 322. See also Buddhas.

Buddha, Gautama (Tib.: sańs-rgyas, pron. *sangyä*): I, 442; II, 159, 286, 341, 528, 531, 533, 549, 554, 555, 557; birth of, announced by vision, I, 92; four truths of, 626; identical to St. Josaphat, 98; II, 579-81; on cessation of caste, I, 435; on poverty, 488; on space & Māyā, 289; overshadowing by, 635; precept of, to King Prasenagit, 599-600; regarded as atheist, 307; shadow of, 600-01; II, 550; teaches how to avoid rebirth, I, 346; transmigrations of, 292; age of, II, 322; antiquity of philosophy of, 169; as 9th avatâra of Vishṇu, 156fn., 274; as restorer of pure religion of *Vedas*, 436fn.; compared to Kṛishṇa & Jesus, 339, 536, 537-39; date of, 537; death of, 571; did not teach annihilation, 319; had esoteric doctrine, 319; high virtues of, 343; and Kashmîr, 509; last words of, 607; legends of, wrought into Gospels, 491-92; moral code of, 339; Müller on death of, 342fn.; never deified, 240; of serpent lineage, 484; on basis of true belief, 559; on sins of world, 547; one of many, 537; taught by Jaina Tîrthaṃkara, 322; taught new birth, 566; teachings of, 123-24; tempted, 513; ten commandments of, and *Matthew*, 553; variations of name of, 30fn.; wonders at incarnation of, 551-52; worshipped by Ṛishi Asita, 518-19fn.

Buddhagosha, *Parables*, etc., II, 540.

Buddhas: before Gautama, II, 322; four, 467; govern 22 universes, 156fn.; not gods, 322.

Buddhasp, II, 291.

Buddhism: and Christianity, I, 347; esoteric doctrine of, 243fn., 316; does not teach atheism, 292; four truths of, 291; and Kabalah, 271; key to, 289; on reality & illusion, 306; ascetics of, & 4th degree of Dhyâna, II, 287-88; as doctrine of Wisdom, 143; based on three principles, 124; believes in creative powers, 264; better understood, 345; and Christianity compared, 288; compared with Romanism, 541-42; does not deny Supreme Being, 323; enjoins individual effort, 288; four schools in, 533; in Ireland, 290fn.; in Palestine & Greece, 492; in Syria & Babylon, 289, 491; legend of, similar to those of Jesus, 550ff.; monastic, & Sermon on Mount, 553; Müller on moral code of, 339; of Nepal close to original, 290, 608; on Dead Sea, 130, 132, 321, 507, on Noble Path, 282; precepts of, 164; prehistoric, universal, 123, 142, 156, 198fn., 322; pre-Vedic, and Brahmanism, 156fn., 169, 436fn., 639; ranks in Tibetan, 631; relation to Jainism, 322-23; religion of earlier *Vedas,* 436fn.; strong in idea of man's *inner* self, 554; two religions in, 607: why flourishes, 239-40.

Buddhists, II, 320.

Buffon, Comte de (1707-88), I, 84-85, 414.
— *Œuvres complètes,* on mirror of Alexandria, I, 528.

Builders: operative, as adepts, II, 392; Master—, 392, 393.

Bulgarian, atrocities, II, 54.

Bull: symbol of life in various religions, II, 235-36, 465.

*Bulletin de l'Académie de Médecine* (art. by Dr. Oudet), I, 166-67fn.

*Bulletin de la Société de Géographie* (art. by Agardt), on blood in water, I, 414.

*Bulletin de pharmacie* (art. by J. J. Virey), on chemical knowledge of ancients, I, 531.

Bulstrode, W. (1650-1724), *Essay of Transmigration,* etc., on Pythagorean doctrines, I, 290.

Bulwer-Lytton, E. (1803-73): on secrets of nature, I, 39; and Dweller of the Threshold, 158, 325.

— *A Strange Story:* I, 360; on immortality, 253; on life-principle, 329; on science, 278, 282.

— *The Coming Race:* on vril, I, 64; on Vril-ya, 296.

— *The Last Days of Pompeii,* on theurgy, I, xliii.

— *Zanoni:* on elemental creatures, I, 285-86; on invocation of Augoeides, 358; on mirror of soul, 73; on perfection of soul, 64; on real medicine, 461; on research, 1; on starry truths, 17.

*Bundahish:* II, 238; on Ahriman, 488fn.

Bunsen, C. C. J. (1791-1860): I, 513; and experiment with rabbit's eye, 607; attacked, II, 366fn.
— *Egypt's Place in Univ. Hist.:* on antiquity of Egypt, I, [16], 33fn., 529; on Cheops Pyramid, 518; on cycles, 32; on date of Menes, 589fn.; on flood, 241; on quarrying, 518; on age of Egyptian religion & *Book of the Dead,* II, 548fn.; on age of Zoroaster & Moses, 432; on cycle of nutation of ecliptic, 366fn.; on date when Israelites left Egypt, 558; on disfigured dates in *Genesis,* 217; on Egyptian funeral ritual and Thoth, 367; on Egyptian history, 448; on Eusebius' forgeries, 327; on hieroglyphs spelling Peter, 92-93; on human sacrifices, 565fn.; on Khamism, 435; on Menes, 361; on mystery of names, 368fn.; on precepts of earliest rituals, 361fn.; on sacred texts unintelligible to later scribes, 415; on Seth & Hittites, 482fn.; on soul's second death, 368.
— *God in History,* on Seth, II, 484, 487fn.
— *Hippolytus und seine Zeit,* on Colarbasus error, II, 248fn.

Burattinus, T. Livius, I, 226, 227, 638.

Burdach, K. F. (1776-1847), I, 384, 387.

Burdett-Coutts, Baroness A. G. (1814-1906), II, iii.

Burdin, and mesmerism, I, 174.

Burges, G. (1786-1864), *The Works of Plato,* misreads Plato, I, 8.

Burgess, Rev. E. See *Sûrya-Siddhânta.*

Burgess, Rev. H. (1808-86), on *Bible,* I, 605fn.

Buri: born of Audhumla, I, 147; first man, father of Bör, 122.

Burial, cases of premature, I, 456.

Burmese, classics, II, 554fn.

Burning: of Arabian MSS., I, 511; of books, II, 29fn.; of heretics, 62ff.

Burnouf, Eugène (1801-52), on ancient traditions & India, II, 259.
— *Introduction,* etc.: on Nirvâṇa, I, 431; on Svâbhâvikas, 250; on Buddha's shadow on cloth, II, 550.
— *Saddharma-puṇḍarika:* II, 164fn.; on Viśodhana, 287.

Burton, R. (1577-1640), *The Anatomy of Melancholy,* II, 445fn.

Bush, burning, II, 438.

Bushby, H. J. (1820- ? ), *Widow-Burning,* etc., I, 541fn., 649.
Butler, A. (1711-1773), *Lives of the Fathers,* etc., on Simeon Stylites, II, 77.
Butler, S. (1612-1680), *Hudibras,* I, 83.
Butler, W. A. (1814?-1848), *Lectures . . . on Philosophy,* on numbers, I, xvi.
Butleroff, A. M. (1828-86): I, 46, 54, 222; and mediumism, 118.
—— *Mediumistic Manifestations,* on scientific facts, II, 3.
Buttmann, Ph. K. (1764-1829), I, 8.
Buxdorf the Elder, J. (1564-1629), *Lexicon Chaldaicum,* etc, II, 445fn.
Byauds, secret, or Brotherhoods, II, 609.
Byron, Lord G. G. (1788-1824), II, 511.
—— *Don Juan,* I, 48.
—— *Giaour,* I, 417.
Bythos (Βυθός): II, 216, 227, 295; as Adam-Kadmon, II, 223; as ever-producing Cosmos, 171, 172; and Propatôr, 210; and Shekhînah, 169, 293.
Byzantines, and red dragon, II, 484.

# C

Cabanis, P. J. G. (1757-1808), *Rapport du physique,* etc., on spiritual perceptions, I, 145.
—— *Histoire de la médecine,* Hippocrates quoted, I, 425, 434.
"Cable-tow," of Brahmans & lamas, II, 393.
Caciques: derivation of word, I, 592; descendants of, survive, 546.
Cadière, Mlle C., victim of sorcery, II, 633-34.
Caelius Aurelianus (end of 4th c. A.D.): I, 226, 638; and the *diacentaureon,* 89.
Caesar, Julius (100-44 B.C.), *Commentarii,* etc.: I, 193; on Druids, 18; on human sacrifice, II, 547.
Cagliostro, Alessandro di: I, xxxiii, 100, 128; and gold, 509; and de Saint-Germain, II, 403.
Cahen, S. (1796-1862), *La Bible,* on Lord & Eternal, II, 401.
Caiaphas, and Annas, II, 522.
Cain (or Kain): and Abel, II, 446; as Ahriman & Taurus, 465; as Aries, 462; generations of, 459-60; Kin & Eva, 225; meaning of, 466; and other murderers in line of descent, 448; son of Adam-Kadmon, 464.

Calchas, II, 7.
Calder, A., II, 597.
Caldwell, R. (1814-1891), *Comparative Grammar,* etc., on Solomon & India, I, 136fn.
Calef, R. (1648-1719), I, 361.
Calendar, of Aztecs & Chaldeans, I, 11.
Calixtus III (ca. 1378-1458), and Halley's comet, II, 509.
Callimachus (ca. 305-ca. 240), golden lamp of, I, 227.
Callisthenes (4th c. B.C.), I, 21.
Calmeil, Dr. J. L. (1798-1895): I, 369, 371; on convulsionnaires, 375.
Calmet, Father A. (1672-1757), II, 346.
—— *Diss. sur les apparitions*: I, 354; on vampirism, 451-52.
Calvin, J. (1509-64), II, 208, 479, 503.
—— *Institutes,* etc., on predestination & grace, II, 547.
Cambodia. *See* Nagkon-Wat.
Cambrai, Archbishop of, *Pastoral* on Ultramontanism, II, 356.
Camerarius, Phil. (1537-1624), *Operas horarum subcisivarum,* etc., on handling burning coals & Jesuits, I, 445.
Camisard, prophets, I, 369, 438.
Campanella, T. (1568-1639), I, 207.
Campanile, II, 5.
Canaan; Beth-el of, I, 550; Heth & Hivites, 546.
Candolle, A. L. P. P. (1806-93): on blood phenomenon in Lake Morat, I, 413; on vital movement, 313.
Canon, N. T.: blunders & falsifications in, II, 133-37, 143-44, 153, 169, 177-83, 192, 199, 203, 247-48; decided by divination, 251-52; plagiarisms in, 237-39, 241-42, 244; revision of, a new "revelation," 252; why *Acts* & *Revelation* so long rejected, 137-38.
Canova, A. (1757-1822), I, 528.
Canton, J. (1718-1772), I, 417.
Capel, Mons. Thos. J. (1836-1911), on Lourdes miracles, I, 119-20.
Capella, Martianus M. F. (*fl.* 5th c.) *Satyra de nuptiis,* etc., on Typhon, II, 490.
Capellus, J. (1570-1624), on Jehovah, II, 400.
Capuchins, Christmas observances of, II, 365-66.
Cardan, G. (1501-76), I, 205, 251, 404.
—— *De varietate rerum,* on projection of astral soul, I, 477.

Cardinals, College of, II, 31fn.
Cariai, village mentioned by Columbus, I, 592.
Carlyle, T. (1795-1881), *Sartor Resartus*, on ever-present, II, 251.
**Carnac, and Karnak, I, 554.**
Carné, L. de (1844-1870), *Voyage en Indo-Chine*, etc., on civilizations of ancients, I, 564.
Carneades, I, 582.
Carnelian, white, II, 351. *See* A-yu.
Carpenter, W. B. (1813-85): I, 55, 234, 248, 410; on spiritual phenomena, 232-33; on laws of nature, II, 587.
—— *Ancient and Modern Egypt*: on irrigation & architecture, I, 517; on Dendera pictures, 440.
Carpini, Joannes de Plano (ca. 1182-1252), I, 247.
**Carpocratians: II, 325; used pictures of religious figures, 150.**
Carré de Montgeron, L. B. (1686-1754), *La Vérité des miracles*, etc., I, 373.
Carrière, J. de (1795-1864): on chronology and reproduction of Jews, II, 558; on Mosaic books, 425fn.
Carthage, antiquity of, I, 520.
Carthagenians, human sacrifices among, II, 565fn.
**Carthusians, II, 546fn.**
**Carwithen**, Rev. J. B. S., on Kṛishṇa & Mathurâ, II, 537.
Casalius, I, 226, 639.
Casley, D. (*fl.* 1734), *Catalogue of the MSS. of the King's Library*, on Christ's descent into Hell, II, 177.
Casmilos (Κάσμιλος), or Cadmilos (Κάδμιλος), and Kabiris, I, 569.
Casnedi, C. A., *Crisis theologica*, on blasphemy & lying, II, 358.
Cassandrus, I, 294fn.
Cassaudière, I, 79.
[**Cassels, W. R., 1826-1907**], *Supernatural Religion*: I, [16], 305; II, 80; on credulity, I, 403; on Basilides, II, 155fn.; on *Clem. Hom.*, 189, 190; on Divine Revelation & Truth, 126; on Emmanuel & Jesus, 166; on *Epitome*, 190; on Epistle of Clement, 248; on false ref. to *Isaiah*, 192; on ignorance of Ch. Fathers, 248fn.; on **Kol-Arbas error, 248fn.**; on **Marcion** & his era, 161fn.; on Marcion & Luke's Gospel, 168; on Marcion's view of Christ, 168; on primitive Christianity, 180-81;
on **Peter & Paul antagonism, 161-63, 161-62fn.**; on Tertullian, 329; on Tertullian's abuse of Marcion, 160; proves Gospels spurious, 125; q. Xenophanes on God in human likeness, 242.
Cassianus, J. M. (*fl.* 4th & 5th c.), *Collationes*, etc., I, 25.
Castaldi, P. (1398-1490?), and printing, I, 513.
Castelfidardo, II, 81.
Castes: promoted by Brahmans, II, 169; seven, 407.
Castor, on Belus, I, 552.
Cataclysms, periodic: I, 31; ante-historical, 266.
Catalepsy: I, 445; cannot be feigned, 166; and death, 484; and vampirism, 449; and dharana, II, 591; and mediumship, 588.
Cataleptics, and vampirism, I, 453.
Catastrophies, Görres on, I, 103.
Catherine of Medici (1519-1589): II, 54; practices sorcery, 55-56.
**Catholic**: *See* **Roman Catholic Church, and Church.**
*Catholic World*, on nagualism, I, 556-57.
Caucasians: I, 576; II, 263, 297, 436-37; dark-skinned, I, 525.
Causality, physical, can be transcended, I, 59.
Cause(s): Great, always invisible, I, xxv-vi; Platonic division of, 393; Supreme, cannot be cognized, 621; farflung effect of a, II, 542-43. *See also* First Cause.
Caution, I, 401, 424, 465.
Cave(s) (κρυπτή): symbol of subterranean, I, xiii-xiv; Illuminator inhabiting a, II, 93; of Mithras, 491.
Cave-men, of Les Eyzies, I, 295.
Cave-temples: I, 573, 590fn.; of Ajanta, 349ff.; Jainas, II, 323.
Cave, Wm. (1637-1713), II, 549.
—— *Apostolici*, etc., on Cyril, II, 253.
Cebes, I, 114, 251.
Cedrênus, G. (11th c.), I, 226, 227, 639.
—— *Compendium historiarum*, on Iaô, II, 297fn.
Cellarius, A. Keller (1638-1707), *Harmonia Macrocosmica*, I, 635.
Cellini, Benvenuto (1500-1571), and sorcery, II, 57.
Celsus, A. C. (*fl.* 1st c.), *De medicina*, on signs of death, I, 479.

Celsus (*fl.* 180 A.D.): accuses Christians, II, 51; and Gnostics, 325; twitting Christians, 520; view of, on Jesus, 530; writings of, concealed on Mt. Athos, 52 & fn.
— *Logos alêthês,* lost, II, 52.
Celsus the Epicurean, II, 52fn.
Celts, origin of, I, 576.
Cemec. *See* Semes.
Cement: and joints in ancient buildings, I, 562; of Egypt, 239, 518, 519.
Cenchrea, and Paul, II, 90.
Censorinus (3rd c. A.D.), *De die natali,* on Great Year, I, 30, 31, 294fn., 633-34.
Cerberus, and Heracles, II, 515.
Cerebration, unconscious, I, 232-33.
Ceres: and Bacchus, II, 139fn., 560; and Hadês, 145 & fn.; passive productive principle, 560fn.; and post-mortem purification of man, 284; symbol of bread, 44, 560.
Ceres-Demeter, occult meaning of, II, 111, 505fn.
Cerinthians. *See* Cerinthus.
Cerinthus (1st or 2nd c. A.D.): disciple of Simon Magus, II, 126, 151, 181, 196-97fn. 215fn.; teachings of, distorted by Irenaeus, 176.
Cévennes, Cévennois: I, 217, 221, 390, 438, 626; convulsionnaires of, 370.
Ceylon, Müller on Pâli books of, II, 576fn.
Chaeremon, I, 416.
Chakhars, land of the, II, 599, 658.
Chakra, II, 217, 220, 301.
Chalcidius (4th or 6th c. A.D.), I, 12.
— *Comm. in Timaeum,* on Berêshîth, II, 35.
Chaldea, or Babylonia, I, 267.
*Chaldean Oracles. See* Opsopäus, *Oracula Sibyllina.*
Chaldeans (Kasdim, Chasîdîm, Kasdeans): I, 535; II, 135, 441; allegory of, about flood, I, 554; astronomy of, 11; defined, *xxviii;* magic of, 66, 459; and Ur, 549; cosmogony of, II, 266ff.; founders of magic art, 233fn.; or Asideans, 135, 441, 481, 501; tribe of Akkadians, 46; worshipped Moon, 48.
Châmpnâ, as magical manipulation, I, 445.
Champollion, J. F. (1790-1832): discoveries of, I, 530; fine intentions of, 24.
— *Lettres,* etc.: on Karnac, I, 523; on Hermes' prophecy, II, 360.
Champollion-Figeac, J. J. (1778-1867), *Égypte ancienne*: on ancient knowledge, I, 406; on Egyptian priests & antiquity of Egypt, 626; on Plato's oath of silence, 409; q. Poimandres on truth & death, 624-25; on chaos & verbum, II, 214; on Hermes, 187; on Neith & child, 50; on Osiris, Isis, 268fn.; on Poimandres, 212, 506; on trinities, 227; q. Hermes on how to conceive God, 579fn.
Chaṇḍâlas, II, 438.
Chandragupta, Maurya (r. 321-296 B.C.), II, 436, 607, 608.
Chaos: and aether, I, *341*; as astral light, 129; as primordial matter, 133; female principle, 61; universe a, to sense, a cosmos to reason, xvi; symbolized by Tiamat, I, 445; and Verbum, 214.
Charaka, I, 619.
——*Usa,* on earth, I, 560.
Charak-pûja, I, xxviii.
Chariot, Plato on, and winged steeds, I, xiii.
Charles II (1630-1685), *Enactment,* etc., on Sabbath, II, 419.
Charmers, of beasts, I, 381.
Charms, dhâranî, I, 471.
Charybdis, I, 545.
Chasîdîm. *See* Chaldeans, Asideans.
Chastity, of Talapoins, II, 321.
Chayla, Abbé du ( ? -1702), and the Cévennois, I, 370.
Chêmeia ($\chi\eta\mu\epsilon\iota\alpha$), I, 405, 648.
Chemi (Chem, Chemmis): ancient Egypt, I, 147, 541, 648; as Coptic term ($\chi\eta\mu\iota$) & Sahidic term ($\kappa\eta\mu\epsilon$), 226fn.
Chemical: groupings, I, 508; knowledge of ancients, 531; symbols, 462.
Chemistry: I, 165; and alchemists, 190ff.; Egypt as birthplace of, 541; and elements of ancients, 50, 343fn.; in archaic India, 619; Kenrick on origin of wood, 541; revolution in, 163.
Cheops: pyramid of, I, 518, 520; ring of, 240.
Cherub, Cherubim: and Evangelists, II, 235fn., 451; in Kabalah & Chaldea, 231, 235; modified form of bulls, 236; nail of, 71; Ezekiel, 451.
Chess, in Egypt and India, I, 544.
Chevreul, Dr. M. E. (1786-1889), I, 60, 116.
*Chhândogyopanishad:* on lightning, I, 528; on the Self, II, 318fn., 342; on Svarga, 566fn.

Chibh-Chondor, I, 470-71, 616.
Chichén-Itzá, I, 561.
Chidambaram, pagoda of, II, 262.
Child, L. Maria (1802-1880), *Progress of Religious Ideas*, etc., on Śiva & sexual emblems, I, 583; on sex emblems in Egypt, II, 445.
Child-birth, and moon, I, 264.
Children: born malformed, I, 386; sacrificed to Moloch, 11; may kill their parents, II, 363.
China: glass in, I, 537; metal work in, 538.
Chinese: II, 49, 554; ideas of, about immortality, I, 214; religions, etc. of, 601ff.
Chingîz-Khân (1162?-1227), tomb of, I, 598-99, 656-57.
Chiretta, medicinal herb, II, 622fn.
Chiton (χιτών), a coat, I, 576; II, 458fn.
Chiun (or Khîyûn): as Śiva, I, 570; is Saturn, II, 236, 296, 524.
Chnuphis [Khnemu]: a "Son of God," II, 187; as Ophis, 295, 512fn.; emblem of divine mind, 506; produces an egg, 226; —serpent, as Logos, 510fn.
Chogor-tan (Ch'u-'khor-tang), II, 605.
Chrêstos (χρηστός): as Good Principle, II, 324; Kṛishṇa & Jesus united to their, 558.
Chrism (χρίσμα), II, 158.
Christ(s): allegedly preaching ten years, II, 305; as Jupiter-Pluto, 335; as Sun, 517; body of, illusion acc. to Marcion, 168; called Aeôn, 219; descent into Hell, 177; hour of birth & St. Bernard, 73; idea of, disfigured, 575; **image of, & Alex. Severus,** 150; modified Kṛishṇa for Hindus, 532; of Paul as embodied idea, 574; phial of blood of, at Westminster, 70-71; pre-Christian, many, 43, 205; reincarnationist, 145; religion of, incoherent dream, 248; second advent of, & avatâras, 535; and Serapis, 336fn.; story of portrait on cloth borrowed from Buddhism, 550; and worship of Jehovah, 527.
Christian(s): accused by Celsus, II, 51; adopted popular view of Jehovah, 525; adopt Platonic metaphysics, 33; antiquity of, terms, 205; as modified Buddhists, 540; borrow myth of Serapis, 336; cheat heathen, 531; dislike cleanliness, 331; doctrine & Buddhism, 540-41; doctrine originated in heathendom, 41ff.; early, community at Pella, 197; and Essenes, 323; farce of, monks, 585; first, poor & ignorant, 175; first were Ebionites, 180-81; force Theodosius to destroy idols, 40; found necessary to kill a God, 242; full of dissension, 4; nominal, 3; outdoing pagans in ferocity, 32; pagan origin of symbolism, 334-35; panic of, & doctrine of emanations, 34-35; Peter Cooper a *practical*, 549fn.; prejudices of, 96-97; real, higher than creed, iii; Saturnalia in, monasteries, 365-66; slaughtered 50 millions, 479; sources of purest teachings, 197-98; Suetonius & Hadrian on, 335-36; *true*, died with Apostles, 10; two schools of, kabalists, 198; vandalism of, 93, 323; why, hate paganism, 51-52.
Christianity: adopts pagan gods, II, 49, 51; appropriates from Lamaism, etc., 211; avoided paganism & fell into Judaism, 526; based on alleged prophecy absent from *Bible*, 50; Bishop Kidder on, 240; blended with Gnosis & Kabalah, 211; bloody record of, 53; breeds crime, 573-74; and Buddhism compared, 288; dead in faith & works, 370; devil as fundamental stone of, 501; differs from teachings of Christ, 374fn.; dilemma of, 166; dire moral effects of, 374; **doctrines of,** allegedly plagiarized by pagans, 346; dogmatic, offspring of pagan sects, 334; early, composed of secret societies, 335; early, fights Eclectic School, 34, 51; **early,** had horror of pictures, 149, 150; early sects of, kabalistic, 127; **ecclesiastical,** cunning, sacrilegious, 180; ecclesiastical, founded upon error, 579; essentially distinct from Judaism, 526; and exoteric pagan symbols, 94ff.; factions in early, 161; facts about first five centuries of, lost, 28; final triumph of, & impending bankruptcy, 249; freely borrowed from pagans, 353, 479; God of, **secondary** power, 264; hatred of, towards pagans, 253; heresy or sect, 123; high- & low-caste, 533; iniquities of, and Kublai-Khân, 581-82; lost the Word, 370; mediaeval, assassin of Master's doctrine 38; misrepresents antiquity, 96; modern, a farce, 366; modern, not that of Paul, 575; Müller on, 10; not evidently true, 358-59; **only half-original document of, 204;** original, only in Syrian heresies, 137; phallicism in, 5; and Platonic Gnosis, 198; Platonism in early, 41; primitive, had

degrees of initiation, 204; St. Thomas engrafts, **on religion of Ḳrishṇa, 539;** skeleton of, formed of pagan myths, 339; Sprengel on, & Platonism, 325; symbols of, of pagan origin, 334-35; theological, opponent of free thought, iv; theology of, *pot-pourri* of pagan mythologies, 525; true, 81fn.

*Christian World, The,* on mediumship, I, 123.

Christism: instead of Christianity, II, 472; true, before Christ, 32.

Christists, as Gnostics, II, 324.

Christmas, with Capuchins, II, 365.

Christos (Χριστός): and Aeôn, II, 176, 177; anointed, or King Messiah, 42, 124, 223; as man's personal spiritual entity, 593; as son of Sophia the elder, 177; and Claudius, 335-36; derivation & meaning of, 158-59; and female Spiritus, 193; Gnostics ideas about, 194, 247; identical with Ophis, 187; and Ḳrishṇa, 173-74; Ophis—, 449; Serpent as Logos or, 505; and Sophia in Gnosticism, 185-86; and Sophia-Akhamôth, **295; suffered spiritually,** 158, 159; unrevealed Logos, 172.

**Chromatius (b. 4th c.-d. 410), and Jerome,** II, 182.

*I Chronicles,* on Satan & the numbering of Israel, II, 481 & fn.

*II Chronicles*: I, 593fn.; II, 440, 441; on Tobo, 517.

*Chronicon de Lanercost,* etc., on Bacchanalian dancing, II, 332.

*Chronique des arts,* etc., on St. Peter's chair, II, 23-25fn.

Chronology: effect of false, **I, 522;** Vedic, 32, 587; Bunsen's, II, 366, 558; **Egyptian,** 33, 448; Egyptian, falsified by Ch. Fathers, 327; **established by Holy Ghost, 558;** fanciful in *Pentateuch,* 443fn.; Hindu, & age of Patriarchs, 464fn.

Chronos (χρόνος): **or Olam, I, 132; and** Anu, II, 423.

Chrysostom, St. John (345-407 A.D.), on Simon, II, 91fn.

Chtonia (Χθονία): **I, 156; and Zeus, 262.**

Chughi, II, 620.

Chukchis, I, 211.

**Church: bane of, and priestcraft, II, 586;** blesses Moslem swords, 511; manages celestial hierarchy as theatrical stars, 242; Mousseaux on, & magic, 76; on lies & deception, 303; persecutes magic, 502-03; two factions in primitive, 161; world needs no sectarian, 635. *See* Roman Catholic.

Church Councils: and divination, II, 21, 641.

Church Fathers: helped themselves to ancient myths, I, 298; criminal record of, II, 304; distort a universal theomythos, 238; eager to avoid paganism, 526; had no key to symbolism, 403; Hilgenfeld on, 161; ignorance of, 477; ignorance of, helps science of religion, 527; ignorant of doctrine of atonement, 546; ignorant of Old Test., 247; mixed upon heretics, 248-49 & fn.; panicky at **doctrine of emanations,** 34-35; resort to forgery when cornered by Gnostics, 329; slander pagan thaumaturgists, 97.

Churchill, Chas. H. (1828-1877), *Mount Lebanon,* etc., on Druzes, II, 315.

Chwol'son, D. A. (1819-1911), *Nabathäische Landwirtschaft,* Maimonides on, II, 197.

—— *Die Ssabier,* etc. on Sabianism, II, 554; q. Shahrastânî, 197.

Cicero, M. T. (106-43 B.C.): on prophecy, I, xxxv; his *quiddam divinum,* 131fn.

—— *De divinatione:* II, 128fn.; on exhalations of earth, I, 200; on long observations by Babylonian priests, 533.

—— *De legibus,* on Mysteries, II, 167.

—— *De natura Deorum*: on fleeting shapes of gods, I, 280, 641-42; on first gods, II, 451; on eucharist, 44; **on water, 458.**

—— *De senectute:* on Sod, I, 301fn.; on Sodalities, 555fn.

—— *Tusculan Disput.,* on Xenocrates, I, xx.

Cideville, manifestations at, **I, 106.**

Cipher, or zero, II, 299-300.

Ciphers, secret, of Masonry, II, 393, 395-97.

Circle: and inscribed cross, I, 508; of necessity (κύκλος ἀνάγκης), 553; of heaven, II, 463; Platonic, decussated, 469, 557.

Circulation: of blood understood in Egypt, I, 544; terrestrial, similar to blood, 503.

Circumcision: and Christian Bishops of Jerusalem, II, 126; in ancient sects, 138; Paul forbids, 180.

Citesius (François Citois, 1572-1652), I, 226, 229, 638.

Cities, mysterious and hidden, I, 547.

Civile, Fr., twice resuscitated, I, 479.

Civilization: **ancient, I, 239;** cycles of, and

barbarism, 5; rise & fall of, 34-35; state of Occidental, ix-x.
Claims, fictitious, II, 381.
Clairaudience, nature of, II, 605-06.
Clairvoyance: cataleptic, I, 484; and epidemics, 278; and phenomena, 199; and prophecy, xxxix, 174; and psychometry, 184; spiritual sight in, 159; and spiritual seership contrasted, II, 591.
Claremont College, of Jesuits and Masonic rites, II, 390.
Clarke, Rev. James Freeman (1810-1888), on theology, II, 30.
*Classical Journal, The,* on Dunbar's work, I, 443.
Claudius, and Christos, II, 335-36.
Clavel, F. T.B. *Histoire . . . de la Francmaçonnerie,* etc. (implied), on Templars, II, 385.
Cleanliness, vain, II, 511fn.
Cleanthes (b. ca. 300 B.C.), on Aristarchus, I, xiiifn.
Clearchus *(fl.* ca. 250 B.C.), *Treatise on Sleep,* on soul, body & resuscitation, I, 364-65.
—— *History,* II, 305.
Clement IV, Pope (r. 1265-1268), II, 581.
Clement XIV (Lorenzo Ganganelli, 1705-74), Pope, & Jesuits, II, 356.
Clement of Alexandria (150?-220?): on Basilides, II, 188, 189; slanders Eleusinia, 100.
—— *Hortatory Address to the Greeks,* II, 108fn.
—— *Paedagogus,* on symbol of fish, II, 256.
—— *Stromateis:* II, 128fn.; on 42 sacred books of Egyptians, I, 33fn.; on Hermetic Books, 3fn.; on Jews, 567; on nature-spirits, 326; on soul of beasts, xix; on Basilides, II, 155; on Berêshîth, 35; on Mysteries, 350; on Nazaratus, 140; on Zardosht, 142; q. Pindar on Initiation, 111; q. Xenophanes on gods, 212, 242.
Clement of Rome (1st c. A.D.), II, 189.
—— *1st Epistle to the Corinthians,* misquotes O.T., II, 248fn.
*Clementine Homilies:* II, 546; date of, 189-90; exhibit doctrine of permutations, 195; on Simon, 162fn., 230; prove existence of secret doctrine of Jesus, 191; regard Jesus only as prophet, 194-95.
*Clementine Recognitions,* on Jesus & magic, II, 148.
Cleonymous, returned after dying, I, 364.

Cleopatra (ca. 68-30 B.C.), I, 517; II, 27, 428.
Clergy: opposes Spiritualism, I, 26; and science, 85; as self-appointed interpreters, II, 430; burned original MSS., 26; Christian, attired in cast-off garb of heathen priesthood, 8; and Church are a farce, 586; crimes of, in USA., 573fn.; engages in exorcisms, 67, 68-69fn.; H.P.B. means by Christianity the, 374fn.; lowest, of India practice vulgar magic, 70; Müller on, 345; muzzled, 25; practices magic, 57, 59ff.; practices *sortes,* 6, 20, 21.
Climate: changes of, I, 31; and psychological powers, 211.
Climer, Dr. Meredith, I, 387.
Clinton, De Witt (1769-1828), II, 383.
Coals, handling burning, I, 444-45, 446.
Coats, Capt., I, 417.
"Coats of skin:" I, 149; II, 458fn.; meaning of, I, 150, 293, 296, 301; worn by priests of Hercules, 575.
Cobija, I, 597.
Cochin-China, heathens of, and their religion, II, 554.
Cocker, B. F. (1821-1883), *Christianity and Greek Philosophy,* I, xii.
Cocles, Horatius, II, 340.
*Codex Claromontanus,* II, 243fn.
*Codex Justinianus:* copies from *Laws of Manu,* I, 586, 587-88; prescribed against sorcery, II, 633, 661.
*Codex Nazaraeus.* See Norberg, M.
*Codex Sinaiticus,* II, 192, 243fn., 648.
Coincidences: I, 274; and scholars, 268.
Coke, E. (1552-1634), *Institutes,* II, 20.
Colarbasus: mistaken by Epiphanius and Hippolytus for heretic, II, 248-49 & fn.
*Colchicum autumnale,* I, 89.
Colebrooke, H. T. (1765-1837): on Plato, II, 39; on the *Vedas,* 269.
Coleman, Chas., *The Mythology of the Hindus:* I, 32fn.; on Japanese patriarchs, II, 79; on 7th Avatâra of Vishnu, 278; on symbolism of Vishnu, 301.
Coleman, W. E., and *Isis Unv.,* I, [18fn.].
Colenso, J. Wm. (1814-1883), II, 4.
Colleges: for teaching prophecy, I, 482; in Egypt, 520; sacerdotal, in antiquity, 590.
Collyridians: and worship of Mary, II, 110, 444fn.
*Collosians,* on worship of angels, II, 206.
Colors: alliance between, and sound,

I, 514; as spiritual numerals, 514; imperishable, in Egypt, 541; influence of, and music, 275; —instinct of Kashmîr girls, 211; and temple of Borsippa, 261; unfading, of Luxor & Tyre, 239.
Colquhoun, J. C. (1785-1854), *An History of Magic*, etc., on the Devil, II, 477.
Colton, G. Q. (1814-98), and nitrous oxide gas, I, 540.
Columbus, Chr. (1446?-1506), I, 71, **542**.
Columella, Lucius J. M. (*fl.* 1st c. A.D.), I, 398.
—— *De re rustica*, on Tarchon, I, 527.
Comes, B. (beg. 16th c.), I, 504.
—— *Lucernam*, etc., I, 647.
Comet(s): and Tycho Brahe, I, 441-42; Halley's, exorcised by the Pope, II, 509.
Cometary, matter, I, 168.
*Commercial Advertiser*, I, [1fn.].
*Commercial Bulletin* (O'Grady), II, 475fn., 532, 574, 614, 629.
Communication(s): objective, with elementals, I, 311; supposed, with the dead, 323; with daemons in Theurgy, 333; with Godlike spirits, II, 115.
Communion, with God, II, 101-02.
Compassion, practiced in Orient, II, 279.
Compensation: law of, and man's destiny, II, 593; law of, never swerves, **545**.
Comte, ventriloquist, I, 100, 101.
Comte, A. (1798-1857): as prophet, I, 76; ideas of, discussed, 77-83; and positivism, II, 3-4.
—— *Catéchisme positiviste*, on woman, I, 78-79.
—— *Cours de phil. positive*: I, 78; on artificial fecundation, 81.
—— *Système de politique positive*, I, 78.
Concealed, the, II, 224.
Confessional, II, 85, 321.
"Conflict of Ages," I, ix.
Confucius (B.C. 551-478), II, 159.
—— *Analects* (Lun-Yü), II, 239, 338.
Conjurer: fired at, I, 378; magical performance by, 473-74.
Conscience, and reason, I, *305*.
Consciousness, quality of the sentient principle, I, 198.
Consequences, Buddhists on, II, 541.
Constantine (288?-337): I, 159fn., 526; a vandal, 436; criminal nature of, II, 304.
*Constitutionel*, I, 103fn.
Consumption, cure of, I, 89.

Contagion, moral, lingers about localities. II, 611.
Contemplation, and prayer, I, 434.
*Contemporary Review*: Müller on Laboulaye & Josaphat, II, 580; on Buddha's virtues, 581.
Continent: great equinoctial, in Pacific, I, 594-95fn.; Jacolliot on submerged, 595-96fn.
Continuity, principle of, universal, I, 114.
Convents: infant skulls exhumed in, II, 58 210; Romish, copied from Tibet, 211.
Conversion, and crime, II, 543.
Convulsionnaires: of Cévennes, I, 370-72; of Saint-Médard, 372-76.
Cooke, J. P. (1827-94), *The New Chemistry*: on chemical affinity, I, xxiii; on chemical groupings, 508; on chemistry, 165; on elements, 190; on light, 137; on scientific truth, 163; on water, oxygen & hydrogen, 464.
Cooper, Peter (1791-1883): II, iii; noble *practical* Christian, 549fn.
Copán, I, 561, 564, 567.
Copernicus, N. (1473-1543), I, 24, 35, 338, 621, 623.
Coptic, term ($\chi\eta\mu\iota$) for Egypt I, 226fn.
*Coptic Legends of the Crucifixion*, on cross of infamy, II, 255.
Copts: remnants of true Egyptian race, II, 404; solitary students of secret doctrine, 306.
Coralillos, Indian snake, II, 622.
Cordilleras, mysterious city in the, I, 546-47.
*I Corinthians*: I, 476; II, 90, 204, 287, 485; on seed, I, 114; misquoted, II, 248; on allegories, 493; on endogamic marriages, 240; on first & second man, 282, 318; on judging angels, 277; on long hair, 140fn., 151; on master-builder, 392; on Principalities, 189fn.; on temple of God, 338; on wife, virgin & marriage, 330; on wisdom, 146.
*II Corinthians*: I, xxxiiifn. 307; II, 485, 556; on Christ, II, 574; on Paul's illumination, 146, 187; on Peter, 161fn.; on temple of living God, 318.
Corona, in Nazarene system, II, 228.
*Corpus Juris Civilis*. See *Codex Justinianus*.
*Correspondant* (Villemarqué), I, 550.
Correspondences, doctrine of, I, 306.
Corson, Prof. Hiram & Mrs., H.P.B. visits, I, [5].

Corson, E. R. (1855- ? ), *Some Unpublished Letters,* etc., on H.P.B. writing *Isis,* I, [5].
Corson, H. (1828-1911), "Dogmatism in Science," on scientific papacy, I, 403-04.
Cortés, H. (1485-1547), I, 546, 559.
Cory, I. P. (1802-42), misunderstands ancients, I, 288.
—— *Ancient Fragments:* I, [16], 188, 287fn. 577fn., 634, 636; on Atlantis, 413; on Berosus & Oannes, 349; on Elion, 554; on hairy savages, 412; on intellectual light, 56; on mundane god, 56; on Oannes, 154; on Orpheus, 532; on Ouranos & Saturn, 578; on Patriarchs, 150; on Plato's nous, 55; on saros & neros, 30fn.; citing: Damascius, 341fn.; Ficino, 336; Lydus, 336; Philo Byblius, 342; Proclus, 321, 396; Psellus, 321, 353, 535; Simplicius on aether, 178; on Berosus' account of creation, II, 271; on deluge, 426; on Divine Triad, 48; on Sanchoniathon's cosmogony, 261; on Taaut, 235; citing Berosus on 12 gods, 448.
Corybantes, I, xxxix.
Cosmas Indicopleustes (522-547), *Cosmae Christiana topographia,* II, 477.
Cosmo and Damiano, Sts. (3rd or 4th c.), phallic ex-votos of, II, 5.
Cosmogony(ies): ancient, based on one irrefutable formula, I, 341; Tyrrhenian, & twelvefold division, 342; diagram of Hindu & Chaldeo-Jewish, discussed, II, 266-71; numbers are keys to, 407.
Cosmos. See Kosmos.
Costaeus, J. ( ? -1603), I, 226.
—— *De universali sirpium natura,* I, 639.
Councils. See Church Councils.
Cousin, V. (1792-1867), *Cours de l'histoire,* etc., I, xvi.
Couto, Diogo do (1542-1616), *Da Asia,* etc., on Josaphat & Barlaam, II, 580-81.
Covercapal, King, II, 509.
Cow, symbol of generation and intellectual nature, I, 147fn.
Cowell. See *Jâtakas.*
Cox, Sergeant E. W., on psychic force and phenomena, I, 195-97, 199, 201, 203.
Crantor (middle of 4th c. B.C.), teachings of, I, xx.
Craterus, I, 365.
Crawfish, and deceased saints, II, 72.
Crawfurd, J. (1783-1868), *Journal of an Embassy,* etc.: on levitation, II, 618; on natives' nakedness, 346.
Creation: II, 107, 260; and Brahmâ, I, 91; by will, 297; double-sexed deities in, myths, 156; in *Bk. of Numbers,* 254; myths of, in *Eddas,* 147, 148, 151-52, 160; myths of, in India, 148; of man, acc. to *Cod. Naz.,* 299-300; of third-race men, 558 & fn.; possible for man, 62; two stories of, in *Genesis,* 575; Augustine on, & rêshîth, II, 35-36; none *ex nihilo,* 220; of man in *Zohar,* 271; of material worlds, 175 & fn.; of worlds in *Zohar,* 271; and procreation, 420, 462; seven days of, 468.
Creative: principle in cosmogenesis, I, 146; principle & Pyramid, 519; Pike on, principle, II, 377; powers, not God, 264.
Creator(s): Demiurgic, I, 130; double-sexed, 156; not the highest God, 309; as Trinity in Kabalah, II, 214, 272; not Supreme Essence, 212-13.
Credner, C. A. (1797-1857), II, 189.
—— *Beiträge,* etc., on Marcion, II, 159, 161fn.
—— *Zur Geschichte des Kanons,* on *Gospel acc. to the Hebrews,* II, 182fn.
Credo, as amended by R. Taylor, II, 522-23.
Credulity, I, 403.
Cretans, I, 264, 545.
Creuzer, G. F. (1771-1858), *Symbolik,* etc., on female Holy Ghost, II, 505.
Crier (κῆρυξ), at Mysteries, II, 101.
Crime(s): compulsion to, I, 276; mediumship & possession, 490; and psychometry, 332; seeds of, 275; and conversion, II, 543.
Crimean War: and Nostradamus, I, 260; prophecy about, by a Shaman, II, 625.
Crispus, Caesar, I, 526.
*Criterio Espiritista, El,* I, xxiv.
Criticism, easy, II, 47-48.
Crocodiles, I, 383; II, 458.
Cromwell, O. (1599-1658), and magic, II, 57, 644.
Crook, origin of episcopal, II, 94.
Crookes, Sir. Wm. (1832-1919): I, 195, 499; and Dialectical Soc., 44-45; former opinions of, 48; on Katie King having no soul, 67; recognizes phenomena but not spirit-agency, 110; weighs light, 281; experiments of, II, 83fn.
—— *Researches,* etc.: I, 199, 202; discusses phenomena observed, 202-03; on de

Gasparin & action of will at distance, 108-09; on Katie King, 48, 49; on phenomena in his house, 129fn.; on result of investigation of psychic force, 44-45; on theories about phenomena, 47; on Thury's ideas, 113; q. Cox, 195, 201; q. Faraday, 43.

Cross: and circle, I, 508; Egyptian, at Palenque, 572; as instrument of torture, II, 255; as male and female principles, 270fn., 392; astronomical, & Zodiac, 452, 453; and avatâras, 453; and circle of heaven, 463; found in Serapeion, 253-54; in ancient religions, 254-55; Irish, at Tuam Asiatic, 538; Kabalistic meaning of, 87; meaning of Templars', 382; mundane, and its reflections, 454; on breast of Nâga, 539; pagodas built as a, 382fn.; Plato on man and circle decussated as a, 469; symbol of threefold powers of creation, 539.

Crosse, A., produces living *acari*, I, 465, 647.

Crowe, C. (1800?-1876), *The Night-Side of Nature*: on ashes retaining form, I, 476; on burial of fakir, 478-79fn.; on Eslinger & voices, 68; on premature burial, 482fn.; on priest of Wimmenthal & spirit-animals, 71; on stigmata, 398; q. Proclus on resuscitations, 364-65.

Crucifixion: Hindus unimpressed by, II, 340; of divine man and Plato, 557.

Cruciform, inscriptions, II, 436, 442.

Cryptographs, Masonic, II, 394-95.

Csoma de Körös. See *Kanjur.*

Ctesias (*fl.* 5th c. B.C.), *Indica,* on lightning in India, I, 528.

Cucoana, Moldavian lady, II, 627.

Cudworth, R. (1617-1688), *The True Intellectual System,* etc., on immortality, I, 251; on Mosheim, II, 39.

*Culla-Niddesa,* on Virgin Avany & first Buddha, II, 322.

Cup: of health, I, 157; consecrated, in Bacchic Mysteries, II, 513.

Cures: magical, I, 532; miraculous, 464.

Curse, refused by priestess of Athena, II, 334.

Cursing: Christian habit, II, 334; strictly forbidden by Buddhist rules, 608.

Cush, I, 150.

Cushite, II, 567fn.

Cuvier, G. L. (1769-1832): incredulity of, I, 223; on skulls of mummies, II, 437fn.

Cuzco, and gold treasures, I, 597-98.

Cybelê (Κυβέλη), I, xxviii; II, 30, 501.

Cycle(s): ancient calculations of, and spiritual progress, I, 32; ascending & descending, 2, 5; and changes of climate, 30-31; do not embrace all mankind, 6; downward, 301; ebb & flow of, in history, 34; example of, 526; and Gobi Desert, 598; Grand, 303; II, 293; Hermetic doctrine of, I, 6; in history, 521; new, about to begin, 38; and numbers, 7; of civilizations, 293-94; of Devachanic rest, 351fn.; of moral & physical epidemics, 274; of planetary motions, 294; of 3,000 years, 297; pictorial representation of, 348-49; Schliemann supports, 6; secret, 32; spiritual evolution in, 34; universality of, 389-90; we are at bottom of a, 247; world moves in, 51; descending, and *man-spirit,* II, 362; ending in first century, 246; in *Avesta,* 221 & fn.; in evolution of earth, 420; and nutation of ecliptic, 366fn.; of manifestation, 264-65, 272-74; of worlds, 219; secret, 156fn.; secret & Essenes, 144 & fn.; twelvefold, earth & man, 455-56; within cycles, 263.

Cyclopes (κύκλωπες): Homer on, I, 332; and Tiryns, 529; ancient Titans, 567; and Râjputs, II, 438.

Cynchris, I, 406.

Cynocephalus, I, 564.

Cyprian, Thascius C. (ca. 200-258), on Tertullian, II, 189fn.

—— *De idolorum vanitate*: on animated statues, I, 615; on the one true God, II, 88.

Cyril of Alexandria, St. (376-444 A.D.): II, 54, 304; anthropomorphizes Isis into Mary, 41; bloodthirsty, 32; and Hypatia, 28, 53, 253, 644.

Cyril of Jerusalem (315?-386), *Catecheses,* on Paul, II, 146, 253, 644.

Czechs, burn Pope's Syllabus, II, 560.

# D

Dactyls (δάκτυλος): I, xxviii; Bart on, 23.

Dâdâbhâi Naurozji, *Catechism of the Pârsis,* on God, II, 579fn.

Daemons: animating statues, I, 614; attendant to Naguals, 556; bad, ambitious to be recognized as supreme God, 219,

332-33; Buddhist views on, 448; def. *xxviii;* evicted by word, 363; Iamblichus on, 321, 345; in desert, 604; malicious, in invisible world, 70; Plutarch on, xix-xx; Porphyry on, 332-33; possession by, & exorcisms of, 356; Proclus on, 312; subjective, and vampires, 353; and sword, 363, 364; three classes of, xxii; Philo on, II, 34fn.
Daêvas: I, 313, 348fn., 456; II, 185, 206, 238fn., 512; and devas, II, 484; origin of term in *Vendîdâd,* 488fn. See also Devas.
Dag, Dagon: at Nagkon-Wat, I, 565; as Kêtos & Jonah, II, 258-59; man-fish, 256; and Vishṇu, 258-59, 298.
Daghestan, H.P.B. in, II, 568fn.
Dagoba, II, 255.
Daguerre, L. J. M. (1789-1851), declared insane, II, 619fn.
Dahshûr, entrance to Pyramid of, II, 26fn.
*Daily Graphic, The* (New York), I, [6], 635.
*Daily News,* on Spiritualism, I, 121.
Daimôn (δαίμων), perverted, meaning of, II, 34, 257.
Daimonia [δαιμόνια]: evocation of, in theurgy, I, xlii-xliii; man influenced by, 276.
Daimonion [δαιμόνιον, neutral of δαιμόνιος], of Socrates, I, xx, 68; II, 117, 283, 284.
Daiteyî: I, 148; daughter of giants, 122.
Daītu, capital of, II, 587.
Daityas: I, 313; as giants, 122; source of legends on Titans, II, 425, 505fn.
Daksha, and Aditi, I, xxxi.
Dâksha-pitaraḥ, fathers of gods, I, xxxi.
Dalai-lama. *See* Taley-lama.
Dalcho, Dr., on Masonry, II, 389.
Dalton, John (1766-1844), I, xxv, 401, 411, 417, 510.
**Damaru, emblem of Śiva, II, 235.**
Damascenus, Nicolaus (1st c. B.C.), II, 406.
Damascius the Syrian (5th & 6th c. A.D.), Neo-Platonist, I, 436.
— *De principiis rerum,* on Dis, I, 341fn.
**Dama-sâdhanâ, of fakirs, II, 590.**
Damiano, St. II, 5.
Damnation (ἁμαρτήματος): II, 475, 507; Augustine on, 546; eternal, disbelieved by Origen, 238fn.; eternal, original with Church, 334; *Mark* on, II, 478fn.
Dan, and Levi, I, 555.

Daniel, Babylonian magi, II, 236.
*Daniel:* I, xxxiv, 270; II, 206; on a trance, I, 494; and *Book of Enoch,* II, 147.
Dance, circle-, as Bacchic frenzy, II, 45, 332.
Dante, A. (1265-1321), I, 564.
— *La Divina Commedia,* II, 502.
Daouthia (?), I, 621.
Dardanus, I, 570.
Darius Hystaspes (558?-486?): established Persian colony in Judaea, II, 441; and magian cult, 128, 141, 306 & fn., 434, 481, 502, 630; vicegerent of Ahura-Mazda, 486fn.; and Zoroaster, 140-41, 220.
Darkness: and light, I, 302; Highest Light in, II, 225.
Darwands, I, 456.
Darwin, Ch. R. (1809-82), starting point of, I, 14-15.
— *On the Origin of Species:* on animal progenitors, I, 153; on lineal descendants, 154; on primordial progenitor, II, 261.
Dasent, Sir G. W. (1817-1896), *The Norsemen in Iceland,* II, 399.
"Daughters of men," *Bk. of Enoch* on, I, 305.
Davenport Brothers, I, 492.
**David (r. 1010-970 B.C.), and Dido, I,** 567fn.; exorcises "evil spirit of God," 215; revitalizes himself by means of a virgin, 217; circle dance of, II, 45; established new religion in Palestine, 439; ignorant of Moses, 45, 401; introduces Jehovah worship, 45; not Mosaic Jew, 297; performs phallic dance, 79; similar to King Arthur, 439.
**Davis, A. J. (1826-1910): Diakka of, I,** 325; visions of, II, 73.
— *The Diakka,* etc., I, 218-19.
Davis, S. (1760-1819), "On the Astronomical Computations of the Hindus," I, 32.
Davkina, II, 171, 444.
Davy, H. (1778-1829), I, 505.
Dead Sea Scrolls, II, 642.
Deane, J. B. (1797-1887), *The Worship of the Serpent,* etc.: on Divine Mind, II, 506; on hawk-headed serpent, 512; on immaculate conception, 505.
— "Observations on Dracontia," I, 550.
**Death: and catalepsy, I, 484; cases of** seeming, 364-66; and immortality, 508; Lévi on vision after, 484; Lévi on, &

life, 480; II, 343; and life, I, 480; nature of, & reanimation, 482-84; never sudden, 480; no sure sign of actual, 479; on signs of, 429; Plato on life &, 114; progress after, 329; second, 329; second, & Proclus, 432; spiritual, 317-18, 328; state of half-, 452-53; Thespesius' vision after, 484; and withdrawal of astral soul, 476; Greek term for, & Mysteries, II, 284; Müller on disdain for, in India, 340; Plutarch on sufferings after, 587; second, & moon, 284; second, in Egyptian beliefs, 368. See *Teleutan*.

Decimal, notation and Pythagoras, II, 300-301.

Defoe, D. (1661?-1731), *The Political Hist. of the Devil*, II, 473.

Deity(ies): double-sexed in myths, I, 156; geometrizes, 318, 508; inactive & creative, 428; manifested, & Manas, 348; man may be as powerful as, 575; only aspect under which, allows itself to be viewed, 424; revealed, and primordial form, 153; unknowable, 291; derived from *deva*, II, 512; Plato on nature of, 344-45; Supreme, infinite & just, 541.

Dekad, meaning of, I, xvi.

Deleuze, J. (1753-1835): I, 164; on Billot, 499; on mesmerizing power of toads, 399.
—— "De l'opinion de van Helmont sur la cause . . . du magnétisme," I, 194.

Delphi, Pythoness of, I, 358.

Delphos, meaning of, I, xxxixfn.

Delphus (δελφύς), womb, abdomen, I, xxxixfn.

Delrio (Delrius), M.A. (1551-1608), I, 226, 639.
—— *Disquisitionum, etc.*: I, 639; on Simon Magus' powers, 471-72.

Deluge: II, 257, 447; myth of, I, 150; ten thousand B.C., 241; esoteric meaning of, II, 458; in Chaldean cosmogony, 422-23 & fn.; and Indian sacred books, 427-28; local, in Central Asia, 424, 426; Noah & Lamech, 466.

Demeter: II, 108, 111; Kabirian, surrounded by electric aura, I, 234; as astral soul, II, 112.

Demi-gods: and atmospheric electricity, I, 261; and saints, II, 159.

Demiurge, Demiurgus, Dêmiourgos: I, *xxviii*, xxxi; II, 297 & fn., 154fn.; and dodecahedron, I, 9; and sun, 131fn., 132; androgyne, of *Talmud*, II, 468; as Bel or El, 170; as Elohim, 419-20; as Ialdabaôth, 175, 206, 228fn., 296; and planetary genii, 157; as Ptaḥ, 368; as seven-rayed god, 417; as Son, 225; Dionysos older than the, 245; rests, 422; Simon Magus on the, 190-91.

Democritus (ca. 470 B.C.): I, 510; an alchemist, xxv; as atomic philosopher, 249; believed in apparitions, 251; and healing by music, 215; on atoms & vacuum, 61, 62; on nothing, 408fn., on magic, 512; on soul & atoms, 401.
—— *Physica et Mystica*, I, 641.

Demon(s): various types of, I, 495-96; Yezîdis on, 459; Augustine on, & magic, II, 67; lying, and saints, 74, 75-76; and Savior, 476. See also Daemons.

Demon-worship, and saint-worship, II, 29.

Demonism, and Spiritualism, II, 5.

Demosthenes (384-322 B.C.), I, 584.

Dendera: figures of, I, 524; pictures, and *Genesis*, 440-41.

Denon, D. V. (1747-1825), *Voyage dans la Basse et la Haute Égypte*, etc.: on Karnak, I, 524; on *tau* at Dendera, II, 454.

Denton, Wm. (1823-1883) & Eliz., *The Soul of Things*, etc., I, 183, 295, 331.

Denys, St. (Dionysius, *fl.* 3rd c. A.D.), and Tau, II, 254.

Derbent, II, 567.

Dervishes: I, *xxviii*; and mesmerism, I, 632; rites and degrees of, 316-17.

*Desâtîr*, on soul-spirit and its shadow, II, 113, 115.

Descartes, R. (1596-1650): I, 417, 427; believed in univ. remedy, 214; on medicine, 71; on space & its fluid, 206.

Descendants, resemble ancestors, I, 385.

Descent: of spirit into matter, I, 285; into hell, 299; II, 177, 515, 517-18, 522.

Desert, magical phenomena in, I, 604-05.

Deshtur, lamp of the, I, xxxix.

Desire(s): Plato on lust &, I, 276; and will, 434; II, 320; aspiration & purity, II, 592; and will in mesmerism, 21.

Despretz, C. M. (1792-1863), I, 505, 509.

Desservant, II, 601.

Destiny, man's self-made, and law of compensation, II, 593.

Deucalion: II, 447; and creation of men, 428, 429; and Vaivasvata, 428.

Deus, daêva and deva, I, 348fn.

*Deus est Daemon inversus*, II, 303.

Deus-Lunus, II, 48.

*Deuteronomy:* I, 87; II, 499; on witches, etc., I, 355, 491; mistranslated word in, II, 34fn.; on burial of Moses, 207; on Kadesh, 45; on Moses' death, 167; on tables of stone, 367.
Devachan, cycle of, I, 351fn.
Devadâsîs, virgins, II, 210.
Devakî, II, 95, 209, 537.
Devas: I, 141; II, 159, 512; age of the, II, 467fn.; became daêvas, 484; degraded into evil potencies, 488; manvantaras, 464fn.; as powers of Brahmâ, 563; and twelve thousand years, 468.
Devatâs, I, 148.
Devil: as chief pillar of faith, I, 103; and Baal, 552; and Catholic Church, 459; de Mirville & Academy, 102; des Mousseaux & the, 614-15; God's business partnership with, 103; personal, 561; so-called —worship, 557; unknown to Orientals, 446ff.; ancients did not believe in personal, II, 483, 506; as basis for Redeemer, 479; challenged by "spirits," 23-24; dogma of, based on two passages in N.T., 480; fundamental stone of Christianity, 501; inventend by Christianity, 507; Müller on, 10-11; no, no Christ, 478-79; no malignant principle, 485, 500; not believed in by Buddhists, 508; offensive smell of, 511, 512; Oriental ideas of, 501; patron genius of Christianity, 478; personal, unknown in antiquity, 506, *Protevangelium* on, 473; and temptation of Jesus, 485. *See also* Satan.
"Devil-worshippers:" falsely so termed, I, 446-47; of Travancore, 135.
Dewal, of Ceylon, I, 448.
*Dhammapada:* II, 282; on being born again, II, 566; on the Path, 282; on virtuous life, 529.
*Dhanurveda,* II, 556fn.
Dhâranâ: II, 590; condition of, affected by brain, 591.
Dhâranî, I, 471.
Dharmâśoka (ca. 272-232 B.C.), greatest king of Mauryas, II, 607-08.
Dhâtrî, same as Venus-Aphrodite, II, 259.
Dhauli, II, 32.
Dhôti, I, xxxii.
Dhyâna: four degrees of, II, 281, 320; fourth degree of, 287.
Dhyâni-Buddhas: as elements, II, 226; five, & Âdi-Buddha & Avatâras, 156.
Diabology, of Milton's work, II, 501-02.

Diabolos. *See* Devil.
Diacentaureon, I, 89.
Diakkas: I, 325; Davis and Porphyry on, 219.
Dialectical Society, and scientists, I, 46, 232, 422.
*Dialectical Society.* See *Report on Spiritualism.*
Diamond, made by Despretz, I, 509.
Diana, I, 264, 265.
Diana-Bhavânî, I, xxx.
Diana-luna, I, 266.
Díaz del Castillo, B. (ca. 1498-1560), *Historia . . . de la Nueva España,* on Aztec civilization, I, 559-60.
Dicastillo, J. de (1584-1653), *De justicia et jure,* etc., on patricide, II, 363.
Dictamnus (diktamnon), somnambulism & childbirth, I, 264.
Dictê, Mount, I, 264.
*Dictionnaire de théologie catholique,* II, 642.
Didier, Alexis, somnambulist, II, 22.
Dido: and Carthage, I, 520; and David, 567fn.; Virgil on, II, 376; and Virgin Mary, 446.
Didron, A. N. (1806-1867), *Iconographie chrétienne,* etc., on scene of Eliz. & Mary, II, 555.
—— *Manuel d'iconographie,* etc., II, 555.
Didymos, or Adam-Kadmon, II, 213.
Diemerbroeck, I. de (1609-1674), *Tractatus de peste,* etc., on suspended animation, I, 479.
Digby, Sir Kenelm (1603-1665), I, 476.
Dignities: II, 205, 206; and Peter & Jude, 207.
*Dii minores,* II, 451.
Dîkshita: Light of the, I, xxxix; or initiate, II, 268, 269, 410.
Diktynna, and Jupiter, I, 264.
Dinos, and Socrates, I, xiifn.
Diocletian (Διοκλητιανός) (245-313 A.D.), burns libraries, I, 405; destroys ancient works, 503.
Diodorus Siculus (*fl.* 1st c. B.C.), I, 234, 466.
—— *Bibliotheca historica:* on Books of Hermes, I, 407; on Isis' healing, 532; on Astarte on prow of ships, II, 258; on Iaô, 301; on Osiris & Dionysos, 165; on tombs of kings, 403-04; on twelve gods, 448; on Typhon, 489fn.

Diogenes (6th c. A.D.), Neo-Platonist, I, 436.
Diogenes Laërtius (3rd c. A.D.), *Lives*: on air & soul, I, 290; on antiquity of Egypt, 33fn.; **on Democritus, 512; on earth,** moon, 256fn.; on Empedocles restoring life, 480; **on Epicurus' ideas of gods,** 436; on Heraclitus, 423; on Stilpo & Phidias' Minerva, 612; on Anaxagoras, II, 282; on Plato's birth, 325; on Pythagoras & Mysteries, 140, 529; on Zoroaster, 142.
Diogenianas, I, 506fn.
Dione, and Typhon, II, 490.
Dionysius Areopagita (1st c. A.D.): I, 26; and Kabalah, II, 38.
**Dionysius Halicarnassus (1st c. B.C.),** *Roman Antiquities,* on sphericity of earth, I, 159.
Dionysus, Dionysos: or night-sun, I, xiv; and Jehovah, II, 165, 302, 526; liberates souls of men, 561fn.; of Indian origin, 560fn.; older than the Demiurge, 245; orgies of, 587; —Sabazius, 491.
Dioscorides Pedacius (*fl.* 1st c.), *Materia Medica* (Peri Hylês Yatrikês), on stone of Memphis, I, 540.
Dioscuri (Διόσκοροι): I, xxxix, 243; and polarities, 235.
Diphilus, substitutes bulls for human victims, II, 565fn.
Dîrghatamas, *Vedic Poems* (implied), II, 411-12, 654.
Dis, Damascius on, I, 341fn.
Disciples of John, II, 290.
Discoverers, opposed and persecuted by science, I, 83.
Discoveries: astounding, to be made, I, 38; great, usually come with a *flash,* 513; of telephone, 126-27; unexpected, II, 26fn., 641.
Diseases, can be communicated by unhealthy healer, I, 217.
Disintegration, cannot be used on living animal organisms, II, 589.
Distance, injury at a, I, 361.
Divination: by meteoric stones, I, 332; and familiar spirits, 355; by lot, & Church Councils, II, 20-21; by wreaths in river, 612; and Jesuits, 354; used by Church, 251-52.
Divine: Mind, II, 506; Triad, 48.
*Divine Book.* See Apollonius Orapius.
Divine Power: **cannot be expressed in hu**man language, I, 307-08; recognized by Theosophists, 29.
Divining, II, 252fn.
Divinity, Robespierre on, I, 73.
Djibtzun-damba-Hutugtu, **high lama, II,** 659, 660.
Docetae, Gnostics called, II, 157.
Dodecahedron: I, xxi, 9, 55; and visible universe, 342; and initiation, II, 392.
Dodona, II, 592.
Dodwell, E. (1767-1832), I, 413.
Dogmas, day of, has reached its gloaming, I, vii.
Dokos, I, 412.
Dolgorukov, Prince Alexey Vladimirovich (1815-47), mesmerizer, I, 166.
—— *Organon,* etc., I, 637-38.
Domes, and lithoi, I, 5.
Dominic, St. (1170-1221): exorcises demon, II, 75-76; **and the flea, 78.**
Domitian (51-96 A.D.), persecutes Kabalists, II, 147 & fn.
Donaldson, J. W. (1811-61), II, 469fn.
—— *Christian Orthodoxy*: on chronology, II, 443fn.; on Masoretes, 431.
Doppelgänger, of entranced medium moved by another intelligence, I, 360.
Doré, G. (1833-1883), *La Sainte Bible,* II, 242.
Dornesius, I, 504.
Dositheans, II, 144.
Double, F. J. (1776-1842), **and mesmerism,** 1, 174.
Double-sexed, deities in myths, I, 156.
Douglas, Bishop, (1721-1807), **I, 372.**
Dove: and Dagon, II, 258; and Noah & Baal, 448fn.
Dozous, P. R., *La Grotte de Lourdes,* etc., on miracles, I, 120.
Dracontia: II, 294, 295; **once covered con**tinents, I, 550, 554.
Dracontian, Aethereal, II, 506.
Dragon: in Mexican & Russian tales, **I, 550;** Oriental in character, 448; sons of the, 553; and Isis, II, 489; in Buddhism; 509; is sun or generative principle, 505fn.; and Lucifer, 501; Michael overcomes, 488; Michael's, an Âryan myth, 486; red, 484; and St. George, 509; Saturn as, of Life, 505; Vasuki as, 490; and Virgin of Sea, 446; Zohâk & the red, 486fn.
Draper, J. W. (1811-82), *History of the Conflict,* etc.: I, [16], 208fn.; erroneous ideas on Bruno, 94; mistaken on an-

cients, 429-31; on ancient optics, 240; on Aristotle's failures, 404; on astronomical knowledge of ancients, 21-22; on burning of Arabian MSS., 511; on clergy & science, 85; on cycles, 6; on early steam engine, 241; on Euclid, 512; on geometers, 7; on ideas, 19-20; on invisible impressions recorded in nature, 186; on memory, 179; on nebular theory, 238; on nirvâṇa, 430; on Roman Church, 27; on testimony for phenomena, 233; on vast knowledge of ancient Persia, 534; on Augustine's role, II, 88, 89; on Bede, 478; on Church Fathers & atonement, 546; on criticism of Bible, 251; on doctrine of atonement, 41; on Eusebius as forger, 327; on exorcising comets, 509; on Torquemada & burning of heretics, 62fn.; q. Augustine, 32.
—— *History of the Intellectual*, etc., I, 521, 582.
Dravidian, words in West Europe, I, 563fn.
Dreams, I, 170, 179, 429, 460.
Drepung (Tib., *ḥBras-sPuṅs*), and College of magicians, II, 617, 660.
Drink, in India, II, 574.
Drower, Mrs. E. S., *The Secret Adam*, II, 651.
Drowning, and magnetism of garments, II, 611-12.
Druids: I, xxix; called serpents, 554; monuments of, 554; practiced magic, 18; structures of, 572; teachings of, 18.
Drummer of Tedworth, I, 123, 363.
Drummond, Sir Wm. (1770?-1828), *Oedipus Judaicus*, on El, I, 13.
Druon, H., *Œuvres de Synésius*, II, 198.
Druses: II, 306, 572; related to Kabalists, 292; and Copts, 169fn., 306; King on, 289; and Lady Ellenborough, 255.
Duad: I, xvii; II, 407; ether & chaos the first, I, 343fn.; Pythagorean, 347.
Dual: Enoch as type of, man, II, 452-53; evolution & Adam, 277.
Dualism: of Abel & Cain, II, 225; of universal forces kept in balance, 463; patriarchal, 459.
*Dublin Quart. Journal of Med. Science* (Fisher), on teratology, I, 392.
Dubois, Jacques (1478-1555), I, 438.
Dubois, Abbé J. A. (1765-1848): on missionaries aping Hindu customs, II, 110; misrepresents Buddhism, 320; denounces missionaries, 532.

—— *Description . . . of India*: on *Atharvaveda*, II, 563; on Brahmans never borrowing any myths, 426-27.
Du Bois-Reymond, Emil H. (1818-96), I, 336.
—— *Grenzen des Naturerkennens*, I, 433-434.
Duchaillu, Paul B. (1831-1903), I, 412.
Duchesne, J. (1546-1609), and form retained in ashes, I, 476.
Dûdâîm, or mandragora, I, 465.
Dufferin, Frederik, Lord (1826-1902), I, 239.
Dugdale, Sir Wm. (1605-1686), II, 544.
Du Halde, J. B. (1674-1743), *Description . . . de la Chine*, etc. (implied), on magic, I, 600.
Dulaure, J. A. (1755-1835), *Histoire abrégée des differens cultes*, on Waldenses' rites, II, 332.
Dumas, J. B. A. (1800-1884), I, 509.
Dunbar, G. (1774-1851), *Inquiry into . . . the Greek and Latin languages*, etc., I, 443.
Duncker, M. W. (1811-1886), *Geschichte des Alterthums*: on souls, I, 270; on white horse & sun, II, 237.
Dunham, I, 540.
Duniyas. *See* Gan-duniyas.
Dunlap, S. F. (1825-1905), *Söd, the Mysteries of Adoni*: I, [16]; on Eumolpus, 130; on Musion, Hercules, etc., 130fn.; 132; on *Söd*, 301fn., 555fn.; on Feast of Tabernacles, II, 44; on Iacchos & Iach, 302.
—— *Söd, the Son of the Man*: I, [16]; on creation of man in *Cod. Naz.*, 299-300; on Saturn, 570fn.; q. Hermes on Spirit of Planets, 255; on age of *Cod. Naz.*, II, 135fn.; on baptism & oil, 134; on Demiurge, 154fn.; on Essenes, 144-45; on Jesus & Logos, 198; on Jordan & Nazarenes, 181; on Logos in India, 204fn.; on *Matthew* & nazaria, 134; on nazaraios, 128; q. Jost on Essenes, 37fn.; q. Nork on *Targum*, 247fn.
—— *Vestiges*, etc.: I, [16]; on analogy between Christian & Buddhist teachings, 347; on Horus, 56; on origin of Hebrews, 569-70; on Saturn, 570fn.; on ancient triads, II, 48; on bread & wine, 513; on highest arcana, 503; on Iaô, 139fn.; on Logos, 506fn.; q. Jerome on Adonis, 139.

Dupanloup, (1802-1878), on Protestants, II, 208.
Duplanty, I, 188.
Du Potet, J. (1796-1881): I, 23, 114, 129, 166, 167; II, 23; accused of sorcery, I, 164; enchanted circle of, 204; on ancient symbols, 378; on organized matter, 144; on pregnant women, 394.
— *Cours de magnétisme,* on nature of magnetic fluid, I, 279.
— *Expériences publiques,* on Academy's investigations, I, 174-75.
— *La Magie dévoilée,* on magic power, I, 142, 279; on spiritual agents, 333-34.
Dupuis, C. F. (1742-1809), I, 347; mistaken, 24.
— *Origine de tous les cultes*: I, 160fn.; on black Isis, II, 490fn.
Durgâ: and active virtue, II, 233, 276, 301; and Ste. Anna, 491fn.
Dust: Longfellow on, & soul, I, 212; of earth to become part of soul, II, 420.
Dweller, of the Threshold, I, 158, 325.
Dyaus: Brahman—, II, 170; Unrevealed God, 273, 298.
Dynamis, II, 156.
Dynasties, two in India, II, 437.

# E

Earth: analogy in gestation of, and embryo, I, 389; as magnet, xxiii, 169, 282, 497; becoming astral planet, 330; early states of, 255; exhalations of, 200; generates own heat, 272; gravitation & shape of, 622-23; Lactantius on, being flat, 526; *living* organism, 189; magnetic force of, 172-73, 282; Plato on regions of punishment beneath, 328; Plutarch on, revolving in space, 238; pre-Adamite, 256; pre-Adamite, made by Theosophist, 505; Proctor on, 253ff.; revolution of, 256fn.; rotation of, known to ancients, 621; spirit of, and cyclic changes, 255; double evolution of, II, 420; earliest shape of, & serpent, 489; hints on twofold structure of, 455; reimbodiment of, 456; spiritual, and previous worlds, 420; transformations of, 464; virgin, & living water, 550-51fn.
Earth, Sphericity of: acc. to Dionysios of Halic., I, 159; acc. to *Edda,* 151; known to ancients, 256fn.; known to Greeks, 526; known to Egypt, 532; known to Hindus, 10; taught by Pythagoras, 532; and Ch. Fathers, II, 477.
Earthly, human race and Plato, I, 428.
Eberhart, *Berliner Monatschrift,* on magic, I, 24.
Ebers, G. M. (1837-1898), *Papyros Ebers,* etc., I, 3, 21, 23-24, 403, 529, 543, 544.
Ebionites, II, 127, 135, 144, 492; followers of Nazarenes, 190; overwhelmed by Church, 307fn.; primitive Christians, 180-81, 182fn.
Ecbatana, many-colored walls of, I, 534.
*Ecclesia non novit sanguinam,* I, 64; II, 58.
*Ecclesiastes* [Koheleth]: II, 476fn.; foreshadowed modern ideas, I, 410; on Olam, II, 218.
Ecclesiastial: history exhibits same plot always II, 640; systems subversive, iv.
*Ecclesiasticus*: on bells, II, 624fn.; on wisdom, 506.
Eclectic School: and early Christianity, II, 32, 34; destroyed by Theophilus, 52-53; identical with earlier mystics, 342-43; taught Oriental Kabalah, 402.
Eclipses, Egyptian records of, I, 33fn.
Ecliptic: obliquity of, known to Egyptians, I, 532; cycle of nutation of, II, 366fn.
Ecpyrosis (ἐκπύρωσις), I, 31.
Ecstasy: power of conversing with deity, I, 121; van Helmont & Paracelsus on, 170; Wilder on Plotinus', def. 486; and will, 500.
"Ectenic:" force, I, 55, 113; and forms created by elementaries, 116.
Ecumenical Council: anathematizes science, II, 1, 560; and immaculate conception, 9; of 1870, 359.
*Edda:* I, 151, 153, 187fn.; creation myths in, 147, 148; on giants, 122; on honeydew, 133
Eddy Brothers, I, 70, 635-36.
Eden, as locality, I, 575, 580fn.
Edessa, or Orfa, seat of College of Magic, II, 550.
*Edinburgh Review:* on crocodiles, I, 383; on missionaries, II, 110, 532.
Edison, T. A. (1847-1931), discovers new force, I, 126.
Edmonds, J. W. (1799-1874), I, 334.
Egg(s): and Bhagavat, I, 347; Brahmâ & universal, 91; and Emepht, 146; mundane, 157; II, 214, 215, 226, 267, 268;

INDEX 697

mundane, & Chemmis, I, 147; Spiritual, & Eros-Phanes, 56; unfructified, hatched by electricity, 465.

Egkosmioi (ἐγκόσμιοι), I, 312.

Ego: knows of God in Nature, I, 36; inner, 476; loss of, 316; personal, cannot die, 432; Spiritual, omnipotent, vi; as sentient soul inseparable from brain, II, 590; immortal, effused from boundless, 218; or Ahaṃkâra, 287; Spiritual, 563; successive existences of the, 320.

Egypt: architecture of, I, 517; art of writing in, 529-30; astronomical knowledge in, 533; called Kemet or Kem, xxv; colleges in, 520; colossal monuments in, 524; downfall of, 16; embalming in, 539; fast communication in, 127; fleet of, & Cape of Good Hope, 542; forty-two sacred books of, 33fn.; glass-blowing in, 543; gods of, 406; Greece's debt to, 521; Herodotus on antiquity of, 515; Herodotus on moving granite blocks, 519; immense antiquity of, 33fn., 529; and India, 515, 627; initiated priests and antiquity of, 626; jewelry in, 537, 543; knowledge & skill of ancient, 515ff.; land of chêmi, 226fn.; language of, & séance at Paris, 610; letters invented in, 532; medicine in, 544-45; music in, 544; no barbarous stage in civilization of, 526; and numerical cycles, 342; papyri of, 16; perfection of early art in, 6; Peebles on temples & geometry in, 522, 531; and pre-Vedic India, 589; units of measures in, 536; age of Menes, II, 520fn.; baptism of blood in, 42; blind of hierogrammatists, 426; composite nature of man in, 367-68; Essenes and, 42; first settlers of, from India, 426; funeral ritual of, 367; Hermetic Brotherhood of, 307; initiatory degrees in, 364-65; Jews in, multiply like herrings, 558; Khamism as language of, 435; Menes & Osiris, 361; mysteries of, 362; no account of deluge in, 426; owes civilization to India, 431, 435-36, 437; periods of history in, 448; Porphyry on learning of, 506; precepts of earliest ritual, 361; prophecy of Hermes about, 360; secret records on hieroglyphics preserved, 403; skulls in, of Caucasian type, 436-37; trinity in, 227; untold antiquity of religious philosophy in, 415, 548fn.

Eighth Sphere: and annihilation, I, 219fn.; and daemons, 353; human spirits of, 355; monad raised from, 357; or Hadês, 352; planet following ours, 328; sacred sleep of neophyte & mysteries of, 357.

Eikon, or Ain-Soph, II, 170.

Eileithyia (Εἰλείθυια), presides over births, I, 264, 265.

Eirenaeus Philalethes (1622?-1665), I, 504.

—— Ripley Reviv'd: on hidden meaning of mystical writings, I, 628; on man's spirit & body, 309.

Ekphantos, I, xx.

El (or Al): I, 13, 554; Sun-God of Syrians, II, 524.

Elam, Eilam, II, 217, 218.

Elam, Dr. Chas. (1824-89), A Physician's Problems: on cycles of moral & physical epidemics, I, 274, 275-76, 276; on imagination of pregnant women, 385; on incendiarism, 277; on mind & matter, 387.

Eleazar, Rabbi, II, 348; expelled demons, 350fn.

—— Comm. on Idrah-Zutah, I, 301fn.

Electricity: active, as Thor, I, 162; and heat of earth, 272; intelligence in, 188; intelligent, and mental photography, 322; known in Mysteries, 234-35; known to ancients, 526ff.; known to Edda, 161; and mineral springs, 162; relation of, to magnetism, 201, 393-94; two kinds of human, 277fn.; higher form of, exists, II, 620.

Electro-biological, power, I, 55.

Electromagnetic: life is, I, 137; currents & psychic force, 201; relations between planets, etc., 161.

Electromagnetism: I, 104; used by Paracelsus, 164.

Element(s): I, 205; ancient & modern ideas about, 190; astral soul formed of, 432; and classes of daemons, 312; and elementals, 311; every creature lives in its own, 343; of ancients, & theurgic power, 342; peopled with beings, 343fn.; primal form of, 505; triune, in nature, 423; emanation of the, II, 272; final struggle of, & deluge, 458; five, & Ptaḥ, 226; five mystic, and Druze doctrine, 310; and four beasts, 451.

Elemental(s): assume likenesses, I, 311; attracted by sorcerers, 141; and bodies of human races, 285; and "Book of Life,"

343; Bulwer-Lytton on, & magic, 286; def. & names, *xxix;* and earth-bound elementaries, 616fn.; evolved by astral light, 285; irresponsible, 158fn.; and magnetic attractions, 313; materialize reflections of human spirits, 359; produce all but subjective phenomena, **xxx**; Augustine on, 158-59fn.; three classes of, *310ff.;* and universal ether, 284-85; various, daemons, 495-96; can enter vacant body, II, 589; unconnected with subjective manifestations, 597; and "miracles," 351fn.; and phenomena of mediumship, 595. See *also* Nature-spirits.

Elementaries: I, 66; construct portrait-statues, 70; danger from, 342; II, 117-18fn., 589; def. I, *xxx;* dread sharp weapons, 359, 362-63, 364; **earth-bound**, & elementals, 616fn.; Homer on, 332; and mediumship, 490; and Nâgas, 448; plates of, in Khunrath, 319; Porphyry on, 332; propitiated by Hindus, 447; role of, in manifestations, 68-69, 116.

Elephanta: I, 590; Mahâdeva of, II, 5.

Eleusinia (τὰ 'Ελευσίνια), II, 138, 245, 306fn.; archons of, 90; as abodes of light, 254; and Feast of Tabernacles, 44; and Heracles, 516; slandered by Clement, 100.

El Ḥay, mighty living one, II, 213, 276.

Eli, Hymn to, II, 506.

Elias, I, 493; II, 38, 237. See *Apocalypsis Eliae.*

Élie de Beaumont, J. B. (1798-1874), *Recherches,* etc. (implied): on knowledge of ancients, I, 189; on terrestrial circulation, 503.

Elihu, I, 74; II, 497 & fn.

Elijah: I, xxxvii, 447, 525; a Nazarene, II, 140; "small voice" of, 344.

Elis, sixteen matrons of, II, 525.

Elisha: I, 475, 482, 485; anointed Jehu, II, 525.

Elivâgar, I, 147.

Elixir vitae, rationale of, I, 502-03.

Elizabeth, Queen (1533-1603): I, 65; and Jesuit Walpole, II, 373fn.; and Mary at Lyons, 555.

Ellenborough, Lady (ca. 1807-81), amulet of, II, 255-56, 649.

Ellora: I, 561, 567, 590, II, 95; hint about, II, 26fn.; and Viśvakarman, 232.

Eloah, II, 213.

Eloaios, genius of the spheres, II, 184, 294.

Elohim: gods or powers, I, 575; real, and the lost "word," 589; and Adam, II, 187fn.; and Spiritual Sun, 213; and "days" of *Genesis,* 421; and Egyptian gods, 448; Jehovah on the, 401; making of man by, 246; powers of nature, 420; and sexes of man, 468; similar to Ptaḥ, 368.

Eloi, II, 154, 207.

El Shaddai, not Jehovah, I, 491fn.

Elyon, El'yon, I, 554.

Emanation(s): doctrine of, I, xvi-xvii; doctrine of, in Buddhism, Pythagoras & Plato, 430; and numbers, 7; odic, of man, 169; and re-absorption, 242, 243; symbolically pictured, 1; three, of the invisible, 302; as "primitive men," II, 176; doctrine of, and panic of Ch. Fathers, 34-35; from First Cause, 159; from spiritual prototypes, 220; and Gnostic Christ, 219; idea of, in Paul, 506; in *Cod. Nazar.,* 174ff.; in Ophite system, 171-72, 174; Kabalistic, 212ff., 222; magnetic, and their effect, 610-11; of Dhyâni-Buddhas, 156; of Elements, 272; of gods & Meru, 233; of *originals* from Unknown, 158; of universe, 156fn.; of worlds & Avatâras, 278; on Son as, 227; origin of doctrine of, 39; out of Emepht, 41; Rees & Augustine on, 35-36; and Second Person of Trinity, 36-37; Sephirôth as, 205fn.

Emanationists, contrasted with Evolutionists, I, xxxii.

Embalming: in Egypt, I, 541; in Mongolia by alchemical art, II, 603-04.

Embla, I, 151.

Embryos: evolution of, I, 303; and imagination of mother, 385; and metempsychosis, 388-89; psychic, 311, relation of, to mother, 401.

Emepht: and Ptaḥ, I, 146, 157, 636; and emanations, II, 41, 49.

Emerald, imitation of, I, 537-38.

Emerson, R. W. (1803-82): on Plato, I, xv; and Truth, **99.**

Emmanuel, not Christ, II, 166 & fn., 440.

Emmerich, Anna K. (1774-1824), stigmata of, I, 398.

Emotions, as changes in magnetic condition, I, 209-10.

Empedocles (*fl.* ca. 444 B.C.): I, 24, 251, 384; II, 406; on two souls, I, 317;

restoring life, 480; arrests a waterspout, II, 597.
Empusa, or ghûl, I, 604.
*Encyclical of 1864*, I, vii.
*Encyclopaedia Britannica* (Bonamy), on Serapeion, II, 29. See also Bonamy.
*Encyclopaedia of Islam*, I, 657.
En-Dor, Obeah woman of, II, 488, 494.
Enemies: of Theosophists, I, viii; Augustine on slaying of, II, 32.
Energy: conservation of, I, 502; lives forever, 114.
Enfield, Wm. (1741-97), I, xv.
Engastrimuthos (ἐγγαστρίμυθος), consultor of spirits, I, 355.
Engelbert, Cardinal, Archbishop of Malines, II, 85.
Englishman: becomes magician in Tibet, II, 618; not a single, penetrated sanctuary of pagodas, 623.
Enigma, *Talmud* on, I, 17.
Ennemoser, J. (1787-1854), *The History of Magic:* I, [16], 242fn.; II, 500fn.; on Descartes, I, 207; on electrified hair, 234; on magnetic sympathy, 207; on myths, 235; on Paracelsus, 52; on religion, visions & dreams, 460; on secrecy of ancients, 24-25; q. Bart on Dactyls, 23; q. Fludd, 171.
Ennius, alleged words of, I, 362.
Ennoia (ἔννοια): II, 505; as *Second* God, 177; as thought of Bythos, 223, 293; and Mano, 295; or Mind, 169; same as Poimandres, 171.
Enoch: I, 150, 182; II, 38, 195, 459, 460, 469, 488; first parent of Masonry, I, 579; and garments of skin, 149-50; identified with Hermes, xxxiii; Masonic "sacred Delta" of, 30, 571-72; II, 371; translated, I, 559; II, 424; age of, & Zodiac, II, 464fn.; as Metatron, 464; and Elias ascending from Hell, 517; is Anak, 450; and Lamech, 457; and Libra, 462, 463; and Seth, 466; type of dual man, 453. See *Book of Enoch.*
*Ens genitale*, I, 51.
En-Soph. See Ain-Soph.
*Ephesians:* II, 230, 231; on Archon & powers, 206; on Principalities, etc., 189fn.
Ephesus, focus of universal secret doctrines, II, 155.
Epi (ἐπί), upon, II, 91.
Epicharmus (ca. 540-450 B.C.), I, 251; II, 406.

Epictetus (ca. 55-135 A.D.), II, 179fn.
Epicurus (b. 342 B.C.): on air & atoms, I, 290; on astral soul, 250-51; on gods, 436; on the soul, 317.
Epidemics: clairvoyant vision and, I, 278; cyclic nature of moral & physical, 274, 275-76; of incendiarism & assassination, 277; psychological & possessions, 370ff.
Epimenides (ca. 500 B.C.): I, 364; quits body at will, II, 597.
Epiphanius, St. (ca. 315-402): delights in accusations, II, 326; reason why, slanders Gnostics, 330; self-confessed infamy of, 249; violates oath, 375fn.
—— *Panarion:* on Carpocratians & pictures, II, 150; on Colarbasus, 249; on descent into Hell, 514; on Ebionites & Jesus, 181, 182fn., 190; on Manes, 208fn.; on Marcion, 160; on Nazarenes, 151, 190, 196; on Parchus, 294fn.; on theurgic eucharist of Marcosians, 513-14; on Typhon as an ass, 484.
*Epistle of Barnabas*, on Council of Nicæa, II, 251.
*Epistle of Clement to the Corinthians*, II, 248.
*Epistle of Jesus Christ and Abgarus*, a forgery & Eusebius, II, 549-50.
*Epistle of Paul to Seneca*, etc., II, 277.
*Epistle of Peter to James*, II, 162fn.
Epistles, of Apostles more genuine than *Acts*, II, 277.
*Epitome* (Clementine), II, 190.
Epoptai (ἐπόπται), I, xxxvii; II, 96, 102, 563, 565.
Epopteia (ἐποπτεία): I, xiv; II, 101; def. II, *90-91, 113;* and Paul, 146.
Equilibrium: and universe, I, 318; and harmony, II, 457, 463, 480-81.
Érard, royal, & spinet, I, 426.
Erasmus, D. (1466?-1536), II, 20.
—— *New Testament*, and the three heavenly witnesses, II, 177, 647.
Erastosthenes (276-ca. 196 B.C.), I, 512; II, 448.
Erech, city of, II, 444.
Ergon (ἔργον), work, I, xlii.
Ericius, I, 226.
Erigena, Joh. ( ? -875?), *De divisione naturae*, on force-correlation, I, 242.
Eritene, II, 236, 649.
Eros-Phanes, I, 56.
Error (ἁμαρτήματος), or damnation, II, 478fn.

Esau: as the sun, II, 402; is red, 489; and Jacob, feminine & masculine principles, 401.

Escobar, A. de (1589-1669), *Liber theologiae moralis,* on use of magic, II, 353-54.

—— *Univ. theol. moralis,* on sinful purpose, II, 355 & fn.

Eskimos, I, 323.

Eslinger, Eliz., and spirit-voices, I, 68.

Eslon, Charles d' (d. 1786), and mesmerism, I, 172.

Esmun-Asclepius, II, 481.

Esoteric: catechism, I, 19; doctrine never written, 271fn.; truths expressed in identical symbols, 577; universal, and ancient monuments, 561; Wisdom of ancients, II, 146fn.

Esotericism: destroyed by Hezekiah, II, 440; students of, scattered and silent, 306-07; symbolized by Zipporah, 551fn.

**Espagnet, Jean d'** (*fl.* 1633-50), on truth & symbolic language of philosophers, I, 628.

Essence: Divine, and Adam, I, 1; immortal, a distinct entity, 315; divine, origin of immortal Self, II, 320; expansion & contraction of Divine, 264-65; Supreme, not the Creator, 212-13; Ultimate, in India, 274fn.; Unknown, is Svayambhû, 214.

Essenes ('Εσσαίοι): II, 99, 127, 137, 140, 145fn., 155, 190, 389, 548fn.; def., I, xxx, 630; give refuge to Egyptian initiates, 16; Gnostics as followers of, 26; angels secret with, II, 196; around Dead Sea, 485; as physicians, 144; Egyptian initiates converted to Buddhism, 42, 132, 139fn., 491; and Gnostics, 324; Jesus an, 37fn.; had no oath, 373; meals of, 147; never used oil, 133; on soul's transmigration, 280; Pythagoreans, 130; semnion of, 196fn.; were Chrêstians, 323.

Esseoua, sorcerers, I, 488.

Etchmiadzin, monastery of, II, 564.

Eternity: and loss of individuality, I, 316; problem of, 9, 184; as Aeôns, def., II, 219; no word for, in Hebrew, 12.

Ether: as Aether of ancients, I, 134; as photographic album, 67; as repository of *spiritual* images, 395; astral, and second sight, 211-12; gross purgations of, 186; known to ancients, 189; made into a personal god, 341; pictures in, 397; races of beings from spiritual part of, 340; scientists on, 186-87; and thought, 273, 327; Universal, and electricity, 393-94; Universal, known to ancients, 128; Universal and *liquor amniae,* 389; Universal, and privation, 310-11; Universal, and psychometry, 182-83; astral, & impress of acts & thought, II, 59; as pure & impure fire, 12fn.

Ethereal (or aethereal): body, I, 281; space, 349.

Ethiopians (Aethiopians): Eastern, came from India, I, 515; and Jews, 567 & fn., more ancient than Egyptians, 406; not a Hamitic race, 525fn.

Etruscans, understood electricity, I, 527.

Etz Ḥaiyim, Tree of Life, II, 267.

Eucharist: and soma, I, xxvii, xl-xli; esoteric meaning of, II, 44, 561; in ancient worships, 513, 551, 578; in Mysteries, 139fn.

Euclid (*fl.* 300 B.C.), I, 17, 251, 461, 512, 531.

—— *Elements* (Stoicheia), derived from Pythagoras, I, 512.

Eudemus (2nd half of 4th c. B.C.), II, 506.

Eudoxus (4th c. B.C.), and Euclid, I, 512.

Eugenics, Plato on, I, 77.

**Eugenius Philalethes (Thomas Vaughan,** 1622-1666): I, xxv, 51, 67, 167, 193, 226, 306, 308; on artificial gold, 504.

—— *Magia Adamica*: on mystic meaning of earth, I, 255-56, 257; on triune man, 309; q. Marcus Antoninus, 257.

Euhemerus (*fl.* ca. 300 B.C.), on myths, II, 406.

**Eulamius (6th c. A.D.), Neo-Platonist,** I, 436.

Euler, L. (1707-1783), on aurora, I, 417.

Eumolpus, Eumolpidae, I, 129-30.

Eunapius (b. 347 A.D.), *Lives of Sophists,* II, 642.

Eupolemus (*fl.* ca. 150 B.C.): I, 31; on Abraham, II, 217.

Euripides (B.C. 480-406): I, 130, 251, 405, 584; on Dionysos, II, 165.

—— *Bacchae,* on Bacchus & Semelê, II, 504.

—— *Chrysippos,* I, 314, 643.

—— *Hippolytus,* on possession by a god, II, 625.

—— *The Madness of Heracles,* and Underworld, II, 517.

Europeans: I, xl, 11, 267, 384, 446; II, 28, 104, 106, 240, 278, 291, 323, 413, 417, 534, 584, 603, 612, 613, 615, 621fn.,

622, 623, 629, 635; cannot see certain colors, I, 211; Hanuman as progenitor of the, 563fn.
Eurydice, as esoteric doctrine, II, 129.
Eurynous, revived, I, 365.
Eusebius, P. (ca. 260-ca. 340): I, 288, 406; on Aethiopians, 567, 651; convicted of forgeries, II, 327-28.
—*Chronicon:* I, 30fn.; on Belus, 552; q. Berosus on Xisuthros, II, 217, 426.
—*Demonstr. evang.,* on Christ as Sun, II, 517.
—*Eccles. Hist.*: on Essenes, I, xxx; on Basilides' book, II, 155; on Christian community at Pella, 197; on circumcised Bishop of Jerusalem, 126; on Jesus & Abgarus & portrait of Christ, 549-50; on Linus, 124; on Papias, 327; on semnion of Essenes, 196fn.; recognizes *Gospel acc. to Hebrews,* 182fn.; stratagems of, 324.
—*Praep. evang.*: I, 31; II, 247fn.; on El, I, 554; on Emepht, 636; on Porphyry & Egyptian magic, 416; q. Philo Byblius, 342; on Essenes, II, 196; on serpent, 489-490; q. Eupolemus on Abraham, 217; q. Philo on Saturn & Israel, 513fn.
Eva(s): affinity with Tetragrammaton, II, 299; bears *Kin,* 225; in Kabalah, 268; the two, and Adonis, 223-24.
Eve: as chaotic matter, I, 582; and Adam, II, 270fn.; Adam & Jehovah, 269; distorted from Sophia, 171fn.; and Eve-Lillith, 445 & fn.; or Ieva, 463.
Everard, A. ( ?-1679), *Mystères physiologiques,* on evolution of embryo, I, 303.
Ever-present, II, 251.
Evil: extreme of good, I, 157; and good, 561; and good balanced, II, 463, 480; as blind force in matter, 483; shadow of light, 480.
Evil-eye, I, 380.
Evocation(s): of larvae, I, 493; of souls objected to, 321; subjective, of spiritual beings, 66; blood, II, 567-68, 569-70; by a fakir, 104-05; Kabalistic, of initiation, 119; magical, in Mysteries, 118; of pitris, 114; particular language of, 46.
Evolution: acc. to *Manu,* I, 620-21; II, 271; ancient & modern ideas on, I, xxx-xxxii, 154; ancient theory of, on slabs, 154; antediluvian, 238; double, 213; double, & Pythagorean numerals, 9; Fludd on, 258; future, of man, 296; and giants, 152-53; and hierarchies, 285; higher meaning of, 153; in *unseen* universe, 295; and metempsychosis, 9; of man & ape, 331; of molecules & forms, 330; spiritual, & instinct, 425-26; spiritual & physical, 352; II, 420; well-known to ancients, I, 134; II, 279; downward, of primitive spiritual man, II, 276-77; humanity passing thru seven stages of, 407fn.; numberless worlds in, 424; symbolized by avatâras of Vishnu, 274-76; thru successive cycles, 455, 456, 458; Vyâsa, Kapila & Darwin on, 261.
*Evolution, The* (A. Wilder), II, 523fn., 527-28.
Exhalations, of earth, I, 200.
*Ex nihilo nihil fit,* I, 8.
Exodus, date of Israelites', from Egypt, II, 558.
*Exodus:* I, 14, 491; II, 44, 95, 129, 214fn., 234, 458fn., 481fn.; on perpetual lamps, I, 228; on river & blood, 414; on witches, 355; on Baal-Zephon, II, 487; on God not being Jehovah, 167; on Jehovah as man of war, 513fn.; on Jehovah's interview with Moses, 429; on Jehova-Nissi, 165; on Lord God of Hebrews, 301; on Moses, 442 & fn., 443; on Moses & well, 550fn.; on Moses & Yeva, 398; on seeing God, 230fn.; on seven daughters of Moses, 551fn.; on smearing with blood, 454; on sound of bells, 624fn.; on tables of stone, 367; spoliation scene of, 33.
Exorcisms: I, 356; 218; by priests, II, 66, 68-69fn., 69; by St. Dominic, 75-76; Kabalistic & Roman, 85-86; of comets, 509; of priests are necromantic evocations, 121.
Expansion, of Divine Essence, II, 213.
Experience, progressively enlarged, I, 403.
Exposures, do not effect rooted beliefs, I, 121.
Extinction, belief in, II, 566.
*Extraits des Assertions,* etc., on Jesuits, II, 353fn.
Ex-votos, traffic in phallic, II, 5.
Eye: mesmeric fluid projected from, I, xxxiifn.; retains last impression at death, 607.
Ezekiel: on "Wheels," II, 299fn., 451, 452; wheels of, exoteric & esoteric, 461-62; and Zodiac, 456.
*Ezekiel:* I, 167, 492; pentacle of, 147; on Ancient of Days, II, 229; on Jewish

worship, 131; on Olam, 218; on *signa thau*, 393; on Son of Man, 232; vision of, 231, 232, 235.
Eznik (5th c.), *Refutation of the Sects*, II, 564, 656.
Ezra: I, 568; compiles *Pentateuch*, 578; and Herodotus, II, 429fn.; as nazar, 128; restores destroyed books, 217, 470; rewrote Mosaic Books, 129.
*Ezra*, II, 441.

# F

Faber, G. H. (1773-1854), *Dissertation on the Mysteries of the Cabiri*, on triple god of Tatars, II, 49.
— *On the Origin of Pagan Idolatry*, on Tanga-tanga, II, 49.
Fables: allegorized geology, etc., I, 122; allegorized natural phenomena, 261.
Fabricius, J. A. (1668-1736), *Bibliotheca Graeca*; q. Psellus, I, 535; q. Pappus on Nicæa, II, 251; q. Porphyry, 115.
— *Codex apocryphus N. T.*, II, 148fn.
Fadeyev, Nadyezhda A. de (1829-1919), II, 603, 658.
Fagundez, F. S. (1577-1645), *In . . . praecepta Decalogi*, on killing parents, II, 348, 363.
Faho. *See* Ferho.
Fairfield, F. G. (1844-1887), *Ten Years with Spiritual Mediums*: I, 117, 145fn.; on spirit-hands, I, 594-95.
Fairies. *See* Elementals.
Faith: phenomena of, I, 323; power of, to heal, 216; rooted in inner senses, 467; based on knowledge, II, 369; Jesuits & breaking, 372fn.; and magical feats, 370; power of human, 120; sincere, & virtuous living, iii-iv; sincere, should be respected, 530; true, as divine charity, 640; will & imagination, 598; and works, 563.
Fakirs: I, xxxii; buried alive, 224, 475, 477-78 & fn.; def. *631;* evoke help of Pitris, 458; and growth of seed, 139; magic of, 470-71, 616-17; **omniscient when entranced**, 141; reanimation of, 484; and scientists, 223; tortures of, xxviii-xxix; will of, and *creation* of matter, 140; mediums, II, 106; cannot reach beyond first initiation, 104; extent of power of, 106; initiation of, & Pitris, 114, 115; Jacolliot on, & evocations, 104-05; mesmeric powers of, 612; phenomena of, 629; and Pitris, 107; psychological wonders of, 583; religious exercises of, 590; taming tigress, 622-23; wash daily, 511fn.
Falconer, Hugh (1808-1865), I, 413fn.
Fall: of man, I, 296, 299-302, 315; of Adam & religious dualism, II, 225; of Earth, 420, 424, 546; of man as Kâlî, 275; meaning of, of Adam, 277.
Falré-Paraplat, Dr. (d. 1838; assumed name Barnard Raymond), II, 384.
Fan, Bacchic, II, 494.
Famines, and missionaries, II, 532.
Fanaticism: I, 615; incurable evil, II, 53, 239.
Fancy: I, *396;* or phantasy, and memory distort vision, II, 591.
Faraday, M. (1791-1867): I, 75, 85, 99, 104fn., 116, 177, 281, 505; and jumping tables, 62-63; on common origin of forces, 126; on "unconscious muscular action," 55; and phenomena, 57; quoted by Crookes, 43.
Farrar, Dr. F. W. (1831-1903), II, 370.
Fascination: at precipice, I, 501; Kircher on, 210; of birds, 380-81; and will, 144.
Fasting, in Mysteries, II, 178.
Fatalism, rejected, II, 593.
Father: as used by Plato, II, 344; in secret, 230; means hierophant, 561; unknown one above, 151.
Father-Spirit, and man's Spiritual Ego, I, vi.
Faustus of Riez ( ? -ca. 490), *The Genealogy of . . . Virgin Mary*, II, 110fn.
Faustus the Manichaean (4th c A.D.), on origin of Gospels, II, 37-38.
Favre, Jules (1809-1880), I, 166, 167.
Fear, fatal at initiation, II, 119.
Félix, Père, *Le Mystère et la Science:* I, 397; on science, attraction & mystery, I, 337-39.
Felt, George H., on geometrical foundations of ancient knowledge, I, 22-23, 633.
Feltre, and Castaldi, I, 513.
Female, and male qualities in Nature, I, 12-13.
Fénelon, F. (1651-1715), *Abrégé des vies,* etc., on Pythagoras & sphericity of earth, I, 256fn., 532.
Fergusson, J. (1808-1886), *Illustrations of the Rock-cut Temples of India*, on age of caves, I, 590fn.
— *Tree and Serpent Worship*, II, 489.
**Ferho: I, 300, 302; as formless life,**

II, 174, 224, 227, 228; and Iaô, 295; or Par'ha Rabba, 294fn.; God of John the Baptist, 290; waters vines, 244.

Feroher [Pahlavi, *fravahr; Av., fravashi*]: II, 495; as ideal conception, 221.

Festus, on *saga*, I, 354.

Fever, treatment of, in India, II, 621-22fn.

Fiacre, St., chair of, and fecundity, II, 333.

Ficino, M. (1433-99): I, 8, 385; and Hermetic Books, 407.

—— *Theologia Platonica*, etc., on revolution of things, I, 336.

See also: *Hermetic Books;* Porphyry; Proclus.

Figuier, G. L. (1819-94), I, 505, 509.

—— *Histoire du merveilleux*, on psychological phenomena & epidemics, I, 369ff.

Findel, J. G. (1828-1905), *Geschichte der Freimaurerei*, etc., on Templars, de Molay & Jesuits, II, 381, 383, 384, 384-85, 394.

Finlayson, II, 618.

Fiords, of Norway and *Odyssey*, I, 549.

Fire: astral ocean of invisible, I, xxv; celestial, pure, of ancients, xxxi, 283; from heaven used on ancient altars, 526, 528; II, 404 & fn.; Heraclitus & Hippocrates on, I, 422-23; Pentecostal, 125; and sun and life, 270; and sword, 247-48; triune nature of, 423; Ether is spirit of, II, 12fn.; and rhythm of flames as key to theologies, 410; temple of perpetual, at Baku, 632fn.; and water, in myths, 156.

Fire-philosophers, I, 165.

First-born. See Protogonos.

First Cause: and spirit, matter & force, I, 428; *in abscondito*, 160; objective proofs of, 613; and androgyne Deity, II, 299; as Svayambhû, 219; denied by Vyâsa & Kapila, 261; emanation from, 159; Eternal Cause is not, 266, 267, 271. *See also* Cause.

Fish(es): and tides, I, 210; —charming in Ceylon, II, 606; origin of symbol, 256-58; pond at Rome filled with skulls, 58; symbol of first avatâra of Vishṇu, 259, 274.

Fisher, G. J. (1825-1893), *Diploteratology*, etc., I, 390ff.

Fiske, J. (1842-1901), *The Unseen World:* I, 185, 240, 428; on effect of thought on ether, 274, 327; on ether, 181-82; on Gehenna, 328; on spirit & proofs of future life, 42.

—— "The Laws of History"; denies superiority of Egypt & India, I, 525; disputes cycles, 521.

Flame: magic effect on, by mendicant, II, 607; sensitive, of Tyndall, 606; and twofold light, 222; visible & invisible, 605.

Flammarion, N. C. (1842-1925): I, 54; on unknown laws of nature, 195. See also *La Nature.*

Fleischer, Anna, I, xxiv.

Flesh, soul *and* spirit, II, 285.

Flood. *See* Deluge.

Florentine, account of a, scientist about reincarnation of a Taley-Lama, I, 437-38.

Flourens, M. J. P. (1794-1867), *Buffon*, etc., on intolerance of scientists, I, 85.

Flower: spiritual, and Land of Enlightenment, I, 601-02; evocation of the soul of, II, 609-10.

Fludd, R. (1574-1637): I, 423fn.; on alchemical gold & light, 511.

—— *Mosaicall Philosophy:* mutual magnetisms, I, 171; on evolution, 258; on invisible creatures & creator, 309-10.

—— *Summum bonum*, I, 165.

Fo, or Fho, name for Buddha, II, 290, 293fn.

Foetus: and metempsychosis, I, 338-89; and mother's imagination, 384-88, 390-91, 392, 394, 397, 399, 402.

Foh-tchou, II, 293-94.

Foissac, P. (1801- ? ), I, 174.

Foraisse, M., Mason, II, 381.

Forbes, J. (1749-1819), *Oriental Memoirs*, on poisonous snakes, I, 383.

Force(s): atomic, & will, I, 61; common origin of all, 126; correlation of, & divine electricity, 271; corr. of, known to ancients, 242, 243, 269; involved in moving tables, 112; and matter, 59; new, discovered by Edison, 126; opposing, & harmony of life, 318-19; psychic, & phenomena, 195ff.; vital, & science, 239, 313; correlation of blind, & anima mundi, II, 402; dual, & Zodiac, 463; generates matter, 320; of nature die & are reborn, 468; trinity of all natural, 606; will develops, 320.

Forlong, General J. G. R. (1824-1904), "Through What Historical Channels, etc.," II, 643.

Form: Aristotle on, I, 312; and ether, 395; in mystical sense, 290-91.

Forner, F., *Panoplia armaturae Dei*, etc., on witchcraft, II, 61.

Forsyth, J. S., *Demonologia*: on H. More, I, 123; on remedies of ancients, 89; on water, 193; on Council forbiding *sortes*, II, 21-22; on false relics, 71-72; on geocentric hell, 13; on Gregory of Tours, 21; on origin of Inquisition, 59; on St. Dominic's exorcism, 75; on St. Francis & wolf, 77; on tomb of Inquisitor, 59.

Fortin, Dr., I, 166.

Fossils, give wrong view of man's ancient status, I, 4.

Foucault, J. B. L. (1819-1868), on levitation, I, 63, 202fn.

Foucaux, P. É. (1811-1894), See *rGya*, etc.

Fouquier, P. E. (1776-1850), and mesmerism, I, 174.

Fourfold: deities, II, 171-72; emanations, 272.

Fourier, J. B. J. (1768-1830), I, 76.

Fournié, É. (1833-86), I, 180, 352.
— *Physiologie*: on effect of molecular motion & pictures in ether, I, 397; on "forbidden ground," 402; on physiology, 407; on van Helmont, 400.

Fox, Kate, I, 203, 439.

Foxius (Sebastián Fox Morcillo, 1528-68), I, 226, 638-39.

Francis, St. (1181-1226): and levitation, I, 115.
— *Life of St. Francis*, and wolf, II, 77.

Franciscus, Erasmus, I, 228fn.

Franck, A. (1809-93), *La Kabbale*: I, xxviii; on Ain-Soph, II, 210; on age of *Sepher Yetzirah*, 298fn.; on brotherhood of Kabalists, 470; on "garden of delight," 119; on Highest One, 210; on initiation & great secret, 99; on its origin, 38; on Jewish thaumaturgists, 357; on nature of Sephîrôth, 40; on Merkabah, 350; on predecessors of Shimon b. Yoḥai, 350.

*Franco-Américain, Le*: I, 475; on fakir performances, 470-71.

Franklin, Benj. (1706-90): I, 85, 146, 234, 417, 424; condemns mesmerism, 410.

Franklin Committee, and mesmerism, I, 171ff.

Fraunhofer lines, and Roscoe, I, 513.

Fredegonde, Queen (d. 597), II, 21.

Freedom, spiritual, I, xlv.

Freemasonry. *See* Masonry.

Freemasons. *See* Masons.

Freund, Wm. (1806-1894), *Wörterbuch der lateinischen Sprache*, on Sodales, I, 301fn., 555fn.

Frigga, II, 11.

Frizius, J. *See* Fludd, *Summ. bonum*.

Fuentes, F. A. de, *Historia de Guatemala*, etc.: I, 552; on Balam Acán, 553; on naguals, 556fn.

Fukarâ-Yogis, and fakirs, II, 104.

Fulton, Robert (1765-1815), I, 85.

Fumigations, of Iachus, I, 406.

Fürst, J. (1805-1873), *Hebräisches und Chaldäisches Handwörterbuch*, etc., on Iaô, II, 297.

## G

Gabet, Father, II, 605.

Gabriel: as Metatron, II, 225; and Isaac, 452; is Hibil-Ziwa, 204, 247; Logos with Gnostics, 193; on Mary, 203; or Michael, 510fn. and Saoshyant, 236; symbol of union of spirit & mortal man, 154, 174.

Gadarenes, I, 604.

Gaffarel, J. (1601-81), II, 199.
— *Curiositéz inouyes*, on form retained by ashes, I, 475-76.
— *Book of Enoch*, II, 470fn.

Galand, A. *See* d'Herbelot.

*Galatians*: I, 575fn.; II, 84, 178, 181; on bondage, 180; on Peter, 162fn.; on Son of God & woman, 576fn.

Gale, I, 34.

Galen, Cl. (130-200?), I, 89, 164, 384.
— *Compos. medicamentorum*, on medicine called Isis, I, 532.
— *De simplicium medicam.*, on Ophis amulet, II, 295fn.

Galileans, Munk on, II, 139, 145, 152.

Galileo, G. (1564-1642): xxxiii, 35, 40, 97, 121, 241, 621; II, 528; and Pythagorean doctrines, I, 159, 238 & fn.

Gallaeus, S. (Servatius Gallé, 1627?-1709), *Sibyllina Oracula*, I, 251fn.; q. Psellus, 535; on Virgin & child, II, 504.
— *Summaria*, etc., on Persian Triad, II, 49.

Gallicanism, II, 356.

Galvani, L. (1737-1798): I, 188, 283; on persecution, 45.

Galvanism, or divine electricity, I, 271.

Gamaliel, II, 339.

## INDEX

Gamgee, Dr. A. (1841-1909), and experiments with rabbit's eye, I, 607.
Ganden (Tib.: *d*Ga-*l*Dan), lamasery of, & manifestation of Tsong-Kha-pa, II, 616.
Gandharva(s), I, xxxvi; II, 107.
*Gāndharvaveda,* II, 556fn.
Gan-duniyas, name of Babylonia, I, 575fn., 651.
Gaṇeśa: II, 439; in Mexican ruins, I, 573.
Ganges, sacred, II, 30.
Gangler, I, 122.
Ganglia, micrographs of cerebral, and astral light, I, 179, 180.
Garden of Delight, story of, II, 119.
Garibaldi, G. (1807-1882): a mason, II, 391; on priests, 347.
Garima, II, 593.
Garlande, de, Bishop of Orléans (12th c.), II, 22.
Garlic, and Hippocrates, I, 20fn.
Garma-khian, and unprogressed spirits, II, 616.
Gasparin, A. E. de (1810-1871), *Tables tournantes:* I, 222; II, 15; on certitude, 108; on de Mirville's work, 102; on effect of will, 109; on Faraday, 111; on fluid from experimenters, 111-12; on motions of tables, 99-100; on scientists, 99; on supernatural, 101; on unprejudiced witnesses, 109.
Gassner, J. J. (1727-79), healer, I, 217, 218.
Gate, and last days, II, 246.
Gaulmin, G. (1585-1665), *Vita et morte Moysis,* etc., I, 25.
Gauls, I, 18; II, 547.
Gautama Buddha. *See* Buddha, Gautama.
Gâyatrî, most sacred verse, II, 410.
*Gazette du Midi,* on Pius IX, I, 27.
Geber (or Jâbir) (721-813), I, xxv, 504.
Geburah: II, 213; and sign of the Cross, II, 87.
Gegen Hutuktu, title of High Lama of Urga & his powers, II, 617, 660.
Gehenna: I, 328, 352; locality outside Jerusalem, II, 11; and Tophet, 507.
Gellius, Aulus (130?-180?), *Noctes Atticae,* on mechanical devices, I, 543.
Gelong (Tib.: *d*Ge-*s*loṅ), of Kalmuck tribe and talisman, II, 600fn.
*Gemara,* II, 350.
Gematria: II, 298; and Zura, 424.
Gemma, C. (1535-1577), I, 386, 645.

Gems, II, 264-65.
Genealogical, trees & apes, I, 40.
Generation: spontaneous, and magic, I, 414; soul descending into, II, 112.
Generative, matter & teratology, I, 392.
Genesis: I, 92, 147, 266, 293, 297, 305, 554, 569; II, 36, 128, 442, 446, 464; and Dendera pictures, I, 440-41; first & second chapt. from different pen, 575; genealogy of, mythical, 554; Higgins on, 284; hist. interpretation of 4th chap., 579; and Kṛishṇa, 579fn.; Maimonides on, 435-36; on coats of skin, 149, 575; II, 458fn.; on creation of light, I, 269; on creation of man, 558; II, 263, 460, 462; on Dan & Levi, I, 555; on four generations of man, 559; on giants, 122; on living soul, 13; on nephesh, xli; II, 362fn.; on three angels, I, 493; second & third chapt. kabalistically, 433; several Adams in, 303; and Swedenborg, 306; appropriated by Jews, II, 217; meaning of the "days" of, 421-22; on Abraham, 216; on age of mankind, 467; on ancient dynasties, 486fn.; on ark, 405; on birth of Cain, 225; on creatures of water, 258; on Dan, 167; on darkness & deep, 214; on Elohim's curse, 420; on enmity between serpent & woman, 50; on generation of Seth & Cain, 459; on Jacob wrestling with the "Lord," 401; on Jehovah-jireh, 167, 301; on Kadesh, 45; on nephilim, 217, 218; on Noah & waters, 423; on Olam, 218; Parkhurst suppresses first word in, 34; part of universal cosmogony, 216; on Penuel, 402; on Shiloh, 244; on sixth day, 421; serpent of, 508.
Genii: of Nazarenes & Meru, II, 233; planetary, 184, 186, 230; planetary, of Nazarenes, 294, 296.
Genius, as Divine Spirit, I, 277.
Gennaro, San (*fl.* 3rd c.), blood-miracle of, I, 613.
Genoa, vase of the, Cathedral, I, 538.
Gentiles, II, 88, 89, 91fn., 139, 150, 162fn., 196, 401, 471, 481, 504, 536fn.
Geocentric system I, x, 621ff.
Geoffroy Saint-Hilaire, E. (1772-1844): I, 384, 387, 390, 395; on horse with fingers, 412.
Geographers, Plutarch on, I, 29.
Geological: ages or phases, II, 464; era & avatâras of Vishṇu, 275.

Geology, disagrees with archaeology, I, 526.
Geometry: as science, I, 7; Felt on, of ancients, 22-23; in Egypt, 531; led to picture writing, 156.
Germ(s): I, 14; *Manu* on Spiritual, II, 270-71.
Germany: depopulated, II, 503; priestesses of, 592.
Gesenius, H. (1786-1842), *Hebrew and English Lexicon of the O.T.*, On Iaô, II, 301; on Olam, 12.
Gesner, J. M. (1691-1761), I, 226, 639.
—— *Orpheôs apanta:* on lodestone, I, 265; q. Orphic Hymn, II, 123.
Gestation: of earths in universal ether, I, 389; and successive shapes of foetus, 388-89.
Ghârâpuri, temple of, II, 49.
Ghariyâl, I, 383fn.
Ghebers, I, xxxvi, 25, 569; II, 632fn.
Ghillany, F. W. (1807-1876), *Menschenopfer*, etc., on O.T., II, 469-70fn.
Ghosts, I, 69, 245, 344.
Ghouls, ghûls, I, 319, 564, 604.
Giants: I, 31fn., 133, 150, 153, 595fn.; II, 275, 422, 449-50, 487; bones of, in Missouri, I, 304-05; in Bible, *Vedas & Eddas,* 122; man descended from, 153; progenitors of Brahmans, 122; or nephilim, II, 218.
Gibbon, Edw. (1737-94), *The Decline and Fall:* on Pharisees & transmigration, I, 347; on forged verse in *I John,* II, 178; on Gnostics, 249, 330; on lives of saints, 78; on Plato's doctrine, 33; on Therapeutes, 324.
Gibeonites, II, 481.
Giborim, I, xxxvi; II, 217, 450.
Gibraltar, and Egyptian fleet, I, 542.
Giddiness, I, 500-01.
Gihon, is Indus, II, 30.
Gilbert, Wm. (1540-1603), *De Magnete,* etc., on globe as magnet, I, 497.
Giles, Rev. C., on spiritual death, I, 317-18.
Gilgûlah, doctrine of, II, 152.
Ginnungagap, as boundless abyss, I, 147, 150, 160.
Ginsburg, C. D. (1831-1914), *Kabbalah,* etc., on Shimon b. Yoḥai's death, II, 348fn.
*Ginzâ,* I, 651.
Girard, Father J.-B. (1680-1733), sorcery of, II, 633-34.
Girnâr, II, 32.

Glaciation, last, and man's antiquity, I, 3, 632.
Gladstone, W. E. (1809-1898), *Rome and the Newest Fashions in Religion,* II, 379; on Papal "flowers of speech," 7; on Pius IX, 4fn.; on Virgin Mary, 110fn.
Glanvill, J. (1636-80), *Sadducismus triumphatus:* on Drummer of Tedworth, I, 123, 363; on ethereal vehicle of souls, 453; on intelligent beings, 74; on Scot, Adie & Webster, 206; q. H. More on apparitions, 54-55; q. More on meaning of witch, 354-55; q. More on Catholicism, II, 560fn.
Glass: and alkahest, I, 51; —blowing in Egypt, 543; malleable, 239; malleable, and cup of Tiberias, 50; malleable, in Tibet, 60; Nero's optical, 240; of Egypt & China, 537, 543.
Glauber, J. R. (1604-1668), I, 191.
Glaucias, disciple of Peter, II, 125, 155.
Gliddon, G. R. (1809-1857), *Ancient Egypt:* on antiq. of Egypt, I, 515; on moving obelisk, 519; on knowledge of Egyptians, 521-22.
—— & Nott, *Types of Mankind,* on Trimûrti, II, 303.
Glycerine, I, 505-06.
Gnosis ($\gamma\nu\hat{\omega}\sigma\iota s$): binary as fundamental cornerstone of, II, 268; Ephesus as focus of, 155; has representatives at all times, 38; lingers still, albeit unknown, 402; Oriental, & early Christianity, 205, 211; Platonic, & Christianity, 198.
Gnosticism: primitive, corrupted, I, 271fn.; borrowed from *Avesta,* II, 221; cosmogony of, 183-85, 186-88; discussed, 155ff.; distorted, 176; H.P.B. defends mainly, 326; Gospels use language of, 205; more logical than Christianity, 174; offshoot of Buddhism, 158, 169.
Gnostics: followers of Essenes, I, 26; Gibbon on, 12; and Celsus, III, 325; distorted by Irenaeus, 176; and doctrine of atonement, 327; high character of, 249, 330; ideas of, on Jupiter, Semelê & immaculate conception, 505; maxim of, 212; persecution of, 37; slandered, 329, 330-31; superior to Jesus' disciples, 208; superseded Essenes, 324.
Gobi Desert: II, 599; malignant beings of, I, 603; once seat of rich empire, 598; prophecy about, 599; "Spirit-voices" in, 606; lost secret buried in, II, 361.

Goblins, elementary, I, 68.

God: as Sephîrâh, I, 270; as Universal Mind, 131, 289; as Universal Soul, vi; belief in, rooted in people, 222; Bruno & Spinoza on, 93; business partnership of, with Devil, 103; cannot be described, 308; def. as intelligent Will, 58; demonstrated by man's own Self, vi; denied by science, 61; fourfold, 508fn.; geometrizing, 506-07fn.; how to prove, vi; idea of, & fire, 423; inner, & endurance of individuality, 316; intelligible, 56; and miracles, 119; More on nature of, 206; *not a thing,* 292; *one,* and polytheism, 132fn.; over all, xii; personal, and Supreme Being, 16; Plato on becoming like, xiii; Poimandres on man becoming a, 625; projection of the personality of masses, 16; Pythagoras on, 287; reflected in man's soul, xviii; some *other* image of 331; the one, idea & Plato, 288; the one-living, vii; Theos. conception of, 36; Voltaire & Volney on, 268-69; II, 288; Bible—, of Israel as tempter, II, 639; Christian, & his Logos, 510; Christian, a secondary power, 264; conception of, depends upon spiritual vision, 567; conception of, in India, 261-62; curses serpent, 512; every man a, 262-63; firstborn of, 195; Hanuman the monkey—, 274, 278; highest, in *Zohar,* 212; incarnate, def. 153; inner Self as Supreme, 566fn.; Jesus made into a, 480; "Lord," a subordinate, 184; Lord, of Hebrews, 301-02; Lord, of Israel was Moloch, 525; made in human likeness, 242; Masonry & Personal, 375, 377; men of, 154; one true, 88; Pârsis on, 579fn.; pictured by Doré, 242-43; possession by a, 625; puerile & absurd term, 265; *Rigveda* on, within, 412; seen by 70 elders, 230fn.; seven-rayed, & souls, 417; Sun-Isaral, 402; Temple of, within us, 635; the *One,* of Chinese, 554; triple, of Tatars, 49; union with our own inner, 318; views about, compared, 541-42.

Gods: and Archangels, not men on our planet, I, 316; as instructors of truths, 122; as occult potencies, *xxxviii;* celestial bodies are images of, xxi; "creation" of, in theurgy, xlii; double-sexed, 156; elementaries desire to be honored as, 332-33; eminent men called, by ancients, 24; fleeting shapes of, & images, 280; and goddesses & electricity, 261-62; Hermes on, & animated statues, 613-14; issuing from a duad & triad, 348; *John* on being, 2; of Egypt, 406; II, 448; Olympic, I, 267; Plato on, 150, 287; priests named after their, 550, 554; sexless, in myths, 303; appearance of, in Mysteries, II, 113; as first principles of Nature, 406; as symbols of creative powers, 402, 410; black & white, of Yakuts, 568-69; creative powers misnamed, 386; and demi—, 536; descend into Hell, 514 & fn.; embody ideas, 413; euhemerized in all ages, 487; initiates are, 287; intermediate, managing the world, 554; Müller on heathen, & Fathers, 480; on earth, 153, 159; of Meru & Sephîrôth, 233; Pagan incarnate, & Jesus, 337; personated occult powers, 143; Plato on seeing the, 146; resurrection of Sun—, 173; and Śaktis, 275-76; seers instructed by, 369; sun— idea dual, 507; symbols of Hindu, 301; twelve great, 448, 450-51; vindication of ancient, 527-28; we are, above; demi-gods below, 112; we are all, 318; Xenophanes on, 212, 242; Zeller on minor, 345.

Godwin, Wm. (1756-1836), *Lives of the Necromancers,* on alchemy, I, 503.

Godwin-Austen, R. A. C. (1808-1884), I, 223.

Goethe, J. W. von (1749-1832), *Faust,* I, 125; II, 501.

Goffridi, Louis (d. 1611), burnt for sorcery, II, 633.

Gogard, Mazdean Tree of Life, I, 297.

Gold: as deposit of light which generates, I, 511; basic matter, 50; Incas', 546, 597; oil of, 51, 224; manufacture of, asserted, 503ff. *See also* Transmutation.

*Golden Legend. See* Jacobus de Voragine.

Goldschmidt, H. (1802-66), I, 54.

Gomates, II, 129.

Good: Plato on Supreme, I, xii, xvi; dogma of sin allegedly cause of greatest, 479; and Evil balanced, 463, 481; Jacolliot on contest of, and Evil, 510; Plato on, and God, 239.

"Good Shepherd," image of, II, 149.

Goodale, Miss Annie ( ? -1877), strange death of, I, 479.

Gopura, of pagodas, II, 584.

Görres, J. J. von (1776-1848). *Die christliche Mystik:* on apparitions, I, 103; on Malabar phantoms, 344.

—— *Gesammelte Schriften,* on man's soul, I, 453.
Gosain (Hind. *gosâin,* from Skt. *gosvâmin*), contests a sorcerer, I, 368.
Gospel(s): one *infaillible,* we recognize, I, 29; why four only, 147; II, 231; apocryphal, II, 539; author of fourth, Alexandrian Gnostic, 476; chosen by *sortes,* 251-52; compared with Oriental & Greek precepts, 338; contradictions in, 133; Faustus on origin of, 37-38; fourth, contradicts Peter, 211; fourth, not written by John, 211; genuine, of Matthew, 181-82; not written by those to whom attributed, 530; secret character of, of Matthew, 182, similar to older Scriptures, 337; stories in, borrowed, 241, 548ff.; system of pious fraud, 133; teem with Gnostic expressions, 205; written by men unacquainted with each other, 246.
*Gospel according to Peter,* II, 181.
*Gospel according to the Hebrews,* II, 182fn., 183, 505.
*Gospel of Nicodemus:* absurdities of, II, 515ff.; Church forced to repudiate, 522; on Jesus & magic, 148; on powers of darkness, 556; on Satan & Jews, 186fn.; plagiarism in, 515-17; spurious scene in Hell, 518-20.
*Gospel of St. Thomas,* II, 539.
*Gospel of the Birth of Mary,* II, 444fn., 556; on death of Zacharias, 523fn.
Goths, I, 576.
Gougenot des Mousseaux, H. R. (1805-78), and de Mirville demonstrate unseen spir. universe, II, 15.
—— *Dieu et les Dieux:* I, 614; on voices of spirits, 68.
—— *La Magie au XIXme siècle:* I, 101, 370, 614; on Huc's story of moon's picture, I, 441; on Figuier, 372, 376; on Regazzoni, 143; q. Plutarch, 200; on Ch. Fathers, II, 447; on exorcisms, 69, 85-86, 87.
—— *Les Hauts Phénomènes de la magie:* I, [16], 76, 101, 614, 635; on "canine hallucinations," 278; on Comte, 78; on Hermes, 551; on Hivim, 554; on Janet's views, 80; on repercussion, 360-61; on vampirism, 450, 451-52; q. Père Félix on science, 337-39; letter of Raulica re Satan, II, 14; on batylos, 5; on demons & Savior, 476; on nimbus, 512; on Saint-Hilaire, 343.

—— *Les Médiateurs,* I, 101.
—— *Mœurs et pratiques des démons:* I, [16], 101; on Devil as pillar of faith, 103; on Görres & catastrophies, 103; on Tertullian, 159; on Church & magic, II, 76; on Devil & Redeemer, 479; on Pope's bull about Spiritualism, 69; on rites & spirits, 71; q. Raulica on dangers of magic, 70.
Gourdain. *See* Woof.
Gout, remedies against, I, 89.
Govinda Svâmin, Jacolliot's fakir, I, 139, 140fn., 147, 458.
Grabe, J. E. (1666-1711), II, 549.
Grace, Highest, II, 224.
Graeco-Russian Church, I, 27.
Graham. *See Quarterly Review.*
Granger, J. (1723-1776), *Biogr. Hist. of England,* on horse burnt for witchcraft, II, 59.
Granville [actually Dr. Augustus Bozzi, 1783-1872], on Egyptian mummies, I, 539.
Graves, K. (1813-1883), *World's Sixteen Crucified Saviors,* etc., unreliable, II, 341-42fn.
Gravitation: and earth's shape, I, 622-23; Kepler on, 207; merely magnetic attraction & repulsion, 271; Plato on, 236-37, 244.
Great Kuren, convent at Urga & its sepulchre, II, 604, 658-59.
Great Year, I, 30, 31, 294fn.
Greatrakes, V. (1629-83), healer, I, 218.
Greece: arts of, from Egypt, I, 521; gods of, from Egypt, 543; mechanical devices of, 543.
Greek: learning derived from Egypt, I, 531; transl. of *Berêshîth Rabbah,* II, 247.
Greek, terms & expressions in, letters: I, xii, xiii, xiv, xvi, xviii, xx, xxviii, xxxv, xxxix, xli, xlii, xliii, 1, 6, 56, 68, 125, 131, 224, 226, 228, 231, 242, 255, 256, 257, 271, 317, 321, 336, 354, 355, 405, 412, 429, 432, 436, 540, 569, 576; II, 12, 38, 48, 52, 91, 93, 95, 97, 101, 111, 144, 146, 155, 158, 191, 193, 213, 231, 233, 258, 280, 282, 283, 284, 293, 297, 298, 301, 324, 328, 344, 352, 423, 482, 484fn., 486, 491fn.
Greeley, H. (1811-1872), *Recoll. of a Busy Life,* on authority, I, x.
Green: corresponds to middle nature, I, 514; and silver, 513.

Greene, Robert (1560?-1592), dramatist, I, 65.
Greenhill, T. (1681-1740?), *Nekrokêdeia* (Νεκροκηδεια), on recipes for perpetual lamps, I, 228, 229fn.; on Grew & asbestos, 231.
Grégoire, Bishop Henri (1750-1831), *Histoire des sectes,* etc., on Templars, II, 381, 384.
Gregory VI (Johannes Gratianus, Pope, 1045-46), magician-pope, II, 56.
Gregory VII (Hildebrand), St. (ca. 1023-1085), magician-pope, II, 56.
Gregory XIII (Ugo Buoncompagno, 1502-1585), Pope, II, 580.
Gregory, Wm. (1803-1858), *Letters . . . on Animal Magnetism,* on catalepsy, I, 484.
Gregory of Nazianzus (325?-389?), II, 633.
— *Epistolae,* writes Jerome on verbiage, II, 183.
Gregory of Tours (538?-593), *Historia Francorum,* on *sortes,* II, 20, 21.
Grew, N., *Catalogue of . . . Gresham College,* and asbestos, I, 231.
Grihastha: II, 103; evocation of Pitris by, I, xlii-xliii.
Grimoire, II, 85.
Gross, J. B. ( ? -1891), *The Heathen Religion:* on vaticination, I, 132; on preformation, 92; on Christian prejudice, II, 96-97.
Grote, Geo. (1794-1871), I, 525.
— *A Hist. of Greece,* on Pythagoras, II, 529.
Grousset, R. (1885— ), *Le Conquérant du monde,* I, 656.
Grove, Wm. R. (1811-1896), *On the Correlation of Physical Forces,* I, 242.
Groves, sacred, II, 316.
Grynaeus, J. J. (1540-1617), *Monumenta S. Patrum,* etc.: II, 517fn., 648; on Lentulus & Jesus, 151.
Guatemala. *See* Fuentes, and Vázquez.
Gueneau de Mussy, and mesmerism, I, 174.
Guibert de Nogent (1053-1124), on *sortes,* II, 21.
Guido d'Arezzo (ca. 990-1050), and Hindu scale, I, 620.
Guigniaut, J. D. (1794-1876), *Religions de l'antiquité,* etc., II, 538fn.
Guillotin, Dr., and mesmerism, I, 171.
Guizot, F. P. G. (1787-1874), q. I, 293.

Gully, Dr., J. M. (1808-73), I, 85.
Guṇî, as snake-charmers, II, 622.
Gunpowder, known to Chinese, I, 241.
Guppy, Mrs., I, 494.
Guru-astara, II, 141.
Gushtasp. *See* Hystaspes, and Vishtâspa.
Gützlaff, K. F. A. (1803-1851), and Buddhism, II, 553.
Gymnosophists: I, xxxix, 113, 205, 347, 442, 475; II, 305, 389, 531; holiness of life of, and profound knowledge of magic, I, 90.

H

H, efficacy of letter, II, 299.
Ḥabir, an associate, I, 569.
Hadês ("Αιδης): Aeneas' descent to, I, 362-63; Christ & Hercules descending to, 132 & fn., 299; and loss of soul, 319; on eighth sphere, 352; Plato on, 328; descent of god into, II, 145, 514-15; differs from Hell, 11; in Gospel, 506; intermediate state of purification, 11.
Hadrian (76-138 A.D.): II, 335; on Christians, 336.
Haeckel, E. (1834-1919), *Anthropogenie,* etc., I, 154.
Haemerobaptists, II, 307fn.
*Ḥagîgâh.* *See* *Talmud.*
Hai-banda, shark-binders, I, 606.
Haideck, Countess, a Mason, II, 391.
Hair: electrified, I, 234; long, of Nazarenes, II, 140, 151; Paul on long, 140fn., 151.
Haiti, bloody rites in, II, 572.
Ḥakhamim, wise men, II, 415.
al-Ḥakîm, and Druzes, II, 310.
Ḥakîm, a physician, II, 328fn.
Hales, W. (1747-1831), *A New Analysis of Chronology,* I, xl.
Halévy, J. (1827-1917), *Mélanges,* etc.; I, 576; on language of Babylon, II, 472.
Halhed, N. B. (1751-1830), on Hindu annals, II, 258.
— *A Code of Gentoo Law,* II, 411fn.
Hall, S. C. (1800-89), on spirits, I, 445.
Hall of Spirits, II, 365.
Haller, Albrecht von (1708-77), I, 391.
Halley, Edm. (1656-1742): on aurora, I, 417; comet of, II, 509.
Hallucination(s): and objective visions, I,

145; pet explanation of scientists, 278; psychological, and epidemics, 370ff.; mesmeric, II, 588-89.
Ham: "accursed" descendants of, I, 556; "Land of," 226fn.; steals Noah's garments, 149-50; treatise ascribed to, 25.
Hamilton, I, 100.
Hamites: I, 567fn., 576; II, 434, 440, 458.
Hamley, Maj.-Gen. Wm., on ancient Egypt, I, 515ff., 647.
Hamlin, Dr. A. C., on Indian arts, I, 538.
H'amza: as Christos, II, 310, 312; and Druzes, 308fn., 310; ethereal form of, at Druze initiation, 312.
Hamzaites. See Druzes.
**Hananyah, Rabbi Joshua ben, II, 357.**
Hand-shaking, and magnetic emanations, II, 611.
Ḥanina, Rabbi, II, 357.
Hanno (ca. 5th c. B.C.), *Periplus*, I, 413.
Hanuman: I, 563 & fn., 564; II, 274; secret meaning of, II, 278.
Har, I, 122.
Hâras, gods of war, II, 513fn.
Hardy, R. S. ( ? -1868), I, 583.
—— *A Manual of Budhism:* **II, 504;** on Buddha's annunciation, II, 555; on his learning, 552; on his being tempted, 513.
—— *Eastern Monachism,* on rebirth, karma & Arhats, I, 346.
Hare, Prof. R. (1781-1858): I, 38, 46, 54, 195, 222, 334; and Amer. Ass'n, 245; denounced at Harvard, 177; and spiritualism, 233.
—— *Experimental Investigations,* I, 79-80.
Hari, and Kula, I, 567.
*Harivaṇśa,* **Gospels copy, II, 241.**
Harmony: I, 184; as equilibrium of opposing forces, 318-19; great law of nature, 330; beneficent effect of, II, 411, and equilibrium, 457, 463, 480-81; law of, & justice, 545.
**Harrison, Wm. (1534-1593),** *Historicall Description,* etc., I, 635.
Hartmann, K. R. E. von (1842-1906), *Philosophie des Unbewussten* (implied), on matter & forces, I, 59, 60-61.
Harvard University, Committee of, on spiritualism, I, 177, 233.
**Harvey, Wm. (1578-1657), I, 85.**
Hasisadra. See Xisuthros.
Hasselquist, F. (1722- 1752), *Voyages,* etc., I, 381.
Hat, square, II, 392-93.

Hathor: **Egyptian primordial element, I, 91;** II, 209.
Hatred, of those injured, II, 330.
**Hauber, E. D. (1695-1765),** *Bibliotheca... Magica,* on burning of heretics, II, 62ff.
Hauffe, Mme. See Prevorst.
Haug, M. (1827-76), *Essays:* on Ahriman & Bull, II, 464-65; on Devil, 486. See also *Aitareya-Brâhmaṇa.*
Haunted house, I, 69.
Hava, or Eve, I, 582.
Haweis, H. R. (1838-1901), *Ashes to Ashes,* etc., on premature burial, I, 456.
Haxthausen, A. von (1792-1866), *Transcaucasia,* on Yezîdi, II, 197.
Hayden, F. V. (1829-1887), *Report of the U. S. Geological Survey,* etc., I, 412.
Hayes (1739-1805), Moses Michael and Royal Arch, II, 393.
Ḥayyôth, holy creatures, II, 299.
Ḥazîm, prophets or seers, I, 482.
*Hazitha.* See *Talmud.*
Head(s): Three, of Kabalah as emanations, I, 160; II, 212-13; 222, 268; oracular, Popes & Albertus Magnus, II, 56.
Healers: natural, I, 464; true and false, 217ff.
Healing: by imagination, I, 216; by music, 215; by Will, 217; and Egyptian Mysteries, 531-32; faith & expectancy essential in, 216; false, by diseased healers, 217; and indulgence, 218; and seers, 347; temple—, magical, II, 502.
Health, disease and magnetism, I, 164, 169.
Hearing, inner, II, 605-06.
Heart, powers of human, I, v.
Heat: and electricity, I, 272; and light, 269; terrestrial, not derived from sun, 272.
Heber, Bishop R. (1783-1826), *Narrative,* etc., on archaic monuments, I, 351fn., 644.
Hebir, astrologer, I, 569.
Hebrew(s), and Aztec languages, I, 553; tribes and their origin, 568-70; contrasted with Jews, II, 526; MSS. of Bible, 430fn. See also Israelites, Jews.
Hebrew, terms & expressions in, letters, I, xxxiv, xxxvi, 13, 181, 226fn., 309, 355, 567fn., 569, 575, 580fn.; II, 12, 29, 34 & fn., 37, 45, 86, 92, 127, 128, 130, 132, 165, 172, 183, 193, 213, 215fn., 217, 218, 220, 222fn., 225, 264-65 (diagrams), 266, 267, 268, 269, 270fn., 271, 276, 280, 297, 298, 301fn., 302,

348, 398, 400, 401, 415, 418, 441, 458fn., 462, 464, 465, 466, 478, 481fn., 482, 488, 491fn. 501, 537fn.
Hebrews: II, 123, 440; contradicts *James*, 84; on Aeôns, 506; on angels as fire, 273fn.; on Jesus & Moses, 37; on Paul & James, 162fn.; on remission through blood, 566.
Hebron: I, 569; II, 297; and Smaragdine Tablet, I, 507; or Kirjath-Arba, II, 171.
Hefele, C. J. von (1809-1893), *Conciliengeschichte*, II, 642.
Hegel, G. W. F. (1770-1831), II, 369.
Heindorf, L. F. (1774-1816), I, 8.
Hekal ahabah, Palace of Love, II, 280.
Hel, or Hela, II, 11.
Helen, and Paris, I, 566.
Hêliacal, year, I, 31.
Heliocentric System: denied, I, 83; in Egypt, 532; known to Philolaus, 238; to Plato, 9-10, 409; to Pythagoras, 9-10; II, 13; taught by Heraclitus, I, xxi; taught in *Vedas*, 9; and Thales, 526; transmitted from India, 31fn.; and Galileo, II, 528.
Heliodorus (4th c.), and Jerome, II, 182.
Heliolatry, return to, proposed by Jesuits, II, 450-51fn.
Hêlios, Adonis & Christ, II, 517.
Heliotrope, and sun, II, 630.
Hell: Apostles' Creed & Fathers on descent into, II, 514; as intermediate state of purification, 11; descent into, & initiation, 177, 514 & fn.; differs from Hadês & Hel, 11; dogma of, as Christian lever, 11; and Gehenna, 507; geocentric, of Augustine, 13; in Sun, 12; invention of Christianity, 507; not Hebrew idea, 506-07; of various nations, 8ff.; Origen denies perpetuity of, 13; scene in, 518-21; Tertullian on his enemies burning in, 250; torments in, 12.
Hellanicus (ca. 496-411 B.C.), and betyli, I, 332.
Helmont, B. van (1577-1644): chemical knowledge of, I, 194; greatest chemist of his age, 192; Fournié on, 400; principle of life of, 400; produces eels & frogs, 414.
—— *Ortus medicinae*: on alkahest & salt, I, 50-51, 148, 191; on elements, 190; on foetus & mother's imagination, 386, 399; on gold, 50; on magnetism & man, 170; on man as mirror of universe, 213; on Paracelsus, 406-07fn.; on Will, 57.

'Hem, or chêmi, I, 226fn.
Hemmann, J. A., *Medizinal-chirurgische Aufsätze*, II, 500fn.; on Paracelsus, I, 52, 164.
Hénin de Cuvillier, E. F. d' (1755-1841), *Archives du magnétisme animal*, I, 173.
Henoch. See Enoch.
Henriquez, E. (ca. 1520-1600), *Summae theologiae moralis*, on murder, II, 363.
Henry, Prof. J.: I, 410; and Prof. Hall, 245.
Heptaktys, II, 417, 419, 487.
Heracleon, II, 248fn., 249.
Heracles ('Ηρακλῆς): as a Savior, liberating Prometheus, II, 515; model for the story of Jesus, 515, 518; opposed to human sacrifices, 565fn. See also Hercules.
Heraclitus ('Ηράκλειτος, ca. 540-475 B.C.): on fighting anger, I, 248; teachings of, xx-xxi; view of, by B. Stewart, 422; on Pythagoras, II, 529.
Herbelot de Molainville, B. d' (1625-95), *Bibliothèque orientale*, on music in desert, I, 604.
Herbs, and dreams, II, 589.
Hercules, Herculeus: II, 123, 451, 512, 513fn.; as "self-born," I, 132; and Hadês, 299; King of Musians, 130fn.; Sanskrit in origin, 567; and Thor, 260; and Typhon, 132; as Sun-god, II, 524; Baal—, and Jesus, 525. See also Heracles.
Herder, J. G. von (1744-1803), *Ideen zur Philosophie*, etc.: I, 250; on India, II, 30.
Heresies: Christian secret sects were, II, 289; early Christianity one of the, 123.
Herford, Rev. Brooke (1830-1903), on evidence of spiritual, I, 222.
Hermeias ('Ερμείας, 6th C. A.D.): Neo-Platonist, I, 436; on chaos, 341.
Hermes ('Ερμῆς): I, xxxiii, 551; II, 187; Homer on, I, 163; on gods & animated statues, 613-14; on Spirit of planets, 255; and Cain, II, 508; and Enoch & Libra, 454, 463; on God, 579fn.; on God the Father, 199; and Prometheus, 514-15; prophecy re Egypt fulfilled, 360; second, or serpent, 508; and Seth, 466.
Hermetic: adept & nature of universe, I, 17; art & man, 309; axiom, 1; science on triune man, II, 362.
*Hermetic Books*: I, 3, 33fn., 406-07, 441, 444, 522, 529, 574, 580, 625; II, 50, 116, 357, 564fn.; key to, missing, I, 551; on Pyramid being on seashore, 520.

—— *Mercurii Trismegisti Liber*, etc., I, 645-46.
—— *Smaragdine Tablet*, I, 506, 507.
—— *Tractatus de transmutationes*, etc., I, 254fn.
See also L. Ménard.
Hermetic Philosophy: I, 306, 307; and condemnation, 437; identical to *Rigveda*, xxxii; most reasonable, 341; on truth & death, 624-25; plea for recognition of, vii, 255, 257, 258; on rebirth, II, 195.
Hermetists: I, 307; on soul, xx.
Hermippus, II, 141.
Hermod, II, 11.
*Hermodactyllus*, I, 89.
Hermodorus, I, 364.
Hermotimus of Clazomenae, and astral soul, I, 476.
Hero, invents steam engine, I, 241.
Herod, and Kansa, II, 199, 537.
Herodotus (484-425 B.C.), *History*: on antiquity of Egypt, I, 515; on bygone glories, 5; on Egyptian fleet sailing around Africa, 542; on Egyptian Labyrinth, 522-23; on Egyptian linen, 536; on Egyptians' 3,000 yr. cycle, 297; on Greek learning derived from Egypt, 531; on lake Moeris, 516; on moving granite blocks, 519; on mummification, 539; on Necho canal, 517; on people sleeping six months, 412; on priestesses of Babylon & aërolites, 331; mentions no Israelites, II, 429fn.; on Bacchic rites, 138; on Eastern Aethiopians, 435; on Hercules, 451.
Herrings, Jews multiply like red, II, 558.
Herschel, Sir John F. W. (1792-1871), on light, I, 137.
Hesed, II, 87, 213.
Hesiod (ca. 9th c. B.C.): I, 151fn., 265, 268; II, 26, 516.
—— *Theogony*, on Titans, I, 567.
—— *Works and Days*, on ash trees & men, I, 558fn.
Heth, I, 546, 554.
Heva, Hevah, I, 579fn., 589; II, 481fn.
Heyne, C. G. (1729-1812), II, 561fn.
Hezekiah: I, 166, 542fn.; role of, II, 440-41.
Hiah, hiah, to be, II, 302.
Hibil-Ziwa, as revealed Logos & Gabriel, II, 154, 174, 204, 236, 247.
Hide, inflated bags of, I, 518.
Hierarchies, and evolution, I, 285.

Hieratic, writings hide concealed meaning, I, 191.
Hiero, I, 364.
Hieroglyphics: I, 156; II, 424; chiselled, I, 524; and Incas' treasure, 597.
Hierophant(s): Egyptian and Babylonian, as Son of Dragon, I, 553; of Atlantis, 593; of India & Tibet, xxxiii; and Peter, *xxxiii*; concealed from candidates, II, 93; cured mediumship, 98; female, of Sabazius, 589; knowledge of, concealed, 113; and life-transfer, 565; of Eleusis, 31fn.; offered his life, 42; often accused of sorcery, 148.
Higgins, G. (1773-1833), I, 347.
—— *Anacalypsis*: I, 32; and *Isis Unveiled*, [2]; on Adam, Enoch & Noah, I, 150; on Aura & Placida, 160; II, 248; on cycles, I, 33-34; on *Genesis*, 284; on black Isis, II, 490; on eucharist, 43-44; on rêshîth as a Principle, 35-36; on Rishis, 305; on sign of Virgo and Albertus Magnus, 490.
—— *Celtic Druids*, on name of Pythagoras, II, 491fn.
Hiketas ('Ικετας), Pythagorean, I, xx, 621.
Hilarion, St. (?-371), on schools of magic, II, 97.
Hildebrand. See Gregory VII.
Hilgenfeld, A. (1823-1907), II, 189fn.
—— *Kritische Untersuchungen*, on view of Ch. Fathers, II, 161.
Hilkiah, and Mosaic books, II, 421, 457, 470, 492.
Hillel, I, xxviii, xxxiii, 482; II, 152, 207, 339, 552, 561, 562.
Himyarites, and Jews, I, 567.
Hindostan, once called Aethiopia, II, 434.
Hindus: astronomical knowledge of, I, 11, 32; and Iranians as Devas & Asuras, 12; philosophies & sciences of, 618-20; II, 27; moral characteristics of, 474 & fn.; more susceptible to magnetism, 611.
Hipparchus (2nd c. B.C.), on violation of oath, II, 374.
—— *Epistles*, on larvae, I, 365, 645.
Hippocrates (5th c. B.C.): I, xxxvii, 384, 423, 584; II, 410; on instinct, I, 434; on nature, 425.
—— *De optima*, etc., on medical pretensions & garlic, I, 20fn.
Hippolytus (3rd c. A.D.), *Philosophumena*: II, 155fn.; on Colarbasus, 249; on Logos among Brahmans, 205.

Hiram: I, 135, 566, 568; II, 297; and Iarchos, I, 19; King, from India, II, 265.
Hiram Abiff, I, 29; II, 138, 349, 388.
Hiraṇyagarbha, and Amrita, I, 265fn.
Hirt, Prof., I, 528.
*Histoire de l'Académie des Inscriptions,* etc., II, 29fn.
History: Fiske on laws of, I, 521, 525; moves in ebb & flow, 34; adepts could explain mysterious pages in, II, 403; Pococke on primitive, 471.
Hitchcock, E. (1793-1864), *Religion of Geology,* etc., on nature's picture-gallery, I, 184-85.
Hitchcock, E. A. (1798-1870), *Remarks upon Alchemy,* etc., on Hermetic art & man, I, 309.
Hittites (Hebr. Ḥittîm, or Benê Ḥêth), I, 568; II, 481-82, 501, 523.
Hiuen-Tsang (ca. 596-664): on magic, I, 599; on virtues of Hindus, II, 474fn.
— *Si-yu-ki,* on Buddha's shadow, I, 600-01. See also Julien, S.
Hivim, and Ḥam, I, 554.
Hivites: I, 568; II, 481fn., 446; and Votan, I, 546.
Hobbes, Thos. (1588-1679), I, 317.
Hobbs, Abigail, I, 361.
Hod, II, 213.
Hodgson, B. H. (1800-1894), *Essays,* etc., on individual effort in Buddhism, II, 288.
Hoffmann, A. W. von (1818-92), I, 54.
Hoffman, E. T. W. (1776-1822), II, 564.
Hohenlohe - Waldenburg - Schillingsfurst, Alexander L. F. E., Prince of (1794-1849), medium & healer, I, 28.
Hoi polloi, ideas of, about God, I, 436, 624.
Ḥokhmah: male principle, II, 213, 215fn.; male Wisdom, 268-69; Supreme Wisdom, 212; —Akhamôth, as androgyne Demiurge, 468; —nistharah, 220, 266, 269.
Ḥokhmôth, wisdom, II, 172.
Holloway, Laura Langford, on James Robinson, I, [10].
Holy Ghost: Aether is, II, 506; as first androgyne duad, 229fn.; and baptism, 135ff.; female principle, I, 130, 299fn.; II, 267fn., 357, 505, feminine, similar to Shekhînah, II, 223, 224, 267fn., 357; finger of, 71; Gnostics on female, or Spiritus, 193; or Nara, 267; and Son of Man, 238; Zoê or female, 226.

Holzmann, M. & H. Bohatta, *Deutsches Anonymen Lexikon,* II, 652.
Home, D. D. (1833-86), I, 45, 202-03.
Homer, *Iliad:* on lying, I, 253; and *Rāmayaṇa,* 566; II, 436.
— *Odyssey:* on Cyclops, I, 567; on elementary beings, 332; on "festival of blood," 362; on Hermes, 163; on maelstrom & icebergs, 549; on Northern days & nights, 545, 549.
*Homeric Hymn XXXI,* to Eli, II, 506.
Homunculi, of Paracelsus, I, 465.
Hone, W. (1780-1842), *The Apocryphal New Testament:* on Christ & Hell, II, 177; on Collyridians, 444fn.; on forged verse in *I John,* 177fn.; on *Gospel of Nicodemus* & Beelzebul, 486; on Paul & Seneca, 277; on *Shepherd of Hermas,* 518; on Zacharias & ass, 523; q. Newton on Paul's text, 178.
Höner, I, 151.
Honey-dew, I, 133.
Honover [corr. of *Ahuna-Vairya*], Persian Logos, I, 560.
Hopkins, on Masonic Oath, II, 375.
Horace (65-8 B.C.), *Ars poetica,* on myths, II, 406, 654.
— *Epistles,* I, 460.
— *Satires,* on evocations, I, 493.
Horaios, genius of the spheres, II, 184, 294.
Horns, or crescent as badge of Lamaic Sovereignty, II, 505fn.
Horse: Spirit—, I, 70; with fingers, 412; burnt for witchcraft, II, 59; white, and Sun, 237, 302.
Horsley, Bishop. See Newton, I.
Horst, G. C. (1578-1636), *Zauber-Bibliothek,* etc., on spirits, I, 457.
Horus: II, 483, 491; elder and younger, I, 56; and dragon, II, 446; and Egyptian Ritual, 367.
*Hosea:* II, 132; on Bosheth, 130; on Kadesh, 45.
Hotṛi: I, xxxviii, 10; II, 409; representative of gods, I, xxvii.
House of Life, and Seven Lives, II, 234.
Hovelaque, A.-A. (1843-96), and Hanuman, II, 274fn.
Howitt, W. (1792-1879), *Hist. of the Supernatural:* on blindness of scientists, I, 409; on Cévennois, 390; on enlightenment, 125; on evocations, 493; on Franklin's skepticism, 409; on scientific errors,

223; on exorcism, II, 66-67; on thunder of Vatican, 57.
Hrimthussar, I, 148.
Hubilgans (also Khubilgans & Khubilhans): I, 631; or Shaberons, as reincarnations, II, 583, 609, 660.
Huc, Abbé É. R. (1813-60): on moon picture in Tibet, I, 441; high opinion for Buddhists, II, 345; on Lama leaving body behind, 604-05; on tomb of Tatar rulers, 604.
—— *Souvenirs d'un voyage*, etc.: I, 302; on Kumbum tree, 440; on reincarnation of a Buddha, 438; on similarities of Lamaism & Catholicism, 345-46fn.; on Lamaism, 582.
Huet, P. D. (1630-1721), *Huetiana*, etc., on vampires, I, 450.
Hufeland, F. (1762-1836), and Paracelsus, I, 52.
—— *Über die Sympathie*, on magnetism, I, 207.
Hukkabaz, juggler, II, 612.
Huldah: and *O. T.*, II, 421fn., 457; dwelt in a College, 525.
Huldrich, J. J. See *Sepher Toldoth Yeshu*.
Hulin. See *Talmud*.
Human: sacrifices an ancient practice, II, 547; sacrifices as perversion of Theurgy, 565fn.
Humanity, seven stages of evolution of, II, 407.
*Human Nature* (P. C. Mitra), on soul's powers, II, 592-93.
Humboldt, F. H. A. von (1769-1859): I, 82; on American natives, 548; on skepticism, 223.
—— *Kosmos*, on Tycho Brahè & Comet, I, 441-42.
Hume, D. (1711-76): I, 83, 314, 402, 403; sophisms of, 195.
—— *An Inquiry*, etc., I, 421.
—— *Philosophical Works*, on Abbé de Pâris, I, 373.
Hungarians, and vampires, I, 449.
Hunt, R. (1807 - 1887), *Researches on Light*, on chemical effect of light, I, 136.
Hunt, Thos. S. (1826-92), I, 162, 189, 509.
—— *The Origin of Metalliferous Deposits*, on water, I, 192.
Huss, John (1369-1415), and Czechs, II, 560.
Husson, Dr.: *eau médicinale* of, I, 89; and mesmerism, 174, 175.

Hutugtu (also Hutughtu & Khutukhtu), as a title, I, 631; II, 617, 618, 622, 660.
Huxley, T. H. (1825-95): on early horse, I, 411; on human testimony, 193; on spiritualism, 232, 422; on the "impossible," 223.
—— *On the Physical Basis of Life*: I, 15, 59; on Comte's philosophy, 82-93; on ignorance of science, 408; summary of, & errors in, 419-21; on positivism, II, 3-4.
—— *On the Study of Biology*, on human testimony, I, 121.
—— "Darwin and Haeckel," I, 153, 155.
Hvergelmer, I, 152.
Hyde, Thos. (1636-1703), *Historia religionis veterum Persarum*, II, 140fn.
Hydrogen: discovered by Paracelsus, I, 169, 192; and oxygen, known to Rosicrucians, 52fn.
Hydrostatics, Roman and Egyptian, I, 516-17.
Hyksôs: II, 27, 438, 481, 523fn.; and Israelites: I, 569, 570; ancestors of Israelites, II, 487.
Hyle (ὕλη), I, 146.
Hynemann, L. (1805-1879), *Ancient York*, etc.: on decadence of Masonry, II, 380; on history of Masonry, 389.
Hypatia ( ? -415 A.D.): II, 28, 249; murder of, 53; and Synesius, 198; why murdered, 253.
Hyper-ouranioi (ὑπερουράνιοι), I, 312.
Hystaspes: blunder about, II, 140-41; visited Kashmîr, 434. See also Darius.
Hysteria: curious properties of, I, 370ff.; and scientific ideas, 278.

# I

Iacchos (Ἴακχος), worship of, II, 135, 245, 302, 518.
Iachus, Egyptian physician, I, 406.
Iâḥ, Iâh, as life, II, 299. See also Yâḥ.
Iahoh, Adoni-Iahoh, II, 131. See also Yâho.
Ialdabaôth: II, 296, 501, 526; as Archon, 206; as Demiurgus, 175, 183-84, 206, 228fn.; and Christos, 185-86, 187-88, 247; dwells in Saturn, 236, 294, 505; and Jehovah, 292; Jewish second Adam, 207; revenge of, 185.
Iamblichus (255?-ca. 333 A.D.): levitated, I, 115; on daemons, 321; on higher

intelligences, 489; on icosagonus, xxi; and Theurgy, xlii; II, 84.
—— *De mysteriis:* on *Books of Hermes,* I, 33fn., 406; on daemons & phantoms creating illusions, 333; on danger of theurgic evocations, 333; on effect of bad daemons, 219; on Egyptian magicians, 416; on Emepht, 636; II, 49; on good and bad spirits, I, 344; on sanctity of Mysteries, II, 101.
—— *Life of Pythagoras:* I, 238fn.; on intuition, 435; q. Heraclitus on anger & self-control, 248; on Pythagoras at Carmel, II, 145.
—— *Protreptics,* II, 338.

Iaô (or Iaho) ('Iaω): I, 61, 184; and Abraxas borrowed from East, II, 233fn.; as Central Sun, 139fn., 293; as quaternary emanation, 207; as secret name, 165, 269; and Egyptian mysteries, 315; *eo* or *ao* as phonetic of, 484, 523fn.; and Ferho, 295; Genius of the Spheres, 184, 294; is over the seven orbits, 417; Kabalistic meaning & derivation of, 299; King on, & engraved stones, 233fn., 351; mysterious, 527; mystery-name, 215fn., 220; of the Mysteries, 184fn.; or Yâho, 297, 298; Phoenician, 481, phonetic counterparts of, 301-02, 484, 523fn.

Iapestos, Assyrian Titan-god, II, 488.
Iarchas, and Hiram, I, 19.
Iberians, I, 576.
Ibn Batûtah (1304-1378), *Voyages:* on demons in desert, I, 604; on magic performance, 473.
Ibn al-Waḥshîya (9th c.), and *Nab. Agriculture,* II, 197.
Icebergs, Homer on, I, 549.
*Icosagonus,* Iamblichus on, I, xxi.
Idaeic, finger, I, 23.
Idea(s): I, 19-20; Divine, of Plato, as will, 61; embodied in symbols, 22; Plutarch on, 250; visible universe built on Divine, 342.
Idiot, and reincarnation, I, 357.
Idolatry, and Jesuits, II, 360.
Idols: destroyed by Theodosius, II, 40; and philosophy in Buddhism, 554; speaking, 583; we build ourselves in our own images, 402.
*Idrah Rabbah:* on Adan, II, 247; on Ancient of Days, 223; on Long Face, 212; on Self, 342; on Shekhînah, 227; on Superior Adam, 224; on superior worlds, 245; on Zeir-Anpin, 234fn.
*Idrah Zutah:* on Concealed, II, 224; on expansion of Divine Essence, 213; on Lord Mano, 224; on Sephîrâh, 214; on three Heads & the Ancient, 222-23; on worlds that perished, 220.
Iessaeans, II, 137, 190.
Ievo ('IETΩ), and Abraxas, II, 296; and Philo Byblius, 301.
Ievo-hevah, Adam and Eve, II, 269, 398.
Igili, celestial beings, II, 452.
IHΣ, Interpretation of, II, 527.
Ikshvâku, II, 488.
Illuminati, I, 257; II, 391.
Illumination, by means of Soma-Mystery, I, xxxv.
Illusion: doctrine of, II, 157-58; Schopenhauer on, 158.
Illusions, created by daemons, I, 333.
Ilon, unrevealed Deity, II, 423.
Ilu, or Ain-Soph, II, 170.
Ilus (or Hylê): I, 146, 342; and Chaos, II, 260, 261, 271fn., 275.
Imagination: as creative faculty, I, 396-97; as creative power of soul, 396; cure by, 216; formidable potency in, 384; of mother & effect on foetus, 384ff.; Paracelsus on, 361fn; plants have, 396; and Will as keys to magic, 62, 140; II, 619; faith and will, II, 598.
Imbibition, property of organic tissues, I, 169.
Immaculate: II, 5; conception of Virgin Mary, 9.
Immorality, said to be caused by religious instinct, I, 83.
Immortality: assurance of man's, I, vi; Chinese ideas of, 214; conditioned, 432; conditions of, 328; and cross circumscribed, 508; and ether & Nirvâṇa, 290; evidence for, in psychometry, 186; idea of, supported by ancients, 251; inner sense of, 424, 425; Maxwell on, 216; and planetary gods, xxi-xxii; serpent as symbol of, 553; skepticism about, a malady, 115; Tatian on the, of man, 13; universal yearning for proof of, 36-37; and earlier cycles of man, II, 362; Jacolliot on man's, 262; and Nirvâṇa, 117, 320; not mentioned in Bible, 117.
Imos, I, 551.
Impressions, invisible, in Nature, I, 186.
Inachienses, II, 438.

Incarnation, of adept into a child's body, II, 601-02.
Incarnations. *See* Avatâras.
Incas: gold ransom of, concealed, I, 546; story about treasure of, as told to H.P.B., 595-96; tomb, 597; treasure and Spanish rule, 598; 654-56; treasures of, II, 26fn.
Incendiarism, I, 276, 277.
Incense, why used, I, 357fn.
Incest, cosmic meaning of, II, 268.
Incredulity, of educated man, I, 409.
Incubi: didactic, and Comte, I, 81; and succubi, 459.
Indecency: alleged of various sects, II, 330-32, 333; of *bas reliefs* on Doors of St. Peter's in Rome, 332; of Christian Scriptures, 79-80, 130-31; of various Christian practices, 332-33.
*Independent,* on ale, I, xlifn.
*Index Expurgatorius,* and scientists, I, 338fn.
India: achievements of ancient, I, 618ff.; ancient literature of, 585ff.; and Egypt, 627; grandeur of thought in ancient, 583-84; pre-Vedic, and Egypt, 589; Alexander did not invade, II, 429; *alma mater* of religions, 30; bathing festivals in, 138; and *Book of the Dead,* 438; and conception of God, 261-62; cosmogony of, 266ff.; disdain of Anglo-Indians for, 613; and Egypt, 431; evils of drinking in, 574; knowledge of Schools of Magic derived from, 361; leading features of philosophy of, 530; mâyâ as basis of metaphysics of, 157-58; mesmeric powers in, 612; and missionaries, 531-33 & fn.; mother-religion of, 413; Müller on, as origin of Zoroastrianism, 143; native doctors & European medicine, 621fn.; psychological powers known in, 584, 585; sacred books of, mistranslated, 417; source of Western schools, 412; and the British, 624; untold antiquity of religions of, 415; virtues of people of, 474fn.; what ancients meant by, 434; Whitney on older creed in, now vanished, 535.
*Indian Antiquary,* on the One God, II, 554.
Indians (Amerindians): I, 6, 248, 304, 551, 556, 564, 592-93, 595-98; II, 254; and mysterious city in Cordilleras, I, 546-47; practice native rites, 557; demoralization of, and Christians, II, 474fn.
*Indica. See* Arrian, *Anabasis.*
Individuality: endurance and loss of, I, 315-16; distinct, and Nirvâṇa, II, 534.

Indra: and Ahura-Mazda, II, 484; degraded, 488; identical with Michael, 510fn.
Indrânî, II, 301.
Induction: and Aristotle, I, 408; and experiment, 393; not usual mode of discoveries, 513.
Inductive, and universal reasoning and science, I, 405.
Infancy, ensnares the Soul, II, 112.
Infants: and reincarnation, I, 351; unborn, how influenced, 395; eaten in Haiti, II, 572.
Initiate(s) ($\tau\epsilon\lambda\epsilon\iota\omega\tau\eta\varsigma$): II, 145; def. I, xxxiii; King—, of Siam, 571; pursues studies in silence, 287; ancient, right, II, 112; brotherhood of, & H.P.B., 306-07; do not divulge secrets, 404; every, becomes a Son of God, 566; Jesus belonged to body of, 337; keep silent, 510; of Galilee, 131; or consecrated, 130; passes the "word" to successor, 42 & fn.; penalties of, for revealing secrets, 99-100, 111; prophets were nazars &, 525.
Initiation: denied to foreigners, I, 556; depends upon man himself, 307; Theon of Smyrna on, xiv; adepts of the third, II, 115; barred to murderers, 363; and descent into underworld, 514fn.; and dodecahedron, 392; Egyptian, and its degrees, 364-65; and freedom of soul, 565; grade of, symbolized by age, 199-200; *Job* as symbolical poem of, 494ff.; MSS. for candidates of, 204; Mithraic, 351-52; of Apuleius & midnight sun, 146; of Druzes, 310, 312ff.; of fakirs, & evocation of Pitris, 114-15; of Paul, 146; ordeals of, tipified by animals in the ark, 447; perfective rite & epopteia, 101; Pindar on, 111; stone of, 351; twofold dangers of, 118-19; virtues required for, 98.
Injury, at a distance, I, 361.
Injustice, and spirit in creatures, I, 331.
Inman, Thos. (1820-76), *Ancient Faiths and Modern:* on Buddha & Supreme Being, II, 533; on differences between Buddhist & Christian doctrines, 540-41; on Christians, 540.
—— *Ancient Faiths embodied,* etc., II, 94fn., 445, 458.
—— *Ancient Pagan and Modern,* etc.: II, 108fn.; on ancient symbols adopted by Christians, 109 & fn.; on dangers of priestcraft, 121-22; on Longinus & Amphibolus, 248; on origin of Catholic

symbols, 94, 96; on paganism in Christianity, 80-81; on Popes & circumcision, 126.
Innocent VIII (Giovanni Battista Cibo, 1432-92), bull of, against magic, II, 69.
Innocent X (Giovanni Battista Pamfili, 1574-1655), Pope, I, 89.
"Innocents:" Kabalistic meaning of, II, 200-01; massacre of the, copied from India, 199, 537.
Inquisition: I, 85, 97; II, 5-6; and magical knowledge, I, 65; Bodin and, II, 55; burns ten thousand persons, 59; destroys Hebrew Bibles, 430; and human sacrifices, 565fn.; and Loyola, 354; slaughter-house of Church killed by Napoleon, 22; standard of, from the Escorial, 59.
INRI, II, 526-27.
Insanity: from spiritualism, II, 7; and possession by vampires, 589.
Inspiration, true and false, I, 201.
Instinct ($\alpha\iota\sigma\theta\eta\tau\iota\kappa\acute{o}\nu$): as spiritual unity of five senses, I, 145; def., *425-26; 432-34;* Hippocrates on, 434; of child and animal, 426; and omniscience, II, 587.
Intellect: divine, veiled in man, I, 247; does not imply spiritual life, 318; revolution in world of, 34.
Intellectual ($\nu o\epsilon\rho\tilde{\varphi}$), I, 56.
Intellectuality ($\nu o\eta\tau\iota\kappa\acute{o}\nu$), I, 432.
Intelligences: apart from mediums, I, 53; astral currents and, 199-200; directing occult powers differ, 492; divine, in all manifestations, 198; extraneous to medium, 196ff.; Kepler on planetary, 208; key to understanding, 54; spiritual & electricity, 322-24; spiritual, *subjectively* evoked, 66.
Intelligible ($\nu o\eta\tau\acute{o}s$), I, 56.
Intolerance, of scientists, I, 85.
Intuition: I, xviii, 61; crown of instinct, 433; discoveries in flashes of, 513; faith rooted in, 467; Iamblichus on, 435; needed to grasp truth, 16; Plotinus on, 434; prescience of women, 434; prior to reason, 61; superior to reason, 435; unerring guide to seer, 433.
Invisible: Sun, I, 302; universe and ether, 187-88; universe inhabited also, 344; worlds, 185.
Invocation: Buddhist, II, 114fn.; by Moldavians, 570; of Apollonius of Tyana, 344; to Brahmâ, 105.
Invulnerability, cases of, I, 378-80.

Iota, a secret password, II, 324.
Iphicles, healed, I, 532.
Iphicrates (4th c. B.C.), stops human sacrifices, II, 565fn.
Irad, II, 466.
Iran, and Turan, I, 576.
Iranians, I, 12.
Ireland: Buddhist missionaries in, II, 290-91; Round Towers of, 290fn.
Irenaeus (130?-202?): I, 289; distorts Jesus' character, II, 137; falsifications of, 304-05, 326.
— *Adversus Haereses:* on *four* Gospels, I, 147; on Holy Ghost being feminine, 299fn.; distorts teachings of Cerinthus, II, 176; mentions no descent into Hell, 514; on Apostolic succession, 326; on Christ preaching for ten years, 305; on Colarbasus, 248fn.; on Ebionites using Gospel acc. to Hebrews, 182fn.; on flesh, soul & spirit, 285; on followers of Basilides, 128; on Gnostics, 325; on Gnostic King Messiah, 223; on Holy Spirit as Life, 193; on Marcion, 168fn.; on Ophites, 172; on Papias, 327; on *Pastor of Hermas,* 243fn.; on Propatôr, 210; on reason for four Gospels, 231; on Simon Magus, 230; on teachings of Basilides, 156-57.
— *Fragments,* on Jesus & the Cherubim, II, 232, 451.
Iron: bronze & steel among ancients, I, 338-39, 589; grooves coated with, in Egypt, 528; in Egypt, 542; in the sun, 513; meteoric in Egypt & India, 538; rust of, and impotency, 532.
Irrigation, Egyptian, I, 517.
*Isaiah:* II, 166, 166fn., 440, 651; on "man of sorrow," I, 574; on manticism, 358; false rf. to, in *Homilies* & Sinaitic *Codex,* II, 192; on Adoni-Iahoh, 131; on dragon of sea, 447; on Lord God as "son of ancient Kings," 400; on Lord of Hosts, 513fn.; on Valley of Hinnom, 507; on well, 550fn.; passage in *Malachi* attributed to, 248, 651; on Virgin & lamb, 556.
Isernia, and phallic ex-votos, II, 5.
Ish Amon, the pleroma, II, 225, 227, 228.
Ishmonia, subterraneous galleries near, filled with MSS., II, 29, 642.
Ishtar: and Chaldean deluge, II, 422, 423fn., 424; or Mylitta, 171; and Virgin Mary, 109fn.

Isiaci, I, 536.
Isidorus of Gaza (6th c. A.D.), I, 436.
Isidorus of Pelusium (4th & 5th c. A.D.), *Epistles*, II, 646.
Isis: as healer, I, 532; lifting the veil of, 408; veil of, hides truth, 16; who will lift veil of, 573; anthropomorphized by Cyril into Mary, II, 41; black image of, 490; Mary inherited emblems of, 95; and Osiris, 268fn.; titles of, 209; veiled in Mysteries, 10.
Isis-Latona, I, 156.
Iśitva, II, 593.
Islamism, spread of, due to fights among Christians, II, 53-54.
Island(s): beauteous, in inland sea, I, 589-90; Jacolliot on, in Pacific, 594-95fn.
Israel: and Hyksôs, I, 569; and Nagkon-Wat, 565ff.; and Saturn, 578; II, 236, 513fn.; and Toltecs, I, 552; tribes of, mythical, 568; II, 429fn.; as primeval Saturn, II, 524; checkered history of, 440-41; derivation of name, 402; Lord God of, was Moloch, 525; prophets dominated, 439; Satan & numbering of, 481fn.
Israelites: intermarried perpetually, I, 568; polytheists, 491fn.; Bunsen on date when, left Egypt, II, 558; cubical stone of, 201-02; had initiated adepts, 135; Hyksôs as ancestors of, 487; not mentioned by Herodotus, 429fn.; origin of, 439fn.; robbed of their sacred books, 186fn.; we are inheritors of, 526; worship Bacchus as Jehovah, 128, 523; and worship of Saturn, 236.
Istar, and astral, I, xxv.
Iśvara, II, 591fn.
Iśvara-prasâda, as grace, II, 591fn.
Itard, J. E. M. G. (1775-1838), and mesmerism, I, 174.
Iurbo-Adonai, II, 185 & fn., 190 & fn., 206fn.
Ivy, or Kissos and Dionysos, II, 561fn.
Ixtlilxóchitl, and *Popol-Vuh,* I, 548, 650.
*Izhe Cheruvim,* Greek Orthodox prayer of, I, 28.

# J

Jabal, I, 579.
Jabe, II, 301.
Jablonski, P. E. (1693-1757), *Pantheon eagyptiorum,* etc., on heliocentric system, I, 532.
Jachin, and Boaz, II, 232, 270fn.
Jackson, Dr. C. T. J. (1805-1850), and the *Letheon,* I, 540.
Jacob, Zouave mesmeric healer, I, 165, 217.
Jacob: as earth, II, 402; and Esau, male & female principles, 401; boxing with the Creator, 429; family of, increases like herrings, 558; pillar of, a liṅga, 445; and Uriel, 452.
Jacobi, M. H. de (1801-74), I, 188.
Jacobins, II, 394.
Jacobus de Voragine (1230?-1298), *The Golden Legend:* II, 73, 74ff., 77, 509, 537, 645; plagiarizes from Buddhism, 579.
Jacolliot, L. (1837-90): I, 222; as a writer, II, 584fn.
—— *Christna et le Christ:* on knowledge of ancients, I, 618-20; on *Manu,* 586; on *Kris,* II, 324; on souls in svarga, 107; on spelling of Christna, 158fn.; and story of Kâlavatî, 241-42; Textor de Ravisi on, 47.
—— *Histoire des Vierges,* on tradition of submerged continents, I, 595-96fn.
—— *La Bible dans l'Inde:* on errors of Orientalists, I, 583; on greatness of ancient India, 584; on India & Egypt, 589fn.; on Krishṇa, 579fn.; on *Manu,* 585-86; on Good & Evil, 510; on Oriental Scriptures & Bible, 556; q. de Carrière on Bible, 425fn.
—— *La Genèse de l'Humanité:* I, 590fn.; on antiquity of *Vedas* & *Manu,* II, 257-58; on deluge & Indian books, 427-28; on man being immortal, 262; on Nirvâṇa, 533; on Turanian fallacy, 48fn.; on Vyâsa's & Kapila's views of evolution, 261; q. Vyâsa on religious dogmas, 242.
—— *Le Spiritisme dans le monde:* on fakir & seed, I, 139; on being refused the mysteries, II, 262; on Brahmans & occult powers, 103, 106-07; on Brahmâtma & his keys, 31; on fakirs, 104-05; on Kabalah, 38; on mystery-language, 46 & fn.; on pre-Vedic religion, 39; on vulgar magic in India, 70.
—— *Les Fils de Dieu:* on Manu-Vina, India & Egypt, I, 627; on farce of monks, II, 585; on mysteries, 262; on night of Brahmâ & pralaya, 273-74; on occult sciences in India, 584-85; on Virgin Avany, 322 & fn.
—— *Les Traditions,* etc.: attacks Müller,

II, 261; on numbers in *Vedas*, 411-12; q. stanzas to Viśvadevas, 412.
— *Voyage au pays des éléphants*, on Talapoins' chastity, II, 321.
— *Voyage au pays des perles*, etc.: on knowledge of ancients, I, 621; on magic of fakirs, 616-17.
Jacquemont, on Sanskrit, I, 582.
Jâdûgar: powers of, II, 69-70; or sâhir, magician, 612.
Jafnar, I, 122.
Jagannâtha: II, 297, 301; car of, and Virgin Mary, 111.
Jahângîr (1569-1627), and magical performances, I, 457-58.
— *Tûzuk-i-Jahângîrî*, on magical feats, I, 474.
Jah-buh-lun, II, 348, 351.
Jahi, demon of lust, II, 488.
Jahve, II, 398.
Jaimini, I, xi.
— *Pûrva-Mîmânsâ-Sûtra*, I, 621; II, 591fn., 657.
Jainas: II, 399fn., 609; and idea of soul, I, 429; books of, on Buddha, II, 318; claim Buddhism as offshoot from themselves, 322-23; humane feelings of, 279.
Jairus: I, 478, 481; resurrection of daughter of, copied from Orient, II, 241.
James: a Pharisee, I, xxx; *Talmud* on, II, 148.
*James:* II, 123; contradicts *Hebrews*, 84; on Jesus, 198fn., 202-03; on Paul & James, 162fn.; on psychical soul, 282.
Janet, Paul (1823-99), I, 80.
Jannaeus (or Alexander Jannaeus, r. 104-78 B.C.), King, & Jesus, II, 201, 386fn.
Jannes, School of, II, 361.
Jansenists, I, 217, 369, 372-76, 378.
Janus: and bread and wine, II, 44; copied in St. Peter, 448-49; keys of, 30.
Japanese: patriarchs of, II, 79; probity of, 573.
Jaquenet, Abbé, on Jewish tribes, I, 566.
Jared, I, 25.
Jastrow, Morris (1861-1921), *The Civiliz. of Babylonia*, etc., II, 423fn.
Jastrow, Marcus (1829-1903), *Dict. of the Targumim*, II, 655.
*Jâtakas*, meaning of stories in, I, 291-92.
Javanese, island-empire, I, 592.
Jebel-Judi, II, 423fn.
Jebusites, I, 568.
Jedker (*pr. sütger*), elemental daemon, II, 626.

Jehoram, I, 494.
Jehovah: castle of, on fire, I, 270; cruel god, 307; Moses & Sun, 13fn.; and Adonai, II, 224, 398; as active principle, 402; as Ialdabaôth, 292, 399, 526; as Ievo-hevah, 269, 398; as Saturn, 236, 294, 512; as work-master, 400; controversy on supremacy of, 188ff.; date of, 398; double-sexed formative power, 401; God is not, 167; ignored by Jesus, 163; Kabalistic nature of, 207; lamas of, 559; mask of Bacchus, 128, 165; not God preached by Jesus, 207; not sacred name, 398; one of the aeôns, 400; or Yava, 478; similar to Śiva, 524; twofold character of, 482; various readings of Hebrew script, 301-02. See Yahweh, Ievo.
Jehovah-jireh, II, 167, 301.
Jehovah-Nissi, II, 165, 526.
Jemshid, I, 576.
Jencken, H. D., and child-medium, I, 439.
Jenkins, Thomas ( ?-1798), II, 564.
Jennings, H. (1817?-1890), *The Rosicrucians:* I, [16], 423; on magic, 35-36; q. Fludd, 258, 511; on Ark & Masonry, II, 444; on Ezekiel's Wheel, 461; on phallic symbols in Christianity, 5; on symbols of Hindu gods, 301.
Jephthah, sacrifices daughter, II, 524.
*Jeremiah:* II, 128fn.; against sacrifices, 525; passage from *Zechariah* attributed to, 247.
Jeroboam, II, 439.
Jerome, St. (340?-420): and authentic *Matthew*, II, 134fn., 181-83; distorts *Job*, 496; and Gregory of Nazianzus, 183.
— *Comm. in Matthaeum*, II, 182.
— *De viris*, II, 181-82.
— *Dialogi contra Pelagianos*, II, 182fn.
— *Epistolae:* cruel precept in, II, 250; on worship of Adonis, 139.
— *Opera omnia:* on Asaph & Isaiah, II, 192; on genuine *Matthew*, 182, 647.
— *Vulgate.* See s.v.
Jerusalem, Temple of, II, 389.
Jervis, Sir J. (1766-1830), *Genesis Elucidated*, on Nabathaeans, II, 127.
Jesse, II, 441.
Jesuitism: banishment of, II, 358; and Masonry, 352, 381, 383, 384, 385, 394; principles & precepts of, 353ff., 371-73; terrible soul of, 352.
Jesuits: handle burning coals, I, 445; and miracles, 372-73; as political assassins, II, 372; attempt to defend sorcery, 634;

attempt to kill Queen Elizabeth, 373fn.; Cleremont Coll. of, & masonic rites, 390; cryptography of, & Masonry, 397; disguised as Talapoins, 371; most powerful at Bamberg & Würzburg, 61; on heliolatry, 450-51fn.; permeate Masonry, 385, 394; and political power in USA, 379; and Templars, 381, 383, 384.

Jesus: and Abgarus, II, 549-50; accused of magic, 148; adept, 150; age of, 135fn.; allegedly profanes mysteries, 202 & fn., 515; Amberley on, 562; Ammonius Saccas on, 249-50; as Chrêstos, 324fn.; as concocted myth, 544; and Ben Peraḥiah, 201; born of snake acc. to Ophites, 484; called "that man" in *Talmud,* 537fn.; claims of, to love & veneration, 337; compared to Kṛishṇa & Śâkyamuni, 536, 537-39; crucifixion of, and Hindus, 340; cry of, on the cross, 154; death of, helped to deify, 339; disfigured, 33-34; doctrine of, not original, 337; educated in Egypt & by Essenes, 548fn.; ethics of, Buddhistic, 337, 339; Father of, 190, 193; Gnostics saw in, Logos, 204; Herakles as model for, 515; high priest, not a God, 566; historical, and mythical Christ, 553; historical proofs of, lacking, 530; ignored by contemporary historians, 329, 335; ignores Jehovah, 163, 165; in *Homilies,* 191, 194-95; initiate, 94, 337; inspired prophet only, 198; killed by his Logos, 510; King on, as magician, 149; lapidated acc. to *Talmud,* 255fn.; and last days, 246; lower than angels, 37, 153fn.; made into a God, 480; man, not a God, 193, 239, 530; Marcion's view of, 162-63; and Mercury, 132; ministry of, twisted by Irenaeus, 305; mission of, & Gautama, 319; Nazar, 132-33, 134, 137, 144, 151, 206fn.; no master of social etiquette, 562; not strictly an Essene, 132, 133; no voluntary sacrifice of, 545; object of, 527; of "the seed of man," 181, 182; on John the Baptist, 203; on wine & bread, 561; origin of, acc. to *Toledoth,* 386fn.; Paul real apostle of, 241; permutation of Gautama, 286; reincarnationist, 145; rejected by men instructed in secret wisdom, 455; relatives of, Ebionites, 181; Renan distorts, 340-41fn., 562; resurrection of, 258; secret hope of, 561; secret doctrine of, 182, 186, 192, 307fn., 324; source of inspiration of, 195-96; story of, meeting woman at well borrowed from Buddhism, 550; teachings of, debased, iv, 303; temptation of, & Diabolos, 485; and transmigration, 152; uses Pythagorean & Essene language, 145, 147; virtues taught by, not practiced, 526; and Viṭhobâ, 557-58; why contempt for, 133; wonders at birth of, 552.

Jettatura, nature of, I, 144.

Jevons, Wm. S. (1835-1882), *The Principles of Science,* & unseen record on atoms, I, 185, 395.

Jewelry, in Egypt, I, 537.

Jews: adopt rites from Egypt, I, 536-37; and Hyksôs, 569; and Indian Kalanis, 567; intermarry & scatter, 568; origin of, 566-67; II, 438-39 & fn.; tribes of, mythical, I, 568; and Yadus, 567; Alexandrian, Kabalists, II, 135; borrowed from *Avesta* & India, 221, 428; called Abortive, 190, 204, 205fn.; carry off ornaments from Egypt, 33; Christian despoil, of their records, 424; faithful to their religion & united, 526; familiar with *tau,* 454-55; human sacrifices of, 524 & fn.; incredible increase of, in Egypt, 558; idolatrous & polytheistic, 269, 302; learned secret doctrine from Magi, 361; lost key to Sacred Books, 430; monotheism of, recent, 526; national history of, not earlier than Moses, 216; no belief in univ. spirit among, 535; orthodox, & Nazarenes, 131; probable age of, 524; and Satan, 186fn.; and seven-day week, 418; worshipping ass & Moloch, 523, 524. See also Israelites, Hebrews.

Jibal Nakía, "Hill of the Bell," I, 605.

Jibal-ul-Thabúl, "Hill of the Drums," I, 605.

Jiménez de Cisneros, Cardinal Francisco (1436?-1517), burns MSS. in Granada, I, 511.

Jinn: I, xxix; reading magic rolls, II, 29.

Jîvan (or Jîva), and Vaikârika, I, 429.

Jîvâtman, nature, interrelations and visions of, II, 590.

Joachim, Bishop Fray, burns books, II, 29fn.

Joannes Laurentius Lydus (490- ? A.D.), *De mensibus:* on Spirit & Triad, I, 336; II, 48, 405; on Iaô, 139fn., 297, 417.

*Job:* I, 74, 133, 225; allegory of initiation, II, 351, 364; on gates of death, 364; trials of, 485-86, 494ff.

Jobard, J. B. (1792-1861), on intelligent electricity, I, 188.
Jobert de Lamballe, A. J. (1799- ? ), I, 102, 104.
*Joel,* I, 494, 613; II, 440.
*Johannesbuch der Mandäer,* II, 651.
John, Disciples of St., *See* Nazarenes.
John, Knights of St., not Masons, II, 383.
John, Apostle, was a virgin, II, 329-30.
*John:* I, 125, 132, 493, 613; II, 133, 205, 234fn., 239, 282, 343, 551, 556; on being gods, I, 2; II, 318; on Jesus having a devil, I, 494; on true vine, 300fn.; forged sentence in, II, 125; Gospel of, written by Gnostic, 91fn.; interpolated verse in, 135; on archê, 37; on being born again, 565; on flesh & blood, 560; on God not seen by anyone, 211; on Jesus & his Father, 193; on killing, 1; on life & light of men, 230; on only-begotten Son, 230; on scene of Cana, 386fn.; on true vine, 244, 561.
*1 John:* on trying spirits, I, 491; forged verse in, II, 178; on devil, 480; on three heavenly witnesses, spurious, 177-78; on two trinities, 334.
*II John,* on antichrist, II, 334.
John Hyrcanus ( ? -105 B.C.), II, 135.
John of Damascus, St. (8th c. A.D.), and Josaphat, II, 580.
John (of Patmos), a Kabalist, II, 147.
John the Baptist (Yôḥânân): anointed, II, 204; doubts of, 519; Ferho was god of, 290; and Ialdabaôth, 185-86; James & Jesus on, 202-03; and Jesus, 135ff., 382fn.; Nazarene himself, 132, 181; and story of Ananda, 555.
Johnston, Vera Vlad. (1864-1923), I, [22fn.].
Jonah: II, 525; and the whale, 258-59.
Jones, Sir Wm. (1746-94), *Dissertations,* on lotus, I, 92.
—— *Institutes:* I, 18, 271-72fn., 585, 586, 587, 588; II, 107, 111 & fn.; on age of *Yajur-Veda,* II, 433.
—— *Works:* I, 92, 585, 586; on Purusha and Nârâyana, II, 214, 267; on what is a Purâna, 492. See also *Mânava-dharma-śâstra* and Loiseleur-Deslongchamps.
Jordan: as Zacchar, II, 550fn.; spiritual, 181, 228, 295.
Jordanus, Dom. friar (*fl.* 1321-30), on virtues of Hindus, II, 474fn.

Jormungand (Old Norse: *jörmungandr*), as Earth-Serpent, I, 151.
Jortin, Jean (1698-1770), II, 78.
Josaphat, St.: I, 98; and Gautama Buddha, II, 579-81.
Joseph: I, 568; became Egyptian, 556; Justinus on, 25; studied in Egypt, 25, 536.
Josephus, F. (37-98? A.D.), on study of virtue, I, 293.
—— *Antiquities:* on exorcism, I, 218; on Moses and allegories, 436; on Solomon, 135; on destruction of Mosaic books, II, 470; on herbal cure, 350fn.; on Nazarenes, 139, 140; on Seth, 466; on transmigration, 152; spurious passages on Jesus, 196, 328, 335, 652.
—— *Contra Apionem:* on the one God, I, 287-88; on Hyksôs, 487fn.; on Jewish human sacrifices, 524fn.
—— *Jewish War:* on lightning rods, I, 528; on thummim, 536; on beliefs & customs of Essenes, II, 133fn., 147, 196, 280.
Joshua: I, 284, 531; II, 244; initiated by Moses, II, 43; and Kanaan, 558.
*Joshua:* I, 149fn.; II, 26; mentions *Book of Jasher,* II, 400; on Valley of Hinnom, 507.
Joshua (Jesus) Navin, II, 244fn., 256-57, 579; as a brigand, I, 545, 551.
Jost, I. M. (1793-1860), *The Israelite Indeed:* II, 203, 469fn.; on books of Moses, 470; on Essenes and Jesus, 37fn.; on Nazarenes, 151; on "wise man," 328fn.
*Journal de médecine,* etc. (Aucante), I, 384.
*Journal des Débats:* I, 99; Foucault on levitation & Faraday, 62-64; Laboulaye on Buddha, II, 286, 343; and Moslems, 82.
*Journal du magnétisme,* on mensabulism, I, 322ff.
*Journal für Freimaurer* (Woog), II, 394.
*Journal of Sacred Literature, The* (H. Burgess), on Bible, I, 605fn.
*Journal of the Amer. Geogr. Soc. of New York* (G. C. Harlbut), on name of America, I, 653.
*Journal of the Royal Asiatic Society of Great Britain and Ireland:* (H. C. Rawlinson), I, 261; II, 465; (E. C. Ravenshaw), on Śri-Yantra, II, 265.
Jowett, B. (1817-93), *The Dialogues of Plato:* imputes lie to Plato, I, 413;

misconstrues Plato, 288; on attraction, 271fn.; on earth's revolution, 256fn.; on knowledge of ancients, 238; on original qualities, 242; on Plato, 236; on scientific points in, 261.

Joy, Algernon, I, 73.

Juarros, D. (1752-1820?), *Compendio*, etc., on origin of Toltecs, I, 552.

Jubal, I, 579.

Judaea, Judaei: history of, a distortion of Indian fable, II, 471; Persian colonies in, 441.

Judaism, erected on identical cosmical myths with other religions, II, 405.

*Jude:* abusive, II, 205; on Dignities, 207; on rebuking the Devil, 482.

Judge, John H., and *Isis Unv.*, I, [10].

Judge, W. Q. (1851-96), on New York Bldg. where *Isis Unv.* was written, I, [7], [9].

*Judges:* legendary book, I, 568; on Teraphim, 570; on circle-dance, II, 45; on Dan & Laish, 167; on Deborah, 525; on Jehovah's name, 165fn.; on Jephthah's daughter, 524; on Samson, 151.

Judson, A. (1788-1850), *Journal*, on Buddhism, II, 553-54 & fn.

Judson, Ann H. (1789-1826), *An Account*, etc., II, 553-54 & fn.

Judgment: H.P.B. fights for right of private, II, 120; of the dead, 364.

Judia, name for Siam, II, 441.

Juggernaut. See Jagannâtha.

Jugglers, Indian, and their feats, I, 73-74.

Jukes, II, 545.

Julian, Emperor (331-363 A.D.): on skeptics, I, 247; initiated, II, 351, 566.

— *Oratio IV in Solem:* I, 130; on Iaô, II, 139fn.

— *Oratio V in Matrem Deorum*, on seven-rayed god, II, 417.

Julien, S. (1797-1873), I, 438.

— *Histoire*, etc., on magic, I, 599.

— *Si-yu-ki*, on Buddha's shadow, I, 600-01.

Julius Africanus (beg. 3rd c. A.D.), I, 406fn.

Juno: I, 264, 266; animated statue of, 614; temple of, and lightning, 527.

Jupiter: as Bel, I, 261; as Peter, 98; in Orphism, 262; knowledge of ancients on, 267-68; symbolized by bull, 262; as serpent & Semelê, II, 505; Capitolinus & bells, 592; and Juno & their derivation, 298; —Pluto as Christ, 335; red as color of, 465. *See also* Zeus.

Jupiter Elicius, I, 527.

Jussieu, Antoine Laurent de (1748-1836), and mesmerism, I, 172.

Justice: and harmony, I, 330-31; advocate, II, 530; atonement a travesty of, 542ff.; taught by ancients, 541.

Justin Martyr (100?-165), unaware of St. Peter, II, 24fn.

— *1st Apology:* on Logos, II, 195, 247; on Socrates, 8; perverts Plato, 469.

— *2nd Apology*, on feminine Holy Ghost, I, 299fn.

— *Cohortatio:* on seven spirits, II, 187fn.; q. Orphic Hymn, 123.

— *Dialogue with Trypho:* on angels & powers, II, 195; on Jesus accused of magic, 148; on Sabbath, 419; on Wisdom & Son, 216.

— *Quaestiones*, etc., on talismans of Apollonius, II, 97.

Justinian I (Flavius Anicius Iustinianus, 483-565): I, 584; a vandal, 436. See *Codex Justinianus.*

Justinus, Marcus Junianius (ca. 3rd c. A.D.), *Historiarum Philippicarum libri XLIV*, on Joseph, I, 25.

Jyotishṭoma, I, xxvii.

# K

K——, his experiences in Tibet, II, 599-602.

Kabala, Kabalah, Kabbalah: I, 25, 26; antiquity of, 1 & fn.; def. *xxxiv;* geometrical figure of, 14; "Living Fire" of, 301; on daemons, 356; on man's spirit & soul, 315; Oriental or Universal, 17; and *shedim*, 313; solves esotericism of religion, 271; agrees with Greek esotericism, II, 144; Ain-Soph & Sephîrôth in, 212-14; at Alexandria, 38; cosmogony of, 266-71; early Christian schools of, 198; expressions from, in Gospels, 205; gematria & temurah in, 298; interprets Bible, 415, 424-25; and Jesus' teachings, 196; joint property of all adepts, 350; numerical systems of, 298-99; on Gilgûlah, 152; on heavenly Adam, 224; on three Heads, 222; Oriental, & Bible, 210; Oriental, & Gnostics, 205, 211; Oriental, & Neo-Platonism, 34, 41; ritual of, 85-87; scoffed at, 402; and *Zohar*, 348-49.

Kabalists: axioms of, I, xxxvii, 301fn., 388; II, 510; brotherhood of, II, 470; deadliest enemies of clergy, 500; glorious thinkers, 389; persecuted by Church, 303; and sacred name, 399.
Kabiri, Kabeiri, Cabiri (Gr.: Κάβειροι; Phoen.: *Qabirim*): I, xxxix, 23; at Angkor Vat, 565, 569; derivation of term, 569; teraphim, 570; as Arba, II, 270; four, 171; number hardly known, 478.
Kaḍal-Kaṭṭi, shark-charmers, I, 606.
Kadesh, Kadeshim: I, 555fn.; II, 131, 395; identical with nautch-girls, II, 45.
Kadmos, I, xxxiii, 254; II, 504.
Kain. See Cain.
Kaiser, I, 313.
Kakodaimôn (κακοδαίμων), I, 133.
Kalani, and Jews, I, 567.
Kalâs, and muhurtas, II, 464fn.
Kalâśas, invocation, II, 108.
Kalâvatî, story of, II, 241-42.
Kaldany, are Manichaeans & Yezîdis, II, 629-30.
Kâlî, emblem of "fall of man," II, 275.
Kâlidâsa, *Meghadûta*, I, 620.
—— *Abhijñâna-śakuntala*, I, 620.
Kâlîya-nâga, II, 447.
Kali-yuga: I, 32, 587, 588; II, 275; and Buddhas, II, 156fn.; and Noah, 443; and Vishṇu, 237.
Kalki, avatâra, II, 237, 274, 275.
Kalmucks: I, 248; II, 575; on higher races, I, 2; H.P.B. among, II, 600fn.; idols of, made of ashes, 603fn.
Kalpas: I, 347; II, 219, 272; and yugas, I, 32, 634.
Kamchadal, I, 248.
Kaṅgâlin: powers of, II, 69-70; witch, 612, 645.
Kânheri, Caves, II, 581.
*Kanjur* (Tib.: *b*Kaḥ-ḥgyur), II, 518fn., 550fn., 555fn.; 617 & fn.
Kanne, J. A. (1773-1824), *Pantheon*, etc., I, 152.
Kaṇsa: King, I, 444; and Herod, II, 199, 537; tyrant of Mathurâ, 537.
*Kansas City Times, The,* on giant bones, I, 304-05.
Kant, I. (1724-1804), I, 58, 621; II, 158.
Kanyâbhâva, II, 209.
Kanyâs, bad virgins, I, 447.
Kapi, monkey, I, 136fn.
Kapila: I, xi, 121, 307; II, 536, 565; and Buddha, I, 580fn.; and Positivism, 98; and Vyâsa, 626; not atheist, II, 531; on evolution, 261; on mâyâ, 158.
—— *Sânkhya-Sûtra,* II, 318, 345; on the eight faculties of the soul, 592-93.
—— *Mukta* and *Baddha,* I, 580.
Kapûrdigiri, II, 32.
Karabtanos: I, 300, 301; II, 175, 187fn.; as matter, I, 582.
Kardecists, I, 197, 345.
Karma (Karman): I, *346;* II, 287; as law of compensation, II, 545, 593; and self-procreations, 320.
Karnak: I, 523-24, 572; and Carnac, 554.
Karth, or Tyre, I, 567.
Kasdean, alleged language, II, 46. See Chaldeans.
Kasdim. See Chaldeans.
Kashmîr; II, 603; girls in, detect 300 color hues, I, 211; magicians of, 505; Nâga worship in, II, 509fn., 608.
Katchi [K'a-chê — Moslems in Lhasa], II, 609.
*Kâthakopanishad,* on Purusha, I, 56.
Katharsis (κάθαρσις), purification, II, 100.
*Kaushîtaki-Brâhmaṇa,* II, 409.
Kazbek, Mt., I, 298.
Kean, Chas (1811-68), I, 485.
Kebar-Ziwa: as third life, I, 300; and seven vines, II, 244.
Kedje, II, 308fn.
Kême (κημε), Sahidic term, I, 226fn.
Kemet (or Kem), name for Egypt, I, xxv, 648.
Kemshead, W. B., *Inorganic Chemistry,* on Paracelsus, I, 52fn.
Kenites, I, xxx.
Kennedy, Maj.-Gen. Vans (1784-1846), *Researches into ... Mythology* (implied), on Babylonia & Brahmans, II, 46fn., 428, 643.
—— *Researches into ... Languages,* as above.
Kennicott, Dr. B. (1718-83), and Bruns, II, 430fn.
Kenrick, J. (1788-1877), *Ancient Egypt,* etc., II, 404; on *chemi,* I, 541; on indestructible cement, 518; on skill of Egyptians, 530; q. Granville on mummies, 539.
Kêphas (Κηφᾶς), or Petros, II, 91.
Kepler, J. (1571-1630): I, xxxiii, 623; believed in planetary intelligences, 208, 253fn.; and exploding stars, 254; on geometrical solids, 208fn.

*Keren happuch,* in *Job,* II, 496.
Kerner, Dr. J. A. C. (1786-1862): I, 68, 71; on astrographs, 398.
— *Die Seherin von Prevorst,* I, 463.
Kêrux (κῆρυξ), crier, II, 101.
Ketch, Jack, II, 58, 59.
Kether, crown, II, 213, 266, 267, 268.
Kêtos (Κῆτος), is Dagon, II, 258.
Ketu, II, 509fn., 655.
Key(s): to Buddhism, I, 289; to symbolism, 573; of Brahmâtma, II, 31; of Peter, 30; *one* turn of the, given in *Isis,* 461; to Ezekiel's Wheel, 461-62; to mysteries lost by Church, 120-21; to philosophies in Hindu works, 227.
Keynes, G. (1630-1659), *Roman Martyrology,* etc., on Barlaam & Josaphat, II, 580.
Keystone: absence of, I, 571; and Masonry, 571-72.
Khaldi. See Chaldeans.
Khalwehs, of Druzes, II, 309.
Kham, Assyrian god, II, 487.
Khamism, language of Egypt, II, 435.
Khansa, and juggling trick, I, 473.
Khe-lans, Brotherhood of, II, 618.
Khîyûn (or Chiun), as Saturn, II, 234, 236, 296, 524.
Khnemu. See Chnuphis.
*Khordah-Avesta.* See *Avesta.*
Khoshuts, and Kalmucks, II, 600fn.
Khotan, wise men of, II, 361.
Khunrath, H. (ca. 1560- ? ): I, xxv, 415.
— *Amphitheatrum,* plates of elementaries in, I, 319, 643.
Kibitka, Kalmuck tent, II, 600fn.
Kidder, Bishop Richard (1633-1703), on Christianity, II, 240.
Kieser, D. G. (1779-1862), *Archiv,* etc., I, 265.
Killing: Alagona on, II, 355; Fagundez on, parents, 348, 363.
Kîlnâ, serpent-mantra, II, 622 & fn.
Kîmiyâ, phenomenon, II, 612.
King, C. W. (1818-88), *The Gnostics and their Remains:* I, [16], 630; on a common religion, II, 198fn.; on Alex. Severus & image of Christ, 510; on Buddhism as origin of later sects, 143; on Cherubim, 232; on Christos, Ialdabaôth & Sophia, 186; on Clement's view of Basilides, 188; on Collyridians & Mary, 110; on doctrine of Sufis, 306; on Druzes, 289; on Essenes, 139fn.; on genii of seven spheres, 184; on Iaô & engraved stones, 233fn., 351; on Isis & Mary, 95; on Jesus as magician, 149; on Lentulus, 151; on Marcosians, 514fn.; on M. Felix's accusations of Christians, 333; on Ophiomorphos, 184; on Ophis amulet, 295fn.; on Ophite cosmogony, 187-88; on phallicism, 5; on picture of Anubis, 149-50; on Pythagorean numerals, 300; on Serapis & Christians, 336; on shady character of Epiphanius, 249; on Solomon's seal, 255fn.; on symbol of fishes, 266fn.; on Tau, 254; on Templars, 331; on value of letters, 233fn.; q. Matter on Ephesus, 155.
King, E. (1795-1837), *The Antiquities of Mexico:* on Aztec & Hebrew languages, I, 553; on Mexican trinity, II, 50-51.
King, John, I, 73, 75, 492; II, 83fn.
King, Katie: I, 43 *et seq.,* 48, 54; II, 83fn.; soulless, I, 67.
King, P. (1669-1734), *Hist. of the Apostles' Creed,* etc., on St. Thomas & *Credo,* II, 514.
King-initiates, and Herodotus, I, 5, 519.
Kingdoms: subordinate, and human monad, I, 357; four, 329-30.
*I Kings:* I, xxx, 136fn., 217; II, 44, 45, 485; on nephesh, II, 362fn.; on seven, II, 447; on "small voice," 344; on Solomon's Temple, 391.
*II Kings:* I, xxx, 568, 593; II, 140, 440; on Brazen Serpent, II, 481; on Hezekiah, 166fn.; on Hilkiah, 421fn.; on Huldah, 525; on Kadeshim, 45, 395fn.
Kingsley, Chas. (1819-1875), *Hypatia,* II, 53.
Kircher, A. (1602-1680): I, 476; on magnetism & nature's sympathies, 209-10; on origin of Ophites, 551.
— *Magnes,* etc.: I, 208fn.; on healing power of music, 215.
— *Oedipus Aegyptiacus;* on perpetual lamps, I, 227; II, 630; q. Avenare on Virgin, II, 167, 491.
— *Sphinx Mystagoga,* II, 41.
Kirchhofer, II, 189fn.
Kirchhoff, G. R. (1824-87), and Roscoe, I, 513.
Kirjath-Arba, II, 171.
Kirub, bull with human face, II, 231.
Kislingbury, Miss Emily, and *Isis Unv.,* I, [20].
Kiss, holy, II, 331.

Kistophoros (κιστοφόρος), degree of neophyte, II, 365.
Kitto, J. (1804-54), *Cyclop. of Biblical Liter.*, II, 649.
Kleucker, J. F. (1749-1827), *Anhang z. Zend-Avesta*, on Sim & Shem, II, 217.
—— *Natur der Emanationslehre:* on Gnostic expressions in Gospels, II, 205; on the First-born, 195, 223.
—— *Zend-Avesta*, on Saoshyant, II, 237-38.
Klikushy, Russian mediums, I, 28.
Klippoth: dwellers of Asiah, I, 141; mischievous beings, II, 210.
Kneph: and egg, I, 256fn.; incubates water, 133; unrevealed deity, 133, 147, 157. *See also* Chnuphis.
Knight, C. (1791-1873), *Old England*, etc., on bishop's *pallium*, II, 94.
Knight, R. P. (1750-1824), *On the Worship of Priapus:* on Augustine & "holy kiss," II, 331; on festivals of Pan, 51; on Gnostics accused by Epiphanius, 331.
—— *Symbolical Language:* on age of Menes, II, 520fn.; on Ceres as passive productive principle, 560fn.; on Serapis & Christ, 336fn.; on wine, 514fn.; Wilder in, on paganism, 179fn.
Knights: cipher of Kadosh & Rose Croix, II, 395-96; of Malta, 383.
Knights-Templars: I, 30; II, 333, 394; and Baphomet, I, 138; II, 302, 331; become branch of Jesuits, II, 383, 384, 385, 390; and blood of Christ, 71; last real, poisoned, 385; and Masonry, 371, 372; and Nazarenes, 382 & fn., 386; origin, object & beliefs of, 381-83, 386; seven-degree-rite of, 377; secret body, 380; and "Word," 349.
Knights of St. John, II, 384.
Knorr von Rosenroth, Chr. (1636-1689), *Kabbala denudata:* II, 33fn.; on Adam-Kadmon, II, 342; on anima mundi, 227; on Kabalistic trinity, 226; on Microprosopus, 210; on Musah as *revolutio*, 195, 447; on Noah as *revolutio* of Adam, 447; on Shekhînah's garment, 245; on the Ancient and three Heads, 222; on transmigration, 152; on Unknown Essence, 212; on virgin earth & living water, 550-51fn.
See also: *Idrah Rabbah, Idrah Zutah, Siphra Dtzeniuthah.*
Knowledge: I, 534; def., 236; of facts, 578; of good & evil, 2; Nârada on ignorance and, 628; real, xi; supplants faith, vi; world-tree of, 574; II, 412; arcane, when sorcery or wisdom, II, 588; based on faith, 369; and ignorance, 41. *See also* Ancient.
Koheleth. *See Ecclesiastes.*
Koinobion (κοινόβιον), living in a community, I, xxx.
Koinobioi (κοινόβιοι), confused with Therapeutae, II, 305, 336.
Kokonor, II, 600fn.
Kol-Arbas. *See* Colarbasus.
Koldun (Russian), sorcerer, II, 43fn.
Koliadovki, Koliadovat', as religious shows & divination, II, 119-20, 646.
Kolob, of the Mormons, II, 2.
Koph, monkey, I, 136fn.
Köppen, K. F. (1808-1863), *Crata Repoa*, etc., on Egyptian initiation, II, 364-65.
Kora, II, 42fn.
*Koran* (Ar. *al-Qur'ân*), II, 317.
Korê (Κόρη): brazen bowls of, II, 592; Indian origin of, 505fn.; and Zagreus, 505; and Zeus, 527.
Korndorf, B., recipe of, for perpetual lamp, I, 229fn.
Koros (Kurios), I, 131.
Kosmos (κόσμος): as God, I, 154; of Plato, 56; and Chronos, II, 423.
Kotzebue, A. F. F. von (1761-1819), *The Stranger*, I, 205.
Krapf, Dr. J. L. (1810-81), I, 412.
Kris, II, 158, 324, 647.
Krische, A. B. (1809-1848), *Forschungen*, etc., on Xenocrates, I, xix.
Krishna: and *Genesis*, I, 579fn.; as avatâra, II, 274, 276; aureole of, 95; and Christna, 158 & fn.; compared to Jesus & Sâkyamuni, 536; crushing serpent, 446, 537; death of, 545-46; Kansa & Herod, 199; legends about, compared with those of Gautama & Jesus, 537-39; Lundy on, 546; raises daughter of Angashuna, 241; same as Christos, 173; united to his Chrêstos, 558; and Viṭhobâ crucified, 557-58.
Krishna Dwaipâya Vyâsa. *See* Vyâsa.
Krita-yuga, I, 587, 588.
Kritya, magical performance, I, xxvii.
Kronos (Cronus), or Saturn, I, 263, 266; II, 235.
Kruptê (κρύπτη), cave, crypt as abode of initiate, II, 93.
Kshatriya(s), I, 148, 435.
Kshatriyânî, I, 148.

Kublai-Khân (1216?-1294): I, 603; II, 616; and Christian missionaries, II, 581-83; and Tissu, 608.
Kudian, magician, II, 631.
Kuen-lun-shan, pilgrimage to, II, 294.
K[uhlwein], Mr., witnesses phenomenon of the incarnation of an adept, II, 599ff.
Kuklos (κύκλος), cycle, II, 293.
Kuklos anankês (κύκλος ἀνάγκης), circle of necessity, I, 553.
Kukushan, medicinal plant, II, 621, 661.
Kula, I, 567.
Kullûka-Bhaṭṭa: I, 586; II, 434.
—— *Hist. of India*, on emigration of Manu-Vena to Egypt, I, 627.
Kumbum (Tib.: sKu-ḥbum), Huc witnesses lama's withdrawal at, II, 604-05.
Kumbum Tree: I, 289, 301; II, 316fn.; character on, I, 440; II, 46; and Tsong-Kha-pa, II, 609.
Kumil-Mâdan, undine, I, 496.
Kurdistan, tribes of, their magian rites, II, 629.
Kurds: magical performance among, II, 630-32; and Yezîdis, 571.
Kurios (κύριος): master, II, 193; and Kora, 42fn.
Kurma-avatâra, II, 300-01.
Kutchi, of Lhasa rescues H.P.B., II, 628.
Kutsa, Ṛishi, I, 11.
Kutti-Shâttan: an imp, I, 495, 567; commanded by juggler, 446.

# L

Labarum, and miracles, II, 304.
Laboulaye, René Lefevre de (1811-83), II, 286, 343, 580.
Labyrinth: and Herodotus, I, 522-23; and King-Initiates, 5.
Lacroix, C. (1652-1714), *Theologia moralis*, etc. on palmistry, II, 354.
Lactantius (ca. 260-ca. 340), *Divine Institutes*: I, 9, 293; on flat earth, 526; on magicians, 167; on earth's sphericity, II, 477.
Lacustrians, I, 545.
Ladâkh, II, 598, 658.
Laestrigonians, I, 549.
Laghiman, II, 593.
La'hash, secret speech, II, 266.
Laing, A. G. (1793-1826), *Travels*, etc., on firing at a conjurer, I, 378.

Lake(s): on sacred precincts, I, 572; of Bacchus, II, 138; of fire & brimstone, 12; purification in, 238.
Lakshmî: II, 209; role of, 173; and Vishṇu, 259.
*Lalitavistara.* See *Rgya tch'er rol pa.*
Lamaism: badge of sovereignty in, II, 505fn.; merely external rites, 608; preserved primitive magic, 616; similar to Catholicism, 345-46fn., 582.
Lama(s) [Tib.: bla-ma]: I, xxxiv, 631; use âkâśa, 113; wonders of, 222, 225; interview with 18-months-old, II, 598. See also Taley-Lama.
"Lamasery," in New York, described, I, [7ff.].
Lambert, Franz, *Weisheit der Aegypter*, II, 653.
Lamech; key to riddle of wives of, I, 579; distorted copy of Manu, II, 468; and Enoch, 457; and Noah, 466; murderer, 447-48.
Lamprias: I, xxxviii; on prophetic powers of the soul, II, 594.
Lampridius, Aelius, on image of Christ, II, 150, 647.
Lamps: old-fashioned in Kurdish rites, II, 630.
Lamps, ever-burning: attributed to devil, I, 227-28; authorities vouching for, 226-32; exist now, 511; ideas of alchemists on, 228-30, 231-32; in tomb of Tulia, 224, 228; in Trevandrum, 225; and B. Stewart, 510.
Lampseans, II, 307fn.
Lanci, M. A. *Paralipomeni*, II, 302fn.
—— *La Sacra Scrittura*, etc., on Azâzêl, II, 303.
Lane, E. W. (1801-76), I, 225.
—— *Arabian Nights*, I, 549.
Lange, *Commentary*, etc., II, 476fn.
Laṅghana-śâstra, secret sect, II, 315-16.
Language, of Babylon, II, 472.
Lankâ: and Râma, II, 278fn; and Sommona-Codom, 576.
*Lankâvatâra Sûtra*, on Nirvâṇa, I, 431.
Lankester, I, 612.
Lankester-Donkin-Slade, persecution of, I, 86, 118, 218.
Lao-tse, I, 600; II, 159.
*Lapis asbestinus.* See Asbestos.
*Lapis Carystius*, I, 231.
Laplace, P. S. de (1749-1827), *Essai philo-*

*sophique,* etc., on animal magnetism, I, 173.
Laplanders, I, 247.
Lara, D. E. de [venerable scholar present at formation of T.S.], I, 502.
Lardner, Dr. N. (1684-1768), *Credibility of Gospel History:* II, 304; on Josephus' spurious passage, 328fn.; on Peter, 125.
Lares, I, 345.
Larmenius, Charter of, II, 384, 385.
Larvae: I, 310, 345, 352; and reincarnation, 357; and resuscitation of dead, 364-65.
Latin Church. See Roman Catholic Church.
Latins, I, 158; II, 473.
Laurence, R. See *Book of Enoch.*
La Valette, Father Antoine de (1708-1767), II, 354.
Lavoisier, A. L. (1743-94), I, 171, 505.
Law(s): balance of forces, I, 341; of harmony are immutable, 146; of history, 521, 525; of nature are eternal, v; of nature as relations of ideas to forms, 55; world sustained by, 318; Immutable, or Anima Mundi, II, 402; of compensation, 545; principles of natural, 587-90.
Lawes, Major, I, 477.
*Laws of Manu.* See *Manu, Laws of.*
Lawson, D., *Christ's Fidelity,* etc., I, 361.
Layard, A. H. (1817-94), slabs excavated by, I, 154.
Lazarus, I, 478, 481; II, 149.
Lazius, W. (1514-1565), I, 226, 639.
Leaves, esoteric meaning of, II, 448.
Lechler, G. V. (1811-88), II, 189fn.
Lecky, W. E. H. (1838-1903), *Hist. of European Morals,* etc., on incredulity of educated men, I, 409.
Le Clerc, J. (1657-1736), on Olam, II, 12.
Le Conte, J. (1823-1901), "Correlation of Vital, etc."; on force, I, 352; on four kingdoms, 329-30; on life-principle, 466-67; on limits of science, 408; on vital force, 313.
Le Fèvre, Dr., I, 503.
Legatus, II, 33, 154, 194.
Legends: identity of, I, 122; Müller on deeper meaning of exoteric, 442.
Leh, in Ladâkh, II, 598.
Lehdoio, and Pthahil, II, 227, 229, 295.
Leibnitz, G. W. (1646-1716), dynamism of, I, 423.
Lemoinne, John-M.-É. (1815-92), Editor of *Journal des Débats,* II, 82.

Lemprière, J. (1765?-1824), *Bibliotheca Classica:* on Aristotle's works, I, 320; on Porphyry, 416fn.; on Pythagoras, 347fn.; unfair about ancient philosophers, 431; on Aethiopians, I, 567, 651; II, 437fn.
Lemprière, Wm. ( ? -1834), *Voyage dans l'Empire de Maroc,* etc., I, 381.
Lemures, I, 345, 352.
Lemuria, I, 592, 654.
*Lenning's Encyclopädie der Freimaurerei,* Count Ramsey on Templars, II, 384.
Lenoir, "Du Dragon de Metz," on Michael, II, 488.
Lenormant, F. (1835-1883), *Première civilisations,* I, 298fn.
—— *Les Sciences occultes en Asie,* Assyrian tablet on seven, II, 408.
Lens, found at Nimrud, I, 240.
Lentulus, forged letter of, on Jesus, II, 151.
Leo, presided by Mahalalel, II, 466fn.
Leopard-skin, used in mysteries, I, 568-69.
*Lepra vestum,* lichen-infusoria, I, 415.
*Lepraria kermasina,* I, 415.
Lepsius, K. R. (1810-84), I, 6, 529.
—— *Denkmäler,* on Hermetic Books, II, 367fn.
—— *Königsbuch,* on Onnofre, II, 324.
Lermontoff, M. Y. (1814-1841), *The Demon,* II, 511fn.
Leroux, and mesmerism, I, 174.
Le Roy, Dr. A., and mesmerism, I, 171.
Les Eyzies, cave men of, I, 295.
Leslie, F. See *Popular Monthly.*
Lesseps, F. M. de (1805-94), I, 517.
Letters: invented in Egypt, I, 532; numerical value of, II, 233.
*Letters,* to H. P. Blavatsky. See O'Grady, Rawson, Sotheran and O'Sullivan.
Leucippus (*fl.* ca. 440 B.C.), I, 61.
Leudastus, Earl of Tour, II, 21.
Levi: caste, not tribe, I, 568; and Simeon, 556.
Lévi, Éliphas (1810-75): on sleep & soul, I, 179; on nature of blood and vital light, II, 567.
—— *Dogme et Rituel:* I, 113; II, 270fn.; on astral light, I, 137-38, 281; on influences of planets, 314; on pregnant women, 395; on Bodin & Inquisition, II, 55; on death, 343; on Ḥokhmah, 215fn.; on Kabalistic meaning of cross, 87; on Lucifer, 473; on Medici's sorcery, 56; on *Nychthêmeron,* 467, 468.
—— *La Science des esprits:* on Azoth, I,

462; on death & life, 480; on mensambulism, 322ff.; on nature's forward march, 481; on reanimation after death, 485; on vision after death, 484; on *Toledoth Yeshu,* 127fn.; q. *Toledoth* on Jesus, 201-02.

Leviathan, symbol of occult wisdom, II, 499.

Levitation: II, 194, 589; Babinet on, I, 202fn., 501; and Crookes, 202; magnetic causes of, 496ff.; of fakirs, 495; of mediums & saints, 491; of natives in Orient, 472; principle of, xxiii-xxiv; proclaimed impossible, 105; and psychic force, 196; Salverte on, of Iamblichus, 115; of King Pia Metak, II, 618.

Levites: I, 536, 555; or Ophites, II, 129, 481fn.

*Leviticus:* on witches, I, 356; on Aaron & goat, II, 513; on Azâzêl, 302; on Lord God & human sacrifice, 525; on Lord as mistranslated, 401; on nephesh, 244, 362fn.

Lewes, Geo. H. (1817-78), on phenomena, I, 232.

Lewis, Rev. E., *The Tinnevelly Shanars,* on propitiating human elementaries, I, 447.

Lewis, G. C. (1806-1863), *An Historical Survey of the Astronomy of the Ancients,* I, 525.

Leylande, antiquary, II, 389.

Leymarie: in prison, I, 494; sentenced, 166.

Lhasa, I, xxxiv; II, 616fn.

Libavius (Libau), A. (1560?-1616), I, 226, 503, 639.

—— *Alchymia,* I, 639.

—— *Works* (implied), on perpetual lamps, I, 229fn.

Liberalia, or St. Patrick's Day, II, 528.

*Liber mysterii.* See Knorr von Rosenroth.

Libra: added later to Zodiac, II, 456; *Genesis* later than invention of, 457; is Enoch, 463; meaning of, 457.

Libra-Hermes-Enoch, II, 454, 463.

Libraries: ancient, destroyed, I, 24-25, 403, 405, 406, 503, 511; II, 27-28, 430; hidden near Ishmonia, II, 29; of Alexandria (see Bruchion); of Attalus III of Pergamos, saved, 28.

Licetus (Liceti), Fortunio (1577-1657), I, 226, 639.

—— *De Lucernis antiquorum,* on perpetual lamps, I, 227, 228-29, 231-32.

—— *De monstrorum causis,* on signatures of foetus, I, 385-86.

Lidzbarski, M. (1868-1928). See *Ginzâ* and *Johannesbuch.*

Liebig, Baron Justus (1803-1873), *New Materialism,* I, on brain & thought, 249-50.

Life: allegedly phenomenon of matter, I, 115; Aristotle on, 320; as electromagnetic phenomena, 137; connected with elements, 343; galvanic battery, 236; Huxley, & protoplasm, 15; intelligent & blind, 302; is light & electricity, 258; magical arcanum as principle of, 506; Paracelsus on, & death, xxvi; physical, 419, 420; principles of, chiefly in astral body, 180-81; Universal, & Yggdrasill, 152; v. Helmont's principle of, 400; battle of, II, 112; Hebrew terms for, 302.

Life-force: active & passive at will, I, 475; and animated statues, 485; hidden in occult powers of nature, 466.

Life-Principle: I, 180-81, 408, 466-67, 480, 482, 485, 506; obeys controlling will, 140; of man & animals, 329; II, 218; role of guided, in animated statues, I, 616-17; above & below, II, 402; in all things, 263; one common, pervades all things, 590; and process of annihilation, 369.

Life-transfer, II, 564-65.

Light: chemical effect of, I, 136; and heat, 269; intellectual, 56; material, 137; originates matter & spirit, 258; perpetual, 510; ponderable, hence matter, 281; sublimated gold, 511; and will, 285; Highest, is Darkness, II, 225; Ptah as principle of, 36; vital, & nature of blood, 567; *Zohar* on garment of heavenly, 277.

*Light,* H.P.B. on her own mediumship, I, [12].

Lightfoot, J. (1602-1675), *Horae Hebraicae,* etc., on Bath-Kôl, I, viifn.; on *Nozari,* II, 128.

Lightning: ancients knew how to handle, I, 527-28; consumes Tullus Hostilius, 527; globular, 107, 108; —photographs, 394-95.

Lillies, same meaning as lotus, I, 92, 93.

Lillith, and Eve, II, 445 & fn.

Lincoln, Bishop of. *See* Tomline, Geo.

Lindsay, Lord, I, 379.

Linen: in Egypt, I, 536; treated, and asbestos, 230-31.

Liṅga: and Arba-il, II, 171; same as pillars

of Patriarchs, 235; and *yoni* in Christianity, 5.
Linigera, I, 536.
Linnaeus, C. von (1707-1778), *Amenitates,* etc., on cure of consumption, I, 89.
Linus, and length of Hêliacal year, I, 31.
Linus, second bishop of Rome, II, 124.
*Lippincott's Gazeteer of the World,* I, 656.
*Liquor amnii,* and universal ether, I, 389.
Lithos, or phallus, II, 5.
Littré, M. P. E. (1801-81), I, 76, 621; on hallucination & collective hysteria, 278.
—— *Paroles de philosophie positive,* on A. Comte, I, 78-79.
Lives, Seven, and Kebar-Ziwa, II, 234.
Livius, Titus (59 B.C.-17 A.D.), *Roman History:* on Juno's animated statue, I, 614; on Tullus, 527.
*Lloyd's Weekly Newspaper,* on a child phenomenon, I, 438-39.
Lobeck, C. A. (1781-1860), *Aglaophamus,* etc., on mysteries, I, xii.
Lodestone, effect of, I, 265.
Lodge(s): Mother, and its branches, II, 315; secret, of India, 584.
Lodur [Old Norse: *Lôthurr*], one of the Aesir, I, 151.
Logia, secret, of Jesus, II, 191.
Logos: I, 271; a, in every mythos, 162; as Phanes, 146; as Prometheus, 298; and avatâras, 291; Honover, Persian, 560; idea of, universal, 298; and Sun, 131fn.; among Brahmans, II, 205; an androgyne, 270fn.; as Savior, 237; called *petra,* 246; in Basilides, 156; intelligible, 223; and Jesus acc. to Nazarenes, 198; Jesus killed by his, 510; Justin Martyr on, 195; and nous, 282; of Philo, 33, 36, 210, 216, 247, 506; Only-Begotten of the Father, 506; or Son, 170; Poimandres as, 212; and Śabda, 241; serpent as, 505, 510fn.; unrevealed, of Ophites, 172, 177, 293; Word becomes, 41.
Loiseleur-Deslongchamps, A. (1805-1840), *Mânava-dharma-śâstra,* etc., I, 590fn.
Lomaśa, I, 133.
Longevity, cases of, II, 564 & fn., 620.
Long Face, II, 212.
Longfellow, H. W. (1807-1882), *A Psalm of Life,* on dust & soul, I, 212.
Longinus, Cassius (ca. 213-273 A.D.), Greek philosopher, II, 118.
Longinus, St., II, 248, 579.

Lord: deeper meaning of, I, 307; and Eternal, II, 401.
Loris-Melikoff, Count M. T. (1826-88), II, 568fn.
Lotâ, brass-pot, II, 629.
Lotharius (795-855), saying of, I, 40, 635.
Lotus: esoteric meaning of, I, 92-93; symbol of Horus and Brahmâ, 91-92.
*Lotus de la Bonne Loi, Le. See* Burnouf, Eugène.
Loubère, S. de la (1642-1729), *A New Historical Relation:* on Chinese & immortality, I, 214; on fishes & tides, 210; on power of Talapoins, 213-14; advises missionaries, II, 577-79; on Sommona-Codom, 576.
Loudun, II, 25.
Lourdes: II, 6; Madonna of, runs away, I, 614, 618; miracles at, 120.
Love, magnetism of, and its conditions, I, 210.
Loyola, I. (1491-1556), and Inquisition, II, 354.
Lucas, P. (1805-1885), *Traité philosophique,* etc., on imagination & childbirth, I, 384.
Lucian (ca. 125-190 A.D.), on Heracles & divine wisdom, II, 515.
—— *De Syria Dea:* on Nazars, II, 131; on number seven, 447.
—— *Philopatris,* on followers of Paul, II, 331.
—— *Philopseudes:* on Democritus & magic, I, 512; on lying, II, 212.
Lucifer: II, 501; Hindu, I, 299; five-pointed star of, II, 448; regenerates, 473.
*Lucifer* (London): I, 346fn., 351fn.; H.P.B. on *Isis Unv.,* I, [5], [34-42], [47-48], [55].
Lucius Piso (ca. 133 B.C.), q. by Pliny, I, 527.
Lucretius (ca. 98-55 B.C.), alleged q. from, on man after death, I, 362, 635.
—— *De rerum natura:* on magnetic stone, I, 163; q. Epicurus on astral soul, 250-51.
Lugo, Card. John de (1583-1660), I, 89.
*Luke:* I, 604; II, 133, 134, 203, 545, 552fn., 556; old Syriac, on Jesus, II, 198; on annunciation, 505; on blaspheming against Holy Ghost, 238; on Jesus' temptation, 485; on key of knowledge, 561; on Satan, 511; on unborn John the Baptist, 555; plagiarized story about

Simeon, 518, 518-19fn.; reputed an Essene, 144.
Lukhsur, and Luxor, II, 308fn.
Lully, R. (1235?-1315), *De angelis opus divinum,* etc., I, 254fn.
Luminous, appearances, I, xliii.
Luna, as Diana, I, 266.
Lunacy, I, 276.
Lunar, dynasty, II, 438.
Lundy, J. P. (1823-92), *Monumental Christianity:* on Apocryphal Gospels, II, 539; on cross, 454, 455; on cross at Tuam, 538; on Kṛishṇa's story, 546; on Viṭhobâ & Kṛishṇa, 557-58; q. O'Brien on Round Towers, 290fn.; q. Plato on decussated circle, 469; twists facts, 447.
Lunus, Deus, II, 48.
Luther, M. (1483-1546): accused of companionship with Devil, II, 503; allegedly worst man in Europe, 200fn.; on blessed sin, 480; on Catholics, 208; why, hated Aristotle, 34-35.
—— *Missa privata,* on demon upbraiding him, II, 74.
—— *Tischreden,* on fishpond at Rome filled with infant skulls, II, 58.
Lutherans, burned as sorcerers, II, 61.
Luxor: I, 541; unfading colors of, 239; Brotherhood of, II, 308fn.
Lybian, Desert, and monks, II, 404.
Lycanthropy, Voltaire on, in Jura, II, 626.
Lydda, Jews of, I, 26.
Lying, I, 253; II, 212, 358.
Lyly, John (1554?-1606), *Euphues,* etc., 635.

# M

Maât, Egyptian goddess, same as Thmei, II, 648.
Macaulay, T. H. (1800-1859), *Essays,* on evidence of immortality, I, 424.
Mac Benae, Masonic term, II, 349.
Maccabees, II, 524.
Macedo, Antoine de (1612-1693), and Inquisition, II, 59.
Macedonians, II, 607.
McEmery, on worked flints, I, 223.
Machagistia: I, 90, 251; or magian religion, II, 306.
MacKenzie, K. R. H., *Royal Masonic Cyclopaedia:* on Azâzêl, II, 303; on Brotherhood of Luxor, 308fn; on Chrêstos, 324; on Druzes, 309; on Jesuits, 355; on Kabalistic pillars, 215fn.; on occult fraternity & its members, 307-08; on soul, 280; q. Capellus on Jehovah, 400.
Macrinius, I, 127.
Macrocosmos: I, 62; II, 276, 456, 458, 461, 464; man as foetus in, I, 212.
Macroprosopus, I, 580fn.; II, 224.
Mâdan, wicked elemental, I, 495.
Madonna(s): of Lourdes runs away, I, 614, 618; —element, II, 110; of Bari in crinoline, 9; of Egyptian origin, 49-50; of Rio décolletée, 9-10; various, 209-10.
Maelstrom, and *Odyssey,* I, 545.
Magadha, Nâga race of, II, 484.
Magao, I, xxxiv.
*Magasin scientifique de Göttingen* (Michaelis), on lightning conductors in Jerusalem temple, I, 528.
Magendie, F. (1783-1855): I, 89, 400, 401; on error & truth, 378.
—— *Précis,* etc.: on foetus & mother's imagination, I, 386-87, 390, 394, 395; on mesmerism, 176.
*Magia Jesu Christi,* II, 148.
Magian: religion or Machagistia, II, 306; rival, schools at Babylon, 128.
Magians (Magi): def. I, *xxxiv, 94-95;* established magic, 25; magnet and, 130; objected to evocation of souls, 321; secret mysteries of, 556; taught evolution of worlds, 255; Chaldean, masters of the Jews, II, 361; mysteries of, never violated, 306fn.; and Orpheus, 130; persecuted by Domitian, 147.
Magic: ancient Colleges of, I, 482; II, 617; and ancient knowledge, I, 35-36; appeared with earliest races, 25; as occult psychology, 612; as old as man, 18-19; at Paris séance, 608-11; basis of, as a science, *244, 247,* 627; black, & necromancy, 321; and Brahmâ, xxvii; Chaldean, 66; cures by, 532; def. *65-66;* difference between, & sorcery, 366; dignity of, 560; divine science, 25, 90, 94; II, 502; Dupotet on, I, 142, 279; highest possibilities of, 282; imitates laws of Nature, 512; in China & Tibet, 599ff.; in Kashmîr, 505; in *Popol-Vuh,* 549-50; mesmerism most important branch of, 129; no transgression of law, v; origin of Black & White, 593; Paracelsus on, 361fn.; II, 500; performances of, I, 456ff.,

468-71, 473, 474; Perty on, 138-39; phenomena of, in desert, 604ff.; and Popes, 617-18; practices in all lands, 18; Proclus on, & sympathies, 243-44; and sharks, 606-07; Spiritualism modern form of, 42; and spontaneous generation, 414; theurgy & benevolent, xliii; universal belief in, 624; unwavering belief in, 414; Vedic sacrifices are ceremonial, xxvii; brooks no rival, II, 630; cornerstone of, is magnetism, 589, 610; Escobar on use of, 353-54; European, in cloisters, 20; in India, 70, 612; Jesus accused of, 148; knowledge of man's inner being, 587; Moors skilled in, 59-60; of Albertus Magnus, 57; of *Zohar*, 350-51; openly practiced by clergy, 20, 57, 59ff.; principles of, 587-88; Schools of, 97, 361; should, replace spiritualism, 634; and Spiritualism, very ancient, 15; spiritual wisdom, 590; theoretical & practical, 617; trinity of nature is lock of, 635; Ventura di Raulica on modern, 70.

*Magic and Mesmerism* (anonymous), II, 634fn.

Magical Power: Agrippa, Cicero & Lévi on, I, 280-81; never possessed by those of vicious indulgence, 218; of fakirs, 616-17; personal purity indispensable for, 320; utilized & denied by British, 607.

Magician(s): called "sons of giants," I, 595fn.; def. *xxxiv;* distinction between, & mediums, 367; Eastern, has power over nature-spirits, 457; Iamblichus on Egyptian, 416; imagination & will make a, 62; and invisible spirits, 66; Lactantius on, 167; natural, & hierophants, 593; passive, xxxvii; performance of, under Jahângîr, 457-58.

Μαγικον *oder das geheime System, etc.* (anonymous), on true mathematics, I, 6-7, 632-33.

*Magnale magnum,* I, 170, 213.

Magna Mater: name of many goddesses, I, 579; cap of, and the Pope, II, 30.

Magnes, I, xxv, 64, 129.

Magnesian, stone, I, 130.

Magnet: concealed power, I, 168; and Dioskuri, 235; globe as a, 497; rediscovered by Paracelsus, 71; the one, of universe, 208.

Magnetic: force of earth, I, 172-73, 282; healing, 215-16; nature of, emanations & fluid, 279, 463, 498; sleep & insensibility, 166-67fn.; sleeper, 532; symbols and, powers, 23; universal, ocean, 282.

Magnetism: action of moon in animal, I, 264; attractive, of thought, 181; Cox on, psychology & scientists, 611-12; derivation of term, 129; and electricity, 201, 293-94; from ideas & physical bodies, 39; and human feelings, 209-10; imparted by one subject to another, 462-63; inquiry about, 171ff.; intelligent streams of, 208; Laplace on, 173; and levitation, 496ff.; Mesmer on, 172-73; and Mysteries, 235; of love, & its conditions, 210; of nature feeds our bodies, 169; Paracelsus on, xxvi, 164; requires positive nature, 109; soul-electricity, 322; sympathetic, in nature, 206ff.; underlies theurgic rites, 130; v. Helmont on, & man, 170; as alphabet of magic, II, 610; communicated by touch, 611; and electricity as cornerstone of magic, 589; impure, and man's shadow, 611; of garments used in finding drowned persons, 611-12; of red-haired people, 611.

Magnetists, in competition with Apostles, II, 22.

Magnetization, two kinds of, I, 178.

Mah, venerable and Masonic Ritual, II, 388.

Mahâ-Bhadra-Kalpa, II, 156fn.

*Mahâbhârata:* I, 578; II, 275, 425, 450, 457, 538, 562; great antiquity of, II, 428.

Mahâdeva, or Śiva, I, 583; II, 5, 434.

Mahâdevasthâna, II, 584.

Mahâkalpa, I, 31-32.

Mahalalel, II, 466.

*Mahâmâyâ,* and Ananda, II, 555.

Mahan-âtma, I, 56.

Mahandû, II, 627.

Mahâ-samudra, II, 234.

Mahâsura, as Lucifer, I, 299.

Mahat, and Prakriti, II, 565.

*Mahâvaṁśa:* on Buddhism in Nepal, II, 290; on King Covercapal, 509.

Mahâyugas, I, 32, 634.

Mahiman, II, 593.

Mahinda, II, 576fn.

Maimonides (1135-1204): on rites of Sheol, I, 493; on *Talmud* & natural science, 17.

—— *Mishnah Torah:* on inner meaning of *Genesis,* I, 435-36; on Shedim & their rites, 449.

—— *Moreh Nebûkhîm:* on Berêshîth, II, 35; on Sabians, 197.

Maiolus (*fl.* 1480), I, 226.
—— *De gradibus medicinarum,* I, 639.
Maistre, J. M. de (1754-1821), *Les Soirées,* etc., on ancients & modern, I, 252.
Maitreya-Buddha: II, 156fn., 275, 286fn., 549; and Fifth Buddha, 260.
Majault, Dr., and mesmerism, I, 171.
Majesty, Hidden, of *Popol-Vuh,* I, 559.
Makara, II, 273.
Malabar, phantoms in, I, 344.
Malacarne, V. G. (1744-1816), *Anatomia cerebrale,* on convolutions of brain, I, 352.
*Malachi,* passage in, attributed to *Isaiah,* II, 248.
Malach-Iho, and Israel, II, 401.
Malagrida, Gabriel (1689-1761), and magic, II, 58. See also *Proceedings.*
Malalas, Joannes (491?-578?), *Historia Chronica,* on Semitic Triad, II, 51.
Malays, island-empire of, I, 592.
Malchu, *Bestia arundinis,* on levitation, I, xxiii, 629.
—— *Conciones,* as above.
Male, and female qualities in Nature, I, 12-13.
Males, rabbit, suckling young, I, 412.
Malebranche, N. de (1638-1715), I, 269.
Malefici, II, 502.
Malformations: Armor on, I, 392; Magendie on, 388.
Malhandrini, H., *Ritual of Initiations,* on Egyptian initiation, II, 365.
Malkhuth: II, 213; Sephîrâh as female counterpart of, II, 224; and sign of the Cross, 87.
Mallet, P. H. (1730-1807), *Northern Antiquities:* on giants in *Edda,* I, 122, 150; on Norse creation-myth, 160; on Balder & Hel, II, 11.
Malocchio, or jettatura, I, 381.
Malouli, in Egyptian cosmogony, II, 268fn.
Malta: rendezvous of last real Templars, II, 385; spurious order of, 383.
Maltebrun, C. (1755-1826), *Géographie mathématique du monde,* I, 412.
Man(Men): affects nature, I, 211; androgynous, & separation of sexes, 297; II, 264; and animal, I, 327; ante-Silurian, 155; and Augoeides, 306; as correlation of forces, 309; as foetus in macrocosmos, 212; as Life, 307; as mirror of universe, 213; as trinity, 212, 309, 341; II, 285, 362, 588, 635; bodies of, produced by elementals, I, 285; can create, 62; casts off body, 149; combines all elements, 343fn.; creation of, 303; II, 429, 558 & fn.; creation of, in *Edda,* I, 138, 151; does not change much, 40, 72; enigma to science, 336; evolution of spiritual, 121-22; and Hermetic art, 309; immense antiquity of, 3-4, 155; inner self of, 316; is our great object in view, 308; loses spirituality, 149; —matter & man-spirit, 157; moral descent of, 39; Müller on past of, 4; Plato on dual, 277; spiritual yearning of, 64; stars and, are one in essence, 168; Tatian on immortality of, 13; to be evolved to completion, 346; triple nature of, key to phenomena, 49; Wallace on development of, 294-95; will be *physically* spiritualized, 296; age of, in various yugas, II, 467-68; astral souls become, in time, 456; composite nature of, acc. to Egyptians, 367-68; and conception of God, 567; conscious withdrawal of inner, 588; divine, crucified, 557; every, a god on earth, 262-63; everything comprised in, acc. to *Zohar,* 276; first races of, spiritual, 276-77; may have existed as non-organic being, 464; and metempsychosis, 279; and nature, 279; personal spiritual entity of, 593; physical, & nature of soul, 362; Plato on earlier stage of, 345; races of, 407fn.; revivified without souls, 564; soulless, 369; spheroidal at first, 469; —spirit & descent into incarnation, 362; triune nature of, & fate after death, 283-84; twofold, 193.
Man-tree, as tree of knowledge, I, 297.
Manas, and Monas, discussed, I, 347-48fn.
Mandaeans, II, 289ff., 650-51. See also Nazareans, Nazarenes.
Mandragora (*dûdâim*), I, 465-66.
Maneros, II, 503, 504.
Manes, anima and umbra, I, 37.
Manes, Mani: as anointed or interpreter, II, 208fn., 221, 286, 294fn.
Manetho: I, 33fn., 415; II, 448; on aërolites, I, 331.
—— *Aegyptiaca,* I, 406, 518, 555, 569; II, 51, 327, 483.
—— *Compendium,* I, 256fn.
Mani. See Manes.
Manichaeans: II, 325, 329, 352; on Jesus as permutation of Gautama, 286.
Manifestation, Manu on, I, 271-72fn.

Manifestations: Billot & Wagner on, I, 499; conditions of objective, 198; genuineness of mediumistic, 320; and mediums, 109; old & modern, 53; produced by elementals, 311; produced by malicious daemons, 70; subjective & objective, 198; subjective, & their origin, 324-25; unconscious will stops, 57; periodical, of the universe, II, 264-65; source of physical & subjective, 597; Spiritualistic, alarm Cath. Church, 16, 23.

Manna, hidden, II, 351.

*Manna benedicta, De* (anonymous), on philosopher's stone, II, 618.

Mano, Lord, I, 300; II, 174, 224, 227, 228, 229, 295, 296.

Mansi, G. D. (1692-1769), *Sacrorum conciliorum*, etc., II, 642.

Mantar phenknâ, magical spell, II, 612.

Manteis (μάντεις), prophets, I, xxxv.

Manthi-cup, I, xxxv.

Manthran, title of Zoroaster, II, 409.

*Mânthra-speñta*, II, 409.

Mantic, frenzy produced by exhalations, I, 531.

Manticism: I, 358; colleges of, 482; def. *xxxiv-xxxv*.

Mantius: I, xxv; magnetic sleeper, 532.

Manto, I, xxxv.

Mantra(s): I, xxxviii, 152; def. *xxxvi*; evidence for, 444-45; and numbers, 9, and sphericity of earth, 10; and will power, xliv; as magic prayer, II, 409; and Vâch, 269-70, 371.

Manu(s): I, 587, many, & races, 590; as races of man, II, 407fn.; mythical, or first man, 269; and Prajâpatis, 427; Rishis & patriarchs, 468; Rishis & Noah, 271fn.

Manu-Vena, as Menes, colonizes Egypt from India, I, 627.

*Manu, Laws of;* I, xvi, xvii, xix, xxxvii, xxxviii, 18, 271; age of, 586ff.; II, 257; genuine & apocryphal, I, 586; Jacolliot on, 585-86; II, 257-58; Jones on, I, 585-86; Moore on, 585, 587; on evolution of beings, 620-21; on manifestation, 271-72fn.; on many Manus & races, 590; ethical code of, higher than *Pentateuch*, II, 535; on age of man in yugas, 468; on Aum, 39; on Brahmâ, 226, 272; on cosmic egg, 267; on creation of various beings, 107, 260; on evolution of species, 271 & fn.; on future Redeemer, 50; on identification with the Supreme, 159; on moral precepts, 338; on muhurtas & kalâs, 464fn.; on Nara, 267fn.; on production of Virâj, 111; on Purusha & Virâj, 270; on soul in plants, 263; on spiritual germ, 270-71; on Supreme Soul, 116; on Supreme Wisdom, 156fn.; on Thought as Lord of World, 116; on virtues for initiation, 98, 163-64; on water, light & earth, 267; silent on deluge, 427.

Manuscripts, burning of, I, 511.

Manvantaras: II, 270; and kalpas, I, 32; almost seven now passed, II, 464fn.

Mar, root of Mary, II, 446.

Marabout, I, xxxvi.

Marathon, battle of, and neighing of horses 400 years later, I, 70.

Marathus, I, 570, 579, 651.

Marbodus (*fl.* 1067-1101), *Liber lapidum*, etc., I, 265.

Marc, and mesmerism, I, 174.

Marcion (*fl.* 2nd c. A.D.): allegedly mutilates Gospel of Luke, II, 160, 192; ascetic, 333; discussed, 159ff.; founded School, 536; on illusion-body of Christ, 168; on Jesus, 166.

—— *Antithesis*, II, 160.

Marcionites, II, 221.

Marcosians, theurgic Gnostic sect & eucharist, II, 513-14.

Marcou, Jules (1824-1898), Letter to the Editor, *Atlantic Monthly*, March, 1875: on origin of America's name, I, 592.

Marcus Aurelius Antoninus (121-180): on matter & creation, I, 257; instructed by the gods, II, 369.

Marcus Damascenes, I, 384, 385.

Margil, Hindus' answer to, on missionary work, II, 573.

Margosa, bark of, and fevers, II, 622fn.

Mariâma, II, 209.

Mariana, Juan de (1536-1624), *De Rege et Regis*, etc., on murder & poisoning, II, 372-73fn.

Marie of Medici (1573-1642), victim of Inquisition, II, 60.

Mariette-Bey, Aug. E. (1821-1881), excavations of, I, 6.

Marin, M. A. (1697-1767), *Les Vie des Pères*, etc., on schools of magic, II, 97.

Marion [N. T. Marion-Dufresne, 1729-1772], on aurora, I, 417.

Mariotte, Edmé (1620?-1684), physicist, I, 188.

*Mark:* II, 44, 125, 338; on Holy Ghost & damnation, 478fn.; on last days, 246; misquotes, 247.
Markland, and Meru, I, 592.
Marmontel, J. E. (1723-1799), *Bélisaire*, II, 8.
Marriage(s): and the convulsionnaires, I, 375; endogamic, II, 240; and virginity, 300.
Mars: day of, II, 418; or Nerig, 296; or Saba, 294.
Marsi, of Italy and power over serpents, I, 381, 467.
Martezzi, *Pagani e Cristiani*, II, 332fn.
Martin, Jean, *Légende de Saint Dñique*, etc., on exorcism, II, 75.
Martineau, I, 86.
Maruts: and storms, I, xxixfn.; Hymns to the, II, 267fn.
Marvin, F. R. (1847-1918), *Philosophy of Spiritualism*, etc., I, 75, 81-82, 83, 117, 187.
Mary. *See* Virgin Mary.
Mary Magdalene, I, 488, 493.
Mason, Osgood, on the Over-Soul & Nature, I, 426.
Masonic: oath & Anti-masonic Convention, II, 375; Ritual, 348; secret ciphers, 393ff.; symbols, 392-93; the "Word" in, Ritual, 387-88.
*Masonic Mirror and Keystone*, II, 380.
Masons (Freemasons): I, 19, 136fn., 579; symbolic language of, & their ignorance, 29-30.
Masonry (Freemasonry): II, 37, 46fn., 99-100, 138, 152, 199, 215fn., 270fn., 289, 302-03, 316, 317, 368fn., 404, 408, 444, 450, 466; and keystone, I, 571; universal, of science & philosophy, 38; a sham, II, 378; attacked & slandered, 372-73, 375; connected with Jesuitism, 352; decadent, 375-77, 380; and early American statesmen, 391; grips of, & Epiphanius, 330; has lost the Word, 371; has nothing worth concealing, 371; and impostor Anderson, 389; and Jesuits, 385; and members of Eastern Brotherhoods, 380; and Negroes, 391; now a corpse, 388; origin of modern, 349-50; and personal God, 375, 377, 380; Sotheran on, 388-91; threats to the candidate in, 99; true & false Templarism and, 381ff.; universal, & occult schools, 305; and white stone, 351.

Masorah: II, 131, 430, 443 & fn., 459fn.; a closed book, 561; completed work of destruction, 470.
Masoretes, disfigure old MSS., II, 430-31, 459fn.
Masoretic Points, II, 301, 302, 398, 430, 471.
Masra, Cairo, I, 627.
Master (κύριος), II, 193.
al-Mas'ûdî (ca. 885-956), *Les Prairies d'or*, on ghûls in desert, I, 604.
Mata, spurious Masonic Order, II, 383.
Mâtaṃgî, woman and Ananda, II, 551.
Matarea, II, 537.
Mateer, S., *The Land of Charity:* on ever-burning lamps, I, 225; on magical incantations, 135-36; on peacocks & monkeys, 136fn.
Materialism: bastard of French Revolution, I, xlv; in Aristotle's day, 15; and key to mysteries, 573; molecules & occult impulse, 87; more bigoted than religion, 86; of ancients, 251; of scientists, 114-15; and phenomena, 624; sickly child, xlv; titanic struggle between, and spiritual aspirations, xlv; ever growing, II, 369; and positivism, 3-4.
Materialization(s): I, 319; as portrait-statues, xxxvi; cases of, in Bible, 493; and Crookes, 220; *personal*, & human spirits, 321; seen by H.P.B., 69-70.
Mathematics: in Egypt, I, 531, 536; in India, 618; Pythagorean & Platonic, 506-07; true, 6-7.
Mather, Cotton, I, 361; II, 503.
Mathurâ: II, 557; Kaṇsa and Kṛishṇa, 199, 537.
Matsya, avatâra, II, 427.
Matter: annihilation of, I, 289; astral, & phantoms, 200; became progressively more dense, 1-2; clings to spirit, 428; cometary, 168; Cosmic, & dual principle, 146, 149, 156; eternal & indestructible in its particles, 328; formless, 256; impregnated with divine influx, xxi; indestructibility of, & ancients, 8, 61, 242-43; infused with life-principle by will of adept, 616; is nothing without spirit, 235, 258, 582; and mind, 387; pre-existent, passed thru million forms, 144; privation, & universal ether, 310-11; produced by will, 140; scientists deify, 59; scientists do not understand, 115; and spirit in *Codex Naz.*, 299-300; and spiritual

essence, 343fn.; sublimated, furnished by elementaries, 116; symbolized by serpent, 297; and thought, 58, 186; Tyndall on, 14; chaos or Tiamat, II, 445; creation of, in *Cod. Naz.*, 175; defied spirit, 420; effect of emanative energy, 35; formation & destruction of, & personified powers, 402; generated by force, will & desire, 320; indestructible, or Prakṛiti, 271; inert, disintegrated by occult means, 589; and mother, 270fn.; thoughts are, 619; transformation from spirit, 268; and woman, 446. *See Also* Substance.

Matter, A. J. (1791-1864), *Hist. critique du Gnosticisme*, etc.: on Ephesus, II, 155; on Ophite cosmogony, 221; on symbol of Bull, 236.

Matteucci, C. (1811-68), I, 188.

*Matthew:* I, 481, 575fn.; II, 12fn., 132, 136, 160, 476, 533, 551, 556; on mysteries of kingdom, I, xii; on prayer, 434; on salt of earth, 148; on unbelief, 57; authentic evangel of, II, 134fn.; compared with ancient Scriptures, 338; Gospel of, a fabrication, 544; Hebrew Gospel of, 181-82 & fn., 191, 204; misquoted, 247; passages identical with *Book of the Dead*, 548-49; on Beelzebul, 487; on binding & loosening, 544; on children, 65; on doubts of John the Baptist, 519; on Elias, 133; on faith & works, 563; on fishers of men, 549; on gates of death, 506; on gates of Hell, 364fn.; on good & God, 238; on heaven taken by violence, 404; on Iota, 324; on Jesus tempted, 513; on John the Baptist, 203; on loving enemies, 163, 479; on Mary's several children, 531; on men as angels, 345; on mysteries of kingdom, 493; on *nazaria*, 134; on parables, 145; on *petra*, 30, 392; on Satan, 473; on secret prayer, 196; on swearing, 196, 373fn.; on the *word*, 387; on virtuous life, 164; on wine & bottles, 163.

Maturantius, F. ( ?-1512 or 1518), I, 226, 227, 228, 639.

Ma-Twan-lin, on desert music, I, 604.

Maudsley, H. (1835-1918), *Body and Mind:* on caution, I, 465; on experiment & induction, 393; on so-called miraculous cures, 464; on positivism, II, 3-4.

Maulet, Jeanne, I, 374.

Maurice, Thos. (1754-1824), on triad, II, 48.

—— *Hist. of Hindostan:* II, 537, 539; on Kalki-avatâra, 237; on Kûrma-avatâra, 300-01; plate of Kṛishṇa crushing serpent, 446, 537.

—— *Indian Antiquities,* on pagodas built as a cross, II, 382fn.

Mauritania Tingitana, I, 545.

Mauritius, and nauscopite, I, 240.

Maury, Comm. M. F. (1806-73), I, 410.

Maximi, the Ephesian, initiates Emp. Julian, II, 566.

Maximus, Valerius (ca. 1st c. A.D.), *De factis,* etc., on statue of Juno, I, 614.

Maxwell, Wm. (17th c.), I, 172.

—— *De medicina magnetica,* on magn. healing and world-soul, I, 215-16.

Mâyâ: I, xiv; II, 300, 476; def. I, *290;* magic performance involving, 473, 474; trinity of, 288 & fn.; Kapila on, II, 158; principle of, & metaphysics, 157-58.

Mâyâdevî, immaculate virgin, II, 537, 555.

Mayas: language of, I, 547; mysterious city of, 547.

Mayer, A. M. (1836-97), I, 162.

—— *The Earth a Great Magnet,* I, 169, 172-73, 282.

Mayerhoff, E. Th., *Life and Times of John Reuchlin,* etc., II, 20fn.

Mazdeans, def. I, *xxxvi.*

Mazzini, Giuseppe (1805-72), Mason, II, 391.

Mead, G. R. S. (1863-1933), *Orpheus,* I, 636.

—— *Thrice-Greatest Hermes,* I, 640.

Meadow saffron, I, 89.

Meaning, hidden, of mystical writers, I, 628.

Mechanical, devices, I, 543.

Meckel, J. F. (1714-74), I, 387.

Medea: II, 376; journey of, through air, I, 366.

Medes, I, 576; II, 141, 435, 486fn.

Mediatorship: and mediumship, I, 487-88; as Logos, II, 238.

Medical: Egyptian, treatise, I, 3; pretentions, 20fn.

*Medical and Surgical Journal* (London), on changes in steel, I, 211.

Medici Family, practiced black art, II, 55.

Medicine: among Egyptians, I, 540, 544-45; classed by Bacon as conjectural, 405; in India, 619; insecure basis of, 180; least exact of sciences, 88; and new curative methods, 88; and Paracelsus, 164;

prejudiced & malicious, 88; purblind & materialistic, 20.

Medina-Sidonia, Don Alonso Pérez de Guzmán el Bueno, 7th Duke of (1550-1615), I, 399.

Medium(s): ancients persecuted *unregulated,* I, 489; as conductor, 201; as nucleus of magnetism, 499; auric & moral condition of, *490;* best, when exercises no will, 109; controlled by elementals, 490; and controlling Intelligence, 199-200; Cox's ideas on, 195-96; developed for physical or spiritual mediumship, 367; and disembodied spirits, 67; distinction between, & magician, 367; double of entranced, moved by another intelligence, 360; —healers & vampirism, 490; healing, and moral defilement, 217; honest, no longer his own master, 360; and Intelligences, 53; Leucken child—, 439; magnetized, and unseen universe, 159, 499-500; nature of spirits evoked by, depends upon morality, 67; passive, has no power, 490; persecuted by clergy, 26-27; phenomena when, is conscious, 113; physical, to be pitied, 488-89; and powerful mesmerizer, 200; psychic force not originating in, 196-97; pure & impure, 325; Russian, & clergy, 28-29; sickly & often morally feeble, 490; II, 595; spiritual phenomena independent of, I, 109; *subjective,* and Augoeides, 321; and writings from planetary spirits, 494; does not exercise will power, II, 596; fakirs are, 106; and greater knowledge of his spiritual entity, 596; and material furnished by elementals & auras of sitters, 595; materializing, & perspiration, 569; nervous system of, generates force for phenomena, 595; not admitted into Mysteries, 117-18; opposite pole of adept, 596; passive instrument, 588; physical brain of, unconscious of phenomena, 595; require extraneous influence to induce trance, 592; Socrates a, 118.

*Medium and Daybreak* (London): on apparition, I, 69; on Jencken child-medium, 439; on vampirism and mediums, 491.

Mediumship: I, 123; case of unreliable, 356 & fn.; genuine, & opinions of Houdin, etc., 359; hereditable, 500; H.P.B.'s own, [12]; many phases of, 320; and mediatorship, 487; nature & qualities of, *487-88;* physical, & its dangers, 490; physical & spiritual, *367;* subjective & objective, 325; treated unfairly at St. Petersburg, 117-18; and catalepsy, II, 588; artificial means of inducing, 592; cured by hierophants, 98; def. *118, 588;* and Mysteries, 117-18.

Megalistor, II, 37.

Megasthenes (*fl.* 300 B.C.), II, 616.
—— *Indica:* I, xl; on Jews & Kalani, 567.

Meghestom, I, xxxiv.

Meipo, miracles & occult arts, II, 159fn., 288, 555, 608, 617, 618.

*Mekhashephah,* as witch, I, 355.

Mela, Pomponius (1st c. A.D.), *De situ orbis,* on Druids, I, 18.

Melampus: I, xxxv; as healer, 532.

Melanchthon, P. (1497-1560), II, 20.

Melanêphoros, third degree, II, 364.

Melchisedek, II, 535, 566.

Meldrum, Chas. (1821-1901), I, 410.

Mel-Karth, I, 567, 568, 575.

Melton, E. *Zeldzaame Reizen,* on boy & rope, I, 474.

Memnon, I, 514.

*Mémoires de l'Académie Celtique* (Lenoir), II, 488.

*Mémoires de la Société des Antiquaires de France* (Münther), I, 19.

Memory: and astral light, I, 178-79; and reincarnation, 179; nature of, 184; of drowning man, 179; and fancy distort visions, II, 591; opposed to seership, 591.

Memphis: catacombs of, I, 553; stone of, 540.

Memra: angel of the Lord, II, 207-08; as "Word," 400.

Menander, Gnostic teacher, II, 294.

Ménard, L. N. (1822-1901), *Hermès Trismégiste:* I, 16; on gods & animated statues, 613-14; on Divine Triad, II, 50; on God, 199, 238; on rebirth, 195.

Mendeleyeff, Prof. D. I. (1834-1907): I, 612; prejudged manifestations, 117-18.

Menephthah, II, 558.

Menes: I, 406-07, 516, 529, 589; II, 548fn., 565fn.; as Manu-Vina, I, 627; five thousand years prior to Adam, II, 520; and worship of Osiris, 361.

Menippus (3rd c. B.C.), I, 19.

Menos, and invention of letters, I, 532.

Mensambulism, I, 322-23.

Mentana, Cains of, II, 81.

Menthu-hetep, Queen, II, 92.

Mephistopheles, II, 511.

*Mercurius vitae,* II, 620.
Mercury: Arnobius on, I, 131; water of, symbol of soul, 309; alchemical meaning of, II, 621; as psychopompos, 335; astrologically, 294fn.; day of, 418; and Jesus, 132; potions of, 620; or Nebo, 132, 296.
Merdasht, II, 630fn.
Meridian, true, known to Egyptians, I, 536.
Merkabah, I, xxxiii; II, 99, 266, 348, 349, 350, 424.
Merle d'Aubigné, J. H. (1794-1872), *Hist. de la réformation,* etc. (implied), q. Luther on sin, II, 480.
Merriam, C. H. (1855- ? ), *Report of the Geological Survey,* etc., on male rabbits suckling young, I, 412.
Meru: I, 156; and America, 591-92; symbolism of Mt., the Sephîrôth and *Cod. Nazar.,* II, 233ff.
Meryon, Dr. C. L. (1783-1877), *Memoirs,* etc., II, 657.
Mesmer, F. A. (1734-1815): II, 23; and magnetism, I, 72; and music as healing, 215; re-discovered animal magnetism, 72; treatment of, by Academy, 171ff.
—— *Lettre,* etc., on principles of magnetism, etc., I, 172-73.
Mesmeric: experiment of Regazzoni, I, 143; eye and, fluid, xxxiifn.
Mesmerism: Academy turns back upon, I, 165; and auto-mesmerism, 500; branded as hallucination, 165; and control of medium, 200; experiments in, 166 & fn.; fluidic influence in, 131; inquiry about, 171ff.; and magic in R. Cath., 617-18; and moon, 264; most important branch of magic, 129; and *ob* & *od,* 158; produces insensibility, 378; requires positive nature, 109; and trance, 113; used on animals, 283; and breathing, II, 632-33; easily becomes sorcery, 634; of fakir by guru, 105; used by Adepts to produce illusory appearances, 588-89.
Mesmerizer: power of, I, 142; will of, II, 21.
Messiah: and conjunction of Saturn & Jupiter in Pisces, II, 256; as the Sun, 450fn.; Gnostic King, 223; and Josephus' spurious sentence, 328; Kabalistic, 226, 244-45, 259; and Vishṇu, 259-60.
Metalline, I, 502.
Metallurgy: of ancients, I, 538; was alchemy in ancient days, 542.
Metals, not simple bodies or true elements, I, 509.

Metatron: II, 33, 154, 225, 238, 400, 420, 576; as seventh Zodiacal Sign, 456; Enoch is, 463-64; and *feroher,* 495; and golden age, 144fn.; in all religions, 454.
Metempsychosis: I, 8-9; believed in by ancients, 12; def. *xxxvi-xxxvii, 290;* in inferior bodies, 346; in Plato, 276-77; Jews believed in, 347; Kabalistic axiom of, 388; of soul as a cycle, 348-49; real meaning of, 289; and reincarnation, 351; and 3,000 year cycle, 297; as discipline, 286; as transformations, 456; distorted by scholars, 534; Druze doctrine of, 310; origin of idea of, 279; and rebirth in Kabala, 195; universally taught, 280ff. *See also* Reincarnation.
Meteoric, iron in Egypt, I, 538.
Meteorology, ancient, I, 410.
Methodius Patarensis (3rd & 4th c. A.D.), *De creatis,* on be-rêshîth, II, 35.
Methuselah: I, 149; and Enoch in Masonry, 571-72.
Mêthis (Μῆτις), I, 156, 262, 263, 266.
Metre: of mantras, II, 409-10; prototype of visible forms, 410.
Mexicans: on lunar eclipses, I, 548; on spirit-abodes, 313.
Mexico, I, 650.
Mezua, I, 164.
*Micah:* II, 166fn., 440, 476; on Bosheth, 130.
Michael: of the Gnostics, I, 300fn.; chief of Aeôns, 510fn.; and Dragon an Âryan myth, 486; gossip between, & Seth, 520; guardian of Jews, 206; identical with Anubis, 488; identical with Indra, 510fn.; meaning of name, 488; one with Enoch, 452; one with the Lord, 482; overcomes Dragon, 488; sweat of preserved, 71; worshipped by Peter & Jude, 207.
Michaelis, Joh. D. (1717-1791), on conductors of lightning in Jerusalem temple, I, 528.
Miche, Bishop of Cambodia, I, 565.
Michelangelo (1475-1564), gem of, I, 240.
Michelet, J. (1798-1874), on Herakles, I, 130fn.
—— & J. E. Quinet (1803-75), *Des Jésuites:* II, 352fn.; on banishment of Jesuits, 358; on Pope's infallibility, 359.
—— *La Sorcière,* on dirt of monks, II, 511fn.
Microprosopus: I, 580fn.; II, 210, 224; as Adam Primus, II, 452.
Microscope, among ancients, I, 240.

Middle Ages, cause of darkness in, II, 253.
Middleton, C. (1560?-1628), *A Free Enquiry*, etc., on Jansenists' marvels, I, 373.
Midgard (Old Norse: *mithgarthr*), the earth and the great serpent, I, 151.
Midianites: II, 470; as wise men, 449.
Midnight Sun, II, 146.
*Midrash* (pl. *Midrashim*). See *Talmud*.
Migne, J. P. (1800-1875), *Patrologiae Cursus Completus:* I, 642; II, 650.
Mikra, minor mysteries, II, 108.
Milano, il Duomo di, its original, II, 5.
Militrissa, with moon on forehead, I, 550.
Mill, J. S. (1806-1873), *A System of Logic*, on miracles, I, 403-04; on *unalterable experience*, 403.
Milman, H. H. (1791-1868), *The History of Christianity*, etc., II, 42fn., 161fn.; on early Christianity, 204.
Milton, J. (1608-1674), *Paradise Lost:* on devil & man, I, 233; on unseen spiritual creatures, 125; diabology of, II, 501-02.
*Mîmân̥sâ*. See Jaimini.
Mimer, I, 151.
Mina, II, 273.
Minarets, phallic, II, 5.
Mind: can create objective forms, I, 62; influence of, over body, 216; and matter, 341, 387; of man & Supreme Mind, xiii; receives indelible impressions, 311; universal, as God, 289; Divine, II, 506.
Mineral: deposits and springs, I, 162; magnetized by man, 209; occult properties in, and plants, II, 589-90.
Minerva: II, 36; Proclus' invocation to, 123.
Miniature, sized *Iliad*, I, 240.
Minucius Felix (2nd-3rd c. A.D.), accuses Christians, II, 333.
Miracles: as natural forces, I, 128; at Lourdes, 120; and credulity, 119; exhibit hidden laws, 512; and God, 119; human testimony of divine, 120; Hume & Wallace on, 421-22; impossible, 340-41; and Jansenists, 119fn.; and mesmerism, 129; Mill on, 402-03; no transgression of natural law, v; *divine*, impossible before theurgists, II, 253; and facts, 304; and indecent practices, 332-33; and meipo, 159fn.; modern challenge to Church, 22-23; none in nature, 587; of Apollonius, 97; performed by *Sepher Yetzirah*, 357; Plato on, 344; Spain & Italy hotbeds of, 19; and the Word, 370; unconscious & at will, 351 & fn.; why no Church— in Russia & Poland, 17-18.
Miraculous conception, legend of Buddhism, II, 504.
Miriam, had several children, II, 537.
Mirror(s): in port of Alexandria, I, 528; magic, 468, 596 & fn.; II, 631-32.
Mirville, J. E.de (1802-73), and des Mousseaux demonstrate unseen universe, II, 15.
—— *Pneumatologie*, I, 101.
—— *Question des esprits:* on Babinet & tables, I, 106; on Faraday & tables, 63; on Gasparin, 100; on globular lightning, 107, 108; on Houdin, 73, 101; on manifestations of Cideville, 106; on Rayer & de Lamballe, 102; on theories of adversaries of Spiritualism, 116; on Thury's ideas, 112-113; on will, 109.
*Mishnah* (pl. *Mishnayôth*). See *Talmud*.
Missionaries: abusive, II, 577; advised how to teach Orientals, 577-79; caused Mutiny of 1857, 476; cause of failure of, 553; consider heathen damned, 474; deceive & despoil Hindus, 532fn.; denounced by Abbé Dubois, 532; Hindus' reply to Margil, 573; and Kublai-Khân, 581-82; lose to Buddhist punghis, 559; O'Grady on the, 475-76; picnics of, 586; slander heathen, 347.
Mitchel, O. M'Knight (1809-62), on ancient Egyptian astronomical skill, I, 521, 533.
Mitchell, Mrs. I. C., Col. Olcott's sister, I, [7].
Mitchell, S. L. (1764-1831), "On Two-Headed Serpents," I, 393.
Mithras, Mithra (Μιθρας): I, 156; II, 223; as Messiah, II, 504; degraded to a devil, 488; rites of, 491; triple god, 46; and Yazatas, 221.
Mithraism: initiation in, II, 351-52; 485; Julian and, 566.
Mithridates, I, 531.
Mitra, Pyârichânda (1814-1883), "The Psychology of the Âryas," II, 592-93.
—— "A Buddhist's Opinions, etc.," II, 597.
—— *On the Soul*, etc., II, 592-93.
Mitrophan of Voronezh, St., (1623-1703), II, 17.
Mizraim, II, 426.
Mnevis, and Hermes, I, 407.
Mnizurin (Μνιζουριν), stone, I, 321.
Mobeds, I, xxxiv, 25.

Mochus: I, 7; Theogony of, 56; and Pythagoras, II, 338.
Models, space filled with, of things, I, 116.
Moderatus (ca. 50-100 A.D.), on Pythagorean numerals, II, 300.
Moeris, artificial lake, I, 516.
Mogh, origin of word, I, xxxiv, 129.
Mohammed (570?-632): I, xliv, 119; II, 239, 582; not a god, II, 575; testimony of, about Jesus, 480.
Mohammedanism: I, 613; and chair of Peter, II, 25fn.; degenerated, 575; outgrowth of Christian cruelty, 53-54; why flourishes, 239. *See also* Moslems.
Mohldenhawer, II, 383.
Moigno, Abbé, François-N.-M. (1804-84), I, 336.
Mokhtana Boha-eddin, and Druzes, II, 308-09fn.
Moksha, II, 116, 566.
Molay, J. B. de (1250?-1314), and Templars, II, 381, 385.
Moldavia, evocations in, II, 569-70.
Molecular, motion and ether, I, 397.
Molecules, evolution of, I, 330.
Molinos, Miguel de (ca. 1640-1697), I, xxxvii.
Molitor, J. J. (1779-1860), *Philosophie der Geschichte*, etc.: on Mysteries & magic of Israel, I, 26; on Paracelsus, 52; II, 500.
Mollien, G. T. (1796-1872), *Voyage*, etc., on pigmies, I, 412.
Moloch-Hercules: Jews worshipped, II, 524, 525; sacrifices to, 11.
Monad: astral, & reincarnation, I, 351; evolutionary progress of, 302-03; generic meaning of Buddha, 291; goes thru subordinate kingdoms, 357; and lower forms of life, 352; of larvae re-enters terrestrial evolution, 357; Pythagorean, 212-13, 347, 507; and scintilla, 302; severance of, from lower vehicles, 315; and Tetraktys, 262, 507; fivefold & tenfold, II, 156; and numeral seven, 407.
Monas: I, xvii; II, 120, 407; and anima mundi, I, 316; evolves the Duad, 347; and Manas, 347-48fn.
Monasteries, Saturnalia in, II, 365-66.
Moncal, I, 188.
*Monde, Le* (Paris), on Pius IX, I, 27.
Money, genuine magicians spurn, I, 488.
Mongolians, and Scyths, I, 576; II, 263, 603.
Monkeys: exhibit intellect, I, 326; and peacocks, 136fn.; universal in symbolism, 564; and Westerners, 563.
Monks: defend filth, II, 511fn.; farce of Christian, 585; none in hell, 75; of Lybian Desert, 404.
Monogenês, name of Proserpine, II, 284.
Monotheism: of ancients, I, 24; of Plato, 287; of ancient systems, II, 219; of Jews recent only, 526.
Monsters: among snakes, I, 393; Fisher on, 390.
Montaigne, Michel E. de (1533-92), I, 621.
Montalboddo, Fracan da, *Paesi novamente retrovati*, etc., I, 652.
Montanes, II, 188fn.
Montanists, Wilder on the, I, xxxv.
Montesquieu, C. L. (1689-1755), *L'Esprit des Lois*, on witnesses, I, 87.
Montezuma (1480?-1520), I, 557.
Montfort, Simon IV de (1160-1218), II, 47.
Montpellier, Faculty of, I, 371.
Monuments, Heber on archaic, I, 351fn.
Moody, D. L. (1837-99): on his son, II, 250; and I. D. Sankey (1840-1908), 7.
Moon: action of, in animal magnetism, I, 264; influence on women, 264; and middle nature & color green, 514; myths about, 266; and oil of asbestos, 505; picture of, in Tibet, 441; tides, etc., 273; dynasty of, II, 438; phases of, & seven, 419; rites of Kurds at new, 630; and second death acc. to Plutarch, 284, 285; worshipped in Babylonia, 48.
Moor, E. (1771-1848), *The Hindoo Pantheon:* I, [16]; on Agni, II, 465; on Devakî & Mary, 95; on Nâga King, 539; picture of Viṭhobâ, 557.
Moore, Rev. Dunlop, on *Manu*, I, 585.
Moors: learned in alchemy, II, 19; skilled in magic, 59-60.
Mora, parsonage of, and burning of children, II, 503.
Morat, blood phenomenon and Lake, I, 413.
More, Henry (1614-87): believed in witchcraft, I, 205; commentaries on *Phaedo*, 139fn.; pious enthusiast, 308; role of, in writing *Isis Unveiled*, [31-32 & fn.].
—— *Antidote against Atheism*, on God & spirit, I, 206.
—— *Divine Dialogues*, I, [32].
—— *Letter to Glanvill:* on apparitions, I, 54-55; on Drummer of Tedworth, 123; on intelligent Beings, 74; on meaning of *witch*, 354-55; on *sheol ob*, 355; on

—— *The Immortality of the Soule:* on astral spirit of man, I, 206; on malformations of foetus, 385-86; on soul distinct from body, 574; q. Paramatus on child-monster, 399-400.

Moreau-Cinti, on genuine mediums, I, 359.

Morgan, Prof. de: I, 46, 54, 222, 245; on scientists, II, 8.

Morgan, murder of, II, 372.

Morin, Dr., I, 321.

*Morituri te salutant,* I, viii, 629.

Mormons, as Polytheists, II, 2.

*Morning Herald,* on suspended animation, I, 479.

Morse, S. F. B. (1791-1872): I, 234; Code of, and Crookes' phenomena, I, 303.

Morton, Dr. W. T. G. (1819-68), and the *Letheon,* I, 539, 540.

Morton, S. G. (1799-1851), *Crania Aegyptiaca,* etc., II, 437fn.

Morzine: I, 217; and Valleyres, II, 16.

Moses: at Sinai, I, 307; Egyptian priest, 555-56; in Egypt, 25; Josephus on, 436; knew the secrets of Egypt, 415; and magicians, 593-94; on man as made of earth & water, 389; secret knowledge of, 26; and serpent of brass, 542fn.; Books of, full of interpolations, II, 167; Bunsen on age of, 432; buried in Moab, 207; destruction of Books of, 470; ex-Egyptian priest, 216; godlike man, 153; and Hobab, 449; initiate, 129; initiated by Reuel, 551fn.; initiates Joshua, 43; laws of, borrowed from *Manu,* 431, 447; laws of, recent, 526; recounts his own death, 167; rod of, 393; and seven daughters, 551fn.; and story of Sargon, 442-43; Zipporah as wife of, 551fn.

Moses, Wm. Stainton (1839-92): and materializations, I, xxxvi; on weaknesses and needs of Spiritualism, II, 638.

Moses de García, and temple of Dagon, II, 258.

Moses Nachmanides (1194-1270), on the first Sephîrôth, II, 36.

Moses of Choren ( ?-489?), *Historiae Armeniacae,* etc., on Hindu learning, II, 27fn.

Mosheim, J. L. von (1694?-1755), *Institutes of Eccl. Hist.:* on views of Ammonius, I, 443-44; on Church & lies, II, 303; on Council of Nicæa, 251; on Druzes, 309; on Philo, 39; q. Ammonius on aim of Christ, 249-50.

Moslems: arms blessed by Pius IX, II, 560; and R. C. Church, 81-82; welcomed by Christians, 575. *See* Mohammedanism.

Môt, or Ilus, I, 342.

Mother: imagination of, & effect on embryo, I, 384-88, 390-91, 392, 394, 397-99, 400; mystic, 257; and matter, II, 270fn.; myth of, & child universal, 491; universal, 444.

Mothers: three, I, 257; in *Codex Nazar.,* 300.

Motion: molecular and ether, I, 397; perpetual, possible, 502.

Mouhot, A. H. (1826-1861), *Voyage,* etc., on Nagkon-Wat, I, 565.

Mounds, yield giant bones, I, 304-05.

Mountain, as symbol, I, 157.

Mousseaux. *See* Gougenot des Mousseaux.

Movable type in China, I, 513.

Movers, F. K. (1806-56), *Die Phönizier:* I, 577fn.; on Abraham & Saturn, 578; II, 216fn.; on Assyrian priest bearing name of his god, II, 554; on Horus & Logos, 56; on Iaô, 61; II, 139fn., 302, 417; on Plato's Nous, I, 55; on Theogony of Mochus, 56; on Typhon, 132; on ancient Triads, II, 48; on Azâzêl & Samael, 512 & fn.; on Chaldean Logos, 506; on Iacchos, 245; on Jehovah & Abram, 236; on Ophion, 512; on Saturn being Israel, 513fn.; on Son as emanation, 227; on the initiated, 130; on twelve gods, 448; on Typhon, 490fn.; on Xisuthros, 457.

Mṛityuloka, I, 148.

*MS. Ex. cod. reg. Gall. gr. No. 2390, fol. 154,* I, 30fn.

Mudalai, I, 383.

Muêsis (μύησις), initiation, II, 101.

Mufti of Aleppo, I, 362.

el-Mughtasilah, or Mandaeans, II, 291 & fn.

Muhurtas, and Kalâs, II, 464fn.

Muir, J. (1810-1862), *Original Sanskrit Texts,* etc., on Primal Essence, II, 274fn.

Mukti, II, 566.

Müller, A., *Die ältesten Spuren:* on age of paper, I, 535; on ancient bronze & iron, 589; on bronze age, 534fn.

Müller, F. Max (1823-1900): I, 248; critical of Whitney, II, 47; estimates number of religionists, 539; Jacolliot attacks, 261; on truth, 529.

—— *Chips from a German Workshop:* I, [16]; on Brâhmaṇas, 580, 582; on Buddha's shadow, 600-601; on creation of man, 558-59; on deeper meaning of exoteric legends, 442; on man's intellect and noble past, 4; on meaning of *Veda*, 354; on Nirvâṇa, 430; II, 432; on Occidental ignorance of Oriental literature, I, 442; on *Popol-Vuh*, 548-49; on religion as national property, 581; on Sanskrit MSS., 587; on sympathy between man & plants, 246; on widow-burning, 541fn., 589fn.; contradictory on *Vedas*, II, 414, 415, 416; confused, 416; on Abraham, 413fn.; on age of *Vedas*, 432; on Aśoka's inscription, 32; on Buddha's death, 342fn.; on Christianity, 10; on cipher being Arab, 300; on clergy & ancient beliefs, 345; on deeper meaning of Hindu myths, 430; on Devil, Pluto and Proserpine, 10-11; on discovering truth, 337; on disdain for death in India, 340; on Dyaus, 298; on Gushtasp, 141fn.; on Heathen gods & Fathers, 480; on Hindu gods as masks, 413; on Huc's ideas about Lamaism & R. Church, 345-46fn.; on India & Zoroastrianism, 143; on Laboulaye, 343; on moral code of Buddhism, 339; on Pâli Books of Ceylon, 576fn.; on Pârsî idea of punishment, 547fn; on Quichés' "hidden majesty," 344; on root *as*, 299; on science of religion & discovery of records, 26; on Self, 317-18fn.; on Vṛitra & Ahriman, 511; on Zend *h* & Skt. *s*, 220fn.; q. Confucius, 338.

—— *Ṛigveda-Saṃhitâ*, etc., I, xxixfn., xxxi, xxxii.
See also: *Contemporary Review* and *Trübner's Amer. & Oriental Lit. Record*.

Müller, J., I, 387.

Müller, K. O. (1797-1840), *Geschichte der griech. Literatur:* I, 56; on Iacchos, II, 245, 302; on Orphic Mysteries, 129.

Mummies: art of bandaging, I, 20, 539; finger-ring of a, 537; surgical skill in preparing, 539; symbol of human race, 297; alchemically prepared, II, 603.

Munk, S. (1803-1867), *Palestine,* etc.: on Essenes, II, 144, 145fn.; 196-97; on Galileans, 139; on Nazar & Nazireate, 131, 139.

Münther, "On the most Ancient Religion of the North, etc.," I, 19.

Münther, Bishop F. (1761-1830), *Noticia codicis graeci*, etc., II, 381.

Muratori, L. A. (1672-1750), and his cuirasse, I, 530.

Murder: condoned by Jesuits, II, 355, 358, 363, 372-73; obstacle to true initiation, 363.

Murderers: II, 13; after Cain, 448.

Murray, H. (1779-1846), *Historical Account,* etc., on Father Barri & heathen symbols, II, 554.

Muru, lamasery at Lhasa & spirit-intercourse, II, 616.

Musah, as a *revolutio,* II, 195, 447. See also Moses.

Musaeus, I, xxxiii; II, 130, 139.

Museo Gregoriano, II, 149.

Music: effect of, on vegetation, I, 514; and Hindu scale, 620; Kircher on healing power of, 215; magic, in desert, 604; and musical instruments in Egypt, 544; of the spheres, 275, 514; produced by magic, 65, 66; Saul cured by, 215; taming snakes by, 382-83.

Musion, and Hercules, I, 130fn., 132.

Muspelsheim (Old Norse: *Mûspellsheimr*), sphere of fire, I, 160.

Mut, as Isis, II, 209.

Mutiny: Indian, caused by missionaries, II, 476; and the British, 624.

Mycenae, I, 598.

Myé-nmo, Burmese for Mt. Meru, II, 232.

Myer, Isaac (1836-1902), *Qabbalah,* II, 649.

Mylitta, I, 579; or Ishtar, II, 171, 173.

Mysteries (τὰ μυστήρια): and animated statues, I, 614; concealed, xiifn.; cures in Egyptian, 531; def. xxxvii; degeneration of, 15; intercourse with invisible beings in, 95; knowledge imparted in, 22; and knowledge of electricity, 234-35; Lobeck on, xii; magnets & aërolites, 282; of magi, 556; of Samothrace, 132, 302; Philo on, 271fn.; Plato on, 132, 287; Plato taught in the, xii; purpose of, xiv; and Pyramid, 519; sublimer scenes of, in the night, xiv; taught heliocentric system, xiiifn.; Theon of Smyrna on, xiv-xv; universal, 561; very ancient, 234; appearance of gods in, II, 113; as old as world, 98; Cicero on, 167; Egyptian, little known, 362; esoteric doctrine of, 146; excluded criminals, 98; gradation of, 101, 115; Grecian, derived from Vedic rites, 91fn.; Greek term for, and death, 284; guarded in all religions, 99; mediumship debars from, 117-18; micra or minor, 108, 111-12; Mithraic, 351; not unfathomable, 121; of Israel & Jesus, 201-02; of magi never violated, 306fn.; Orphic, 129; Plotinus on visions in, 118; popular, at Byblus, 131; refused to Jacolliot, 262; some, superceded by others, 491-92; and transfer of life from hierophant to candidate, 563; two classes of participants in, 145; and underworld, 494; various sects as followers of theurgic, 144; veneration for, by ancients, 100; wine & bread in the, 561.

Mystery: and science, I, 337ff.; no, of Nature is inscrutable, 402; of ancient symbolism *must be* unveiled some day, 573; *one* turn of the key to the, given in *Isis*, II, 461.

Mystery-language: in Babylonia, II, 46; on Kumbum tree, 46.

Mystery-names, in Egypt, II, 368fn., 369.

Mystês (μύστης): one initiated, I, xl; II, 96, 111, 114.

Mystic, mother, I, 257.

Mystical, hidden meaning of, writers, I, 628.

Mystics, I, xxxvii. See also Mystês.

Mysticism, Oriental, I, 297.

Mythologies, concurrent design in, I, 152.

Myths: about double-sexed deities, I, 156; about moon, 266; allegorized truths, 122; a logos in every, 162; ancient, & natural facts, 261-62, 263; ancient, borrowed by Ch. Fathers, 298; Biblical, & Āryan mixed, 569; similarity of, 578; similarity of American & Biblical, 588; similarity of Russian & Mexican, 550; universality of, & Bible, 570; vehicles of great truths, xiii; absurd without key, II, 429; and allegories, euhemerized, 406; as method of teaching, 493, 576; Babrias on, 550; deeper meaning of Hindu, 430; and history, 431; identity of ancient, 438; of Israel history, 439-40; rejection of, by Christians, 431.

# N

N. brothers, travel with H.P.B. in Ladâkh, II, 599.

Naba, speak from inspiration, prophesy, II, 127, 132.

Nabae, to wander, II, 127.

Nabathaeans: II, 127, 135; similar to Nazarenes, 197.

*Nâbhânedishṭha Hymn*, I, xxxix.

Nablus (anc. Shechem), II, 197.

Nachmanides. See Moses Nachmanides.

al-Nadîm [Muhammad ibn Ishâq al-Nadîm, 9th & 10th c.], *Fihrist al-'ulûm*, II, 650.

Nadir Shâh, II, 608.

Nâga(s): I, 448; II, 107, 234; and Apollonius, II, 434; and Nagual, 509fn.; of Kashmîr converted to Buddhism, 608; of Magadha, 484; with cross on breast, 539.

Nâga-râjâ, I, 448.

Nagkon-Wat (Angkor Vat): I, 239; 561ff.; and Kabiri, 569; origin of, 566.

Nagual, I, 556.

Nagualism: II, 572, 573; secret, I, 557.

Nahardea, College of, II, 207.

Nahash, brazen serpent, II, 165.

Nahuatl, language and radical *a*, *atl*, I, 591.

Naiḥśreyasa, and initiation, II, 566.

Nain. See Tillemont.

Nakedness, of natives, II, 346.

Name(s): and Brahmātmā, II, 398-99; ineffable, 153, 289, 368fn., 401, 409; in heart of every man, 343; mirific, 344, 450; mystery, in Egypt, 368fn., 369; power of, 370; sacred, and Moses, 398; vocalization of mystery—, 400.

Nammada-Nârada, II, 509.

Nampûtiris, Chief of, II, 138fn.

Nandi, bull of Śiva, and Apis, II, 235-36.

Napier, Sir Chas. J. (1782-1853), I, 225, 477.

Naples, bas-relief at, of God as a serpent, II, 492fn.

Napoleon, B. (1769-1821): I, 538; and Alexander as reflexed images of former types, 35; and ancient principles of war, 612; killed Inquisition, II, 22.

Nara: as Father-Mother, II, 268; as Sephîrâh, 214; and Nârî, 111, 174, 210; and Svayambhû, 214, 215; Svâyambhuva—, & mother-principle, 226; or Holy Ghost, 267.

Nârada: I, 585; on ignorance and knowledge, 628.

Nârâyaṇa, II, 214, 267; Brahmâ as, I, 91.

Nârî: androgyne, II, 268; immortal virgin, 226; or Yâmî, 234.

Nasr-Allah, and Druze scriptures, II, 309.

Nasse, on projection of double, I, 477.

National Ass'n of Spiritualists, II, 596fn.

*National Geographic*, I, 656; II, 659.

*National Quarterly Review:* on Carthage, I, 520; on Phoenicians, 545; on thinkers and scientists, 249ff.
Nattig, with eagle's head, II, 231.
*Natura naturans,* II, 40.
Natural Selection: I, 296; philosophy and magic, 235.
Nature: affected by man's atmosphere, I, 211; as temple, 426; ensouled, 207; ever progressing, 296; forces of, personified by ancients, 261-62; forward march of, 481; man and, 501; "mother that makes many things," 257; never leaves work unfinished, 345-46; pervaded by intelligent will, 58; picture-gallery of, 184-85, 186; reveals all arts, 424-25; secrets of, 513; seven powers in, 466; two eternal qualities in, 12-13; first principles of, may be considered as gods, II, 406; physical, & evolution of man, 279; servant of magician, 590; triune, 587-88.
Nature-Spirits: I, 326, 349, 357, 362; influenced by superior intelligences, 325; or cosmic elementaries, 325; physical phenomena produced by, 320; role of, in animating statues, 616.
*Nature, La* (Paris), Flammarion on Jesuit heliolatry, II, 450-51fn.
Naudé, G. (1600-1653), *Apologie,* etc., I, 207.
Naumachius (2nd c. A.D.), historian, I, 364.
Nauscopite, I, 240.
Nautches, rarely seen, II, 613.
Navarette, F. ( ? -1689), *Tratados históricos,* etc., on Sanpao idol, II, 49.
Navel: mystic nature of, and second sight, I, xxxix; corresponds to the ark, II, 444; of Jesus, 71.
Nazar(s): ascetic initiates, II, 130ff.; belonged to pagan mysteries, 140; Hindostânî meaning of, 142; long hair of, 90; meaning of, 128, 134; or prophets, 129; prophets were, and initiates, 525; similar to *mag,* 142.
Nazara, II, 131.
Nazarân, II, 142.
Nazaratus, II, 140.
Nazar-bandî, II, 142.
Nazarene(s), Nazarean(s): I, 300fn.; anti-Bacchus sect, II, 129; cosmogony of, 174-75, 187fn., 224, 225, 227-29, 247, 295-96; derived from Chaldean theurgy, 134; hated orthodox Jews, 131; Jesus a, 151; and John the Baptist, 204, 290ff.; kept religious tenets secret, 190; location of, 181, 289; oldest, were Kabalists, 132, 133; on Jordan, 139; or al-Mughtasilah, 291 & fn., 650-51; Paul a, 137; Peter a, 127, 181; similar to Nabathaeans, 197; stellars of, 234; and Templars, 382 & fn.; three lives of, 226; trinities of, 227-29; wore hair long, 140.
Nazareth, II, 128fn., 133, 134, 137, 150, 151.
Nazaria, II, 131, 133, 134, 137, 144, 151.
Na-zaruan, Ancient of Days, II, 142.
Nazireate, II, 139.
Neander, J. A. W. (1789-1850), *Allgemeine Geshichte,* etc., II, 161fn.; 644; on Manichaeans' view of Jesus, 286.
Nebiah, a clairvoyant, I, xxxvii.
Nebipoel, one possessing magic powers, I, xxxvii.
Nebo (or Nebu): god of wisdom, I, xxxvii; oracular wisdom, II, 43; or Mercury, 132, 296 & fn.
Nebuah, seership, soothsaying, I, xxxvii.
Nebuchadrezzar, I, 261.
Nebular Theory, ancient, I, 238.
Necessity: circle of, I, 296, 303, 346; and Law, 420-21; man a toy of, 276.
Nechapso, King, II, 295fn.
Necho: canal of, I, 517; fleet of, 542; King of Egypt, 406.
Necromancy: condemned by ancients, I, 492-93; universally diffused, 205.
Needham, J. T. (1713-81), and Buffon, I, 414.
Nègre, Jacques de, II, 380.
Negroes, and Masonry, II, 391.
Neith, celestial virgin with child, II, 50, 209.
Neleus, I, 320.
Neocoris (νεωκόροι), second degree, II, 364.
Neophyte: II, 93; sacred sleep of, I, 357-58.
Neo-Platonism: II, 32, 33; doomed to destruction when sided with Aristotle, 252; end of, 53; greatness of, at its end-period, 41; in early Christianity, 84-85; and Oriental Kabala, 34, 41; teachers of, not mediums, 118.
Neo-Platonists, remnant group of, fled to Persia, I, 436, 646.
Nephesh: I, xli, 181; and blood, II, 244; sentient life-principle, 362 & fn.
Nephilim, I, 559; II, 217, 218.
Neqebah, sheath, II, 270.

Nergal; I, 556; human-headed lion, II, 231.
Nergal-Sharezer, I, 556.
Nerig, or Mars, II, 296.
Nero: ring of, I, 240; II, 24fn.; murders Agrippina, 363.
Neros(es): I, 31; errors in calculating by, 33-34; great, 33; secret cycles, II, 272.
Nervous disorders: at Spiritualistic circles, I, 343; and mediumism, 117; specialty in Egypt, 529, treated by music, 544.
Netubto, II, 296.
Netzaḥ, II, 186, 213.
Neubauer, A. (1832-1907), *Catalogue of the Hebrew MSS.*, etc., II, 654.
*New American Cyclopaedia* (Appleton's): II, 614fn.; on Manu, I, 587; on Druzes, II, 311.
*New Century Path* (Point Loma, Calif.), & *Isis Unv.*, I, [56].
Newcome, Archbishop, II, 178.
*New Era* (New York), I, 83fn.
New Jersey, Negroes burnt for witchcraft at, II, 18fn.
*New Testament:* and *Book of the Dead*, I, 518; II, 548; age of, II, 42; compared with ancient precepts, 338, 556; disfigured, 507; Erasmus', 177.
Newton, Sir I. (1642-1727): I, x, 98; gravitation of, 271 & fn., 281; and light, 281; on Paul's text, II, 178.
—— *Mathematical Principles,* on universal agent, I, 177-78.
—— *Opera omnia:* ed. by Horsley falsified, II, 177; withheld theory for 17 years, 637.
Newton, Bishop J. (1725-1807), II, 120, 233.
—— *Review of Eccl. Hist.* (implied), on Paganism & Popery, II, 29.
Newton, John R., American healer, I, 165, 217, 218; II, 23.
*New York Advocate,* and Sotheran, II, 388.
*New York Tribune,* I, 3, 21.
Nicæa, Council of: II, 257; and Gospels, II, 251-52.
Nicaragua, and de Avila, I, 592.
Nicephorus (ca. 758-829), *Stichometria,* II, 182fn.
Nicholas of Basel ( ?-1397), I, xxxvii.
Nicodemus, I, 132.
Nicolaitans, accused of heresy, II, 329, 333.
Nicolas, II, 189fn.
Nicolini, G. B. (1782-1861), *History of the Jesuits:* on Jesuit constitutions, II, 354; on Saturnalia in monasteries, 365-66.
—— *Hist. of the Pontificate of Pius IX,* II, 365fn.
—— *The Life of Father A. Gavazzi,* II, 365fn.
Nifelheim (Old Norse: *Niflheimr*), as Mist-Region, I, 147.
Nihaṅg, I, 383fn.
Nikiforovitch, I, 477.
Nîlgiri, and the Tôdas, II, 613, 615.
Nimbus: and highly-developed men, I, 487; Mousseaux on, II, 512; and tonsure as solar emblems, 94.
Nimrod: I, 150; as Bacchus, 568.
Nimrud, lens found at, I, 240.
Nin, I, 551.
Nineveh: destruction of, I, 403; size of, 241.
Ninevites, I, 552.
Ninus, and Bel, I, 551-52.
Nirguṇa, II, 539.
Nirvâna: I, xviii, 242, 243fn., 290; II, 280, 282, 319, 566; def., I, *290-91, 346;* II, *116-17, 286;* real meaning of, I, 430-31, 626; Jacolliot on, II, 533; Müller on, 432; not annihilation, 320, 533; ocean to which all religions tend, 639.
Nisan, II, 165.
Nisard, D. (1806-1888), *Pétrone,* etc., I, 644.
Nissa, and Sinai, II, 165.
Nisus, Thyônê and Bacchus, II, 560fn.
Nitria, Desert, traditions in, II, 27.
Nivṛitti, I, 243fn.
Nizir, II, 423fn.
Noah (or Nuah): I, 25, 149-50, 554, 593; II, 195, 244; Adam as prototype of, II, 449; as *revolutio* of Adam, 447; as spirit of waters, 451; borrowed from Egypt, 447; and deluge, 422; and dove, 448fn.; esoteric meaning of, 423-24; and Iron Age, 443; and Lamech, 466; Lenormant on, 423, 424; and Manu, 271fn.; should have been washed overboard, 435; stands for Pisces and Adam, 465; stands for Svayambhû, 443; and Vaivasvata, 425, 428; and Zodiacal trigons, 460.
Nobili, Leopold (1784-1835), I, 188.
Noerô (νοερῷ), intellectual, I, 56.
Noêtikon (νοητικόν), intellectuality, I, 432.
Noêtos (νοητός), intelligible, I, 56.
Nogent, Guibert de (1053-1124), and the Savior's tooth, II, 71.

## INDEX

Nokeb, meaning of, II, 400-01.
Nonna, as a term, II, 95.
Nonnains, epidemic of the, I, 374.
Nonnus (5th c. A.D.), *Dionysiacs:* on Bacchus & Aura Placida, I, 160; on Korê & Zagreus, II, 505.
Norberg, M. (1747-1826), *Codex Nazaraeus:* I, 570, 580, 582; on Bahâk-Ziwa & creation of Adam, 298; 299-300; on Karabtanos, 300, 301; age of, II, 135fn.; on Bahâk-Ziwa, 134; on creation of material worlds, 175 & fn.; on Ebionites, 181; on Ferho, 224; on Gabriel & Hibil-Ziwa, 154, 204, 247; on Gate of House of Life, 245; on Iurbo-Adunai, 185fn.; on Jesus, 132; on Jews as Abortive, 190; on John Abo Sabo, 203, 204; on John the Baptist, 135; on Mano & Ferho, 174; on Nazara, 131; on Nazarene pantheon, 228-29; on Pthahil & Abathur, 229-30; on role of Christ, 154; on Seven Lives, 234; on seven stellars, 187fn., 296; on seven vines, 244; on Spiritus & stellars, 193; on Tobo & Adam, 517; on worship of Adunai, 131.
—— *Onomasticon:* II, 132fn.; on Par'ha, 294fn.
Nork, F. N. (pseud. of Selig Korn, 1803-50), *Biblische Mythologie,* on Saoshyant, II, 237.
—— *Hundert und eine Frage:* on Greek tr. of Hebrew books, II, 247; on King Messiah, 244.
Norns, I, 151-52.
Norris, Rev. H. H. (1771-1850), *The Principles of the Jesuits,* II, 353ff.
*North American Review, The* (Fiske), I, 521, 525.
Northern, Homer on, days and nights, I, 545, 549.
Nostradamus, M. (1503-1566), I, 260, 641.
Nothing, as *not a thing,* I, 292.
*Notice . . . de l'Académie du Gard* (La Boëssière), on Juno temple & lightning, I, 527.
Noumena, and nous, II, 283.
Nourishment, through magnetic forces in nature, I, 169.
Nous (νοῦς): I, xii, xiii, xiv, xli, 55, 139fn.; God-Mind, 131, 317; or pneuma, 401fn.; and thumos, 429; and anoia, II, 286; in Basilides, 156, 157; of Anaxagoras & Nout, 282; or rational soul, 279; Plutarch on, 283-84.

Nout, Divine Spirit, II, 282, 297fn.
*Nouveau Journal Asiatique* (Paris), II, 114fn.
Nozari, II, 128, 133.
Nuah. *See* Noah.
Nubia, rock-temples of, I, 542.
Numa Pompilius (715-673 B.C.): I, 238fn.; books of, 24-25, 527; built temple of Vesta, 159; esoteric learning of, 527.
Numbers: and ancient structures, I, 572; doctrine of, xv-xvi, xxi; and double evolution, 9; esoteric combinations of, 7; and mantras, 9; and Pythagoras, xv, 7; II, 409; in *Vedas,* II, 411; and origin of decimal notation, 300-01; and prototypes in world of causes, 269fn.; represent philosophical ideas, 407.
*Numbers:* I, 558; II, 139, 481fn.; on angel of Lord as Satan, II, 485fn.; on Hobab, 449; on long hair of nazars, 151; on Nazarenes, 133; on nazars, 131; on seven, 405; on sons of Anak, 450; on sun- & serpent-worship, 129.
Numerals: Porphyry on Pythagorean, I, 35; spiritual, 514; King on Pythagorean, II, 300.
Nummulitic limestone, and Pyramid, I, 519.
Nun: Joshua son of, I, 545, 551; Egyptian term, II, 95.
Núñez de la Vega, F., *Constituciones,* etc., on Nin & Tzendales, I, 551.
Nuns, of various virgin-mothers, II, 210.
Nyagrodha, plant, I, xl.
*Nychthêmeron* (Νυχθήμερον), symbolism of, II, 467, 468.
Nys (or Nysa): as Sinai & Dionysos, II, 165, 526; Mt. in India, 560fn. *See also* Nissa.

## O

Oak, sacred, I, 297-98.
Oannes: man-fish, I, 349; II, 257, 457; or Dagon, I, 133, 154; emblem of esoteric wisdom, II, 458; four, or suns, 467.
Oath: Sodalian, I, 409; Jesuitical views of, II, 373; and personal responsibility, 374; and Peruvians, 374fn.
Ob: I, 489, 594; as astral light, 158.
*Obadiah,* II, 440.
Obeah: I, 81, 361, 488, 494; women and snakes, 483.
Obelisk, moving, in Egypt, I, 519.

Obongos, I, 412.
O'Brien, H. (1808-1835), *Round Towers of Ireland:* built by Buddhists, II, 290fn.; on cross at Tuam, 538.
*Observer* (London), on Aurangâbâd & Ajanta, I, 349-51.
Obsession(s): I, 276, 355-56, 374; and mediumship, 488, 490; and possession, II, 16.
Occult: colleges of, sciences, I, 482; forces & animated statues, 485; Porta on, powers, 66; powers the same, but directing intelligences differ, 492; properties of plants & minerals, 466; II, 589; property of protoplasm to differentiate, I, 420; protection of pure natures, 460; fraternities, II, 306-08; powers by inheritance, 635-36.
Occultism: ABC of, I, 243; physical or therapeutics, 19; psychomatics of, *344;* practical of *Zohar,* II, 350; and Spiritualists, 636.
Occultist, I, *xxxvii;* II, 400.
Ocean-beds, disturbed, I, 31.
Ocosingo, and keystone, I, 571.
Od, as universal agent, I, 125, 146, 158, 163, 594.
Odic, or psychic force, I, 67.
Odin (Old Norse: Ōthinn): I, 19, 160; meaning of, 151-52.
Odoric, Friar (ca. 1286-1331), on "flowing sands" or Reg Ruwán, I, 605.
Odors, and fragrances produced by magic, I, 65, 66.
Oersted, H. Chr. (1777-1851): and magnetic needle, I, 104; and Paracelsus, 164; on laws of nature, 506-07.
Oetinger, F. C. (1702-1782), *Thoughts on the Birth,* etc., on form retained in ashes, I, 476.
Offenbach, Jacques (1819-80): Calchas of, II, 7; Gen. Boum of, 378.
Ogdoad, II, 410.
O'Grady, W. L. D., "Indian Sketches, etc.": II, 475; on evils of drink in India, 574; on missionaries in India, 532; on phenomena of fakirs, 629; on Tôḍas, 614.
Oida (οἶδα), I know, I, 354.
Oil: and Essenes, II, 133fn.; monuments anointed with, 134.
Olam: I, 56; II, 266; or Chronos, I, 132; as Aiôn, II, 216; does not mean eternity, 12; immortal Ego effused from, 218; or Eilam, 217; ——Ach, 468.

Olcott, Col. Henry Steel (1832-1907), art. in *Daily Graphic,* I, 635.
—— *Old Diary Leaves:* I, [2fn.], [3], [4-5], [7-8], [8-9], [12fn.], [14-21], [24-25], [26-33], [34], [34fn.], [39fn.], [40fn.], [54], [55], [60-61], 633, 640; II, 645.
—— *People from the Other World:* on materialized squirrel, I, 329; on pole-climbing feat, 495; and Spiritualistic phenomena, 635.
Oldham, J. (1653-1683), *Satires upon the Jesuits,* etc., II, 55.
"Old Parr" (Thos. Parr, 1483-1635), II, 564.
*Old Testament:* age of, II, 469-70fn.; allegorical, 493; compared to *Atharva-Veda,* 556; disfigured, 265, 431, 467; immoral without esoteric key, 413fn., 430; no real history in, 441; oldest MSS. of, 430 & fn., 443; origin of, 135; revelation of a subordinate deity, 169; Satan in, 481; starting point of, 175; translators made jumble of, 362fn.
Oliver, Rev. Dr. Geo. (1782-1867), on Masonry, II, 389.
Olmstead, D. (1791-1859), on auroras, I, 418.
Olshausen, H. (1796-1839), *Biblischen Commentar,* etc., on age of N.T., II, 42.
—— *Nachweis der Echtheit,* etc., on Gospel of Matthew, II, 182fn.
Olybius, Maximus, I, 227.
Olympic, gods relate to physics, etc., I, 261.
Olympiodorus (2nd c. B.C.), *On the Phaedo of Plato,* on phantasy & seership, II, 591-92.
Omniscience: and instinct, II, 587; of the spirit and astral light, 588.
Omphalos (ὀμφαλός), I, xxxixfn.
On-ati, II, 500.
One: in three, I, 258; Higher, of Hebrews, II, 210; only good, 238, 413; and ten, 298.
Onkelos: II, 400; and *Pentateuch,* 207; *Targûm* of, 244, 247fn.
Only-begotten sons, II, 171, 176, 205.
Onnofer, Nofer [Un-nefer] as Chrêstos, II, 324.
Ookshan, and Pâlistân, II, 439fn.
Ootacamund, II, 614.
*Open Court, The,* II, 645.
Ophanim, wheels of creation, II, 268.

Ophiogenes, in Cyprus have power over reptiles, I, 381.
Ophiomorphos (ὀφιόμορφος); and Ialdabaôth, II, 184, 206; symbol of matter, 225, 449.
Ophion, II, 512.
Ophis (ὄφις): as Adam-Kadmon, II, 225; as Agathodaimôn, 293, 295; —Christos, 449; divine wisdom, 172, 225, 449; and Lord Jordan, 295; same as Chnuphis & Christos, 187; and Sophia-Akhamôth, 185.
Ophites: priests of, named after their gods, I, 550; accused of licentious rites, II, 325; and Adonai, 190fn.; cosmogony of, 187-88; cosmogony of, comp. to Nazarene, 295-96; eucharist of, 513; and Jews, 206; origin & teachings of, 168ff., 293ff.; or Levites, 129, 481fn.; rejected O.T., 147; serpent of, as wisdom, 223, 484; true teachings of, preserved, 221; two serpents of, 225; worship transmuted into Christian symbolism, 505.
Oporinus, accuses Paracelsus, I, 164.
Opsopäus, Johannes (1556-1596), *Oracula Sibyllina*, etc.: I, 56, 251; on Divine Triad, II, 48.
Optics, advanced, of ancients, I, 240.
Optomai (ὄπτομαι), to be an overseer, II, 91.
Or: meaning of, I, 158; as light, II, 266.
Orabio, and Inquisition, II, 59.
Oracles, and sacred sleep of neophyte, I, 358.
Oracular, heads, II, 56.
Orange, Prince of, I, 378.
Orangoutang, brain capacities of, I, 326.
Orant, Egyptian, II, 446, 655.
Orbiney, Papyrus d', I, 403.
Orcus, I, 299.
Ordóñez y Agiar, D. Damón de, *Historia del cielo y de la tierra*, I, 650.
Organisms, living animal, cannot be disintegrated, II, 589.
Oribasius, I, 89.
Oriental: Occidentals ignorant of, literature, I, 442; fundamental propositions of, philosophy, II, 58ff.
Orientals, acute senses of, I, 211.
Orientalists: Jacolliot on errors of, I, 583; assumptions & denials of, II, 322-23; disagreement of, about Sanskrit, 47; misjudge Indian metaphysics, 103.
Origen (185?-254?): I, 316; believed in metempsychosis, 12; on daemons, 353; on Moses' secret knowledge, 26; fails to answer Celsus, II, 51.
— *Comm. in Epist. B. Pauli ad Romanos*, on threefold nature of man, II, 285.
— *Comm. in Evang. Joannis*, on female Holy Ghost, II, 267fn.; 357, 505, 650.
— *Comm. in Matthaeum*, on Rev. of Elias, II, 248.
— *Contra Celsum*: I, xxxiifn.; on Brahmans curing by words, 444; Celsus' views of Jesus & magic, II, 148; on Ophite cosmogony, 221.
— *De principiis*: denies perpetuity of Hell, II, 13; mentions no descent into Hell, 514; on Be-rêshîth, 35; on forgiveness of devils, 238fn.
— *Homiliae in Lucam*, on John the Baptist, II, 204.
Originals, Wilder on, II, 567.
Orioli, A. & F., *Fatti relativi a mesmerismo*, etc.: on cures by words, I, 444; on power of mesmerist, 142.
Ormazd: I, 274; II, 36; and Ahriman, II, 237; and Zeruana, 221. See also Ahura-Mazda.
Orohippus: I, 411; Eocene, and Huxley, 74.
Orosius, P. (*fl.* 413-415), *Historiarum adversus Paganos*, etc., on Serapeion, II, 29fn., 642.
Orpheus ('Ορφεύς): I, 24, 263; II, 536, 539; as healer, I, 532; on cycles, 294fn.; on lodestone, 265; on nature, 257; brought Bacchic Mysteries from Edessa, II, 550; came from India, 130, 561; descends into underworld, 514 & fn.; meaning of fate of, 129-30; tawny-colored, 561fn.
Orphic, line on sixth race in Plato, I, 8.
*Orphic Hymn*, on Hercules, I, 132; II, 123.
Orphikoi ('Ορφικοί or 'Ορφεῖοί), II, 129, 553.
Orphism, II, 35, 129.
Orphnos (ὀρφνός), and Orpheus, II, 561fn.
Osarsiph, or Moses, I, 555.
Osborne, Lord Wm. G. (1804-1888), *Court and Camp of Runjeet Sing*, on burial of fakir, I, 477-78.
*Oscillatoria rubescens*, I, 413.
Oshaia, Rabbi, II, 357.
Oshêdar-Bâmî, II, 467.
Oshêdar-Mâh, II, 467.
Osiris: I, 93, 156, 555; eye of, as sun,

506; nature of, 262; one with Typhon & Apollo, 550; as the sun, II, 517; cut into fourteen pieces, 487; and Dionysos, 165; or Hisir, 478; Indian origin of, 438; in scene of Judgment, 493-94; and Isis, 268fn.; Pococke on, 435-36; and Serapis, 491; and Śiva & Jehovah as active principles in nature, 402; and Typhon, 507; worship of, pre-Menite, 361.
Osiris-Horus, and Virgin Mary, II, 173, 268fn.
Osthanes, a magi, I, 641; II, 88, 361, 645.
O'Sullivan, Hon. J. L.: H.P.B. receives from, Jacolliot's works, I, 594fn.; letter from, on magical séance in Paris, 608-11.
Oudet, Dr., on magnetic sleep and insensibility, I, 166-67fn.
Ouranos (Οὐρανός): father of Saturn, I, 267, 578; Kronos maiming, II, 429.
Ou-Tay, lamasery of, II, 603, 658.
Over-Soul, and Nature, I, 426.
Ovid (43 B.C.-17 A.D.), *Fasti:* on Jupiter, I, 527; on Dione & Typhon, II, 490; on heaven's perpetual axis, 405.
—— *Metamorphoses,* on Medea, II, 376.
—— [Source unknown]: on manes, anima & umbra, I, 37.
Ovule, becomes independent of mother, I, 401.
Ovum, evolution of, I, 389.
Owen, R. D. (1801-77), I, 245, 334, 603.
—— *The Debatable Land,* on worship of words, II, 560.
Ox: and Ookshan, II, 439fn.; sacrificed at Bacchic Mysteries, 524fn.
Oxus, tribes of, II, 439fn.
Oxygen: Cooke on, I, 464; and hydrogen known to Rosicrucians, 52fn.
Ozarim, Essene initiates, I, 507; II, 42. 154.

P

Padma-Sambhava, I, 599.
Paganism: ancient wisdom replete with Deity, II, 639; def. *179fn.;* in Christianity, 49, 80-81.
Pagan: custodians of, lore, act when timely, II, 26fn.; Tillemont on, 8.
Pagodas, built as a cross, II, 382fn.
Pa'had, II, 213.
"Palace of Love," II, 280.
Palaśa, flower, I, 438.

Palenque: I, 545, 571, 572; bas-reliefs of, 553.
Palestine: domain of Seth, II, 482 & fn.; origin of word, 439fn.
Paley, I, 511.
Pâli, books of Ceylon, II, 576fn.
*Pâli-Buddhistical Annals:* on learning of Buddha, II, 552; on Mâyâdevî, 555.
Pâli-shepherds, and Hyksôs, I, 569, 578; II, 439fn.
Palindromia (παλινδρομία), returning back to mortal bodies, II, 280.
Pâlistân, II, 439fn.
Palissy, Bernard de (1510-1589), I, 85, 404.
Palît, human phantom, II, 107.
Pallas, on Banyan colony, II, 474fn.
Pallegois, J. B., *Description du royaume Thai,* etc., I, 565.
Pallium, or stole, a feminine sign, II, 94.
Palm, Baron de: I, [36], 585.
Palmistry, Jesuits on, II, 354.
Pamphilius, and Caesarea library, II, 181.
Pan, festivals of, adopted by Christianity, II, 51.
Panchen-Rimpoche [Tib.: *pan-chhen rin-po-chhe,* Precious Jewel of Learning], II, 618.
Panciroli, G. (1523-99), I, 226, 639.
—— *Rerum memorabilium,* on perpetual lamp, I, 228.
Pancoast, J. (1823-1889), *Blue and Red Light,* etc., on Pythagoras, II, 289.
Pandora, I, 488.
Pangenesis, of Darwin, I, 14.
Pantheism, I, 152.
Pantheon, Grecian, contained Egyptian gods, I, 543.
Panthera (Pandira), II, 386fn.
Papacy, danger of scientific, I, 403.
Paper, art of preparation, I, 529.
Papias (1st & 2nd c. A.D.): did not know St. John, II, 327; and *Gospel of Matthew,* 204.
Pappus, Joh. (1549-1610), *Libellus synodicus,* etc., on choosing of Gospels at Nicæa, II, 251.
Papyri: as old as Menes, I, 529; hide truth to be revealed by intuition, 16; and tile-libraries, 403.
Parables, in work of Jesus, II, 145.
Parabrahman: I, 91; nature of, II, 266, 270.
*Parabrahman, aham eva,* II, 262.
Paracelsus, P. T. (1490?-1541): founder of

School of Animal Magnetism, I, 164; v. Helmont on, 406-07fn.; homunculi of, 465; on healing, 217; on identity of men & stars, 168; on imagination, faith & will, 57; II, 597-98; on influences upon germinal development, I, 314; on magnetism of ill health, 164; on sidereal light, xxvi; on sleep & astral body, 179; on study of nature, 164; opinions about science of, 52; re-discovered hydrogen, 52fn., 169, 192; ridiculed, 168; used secret terms, 191; cured possessed, II, 625; initiated alchemist, 349; on magic & clergy, 500; on occult power of blood, 567; "sleeps in his grave," 500.
—— *Archidoxa*, etc., on concealed power of magnets, I, 168.
—— *De ente astrorum*, I, xxvi, 168.
—— *De ente Dei*, I, 168.
—— *De ente spirituali*, on stars as a shell, I, xxvi.
—— *Opera omnia*: on astral body & dreams, I, 170; on man as product of three worlds, 212; on powers of inner man & imagination, 361fn.; on salt, 148; on *mercurius vitae*, II, 620.
Paradinus, G. (1510-1590), I, 385, 645.
Paraeus (Ambroise Paré, 1517-90), I, 385, 645.
Paramâtman: or Para-Purusha, I, xvi; Universal Soul, II, 108, 463.
Para-Purusha, I, xvi.
Paraśu-Râma, II, 276.
Paravidyâ, secret prayer, II, 565fn.
Parchment, durability of, I, 529.
Parḥa Rabba, II, 294fn.
Pariahs, or Chaṇḍâlas, and origin of Jews, II, 438.
Paris, and Helen, similar to Râvaṇa and Sîtâ, I, 566.
Pâris, Abbé François de (1690-1727): I, 369; phenomena at tomb of, 372.
Parker, Dr., II, 549.
Parker, Rev., on Protestants & Bible, II, 200fn.
Parkhurst, J. (1728-1797), *Hebrew and English Lexicon*: I, 140fn.; and first word in *Genesis*, II, 34.
Parmenides (5th c. B.C.), I, 24; II, 410.
Parodi, Maria Teresa, I, 392.
Parr, Thos. (1483-1635), longevity of, II, 564, 656.
Pârsîs: I, xxxiv, xxxvi, 25, 443, 459; II, 135, 141, 390, 409, 441; on Dashtur or flame in navel, I, xxxix; ideas of, on punishment, II, 547fn.; inoculate Jews with horror for images, 149.
Partzuphim, Kabalistic Faces, II, 226
Pârvatî, II, 301.
Pase-Buddhu, ascetic, II, 599.
Pashai, or Udyâna, I, 599.
Pashley, Rob. (1805-59), on vampires, I, 450.
Pasquale de Franciscis, *Discorsi*, etc.: II, 4fn., 7, 379; on Virgin Mary, 110.
Pasquier, É. (1529-1615), *Le Catéchisme des Jésuites*, etc., on Squire & Walpole, II, 373fn.
Passports, to heaven, II, 243.
Pasteur, Louis (1822-95), I, 414.
Pastophoros (παστοφόρος), first degree, II, 364.
Patah, and Pytho, II, 491fn., 655.
Pâtâla, I, 148.
Patar: as interpreter, II, 93; and Petra, 392.
Patara, in Lycia, I, 331.
Pater (πατήρ), I, 271; II, 48.
Pateres (or pateras), II, 29.
Path, to liberation, II, 282.
*Path, The*: I, [46]; on New York Bldg. where *Isis Unv.* was written, [7], [9]; citing H.P.B. on writing *Isis*, [22-23], [55]; on interest from *Isis*, [56].
Paṭhâns, I, 351fn.
Patriarchs: symbolize races, I, 150; ages of the, & Hindu calculations, II, 464fn.; as antediluvian races, 466; as myths, 455; as Zodiacal Signs, 460; copied from ancient pantheons, 185; controversy about, 191; and Manu, 271fn.; and Prajâpatis, 413, 450, 459, 463; prediluvian, 463; and twelve gods, 448, 450-51.
Paul, St.: in garden of delight, I, xxxiiifn.; schismatic, xxx; as master-builder, II, 90; antagonism of Peter and, 84, 161, 161-62fn., 175-76, 179, 180; Christ of, as embodied idea, 574, 576; Cyril on, 146, 253; head of, shorn, 90; initiate, 89-90, 277, 574; Lucian on followers of, 331; Nazarene, 137; on Jesus as lower than angels, 37; on long hair, 140fn.; only real Apostle of Jesus, 241; on trine human entity, 281-82; real founder of Christianity, 574; real name of, 536fn.; and Seneca, 277; shared Gnostic views, 206-07; text of, on *theos*, 178; writings of, distorted, 536.
Paul III (1468-1549), Pope, I, 224, 228.

Paulicians, II, 325.
Paulin de Saint-Barthélemy, J. P. (1748-1806), *Voyage aux Indes Orientales,* on widow-burning, I, 541.
Pauly-Wissowa, *Real-Encyclopaedie,* I, 641; II, 645.
Pausanias (*fl.* ca. 150 A.D.), *Itinerary:* on perpetual lamp, I, 227, 231; on rites of magi, 130; on spirit-horses, 70; on Zeus, 125; on women-colleges, II, 524-25.
Pauthier, J. P. G. (1801- ? ), *La Chine,* on Confucius' precepts, II, 239.
Payens, Hugues des ( ? -ca. 1129), II, 381.
Pay'quina, and gold, I, 597, 598.
Pazen [Tib.: *spags-zen,* pr. in Lhasa as *pak-zeen*], II, 600fn.
Pearson, J. (1613-1686), *An Exposition of the Creed,* on descent into Hell, II, 514.
*Pedactyl equus,* I, 411.
Peebles, J. M. (1822- ? ), *Around the World:* on Egyptian geometry, I, 531; on Egyptian temples, 522; q. Mitchel on astronomy in Egypt, 520-21.
—— *Jesus: Myth, Man, or God,* II, 240.
Peh-ling, foreigner, becomes magician in Tibet, II, 618; def. *660.*
Peifam, curé of, and sorcery, II, 633.
Peisse, Dr. L. (1803-80), and transmutation, I, 505.
—— *La Médecine,* on alchemy, I, 508-09.
Pélissier, Jacques, kills birds by will, I, 380, 399.
Pella, refuge for early Christian community, II, 197.
Pengelly, Wm. (1812-1894), *Ancient Cave Men of Devon,* on meteoric iron in Egypt, I, 538.
Penotus (B. Georges Penot, 1522-1620), I, 504.
—— *Theatrum chemicum,* I, 647.
Pentacle, Vedic and Pythagorean, II, 451-53.
*Pentateuch:* compiled by Ezra, I, 578; age of, II, 433; a *purâna,* 492; destroyed in Jerusalem, 470; ethics of *Manu* higher than, 535; gross materialism in, 454fn.; not written by Moses, 167; of quite recent date, 526; Samaritan, more ancient than *Septuagint,* 471; version of Onkelos, 207.
Pentheus, II, 492.
Penumbra, planet in earth's, I, 328.
Pepper, Prof., and artificial phantoms, I, 359.

Peraḥiah, Yehôshûah ben-, and Jesus, II, 201.
Peramatus, I, 399.
Perdonnet, A.-A. (1801-67), I, 85.
Père Félix, on science, I, 337-39.
Perictionê (Περικτιόνη): II, 576; and Apollo, 325.
Peripatetics (Περιπατητίκοι), I, 61.
Périsprit: I, 197-98, 301fn.; as astral soul, 289.
Perizzites, I, 568.
Permutation: doctrine of, II, 152; in *Clement. Hom.,* 195.
Perpetual, motion, I, 501, 502.
Perring, J. S. (1813-1869), *The Pyramids of Gizeh* (implied), on hidden entrance, II, 26fn.
Persephonê (Περσεφόνη or Περσεφόνεια): temple of, I, 130; Queen of Hadês & Ste. Anna, II, 491; and Zagreus, 505fn. *See also* Proserpine.
Persepolis: marvels of, I, 534; ancient Istakhr, II, 630fn.; inscriptions of, 436.
Persia, vast knowledge & skill of ancient, I, 534.
Persians: I, 156, 313, 576; II, 27fn., 36, 42, 141, 206, 236, 291, 306, 405, 441, 486, 495, 503, 632.
Personality: and loss of soul, I, 317-18; and reincarnation, 351.
Personation: by goblins assuming pompous names, I, 68-69; by spirits, 55.
Perty, J. A. M. (1804-84), I, 222.
—— *Mystischen Erscheinungen:* on levitation, I, xxiv, 225; on magic, 138-39.
Peru: and Incas' treasure, I, 595-98, 654-56; Indians of, 546; native priests of, & H.P.B., 547; longevity in, II, 564.
Peruvian: bark, I, 89; mythology, II, 49, 259.
Peshâwar. *See* Pashai.
Peter, St.: I, ix; II, 8, 38, 189, 448, 544; Jupiter on Capitol as, I, 98; spurns money, 488; alleged succession of, II, 326-27, 335; antagonism of, and Paul, 84, 161, 161-62 fn., 175-76, 179, 180; as pictured in *Toledoth Yeshu,* 127; as thaumaturgist, 194; as ticket-taker to Trinity, 243; contradicted by John, 211; copy of Janus, 448-49; derivation of, 92-93; and Dignities, 207; and heavenly passports, 243; holds to Law, 190-91; ideas of, acc. to *Clement. Hom.,* 195; in Babylon, 127; keys of, & Brahmâtma, 31; knew nothing

of atonement, 546; martyrdom at Rome suspect, 124; mystery-name, 29; Nazarene, 127; never at Rome, 24fn., 30, 91-92, 124-25, 357; no relation to Church of Rome, 126; not mentioned until Ireneus, 24fn., 91; R.C. Church imposed herself on, 89; and Simon, 357; and Tartarus, 507; two chairs of, 23-25fn,; vocabulary of, 205, 208. See also Patar, Petra, Peter-ref-su.
Peter I, the Great (1672-1725), stopped spurious miracles, II, 17.
Peter of Blois (ca. 1135-ca. 1205), Epistolae, I, 22.
Peter-ref-su, mystery-word on coffin, II, 92-93, 646.
Peter's Cathedral, St., obscene bas-reliefs on door of, II, 332.
Peter the Reader, and Hypatia, II, 53.
I Peter, on Lord Chrêstos, II, 324fn.
II Peter: abusive language of, II, 205 & fn.; on Dignities, 207; on liberty and bondage, 180; on Tartarus, 507.
Petermann, H. (1801-1876), Thesaurus, etc., II, 653.
Pether: I, xxxiii; interpreter, II, 29, 92, 246.
Pétis de la Croix (1653-1713), and Druze scriptures, II, 309.
Petra: as Christian Mysteries, II, 30; as Logos, 246; as rock-temple, 30, 139, 392, 544.
Petrie, W. M. Flinders (1853-1942), The Pyramids and Temples of Gizeh, I, 648.
Petroma (πέτρωμα): II, 25fn., 30, 544, 561; as stone-tablets, 91-92, 392; and initiation, 499.
Petronius, Satyricon, on Democritus, I, 512.
Petrovsk, sorcery at, II, 568fn.
Pey, as ghost, I, 447.
Pfaff, J. W. A. (1774-1835), Astrologie: II, 500fn.; on Paracelsus, I, 52.
Pflaumerus, I, 228fn.
Phallicism, in Christian symbols, II, 5.
Phallus, or lithos, II, 5.
Phanês (Φάνης), as logos, I, 146, 636.
Phantasmal, duplicate, I, 360.
Phantasy: impairs Divine inspiration, II, 591-92; and mâyâ, 158.
Phantom(s): ethereal, I, 281, 333; in Malabar, 344; nature of, 200; Pliny on, in desert, 604; evoked by fumes of blood, II, 567-68, 569.
Pharaoh, I, 25, 414, 491, 549, 556.

Pharisees: I, xxx, 553; II, 132, 135, 179, 198, 202, 339, 441, 502, 538; Gibbon on, & transmigration, I, 347; Jesus a, II, 148; and transmigration, 152.
[Pharmaceutical, symbols], I, 229.
Pharmacology, in ancient India, I, 619.
Pharsi, II, 441, 501. See also Pârsîs.
Phasmata (φασματα), I, xliii.
Phelps, J. W. (1813-1885), Force Electrically Exhibited, on whirlwinds, I, 498fn.
Phenomena: child, I, 438-39; Cox's views on mediums and, 195-97; Crookes on, 45, 47, 48, 49, 202-03; due to occult forces under control, 128; and elementals, xxx; few physical, caused by human spirits, 73; and fraudulent messages, 41; idle to deny, 40; in every age, 53; and intelligence, 198-99; lack philosophy, 220; magnetic & spiritual, 109; many, are frauds, 52; many scientists believe in, 54; and mental photography, 322-23; physical, 66, 218; physical, produced by nature-spirits, 320; problems of, explained by ancient philosophies, xi; proved to exist, 624; and séance at Paris, 608-11; should be studied, 49; stopped by skepticism, 57; subjective, and their origin, 324-25; II, 597; Tyndall on spiritual, 176; when medium is conscious, 113; at Tambov, II, 17-18fn.; force in real, generated in medium's nervous system, 595; and healthy magnetism, 18; occult, help science, 25; occult, in India, 584-85; of Lamas & Talapoins, 370; utilize material from elementals & aura of sitters, 595, 596.
Pherecydes (fl. ca. 550 B.C.), Theogony, I, 157, 298.
Phidias (ca. 490-417 B.C.): I, 262, 397, 528, 564, 621; II, 614; Minerva of, I, 612.
Philadelphia Press, on Isis Unv., I, [2].
Philaletheians (φιλαλήθεις), I, xvii, 436; II, 249, 402.
Philalethes. See Eirenaeus.
Philastrius, II, 248fn.
Philhellenes (φιλέλληνες), II, 553.
Philip: aerial flight of, I, 494; first martyr, II, 329fn.
Philistines, II, 45, 297.
Phillipians, on being perfect, II, 287.
Phillips, W. (1811-1884), The Lost Arts: on acute senses of Orientals, I, 211; on glass of ancients, 537; on imitation of

emerald, 538; on knowledge, 534; on malleable glass, 50; on metallurgy of ancients, 538; on optical knowledge of ancients, 240.

Philo Herennius Byblius (1st c. A.D.): on Sanchoniathon's cosmogony, I, 342; on Iaô, II, 301.

Philo Judaeus (20 or 10 B.C.-45 A.D.): conceals true doctrine, II, 39; echoes Plato, 84; father of Neo-Platonism, 144; Kabalist, 33; q. by Eusebius, 513fn.
— *De cherubim,* on Adam-Kadmon, II, 216.
— *De confus. ling.,* on active Logos, II, 506.
— *De fuga et inventione,* on Logos, II, 216.
— *De gigantibus:* on invisible spirits in air, I, 2; on daemons, II, 34fn.; on metempsychosis, 280.
— *De migratione Abrahami,* on Kosmos, I, 154.
— *De opificio mundi:* on spirits in air, I, 2; on incorporeal world, 56; on daemons, II, 34fn.
— *De sacrificiis,* on mysteries, I, 271fn.
— *De somniis,* on metempsychosis, II, 280.
— *De specialibus legibus,* on magic, I, 25.
— *De vita contemplativa:* I, xxxfn.; on Therapeutae, II, 144, 196, 324.
— *Fragmenta* on Logos, II, 247fn.
— *Legum allegoriae,* on Logos, II, 247fn.
— *Quaestiones,* etc., on Logos as second God, II, 210, 247, 506.
— *Quod omnis probus,* on Essenes, II, 196.

Philolaus, I, xv, xvii, 159, 238.
Philology, linking Orient & Occident, I, 550.
Philonaea, revives, I, 365.
Philosopher's Stone: II, 618; and King of Siam, I, 571; and Voltaire, 268; two meanings of, 308.
Philosopher's tree, I, xxxii, 630.
Philosophers: ancient, misunderstood by scholars, I, 8; ancient, sworn to silence, 8; use figurative language, 307-08; their consignment to hell desired, II, 250.
Philosophy (ies): in archaic India, I, 618; modern, dug from Oriental mines, 98; all similar, II, 84; archaic religious, universal, 557; essence of all religions, 124; fundamental principles of Oriental, outlined, 587-90; grandeur of ancient, 38; H.P.B. intends to defend ancient, 120; occult, & spiritualism, 636; true, is divine truth, 121.

Philostratus (ca. 170-245), *The Life of Apollonius of Tyana:* on Brahmans, I, xxxiifn.; on ghûls in desert, 604; on Memnon, 514; on precious stones, 265; on resuscitation of Roman bride, 481; on Aethiopians & India, II, 437fn.

Phipson, T. L. (1833-1908), *Phosphorescence,* etc., I, 82.
Phliasians, I, 444.
Phoenicians (Φοίνικες): I, 572; II, 94, 134, 438, 440; Aethiopian race, I, 566-67; and Carthage, 567; derivation of term, 569; and Hyksôs, 569; and Israelites, 555; and Jews, 567; language of, 568; navigators & colonizers, 239, 545; called Kronos-Saturn Israel, II, 513fn.; colonized Ireland, 290fn.
Phoroneus, most ancient King of Greece, I, 532.
Photius (815?-891), *Bibliotheca,* q. Methodius, II, 35.
Photography: and âkâśic film condensed on metal, I, 463-64; electrical, 395; mental, & phenomena, 322-23; spiritual, 486; astral, II, 588; and projection of thought, 619.
Phra Pathum Suriving, King, I, 565.
Phrên (φρήν), II, 283, 286.
Phronêsis (φρονησις), II, 156.
Phrygian, Dactyls, I, 23.
Phylacteries (φιλακτήρια), Hebrew and Aztec, I, 553; II, 352.
Physicians: prejudiced and dogmatic, I, 88; and native doctors, II, 621fn.; wash their hands on leaving patient, 611.
Physics, in archaic India, I, 619.
Physiology: cyclic nature of, I, 7; Fournié on, 407; least advanced of sciences, 352.
Pia-Metak, and levitation, II, 618.
Pichalpâî, female phantom, II, 107.
Pico della Mirándola, Count Giovanni (1463-1494), as kabalist & mystic, I, 226; II, 20.
Pico della Mirándola, G. F. (ca. 1469-1553), *Libri tres de auro,* on transmutation, I, 504.
Picture-gallery, of nature, I, 184-85.
Picture-writing, I, 155, 156.
Pictures, horror of, in early Christianity, II, 149-50.

INDEX 753

Piérart, on vampires, I, 449-50, 453.
Pierrard, I, 166.
Pietro, Friar (14th c.), presents demon Zequiel to Torralva, II, 60.
Pigmies, existence of, confirmed, I, 412.
Pike, Gen. A. (1809-1891), *Proceedings of the Supreme Council,* etc., on personal God & creative principle, II, 377.
Pilate: convokes assembly of Jews, II, 522; never heard of Jesus, 335.
Pillars: in Kabalah, II, 215fn.; of Patriarchs & Śiva's liṅga, 235.
Pindar (ca. 522-443 B.C.), *Dirges:* on Bacchus & Zeus, II, 165; on vision of underworld, 111.
Pino, Don Pedro Baptista, on *Artufas,* I, 557.
Pippala tree [Hindî: *pîpal*], II, 412.
*Pirke Aboth.* See *Talmud.*
Piron, and sorcery in Cuba, II, 572-73.
Piśâcha(s), as ghost, I, 447; II, 107.
Pisces: II, 456, 461-62; conjunction of Saturn & Jupiter in, 256; Noah stands for, 465.
Piso, Lucius, on Tullus invoking Jupiter, I, 527.
*Pitakattayan,* on attainment of Bodhi, II, 164.
Pitarâî, kinsmen, II, 107.
Pitṛis: II, 104, 105, 106; def. I, *xxxviii, xlii-xliii;* evoked by fakirs, I, 458; II, 107-08, 114; no relation to exhibition of magic, I, 495; pure beings attracted by ascetics, 141; reincarnate, 346; distinct race of spirits, II, 107; reflection of, on astral light, 115; seat of the, 308; worship of, 639.
Pius VII (1740-1823), Pope, and Jesuits, II, 356.
Pius IX (1792-1878), Pope: I, 54; II, 9, 110; and *Encyclical* of 1864, I, vii; jetattore, 618; and Russian Emperor, 27; visions or fits of, 27; echo of Jesuits, II, 359; on his rights, 4fn.; vituperations of, 7.
Pizarro, F. (ca. 1471 or 1475-1541), I, 546, 596.
Planchette, I, 199.
Planets: as magnets, I, 282; astral, 330; colors of, known to Babylonians, 261; electromagnetic relations between, 161; emplacement of, 35; ethereal, 255; Hermes, on Spirit of, 255; in earth's penumbra, 328; influence of, 273; impulses of, on astral light, 275; motions of, & elementals, 284-85; motions of, regulated by magnetism, 271; and "music of the spheres," 275; reciprocal influences of, 269, 314; seven, & walls of Ecbatana, 534; all, are inhabited, II, 421; seven, of the Ophites, 294.
Planetary: aspects & elementals, I, 313; chambers & soul, 297; death, 254; influences, 259, 284; orbits & the five regular solids, 208; Plato on, Gods & immortality, xxi-xxii; genii of seven, spheres, II, 184-85, 230, 234, 296.
Planetary Spirit(s): descend occasionally to our sphere influencing sensitives, I, 158; of earth, 255.
Plants: ancients on nature of, I, 267-68; Chaldean ideas about, 254-55; inner nature of, 466; rotatory motion of, 244; sympathies of, 209, 246; *Manu* on soul in, II, 263; medicinal, in Orient, 621fn.; mystical properties of, 589.
Pla-out, and pla-cadi, I, 210.
Plato (427?-347 B.C.): and Atlantis, I, 591; Augustine on, xii; division of causes, 393; knowledge of, imparted to disciples, 406; methods of, & Aristotle, 7, mirrored Vedic philosophers, xi; misunderstood by scholars, 8, 307-08; not appreciated by moderns, 236; and oath of silence, 409; on *epopteia,* xiv; on fertile & barren periods, 247; on intellectual Light, 56; on numbers, xv-xvi; on real knowledge & Nous, xi-xii; on true philosophy, xiii; on Universal Archaeus, 14; philosophy of, 238-39; spirit of, cannot be altered, 560; taught justice, xi; vast knowledge of, 237; world's interpreter, xi; Gibbon on, II, 33; hides higher teachings, 39; on psychê, anoia & nous, 282; on seership, 591; taught by Pythagoras, 338; teachings of, derived from Orient, 39; virgin birth of, 325.
—— *Banquet:* I, 287; on spirit as interpreter, II, 635.
—— *Cratylus:* I, 287; on Koros, 131.
—— *Epinomis,* on immortality & planetary gods, I, xxi-xxii.
—— *Epistles:* on secrecy, I, 287fn.; on Supreme, 308.
—— *Euthyphron,* on unbelief, II, 16.
—— *First Alcibiades,* on Darius, II, 128.
—— *Gorgias:* on mortal soul, I, 327; on myths, xiii.

—— *Ion,* on magnesian stone, I, 130.
—— *Laws:* on Deity, II, 344; on nature of soul, 285-86; on retribution, 344, 345.
—— *Parmenides:* I, 287; on Nous, 55; on the One, xviii.
—— *Phaedo:* on chariot & winged steeds, I, xiii; on escaping prison of body, 139fn.; on Hadês & souls, 328; on life & death, 114; on mysteries, 132, 287; on myths, xiii; on recollection of reality, xiv; on regions of punishment beneath earth, 328; on winged races, 2.
—— *Phaedrus:* on body as shell, II, 114; on conditions of seeing gods, 146; on Deity, 344, 345; on earlier stage of man, 345; on *epopteia,* 113.
—— *Politicus:* on *earthly* human race, I, 428; on Deity, II, 344.
—— *Protagoras,* on good & God, II, 239.
—— *Republic:* II, 142; on eugenics, I, 77; on subterranean cave, xiii-xiv; on Deity, II, 344; on divine man crucified, 557; on miracles, 344; on retribution, 344.
—— *Theaetetus:* on becoming like God, I, xiii; on miracle, II, 344.
—— *Theages,* on Socrates & animal magnetism, I, 131.
—— *Timaeus:* I, 299, 327; and earth's revolution, 256fn.; and world tree, 297; on antiquity of Sais, 515; on astral soul assuming animal form, 328; on attraction, 244, 281; on causes of lusts, 276; on circulation of blood & gravitation, 236-37; on dodecahedron, 9, 55, 342; on dual man & invisible influences for evil, 277; on forms & numbers, xvi; on minor gods, 150; on monad becoming senseless, 303; on prophecy, 201; on Solon, 31; on soul's transformations from actions, 277; on sun, 258; on will, 55; echoes Oriental thought, II, 40; on circle of heaven, 463; on early men as pure spirits, 345; on ideal of Deity, 344; on man & circle decussated as a cross, 469, 557; on principles of man, 283; purposely confused, 39.

Platonists, misrepresented by modern scholars, I, 431.

Plautus, M. A. (ca. 254-184 B.C.), I, 584.

Playfair, Prof. Lyon (1818-98), I, 249.

Pleasonton, Gen. A. J. (1808-1894), *Influence of the Blue Ray,* etc.: I, 137, 171, 209, 264; on alcoholism & electrical polarity, 277fn.; on heat, electricity & light, 272, 273fn.; on sun as lens, 271fn.

Pleroma ($\pi\lambda\acute{\eta}\rho\omega\mu\alpha$): II, 226; three degrees of, I, 302.

Pletho: I, 353fn.; comments on *Chaldean Oracles,* 251.

Pleyte, W. (1836-1903), *La Religion des pré-Israélites,* on El, II, 524.

Pliny (ca. 23-79 A.D.), *Natural History:* on asbestos, I, 230; on Druids, 18; on Essenes, xxx; II, 130, 139, 485; on glass cup & Tiberias, 50; on letters, 532; on linen of Egypt, 536; on miniature *Iliad,* 240; on moving obelisk, 519; on Nero's optical glass, 240; on phantoms in desert, 604; on signs of death, 479; on stone of Memphis, 540; on trance & second soul, 476; on Thessalian priests, 366; on Tullus & lightning, 527; on Zoroaster, 19; on age of Zoroaster, II, 141-42; on artificial help to trance, 592; on Astartê on prow of ships, 258; on three schools of magic, 361; on virtues of engraved stones, 233fn.

Plot, R. (1640-1696), *The Natural Hist. of Staffordshire,* on Masonry, II, 349.

Plotinus (205-270): on ecstasy, I, 486; on intuition, 434; on public worship of gods, 489; united to his "god" four times, 292fn.; II, 115, 591.
—— *Enneads:* on soul descending into generation, II, 112; and visions in Mysteries, 118.

Plutarch ( 46 - 120 ), on oracular vapors, I, 200.
—— *Adversus Colotem,* on soul & substances in space, I, 401.
—— *Alcibiades,* on refusal to curse, II, 334.
—— *Consolatio ad Apollonium,* on sufferings of soul after death, II, 587.
—— *De defectu oraculorum:* on perpetual lamp, I, 227, 231; q. Lamprias on prophetic powers of soul, II, 594.
—— *De genio Socratis:* on second soul's journeys, I, 476, 477; on nous & soul, II, 284-85.
—— *De Iside et Osiride:* on daemons, I, xix-xx; on Plato's cosmos, 56; on Jupiter & Egypt, II, 505fn.; on Maneros, 504; on Persian Triad, 49; on Seth or Typhon, 482fn., 483, 489, 570fn.; on Thueris & dragon, 490; q. Euhemerus on myths, 406.

— *De placitis philosophorum:* on ideas, I, 250; on Plato's & Pythagoras' ideas on dual soul, II, 283.
— *Laconic Apophthegms,* on god & man, II, 212.
— *On Divine Punishment,* on Thespesius' vision after death, I, 484.
— *On the Face in the Orb of the Moon:* on brazen bowls of Korê, II, 592; on compound nature of man & post-mortem purification, 283-84, 285.
— *Roman Questions,* on refusal to curse, II, 334.
— *Symposiacs:* on bird & egg, I, 426; on God geometrizing, 506-07fn.; on Plato's birth, II, 325.
— *Vitae:* on earth being round, I, 159; on earth revolving in space, 238; on geographers, 29; on Pythagoras, II, 529.
Pluto: meadows of, II, 284; Müller on, 10-11; realm of, and Heracles, 515.
Pneuma (πνεῦμα): I, 132, 139fn.; II, 190, 230, 267, 357, 505, 551fn.; or nous, I, 401fn.; and Ophis, II, 172.
Pneuma Pythônos (πνεῦμα πύθωνος), I, 355.
Pneumata (πνεύματα), II, 231.
Pococke, E. (1648-1727), *India in Greece,* I, 651; on Aethiopians & India, II, 437fn.; on Indian origin of Osiris & Serapis, 438; on Korê & Zagreus, 505fn.; on Mary and Juggernaut, 110; on myths & history, 431; on name of Pythagoras, 491fn.; on Oxus, Ooksha & Pâlistân, 439fn.; on primitive history, 471; on struggle of solar & lunar chiefs, 435-36; on variations of name of Buddha, 30fn.
Podocatharo, *De rebus Cypriis,* on asbestos, I, 230.
Podolia, wonders in, II, 332.
Poetry, in archaic India, I, 619-20.
Poimandrês (Ποιμάνδρης): I, 298, 642; on truth & death, 624-25; root of Egyptian sun-gods, 93; Egyptian Logos, II, 212, 506; on Divine Triad, 50; same as Ennoia, 171, 223.
Polancus, and Jesuit constitutions, II, 354.
Polar lights, and earth's magnetism, I, 282.
Polarities, electrical, and use of alcohol, I, 277fn.
Pole-climbing, I, 495.
Policritus, returned after dying, I, 364.
Polier, M. E. de (1742-1817), *La Mythologie des Indous,* on creation & Brahmâ, I, 91; on origin of Brâhmans, 122.

Pollok, R. (1798-1827), *The Course of Time,* II, 502.
Polo, Marco (1254?-1324). *See* Yule, Sir Henry.
Polycarp, II, 196fn.
Polygamy, and Positivists, I, 78.
Polynesians, I, 594-95.
Polytheism, I, 183 & fn.
Pompeii, room full of glass at, I, 537.
Pomponazzi, Pietro (1462-1525?), I, 251.
Pontifex Maximus, and the Pope, II, 30.
Pope(s): and *Encyclical* of 1864, I, vii; as usurpers of hierophant power, II, 30; bull of, against Halley's comet, 509; and circumcision, 126; conversant with occult sciences, 19-20; "flowers of speech" of, 7; infallibility of, 359, 444fn.; Pius IX blesses Moslem arms, 560; sorcerers & magicians among, 56; sympathizes with Turks, 81-82.
Pope, A. (1688-1744), *Essay on Criticism,* I, 39.
— *Essay on Man,* I, 390, 427.
— *The Universal Prayer,* I, 205.
*Popol-Vuh. See* Brasseur de Bourbourg.
*Popular Monthly* (Frank Leslie's), art. about H.P.B., II, 654.
*Popular Science Monthly, The:* (M. Bond), I, 412; (T. H. Huxley), I, 153, 155; (Le Conte), I, 313, 329-30, 352, 408, 466-67; (O. Mason), I, 426; (A. L. Rawson), II, 654; (J. Tyndall), I, 418.
Porcacchi, T. (1530?-1585), *Funerali antichi,* etc., on asbestos, I, 230.
Porchetus de Salvaticis, *Victoria Porcheti adversus impios Hebreos,* II, 127fn.
Porphyry (233-305?): and Egyptian magic, I, 416; on chastity & purity, 432; on ignorance of *hoi polloi,* 624; on Plato & Mysteries, xii; united to God twice, 292fn.; on ancient systems, II, 198fn.
— *De abstinentia:* on daemons ambitious to be recognized as Supreme God, I, 219, 332-33; on divinely-luminous appearances, xliii; on elementaries, 332; on malicious daemons, 70; on soul's affinity to body & blood, 344, 493; on Amosis & wax figures, II, 565fn.; on learning of Egypt, 506.
— *De vita Pythagorae,* on numerals, I, 35; II, 300.
— *Letter to Anebo. See* Iamblichus, *De mysteriis.*
— *Plotini vita:* on Plotinus' guardian

angel, I, xliii; II, 115; on superiority of spirits, I, 489.
Porson, R. (1759-1808), *Letter to Mr. Archdeacon Travis,* on forged verse in *1 John,* II, 178.
Porta, G. Baptista della (1540?-1615): I, 226, 504; on asbestos, 230.
— *Magia naturalis:* on astral light, I, 208; on occult powers, 66.
Porter, R. K. (1777-1842), *Travels in Georgia,* etc., on figure of *feroher,* II, 495.
Portrait-gallery: I, xxxvi; constructed by elementaries, 70.
Poruthû Mâdan, daemon, I, 496.
Poseidon, I, 413, 565.
Positivism: II, 3-4; borrowed from Kapila, I, 98; discussed, 76-83; found in Vyâsa, 621.
Possession(s): and crimes, I, 490; demoniacal, 274; and elementaries, 355; epidemic of, in Germany, 374; and exorcism, 356; and mediumship, 488; as psychological epidemic, II, 625-26; by a god, 625; by vampires, 589; of Morzine, Valleyre, etc., 16.
Postel, G. (1510-1581), II, 470.
Potala: II, 616fn.; and scepter of Bodhisattva, 616-17.
Potency, occult, as a god, I, xxxviii.
Pothos, (πόθος), I, 342.
Poudot, house of, beset by elemental, I, 364.
Powers: Porta on occult, I, 66; arcane, can be developed, II, 113; attached to names, 370; and Dignities, 205-07; euhemerized, 407fn.; generative, & ancient goddesses, 444; gods are personated occult, 143; infinitude of creative, 264; latent, in man prove his inner god, 567; magical, exist in all men, 635; occult, awakened by Vâch, 410; of occultists at Kublai-Khân's Court, 583; of the soul, 592-93; personified, in religions, 402; psychological, natural to every man, 584; seven occult, & Moses, 551fn.; various, in Tibet, 616ff.
Powers, H. (1805-73), I, 528.
Prachidas, II, 255.
Prajâpatis: as antediluvian races, II, 466; dynasties of, 467fn.; and *Manu,* 427; and Patriarchs, 413, 450, 459, 463; and Sephîrôth, 40, 215, 271, 407fn.
Prajñâ-Pâramitâ, as perfect wisdom, I, 98.

*Prajñâ-Pâramitâ,* on four truths, I, 291.
Prâkâmya, II, 593.
Prakṛiti: fetters of, II, 565; indestructible matter, 271.
Pralaya(s): and emanation, I, xvi; description of, II, 273-74; and Noah, 466; and Svayambhû, 219; two kinds of, 424.
Pra-Mogla, II, 576, 578.
Pra-Narotte, II, 576.
Prâṇâyâma, II, 590.
Prapti, II, 593.
Pra-Scaribout, II, 576, 578.
Prasenajit, King, and Gautama's precept, I, 599-600.
*Prâtimoksha-Sûtra,* on Sermon on the Mount, II, 553; on virtues, 164.
Pratyâhâra, II, 590.
Pravṛitti, I, 243fn.
Praxiteles (4th c. B.C.), I, 621; II, 614.
Prayâga, II, 438.
Prayer, desire & will, I, 434; II, 566fn.
Pre-Adamite: men, I, 295, 305; potency in, earth, 256, 505.
Precepts, *Manu* on moral, II, 338.
Precognition, I, 144-45.
Predestination, II, 546 & fn., 547.
Pre-existence: both spirit & soul have, I, 317; of germ of present race, 152; of human spirit, 251; of law of form, 420; of spirit or nous, xiii; of worlds & beings, II, 455-56; universally taught by ancients, 280.
Preformation, I, 92.
Pregnancy: false, and unconscious will, I, 402; and influences on foetus, 394-95.
Prejudice, of investigators, I, 118; and truth, 615.
Preller, L. (1801-1861), *Griechische Mytologie:* on Hercules & Hadês, I, 132; II, 516; on Bacchus, II, 134; on Iacchos, 245.
Prenatal, conditions, I, 384ff.
*Presbyterian Banner* (D. Moore), on Manu, I, 585, 587.
Prescience, I, 179-80.
Preston, Rev., on role of Mary, II, 172-73.
Pre-Vedic, *Bhagavad-Gîtâ* is, II, 562-63.
Prevorst (Mrs. Hauffe), Seeress of: I, xxiv; a magnetic vampire, 463.
Priest(s): Assyrian, bore name of his god, I, 554; of Egypt, 626; of Thessaly, 366; cast off garb of, worn by scientists, II, 8; —sorcerers, 57; Synesius on being, & philosopher, 198-99.

Priestcraft: bane of, & Church, II, 586; dangers of, 121-22; Garibaldi on, 347; two orders of, in Japan & Siam, 602.

Priestess(es): ancient, hypnotized themselves, II, 592; of Apollo, 507.

Priestley, J. (1733-1804), discovered oxygen, II, 250.

—— *General History*, etc., on divinity of Jesus, II, 239.

—— *Hist. of Early Opinions*, etc., II, 239fn.

Primordial: substance and alchemy, I, 133; progenitor of Darwin, II, 261.

Principes (princes), or Sons of Light, I, 300.

Principle: Divine, I, 97; male & female, 61, 156, 161; primeval, 341; sentient, & consciousness, 198; active, & its reflection, II, 444; active, in nature, 402; as Rêshîth, 35-36; Ceres as passive, productive, 560fn.; creative, and term God, 265; creative, as Adam & Eve, 276fn.; creative, in Masonry, 377; Esau & Jacob as male & female, 401; female, in Trinity, 172; no Evil, 480.

Principles: first, of nature as Gods, II, 406; fundamental, of Oriental philosophy, 587-90; Plato on, of man, 283; seven, in man taught in Egypt, 367, 653.

Printing, in ancient China, I, 513.

Priscianus (6th c. A.D.), Neo-Platonist, I, 436.

Privation: and universal ether, I, 310-11; and mâyâ, II, 157.

Priyadarśin, title of Dharmâśoka, II, 608.

*Proceedings . . . against G. Malagrida*, etc., II, 58.

*Proceedings of Soc. of Bibl. Arch.*, II, 655.

Proclus (410-485): on attainment of divine power, I, 489; on hierarchies of daemons & beings, 312; on Intelligible Triad, 212; on second death, 432.

—— *De anima ac daemone*, on magic & doctrine of sympathies, I, 243-44.

—— *On Plato's Republic*: on seeming death & withdrawal, I, 365-66; on appearance of gods, II, 113.

—— *On the Cratylus*, on mirific name, II, 344.

—— *On the First Alcibiade*: on evocations, I, 321; on seduction of souls & initiated body, 321; on strong souls perceiving truth, 336; on Iaô, II, 139fn.

—— *On the Parmenides*, I, 55.

—— *On the Theology of Plato*, on mysteries, II, 101.

—— *On the Timaeus*: I, 636; on Atlantis, 413; on Isis & Sun brought forth by her, [1].

—— *To Minerva*, invocation, II, 123.

Procopius (4th & 5th c. A.D.), *De bello vandalico*, on Joshua, I, 545, 551.

Proctor, R. A. (1837-88), *Borderland of Science*, on ghost-stories, I, 245.

—— *Our Place Among Infinities*: I, 249, 275, 386, 401; on ancients & earth, 253-54, 255; 258; on astrology, 259; on ideas of ancients about planetary influences, 269; on Saturn's rings, 260; on the thummim, 537.

Prodigies, in *Atharva-Veda*, I, 91.

Proetus, King of Argos, I, xxv.

Projection: I, 477; electrical, of the astral, II, 620.

Prometheus: brings down lightning, I, 526; myth of, 298; pangs of, and descent of a god into Hadês, II, 514-15.

Propatôr (προπάτωρ), II, 210.

Prophecy: II, 360-61, 404; Aristotle on, I, 430; and astral emanations, 200-01; by newly-born child, 438-39; colleges of, 482; and Divine inspiration, 306; last stage of scientific growth, 533; of Nostradamus, 260; Plato on, 201; and priestesses of Babylon, 331; about future discoveries, II, 26 & fn.; of *Atharvaveda* compared to Bible, 556; power of, inherent in soul, 594; spurious, in Christianity, 50.

*Prophecies, Book of*, ed. of 1453, I, 260.

Prophets: and circle-dance, II, 45; denounce Jews for idolatry, 524, 525; hold to secret doctrine, 525; oppose orthodox Jews, 129, 131; oppose priests, 525; or nazars, 129, 525; role of, among Israel, 439-41; "sons of the," 130, 132, 139fn.

Proselênoi (προσεληναῖος), pre-Selênic, I, xxxix.

Proserpine: and after-death states, II, 284; Müller on, 10-11. *See also* Persephonê.

Protagoras (5th c. B.C.), I, 308.

Protestantism: desolate creed of, I, 435; and Bible, II, 200fn.; as cruel as Catholicism, 503; doctrine of, 296fn.; dogmatic & intolerant, 180; nature of, 501.

*Protevangelion, The*: on Devil, II, 473; on wonders of Jesus' birth, 552; on Zacharias, 523fn.

Protogonos (πρωτόγονος): I, 341, 342; II, 195; four-headed, I, 146-47; Adam-Kadmon as, II, 213, 268 & fn.; as oldest Aeôn, 216fn.; or Heavenly Man, 276.

Protoplasm: an old idea, I, 251; as new God, 222; and Huxley, 15; taught by Seneca, 249.

Prototypes: reflect themselves in later history, I, 35; in world of causes and numbers, II, 269fn.; spiritual, and emanation of worlds, 220.

Prounikos (προύνικος), and Aeôns, II, 187.

*Proverbs:* II, 67, 440; on lots, 252; on Olam & Rosh, 218; on sons of man & higher life, 218-19.

*Psalms:* I, 541, 555fn., 629; II, 153, 513fn.; on *chemi,* I, 226fn.; and *Isaiah,* II, 192; on gods as idols, 510, 527; on Iach, 302; on Israel & Jehovah, 513fn.; on Kadesh, 45; on "Lord," 401; on Sod of the Kadeshim, 131.

Psellus, M. C. (1018-ca. 1079), I, 321, 353, 535; II, 49.

—— *Chaldean Oracles:* on evocation of soul, I, 321; on seven-step abyss below earth, 353; on stone Mnizurin, 321; on sun, moon, stars & wisdom, 535.

—— *Dialogus de daemonum,* etc., on evicting daemons by sword, I, 363, 642.

—— *Graecorum opiniones de daemonibus,* on nature of magic, I, 282-83, 642.

Psychê (ψυχή): I, xli, 139fn., 317, 632; as soul, 401fn.; as astral soul, xxxix; anoia & nous, II, 282; Plutarch on, & nous, 283-84.

Psychic: I, 203, 204; currents of, force & undines & sylphs, 67; embryos, 311; force & electromagnetism, 44-45, 196-97, 201, 497; nature is not divine spirit, 429; or ectenic force & elementaries, 116.

Psychicos (ψυχικός), meaning of, smothered, II, 281.

Psychode, of Thury, I, 55, 113.

Psychography: I, 203; case of Sanskrit, 368; def. 367; of gosain and juggler, 369.

Psychological: powers alter with climate, I, 211; science retarded by public opinion, 75.

Psychology: def. *xxvii-xxviii;* future discoveries in, contingent upon recognition of facts known to theurgists, 335; in archaic Egypt, 531; in archaic India, 620; magic is occult, 612; magic unlocks secrets of, 282; neglected by scientists, 88; *terra incognita* to modern science, 46; understood only in the East, xlv; what, lacks today, 124.

Psychomatics, of occultism, I, *344.*

Psychometry: I, 14, 462-63; future of, 331; and mesmerizer's control, 184; nature of, 182-84; on stone age of man; 295; shows harmony in nature, 330.

Psychophobia, scientific, I, 46.

Psylli: Libyan serpent-charmers, I, 606fn.; powers of, over snakes, 381, 467.

Ptah: I, 125, 257; as Aesculapius, 130fn.; and Emepht, 146; produces Râ, 157; water of, 64; and astral soul in Egypt, II, 368; and Atum, 500fn.; as Principle of Light, 36; as universal germ, 226.

Ptar (videus), Rougé on meaning of, II, 93fn.

Pthahil: I, 298, 299, 300 & fn.; and Abathur, II, 224, 225, 227, 228, 229-30; and Akhamôth, 174, 175 & fn.; and Lehdoio, 295.

Ptolemaeus: II, 248fn.; Gnostic argument of, with Irenaeus, 305.

Ptolomaeus II Philadelphus (309-246 B.C.), obelisk of, at Alexandria, I, 519.

Ptolemies, I, 6.

Ptolemy [Ptolemaeus], Claudius (*fl.* 127-151 A.D.), I, 21, 182, 512.

Public, docile and pious child, easily lead, I, 167.

Pufendorf, S. von (1632-1694), *Le Droit de la nature,* etc., on oath, II, 373.

Pu-lu [Tib.: *bubs-lug;* pr. in Lhasa as *pu-luk*], sheep's woollen fabric, II, 600fn.

Pulwâr, II, 630fn.

Pumbeditha, College of, II, 207.

Punch-and-Judy, boxes, II, 119.

Punghi, learned man, II, 320, 508, 559.

Punishment: regions of, beneath earth, I, 328; eternal, II, 12; Pârsîs on, 547fn.

Puñjâb, race of, hybridized with Asiatic Aethiopians, I, 567.

Purâna: sacred tradition, I, 590fn.; what constitutes a, II, 492.

*Pur asbeston* (πῦρ ἄσβεστον), I, 125.

Puritans, and Sabbath, II, 419.

Purity, and illumination, I, 18.

Purohita, public priest, II, 98, 103.

Purple, Tyrian, I, 239.

Purpose, Escobar on sinful, II, 355 & fn.

Purusha: I, 56; II, 214; Brahmâ or, I, xvi,

xvii; Para—, xvi; as divine male, II, 270; gestation of, 267.
Pûtam, haunting spooks, I, 447.
Putnam, Israel (1718-90), I, 176.
Puységur, A. M. J. de (1751-1825), I, 166, 500.
—— *Mémoires,* I, 173.
Pygmies, in Africa, I, 412.
Pyramids: I, 239; II, 26; iron in, I, 542; majestic fane, 519; numulitic limestone of, 519, 647-48; sarcophagus in, 519; seven chambers of, 296; similar to mundane tree idea, 154; standing on seashore, 520; symbology of, 296-97.
Pyrrho (ca. 360-270 B.C.), I, 621; II, 261; reflects Hindu philosophy, II, 55, 530-31.
Pythagoras (6th c. B.C.): I, 307; derived knowledge from Hermetic Books, 444; and earth's revolution, 256fn.; and Euclid, 512; and Galileo, 238 & fn.; greatness of, 7; influenced by *Manu,* xvii; influenced Plato, xv; key to, xvi; on God, 287; on precious stones, 265; on universal mind, 131; reflects Buddhist tenets, 289; and Reuchlin, 238; taught in India, 347fn.; taught mathematical universe, 318; taught sphericity of earth, 532; teachings of, grounded on Buddhism, 290, 430; theory of numerals of, xv, 7, 9, 35; II, 300, 409, 410, 418; used mesmerism, I, 283; cipher of, II, 299; Heraclitus & Timon on, 529; Iamblichus on, 145; initiate, 338; instructed by Zoroaster, 140, 141; on his own initiation, 101fn.; on nous, phrên & thumos, 283, 286; on sun & heliocentric system, 13, 194; origin of name, 491fn.; Pancoast on, 289; and Zar-adas, 128.
—— *Ethical Fragments,* I, 320.
Pythia (πυθία, fem. of πύθιος), and Pythoness, def. I, *xxxviii-xxxix.*
*Pythii vates,* I, 355.
Pytho (Πυθό), or Ob, I, 355.
Python (Πύθων): original meaning of, I, 355; and Apollo, II, 447.
Pythoness: of Cumae, I, 531; of Delphi, 358; seership of, II, 590.

## Q

Qabbalah. *See* Kabala.
Quaritch, Bernard (1819-99), and *Isis Unv.,* I, [3 & fn.].
—— *General Catalogue,* I, [3 fn.].
Quarrying, in Egypt, I, 518.
*Quarterly Journal of Science* (Dublin), I, 108.
*Quarterly Review:* Graham on giant buildings, I, 123fn.; attacks Bunsen, II, 366fn.
Quaternary: II, 407, 418; and trinity, I, 508.
Quenouillet, I, 477.
Quercetanus (J. Duchesne, 1546-1609), I, 504, 647.
Quetzalcohuatl: and Moses, I, 558; and Solomon, 546; and Votan, 554.
Quiché: traditions of, I, 55ff., 596fn.; "Hidden Majesty" of the, II, 344.
Quicksilver: liquor of, and perpetual lamps, I, 229; and antimony, II, 620.
*Quiddam divinum,* of Cicero, I, 131fn.
Quincey, Thos. de (1785-1859), on Essenes, I, xxx.
—— *Murder,* etc., on epidemics of assassination, I, 277-78.

## R

Rabbis (Rabbins): II, 27, 119, 224, 386, 430, 443, 457, 478, 515, 552; Consistory of, I, 149fn. College of, at Venice, II, 399.
Rabbits, species of male, suckling young, I, 412.
Rab-Mag, I, 556.
Race(s): II, 466-67; alleged barbarism of early, I, 4; *eārthly* human, & Plato, 428; fourth, of *Popol-Vuh,* 593; human, could live in several elements, 589; invisible, 340; many earlier, 590; many human, before Adam, 2; more spiritual, than ours, 2; of spiritual beings filling universe, 2; pre-Adamite, 305; sixth, 8; sprung from hierophants, 593; differ in spiritual gifts, II, 588; represented by Manus, 407fn.; represented by Patriarchs, 450.
Rachel, I, 465.
Raderus, M., *M. V. Martialis Epigrammaton,* etc.: on asbestos, I, 231.
Radziwill, Prince, and false relics, II, 72.
Raffles, T. S., (1781-1826), II, 79.
Raguel-Jethro, and sapphire-stick, I, 558.
Rahats, II, *288.*
Râhu, Ceylon demon, II, 509, 655.
Rain, and Bahâk-Ziwa, II, 134.

*Rāja-Yoga Messenger,* on John H. Judge, I, [10].
Rakíy, grape-whiskey, II, 570.
Rākshasas, and Rāma, I, 563fn.; and Vāch, II, 410.
Ram, identical with Amen, I, 262.
Rāma: I, 266; and Hanuman, 563fn.; and Lankā, II, 278fn., 436; Paraśu—, 274.
Ramana(?), I, 621.
Ramatsariar, *Prophecies:* similar to *Genesis,* I, 579fn.; on blood, II, 567.
Rāma Vurmah, Rāja of Travancore, II, 437fn.
*Rāmāyaṇa:* II, 274, 278, 436; on Hanuman, I, 563 & fn.; and *Iliad,* 566.
Rameses the Second, I, 542.
Ramsay, Baron M. A. (1686-1743), on Templars, II, 384, 390.
Ramusio, G. B. (1485-1577), and Kublai-Khân, II, 581.
Randolph, P. B. (1825-1875), *Pre-Adamite Man,* on instant communication in Egypt, I, 127.
Ranjit Singh (1780-1839), fakir at Court of, I, 477.
Ranke, L. von (1795-1886), *Römischen Päpste,* etc., I, 424.
Raoul-Rochette, D. (1799-1854), *Monumens inédits,* etc., on electrified hair, I, 234.
Raphael, Sanzio (1483-1520), I, 564.
Rapin-Thoyras, Paul de (1661-1725), *Histoire d'Angleterre,* on Squire & Walpole, II, 373fn.
Raps: Babinet on, I, 105-06; Comte on, 101.
Rāśi-chakra, zodiac, II, 273.
Rastā Khez, II, 547.
Rathke, M. H. (1793-1860), I, 387.
Rational, soul, I, 251.
Raulica. *See* Ventura di Raulica.
Rāvana, I, 566; II, 301, 436.
Ravenshaw, E. C., "Note on the Sri Jantra, etc.," II, 265.
Rawlinson, Canon George (1812-1902), *The History of Herodotus:* on Labyrinth of Egypt, I, 523; on Āryans, II, 433; on Seth, 523.
Rawlinson, Sir H. C. (1810-1895): finds city of Martu, I, 579; on Akkadians from Armenia, 263, 578; II, 457; on stone with treatise on mathematics, I, 240.
—— "On the Birs Nimrud": I, 261; on red as Jupiter's color, II, 465.

Rawson, A. L. (1829-1902): article on H.P.B., II, 652; describes initiation into Druze Order, 313-15.
Rayer, Dr. P. F. O. (1793-?), I, 102, 104.
Razors, and African tribes, I, 538.
Reade, W. Winwood (1838-1875), *The Veil of Isis,* and Bouton, I, [43].
Reality, and illusion, II, 157-58.
Re-animation, of bodies, I, 475, 477-78, 485.
Reason: and conscience, I, *305;* def. *425, 432-33;* emanation of finite mind, 36; incapable of acquiring knowledge of spirit, 433; and instinct, 145, 432-33; insufficient for understanding universe, 87; and intuition, 61, 467; educated, and spiritual man, II, 636.
Reber, Geo., *The Christ of Paul:* on Irenaeus, II, 326; on Peter in Rome, 24fn., 124-25.
Rebirth: II, 195; and Buddha's teaching, 566; and Nicodemus explained in Hindu Scripture, 565.
Rebold, E., *Hist. générale de la Francmaçonnerie:* II, 389; on colleges of Egypt, I, 520; on occult science, II, 305-06.
*Rebus,* Zhelihovsky's articles on H.P.B., I, [22]fn., [24]fn.
*Receuil général,* etc., II, 634.
Recollection, of ante-natal state of bliss, I, xiv.
Records: secret, of solitary students, I, 557-58; imperishable, II, 542; Müller on unexpected recovery of, 26; secret, preserved by Brotherhood, 26-27, 117, 403.
Redeemer: and Devil, II, 479; prophecied in *Manu,* 50.
Red-haired, man and his shadow, I, 610.
Rees, O. (1743-1825), *The Cyclopaedia,* on emanations, II, 35.
Reformation: double meaning of, II, 180; seed of, 84.
Reformers: persecuted by science, I, 83; as bloodthirsty as Catholics, II, 503.
Regazzoni: I, 23, 114, 129, 166, 204, 283; experiments of, on sensitives, 143.
Reghellini de Scio, M. (1780?-1855), II, 383.
Regicide, Jesuits on, II, 372fn.
Reg Ruwán, I, 605.
Reichenbach, Baron K. von (1788-1869): I, 54, 125; II, 611; *od* of, I, 146, 163, 169; on pregnant women, 394, 395.

—— *Physic.-physiol. Untersuchungen,* I, 169.
Reincarnation: evolution through, I, 368; how to avoid, 346; and memory, 179-80; of astral monad, 351; of larvae, 357; and transmigration in inferior bodies, 346; desire, will & force condition, II, 320; and Jesus, 145; of Tibetan lamas, 563; or rebirth & triune man, 195; and permutation, 152-53, 195; and skandhas, 287. *See* Metempsychosis.
Relics, false, II, 71-72.
Religion(s): all, built on God & immortal spirit, I, 467; Ammonius Saccas on, 443-44; ancient, alone in harmony with nature, 38; ancient, misunderstood, 581-82; as opposed to *knowledge,* 613; Augustine on, 443; every true, based on knowledge of occult powers, 25; heliolatrous, once universal, 550-51; of ancients is religion of future, 613; Oriental, unknown in West until very recently, 442-43; sectarian beliefs of, will yield to rush of *facts,* 613; state, and *true* worship, 535; Tyndall on, and spiritualism, 417, 419; universal, 560; become adulterated through priests, II, 536; compulsory, breeds deceit, 573; essence of all, 124; fairytales transformed into, 406; fragments of divine truth, 639; identical at starting point, 215; indispensable to average man, 25; Jacolliot on pre-Vedic, 39; key to ancient, 399; King on a common, 198fn.; monotheism of ancient, 219; numerical strength of three, 539; once universal, of pre-Vedic age, 123; one, possible, but forfeited, 148; powerless without science, 264; science of, & unexpected recovery of records, 26; and Secret Doctrine, 292; true & false, 81fn., 121; wisdom-doctrine underlying all, 99.
Religious, instinct productive of sexual immorality, I, 83.
*Religious Statistics of the USA.,* on clergy & expenses, II, 1-2.
Rêmata (ῥήματα), arcane utterances, II, 560.
Remedies: known to ancients, I, 89; old, ignored by modern physicians, 20.
Reminiscence, of higher worlds, I, xiv.
Rémusat, J. B. A. (1788-1832), *Hist. de la ville de Khotan,* etc., on singing sands, I, 605.
Renan, E. (1823-92), "Des Religions, etc.," on pagan origin of Christian symbolism, II, 334-35; on Philo & Josephus ignoring Jesus, 335.
—— *La Vie de Jésus:* distorts outline of Jesus, II, 340-41fn., 562; on Mandaeans, 291fn.; on spurious sentence in Josephus re Jesus, 328; wrong on Jesus, 336-37.
Repentance, possible even in eighth sphere, I, 352.
Repercussion: between astral light and pregnant woman, I, 397; phenomenon of, 360-61.
Rephaim, giants, I, 133.
*Réponse aux Assertions,* II, 353fn.
*Report on Spiritualism,* etc., I, 232.
Rêshîth: esoteric meaning of, II, 34, 35, 36, 37.
Resistance, to blows, etc., I, 375-76.
Resurrection: bodily, and Jerome, II, 496; and Heracles in Hadês, 518; meaning of, of slaughtered sun-gods, 173.
Resuscitation: of Roman bride, I, 481; Proclus on, 364-65. *See also* Animation.
Retina. *See* Eye.
Retribution: moral, I, 88; overtaking Roman Church, II, 121; Plato on, 344, 345.
Reuben, I, 465.
Reuchlin, J. (1455-1522): and fragments of Pythagoras, I, 238; an occultist, II, 20.
—— *De Verbo mirifico:* II, 20; on Divine Breath, 419.
Reuel, or Jethro, initiator of Moses, II, 551fn.
Reuss, É. G. E. (1804-91), II, 189fn., 328, 329.
Reuvens, C. J. C. (1793-1837), on Typhon-Seth, II, 484.
*Revelación, La,* and burning of books, II, 29fn.
Revelation: religious, I, 287; double source of Biblical, II, 457.
*Revelation* (Apocalypse): II, 6; seven spirits of, & occult powers, I, 461; II, 187fn.; allegory of initiation, II, 351; authority of, 92fn.; describes Śiva, 235; exhibits Buddhist ideas, 508; Kabalistic allegory on 4th angel & sun, 12; Kabalistic in nature, 147; kept out of Canon, 138; key to all wisdom, 38; on Alpha & Omega, 277; on Lake of fire, 12; on Michael & Dragon, 488; on Nicolaitans, 329; on Satan, 480; on second death, 368; on seven lamps of fire, 229; on sign of cross, 393; on Son of Man &

seven stars, 295; on Tau, 254; on virgins, 330; on white horse, 237; on white stone, 351; on word, 147; and Pythagorean pentacle, 451; seven seals of, 352.

Revivals, rationale of religious, I, 498.

Revolution: of earth, I, 256fn.; of things, 336.

Revolution, French, swept out ecclesiastical tyranny, II, 22.

*Revue Britannique:* Burton on Lady Ellenborough, II, 649; Pashley on vampires, I, 450.

*Revue des Deux Mondes:* (Babinet), I, 104-05, 105-06, 202fn., 505; (Chevreul), 60; (P. Janet), 80; (Littré), 278; (Renan), 334-35.

*Revue de théologie* (Reuss), on Tertullian, II, 329.

*Revue encyclopédique:* on blood in lake Morat (de Candolle), I, 413; on bloodred snow & water, 414.

*Revue spirite, La,* I, 166.

*Revue spiritualiste:* on taming birds by will power (d'Alger), I, 380-81; on vampirism (Jobard & Piérart), 449-50, 453.

*Rgya tch'er rol pa* (Lalitavistara): on Buddha's gestation, II, 555; on original of Simeon story, 518-19fn.; on wonders at Buddha's birth, 551-52.

Rhazes, I, 164.

Rhea Sylvia, and Mars, II, 325.

Rhythm, influence of, II, 410, 411.

Rib, of the Word, preserved as relic, II, 71.

Richardson, Dr. B. W. (1828-96), quoted, I, 180.

Richardson, J. (1741-1811?), *Persian, Arabic, and English Lexicon,* on Bahāk, II, 134.

Richardson, Dr. R. (1779-1847), *Travels,* etc., on Dendera, I, 524.

Richter, J. D. G., *Berosi Chald. Historiae,* etc., on Zeru-an, II, 217.

Richter, S. *Sincerus Renatus,* Jesuitical, II, 394.

Ricold of Monte Croce (1242-1320), *Itinerary,* on levitation, I, 472.

Ṛigveda: II, 409; ideas in, identical with Hermetic philosophy, I, xxxii; on Agni as sun, 270; on evolution from Notbeing, xxxi; on widow-burning, 541fn.; age of, II, 433; *Brâhmaṇas* as key to, 415; Müller on, 414; on Aditi, 267fn.; on Being from not-Being, 269; on god within, 412; on importance of astral body & immortal Spirit, 534; on numbers, 411, 412; on Self; 318fn.; on Soma & Sun, 167; on the One, 413.

Riley, J. (1777-1840), *Authentic Narrative,* etc., on longevity in Africa, II, 564fn.

Rings, signet, of ancients, I, 240.

Rio de Janeiro, Madonna & Jesus dressed up at, II, 9-10.

Ṛishi Kutsa, *Nivids,* I, 11.

Ṛishis: pre-Vedic, I, 90fn.; Higgins on, II, 305; and Manus, 271fn.; and patriarchs, 468; and Prajâpatis, 407fn.; seven, 296; and supersensuous source of knowledge, 593.

Rites: holy, of magi, I, 130; and ceremonial dress of clergy similar to ancients, II, 94-95; Mousseaux on, and spirits, 71; perfective ($\tau\epsilon\lambda\epsilon\tau\acute{\eta}$), 101.

Ritschl, F. W. (1806-76), II, 189fn.

Ritter, H. (1791-1869), on Pythagoras, I, xv.

Ritual: funeral, in Egypt, II, 361, 367; Kabalistic, 85-87; of exorcism, 69.

*Rituale Romanum* (Paris): and kabalistic ritual, II, 85-87; on exorcism, 76; recently republished, 69.

Rive, A. de la, on aurora, I, 418.

Robert-Houdin, Jean-Eugène (1805-71): I, 73-74, 100, 101, 470; cheats natives, 379; on genuine mediums, 358-59.

Robertson, J. B. (1800-1879), *Lectures,* etc., on dangers of Masonry, II, 373, 375.

Robespierre, M. M. I. (1758-1794), *Discours sur la Constitution,* on Divinity, I, 73.

Robinson, James, and *Isis Unv.,* I, [10].

Robison, apostate-Mason, II, 373, 374, 375.

Rochester: rappings at, I, 36; Cathedral, its originals, II, 5.

Rock-temples, of Abu Simbel, I, 542.

Rock-works, ancient, I, 570-71.

Rod: or wand used by magicians, I, 415-16; of Moses, the *crux ansata,* II, 455.

Roger, Mme., trial of, I, 166.

Rohan, Louis René Édouard, Card. de (1734-1803), I, 509.

Rokitansky, Karl von (1804-78), I, 387.

Roma, founder of Angkor in Cambodian tradition, I, 566.

Roman Catholic Church: insolent claims of, I, 27; kills mediums, 100; why vindictive to arcane science, xxxiii; anathematizes occult phenomena, II, 6; blocks the way, 292; and cases of sorcery, 633-34; cunning devices of, 85; deprived herself of key to mysteries, 120-21; desires to crush last vestiges of old philosophies, 303; dogmas of, rest upon assumption, 329; falsifications of, a necessity, 504; familiar with Kabalistic learning, 450fn; fetish-worshippers, 80; and Jesuitism, 356; misuses occult knowledge & kills competitors, 58; and Moslems, 82; not build by Peter, 126; and political power in USA, 379; revenges herself, 6-7; rites & ceremonies of, derived from Pagans, 504; rituals of exorcism in, 85-86; self-doomed, 121; similarities of Cochin-China religion and, 554; similarities of Lamaism and, 345-46fn.; and spilling of blood, 58; symbol of, 94, 96; two great enemies of, 30; unverifiable assumption of, re Peter, 89; yearns for return of dark ages, 4.

*Romans:* I, xvi; on goat & evil, II, 303, 652; on Principalities, 189fn.; on the Word, 370; on Zion, 286fn.

Rome, Varro on building of, II, 588.

Romulus, virgin birth of, II, 325.

Ronsaeus, B., I, 385.

Rope, and boy phenomenon, I, 474.

Rosaries, ancient, II, 95.

Roscoe, H. E. (1833-1915), *Spectrum Analysis,* on iron in the sun & nature's secrets, I, 513.

Rose-Croix, American Order of, II, 386.

Rosellini, I. (1800-43), on mummies, I, 539.

Rosh, and Olam, II, 218, 219.

Rosicrucians: I, 67, 511; II, 37, 372, 410; burned by Church, I, 64; and Kabalist of 17th cent., I, 343; Ashmole the last of the, II, 349; and Catholicism, 394; on creation of woman, 445; motto of, & meaning of INRI, 526-27; seventh rule of, 404; true, still unknown, 380.

Rosie-Cross, brothers of the, live only in name, I, 29.

Ross, Sir James Clark (1800-1862), and red snow, I, 413-14.

Rossi, G. B. de (1822-94), *Compendio,* on errors of the Masorah, II, 459fn.

—— *Introd. alla Sacra Scrittura,* on Hebrew MSS. of Bible, II, 430fn.

—— *La Roma sotterranea,* on Chrêstos, II, 324.

Roth, R. von (1821-1895), "The Burial in India," I, 589fn.

—— & O. Böhtlingk, *Sanskrit Wörterbuch,* II, 47.

Rougé, E. de (1811-1872), *Stele,* on Ptar, II, 93.

Round, earth is, acc. to Dionysius, I, 159.

Round Towers: Irish, of Buddhist origin, II, 290-91; of Bhagalpur, 5.

Rousseaux, J. J. (1712-1778), kills toads by glance, I, 399.

Royal Arch: cipher of, II, 396-97; password of, 393.

Ruad, I, 570, 651.

Ruaḥ, wind, breath, spirit, I, 140fn., 181.

Rubeus, I, 504.

Ruc (Roc), I, 603.

Rufinus, T. (ca. 340-410), and Sextus, I, 238fn.

—— *Expositio,* on descent to Hell, II, 514.

Ruins, I, 239.

Rûkh-chaḍhâ, monkey, I, 470fn.

Rule, Margaret, case of, I, xxiv.

Rungius, J., I, 504.

Rûpa-lokas, II, 286.

Ruscellius, G. (beg. 16th c.-1566), I, 226.

—— *Segreti nuovi,* I, 639.

Russell, Lady, revives, I, 479.

Russia: case of a sorcerer's death in, II, 43-44fn.; no false miracles in, 17.

Russians: tales & traditions of, I, 550; before Vladimir's day, II, 572; missionaries, 599; Pope cursing, 560; residents in Siberia & Shamans, 624; traditions of, about wizard's death, 42-43fn.

*Russkiy Vestnik* (Russ. Messenger, Moscow), II, 659.

*Russkoye Obozreniye,* Zhelihovsky's art. on H.P.B., I, [21-22 & fn.].

Ryan, C. J. (1865-1949), "Precipitation of Astral-Forms or — What?," I, 647.

# S

Sá, M. de (1530-1596), *Aphorismi,* etc., on regicide, II, 372fn.

Saar-Louis, prophecy of, I, 439.

Sabaean: II, 450; astrological doctrine, 456; worship, 45.

Sabaeanism: I, 13; II, 438, 451fn., 494; and Shahrastânî, II, 554.

Sabaït, or Badir, II, 600fn.

Sabazian, worship, II, 45.

Sabazius: mysteries of Dionysus—, II, 491; torn into seven pieces, 487.
Sabbath: II, 407, 422; Man is lord of the, I, 489; and adepts, II, 419; and enactment of Charles II, 419; and seven-day week, 418.
Śabda, and Logos, II, 241.
Sabians, II, 197, 203, 307fn., 650-51. *See also* Nazarenes.
Sabinus, Bishop of Heraclea, II, 251.
Sacerdotal: caste ambitious and jealous, II, 154; function of, caste, 99.
Sacrifice: as yajña, I, xliv; ceremonial magic, xxvii; abolished by various rulers, II, 565fn.; human, 547; of hierophant, 42; perversion of theurgy, 565fn.; prophets opposed human, 525.
Sacy. *See* Silvestre de Sacy.
Sadasya, and âkâśa, I, xxvii.
*Saddharma-puṇḍarîka*. See Burnouf, Eugène.
Sadducees: I, xxx; II, 135; crucified Jesus, II, 148fn.; Jesus opposed, 339; nihilism of, 179; or Zadokites, 297; rejected resurrection, 152; unbelievers, 194.
Saga, meaning of, I, 354.
Sage, B. G. (1740-1824), *Dict. général des tissues,* on asbestos, I, 504.
Sages, of the Orient, I, vi.
Sagittarius, II, 451, 456, 461-62, 465.
Sahamaraṇa, cremation, I, 540-41 & fn.
Sahân, II, 320.
Sahara: once a sea bed, I, 592; upheaval of, and age of Pyramids, 520.
Saharoff, I. P. (1807-1863), *Tales and Traditions,* etc., I, 550.
Saint-Adhémar, Geoffroy de, II, 382.
Saint-Barthélemy. *See* Paulin de Saint-Barthélemy.
St.-Foix, on a tomb with Moors chained, II, 59.
Saint-Germain, Count de: and Cagliostro, II, 403; Rosicrucian MS. of, I, 575.
Saint-Hilaire. *See* Barthélemy Saint-Hilaire.
Saint-Ménard, fanatics of, I, 375.
St. Paul's Cathedral, double *lithoi* of, II, 5.
St. Petersburg Scientific Committee: most unfair to mediums, I, 117-18; prearranged report of, 42.
Saints: body of, and crawfish, II, 72; fictitious, 510-11; lives of, 78; and Madonnas guadily dressed, 532fn.; mediums versus orthodox, 76; rescued from Hell, 517; sanctity of Buddhist & Lamaic, 608.

Sais, antiquity of, II, 515.
Śakti(s): as active energies of the gods, II, 276; —trimûrti, 444.
Śâkyamuni, II, 130.
Salamander, asbestos, I, 504.
Sâla-tree, II, 607.
Salem, witchcraft at, I, 71, 361; II, 18, 25.
Salisbury, Earl of, II, 532fn.
Sallin, Dr., and mesmerism, I, 171.
Sallust (86-34 B.C.), I, 584.
Salsette, Isle of, and Kânheri caves, I, 581.
Salt(s): alchemical meaning of, I, 191; nature of, 147-48; "spirits" and chemical, 356-57fn.; creature of, II, 85fn.
Salverte, E. (1771-1837), *The Philosophy of Magic:* I, [16]; cases of suspended animation, 479; on Apollonius of Tyana, 481; on cure by imagination, 216; on electricity & ancients, 528; on firing at men protected by amulet, 378-79; on knowledge of ancients, 25; on levitation, 115; on mechanical skill of Egyptians, 516; on taming beasts by will power, 381-82; on Tullus & lightning, 527, résumé of, 115; T. Thomson on signs of death, 429.
Samâdhi: and jîvâtman, II, 590; far above clairvoyance, 591.
Samael: II, 402; and Azâzêl, 512; name for Simoom, 483; same as Satan, 483.
Samaneans. *See* Shamans.
Sâmanêra, II, *321fn.,* 508.
Samaria, woman of, original of story, II, 550-51.
Samaritans: II, 301, 399, 448fn.; recognized only books of Moses & Joshua, 470.
*Sâmaveda-Saṃhitâ,* II, 415.
Sambuke, Egyptian lyre, I, 544.
Saṃdhyâ, Saṃdhyânśa, I, 32, 634.
Samothrace: electricity & magnetism known to theurgists of, I, 234; Mysteries of, 23, 132, 302; and worship of Kabiri, xxxix, 570.
Samothraces, same as Kabiri, I, xxxix.
Samson: a nazar, II, 128, 151; mythical, 439.
Saṃtushita, and Mahâ-mâyâ, II, 555.
Samuel: I, 55, 206, 492; and institution at Ramah, 482; a nazar, II, 128; mythical, 439.
*I Samuel:* I, 215, 494; against burnt offerings, II, 525; on age of Saul, 200; on David & foreskins, 79.
*II Samuel:* I, 149fn.; II, 297; on *Book of*

*Jasher,* II, 400; on David's dance, 45; on numbering Israel, 481fn.; on wise women, 525.
Sanang Setsen, on Daïtu, II, 587.
—— *Geschichte der Ost-Mongolen,* on nature-spirits in deserts, I, 603.
Sanchoniathon: I, 234, 341; II, 48, 260, 261, 275.
—— *Cosmogony:* on generation of universe, I, 342; on Taaut, II, 235.
Sand: musical, in California, I, 605; singing, in Lop desert, 605.
Sannyâsin, life of a, II, 98, 104, 107.
Sanpao, II, 49.
Sanskrit: age of, I, 347-48fn; ancient, literature, 585, 626; ancient, or Senzar in Kumbum, 440; II, 46; books in, written by child-medium, I, 368; derived from the Rutas, 594fn.; and Greek, 443; hidden meaning of, words, 581; impressions by fakirs on leaves, 368-69; MSS. translated into Asiatic languages, 578; Müller on, MSS., 587; antiquity of, II, 411; no inscription in, older than Chandragupta, 436; not yet understood, 103; vernacular of Akkadians, 46.
Santa Croce, figure of Christ at, with square in hand, II, 393.
Santa Cruz del Quiché: and keystone of arches, I, 571; lake at, 572; and mysterious city in Yucatan, 547; *terra cottas* from, 553.
Santanelli, I, 172.
Saoshyant: and Maitreya, II, 156fn.; and other Saviors, 236-38, 467, 503.
Sapphire, properties of, and somnambulism, I, 264, 265.
Sapta-Kulas, II, 407.
Sapta-lokas, II, 294, 407.
Saptarishis, II, 296, 407.
Sar, circle, II, 217.
Saracens, I, 20; II, 582.
*Sâranga-sâra-kâvya,* I, 620.
Sarasvatî: II, 209; and Sophia, 42; and Vâch, 409.
Sarcophagus, porphyry, in Great Pyramid, I, 519.
Sargent, E. (1813-1880), *Materialism's Last Assault,* I, 419fn.
—— *Proof Palpable,* etc., on materialized spirits, I, 220-21.
Sargon I, history of, and Moses, II, 442.
Sarîra, as manifested visible form, I, xvii.
Sarles, Rev. J. W., on heathen being damned, II, 474.

Saros: I, 21, 30; and neros, 30fn., 31, 34; or age, II, 466; length of, 467fn.
Sarpa-râjñî: and rotundity of earth, I, 10; earth as, II, 489, 490.
Sarpas, II, 107.
Sarvamedha, as sacrifice, II, 558.
Satan (Shatan): and Seth, I, 554; a son of God, II, 492; an angel before his fall, 207; and Azhi-Dahâka, 486; as public accuser, 494; as Samael & Azâzêl, 402; as Samael & Typhon, 483; declared fundamental, 14; derivation of name, 481fn., 487fn.; in the *O.T.,* 481; and Jews, 186fn., 501; made dogma of Church, 13; mainstay of sacerdotalism, 480; or Set of Hittites, 481, 482fn.; plagiarized, 515-17; tests Job, 485; Waterloo of, 517.
Satanism, def. by V. di Raulica, II, *14.*
*Śatapatha-Brâhmaṇa:* II, 425, 428; on births of man, 565; prior to Cyrus, 428.
Satî, and widow-burning, I, 541 & fn., 648-49.
Sattra, imitation of the course of the sun, I, 11.
Saturn: I, 570fn.; Abraham as, 578; II, 216; in ancient myths, I, 267; rings of, 260, 263, 266; temple of, at Carthage, 413fn.; as Ialdabaôth, II, 505; as Taaut, 235; conjunction of, & Jupiter in Pisces, 256; El as primeval, 524; is Bel-Moloch, 513fn.; and Israel, 236, 513fn.; same as Jehovah, 236, 294, 512; same as Khîyûn, 524.
Saturnalia: Christian, II, 532; in monasteries, 365-66.
Satya. See Kṛita.
Satyrs, pickled, I, 159fn.
Saul: I, 488, 493, 567fn.; II, 199-200; obsessed, I, 215.
Saurya, sect, II, 399fn.
Sautrântikas, teach intuitional perception, II, 607.
Savages, hairy, I, 412.
Savary. C. É. (1750 - 1788), *Lettres sur l'Égypte,* on colossal monuments, I, 524.
Saviors: all dual, II, 508; in mythologies, 236ff.; legends of the three compared, 537-39; of Siam, 576ff.; philosophical idea of, 276; periodical appearance of, 535.
Sâyana, II, 415.
Sayce, A. H. (1845-1933), *Records of the Past,* II, 649.
—— *Chaldean Account of Genesis,* II, 655.

Sayer, Anthony ( ? -1742), Grand Master, II, 350.
Sayn-Wittgenstein, Prince E. (1824-78), I, 380, 645.
Sâyujya, identity with Universal Soul, II, 108.
Scaevola, G. Mucius (6th c. B.C.), II, 340.
Scaife, W. B., *America, its Georgr. History,* I, 653.
Scapegoat, origin of, II, 547.
Scardeonius, B., I, 226, 639.
— *Antiquitate* (implied), on perpetual lamps, II, 227.
*Sceau rompu,* on Knights of St. John, II, 384.
Scepter of the Father, a password, II, 324.
Schatta, M., I, 227.
Schelling, F. W. J. (1775-1854), II, 158.
Schenk, Prof., on Ebers MSS., I, 3.
Schiller, and Bayer, Jesuits on heliolatry, II, 450-51fn.
Schindler, V. ( ? -1610), *Lexicon Pentaglotton,* on Sod, I, 555fn.
Schlagintweit, E. (1835-1904), *Buddhism in Tibet,* on Buddha's bait, II, 549.
Schleicher, and Hanuman, II, 274fn.
Schleiermacher, F. D. E. (1768-1834), I, 8.
— *Einleitung,* etc., on Marcion, II, 159.
— *Sämtliche Werke,* on Marcion, II, 159.
Schliemann, A., *Die Clementinen,* etc., on nature of Jesus, II, 194-95.
Schliemann, Heinrich (1822-90): evidence of, on cycles, I, 6; and Mycenae, 598.
Schmidt, I. J. (1779-1847), *Der Weise und der Thor:* II, 504; on Buddhist & Gospel ideas, 549; on virtuous action, 551.
— *Geschichte der Ost-Mongolen,* on nature-spirits in deserts, I, 603.
Schneider, II, 561fn.
*Scholia in Apollonium Rhodium.* See Apollonius Rhodius.
Schopenhauer, A. (1788-1860), *Parerga und Paralipomena:* on higher order of nature & will, I, 59-60; on nature of matter, spirit & thought, 58; on nature as illusion, II, 158.
— *Über den Willen,* on will, I, 60.
Schöpffer, C., *Die Erde steht fest,* on immovable earth, I, 621-23.
Schopheim, *Traditions,* on Paracelsus, II, 500.
Schott, W. (1807-1889), *Über den Buddhaismus:* on Land of Spiritual Flowers, I, 601-02; on religiousness of Chinese, 602; on Shên-hsien, II, 618, 620.

Schwartz, Barthold ( ? -1384), and gunpowder, I, 241.
Schwegler, Albert (1819-57), II, 189fn., 328.
Schweigger, J. S. C. (1779-1857), *Einleitung in die Mythologie:* I, 281; on Dioscuri, 243; on lost mysteries of antiquity, 235; on occult properties of electricity & ancients, 234; on symbols & magnetic powers, 23.
Schweinfurth, G. A. (1836-1925), I, 412.
Science: American pretenders to, I, 75; and authority, 396; cannot stifle voice of nature, 222; and clergy, 85; conflict of, & spirituality, 627; conflict of, with theology, ix-x, 103; II, 23-25; Corson on Papacy in, I, 403-04; def. by Webster, 88; and discoveries in a *flash,* 513; dogmatism of, 84; full of guesswork, 407-08; inductive method of, 405; infallibility of, 223-24; and knowledge of ancients, 189, 406; limitations of, 408ff., 421; modern, & Hindu sages, 98; modern, compared with ancient, 239; and mystery, 337ff.; noblest of, that of spiritual man, xliv; no reason boasting of originality, 618, 623; of sanctuary veiled in secrecy, 7; on wrong track, 13-14; Tait on mysteries of, 187; three stages of every, 533; Tyndall on, & theology, vii; Tyndall on, & universe, xxii; tyranny of, and theology, xlv; Wallace on errors in, 223; factors required by genuine, II, 637; and facts, 3; occult, cannot be studied now on wide scale, 634; powerless without religion, 264; relation of, to state religion, 529.
*Scientific American* (New York): I, 117; on Crosse & *acaris,* 465.
Scientists: are *soul-blind,* I, 387; aroused to retaliation, 46; cause of their discomfiture, 61; credulous, 116; give various names to "psychic force," 55; have no appreciation of ancient philosophies, 581-82; inconsistent & morally oblique, 43; intolerance & despotism of, 85-86; many, are animate corpses, 318; many, believe in phenomena, 54; may be regarded later as *know-no-things,* 51; misunderstand Plato, 236-37; not same as science, 5; opinions of, in *Rep. on Spirit.,* 232; play hide-and-seek, 235; prejudice in, 5, 49, 88, 114, 222, 223-24; pull down spiritual things, 222; reject what they accept later, 146, 204; reject opportunities, 223-24;

INDEX 767

shun spiritualistic phenomena, 41; skepticism of, 409, 410-11; suspected & ridiculed by their own kind, 176-77; thinkers of the past & modern, 249-50ff.; useful as collectors of facts, 422; unfair, 417-18; weird experiments of, 117; disagree on ancient races, II, 472; Hanoverian, on man & ape, 278fn.; might end as *simiae* rather than *seraphs*, 279fn.
Scîn-lâc: as astral spirit & animated statues, I, 616, 657; phantasmal duplicate, 363; of medium, II, 597; spiritual double, 104.
Scintilla: and monad, I, 302; Kabalah on, II, 452.
Scorpio, esoteric meaning of, II, 457, 463, 465fn.
Scott, Walter (1771-1832), *The Lay of the Last Minstrel*, I, 461.
Scottish Rite, and Jesuits, II, 381, 390.
*Scriptores historiae Augustae*, II, 336fn., 647.
Scriptures, blunders in, II, 133-34.
Sculpture, titanic, of ancients, I, 542.
Scythopolis, or Beth-San, II, 165.
Scyths, probably same as Mongolians, I, 576.
Sea, inland, north of Himâlayas, I, 589.
Seal, Solomon's, from India, I, 135.
*Séance de l'Académie de Paris* (Geoffroy Saint-Hilaire), on horse with fingers, I, 412.
Second sight: as intuition & the Bible, I, 435; rationale of, 211-12.
Secrecy: of expressions of ancients, I, 37; on arcane sciences, 7; Plato on, 287fn.; reasons for, xiifn.; *Atharvaveda* preserved in, II, 563; regarding the mystery, 40; regarding name of the gods, 478.
Secret: fraternity holds keys to ancient symbols, I, 573; records of solitary students, 557-58; II, 26-27, 117, 403; treatises, I, 580; consequences of revealing, knowledge, II, 99, 100; discourses (ἀπόρρητα), 191; first Christian communities were, 395; science not to be profaned, 317; science & silent students, 306-07.
Secrets: of nature, I, 513; long kept may be revealed, 38; not divulged by disciples, II, 404; of ancient brotherhoods not revealed, 394.
*Secret Book*, I, 591.
Secret Doctrine: alpha & omega of universal science, I, 511; as Lost Word, 580; esoteric key to all religious monuments, 561; groundwork for all religious works, 580; identical in every country, 38, 444; II, 142; symbolical and Isaiah's "man of sorrow," I, 574; known ages ago, 436, 444; one and the same, on all monuments, 571; origin in India, 136fn.; world-tree of knowledge, 574; basic propositions of the, II, 455-56; basis of Zoroastrianism, 236; identical in all religions, 99, 410; is Truth, 292; misunderstood by Orientalists, 262; of Jesus acc. to Gnostics, 186; of Jesus acc. to *Homilies*, 191; of Jesus based on *Gnosis*, 192; of Jesus preserved, 307fn.; symbolized by a well, 551fn; taught by Gautama, 319.
Sects: and enforced dogma, II, 121; H.P.B. defends Gnostic, 326; many, accused of licentiousness, 325, 331-32; of Lebanon, 221; of sorcerers evoking phantoms with blood, 567-68; Oriental, cultivating powers, 618; Pagan, gave birth to dogmatic Christianity, 334; Saurya, 399fn.; time engulfed many, 289; virtues of early Christian, 144-45.
Secundus, II, 248fn.
Sedecla, and Saul, I, 494.
Seduction, of souls, I, 321.
Seed: accelerated growth of, & its rationale, I, 139-40, 141-42; or cosmic germ, II, 226.
Seer(s): Mantius the, I, xxxv; or *epoptai*, xxxvii; spirit in the illuminated, shines like noonday sun, xvii.
Seeress of Prevorst, a magnetic vampire, I, 463.
Seership: and invisible universe, I, 467; or Nabia, xxxvii; clairvoyance & spiritual, contrasted, II, 591; not mediumship, 118; two kinds of, 590.
Seleucus, I, 406; II, 182.
Self: man's immortal, demonstrates God, I, vi; divine, overshadows men, II, 153, 320; higher or lower, must prevail, 593; inner, & initiation, 114-15; inner, as Supreme God, 566fn.; and Karma, 287; Müller & *Vedas* on, 317-18fn., 342.
Self-conquest, I, xx.
Self-consciousness, I, 368.
Self-control, and anger, I, 248.
Self-incence, I, 43.
Semedo, Álvaro (1585-1658), *Relação*, etc., on sect of Taossé, II, 618-19.
Semelê, II, 504, 505.
Semes Eilam Abrasax, II, 293.
Seminal virtues, I, 191.

Seminarist, term of Buddhist origin, II, 321fn.
Semiramis, and Ninus, I, 552.
Semites: as Assyrians, I, 576; races, 570, 579; II, 408, 411, 426, 483, 484, 524; Iaô as supreme deity of, II, 297; language of, 436; least spiritual people of human family, *434-35.*
Semnion, of Essenes, II, 196fn.
Semothees, Druids, I, 18.
Sendivogius, M. (1566?-1646), *A New Light of Alchymie,* I, 461.
Seneca (54 B.C.-39 A.D.), I, 249; II, 277.
—— *Naturalium quaestionum,* on length of Great Year, I, 31.
Sennertus, D. (1572-1637), I, 386, 645.
Senses: higher, and reason, I, 145; revelations of spiritual, in man, 424-25.
Sensitive(s): and astral emanations, I, 200; *unconscious* use by, of powers, 128; and subjective communications, II, 115.
Senzar: characters in, and Kumbum tree, I, 440; hinted at, II, 46.
*Sepher Toldoth Yeshu:* on Jesus & Jannaeus, II, 201, 386fn.; on Jesus stealing mysteries, 202, 515; on Peter, 127; text of, 127fn.
*Sepher Yetzîrah:* I, 580; on *arba-il,* 508fn.; age of, II, 298fn.; miracles performed by, 357; on emanation of elements, 272; on *hayyôth,* 299; on secrecy, 40; on the One, 298.
Sephîrâh: I, 160, 258, 263, 270, 272; II, 36, 176, 220, 223; and emanations, II, 35; emergence of androgyne, 267-68, 421; first, 213, 214; is Nara, 214.
Sephîrôth: concealed wisdom, their father, I, 258; Adam-Kadmon in their totality, II, 213; as emanations of Adam-Kadmon, 205fn., 213, 267ff.; first three, & Christian Trinity, 36; Franck on nature of, 40; and Heavenly man, 276; and Mt. Meru, 233; and Patriarchs, 459, 460, 463, 465; represented by circles, 232; same as Prajâpatis, 215, 271, 459; and triple Trimûrti, 40.
*Septuagint:* II, 470; more recent than Samaritan *Pentateuch,* 471; translated passages from *Job,* 495.
Serapeion (Σεραπεῖον): II, 28, 29; cross found in, 253.
Seraphs, fiery serpents, II, 71, 232, 481fn.
Serapis (Σέραπις or Σάραπις): II, 502; and source of vowels, I, 574; borrowed by Christians, II, 336; Indian origin of, 438; and serpent symbol, 490; stood for Anima Mundi, 336; usurps place of Osiris, 491.
Serbians, I, 449, 451; II, 7, 368.
Sermon on the Mount: II, 145, 163; essential principles of monastic Buddhism, II, 553; practiced only by Buddhist ascetics & fakirs, 526; precepts of, identical with Egyptian, 361; repudiated by Christians, 575.
Serpent(s): I, 382; brazen, 556; II, 165; catacombs of, I, 553; compared to man, 149; and Dragons, 550ff.; II, 446-47; earth as Queen of the, I, 10; Egyptian symbol of, 149; in Gogard tree, 298; symbol of astral fire, 137; symbol of matter, 297; symbol of wisdom & immortality, 553; 570; II, 223, 225, 449, 484, 489, 510; and teraphim, I, 570; as first manifestation, II, 226; as Logos of Gnostics, 505; as second Hermes, 508; as symbol of destruction, 510; Chnuphis—, as Logos, 510fn.; crushed by three Saviors, 538; and early shape of earth, 489; emblem of sun-god, 129; esoteric reason why sacred, 489-90, 510; God the Father as beguiling, 492fn.; hawk-headed, 512; King—, 234; Krishna crushing head of, 446; reared with children in India, 490; seven-headed, 489; skin of, magnetic, 507; symbol of Divine Intelligence, 398; with tail in mouth, 489-90. See also Snakes.
Serpent-charmers: I, xxxii, 43, 381-83, 470-71; cannot fascinate humans, II, 612; gunîs as, 622; powers of, 622.
Serpent-gods, Mexican, I, 572.
Serpent-monsters, I, 393.
Serpent-worship, I, 555; II, 489.
Serpent-worshippers, converted to Buddhism, II, 608.
Serres, É. R. A. (1786-1868), *Recherches d'anatomie,* etc., on teratology, I, 392.
Servius Maurus Honoratus (4th c. A.D.), I, 207.
—— *Comm. on Virgil:* on heavenly fire, I, 526; on divination, II, 592.
Sesostris, I, 530; II, 51.
Seth: I, xxxiii, 25; is Hermes, 554; begotten by Adam, II, 464; and Ezekiel's Wheel, 462; generations of, 459-60; one with Hermes & Enoch, 466; same as Typhon, 482fn., 484, 487fn., 523; tutelary god of Hittites, 482.
Sethianites, II, 176.
Seven: as radiations of Unity, I, 514; as

trinity completed by quaternary, 508; continents in Hindu tradition, 591; descent of, steps below earth, 353; powers in nature, 466; spirits of *Apocalypse* & seven occult powers, 461; spirits begotten by Karabtanos, 301; stellars, 300; II, 187fn., 296; and adepts, II, 419; Aeôns, 229, 296; daughters of Priest of Midian, 551fn.; days of creation, 468; Heavens of Hindus, 564fn.; in Âryan myths, 407; in Chaldea, 408; in *Genesis* & Christianity, 408; in Nazarene cosmogony, 296; in *Vedas,* 411; keys, but one given in *Isis,* 461; lamps of fire, 229; Lives & House of Life, 234; and Moon's phases, 419; most sacred of numbers, 407; mysteries, 351-52; number, & the Ark, 447; Prajâpatis, 427; Rishis, 296; seals of *Revelation,* 352; sins, halls & staircases, & the soul, 564; spirits, 187fn.; spirits of planets, 294; stages or spheres of emanation, 184, 233; and three in spectrum, 417-18; turns of the key & Ezekiel's Wheel, 461; vines, 244; weeks of days with Jesus & Romans, 418; worlds & spiritual earth, 420.

Sevenfold, man, in all faiths, II, 367.

Severus, Sulpicius (4th c. A.D.), *Chronica,* II, 126fn.

Sex(es): emblems of, in religions, I, 583; and gods of mythologies, 303; separation into, 297; and ancient symbolism, II, 108ff., 445; double-sexed deities, 170, 268-70, 270fn., 401; of man, 468; and religious instinct, 83.

Sextus: Pythagoric sentences of, and Rufinus' role, I, 238fn.; precepts of, II, 338.

Sextus Empiricus (2nd c. A.D.), on Timon, II, 531.

—— *Against the Mathematicians,* on Speusippus, I, xviii.

Shaberon(s): II, 604, 618; and Qubilgans, 583, 609; rescued H.P.B., 628; Taley-Lama a, 616fn.

Shad-belly, coat of Babylonians, II, 458.

Shadow: of Buddha, II, 312, 550; repugnance of stepping across, 610, 611.

Shahrastânî, q. by Chwolson on Sabaeanism, II, 197, 554.

Shakers, and phenomena, II, 18.

Shakespeare, Wm. (1564-1616), *All's Well That Ends Well,* II, 123.

—— *King Henry IV,* II, 473.

—— *King Henry VI,* I, ix; II, 1, 55.

—— *King Richard III,* I, 28.

—— *The Tempest,* I, 574.

Shalom, peace, II, 441.

Shaman(s): Kalmucks on, I, 3; lose power in the West, 211; mediums, xl, 631; conveys astrally message to Kutchi, II, 628; magic performance of a, at H.P.B.'s bidding, 626-28; prophecies about Crimean War, 625; rites performed at Winter Solstice, 624; some, are magicians, 625, 626; Tatar, & H.P.B.'s travel in Ladâkh, 598-99.

Shamanism: I, 631; II, 321, 370; degenerate in Siberia, 616; divination by spirits in, 625; offshoot of theurgy, 615.

Shamas, god of Assyria, II, 487.

Shamhal of Tarkov, II, 568fn., 656.

Shammai, II, 339.

Shamsudin-Khân, Prince, II, 568fn., 657.

Shapar, to shine, II, 551fn.

Shark-charmers, I, 606-07.

Sharpe, S. (1799-1881), *Egyptian Mythology,* etc., on Sinai & Nissa, II, 165.

Shâtana, to be adverse, II, 483. *See also* Satan & Sheitans.

Sheath, II, 270fn.

Shebang, age or cycle, II, 418.

Shedim: four classes of, I, 313, 449; and Jinn, 456.

Sheitans, daemons, II, 569, 572.

Shekhînah: II, 243, 245, 267fn.; as Grace, 224; as female counterpart of Malkhuth, 224; as secret wisdom, 269; as veil of Ain-Soph, 223, 293; and Bythos, 169; and Cherubim, 231; elder Sophia is, 227; female virtue, 176, 223; and Śakti, 276.

Shell, impenetrable, formed of astral fluid, I, 378-80.

Shem: Ham and Japhet, II, 434, 487-88; and Sim, 217.

Shem ha-Mephorash, II, 147, 201.

Shên-hsien: powers of, II, 620; terrestrial beati, 618.

Sheol, and larvae, I, 493.

*Shepherd of Hermas:* data on, II, 243fn.; Fathers' contradictory opinions on, 518; on Gate & last days, 246; similar to Kabalah & *Codex Nazar.,* 243-45.

*Shi-King,* I, 11.

Shiloh, II, 45, 244.

Shimeon, and Patar, II, 93.

Shimon ben-Shetah, system of, II, 299.

Shimon ben-Yoḥai: I, 263, 302; II, 152, 210, 298fn., 350; on androgyne beings, II, 469; and *Zohar,* 348-49 & fn.

Shiraz, II, 630fn.
Shoel ob, as consultor of spirits, I, 355.
Shuckford, Rev. Sam.( ? -1754), & Church Fathers, II, 477.
Shudâla-Mâdan, a ghoul, I, 495-96.
*Shu-King,* I, 11.
Shûla-Mâdan, a spook, I, 496.
Siam: fresh-water fish in, I, 210; king-initiates in, 571; levitation in, 495; Talapoins of, 213-14; King Pia Metak of, II, 618; Mt. Sineru of, 232.
Siamese: missionaries cheat, II, 371; Savior Sommona-Codom, 576ff.
Sibyls: II, 22, 51; among Jews, 525.
Sidereal: force, I, 168; influences, 170-71; light, 125.
Si-dzang, II, 618.
*Siècle, Le,* I, 359.
Sigê (σιγή), silence, II, 171, 172, 176, 294.
Signature, of foetus, I, 385.
Signum Tau, II, 254, 393. *See also* Tau.
Siljeström, P. A. (1815- ? ), *Minnefest,* etc., I, 411.
*Silliman's Journal of Science and Art* (S. L. Mitchell), on snake monsters, I, 393.
Silver: associated with green, I, 513; tipifies female principle, 161; aura of, and mercury, II, 621.
Silvery, spark in brain, I, 329.
Silvestre de Sacy, A. I. (1758-1838), *Exposé de la religion des Druzes,* etc., unreliable, II, 309.
Simeon: tribe of, I, 555, 568; plagiarized from Buddhism, II, 518-19fn.
Simeon Stylites, St. (390-459): II, 509, 617; and dragon, 77.
Simon Magus: I, xxiii, 471, 496; II, 87, 89, 97, 176, 194, 215fn., 294; argues with Peter, II, 191; as "Son of God," 566; distinct from Paul, 91fn.; flies off in the air, 597; miracles of, 341; on Demiurge, 190-91; and Peter, 161-62fn.; preached Father unknown to all, 230; testimony about his powers, 357.
Simon the Cyrenian, II, 157.
Simoom (Ar.: *samûm*), same as Samuel, II, 483.
Simplicius (6th c. A.D.), I, 256fn., 436.
—— *Physica auscultatio,* on pictures in aether, I, 178.
Simpson, I, 387.
Simpson, Sir James Y. (1811-70), and chloroform, I, 540.
Sin, or Luna, II, 296.

Sinai: scoriae at Mt., I, 542; and Nissa, II, 165.
Sineru, Mt., II, 232.
Singhalese, remarkable relics, I, 577; II, 508-09.
Singing sands, I, 605.
Sinnett, A. P. (1840-1921), *Incidents,* etc.: I, [24fn.], [26], [32]; 1fn.
—— *The Mahatma Letters:* on *Isis Unv.,* I, [6], [15fn.], [20fn], [33], [49 - 50], [50]; on Spirit and Matter, 632; on soulless beings, II, 653.
Sins, the five, II, 608.
Sioux Indians, and fire, I, 248.
*Siphra Dtzeniuthah:* II, 174, 205fn.; compiled from very old book, I, 1.
Sippara: II, 442; city of the Sun, 551fn.
Sister, son of, inheriting Aethiopian crown, II, 437.
Sistra, at Israelitish festival, II, 45.
Sîtâ, Râma's wife, I, 566.
Sitügtü, monastery of, has school of magic, II, 609.
Śiva: I, xvii, 348, 446, 590; II, 39, 114, 170, 268-69, 277, 303, 490, 492; and Andhera, I, 299; II, 11, 238; as fire-god is Babylonian Bel, I, 263; II, 524; is Kîyûn, I, 570; and Mahâsura, 299; sacrificing his son, 576-77; and sexual emblems, 583; as Regenerator, II, 448; dual nature of, 524; emblems of, 235-36; has attributes of Jehovah, 234; and Jehovah & Osiris as active principle in nature, 402; linga of, & pillars of Patriarchs, 235; not Vedic, 48fn., 483fn.; same as Tsabaôth & Sabazios, 487.
Śivaites (or Shaivas), II, 332.
*Śiva-Purâna,* on races of man, I, 590.
Śiva-Râtri, festival of, and Tamil juggler, I, 446.
Six: races in *Manu,* I, 590; thousand "years" as Egyptian cycle, 342; days of evolution, II, 422; principles of man in Egypt, 367; sacred syllables & powers from Buddha, 616fn.
Sixth: race, I, 8; degree, II, 365.
Sixtus V (1521-90), Pope, and magic, I, 617.
Skandhas, incarnate, II, 287.
Skene, Wm. F., *The Four Ancient Books of Wales,* I, 651.
Skeleton, of triple man, I, 4.
Skepticism: II, 531; as opposing force, I, 57; impotence of, 43; Lecky on, 409; of immortality as a malady, 115.

Skulls: Egyptian, of Caucasian type, II, 436-37; exhumed in convents, 210; infant, in fish-pond at Rome, 58.
Slade, Dr. Henry ( ? -1905): I, 86, 224, 638; in London, 118; medium, II, 354fn.
Slavonian: form of word *witch*, I, 354; Christians assailed by Catholics, II, 81.
Slavonians, I, 451, 576; and Koldun's mystic word, II, 42-43fn.
Sleeman, Sir Wm. H. (1788-1856), on Hindus, II, 474fn.
Sleep: and dreams, etc., I, 179-80; magnetic, and insensibility, 166-67fn; sacred, of neophyte, 357-58; six-months long, and Herodotus, 412; Spirit protects body in, 460.
*Smaragdine Tablet:* I, xxxi-xxxii, 506; found at Hebron, 507. *See also* Hermes.
Smith, Geo. (1840-76), *Assyrian Discoveries:* on destruction of sixth world, II, 422-23 & fn.; on Sargon, 442.
—— *Chaldean Account of Genesis:* on Akkadian cosmogony, II, 267fn.; on Sargon, 442, 443.
Smith, V. A. (1848-1920), *The Edicts of Aśoka,* II, 644.
Smith, Sir Wm. (1813-1893) & Henry Wace (1836-1924), *A Dict. of Christian Biography,* II, 518.
—— *A Dict. of Greek & Roman Antiquities:* on Apollonides, I, 645; on Samothracian mysteries, 132; on ox of Dionysos, II, 524fn.
Smṛiti, tradition, I, 444, 588.
Smyth, Chas. Piazzi (1819-1900), *Our Inheritance in the Great Pyramid* (implied), I, 519; and Egyptian geometry, 531.
Snake(s): charmed by music, I, 382-83; charmed by will, 370-71; hole of, 553; many meanings of, 157; mundane, in *Edda,* 151; symbol of, 146-47, 149; in mosques, II, 490; skin of, magnetic, 507. *See also* Serpent.
Snout, of seraph as relic, II, 71.
Snow, and blood, I, 413-15.
Snow-flakes, I, 508.
Socrates (469-399 B.C.): I, xv, xvii, xxi, 12, 114, 256fn., 276, 327, 482, 564, 582, 584, 621; II, 406; accusations against, xii-xiiifn.; daimonion of, xx, 131, 276; a medium, II, 117-18; ideas of, 283, 284; not altogether in hell, 8.
Socrates Scholasticus (ca. 380-ca. 440), *Ecclesiastical History:* and descent into Hell, II, 514; on Eusebius' forgeries, 327; on Nicæa, 251.
Sod: a religious Mystery, I, 301fn.; meaning of, 555 & fn. of the Kadeshim, II, 131.
Sodales: I, 301fn.; priest-colleges, 555-56 & fn.
Sodalian, oath, I, 409.
Sodalities, of Greece & Rome, II, 389.
Sodium-carbonate, formula for, I, 462.
Sodom, and Gomorrah, suffering eternal fire, II, 12.
Solar: dynasty in India, II, 437-38; spectrum and three primary rays, 417-18; struggle of, and lunar chiefs, 435-36.
Soldan, W. G. ( ? -1869), *Geschichte der Hexenprocesse,* etc., on witchcraft & Jesuits, II, 61.
Solinus, I, 226, 230, 640.
Sol-Mithra, image of Father, II, 506.
Solomon: I, 19, 97, 147, 256, 410, 503, 580; II, 389, 439, 444, 525; knowledge of, from India, I, 135; seal of, 135-36, 147; II, 255fn., 265; sent navy to India, I, 136fn.; and Votan, 546, 650; brazen bowls of, II, 592; not a Mosaic Jew, 297; on man as temple of God, 230; on sons of men & higher life, 218-19; temple of, its mystic meaning, 391-92.
Solon (7th & 6th c. B.C.), I, 31, 532, 543, 557, 591.
Solovyov, V. S. (1849-1903), *A Modern Priestess of Isis,* citing H.P.B. on appearance of *Isis,* I, [1fn.].
Solvent, universal, I, 192.
Soma: I, xxxi, 157, 348; —mystery & illumination, xxxv; produces trance, 357; true nature of, xl-xli; and Eleusinia, II, 91fn.; and occult properties of plants, 590; purpose of, 117; and Sun, 167; and Vâch, 409.
Somavanśa, I, 627.
Sommona-Codom (Somona-Kodom), Siamese savior, I, 577; II, 576, 577.
Somnambulism: and dictamnus, I, 264; and levitation, xxiv, 174; and sapphire, 264; and mediumship, II, 596.
Somnambulist, and unseen universe, I, 159.
Son: as emanation, II, 227; First-born, 195, 205; in Kabalah, 226; in Nazarene system, 225; of man, as title, 176, 231-32, 238; of the Sun, 438; "Only-Begotten," in mythologies, 171, 176, 211, 228, 230, 492, 527.
"Sons of Giants," as magicians, I, 595fn.

"Sons of God": I, 2, 31, 122, 149, 151, 155, 213, 296, 299, 303, 305, 559, 593, 595fn.; II, 50, 159, 187, 193, 195, 422, 448, 467, 485, 492, 494, 566, 635; or Elohim & their mysterious island, I, 589.

Soolimas, I, 378.

Sophia: II, 156, 169, 267fn., 295, 505; female principle as Holy Ghost, I, 130; same as Sephîrâh & Mêtis, 263; corresponds to Shekhînah, II, 223, 227; identical with Binah-Yehovah, 215fn.; or Binah, 193; spiritual Eve, 171fn.; and third Sephîrôth, 42; two meanings of, 172, 175, 185.

Sophia-Akhamôth: I, 583; II, 172, 173; as sister of Christos, II, 226-27; 295; efforts of, to create visible forms, 175, 183, 184, 185; emanates Ialdabaôth, 296 & fn.; mixed in nature, 174; and Mt. Meru, 234; and Ophis, 293; and Pthahil, 174.

Sophocles (ca. 496-406 B.C.), I, 564, 584; q., 293.

Sorcerer(s): as Nâgas, I, 448; attracts elementals, 141; impervious to bullets, 379; Naguals as, 556; burnt when not priests, II, 58; can enter deserted body, 589; use breath for enchantment, 633.

Sorcery: II, 65, 353, 571-73; difference between, & magic, I, 279, 366; among Popes, II, 56; approved by Augustine, 20; as public danger, 634; by blood, 567-68; and Catherine of Medici, 55-56; def. 588; hierophants accused of, 148; in Russia, 42-44fn.; in Vatican, 6, 19-20; and mediumship, 118; of various sects, 571ff.; practiced by clergy, 633-34; and stigmata, 633-34.

Sortilegium, Sortes: forbidden by Councils, II, 21-22; practiced by clergy, 6, 20, 21; used to choose Gospels at Nicæa, 251-52.

Sosigenes (*fl.* 1st c. B.C.), and Calendar, I, 11.

Sossus, I, 30fn.

Sotheran, Chas. (1847-1902): II, 654; on Buddhism in Ireland, II, 291fn.; on modern Masonry & its true objectives, 388-91.

Soul(s): activity of, apart from body, I, 198; ancient ideas on, 317; apparition of, in material form, 493; Aristotle on double, 319; as luminous essence in Milky Way, xxi; as psychê, 401fn.; as self-moved number, xix; astral, & thoughts of living men, 292; astral light & envelope of the, 281; astral, not immortal, 432; can be recalled to life in body, 475-76; classes of, xxii; differs from spirit, 180; Duncker on, 270; dwells in body as in grave, xiii; —electricity, 322; evocation of, in theurgy, 321; evolution of, through reincarnation, 368; fate of, if not illumined by spirit, 432; forces are manifestations of, 58; *Genesis* on living, 13; and gods, 348; Görres on, 453; human, attracts in sleep congenial beings, 460; human, merges with parent-spirit, 292; immortal, & animals, 427; II, 279; irrational, of Plato, I, 181; Kabalists on spirit and, 315; leaves body and re-enters through magic, 365-66; loss of, 317-18, 328, 352, 357, 422; lusts of, 276; and memory, 179; of beasts, lxi; II, 281; of man proves God, I, vi; of world, 129, 280, 508; partakes of demiurgic powers, 396; and passages through seven spheres, 297; Plutarch on journeys of second, 476, 477; Porphyry, Iamblichus & Apuleius on, lemures & lares, 344-45; Proclus on astral, 432; projection of astral, 477; rational & irrational or astral, 251, 306; recollection of past by, xiv; science of the, 340; and Spirit, *xli;* triple, 429; two, in man & transmigration, 12; all, become men, II, 456; annihilation of, 368-69; as emanations from First Cause, 159; astral, as Demeter, 112; astral, untrustworthy, 117; *Avesta* on the, 635; def. *320;* dual, acc. to Greeks, 283ff.; earth & water required to make a, 267, 551fn.; ensnared in body, 112; evocation of the, 609-10; freed from flesh through initiation, 565; in plants, 263, 279; Jewish doctrine of "whirling of," 152; magical release of astral, from ashes, 603; *Manu* on Supreme, 116; not eternal or divine *per se,* 362; not knit to flesh, 565; often abandons body, esp. in insanity, 589; and Origen, 285; Plato on nature of, 285-86; powers of, 592-93; and prophecy, 594; rational, or nous, 279; reunion of, with spirit, 281; second death of, 368; seven-rayed God lifting the, through Him, 417; —spirit & its shadow, 113; transmigration of, 280ff.; *Vendîdâd* on the, 529.

Soul-death, II, 369.

Soulless, men & women, II, 369.

Sound(s): alliance between color and, I,

514; as spiritual numeral, 514; due to vibration of ether, 275; and clairaudience, II, 605-06; awakens another in invisible world, 411.
South Carolina, statutes on death penalty for witchcraft, II, 18.
Southey, R. (1774-1843), *Thalaba*, etc., on vampires, II, 80-81.
Sozomen, H. S. (ca. 400-443 A.D.), *Ecclesiastical History*, on cross found in Serapeion, II, 254 & fn.
Space: Descartes on fluid of, I, 206-07; infinite & boundless, 289; reservoir filled with models of beings, 116, 295, 312, 343-44; shoreless ocean, 114; and time, 184; worlds floating in electric, 302.
Spallanzani, L. (1729-99), I, 414.
Sparks, or old worlds that perished, II, 421.
Speaking, images, I, 505.
*Spectator* (London), on prejudiced investigators, I, 118.
Spectroscope: and Roscoe, I, 513; supports Paracelsus' ideas, 168-69.
Spectrum: solar, II, 417-18; solar, and religions as fragments of One Truth, 639.
Speculative, class of neophytes, II, 392.
Speech, metrical, of *Vedas*, I, 9.
Spell, evil, and wind, II, 632-33.
Spencer, H. (1820-903): I, 248, 249, 339fn. 340, 426; on hypothesis, 378.
Spencer, E. (1552?-1599), *Faerie Queene*, II, 606, 607.
Speusippus (4th c. B.C.), *Theologumena arithmetica*, on Pythagorean numerals, I, xv; on elements, xvii-xviii.
Sphere(s): eighth, & lost souls, I, 352-53; eighth, in earth's penumbra, 328; invisible, 611; music of the, 275; seven planetary, & soul's passage, 297; seven planetary, and genii, II, 184, 294, 295.
Sphericity. See Earth, Sphericity of.
*Sphinx*, Leipzig, II, 653.
Spiegel, Fr. von (1820-1905). See *Avesta*.
—— *Êrân*, etc., on Ahura, II, 297.
Spina, Alph. a, *Fortalitium fidei*, on Jesus & Mercury, II, 132.
Spinoza, Benedictus de (1632-77): I, 308, 317; and Bruno, 93-94; not an atheist, II, 531.
Spirit: as energizing principle, I, 340; astral, of man & cometary matter, 168; —birds, 71; brooding over waters, 133, 134; co-eternal with sublimated matter, 429; divine, *knows*, 305-06; divine, neither punished nor rewarded, 327; each human, a scintilla of light, 292; every particle contains spark of, 258; everything is materialization of, 428; Father— & spiritual ego, vi; has no form, 291; human, as emanation of First Cause, 436; II, 153; human, knows neither past nor future, I, 185; immortal, in every creature, 330-31; Intelligence beyond finite existences, xii; Kabalists on man's, 315; and matter as first two principles, 61, 341; Maxwell on universal, & healing, 215-16; moves every atom, 384; neither space nor time for, 141; no mâyâ, 289-90; or *inner self* & astral soul, 316; pervades all things, 244, 292; planetary, never embodied, 158; pre-existence & godlike powers of, 251; and proof of future life, 42; scintilla from central sun, 502; snapping of thread between, & soul, 315; and soul, xli, 180-81, 429; II, 281; Will & Âkâśa, 616; as interpreter, II, 635; as source of all forces, 587-88; and Cause, 402; creative, 398; must subject reason for study of magic, 636; powers of human, 638; and soul acc. to Paul, 281-82; vivifying, and water, 458.

Spirit-flowers, produced by a bhikshuṇî, II, 609.
Spirit-hands, phenomena of, II, 594-95.
Spirit-horses, I, 70.
Spirit-matter, and evolution of universe, I, 428-29.
"Spirit-voices:" audible, I, 220; not articulate, 68.
Spirits: and air, I, 290; Augustine on mischievous, 158-59fn.; II, 70; and chemical salts, I, 356-57fn.; conditions which attract, 69; controlled by initiated philosophers, 489; controlling mediums, 490; difference between apparitions of, 69; disembodied, & mediums, 67-68; earthbound, & animated statues, 616; elementals materialize reflections of human, 359; evil, & stone mnizurin, 321; few physical phenomena caused by human, 73; fluidic body of, & vampirism, 453; good & bad, 446-47; higher, 53; human, *never* materialize *in propria persona*, 67; human, can project aethereal reflection, 67; human, propitiated in India, 447; and intelligent electricity, 322-23; low & high, 487-88; magician commands, 367; may animate forms with help of elementaries, 116; nature of, discussed, 220-21; no relation to phenomena of magicians,

457; not all communicating, are elementals or elementaries, 67; numerous kinds of, in invisible universe, 344, 460; of eighth sphere, 353-55; of suicides & murderers, 344; or ghosts, hurt by weapons, 363; personated by elementaries, 68; pure, disembodied & phenomena, 321; should be discriminated, 53; talking in desert, 604; three, in man, 212; Thury on intervention of, 110; trying the, 491-92; universe filled with, 2; voices of, 68; without conscience, 53; challenge the Church, II, 23; disembodied, an inadequate theory, 637; and fakirs, 107-08, 114-15; and fumes of blood, 567-68; individual planetary, overshadow men, 159; —intercourse account at Muru, 616; Justin on seven, 187fn.; may possess body in absence of soul, 589; pure, *cannot* appear objectively, 595; and Shamanism, 615-16.

Spiritual: agents, I, 333; as noëtic element, xiii; Central, Sun, 29, 132, 243; and magnetic phenomena, 109; man as, entity, 39; nature, work of spiritual sun, 132; prototypes, 158; II, 220; scientists have no, sight, I, 318; sounds & colors are, numerals, 514; vision, 145; yearning inherent in every man, 64; aspirations promoted by ancient precepts, II, 635; emission of, substance, 213; universal belief in personal, entity, 593.

Spiritualism: I, 121, 436, 486; alphabet of, passivity, 109; Crookes' theories about, 47; and Dialectical Soc., 232-33; drifting towards Church, 53-54; and evocation of spirits, 67; fraudulent nature of some phenomena, 41; Huxley on, 422; key of, in the East, xlv; last refuge of compromise between religion & materialism, x; materializations of, xxxvi; modern, & phenomena, 40; modern form of magic, 42; phenomena of, analyzed, 195-204, 221; phenomena of, dangerous, 218; phenomena of, imitated by jugglers, 166; pronounced a delusion in Russia, 118; ridiculed by Positivists, 76-77, 80-81; science or philosophy, 83; seers & martyrs of, 494; self-complacency of, 334; and short-lived communities, 77; theories of adversaries of, 116; Tyndall on, 176, 417ff.; universally diffused, 205; vitality of, survives ridicule, 75; weakness of philosophy of, 220; what it has proved, 624; II, 584; Bishop of Toulouse on Protestants and, II, 7-8; Butleroff on, 3; denial of facts of, 369; identified with demonism by R. Church, 5; and magic very ancient, 15; offspring of theology, 120; Pope's Bull about, 69; Protestants hate, 4; Stainton Moses on, 638; suicide & insanity caused by, 7; weaknesses & needs of, 636-38; and worship of *piṭris,* 639.

*Spiritualism and Charlatanism,* on Positivism, I, 79.

*Spiritualist, The* (London): on Maruts, I, xxixfn.; on scientists, 85; (Cox) on phenomena, 624; on psychology, 611-12; on truth & prejudice, 615; (Moses) on weaknesses of Spiritualism, II, 638; (Varley) on "spirits" & chemical salts, I, 356-57.

Spiritualists: I, x, xxxvi, 36, 67; should study ancients for true philosophy, 334; back-door Nicodemuses, II, 2; iconoclasts, 637; start with a fallacy, 638; take no part in formulating a philosophy, 637.

*Spiritual Scientist,* I, [6].

*Spiritual Telegraph,* on Prof. Hare & roosters, I, 245-46.

Spiritus: and Mother, I, 300; of the Nazarenes, 582-83; II, 174-75, 187, 226-27; or female Holy Ghost with Gnostics, II, 193.

Spon, J. (1647-1685), *Miscellanea,* etc., on Chrêstos, II, 324.

Spontaneous generation, I, 414-15.

Sprengel, K. (1766-1833), *Geschichte der Arzneikunde:* I, 89; on magical cures, 532; wrong on v. Helmont, 406fn.; on Platonism & Christianity, II, 325.

Sprenger, J. (1436-1495), *Malleus maleficarum:* I, 353; on vain cleanliness, II, 511fn.

Springs, mineral, and electricity, I, 162.

Spurious, passages in *I John,* II, 177.

Square, emblem of justice, I, 9.

Squire, and Queen Elizabeth, II, 373fn.

Squirrel, materialized, I, 329.

Śraddha (Pâli: *saddha*), faith, II, 591fn.

Śrâvakas, books of the II, 323.

Srî-yantra, and design of pagodas, II, 265.

Songtsen Gampo (Tib.: Srong-*b*tsan Gampo), King, II, 616.

Śrotriya, I, 581.

Śruti, revelation, I, 444, 588; II, 431.

Stahl, G. E. (1660-1734), I, 194.

Stallbaum, L. G. (1793-1861), I, 8.

Stanhope, Lady Hester Lucy (1776-1839), and Yezîdis, II, 572, 657.
Stanley, A. P. (1815-1881), *Lectures,* etc. II, 17.
Stapleton, Wm., conjurer, II, 57.
Star(s): as shell around earth, I, xxvi; emanation from, 168; have souls, xxi; Kepler & souls of, 253fn.; man in direct affinity with, 169, 170, 259, 273, 275, 314; inhabited, II, 421; five-pointed, 270fn., 448; rays of Bethlehem, as relic, 71.
Statues: animated, I, 283, 464, 471, 485, 612, 613-14, 615-16; magnetized, & talismans, 283; portrait— produced at mediumistic séances, 70; speaking, 504.
Steam-engine, invented by Hero, I, 241.
Stedingers, accused of magic, II, 331.
Stedman, J. G. (1744-1797), *Narrative,* etc., I, 383.
Steel: in India, I, 538; and iron, 499-500; oxidizes quickly in Orient, 211.
Stellars, seven, of Nazarenes, II, 175, 187fn., 193, 234, 296.
Stephanus, H. (1528-1598), *L'Introduction au Traité,* etc., on false relics, II, 71.
Stephen, on Jewish religion, II, 526.
Stephens, J. L. (1805-1852), *Incidents of Travel in Central America:* on apes as symbols in the ruins of Copán, 564; on keystones & arches, 571; on mysterious city seen from Cordilleras, 546, 547; on Toltecs, 552.
—— *Incidents of Travel in Egypt,* on grooves coated with iron, I, 528.
Stevenson, J. See *Chronicon.*
Stewart, Balfour (1828-87), *The Conservation of Energy:* 1, 172; confused on perpetual light, 509-10; and electrobiological power, 55; on being cautious, 401, 424; on Heraclitus, 422; on man & nature, 501; on matter, 485.
—— *The Sun and the Earth:* I, 169; on attraction, xxiii; on sun-spots and potato disease, 267.
—— *The Unseen Universe.* See Tait, O. G.
*Sthâpatyaveda,* II, 556fn.
Sthâviras, II, 608.
Stigmata: I, 384ff.; and sorcery, II, 633-34.
Stilpo, and Phidias' Minerva, I, 612.
Stobaeus, J. (5th c. A.D.), *Eclogae:* I, xviii, xix: on Zeus, 263.
Stoddard, missionary, II, 474-75.
Stoic: I, 12, 13; not materialists, 317.
Stone(s): Lucretius on magnetic, I, 163; magnesian, 130; meteoric, 331, 332; of Memphis & anesthesia, 540; precious, & electric polarities, 265; engraved, II, 233fn., 351; yu, of lamas, 393.
Stone Age, man of, I, 295.
Stonehenge: and Delphi, I, 550; Dr. Stukeley on, 572.
Storozhenko, a vampire, I, 454, 646.
Stow, on fanatics, I, 218.
Strabo (63 B.C.-after 21 A.D.), *Geography:* on Aristotle, I, 643; on Niveveh, 241; on Samaneans, xlfn.
Strange, I, 583.
Strauss, D. F. (1808-1874), *Das Leben Jesu,* compared to Renan's work, II, 340-41fn.
Stukeley, Wm. (1687-1765), *Stonehenge,* etc., I, 572.
Subjective: mediums, I, 321; communications, how taught, II, 115; only world of reality is the, 639.
Substance: primordial, and its symbolism, I, 133; Plutarch on, in space, 401; eternal, of inscrutable essence, II, 264, 269.
Subterranean: passages and the fair island on inland sea, I, 590; passages in Peru, used by magicians also, 595.
Succession, Apostolic, a gross and palpable fraud, II, 544.
Sûdras: I, 435; and Brahmâ, II, 407fn.
Suetonius (*fl.* ca. 100 A.D.), *Lives of the Caesars:* I, 629; blunders about Christians, II, 142; on bells of Jupiter Capitolinus, 592; on Claudius & Christos, 335-36; on Domitian, 147fn.; on expectation of avatâra, 503.
Suez Canal, building of, I, 517.
Sufis, origin of their esoteric doctrine, II, 306.
Suicides: spirits of, and murderers, I, 344; and insanity caused by Spiritualism, II, 7.
Suidas, *Greek Lexicon:* on Medea's journey through air, I, 366; on Tyrrhenian cosmogony, 342.
Śukra-cup, I, xxxv.
Sulanuth, I, 325.
Sulla Felix, Cornelius (138-78 B.C.), I, 183.
Sulphur: secret fire of alchemists, I, 309; as curative remedy, II, 621.
Sumati, I, xi, 585.
Sümé, lamasery, II, 628.
Sumerians, II, 472.
Sun: I, 212, 255; as focus or lens, 258; as incandescent globe, 168fn.; Central Spiritual, 29, 132, 270, 302, 342; II, 13,

295; emblem of —God, I, 270; in Aries, 262; iron in the, 513; and Kircher, 208-09; not source of light & heat, 272, 281; one of *magnets* in space, 271; Osiris & Principle of Life, 506; Psellus on, 535; soul of all things, 270; source of seven powers in nature, 514; source of souls, 270; stars and, affect man, 169-70; storehouse of magnetism, 131, 271; symbolized by El, 13; and sympathy of planets, 209; temples of the, & Dracontia, 550-51; visible, as agent of Logos, 131fn.; visible, emblem of spiritual, 13fn.; as Jupiter's prison, II, 13fn.; as sphere of purification, 12-13; Christ as, 517; —God Isaral, 402; Iaô as central, 139fn., 293; increases magnetic emanations, 611; and Pythagoras, 13; races of, and of moon, 437-38; seeing the, at midnight, 146; and Soma, 167; "Sons of the," 438; with Ophites, 294fn.

Sun-gods: create physical nature only, I, 132; no relation to invisible universes, 131fn.; slaughtered, II, 173.

Sun-spots, and potato disease, I, 267.

Sun-worship: among Israelites, I, 555; in Mosaic religion, II, 129, 400; once contemplated by Catholics, 450; universal at one time, 438; and white horse, 237; and Zoroaster, 141.

*Sun, The* (New York): on Rev. Sarles & damned heathens, II, 474; on Talmage, 102fn.

*Sunday Herald* (Boston), on Protestant hatred of spiritualism, II, 4.

Sunrise, and sunset, reason for, I, 10.

Suparṇas, I, 107.

Supernatural: Brierre on, I, 71; recognized by science, 116.

Superstition: and prejudice, I, 39; Vyasa-Maya on, II, 242.

Supralapsarians, on predestination, II, 546fn.

Supreme: Plato on the, I, 308; *Manu* on identification with the, II, 159.

Sura, College of, II, 207.

Sûran, blood-miracle of, I, 613.

Surgery: in archaic India, I, 619; of Yogis and Talapoins, II, 621.

Sûrya, II, 438, 483fn.

*Sûrya-Siddhânta*, I, 619.

Susinians, I, 567.

Suśruta, I, 619.

*Sûtra of the Foundation,* etc., II, 281.

Suttee. *See* Widow-burning.

Svabhâva, I, 93, 250.

Svabhavat: not a person, I, 292; and Unknown Essence, II, 264, 266.

Svâbhâvikas: I, 250; doctrine and beliefs of, 93; II, 220, 264, 271, 530.

Svarga, I, 148; II, 107, 539, 566fn.

Svayambhû: I, xvi, 590, 629; II, 170, 271fn.; and cosmic time-periods, II, 219; emits Nara & Nârî, 214-15; and first Manu, 169; identical with Ain-Soph, 214; impelled to manifest, 225-26, 269; Manu, son of, 468; and spiritual germ, 270-71; and triple Trimûrti, 39-40, 443-44.

Svâyambhuva: I, xvi, 443, 590, 629; —Nara, II, 226.

Swearing, forbidden by Jews, II, 373.

Swedenborg, E. (1688-1772): I, 308; miraculous cures by father of, 464; natural-born magician, 306; personated by a Diakka, 219; tells where to seek *lost word,* 580; II, 470, 471; great seer, II, 73; rite of, Jesuitical product, 390.

—— *Arcana caelestia,* interprets *Genesis* correctly, I, 306.

—— *True Christian Religion,* on image of God, I, 308.

Swedenborgians, believe in soul's withdrawal from body, II, 589.

Swinden, Rev. T. ( ? -1719), *Inquiry,* etc., on Hell's location, II, 12, 13.

Sword: II, 270fn.; elementaries afraid of, I, 359, 362ff.; and fire, 247-48.

Sydenham, Floyer (1710-87), I, 8.

*Syllabus,* affinities of, with *Koran,* II, 82.

Sylvester II, Pope (r. 999-1003), sorcerer, II, 56.

Symbolic: language of ancients, I, 37; meaning of mystical writings, 628.

Symbolism, of *Nychthêmeron,* II, 467, 468.

Symbols: ancient, universal, I, 572-73; apes as, 564; as embodying ideas, 22; as representing esoteric principles, 24; exoteric & universal religion, 560; identical, for same esoteric truths, 577-78; key to ancient, in secret fraternity, 573; misunderstood, 582-83; ancient sex, taken over by Christians, II, 109; Christian, of pagan origin, 94, 96, 334-35; enemy of clerical pretence, 254; heathen religious, 554; key to secret of, unknown to Ch. Fathers, 403; modern scholars see only physical aspect of, 120; myths & allegories identical in various systems, 405; of Hindu gods, 301; pagan paterni-

ty of Christian, 120; Roman C. dignitaries aware of real meaning of ancient, 110-11.
Sympathy: between man & nature, I, 247; between man & tree, 246; offspring of light, 309; Proclus on, 243-44; universal magnetic, 206ff.
Synagogue, best behaved of Churches, II, 477.
Syncellus, Georgius (8th & 9th c. A.D.): accuses Eusebius, II, 327; falsifies himself, 327.
Synesius (ca. 370-430): I, 251; II, 53, 84; believed spirit pre-existed, I, 316; on books of stone, 257, 641; most unfortunate Christian, II, 198.
—— *Hymn III*, on Artificer of the gods, II, 198.
—— *Letter to Brother*, on being philosopher & priest, II, 198-99.
—— *Letter to Hypatia*, II, 53.
Syrian, heresies are original Christianity, II, 137.
Syrians: II, 306, 418, 482fn., 524, 550; and Pythagoras, I, 284.

T

Taaut, or Saturn, II, 235.
Tabasun-Nor, and tomb of Chingîz-Khân, I, 598-99, 656-57.
Taberna, J. B. (1622-1686), *Synopsis theologiae*, etc., on bribe, II, 356.
Tabernacles, Feast of, and Eleusinia, II, 44.
Tables: intelligent replies given by, I, 112; levitated, tipping, etc., 99, 105; made immovable, 99, 204; moving, and Babinet's explanation, 60-61; moving, and intelligent electricity, 322-23.
*Tablet 562*, British Museum, II, 361.
Tachenius, Otto ( ? -1670), I, 193.
Tacitus (55?-after 117 A.D.), *Annals:* on Memnon, I, 514; on expectations of avatâra, II, 503; on worship of ass, 523fn.
Tafel, Dr. R. L., on Swedenborg, II, 471.
Tailapaca, a bird, I, 470.
Tait, P. G. (1831-1901) & B. Stewart, *The Unseen Universe:* I, 159, 185, 189; on ether & inv. universe, 67, 187-88, 395; on mysteries of science, 187; on thought & matter, 186; q. Young, 185.
*Taittirîya-Âranyaka,* I, 649.
*Taittirîya-Brâhmaṇa,* on magic, I, xxvii.

Talapat Nang, Mongolian sacred fan, II, 603.
Talapoins: power of, I, 213-14; of Siam, 577; and treated linen, 231; curative means of, II, 621; Jesuits disguised as, 371, 577fn.; long-lived, 620; strict morality of, 321, 531.
Taley-lama [rGyalpo-Rinpoche]: I, xxxiii, xxxiv, 442; reincarnation of a, 437-38; and mysteries of Lamaism, II, 93; palace of, 616fn.; and the A-yu talisman, 600fn.; and tiara of Popes, 30fn.
Taliesin, a Druid & Serpent, I, 554, 651.
Talisman: I, 462, 464; and amulets, II, 351-52; and Tibetans, 600; of Apollonius of Tyana ($\tau\epsilon\lambda\acute{\epsilon}\sigma\mu\alpha\tau\alpha$), 97; of Lady Ellenborough, 255-56; of Shamans, 626.
Talmage, Rev. Dr., blasphemes, II, 102.
*Talmud:* an enigma, I, 17; Maimonides on, 17; borrowed from *Avesta*, II, 206; calls Jesus "that man," 537fn.; on garden of delight, 119; on James, 148; on Paul, 537; on Peter, 127; on Rabbi Hananyah's miracles, 357; on thirteen murderers after Cain, 448.
—— *Midrash Berêshîth Rabbah:* II, 424; Greek transl. of, 247; on Elohim being pleased, 421; on worlds destroyed, 220.
—— *Midrash Ḥazitha*, on Israel and new gate, II, 245.
—— *Midrash Rabboth*, and Ch. Fathers, II, 247.
—— *Midrashim*, II, 247fn.
—— *Mishnah*, on Ḥokhmah-Akhamôth, II, 468.
—— *Mishnah Ḥagîgâh:* on the four Tannaim, II, 119; on the Merkabah, 350.
—— *Mishnah Hulin*, on Noah & dove, II, 448fn.
—— *Mishnah Nazir*, on Nazarenes, II, 151fn.
—— *Mishnah Pirke Aboth:* and Gospels, II, 338fn.; on soul, 280.
—— *Mishnah Sanhedrin*, on lapidation of Jesus, II, 255fn.
—— *Mishnah Sotah*, on Jesus in Egypt, II, 201.
—— *Mishnah Sukkah*, on pouring water seven days, II, 550fn.
—— *Torah Kethubim & Nebiim*, II, 430.
—— *Yôḥânân*, II, 148.
Tambov, portrait-phenomenon at, II, 17-18fn.
Tamil Hindus, and Kutti-Shattan, I, 567.
al-Tamîmî, divine soul of Druzes, II, 310.

Taming, wild beasts by will power and music, I, 381-84.
Tanga-tanga, II, 49.
*Tanjur* (Tib.: *bs*Tan-ḥgyur), I, 580 & fn.
Tanmâtra: II, 209; and five elements, 226.
Tannaim: I, 136fn., 580; II, 154, 155, 206, 207, 260, 349, 350, 352, 357, 470, 561; as Kabalists, I, xxxiv; are blameless, II, 220; four, & Garden of Delight, 119; Jewish, School, 198.
Taossé, II, 618-19, 620.
Ta perierga (τὰ περίεργα), "curious arts," II, 155.
Tappan, Cora L. V., on Moses & witches, I, 356fn.
Tarchon, and lightning, I, 527.
*Targûm of Jerusalem,* on Be-rêshîth, II, 35.
*Targûm of Onkelos:* on King Messiah, II, 244; and *New Test.,* 247fn.
*Targûmim,* on Shekhînah, II, 224.
Tarkov, Shamhal of, II, 568fn., 656.
Taro, as symbol, I, 462.
Tartarus: descent of a god into, II, 514-15; and Gehenna, 507.
Tartary: I, 598, 599; II, 603, 632; happy and heathen, II, 240.
Tashi-Lhünpo (Tib.: *bk*ra-śis-lhün-po), II, 618.
Tasso, T. (1544-1595), *La Gerusalemme liberata,* I, 253.
Tatars: I, 214; II, 631, 632; and Laplanders, I, 247; and Shamans, xxxix-xl; triple god of Northern, II, 49.
Tathâgata, def., II, *550fn.*
Tatian (120?- ? ), disciple of Justin Martyr, II, 182fn.
— *Oratio adversus Graecos,* on man being as immortal as God, I, 13.
Tau: II, 94, 293, 365; at Palenque, I, 572; as tree of life, II, 256; at Dendera, 454; attribute of Isis, 392-93; known to Jews, 454-55; magic talisman, 254-55; symbol of dual generative power, 254.
Taurus: I, 262; II, 456, 461-62; and Kain, II, 465.
Taylor, Bayard (1825-78): I, 412; on Greek statues, 6.
Taylor, John (1580-1653), *Old, Old, Very Old Man,* II, 656.
Taylor, R. (1784-1844), Credo of, II, 522-23.
— *The Diegesis,* II, 331fn.
Taylor, Thos. (1758-1835): unceremonious with Mosaic God, I, 288; brave defender of ancient faith, II, 108-09; on philology & philosophy, 414; Wilder on, as scholar, 109.
— *Iamblichus' Life of Pythagoras:* on magic powers of Pythagoras, I, 283, 284; q. Sextus' precepts, II, 338. See Iamblichus.
— *Iamblichus on the Mysteries,* I, 219, 345, 416. See Iamblichus.
— *Mystical Hymns of Orpheus,* on Zeus, I, 263, 636.
— *Proclus on the Theology of Plato.* See Proclus.
— *Select Works of Plotinus:* I, 16; q. Asclepian Dialogue, 247, 640.
— *Select Works of Porphyry:* I, 638; on divinely-luminous appearances, I, xliii; on phantasy, II, 591-92.
— *The Descr. of Greece by Pausanias:* on perpetual lamps, I, 227; q. Psellus on magic, 282-83.
— *The Eleusinian and Bacchic Mysteries:* II, 123fn., 495; q. Psellus on magic, I, 282-83; q. Theon on initiation, xiv; hymn to Athena, II, 123; on Archons & *basileus,* 90; on criminals excluded from Mysteries, 98; on epopteia, 113; on esoteric wisdom of ancients, 146fn.; on faith, 120; on gradations in Mysteries, 101; on magical evocations, 118; on meaning of Lesser Mysteries, 111-12; on parables, 145; on Peter & Pether, 92.
— *Theoretic Arithmetic,* on the elements, I, xvii.
— *The Works of Plato:* II, 113fn., 469; App. to *Timaeus* q. I, xix; on seeing death & re-entry of soul, 365-66; q. Proclus on resuscitations, 364-65.
Tcherno-bog, black god of Variago-Russ, II, 572.
Tee, of pagodas and the cross, II, 270fn.
Teḥuti (or Thoth), I, 254.
*Telegraphic Journal,* on scientific prophecy, I, 533.
Telegraphy, neurological, I, 324.
Telein (τελεῖν), Mysteries, II, 284.
Teleiôtês (τελειωτής), initiate, finisher, perfecter, II, 93.
Telepathy, as power of soul, I, 280.
Telephone: II, 605, 619; discovery of, I, 126-27.
Telescope, in lighthouse at Alexandria, I, 528.
Telesmata (τελέσματα), talisman, II, 97.
Teletê (τελετή; τελεται), perfective rite, initiation, II, 101.

Teleutan (τελευτᾶν), to die, II, 284.
Temir-Khân-Shura: II, 568 fn., 656; sect near, evokes phantoms through blood, 567-68.
Templars. *See* Knights-Templar.
Templarism, is Jesuitism, II, 390.
Temple(s): ancient, their message to man, I, 573; keystones of, 572; rock-cut, 590; secret knowledge confined to, 25; sun & dragon, 550.
Temple of Solomon: Hebrew prophets did not care for, II, 525; mystic meaning of, 391-92; not very ancient, 389.
*Tempora mutantur*, etc., I, 40.
Temurah, II, 298.
Ten: Hermetic ideas on one and, II, 298; Pythagorean, 171; virtues cited by Manu, 98.
Terah, and Abraham, I, 570, 579; II, 38.
Teraphim, are Kabiri, I, 570.
Teratology: among animals, I, 397-98; and birth marks, 390ff., 399-400; and reincarnation, 351.
Terrestrial: circulation of, fluids, I, 503; or earthly elementaries, 319; immortality, II, 620.
Tertullian (ca. 155-ca. 222): on devils, I, 159; on elementals, 311; on "monkey of God," 46; on soul being corporeal, 317; becomes Montanist, II, 157fn., 188; bigotry of, 166; expelled from Ch. of Rome, 188-89fn.; patristic firebrand, 329; Reuss on, 329.
—— *Adv. Marcionem*: abuses Marcion, II, 160, 166; on Marcion's view of Christ, 168.
—— *Adv. Praxeam*, mentions no descent into Hell, II, 514.
—— *Apologeticus*: on madness, I, 293; falsifies pagans, II, 510.
—— *De oratione*, on *Pastor*, II, 243fn.
—— *De praescr. haeret.*: II, 24fn., 648; mentions no descent into Hell, 514; on Basilides, 189; on eucharist, 44fn.; on Valentinus, 333fn.
—— *De pudicitia*, on "Good Shepherd" picture, II, 149.
—— *De spectaculis*, on his enemies burning in Hell, II, 250.
Tertullus, accuses Paul, II, 137.
Teste, A.: I, 166; on being suspected as dupe, 176.
Testimony: human, I, 120-21; 193-94; Voltaire on, 99.
Tê. *See* Thoth.

Tetragram, sacred, I, 507.
Tetragrammaton, II, 255, 297, 299, 302, 398, 462, 478, 482, 501.
Tetraktys (τετρακτύς): I, 9, 320; & Monad, 507; II, 419; and Zeus, I, 262; or Arba, II, 171; Theon on, 405; and Trinity, 36; with Ophites, 171.
Textor de Ravisi (1822-1902): on Jacolliot, II, 47; on Krishṇa, I, 586; II, 158fn.
Texts, Egyptian, unintelligible to later scribes, II, 415.
Thales (6th c. B.C.): I, 189, 512; and amber, 234; and heliocentric system, 526; and watery principle, 134; II, 458.
Tharshish, in India, I, 136fn.
Thaumaturgist(s): good health of, I, 490; use Ākâśa, 113; Jewish, II, 357; power of, over body, 588.
Thaums, of Jesus, II, 194.
Théâtre Porte St.-Martin, and intelligent echo, I, 606.
Thebes (or Tha-ba): I, 564, 565, 626; serpent's catacombs at, 553; Memphis & Karnak, 523; origin of word, II, 448; twelve tortures of, 364.
Themis, blindfold, II, 54.
Theocletes, grand-Pontiff, II, 382.
Theodas, *Alexandrian MS.* (unavailable), about Bruchion, II, 27.
Theodikê (θεοδίκη), as divine justice, I, 561.
Theodoret (ca. 386-ca. 457 A.D.): falsified Gnostic teachings, II, 177; on Simon, 91fn.
—— *Eccles. History*, on descent into Hell, II, 514.
—— *Haeret. fabul.*: confused on Gnostics, II, 176; on Gnostic Delegatus, 194; on Jesus, 193; on Nazarenes & Peter, 127, 181; on Ophite cosmogony, 187-88.
—— *Quaest. in Exodum*, on Iaô, II, 301.
Theodosius, Emperor (ca. 346-395), a murderer, II, 528.
Theology(ies): conflict of, with science, I, ix-x, xlv; cramped idea of history, 522; disfigured Scriptures, 13 & fn.; Christian, breeds crime, II, 586; and one truth, 639; science of comparative, 25, 531; subversive & evil, 639.
Theomania, ecstatic, of Calvinists & its cause, I, 371.
Theomythos, and electromagnetic powers, I, 23.
Theon of Alexandria (1st c. A.D.), fragment of, I, 30fn.

Theon of Smyrna (*fl.* ca. 115-140 A.D.), on philosophy & Mysteries, I, xiv-xv.
—— *Mathematica:* on gradation in Mysteries, II, 101; on Tetraktys, 405.
Theophilus of Alexandria: II, 304; bribing slaves, 28; destroys the Eclectic School, 52-53.
Theophilus of Antioch ( ? -ca. 182 A.D.), *Ad Autolycum,* on gods of Egypt, I, 406.
Theophrastus, I, xix, 320.
Theopoiia (θεοποιία): as a science, and animated statues, I, 615-16; and theurgy, xlii.
Theos (ὁ θεός): I, xii, xliii; alteration of, II, 178.
Theosebeia, wise men, II, 415.
*Theosophical Path, The* (Point Loma), I, 647.
Theosophical Society: I, 51, 66, 325; original objects, xli-xlii.
Theosophist(s): I, 426, 587; II, 41, 380; def. *xli;* makes pre-Adamic earth, I, 505; must meet world at large, 36; originated in Germany, II, 20.
*Theosophist, The* (Adyar), I, 43-44, 44, 44-45, 46, 50, 55, 629, 633.
Theosophy, Oriental Kabala & Neo-Platonists, II, 34.
Therapeutae (θεραπευτής): II, 41, 127, 144, 196; defiled by contact with money, I, 488; derivation of name, 491fn.; forefathers of later hermits, 33; and Koinobioi, 305; neither Christians nor monks, 324; offspring of Essenes, 37fn., 144; probably Buddhists, 491.
Thermouthis (or Ernutet), daughter of Pharaoh, I, 556.
*Thesis propugnata,* etc.: on Christian religion not evidently true, II, 358-59; on Jesuits disguised as Talapoins, 371, 577fn.
Thespesius, apparently dead for three days and his experiences, I, 484.
Thessaly: priests of, I, 366; sorcery in, II, 568, 589.
Theurgists: I, *xlii,* 128-29, 205, 219; II, 3, 51, 90, 97, 118, 121, 128, 352, 370, 477, 502; not "spirit-mediums," II, 118; persecuted by Christians, 34.
Theurgy (θευργία): I, 243, 284, 485, 489, 512, 527; II, 58, 113; and bad daemons, I, 219, 333; evocation of souls in, 321; keys left by, & future psychology, 334-35; last expression of occult science, 281; and magnetism, 130; phenomena of, produced by magnetism, 23; and *subjective* evocations, 66; human sacrifices as perversion of, II, 565fn.; known to Hypatia, 253; seventh rite of, 564-65.
Thevetat: II, 576; King, and Atlantis magicians, I, 593.
Thibault de Chanvalon, J.-B. (1725?-1785), *Voyage à la Martinique,* on serpents, I, 382.
Thief, on the cross, original source of, II, 546.
Thillaye, and mesmerism, I, 174.
Thilorier, I, 188.
Things ineffable (ἄρρητα ῥήματα), II, 146.
Third: Adam or *nephilim,* I, 559; emanation and physical matter, 302; race of men in Hesiod, 558fn.
Thirteen, Mexican serpent-gods, I, 572.
Thlinkithians, I, 593.
Thmei: I, 537; II, 209, 648; genius of Truth, II, 494.
Thomas, St.: and *Credo,* II, 514; engrafted Christian heresy on religion of Krishna, 539.
Thompson, A. Todd, I, 25, 115, 479.
Thompson, Elizabeth, II, iii.
Thompson, R. W. (1809-1900), *The Papacy,* etc., II, 378.
Thomson, Allen, (1809-84), I, 387.
Thomson, Sir Wm. (Lord Kelvin, 1824-1907), *Address,* on science, I, 223.
Thor: and cosmic electricity, I, 160-62, 262; bruises head of serpent, II, 447.
Thory, C. A. (1759-1827), *Histoire de la Fondation,* etc., II, 384.
Thoth (Tehuti, Tat, Têt, etc.): I, xxxiii, 554; meaning of, 444; as a snake, II, 484; and Egyptian Ritual, 367.
Thoth-Hermes, I, 131.
Thought(s): affecting other planes, I, 186; and cyclic epidemics of ideas, 274; Divine, & Brahmâ, 92; give rise to astral forms, 292; guided by spiritual beings, 366; and matter, 186, 327; power & magnetic attractions of, 181; projected on astral light, 395; and production of matter, 310-11; concealed the world in silence, II, 116; and desire can assume objective appearance, 410-11; Divine, & concealed Wisdom, 41; Divine & Unknown Essence, 265; Father as latent, 506; impressed upon astral ether, 59; may become corporealized by will, 619; and Poimandres, 50; power of, & phenomena, 320; same as Ennoia, 171.

Thought-transference, by Shaman with a stone, II, 627.
Thouret, M. A. (1749-1810), *Recherches*, etc., I, 172.
Thraêtona, II, 486 & fn.
Three: kabalistic faces, etc., I, 302; degrees of communication with spirits, II, 115; heavenly witnesses, 177-78.
Threefold: nature of man in *Edda*, I, 151; Origen on, nature of man, II, 285.
Thrum-stone, or *asbestinus*, I, 231.
Thuêris [Ta-urt], same as Isis, II, 490.
Thummin, I, 536, 537.
Thumoeides (θυμοειδές), and thumos, I, xiii.
Thumos (θυμός): II, 283, 286; and nous, I, 429; and thumoeides, xiii.
Thury: I, 54, 55, 125, 222; on alleged intervention of spirits in phenomena, 110; on levitation, 112; on psychode and ectenic force, 113.
Thyônê (Θυώνη), and Nisus, II, 560fn.
Tiamat, II, 267fn., 444, 445.
Tiara: of Popes & of Taley-Lama, II, 30fn.; origin of Papal, 94.
Tiberias, Jews of, I, 26.
Tiberius (42 B.C.-37A.D.), and glass cup, I, 50.
Tibet (or Tu-phoo): Eastern, and Kokonor, II, 600fn.; magic in, 616ff.
Tibetan(s): I, 580, 599; II, 95, 290, 603, 626; and mundane egg, I, 152; ranks of, Buddhist Order, 631; intuitive perception of occult forces in, II, 636; lamas, 563; talisman of, 600.
Tibullus, Albius (48?-19 B.C.), *Elegies*, on bronze bells & enchantment, II, 624fn.
Tides: and fishes, I, 210; and moon, 273.
T'ien-t'ân, Peking temple, II, 554.
Tiffereau, G. T. (b. 1819), *L'Or et la transmutation des métaux*, on making gold, I, 509, 647.
Tiger: ant higher than, I, 433; mesmerized, 467; II, 623.
Tikkun, the first-born engenders Adam, II, 276.
Tillemont, L. S. le Nain de (1637 - 1698), *Mémoires*, etc., on pagans condemned to Hell, II, 8.
Tillotson, J. (1630-1694), *Works*, on eternal punishment, II, 12.
Timaeus Locrius, *On the Soul*, I, 55fn., 316.
Time: and space, I, 184; boundless, II, 220-21; and space no obstacle to inner man, 588.
*Times* (Chicago), II, 543.
*Times* (London): on exorcism in Barcelona, II, 68-69fn.; (Capel) on miracles at Lourdes, I, 120; (Müller) on Nirvâṇa, II, 432.
*Times* (New York), on suspended animation, I, 479.
*I Timothy*, II, 91fn., 485.
Tiphereth, II, 213.
Tiresias, I, 448.
Tîrthaṃkâra, and tuition of Buddha, II, 322.
Tîrthikas, and Nirvâṇa, I, 431.
Tiryns, and Cyclops, I, 529.
Tischendorf, L. F. K. von (1815-1874): II, 159, 650; and Syrian Gospels, 137.
Tissu, as spiritual teacher, II, 608-09.
Titans: I, 122, 567; II, 217-18, 425, 487, 488.
Titanic, power and divine magnetic spirit, I, 132.
Tithymallus, and sun, I, 209.
Titis, Placidus de (middle of 17th c.), *Tabulae*, etc., on Venus' bluish lustre, II, 294fn., 651-52.
Tobo, and Adam, II, 517.
Tôḍas: fulfill a high purpose, II, 615; nature and character of, 613-15, 659.
Toghon-Temur, verses by, on Daïtu, II, 587.
Tokei, peacock, I, 136fn.
Tollenare, J. de, *Imago primi*, etc., on Jesuitism & Jesus, II, 355.
Toltecs, and Israel, I, 552.
Tombs, hidden, of Egyptian Kings, II, 403-04.
Tomline, Geo. (1750-1827), *Elements of Christian Theology*, on forged verse in *1 John*, II, 178.
To on (τὸ ὄν): II, 38; and emanation, I, 242.
Tooth, and other relics of Jesus, II, 71.
Tophet: and Hinnom, II, 11; not a place of endless woe, 507.
*Torah*. See *Talmud*.
Torches, as emblems of resurrection, II, 518.
Torphaeus, T. (1636-1719), *Historia Vinlandiae*, etc., on Markland, I, 592.
Torquemada, Thos. de (1420-98): burnings of, II, 62fn.; destroys Hebrew Bibles, 430; and Inquisition, 59.
Torralva, Dr. E., trial of, II, 60-61.

Torres, Don Juan, *Manuscript*, I, 552.
Toulouse, Bishop of, on Spiritualism, II, 7-8.
Townshend, Col., and suspended animation, I, 483.
Tradition(s): identity of, & ceremonies, I, 557; oldest, supported by modern discoveries, 3; secret, 557-58; uniform religious, 152.
Traividyâ: I, xliv; sacred science, II, 269-270.
Trance: I, 201, 476, 477, 479, 481ff., 494; depth of, and soul-powers, 181; in mesmerization, 113; medium in, not his own master, 360; and quasi-omniscience, 141; subject in, may be killed by contact, 140fn.; subject in, never hurt, 166; Pliny on artificial help to, II, 592.
*Transactions of Med. Soc. of N.Y.* (G. J. Fisher): on authority, I, 396; on monsters, 390.
*Transactions of Royal Asiatic Soc.* (H. T. Colebrooke), II, 39fn.
*Transactions of Soc. of Bibl. Arch.* (Geo. Smith), II, 442.
Transmigration: I, 448-49; and Pharisees, 347; or *revolutio* & Gilgûlah, II, 152; universally taught, 280ff. *See also* Metempsychosis.
Transmutation: and elements, I, 503ff.; men who testified to, 504; Peisse & Tiffereau on, 509.
Transubstantiation: II, 560-61; origin of, I, xxvii.
Trapaca, I, 597.
Travancore: perpetual lamp in, I, 225; proverb on moon, 273.
Treason, and lies, II, 330.
Treasures: buried in Gobi, I, 598; of Incas, 596ff.
Trediakovsky, V. K. (1703-1769), I, 46.
Tree: Gogard, I, 297; Kumbum, 289, 302, 440; II, 46, 609; mundane, in *Edda,* India & Tibet, I, 151, 152, 153, 157; and pyramid, 154; Tsité, & Third Race men, 558; world—, 297; Yggdrasill, 133, 151-52; of Knowledge & Life, II, 264, 267, 269, 293-94; Pippala, 412.
Triad: I, 336; II, 405; demiurgic, I, 262; duad becomes a, 348; human, xli, 212; II, 114-15; Vedic, I, xvii; and battle of life, II, 112; *Books of Hermes* on, 50; Chaldean, 48; complete man a, 195, 362; divine, 48, 50; first abstract, 267, 268; Kabalistic, 169; Kabalistic, & trigons, 465; mystery of, cannot be revealed, 115; of gods, 171; Persian, 59; primitive, in all theogonies, 454; second, 268; Semitic, 51.
Triangle: double, of Masons, II, 270fn.; meaning of, in symbolism, 270.
Tribes, of Israel, mythical, I, 568; II, 429fn.
*Tribune* (New York): I, 636; on *Ebers Papyrus,* 3, 21.
Tridandin, I, xvii.
Tridi, I, 122.
Trigonocephali, deadly in India, II, 622.
Trigons, II, 465, 466.
Triguṇa, Virgin, II, 209.
Trimûrti: I, xvii, 93, 160; II, 169, 171, 213, 276, 537; and double triangle, II, 270; habitation of, 234; indivisible as abstraction, 303; male & female, 444; primordial secret, 268; triple manifested, 227; triple, & Svayambhû, 39-40, 444.
Trincomalee, II, 622.
Trinities: II, 238, 268; Brahmanical, 173; Chaldean & Ophite, 169-72, 295-96; Hindu, is a unity & convertible, 278, 444; in ancient pantheons, 48-51, 212-15, 226ff.; Kabalistic, 222, 226; metaphysical, 39-40; of initiates, 38; two, in *1 John,* 334.
Trinity: II, 238, 407, 419, 506; Hindu, explained, I, xvi-xvii, 93; man as a, 212, 327, 328; II, 114-15fn., 195, 587-88; mystical, of Orphism, I, 262; of fire, 423; Plato's, 56; real meaning of, 160; universal, & man, 341; ancient origin of, II, 46; dogma of, not in *O.T.* or *N.T.,* 522; female principle of, 172; in Chaos & manifested, 212; Kabalistic, model for Christian, 222, 272; of man as key to magic, 635; of workers in every cosmogony, 420; origin of Christian doctrine of, 33-34, 36, 41, 49, 171, 177-78, 226; second person of, untenable, 37; and Sesostris, 51; solar, 417.
*Tripiṭaka* (Pâli: *Tipitaka*), I, 442, 565.
Trismegisti: in history, II, 38.
Trithemius [Tritheim], Joh. (1462-1516): II, 20; recipe of, for perpetual lamp, I, 229fn.
—— *Annales de origine gentis Francorum,* II, 641.
—— *Annales Hirsangiensis,* II, 641.
—— *Polygraphia,* II, 641.
—— *De scriptoribus eccles.,* II, 641.

—— *Steganographia*, II, 64; on projection of astral soul, I, 476-77.
Trizna, ancient "feast for the dead," II, 569-70.
Trojan, war counterpart of that in *Rāmāyana*, I, 566.
Trolls, and bells of churches, II, 624fn.
Troy, and worship of Kabiri, I, 570.
*Trübner's Amer. & Oriental Lit. Record* (M. Müller), on Nirvāṇa, II, 432.
Truth(s): adepts as safekeepers of, I, 37; compromise, 176; Espagnet on, 628; eternal, never destroyed, 560; four, 291; growing body of, 405; must have proper soil, 219; Plato on love of, xiii; Poimandres on, & death, 624-25; and prejudice, 615; Proclus on perceiving, 336; scientific, 163; Cassels on need of, II, 126; divine, is true philosophy, 121; is everywhere, 337; One, one Church as temple within us, 635; one universal, 639; unveiled, 640; what is, 2.
Tsabaôth: II, 66, 131, 207, 417, 487, 518; genius of the spheres, 184, 294.
Tschudi, J. J. von (1818-1889), and hidden treasure of Incas, II, 26fn.
—— *Antigüedades Peruanas*, on Incas' treasure, I, 546, 596.
Tshiddy-Parvâdy [?], I, xxviii.
Tsité, and third race men, I, 558fn.
Tsong-Kha-pa (1358-1419): and Kumbum tree, II, 609; manifests at Dga'-ldan, 616.
Tuam, Irish cross at, Asiatic, II, 538.
Tubal-Cain, I, 579.
Tughlak, Muḥammad ibn (r. 1325-51), and levitation, I, 472.
Tukki, peacock, I, 136fn.
Tukt-i-Sulaiman, II, 439.
Tula, I, 552.
Tulku, doctrine of, I, [11ff.], 631; II, 660.
Tullia, lamp burning in tomb of, I, 224, 228.
Tullus Hostilius (673-642 B.C.), consumed by lightning, I, 527.
Tum, devotees of, II, 387.
Tumen', Prince: and figurines made of ashes, II, 603fn.; hospitable to H.P.B., 600fn.
Tunnel, from Cuzco to Lima, I, 597-98.
Turanians: I, 570, 579; II, 46, 48fn., 472; and Assyrians, I, 576.
Turkey, wars with Russia, I, 260.
Turks, I, 451; II, 81.
Turner, S. (1749?-1802), *An Account of an Embassy*, etc., II, 598.

—— "Letter of S. Turner to the Governor General," on interviewing 18-month old lama, II, 598.
Turu, II, 500.
Twelve: fable of the, Houses, I, 267; law of, tables and its date, 588; thousand divine years, I, 342; II, 468; Dii minores, II, 451; disciples sent out by Jehoshaphat, 577; great gods & Zodiac, 448; labors of adeptship, 564; labors of Hercules on chair of Peter, 25fn.; tortures of Theban initiation, 364; tortures of Mithraic mysteries, 351; transformations of earth, 455.
Two: primeval principles, I, 341; souls taught by philosophers, 12, 317; tale of the, brothers of Central America, 550; Brothers in Bible, II, 489; doctrine of, principles brought from Persia, 501.
Tylor, E. B. (1832-1917), *Researches*, etc.: I, 246; on fire & sword, 247-48.
Tyndall, J. (1820-93): I, 4, 43, 57, 135, 137, 188, 242, 256, 285, 336, 340, 396, 404, 427, 439; Belfast address of, 314, 418; borrowing ideas of earlier thinkers, 250; and Dialectical Soc., 232; and Gen. Pleasonton, 273fn.; on supersensual beings, 314; on factors required by genuine science, II, 637.
—— *Fragments of Science*: I, xxv; on brain & consciousness, 86; on Emerson & truth, 99; on mysteries of matter, 14; on religion & spiritualism, 417, 419; on science & theology, vii; on science & universe, xxii; on scientists as cowards, 418; on spiritualistic phenomena, 176; on Ultramontane mind, 87; on vapors assuming weird shapes, 128; on what is allegedly impossible, 417.
—— *Sound*, on sensitive flame, II, 606.
Type, Chinese movable, I, 513.
Types: human, reproduced from age to age, I, 35; lower, concrete images of higher, 14.
Typhon: I, 132; II, 478, 518, 547; as Seth or Satan, I, 554; II, 482fn., 484, 487, 494, 523; one with Apollo & Osiris, I, 550; androgynous at first, II, 524; begat Hierosolymus & Judaeus, 487-88; becomes an evil demon, 487, 488; chasing divine boy, 490; character of, in Egypt, 483; dark shadow of Osiris, 507; or Apophis & Horus, 446; red-skinned, 489, 507fn.; and symbol of ass, 483.

Tyrian, worship & Ahab of Israel, II, 525.
Tyrrhenian, cosmogony, I, 342.
Tzendales, Nin or Imos of the, I, 551, 552.

## U

Udumbara, flower, I, 438.
Udyâna (or Pashai), land of sorcery, I, 599.
Ultramontanes: of Cath. Church side with Mohammedans, II, 82; one with Jesuitism, 356.
Ultramontanism, in science, I, 87.
Ulysses: adventures of, and Norway, I, 549; frightens phantoms with sword, 362.
Umbilical, chord ruptured and cicatrized, I, 386-87.
Umbilicus, represented by the Arc, II, 444.
*Umbra, manes* and *anima*, I, 37.
Unavoidable Cycle. *See* Circle of Necessity.
Unconscious: cerebration, I, 45, 55, 232; ventriloquism, 101.
Underworld: and the *manes*, I, 37; Euripides on, II, 517; and initiation, 514fn.; Pindar on, 111.
Undines, and sylphs, I, 17.
Unitarians, God of, a bachelor, II, 2.
United States: a Catholic, II, 379; Brotherhood of Luxor in, 308fn.; statistics on clergy in, 1-2.
Unity, Supreme, of three trinities, II, 39-40.
Universal: Archaeal, soul, I, 130; doctrine of, of mind in all philosophies, 289; Newton on, agent, 177-78; relation of, soul to animal soul, 316-17; solvent, 50, 133, 189; Soul or Astral Light, 56.
*Universal History, An,* etc., on Zacchar & Jordan, II, 550fn.
Universality, of doctrine on monuments, I, 571.
Universe: as body, spirit & soul of *Invisible Central Sun,* I, 302; beginnings of, 428-29; chaos to senses, cosmos to reason, xvi; double, 324; filled with spiritual beings, 2, 603; II, 15; invisible, inhabited also, I, 344; unseen, & evolution of forms, 295-96; visible, concrete image of ideal abstraction, 342; whole, as musical instrument, 514; abstract, II, 214; dissolution & re-appearance of, 219, 265; emanation of, 272; evolved from pre-existent matter, 455; four ages of, 421; present, one of infinite series, 265, 270;

twenty-two, of Buddhism, 156fn.; unseen, or astral light & its records, 588.
Unknown: craving for, congenital to man, I, 76; as future self of man, II, 115; One above, 150, 242; Presence witnessed by disciple, 114.
Un-nefer, II, 324.
Upâdâna, longing for life, II, 320.
Upâsakas, and Upâsikâs, their rules of life, II, 608.
Upasampadâ, II, 321 & fn.
Upasampanna, II, 508.
*Upaveda,* II, 556fn.
Upham, C. W. (1802-1875), *Salem Witchcraft,* etc.: I, xxiv; on spirit-birds, 71; on causing injury at distance, 361.
Upham, E. (1776-1834), *Hist. and Doctrine of Buddhism:* on Samaneans, I, xlfn.; on transmigration, 48-49; on Dr. Judson & Buddhism, II, 553-54.
—— *Mahâvansi,* etc., on Rahu, II, 509.
'Uqqâls, Druze initiates, II, 292, 309 & fn., 311fn., 315, 572.
Ur: and America, I, 549; meaning of, 579.
Urabá, Gulf of, and Atlan, I, 591.
Uranus: in myths & astronomy, I, 267. *See also* Ouranos.
Urban VIII (1568-1644), Pope, II, 580.
Urbs (city), Rome, II, 448.
Urdhar: I, 151, 188fn.; and mineral springs, 162; secret meaning of, hinted at, 161.
Ūrdhwa-bâhu, posture of fakirs, II, 612.
Uri, J. (1726-96), *Catalogus . . . Bodleianae,* II, 654.
Ushas, I, 265.
Ustur, Sphinx-man, II, 231.
Utatlán, I, 553.
Uttânapâda, I, xxxi.
Uttara-mîmânsâ. *See* Mîmânsâ.

## V

Vâch: & mantras, I, xxxvi, xxxviii; awakens occult powers, II, 410-11; as magic power, 269-70; as Sarasvatî, 409; as secret wisdom, 269; as transformation of Aditi, 269; and metre, 409-10; same as Shekhînah, 269; spirit of matter, 266; and "Word," 371.
Vacuum, as latent Deity, I, 61.
Vaguḍâ, I, xxxii.
Vaibhâshikas, II, 531.
Vaikârika, as divine spirit, I, 429.

Vaikuṇṭhā, Paradise of Vishṇu, II, 538.
Vairo, Leonardo (1540?-1603), *Trois livres des charmes*, on walking on burning coal, I, 444-45.
Vaishnavas, II, 275.
Vaiśya, I, 148, 435.
Vaivasvata: I, 593; and deluge, II, 425, 428; Hindu Noah, 257, 450.
Valas, Völvas, I, 19.
Valentijn, F. (1666-1727), *Oud en nieuw Oost-Indien*, on levitation, I, 472.
Valentinians, II, 210, 221.
Valentinus, II, 123, 210, 236, 248, 333 & fn.
Valentyn, Dominic, and Josaphat, II, 580.
Vallemont, I, 476.
Vâmadeva Modaliyar, on pralaya, II, 273.
Vámbery, A. (1832-1913), *Travels in Central Asia*, on Kashmîr magic, I, 505.
Vampires: and astral soul, I, 459; as earthly elementaries, 319; Blanc on, 452; and daemons & their occult origin, 353; practices connected with, 449ff.; renowned case of, in Russia, 454-55, 646; seeress of Prevorst a magnetic, 463; as wandering astral souls, II, 564; possess insane, 589.
Vampirism: I, 217, 365, 449ff.; and medium-healers, 490.
Vanaprasthas, II, 107.
Vaner, I, 151.
Vanity, at root of scientific denials, I, 115.
Vannus, symbol of justice, II, 548.
Vapereau, L. G. (1819-1906), on Littré, I, 76.
Vapors, assuming weird shapes, I, 128.
Variago-Russ: II, 572; had mysteries, 42-43fn.
Varley, C. F. (1828-1883), I, 44, 46, 54, 232.
Varnhagen, F. A. de (1816-1878), *Amerigo Vespucci*, etc., I, 652.
Varro, M. Terentius (116-28 B.C.), *De re rustica* (implied), on building Rome, I, 588.
*Vas electionis*, and Manes, II, 208.
Vases: of Egypt and Greece, I, 541-42; of Genoa Cathedral of unknown material, 537-38.
Vaśitva, as power of mesmerizing, II, 593.
Vâsuki: II, 510fn.; and Śiva, 490.
Vatican: abuses heretics, II, 189fn.; despotic pretensions of, iv; plays politics, 81; secret libraries in, 18; sorcery in, 6; storehouse of ancient MSS., 16, 19; thunder of, 57; whitewashes sinners, 321.

Vaticination, gift of, I, 132.
Vatû, candidate, II, 98, 114, 115.
Vaughan, Thos. See Eugenius Philalethes.
Vay, Baroness Adelma von (1840- ? ), a good medium, I, 325.
Vâyu, I, 348.
Vázquez, F. (1647-1713?), *Crónica . . . de Guatemala*, I, 552.
Vázquez, G. (1551?-1604), *De culto adorationis*, on idolatry, II, 360.
*Vedāṅgas*, compared to Gospels, II, 556.
Vedânta, on nature of soul, I, 429-30.
Vedas: I, 17, 152, 153, 306; II, 432-34; antedate Bible, I, 91; antiquity of, II, 588; II, 257, 427; as sacred knowledge, I, 122; and Hermetic Books, 444; meaning of, 354; "metrical speech" of, 9; *Avesta* as spirit of, II, 220fn.; belong to "those who know," 415; Jacolliot on antiquity of, 257-58; Jacolliot on numbers in, 411-12; Müller contradictory on, 413-14; not as immodest as Bible, 80; parents of later philosophies, 411; silent on deluge, 427.
See also: *Atharvaveda; Ayurveda; Dhanurveda; Gândharvaveda; Sthâpatyaveda; Ṛigveda; Upaveda; Yajurveda.*
Veda-Vyâsa. See Vyâsa.
Vedic: influence in Babylon, II, 298; origin of, rites, 91fn.; religion & *Avesta*, 129; religion monotheistic, 413; views of soul, 263.
Vegetarianism, Xenocrates on, I, xx.
Vegetation: influence of moon on, I, 273; influenced by musical tones, 514.
*Vendîdâd*. See *Avesta*.
Ventriloquism, Ventriloquist (ἐγγαστρίμυθος), and Pythiae, I, 355.
Ventura di Raulica, Card. G. (1792-1861): letter of, on Satan, II, 14, 479; letter of, on modern magic, 70.
—— *Conférences*, misrepresents Augustine, II, 88.
Venus: II, 257, 439; day of, 418; dove sacred to, 258, 424; Placidus de Titis on bluish lustre of, 294fn., 651-52.
Venus-Aphrodite: and Belita, II, 444; and Lakshmî, 259.
Venus-Erycina, II, 446fn.
Verbum: issuing from the Void, II, 214; Latin, and Virâj, 159.
Verdi, G. F. F. (1813-1901), *Ernani*, I, 29.
*Vesica piscis*, I, 255.
Vespuccio, Amerigo (1454-1512), I, 71, 591, 592.

— *Mundus Novus,* I, 652.
Vesta, as earth, I, 159, 262, 637.
Vianney. *See* Ars, Curé d'.
Vicarious atonement: doctrine of, I, 542ff.; pernicious, 316.
Vice, seeds of, and crime, I, 275.
*Vidma* [Skt.], we know, I, 354.
Viero, I, 142.
Vigil-night, of Śiva, I, 446.
Vigilius Tapsensis, forges verse in *I John,* II, 77fn.
Vignaud, J. Henri (1830-1922), *Améric Vespuce 1451-1512,* etc., I, 652.
Villanova, A. de (1230?-1313), *Rosarius,* etc., I, 254fn.
Villemarqué, T. H. de la (1815-1895), "Poésie des cloîtres Celtiques," on philology, I, 550.
Villianûr, pagoda of, II, 262, 322fn.
Vina-Snati: II, 438; on Nara and Nârî, II, 251.
Vincent, F. (1848-1916), *The Land of the White Elephant,* etc., on Nagkon-Wat, I, 561ff.; on keystone, 571.
Vincent de Beauvais (ca. 1190-ca. 1264), *Speculum historiale,* on Josaphat, II, 580.
Vincent of Lerins, St., (d. ca. 450 A.D.), on Tertullian, II, 189fn.
Vine(s), vineyard: Jesus as true, II, 561; seven, from Kebar-Ziwa, 244; symbol used in various religions, 244.
Viññāna-skandha, II, 287.
Viracocha, of Peru, II, 259.
Virâj: I, xvii; II, 111, 159, 170, 215, 268, 270, 407fn.
Virey, J. J., (1775-1846), on chemical knowledge of ancients, I, 531.
Virgil (70-19 B.C.), I, 251, 492, 526fn.
—— *Aeneid:* on Aeneas' descent into Hadês, I, 362-63; on Divine Principle, 97; on Dido, II, 376; on Heracles, 518; on Spirit, Water & Matter, 458.
—— *Fourth Eclogue:* on Metatron, II, 144fn.; on serpent, 490.
—— *Georgica:* on Zeus, I, 158; on Eurydice, II, 129; on Vannus, 548fn.
Virgin(s): milk of celestial, I, 64; black, II, 95; celestial, pursued by dragon, 489, 490; and child, 167, 504; Devakî & Mâyâdevî as immaculate, 537; and ears of wheat, 491; of the sea, crushing Dragon, 446; of Zodiac, & Dec. 25th, 490; were almeh, 491fn. *See also* Avany, Perictione, Rhea Sylvia.
Virgin birth: alleged, of Plato and Perictione, II, 325; of Devakî and Mâyâdevî, 537; of Jesus, 504, 505.
Virgin Mary: materializing at Lourdes, I, 119; almost became a "demon," II, 32; bleeding cheek of, 17; and Collyridians, 110; dressed up at Bari, 9; and Elizabeth at Lyons, 555; and Gnostics, 444fn.; immaculate conception of, 9, 110; inherited emblems of Isis, 95; and Ishtar, 109fn.; and Isis, 49; and Jesus dressed up at Rio, 9-10; letters from, 8, 82-83; made into goddess, 203; mediatrix, 9; and Neith, 50; on crescent moon, 96; origin of, & Cyril, 41; overshadowed by Ialdabaôth, acc. to Gnostics, 247; patroness of sailors like Dido, 446; thrashing a demoniac, 76; titles of, compared with other goddesses, 209ff.; visited by Agathodaimôn, 505. *See also* Miriam.
Virgin Mother(s): Isis as, II, 10; of India & Egypt compared with Mary, 209ff.; of several great men, 325; Nârî as, 226; Sibylline oracles on, 504; universal myth, 489, 491.
Virginity, and marriage, II, 330.
Virgo: and boy-child, II, 491; Sign of, and Dec. 25th, 490; and Virgo-Scorpio, 445, 449, 456, 461, 463.
Virtue(s): II, 163-64, 541; active, and Durgâ, 233; as basis for initiation, 98; life of, 529; magic, of engraved stones, 233fn.
Visdelou, C. de (1656-1737). *See* d'Herbelot.
Vishṇu: I, xxvii; II, 39, 48, 114, 170, 173, 227, 255fn., 257, 268-69, 293, 322, 484, 557; as expression of universe, 277; as life-giver, 303; as water-god, 259; avatâras of, & decimal symbols, 300-01; avatâras of, geological eras & ages, 274-76, 277, 278; and Dagon, 258-59, 298; first avatâra of, fish & Vaivasvata, 257, 425, 457; Kṛishṇa as incarnation of, 537; ninth avatâra of, 156fn.; same as Adam-Kadmon, 259; same as Oannes, 257; seventh avatâra of, 278; tenth avatâra of, 237, 238, 260.
Vishṇu-flower, sweet basil, I, 468.
*Vishṇu-Purâṇa,* on Kṛishṇa's death, II, 538, 545-46.
Vishtâspa (Gushtasp), and Zoroaster, II, 141.
Vishuvan, equator, I, 11.
Visions: of sensitives, I, 145; divine, in Mysteries, II, 118; highest, & initiation,

114; induced by Soma-drink, 117; pagan & Christian, 108; produced by sorcery, 633; psychic & spiritual, *591;* reliability of, 73.
Viśodhana, perfection, II, 287.
Viśvadevas, II, 412.
Viśvakarman, at Ellora, II, 232.
Viśvamitra: and Egypt, I, 627; and *Upaveda,* II, 556fn.
Vital, force, I, 313, 408, 466, 485.
Viṭhobâ, crucified in space, II, 557-58.
Vitim, river, and Yakuts, II, 568.
Vitriol, nitre and "spirits," I, 357fn.
Vitruvius Pollio, M. (1st c. B.C.), *De architectura,* on Democritus, I, 512.
Vitus, St., dance of, II, 625.
Vivasvat, II, 427, 428.
Vives, J. L. (1492-1540), I, 226, 639.
—— *Comm. in Civitatem Dei,* on lamps, I, 230, 231.
Vlkodlak [Czech], I, 451.
Vogelius, I, 504.
Voice(s): divine, I, viifn., 246-47; in the desert, 604-06; nature of, from spirits, 68; of spirits not articulated, 68, 220-21.
Volaterranus (Raphael Maffei, 1452-1522), I, 226, 640.
—— *Commentarii urbani,* I, 640.
Volcanos, springs and electric currents, I, 162.
Volkmar, G. (1809-93), "Die Colarbasus-Gnosis," II, 249.
Volney, C. F. (1757-1820): I, 347; mistaken, 24; on God, II, 288; on Zoroaster, 142.
—— *La Loi naturelle,* on God, I, 268.
—— *Ruins of Empires,* on date of origin of Zodiac, II, 456fn.
Voltaire, F.M.A. de (1694-1778): on philosopher's stone, I, 268; on lycanthropy in Jura, II. 626.
—— *Dict. philos.:* on testimony, I, 99; on God & mathematical laws, 268-69.
*Völuspa,* I, 147, 151, 153, 187fn. See also *Edda.*
Völvas, Valas (Old Norse: *völur*), I, 19.
Voodoos, in Cuba, II, 573.
Vopiscus, Flavius, *Vita Saturnini,* on Hadrian & Christians, II, 336.
Voss, II, 561fn.
Votan: and serpent's crypt, I, 553; and Solomon, 546, 650; supposed to be descendant of Ham, 554.
—— *Proof that I am a Serpent,* I, 650.
Vowels, seven, I, 514.

*Vṛiddha-Manava,* I, 585, 586.
Vril, in Bulwer-Lytton, I, 64, 125.
Vril-ya, coming race in Bulwer-Lytton, I, 296.
Vṛitra, II, 478, 511.
Vrolik, G. (1775-1857) & W. (1801-63), I, 387.
Vulcan, at Nagkon-Wat, I, 565.
Vulcan-Hephaistos, II, 501.
*Vulgate,* II, 183, 239, 495.
Vurdalak, vampire, I, 451; II, 368.
Vyâsa: I, xi, 621, 626; II, 428, 438, 531, 591fn.; and Kapila on evolution, II, 261; on religious dogmas, 242.
Vyed'ma, witch, I, 354.
Vyed'mak, wizard, I, 354.
Vyse, Col. H. (1784 - 1853), *Operations,* etc.: on Egypt, I, 538; on iron in Pyramids, 542, 649.

## W

Wachtmeister, Countess Constance (1838-1910), *Reminiscences,* etc.: citing H.P.B. on creating vacuum, I, [17-18fn.]; on Judge at Enghien & *Isis Unv.,* [54].
Wade, Sir Claude Mortine (1794-1861), on burial of fakir, I, 477-78.
Wagenseil, J. C. (1633-1708), *Tela ignea Satanae,* II, 127fn., 201.
Wagner, N. P. (1829-1907): I, 54, 222; on psychic force, 497; ridiculed, 177.
—— *Mediumistic Phenomena,* I, 499.
Wake, C. S. (1835-1910), *Serpent-Worship,* etc., II, 499. See also Westropp.
Waldenses: II, 502; pagan rites of, 332.
Waldseemüller, M. (1470?-ca. 1522), *Cosmographiae Introductio,* I, 653-54.
Walker, G. A. (1807 - 1884), *Gatherings from Graveyards,* etc., I, 456.
Wallace, A. R. (1823-1913): I, 38, 42, 46, 54, 55, 118, 222, 245, 334, 407, 428; on apes, 326; ridiculed, 177.
—— *Contribution,* etc.: on brain of savages, I, 331; on man's evolution, 294-95, 296.
—— *Geographical Distribution,* etc., on man's past, I, 155.
—— *On Miracles:* II, 22; on facts, I, 194; on superhuman intelligences, 421-22; on scientific errors, 223.
Wallachian, simulacrum of, lady sent to Mongolia, II, 627-28.
Walpole, and Queen Elizabeth, II, 373fn.

Wanderoo, lion-monkey, I, 468.
War, of Michael & Dragon, II, 486.
Warburton, Wm. (1698-1779), *Divine Legation of Moses,* etc., on Mysteries, II, 101.
Warring, C. B., on Peruvian bark, I, 88.
Warton, Dr. Thos., on dragons, I, 448.
Wasawarti-Mâra, tempts Buddha, II, 513.
Washing, of idols, II, 138.
Water: as primordial substance, I, 133; as universal solvent, 133, 189, 192-93; existtence of oxygen & hydrogen in, 464; and fire in myths, 156; Hunt on, 192; of mercury & alchemy, 309; of Ptaḥ, 64; and spirit brooding over, 134; turned to blood, 413, 415; as first created element, II, 458; ceremony of pouring, 550fn.; female as chaos, 550fn.; greatest purifier, 138; light & earth, 267; male principle in spiritual sense, 550fn.
Water-lillies, of Gabriel, I, 93.
Wave-theory, of light, I, 137.
Weber, A. F. (1825-1901), I, 583.
—— *Akadem. Vorlesungen,* on Purusha, I, 56.
—— *Indische Studien,* on the sun, I, 270.
Webster, John (1610-1682), *The Saints Guide,* etc., I, 353.
Webster, Noah (1758-1843), I, xxxviii, 30fn., 139, 603; def. science, 88.
—— *Amer. Dict. of English Language,* I, 88.
Week, origin of seven-day, II, 418.
Weekman, Mr., reputed first believer in spiritualistic phenomena in USA., I, 106.
Weeks, and *acari,* I, 465.
Weidenfeld, J. S., *De secretis adeptorum,* I, 191fn.
Weight, augmented, I, 204.
Well, and water symbolism, II, 550-51fn.
Wells, Dr. Horace (1815-48), I, 539.
Weninger, F. X. (1805-88), *Reply to Hon. R. W. Thompson,* etc., on Catholic USA., II, 379.
Wesermann, power of, to influence dreams of others, etc., I, 477.
West, Judge E. P., and giant bones, I, 204-05.
Westcott, B. F. (1825-1901), II, 159, 370.
—— *A General Survey,* etc.: on *Hermas,* II, 243, 245; on Peter & Paul, 161fn.
*Westminster Review,* on longevity, II, 564.
Westropp, H. M. (1820-1884) & C. S. Wake, *Ancient Symbol Worship:* on El & Śiva, II, 524; on Peter's chair, 25fn.

Whirlwinds, I, 498fn.
White-skinned, people unfit for magical powers, II, 635.
Whitney, Wm. D. (1827-94), II, 472.
—— *Oriental and Linguistic Studies:* critical of Müller, II, 47; on *Atharvaveda,* 415fn.; on ease of criticism, 47-48; on older creed of India, 535; q. *Ṛigveda* on astral body and spirit, 534.
Widow-burning, I, 540-41 & fn., 588-89.
Wier, Joh. (1515-1588), *De praestigiis Daemonum,* on teratology, I, 399.
—— *Pseudomonarchia daemonum,* on infernal court, II, 572.
Wigand, J. W. A. (1821-1886), *Über die Auflösung der Arten,* etc., II, 278fn., 650.
Wilke, W. F., *Templerei,* etc., on fictitious claims, II, 381.
Wilde, and electric machine, I, 497.
Wilder, Dr. A. (1823-1908): and *Isis Unveiled,* I, [16], [39 & fn.], [41], [51-52]; II, 641, 645; on Aethiopians & Cushites, 567fn.; on Ak-ad & Ad, 579; on *Americ & Atlan,* 592; on Gan-duniyas or Babylonia, 575fn.; on softening of *s* into *h*, 570fn.; on Turanians & Mongolians, 576; on coats of skin, II, 458fn.; on Jupiter & Juno, 298; on magic, intuition & omniscience, 587; on meaning of Paganism, 179fn.; on parables, 145; on Peter's chair, 25fn.; on Peter & Pether, 92; on power of faith, 120; on T. Taylor as scholar, 109; on Zeruana, 142; on Zorobabel, 441.
—— "Bacchus, the Prophet-God:" on degradation of Bacchus, II, 527-28; on Tacitus & worship of ass, 523fn.
—— *New Platonism,* etc.: on alchemy, I, 502; on ecstasy & spir. photography, 486; on Hermetic phil., 437; on primal form of elements, 505; on Proclus & divine power, 489; on Roger Bacon, 413; on Thoth, Yadus & Hermetic Books, 444.
—— "Paul and Plato:" on Neo-Platonic ideas in early Christianity, II, 84-85; on Paul as an initiate, 90.
—— "Paul, the Founder of Christianity:" on figure of Christ disfigured, II, 576; on Moslems welcomed by Christians, 575; on Paul as real founder, 574; on Paul's real name, 536fn.; on Sermon on the Mount being repudiated, 575.
—— "Prophecy, Ancient and Modern:" I, xxxv; on originals & counterfeits, II, 567.
Wilkins, Chas. (1749?-1836), II, 563fn.

Wilkinson, J. G. (1798-1875), *Manners and Customs,* etc.: I, 529; on absence of barbarous stage in Egypt, 526; on asp & Isis, 556; on astronomical knowledge in Egypt, 533; on glass-blowing, 543; on Menes, 516; on Thummim, 537; q. Reuvens on Typhon-Seth, II, 484.

Wilkinson, Dr. J. J. G., on temperament, I, 234.

Will: action of, at distance, I, 109; adepts sole masters of their, 464, 496; and creative deity, 146; and current of force, 198, 500; effect of human, on âkâśa, 463, 471, 616; formidable potency in human, 384; greatest of magnets, 462, 472; imperious, 62; in motion is force & *creates,* 140, 297, 613; key to magic, 59, 62; latent Deity and, 61; light, force and, 285; magnetizer, 178; II, 21; mediumship and, I, 109; II, 596; nature of, I, 144; organizes matter, 57; Paracelsus & v. Helmont on, 57, 170; pervading all nature, 58; physical condition depends upon, xxiv; Plato on, 55, 61; and prayer, 434; and senses, 199; as magician & corporealization of thought, II, 619; determined, & purity of purpose, 617; faith & imagination, 598; —force, & soul-power, 565; intense desire produces, 320; man's conditions and, 593.

Will Power: active & passive, I, 57; controls currents of astral light, 129; impulse of, in yajña, xliv; indispensable for magical powers, 320; taming birds by, 380; as prayer, 592; highest form of prayer, II, 592; and mediumship, 596; of Yogis, 565; sole requisite of adept, 592.

Williams, W., *Primitive History,* etc., II, 503fn., 504.

Wilson, H. H. (1786-1860), II, 345, 428.
—— "On . . . Vaidik Authority for . . . Burning of . . . Widows," I, 541fn., 589fn., 649. See also *Ṛigveda* & *Vishṇu-Purâṇa.*

Wilson, John, *Hist. of the Suppression of Infanticide in India,* I, 649.

Wind(s): and evil spells, II, 632-33; four general, 231.

Wine: II, 449; sacred in Mysteries of Bacchus, 514fn., 560-61; symbol used in various religions, 244, 513.

Winged: men of *Phaedrus,* I, 2; steeds of Plato, xiii.

Wirdig, S. (1613-1687), *Nova medicina spirituum,* etc., on nature & magnetism, I, 207.

Wisdom: ancient, slowly degenerated, I, 436; of ancients, 444; of gymnosophists, 442; serpent as symbol of, 553; as a cloud, II, 506; as esoteric doctrine, 146 & fn.; as first Principle, 36, 37; concealed, & Divine Thought, 41; concealed, & the Ancient, 222, 224; def. *588;* fruit of esoteric, 412; hidden, identical all over world, 337; Ḥokhmah, as Supreme, 212; and Job, 497, 498, 499; Justin on, & Son, 216; occult, symb. by Leviathan, 499; origin of, 218; primitive, survives & is attainable, 586; secret, as magianism, 220; serpent as symbol of divine, 484; spiritual, is magic, 590; Supreme, 156fn.; Zipporah as symbol of esoteric, 551fn.

Wisdom-doctrine: one & identical throughout the world, II, 99, 142, 143; exists as before, 535.

Wisdom-Religion: classes arrayed against it, I, viii; key to Absolute in science & theology, vii; esoteric, of ancients, II, 146fn.; on evolution, 457; parent of all religions, 216; and pre-Vedic Brahmanism & Buddhism, 639; principal tenets of, 116; sacred books of, 417; universal, 39, 142.

*Wisdom of Solomon,* on formless matter, I, 256.

Wise, Rabbi I. M. (1819-1900), on Hebrew Scriptures, I, 444.

Witch(es): I, 489; Moses' & Jesus' attitude to, 353; occult explanation of, 353; on *kaṅgâlin,* II, 612; votaries of a proscribed worship, 502.

Witch-burning, II, 58, 61, 62-65.

Witches' Sabbath, and orgies of Bacchus, II, 528.

Witchcraft: I, 71, 353-56, 642; abundantly proven, 366; at Salem, 361; an offence among ancients, II, 98; executions for, 18fn., 59ff., 502-03; and mysteries, 117, nature of, 117-18fn.; and witches' Sabbath, 528.

Withdrawal: of inner from outer man, I, 476; of astral soul from ashes, II, 603; of consciousness from outer body, 588, 604-05; of Shaman from body, 626-28.

Witnesses: Montesquieu on, I, 87; verse on three heavenly, spurious, II, 177-78.

Wizard, as wise man, I, 354.

Wolf, converted by St. Francis, II, 77.

Wolff, K. F. (1733-94), I, 387.

Wolsey, Cardinal Thomas (1475-1530), practices magic, II, 57.
Woman (Women): artificial fecundation of, I, 81; as matter & great deep, 575; II, 446; Comte on, of future, I, 76-78; electrical polarity & alcohol, 277fn.; evolved out of lusts of matter, 433; exudes odic emanation when pregnant, 395; highly impressionable when pregnant, 394, 395; magnetically influenced by moon, 264; separation of, & man, 297; clothed with the Sun, as Isis, II, 489; hierophants of Sabazius, 589; sacred colleges for, 525; and snake, 449.
Wong-Ching-Foo, Chinese orator in USA, on Nirvâna, II, 319-20.
Woof, R. (1822-1877), *A Sketch of the Knights-Templar*, etc., on spurious Order of Malta, II, 383.
Woog, Prof., *Journal für Freimaurer*, on Rosicrucian Order, II, 394.
Wool, mantle of, and Apollonius of Tyana, II, 344.
Word: and eviction of daemons, I, 363; Lost, xliv, 580, 589-90; II, 370, 371; or Verbum, I, 324; as Logos, II, 41, 50; as *Memra*, 400; ineffable, the seventh, 368fn., 387, 418; Masonic lost, & substitutes, 349, 387-88; of God, 147; Omnific, of Enoch, 371; only possessors of the, 393; or Logos & death of Jesus, 510; passed by Initiate to successor, 42 & fn., 571; sacrificial, 409; and secret books, 470; used by Jesus, 387; and white stone of initiation, 351.
Words: magic power of, I, 444; destructive power of, II, 411; express things in invisible world, 410; worship of, 560.
*Word, The:* Holloway on James Robinson, I, [10]; A. Wilder on *Isis Unv.*, [51-52]; Judge on *Isis Unv.*, [54].
Wordsworth, W. (1770-1850), *Lyrical Ballad*, I, 396.
World(s): age of, I, 587; how called into existence, 341; invisible, interpenetrating, 185; creation of, 4004 B.C., II, 361; creation of material, 175 & fn.; destruction of sixth, 422-23 & fn.; previous, destroyed, 220, 271, 420, 421, 424; seven, 294, 420, 468; superior, in *Zohar*, 245; supernal, can be entered by initiates, 565; three, of Kabalah, 213.
World-Soul: I, 208, 342; as Chaos, 129; as life-spirit, 215; not Deity itself, xviii, xix; soul derived from, 316.
World-tree: I, 297; of knowledge, 574.
Worship: elementaries desire, I, 332-33; of sun & serpent by Israelites, 555; of spiritual portion of mankind, II, 639; of words, denounced, 560.
Worsley, E. (1605-1676), *Discourse of Miracles*, etc., II, 82.
Wounds, mortal, self-inflicted and healed, I, 224.
Wrangel, Baron Ferdinand von (1794-1870), I, 415.
Wreaths, of green leaves for oracles, II, 612.
Wren, Sir Christopher (1632-1723), and Masonry, II, 390.
Wright, Thos. (1810-77), *Narratives of Sorcery*: on nature of magic, I, 366; on Roger Bacon, 65; on Bishop of Bamberg & witchcraft, II, 61; on burning of witches, 58, 65; on Cellini & magic, 57; on curé of Bogota's sorcery, 60; on Friar Pietro & Dr. Torralva, 60-61; on Wolsey & Cromwell, 57; q. Hauber on burning of heretics, 62ff.
Writing: art of, in Egypt, I, 529-30, 532; direct, by spirits, 221.
Writings: of antiquity as safest guides, II, 635; under ban, 8.
Wuttke, C. F. A. (1819-1870), *Geschichte des Heidenthums*, etc., on sun, I, 270.

# X

X, Dr. and extraordinary scenes at séance, I, 608-11.
X, decussation of circle, II, 469.
Xanthus of Lydia (5th c. B.C.), and Zoroaster, II, 142, 646.
Xavier, Francisco de (1506-1552), on Japanese virtue, II, 573.
Xenocrates (4th c. B.C.), I, xv, xix, xx, 568; teachings of, xviii-xx.
Xenophanes (6th c. B.C.), *Fragments*, on nature of gods, II, 212, 242.
Xerxes, instructed by Magi at Abdera, I, 512.
Xisuthros: and flood, I, 554; identical with Great Father of Guatemalans, 593; as Sun in Zodiac, II, 457; legend of, 217, 424.
Xynoris, fictitious Saint, II, 510-11.

# Y

Yadu, and patriarchs, II, 488.
Yadus [Yâdavas]: came from Afghânistân to Egypt, I, 567; and *Vedas*, 444.
Yâḥ (or Iâh): and Jehovah, II, 215fn.; God of Life, 302; or Ḥokhmah, 213, 268. See also Iâḥ.
Yâho, Semitic mystery-name for Supreme, II, 297. See also Iahoh.
Yahweh, Yahveh, Yahve, Yehovah: not Yod-heva, II, 268; or Binah, 213, 215fn.; the Existing One, 400. See also Jehovah.
Yajña, I, xliii-xliv; II, 269.
*Yajurveda:* II, 415; age of, 433.
Yajus: I, xliv; sacrificial mysteries, II, 270.
Yakshas: II, 107; aerial spirits, 572.
Yakuts, beliefs and sacrifices of, II, 568-69.
Yale, Scientific Club, I, 282.
Yama, I, 270.
Yâmî, or Nârî, II, 234.
Yangkie, and Mahu, I, 601-02.
Yarker, J. (1833- ? ), *Notes on the ... Mysteries,* etc.: on decadence of Masonry, II, 376; on Dervish rites, 316-17; on English Templar Rite, 377; on Masonic bodies, 394; on violation of oath in Greece, 374fn.
Yarkhun, river, II, 600.
*Yashts.* See *Avesta.*
Yâska, II, 415.
*Yaśna.* See *Avesta.*
Yava, or Iaô, II, 165.
Yava-Aleim: II, 293, 458fn.; hierophant, I, 575; and Sacerdotal Colleges, 590.
Yawar-Ziwa, first vine, II, 244.
Yazatas: I, 457; and Mithras, II, 221.
Years(s): great, and floods, I, 30, 294fn.; hêliacal, 31, 633-34; often meant ages, 30-32, 342.
Yehôshûah. See Jesus and Peraḥiah.
Yesod, II, 213.
Yetzîrah, third Kabalistic world, II, 210.
Yeva, and Jehovah, II, 398.
Yezîdis: ideas of, on demons, I, 459; sect of sorcerers and their rites, II, 571-72; some Kaldany are, 630; teachings of, 197.
Yggdrasill: bees of, I, 133; myth and meaning of, 151-52.
Yiddeoni, I, 356.
Yin-yuan, and annihilation of soul, I, 319.
Ymir: I, 147, 148; meaning of, 150-51.
Yod, male principle, II, 268.

Yod-heva: as Adam-Kadmon, II, 463; not Yehovah, 268; and tetragram, 462.
Yogins (Yogis): I, 442, 580fn.; II, 346, 591; Brahman—, & mystical visions, I, 307; ecstatic, claim seeing Deity, 121; spirit of, shines like sun in ecstasy, xviii; communicate with supernal worlds, II, 565; curative remedies of, 621; Fukarâ—, & fakirs, 104; longevity, of, 620; some, regarded as demi-gods, 612.
Yôḥânân, and Mariam, II, 386fn. See also John the Baptist.
*Yôḥânân.* See *Talmud.*
Yonge, *The Works of Philo Judaeus,* II, 653.
*Yonim agne,* and widow-burning, I, 541fn.
Youatt, Wm. (1776-1847), I, 398.
Youmans, E. L. (1821-1887), *A Class-Book of Chemistry:* I, 172, 192; on growing body of truth, 405; on snowflakes, 508; on sun & stars, 169.
Young, Edw. (1683-1765), I, 336.
Young, Thos. (1773-1829), *A Syllabus of Lectures,* etc. (implied), on invisible worlds, I, 185.
Youth, regaining, II, 618.
Yowahoos, elementaries known to African tribes, I, 313.
Yucatán: I, 561; and mysterious city, 547.
Yugaṃdhara, Mount, I, 448.
Yugas: I, 587, 588; II, 275, 443, 467fn., 468; and Kalpas, I, 32; scholars had no key to, 347; series of cycles or, 293.
Yuh-Hwang Shang-ti, II, 554.
Yule, Sir Henry (1820-89), *The Book of Ser Marco Polo:* I, [16]; on Abraiamans & fish charmers, 606; on boy & rope, 474; on Chinese movable type, 513; on desert music, 604; on dhâraṇî & Simon Magus, 471; on Kashmîr speaking idols, 505; on Land of Spiritual Flowers, 601-02 & fn.; on levitation in Orient, 472; on performance of boy & thong, 473; on salamander or asbestos, 504; on veracity of Marco Polo, 603; q. Du Halde on magic, 600; q. Marco Polo on Pashai magic, 599; on Barlaam & Josaphat, II, 580; on Chinese Emperor & the One God, 554; on Chughi, 620; on Kublai-Khân & missionaries, 581-83; on virtues of Brahmans, 474fn.; q. Bernier, 620; q. Crawfurd, 346; q. Müller on Buddha, 581; q. Semedo on Taosse, 618-19; q. Toghon Temur on Daïtu, 587.
—— *Cathay,* etc., on musical sands, I, 605.

—— & A. C. Burnell (1840-82), *Dict. of Anglo-Indian,* II, 661.
Yurodiviy, Russian mediums, I, 28.
Yurta, Tatar tent, II, 626.
Yu-stone, of lamas, II, 393.

# Z

Zacharias: meaning of term, II, 550fn.; sees the ass in temple and is killed, 523fn.
Zadokites: persecuted Christians, I, xxx; assert sacerdotal rule, II, 135; David & the, 297; prophets opposed, 166fn.; and Sadducees, 148fn.
Zagreus: Dionysos—, of Hindu origin, II, 561fn.; and Korê, 505 & fn.; name of Bacchus and water, 550fn.
Zakar, sword, II, 270.
Zampun, Tibetan tree of life, I, 152.
Zamzummim, or Anakim, I, 567.
Zar-adas, and Pythagoras, II, 128.
Zarathushtra, II, 141, 467. *See also* Zoroaster.
Zarathushtra-Spitama, of untold antiquity, I, 12.
*Zechariah:* on coming of the King, II, 556; on Satan, 481; passage in, attributed to *Jeremiah,* 247.
Zedler, J. H. (1706-1763), *Lexicon,* I, 629.
Zeir-Anpin: Anointed, II, 230; as third god, 247; numbers of his figure, 232; and Sol-Mithra, 506; and symbolism of Mt. Meru, 234.
*Zeitschrift für Psychische Ärzte* (Nasse), on projection of double, I, 477.
*Zeitschrift für Hist. Theol.* (Volkmar), II, 249fn.
Zeller, E. (1814-1908), and Church Fathers, I, 288.
—— *Plato and the Older Academy:* on Xenocrates, I, xx; on minor gods, II, 345.
Zend, and Sanskrit, II, 220fn.
Zeno, teachings of, I, 12-13.
Zequiel, II, 61.
Zero: and chakra as universal symbols, II, 220; and the One, 407.
Zeruana, Zeruan: Abraham an alias of, II, 216; as Boundless Time, 185, 221; Berosus on, 217; and chakra, 217, 220; not in *Avesta,* 142; Sim called, 217.
Zeruana-Akarana, II, 221.
Zeus: II, 401, 438, 504, 527; as Dionysus & Poseidon, I, 262; double-sexed, 263; nature of, in Orphism, 262; Pausanias on, 125; Virgil on, as Aether, 158; as Dyaus or sky, II, 298; and Heracles, 515; Jupiter—, 505fn.; and Korê, 527; Pelasgian, 592. *See also* Jupiter.
Zeus-Akrios, I, 268.
Zeus-Dionysus, I, 262.
Zeus-Kataibates, I, 125.
Zeus-Pluvius, I, 268.
Zeus-Poseidon, I, 262.
Zeus-Zên, I, 156, 157.
Zhelihovsky, Vera Petrovna de (1835-96), "H. P. Blavatsky, etc.," I, [21-22 & fn.].
—— "The Truth about H. P. Blavatsky," I, [22fn.], [23-24].
Zhizhkov, Mt., and burning of Pope's Syllabus, II, 560.
Zibak, and creation of woman, I, 558.
Zimmer, Dr. H. (1851-1910), *Aśoka,* etc., II, 644.
—— *Philosophies of India,* II, 644.
Zion, II, 286 & fn.
Zipporah, symbol of esoteric wisdom, II, 551fn.
Ziwa. *See* Bahâk-Ziwa, Hibil-Ziwa, Kabar-Ziwa, Yavar-Ziwa.
Zmei Gorinich, Slavonian Dragon, I, 550.
Znahar', znaharka: as witch, I, 354; and the "Word," II, 43-44fn., 571.
Zodiac: with Chaldeans, I, 533; and age of Enoch, II, 464fn.; Brahmanical, & gods, 465fn.; date of origin of, 456fn.; and evolution of world, 456; and Ezekiel's Wheel, 456, 461-62; Houses of, & their correspondences, 460; later alterations in, 456-57; Patriarchs as Signs of, 450fn., 460; ten signs of, at first, 456.
Zodiacal: symbolism, I, 262, 267; Chronology, II, 278fn., 322fn., 366, 426, 432, 443, 464fn.
Zoê (Ζωή), female Holy Ghost, II, 226.
Zohak: and Jemshid, I, 576; and the dragon, II, 486fn.
*Zohar:* on the invisible, I, 302; on the three heads, 160; age of, II, 42; on Adonai, 224; on Aged of the Aged, 213; on creation of man, 246; on creation of worlds, 271; on Deity as Three Heads, 212, 222-23; on emanation from spiritual prototypes, 220, 272; on garment of heavenly light, 277; on Jehovah as workmaster, 400; on King Messiah, 245; on man as including everything, 276, 277; on metempsychosis, 280; on nature of

soul & its reunion with spirit, 281; on one flame and twofold lights, 222; on Shimon ben-Yoḥai's death, 348fn.; on souls & cherubim, 231; on the Legatus, 33; on transmigration, 152; on wine from above, 244; on worlds that perished, 220, 271, 421; teaches practical occultism, 350. See also *Auszüge,* etc.

Zonaras, Joannes ( ? -1130), *Chronicon* (implied), on Egypt & Greece, I, 543.

Zoomagnetism, or animal magnetism, I, 209.

Zoroaster: I, xxxiv, xxxvi, 178, 251, 271; II, 38; age of, & *Vedas,* II, 432-33; as *nazar,* 128; and Brahmans, 237fn.; and deities of *Vedas,* 217-18; derivation of term, 141; relation to India, 143; religion of, based on secret doctrine, 236; several teachers named, 141-42. See also Zarathushtra.

—— *Chaldean Oracles.* See Psellus.

Zoroastrianism: affinity with Judaism & Christianity, II, 486; and gods of *Vedas,* 143; prophets of, 467; teachings of, 221.

Zoro-Babel, II, 128, 441.

Zoro-Ishtar, Magian hierophant, II, 129.

Zura, figurative Gematria, II, 424.

Zweig, Stefan (1881-1942), *Amerigo,* etc., I, 652.

Zwingli, H. (1484-1531), I, 132.

# BIBLIOGRAPHY

## EXPLANATORY NOTE

This Bibliography is intended to provide succinct information on the various editions of works quoted from or referred to in *Isis Unveiled*, and gives brief explanation of certain writings less familiar to students. For the pages where any of the works are cited, consult the General Index under the author's name, or the title of the work, if no author is known. All Biblical works are to be found in the General Index only.

Most of the Greek and Latin Classics quoted in *Isis Unveiled* may be conveniently consulted in *The Loeb Classical Library*, a uniform series of Classical texts in their original, with parallel English translation. Greek volumes are bound in green; Latin volumes in red.

Works not included in *Loeb* are listed below with pertinent information on editions.

Original texts of the Church Fathers may be consulted, in most cases, in Jacques Paul Migne's monumental *Patrologiae Cursus Completus* (PCC) listed below. Works not included in that Series may be found in the present Bibliography with all available data.

English translations of many of the Church Fathers may be found in: (a) *The Ante-Nicene Christian Library* (ANF), Edinburgh, 1867-72, 24 vols. 8vo.; or ed. A. Cleveland Coxe, Buffalo, 1884-86, 8 vols., 8vo., with original Bibliographical Synopsis of great value and General Index (1887). An additional volume (Vol. X) occurs in the American edition of 1965-66 (Grand Rapids, Mich., Wm. B. Eerdmans); and in (b) *A Select Library of the Nicene and Post-Nicene Fathers* (NPNF), ed. by Philip Schaff, New York, Scribner, 1868-1909, and 1898-1900, in 14 volumes.

Initials *SBE* stand for the Series of the *Sacred Books of the East*, edited by F. Max Müller. Initials *PCC* indicate J. P. Migne's *Patrologiae Cursus Completus*.

Asterisks are appended to titles of works which have not been traced or identified, and the whereabouts of which are unknown.

Except for a very few special cases, Journals, Magazines and other Periodicals are not listed in this Bibliography, and may be found in the General Index.

# BIBLIOGRAPHY

## A

*Abhidharma* (Pâli, *Abhidhamma*). See *Tripiṭaka*.

*Abrégé des vies des anciens philosophes, avec un recueil de leurs plus belles maximes* (F. Fénelon), Paris, 1726, 1740, 1822, 1823.

*Abstinentia ab usu animalium, De* (Porphyry). Gr. & Lat., J. J. Reiskii. Trajecti ad Rhenum, 1767, 4to. Eng tr. by S. Hibberd, London, 1851, 8vo.; and by Thos. Taylor in *Select Works of Porphyry*, q.v.

*Account of an Embassy to the Court of the Teshoo Lama of Tibet, An* (S. Turner): containing a narrative of a Journey through Bootan and part of Tibet, London, 1800, 4to.

*Account of the American Baptist Mission to the Burman Empire* (Ann Hasseltine Judson), 2nd ed., London, J. Butterworth, 1827. Includes *Diaries* or *Journal* of Dr. Adoniram Judson.

\**Account of the Origin and Attributes of the True Rosicrucians*, MS.

*Acta Sanctorum*, etc. (John Bolland, or Bollandus, and others). Orig. ed., Antwerp, 1643-1794, in 54 vols.; work resumed in 1838 by the new Bollandists; latest ed. is by G. J. Camadet, Paris & Rome, 1863-83, in 61 vols.

\**Adumbratio Kabb. Chr.* (Knorr von Rosenroth). Possibly in his *Kabbala denudata*.

*Aegyptiaca* (Manetho). From the Armenian version of Eusebius' *Chronica*. Loeb Classical Library. Also in Cory's *Ancient Fragments*, q.v.

*Aethici Cosmographia* (Ister Aethicus). Geographical work by a Roman writer of the fourth century. Ed. princeps by Simler, Basel, 1575; the best ed. is by Gronovius in his ed. of Pomponius Mela, Leyden, 1722.

*Aglaophamus, sive de theologiae mysticae Graecorum causis* (C. A. Lobeck), Regiomontii Prussorum, 1829, 2 vols.

*Agriculture*. See *Nabathäische Landwirtschaft* (D. A. Chwol'son).

\**Agrushada Parikshai*.

*Aitareya Brâhmaṇam of the Ṛigveda* . . . Edited, translated and explained by Martin Haug, Bombay, 1863, 2 vols. Reprint of translation in *Sacred Books of the Hindus*.

*Akademische Vorlesungen über indische Literaturgeschichte* (A. F. Weber), Berlin, 1852; 2nd ed., 1876.

*Alchymia* (A. Libavius), Frankfurt, 1595, 1606.

*Alcibiade, On the First* (Proclus). Quoted in Cory's *Ancient Fragments*.

\**Alexandrian MS.* (Theodas).

*Allgemeine Geschichte der christlichen Religion und Kirche* (J. A. W. Neander), Hamburg, 1825-52, 6 vols. — Engl. transl. from 2nd German ed., by J. Torrey as *General History of the Christian Religion and Church*, London, 1847-55. 9 vols.; London, Bohn's Standard Library, 1846, etc.

*Ältesten Spuren des Menschen in Europa, Die* (A. Müller), 1871; in *Öffentliche Vorträge gehalten in der Schweitz*, Heft 3; 2nd ed., 1876.

*Amenitates Academicae*, etc. (C. Linnaeus), Erlangen, 1787, 85-90, 10 vols.

*Améric Vespuce 1451-1512*, etc. (H. Vignaud), Paris, 1917.

*America, Its Geographical History, 1492-1892* (W. B. Scaife). Baltimore, 1892.

*Amerigo*. A Comedy of Errors, etc. (S. Zweig). Transl. from German by A. St. James, New York, 1942.

*Amerigo and the New World* (G. Arciniegas), Transl. from Spanish by Harriet de Onís, New York, 1955.

*Amerigo Vespucci*. Son caractère, ses écrits, etc. (F. A. de Varnhagen), Lima, 1865.

*Amphitheatrum sapientiae aeternae solius verae, christiano-kabalisticum, divino-magicum,* etc. (H. Khunrath), Hanoviae, 1609; also Magdeburg, 1608, and Hamburg, 1611; the 1619 ed. contains twelve plates; an early German ed. of 1602 is known also.

*Anacalypsis, an Attempt to draw aside the Veil of the Saitic Isis; or an Inquiry into the Origin of Languages, Nations, and Religions* (G. Higgins), London, 1836, 2 vols., 4to; 2nd ed., Glasgow, 1878, 8vo.

*Analects* (Lun-Yü) (Confucius). W. E. Soothill, 1910. J. Legge, *The Life and Teachings of Confucius*, Vol. I of *The Chinese Classics*, 1861-72, 3 vols.; 2nd ed., 1869-76. Also in G. Pauthier, *Les Livres Sacrés de l'Orient*, etc., Paris, 1840.

*Analysis of Religious Beliefs, An* (Viscount John Amberley), London, 1876, 2 vols.

\**Anatomia cerebrale* (V. G. Malacarne), Milan.

*Anatomy of Melancholy, The* (R. Burton), 1621; many subs. editions.

*Ancient America* (J. D. Baldwin), London, 1869, 1872; New York, 1869, 1874, 1896.

*Ancient and Modern Egypt, or, the Pyramids and the Suez Canal*. A Lecture, etc. (W. B. Carpenter), 1866.

*Ancient Cave Men of Devon* (Wm. Pengelly). Report of Two Lectures delivered at Worcester and Malvern, on Wed., Jan. 26, and Friday, Jan. 28, 1870, etc., Worcester, 1870.

*Ancient Egypt. Her Monuments, hieroglyphics, history and archaeology* (G. R. Gliddon), New York, 1843; 10th ed., 1847; 12th ed., Philad., 1848.

*Ancient Egypt under the Pharaohs* (J. Kenrick), London, 1850, 2 vols.

*Ancient Faiths and Modern* (Thos. Inman), New York, 1876, 8vo.

*Ancient Faiths, embodied in Ancient Names* (Thos. Inman), London, 1868-69; 2nd. ed., 1872-73. 2 vols.

*Ancient Fragments of the Phoenician, Chaldean, Egyptian, Tyrian, Carthaginian, Indian, Persian, and other Writers* (I. P. Cory), London: Wm. Pickering, 1828, 8vo; 2nd ed., 1832; lix, 361 pp. Greek, Latin and Engl. texts; *the most valuable edition.* — New & enlarged ed. by E. Richmond Hodges, London, Reeves & Turner, 1876 (xxxvi, 214 pp.); introduces various Editorial Comments of some historical value, but eliminates the famous *Chaldean Oracles*.

*Ancient Pagan and Modern Christian Symbolism exposed and explained* (Thos. Inman), London, 1869; 2nd ed., New York, 1871.

"Ancient Religion of the North before the Time of Odin, On the most" (Münther), in *Mémoires de la Société des Antiquaires de France*, tome II.

*Ancient Symbol Worship*. Influence of the Phallic Idea in the Religions of Antiquity (H. M. Westropp & C. S. Wake), New York, 1874, 8vo; 2nd ed., 1875.

*Ancient York and London Grand Lodges.* A review of Freemasonry in England from 1567 to 1813 (Leon Hyneman). Philadelphia, Pa., Mrs. W. Curtis, 1872. 8vo.

*Angelis opus divinum de quinta essentia, De* (R. Lully). No date.

*Anhang sum Zend-Avesta* (J. F. Kleuker), Leipzig & Riga, 1781. 2 vols.

*Anima ac daemone, de sacrificio et magia, De* (Proclus). Transl. M. Ficino, Venice, 1497; also Basel, 1576. See also *Procli Opera,* ed. Cousin, Paris, 1820-27, III, 278; and Kroll, *Analecta Graeca,* Greisswald, 1901, where a Greek transl. accompanies the Latin text.

*Annales de origine gentis Francorum* (Joh. Trithemius), 1574 fol., 1673 & 1713.

*Annales ecclesiastici a Chr. nato ad an. 1198* (Ceasar, Cardinal Baronius), Rome, 1588-1607, 12 vols. Continued later by several scholars; one of the later editions is that of Augustin Theiner, Paris, 1864—, 4to (to run into some 50 vols.).

*Annales Hirsangiensis* (Joh. Trithemius), 1514.

*Anthropogenie, oder Entwickelungsgeschichte des Menschen* (E. Haeckel), 2nd ed., Leipzig, 1874.

*Antidote against Atheism, An* (H. More), London, 1653.

*Antigüedades Peruanas* (J. J. von Tschudi & M. E. de Rivero), 1851, 4to.

*Antiquitate urbis Patavii et claris civibus Patavinis libri tres,* etc. (Bernardino Scardeone or Scardeonius), Basileae, apud N. Episcopium juniorum, 1560, fol., 437 pp. Index.

*Antiquities of Mexico, The* (E. King, Viscount Kingsborough, in collab. with Agostino Aglio), London, 1830-48, 9 vols.

*\*Antitheses* (Marcion).

*Aphorismi confessariorum ex doctorum sententiis collecti,* etc. (E. Sa), Coloniae, 1612, 1615.

*Apocalypsis Eliae* (Revelation of Elias). Mentioned by Origen in *Comm. in Matthaeum,* tom. X, p. 465.

*\*Apocrypha* [Secret Books of the Alexandrian Jews — unobtainable].

*Apocryphal New Testament translated from the Original Tongues, The* (W. Hone), London, 1820, 1821; many reprints.

*Apologie pour tous les grands personnages qui ont été faussement soupçonnés de magie* (G. Naudé), Paris, 1625; The Hague, 1653; Amsterdam, 1712; Engl. tr., London, 1657.

*Apostolici;* or History of the Apostles and Fathers in the First Three Centuries of the Church (W. Cave), London, 1677; 2nd ed., corr., 1682. — New ed. rev. by Henry Cary, Oxford, 1840, 3 vols. as *Lives of the most eminent fathers,* etc.; includes the 4th century.

*Arabian Nights Entertainments* (E. Wm. Lane), 1838-40. With Notes and Ill. designed to make the work an encyclop. of Eastern manners; 3 vols.

*Arabic Gospel of the Infancy, The.* ANF, 1873.

*Arcana caelestia* (E. Swedenborg), 1749-56, 4to.

*Archaeologia, or Miscellaneous Tracts relating to Antiquity,* publ. by the Society of Antiquarians of London. Letter from William Hamilton entitled: "Remarks on the Fortresses of Ancient Greece," Vol. XV (1806), pp. 315-25; Vol. XXV (1834), p. 220.

*Archidoxorum libri decem, sive Lux Lucens in Tenebris et Clavis Librorum Paracelsi* (Paracelsus), 1681.

*Archiv für den thierischen Magnetismus* (ed. by D. G. Kieser), 1831.

*Archives du magnétisme animal* (d'Hénin de Cuvillier), Paris, 1820-23, 8 vols.

*Argonautica* (Apollonius Rhodius). This poem in Greek on the expedition of the Argonauts was based on the rich material of the Alexandrian library. It elicited many Commentaries by various writers and became very popular. Consult *Scholia in Apollonium Rhodium Vetera*, recensuit Carolus Wendel, Berlin, 1935.

*Around the World: or, Travels in Polynesia, China, India, Arabia*, etc. (J. M. Peebles), 4th ed., Boston, 1880.

*Arrest du Parlement du 5 mars, 1762.* Consult Vol. IX of Blavatsky's *Collected Writings*, pp. 308-310, for further data on this *Arrest*.

*Ars Geometriae* (A. M. S. Boethius), 1507. Migne, *Patrol.*, lxiii-lxiv, 1847; G. Friedlein, Leipzig, 1867. See also *Theoretic Arithmetic* (Thos. Taylor).

*Art Magic; or, Mundane, Sub-Mundane and Supermundane Spiritism* (E. H. Britten), New York, 1876.

*Asclepian Dialogue.* See *Hermes, Books of.*

*Ashes to Ashes: A Cremation Prelude* (H. R. Haweis), London, 1874.

*Asia, Da,* etc. (Diogo do Couto), Lisbon, 1780.

*Asiatic Journal* (London). Vols. 1-25, 1816-28; vols. 26-28, 1828-29; New Ser., 1830-43; 3rd Ser., 1843-45; 4th Ser., 1845.

*Asiatick Researches;* or, Transactions of the Society instituted in Bengal, for inquiring into the History and Antiquities, the Arts, Sciences, and Literature, of Asia. Calcutta, 1788-1839; 20 vols., 4to.; London, 1801-12, 11 vols., 8vo.; new ed., Calcutta, 1875, etc. — Index to first 18 vols., Calc., 1835.
See *Vedas* (Colebrooke); "Astron. Computations" (Samuel Davis); "Letter of S. Turner, etc."

*Assyrian Discoveries* (Geo. Smith), New York, 1875.

*Astrologie* (J. W. A. Pfaff), Nürnberg, 1816, 8vo.

"Astronomical Computations of the Hindus, On the" (Samuel Davis), dated 1789, in *Asiatick Researches,* etc., Vol. II (1799), pp. 225-87.

*Atharva-Veda.* Fourth *Veda,* said to have been composed by Atharvan, alleged to have been the first to institute the worship of fire and offer Soma. Consists chiefly of formulae and spells intended to counteract diseases and calamities. — *Atharva-Veda Sanhitâ,* ed. by R. Roth and W. D. Whitney, Berlin, 1855-56. — With the Comm. of Sâyanâchârya. Ed. by Shankar Pândurant Pandit, Bombay, 1895-98, 4 vols. — Translated into Engl. verse by Ralph T. H. Griffith, Benares, 1895-96, 2 vols. — Trans. by W. D. Whitney; rev. & ed. by C. R. Lanman, Cambridge, Mass., 1905. — Transl. into Engl. prose by M. Bloomfield, Oxford, 1897, in *SBE,* Vol. XLII.

*Auro, Libri Tres de* (Giovanni Francesco Pico della Mirándola, ca. 1469-1533), Ursellis, Impensis C. Sutorii, 1598. Also in Zetzner, *Theatrum Chemicum,* Vol. II, pp. 312ff.; and in Manget, *Bibliotheca Chemica,* Vol. II, pp. 558ff.

*Auszüge aus dem Buche Sohar mit deutschen Übersetzung* (anonymous); 3rd rev. ed., Berlin, 1857, 8vo., 46 pp.

*Authentic Narrative of the Loss of the American Brig Commerce . . . wrecked . . . Aug., 1815, An* (J. Riley), New York, 1817, 8vo.

*Avesta: The Religious Books of the Parsees* (F. Spiegel). From Prof. Spiegel's German Translation of the Original Manuscript, by A. H. Bleeck. Hertford, 1864 [*Vendîdâd, Vispered, Yaśna* and *Khordah-Avesta*]. — Consult also *The Zend-Avesta.* Transl. by James Darmesteter. Parts I, II & III (tr. by L. H. Mills). Oxford: Clarendon Press,

*SBE* IV, XXIII, XXXI. Orig. ed. is of 1880; 2nd ed. of 1895, somewhat abbreviated as far as Introduction goes. His French transl. is 1892-93, in the *Annales du Musée Guimet*, Vols. 21, 22, 24.

\*Âvrita. Untraced.

*Âyurveda.* The science of health or medicine, considered by some as a supplement of the *Atharvaveda*, by others as appended to the *Rigveda*, and containing eight departments. See *Upaveda.*

B

"Bacchus the Prophet-God" (Dr. A. Wilder), in *The Evolution*, New York, June, 1877.

*Bampton Lectures*, 1809: "A View of the Brahmanical Religion, etc.," by Rev. J. B. S. Carwithen, London, 1810.

*Baptismo contra Donatistas, De* (St. Augustine). *Works*, ed. by M. Dods, Edinburgh, 1872-76.

*Beiträge zur Einleitung in die biblische Schriften* (C. A. Credner), Halle, 1832-38, 2 vols.

*Belfast Address* (J. Tyndall). Inaugural Address before the British Ass'n. at Belfast. *Popular Science Monthly*, Vol. V, October, 1874.

*Bélisaire* (J. F. Marmontel), 1767.

*Bello vandalico, De* (Procopius). *Loeb Class. Library.*

*Berosi Chald. Historiae quae supersunt; cum Comment. de Berosi Vita*, etc., ed. by J. D. G. Richter, Lips., 1825, 8vo. This is the best collection of fragments of Berosus' *Babylonica* that has come down to our time.

*Bestia Arundinis* (Malchu). See Vol. I, p. 629, Note 3.

*Bhagavad-Gîtâ, or Dialogues of Krishna and Arjuna.* Transl. by Charles Wilkins. London: C. Nourse, 1785. Repr. New York: G. P. Philes, 1867. Repr. for the Bombay Theos. Publ. Fund, Bombay, Tookaram Tatya, 1887.
  Innumerable other editions, though H. P. B. specifically refers to Chas. Wilkins' transl. See also *Mahâbhârata.*

*Bhâgavata-Purâna.* Edited by Bâlakrishna Sâstrî Yogi, 2nd ed., Bombay, 1898. — Prose Eng. tr., ed. and publ. by M. Nath Dutt, Calcutta, 1895-96. — *Srimad Bhâgavatam.* Tr. by S. Subba Rau, Tirupati, 1928. — French tr. by Eugène Burnouf, Paris, 1840, 44, 47, and (vols. 4, 5) 1884, 1898.

*Bible, La* (S. Cahen): Trad. nouvelle, avec l'Hébreu en regard. Avec Notes. Paris, 1832.

*Bible dans l'Inde, La. Vie de Iezeus Christna* (L. Jacolliot), 1869. Engl. tr. as *The Bible in India*, London, 1870.

*Bibliotheca, Acta et Scripta Magica* (E. D. Hauber), Lemgo, 1739-38-45, 8vo.

*Bibliotheca Classica; or, a Classical Dictionary, containing a full account of all the proper names mentioned in ancient authors*, etc. (J. Lemprière), Reading, 1788, 8vo; many later ed.; French tr., 1805.

*Bibliotheca Graeca* (J. A. Fabricius), Hamburg, 1705-28, 12 vols.; rev. and continued by T. C. Harless, 4th ed., Hamburg: Carolum Ernestum Bohn, 1790-1812. — Photographic reproduction of the latter ed. in 11 vols. publ. at Hildesheim: Georg Olms, 1966.

*Bibliotheca* or *Myriobiblon* (Photius, Patriarch of Constantinople, 858-67 and 878-86), Gr. ed. by I. Bekker, 1824-25; it is a collection of excerpts from, and abridgments of,

280 vols. of classical authors (usually cited as *Codices*), the originals of which are now to a great extent lost. To Photius we are indebted for almost all we possess of Ctesias, Memnon, Conon, the lost books of Diodorus Siculus, and the lost writings or Arrian. — Engl. tr. by J. H. Freese, New York, McMillan, 1920.

*Bibliothèque du Magnétisme animal* (by the Members of the Société du Magnétisme), Paris, 1817-18, 4 vols.

*Bibliothèque orientale, ou dictionnaire universel contenant tout ce qui regarde la connaissance des peuples de l'Orient* (B. d'Herbelot de Molainville). Based mainly on the Arabic dictionary of Hadji Khalfa. Completed in 1697 by A. Galland. Printed at Maestricht in 1776, and The Hague in 1777-99 (4 vols.). The latter ed. contains Supplements by C. de Visdelou and A. Galland.

*Biblische Mythologie des alten und neuen Testaments* (F. N. Nork), Stuttgart, 1842-43.

*Biblischen Commentar über sämtliche Schriften des Neuen Testaments* (H. Olshausen), Königsberg, 1830 *et seq.*, 4 vols.; rev. ed., Reutlingen, 1834-62, 7 vols.; Engl. tr., New York, 1861-63, 6 vols.

*Biographical History of England, from Egbert the Great to the Revolution, A* (J. Granger), London, 1769-74, 3 vols., 4to.

*Blackwood's Edinburgh Magazine,* Vol. 108, August, 1870; art. by Maj.-Gen. Wm. Hamley, on "What the Old Egyptians Knew."

*Blavatsky, Tibet and Tulku, H. P.* (G. A. Barborka), Adyar, Madras, India, 1966; 2nd ed., 1970.

"Blavatsky, Yelena Petrovna" (Vera P. de Zhelihovsky). Essay publ. in *Russkoye Obozreniye* (Russian Review), Vol. VI, Nov. & Dec., 1891.

*Blue and Red Light: or, Light and its Rays as Medicine* (J. Pancoast), Philadelphia, 1877, 8vo.

*Bodleian Codex.* Entry No. 37 of the year 1104 in Joannes Uri's *Catalogus Codicum Manuscriptorum Orientalium Bibliothecae Bodleianae,* 1781, in 3 vols. No. 1 in Adolf Neubauer's *Catalogue of the Hebrew Manuscripts in the Bodleian Library,* etc., 1886, 1906, in 2 vols.

*Body and Mind* (H. Maudsley), London, 1870, 1873, 1880.

\*Book of Brahmanical Evocations.

\*Book of Common Prayer (Justice Bailey), 1813.

\*Book of Enoch (J. Gaffarel).

*Book of Enoch the Prophet . . .* now first translated from an Ethiopic MS. in the Bodleian Library (R. Laurence), Oxford, 1821; 2nd ed., 1832, 1833; 3rd ed. 1838; also later ed.

\*Book of Evocations.

*Book of Jasher.* See Vol. I, p. 637, Note 26, for comprehensive information regarding this work.

\*Book of Numbers, Chaldean. Unavailable.

*Book of Ser Marco Polo, the Venetian, Concerning the Kingdoms and Marvels of the East* (Marco Polo). Newly translated and Edited, with Notes, by Col. Henry Yule. London: J. Murray, 1871; 2nd ed., 1875; 3rd ed., 1902; repr., 1929; also in *Universal Library,* New York, Grosset and Dunlap, 1931.

*Book of Shet.* See *Desâtîr.*

\*Book of the Babylonian Companions.

*Book of the Dead* [Reu-nu-pert-em-hru, "Chapters of the Coming Forth into Day"]. H.P.B. uses in *Isis Unveiled* portions of the translation by Samuel Birch, as published in C. C. J. von Bunsen's *Egypt's Place in Universal History* (London, 1848-67, in 5 vols.) which is the Engl. tr. by C. H. Cottrell of Bunsen's *Aegypten's Stelle in der Weltgeschichte* (Hamburg: Gotha, 1845-57, 8vo.). See also Vol. X of the *Coll. Writings*, pp. 413-15, for Bibliogr. data concerning the *Book of the Dead*.

*Book of the Historical Zodiacs.

*Book of the Keys.

*Book of the Wisdom of Solomon.* One of the so-called Apocrypha of the Old Testament. An essay on Wisdom as divine agent in the creation and government of the world. Emanates most likely from intellectual circles of the Jewish Diaspora in Alexandria, and is not earlier than about 150 B.C. Exhibits Platonic and Pythagorean tendencies. See R. H. Charles' *Apocrypha and Pseudepigrapha of the Old Testament*, Oxford, 1963-64.

*Books of Hermes.* See *Hermes, Books of*.

*Borderland of Science, The* (R. A. Proctor). A Series of Familiar Dissertations on Stars, Planets, etc., etc., London, 1873.

*Bouddha et sa religion, Le* (J. Barthélemy Saint-Hilaire), Paris, 1860.

*Brâhmaṇas.* Ancient Sanskrit prose treatises in close relation to the *Vedas;* ritual textbooks the main object of which is to explain the sacred significance of the ritual of sacrifice to those who are already more or less familiar with it. Their contents may be classified under the three heads of practical sacrificial directions (*vidhi*), explanations (*arthavâda*), exegetical, mythological, or polemical, and theological or philosophical speculations on the nature of things (*upanishads*). At the end of the *Brâhmaṇas* may be found the *Âraṇyakas* or "Forest Treatises," with their corresponding *Upanishads* which are either imbedded in them or form their concluding portion. These are the most mystical and esoteric treatises of ancient Hindu lore.

*Bṛihad-Âraṇyaka* and *Bṛihadâraṇyakopanishad. The Twelve Principal Upanishads* (Eng. transl.), with Notes from the Comm. of Śâṃkarâchârya and the gloss of Ânandagiri. Publ. by Tookaram Tatya. Bombay: Theos. Publ. Fund, 1891. Repr. 1906. — *The Upanishads,* Tr. by F. Max Müller. Oxford: Clarendon Press, 1884. Part II, *SBE* 15.

*Buddhism in Tibet,* etc. (E. Schlagintweit), Leipzig, 1863.

*Buarth Beirdd — The Cattlepen of the Bards.* In Wm. F. Skene's *The Four Ancient Books of Wales,* etc., Edinburgh, 1868. Contains "The Book of Taliesin."

"Buddhist's Opinions of the Spiritual States, A." (P. C. Mitra). In *The Spiritualist,* London, May 25th, 1877, p. 246. A Letter addressed to Alexander Calder.

*Buffon: histoire des ses travaux et de ses idées* (M. J. P. Flourens), Paris, 1844.

*Bundahish.* In Pahlavi *Bûndahishar*. A Pahlavi text on creation, cosmogony, etc.; one of the Scriptures of the Pârsîs. Translated by E. W. West in *SBE,* V.

"Burial in India, The" (R. von Roth), 1867. Source untraced.

# C

*Cartas* (Brasseur de Bourbourg). See *Lettres*.

*Catalogue of Curiosities at Gresham College* (N. Grew), London, 1681.

*Catalogue of the Hebrew Manuscripts in the Bodleian Library and in the College Libraries of Oxford* (A. Neubauer), 1886, 1906; 2 vols.

*Catalogue of the Manuscripts of the King's Library, A* (D. Casley), London, 1734.

*Catalogus Codicum Manuscriptorum Orientalium Bibliothecae Bodleianae* (Joannes Uri), 1781, 3 vols.

*Catecheses* (Cyril of Jerusalem). Text in Migne, *PCC*, Ser. Gr.-Lat. XXXIII. Engl. tr. in *Oxford Library of Fathers*, 1838.

*Catechism of the Pârsîs.* Tr. by Dâdâbhâi Naurozjî.

*Catéchisme des Jésuites, ou le Mystère d'Iniquité, etc., Le* (É. Pasquier), 1602; Villefranche, 1677.

*Catéchisme positiviste, ou sommaire exposition de la religion universelle,* etc. (A. Comte), Paris, 1852; also 1874, 1890; 1891; Engl. tr. by Rich. Congreve as *The Catechism of Positivist Religion,* London, 1858.

*Cathay, and the Way Thither,* etc. (Col. H. Yule), London, 1866; also 1913-16.

*Catholic World,* New York, 1865-86, 44 vols.

*Causa, Principio ed Uno, Della* (G. Bruno), 1584.

*Celtic Druids (The); or, an Attempt to shew, that the Druids were the Priests of Oriental Colonies who emigrated from India,* etc. (G. Higgins), London, 1829.

*Centrum naturae concentratum; or, the salt of nature regenerated.* Improperly called the philosopher's stone. Written in Arabick by Alipili, a Mauretanian, published in Low Dutch and now done into English (by E. Price), London, 1696.

*Chaldean Account of Genesis, The,* (Geo. Smith), New York, 1876.

*Chaldean Book of Numbers.* See *Book of Numbers.*

*Chaldean Oracles* (Psellus). See *Oracula Sibyllina* (J. Opsopäus).

*Chhândogyopanishad.* See *The Twelve Principal Upanishads* (Engl. tr.), publ. by Tookaram Tatya. Bombay: Theos. Public. Fund, 1891; repr. 1906. — *The Upanishads.* Tr. by F. Max Müller, Oxford: Clarendon Press. Part I, 1879. *SBE* I.

*Chine, La* (J. P. G. Pauthier), Paris, 1857, 2 vols.

*Chips from a German Workshop* (F. Max Müller), New York, 1867.

*Christ's Fidelity the only Shield against Satan's Malignity* (D. Lawson), London, 1704.

*Christ of Paul; or the Enigmas of Christianity, The* (Geo. Reber), New York, 1876.

*Christian Orthodoxy reconciled with the conclusions of modern Biblical Learning* (J. W. Donaldson), London, 1857.

*Christianity and Greek Philosophy* (B. F. Cocker), New York, 1870.

*Christliche Mystik, Die* (J. J. von Görres), Regensburg and Landhut, 1836-42, 4 vols.; 1854; new ed., Regensburg, 1879-80, 5 vols.

*Christna et le Christ,* etc. (L. Jacolliot), Paris, 1874.

*Chronica* (Sulpicius Severus). Editio princeps publ. by Flacius Illyricus, 1556. Complete works ed. by Halm in Vol. I of the *Corpus scriptorum ecclesiasticorum Latinorum,* Vienna, 1866. Also in *NPNF.*

*Chronicon,* or *Annales* (Joannes Zonaras). Compiled from various Greek authors by this Byzantine historian of the 12th century. First ed. by H. Wolf, Basel, 1557, 3 vols.; best ed. is by Pinder, Bonn, 1841, etc., 8vo., in the Bonn collection of Byzantine writers.

*Chronicon de Lanercost, 1201-1346,* etc. (ed. by J. Stevenson) [E codice Cottoniano nunc primum typis mandatum], Edinburgh, 1839.

*Chrysippos* (Euripides). Fragments only of a trilogy: *Phoenicians - Oinomaos—Chrysippos*, which has not come down to us. See Pauly-Wissowa for data.

*Civilization of Babylonia and Assyria, The* (M. Jastrow), Philadelphia, 1915.

*Class-Book of Chemistry, on the Basis of the new System, A* (E. L. Youmans), New York, 1852; rewritten in 1863; rev. ed., 1875; also London, 1876. Rewritten and rev., New York: D. Appleton & Co., 1880.

*Classical Dictionary, etc., A* (Charles Anthon). New York: Harper & Brothers, 1841, 8vo., viii, 1423 pp.; 4th ed., 1843; many subsequent editions.

*Classical Journal, The.* London, 1810-29, 40 vols., 8vo. Vol. LXXIII, March, 1828.

*Clementinen nebst den verwandten Schriften und der Ebionitismus, Die* (A. Schliemann). Ein Beitrag zur Kirchen- und Dogmengeschichte der ersten Jahrhunderte. Hamburg, 1844.

*Code of Gentoo* [Hindu] *Law, A.* Or Ordinations of the Pandits, from a Persian translation, made from the original written in the Shanscrit language (N. B. Halhed), 1776.

*Codex apocryphus Novi Testamenti, collectus, etc.* (J. A. Fabricius), Hamburg, 1703, 2 vols.; 1719, 1743.

*Codex Claromontanus.* One of the bilingual MSS. of the New Testament, containing the Greco-Latin text of Paul's *Epistles.* It is deposited in the Bibliothèque Nationale of Paris and is supposed to date from about the VIth century. It is written in uncials and is designated as *D* for the Greek portion, and as *d* for the Latin. It was found by Theodor de Bèze in the Claremont Monastery, in the diocese of Beauvais, France. Integrally published by Tischendorf, Leipzig, 1852.

*Codex Justinianus,* in *Corpus Juris Civilis,* ed. of the Brothers Kriegel, Leipzig, 1840; ed. Krüger, Berlin, 1906. — Tr. by J. B. Moyle, Oxford, 1937; also By C. H. Munro, Cambridge, 1909, 2 vols. Book I.

*Codex Nazaraeus 'Liber Adami' appelatus Syriace transcriptus* . . . Latineque redditus, etc. (M. Norberg), London, 1815, 16, 4to, 3 vols. Text transcribed into Syrian characters, and the Mandaeans dialect of the original is mostly translated into High Syrian.

*Codex Sinaiticus.* See Vol. II, p. 648, Note 29. Consult also *The Codex Sinaiticus and the Codex Alexandrinus,* by H. J. M. Milne and T. C. Skeat. Publ. by the Trustees of the British Museum, 2nd. ed., London, 1955.

"Colarbasus-Gnosis, Die" (Volkmar), in *Zeitschr. Hist. Theol.*

*Collected Writings* (H. P. Blavatsky). Comprehensive edition published by The Theosophical Publishing House, Adyar, London & Wheaton, Ill. Large octavos, illustrated and fully indexed. Volumes I through X, covering period 1874-89, publ. to date. Other volumes forthcoming. Present ed. of *Isis Unveiled* is an integral part thereof.

*Coming Race, The* (Bulwer-Lytton), 1871.

*Commentaries on Virgil* (Servius Honoratus). Best text is in Burmann's ed. of Virgil, 1746.

*Commentarii urbani* (Volaterranus), in *Opera omnia,* Rome, 1506; Paris, 1526.

*Comment. in Civitatem Dei* (Joannes Ludovicus Vives), 1522 fol., 1555 fol., 1610, 8vo., 1661, 4to.; Engl. transl., 1610.

*Comment. in Timaeum* (Chalcidius); also as: *Interpretatis Latina partis prioris Timaei Platonici.* First printed by Badius Ascensius, Paris, 1520, fol.; the best ed. is that of J. A. Fabricius, Hamburg, 1718, fol.

\**Commentary on Idrah-Zutah* (Rabbi Eleazar). Untraced.

*Commentary on the Old Testament* (Lange), Edinburgh, 1870: *Ecclesiastes,* transl. by Wm. Wells; ed. by Tayler Lewis.

*Commercial Bulletin,* Boston; art. by Hadji Nicka Bauker Kahn (pseud. of Capt. W. L. D. O'Grady), "Indian Sketches; or Rubs of a Rolling Stone." Published in 1876-77.

*Comparative Grammar of the Dravidian or South-Indian Family of Languages, A* (R. Caldwell), London, 1856; 2nd ed., 1875.

*Compendio de la Historia de la ciudad de Guatemala* (D. Juarros), Guatemala, 1808-18, 2 Vols.; 3rd ed.: Biblioteca Payo de Rivera, 1936, 2 vols. in one. Engl. tr. by J. Baily as *A Statistical and Commercial History of the Kingdom of Guatemala,* etc., London, 1823.

*Compendio di Critica Sacra dei difetti e delle emendazione del sacro testo* (G. B. de Rossi), Parma, 1811.

*Compendium of Natural Philosophy* (Manetho). This work, with its Greek title of *Tôn physikôn epitomê,* has been ascribed to the Egyptian priest Manetho who lived in the reign of the Ptolemies, by Diogenes Laertius, who gives excerpts from it.

*Compositione medicamentorum per genera, De* (Galen). Ed. by C. G. Kühn, Leipzig, 1821-33, 20 vols.

*Concertatio Ecclesiae Catholicae in Angliâ adversus Calvino Papistas* (J. Bridgewater, or Joannes Aquipontanus), 1589, etc., 4to.

*Conciliengeschichte* (C. J. von Hefele), Freiburg, 1855-74.

*Conférences, sermons et homélies* (Gioacchino Ventura di Raulica); posthumously issued, Paris, 1862 and 1865.

*Conquérant du monde, Le* (R. Grousset), Paris, 1944.

*Consensu evangelistarum, De* (St. Augustine). *Works,* ed. by M. Dods, Edinb., 1872-76.

*Conservation of Energy, The* (Balfour Stewart), New York, 1875.

*Constituciones diocesanas de Chiapa* (Francisco Núñez de la Vega), Rome, 1702.

*Constitutions for Freemasons, The Book of* (Dr. James Anderson), London, 1723.

*Contra Faustum Manichaeum* (St. Augustine). *Works,* ed. by M. Dods, Edinb., 1872-76.

*Contribution à l'histoire de la Société Théosophique en France* (Charles Blech), Paris: Éditions Adyar, 1933, 215 pp.

*Contribution to the Theory of Natural Selection* (A. R. Wallace), 2nd ed., London, 1871.

\**Coptic Legends of the Crucifixion.*

*Corpus Juris Civilis.* See *Codex Justinianus.*

"Correlation of Nervous and Mental Forces" (Alex. Bain). Possibly a paper.

*Correlation of Physical Forces, On the* (Wm. R. Grove); being the substance of a course of lectures delivered in 1843. London, 1843, 1846, 1850, 1855, 1862.

*Cosmae Christiana topographia* (Cosmas Indicopleustes), 1706, fol., Gr. and Lat.

*Cosmogony* (Sanchoniathon). Ancient Phoenician writer whose identity has never been fully established. His work, known also as *Theologia* is supposed to have been translated into Greek by Philo Byblius; a considerable fragment of this transl. is preserved by Eusebius in the first book of his *Praeparatio evangelica.*

*Cosmographiae Introductio* (Martin Waldseemüller), St. Die, May, 1507.

*Cours de l'Histoire de la philosophie moderne* (Victor Cousin), Ser. 2, new ed., Paris, 1847.

*Cours de Magnétisme* (J. Dupotet), Paris, 1834, 1840.

*Cours de Philosophie positive* (A. Comte), Paris, 1830-42; 6 vols.; 2nd ed., 1864 (Preface by Littré); Engl. tr. by Harriet Martineau, 1853.

*Course of Time, The* (R. Pollok). A Poem in Ten Books. London, 1827, 2 vols.

*Court and Camp of Runjeet Sing*, etc. (Wm. G. Osborne), London, 1840, 8vo.

*Crania Aegyptiaca; or, Observations on Egyptian Ethnography, derived from Anatomy, History and the Monuments* (S. G. Morton), Philadelphia; London, 1844. (From the *Transactions* of the American Philosophical Society, Vol. IX).

*Crata Repoa oder Einweihungen in der alten geheimen Gesellshaft der Egyptischen Priester* (Carl Friedrich Köppen), Berlin, 1770. Reprinted by Christian Ludwig Stahlbaum, Berlin, 1778. — French transl. by Ant. Bailleul, Paris, 1821, 8vo. — English transl. by John Yarker from French version; see Manly P. Hall's ed., Los Angeles, 1937. — Engl. transl. by Philip A. Malpas, as unpublished MS.

*Cratylus, On the* (Proclus). Ed. by Boissonade, Lips. 1820.

*Creatis, De* (Methodius Patarensis), in Photius, *Bibliotheca*. Text in Migne, *PCC*, Ser. Gr.-Lat., CIII-CIV.

*Credibility of the Gospel History, The* (N. Lardner), London, 1727-55; 2 parts in 17 vols.

*Crisis theologica* (C. A. Casnedi), Ulyssipone, 1711.

*Crónica de la provincia del santísimo nombre de Jesús de Guatemala*, etc. (Francisco Vázquez, the Franciscan), 1714-16.

*Culla-Niddesa*. Commentary on the *Parayana-vagga* and the *Khaggavisanna-sutta;* together with the *Mahâ-Niddesa*, a comm. on the *Atthaka-vagga* of the *Sutta-Nipâta*, forming the *Niddesa*, a Buddhist Scripture. Publ. by the Pâli Text Society, London.

*Culto Adorationis libri tres, De* (G. Vázquez), Alcalá, 1594; Mainz, 1601, 1604.

*Curiositéz inouyes, sur la Sculpture talismanique des Persans. Horoscope des Patriarches. Et lectures des Estoilles* (J. Gaffarel), Paris, 1629, 8vo.; Rouen, 1631; Engl. tr. by E. Chilmead, as *Unheard-of Curiosities*, etc., London, 1650.

*Cursus theologicae juxta scholasticum hujus temporis Societatis Jesu methodum* (F. Amico), Duaci, 1640-49, 9 Vols.; Antwerp. 1650.

*Cyclopaedia, The* (A. Rees), London, 1819, 39 vols., 4to.

*Cyclopaedia of Biblical Literature, A* (ed. by J. Kitto), 1843-45, 2 vols.; 3rd ed. Edinb., 1862-66, 3 vols.


D

*Debatable Land between this World and the Next, The* (R. D. Owen), London, 1871.

*Decameron* (G. Boccaccio); 1st dated ed., Venice, 1471.

*Decline and Fall of the Roman Empire, The* (E. Gibbon); Vol. I, 1776; Vols. II & III, 1781; Vols. IV-VI, 1788, 4to; many subs. ed.

*Defence of Masonry* (Dr. James Anderson). In Geo. Oliver's *The Golden Remains of the Early Masonic Writers*, etc. (5 vols. London, 1847-50), Vol. I, 1847.

*Demon, The* (M. Y. Lermontov). Russian text, Berlin, 1856. Eng. tr. by A. C. Stephen, London, 1875, 1881, etc.

*Demonologia, or natural knowledge revealed; being an exposé of ancient and modern Superstitions*, etc (J. B. Forsyth), London: John Bumpus, 1827; also 1831, 8vo.

*Démonomanie, ou traité des sorciers, De la* (J. Bodin), Paris, 1580 (Vol. II, 1587).

*Denkmäler aus Ägypten und Aethiopien*, etc. (C. R. Lepsius), Berlin, 1849-58, 12 vols. fol. (904 plates).

*Deo Socratis liber, De* (Apuleius), in *Pétrone, Apulée, Aulu-Gelle. Œuvres complètes,* etc., ed. of Désiré Nisard, Paris, 1850. Latin and French. Engl. tr. in *Bohn's Class. Library*, London, 1853.

*Desâtîr or the Sacred Writings of the Ancient Persian Prophets, The.* With the Commentary of the Fifth Sasan, and English transl. by Mulla Firuz Ben Kaus. Bombay, 1818. 2 vols. — Edited and republished by D. J. Medhora, Bombay, 1888, 8vo. ii. 13, 190 pp.

*Description du royaume Thaï ou Siam*, etc. (J. B. Pallegois), Paris, 1854, 12°.

*Description géographique, historique, chronologique et physique de l'Empire de la Chine et de la Tartarie chinoise* (J. B. Du Halde), Paris, 1735. 4 tom. fol. — Eng. tr., London, 1736, 8vo.

*Description of Greece by Pausanias, The* (Thos. Taylor). Transl. from the Greek. With Notes, etc. Ill. with maps and views. London, 1794, 3 vols., 8vo.; 2nd ed., with consid. augmentations, London, 1824 [publ. anonymously], 3 vols.

*Description of the Character, Manners, and Customs of the People of India; and of their Institutions, religious and civil* (Abbé J. A. Dubois). Tr. from French MSS., Philad., 1818, 2 vols.

*Deutsches Anonymen Lexicon* (Hanns Bohatta & M. Holzmann), Hildesheim, 1961.

*Dhammapada.* The Path or Way of the Buddha's *Dhamma* (Pâli) or Teaching. The most famous scripture in the Pâli Canon, a collection of 423 verses comprising a noble system of moral philosophy. Numerous translations into various languages.

*Dhanurveda.* The science of archery, a treatise regarded as an *Upaveda* connected with the *Yajurveda*, and derived from Viśvâmitra or Bhṛigu. See *Upaveda*.

*Diakka and their Earthly Victims, The* (A. J. Davis), New York, 1873.

*Dialectical Society*, etc. See *Report on Spiritualism.*

*Dialogues of Plato, The* (M. A. Jowett), Oxford, 1871; many later editions.

*Dialogus de daemonum energia seu operatione* (Peri energeias daimonon dialogus) (M. Psellus). Gr. ed. of G. Gaulminus, Paris, 1615, in Migne, *PCC*, Ser. Gr. CXXII, col. 819-876 (Paris, 1889), together with Gaulminus' Notes. — Gr. text with Notes in Latin, Nürnberg, 1838; repr., Amsterdam, 1964. 348 pp. — Engl. tr. and Notes by Marcus Collisson as *Dialogue on the operation of Daemons*, etc. Sydney; J. Tegg, 1843. 49 pp. — French tr. by P. Moreau. Paris: Guillaume Chaudière, 1573.

*Dictionary of Anglo-Indian Words and Phrases* (Col. H. Yule & A. C. Burnell), 1886. Known as *Hobson-Jobson*.

*Dictionary of Christian Biography, Literature, Sects and Doctrines, A* (ed. by Sir Wm. Smith & Henry Wace), Boston: Little, Brown & Co., 1877-87, 4 vols.

*Dictionary of Greek and Roman Antiquities, A* (Ed. by Sir Wm. Smith), London, 1842; 2nd ed., 1848; many impressions; 3rd ed., rev. & enl., London: John Murray, 1890-91, 2 vols.

*Dictionary of the English Language, An American* (Noah Webster), Revised & Enlarged by Chauncey A. Goodrich & Noah Porter, Springfield, Mass., 1879.

*Dictionary of the Targumim, etc., A* (M. Jastrow), London, 1886-1903, 2 vols., 4to.

*Dictionnaire de théologie catholique.* Paris: Letouzey et Ané, Editors, 1903, etc. Vol. III, 886; Vol. V, 2188.

*Dictionnaire général des tissues* (B. G. Sage), 2nd ed., Lyon, 1859.

*Dictionnaire historique et critique* (P. Bayle), London, Rotterdam, etc., 1697, fol.; Engl. tr., 1734-41, fol., 10 vols.

*Dictionnaire philosophique* (Voltaire), London [Geneva], 1764, 8vo.

*Dictionnaire universelle des contemporains* (L.-G. Vapereau), Paris: L. Hachette, 1858; many subsequent editions.

*Diegesis, The* (R. Taylor): being a discovery of the origin, evidences, and early history of Christianity, etc., London, 1829, 8vo.

*Die natali, De* (Censorinus). Ed. princeps is in 4to. and without date, place or printer's name; 2nd ed. appeared in Bologna, fol., 1497; first critical ed. is that by Vinetus, Pictav. 4to, 1568, followed by those of Aldus Manutius, Venet. 8vo., 1581, and Carrio, Luet. 8vo., 1583. The most complete and valuable is that by Havercamp, Lugd. Bat. 8vo., 1743.

*Dieu et les Dieux ou un Voyageur Chrétien devant les objects primitifs des cultes anciens,* etc. (H.-R. Gougenot des Mousseaux), Paris, 1854.

*Diploteratology; an Essay on Compound Human Monsters* (G. J. Fisher), Albany, van Benthuysen's Press, 1866; also 1868.

*Discorsi del Sommo Pontefice Pio IX pronunziati in Vaticano,* etc. (Pasquale de Franciscis), 1872, etc.

*Discours sur la Constitution,* May 7, 1794 (M. M. I. Robespierre). Séance du 18 Floréal; In *Bibliothèque historique de la révolution,* 1793.

*Discourse of Miracles Wrought in the Roman Catholick Church, A,* (E. Worsley), Antwerp, 1676.

*Discourse on the Worship of Priapus, and its connection with the Mystic Theology of the Ancients, A* (R. Payne Knight). To which is added an Essay on the Worship of the Generative Powers during the Middle Ages of Western Europe. London: Privately printed, 1865; also 1871.

*Disquisitions relating to Matter and Spirit* (J. Priestley), London, 1777, 8vo.; Northumberland, 1802, 1803.

*Disquisitionum magicarum libri sex* (Marcino Delrio), Lovanii, 1599, 1600, 4to; Lugduni, 1608.

"Dissertaton historique sur la Bibliothèque d'Alexandrie" (P. N. Bonamy), in *Histoire de l'Académie Royale des Inscriptions et Belles Lettres,* 1736, Vol. 9, pp. 414 *et seq.*

*Dissertation on the Mysteries of the Cabiri, A* (G. S. Faber), Oxford, 1803, 2 Vols., 8vo.

*Dissertations sur les apparitions des anges, des démons et des esprits,* etc. (A. Calmet), Paris, 1746; 1759, 2 vols.; Engl. tr., London, 1759, 1850.

*Divina Commedia, La* (Dante Alighieri). The first three editions were printed in 1472 at Foligno, Manua and Jesi.

*Divine Book, The.* See *Semenuthi.*

*Divine Legation of Moses Demonstrated, on the Principles of a Religious Deist, from the*

*Omission of the Doctrine of a Future State of Reward and Punishment in the Jewish Dispensation* (Wm. Warburton, Bishop of Gloucester). London, 1738-41, 2 vols.; 2nd ed., 1742; 10th ed., 1846, 3 vols.

*Divisione naturae, De* (Joh. Erigena), Oxford, 1681; Münster, 1838.

*"Dogmatism in Science," (H. Corson).

*Dogme et rituel de la haute magie* (É. Lévi), Paris, 1856, 2 vols.

*Don Juan* (Byron), 1818-23.

*Dono perseverantiae, De* (St. Augustine). *Works*, ed. by M. Dods, Edinb., 1872-76.

"Dragon de Metz, Du" (Lenoir), in *Mémoires de l'Académie Celtique*, I, 11, 12.

*Drei Programmen über die Abraxas-gemmen* (J. J. Bellermann), Berlin, 1820-22.

*Droit de la nature et des gens, Le* (S. von Pufendorf). Traduit par J. Barbeyrac, Amsterdam, 1706, 4to; 2nd ed., 1712; 6th ed., 1750.

*Druze MSS.* (transl. by Pétis de la Croix, 1701).

# E

*Earth a Great Magnet, The* (A. M. Mayer). A lecture. New York, 1872, 8vo.

*Eastern Monachism* (R. Spence Hardy), London, 1860.

*Ecclesiasticus;* also known as *The Wisdom of Jesus, the Son of Sirach,* and *The Wisdom of Iaseous.* See *The Apocrypha or Non-Canonical Books of the Bible,* ed. by Manuel Komroff. New York, 1936, 1937.

*Eclogae* (Joannes Stobaeus). Ed. princeps of all the works of the author is that publ. at Geneva in 1609, fol.; best ed. of the *Eclogae* are those of T. Gaisford, 1822, and A. Meinecke, 1860-64.

*Edda,* or *Eddas.* Either of two works in the Old Norse or Icelandic language: a) The *Younger* or *Prose Edda,* or *Edda of Snorri Sturluson,* a prose work treating of Norse mythology and the language and modes of composition of the skalds. Its most remarkable portion is the *Gylfaginning,* or the Delusion of Gylfi, which is a compendium of the mythological system of the ancient Nordic people. While written by Sturluson (1178-1241), it embodies traditions of earlier ageess; b) The *Elder* or *Poetic Edda,* also known as *Edda of Saemund the Wise,* which is a collection of heroic chants and mythical legends of great antiquity, reduced to their present form between the 9th and the 12th centuries, and discovered in 1643 by Brynjólfr Sveinsson, Icelandic Bishop of Skálaholt, who erroneously ascribed them to Saemundr Sigfússon (1656-1133). The most remarkable of the poems in this collection is the *Völuspá,* or prophecy of the Völva or Sibyl, containing some of the ancient cosmogonic ideas.

The *Prose Edda* has been partially tr. into Engl. by T. Percy in his *Northern Antiquities* (q.v.) from the French of P. H. Mallett (1770); by G. Webbe Dasent (Stockholm, 1842); by R. B. Anderson (Chicago, 1880); by A. G. Brodeur (1916). The first Engl. tr. of the *Poetic Edda* was that publ. by Benjamin Thorpe in 1886; more recent versions are those of Olive Bray (1908) and H. A. Bellows (1923).

*Edward Meltons, Engelsh Edelmans, Zeldzaame en Gedenkwaardige Zee en Land Reizen,* etc. (E. Melton), Amsterdam, 1702.

*Égypte ancienne* (J. J. Champollion-Figeac), Paris, 1839, 1847.

*Egyptian Medical Treatise.* See *Papyros Ebers.*

*Egyptian Mythology and Egyptian Christianity, with their Influence on the Opinions of Modern Christendom* (S. Sharpe), London, 1863.

*Egypt's Place in Universal History* (C. C. J. Bunsen). Engl. tr. by C. H. Cottrell, (London, 1848-67, 5 Vols.) of the German text: *Aegypten's Stelle in der Weltgeschichte.* Hamburg: Gotha, 1845-57, 8vo.

*Einleitung in die Mythologie auf dem Standtpunkte der Naturwissenschaft,* etc. (J. S. C. Schweiger), Halle, 1836.

\*Einl. in N. T. (untraced).

*Elements* (Stoicheia) (Euclid). Best edition of the text is that of *Euclidis opera omnia,* ed. by Heiberg and Menge, Leipzig, 1883-1916, 8 vols.; vols. i-v contain the *Elements* with Latin transl. — Engl. tr.: T. L. Heath, *The Thirteen Books of Euclid's Elements,* transl. from the text of Heiberg, with Introd. and Comm., Cambridge, 1908, 3 vols.; 2nd ed. rev., 1926. Also *Loeb Class. Libr.*

*Elements of Christian Theology containing proofs of the authenticity and inspiration of the Holy Scriptures* . . . (George Tomline, Lord Bishop of Lincoln), 1799; 9th ed., 1818; 12th ed., 1826.

*Eleusinian and Bacchic Mysteries, a Dissertation, The* (Thomas Taylor). Amsterdam, 1790 (most likely printed in London); 2nd ed., with additions, appeared in *The Pamphleteer,* Vol. VIII, 1816; 3rd ed., edited, with Introd., Notes, Emendations and Glossary by Dr. Alexander Wilder, New York, J. W. Bouton, 1875; 4th Ed., New York, 1891. With 85 ill. by A. L. Rawson.

*Enactment* (Charles II): 29 Car. II, c. 7 (1676).

*Encyclopaedia of Islam, The.* Ed. by M. Th. Houtsma, T. W. Arnold, R. Basset & R. Hartmann. Leyden & London, new ed., 1960, 3 vols.

*Enneads* (Plotinus). The best ed. of the original Greek text is that of F. Creuzer, with the Latin transl. and commentaries of Ficinus appended. Oxford, 1835, 3 vols., 4to. Among the partial translations into English, mention should be made of Thos. Taylor's *Concerning the Beautiful* (London, 1787 & 1792); *Five Books of Plotinus* (London, 1794, 8vo.); *On Suicide* (London, 1834, 8vo.); and his *Select Works of Plotinus,* q.v. — *Complete Works,* tr. with biogr. by Porphyry, etc., by Kenneth S. Guthrie, Alpine, N.J., Platonist Press, 1918, 4 vols.; *Plotinus . . . with Porphyry's Life of Plotinus,* tr. by S. Mackenna, London, P. L. Warren, 1917-30, fol., 5 vols. (Libr. of Philos. Translations, vols. 1-5).

*Ente astrorum, De.* — *De Ente Dei.* — *De Ente spirituali* (Paracelsus). See his *Opera omnia.*

*Epistle of Barnabas, The General,* in W. Hone, *Apocryphal New Testament,* etc. (q.v.).

*1st Epistle of Clement to the Corinthians.* In W. Hone, *Apocryphal New Testament,* and *The Ante-Nicene Fathers,* Vol. X.

*Epistle of Jesus Christ and Abgarus, King of Edessa;* in M. R. James, *The Apocryphal New Testament,* 1924.

\*Epistle of Peter to James.

*Epistle II to Januarius* (St. Augustine). *Works,* ed. by M. Dods, Edinb., 1872-76.

*Epistles* (Hipparchus), Rf. to in Proclus, *On Plato's Republic.* See Thos. Taylor, *Works of Plato,* I, 467-68.

*Epistles* (Isidorus of Pelusium), Paris, 1638, fol.; ed. J. Billins, Paris, 1585.

*Epistles of Paul to Seneca, and Seneca to Paul.* In Hone's *Apocryphal New Testament,* London, 1820, 1821; many reprints.

*Epistles to Philip* (Arrhidaeus). Rf. to in Proclus, *On Plato's Republic;* see Thos. Taylor, *Works of Plato,* I, 467-68.

*Epistolae* (Jerome): 1) *Ad Paulinum altera* (2nd Letter to Paulinus of Nola). Engl. tr. in *NPNF,* 2nd Ser., Vol. 6, Letter No. LVIII.; 2) *Epistola XIV: Ad Heliodorum Monachum.* See *Corpus Scriptorum Ecclesiasticorum Latinorum,* Vol. 54, Pars I, pp. 46-47 (Ed. Isidorus Hilberg).

*Epistolae* (Peter of Blois, or Petrus Blesensis). See his works in J. P. Migne's *Patrologia* and A. Duchesne's *Historiae francorum scriptores;* also the ed. of Pierre de Goussainville (Paris, 1667) and J. A. Giles (Oxford, 1846-47).

*Epitome* (Clementine Literature). First publ. by Turnebus, Paris, 1555, then by Cotelerius in his *Patres Apostolici.* It is an extract from the *Homilies,* with the addition of a portion of Clement's Letter to James, etc.; also publ. by Dressel, Leipzig, 1859.

*Êrân, das Land zwischen dem Indus und Tigris* (F. Spiegel), Berlin, 1863.

*Erde steht fest, Die* (C. Schöpffer). Beweise, dass die Erde sich weder am ihre Achse noch um die Sonne dreht. Lecture delivered in Berlin; 5th ed., 1854.

*Ernani* (G. F. F. Verdi), 1844.

*Esprit des Lois, L'* (C. L. Montesquieu), 1748.

*Essai philosophique sur les probabilités* (P. S. de Laplace), Paris, 1814, and later ed.

*Essay of Transmigration in defence of Pythagoras; or a Discourse of Natural Philosophy, An* (W. Bulstrode), London, 1692.

*Essay on Classification, An* (L. Agassiz), London, 1859.

*Essay on Criticism* (A. Pope), 1711.

*Essay on Man* (Pope), 1733.

*Essays* (T. H. Macauley), 1841-44, etc.

*Essays on the Languages, Literature, and Religion of Nepal and Tibet,* etc. (B. H. Hodgson), London, 1874.

*Essays on the Sacred Language, Writings, and Religion of the Parsees* (M. Haug), Bombay, 1862; 2nd & 3rd ed., 1878.

*Ethical Fragments* (Pythagoras). See *Iamblichus' Life of Pythagoras* (Thos. Taylor).

*Euphues, or the Anatomy of Wit* (John Lyly, or Lilly, or Lylie), 1578.

*Examen de la doctrine médicale généralement adoptée* (F. J. V. Broussais), Paris, 1816.

*Expériences publiques sur le magnétisme animal* (J. Dupotet), 2nd ed., Paris, 1826.

*Experimental Investigation of the Spirit Manifestations,* etc. (Robert Hare), New York, 1855.

*Exposé de la religion des Druzes, tiré des livres religieux de cette secte,* etc. (A. I. Silvestre de Sacy), Paris, 1838.

*Expositio in symbolum apostolorum* (Rufinus), 1682.

*Exposition of the Creed, An* (J. Pearson), London, 1659, 1676, etc. Burton's rev. & corr. ed., 3rd, Oxford, 1847, 3 vols.

*Extraits des Assertions dangereuses et pernicieuses en tout genre, que les soi-disans Jésuites ont, dans tous les temps & persévéramment, soutenues, enseignées & publiées dans leurs livres, avec l'approbation de leurs Supérieurs et Généraux* (compiled by the "Commissaires du Parlement"), Paris, 1762, 4 tomes, 12°; also a single 4to ed.; 5th ed., Amsterdam, 1763, 3 vols., 8vo. See also *Collected Writings,* Vol. IX, pp. 308-10, for data.

## F

*Factis dictisque memorabilibus, De* (Valerius Maximus). Often spoken of as *Memorable Deeds*. Ed. princeps by J. Mentelin, Strassburg, ca. 1470. Engl. tr. as *The History of the Acts and Sayings of the Ancient Romans*, etc., by W. Speed, London, 1678.

*Faerie Queene* (E. Spencer), 1617.

*Fatti relativi a mesmerismo e cure mesmeriche*, etc. (A. & F. Orioli), Corfu, 1842, 8vo.

*Faust* (Goethe). First Part publ. in 1808.

*Faustus*, apud *Augustine*. Excerpts from the writings of an African Bishop of the Manichaeans in Vol. VIII of the Benedictine ed. of St. Augustine.

*Festus* (Ph. J. Bailey), 1839.

*Fide et symbole, De* (St. Augustine). Engl. tr. in *Library of Christian Classics*, John H. S. Burleigh, London, SCM Press, 1953.

*Fihrist al-'ulûm* (Abu'l-Faraj Muḥammad b. Abî Ya'qûb Isḥâk al-Warrâq al-Nadîm al-Baghdâdî). The title means *Catalog;* the work was compiled by an Arab bibliographer of the 4th c. Two recensions are known. Arab text with German translation by G. Flügel, as *Das Kitâb al-Fihrist*, Leipzig, 1871-72, 2 vols.

*Fils de Dieu, Les* (L. Jacolliot), Paris, 1873, 1875, 1882.

*Florida* (Apuleius). Eng. tr. in *Bohn's Class. Library*.

*Force Electrically Exhibited* (J. W. Phelps), 1879.

*Forschungen auf dem Gebiete der alten Philosophie* (A. B. Krische). Vol. I (Die theologischen Lehren der griechischen Denker), Göttingen, 1840, 8vo.

*Fortalitium fidei* (Alph. a Spina), Strassburg, 1473, fol.; Basel, 1475; Nürnberg, 1485, 1487; Lugduni, 1500.

*Foudre, considérée au point de vue de l'histoire, de la médecine légale et de l'hygiène publique, De la* (J. C. Boudin). Paris, J.-B. Baillière, 1855.

*Four Ancient Books of Wales, The* (Wm. F. Skene), Edinb., 1868.

\**Fragment* from the writings of Marcus Aurelius. Unidentified.

*Fragment* (Hermeias). Quoted by Cory in *Ancient Fragments*, p. 295, q.v.

*Fragment* (Theon of Alexandria). In MS. Ex. cod. reg. Gall. gr. No. 2390, fol. 154.

\**Fragment* (Vyâsa-Maya).

*Framents* (Xenophanes). Quoted in the *Stromateis* of Clemens Alexandrinus.

*Fragments of Science* (J. Tyndall), 1872; 5th ed. 1876.

*Free Enquiry into the Miraculous Powers, etc., A* (C. Middleton), London, 1749, 4to.

*Funerali antichi di diversi popoli et nationi* (T. Porcacchi), Venice, 1574, 1591.

## G

*Gândharvaveda*. The *Veda* of music, considered as an Appendix to the *Sâmaveda* and ascribed to Bharata.

*Gatherings from Graveyards*, etc. (G. A. Walker), London, 1839, 8vo.

\**Genealogy of the Blessed Virgin Mary* (Faustus, Bishop of Riez).

*General Catalogue of Old Books and Manuscripts* (B. Quaritch). London, 1887-88, Index 1892; 7 vols. 8vo., with portraits.

*General History of the Christian Church from the Fall of the Western Empire to the Present Time,* (J. Priestley), Northumberland (Penn.), 1802, 1803, 4 vols.

*General History of the Christian Church to the Fall of the Western Empire* (J. Priestley), Birmingham, 1790, 2 vols., 8vo.; 2nd ed., 1808.

*General Survey of the History of the Canon of the New Testament, A* (B. W. Westcott), London, 1855, 1866, 1870; 4th ed., 1875; 5th ed., 1881.

*Genèse de l'humanité, La. Fétichisme, polythéisme, monothéisme* (L. Jacolliot), Paris, 1875, 1876, 1877, 8vo.

*Genesis Elucidated* (J. Jervis-White Jervis). A new Translation from the Hebrew compared with the Samaritan Text and the Septuagint and Syriac versions, with Notes by J. J.-W. J., London, 1852.

*Geographical Distribution of Animals, etc., The* (A. R. Wallace), London, 1876, 2 vols.

*Géographie mathématique du monde* (Conrad Maltebrun), 1803-07, 16 vols.

*Gerusalemme liberata, La* (T. Tasso), 1580-81.

*Gesammelte Schriften* (J. V. von Görres), Augsburg, 1854, etc.

*Geschichte der Freimaurerei von der Zeit ihres Entstehens bis auf die Gegenwart* (J. G. Findel), Leipzig, 1861, 1862, 2 vols.; 2nd ed., 1863. Eng. tr. as *History of Freemasonry,* etc., Leipzig, 1866; 2nd rev. ed., London, 1869.

*Geschichte der griechischen Literatur bis auf das Zeitalter Alexanders* (K. O. Müller), Breslau, 1841, 1857, 1875, 2 Vols.; Engl. tr. as *A Hist. of the Liter. of Ancient Greece,* London, 1858, 3 vols.

*Geschichte der Hexenprocesse. Aus den Quellen dargestellt* (W. G. Soldan), Stuttgart, 1843, 8vo.

*Geschichte der Ost-Mongolen und ihrer Fürstenhäuser,* etc. (Sanang Setsen). Translated from the Mongolian into German by I. I. Schmidt. Mongolian & German texts. St. Petersburg, 1829. 4to. Photographic reprod. [1935?], St. Petersburg, Leipzig. xxiv, 509. This work is a transl. of Sanang Setsen's Mongolian Chronicles of 1662. He was the Chungtaidschi of the Ordos.

*Geschichte des Alterthums* (M. W. Duncker), Berlin, 1852-57, 4 vols.

*Geschichte des Heidenthums in Beziehung, auf Religion, Wissen, Kunst, Sittlichkeit und Staatsleben* (C. F. A. Wuttke), Breslau, 1852-53, 2 vols.

*Geschichte des Kanons, Zur* (C. A. Credner), Halle, 1847; ed. Volkmar, Berlin, 1860.

*Ghost Land; or Researches into the Mysteries of Occultism* (E. H. Britten), Boston, 1876.

*Giaour, The* (Byron), 1813.

*Ginzâ* ("Treasure"): *der Schatz oder das grosse Buch der Mandäer.* German transl. by M. Lidzbarski. Göttingen, 1925.

*Gnostics and their Remains, The* (C. W. King), London, 1864; 2nd ed., 1887.

*God in History or the Progress of Man's Faith in the Moral Order of the World* (C. C. J. Bunsen). Transl. by Susanna Winkworth from the German text: *Gott in der Geschichte, oder der Fortschritt des Glaubens an eine sittliche Weltordnung,* Leipzig, 1857-58, in six books.

*Golden Legend* (Legenda aurea, vulgo Historia lombardica dicta, ad oppt. libr. fidem recensuit Dr. Th. Graesse) (Jacobus de Voragine), Dresdae et Lips., 1846, 8vo. This is the most convenient ed., and the French of Gustave Brunet (Paris, 1843, 2 vols.) the best translation. Written originally as *Historia lombardica*, it was publ. variously under this title, or as *Legendae sanctorum, De vitis sanctorum*, or *Legenda aurea*. See also *Lives* (Alban Butler).

*Gospel According to Peter.* Since 1877, when *Isis Unveiled* was written, a fragment of this Gospel was discovered by the French Archaeological Mission in Cairo, in 1886, in a grave of an ancient cemetery at Akhmîm (Panopolis), in Upper Egypt. See for translation *The Ante-Nicene Fathers*, Vol. X.

*Gospel According to the Hebrews.* One of the Gospels mentioned by several Church Fathers but which has not come down to us.

*Gospel of Nicodemus* (Acta Pilate). In W. Hone, *Apocryphal New Testament*, etc., London, 1820, 1821, 1846, where it is trans. from Grynaeus' *Orthodoxographa*, 1569, Vol. I, tom. ii, p. 643. Also in *ANF*.

*Gospel of St. Thomas.* Greek apocryphal work whose more exact title was *The Gospel of Thomas the Israelite Philosopher*. It is a rather mediocre apocryphon consisting of naive legends about the Savior's boyhood which later became scattered among the "Infancy Gospels." Not to be confused with the recently discovered *Gospel According to Thomas*, the Coptic text of which was found at Chenoboskion, Egypt.

*Gospel of the Birth of Mary.* In W. Hone, *Apocryphal New Testament*, etc. (q.v.). Also in *ANF*.

*Gradibus medicinarum, De* (Maiolus), Venice, 1497.

*Greacorum opiniones de daemonibus* (M. Psellus), or *Concerning daimons according to the Dogmata of the Greeks;* in Thos. Taylor. *The Description of Greece by Pausanias,* Vol. III, pp. 292-93 (Greek and Engl.); also in Migne, *PCC*, Ser. Gr., CXXII, Paris, 1889 (Gr. and Latin).

\**Great Book, The* (untraced).

*Greek Lexicon* (Suidas). Best ed. are those of T. Gaisford (without Latin version), Oxford, 1834, 3 vols., and of G. Bernhardy, Halle, 1834, which embodies the Latin version as well.

*Griechische Mythologie* (L. Preller), Leipzig, 1854, 2 vols.

*Grotte de Lourdes, sa fontaine, ses guérisons, La* (P.-R. Dozous), Paris, 1874.

# H

*Hallucinations, Des* (A.-J.-F. Brierre de Boismont): ou histoire raisonnée des apparitions, des visions, des songes, de l'extase, du magnétisme et du somnambulisme. Paris, 1845, 1852, 1862; Engl. tr., London, 1859; Philad., 1853.

*Harivaṇśa.* See *Mahâbhârata*.

*Harmonia Macrocosmica* (Andreas Cellarius), Amsterdam, 1660, 1661, 1708.

*Hauts Phénomènes de la magie, précédés du spiritisme antique, Les* (H.-R. Gougenot des Mousseaux), Paris, 1864.

*Heathen Religion in its Popular and Symbolical Development, The* (J. B. Gross), Boston, New York, 1856.

*Hebräisches und Chaldäisches Handwörterbuch über das Alte Testament* (J. Fürst), Leipzig, 1851-61, 2 vols.; Engl. tr. by S. Davidson, London, 1867, 1871.

*Hebrew and English Lexicon, An* (without points) (John Parkhurst), London, 1762; 7th ed., 1813; also 1823, 1829.

*Hebrew and English Lexicon of the Old Testament, A* (H. Gesenius). Transl. from the Latin of Gesenius by E. Robinson, Boston, 1836; also 1844, 1892.

*Hercule et Cacus, étude de mythologie comparée* (M. Bréal), Paris, 1863.

*Hermes, Books of.* Consult G. R. S. Mead's *Thrice-Greatest Hermes* (3rd impr., rev., London, J. M. Watkins, 1964) for the *Asclepius* and the *Poimandrês*. The *Smaragdine Tablet* (q.v.) is somewhat questionable as to genuineness. The *Tractatus de transmutatione metallorum* likewise.

*Hermès Trismégiste* (L. Ménard). Traduction précédée d'une étude sur l'origine des livres hermétiques. Paris, 1866, 8vo.

*Hindoo Pantheon, The* (E. Moor), 1810, 4to; new ed., cond. and annot. by W. O. Simpson, Madras, 1864, 8vo. lacks the plates.

*Hippolytus und seine Zeit* (C. C. J. Bunsen), Leipzig, 1852-53, 2 pts.; Engl. tr. as *Hippolytus and his Age*, London, 1852, 4 vols.

*Histoire abréguée des differens cultes* (J. A. Dulaure), 2nd ed., Paris, 1825, 2 vols.

*Histoire critique de Manichée et du Manichéisme* (I. de Beausobre), Amsterdam, 1734-39, 2 vols.

*Histoire critique du Gnosticisme, et de son influence sur les sectes religieuses et philosophiques des six premiers siècles de l'Ère Chrétienne* (A. Jacques Matter), Paris, 1828, 2 vols.; 2nd ed., Strasbourg, 1843-44, 3 vols.

*Histoire d'Angleterre* (De Rapin-Thoryas), The Hague, 1724-36, 4to, 13 tom.; 2nd ed., 1733.

*Histoire de l'Académie Royale des Inscriptions et Belles Lettres.* See "Dissertation," etc. (Bonamy).

*Histoire de la fondation du Grand Orient de France* (C. A. Thory), Paris, 1812.

*Histoire de la médecine, Rapport du physique et du moral de l'homme* (P. J. G. Cabanis). New ed., with a biography of the author. Paris, 1824.

*Histoire de la réformation du XVIme siècle* (J. H. Merle d'Aubigné), Paris, 1835-53, 5 vols., 8vo.; also 1877-78; Engl. tr., 1840.

*Histoire de la ville de Khotan, tirée des Annales de la Chine et traduite du chinois,* etc. (Abel Rémusat), Paris, 1820, 8vo.

*Histoire des Juifs, depuis Jésus Christ jusqu'à présent* (J. Basnage de Beauval), Rotterdam, 1706; The Hague, 1716, 9 vols.; Eng. tr., 1708.

*Histoire des nations civilisées du Mexique* (C. E. Brasseur de Bourbourg), Paris, 1857-59, 4 vols.

*Histoire des sectes religieuses,* etc. (Bishop Henri Grégoire), Paris, 1828-45, 6 vols.

*Histoire des Vierges — Les Peuples et les Continents disparus* (L. Jacolliot), 1874; another copy with new title-page, 1879.

*Histoire du merveilleux dans les temps modernes* (Guillaume-Louis Figuier), Paris, 1860, 4 vols.

*Histoire générale de la Francmaçonnerie* (E. Rebold), Paris, 1851; Engr. tr. by J. Fletcher as *A General History of Freemasonry in Europe,* Cincinnati, 1861.

*Histoire pittoresque de la Francmaçonnerie et des sociétés secrètes anciennes et modernes* (F. T. B. Clavel), 2nd ed., Paris, 1843, 8vo.

## BIBLIOGRAPHY 815

*Historia Chichimeca.— Relaciones* (Fernando de Alva Ixtlilxóchitl), 1848.

*Historia Chronica* (Joannes Malala), Oxonii, 1691, 8vo; Greek and Latin; later ed.

*Historia de Guatemala o Recordación florida,* etc. (Francisco Antonio de Fuentes y Guzmán). Madrid, 1882, 83, 2 vols.; also Guatemala, 1932-33, 3 vols.

*Historia del cielo y de la tierra* (D. R. de Ordóñez y Aguiar). Written ca. 1794, but unpublished.

*Historia Francorum* (St. Gregory of Tours), Paris, 1561, 8vo; Basel, 1568; ed. of T. Ruinart, Paris, 1699; ed. of Guadet and Taranne, in the *Soc. de l'hist. de France* (4 vols., with French tr., 1836-38); Engl. tr. by O. M. Dalton. Oxford: Clarendon Press, 1927, 2 vols.

*Historia religionis veterum Persarum* (Thos. Hyde), Oxoniae, 1700, 4to; 2nd ed., 1760, 4to.

*Historia verdadera de la Conquista de la Nueva-España,* etc. (B. Díaz del Castillo), Madrid [1632], fol.; Madrid, 1795, 4to; Mexico, 1854, 4to; Engl. tr. by M. Keatinge, London, 1800; and by Maudsley, 1908, 3 vols.

*Historia Vinlandiae antiquae, seu partis Americae Septentrionales,* etc. (T. Torphaeus or Thormod Torfason), *Hanniae,* 1705; also 1715. Engl. tr. by Chas. G. Herbermann, as *The History of Ancient Vinland,* etc. New York: J. G. Shea, 1891, 8vo., 83 pp.

*Historiae Armeniacae libri III* (Moses of Choren), Londini, 1736, 4to.; Armenian and Latin; Moise de Khorène, *Histoire d'Arménie,* Arm. text and French transl, by P. E. le Vaillant de Florival, Venice, 1841. — Engr. tr. in *ANF.*

*Historiarum adversus Paganos libri VII* (P. Orosius); ed. pr., Vienna (J. Schüssler), 1471, fol.; Venice ed., 1483, 1484, 1499, 1500; ed. of Havercamp, Lug. Bat., 1738, 4to; Eng. tr., London, 1773, 8vo.

*Historiarum Philippicarum libri XLIV* (Justinus). An abridgment of the *Universal History* composed in Latin by Trogus Pompeius. Ed. princeps was printed by Jensen at Venice, 1470, followed by a great many others; Engl. tr. by Turnbull, London, 1746; and by Rev. John S. Watson (incl. Cornelius Nepos and Eutropius), London, 1872, 1890.

*Historical Account of Discoveries and Travels in Asia from the Earliest Ages to the Present Time* (H. Murray), Edinburgh, 1820.

*Historicall Description of the Islande of Britayne,* etc. (Wm. Harrison), 1577, fol. Incl. *The Description of Scotlande,* by H. Boethius, transl. by Wm. H.

*Historical Survey of the Astronomy of the Ancients, An* (G. C. Lewis), London, 1862.

*History and Doctrine of Buddhism, Popularly illustrated, The* (E. Upham). With notices of the Kappooism, or Demon Worship, and of the Bali, or Planetary Incantations of Ceylon. London, 1829.

*History of Barlaam and Josaphat.* Aside from the works of John of Damascus, the Greek text with an English transl. is given in *Barlaam and Ioasaph,* by G. R. Woodward and H. Mattingly, 1914.

*History of Christianity, from the Birth of Christ to the Abolition of Paganism in the Roman Empire, The* (H. H. Milman), London, 1840, 3 vols.; also 1863, 1867; New York, 1881, 3 vols.

*History of Early Opinions concerning Jesus Christ, compiled from original writers,* etc. (J. Priestley), Birmingham, 1786, 4 vols.

*History of Egypt* (Manetho). Passages quoted in Eusebius and Julius Africanus; also *Ancient Fragments* (Cory).

*History of European Morals from Augustus to Charlemagne* (W. E. H. Lecky), London, 1869, 2 vols.; 3rd ed., 1877.

*History of Greece, A* (Geo. Grote); first 2 vols., London, 1846; other 10 vols., 1847-56; new ed., 1862, 8 vols.

*History of Herodotus, The* (Geo. Rawlinson), London, 1858, 4 vols.

*History of Hindostan, its Arts and its Sciences,* etc., The (Thos. Maurice), London, 1795-98, 2 vols., 4to (bound in three); 2nd ed., 1820, 4to.

\**History of India* (Kullûka-Bhaṭṭa).

*History of Magic, The* (Joseph Ennemoser). Transl. by Howitt from the German original *Geschichte der Magie* (Leipzig, 1844, 8vo.), with Appendix on Apparitions, etc., London, 1854.

*History of Magic, witchcraft and animal magnetism, An* (J. C. Colquhoun), London, 1851, 2 vols.

*History of the Apostles' Creed, with critical observations on its several articles* (Peter King [Lord King]), London, 1703, 1711, 1719, 1738.

*History of the Conflict between Religion and Science* (J. W. Draper), New York, 1874.

*History of the Intellectual Development of Europe* (J. W. Draper), New York, 1863.

*History of the Jesuits; their origin, progress, doctrines and designs* (G. B. Nicolini), 1854; London, 1879; also in Bohn's ill. library.

*History of the Pontificate of Pius IX, The* (G. B. Nicolini), London, 1851, 8vo.

*History of the Popes, from the foundation of the See of Rome to the present Time, The* (A. Bower), London, 1748-66; Dublin, 1749-68; London, 1750-66; Philad., 1844-45. 7 vols.

*History of the Supernatural* (W. Howitt), London, 1863, 2 vols.

*History of the Suppression of Infanticide in Western India under the Government of Bombay* (John Wilson), 1855.

*Horae Hebraicae et Talmudicae,* etc. (J. Lightfoot), Cambridge, 1663, 4to.; 1671, 1674; ed. by Rev. R. Gandell, Oxford, 1859, 4 vols.

*Hortatory Address to the Greeks* (*Protreptikos pros Hellênas*) (Clement of Alex.), French transl. as *Le Protreptique* by Claude Mondésert. 2nd ed. with Greek text, Paris, 1949, 8vo.

*Hudibras* (S. Butler), 1663, 1664, 1678.

*Huetiana; ou pensées diverses de H. Huet, Évêsque d'Avranches* (P. D. Huet), Paris, 1722.

\**Hundert und eine Frage* (F. N. Nork).

*Hypatia* (Chas. Kingsley), 1853.

I

*Iamblichus' Life of Pythagoras, or Pythagoric Life* (Thos. Taylor). Accompanied by Fragments of the Ethical Writings of certain Pythagoreans in the Doric dialect; and a Collection of Pythagoric Sentences from Stobaeus and others. London, 1818, 8vo. Repr. by J. M. Watkins, 1965.

*Iamblichus on the Mysteries of the Egyptians, Chaldeans, and Assyrians.* Transl. from the Greek by Thos. Taylor, Chiswick, 1821, 8vo.; 2nd ed., London, 1895, 8vo.; 3rd ed., 1968.

*Iconographie chrétienne. Histoire de Dieu* (A. N. Didron), Paris, 1843; in *Collection de documents inédits sur l'histoire de France,* 3me. série, 1835, etc. — Eng. tr. in 2 vols., 1851.

*Ideen zur Philosophie der Geschichte der Menschheit* (J. G. von Herder), Riga, Leipzig, 1784-91, 4 pts.

*Index Expurgatorius.* More correctly, *Index Librorum Prohibitorum,* which was the title of the official list of books which, until 1966, were forbidden by ecclesiastical authority to members of the Roman Catholic Church. In June 1966, through an express declaration by authority of Pope Paul VI, the *Index* lost all obligatory binding force. Canons 1399 and 2318, declaring certain penalties against those who violate laws concerning the censure and prohibition of books, were explicitly abrogated Nov. 15, 1966. Both revocations are retroactive.

*Idrah Rabbah* (Great Holy Assembly, incl. in Knorr von Rosenroth's *Kabbala denudata,* q.v.).

*Idrah Zutah* (Lesser Holy Assembly, incl. in Knorr von Rosenroth's *Kabbala denudata,* q.v.).

*Illustrations of the Rock-cut Temples of India* (James Fergusson), Text to accompany the folio volume of Plates. London, 1845.

*Imago primi saeculi Societatis Jesu, à Provinciâ Flandro-Belgicâ ejusdem Societatis repraesentata* (ascribed to Jean de Tollenare), Antwerp, 1650.

*Immortality of the Soule, The* (H. More), London, 1659.

*Incidents in the Life of Madame Blavatsky* (A. P. Sinnett). London: George Redway, 1886, xii, 324 pp.; 2nd ed., London: Theos. Publ. House, 1913, 256 pp. Somewhat abbreviated.

*Incidents of Travel in Central America, Chiapas, and Yucatan* (J. L. Stephens), London, 1841, 2 vols.; 12th ed., 1846.

*Incidents of Travel in Egypt, Arabia Petraea and the Holy Land* (J. L. Stephens), New York, 1837.

*India in Greece; or, Truth in Mythology,* etc. (E. Pococke), London, 1852, 8vo.

*Indian Antiquary.* A Journal of Oriental Research, Bombay, 1872.

*Indian Antiquities* (Thos. Maurice), London, 1793-1800, 7 vols., 8vo. (intended as Introduction to *The Hist. of Hindostan*); also 1794-1800, and 1806.

"Indian Sketches; or Rubs of a Rolling Stone," by Hadji Nicka Bauker Khan (W. L. D. O'Grady), *Commercial Bulletin,* Boston, Mass.; series consisting of 49 chapters, from March 13, 1876 to April 14, 1877.

*Indica.* Same as Book VIII of Arrian's *Anabasis,* q.v.

*Indica* (Ctesias). Treatise on India the material for which this Greek writer collected during his stay in Persia. Known only as an abridgment in Photius' *Bibliotheca,* q.v.

*Indica* (Megasthenes): *Ancient India as described by Megasthenês and Arrian,* etc., by J. W. McCrindle, London, 1877.

*Indische Studien,* ed. by Dr. Albrecht Weber, 1850-98, 18 vols.

*Infinito, Universo e Mondi Innumerabili, Del'* (G. Bruno), 1584.

*Influence of the Blue Ray of the Sunlight and of the Blue Color of the Sky, The* (Gen. A. J. Pleasonton). Address to the Philadelphia Society for Promoting Agriculture. Philadelpia, 1876.

*Inorganic Chemistry* (W. B. Kemshead), 1872; enl. ed., 1881; 4th ed., 1885.

*In quinque priora praecepta Decalogi* (F. S. Fagundez), Lyon, 1640.

*Inquiry into Human Understanding, An* (D. Hume), London, 1861.

*Inquiry into the Nature and Place of Hell, An* (Rev. T. Swinden), London, 1714; 2nd ed., 1727.

*Inquiry into the Structure and Affinity of the Greek and Latin languages, etc., An* (Geo. Dunbar), Edinburgh, 1828.

*Inspiration des Camisards, De l'* (H. Blanc), Recherches nouvelles sur les phénomènes extraordinaires observés parmi les Protestants des Cévennes à la fin du XVIIme siècle, etc. Paris, 1859.

*Institutes* (Edward Coke), 1628, etc., fol.; many later ed.

*Institutes of Hindu Law: or, The Ordinances of Menu, according to the Gloss of Culluca. Comprising the Indian System of Duties, Religious and Civil.* Verbally translated from the Original Sanskrit. With a Preface, by Sir William Jones. In *The Works of Sir William Jones* (six vols.), London, 1799.

*Institutes of the Christian Religion* (J. Calvin); 1st Latin ed., 1536; 1st French ed., 1540.

*Institutiones physiologicae* (J. F. Blumenbach), Göttingen, 1787; London, 1807; Engl. tr., by John Elliotson, London, 1820.

*Institutionum historiae ecclesiasticae libri IV* (J. L. von Mosheim), 1726; Engl. tr. by J. Murdock and H. Soame, as *Institutes of Eccles. History, Ancient and Modern*, London, 1863, 3 vols.

*Introductio in Chaldaicam linguam, Syriacam atque Armenicam et decem alias linguas* (Theseus Ambrosius), Pavia, 1539.

*Introduction à l'Histoire du Bouddhisme indien* (Eugène Burnouf), Paris, 1844; 2nd ed., 1876.

*Introduction au Traité de la Conformité des merveilles anciennes avec les modernes, ou Traité préparatif à l'Apologie pour Hérodote* (H. Stephanus), Geneva, 1566, etc.; new ed., Paris, 1879, 2 vols.

*Introduzione alla Sacra Scrittura* (G. B. de Rossi), 1817.

*Isbrandi de Diemerbroeck tractatus de peste . . . ab auctore audanctus* (I. de Diemerbroeck), 4. lib. Amsteladami, 1665; *A Treatise concerning Pestilence*, etc., abridged and transl. by G. Stanton, 1722.

*Isis Unveiled* (H. P. Blavatsky), Orig. ed., New York, J. W. Bouton, 1877. Many subsequent editions. As part of the *Collected Writings*, 1972.

\*Israelite Indeed, The (I. M. Jost).

*Itinerary* (Ricold of Monte Croce), Paris, 1511, 4to.; also known as *De Vita et moribus Turcorum;* best ed. is by J. C. M. Laurent, in *Peregrinatores Medii Aevi Quatuor*, pp. 105-41, Leipzig, 1864 and 1873.

*Itinerary* or *Description of Greece* (Pausanias). *LCL*. See *Description of Greece by Pausanias* (Thos. Taylor) for Engl. transl.

## J

\*Jaina Books of Pattana.

Jātakas. Stories of Buddha's former births. The Jātaka together with its commentary, etc. Edited by V. Fausböll [Roman translit.]. London: Trübner & Co., 1877-1897. 7 vols. — The Jātaka, or stories of the Buddha's former births. Trans. under the ed. of Prof. E. B. Cowell. Cambridge Univ. Press, 1895-1913, 7 vols.

Jésuites, Des (J. Michelet & J. E. Quinet), 6th ed., Paris, 1844; Eng. tr. by G. H. Smith, London, 1846; and by C. Cock, London, 1846.

Jesus: Myth, Man, or God; or, The Popular Theology and the Positive Religion Contrasted (J. M. Peebles), London, 1870; 3rd. ed., 1878.

Johann Reuchlin und seine Zeit (E. T. Mayerhoff), Berlin, 1830, 8vo.; Engl. tr. by Francis Barham as The Life and Times of John Reuchlin, or Capnion, the Father of the German Reformation, London: Whittaker & Co., 1843.

Johannesbuch der Mandäer, Das. Text and transl. by M. Lidzbarski. Giessen, 1915. 2 vols.

Journal (A. Judson). See under Account of . . . Baptist Mission, etc. (Ann H. Judson).

Journal du magnétisme. Monthly founded at Paris by Baron du Potet in 1845; ed. by H. Durville.

\*Journal für Freimaurer (Woog), Vienna, 5786.

Journal of an Embassy from the Governor General of India to the Courts of Siam and Cochin-China (J. Crawfurd), London, 1828, 4to.

Justicia et jure ceterisque virtutibus cardinalibus libri duo, De (J. de Dicastillo), Antwerp, 1641.

## K

Kabbala denudata seu doctrina Hebraeorum transcendentalis et metaphysica adque theologica, etc. (Knorr von Rosenroth); Vol. I, Sulzbach, 1677-78; Vol. II, Frankfurt a. M., 1684. Contains also: Idrah Rabbah (Greater Holy Assembly), Idrah Zutah (Lesser Holy Assembly), and Siphra Dtzeniuthah (Book of the Concealed Mystery), q.v. — See Vol. VII of the Collected Writings, pp. 269-71, for additional data on translations, etc.

Kabbalah: its doctrines, development, and literature, The (C. D. Ginsburg), London, 1863, 1866, 1925, 1955.

Kabbale, ou la philosophie religieuse des Hébreux, La (A. Franck), Paris, 1843, iv, 412 pp. 8vo.; 2nd ed., Paris, 1889, vi, 314 pp. 8vo.; 3rd ed. 1892. — Also Adolf Jellinek, Beiträge zur Geschichte der Kabbala, Leipzig, 1851.

Kabiren in Teutschland, Die (C. C. Bart), Erlangen, 1832.

Kanjur (Tib. sp. bKah-hgyur). "Translation of the Word," the first part of the Tibetan Buddhist Canon. It contains 108 volumes, some of which concern the Vinaya or monastic discipline, while others set forth the prajñā-pāramitā philosophy and expound the Trikāya and the ālaya vijñāna doctrines. The second part of the Tibetan Canon is the Tanjur (Tib. sp. bStan-hgyur) or "Translation of Treatises"; this collection contains 225 volumes of works by Indian masters, being partly comm. on the Sūtras and partly on the Tantras. The Tibetan Canon consists mainly of translations from the Sanskrit and the Chinese collected and arranged into the above two groups by Bu-ston, a Tibetan scholar (1290-1394). Only partial translations into English are available such as the Analysis of the Dulva, by Alex. Csoma de Körös, 1836, 39.

*Kâṭhakopanishad.* Same as *Kâṭhopanishad.* See for bibliogr. data *Chhandogyopanishad.*

*Kaushîtaki-Brâhmaṇa* or *Kaushîtakibrâhmaṇopanishad.* Ed. with Engl. tr. by E. B. Cowell. Calcutta: As. Soc. of Bengal, 1861. *Bibl. Ind.* 39. — *The Upanishads.* Tr. by F. Max Müller. Oxford: Clarendon Press, 1879, 1884. *SBE* I & XV. — *The Twelve Principal Upanishads* (Eng. tr.), Tookaram Tatya. Bombay: Bombay Theos. Public. Fund, 1899.

*Key to Theosophy, The* (H. P. Blavatsky). Orig. ed., London, 1889; 2nd ed., with Glossary, 1890; many subsequent ed.

*Khordah-Avesta.* See *Avesta.*

*Königsbuch der alten Ägypter* (K. R. Lepsius), Berlin, 1858, 4to.

*Koran* (Ar. *al-Qur'ân* meaning recitation). Sacred Scripture of Islam containing the professed revelations of Mohammed. It is in Arabic, and is divided into 114 *suras* or chapters; it is the basis for the religious, social, civil, commercial, military and legal regulations of the Mohammedan world. — Translations by G. Sale (1734, etc.), J. M. Rodwell (1876, etc., arranged chronol.), E. H. Palmer (1880, etc., *SBE,* 6 & 9), Muḥammad 'Alî (1917). Rodwell's tr. is in *Everyman's Library,* London, 1909.

*Kosmos. Entwurf einer physischen Weltbeschreibung* (F. H. A. von Humboldt), Stuttgart and Tübingen, 1845-62, 5 vols.

*Kritische Untersuchungen über die Evangelien Justin's, der Clementinischen Homilien und Marcion's* (A. Hilgenfeld), Halle, 1850.

L

*Lalitavistara.* See *Rgya tch'er rol pa.*

*Land of Charity, The* (S. Mateer). A descriptive Account of Travancore and its People, etc., London, 1871, 8vo.

*Land of the While Elephant, etc., The* (F. Vincent), London, 1873.

*Lankâvatâra Sûtra.* A scripture of the Yogâchâra School of Mahâyâna Buddhism, written in Sanskrit in India (ca. 350 A.D.); contains an epitome of nearly all Mahâyâna teachings. Expounds subjective idealism based on Buddha's enlightenment, and the doctrines of Sûnyatâ and Mind-Only. Said to have been given by Bodhidharma to his disciple, the Second Patriarch, Hui-K'o. For trans. see D. Suzuki, *The Lankâvatâra Sûtra* (1932) and his companion vol. *Studies in the Lankâvatâra Sûtra* (1930).

*Last Days of Pompeii, The* (Bulwer-Lytton), 1834.

*Lay of the Last Minstrel, The* (Walter Scott), 1805.

*Leben Jesu, Das* (D. F. Strauss), 2nd ed., Tübingen, 1837, 2 vols.; Engl. tr. by Marian Evans as *The Life of Jesus,* London, 1846, 3 vols.

*Lectures on Some Subjects of Modern History and Biography* (J. B. Robertson), Dublin, 1864.

*Lectures on the History of Ancient Philosophy* (W. A. Butler), Cambridge, 1856, 1874.

*Lectures on the History of the Eastern Church* (A. P. Stanley). With an Introd. to the Study of Ecclesiastical History. London, 1861; 2nd ed., 1862; also 1869, 1883.

*Légende de monseigneur Saint Dñique Père et premier fondateur de l'ordre des frères prescheurs, La* (trāslate d'latin en Francoys par Jean Martin), Paris, [1510- ? ], 4to.

*Lenning's Encyclopädie der Freimaurerei, etc.* (ed. by Mossdorf), Leipzig, 1822-28, 3 vols.

"Letter of S. Turner to the Governor General," *Asiatick Researches*, Vol. I, 1801, pp. 197-205.

*Letter to Anebo* (Porphyry). In Iamblichus' *On the Mysteries*, etc., q.v.

"Letter to Glanvill" (Henry More). See *Sadducismus*, etc.

*Letter to Mr. Archdeacon Travis, in Answer to his Defence of the Three Heavenly Witnesses*, etc. (R. Porson), London, 1790.

*Letters from the Masters of the Wisdom.* Transcribed and Annotated by C. Jinarâjadâsa. With a Foreword by Annie Besant. 1st Series, Adyar: Theos. Publ. House, 1919; 2nd. ed., 1923; 3rd ed., 1945; 4th ed., with addit. letters (1870-1900), 1948. — 2nd Series, Adyar, 1925, and Chicago, 1926.

*Letters of H. P. Blavatsky to A. P. Sinnett, The.* Transcribed, Compiled, and with an Introduction by A. T. Barker. New York: Frederick A. Stokes; and London: T. F. Unwin, 1925, 8vo.

*Letters to a candid inquirer on Animal Magnetism* (Wm. Gregory), London, 1851.

*Lettre à un médecin étranger* (A. Mesmer), in *Le Nouveau Mercure Savant*, Altona, Jan. 5, 1775; also as pamphlet, 22 pp. (Caillet 7418).

*Lettres écrites d'Égypte et de Nubie, en 1828 et 1829* (J. F. Champollion), Paris, 1833.

*Lettres pour servir d'introduction à l'histoire primitive des nations civilisées de l'Amérique Septentrionale. Cartas*, etc. (Brasseur de Bourbourg), Mexico, 1851, 4to. [French and Spanish].

*Lettres sur l'Égypte*, etc. (C. É. Savary), Paris, 1785, 8vo.; 2nd ed., 1786, 3 vols. Engl. transl., London, 1787, 2 vols.

*Lexicon* (J. H. Zedler), 1732-54.

*Lexicon Chaldaicum, Talmudicum et Rabbinicum*, etc. (J. Buxtorf the Elder), Basileae, 1639 fol.; Lipsiae, 1869-75, 4to.

*Lexicon Pentaglotton:* Hebrew, Chaldean, Syriac, Talmudo-Rabbinical, Arabic (V. Schindler), Hanoviae, 1612, 1653, fol.

*Libellus synodicus, omnes Synodos, tam orthodoxas, quam haereticas . . . continens*, etc. (Joh. Pappus). Greek and Latin, in J. A. Fabricius, *Bibl. Graeca*, etc., Vol. II, Hamburg, 1722.

*Liber lapidum seu de gemmis* (Marbodus), ed. Beckman, Göttingen, 1799; also in Migne, *PCC*, Ser. Lat., Vol. 171, with a Life of Marbod, Bishop of Rennes.

*Liber mysterii.* See *Kabbalah Denudata*.

*Life and Times of John Reuchlin, or Capnion, the Father of the German Reformation.* Engl. tr. by F. Barham (London, 1843) of Ernst Theodor Mayerhoff's *Johann Reuchlin and seine Zeit*, Berlin, 1830.

*Life of Apollonius of Tyana, The* (Philostratus). Translated from the Greek, with Notes and Illustrations, by the Rev. Edward Berwick, London, 1809.

*Life of Father Alessandro Gavazzi, The* (G. B. Nicolini), Edinburgh, 1851.

*Life of Plotinus* (Porphyry). In Thos. Taylor, *Select Works of Plotinus*, q.v.

*Life of St. Francis.* The official account is St. Bonaventura's *Legenda*, publ. by the Franciscans of Quaracchi (1898) and tr. into Engl. in *Everyman's Library* (1910).

*Light:* A Journal of Spiritual Progress and Psychic Research, London. Founded by E. Dawson Rogers. Edited for some years by Rev. Wm. Stainton Moses (*pseud.* "M. A., Oxon."). First issue, January, 1881. In progress.

*Lives.* See *Apostolici.*

*Lives of the Fathers, Martyrs, and other Principal Saints, The* (Alban Butler), 2nd ed., Dublin, 1779, 12 vols.; 3rd ed., Edinburgh, 1798-1800; many other ed.

*Lives of the Necromancers* (Wm. Godwin), London, 1834, 1876.

*Lives of the Sophists* (Eunapius), Antwerp, 1568; ed. Boissonade, Amsterdam, 1822.

*Lloyd's Weekly Newspaper,* March, 1875.

*Loco Purgatorii, De* (R. Bellarmin). This is Chapter 6 of Book II (De Circumstanciis Purgatorii), of Vol. II of his *De Controversiis Christianae Fidei.* Tertia Controversia Generales, de Ecclesia, quae est in Purgatorio. This is in the 1619 ed. of Bellarmin's *Opera,* Col. Agrippinae. It can also be found in Bellarmin's Catechism: *An Ample Declaration of the Christian Doctrine,* transl. by Richard Hadock, Roan, ca. 1610.

*Logos alêthês* (True Doctrine), by Celsus the Epicurean; known only through the writings of Origen.

*Loi naturelle, ou catéchisme du citoyen Français, La* (C. F. Chasseboeuf de Volney), Paris, 1793, 1794.

*Lost Arts, The* (W. Phillips). Redpath Lyceum Lecture, Boston, Mass. Delivered several hundred times in the 19th century.

*Lotus de la Bonne Loi, Le.* See *Saddharma-puṇḍarîka.*

*Louis XI* (Dionysius Lardner Boucicault, formerly Bourcicault), ca. 1841.

*Lucernam inquisitorum haeretici pravitatis* (B. Comes), 1566.

*Lucernis antiquorum reconditis libri sex, De* (F. Licetus), Utini, 1653, fol.; Venetiis, 1621, 4to.

*Lucifer.* A Theosophical Magazine, Designed to "Bring to Light the Hidden Things of Darkness." Edited by H. P. Blavatsky and Mabel Collins (later by Annie Besant & G. R. S. Mead). London: The Theosophical Publishing Co., Ltd., London, Vols. I-XX, September, 1887 - August, 1897. Continued serially as *Theosophical Review.*

*Lun-Yü.* See *Analects* (Confucius).

*Lyrical Ballads* (W. Wordsworth), 1798.

# M

*Magia Adamica: or the Antiquities of Magic* (Eugenius Philalethes), London, 1650.

*Magia Jesu Christi.* Attributed to Jesus himself in Augustine, *De consensu evang.,* Bk. I, ch. ix.

*Magiae naturalis, sive de miraculis rerum naturalium libri iiii* (G. della Porta), Neapoli, 1558; Lugduni, 1569. Engl. tr., 1658.

*Magic and Mesmerism.* An Episode of the Eighteenth Century, and Other Tales. (Anonymous). London, 1843, 3 vols. bound together.

*Magie au XIXme siècle, ses agents, ses vérités, ses mensonges, La* (H.-R. Gougenot des Mousseaux), Paris, 1860; 2nd ed., 1864.

*Magie dévoilée, ou principes de science occulte, La* (J. Dupotet), Paris, 1852, 4to.

Μαγικον *oder das geheime System einer Gesellschaft unbekannter Philosophen,* etc. Von einem unbekannten des Quadratscheins, der weder Zeichendeuter noch Epopt ist., Frankfurt und Leipzig, 1784, 8vo.

*Magnes; sive de arte magnetica opus tripartitum*, etc. (A. Kircher), Rome, 1641, 4to.; Coloniae Agripp., 1643, 4to.

*Magnete, magneticisque corporibus, et de magno magnete tellure, De* (Wm. Gilbert), London, 1600; Stettin, 1628, 1633; Frankfurt, 1629, 1638.

*Magnétisme animal en France*, etc., *Du* (A.-J.-F. Bertrand), Paris, 1826.

*Mahâbhârata*, meaning "Great War of the Bharatas." One of the two great epics of the Hindus, the other being the *Râmâyaṇa*. The poem consists of about 215,000 ślokas and describes the acts and contests of the sons of the two brothers Dhṛita-râshṭra and Pâṇḍu, descendants of Bharata who were of the lunar line of kings reigning in the neighborhood of Hastinâpura. It contains a mass of speculative, social and ethical discourse, notably the 18 chapters of the *Bhagavad-Gîtâ*, or the Song of the Blessed One, meaning Kṛishṇa, containing the renowned dialogue between the latter and Arjuna on some of the most vital subjects of the spiritual life. It teaches the bhakti yoga of devotion and the karma yoga doctrine of action. — The *Mahâbhârata* has been attributed to Vyâsa, a name which in reality means "Arranger." — Edited (with the *Harivaṇśa*, its Supplemental portion) for the Asiatic Soc. of Bengal, Calcutta, 1834-39. — Transl. by K. M. Ganguli and Pratap Chandra Roy. Calcutta: Bharata Press, 1883-96, 12 vols.; 2nd ed. Calcutta: Datta N. Bose & Co., 1923, etc. — Transl. by M. N. Dutt. Calcutta: Elysium Press, 1895-1905, 18 vols.

*Mahatma Letters to A. P. Sinnett, The* (from the Mahatmas M. and K. H.) (A. P. Sinnett). Transcribed, Compiled and with an Introduction by A. T. Barker (1893-1941). London: T. Fisher Unwin, December, 1923; New York: Frederick A. Stokes; xxxv, 492; 2nd rev. ed., London: Rider & Co., 1926; 8th impr., London, 1948; 3rd & rev. ed., Adyar, Madras: Theosophical Publ. House, 1962.

*Mahâvaṇśa*. The Sinhalese Pâli chronicle; a record in verse of the early history of Ceylon, incl. its religious history. Compiled in the 5th or 6th century. — Rev. and edited by H. Sumangala, Colombo, 1877; ed. by Wm. Geiger. London, for Pâli Text Society by Oxford Univ. Press, 1908 [Roman]. *PTS* 63. — Transl. by H. Sumangala, Colombo, 1883; transl. by Wm. Geiger and Mabel Bode, London, for Pâli Text Soc. by Oxford Univ. Press, 1912. *PTS*. tr. ser.. 3.

*Mahâvansi, the Râjâ-Ratnâcari, and the Râjâvali, forming the Sacred and Historical Books of Ceylon, The* (tr. and ed. by E. Upham), London, 1833, 3 vols.

*Malleus maleficarum — The Witches' Hammer* (J. Sprenger), 1487; Venice, 1574.

*Mânavadharmaśâstra* or *Manusmṛiti*. The most important and earliest of the metrical Smṛitis, probably based on a *Mânavadharmasûtra*. Closely connected with the *Mahâbhârata*, of which three books alone (iii, xii, xvi), contain as many as 260 of its 2684 ślokas. Text crit. ed. by J. Jolly. London: Trübner's Oriental Series, 1887. Trans. by G. Bühler. Oxford: Clarendon Press, 1886. *SBE* XXV — *Mânava-dharma-śâstra. Lois de Menou . . . traduites du sanscrit*, etc. (A. Loiseleur-Deslongchamps), Paris, 1833; also 1850.

*Manna benedicta, De* (no author). In a collection of 14 Treatises by John Frederick Houpreght entitled: *Aurifontina Chymica*, London: Printed for Wm. Cooper, 1680.

*Manners and Customs of the Ancient Egyptians* (J. G. Wilkinson), London, 1837-41, 8vo., 3 vols. ill.; 2nd Series under same title and date, in 3 vols.; 3rd ed., London, 1847, 8vo. New & rev. ed. by S. Birch, London, 1878, 3 vols.

*Manual of Budhism, in its modern Development, A* (R. Spence Hardy). Translated from Sinhalese MSS., London, 1853.

*Manuel d'iconographie chrétienne, grecque et latine,* etc. (Denys, moine de Fourna-Agrapha, ed. and annot. by A. N. Didron), Paris, 1845. 8vo. Transl. from the Byzantine MS "Le Guide de la painture."

*MS. Ex. cod. reg. Gall. gr.* No. 2390, fol 154.

\**Manuscript* (Don Juan Torres).

*Martialis Epigrammaton libri omnes, novis commentariis . . . illustrati . . . a M. Radero,* etc. (M. Raderus), 1602, fol., 1615, 1626, 1627.

*Materialism's Last Assault. Does Matter Do it All?* (E. Sargent), Boston, 1876.

*Materia medica* (Peri Hylês Yatrikês) (Dioscorides Pedacius). A work of great labor and research, in five books, which for a long time was considered of high standard, and replete with most valuable information on herbal medicine. One of the best ed. is that of C. Sprengel, Lips., 1829-30, 2 vols. 8vo., in Greek and Latin, with useful commentary, forming Vols. 25 & 26 of Kühn's Collection of the Greek Medical Writers.

*Mathematica* (Theon of Smyrna). See *Theoretic Arithmetic* (Thos. Taylor).

*Mathematical Principles of Natural Philosophy* (I. Newton), 1687.

*Médecine et les Médecins, La* (L. Peisse): philosophie, doctrines, institutions critiques, mœurs et biographies médicales, Paris, 1857, 2 vols.

*Médiateurs et les moyens de la magie, Les* (H.-R. Gougenot des Mousseaux), Paris, 1863.

*Medicina magnetica, De* (Wm. Maxwell), Francof., 1679.

\**Mediumistic Manifestations* (Prof. A. M. Butlerov), pamphlet.

\**Mediumistic Phenomena* (N. P. Wagner).

*Medizinal-chirurgische Aufsätze* (J. A. Hemmann), Berlin, 1778; 2nd ed., 1791.

*Meghadûta* or "Cloud Messenger." Kâlidâsa's lyrical gem of the Sanskrit lyrical poetry, the theme of which is a message which an exile sends by a cloud to his wife dwelling far away. — Transl. into Engl. verse by H. H. Wilson. 3rd ed., London, 1867. — Transl. by Thos. Clark, London, 1882.

*Mélanges d'épigraphie et d'archéologie sémitique* (J. Halévy), Paris, 1874.

*Mémoires pour servir à l'histoire ecclésiastique des six premiers siècles,* etc. (L.-S. le Nain de Tillemont), Paris, 1693-1712, 16 vols. 4to.; Venice, 1732. Engl. tr. London, 1733-35, 2 vols. (Only to year 177 A.D.).

*Mémoires pour servir à l'histoire du Jacobinisme* (A. Barruel), Paris, 1797-98, 4 vols.; Engl. tr. by R. Clifford, London, 1797-98.

*Mémoires pour servir à l'histoire et l'établissement du magnétisme animal,* etc. (A. M. J. de Puységur), [Paris], 1784, 232 pp., 8vo.; 1786; 2nd ed., 1809.

*Menschenopfer der alten Hebräer, Die* (F. W. Ghillany), Nürnberg, 1842.

*Mensibus, De* (Joannes Laurentius of Philadelphia, the Lydian; or Joannes Lydus). Only two epitomae or summeries and a fragment of this work are extant. It is an historical commentary on the Roman calendar, with an account of its various festivals, etc., derived from authorities most of which have perished. Publ. by N. Schow, Leipzig, 1794; with Latin version, publ. by Roether, Leipzig & Darmstadt, 1827. Edited by R. Wünsch, 1898-1903. All the extant portions of the works of Joannes Lydus, with text rev. by Imm. Bekker (Bonn, 1837), form one of the volumes of the reprint of the *Corpus Scriptorum Historiae Byzantinae.*

*Mercurii Trismegisti Liber de Potestate et Sapientia Dei* (Latin transl. of *Poimandrês* by Marsiglio Ficino), Treviso, 1471. 4to. See also *Thrice-Greatest Hermes* (G. R. S. Mead).

*Midrash, pl. Midrashim.* See *Talmud.*

*Mîmânsâ.* Meaning profound thought, reflection, examination, inquiry. Name of one of the great Schools of Hindu philosophy. It is divided into two systems: the *Pûrva-mîmânsâ,* or "First Inquiry," also called *Karma-mîmânsâ* or simply *Mîmânsâ,* founded by Jaimini and concerning itself chiefly with the correct interpretation of Vedic ritual and text; and the *Uttara-mîmânsâ* or "Second Inquiry," usually termed *Vedânta* or "End of the Veda," dealing chiefly with the nature of Brahma or the one universal Spirit.

Jaimini's system is set forth in the *Jaiminisûtra.* Transl. (with text) by Pandit Mohan Lal Sandal, Allâhâbâd, 1923-25, *SBH* 27. Consult also the commentaries of Śabarasvâmin and Mâdhava. As to the doctrines of the Vedânta, they are laid down in the *Brahmasûtras* of Bâdarâyaṇa and the famous *bhâshyas* or Commentaries of Saṃkarâchârya. Consult Engl. transl. in Volumes 34, 38 & 48 of the *SBE.*

*Minerva, To* (Proclus). Transl. by Thos. Taylor in his *Dissertation on the Eleusinian and Bacchic Mysteries,* q.v.

*Minnefest öfver J. J. Berzelius,* etc. (P. A. Siljeström). Minnestal af P. S. S.; Stockholm, 1849.

*Mirabili Potestate Artis et Naturae, De* (R. Bacon), 1542. 4to.; 1618. 8vo.; 1732. Engl. tr. by T. M. as *Friar Bacon, his Discovery of the Miracles of Art, Nature and Magick,* London, 1659.

*Miracles and Modern Spiritualism, On* (A. R. Wallace), 3 Essays. London, 1875; 2nd ed., 1881.

*Miscellanea eruditae antiquitatis* (J. Spon), Lugduni, 1685, fol.

*Mishnah, pl. Mishnayoth,* meaning instruction, oral law, from Hebrew *shânâh,* to repeat; in post-Biblical Hebrew, to teach, to learn. See *Talmud* for further data.

*Mishnah Torah* (Maimonides or Abraham ben Moses ben Maimon). A compilation from the *Talmud* on the Second Law. Constantinople, 1509 fol.; Venice, 1524, 1550, 1574-75; Amsterdam, 1702; Leipzig, 1862. Partial Engl. transl. by E. Soloweyczik, 1863.

*Missa privata et unctione sacerdotum libellus, De* (M. Luther), *Vitebergae,* 1534; many transl. and ed.

*Modern American Spiritualism* (E. H. Britten), New York, 1870.

*Modern Priestess of Isis, A* (V. S. Solovyov). 2nd Russian ed., St. Petersburg, 1904; Engl. tr., London, 1895.

*Mœurs et les femmes de l'extrême Orient, Les.—Voyage au pays des Bayadères . . . (Voyage au pays des Perles),* (L. Jacolliot), Paris, 1873, 1874, 1875, 1876, 8vo.

*Mœurs et pratiques des démons* (H.-R. Gougenot des Mousseaux), Paris, 1854; 2nd ed., 1865.

*Monstrorum causis, natura, et differentis, De* (R. Licetus), Patavii, 1616, 4to.; 2nd ed., 1634, 4to.; also as *De Monstris.* Ex recensione G. Blasii . . . Amsterdam, Sumptibus A. Frisii, 1665, 4to.; and Patavii, 1668, 4to.

*Monumens inédits d'antiquité figurée, grecque, etrusque et romaine* (D. Raoul-Rochette), Paris, 1833, fol.

*Monumenta S. Patrum Orthodoxographa,* etc. (J. J. Grynaeus), Basileae, 1569, fol., 3 vols.

*Monumental Christianity* (J. P. Lundy): or the Art and Symbolism of the Primitive Church as Witnesses and Teachers of the one Catholic Faith and Practice. New York, 1876.

*More Nebûkhîm* (Maimonides). Known as *Guide to the Perplexed* (Ar. Dalalat al-Ḥa'irin). Completed about 1190; transl. into Hebrew about 1480. Publ. by S. Munk, Paris, 1856-66, 3 vols.; Engl. tr. by M. Friedländer, London, 1889, 3 vols. Repr. in one vol., 1925.

*Mosaicall Philosophy: Grounded upon the Essentiall Truth or Eternal Sapience* (Robert Fludd). Written first in Latin [*Philosophia Mosaica*], and afterwards thus rendered into English. London, 1659.

*Mount Lebanon. A ten Years' Residence from 1842 to 1852*, etc. (Chas. H. Churchill), London, 1853, 3 vols.

\**Mukta* and *Baddha*. Attributed to Kapila.

*Mundus Novus* (Amerigo Vespucci), 3rd ed., Augsburg, 1504. See Vol. I, pp. 651-52, Note 73.

*Murder Considered as one of the Fine Arts* (Thos. de Quincey). First publ. in *Blackwood Magazine*, February, 1827. See his *Miscellaneous Essays*.

*Mystère et la science, Le* (Père Félix), Paris, 1863.

\**Mystères physiologiques* (A. Everard). Untraced.

*Mysteriis, Liber de* (Iamblichus). Often referred to as *On the Mysteries of the Egyptians, Chaldeans and Assyrians*. An Egyptian priest called Abammon is there introduced as replying to a letter of Porphyry. He endeavors to refute various doubts respecting the truth and purity of the Egyptian religion and worship, and to prove the divine origin of the ancient teachings, and also that men, through theurgic rites, may commune with the Deity. Greek text has been edited by Ficinus (Venice, 1483, 4to., with Latin transl.), N. Scutelius (Rome, 1556, 4to.), Thos. Gale (Oxford, 1678, fol., with Latin tr.), and G. Parthey (Berlin, 1857).

See *Iamblichus on the Mysteries*, etc., by Thos. Taylor, for Engl. transl.

*Mystical Initiations; or Hymns of Orpheus, The* (Thomas Taylor). With a Preliminary Dissertation on the Life and Theology of Orpheus. London, 1787, 12mo.; reprinted as *The Hymns*, etc., 1792, 8vo.; new and enl. ed., entitled *The Mystical Hymns of Orpheus*. Demonstrated to be the Invocations which were used in the Eleusinian Mysteries. Chiswick, 1824, 8vo.; repr., London, 1896.

*Mystischen Erscheinungen der menschlichen Natur, Die* (J. A. M. Perty), Leipzig and Heidelberg, 1861, 8vo.

*Mythologie des Indous, La* (Marie E. de Polier), Paris, 1809, 2 vols.

*Mythology of the Hindus, The* (Chas. Coleman), London, 1832.

*Myths* (Babrius or Gabrias). A work in which this Greek poet turned Aesopean fables into verse, and which, acc. to Suidas, comprised ten books, most of which have been lost. Several complete poems have been discovered later and publ. by de Furia (Florence, 1809). Others were ed. by J. Gl. Schneider (Vratislava, 1812), by Berger (Monach., 1816), and Knoch, 1835.

# N

*Nabathäische Landwirtschaft* or *The Book of Nabathean Agriculture* (tr. from the Arabic by D. A. Chwol'son). See Chwol'son's *Über die Überreste der altbabylonischen Literatur*, etc. in *Mémoires des savants étrangers*, Vol. VIII. St. Petersburg: Imp. Acad. of Science, 1859.

*Nâbhânedishtha Hymn.* In M. Haug's *Aitareya Brâhmaṇam* (q.v.).

*Nachweis der Echtheit der sämlichen Schriften des Neuen Testaments* (H. Olshausen), Hamburg, 1832; Engl. tr. by D. Fosdick as *Proof of the Genuineness of the Writings of the New Testament,* Andover, 1838.

*Narrative of a Five Years Expedition against the revolted Negroes in Surinam* (J. G. Stedman), London, 1796, 4to.

*Narrative of a Journey through the Upper Provinces of India, from Calcutta to Bombay, 1824-1825,* etc. (Bishop Reginald Heber). London: John Murray, 1828.

*Narratives of Sorcery and Magic, from the most authentic Sources* (Thos. Wright), 2nd ed., London, 1851.

*Narratives of the Operations and Recent Discoveries within the Pyramids, Temples, Tombs, and Excavations, in Egypt and Nubia,* etc. (G. B. Belzoni), London, 1820, 1821, 1822.

*National Quarterly Review,* Dec., 1875; Vol. XXXII, No. lxiii: articles entitled "The Phoenicians and their Voyages," pp. 123-34, and "Our Sensational Present-Day Philosophers," pp. 76-96.

*Natur und den Ursprung der Emanationslehre bei den Kabbalisten, etc., Über die* (J. F. Kleucker), Riga, 1786, 8vo.

*Natural History of Staffordshire, The* (R. Plot), Oxford, 1686, fol.

*Naturalist in Nicaragua, The* (Thomas Belt): a Narrative of a Residence at the Gold Mines of Chontales, and Journeys in the Savannahs and Forests. London: John Murray, 1874; 2nd rev. & corr. ed., London: E. Bumpus, 1888.

*Naturalium quaestionum libri VII* (Seneca). Eng. tr. as *Physical Science in the Time of Nero,* by John Clarke, London, 1910, 8vo.

*Nekrokêdeia* (Νεκροκηδεια),*or the Art of Embalming,* etc. (Thos. Greenhill), London, 1705, 4to.

*New American Cyclopaedia.* Publ. by Daniel Appleton & Co. Ed. by George Ripley and Chas. A. Dana. 1858-63, 16 vols. Called *American Cyclopaedia* after 1868. New ed. prepared by same Editors, 1873-76, 16 vols.

*New Analysis of Chronology, A* (W. Hales), London, 1809-12, 4 vols.; 2nd ed., 1830.

*New Century Path.* Point Loma, Calif. Started as *The New Century,* Vol. I, Sept. 30, 1897, publ. then at New York; called *New Century Path* from May, 1903, to May, 1908, when it became *The Century Path.*

*New Chemistry, The* (J. Cooke), 2nd ed., London, 1874.

*New Historical Relation of the Kingdom of Siam, A* (S. de la Loubère); tr. from the French by A. P., London, 1693, fol.

*New Light of Alchymie, A* (M. Sendivogius); transl. from Latin by J. F. M. D., London, 1650, 4to. Consult also *The Hermetic Museum, restored and enlarged* . . . Now first done into Engl. [by A. E. Waite] from the Latin and publ. at Frankfort, 1678, etc., 2 vols.; London, Elliott & Co., 1893; and John M. Watkins, 1953.

*\*New Materialism* (J. Liebig).

*New Platonism and Alchemy* (Dr. A. Wilder), Albany, 1869, 30 pp.

*New System, or, an Analysis of Ancient Mythology, A* (J. Bryant), London, 1774-76, 3 vols.; 1807, 6 vols.

*New Testament* (Erasmus), 1st and 2nd ed., 1516 and 1519.

*Newtoni opera quae extant omnia, Isaaci* (ed. by Bishop Horsley), London, 1779-85, 4 vols.

*Night-Side of Nature, or Ghosts and Ghost Seers, The* (C. Crowe), London, 1848, 2 vols.; also 1852, 1882, 1904.

\**Nivids* (Ṛishi Kutsa). No further data available.

*Norsemen in Iceland, The* (G. W. Dasent), London, 1855.

*Northern Antiquities* (P. H. Mallett), London, 1770, 8vo., 2 vols.; also Bohn's ed.; this is an Engl. tr. by T. Percy of the French orig. work entitled *Introduction à l'histoire du Dannemarc*, Copenhagen, 1755, 56, 4to.

*Notes on the Scientific and Religious Mysteries of Antiquity* (J. Yarker), 2nd ed., New York, 1878.

*Notice sur les travaux de l'Académie du Gard* (art. by La Boëssière), Nismes, 1822.

*Notitia codicis graeci evangelium Johannis variatum continentis* (Bishop F. Münther), Havniae, 1828.

*Nouveau Journal Asiatique*, ou Recueil de Mémoires, d'Extraits et de Notices relatifs à l'Histoire, à la Philosophie, aux Langues et à la Littérature des Peuples Orientaux. Published in Paris by the Société Asiatique. Tome VII, March, 1831. Art. by Abel-Rémusat.

*Nova medicina spirituum*, etc. (S. Wirdig), Hamburg, 1673, 2 pts.; Frankfurt and Leipzig, 1707.

*Novum Organum* (F. Bacon), 1620.

*Nychthêmeron*. See Éliphas Lévi's *Dogme et Rituel*, etc.

## O

*Observations on Trance; or Human Hibernation* (J. Braid), London, 1850, 72 pp.

*Occulta philosophia, De* (Cornelius Agrippa). [Cologne] 1533 fol.; Beringo Fratres, Lugduni [1600], 3 vols., 8vo. Vol. I of this work was publ. as early as 1531. — Engl. transl. by J. F. [John French] as *Three Books of Occult Philosophy*. London: R. W. for Gregory Moule, 1651, 4to.

*Oedipus Aegyptiacus; hoc est, Universalis Hieroglyphicae veterum doctrinae temporum injuria abolitae instauratio*, etc. (A. Kircher), Rome, 1652-54, fol.

*Oedipus Judaicus* (Wm. Drummond), London, 1811.

*Œuvres complètes* (D.-F. J. Arago). Publ. under the direction of J. A. Barral. Paris, Leipzig, 1854-62, 17 vols.

*Œuvres complètes de Buffon*, etc. (Buffon), Paris, 1835, 9 vols.

*Œuvres de Synésius* (H. Druon), Paris, 1878.

*Old, Old, Very Old Man: or, the Age and Long Life of Thomas Parr* (John Taylor). In verse, 1635, 4to.; 3rd ed., 1700; repr. in *Harleian Miscellany*, Vol. VII, 1774, etc., and in James Caulfield's *Edition of Curious Tracts*, 1794.

*Old Diary Leaves*. The True History of The Theosophical Society (Col. Henry Steel Olcott). First Series: New York & London, G. P. Putnam's Sons, 1895, xii, 491, ill.;

2nd ed., Adyar, Theos. Publ. House, 1941. — Six vols. altogether have been published under that title, dealing with subsequent years of the T. S. Before being published in book form, the text appeared in the pages of *The Theosophist*, starting with Vol. XIII, March, 1892. While unquestionably of great historical value, it contains many inaccuracies. A number of passages unfortunately display considerable bias and a misunderstanding of the personality of both H.P.B. and William Q. Judge.

*Old England: a pictorial museum of regal, ecclesiastical . . . antiquities* (ed. by C. Knight), London, 1845 [1846], 2 vols.

*Onomasticon*, etc. *Lexidion Codicis Nasaraei, cui "Liber Adami" nomen, edidit M. N.* (M. Norberg), London, 1816, 17, 4to., 2 vols.

\*On the Study of Biology (T. H. Huxley) No definite information.

*Open Court, The.* Art. by Gen. J. G. R. Forlong: "Through what Historical Channels did Buddhism Influence Early Christianity," Aug. 18 and Sept. 1 and 18, 1887.

*Opera* (St. Jerome). Ed. Johannes Martianay. Paris: Ludovicus Roulland, 1693-1706, 5 vols. — Ed. N. & E. Episcopios, Basileae, 1565, 9 vols.

*Opera omnia, medico-chemico-chirurgica, tribus voluminibus comprehensa* (A. P. Th. Paracelsus), Geneva, 1658, 3 tomes in 2 vols. fol.

*Operae horarum subcisivarum sive meditationes historicae,* etc. (Philippus Camerarius), Francofurti, 1602, 4to; also 1606, 1609, 1644; Engl. tr. as *The Walking Library or Meditations,* 1621.

*Operations carried on at the Pyramids of Gizeh in 1837* (Col. H. Vyse), London, 1840-42, 2 vols., 4to.

"Opinion de van Helmont sur la cause, la nature et les effets du magnétisme" (J. Deleuze), in *Bibliothèque du magnétisme animal,* Paris, 1817.

*Optima, etc., De* (Hippocrates). The only complete translation of the Hippocratic collection is Émile Littré's *Œuvres complètes d'Hippocrate,* in 10 vols., Paris, 1839-69.

*Or et la transmutation des métaux, l'* (G. Théodore Tiffereau), Paris, Chacornac Frères, 1924.

*Oracula Sibyllina,* etc. (Johannes Opsopäus) Fr. text with Latin tr. by Sebastian Castationis. Paris, 1607, 3 pts. in 1 vol., ill. Contains: *Oracula magica Zoroastriis cum scholiis Plethonis et Pselli.*

*Organon of Animal Magnetism* (Organon zhivotnago magnetizma) (Prince Alexey Vladimirovich Dolgorukov), St. Petersburg, 1860, Russian text.

*Oriental and Linguistic Studies* (Wm. D. Whitney), 2 Series, London, Cambridge, 1873-75.

*Oriental Memoirs: selected and abridged from a series of familiar letters written during seventeen years' residence in India,* etc. (J. Forbes), Paris, 1813, 4 vols.

*Origin of Metalliferous Deposits, The* (Thos. Sterry Hunt). An address before the Polytechnic Association of the American Institute of New York. No. 15 in *Half-Hour Recreations in Popular Science.* Ed. by Dana Estes. First Series, Boston, 1874. Also in *Van Nostrand's Eclectic Engineering Magazine,* Vol. XI, No. LXX, October, 1874, pp. 326-34.

*Origin of Pagan Idolatry, On the* (G. S. Faber), London, 1816, 3 vols., 4to.

*Origin of Species by Means of Natural Selection, On the,* etc. (Chas. R. Darwin), 1859.

"Origin of the Name 'America,' The," (Geo. C. Harlbut), in *Journal of the American Geographical Society of New York,* Vol. XVIII, 1886, pp. 301-16.

*Original Sanskrit Texts, on the origin and history and progress of the religion and institutions of India* (J. Muir), London, Oxford, 1858; 2nd ed., London, 1868-70, 5 vols.

*Origine de tous les cultes, ou religion universelle* (C.-F. Dupuis), Paris, 1795, 7 vols.; new ed. with Zodiac of Denderah, 1822; 1835, 10 vols.

*Orphêos apanta: Orphei argonautica hymni libellus de lapidibus et fragmenta,* etc. (Matthias Gesnerus), Lipsiae, 1764.

*Orpheus* (G. R. S. Mead), London, 1896; 2nd ed., J. M. Watkins, 1965.

*Orphica* (E. Abel), Lipsiae, 1885.

*Ortus medicinae* (B. van Helmont), Amsterdam, 1652, 4 vols.

*Oud en nieuw Oost-Indien,* etc. (F. Valentijn), Amsterdam, 1724-26, fol., 5 Pts.

*Oupnek'-hat, id est, Secretum tegendum* . . . (A. B. Anquetil-Duperron), Argentorati, 1801-02, 2 vols., 4to.

*Our Inheritance in the Great Pyramid* (Chas. Piazzi Smyth), London, 1864, 1874, etc.

*Our Place among Infinities,* etc. (R. A. Proctor). To which are added essays on astrology and the Jewish Sabbath. London, 1875, 8vo., New York, 1876.

*Outlines of lectures on the neurological system of anthropology,* etc. (J. R. Buchanan), Cincinnati, 1854.


P

*Paesi novamente retrovati, e Novo Mondo da Alberico Vesputio Florentino intitulato* (F. Montalboddo), 1507.

\**Pagani e Cristiani* (Martezzi).

*Palestine. Description géographique, historique et archéologique* (Salomon Munk), in *l'Univers: histoire et description de tous les peuples,* 1835, etc.

\**Pâli-Buddhistical Annals.*

*Panoplia armaturae Dei adversus omnem superstitionum* . . . *daemonolatriam* . . . *concionibus, Bambergae habitis, instructa,* etc. (Fred. Forner), Typis 9, Haenlini: Ingolstadii, 1625.

*Pantheon, The; or Ancient History of the Gods of Greece and Rome,* for the use of schools, etc. (Edward Baldwin). London, 1806; 2nd ed., 1809; 3rd ed., 1810; 4th ed., 1814. The author's real name was William Godwin (1756-1836), and he says in the Preface that the book was originally known as *Took's Pantheon* and was publ. about 100 years previously by one of the Masters of the Charter-House School.

*Pantheon aegyptiorum, sive de diis eorum commentarius, cum Prolegomenis de Religione et Theologia Aegyptiorum* (P. E. Jablonski), Francofurti ad Viadrum, 1750-52, 8vo.

*Pantheon der Naturphilosophie, die Religion aller Völker* (J. A. Kanne), Tübingen, 1811, 8vo.

*Papacy and the Civil Power, The* (R. W. Thompson), New York, 1877.

*Papyros Ebers, das hermetische Buch über die Arzeneimittel der alten Aekypter in hieratischen Schrift* (G. M. Ebers), Leipzig, 1875, 2 vols. fol. — Engl. tr. by Cyril P. Bryan, London, 1930; and by B. Ebbell, London, 1937.

*Papyrus Anastasi* and *Papyrus d'Orbiney*. Consult lists of Egyptological sources and material.

*Parables* (Buddhaghosa). Contained in his Commentary on the *Dhammapada*. Translated [from Pâli into Burmese and] from Burmese by T. Rogers [Col. H. T. Rogers]. With an Introduction containing Buddha's *Dhammapada*, or "Path of Virtue," translated from Pâli by F. Max Müller. London, 1870, 8vo.

*Paradise Lost* (J. Milton), 1668.

*Paralipomeni alla illustrazione della Sacra Scrittura* (M. A. Lanci), Paris, 1845.

*Parerga und Paralipomena. Kleine philosophische Schriften* (A. Schopenhauer), Berlin, 1851.

*Parmenides, On the* (Proclus). Publ. in Stallbaum's edition of that Dialogue.

*Paroles de philosophie positive* (P. M. E. Littré), Paris, 1859.

*Passages from the Life of a Philosopher* (Chas. Babbage), London, 1864.

"Paul and Plato" (Dr. A. Wilder). Source uncertain.

"Paul, the Founder of Christianity" (Dr. A. Wilder), in *The Evolution*, N.Y., Sept., 1877.

*Path, The* (New York). Monthly magazine edited & publ. by W. Q. Judge: Vols. I-X, April, 1886 - March, 1896. Continued as *Theosophy*.

*Patrologiae Cursus Completus* (ed. by Jacques Paul Migne). *Series latina* (221 vols., Paris, 1844-64) covers Latin authors from Tertullian to Innocent III (A.D. 200-1216). *Series graeca* (161 vols., Petit-Montrouge, 1857-66) comprises Greek and Latin texts of authors from the Pseudo-Barnabas to the Council of Florence (A.D. 120-1438) and 81 vols. (1856-67) of the Latin text only of the Greek Fathers.

*People from the Other World* (H. S. Olcott), Hartford, Conn., American Publishing Co., 1875; xvi, 492, ill.

*Periplus* (Hanno). In I. P. Cory, *Ancient Fragments*, pp. 203ff., ed. 1832. Also: Dr. Const. Simonides, *The Periplus of Hannon, King of the Karchedonians*, 1864; 2 fcs., 82 pp., 4to.

*Persian, Arabic, and English Lexicon* (J. Richardson), Oxford, 1777, 1780, fol., 2 vols.; 1800, fol.; 1806-10, 4to.

*Pétrone, Apulée, Aulu-Gelle. Œuvres complètes* (ed. by Désiré Nisard), Paris, 1842.

*Phaedo of Plato, On the* (Olympiodorus). In Thos. Taylor, *Select Works of Porphyry*, London, 1823, q.v.

\**Phenomena of Mediumism* (A. N. Aksakov).

Φιλόλογος (*Philologos*) (N. Bailey), London, 1731.

*Philosophical Works* (D. Hume), Edinburgh, 1826; Cambridge, Mass., 1854; London, 1874-75; 4 vols.

*Philosophie der Geschichte, oder über die Tradition in dem alten Bunde und ihre Beziehung zur Kirche des neuen Bundes* (F. J. Molitor), Frankfurt a. M., 1827-55, 4 pts. [Engl. transl. by Howitt — untraced.]

*Philosophie des Unbewussten* (K. R. E. von Hartmann), 2nd ed., Berlin, 1870.

*Philosophumena* or *Refutation of All Heresies* (Hippolytus). Text in Migne, *PCC*, Ser. Gr.-Lat., XVI-3. Greek and Latin text ed. by Patricius Cruice, Paris, Impr. Royale, 1860. Engl. tr. in *ANF*.

*Philosophy of Magic, The* (E. Salverte). Engl. tr., London, 1846, 2 vols.

*Philosophy of Spiritualism and the Pathology and Treatment of Mediomania, The* (F. Marvin). Two lectures, read before the New York Liberal Club, Mch. 20, 27, 1874. New York, 1874.

"Philosophy of the Hindus, On the," (Colebrooke), in *Trans. of the Royal Asiatic Soc.,* London, 1827, Vol. I, xxxiii.

*Phönizier, Die* (F. C. Movers), Bonn, 1841 and 1856, 2 vols.

*Phosphorescence, or, the Emission of Light by minerals, plants and animals* (Thos. L. Phipson), London, 1862.

*Physica auscultatio* (Simplicius). A Commentary on Aristotle's work by one of the last Neo-Platonic teachers of Athens, who, together with six others, incl. Damascius, had found for a while refuge in Persia. Edited by Franciscus Asulanus in 1526; also by H. Diels, Berlin, 1882, 2 vols.

\**Physica et Mystica* (attrib. to Democritus).

*Physical Basis of Life, On the* (T. H. Huxley). Lay Sermon delivered in Edinburgh, Sunday, Nov. 8, 1868. Subsequently published in the *Fortnightly Review* and as *Protoplasm: the Physical Basis of Life*, Melbourne, 1869.

*Physicalisch-physiologische Untersuchungen über die Dynamide des Magnetismus* (Baron K. von Reichenbach), Braunschweig, 1845, 2 vols.; 2nd ed., 1849; Engl. transl. by Wm. Gregory, as *Researches*, etc., London, 1850.

*Physician's Problems, A* (Chas. Elam), London, 1869.

*Physiologie du système nerveux cérébro-spinal d'après l'analyse physiologique des mouvements de la vie* (É. Fournié), Paris, 1872.

*Pitakattayan.* Referred to by Spence Hardy in his *The Legends and Theories of the Buddhists*, p. 66, as being a generic term for Buddhist writings (*Pitakattaya* — Pâli; and *Pitakatraya* — Sinhalese).

*Plaidoyez et Arrests de la Cour de Parlement, Aydes et Finances de Dauphine, sur plusieurs questions notables, tant en Matières Bénéficiales, que Civiles, et Criminelles* (Jean-Guy Basset), Paris, Jacques Collombat, 1695, 2 vols.

*Plato, The Works of* (G. Burges), *Bohn's Class. Library.*

*Plato and the older Academy* (E. Zeller), being Engl. tr. of Vol. II, Sect. 2, Part II, of Zeller's *Philosophie der Griechen*, from the 3rd and rev. ed. of the latter. By Miss Alleyne and Alfred Goodwin. London, 1888 (new ed.); also New York, Russell & Russell, 1962.

*Plato's Republic, MS. Commentary on* (Proclus). In Thos. Taylor, *The Works of Plato*, London, 1804, Vol. III, p. 328 footnote; also Vol. I, pp. 468-69.

*Pneumatologie. Des Esprits et de leurs manifestations diverses* (J.-E. de Mirville); Vols. I-V, Paris, H. Vrayet de Surcy, 1863-64, 8vo.; Vol. VI, Paris, F. Wattelier, 1868.

*Poimandrês.* See *Hermes, Books of.*

*Political History of the Devil, The* (D. Defoe), 1726.

*Polygraphia* (Joh. Trithemius), 1518.

*Popol-Vuh. Le Livre sacré et les mythes de l'antiquité américaine* . . . Texte Quiché et trad. française . . . accompagnée de notes . . . (Brasseur de Bourbourg). In *Collection de documents dans les langues indigènes,* etc., Vol. I, 1861. — Eng. tr. by Philip A. Malpas in *The Theosophical Path*, Point Loma, Calif., Vols. XXXVII-XXXIX, March, 1930-April, 1931. — Partial Eng. tr. by Aretas, *Lucifer*, London, Vol. XV, Sept., 1894 - Feb., 1895. — Adrian Recinos, *Popol-Vuh: las antiguas historias del Quiché*.

Spanish tr. of original text with introd. & notes. Mexico City, 1947.—English version of Recino's tr. by Delia Goetz & Sylvanus G. Morley. Norman: University of Oklahoma Press, 1957.

*Popular Monthly,* ed. by Frank Leslie, Vol. XXXIII, Feb., 1892. Art.: "Madame Blavatsky: A Theosophical Occult Apology."

*Praestigiis daemonum, De* (Joh. Wier), Basel, 1563, 1564, 1583.

*Prairies d'Or, Les* (al-Mas'ûdî). Arabic title of this work is *Murûj udn-Dhahab wa Ma'âdin ul-Jawâhir,* "Meadows of Gold and Mines of Precious Stones." It was completed in 947, with a 2nd ed. in 956. French transl. of Barbier de Maynard and Pavet de Courteille in nine vols., Paris, 1861-77.

*Prajñâ-Pâramitâ.* Most likely the *Mahâprajñâpâramitâhridaya-sûtra,* also known as the *Heart Sûtra.* Together with the *Diamond Sûtra,* it is the most popular of the many Scriptures contained in the vast *Prajñâ-Pâramitâ* literature. For transl. see D. T. Suzuki, *Manual of Zen Buddhism* (with Chin. text), 1935, and E. Conze, *Buddhist Wisdom Books* (with comment.), 1958.

*Prâtimoksha-Sûtra* (Pâli, *Pâtimokkha*). The 227 disciplinary rules binding on the Buddhist Bhikkhu, and recited on *Uposatha* days or days of the four phases of the Moon. They are enumerated in the *Suttavibhanga,* the first part of the *Vinaya Piṭaka.* See SBE 13.

*Pre-Adamite Man* (P. B. Randolph), 2nd ed., New York, 1863; 4th ed., 1869.

*Précis élémentaire de physiologie* (F. Magendie), Paris, 1816, 17, 2 vols.; 3rd ed., 1833; Engl. tr., 1826, 1829, 1831.

*Preheminence of Women* (H. Cornelius Agrippa); Latin orig.: *H. C. A. de nobilitate et Praecellentia foeminei sexus, Coloniae,* 1532; Lugduni Batav., 1643; Engl. tr. by E. Fleetwood, as *The Glory of Women,* etc., London, 1651.

*Premières civilisations: études d'histoire et d'archéologie, Les* (F. Lenormant), Paris, 1874, 2 vols.

*Primitive History: from the Creation to Cadmus* (W. Williams), Chichester, 1789.

*Principiis rerum, De* (Damascius). This work by the last of the renowned teachers of Neo-Platonism at Athens is also known as "Doubts and Solutions of the First Principles" and was of course in Greek. It was publ. in an incomplete form by J. Kopp, Frankf., 1828, 8vo.

*Principles of Science, The* (Wm. S. Jevons), London, 1874.

*Principles of the Jesuits, The.* Developed in a Collection of Extracts from their own Authors. [Rev. H. H. Norris, although published anonymously.] London: J. G. Rivington, 1839. xvi, 277.

*Proceedings and sentence of the spiritual Court of Inquisition of Portugal, against Gabriele Malagrida, Jesuit, etc., The.* Transl. from the original Portuguese. London, 1762, 4to.

*Proceedings of the Supreme Council,* etc. (Gen. A. Pike), 1876.

*Progress of Religious Ideas, through successive Ages, The* (L. Maria Child), New York, 1855.

*Proof Palpable of Immortality,* etc., *The* (Epes Sargent), Boston, 1875, 8vo.

\**Proofs that I am a Serpent* (attrib. to Votan).

\**Prophecies* (Ramatsariar).

\**Prophecies, Book of,* ed. of 1453. Untraced.

"Prophecy, Ancient and Modern" (Dr. A. Wilder), in *Phrenological Journal*.

*Protevangelion, The.* In. W. Hone, *Apocryphal New Testament*, etc., London, 1820, 1821, 1846. Also in *ANF*.

*Protreptics* (Iamblichus). The Second book of a ten-book series on Pythagoras, of which only five books have survived. First ed. is by J. Arcerius Theodoretus, and the best that of Th. Kiessling, Leipzig, 1813, 8vo. See *Pythagoras*.

*Psalm of Life, A* (H. W. Longfellow), 1775-76.

*Pseudodoxia Epidemica: or, Enquiries into very many received Tenents and commonly presumed Truth* (Sir Thos. Browne), London, 1646.

*Pseudomonarchia daemonum* (J. Wier), 3rd ed., Basileae, 1566, 8vo.

"Psychology of the Âryas, The" (Pyârichânda Mitra), *Human Nature*, March, 1877; also in his *On the Soul: Its Nature and Development*, Calcutta, 1881.

*Pûrva-Mîmânsâ-Sûtra.* (Jaimini). Also known as *Jaiminisûtra* or simply *Mîmânsâ-Sûtra*. Transl. with text by M. L. Sandal, Allâhâbâd, 1923-25.

*Pyramids and Temples of Gizeh, The* (W. M. Flinders Petrie), London, 1883.

*Pyramids of Gizeh, etc., The* (J. S. Perring), London, 1839-42, 3 pts., obl. fol.

*Pythagoras, Life of* (Iamblichus). The first book of a Series of ten which expounded the philosophy of Pythagoras, as a preparation for the study of Plato. Only five of these books are extant, the second one being *Protreptics* (q.v.). The *Life of Pythagoras* was first edited in Greek and Latin by J. Arcerius Theodoretus, Franecker, 1598, 4to.; later by L. Kuster (Amsterdam, 1707, 4to.), and T. H. Kiessling (Leipzig, 1815, 2 vols. 8vo.); also A. Nauck (St. Petersburg, 1884). — See *Iamblichus' Life of Pythagoras*, by Thos. Taylor, for Engl. transl.

## Q

*Quaestiones et Responsiones ad Orthodoxos* (Justin Martyr). Sometimes attributed to Diodorus of Tarsus. *PCC*, Ser. Gr., VI. Also *Opera*, ed. Otto, 2nd ed., Jena, 1849.

*Question des esprits et de leurs manifestations diverses* (J.-E. de Mirville). Appendices complémentaires et défenses des Mémoires publiés. Paris. 1863.

*Qabbalah. The Philosophical Writings of . . . Ibn Gebirol* (Isaac Myer). Publ. by the Author (350 cop. only). Philadelphia, 1888. xxiv, 499 pp.

## R

*Râmâyana*. Renowned Sanskrit epic which details the life and adventures of Râmachandra, his winning of Sîtâ for wife, the rape of the latter by the demon-king Râvana of Ceylon, her rescue by Râma and the latter's final translation to heaven. It has been ascribed to Vâlmîki. In its present form, it consists of about 24,000 ślokas, and is divided into seven books. It has been preserved in three distinct recensions, the West Indian, the Bengal, and the Bombay. — Translated into Engl. verse by R. T. H. Griffith. London: Trübner & Co., 1870-74; Benares, 1895. — Translated into Engl. prose by M. N. Dutt, Calcutta, 1891-94.

*Rapport du Physique et du Moral de l'Homme* (P. J. G. Cabanis): Seventh Memoir: "De l'influence des maladies sur la formation des idées et des affections morales," § ix. Paris, 1802. See his *Œuvres Complètes*, tome III, 1824.

*Rebus* (St. Petersburg), Vols. 1-18, 1882-1899. Edited by V. Pribitkov. Appeared on Sundays. At fist a sheet of riddles, but later the organ of Spiritualism and Mediumship in Russia.

*Rebus Cypriis, De* (Hett. Podocatharo or Podocattarus), 1560 (acc. to Greenhill).

*Recherches d'anatomie transcendante et pathologique,* etc. (A.-E. Serres), Paris, 1832.

*Recherches et doutes sur le magnétisme animal* (M. A. Thouret), Paris, 1784.

*Recherches psychologiques sur la cause des phénomènes, etc.* (G. P. Billot), Paris, 1839.

*Recherches sur quelques unes des révolutions de la surface du globe* (J. B. A. L. L. Élie de Beaumont); Mémoire lut par extrait à l'Académie des Sciences, le 22 juin, 1829; Paris, 1829-30.

*Recollections of a Busy Life* (H. Greeley), New York, 1868.

*Recueil général des pièces contenues an procèz due père Jean-Baptiste Girard, Jésuite, et de Demoiselle C. Cadière,* etc., Aix, 1731, and other ed.

*Refutation of the Sects* (Eznik, Bishop of Bagrevand and Arsharunik, Vth cent.). Armenian orig. ed. publ. at Constantinople, 1763; in Smyrna, 1772; in Venice, 1826 and 1863. French tr., Paris, 1853. German tr. as *Wider die Irrlehren,* 1927. Also in *Patrologia Orientalis,* Vol. XXVIII, Nos. 3-4.

*Rege et Regis Institutione libri tres, De* (Juan de Mariana), Toleti, 1599; Moguntiae, 1605, 1611, 1640.

*Relaçao da Propagaçao da Fé no Reino da China* (Álvaro Semedo), 1638; Engl. tr. as *The History . . . of China,* London, 1655 fol.; French tr. as *Histoire universelle du Grand Royaume de la Chine,* Paris, 1645, 4to.

*Religion des pré-Israélites, La* (Willem Pleyte). Recherches sur le dieu Seth, Utrecht, 1862; Leide, 1865.

*Religion of Geology and its Connected Sciences, The* (E. Hitchcock), Boston, 1851; Glasgow, 1856; London, 1860.

*Religions de l'antiquité, considérées principalement dans leurs formes symboliques et mythologiques, Les* (J.-D. Guigniaut), Paris, 1825-39, 10 vols. Annotated and expanded translation of Georg Fr. Creuzer's *Symbolik.*

"Religions de l'antiquité et de leurs derniers historiens, Des" (E. Renan), in *Revue des Deux Mondes,* May 15, 1853.

*Religions of Tibet, The* (Helmut Hoffmann), London, 1961; Engl. tr. of the original German *Quellen zur Geschichte des tibetischen Bon-Religion,* Wiesbaden, 1950.

*Religious Statistics of the United States,* 1871.

*Remarks upon Alchemy and the Alchemists* (E. A. Hitchcock), Boston, 1857.

*Reminiscences of H. P. Blavatsky and "The Secret Doctrine"* (Countess C. Wachtmeister), London: Theos. Publ. Soc., 1893, 162 pp.

*Reply to Hon. R. W. Thompson . . . addressed to the American People* (F. X. Weninger), New York, 1877.

*Réponse aux Assertions.* See *Collected Writings,* Vol. IX, p. 297 footnote.

*Report of the U.S. Geological Survey of the Territories* (F. V. Hayden & C. H. Merriam), Washington, 1872 & 1873-90.

*Report on Spiritualism, of the Committee of the London Dialectical Society, together with the evidence . . . and a collection from the correspondence,* London, 1871; xi, 412 pp.

*Rerum memorabilium,* etc. (G. Panciroli), Ambergiae, 1599, 8vo.; 1607, 1612, 1622; Frankfurt, 1629-31; 1660. Engl. transl. as *The Hist. of Many Memorable Things which were in Use among the Ancients,* London, 1715, 1727, 2 vols.

*Re rustica, De* (L. Junius Moderatus Columella). Ed. princ., Nic. Jenson, Venice, 1472, fol., in *Rei rusticae scriptores.* Latin and Engl. in *LCL.*

*Re rustica, De* (M. Terentius Varro). Best ed. in *Scriptores Rei Rusticae veteres Latini* of J. M. Gesner, Lips. 1735, 2 vols., and of J. G. Schneider, Lips. 1794-97, 4 vols.

*Researches in the Phenomena of Spiritualism* (Sir Wm. Crookes). Reprinted from the *Quarterly Journal of Science.* London, 1874, 8vo. Also Rochester, N. Y.: The Austin Pub. Co., 1904.

*Researches into the Early History of Mankind and the Development of Civilization* (E. B. Tylor), London, 1865; 3rd ed., 1878.

*Researches into the Nature and Affinity of Ancient and Hindu Mythology* (Col. Vans Kennedy), London, 1831, 4to.

*Researches into the Origin and Affinity of the principal Languages of Asia and Europe* (Col. Vans Kennedy), London, 1828.

*Researches on Light:* An Examination of all the Phenomena connected with the Chemical and Molecular Changes produced by the Influence of the Solar Rays, etc. (Robert Hunt), London, 1844.

*Review of Ecclesiastical History, A* (Bishop J. Newton), London, 1770.

*Rgya tch'er rol pa* [rGya-chher-rol-pa]; ou, Développement des Jeux, contenant l'histoire du Bouddha Cakya-Mouni, traduit sur la version tibétaine du Bkah hgyour, et revu sur l'original sanscrit (Lalitavistara) par Ph. Ed. Foucaux, Paris, 1847-48. Vol. I, Tibetan; Vol. II, French transl. This work in Tibetan is in the Second Volume of the Fifth Section of the *Kanjur.*

*R̥gveda-Saṃhitā.* Ed. by F. Max Müller (Saṃhitā and pada texts in nâgarî). 2nd ed., London: Trübner & Co., 1877; 2 vols. — Ed. by Theod. Aufrecht (Saṃhitā text in transliteration). 2nd. ed., Bonn: Adolf Marcus, 1877; 2 vols. — Trans. by H. H. Wilson. London: Trübner & Co., and Wm. H. Allen & Co., 1850, 54, 57, 66, 88. — Transl. by R. T. H. Griffith. Benares: E. J. Lazarus & Co., 1889-92. — Trans. by F. Max Müller and Hermann Oldenberg. Oxford: Clarendon Press, 1891, 1897. *SBE* 32, 46.

*Ripley Reviv'd: or, an Exposition upon Sir George Ripley's Hermetico-Poetical Works,* etc. (Eirenaeus Philalethes), London, 1678; author also known as Cosmopolita, actually George Starkey.

*Ritual of Initiations* (H. Malhandrini), Venice, 1657.

*Rituale Romanum,* Paris, 1851 and 1852.

*Roma sotterranea Cristiana, etc., La* (G. B. de Rossi), Rome, 1864, etc., 4to.

*Roman Martyrology, according to the Reformed Calendar* (G. Keynes). Faithfully translated out of Latin into English, by G. K. of the Society of Jesus. 1627; re-edited by W. N. Skelly, London, 1847.

*Rome and the Newest Fashions in Religion* (W. E. Gladstone), London, 1875.

*Römischen Päpste, ihre Kirche und ihr Staat im 16 und 17 Jahrhundert* (L. von Ranke), 1834-36, 3 vols. (many other ed.). Eng. tr. as *History of the Popes during the 16 and 17th Centuries,* by S. Austin, 1840, 1841, 1847; by W. K. Kelly, 1843; and E. Foster, 1847-53.

*Rosarius philosophorum, correctus* (Arnaldus de Villa Nova), in *Opera Omnia*, Basileae, 1585, fol.

\**Rosicrucian MS.* (Count de Saint-Germain). Said to have been written in cipher.

*Rosicrucians, their Rites and Mysteries, The* (H. Jennings), London, 1870. 8vo.; 2nd ed., rev., corr. & enl., London, 1879; 3rd ed., newly rev., 1887.

*Round Towers of Ireland; or, the Mysteries of Freemasonry, of Sabaism, and of Buddhism, for the first time unveiled, The* (H. O'Brien), London, 1834, 1898.

*Royal Masonic Cyclopaedia of History, Rites, Symbolism and Biography, The* (ed. by Kenneth Robert Henderson MacKenzie, known as "Cryptonymus." London, 1877 [1875-77], 8vo.

*Ruins: or a Survey of the Revolutions of Empires* (C. F. de Volney). Transl. from French, 2nd ed., London, 1795, 8vo.

*Russkiy Vestnik* (Russian Messenger). Monthly (at first twice a month), Moscow; founded by M. N. Katkov, 1856. After his death (1887), publ. by his widow, & ed. by Prince D. N. Tsertelev.

*Russkoye Obozreniye* (Moscow). Monthly. Vols. 1-9, 1890-98. Ed. by Prince D. N. Tsertelev.

S

*Sacra scrittura illustrata con monumenti fenico-assirj ed egiziani, La* (M. A. Lanci), Rome, 1827.

*Sacrorum conciliorum nova et emplissima collectio* (J. D. Mansi), Florence, 1759-98.

*Saddharma-puṇḍarîka. Le Lotus de la Bonne Loi.* Transl. from the Skt. and with Commentaries, etc. (Eugène Burnouf), 1852. 4to.; 1925. 8vo.

*Sadducismus Triumphatus: or, Full and Plain Evidence concerning Witches and Apparitions* (J. Glanvill). Done into English by A. Horneck, London, 1681, 8vo. Includes Henry More's "Letter to Glanvill."

*Sainte Bible, La* (Illustrated by Gustave Doré), 1866 fol.

*Saints Guide. Displaying of supposed Witchcraft, etc., The* (John Webster), London, 1677.

*Sakuntala* (or *Abhijñâna-śakuntala*) (Kâlidâsa). Devanâgarî recension of the text edited, and with literal Engl. tr. by Monier Williams; 2nd ed., London, Oxford Univ. Press, 1876.

*Salem Witchcraft; with an Account of Salem Village, and a History of Opinions on Witchcraft and kindred Subjects* (C. W. Upham), Boston, 1867, 2 vols.

*Sâmaveda-Saṃhitâ.* Ed. with Comm. by Sâyaṇâchârya by Satyavrata Sâmaśramî. Calcutta: As. Soc. of Bengal, 1874, 76, 77, 78; 5 vols. *Bibl. Ind.* 71, New Ser. Transl. by R. T. H. Griffith. Benares: E. J. Lazarus & Co., 1893; 2nd ed., 1907.

*Sämtliche Werke* (F. X. von Baader), Leipzig, 1850-54; 1851-60; 18 vols.

*Sämtliche Werke* (F. D. E. Schleiermacher), 1835-64, in 32 vols.

*Sânkhya-Sûtra* (attributed to Kapila). Ed. and trans. by R. Garbe. Calcutta: Asiatic Society of Bengal, *Bibl. Ind.*, 122, 131.

*Sanskrit Wörterbuch* (R. Roth & Otto Böhtlingk). St. Petersburg, 1855-75, 7 vols.

*Sâraṅga. Possibly the *Sâraṅga-sâra,* a poem.

*Sartor Resartus* (T. Carlyle), 1838, 1849.

*Śatapatha-Brâhmaṇa, SBE,* XII, XXVI, XLI.

*Satires upon the Jesuits,* etc. (J. Oldham), London, 1678, 1681.

*Satyra de nuptiis philologiae et Mercurii* (Martianus M. F. Capella). A voluminous compilation forming a sort of cyclopaedia of the polite learning of the Middle Ages, divided into nine books. Much of the learning is doubtless derived from sources which have long since perished. In Bk. VIII, para. 857, a remarkable passage distinctly states that the planets Mercury and Venus revolve around the Sun, and their position with regard to the Sun and the Earth, as well as to each other, is so correctly described, that one could easily assume that Copernicus, who quotes Martianus, may have derived the first germ of his ideas from this source. Ed. princeps was printed at Vicenza by H. de S. Urso, 1499, fol.; the best ed. are those of Hugo Grotius, Leyden, 1599, and of U. F. Kopp, Frankf., 1836.

*Sceau rompu,* 1745.

*Scholia in Apollonium Rhodium.* See *Argonautica.*

*Science and Practice of Medicine, The* (Wm. Aitken), 2nd ed., London, 1863, 2 vols.; 6th ed., London, 1872; American ed., from the 4th London ed., with additional material by Dr. Meredith Clymer, Philadelphia, 1866, 68, 72, 2 vols.

*Science des esprits, La* (É. Lévi), Paris, 1865.

*Sciences occultes en Asie, Les* (François Lenormant); consists of two parts separately issued: *La Magie chez les chaldéens et les origines accadiennes,* Paris, Malmaison, 1874, x, 363 (tr. into Engl. by W. R. Cooper, with addit. notes by the author, as *Chaldean Magic: its Origin and Development,* London, 1878); and *La Divination et la science des présages chez les chaldéens,* Paris, 1875, 236 pp.

*Scriptoribus ecclesiasticis, De* (Joh. Trithemius), 1494.

*Séance de l'Académie de Paris,* Aug. 13, 1807 (Geoffroy Saint-Hilaire).

*Secret Adam, The* (E. S. Drower), Oxford, 1960.

*Secret Book* (unknown).

*Secretis adeptorum, De* (J. S. Weidenfeld), London, 1684, 4to.; Hamburg, 1685; Tr. from Latin by G. C., London, 1685.

"Seeming Discrepancies" (H. P. Blavatsky), in *Collected Writings,* Vol. VI.

*Secreti nuovi* (G. Ruscellius), 1567.

*Seherin von Prevorst, Die* (J. A. C. Kerner), 1829; 6th ed., 1892; Engl. tr. by Mrs. Crowe as *The Seeress of Prevorst,* London, 1845; New York, 1859.

*Select Works of Plotinus, and Extracts from the Treatise of Synesius on Providence* (Thomas Taylor). With an Introduction containing the substance of Porphyry's Life of Plotinus. London, 1817, 8vo.; repr. in *Bohn's Philosophical Library,* 1895 where it is edited, with Preface and Bibliography, by G. R. S. Mead; repr. in 1909, 1912 & 1929.

*Select Works of Porphyry* (Thos. Taylor); containing his Four Books on *Abstinence from Animal Food;* his treatise on *The Homeric Cave of the Nymphs;* and his *Auxiliaries to the Perception of Intelligible Natures.* Translated from the Greek by Thos. Taylor. With an Appendix, explaining the Allegory of the Wanderings of Ulysses. By the Translator. London: printed for Thos. Rodd, 17, Great Newport St., 1823, xx, 271, 8vo.

*Semenuthi* (Divine Book) (Apollonides Orapius). Rf. to in Theophilus Antiochenus, *Ad Autolycum,* ii, 6.

*Sepher Toldoth Jeschua ha-Notzri* [in Hebrew letters], *Historia Jeschuae Nazareni, a Judaeis blasphemè corrupta, ex Manuscripto hactenus inedito nunc demum edita, ac Versione et Notis . . . illustrata* (Joh. Jac. Huldrich [Huldricus]), Leyden, 1705.

*Sepher Yetzîrah* or *Book of Formation.* Reputed to be the oldest Kabbalistic work, attributed to Rabbi Akiba. It deals with permutations of numbers and letters, and is our first source for the doctrine of emanations and the *sephirôth.* The *editio princeps* is that of Mantua, 1562, with several subsequent ones. Translated and Annotated by P. Davidson. Loudsville, Georgia & Glasgow, Scotland, 1896, xvii, 27. — Text & Comm. by Dunash ben Tamim have been publ. by M. Grossberg, London, 1902; also by W. Wynn Westcott, 1887, and by Stenring (with Pref. by Waite).

*Septuagint.* Greek version of the Old Testament still in use in the Eastern Church. So called from the legend preserved in the Letters of Aristeas, that the *Pentateuch* was translated at Alexandria by seventy-two emissaries from Jerusalem at the request of Ptolemy II. Church Fathers extended the tradition to the whole of the Greek O.T. The *Septuagint,* usually ref. to by the symbol LXX, differs from the Masoretic text, and is the version cited by Philo, Josephus, and in the New Testament.

*Sermones* (St. Augustine). In Vol. V of the Benedictine ed. of his *Works,* Paris, 1679-1700; a Selection from them was publ. at Oxford in 1844, 1845; transl. by R. G. Macmullen, and is incl. in the *Library of the Fathers of the Holy Catholic Church;* also a Selection transl. and ed. by Q. Howe, New York, 1966.

*Serpent-Worship, and other Essays with a Chapter on Totemism* (C. S. Wake), New York, 1877.

*Shepherd of Hermas* or *Pastor of Hermas.* One of the works representing the so-called Apostolic Fathers and dealing with the problem of the forgiveness of sins committed after baptism. Text and Eng. tr. in *Loeb Classical Library.* Transl. in W. Hone. *Apocryphal New Test.,* q.v.

*Shi-King* SBE III.

*Shu-King.* SBE III.

*Sibyllina Oracula. Ex veteribus codicibus emendata,* etc. (S. Gallaeus), Amsterdam, 1689.

*Silliman's Journal of Science and Art,* Vol. X; art. by Dr. Samuel L. Mitchell "On Two-Headed Serpents."

*Simplicium medicamentorum facultatibus, De* (C. Galen), Paris, 1530. fol.; Lugduni, 1561, 8vo.

*Sincerus Renatus* (S. Richter), Berlin, 1714.

*Siphra Dtzeniuthah* (Book of Concealed Mystery). Incl. in Knorr von Rosenroth's *Kabbala denudata,* q.v.

*Situ orbis, De* (or *Chorographia*) (Pomponius Mela); ed. Tzschukke, Leipzig, 1807; Parthey, Berlin, 1867; Finck, Leipzig, 1880.

*Siva-Purâṇa.* Consult *Die Legende vom Devadâruvana im Siva-Purâṇa,* by Wilhelm Jahn, in ZDMG, 71 (1917); Roman text and translation.

*Si-yu-ki* (Hiuen-Thsang). See *Voyages* (S. Julien). Spelling of the famous traveller's name varies greatly: Hsüan-Tsang, Hiwen T'Sang, Yüan-Tsang, Yuan-Chwang.

*Sketch of the Knights-Templar and the Knights Hospitallers of St. John of Jerusalem, A* (R. Woof), London, 1865.

*Sleep, Treatise on* (Clearchus). Ref. to by Proclus in *Comm. on Plato's Republic;* see Thos. Taylor. *The Works of Plato,* Vol. I, p. 469.

*Smaragdine Tablet.* Translated by Dr. Everard and others, the Smaragdine, or Emerald Tablet, attributed to Hermes, has puzzled scholars for centuries past. Tradition has it that Alexander of Macedonia discovered the tomb of Hermes in a cave near Hebron. In the tomb was found an emerald slab which "Sarah, Abraham's wife," had taken from the dead Hermes. The story is most improbable, but the text of the traditional Smaragdine Tablet is replete with occult precepts. Consult *Tabula Smaragdina,* by Julius F. Ruska, Heidelberg, 1926.

*Sōd: The Mysteries of Adoni* (S. F. Dunlap), London and Edinburgh, 1861, xvii, 216.

*Sōd: The Son of the Man* (S. F. Dunlap), London & Edinburgh, 1861, xxxiv, 152.

*Soirées de Saint-Petersbourg, Les* (J. M. de Maistre), Paris, Lyon, 1822.

*Some Unpublished Letters of Helena Petrovna Blavatsky* (E. R. Corson). With an Introduction and Commentary. London: Rider & Co. [1929], 255 pp., facs. & ill.

*Sorcière, La* (J. Michelet), 1862; 2nd. ed., 1863; also 1867.

*Soul, On the* (Timaeus Locrius). Best ed. is by J. J. de Gelder, Leyden, 1836; also (with Plato's *Timaeus*) by C. F. Herman, Leipzig, 1852.

*Soul: Its Nature and Development, On the* (Peary Chand Mitra [Pyârichânda Mitra]), Calcutta, 1881.

*Soul of Things, or Psychometric Researches and Discoveries, The* (Wm. & Eliz. Denton). First ed. titled: *Nature's Secrets, or, Psychometric Researches.* Ed. and with an Introd. by a Clergyman of the Church of England, 1863, xvi, liii, 55, 335 pp.; 3rd rev. ed., Boston, 1866; also 1873 and 1881-84.

*Sound* (John Tyndall). New York: Appleton, 1867 & 1885; 3rd rev. & enl. ed., 1894.

*Souvenirs d'un voyage dans la Tartarie, le Thibet et la Chine pendant les années 1844, 1845, et 1846* (Abbé É. R. Huc), Paris: A. Le Clère, 1850, 2 vols. 8vo.; 4th ed., Paris: Gaume frères et J. Dupray, 1860; new annotated ed. by J.-M. Planchet, Peking, 1924. Engl. transl. by W. Hazlitt as *Travels,* etc., 1852; abbrev. ed. by M. Jones, 1867.

*Spectrum Analysis Explained,* etc. (H. E. Roscoe), New York, 1869.

*Speculum historiale* (Vincent de Beauvais or Vincentius Bellovacensis), Venice, 1494.

*Sphinx mystagoga* (A. Kircher), Amsterdam, 1676.

*Spiritisme dans le monde, Le. L'Initiation et les sciences occultes dans l'Inde et chez tous les peuples de l'antiquité* (L. Jacolliot), Paris, 1875, 1879, 1892, 8vo.

*Spiritual Scientist, The.* Publ. in Boston, Mass. Vols. 1-7, Sept. 10, 1874—July, 1878. Weekly until last vol., which is monthly. Ed. by E. Gerry Brown.

\**Spiritualism and Charlatanism.*

*Ssabier und der Ssabismus, Die* (D. A. Chwol'son or Khvolson), St. Petersburg, 1856, 2 vols.

*Steganographia* (Joh. Trithemius), Francofurti, 1606, 4to.; Darmstadt, 1621, 1635.

*Stèle* (E. de Rougé). Possibly *Étude sur une stèle égyptienne,* etc., Paris, 1858.

*Stellung des Menschen in der Natur in Vergangenheit, Gegenwart und Zukunft, etc., Die* (F. C. C. Büchner), Leipzig, 1869-70; Engl. tr. by W. S. Dallas, London, 1872.

*Sthâpatyaveda.* The science of architecture, considered as an appendix to the *Atharvaveda,* at least by some authorities. See *Upaveda.*

*Stichometria* (Nicephorus Patriarcha); text and transl. by Anastasius Bibliothecarius, in Petri Pithoei *Opera posthuma,* Paris, 1609, 4to.

*Stonehenge, a Temple Restor'd to the British Druids* (Dr. Wm. Stukeley). London: W. Innys & R. Manby, 1740, fol.

*Strange Story, A* (Bulwer-Lytton), 1862.

*Stranger, The* (A. F. F. von Kotzebue). A drama in 5 acts, tr. by Benj. Thompson, 1849. Orig. German title was *Menschenhass und Reue,* 1788, etc.

*Summa theologica* (Thos. Aquinas). Engl. tr. by the English Dominican Province, New York, Benziger Bros., Inc., 1947, 3 vols.

*Summae theologiae moralis* (E. Henriquez), Venice, 1600, fol.

*Summaria et brevis dogmatum Chaldaicorum* (Pselli expos.), in App. to *Sibyllina Oracula* (S. Gallaeus), Amsterdam, 1689.

*Summun bonum* (ascribed to Robert Fludd, but bearing name of Joachimus Frizius), Frankfurt, 1629.

*Sun and the Earth, The* (Balfour Stewart). Lecture delivered in Manchester, Nov. 13, 1872. In *Science Lectures for the People,* Fourth Series, 1872-73; also in D. Estes, *Half-hour Recreations in Popular Science,* Ser. 2, Boston, 1874, etc.

*Supernatural Religion: An Inquiry into the Reality of Divine Revelation* (Anonymously publ.) [W. R. Cassels], London, 1874, 2 vols.; 6th ed., 1875; 3rd Vol. publ. in 1877; rev. ed. of complete work, 1879.

"Supposed Vaidik Authority for the Burning of Hindu Widows, On the" (H. H. Wilson), in *Journal of the Royal Asiatic Society,* Vol. XVI (1854), pp. 201-14.

*Sûrya-Siddhânta.* Transl. by Rev. Ebenezer Burgess, former missionary in India; New Haven, Conn., 1860, iii, 356.

*Sûtra of the Foundation of the Kingdom of Righteousness* (Dhamma-chakka-ppavatana Sutta, meaning "Setting in motion the Wheel of the Law"). Woodward's transl. in the Pâli Text Series; also in Christmas Humphreys' *Wisdom of Buddhism,* No. 13; and in *SBE,* XI, ed. by F. Max Müller, 1881.

*Syllabus of Lectures on Natural and Experimental Philosophy, A.* (Thos. Young), London, 1802, 8vo.

*Symbolical Language of Ancient Art and Mythology, The* (R. P. Knight). An Inquiry. New ed., with introd., additions, notes and a new index, by Dr. A. Wilder. New York, 1876. — Orig. ed. was entitled *An Inquiry into the Symbolical,* etc., London, 1818, 8vo.; 2nd ed., 1835.

*Symbolik und Mythologie der alten Völker, besonders der Griechen* (Georg. Fr. Creuzer), Leipzig und Darmstadt, 1810-23, 6 vols. See *Religions de l'antiquité,* etc.

*Synopsis Historiôn* (Georgius Cedrênus), or *Compendium historiarum ab orbe condita ad Isaacum Comnenum (1057);* 1st ed., by Xylander, Basel, 1506, fol., with Latin tr.; by Goar and Fabrot, Paris, 1647, 2 vols., fol.; by I. Bekker, Bonn, 1838-39, 2 vols., 8vo.

*Synopsis theologiae practicae,* etc. (J.-B. Taberna or Taverne), Douai, 1698, 3 vols.; six ed. at Cologne between 1700 and 1754.

*System of Logic, A* (J. S. Mill), 8th ed., London, 1872, 8vo.

*Système de politique positive ou traité de sociologie* (A. Comte), 1852-54; Engl. tr. by Bridges, etc., 1875-79.

## T

*Tables tournantes, du surnaturel en général et des esprits, Des* (A. E. de Gasparin), Paris, 1854, 2 vols.; 2nd ed. (incomplete), Paris, 1888, with portrait of author. Engl. tr. as *Science versus Modern Spiritualism*. A Treatise on turning tables, the supernatural in general, and spirits. Tr. by E. W. Robert, with an Introd. by Rev. R. Baird. New York, 1857, 2 vols.

*Tablet, British Museum*, 562. Quoted by Bunsen in *Egypt's Place in Univ. Hist.*

*Tabulae Primi Mobilis . . . Juxta principia . . . in sua Caelesti Philosophia exposita,* etc. (Placidus de Titis), Vatavii, Typis Pauli Frambotti, 1657, 4to. — Revised by M. Sibly, London, W. Justins, 1789, 8vo. — Engl. tr. by John Cooper as *Astronomy and Elementary Philosophy*, "corrected from the best Latin editions," London, Davis & Dickson, 1814, 8vo.

*Taittirîya-Âraṇyaka*. Belongs to the Black *Yajurveda*. Ed. with the Comm. of Sâyaṇâchârya by Râjendralâla Mitra, in *Bibl. Ind.*, 1872.

*Taittirîya-Brâhmaṇa*. Belongs to the Black *Yajurveda*. Ed. with the Comm. of Sâyaṇâchârya by Râjendralâla Mitra, in 3 vols., Asiatic Soc. of Bengal, 1859, 1862, 1890.

*Tales and Traditions of the Russian People* (I. P. Saharoff), Moscow, 1836-37; 2nd ed., 1837; 3rd ed., St. Petersburg, 1841-49 [Russian text].

\**Tales of the Impious Khalif* (Barrachias- Hassan-Oglu).

*Talmud:* including *Midrashim: Berêshîth Rabbah, Hazitha, Rabboth; Mishnayoth: Hagigâh, Hulin, Nazir, Pirke Aboth, Sanhedrin, Sotah, Sukkah; Torah Khethubim* (Hagiographa); *Yôhânân.* — Consult *The Babylonian Talmud*. Translated under the editorship of I. Epstein. London, Soncino Press, 1935-48, 34 vols.

*Tanjur.* See *Kanjur.*

*Targûm* (pl. Targûmim or Targûms). Aramaic term meaning "interpretation." A translation or paraphrase of some portions of the Old Testament in the Aramaic of Judaea or Galilee (formerly erroneously called *Chaldee*), mostly dating in the present form from the Geonic period, but in part based on oral tradition of the pre-Christian Roman period. Among the important Targûms now extant are: for the *Pentateuch* — the *Targûm of Onkelos*, or *Babylonian Targûm*, and the *Targûm of Jonathan*, or *Targûm of Jerusalem;* for the *Prophets* — the *Targûm of Jonathan bar Uzziel*.

*Tela ignea Satanae. Hoc est: Arcani et horribiles Judaeorum adversus Christum Deum et Christianam Religionem Libri anekdotoi* (Joh. Christophorus Wagenseil, or Wagenseilius), Altdorfi Noricum, 1681, 2 vols. 4to., containing six treatises, of which the last is "Libellus Toldos Jeschu." Text with German transl. in J. A. Eisenmenger's *Entdecktes Judenthum*, Frankfurt, 1700, and Dresden, 1893.

*Templerei oder das innere Wesen des alten und neuen Ordens der Tempelherrn, Die* (W. F. Wilcke), Leipzig, 1826, 1827, 1835; Engl. as *History of the Order of Knights Templar*, Halle, 1860.

*Ten Years with Spiritual Mediums*. An Inquiry concerning the etiology of certain phenomena called spiritual (F. G. Fairfield), New York, 1875.

*Textbook of Physiology, General, Special and Practical* (J. H. Bennettt), Edinburgh, 1870.

*Thalaba the Destroyer* (R. Southey), 1801.

*Theatrum chemicum* (B. G. Penotus), 1616.

*Theogony* (Pherecydes). Also known as *Theocrasy* and *Heptamuchos*. A work which has not come down to our times and is known only through other ancient authorities that quote from it.

*Theologia moralis* . . . *nunc pluribus partibus aucta a C. la Croix* (Claude Lacroix), Coloniae Agrippinae, 1707-14, 9 vols.; also 1733; Montauzon ed., 1729, and 1757, 2 vols. fol. Mainly a Commentary on H. Busembaum's *Medulla*, etc.

*Theologia Platonica de immortalitate animae* (M. Ficino), 1482.

*Theologia tripartita universa*, etc. (Richard Arsdekin, or Archdekin), Dilingae, 1687, fol.; Coloniae, 1744.

*Theologiae moralis, Liber*, etc. (A. de Escobar y Mendoza), Lyon, 1650; Venice, 1650; Brussels, 1651; Paris, 1656.

\**Theologumena arithmetica* (Speusippus).

*Thology of Plato. The Six Books of Proclus, the Platonic Successor, On the* (Thos. Taylor), London, 1816, 2 vols. in one, 4to.

*Theoretic Arithmetic in Three Books* (Thos. Taylor). Containing the substance of all that has been written on this subject by Theon of Smyrna, Nichomachus, Iamblichus and Boëthius, London, 1816, 8vo.

*Theosophical Path, The.* Art. by Dr. C. J. Ryan: "Precipitation of Astral-Forms or — What?", Vol. XLIV, Jan. & April, 1935.

*Theosophist, The.* A Monthly Journal devoted to Oriental Philosophy, Art, Literature and Occultism. Started in Bombay, India, October, 1879, and conducted originally by H. P. Blavatsky herself. Later edited from Adyar, Madras, India. *In progress.*

*Theasaurus Liber Magnus vulgo "Liber Adami" appellatus*, etc. (H. Petermann), Leipzig, 1867, 2 vols.

*Thesis propugnata in regio Soc. Jes. Collegio celeberrimae Academiae Cadomensis, die Veneris, 30 Jan., 1693* (Cadomi, 1693).

*S. Thomae Aquinatus theologicae summae compendium* (P. Alagona), Rome, 1619, 1620; Lyons, 1619; Würzburg and Cologne, 1620; Paris, 1621; Venice, 1762; Turin, 1891.

\**Thoughts on the Birth and Generation of Things* (F. C. Oetinger).

*Thrice-Greatest Hermes* (G. R. S. Mead). London & Benares, Theos. Publ. House, 1906; 2nd impr., 1949; 3rd impr. (revised), London: J. M. Watkins, 1964, 3 vols.

*Timaeus, On the* (Proclus). Transl. by Thos. Taylor, 1820, 2 vols., 4to.

\**Tinnevelly Shanars, The* (E. Lewis).

*Tischreden* (M. Luther), Eisleben, 1566; Leipzig: Andreas Zeidler, 1700.

*Torah Khethubim.* See *Talmud.*

*Tractat de lapide philosophorum sive summa rosarii philosophorum* (Arnolphinus Franciscus Lucensis). In C. von Hellwig, *Fasciculus Unterschiedlicher . . . philosophischen Schriften*, etc., Leipzig and Bremen, 1719.

*Tractatus de transmutatione metallorum.* See *Hermes, Books of.*

\**Traditions* (Schopheim).

*Traditions Indo-Européennes et Africaines, Les* (L. Jacolliot), Paris, 1876, 8vo.

*Traité philosophique et physiologique de l'hérédité nouvelle*, etc. (P. Lucas), Paris, 1847-50, 8vo.

*Transactions of the Society of Biblical Archaeology*, Vol. I, 1872, Pt. i, p. 46 (art. by Geo. Smith). Periodical publ. in London, 1872-93, 9 vols.

*Transcaucasia* (A. von Haxthausen), Leipzig, 1856, 2 vols.

*Tratados históricos . . . de China,* etc. (F. Navarette), Madrid, 1676, fol.

*Travels along the Mediterranean . . . during the years 1816-17-18* (R. Richardson), London, 1822.

*Travels in Central Asia* (A. Vámbery), Being an Account of a Journey from Teheran across the Turkoman Desert, on the Eastern Shore of the Caspian, to Khiva, Bokhara, and Samarkand, performed in the year 1863, etc., London, 1864, 8vo.

*Travels in Georgia, Persia, Armenia, ancient Babylonia . . . during the years 1817, 1818, 1819 and 1820* (R. K. Porter), London, 1821-22, 2 vols., 4to.

*Travels in Timmannee, Kooranko, and Soolima Countries in Western Africa* (A. G. Laing), London, 1825.

*Travels to Discover the Source of the Nile, in the years 1768-73* (J. Bruce), Edinburgh, 1790, 5 vols.; 2nd ed., 1805; 3rd ed., 1813.

*Treatise on Optics, A* (D. Brewster), London, 1831.

*Tree and Serpent Worship* (J. Fergusson), London, 1873.

*Tripiṭaka* (Pâli, *Tipiṭaka,* meaning "Three Baskets"). Chief Scripture of the Theravâda School of Buddhism, consisting of the *Vinaya-Piṭaka,* or Rules of Discipline governing the Sangha; the *Sutta-Piṭaka,* or Dialogues and Discourses of the Buddha, containing the five *Nikâyas;* and the *Abbidhamma-Piṭaka* (lit. "Higher Dhamma"), mainly a comm. on the *Sutta-Piṭaka.* Issued by the Pâli Text Society. — Consult also *SBE* X, XI, XIII, XVII, XX.

*Trois livres des charmes, sorcelages, ou enchantemens* (Leonardo Vairo), Paris, 1583. 8vo. Translation by Julien Baudon d'Anvers of the Latin original: *De fascino libri tres,* etc., Paris, Chesneau, 1583. 4to., and 2nd ed., Venice, 1589.

*Trübner's American and Oriental Literary Record,* Oct. 16, 1869: Lect. by F. Max Müller.

*True Christian Religion,* (E. Swedenborg); containing the universal theology of the New Church, etc., transl. from the Latin. 3rd. ed., London, 1795; 6th ed., 1837; also 1855.

*True Intellectual System of the Universe, The* (R. Cudworth), London, 1668; 2nd ed., 1743; also 1845.

"Truth About H. P. Blavatsky, The" (Vera P. de Zhelihovsky). Essay publ. in *Rebus* (Puzzle), Vol. II, 1883.

*Tûzuk-i-Jahângîrî, or, Memoirs of Jahângîr.* Tr. by Alexander Rogers . . . Ed. by Henry Beveridge (with portrait of Jahângîr), London, 1909. *Oriental Translation Fund,* New Ser., Vol. 19.

*Types of Mankind: or, Ethnological Researches* (G. R. Gliddon and J. C. Nott), London, 1854.

# U

*Über den Buddhaismus in Hochasien und in China* (W. Schott); Address given at the Prussian Academy of Sciences, Feb. 1, 1844. Berlin, 1846, 8vo.

*Über den Willen in der Natur* (A. Schopenhauer). Eine Erörterung der Bestätigungen welche die Philosophie des Verfassers, seit ihrem Auftreten, durch die empirischen Wissenshaften, erhalten hat. Frankfurt a. M., 1836.

*Über die Auflösung der Arten durch natürliche Zuchtwahl oder die Zukunft des organischen Reiches mit Rücksicht auf die Cultur Geschichte.* Von einem Unbekannten. Hannover, 1872, v, 72 pp. Published by Rümpler, and actually authored by J. Wiegand. Cf. Heinsius, *Allgemeines Bücher-Lexicon,* 1868-74.

*Über die Grenzen des Naturerkenntnis* (Du Bois-Reymond), Leipzig, 1872, 1882, 1898.

*Über die Sympathie* (F. Hufeland), Berlin, 1817.

*Universae theologiae moralis receptiores absque lite sententiae* (A. de Escobar y Mendoza), Lyons, 1652-63, 7 vols.

*Universal History, from the Earliest Account of Time, An* (Compiled from original authors), London, 1747-54, 21 vols.

*Universal Prayer, The* (Pope), 1738, fol.

*Universali stirpium natura, De* (J. Costaeus), Turin, 1578.

*Unseen Universe, The* (P. G. Tait & B. Stewart), 4th ed., London, 1876.

*Unseen World and Other Essays, The* (John Fiske), 5th ed., Boston, 1876.

*Upaveda,* meaning "secondary knowledge." Name of a class of writings subordinate or appended to the four *Vedas.* It includes the *Âyurveda* or science of medicine appended to the *Ṛigveda;* the *Dhanurveda* or science of archery app. to the *Yajurveda;* the *Gândharvaveda* or science of music, app. to the *Sâmaveda;* and the *Sthâpatyaveda* or science of architecture, app. to the *Atharvaveda.*

*\*Usa* (Charaka).

V

*Varietate rerum, De* (G. Cardanus), Basel, 1557.

*Vedângas,* lit. "limbs of the Vedas." Any one of six classes of Sanskrit works written in the *sûtra* style, including phonetics, meter, grammar, etymology, religious ceremony, and the ritualistic calendar. They are designed to teach how to recite, understand, and apply Vedic texts. — The Skt. text has been publ. in Bombay: Tattvavivechaka Press, 1892.

*Vedânta.* See *Mîmânsâ.*

*Vedas.* See *Atharvaveda, Ṛigveda, Sâmaveda, Yajurveda,* and *Upaveda.*

"Vedas, On the" (Colebrooke). *Asiatick Researches,* Vol. VIII, pp. 391-92, ed. 1805.

*Vedic Hymns* (Dîrghatamas). See Vol. II, p. 654, note 56.

*Veil of Isis, The* (W. Winwood Reade). The Mysteries of the Druids. London: Chas. J. Skeet, 1861, 250 pp.

*Vendîdâd.* See *Avesta.*

*Verbo mirifico, De* (J. Reuchlin), Basel, 1480, fol.; Coloniae, 1532, 8vo.; Lugduni, 1552.

*Vérité des miracles opérés à l'intercession de M. de Pâris . . . démontrée contre l'Archevêque de Sens, La* (L. B. Carré de Montgeron), Paris, 1737, 4to.

*Versuch einer pragmatischen Geschichte der Arzneikunde* (K. Sprengel), Halle, 1800, 1821, 1844, 1846.

*Vestiges of the Spirit-History of Man* (S. F. Dunlap), New York, 1858, vi, 404.

*Victoria Porcheti adversus impios Hebreos* (Porchetus Salvagus, or de Salvaticis, or Salvaticensis), ed. by R. P. A. Justiniani, Paris, 1520, fol.

*Vie de Jésus, La* (E. Renan), Paris, 1863; being Vol. I of his *Histoire des origines du Christianisme,* Paris, 1863-83, 8 vols.

*Vies des Pères des déserts d'Orient, Les* (M. A. Marin), Avignon, 1761.

*Vishṇu-Purâṇa.* Ed. by Jîvânanda Vidyâsagâra. Calcutta: Sarasvatî Press, 1882. — Transl. by H. H. Wilson. Ed. by Fitzedward Hall. London: Trübner & Co., 1864, 65, 66, 68, 70. Also in *Works by the late H. H. Wilson.*

*Vita di Giordano Bruno da Nola,* etc. (D. Berti), Firenze, Milano, 1868.

*Vita e lettere di Amerigo Vespucci* (A. M. Bandini), Florence, 1868. With Notes by G. Uzielli.

*Vita et morte Moysis libri tres, cum observationibus, De* (G. Gaulmin), 1714.

*Vita Pythagorae, De* (Porphyry), Greek and Latin. Amsterdam, 1707; ed. Kiessling, Leipzig, 1816.

*Vitis philosophorum libri X, De* (Diogenes Laertius); also known as *De clarorum philosophorum vitis, dogmatibus et apophthegmatibus libri decem.* Editio princeps, Basel, 1533, ap. Frobenium; best modern ed.: H. Hübner and C. Jacobitz, 1828-33, 2 vols., with critical notes. Text and Engl. transl. as *The Lives and Opinions of Eminent Philosophers,* in *Loeb Class. Libr.;* Engl. tr. alone, by C. D. Yonge, in *Bohn's Class. Libr.*

*Völker des östlichen Asien, Die* (A. Bastian), Jena, 1866-1871, 8vo.

*Völuspá.* See *Edda.*

*Voyage à la Martinique,* etc. (J.-B. Thibault de Chanvalon), Paris, 1763, 4to.

*Voyage au pays des éléphants* (L. Jacolliot), Paris, 1876, 12°.

*Voyage aux Indes Orientales* (J. P. Paulin de St. Barthélemy). Trans. from Italian. Paris, 1808, 3 vols. (Orig. in Latin, Rome, 1794, 4to.)

*Voyage dans la Basse et la Haute Égypte, pendant les campagnes du général Bonaparte* D. V. Denon); 4th ed., Paris, 1803, 3 vols.; Engl. tr., London, 1802, 2 vols.

*Voyage dans l'Empire de Maroc et le royaume de Fez fait pendant les années 1790-1* (Wm. Lemprière); tr. from the English by de Sainte-Suzanne, Paris, 1801, 8vo., the orig. Engl. work being: *A Tour from Gibraltar to Tangier . . . over Mount Atlas to Morocco,* London, 1791; 2nd ed., 1793; 3rd ed., 1800.

*Voyage dans l'intérieur de l'Afrique,* etc. (G. T. Mollien), Paris, 1820, 2 vols., also 1840.

*Voyage dans les royaumes de Siam, de Cambodge, de Laos et autres parties centrales de l'Indo-Chine,* etc. (A. H. Mouhot), Paris, 1868; Engl. tr., London, 1864.

*Voyage en Indo-Chine et dans l'empire chinois,* etc. (L. de Carné), Paris, 1872.

*Voyages and Travels in the Levant, in the Years 1749-52, etc.* (F. Hasselquist), Engl. transl. London, 1766, 8vo. Original work was titled: *Iter Palaestinum el. Resa til Heliga Landet,* publ. by Linné, 1757.

*Voyages, contenant la description des états du Grand Mogol, de l'Hindoustan,* etc. (F. Bernier), Amsterdam, 1699, 2 vols.

*Voyages des Pèlerins Bouddhistes* (Stanislas A. Julien): Vol. I — *Histoire de la vie de Hiouen-Thsang et de ses voyages dans l'Inde, depuis l'an 629 jusqu'en 645,* par Hoeili et Yen-thsong; traduite du Chinois par Stanislas Julien. Paris, 1853. — Vol. II — *Si-yu-ki. Mémoires sur les contrées occidentales,* traduits du Sanskrit en Chinois, en

l'an 648, par Hiouen-Thsang, et du Chinois en Français, par S. Julien. Paris, 1857-58. 2 vols.
 The *Si-yu-ki* or *Ta-T'ang-Si-yu-ki* was compiled under the traveller's own supervision by order of the great Emperor Tai-Tsung.

*Voyages d'Ibn Batoutah* (Muḥammad ibn 'Abd Allâh, called Ibn Batûtah). Texte Arabe accompagné d'une traduction, etc., Paris, 1853-58, 4 vols., 8vo. — *The Travels of Ibn Batûta*, tr. by S. Lee, 1829, 4to. Oriental Translation Fund.

*Vṛiddha-Mânava.* The "Older Manu" or an older recension of Manu's *Laws*.

*Vulgate.* Latin version of the Scriptures, in the main the work of St. Jerome in the 4th cent. The name was taken from that of the earlier Latin translations of the Septuagint, and was first used in the modern sense by Roger Bacon in the 13th cent. The O.T. was transl. directly from the Hebrew with the aid of the Septuagint and other Greek and Latin versions. Declared by the Council of Trent in 1546 to be the standard for the services of the Roman Ch. Standard text is that of Pope Clement VII of 1592. The Engl. version from the Vulgate is known as the *Douay Bible;* N.T. was publ. at Reims, 1582; O.T. at Douay, France, 1609-10. Various rev. ed. exist.

## W

*Weise und der Thor, Der* (I. J. Schmidt), St. Petersburg, 1843. Tibetan orig. and transl. See also *Geschichte der Ost-Mongolen.*

*Westminster Review:* "Septenary Institutions," Vol. LIV, October, 1850.

*Wheel of the Law, The* (H. Alabaster). Buddhism Illustrated from Siamese Sources by The Modern Buddhist; A Life of Buddha, and An Account of the Phrabat. London, 1871. [Pt. I is called: "The Modern Buddhist; being the Views of a Siamese Minister of State on His Own and Other Religions."]

*Widow-Burning. A Narrative* (H. J. Bushby), London, 1855, 8vo.

*Word, The* (New York). Monthly edited by H. W. Percival. New York: The Theos. Publ. House, Vols. I-XXV, Oct., 1904 - Sept., 1917.

*Works* (A. Libavius), Halle, 1600.

*Works of Philo Judaeus, The* (ed. Chas. D. Yonge), Transl. from the Greek. Bohn Eccles. Library, 1854-55, 4 vols.

*Works of Plato, The* (Thos. Taylor). Fifty-five Dialogues and Twelve Epistles translated from the Greek. London, 1804, 5 vols., 8vo.

*Works of Robert Boyle, The* (R. Boyle), London, 1744, fol., 5 vols. (ed. by Thos. Birch); 1772, 6 vols.

*Works of Sir William Jones, The,* London, 1799, 6 vols.

*Works of the most Reverend Dr. John Tillotson . . . containing Fifty-Four Sermons and Discourses, on Several Occasions, together with The Rule of Faith* (John Tillotson), 3rd ed., London, 1701.

*World's Sixteen Crucified Saviors; or Christianity before Christ* (K. Graves), 2nd. ed., Boston, 1875.

*Worship of the Serpent traced throughout the World, The* (J. B. Deane), London, 1830; 2nd enl. ed., 1833.

*Wörterbuch der lateinischen Sprache* (Wm. Freund), Leipzig; Hahn, 1834-40, 4 vols., 8vo. (French tr. by N. Theil, Paris, 1855-65, 3 vols.)

## Y

*Yajur-Veda.* Meaning the "Sacrificial Veda," a collection of sacred mantras, liturgical and ritualistic formulae in verse and prose. It is divided into two distinct collections: the Taittirîya-saṃhitâ called Kṛishṇa or "black" because in it the Saṃhitâ and Brâhmaṇa portions are confused; and the Vâjasaneyi-saṃhitâ called Śukla or "white" because in this the Saṃhitâ is cleared from confusion and is orderly. Consult: 1) Black *Yajurveda.* Trans. by A. B. Keith. Cambridge, Mass.: Harvard Univ., 1914. *HSO,* 18, 19; 2) White *Yajurveda.* Trans. by R. T. H. Griffith. Benares: E. J. Lazarus & Co., 1899.

*Yashts.* See *Avesta.*

*Yaśna* (F. Spiegel). See *Avesta.*

*Yôḥânân.* See *Talmud.*

## Z

*Zanoni* (E. G. Bulwer-Lytton), 1842.

*Zauber-Bibliothek, oder von Zauberei, Theurgia und Mantik,* etc. (G. C. Horst), Mainz, 1821-26, 6 Parts, 8vo.

*Zend-Avesta, Zoroaster's lebendiges Wort.* Tr. from the French of Anquetil by J. F. Kleucker, 1776, 1777, 4to. See also *Avesta.*

*Zohar* (Heb.: *zôhar,* meaning *splendor*), spoken of also as *Midrâsh ha-Zohar* and *Sepher ha-Zohar.* The great storehouse of ancient Hebrew Theosophy. See for comprehensive account Vol. VII of the *Collected Writings,* pp. 269-71, where bibliographical data may be found.

# H. P. BLAVATSKY
# COLLECTED WRITINGS

*Comprehensive Edition published by*

## THE THEOSOPHICAL PUBLISHING HOUSE

WHEATON, IL, U.S.A. — ADYAR, MADRAS, INDIA — LONDON, ENGLAND

Large octavos; illustrated with rare portraits;
cloth bound; fully indexed.

Vol. I (1874–78) lxxx + 570 pp.
Vol. II (1879–80) xlvi + 590 pp.
Vol. III (1881–82) xxxviii + 583 pp.
Vol. IV (1882–83) xliv + 718 pp.
Vol. V (1883) xxxii + 416 pp.
Vol. VI (1883–85) liv + 481 pp.
Vol. VII (1886–87) xxxiv + 433 pp.

Vol. VIII (1887) xxviii + 507 pp.
Vol. XI (1888) xxx + 487 pp.
Vol. X (1888–89) xxxvi + 461 pp.
Vol. XI (1889) xxxvi + 632 pp.
Vol. XII (1889-90) xxx + 859 pp.
Vol. XIII (1890-91) xxxii + 465 pp.
Vol. XIV (Miscellaneous) xlviii + 734 pp.

Vol. XV (Cumulative Index) + 633 pp.

*From the Caves and Jungles of Hindostan* (1883–86) lxviii + 719 pp.

*Isis Unveiled* (1877): Vol. I, [64] + xlvi + (6) + 657 pp.; Vol. II, iv + (6) + 848 pp.

Information concerning further volumes of this series,
which are in preparation, available on request.

OTHER TITLES IN PRINT

*The Key to Theosophy*
*The Voice of the Silence*

Available in various editions.